MARKETING MANAGEMENT

SECOND EDITION

Peter R. Dickson

Arthur C. Nielsen Jr. Chair of Marketing Research
University of Wisconsin—Madison

THE DRYDEN PRESS
HARCOURT BRACE COLLEGE PUBLISHERS

Fort Worth Philadelphia San Diego New York Orlando Austin San Antonio
Toronto Montreal London Sydney Tokyo

Executive Editor	Lyn Hastert Maize
Acquisitions Editor	Bill Schoof
Developmental Editor	Tracy Morse
Project Editor	Sandy Walton
Production Manager	Jessica Iven Wyatt
Product Manager	Lisé Johnson
Art Director	Bill Brammer
Art & Literary Rights Editor	Adele Krause
Copy Editor	Kay Kaylor
Proofreader	Roberta Kirchhoff
Indexer	Leoni McVey
Compositor	TSI Graphics, Inc.
Text Type	10/12 Janson
Cover Image	by Nick Welch

Address for Editorial Correspondence
The Dryden Press, 301 Commerce Street, Suite 3700, Fort Worth, TX 76102

Address for Orders
The Dryden Press, 6277 Sea Harbor Drive, Orlando, FL 32887
1-800-782-4479, or 1-800-433-0001 (in Florida)

ISBN: 0-03-017742-1

Library of Congress Catalog Card Number: 96-83162

Printed in the United States of America

6 7 8 9 0 1 2 3 4 5 032 9 8 7 6 5 4 3 2 1

The Dryden Press
Harcourt Brace College Publishers

DEDICATION

To Diana

The Dryden Press Series in Marketing

Avila, Williams, Ingram, and LaForge
The Professional Selling Skills Workbook

Bateson
Managing Services Marketing: Text and Readings
Third Edition

Blackwell, Blackwell, and Talarzyk
Contemporary Cases in Consumer Behavior
Fourth Edition

Boone and Kurtz
Contemporary Marketing Plus
Eighth Edition

Churchill
Basic Marketing Research
Third Edition

Churchill
Marketing Research: Methodological Foundations
Sixth Edition

Czinkota and Ronkainen
Global Marketing

Czinkota and Ronkainen
International Marketing
Fourth Edition

Czinkota and Ronkainen
International Marketing Strategy: Environmental Assessment and Entry Strategies

Dickson
Marketing Management
Second Edition

Engel, Blackwell, and Miniard
Consumer Behavior
Eighth Edition

Futrell
Sales Management
Fourth Edition

Grover
Theory & Simulation of Market-Focused Management

Ghosh
Retail Management
Second Edition

Hassan and Blackwell
Global Marketing: Managerial Dimensions and Cases

Hoffman
Essentials of Services Marketing

Hutt and Speh
Business Marketing Management: A Strategic View of Industrial and Organizational Markets
Fifth Edition

Ingram and LaForge
Sales Management: Analysis and Decision Making
Third Edition

Lewison
Marketing Management: An Overview

Lindgren and Shimp
Marketing: An Interactive Learning System

Krugman, Reid, Dunn, and Barban
Advertising: Its Role in Modern Marketing
Eighth Edition

Oberhaus, Ratliffe, and Stauble
Professional Selling: A Relationship Process
Second Edition

Parente, Vanden Bergh, Barban, and Marra
Advertising Campaign Strategy: A Guide to Marketing Communication Plans

Rachman
Marketing Today
Third Edition

Rosenbloom
Marketing Channels: A Management View
Fifth Edition

Schaffer
Applying Marketing Principles Software

Schellinck and Maddox
Marketing Research: A Computer-Assisted Approach

Schnaars
MICROSIM
Marketing simulation available for IBM PC and Apple

Schuster and Copeland
Global Business: Planning for Sales and Negotiations

Shimp
Advertising, Promotion, and Supplemental Aspects of Integrated Marketing Communications
Fourth Edition

Talarzyk
Cases and Exercises in Marketing

Terpstra and Sarathy
International Marketing
Seventh Edition

Weitz and Wensley
Readings in Strategic Marketing Analysis, Planning, and Implementation

Zikmund
Exploring Marketing Research
Sixth Edition

Harcourt Brace College Outline Series

Peterson
Principles of Marketing

PREFACE

We are living in a time of extraordinary change. The economic and ecological threat is stark, simple, and very real. U.S. firms must design and make better products and services and find better ways to market them. This demands that we challenge the ways we have come to think about marketing management. What was once good enough is no longer competitive. What were once limitless resources now have to be used ever more efficiently. Today, either a company is on the leading edge, or it is on the bleeding edge. Companies are halving the time it takes to develop and launch a new product, and the quality of the resulting new products is dramatically higher. Marketing management innovations have also reduced the costs of physical distribution by at least one-third over the last decade and, in addition, increased the reliability and speed of distribution services. These dramatic process improvements in making and marketing products and services has been achieved by throwing away the old standard operating procedures, inventing new marketing-management procedures and practices, and then continually improving them.

It is hard enough to keep up with these changes, let alone try to lead them, even though leading them is what marketing education must do if it is to produce graduates who are able to become productive change agents in the businesses and markets that they manage. Teaching students marketing-management practices that were competitive ten to twenty years ago is not preparing them for the marketing management of the next twenty years. Thus the mission of this Second Edition is to continue to present the leading edge rather than the bleeding edge.

At the same time, a major effort has been made to make the new edition a great deal more user-friendly. This Second Edition is much tighter in its structuring of material and topics. It gives greater and more balanced coverage to the marketing-management processes and practices that have become the dominant drivers of success in many markets today: product development and relationship development.

Marketing Management emphasizes getting the most out of people (now called empowering) by developing a learning culture, encouraging personal creativity and activity-scheduling discipline, using cross-functional product development and selling teams, developing win–win trading alliances and relationships, and greatly improving the information and decision support systems. In short, this marketing management text emphasizes competitive rationality, which is thinking and acting smarter, faster. It offers many ways of thinking about the market called mental models. Hopefully, some of the mental models in this book will form the foundation for the way future generations of marketing executives will come to think about the market and marketing management. Throughout my career I have learned from my teachers and colleagues that if we are to master a topic, we must develop simple but powerful frameworks (mental models) around which we learn and think about a topic.

The education priorities of this text continues to closely follow the recent guidelines of the American Assembly of Collegiate Schools of Business (AACSB). The table on the following page outlines how *Marketing Management* addresses these key educational priorities.

How This Text Addresses the Education Priority

1. Global Marketing*	Almost every chapter in *Marketing Management* concludes with a discussion of global marketing issues. Many of the discussion questions deal with global marketing issues and supply chains, particularly the impact of technologies such as the World Wide Web (www) on global marketing.
2. Cross-Functional Team Management*	The textbook assumes that marketing management is primarily a cross-functional activity. Cross-functional team management is discussed in detail in Chapters 2, 3, 4, 10, 13, and 17.
3. Ethics, Environment, Diversity Issues*	Chapter 8 on public policy and ethics presents a framework for making ethical decisions. The extensive selection of questions at the end of the chapter cover ethical dilemmas, the environment, and minority rights.
4. Total Quality Management and Customer Satisfaction	The total quality management and continuous improvement of marketing processes is discussed throughout the text but particularly in Chapters 1, 2, 4, 6, 9, 10, 11, 12, 17, and 19.
5. Relationship Marketing	Relationship marketing is explored in detail in the section on supply-chain management in Chapter 5; the section on analyzing relationship market-share in Chapter 6; all of Chapter 7 on channel analysis; all of Chapters 11 through 13 on relationship strategy, relationship logistics, and relationship selling; and, finally, the section on organizing alliances and networks in Chapter 17.
6. Integration with Computer Decision Support Systems and Software	This textbook introduces the concept of Marketing Intelligence E-Mailboxes (MIEMs) that deliver information to a decision support system. Such a decision support system, *Stratmesh 2.0*, is described including its use in meshing strategy to the environment, in capital budgeting and product portfolio analysis, in tracking relationship market share, as a project organizer for product development, and in creating benefit × feature quality function deployment matrices. Some twenty spreadsheet templates/frameworks are integrated into the chapter materials and end-of-chapter questions. A disk of these spreadsheet templates is available with the book.
7. Integration with Cost and Financial Accounting	Capital budgeting and cost and financial accounting are discussed in Chapters 4, 9, 12, 16, 18, and 19. Many of the spreadsheet templates present standard management accounting tools that can be applied to marketing management.
8. Encouraging Creative Problem Solving	Individual and team creative problem solving is discussed in Appendix 1, which includes a number of classic creative problem-solving exercises.

*Mandated by the new 1992 AACSB requirements for accreditation.

ABOUT THE BOOK

You are holding a book that in its first edition impacted the market so greatly that long-standing traditional marketing management textbooks are changing to imitate the innovative characteristics of this text and its package. Now in its Second Edition you will find, once again, a book which is shaping the market. This textbook was written with the future of marketing management in mind, not the past.

As with the First Edition, this edition emphasizes such important topics as global marketing, cross-functional team management, total quality management, and ethics. But consistent with the theory of competitive rationality that underlies this text, a major effort has been made to improve the product and to lead change in teaching marketing management. Responding to the extensive feedback of the many users of the text—teachers, students, and practitioners—the new edition gives more emphasis to certain topics and also is designed and written to be ever more user-friendly.

Focus on Product and Relationship Positioning

This book further differentiates itself from other textbooks by focusing on two types of marketing management processes that arguably constitute the core competence of the firm and are, hence, truly strategic. They are the way a firm develops its product and service competitive positioning and the way a firm develops its trading relationship positioning.

The product positioning process is described in Chapter 9 and the process to implement such a product positioning strategy using product and brand development tools, techniques, and processes is discussed in Chapter 10. This chapter is the implementation *ying* to Chapter 9's strategic *yang*. Chapter 11 starts off with a discussion of relationship strategy followed by Chapter 12 and 13's discussions on how to implement the strategy using innovations in logistics' processes and personal selling processes.

As the first century of modern marketing management comes to a close it is a time when many popular pricing tactics and advertising/promotion practices are being criticized for having little beneficial effect on demand. They are also often very expensive, driving up the costs of manufacturing and distribution by 20–30%, sometimes even higher. This edition recognizes such criticisms by promoting the search for a TQM (Total Quality Management) solution. A TQM solution increases customer satisfaction, reduces costs and speeds up the process (increases process velocity) *all at the same time.* Such an advance in indisputably able to increase the competitiveness and profitability of the firm. It is competitively rational. In many places throughout the book you will find examples of such TQM solutions, particularly as applied to product development and distribution processes and practices.

What You Can Expect

Completely current, this text presents cutting-edge marketing management concepts in a traditional format, supplemented by the market's most innovative teaching tools. Extremely student-friendly, the text includes many real-world examples and emphasizes on such important topics as international marketing, ethics, cross-functional teams, and quality. Additionally, you will find that the internet and technology play an important role in this Second Edition and are integrated throughout the text and ancillary package.

Features

- International topics are integrated throughout the text. Most chapters conclude with an extensive application of global marketing, while many of the mini-cases and discussion questions also deal with global marketing issues.
- Total quality issues related to marketing management are integrated throughout the text. Comprehensive coverage on understanding and measuring customer satisfaction and quality is included as well.
- An entire chapter is devoted to public policy and ethics, which presents a framework for making ethical decisions. The chapter ends with questions covering ethics, the environment, and minority rights.
- Reflecting today's team-oriented work environment, cross-functional team management topics are discussed in detail in four chapters.

Key Changes

The second edition of *Marketing Management* reflects many changes. To make this textbook more student-friendly, we have carefully revised the textual material and organization of the chapters. Also, we have greatly enhanced the supplemental package that accompanies this text for both the student and the instructors. Examples of such changes are:

- Each chapter opens with a real-life scenario that illustrates and introduces what will be discussed in the chapter. Providing such vivid and concrete case studies increases student interest and provides an anchor for remembering the more abstract content of the chapter. For examples, see Sam Walton's market research discussed on page 69, competition between high definition television technology discussed on page 207, the remarkable success of the disposable camera discussed on page 155, Ford's risky new product development strategy discussed on page 377, and how Nike's marketing relationship with Foot Locker was superior to Reebock's discussed on page 427.
- The organization of each environment analysis and strategy chapter is described at the beginning of each chapter through the use of a chapter organization figure. These figures help to frame the chapters' organization for teaching purposes and aid the students' learning process. In a sense it is a mental model—a way of thinking about the topic.
- Chapter 1 has been expanded and divided into two chapters, which provide added information and examples to help ease students into text material. Chapter 1 introduces what marketing management is—the delta paradigm and competitive rationality. Chapter 2 focuses solely on marketing decision making. The two new chapters include many interesting and helpful examples, such as the characteristic behavior of hypercompetitive markets on page 13 and innovation cycles and imitation paths on page 27.
- A much stronger emphasis on technology and its impact on marketing management is evident in the New Product Development chapter and the Relationship Logistic's chapter.
- The chapters on distribution, selling, and advertising have been significantly revised and updated with the latest trends and issues. Examples include coverage of the Intranet in relationship marketing, the use of the World Wide Web in integrated marketing communications and the future of Internet shopping in the Chapter 7 opener.

A Premier Instructional Resource Package

The learning package provided with *Marketing Management* is specifically designed to meet the needs of instructors facing a variety of teaching conditions and designed to enhance students' experience of the subject. This textbook has attempted to address both the traditional and the innovative classroom environment by providing an array of quality, fundamental, and technologically advanced items, to bring a contemporary, real-world feel to the study of marketing management.

Instructor's Manual

This comprehensive and valuable teaching aid includes all answers to the mini-cases and discussion questions, additional extended mini-case problems, suggested lecture outlines and teaching notes, sample syllabi, and suggestions for integrating other supplementary items into the course. The Instructor's Manual also serves as a resource to the PowerPoint Presentation Software. Each copy of the Instructor's Manual will also include a copy of Stratmesh 2.0.

Testing Resources

This valuable resource provides testing items for instructors' reference and use. The test bank contains over 1,500 multiple-choice, true/false, short answer, and extended essay questions in varying difficulty levels. The test items are also available in a computerized format, allowing instructors to select problems at random by level of difficulty or type, customize or add test questions, and scramble questions to create up to 99 versions of the same test. This is available in DOS, Mac, or Windows formats. The RequestTest phone-in testing service is also available to all adopters. Individual tests can be ordered by question number via fax, mail, phone, or e-mail with a 48-hour turn-around period. Finally, The Dryden Press can provide instructors with software for installing their own on-line testing program which allows tests to be administered over network or individual terminals. This program allows instructors to grade tests and store results with greater flexibility and convenience.

Overhead Transparencies

Available in acetate form are one hundred full-color teaching transparencies which highlight key concepts for presentation in the classroom. In addition to including many important visuals presented in the text, this package contains other supplemental exhibits not found in the text. This transparency package provides an easy display format to reinforce important concepts to students. Notes explaining transparency content and where to use it are found in the Instructor's Manual.

NEW! PowerPoint Presentation Software

New to this edition, for use by adopters, this classroom presentation software in PowerPoint includes graphs, charts, figures, and other information from the text and end-of-chapter discussion questions in an easy-to-use format to enhance lectures and classroom discussions. This innovative PowerPoint package, covers all of the material found in the textbook in addition to numerous other outside supplemental examples and materials. An entire course can be developed around this powerful presentation tool. The software has been prepared in a PowerPoint format to be easily supplemented by instructors who wish to introduce additional materials. Clear instructions on how to mix and match presentations, pull-in discussion questions, and ad material and print-lecture outlines are provided as well.

NEW! Video Package

This new nine-segment video package has been prepared to provide a relevant and interesting visual teaching tool for the classroom. Each video segment is relevant to chapter material and gives students the opportunity to apply what they are learning to real-world situations. The video material enables instructors to better illustrate concepts to students. The videos, which were edited specifically for use with this text, feature companies such as AT&T (new), Dow Distribution (new), Walker Group (new), Rogaine by Upjohn, Marriott Corporation, and Cadillac Motor Company and others in situations that illustrate concepts found in the text.

NEW! Stratmesh 2.0 Software

An entirely new marketing decision support software developed by Scott Stephens and Peter Dickson is available with this Second Edition. What exactly is Stratmesh 2.0? It is an **all new** Windows-based marketing decision support software that improves the quality, reduces the cost, and increases the speed and adaptability of a firm's competitive decision making and implementation. The innovative new software can also evaluate the competitiveness of market trading relationship, track the product/service development process, segment consumer demand, and mesh customer benefits to product engineering specifications. It supports and can access a wide variety of databases, including blueprints, spreadsheets, multimedia kits of advertising, merchandising formats, and product/service prototypes. This software has an exciting future ahead. During the next year it will be beta tested by companies such as General Mills, 3M, and Compaq. Beginning in late 1997, this software will be sold to companies globally. This software will be available to instructors to use themselves, to install in computer labs, and to give the students to use in course-related exercises, cases, and projects.

Custom Cases

The "Dryden Request" Cases in Marketing Management offers numerous cases for custom ordering. Cases profile such companies as Nike, Kellogg, Gillette, Rubbermaid, Hershey Foods, Land's End, Wal-Mart, Anheuser-Busch, Harley-Davidson, and many others. Abstracts and partial text can be viewed at The Dryden Press' website (http://www.dryden.com). Print an order form and customize your own casebook.

NEW! Darden Custom Cases

Through a recent licensing agreement, Dryden will offer top Darden cases for custom ordering via our website. You will find case titles, abstracts, partial/full text in a secured environment, as well as, ordering information. Ordering Darden cases has never been easier.

NEW! Internet Support

Visit the Dryden website at http://www.dryden.com for the latest support material for our marketing list. Look for our useful instructor resources including annotated articles, resource links, cases, and other pedagogical aids which will be constantly updated.

The Dryden Press will provide complimentary supplements or supplement packages to those adopters qualified under our adoption policy. Please contact your sales representative to learn how you may qualify. If as an adopter or potential user you receive supplements you do not need, please return them to your sales representative or send them to:

Attn: Returns Department
Troy Warehouse
465 South Lincoln Drive
Troy, MO 63379

Acknowledgments

Many people have helped with this Second Edition, but none more than Alan Sawyer (University of Florida) who through both editions read and reread material making many useful suggestions about content and structure. Thank you, Alan, for giving so much of your mind and time. Several other friends and colleagues made important contributions to revising and restructuring chapters. Joe Giglierana (San Jose State) helped with the product development and relationship strategy chapters, Diana Haytko (University of Illinois) with the integrated marketing communication and advertising management chapters, Leslie M. Fine (The Ohio State University) the relationship selling and sales management chapter, and Joe Urbany (University of Notre Dame) the pricing management chapter, and Alan Malter (University of Wisconsin-Madison) the organization chapter. Thank you to David Hartman for preparing the Test Bank to accompany this book. The following reviewers also made many and varied useful suggestions:

Reviewers for Second Edition

Frank Acito	Indiana University
Mark I. Alpert	The University of Texas—Austin
Jeffry L. Bradford	Bowling Green University
William G. Browne	Oregon State University
Randolph E. Bucklin	University of California—Los Angeles
Melvin R. Crask	University of Georgia
Jehoshua Eliashberg	University of Pennsylvania—Wharton School
Marian Friestad	University of Oregon
Shankar Ganesan	Virginia Tech
David E. Griffith	University of Oklahoma
Janice Gygi	University of North Texas
Jan B. Heide	University of Wisconsin—Madison
Moonkyu Lee	University of Colorado—Denver
Morgan P. Miles	Georgia State University
Robert M. Morgan	University of Alabama
John W. Nelson	University of Nebraska—Kearney
Michael P. Peters	Boston College
Richard E. Plank	Western Michigan University
John R. Ronchetto, Jr.	University of California—San Diego
Bob Rothberg	Rutgers University
Alan Sawyer	University of Florida
Edward W. Schmitt	Villanova University
Allan D. Shocker	University of Minnesota—Twin Cities
Billy Thorton	Colorado State University
Russell G. Wahlers	Ball State University
John Wong	Iowa State University

Reviewers for First Edition

Mark Alpert, The University of Texas at Austin
Danny R. Arnold, Mississippi State University
Neeraj Arora, The Ohio State University
Rosemary Avery, Cornell University
Steve Bell, New York University
Al Belskus, Eastern Michigan University
Gordon Berkstresser, North Carolina State University
Greg Boller, Memphis State University
William Browne, Oregon State University
Dianne S. P. Cermak, Northeastern University
Michael Dotson, Appalachian State University
Jehoshua Eliashberg, University of Pennsylvania
Dale Falcinelli, DF Falcinelli Inc.
Leslie Fine, The Ohio State University
Neil Ford, University of Wisconsin
Marian Friestad, University of Oregon
Joe Giglierano, San Jose State University

Peter Gordon, Southeast Missouri State University
John Grabner, The Ohio State University
Alicia Gresham, Stephen F. Austin University
David Griffith, University of Oklahoma
Jim Grimm, Illinois State University
Janice Gygi, University of North Texas
Linda Hayes, University of Houston
Michael Hutt, Arizona State University
Bernie Jaworski, University of Southern California
Rosemary Kalapurakal, The London Business School
Meir Karlinsky, The Open University of Israel
Buddy Laforge, University of Louisville
Bud LaLonde, The Ohio State University
JoAnn Linrud, Mankato State University
Max Lupul, California State University—Northridge
James McAlexander, Oregon State University
Dan McQuiston, Butler University
Paul Miniard, University of South Carolina
Mark Mitchell, Mississippi State University
Bradley O'Hara, Southeastern Louisiana University
Michael Peters, Boston College
Chris Puto, University of Arizona
John Quelch, Harvard University
Brian Ratchford, SUNY—Buffalo
Robert Roe, University of Wyoming
John Ronchetto, University of San Diego
Alan Sawyer, University of Florida
Wendy Schneier, The Ohio State University
Terry Shimp, University of South Carolina
Kimberly Scott, The Ohio State University
Shannon Shipp, Texas Christian University
Allan Shocker, University of Minnesota
Hugh Sloan, University of Mississippi
Ravi Sohi, University of Nebraska
Roger Strang, Quinnipiac College
Donnie Sullivan, The Ohio State University
Eugene Teeple, University of Central Florida
William Thornton, Colorado State University
Dillard Tinsley, Stephen F. Austin University
Roa Unnava, The Ohio State University
Joe Urbany, University of Notre Dame
Russell Wahlers, Ball State University
Bill Wilkie, University of Notre Dame
Dale Wilson, Michigan State University
Gordon Wise, Wright State University

I also wish to thank the excellent editorial team assembled at The Dryden Press who worked on this Second Edition: development editors, R. Paul Stewart and Tracy Morse; acquisition editor, Bill Schoof; executive editor, Lyn Maize; project editor,

Sandy Walton; production manager, Jessica Wyatt; copy editor, Kay Kaylor; proofreader, Roberta Kirchhoff; prerevision reviews, Molly Severson; art and literary rights editor, Adele Krause; art director, Bill Brammer; product manager, Lisé Johnson. Thank you all for your creativity, hard work, and infinite patience. The editor to author ratio of seven to one suggests that my English teacher was right in his prophetic remarks on my tenth grade report card: "His thoughts and actions need disciplining," and it is still a mighty task. At my end, I wish to thank proofreader, Bharath Lokkur, and my administrative specialist and woman friday, Janet Christopher, who worked tirelessly on the project. Thank you all for going above and beyond your duties to improve and polish this edition.

ABOUT THE AUTHOR

Dr. Peter R. Dickson is the Arthur C. Nielsen Jr. Chair of Marketing Research at the University of Wisconsin—Madison. He has written some 70 articles, monographs, and books on buyer and seller behavior, particularly on pricing, market segmentation, competitive rationality (thinking), process learning, and hypercompetitive market research. Peter Dickson was previously The Crane Professor of Strategic Marketing and an adjunct professor of Industrial Design at The Ohio State University. He is the founder of two start-up companies (Stratmesh Software and National Family Archives) and a vice-president of marketing in a third highly successful venture. He has received several awards for his teaching, research, and writing. Born in New Zealand, he has two grown children, Chris and Sarah, and is descended from an early, somewhat reluctant settler on Norfolk Island, a ship's mate turned gold prospector, and John Glover, the renown Australian artist.

CONTENTS

DETAILED CONTENTS

MARKETING MANAGEMENT

SECOND EDITION

The greater thing in this world is not so much where we stand as in what direction we are going.

Oliver Wendell Holmes

Today, loving change, tumult, even chaos is a prerequisite for survival, let alone success.

Thomas J. Peters

CHAPTER ONE

Marketing Management Thinking

Marketing is sometimes accused of trying to persuade consumers to want things they really do not need. When this happens it is bad marketing and the product or service ultimately fails. On the other hand, good marketing management does have the objective of creating a *want* for a particular product. This *want* is actually the consumer's belief that the product satisfies a basic need better than the currently marketed products. Often consumers may not know they really wanted a product until years after the product was invented.

Television technology was invented in the 1920s and the first programming was transmitted in the 1930s. At first the attitude of investors and consumers was, "What is it?", and then "Who needs it?" It took until the early 1950s for demand for television sets to take off. The transmission technology had to be invented, marketed, and commercialized. Television stations that could transmit the programming had to be invented, marketed to investors, and then marketed to consumers. Each program then had to be invented and targeted to a particular audience segment. When television did take off, it took over our culture.

The invention and marketing of television has had an immense impact on the world.

The average American spends more time watching television than any other waking activity besides work. We are now a watching rather than a reading culture. Television dominates our culture, as well as many other cultures. On the one hand, it is criticized for corrupting the values and ambitions of our children, while on the other hand it is praised for playing a major role in changing the values and ambitions of citizens in the old totalitarian communist countries, creating millions of freedom revolutionaries.

The role of marketing management in developing the television industry has been tremendous. In the 1950s marketing was used to develop and sell a stream of innovations in the actual television set design promising that "television programs never before looked so real and sounded so lifelike." Today's "surround sound" color television sets are far better and less expensive for the value they provide because of approximately fifty years of marketing of new features. Marketing management also had to learn how to effectively advertise on television. As we shall see in the chapter on advertising management, marketing management may still have much to learn about television advertising.

Today, one of the latest television-related, marketing-management issues is the creation of global news, sports, music, movie, documentary, and arts networks. There is a race to sign up viewers around the world. Will Rupert Murdoch's Sky come to dominate, or will Japan's NHK or some other yet to be launched new satellite network service dominate? Will it be Time Warner Cable expanding its Full Service Network out of test markets and to the entire nation? Will it be AT&T launching its 170 channel television service in several markets in April 1996? Perhaps the hottest competition is ITV, the software side of television. The innovations in programming that will be coupled with 100 plus television channels include video, news, and sports programming on demand; interactive shopping and games; banking services; vocational training and home education programs; and even pizza delivery. The marketing of television's endless stream of hardware and software innovations has, in total, changed the world for the good and promises to do so long into the future.

Television being only one of a thousand product-market histories from pain killers to cancer killers and from air travel to telephone communication services that has a positive and progressive innovation story to tell. The pursuit of life, liberty, and happiness has been greatly advanced by marketing management, which identifies and designs product and service features that customers want, and sells and delivers the product or service in the most convenient way at a cost that they can afford. ■

The most fundamental evolutionary law of modern economics is that the future economic prosperity and survival of countries and cultures depends on their ability to make and market the right products and services. The firms and countries that make and market the right products and services will deliver a higher standard of living to their employees, owners, and citizens. Their economic rivals that lose out will not.

Marketing management is the management of the innovative and imitative processes that firms use to identify and satisfy customers while being more cost effective than their rivals. It involves understanding what benefits consumers want and how the consumer behaves. It involves the study and anticipation of competitor behavior, the development of new competitive products and services, and the management of a network of trading relationships with suppliers and distributors. These processes vary depending on whether the firm's customers are other businesses or households, and whether the firm is manufacturing a product or providing a service—such as those provided by banks and insurance companies.

Competitive marketing management between firms also makes the market economy work better than any other system of political economics. Superior marketing management not only contributes to the success of an enterprise, but it influences the wealth and health of the society within which the enterprise is undertaken. It is also a lot of fun developing and marketing new products and services that make a difference in people's lives.

Marketing management is exciting because first, the new technologies used to improve products and service are often inherently interesting and second, competing against rivals for consumer loyalty is a very risky game of who can serve the customer best—most effectively and efficiently. Indeed, marketing management has many of the characteristics of a high-tech competitive sport, except the stakes are much higher—such as possible loss of jobs, possible non-growth of the standard of living, possible inefficient use of the world's limited resources, and possible ineffective recycling of these resources.

In this first chapter we describe how markets evolve in an endless series of cycles of product and service innovation/imitation. An *innovation* in a market is where an adventurous marketer introduces a new product or distribution technology into the market. If the new idea increases customer satisfaction or profitability, the competing firms will notice the innovation's effect on their sales or will hear about the increased profits that the innovator is earning from its experiment. This leads to a flurry of catch-up learning and imitating, with some rivals learning and imitating faster than others. *Imitation* is copying behavior. It has also been colorfully described as swiping others' ideas. For example, Anita Roddick, a seaside hotel manager in England, thought up the idea of making "natural" cosmetics out of fruit and vegetable oils rather than animal fats. She launched Body Shop in 1976 which now has some 1,000 stores around the world. But she was slow to open stores in the United States and this allowed the cosmetic firm Estee Lauder and the clothing firm, The Limited to launch their successful imitations. They win, she loses.

Often when a firm duplicates another firm's behavior it tries to advance and improve on the initial innovation. It imitates but it also adds a little innovation of its own. Care has to be taken in defining who is an innovator. Micro Instrumentation and Telemetry Systems invented the PC in the 1970s, but it was Apple Computer that make the first commercially successful personal computer with word-processing and spreadsheet capabilities. Royal Crown was first to the market with a diet cola for diabetics, but it took Coca-Cola only a year to establish its market leadership and to start creating today's huge diet segment. Often it is the early imitators with a great deal of

Table 1.1 What-To-Do Lists from the First Marketing Management Textbook[a]

How to Study the Market
Who are the people that make up the market?
Consideration of those who buy and those who influence the buyer.
  Men, women, or children?
  Rich or poor?
  Occupations.
  Environment-city, town, or country dwellers.
Where do they live?
  Is market international, national, sectional, or local?
  What limits it?
  Can it be extended?
  Climatic influence.
When do they buy?
  Buying seasons.
  Extending the seasons.
  When do buyers enter the market?
How do they buy?
  Is it hard or easy to change buying habits?
  Do they buy from dealers or from manufacturers?
  Do they expect credit?
  Do they buy in large or small quantities?
How much will they buy?
  Total consumption of all competing products.
  Is the market growing or shrinking?
  Total consumption in restricted territory.
  Per capita consumption.

[a] Ralph Starr Butler, *Marketing Methods and Salesmanship, Part I: Marketing Methods* (New York: Alexander Hamilton Institute, 1914), pp. 177–78, 195. This work was first published as a series of six pamphlets in 1910 for a marketing management course taught at the University of Wisconsin—Madison. It appears to be the first published educational material on the topic of marketing management. See Robert Bartels, *The History of Marketing Thought* (Columbus, OH: Publishing Horizons Inc., 1987), p. 25.

manufacturing or distribution clout and who are prepared to take the risk of a major market development that make the market, later being perceived as the market innovators. In short, the first mover does not always come to dominate a market.[1] The winner is often the early mover with the most resources, the most drive to risk their resources in developing the market, and the most drive to keep learning and improving its product and processes. They may not be the product innovator, but they become the market innovator.

The *study of marketing management* is the study of the innovative and imitative ways that firms identify and satisfy customers. Think how important it is to have drug companies innovate and imitate vigorously to get the very latest miracle drugs to cancer patients at as low a cost as possible. In such markets, the government attempts to actively encourage innovation by giving a stamp of approval declaring that a particular drug cures a certain type of cancer and also by undertaking comparative benchmark tests called clinical trials. In April 1996 the Federal Drug Administration introduced a

[1] Gerard Tellis and Peter Golder, "First to Market, First to Fail? Real Causes of Enduring Market Leadership," *Sloan Management Review*, 37.2 (Winter 1996), 65–75.

(continued)

Comparison of consumption and production.
From whom do they buy?
Total number of competitors.
Resources of each.
Relative strength of competitors.
Prosperity and goodwill of each.
Marketing methods of competitors.
Sales channels.
Prices and profits.
Transportation problems.
Influence on size of market.
Influence on prices, profits, and other selling factors.

Steps in Reaching the Market

1. Selection of trade channels.
2. Determination of sales policies.
    Advertising.
    Credit.
    Price maintenance.
    Returned goods.
    Guarantees.
    Treatment of customers.
3. Charting the cost of marketing.
    Complete budget of estimated expenditures, sales, and profits.
4. Organization of salesmen and of advertising.
    Definite schedules of all forms of selling activity.
5. Coordinating the salesmanship and advertising.
6. Getting distribution and cooperating with dealers.
7. Plan for detailed records of actual expenditure, sales, and profits.

number of new innovations into its approval processes to speed up this stamp of approval. In economic terms this is known as making the market more efficient.

Obviously, not every product is a cure for cancer, and, in fact, most are much more humble products. However, the general principle applies to all products, great and small: consumer satisfaction with products increases at a faster rate in markets where there is a lot of innovation and imitation, that is, a lot of successful marketing management.

The Evolution of Marketing-Management Thought

The study and teaching of marketing management has followed its own evolutionary process of innovation and imitation. About one hundred years ago a small group of economists, frustrated with mainstream economic thinkers who were not interested in studying the rapid development of new marketing channels occurring in the "real" world, founded the modern study of marketing management. They combined the "what-to-do" lists of tasks and rules that trade schools for selling and merchandising taught (see Table 1.1) with their academic study of the new types of wholesaling and retailing institutions, such as department stores and chain stores.

To the rules of selling and merchandising (that had been handed down for hundreds of years from one generation of merchants to the next) was added advertising principles and practices learned by the founders of the modern advertising agency. From the study of and teaching of department and chain-store retailing and mail-order selling grew distribution and logistics management. To cost-plus-pricing principles was added demand elasticity-based pricing. From consumer motivation research grew new product development management.

In the late 1950s and early 1960s, innovative marketing management textbook writers such as Jerome McCarthy, John Howard, and Philip Kotler started to integrate all of the aspects of product, place, promotion, and price (the four *P*'s of marketing) into a general subject and a single textbook.[2] These early marketing management books emphasized three concepts that are almost always taught in today's introductory marketing courses and are worth reviewing: (1) serving the customer, (2) achieving synergies among the marketing programs, and (3) the product life cycle.

Serving-the-Customer Concept

It may seem obvious that the fundamental goal of a firm is to identify and satisfy customer needs. However, hundreds of case studies taught in business schools for the past seventy years have identified that firms often fail to *continue* to successfully identify and satisfy customer needs. Instead, they take their eyes off the customers and focus on other goals, such as achieving internal organization efficiencies, developing new technology for its own sake, or settling internal political fights among individuals, functions, or divisions.

Sometimes firms focus on customers but not their customers' most important need. For example, BIC has emphasized razor disposability. But disposability is not the *most important* reason for buying a razor. People do not buy a shaver primarily for its convenience. They buy a shaver to shave. Gillette understood this in introducing its reusable Sensor razor in 1989—"the best [shave] a man can get." Using the same advertising appeal around the world, this product innovation has increased sales by 50 percent and profits by 30 percent. It cannot be easily imitated because it has product and process patent protection and is being constantly improved (see Figure 1.1). Gillette also created a Sensor for Women. Its key advertised benefit, in addition to the quality of the blade, is a flat handle with grip that works better in the shower.

The concept of never taking your eyes off the customers is deemed so fundamental to a company's survival and success that it has become known as *the* marketing concept. Of course, merchants have been applying the concept for thousands of years without phrasing it this way. The early Dutch and Spanish explorers applied the marketing concept before setting out on their global trading missions. They learned to fill the holds of their ships with chests full of mirrors, scissors, medicines, ribbons, and bolts of cloth of the "right" color. Solomon's riches were made from his "marketing manager's" shrewd appreciation of how much his Phoenician world-trading neighbors needed his timber and grain. The most successful Neolithic traders presumably also applied the concept.

Some modern writers have elevated this marketing concept to a moral maxim: The only correct and ethical way to earn profits is to earn them through maximizing

[2] See Robert Bartels, *The History of Marketing Thought* (Columbus, OH: Publishing Horizons, Inc., 1987), Chapter 11.

Figure 1.1 **Gillette's Continuous Shaving Innovations**

During the past ninety years the Gillette company launched the safety razor, the stainless steel razor blade, the disposable plastic razor, the twin blade, the Sensor, and now the SensorExcel. Hundreds of millions of dollars spent on product development and consumer shaving tests support and substantiate the company claim that Gillette products provide a shave that is "the best a man can get."

customer satisfaction. But as you shall soon see, it is not the essential moral goodness of managers that leads them to try to outdo each other in satisfying the customer; it is the harsh reality of competition. The greater the competition, the harder a firm must work at increasing customer satisfaction. It is a matter of survival. If any laws govern marketing management, the first law is that *competition forces sellers to focus on satisfying the customer.*

You will also see that focusing on changes in customer behavior (a customer orientation) is ever more important today, but it is not sufficient. To succeed, the modern firm, large or small, must also study changes in competitor behavior, changes in wholesaler and retailer behavior, and changes in government regulations. It must be market oriented. To be *market oriented* is to be alert to and respond to any important changes in the market, including changes in customer behavior.

The Synergy Concept

Synergy is combining actions so their cumulative effect is more than the sum of the effects of the actions when undertaken separately; that is, a positive interaction occurs among the actions. For example, synergy is often achieved by combining the following actions: selecting retailers whose business and reputation are growing, offering financing terms to these retailers, mentioning the retailers' names in advertising if they contribute to advertising the product, and, finally, training and motivating company sales representatives to sell this package of tactics. The underlying principle is that *the firm that creates marketing tactics that fit together well and coordinates their implementation in the right order will do much better than the firm whose tactics and implementation are confused and disjointed.* This principle is so fundamental and has proven to be so true over the years that it also qualifies as a law of marketing management. One of the major reasons why marketing management departments were created in firms and why brand and product managers were hired in large numbers in the 1960s and 1970s was to plan and implement synergies among marketing programs. Today, the use of the synergy principle has advanced far beyond the integration and coordination of marketing tactics. It is now applied to coordinating all of the value-added processes of the firm, such as procurement, manufacturing, order processing, distribution, selling, and after-sales service. This search for synergy efficiency and effectiveness among organization processes and programs is now often undertaken by cross-functional teams and is called total quality management (TQM).

The Product Life-Cycle Concept

The product life-cycle concept likens the life of a product to that of a living organism, with a birth stage, a growth stage, a mature stage, and a decline (death) stage. Figure 1.2 presents these stages and some "what-to-do" lists at each stage. The product life cycle can be studied at various levels, from the life cycle of a single model of a specific product to the life cycle of a whole industry. It is probably most useful to think of the life cycle for product forms, such as supercomputers, photocopiers, or handheld calculators. Life cycles for product forms include definable groups of direct competitors, a core technology, and broad groups of users/buyers. These characteristics make life cycles for product forms easier to identify and analyze.

However, the analogy has its limitations. Most products and services go through many innovation/imitation life cycles. Only fad products like Hoola-Hoops have a single life cycle. Each new, clever innovation in product design or distribution also has its own path of introduction, acceptance, and imitation. Thus a market is full of innovations in products and processes at various stages in their path through introduction, growth, imitation, maturity, and death. The combination of all of these paths is the product-market life cycle. The basic point to remember is that types of products and methods of distribution come and go, but the basic benefits they provide consumers remain the same.

Toward a New Theory of Marketing Management

Is marketing management more than lists of what-to-do supported by some concepts and principles? Does it have its own underlying theory? Some people believe it does,

Figure 1.2 **Product Life-Cycle Stages and Marketing Tactics**

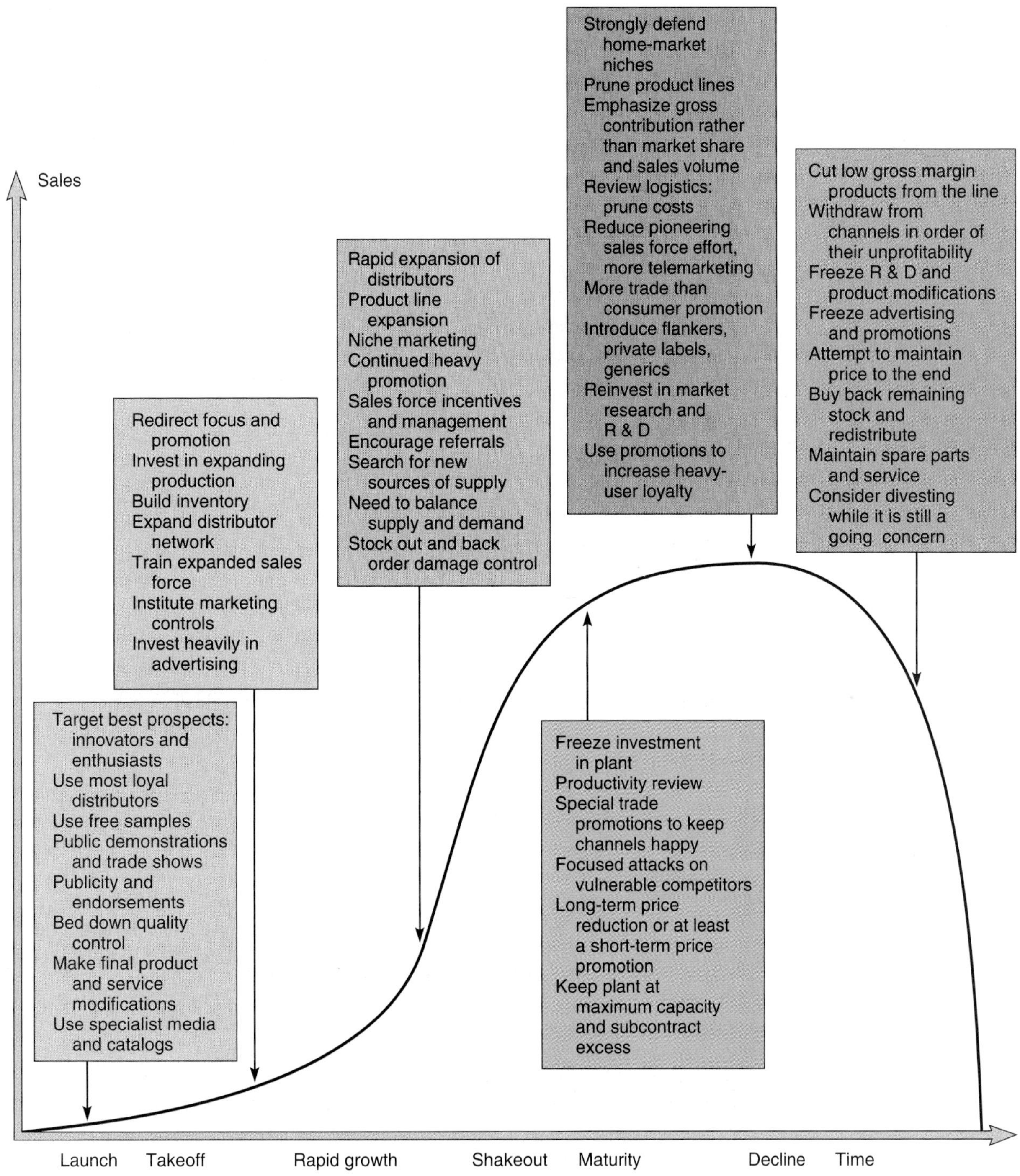

Some of the commonly prescribed competitive tactics are listed at each stage of the innovation/imitation life cycle. The figure illustrates that marketing programs should fit the competitive situation and that marketing programs also determine the next stage of the market.

but most academics and practitioners probably would be hard-pressed to describe their theory of marketing management. But the prospect of marketing management developing its own theory is quite promising.

Today we have broad and in-depth theories of consumer behavior, information processing, information economics, managerial decision making, organization economics, and evolutionary economics that can be used to weave together a richer and more realistic general theory of marketing management. Creating such a cloth that practitioners can cut to fit their thinking and management is in the tradition of Wroe Alderson, whose extraordinary creative thinking in the early 1950s was based on theories of continuous market adaptation and evolution, particularly, evolving channel relationships.[3] Alderson's thinking was much closer to the path that the Austrian economists Ludwig Von Mises, Joseph Schumpeter, and Friedrich August Von Hayek took that emphasized innovation and market learning rather than price equilibrium analysis.

The Delta (Δ) Paradigm

A *paradigm* is a way of looking at and thinking about something—a different perspective that focuses on a different unit of analysis and uses a set of theories to explain different new concepts and phenomena. Marketing-management writing and teaching is going through a paradigm shift. It is changing its focus from *equilibrium management*—why and how markets settle down into a comfortable state of competitive equilibrium. It is shifting its focus to *disequilibrium management*—why and how markets are constantly changing through the continual development of more competitive products and production processes. It is changing its focus from studying static exchange to studying dynamic relationships—how developments in communication and transportation are changing future (it is hoped long-term) trading relationships. It is called the delta paradigm because in calculus a delta (Δ) is used to represent change in a variable.

The new paradigm says do not ask about customer satisfaction; ask about change in customer satisfaction. Do not ask about company culture; ask about change in company culture. Do not ask about law; ask about change in law. Do not ask about distribution channels; ask about change in distribution channels. Do not ask about market share; ask about change in market share. Do not ask about costs; ask about change in costs. And do not ask about the time it takes; ask about change in the time it takes. Opportunities and threats come from a changing environment; company strengths and weaknesses come from changing the organization.

The reason for this paradigmatic shift in thinking is simple. Yesterday's lists of what-to-do and how-to-do-it are not good enough for today, let alone tomorrow. Perhaps in the past a successful marketing executive could be a walking and talking book of lists. This is certainly not so today. Today's marketing executive must be a creative breaker of rules on how things should be done, a driven advocate for change, and a player in a team whose purpose is to create change. The next section describes why this is so.

[3] See Wroe Alderson, *Marketing Behavior and Executive Action: A Functionalist Approach to Marketing Theory* (Homewood, IL: Richard D. Irwin, 1957).

Hypercompetition: Coping with Rapid Change

For several centuries Western cultures had such a technological lead that they possessed most of the options and hence most of the trading power. For example, when Britain "ruled the waves," its mighty navy and merchant fleet enabled it to control most of the world's commerce. Now no single nation "rules the waves," be they sea waves or airwaves. The services of the Internet and international airlines are available to any firm in every nation. The United States is undoubtedly the world's mightiest military power. But in a world of open, free markets, economic power is no longer tied to military power as it has been in the past. Thus, as the whole world joins and enjoys the modern global manufacturing, distribution, and communication economy, buyers have many more options, and they are free to exercise them. All markets are becoming more competitive, and trading relationships are harder to maintain. Customer relationships need to be supported by steadily improved service and consideration. Customers are less forgiving of design mistakes, delivery delays, or exaggerated claims. They are less forgiving because they have plenty of attractive alternatives. As services and product quality increase, customers expect markets to be more efficient in serving their needs—and these expectations are ever increasing.

The political and technological advances of the past twenty years have created a state of hypercompetition in an increasing number of product and service markets. *Hypercompetition* is when several sellers are aggressively innovating new products, distribution channels, and cost-cutting programs and quickly imitating each others' innovations.[4] An example of a hypercompetitive market is the personal computer market from about 1990 on. As the amount of innovation in products and processes increases in a market, the amount of improvisation behavior also increases. *Improvisation behavior* is deliberate, purposeful, impromptu action taken in response to an unexpected event in the market or within the company.[5] It often involves the fast imitation of an innovator's product or process or cutting the price of a now obsolete product. Some very interesting things happen in hypercompetitive markets with a lot of innovation and improvised imitation.

Characteristic Behavior of Hypercompetitive Markets

1. *Advantages do not last.* Any competitive advantage created by innovation in a hypercompetitive market does not last long because it is rapidly imitated or in some other way countered. This explains why the financial guru Warren Buffet has said, "Major sustainable competitive advantages are almost non-existent in the field of financial services" and why the chief executive officer (CEO) of American Airlines, Robert Crandall, said, "This business is intensely, vigorously, bitterly, savagely competitive." Many service markets are hypercompetitive because a new service innovation can be very quickly imitated, much faster than a new product design.

   In effect, hypercompetition changes the rules of the marketplace. According to Richard D'Aveni, "The only enduring advantage results from the ability to generate new advantages . . . the skill of generating new cost and quality advantages *is* sustainable." In his book *The Competitive Advantage of Nations,* Michael Porter says, "A firm's ability to sustain its success is most likely a result of constant innovation to adapt to changing

[4] Richard A. D'Aveni, *Hypercompetition* (New York: The Free Press, 1994).
[5] See Christine Moorman and Anne S. Miner, "The Role of Improvisation in Product Development and the Evolution of Markets," Graduate School of Business, University of Wisconsin—Madison, 9-94-14.

circumstance."[6] The notion that a firm's core competitive competence is its ability to be constantly improving its products and customer services is also supported by experts who study the evolution of technology:

> The failure to keep up with innovation is really the failure to develop and focus core competencies in the direction of change and progress. And that direction is often unclear except in hindsight. The U.S. tire industry represents a case in which firms increased their core competence, but not in the direction [the technological path] that had a promising future. Tire producers continued to develop their ability to manufacture bias-ply tires when they should have been learning to design and manufacture the new radials being produced in Europe."[7]

2. *New market segments are created.* Not all change in a hypercompetitive market is produced by sharp break advances in technology. It often comes about by targeting and serving (creating) new market segments or niches in seemingly stable markets. For example, several years ago the $1 billion cat food market was invigorated by new entrants providing gourmet cat foods, diet cat foods, and foods for different cat life stages, such as for kittens. All of these new segments earned higher profit margins, but new entrants and the resulting fight for shelf space in the supermarket have made the market hypercompetitive.
3. *Distribution innovations are very important.* Innovations in how a product is distributed have revolutionized marketing in many markets. For example, Gateway and Dell specialize in mail-order selling of high-end computers to experienced users. Such users know what they want and are willing to buy sight unseen. They can be sold by telemarketing computer techies like themselves. In addition to the cost savings in eliminating the intermediary, because they can build to order and deliver often within forty-eight hours they do not need to carry as much finished goods inventory. They can also launch new models with the latest processors and disk drives up to three months faster than rivals who sell through traditional dealers or mass merchants.[8]
4. *Hypercompetitive markets feed on themselves.* Hypercompetitive markets that have a great deal of innovation in product design and distribution can develop a momentum that makes them even more competitive. In a hypercompetitive market, one firm's improvised response to a rival's unexpected innovative behavior is yet another firm's unexpected event that itself requires an improvised response. Thus improvisation triggers further improvisation that leads to further unexpected changes in the market that require another improvised response. Thus the amount of innovation/imitation in a market can build. In such a market, a firm's ability to keep up with the change, let alone lead it, can be sorely tested, and often firms end up "shooting themselves in the foot." It is not the competitors who hurt them; they hurt themselves by making bad improvisation decisions. For example, in 1989 Toshiba, the leader in U.S. laptop computer sales, did not respond effectively to Compaq's introduction of the even smaller and yet more powerful notepad computer. Toshiba's disastrous improvised response was to fire its master distributor (only to switch back to it a year later). This opened up the opportunity for other rivals, such as Compaq, IBM, AST, and Dell, to strengthen their position in the market by leapfrogging each other with improvements in processor speed and memory storage. It took until 1994 for Toshiba to regain some of its innovation leadership back from Compaq by introducing notepads with a very fast, cool running chip that eliminated a noisy fan (and extended battery life) and with a vibrant color display.[9]

---

[6] Michael E. Porter, *The Competitive Advantage of Nations* (New York: The Free Press, 1991), 65.
[7] James M. Utterback, *Mastering the Dynamics of Innovation* (Boston, MA: Harvard Business School Press, 1994) 219–20.
[8] Peter Burrows, "The Computer Is in the Mail (Really)," *Business Week*, January 23, 1995, 76–77.
[9] Larry Holyoke, "How Toshiba's Laptops Retook the Heights," *Business Week*, January 16, 1995, 86.

Such pell-mell acceleration in the rate of change as has occurred in the notepad personal computer (PC) market finally dies down as technological cost or customer satisfaction improvements become only incremental and less profitable. The need to respond is less, so a cycle of improvised innovation and imitation is completed until the next technological breakthrough is made (such as a low-cost read-and-write CD-ROM for notepads or built-in cellular digital communication that enables wireless access to the Internet).

5. *Price wars are common.* Finally, not all hypercompetition is innovation. Sometimes it is combined with an old-fashioned price war such as occurred in 1992 in the U.S. television market. Prices for a twenty-seven-inch set dropped from around $800 to as low as $400. In such markets, low "sale" prices that attract economy shoppers may become the permanent name of the game for product models made obsolete by new innovations.

How to Think about a Hypercompetitive Market

Imagine you are working for a company that is competing in a market that is heating up to a hypercompetitive level. How are you going to organize your thinking about how the market works? Does it even matter how you organize your thinking? The answer is "no" if you are happy being a low-level executive whose job is most at risk. The answer is "yes" if you wish to help make your firm more competitive and keep your job by *thinking* about what you are doing on the job! It will also help you get promoted to a job where your thinking earns you tens of thousands of dollars more. So, to think about how a market works, you need to develop your own mental model of how competitive markets work. A *mental model* is used to organize our thinking about something, to explain how it works, and to forecast what is likely to happen next. It might take the form of a diagram, figure, or formula that we visualize in our head. Whatever it is, it forms the basis for intuitive understanding, hypotheses, conjectures, and decision making. Later in this chapter, such a mental model of how competitive markets work is developed. It is a theory that describes how markets change. But first some inspiring examples of great marketing-management thinking are presented that illustrate how the theory has been used by practitioners.

Great Marketing-Management Thinking

The free-market economy's central principle and driving force is competition among the minds of company leaders to more efficiently serve and satisfy consumers in the global marketplace. *Competitive rationality* is the marketing decision making of a firm in a competitive market.[10] It is competitive because the firm operates in a market with many firms making similar decisions. It is rational in that the firm attempts to be logical in developing and servicing exchanges with customers in an evolving market.

Stories about great marketing entrepreneurs such as Cyrus McCormick (farm equipment), DeWitt Wallace *(Reader's Digest)*, Ray Kroc (McDonald's), Tom Watson (IBM), Mary Kay (cosmetics), Bill Gates (Microsoft), and Sam Walton (Wal-Mart) are both fascinating and inspirational (see the Rationality in Practice box). The similarities in their methods of competitive rationality are striking. Accomplished marketing entrepreneurs develop extraordinary insight, often based on years of studying a particular market. They also develop and execute marketing strategies that fit the

[10] Peter Reid Dickson, "Toward a General Theory of Competitive Rationality," *Journal of Marketing* 56 (January 1992): 69–83.

Rationality in Practice

DeWitt Wallace and Reader's Digest

Like many great entrepreneurial ventures, the story of DeWitt Wallace is one of triumph over adversity. Many publishing houses had turned down Wallace's idea for a new type of magazine. They told him that publishing condensed, secondhand articles from other magazines would never fly. So in 1922, Wallace launched the venture himself using a direct-marketing campaign aimed at potential subscribers. The following are some of the brilliant insights and strategies that have made *Reader's Digest* such a success.

- Wallace observed that even people who were bored still skimmed magazine articles. He recognized what later academic research demonstrated: Even good writing can be condensed with little loss of information and *increased* reader satisfaction.
- Many magazines adopt a theme and a style that fit the times (for example, *Playboy* in the 1950s and 1960s), but they become dated as societal values change. The articles in *Reader's Digest* are often about freedom, optimism, faith in the goodness of other people, compassion, love, and personal development. These themes are universal and enduring. Maintaining this focus allowed *Reader's Digest* subscriptions to grow throughout the Roaring Twenties, the depression years of the thirties, and the war years of the forties.

THE READER'S DIGEST

THIRTY-ONE ARTICLES EACH MONTH FROM LEADING MAGAZINES • EACH ARTICLE OF ENDURING VALUE AND INTEREST, IN CONDENSED AND COMPACT FORM

The front page of the first issue of *Reader's Digest* reveals its positioning.

business environment. Almost all made decisions based on intuition. Few of them left written marketing plans behind to show business historians how these successful decisions were made. They had it all in their heads, or at least a good deal of it.

Great marketing entrepreneurs know how to come up with an idea, run it by the known market facts, and make it work. One of the singular advantages of the driven, autocratic entrepreneur is that his or her visions, personal objectives, or plans clearly define the self-interests of the enterprise and direct its behavior. The entrepreneur's personal drive is infectious and energizes the whole enterprise to strive to become more competitive. Sometimes companies that are not led by the founder or an entrepreneurial chief executive cannot even manage to define their self-interests. When this happens, decision making and management can become

A recent issue of *Reader's Digest.*

- Many magazines are directed at either men or women. *Reader's Digest* positioned itself as a family magazine. Wallace's wife was the copublisher, and they balanced the content to be of interest to both husbands and wives. This positioning became extremely valuable in later years when it came to selling advertising to companies marketing products to *both* spouses.
- Wallace recognized that he was vitally dependent on his suppliers—competing magazines. Initially, other magazines were happy to receive the free publicity that came from the publication of their articles in condensed form. They let Wallace publish their articles for free, keeping his production costs very low. Wallace could choose the best articles from one hundred or more magazines. Perhaps his most brilliant strategy was to refuse to accept outside advertising for the first thirty years of the magazine's existence. It was a great selling point to his consumers and to his suppliers, who were in competition for the advertising revenue. It also meant that *Reader's Digest* could keep a low competitive profile because it did not have to publish its circulation figures.

DeWitt Wallace possessed a unique understanding of magazine readers and their reading behavior. He also understood how to handle his competitors so well that they became the low-cost suppliers of his stories. Few marketers have been able to achieve such a feat.

SOURCES: Charles W. Ferguson, "Unforgettable DeWitt Wallace," *Reader's Digest*, February 1987, 1–20; and Samuel A. Schreiner Jr., *The Condensed World of the Reader's Digest* (New York: Stein and Day, 1977).

hopelessly mired in political squabbles among the various factions within an enterprise. Many large U.S. companies have had such leadership problems.

But successful marketing entrepreneurs do more than invent and market new products and services. They build enterprises that enable them to mass produce and market their products and services. The entrepreneur's creative genius combines with energy, courage, and the ability to lead and manage others to create one of the most important entrepreneurial skills—the ability to implement strategy. Entrepreneurs are able to coordinate and schedule the many activities involved in executing their innovative ideas. Other common planning characteristics are listed in Table 1.2. Marketing entrepreneurs also energize the market economy. They change the behavior of consumers and teach rivals to either change their behavior or lose customers, income, and profits.

Table 1.2 **Common Elements in the Marketing Skills of Great Entrepreneurs**

1. They possess unique environmental insight, which they use to spot opportunities that others overlook or view as problems.
2. They develop new marketing strategies that draw on their unique insights. They view the status quo and conventional wisdom as something to be challenged.
3. They take risks that others, lacking their vision, consider foolish.
4. They live in fear of being preempted in the market.
5. They are fiercely competitive.
6. They think through the implications of any proposed strategy, screening it against their knowledge of how the marketplace functions. They identify and solve problems that others do not even recognize.
7. They are meticulous about details and are always in search of new competitive advantages in quality and cost reduction, however small.
8. They lead from the front, executing their management strategies enthusiastically and autocratically. They maintain close information control when they delegate.
9. They drive themselves and their subordinates.
10. They are prepared to adapt their strategies quickly and to keep adapting them until they work. They persevere long after others have given up.
11. They have clear visions of what they want to achieve next. They can see further down the road than the average manager can see.

A General Theory of Competitive Rationality

The basic premise of the theory of competitive rationality is that different types of sellers and buyers exist; some buyers and sellers are innovators, most are followers, and yet others are laggards. Variations in the response rate of buyers *and* sellers to changes in supply and demand create opportunities that can be exploited by the innovators or being an innovator would have no advantage. If every buyer responded in the same way, at the same time and every seller responded in the same way, at the same time, economic competition would be very different from what we observe. Figure 1.3 is a model of the dynamic competitive process in a typical oligopolistic market (a market with only a few major sellers). The model applies to any market, from one as small as a rural town in Georgia to one as large as the entire global economy. It is a model that can be used to mentally visualize market dynamics.

The Macro Theory of Competitive Rationality

According to the *Bicycle Institute of America* and the *Bicycle Manufacturers Association*, in 1987 46 percent of the bikes sold were lightweight adult bikes, 42 percent were children's bikes, and 12 percent were mountain bikes. In 1992 58 percent sold were mountain bikes, 35 percent were children's bikes and 7 percent were lightweight bikes. What happened? Did consumer demand change on its own? No. An innovative supplier experimented with making and marketing what became known as "mountain bikes." Other manufacturers quickly imitated and added their own innovative improvements. Retailers reduced their orders for ten-speed racing bikes and increased their orders for the new mountain bikes. The new designs changed consumer preferences, and everyone making lightweight bikes had to quickly imitate. Note that it was not just a children's fad. The greatest change in demand occurred among adults.

The next Rationality in Practice box describes how one company, Bausch & Lomb, shaped its competitive environment. These two examples demonstrate how a market can be impacted by substantial improvements in product design, reductions in

Figure 1.3 **The Macro and Micro Theories of Competitive Rationality**

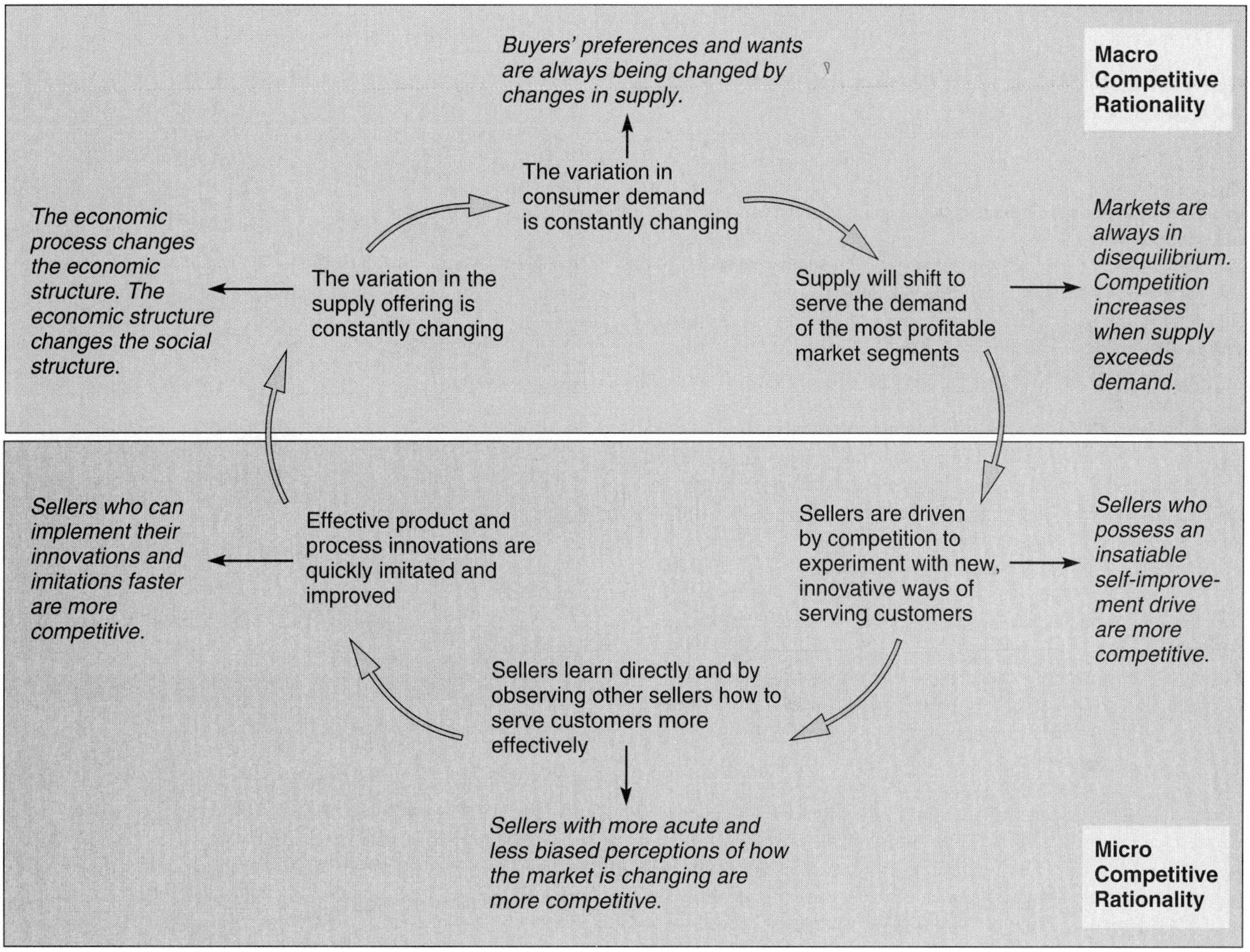
Macro Competitive Rationality
Buyers' preferences and wants are always being changed by changes in supply.
The variation in consumer demand is constantly changing
The economic process changes the economic structure. The economic structure changes the social structure.
The variation in the supply offering is constantly changing
Supply will shift to serve the demand of the most profitable market segments
Markets are always in disequilibrium. Competition increases when supply exceeds demand.
Sellers who can implement their innovations and imitations faster are more competitive.
Effective product and process innovations are quickly imitated and improved
Sellers are driven by competition to experiment with new, innovative ways of serving customers
Sellers who possess an insatiable self-improvement drive are more competitive.
Sellers learn directly and by observing other sellers how to serve customers more effectively
Sellers with more acute and less biased perceptions of how the market is changing are more competitive.
Micro Competitive Rationality

The top half of the figure describes macro market behavior; the bottom half describes an individual firm's micro behavior. The logical consequences and implications of the theoretical propositions are *italicized.* Each proposition serves as a basis for the next proposition. For example, the constantly changing variation in supply leads to a constantly changing variation in demand, which leads to supply shifting to serve the demand of the more profitable market segments, which creates a drive to try new ways of better serving the segments. This leads to new learning, which leads to more effective and faster imitation, which creates the constantly changing variation in supply. Unlike most theories, each proposition serves as a premise for a following proposition. This explains why there is not an obvious starting point in the figure. It also explains why competitive rationality is a dynamic theory of endless innovation/imitation cycles of product forms, distribution channels, and market behaviors, ever advancing along new efficiency and effectiveness learning paths.

production costs, and changes in distribution channels and competition. Consumer attitudes can be altered, public opinion shifted, laws changed, competitors driven away or acquired, and new channels established that change customer relationships. Other examples of how sellers change demand are Sony's introduction of the transistor radio

Rationality in Practice

How Bausch & Lomb Shaped the Soft-Contact-Lens Market

In 1971 Bausch & Lomb (B&L) developed and improved on a Czechoslovakian technique and began making and marketing a soft contact lens through ophthalmologists, optometrists, and opticians. For three years the company had the market to itself (a 100 percent market share) and behaved somewhat like the traditional monopolist. It charged high prices and upset some eye professionals. B&L charged them $25 to attend classes that taught how to fit soft lenses and required them to pay up front for large inventories. When competitors, who offered some design improvements and price cuts, entered the market, many of B&L's clients were eager to do business with the new rivals. By 1978, Bausch & Lomb's market share had plunged to 50 percent. In 1979 B&L's new chief executive introduced "new, improved" models, soothed upset customers, and cut prices by 28 percent. B&L had claimed that its secret production process was able to injection spin and cast a lens for $2, compared to the $5–$7 it cost the competition to manufacture a lathed lens. In addition, lathed lenses could not be reproduced with the same precision, which was important because the new soft lenses lasted only eighteen months on average, and individual refitting was expensive and time consuming for the customer.

A price-cutting war ensued, a Federal Trade Commission decision allowed the advertising of contact lens prices, and manufacturers granted big cooperative advertising allowances to retailers. These factors galvanized the large optical chains, such as Pearle and Sterling Optical. The retail price of a pair of contact lenses fell from $300 to less than $100. The number of wearers doubled in just two years to 5 million. Two-thirds of the new sales went to Bausch & Lomb. However, its competitive onslaught crippled a number of competitors and drove them into the arms of bigger, more market-oriented companies, such as Revlon and Johnson & Johnson. B&L's developing relationships with the emerging optical chains also infuriated the traditional channels, the independent optometrists, and opticians.

In 1981, Revlon and Cooper Vision introduced extended-wear lenses that could be worn continuously for a whole month. It took until 1983 for B&L to launch its extended-wear lens, but, when it did, it did so with a vengeance. Within four months, it had its product in 90 percent of the 12,000 eye-care outlets across the United States and claimed 37 percent of the extended-wear market. Its entry wholesale price of $20 was 50 percent or more below the industry average price for such lenses. Bausch & Lomb's production cost was estimated to have dropped to $1.10 per lens. Cooper Vision responded with a $15 price for its top-quality lens, and B&L reacted by dropping its premium product to $10–$15, depending on the distributor volume (thus giving the chains an advantage over the independents). Its sales immediately tripled.

By 1984 the replacement market had become very large, and market saturation was nowhere near in sight. While only a quarter of the 47 million Americans who needed vision correction were wearing soft lenses, many more millions were expected to enter the market when soft-lens bifocals were introduced and age caught up with the baby boomers. Also, tinted lenses have opened up a fashion market, with many users owning a pair of clear lenses *and* a pair of tinted lenses.

In 1987, Viskaton, a small division of Johnson & Johnson, beat Bausch & Lomb to the market with disposable contact lenses

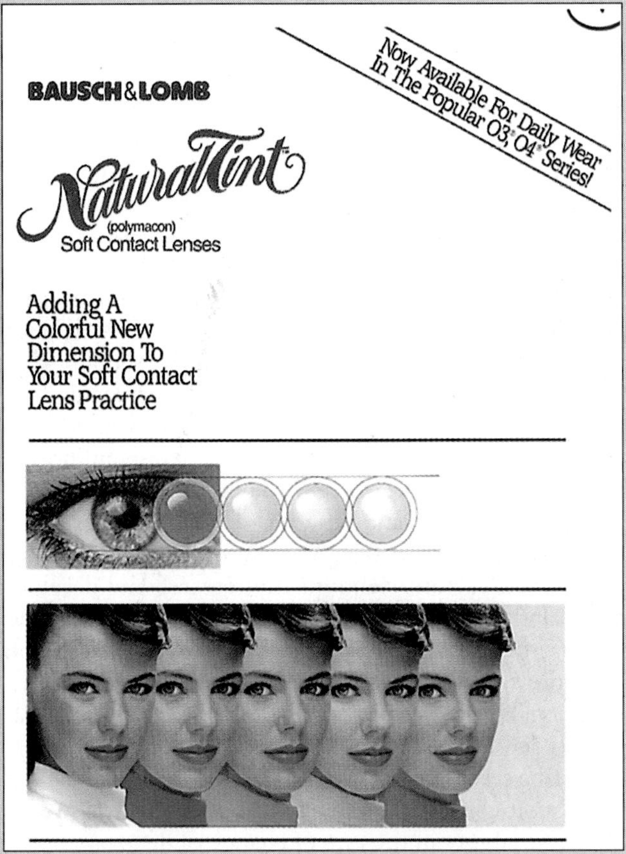

Colored soft contact lenses increased demand among existing contact users.

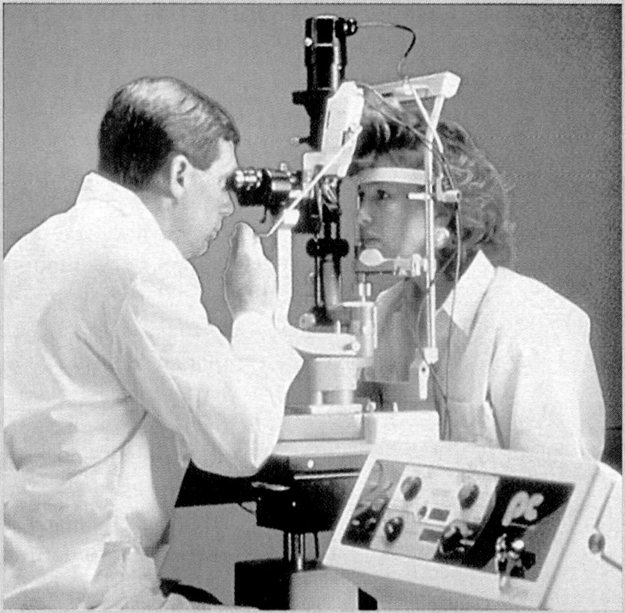

The 30-second laser refractive surgery in process.

that cost $250 per year but do not require the cleaning solutions that cost about $100 per year. Profits were high, and in 1990 the U.S. Department of Justice started an investigation of competitive practices.

However, the eye-care industry was about to undergo another turbulent period for two reasons. First, Wal-Mart and Kmart (working with Lenscrafters) entered the retail market by opening hundreds of full-service outlets within their stores by 1992. Second, corneal sculpting was developed in 1988 to permanently correct nearsightedness, farsightedness, and astigmatism. The laser refractive surgical procedure takes twenty to thirty seconds, and the entire operation takes about thirty minutes per eye, all at a cost of $1,000 to $2,000. Tens of thousands of consumers have had the surgery, and improved procedures are constantly being developed that reduce any slight risks, the cost, and the price. Meanwhile, Bausch & Lomb has lost much of its early control of the contact-lens market, and it appears likely that the new surgical service (which is certain to come down in price) will make glasses and contact lenses obsolete.

This history demonstrates how changes in technology, competition, distribution channels, and public policy influenced B&L's strategy. It also describes how B&L's strategy changed the competitive marketplace for both manufacturers and retailers, but it could not control the impact of the new eye surgery service on its products' long-term sales prospects.

SOURCES: This case was mainly based on the following articles: "Bausch & Lomb: Hardball Pricing Helps It to Regain Its Grip in Contact Lenses," *Business Week*, July 16, 1984, 78–80; Hugh D. Menzies, "The Hard Fight in Soft Lenses," *Fortune*, July 27, 1981, 56–60; "New Disposable Contact Lenses," *New York Times*, July 15, 1987, D4; Rebecca Perl, "Lasers May Mean Sight for Poor Eyes," *Atlanta Constitution*, October 3, 1991, C3; and Iving Arons, *Laser Focus World*, March 1992, 53–62.

and the Walkman. According to the Battelle Technology Management Group, in the next ten years we can expect new powerful, long-lasting batteries and anti-aging products to radically change consumer demand.

Innovations, such as color television, create demand but not uniformly across the whole market of interested consumers. Different potential buyers respond in various ways and at different rates to a new product or service innovation. Such variability in the response of buyers to a change in the offering often creates submarkets called market segments. *Market segments* are groups of consumers who seek the same benefits from a product or service (demand segments) or who have similar buying habits (shopping segments). Market segment analysis is discussed in detail in Chapter 5.

Changing supply changes demand, which further changes supply, which again changes demand, which further changes supply, as illustrated in Figure 1.4. Thus a market keeps evolving and evolves most in market segments where the suppliers believe they can make the most profits. Whether or not these beliefs are correct (and for markets to be efficient, it is hoped they are correct), that is the way markets work—always changing, sometimes a little and sometimes a lot, and always in disequilibrium. Entrepreneurial firms thrive on creating such disequilibrium. It plays to their strengths, which are dealing with uncertainty and reacting quickly.[11] Conversely, companies sometimes hurt themselves in panic, making poor improvised decisions—such as cutting prices and cutting back on feature and quality research and development (R & D), squeezing suppliers and distributors, or, worse, switching suppliers and distributors. The end result is that crucial trading relationships are destroyed and consumer trust and goodwill lost forever.

The theory of competitive rationality also answers a fundamental question: What are the minimum requirements needed to create and sustain a competitive, progressive market economy? There must be freedom of buyer and seller choice (including the absence of autocrats or cabals that constrain behavior), variability in the rate of change of supply among suppliers, variability in the rate of change of demand among buyers, and the desire for more profits rather than less profits. Under such conditions, a market will continue to increase customer satisfaction and the efficient use of resources. In a sense, the market becomes a perpetual motion machine, with each new state of disequilibrium changing seller behavior, which, in turn, creates a new state of disequilibrium. Markets do not mature; they rather ebb and flow in their rate of seller-driven change.[12]

This theory points out the limitations of being customer led. In the ten years that Harl Sperlich spent developing the minivan, first at Ford, which canned the project, and then Chrysler, neither firm ever received a letter from a consumer asking it to invent the minivan. The same situation applied to fax machines, ATMs, MTV, and CNN. As management experts Professor Gary Hamel and C.K. Prahalad have cleverly put it, U.S. companies often follow their customers, but their customers are following more imaginative foreign competitors.[13] They conclude that what is needed is

[11] Tom Peters, *Thriving on Chaos* (New York: Harper & Row, 1987).

[12] It also has been argued that it is not the "maturity" of an industry that determines the long-term profitability of a firm but rather the vitality and innovation of firms in an industry (that is, their competitive rationality) that determines the vitality and profitability of a market or industry. See Charles Baden-Fuller and John Stopford, *Rejuvenating the Mature Business* (London: Routledge, 1992), and Peter Reid Dickson, "Toward a General Theory of Competitive Rationality," *Journal of Marketing* 56 (January 1992).

[13] See Gary Hamel and C.K. Prahalad, "Seeing the Future First," *Fortune*, September 5, 1994, 64–70.

Figure 1.4 **The Perpetual Motion Machine That Increases the Efficiency of Free Markets**

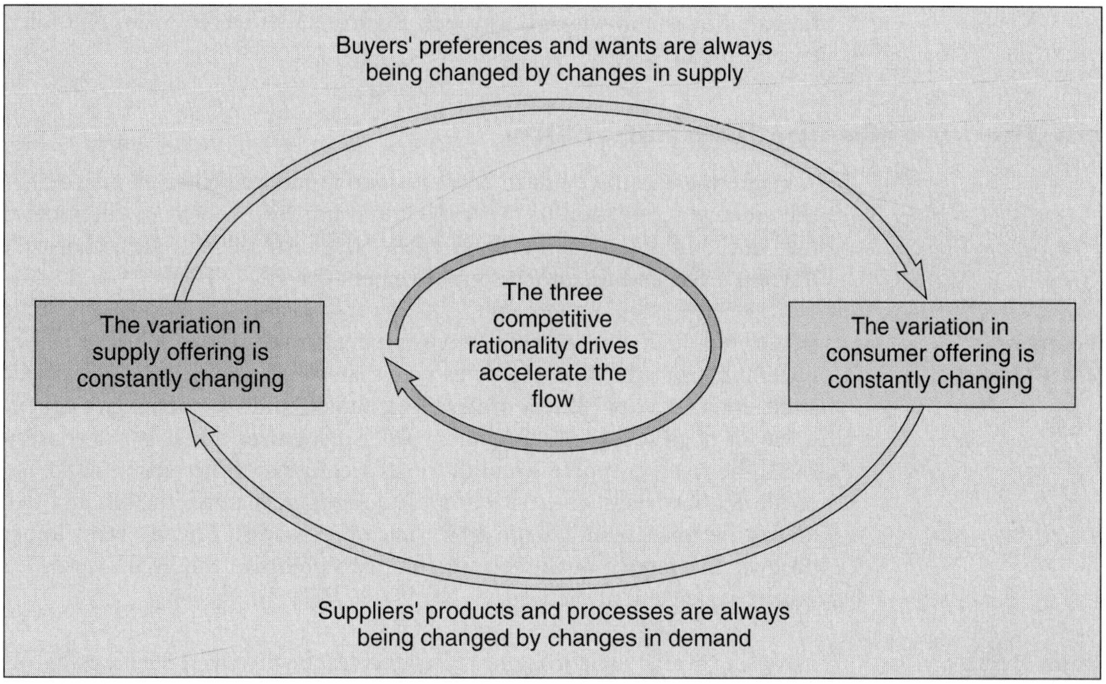
Buyers' preferences and wants are always being changed by changes in supply
The variation in supply offering is constantly changing
The three competitive rationality drives accelerate the flow
The variation in consumer offering is constantly changing
Suppliers' products and processes are always being changed by changes in demand

The constant two-way relationship between changing supply and demand is portrayed as a circular flow of influence. As mentioned in the section on hypercompetitive markets, the rate of change sometimes occurs in fast cycles and then decreases to a slow cycle. But as firms in the industry increase their experimentation, innovation/imitation alertness, and process implementation skills, the long-run trend will be for this circular flow to speed up (leading to ever-shorter life cycles for product models and distribution innovations). Remember that to survive, firms must compete on their ability to outthink the competition in terms of continuously improving (1) customer satisfaction, (2) reducing costs, and (3) increasing process-added value, speed, and efficiency. This dynamic improvement process is the essence of the theory of competitive rationality, and as shown, these three drives (continuously increasing customer satisfaction, reducing costs, and increasing process added value, speed, and efficiency) provide the forces that accelerate the circular flow. This is in effect an economic perpetual motion machine that is accelerating in its rate of change of supply and demand.

market foresight based on understanding trends in technology, consumer behavior, and other features of the market. But more than market foresight is needed. What is needed, as noted earlier, is the entrepreneurial drive to test such visionary foresight.

Because sellers want to increase profits, they will target their marketing efforts toward what they believe will become the most rewarding market segments to serve. This shifting of sellers' resources and marketing efforts to, for example, serving a new country, working women, or even overweight cats creates an imbalance of supply and demand in existing market segments (a market disequilibrium). Initially, the targeting of a new segment by a firm that has a superior fit to that segment results in more demand (a demand shift disequilibrium) for the firm's products or service. This increase in demand should result in greater profits for the firm compared to what it earned before it targeted the segment. Later on rivals learn about the segment and of the profits from serving that segment, some learning later than others. They then imitate, adding their own feature and service innovations, or lowering the price. This new excess supply (a supply shift disequilibrium) intensifies the rivalry to serve and satisfy consumers, which leads us into the micro theory of competitive rationality (illustrated by the downward arrow in Figure 1.3 between macro and micro competitive rationality).

The Micro Theory of Competitive Rationality

A marketing executive has to become good at innovation and imitation. It starts with the creative motivation to experiment and improve, which involves the three drives introduced in the caption of Figure 1.4—the customer satisfaction drive, the cost reduction drive, and the process improvement drive.

The Customer Satisfaction Drive

In a changing and competitive environment, in which the behavior of competitors is uncertain, can a decision maker be sure that what is being done today will, indeed, be sufficient tomorrow? Buyer preferences, choice, and satisfaction are dependent on the behavior of all sellers. An intelligent seller recognizes that it is in a contest with its rivals. The rivals compete to fulfill the expectations of the target market segment and create higher levels of satisfaction by designing, manufacturing, and delivering the quality performance that the target customer wants. The constant improvement of product and service quality are the first two points in the W. Edwards Deming total quality management method.[14]

The Process Cost Reduction Drive

Lowering average and marginal costs enables the firm to reduce a price, or to increase profits at the current price, and allows more options in decision making. Cost-cutting innovations are particularly attractive, because their resulting effects are more predictable than other innovations. Moreover, a firm has greater control over costs than it does over other aspects of its marketing. Cost innovations are also less likely to be detected and immediately imitated than are product or marketing program innovations. The simple and rational desire for greater profits leads decision makers to constantly seek new ways of reducing costs *without* affecting the potency of the output.[15] Modern information systems, which provide accurate and prompt feedback on price-reduction innovations, have made cost reduction more feasible.[16]

Modern management accounting is also in tune with the emphasis in the theory of competitive rationality on understanding and improving processes, as indicated by the following quote:

> Companies need to map and improve customer-focused processes. . . . The long-run global imperative, of course, is to find ways to reduce costs (primarily by removing constraints that cause delay, excess, and variation) of producing what the customer wants in the form the customer wants it. . . . I envision a business as a system of interre-

[14] Mary Walton, *The Deming Management Method* (New York: Putnam, 1986). Almost all of the total-quality-movement gurus emphasize the relentless drive to improve customer satisfaction.

[15] As will be discussed later, the total-quality-management approach is often able to achieve an increase in quality and a reduction in costs at the same time. It is true, however, that a firm has to be careful not to lower costs that will lead to a reduction in product or service quality that consumers notice.

[16] B. Charles Ames and James D. Hlavacek, "Vital Truths about Managing Your Costs," *Harvard Business Review*, January/February 1990, 140–47.

lated processes in which people are continually learning and inventing more fulfilling ways to profitably exceed the expectations of customers (internal and external).[17]

The bottom line for cost managers is that, like all other managers in the modern firm, they must understand processes and be *process thinkers*. Companies have learned the following three important principles of cost management to drive costs down:

1. Costs that are traceable to a process are controllable.
2. Cost managers measure costs better when they understand the processes that generate the costs.
3. The better the measures of process costs, the better is the knowledge of how to reduce costs.

The Process Improvement Drive

The competitively rational firm also relentlessly strives to improve its implementation and decision-making routines by using new information technologies and analytical tools and by moving from bureaucratic decision making to the new, cross-functional decision making.[18] The advantage of this drive is that it leads to new decision-making and implementation processes that create a unique, competitive organizational culture that is difficult to imitate. It also eliminates production and decision-making processes that add little or no value.

Figure 1.5 illustrates the changing competitive rationality of IBM in the personal computer market. In the early 1980s, IBM made the market with superb launches of its PC, XT, and AT models. However, by the middle to late 1980s, the quality of IBM's competitive rationality had clearly slipped. Several factors contributed to this decline: bureaucratic complacency, internal pressure from the powerful midsize and mainframe divisions to slow down further performance innovations that would cannibalize their sales, an inadequate awareness of the evolving market segments, and the innovations of competitors such as Compaq, Apple, Dell, and Toshiba.[19]

As part of its general effort to become more competitive, IBM has embarked on a massive business process-reengineering project. As explained in greater detail in Chapter 4, process engineering involves identifying the key competitive processes of the firm and then redesigning them to increase their productivity and speed. IBM identified seventeen such processes in 1990, but the effort to engineer them got bogged down by organization politics and defensive bureaucrats. A new process reengineering effort was launched by the new CEO, Lou Gerstner, and its success is most evident in the IBM PC Division. New product development time was cut from three years to two months, and the time to make a price change was cut from ninety days to twenty-four hours. The division is now organized into five teams in charge of

---

[17] H. Thomas Johnson, "It's Time to Stop Overselling Activity-Based Concepts," *Management Accounting*, September, 1992, 27–35, and in a reply to letters to the editor.

[18] William G. Ouchi, "A Conceptual Framework for the Design of Organizational Control Mechanisms," *Management Science* 25 (September 1979): 833–47; and "Markets, Bureaucracies, and Clans," *Administrative Science Quarterly* 25 (March 1990): 129–41.

[19] It is reasonable to assume that IBM was well aware of the parallels between the evolution of the calculator market and that of the PC market: Given the geometric increases in the power of the chips, the new generations of PCs that followed the original PC, the XT, and the AT would ultimately cannibalize the market for midrange and mainframe computers. IBM's fundamental competitive irrationality was that it did not allow the new generations of its PCs to aggressively attack its big-machine markets. The long-term consequence was that competitors were able to enter these markets by offering networks of PCs linked to a server. This outcome for IBM was even worse than the painful cannibalizing of its highly profitable midrange and mainframe products.

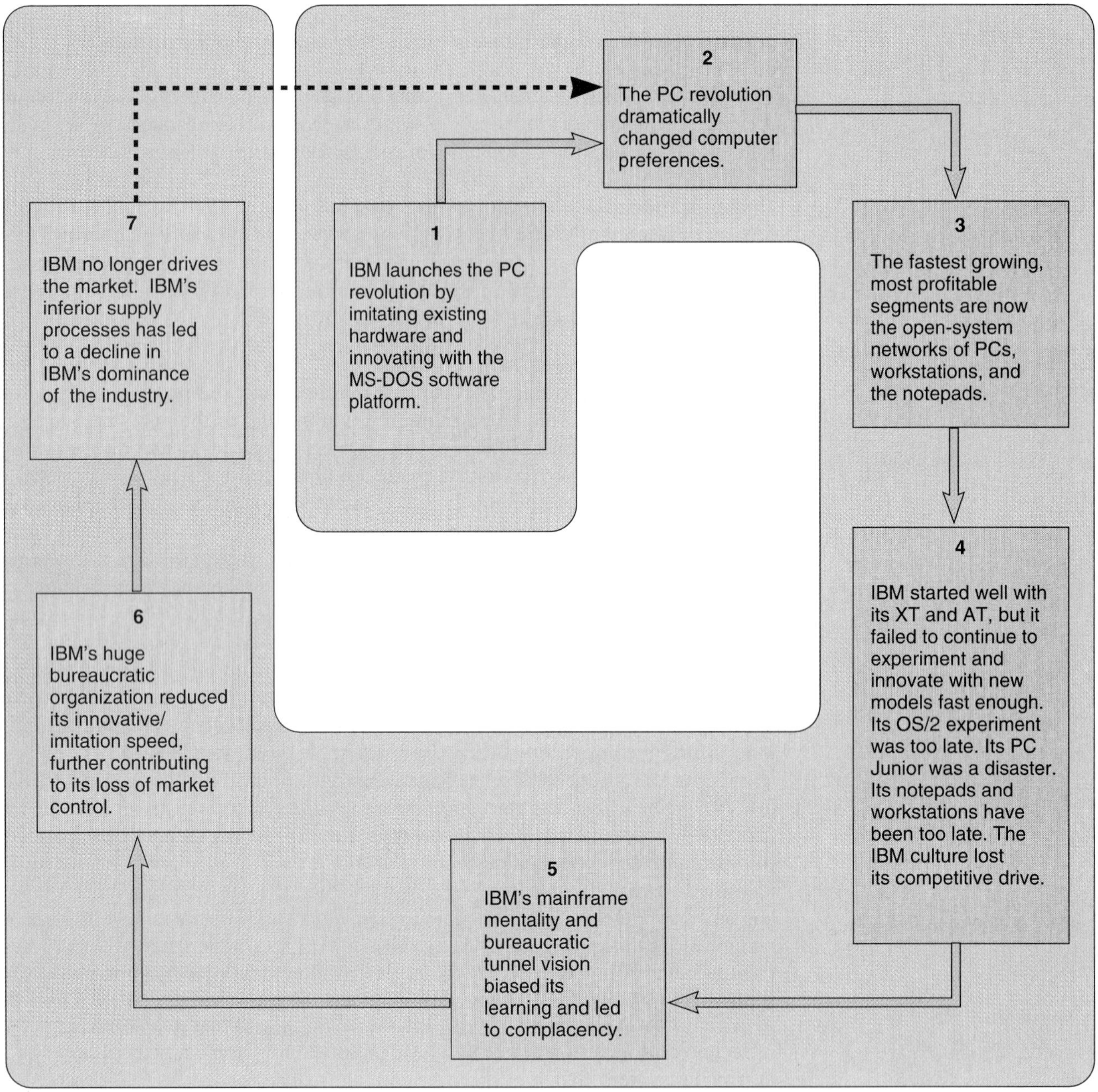
2
The PC revolution dramatically changed computer preferences.
3
The fastest growing, most profitable segments are now the open-system networks of PCs, workstations, and the notepads.
4
IBM started well with its XT and AT, but it failed to continue to experiment and innovate with new models fast enough. Its OS/2 experiment was too late. Its PC Junior was a disaster. Its notepads and workstations have been too late. The IBM culture lost its competitive drive.
5
IBM's mainframe mentality and bureaucratic tunnel vision biased its learning and led to complacency.
6
IBM's huge bureaucratic organization reduced its innovative/ imitation speed, further contributing to its loss of market control.
7
IBM no longer drives the market. IBM's inferior supply processes has led to a decline in IBM's dominance of the industry.
1
IBM launches the PC revolution by imitating existing hardware and innovating with the MS-DOS software platform.

Figure 1.5

The figure traces the hugely successful competitive rationality of IBM in its early years and its later competitive irrationality. Why IBM faltered is still unclear, but it had a lot to do with internal organizational resistance to the continued development of new super-powerful, networkable PCs, which threatened IBM's highly profitable midsize and mainframe product lines.

five different brands: the low-cost Value Point brand; Ambra, another line of low-cost PCs built in Asia by a subcontractor and sold mainly in Europe; the PS/1, targeted at the small-business and home user; the high performance PS/2; and, finally, the ThinkPad notepads.

The PC division's new products are also designed around some twenty modules that can be used across all of the brands. Modular product design has many advantages. It forces closer cooperation with suppliers and among suppliers; it encourages simpler, standardized designs with fewer parts and defects; and it enables lean, make-to-order manufacturing, which reduces inventory and unsold obsolete stock. The result has been the launch of outstandingly successful products, such as the ThinkPad 700, and an almost doubling of worldwide market share, up from a low of 10 percent in 1992. IBM does appear to be regaining the initiative in the PC market.

The firms with organizational cultures energized by the three micro drives strive the hardest in their search for new ways to efficiently serve consumers. These firms are constantly experimenting with new approaches that increase customer satisfaction, reduce costs, or increase the quality and speed of the firm's decision making and implementation. This ceaseless motivation to improve encourages sellers to learn from their own trial-and-error experiments, rivals' experiments, and the experiments of sellers in very different markets. The sellers that are most alert and able to learn from all three type of experiments are the most competitive. Alertness requires an acute, unbiased perception of change and the insightful consideration of its impact on all aspects of market decision making. However, it is normally not enough to be alert.

The mere formulation of creative new ideas is also insufficient. As mentioned earlier, the enterprise has to implement product and marketing strategies and tactics that are imitations and improvements on what has been learned from studying the market. Companies that are excellent at implementing have an inherent competitive advantage. They are able to change and adapt faster. That is why so much emphasis is being given these days to increasing the speed of new product development (see Table 1.3).[20] If several sellers are equally driven and equally knowledgeable, the firm that is fastest at implementation will win. Economic competition does have some parallels with natural evolution and the deployment of resources in military strategy.

Innovation Cycles and Imitation Paths

At any time, some sellers are changing their products/services, production, distribution, and marketing processes faster than others. In some mature markets, the rate at which suppliers change can be slow. In other high-growth markets, where a great deal of technological innovation (such as the personal computer market) occurs, the rate at which suppliers change is much faster. To visualize this in Figures 1.3 and 1.4, in mature markets the rate at which the arrows move in the figure is slow; in high-growth or hypercompetitive markets, the arrows move at a fast speed. In a sense, the speed of the circular flow in the figure represents the speed of individual firm and market learning. If market efficiency is related to the speed with which a market

[20] Brian Dumaine, "How Managers Can Succeed Through Speed," *Fortune*, February 13, 1989, 54–59; Joseph L. Bower and Thomas M. Hout, "Fast-Cycle Capability for Competitive Power," *Harvard Business Review*, November/December 1988, 110–18; George Stalk, "Time—The Best Source of Competitive Advantage," *Harvard Business Review*, July/August 1988, 41–51; and Murray R. Millson, S. P. Raj, and David Wilemon, "A Survey of Major Approaches for Accelerating New Product Development," *Journal of Product Innovation Management* 9 (1992): 53–69.

Table 1.3 Previous and New Product Development Time in Months

Jet engine	General Electric	84 to 48
Medical imaging	Polaroid	72 to 36
Trucks	Navistar	60 to 30
Printers	Hewlett-Packard	54 to 22
PCs	IBM	48 to 14
Thermostat	Honeywell	48 to 10
Checkout terminals	NCR	44 to 22
Airpowered grinders	Ingersoll-Rand	40 to 15
Phone switchers	AT&T	36 to 18
Electric clutch brake	Warner	36 to 9
Electronic pager	Motorola	36 to 18
Machining center	Cin. Milacron	30 to 12
Pampers phases	Procter & Gamble	27 to 12
Gas lantern	Coleman	24 to 12
Cordless phone	AT&T	24 to 12
Wedding rings	Feature Enterprises	4 to 0.25

SOURCE: Abbie Griffin, *Modeling and Measuring Product Development Cycle Time Across Industries*, Report No. 95–117, Cambridge, Mass.: Marketing Science Institute, 1995.

learns to improve customer satisfaction, reduce costs, and speed up processes, then an efficient market can be represented by faster circular flows of seller and buyer innovation/imitation.

The proposition that free markets are constantly evolving through an innovation/imitation process that accelerates, slows down to a trickle, and surges again assumes that product markets go through many cycles. Competitive rationality is a theory of endless innovation/imitation cycles, but some patterns in these cycles have been detected by business historians (see Chapter 6, "Competitive Analysis").

Markets go through cycles of turbulent innovation, followed by periods of slower change, of consolidation, and of relative stability. A cycle starts with pioneering product innovation, followed by a period of fluid trial and error until a dominant standard design emerges. A dominant design defines the way a product should look and perform in the minds of users, distributors, and producers. Certain performance features, such as the speed of a computer or its amount of memory, become the focus of competitive innovation and quick imitation. The realities of mass marketing, distribution, and service maintenance enforce greater standardization. When this happens, small, continuous improvements in product quality and product features occur, but the competitive focus switches to manufacturing and distribution process innovation—ways of reducing costs while increasing reliability and maintaining quality. Successful incremental improvement requires a persistent drive to measure product and process performance, and seek improvement from any and every source. But often the early choices in product and manufacturing process design often determine the development path that the market takes. This is called *path dependency*, such as occurred with typewriters, videocassette recorders (VCRs), and personal computers.

The fact that a computer store has three walls of software for DOS- and Windows-based PCs and only one for Apple Macintoshes is the result of a path dependency. In 1984 the Apple Macintosh's operating system was considered much better than the Microsoft DOS system. It was able to edit sound and pictures and to desktop publish and was an immediate hit with artists, designers, and academics. But Apple did not make its operating system available to other computer manufacturers, who by default used Microsoft DOS to imitate the performance of the IBM PC. The industry standard became DOS and then Windows and the development paths that most PC hardware and software manufacturers have taken. Apple is now trying to license its operating system, but it is proving difficult because it is so tied to Apple's unique "plug and play" hardware configurations. As commentators have pointed out, most companies would "kill" to own a $10 billion market niche with profit margins of more than 20 percent.[21] But is Apple facing the same path dependency outcome that Sony's Betamax faced when video rental stores offered three walls of VHS tapes for rent and one wall of Beta tapes for rent? If so, it would be a sad outcome for a company with a great record for product innovation. The lesson is that sometimes it is not enough to be a leader in technological innovation; marketers also have to know when to share the product in order to make it the industry standard and thus direct a market's development.

Cycles of innovation and imitation are not limited to improvements in product or service features. They occur in all aspects of marketing. For example, innovation and imitation in distribution have led to extraordinary increases in speed and reliability of physical distribution over the past ten years. At the same time that the *quality* of distribution services have dramatically increased, the *cost* of distribution of all products and services in the United States economy has been reduced by one-third, saving hundreds of billions of dollars in scarce resources! This cycle of physical distribution innovation and imitation has been one of marketing management's most important contribution to the modern world. Other less significant but more visible cycles of innovation in marketing practices have been the introduction of frequent-user promotions (starting in the airline industry), the introduction of comparative advertising, and the continuous use of customer satisfaction surveys.

Organization of the Text

The figure on the next page illustrates how the following chapters logically flow from one to the next. Our basic objective is to fit a firm's positioning, tactics, and programs to the realities of the market. Chapter 2 presents a STRATMESH decision-making procedure that helps design such a fit (and continue to improve the fit) between strategy, programs, and an ever-changing competitive environment. A firm uses its market research and decision-making processes to develop and continuously update the positioning and tactical programs of a product or service. A firm uses its organization, budgeting, and control to implement its positioning and programs. This explains why *Marketing Management* starts with a discussion of decision making and information gathering, moves on to an analysis of the market, positioning, and tactical programs, and ends with an examination of organization, implementation, and control.

At the heart of the text is Chapter 9, which explains how to position and develop a product or service that is better than the rival's product or service. Firms that are best at positioning and developing innovative new programs understand their markets better than do their rivals. Their competitive rationality (learning, decision making, and implementation) is better than their rivals. Superior thinking starts with analyzing

[21] "Paradise Lost," *The Economist*, December 10, 1994, 19–21.

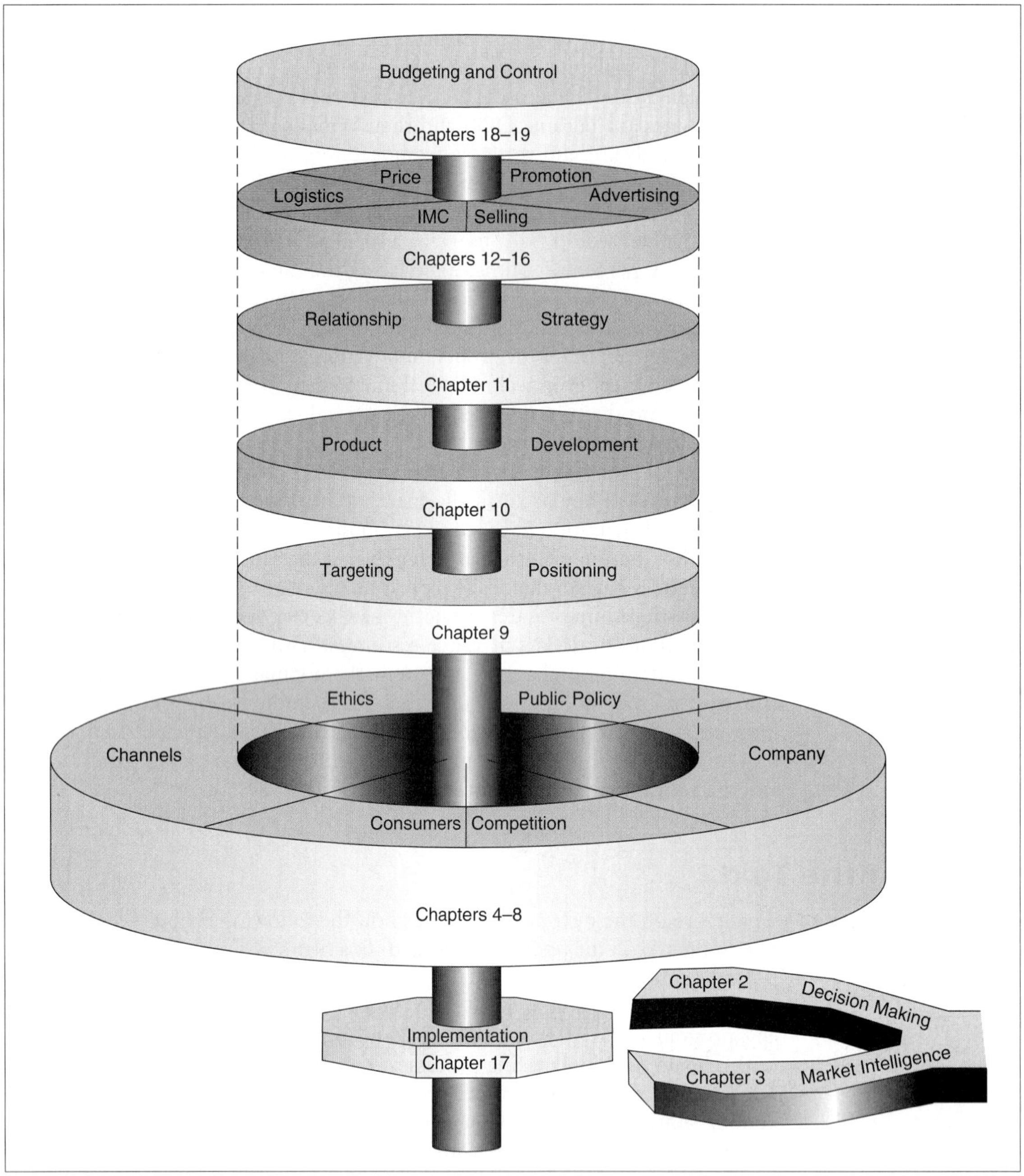

The book has a simple internal structure: five analysis chapters frame the positioning decision chapter, which, in turn, forms the foundation for the seven management chapters. The mental models, techniques, rules, and procedures described are decision-making frameworks and routines that, when used, increase a firm's competitive advantage by improving the firm's competitive thinking. The decision maker or cross-functional team has to fit the basic targeting positioning strategy to the five basic elements of the market environment. On top of the targeting-positioning level are the marketing management programs. The whole system is clamped together by implementing, budgeting, and controlling processes.

all of the elements that make up a market, which is why five chapters (Chapters 4 through 8) explore how to analyze buyers, competition, trading channels, public policy, the law and ethics, and the goals, strengths, and weaknesses of the firm.

Finally, in a world of continuous improvement, organization and implementation skills are crucial. One study revealed that recruiters believe that marketing programs should emphasize teaching students organization and implementation strategies (Chapter 17), ahead of interpersonal, planning, and decision-making techniques. The last chapters (Chapters 18 and 19) discuss how to forecast, budget, and control, using spreadsheets and databases.

Discussion Questions

1. Which of the following metaphors do you think best describes a competitive market: (1) a market is a car that is fueled by capital investments, or (2) a market is a perpetual motion machine. Please explain.
2. Why do firms adopt the marketing concept of focusing on and serving and satisfying the customer?
3. Karl Marx argued that the economic process is constantly changing and undermining the economic and political establishments. His mistake was to assume that the major driver of the economic process would be a worker revolution—the revolt of the proletariat. Use the theory of competitive rationality to analyze and explain this mistake.
4. The citizen army of Napoleon marched and fought at a quick step of 120 paces a minute rather than the orthodox 70 paces of Napoleon's adversaries. Perhaps more important, it was the first modern army to be organized into self-contained divisions. It lived on the country instead of traveling with a large supply train of food wagons, and it had a very effective habit of striking at the opponent's supply wagons and lines of supply.[22] Relate these innovations to the theory of competitive rationality in the global market.
5. In the mid-1980s, the running fad died and was replaced by aerobics. Soft-leather athletic shoes replaced the clunky jogging shoe both as an exercise and casual fashion shoe. Reebok led the market with its line of aerobic shoes for women. Nike did not recognize the new trend soon enough and was slow to respond. What was the basic problem with Nike's competitive rationality at that time?
6. In 1992, two hundred CEOs of high-growth companies were asked this question: Which of the following would *most* increase your ability to compete against your domestic and global competition?
   a. Buying new manufacturing equipment and a new plant.
   b. Using your current equipment and plant more efficiently by adopting the new approaches to manufacturing.
   c. Adopting the new fast-track quality approaches to designing new products and modifying old products.

   What percentage do you think answered a, b, and c? Why?
7. What impact do you think the current innovations and cost reductions in hardware for personal computers are having on software for personal computers?
8. An important component of the infrastructure that supports a healthy economy is an efficient and effective legal system to deal with business litigation such as disputes over exchange contracts and private and civil wrongs between competitors and between buyers and sellers (see Chapter 8). Modern governments are expected to provide such a legal system, just as they are expected to provide other types of trading infrastructures such as efficient and effective highways and airports.

[22] See B. H. Liddell Hart, *Strategy* (New York: Meridian, 1991).

Unfortunately, the effectiveness (fairness) of the courts that deal with commercial law in the United States can be questioned.[23] For example, judges of the Texas Supreme court are elected in campaigns primarily funded by the lawyers who appear in their courts. In 1985, the lawyer who won Pennzoil damages of over $10 billion dollars against Texaco for buying a company that Pennzoil wanted to buy made a $10,000 campaign contribution to the judge who presided over the case a few days *after* the judge was assigned the case. The inefficiency of the courts is also scandalous. Everyone agrees that it takes absurdly long for cases to be settled and that the lawyer's fees are often absurdly large.

How might the free market and competitive rationality be used to address this problem/opportunity? Explain the businesses that entrepreneurs and innovators might start, what the keys to success would be, and what effect such businesses might have on the traditional legal system that deals with accidents and product liability suits?

9. FX (foreign exchange) speculation exists because governments pursue macroeconomic tactics (such as changing central bank interest rates) that are attempts to create a global trading advantage by manipulating exchange rates between currencies (such as between the dollar and the yen).[24] These heavy-handed tactics are immediately arbitraged by FX traders and greatly nullified. The certain result is that the traders will make huge profits, which is like adding a costly friction to the smoothness and efficiency of world trade in products and services that create employment. What macro-economic policy should governments pursue that might be a much more effective way of creating global trading advantages for its firms and a growth in employment?

10. According to *The Economist* (April 17, 1993, kp. 57), in 1992 Japanese companies and individuals filed over 200,000 new patent applications for new products and production processes. Sixty thousand new patent applications were filed by Americans; 30,000 by Germans. Are these differences important? What does this tell us about the competitiveness and competitive rationality of firms in Japan, the United States and Germany? What should the U.S. government do about it, if anything? How should U.S. universities and business schools react to this information?

---

[23] David Frum, "Here Come the Lawsuits," *Forbes*, December 7, 1992, 72.

[24] See Kenichi Ohmae, *The Borderless World* (New York: Harper Business, 1990); and "World Economy Survey," *The Economist*, September 19, 1992.

The will to win is important,
but the will to prepare is vital.
Joe Paterno

Not to decide is to decide.
Harvey Cox

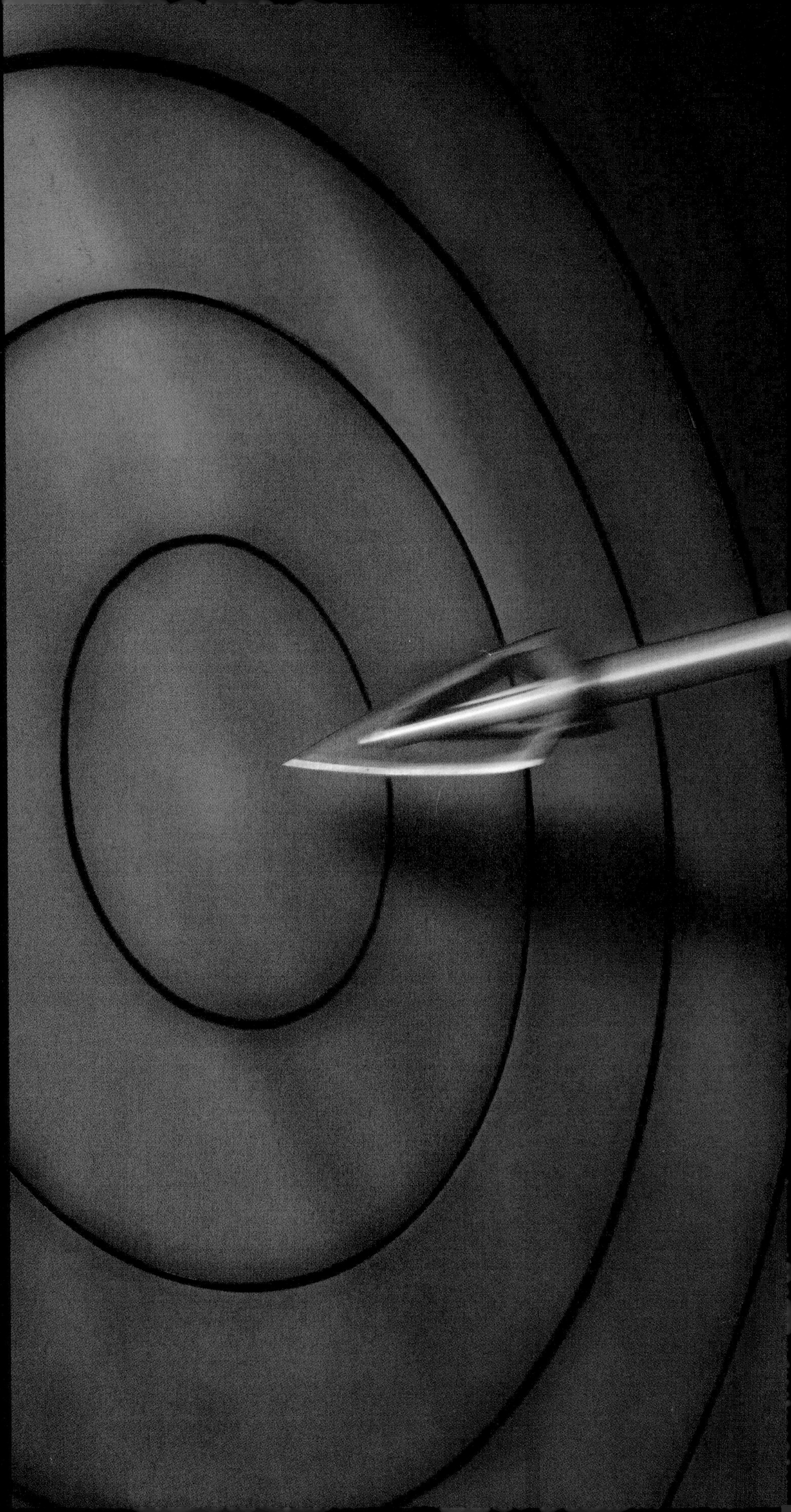

CHAPTER TWO

Market Decision Making

Why does senior management need to institutionalize in the firm a marketing decision-making process that inherently demands alertness and adaptability? Isn't it enough just to have sharp, alert managers? The decision-making routines in a firm are its "genes" that determine its long-term survival. It is important that senior management determine these routines/genes, rather than letting junior executives choose their own, and that senior executives make sure the prescribed decision-making routines are followed by making them standard operating procedures.

Although sharp and alert people are also important determinants of a firm's competitive rationality, if a firm relies on just hiring smart people, its competitive rationality depends on keeping them. If they leave, as they eventually will, and are replaced by less capable people, the firm may lack decision-making routines that would quickly reveal the limited thinking capabilities of the new decision makers. Limited minds are often good at hiding their lack of flair, insight, and alertness. High-quality decision-making routines make everyone perform better. They improve the thinking of excellent minds, and they screen out the foolish thinking of those less capable. They are worth inventing and instituting in all firms competing in a market economy.

This chapter starts off with a discussion of cross-functional team decision making, particularly in new product development and then in a continuous marketing decision-making process. A STRATMESH approach to annual marketing planning is introduced that uses software to help mesh proposed strategy and action programs to business environment facts. ■

Marketing Decision Making

Competitive decision making can be characterized as a process routine that produces strategy and tactics used against or to counter competitors. Consequently, the study of the competitive rationality of an individual firm boils down to the study of its decision-making routines. It is a crucial first step to improving the quality of management. As noted, such routines are the genes of the firm on which its long-term success and survival depend.[1] These decision-making routines are little understood, having been largely neglected by economists and psychologists, despite their tremendous importance to the competitiveness of firms. But even firms themselves often do not have clear, written, standard operating procedures for decision making or planning. This is true even though it has been shown that the credibility and use of marketing plans are increased by having clearly specified rules and procedures and by the wide participation of relevant personnel in the planning process (that is, the use of cross-functional teams).[2]

What exactly is the nature of such decision-making routines, and what components most increase the competitive rationality of the firm? The theory of competitive rationality proposes that a clear competitive advantage is to make informed decisions *quickly.* Thus, one of the first and most interesting concerns is determining how firms update their planned strategies and tactics. In a recent study of major companies, only *half* of the respondents reported that their marketing plans were continuously reviewed and adapted throughout the year.[3] At best, this result suggests that many markets are stable and have very little innovation/imitation; hence, firms do not have to adapt their planned market behavior. At worst, it suggests a mental standstill—a woodenheaded refusal to keep up with changes in the marketplace and a lack of the drive to improve. According to Peter Drucker's theory of business, the crises organizations face occur because "the assumptions on which the organization has been built and is being run no longer fit reality."[4] Consequently, the fit among the company

---

[1] Richard R. Nelson and Sidney G. Winter, *An Evolutionary Theory of Economic Change* (Cambridge, MA: Harvard University Press, 1982).

[2] George John and John Martin, "Effects of Organizational Structure of Marketing Planning on Credibility and Utilization of Plan Output," *Journal of Marketing Research* 21 (May 1984):170–83.

[3] Peter R. Dickson and Rosemary Kalapurakal, "The 'What to Market' and 'How to Market' Decision-Making Process," working paper, no. 92–49 (Columbus: Ohio State University, 1992).

[4] Peter F. Drucker, "The Theory of the Business," *Harvard Business Review*, September-October, 1994, 95.

mission, goals, strategy, product positioning, program and action plans, and market environment has to be tested constantly.

An organization's survival depends on its ability to learn and adapt quickly; in practice, this means that plans often must be altered at the very time they are being implemented. But such changes must be carefully considered and reasoned. Tinkering with plans destroys an organization's ability to execute any coherent strategy. The dilemma then is how to effectively implement strategy and yet remain responsive to new market realities. The decision-making and planning routine described in Figure 2.1 addresses this fundamental dilemma.[5] It has two important features. The first is the involvement of key executives of the company (or the division of a large company) in making marketing decisions—not just approving them. The second is the continual updating of decisions, plans, and programs. The continual revision of decision making is consistent with the dynamics of competitive rationality described earlier. It also reflects a constant strive to do better, a key element of competitive rationality.

Cross-Functional Decision-Making Teams

In the routine described in Figure 2.1, the division manager or chief operating officer chairs an executive committee made up of the managers of the major departments or functions (from here on called a *team*).[6] This team prepares, approves, and oversees the implementation of all functional plans, including the marketing plan. All of the functional plans are integrated into the divisional business plan. This approach is not as radical as it first appears. Senior executive committees have always explicitly addressed major marketing decisions, such as long-term target markets, product positioning, and pricing (see Figure 2.2). Their planning has always involved decisions about new products, the vertical integration of distribution, alliances with suppliers, and other strategic mergers and acquisitions. These are all major marketing strategy decisions. New marketing strategies are also often implicit in major plant expansion decisions. Each of these long-term marketing decisions somewhat constrains succeeding shorter term marketing strategies and tactics. It is, thus, not a huge step to involve the senior executive team in all market decisions. This involvement can be facilitated by the removal of layers of gatekeeping middle management, thereby increasing the informal contact between senior executives and frontline managers. Another advantage of this approach is that it helps to better integrate marketing strategy with company production and financial strategies.[7]

---

[5] This model is based on the following research: H. Mintzberg, D. Raisinhani, and A. Theoret, "The Structure of Unstructured Decision Processes," *Administrative Science Quarterly* (June 1976), 246-75; Henry Mintzberg and James A. Waters, "Of Strategies, Deliberate and Emergent," *Strategic Management Journal*, 6 (1985), 257-72; J. B. Quinn, *Strategies for Change: Logical Incrementalism* (Homewood, IL: Irwin, 1980); Frederick Webster, "Top Management's Concerns about Marketing: Issues for the 1980s," *Journal of Marketing*, 45 (Summer 1981), 9-16, 45; Michael D. Hutt, Peter H. Reingen, and John R. Ronchetto Jr., "Tracing Emergent Processes in Marketing Strategy Formation," *Journal of Marketing*, 52 (January 1988), 4-19; Peter R. Dickson and Rosemary Kalapurakal, "The 'What to Market' and 'How to Market' Decision-Making Process" (Working Paper, Columbus: Ohio State University, 1992).

[6] For a detailed discussion of team decision making and management, see Appendix 1 and Jon R. Katzenbach and Douglas K. Smith, *The Wisdom of Teams: Creating the High Performance Organization* (Cambridge, MA: Harvard Business School, 1993).

[7] Frederick E. Webster, *It's 1990—Do You Know Where Your Marketing Is?* MSI White Paper (Cambridge, MA: Marketing Science Institute, 1989).

Figure 2.1 Continuous Marketing Decision Making

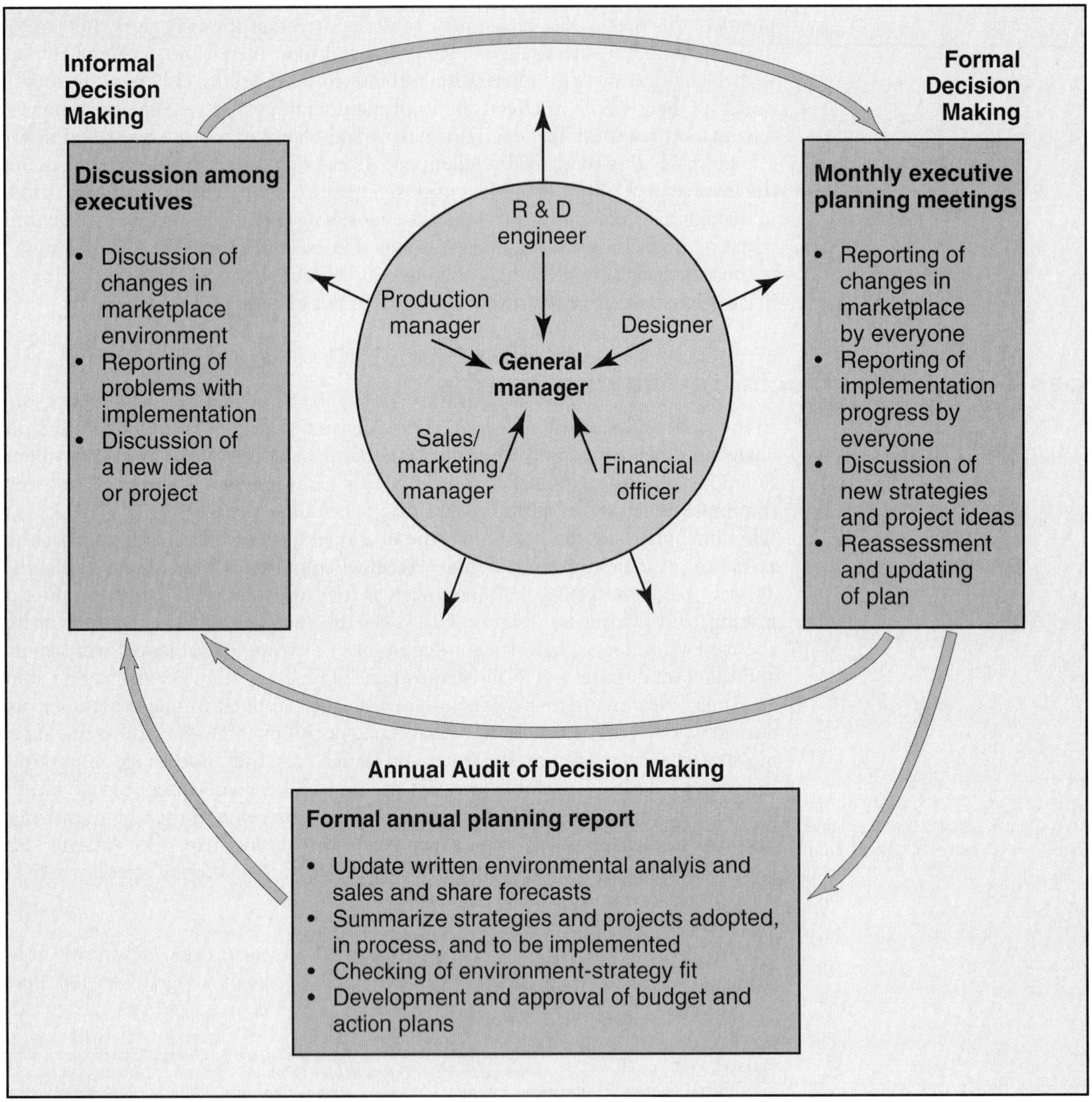
Informal Decision Making
Discussion among executives
• Discussion of changes in marketplace environment
• Reporting of problems with implementation
• Discussion of a new idea or project
Formal Decision Making
Monthly executive planning meetings
• Reporting of changes in marketplace by everyone
• Reporting of implementation progress by everyone
• Discussion of new strategies and project ideas
• Reassessment and updating of plan
R & D engineer
Production manager
Designer
General manager
Sales/ marketing manager
Financial officer
Annual Audit of Decision Making
Formal annual planning report
• Update written environmental analyis and sales and share forecasts
• Summarize strategies and projects adopted, in process, and to be implemented
• Checking of environment-strategy fit
• Development and approval of budget and action plans

Throughout the year, informal decisions impact and are impacted by the more formal decisions made in cross-functional team meetings. The decisions made in these meetings throughout the year are summarized and reviewed in the annual marketing plan. Once established, this plan forms the foundation for decision making in the new year. At the center of this decision-making plan in an entrepreneurial organization is a cross-functional team made up of senior management. In a larger organization, the continuous decision-making process flows around a cross-functional product team.

Figure 2.2 **Goal Setting and Top-Down Directions by Senior Management**

	1980	1990
Broad strategic objectives for marketing are determined by senior management before the plan is prepared.	71.5%	84.5%

1990 Study: Topics checked as included in this top-down instruction.

Goals and Constraints	
Profit goals	74.4 %
Budget constraints	62.6
Sales goals	58.1
Market-share goals	44.8
Cash-flow goals	29.6
Production constraints	22.2
Marketing Strategy	
Choice of target markets	42.4 %
New product/service development	38.9
Market penetration strategy	27.6
Pricing strategy	44.8
Product/service positioning	35.0
Distribution strategy	27.6
Advertising strategy	26.1

These percentages indicate that most marketing planners have profit goals. Some planners are also given explicit sales, market-share, and cash-flow goals, which further constrain their options. Furthermore, in about one in four companies, senior management prescribes the marketing strategy that should be pursued *before* the marketing plan is put together. It is hoped that this direction does not come as a surprise to the marketing planner and is the result of earlier consultations.

It is not suggested that the marketing function in the firm be eliminated. It is still responsible for market analysis, preparing environment reports, suggesting new strategies and tactics, developing the marketing *action* plans and programs, and implementing them. Moreover, the marketing philosophy of making sales and profits by satisfying targeted customers better than competitors do has become accepted by all firms facing vigorous competition. The reason is simple. Competition has forced the adoption of such a philosophy in the same way that competition has forced an emphasis on quality and efficiency in every element of a firm's behavior, including its decision making.

Senior executives who have become steeped in a product market often have an intuitive ability to scan the total business environment and identify significant changes in the marketplace. They are also skilled at drawing higher order strategic implications from such new information. In particular, they are adept at interpreting information from many different perspectives and are therefore less subject to problem framing biases.[8] They are more alert because they are more skilled problem finders and more skilled at recognizing opportunities. Of course, they are not perfect decision makers, but they do not have to be perfect, just better than the competition. Decision making is still chancy, but chance favors the prepared mind, and the minds of senior executives with market experience are better prepared. Senior managers are also able to implement ideas quickly and correctly the first time. Their active involvement in marketing management increases the competitive rationality of the firm because it increases the drive to improve, elevates the alertness and learning of the firm, and improves the quality and speed of implementation.

The major problems with team decision making are twofold.[9] The first risk is that "meetingitis" can develop—the calling of meetings too frequently when informal discussion or individual decision making can deal with the issue. The second hazard is that too much time can be spent in meetings. The best way to prevent these problems is to have strong team leadership that schedules a formal meeting only when necessary, (see Figure 2.1), rather than on a whim, making sure such meetings proceed at a pace, following an agenda that is circulated beforehand. Team members also need to be trained to continuously improve their meeting process skills (see Appendix 1). Like other important management skills, such as writing, using spreadsheets, and mentoring, meeting skills need to be taught.

New Product Development Decision Making

New product development decision making requires a great amount of engineering and design expertise. As a result, many U.S. companies now create special cross-functional teams to plan and develop new products. This team is usually made up of talented, younger marketers, designers, engineers, operations experts, and logistics executives, all eager to make a name for themselves in new product development. Success in new product development is often the fast track to senior management. These teams operate in a manner very similar to that illustrated in Figure 2.1. The group meets constantly to report on progress and the new decisions that have to be made. The meetings are also held as needed, rather than by the calendar. In most cases, the senior management executive committee in a division will be kept informed by a senior manager who is championing, if not heading up, the new product development team. Senior management will also ultimately make the "go" decision, thereby approving the proposed competitive positioning strategy and implementation programs.

Cross-Functional Product Development

For a product idea or concept to advance, it helps if it is championed by an individual who is constantly hustling inside and outside the company to keep up the enthusiasm

---

[8] Michael J. Prietula and Herbert A. Simon, "The Experts in Your Midst," *Harvard Business Review*, January/February 1989, 120–24; Walter Keichel, "How Executives Think" *Fortune*, February 4, 1985, 127–28; and Daniel J. Isenberg, "How Senior Managers Think," *Harvard Business Review*, November/December 1984, 81–90. See Appendix 1, "A Guide to Creative Decision Making," for further discussion of the thinking skills of experts. As explained in Chapter 3, these skills should be applied to specifying the environment report outline.

[9] John W. Henke, A. Richard Krachenberg, and Thomas F. Lyons, "Cross-Functional Teams: Good Concept, Poor Implementation," *Journal of Product Innovation Management*, 10 (June 1993):216–29.

and momentum.[10] She or he also must have the support of an influential senior manager. The problem is that although such a product champion must believe in the new product idea, he or she also must be impartial enough to assess the risks and problems that may cause the project to be abandoned. Even while representing the concept, the champion must be responsible for seeing that a balanced environmental analysis is used to assess the product's opportunities and potential problems.

To help the product champion keep perspective, a cross-functional team should be assembled with the following skills: product design and engineering, market research, marketing, production, purchasing, and cost accounting. The major advantage of such team decision making is the constant, frank interaction among members of the group with different skills that enables marketing, design, operational, and cost problems to be solved at the same time, rather than sequentially.[11] Such teamwork greatly increases the shared insights, learning, and control, and, most important, reduces the time it takes from when a product is conceived to when it breaks even in the marketplace.

Cross-functional product development breaks down the so-called silo mentality of the bureaucratic organization.[12] These silos are the different organizational departments (such as finance, production, engineering, design, marketing, sales, and management information systems) that end up as political fiefdoms. Each one follows and serves its own traditions and legends, its own values created by its professional training and specialized responsibilities, and its own external constituencies.[13] The adoption of the cross-functional management approach goes a long way toward improving a firm's competitive rationality. It allows the collective inculcation of the three drives that are the foundation of competitive rationality: the drive to increase customer satisfaction, the drive to reduce costs, and the drive to improve the enterprise's decision-making and implementation behavior. Cross-functional team management also will increase the number and success of innovation experiments, increase learning from the experiments, and increase the ability of the firm to detect changes in the market environment. For all of these reasons, cross-functional team management of the product development process is superior to the various forms of bureaucratic, functional management that are still common in large U.S. firms.[14] Cross-functional teams are particularly suited to projects involving concepts and technology new to the firm.[15]

---

[10] This suggests that companies should create legends out of product champions who successfully fight the naysayers. Such champions also should be financially rewarded. Such economic and status rewards will spur inventive ways of breaking down institutional blindness and barriers to change.

[11] Hirotaka Takeuchi and Ikujiro Nonaka, "The New Product Development Game," *Harvard Business Review*, January/February 1986, 137–46.

[12] Frederick E. Webster, *It's 1990—Do You Know Where Your Marketing Is?* MSI White Paper (Cambridge, MA: Marketing Science Institute, 1989).

[13] Paul F. Anderson, "Marketing, Strategic Planning and the Theory of the Firm," *Journal of Marketing*, 46 (Spring 1982), 15–26.

[14] Eric W. Larson and David Wileman, "Organizing for Product Development Projects," *Journal of Product Innovation Management* 4 (1989), 284–97; F. Axel Johne and Patricia A. Snelson, "Success Factors in Product Innovation: A Selective Review of the Literature," *Journal of Product Innovation Management* 5 (1988), 114–28.

[15] Eric M. Olson, Orville C. Walker Jr., and Robert W. Ruekert, "Organizing for Effective New Product Development: The Moderating Role of Product Innovativeness," *Journal of Marketing* 59 (January 1995), 48–62. Interestingly, these researchers found that traditional bureaucratic new-product development processes work better for more straightforward existing product modifications and line extensions. Perhaps this is because the creation of a cross-functional team in a traditional bureaucratic culture takes some time and extra effort that hinders progress.

Japanese Product Development Decision Making

A word needs to be said at this point about product costs and profitability and how these factors are incorporated into decision making for new products.[16] The favored model in the West used to be to design the product, build the prototype, and then estimate what it will cost to make such a product. The company then examined whether the product could be sold for a price that incorporated this cost, plus a desired profit margin (cost plus pricing). If the answer was no, then the product was redesigned or killed.

Japanese companies take a much simpler approach (see Figure 2.3). At an early stage, a target price for the new product is determined, based on an understanding of customers and a competitive analysis that determines what price range the product will have to sell for. Target profitability is determined based on the company's financial requirements. Working backward, target costs are set for the new product. Manufacturing and distribution are then designed to meet these target costs. This process involves considerable negotiation among representatives of the various functions of the company, as well as with the company's suppliers. In such a process, a cross-functional team approach is clearly superior.

The resulting product not only meets customer needs, but it is also usually a cost leader. Considering the time it takes Western companies to redesign if initial cost estimates are unsatisfactory, the Japanese approach can be much faster. A further difference between the Japanese approach and the past Western approach lies in the go/no-go decisions based on expected profitability. Western companies tended to kill products based on projections of the individual product's profitability. Often such expected profitability calculations are really no more than creative fiction based on imprecise cost and revenue projections. Japanese companies seem to be much more willing to look at the total picture, seeing the product's likely contribution to an overall strategic position. Consequently, many more products are introduced because they are viewed to play a specific role in a product line or in the company's total offering (see Chapter 9).

This discussion reinforces two considerations that marketing managers should keep in mind when developing new products; an understanding of the customers and the role of an individual product in the company's total offering. If the team knows how customers will value a product, it can have a better sense of the correct trade-off between input quality and costs in the design process. Having contact with customers also will help thinking about the company's total offering and an individual product's role in that offering. Such contact can give the manager an understanding of how the whole offering is perceived, and the manager will have a better sense of the quality differences among the products offered by the company. The positioning procedure described in Chapter 9 combines the best features of Japanese and Western approaches to new product development.

Team Leadership and Continuity

To make the product development team function effectively, top management should appoint a team leader. Without such leadership, the team may flounder, wasting the time, skills, and patience of the team members. The team leader preferably should be

[16] Ford S. Worthy, "Japan's Smart Secret Weapon," *Fortune*, August 12, 1991, 72–75.

Figure 2.3 **Design and Development the Japanese Way**

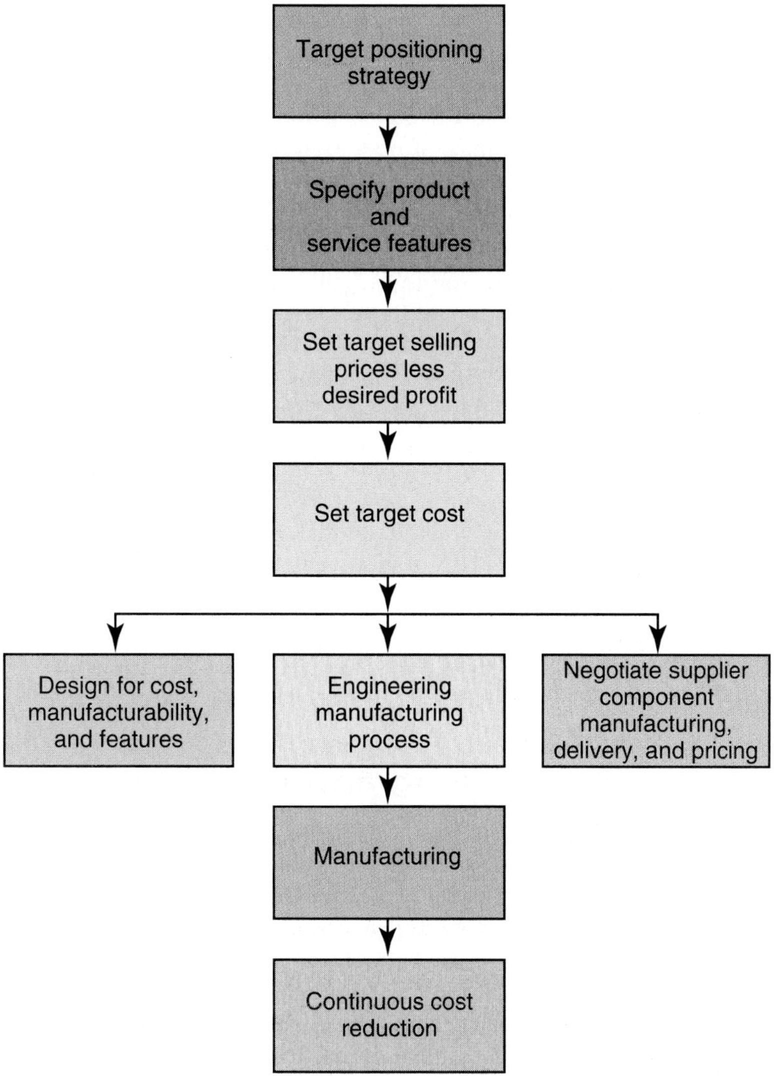

In the traditional approach followed by many U.S. companies, cost is considered too late in the new product development process. Japanese firms often use price, along with other product features, to position the product. They then set a profit margin and subtract it to determine the target direct cost. This target cost, along with QFD-determined features, drives the concurrent engineering process. Afterward, the drive to reduce costs continues unabated.

SOURCE: Reproduced with permission from Ford W. Worthy, "Japan's Smart Secret Weapon," *Fortune*, August 12, 1991, 72–75.

someone with a broad experience and business outlook, but, most important, the leader should have the confidence of the team and be its *informal*, as well as *formal*, leader. This leader should have the authority to make crucial decisions and the willingness to make tough decisions. To provide the incentive necessary to compensate and motivate, many companies give a team leader a stake in the outcome. The team also often receives compensation based on the outcome. Many companies, such as 3M, leave the team intact after its introduction to run the new product as a fledgling business (see also Chapter 17). Some disagree on whether this is always useful. Working out the format for operation of the new business unit may take away effort that could be spent bringing the product to market.[17] However, if the members of the team are to move on to other assignments, the potential for marketing mistakes when the project is handed to an existing operating unit exists.

Furthermore, while it is important to note the unique composition and behavior of cross-functional teams assembled to develop a new product, it is equally important to note that not much difference exists between new product management and mature product marketing management. New product management is the management of innovation/imitation, with an emphasis on innovation. But marketing management is also managing innovation/imitation. An aggressive, driven firm is likely to create the same sort of cross-functional teams to manage all of its products, whether new or established. This is because a cross-functional product development team probably will invent innovations that even make an established product "new." In fact, three out of five marketing plans of industrial and consumer-goods companies contain new product action programs. Almost 80 percent of service-firm marketing plans contain new service development action programs.[18] In short, marketing management is being undertaken by the product development team, which evolves into a product-market business team that continues to make the important decisions.

Continuous Team Decision Making and Improvement

Continuous team decision making takes two forms that vary in formality. The first is the casual discussion among executives, during which new information and ideas are shared and evaluated (this discussion is usually followed by a memo that proposes a change in plans). The proposal is then discussed at formal meetings held regularly throughout the year to monitor progress in implementing the plan and to discuss emerging issues and new strategies or tactics (see Figure 2.1). Continuous decision making does not occur spontaneously. It is driven by a company culture that is itself driven by the three competitive drives. Continuous decision making is demanding and can be time consuming, but the process results in the *perception* of a better plan. This raises morale and the esprit de corps needed for successful implementation.

Informal Processes

In many firms, a great deal of information is sought and disseminated on a seemingly casual basis. This crucial determinant of the firm's competitive rationality serves many

[17] Preston G. Smith and Donald G. Reinertsen, *Developing Products in Half the Time* (New York: Van Nostrand Reinhold, 1991).

[18] Howard Sutton, *Marketing Planning* (New York: The Conference Board, 1990).

purposes. It is used to overcome political obstacles and gain cooperation, resources, and control. It often results in the suggestion and enhancement of new tactics and competitive strategy. This emergent process is dynamic, evolving as it goes, depending on what is learned and the behavior of different interest groups and organizational functions. The strategy emerges as a stream of decisions and en route adaptations to changes in the market environment or to performance feedback.[19] This informal process seems to describe particularly the behavior of the new product development teams that employ concurrent engineering. *Concurrent engineering*, also called *parallel* or *simultaneous engineering*, involves the design, manufacturing, and marketing departments and suppliers working together on each of their functions concurrently, rather than in sequence. Such simultaneous engineering requires considerable informal cooperation and decision making (see Chapter 10).

A high-tech firm's decision to launch a new avionics product is typical of such an unstructured decision process.[20] Research revealed that key information from a salesperson triggered the innovation initiative, followed by a great deal of informal information gathering and decision making between R&D and marketing and by close, back-and-forth consultations with customers. All of this interaction was driven and led by the executive who championed the product.

A similar stream of research has described market decision making more generally as one of "logical incrementalism," in which decisions, events, and new information flow together over time to create a consensus for action among the members of an executive committee or cross-functional team.[21] The competitive positioning strategy emerges incrementally, in a way very different from the step-by-step formal planning process described in many marketing textbooks. The process is more than simply muddling through, because it involves a systematic information search and the use of several total quality management (TQM) procedures. This informal planning process is constantly alert to changes in the product market, and it adjusts action plans to the new competitive, consumer, or channel circumstances. It is likely to be less subject to serious decision-making biases and, hence, will be more competitive and more profitable.[22] A potential problem with emergent strategy, however, is that it can become *too* responsive to the environment. A computer simulation found that reacting to every perceived change in the market is less profitable than reacting to only apparently fundamental trends.[23] In such circumstances, the steadying hand of a senior executive is particularly valuable.

As illustrated in Figure 2.1, the annual marketing report still plays a vital role in such continuous decision making. First, its environmental analysis updates everyone about the current important issues, the emerging issues, and what has been learned

---

[19] Henry Mintzberg and James A. Waters, "Of Strategies, Deliberate and Emergent," *Strategic Management Journal* 6 (1985):257–72; H. Mintzberg, D. Raisinghani, and A. Theoret, "The Structure of Unstructured Decision Processes," *Administrative Science Quarterly* (June 1976), 246–75; and Henry Mintzberg, "Patterns in Strategy Formulation," *Management Science* 24 (May 1978):934–48.

[20] Michael D. Hutt, Peter H. Reingen, and John R. Ronchetto Jr., "Tracing Emergent Processes in Marketing Strategy Formation," *Journal of Marketing* 52 (January 1988):4–19.

[21] James Brian Quinn, *Strategies for Change: Logical Incrementalism* (Homewood, IL: R. D. Irwin, 1980), and "Formulating Strategy One Step at a Time," *Journal of Business Strategy* 1 (Winter 1981):42–63.

[22] Robin M. Hogarth, "Beyond Discrete Biases: Functional and Dysfunctional Aspects of Judgmental Heuristics," *Psychological Bulletin* 90.2 (1981):197–217.

[23] Donald Gerwin and Francis D. Tuggle, "Modeling Organizational Decisions Using the Human Problem Solving Paradigm," *Academy of Management Review* (October 1978), 762–73.

during the year. Annual marketing planning allows for a review of the new strategies and tactics. It also checks the fit between current and proposed strategy and the changing market environment. Finally, it serves to remind the executive committee and others throughout the year of the goals, environmental assumptions, and the priority projects. Much of a firm's competitive rationality depends on the quality of its annual marketing plan.

Annual Marketing Planning

The STRATMESH decision-making process described in Figure 2.4 results in the preparation of the formal annual planning document. It is based on planning approaches used by many leading companies.[24] The routine is called STRATMESH because the distinctive feature of the planning routine is the careful *meshing* of the proposed *strategy* (product positioning and programs) with key facts about the environment.

The process starts with an understanding of the firm's current strategy and tactical programs. It then determines whether or not the firm kept to its plan or why it deviated from the plan. This procedure has two benefits. First, it briefs the team about the firm's current strategy, which must now be adapted to new environmental realities. Second, the deviations from what was planned identify (1) the planned programs that were based on incorrect assumptions about the environment, (2) changes that have occurred in the environment during the last planning period that necessitated changes in strategy, and (3) the implementation of unauthorized strategy and programs. Only about one in four of the marketing plans written by divisions of *Fortune* 500 companies report on implementation of the previous plan.[25] The next step, which can be started at the same time, is the analysis of the different marketplace environments, as described in Chapter 3 and detailed in Chapters 4 through 8.

Developing the Initial Strategy

A team is likely to develop the initial marketing strategy under general headings such as positioning, product, distribution, logistics, sales management, advertising and publicity, promotions, and price (see Chapters 9 through 16). If the consumer segmentation analysis suggests clearly differentiated strategies for different segments, then a separate marketing plan and planning process may be undertaken for each segment. These can be integrated by recognizing such concerns in the company section of the environmental analysis.

The initial strategy should be based on the current strategy described in the first step of the STRATMESH planning process, assuming the product has already been launched. For a new product, the reality is that during the environment analyses, various product, distribution, promotion, and price tactics will suggest themselves to the team.[26] These ideas should be noted in a planning workbook. Consequently, it is

[24] Howard Sutton, *Marketing Planning* (New York: The Conference Board, 1990).
[25] Sutton, *Marketing Planning.*
[26] Most of these will be imitations of competitor tactics or tactics that have worked in other product markets or foreign markets.

Figure 2.4 The Annual Planning Process

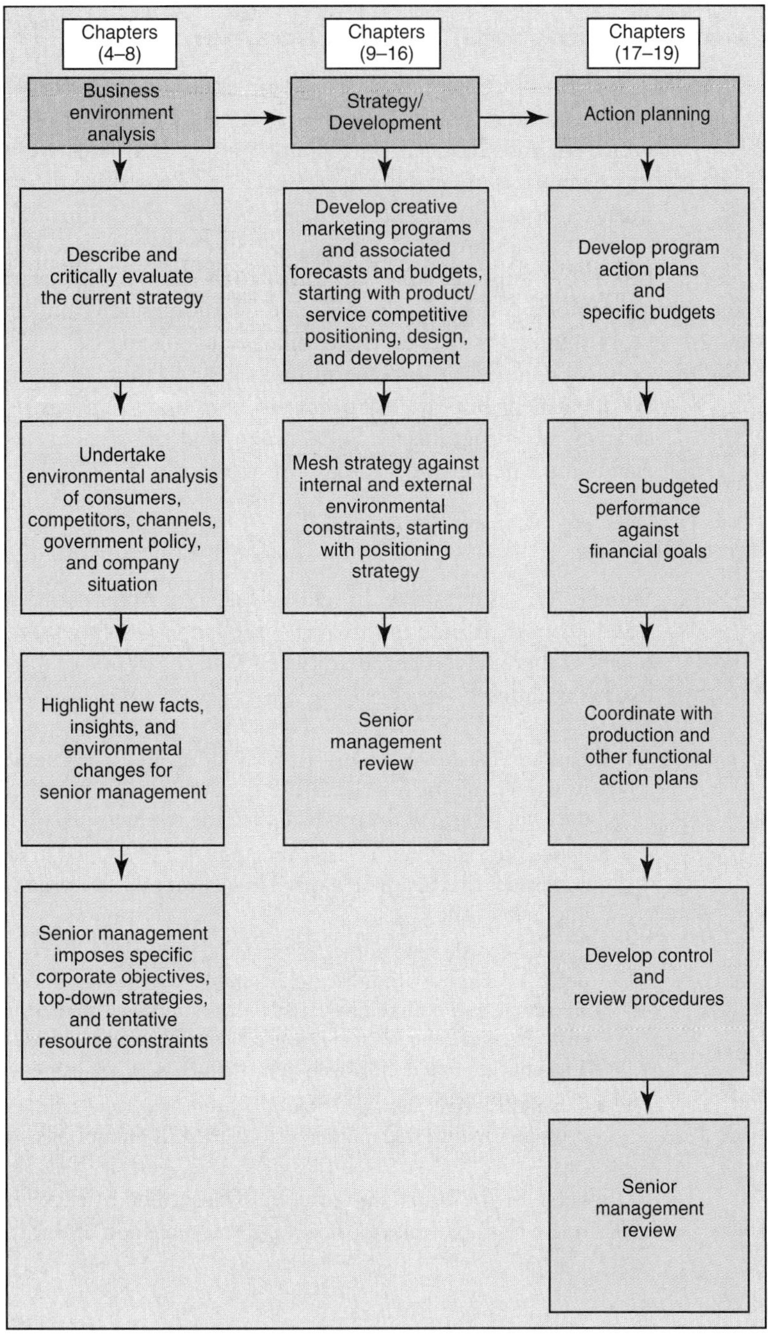

The arrows indicate the process involved in preparing and writing an annual marketing plan. For the sake of clarity, the feedback loops and decision recycling that occurs as a result of senior management review or action-planning problems are not included.

fairly easy to produce a starting strategy, particularly when the team knows that the plan will be fleshed out and even changed in a major way during the meshing stage.

Meshing Strategy and Programs with the Environment

The first objective of market decision making is to avoid any serious allocation or implementation mistakes. If the decision making cannot at least do this, then the process is flawed, and the decision-making routine is a defective gene. Some argue that the most any decision-making approach can do is reduce the chances of making a serious mistake, because no decision-making approach can produce the one best strategy or most creative strategy.[27] Marketplace information is too limited and imperfect, the future is too unpredictable, company goals are too inconstant, and human judgment is too fallible. The research of human decision making undertaken over the past twenty years suggests that even the avoidance of mistakes is a challenging task. This is because of a common information processing failure: Key new facts about the market are identified, but the team fails to consider them when proposing and evaluating strategy and programs.[28] The strategy and the facts are not fitted when the team is evaluating whether the strategy will work or not.

Minimizing Marketing Misfits

Some of the competitive difficulties faced by American firms in recent years have resulted from their inability to adapt to changing competitive markets. In the history of business there have been many blunders, the result of a misfit between strategy and market realities:

- DuPont failed to consider that retail stores and shoe salespeople might not recommend its Corfam plastic over leather. If the distribution channel necessary to sell the product does not believe in the product, then the product will fail.
- Time, Inc., launched a television guide that it planned to sell to cable television companies that competed with Time's own cable television network. It was an impossible sell.
- The Concorde supersonic passenger jet struggled to survive, not just because of public policy problems with noise pollution but also because its airport-to-airport timesaving advantage was nullified by travel delays at either end of a trip (stacking, boarding, customs, taxis, and so on). It was a beautiful design and used pioneering technology. The concept failed, however, because too few fliers gained any real utility.
- General Electric thought it had the production and selling resources to compete in the computer mainframe market against IBM. It did not.

Twelve of the fourteen companies described as excellent American companies of 1982 in the classic book *In Search of Excellence* soon after stumbled because they failed

---

[27] Herbert A. Simon, "Rational Decision Making in Business Organizations," *American Economic Review*, September 1979, 493–512; "Rationality As Process and As Product of Thought," *American Economic Review* 68.2 (May 1978):1–16; "From Substantive to Procedural Rationality," in *Method and Appraisal in Economics*, ed. Spiro J. Latsis (Cambridge: Cambridge University Press, 1976), 129–48; and "On the Concept of Organizational Goal," *Administrative Science Quarterly* 9 (June 1964):1–22.

[28] James K. Brown, *This Business of Issues: Coping with the Company's Environments* (New York: The Conference Board, 1979).

Figure 2.5 **Reasons for New Product Success**

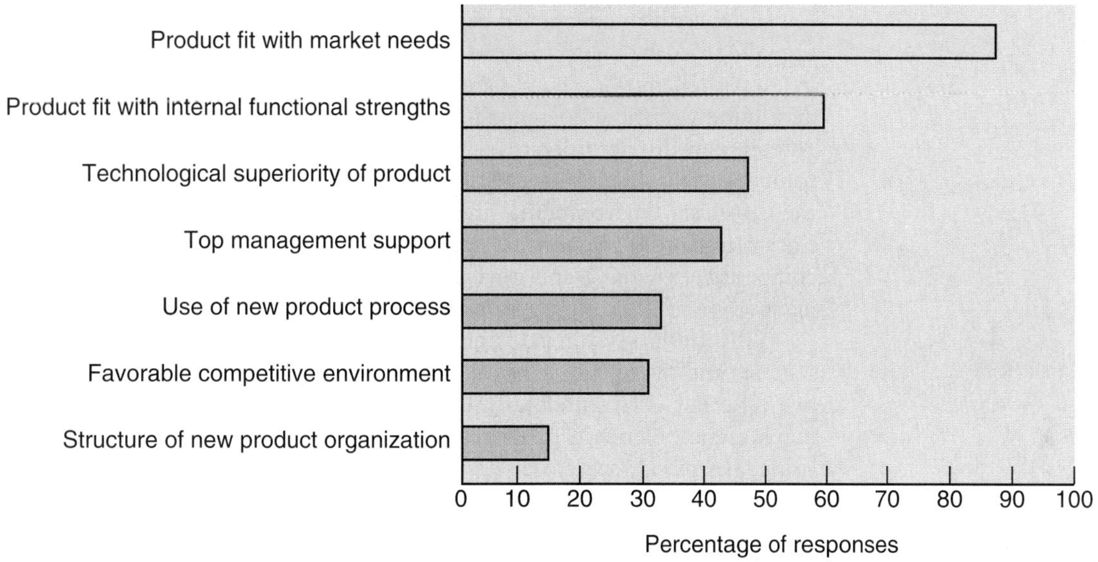

The two most important determinants of new product success are whether the product fits market needs (external fit) and whether the product fits organization strengths (internal fit).

Source: Reproduced with permission from Booz, Allen and Hamilton, *New Products Management for the 1980s* (New York: Booz, Allen and Hamilton, 1982).

to adapt to changes in their environments.[29] Between 1973 and 1988, the great marketing company Procter & Gamble lost an estimated quarter of a billion dollars doing business in Japan. It has been claimed that the company's marketing strategy did not fit consumer values, perceptions, and behavior; did not fit the distribution realities; did not respond to public policy environmental concerns; and underestimated competition.[30] It is easy to second-guess these decisions. It is impossible to know exactly what went wrong and whether the mistakes could have been avoided. However, it does appear that the strategic failures listed occurred because of a critical weakness in team decision making. The product or marketing strategy failed to fit the environment. Certain facts about the external marketplace or the company should have been known and heeded by the team. Figure 2.5 graphs the results of a study on what determines new product development success. It dramatically underlines the importance of making sure a new product fits market needs and organizational strengths.

[29] Thomas J. Peters and Robert H. Waterman, *In Search of Excellence* (New York: Harper Row, 1982), and the follow-up study in *Business Week*, November 5, 1984.
[30] *Forbes*, December 15, 1986.

Marketing decision making can increase the fit between a proposed behavior and market realities by using a meshing exercise. The proposed marketing strategy and tactics are meshed with what is known about each of the marketplace environments. For instance, if the proposed price does not meet the company's financial objectives, then the price may have to be adjusted and then rechecked to make sure the new price fits the other environmental facts. It now may not. It if it discovered that the proposed distribution strategy does not fit the channel environment, then it must be adjusted and the new distribution strategy checked for its fit with the other marketplace environments. It is best to start with the facts in the environmental analysis that describe the consumer environment. These facts act as prompts to help the planner evaluate the strategy from the consumer perspective. The strategy is then evaluated from the competitive, channel, and government perspectives. Finally, it is evaluated from the perspective of all interest groups in the company.

This meshing exercise is no small task. If the environment report contains five sections and the proposed strategy contains five sections (or programs), then twenty-five different environment-strategy combinations have to be reviewed. Each of the major tactical elements of strategy, or programs (product, distribution, selling, advertising, and price), have to be reviewed from the perspective of each of the major market players or environments. The task is made easier by constructing a strategy environment matrix where the fit of each proposed element of strategy can be evaluated by color code against important new and old environmental facts (see Figure 2.6). Another meshing tool can be established by creating a "meshing machine," which has two rotating disks made of transparent film, one on top of the other. The new strategy and program ideas are partitioned on a central gear on the inner disk, and each new market reality is partitioned on gears meshing with the central gear on the outer disk. Each new idea then can be systematically rotated by each of the key facts, as described in Figure 2.7. The STRATMESH 2.0 chapter appendix starting on page 60 describes a Windows program that helps mesh strategy and action plans against the environment.

STRATMESH emphasizes the meshing step. The word *meshing* is used because this is not just a screening stage. The objective is to fit strategy to the environment. But sometimes a firm will plan to execute a bold strategy that will change an aspect of the environment to fit the firm's strategy. Meshing is also a stage for coming up with an even better marketing strategy than the proposed approach. Screening implies simply evaluating the proposed strategy to make sure it fits the facts. Meshing suggests a more creative and positive fitting process. If a good strategy-environment fit cannot be found, then the venture may have to be abandoned. But the planning process will still have fulfilled its function by stopping the firm from wasting its resources. A tactic or component of marketing strategy becomes a *problem* or a weakness and an environmental fact becomes an *issue* or a threat when the two do not seem to fit. Five ways to respond when this occurs are: (1) A different or additional strategy can be proposed that resolves the problem; (2) the environmental fact can be flagged for study to ensure that it is correct; (3) the internally imposed constraints can be relaxed if they are the problem; (4) the misfit can be tolerated and the problem watched very carefully; or (5) the project can be abandoned. It is ultimately up to senior management to determine which environmental/strategy problems, if any, should be tolerated. On the positive side, new tactics are almost certain to spring to mind when reviewing the current strategy against the facts.

Figure 2.6 **Painting the Matrix**

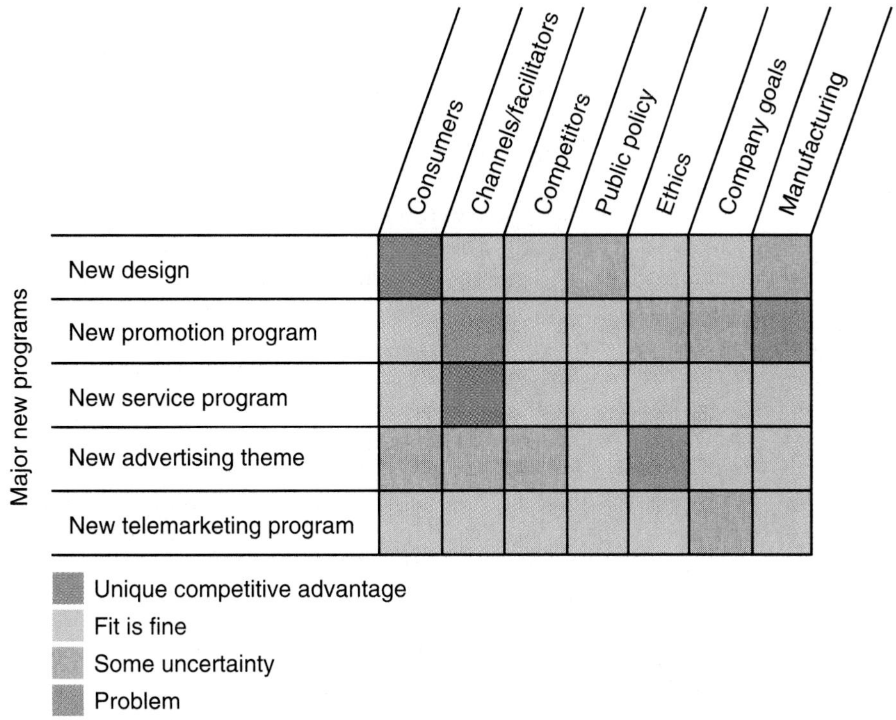

A strategy × environment matrix can be used to indicate misfit problems. In this example, purple indicates a fit that creates a unique competitive advantage, green indicates the fit is fine, yellow indicates some uncertainty, and red indicates a problem.

This meshing approach also can be used in informal, continuous decision making (see the appendix at the end of chapter describing STRATMESH 2.0). It contributes to the competitive rationality of both informal decision making and formal planning. For example, when managers face a crisis such as an unexpected external or internal event, the event that precipitated the crisis must be understood by assessing the effects of the event on all of the players. The decision-making team must quickly, but thoroughly, evaluate the effect of the event on existing strategy and propose new solutions. This is done by meshing the existing strategy against the new realities detailed in a special report that describes the nature and extent of the crisis. This will identify the new problems, focus discussion on understanding why they are problems, and lead to solutions that are themselves meshed against the new and old realities.

Avoiding Repercussion Mistakes

When strategy is changed, the new strategy should be checked for its fit against all environmental facts. This further screening avoids a repercussion mistake, which is similar to what occurs when a doctor prescribes a drug to treat an illness, only to discover

Figure 2.7 **Meshing Strategy and Tactical Programs with Business Environmental Facts**

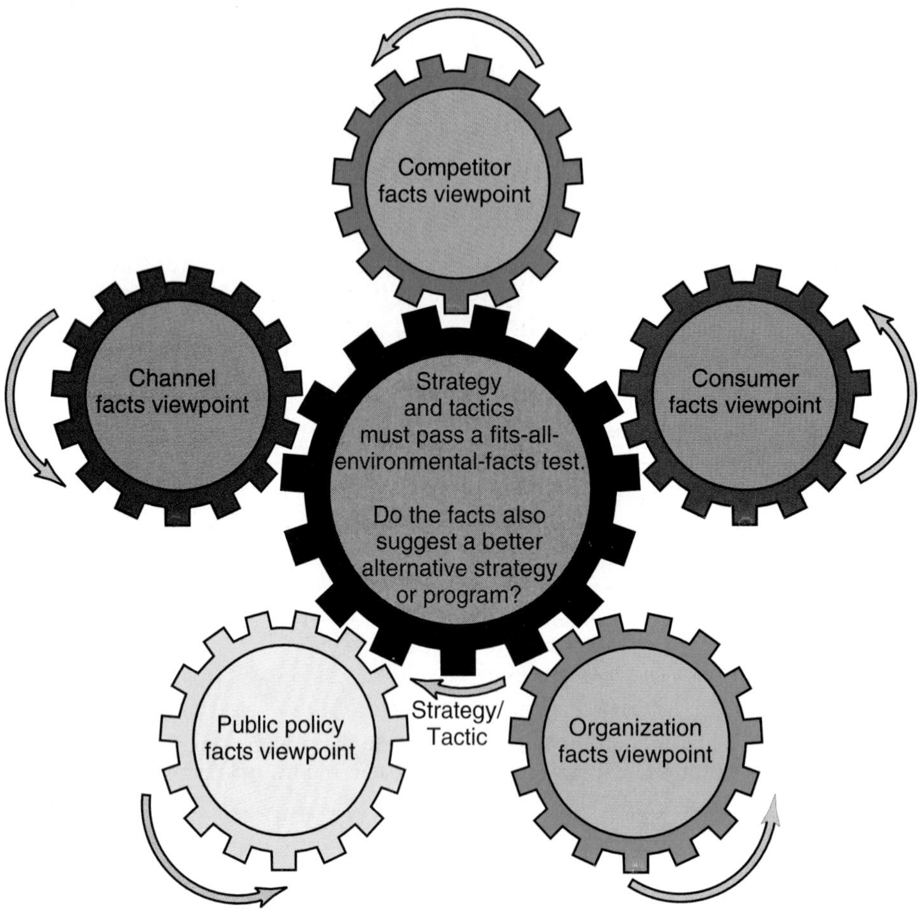

A strategy or tactical program that does not mesh with the environment facts is adapted until it meshes with the facts by considering the strategy from each environmental viewpoint. An environment fact becomes a *threat* if any one of the viewpoints reveals a problem with the fit. An environment fact becomes an *opportunity* if, in considering the fact, it suggests a better strategy or program. If several alternative strategies or programs pass the meshing test, then the most potent alternative (one that will achieve the organization's major objectives most cost efficiently) should be chosen. In the theory of competitive rationality, this is called *bounded optimization.* Bounded optimization is defined as choosing the best option within the bounds of the limited information available, the viewpoints considered, and the current preeminent objectives of the organization.

that the drug's side effects kill the patient. Similarly, a firm may alter its pricing to cater to the demands of an important customer or customer segment, only to discover that this precipitates a price war or that it alienates distributors. This is a repercussion mistake that can be reduced by considering any change in strategy or in a program from the perspective of each interested player.

If the marketing plan is important enough to the future of the enterprise, a final precautionary screening can be undertaken. The components of the suggested strategy are reviewed against each environmental sector, and the following questions are asked: What change in this business environmental sector would greatly reduce the effectiveness of the strategy (perhaps even make it a foolhardy one), and how likely is it that this could happen? This contingency planning approach tests the sensitivity of the strategy to changes in the business environment and gives the team a sense of the uncontrollable, downside risk involved in pursuing the strategy.

After the business environment/strategy meshing is completed, the adapted strategy is presented to senior management for formal approval. If the decision-making team is the senior executive committee, then obviously this step is not needed. Such a review is also likely to result in a further alteration of strategy. However, the suggested changes proposed by senior executives should be treated the same way as any suggested changes: They should be scrutinized using the STRATMESH evaluation and then tactfully reviewed again with senior management. In the STRATMESH planning process, everyone on the planning team reviews the suggested strategy. If adopted, it then becomes everyone's strategy, and everyone learns from its success or failure.

Implementation Planning

Just as the variance in knowledge of sellers and buyers presents opportunities for the marketing entrepreneur, the variance in ability to act or react quickly also presents opportunities. Even in a market with perfect information, where all rivals learn at the same rate, entrepreneurial opportunities would still be created by the differential implementation abilities of sellers. Conversely, the faster the competition, the fewer are the opportunities for exploiting knowledge and response imperfections. As noted earlier competition is more than just learning; it also involves developing the ability to implement quickly (see Chapter 1). This hustle view of competitive advantage requires a top-gun mentality:

> Toyota and other fast-cycle companies resemble the World War II fighter pilots who consistently won dogfights, even when flying in technologically inferior planes. The U.S. Air Force found that the winning pilots completed the so-called OODA loop—Observation, Orientation, Decision, Action—faster than their opponents. Winning pilots sized up the dynamics in each new encounter, read its opportunities, decided what to do, and acted before their opponents could.[31]

Consistent with this view, the CEO of Hewlett-Packard, John Young, introduced a new term, BET (break-even time: the time from concept development to the break-even point in the marketplace), in his attempts to improve his company's speed. Many companies are reaching out to firms in other industries to learn how they are able to implement faster. This is a form of technology transfer across industries, the transfer of how to get things done.

[31] Joseph L. Bower and Thomas M. Hout, "Fast-Cycle Capability for Competitive Power," *Harvard Business Review*, November/December 1988, 112; also see George Stalk, "Time—The Best Source of Competitive Advantage," *Harvard Business Review*, July/August 1988, 41–51; and Murray R. Millson, S. P. Raj, and David Wilemon, "A Survey of Major Approaches for Accelerating New Product Development," *Journal of Product Innovation Management* 9 (1992):53–69.

Routine Rigidity

Organizations can be trapped by prevailing operational routines that limit their ability to innovate, imitate, and implement. Many of these routines add little value to the competitiveness of a firm's products or services. Such functional rigidity can be psychological, intraorganizational, or interorganizational. One of the most powerful psychological human behaviors is the inability to mentally shift from a successful, but inefficient, habitual activity to a more efficient way of solving a problem or achieving a goal.

Such mental inertia is due to more than just habit. It comes from a lack of motivation and the absence of an economic incentive to change behavior. The drive to continue to innovate will be reduced to the extent that innovation is perceived to threaten the sales and profits from past innovations. Thus, a highly profitable firm may be most vulnerable to attack because cautious insiders (often called "tree huggers") are not willing to change their behavior or the firm's behavior. Changing routines within an organization also may be resisted for fear that it would provoke conflict between functions and factions. Here again, the cross-functional decision-making team reduces such conflict.

The need for speed and the habitual tendencies of individuals and organizations require that formal market planning include completion-date deadlines, and activity schedules. The final senior management operational review approves these action programs (see Figure 2.4). Sometimes it is discovered at this late stage that the company simply does not have the resources, or the time, to implement the proposed strategy in the plan. This may require a major revision of the planned strategy and tactics.

Table 2.1 presents The Conference Board findings about what types of action programs are most frequently included in marketing plans. First, it is clear that many marketing plans are dominated by sales management and promotion action programs, such as field sales, major account sales, sales training, customer service, distributor/dealer relations, regional sales, promotion, and telemarketing programs. Marketing plans are more concerned with sales action programs than with advertising campaigns. Second, as mentioned earlier, most marketing plans include new product development action programs. Third, some logical differences exist among the marketing plans of industrial product companies, consumer product companies, and service firms. The plans of business-to-business firms include more action programs directed at major accounts and export sales. Service firms give more emphasis to new service programs, sales training (presumably because the provider of the service is often also the most influential salesperson), customer service, and telemarketing. Overall, however, the results of the study do not suggest that the marketing decision making of these different types of firms (as reflected in their written marketing plans) are radically different.

It is also evident that many tactical marketing decisions and execution details (such as advertising themes, physical distribution, and packaging) are not included in the marketing plan. Presumably, if they exist, they are specified as the year progresses, often emerging in response to new environmental information about competitor behavior and the success of other company initiatives. Moreover, this process suggests that strategy sometimes opportunistically evolves from tactics, in addition to the conventional evolution of tactics from strategy.

The fact some firms do not provide action plans for all of their programs in the marketing plan may frustrate efforts to speed up the implementation of decisions. If a

Table 2.1 Action Programs Usually Included in the Marketing Plan

	INDUSTRIAL PRODUCTS	CONSUMER PRODUCTS	SERVICE FIRMS
Field sales effort	66%	67%	73%
New product/service development	63	64	79
Sales to major accounts	63	44	50
Sales promotions	61	73	75
Pricing policy	52	42	46
Sales training	49	42	69
Export sales	46	21	10
Customer/product service	44	39	75
Product quality	41	39	50
Distributor/dealer relations	39	39	31
Inventories/physical distribution	39	35	17
Advertising themes	35	52	56
Regional selling and promotion	32	53	52
Packaging	23	44	23
Telemarketing	21	26	58
Other overseas marketing programs	22	12	17

SOURCE: Howard Sutton, *Marketing Planning* (New York: The Conference Board, 1990), Table 8.

major goal of the marketing planning effort is to reduce BET, then habitual implementation practices have to be replaced by new, fast-track action plans, which require time-tagged activity sequences that must be documented, circulated, and used as control charts to achieve the deadlines.[32] The natural place for such new fast-cycle action programs would be in the annual marketing plan. Such detailed action planning is described in Chapter 17.

In conclusion, Table 2.2 is the outline of a typical annual marketing plan. An example of an environment report and strategy report in a format that enables them to be meshed using the STRATMESH 2.0 software is presented in Appendix 2. The unique characteristics of the product or service development process is further described in Chapter 10.

Global Marketing Decision Making

As emphasized in this textbook, competitive rationality stresses understanding the business environment and responding to changes quickly. The only reason to not decentralize decision making to the local executive team managing a regional or country market is that headquarter's decision-making skills are so much better that they more

[32] Murray R. Millson, S. P. Raj, and David Wilemon, "A Survey of Major Approaches for Accelerating New Product Development," *Journal of Product Innovation Management* 9 (1992):53–69.

Table 2.2 The Typical Contents of an Annual Marketing Plan

CONTENTS	PAGES
Executive Summary	1
Environment Report	2–7
Consumer Analysis	
Competitor Analysis	
Channel Analysis	
Public Policy Analysis	
Company Analysis	
Strategy Report	8–12
Positioning Strategy	
Product Programs	
Pricing/Promotion Programs	
Distribution/Sales Programs	
Advertising/Publicity Programs	
Control Programs	
Forecasts and Budgets	13–15

than compensate for the advantages of decentralized decision making. There are four major advantages to decentralized decision making by local teams: The teams are closer to the foreign market, they are able to understand changes in the foreign market faster, they can develop a better fit between marketing strategy and programs and the foreign market realities, and they are able to implement faster. Seldom do the superior skills of senior management outweigh these advantages. Marketing management must fit the competitive realities of a market, which often vary across foreign markets. Centralized, global decision making can create suffocating and burdensome bureaucracies, and the siren lure of international jet-setting can encourage decision making during only brief visits to the market. Continuous decision making cannot be made at arm's length. Decentralized decision making is essential in countries or regions where the pace of innovation/imitation and the growth rate of the market are high.

Accepting that the norm should be to allow marketing strategy and programs to vary across global markets, what is the role of the head office in decision making? It can manage at least three programs: (1) the transfer of information and good ideas among markets; (2) the institution, promotion, and standardization of high-quality decision-making routines in all of its foreign markets; and (3) the global coordination and rationalization of production activities, such as financing, procurement, manufacturing, and advertising creatives, when appropriate. Each of these three activities will be discussed in detail now.

Consistent with the innovation/imitation principle of the theory of competitive rationality, it is important that the head office facilitates the global transfer of good ideas. A communications system needs to be developed by which good ideas about competitive positioning, strategy, cost reduction, and implementation are quickly shared across the different international markets. In practice, this means the use of teleconferences, confidential newsletters, global electronic bulletin boards, the use of Internet MIEMS (market intelligence E-mailboxes), and periodic meetings at corporate headquarters where problems, opportunities, and ideas are shared. If Wal-Mart can use a satellite network to hold teleconferences with all store managers every Saturday, then the same technology can be used to manage a global organization. Experts have stressed that the profits from global marketing come from sharing what is learned from experiments and initiatives in one market with similar markets. The result is an exchange of not just technology but good marketing ideas among all the global markets the firm competes in.[33] This process of voluntarily acccpting good ideas from other markets may lead to the development of global standards. The important point is that this standardization occurs not because it was imposed by the head office but because the voluntary acceptance of the idea was universal among the foreign decision-making teams.

Corporate management can standardize the informal decision-making processes and the formal planning process, including the reports, so the decision-making routines are the same among foreign markets, even if the output is not the same. The key elements of the competitive rationality process are the same in all markets. The standardized decision-making routine should encourage experimentation and creativity and should make sure everyone learns from the experiments. It also needs to include the careful and deliberate meshing of the new programs with changing market realities. Most important, the disciplines of total quality management and fast implementation need to be introduced in all foreign markets—an easier task in some cultures than in others.

Finally, global marketing is often concerned with achieving a competitive advantage by obtaining supplies from the least expensive and highest quality global sources. This applies to more than raw materials and manufacturing subassembly. It applies to finding the cheapest global sources of funds for expansion and to finding the best marketing and advertising consulting advice. When such advantages exist, then such operations can be regionalized or even globalized. The acid test is whether the foreign managers themselves clearly see the advantages of such sourcing strategies, because the competitive advantages are readily apparent in terms of higher customer satisfaction, lower costs, faster implementation, and bottom-line profits.

Discussion Questions and Minicases

1. What feature of the STRATMESH planning process is likely to increase the quality of intelligence gathering and environmental analysis in a firm? Develop a step-by-step diagram that describes the evolution of high-quality environmental analysis. Theoretically, what does increasing the quality of environmental analysis do?
2. Why does senior management need to institutionalize a marketing decision-making process in the firm that inherently demands alertness and adaptability? Isn't it enough just to have sharp, alert people?
3. In 1979, the U.S. Mint first issued the Susan B. Anthony $1 coins. The Mint produced millions of these coins for general circulation, but found that no one wanted to use them because they were the same size as the quarter. This created confusion for consumers and retailers, particularly the vending industry. By 1981, the Mint stopped minting them. How might the STRATMESH process have spared the U.S. Mint, which has been in the sole business of making coins and paper money for two hundred years, from the Susan B. Anthony blunder? What *further* mistake did the U.S. Mint make on this project?
4. Why do you think experts such as Mintzberg and Quinn argue that strategy often opportunistically evolves or emerges from tactics rather than tactics evolving from strategy? Relate your answer to the planning processes described in the chapter.

[33] John A. Quelch and Edward J. Hoff, "Customizing Global Marketing," *Harvard Business Review*, May/June 1986, 59–68.

5. Describe the marketplace constituencies that might be studied in an environmental analysis conducted by a university developing a marketing plan to attract more students.
6. Twelve of the fourteen companies described as excellent in the 1982 Peters and Waterman classic *In Search of Excellence* stumbled because they failed to adapt to changes in their environments. A major conclusion of an earlier Conference Board report on marketing planning practices in large companies emphasized the "failure of senior and operating executives to give issues adequate heed in arriving at investment or marketing decisions." What seems to be wrong with such companies' planning?
7. The accompanying Rationality in Practice box describes what often happens when a firm faces a major external economic or political crisis. The decisions made under crisis can have worse effects than the initial crisis. How does institutionalization of the STRATMESH planning process help in a crisis?
8. The marketing planning process often involves a lot of organizational politics. The risk is that the marketing plan itself becomes a political document, rather than a decision-making document. List all the possible effects on the content and use of the marketing plan when it becomes a political document. What influence do you think politics play in the decision making of U.S. firms?
9. Few organizations undertake marketing planning and produce marketing plans the way most textbooks say planning should be done. Many written marketing plans are nothing more than forecasts of future sales and a budget statement. The presentation of the information in dramatic computer-generated graphics is often very impressive and the written statement may make the reader feel good, but too often it is a triumph of form over function. Although a slick presentation can go a long way in communicating information, it can also mask the superficiality of a marketing plan. Such plans often do not describe the environment or the proposed strategy, nor do they provide implementation directions. This is not to say the company does not have plans. It does, but the plans are in the minds of the decision-making executives. The problem is that the plans are not readily available for scrutiny, improvement, and execution by other executives in the organization. A written plan helps us to remember, make decisions, give directions, and implement. Why then do firms not prepare better marketing plans? Please state and explain all the possible reasons.
10. The following example of marketing decision making is a composite of decisions and actions commonly seen in small and large firms launching a new product to be sold to other businesses.

An Example of Marketing Decision Making—How *Not* to Do It

Suppose that a relatively large company that sells products to other businesses is preparing to launch a new product. The product is one whose genesis was in the research and development department of the firm. Developers have talked with potential customers early in the design process, but shortly after the new idea gained some momentum, it was decided by upper-level management to cease talking with all but one customer for fear of divulging information to competitors. The one principal customer has signed a nondisclosure-noncompetition agreement in exchange for receiving proprietary first versions of the product. This principal customer is providing some of the financing for the research and development effort. An initial analysis of secondary data suggests that there is a large potential market for a generic version of the new product. The project gets the go-ahead.

After a year of successive development advances, the company begins work on the generic version of the product. The product manager is still hesitant to talk to potential customers and so does an updated analysis of secondary data and concludes that market potential is still quite large. Planning proceeds on the generic version of the product. Trials with the principal customer are well under way. The product passes through several "go/no-go" reviews and passes, largely because technical progress is being made. The project builds a momentum of its own.

A launch date is set for the generic version of the new product. The product manager provides preliminary specifications of the product to manufacturing. He provides these specifications and the desired positioning of the product to the marketing department and the sales force. The product manager finds he is spending most of his time refining the product's features with R&D and working on pricing.

Upper-level management is getting excited about the new product. Between the principal customer and the broader market, they feel the new product will fill a large role in the company's future over the next three to five years. They tell the director of marketing, who in turn tells the product manager.

The launch date is approaching. The principal customer is very pleased with the product but is using it less than first anticipated. The product manager is getting anxious about the prospects for the new product, so a market research consultant is called in to verify the size of the market and the chosen target segments, help refine the product's positioning, and forecast the sales of the product. The manufacturing department says that it can probably produce the product for a reasonable cost, somewhere near the cost target. However, the manufacturing department needs updated product specifications and solid sales estimates so that it can plan better. The marketing department says that it needs final specifications and that it has called in its advertising agency to help produce the launch campaign. This will add to the startup cost. The sales force says that it is ready when the product is but will need training on how to sell the product.

The launch date is getting closer. The product manager is still working with engineering to get the product features refined. The preliminary market research results are somewhat ambivalent. Discussions with manufacturing have become heated. The manufacturing cost estimates are going up, and the manufacturing department does not feel comfortable with the lack of details in the product specifications. The sales force is waiting patiently, or as patiently as a sales force can wait. The ad agency has come up with a new idea for positioning the product and the marketing department believes it has merit. Meanwhile, marketing has gone ahead with press conference scheduling and booth design for the industry's major trade show, which will coincide with the product launch.

The launch date is imminent. New market research is now fairly negative and the researchers' suggestions for "re"-positioning the product are judged to be too far afield to be of use. To ensure that the product will reach sales targets, top-level management and the product manager decide to target the product to a broader market than originally intended. Because manufacturing costs appear to be higher than anticipated, the price of the product is raised to maintain the desired profit margin. As positioning has become very vague at this point, the product manager instructs marketing to focus communications on product features. It is rationalized that customers will easily be able to translate for themselves how the product will be useful for them. There is not enough time or money now to produce a full-blown sales training program. Accordingly, the sales force is told that sales techniques used for existing products will work well enough for the new product. Product briefings will be held for the sales force shortly before the trade show.

Shortly afterward, R&D informs the product manager that the first product shipped will have to be a "watered down" version of the original conception of the generic product. R&D is still working on finding ways to provide some features at a cost that "won't break the bank." It is too late to change the advertising or the trade show booth. The sales force is instructed that the first version of the product will not live up to its billing and that it can offer a discount if the customer is unwilling to wait for the upgraded version.

The launch actually goes smoothly, all in all. Early sales figures are somewhat disappointing. The product manager is actually temporarily relieved at this, since manufacturing ran into problems handling the last-minute product changes, so deliveries

Rationality in Practice

Organization Decision Making in a Crisis

STAGE	PLANNING BEHAVIOR	STAGE	PLANNING BEHAVIOR
Shock	There is general confusion, panic, and inability to understand the situation. The organization is incapable of reasoned planning. It sometimes reacts impulsively, without exploring alternatives or fully understanding the event.	**Defensive Retreat**	The threat is minimized, sometimes even dismissed. There is a retreat to old, "tried and true," top-down decision making. Open planning processes are abandoned. Accusations and blaming politicize decision making. The planning team splinters and the decision-making structure disintegrates. The organization then becomes very defensive: programs are cut, budgets are tightly controlled, and all decisions become short term.

are slower than anticipated. The product manager decides to get some post-launch evaluative information to try to pinpoint why the product is not moving as well as desired. Other than sales figures, there is no real data on how the company is doing, except for salesperson call reports. Upon examining the early call reports, the product manager realizes that no one told the salespeople what information to include in their call reports.

At this point, this process can go in any direction. Indeed, the company may have a winner on its hands. More likely, the results will probably be somewhat disappointing and perhaps even disastrous. The point is that there are better ways to handle a product launch that will minimize the chances of making mistakes. The process described in this chapter and discussed in detail throughout this book, if followed, will help keep an organization's marketing efforts focused on the important issues and will help ensure that these efforts are coordinated and move along on a reasonable schedule. Please critique the process described in the example.

Appendix 2-1

STRATMESH 2.0™

STRATMESH 2.0 is a Windows-based software built using POWERBUILDER 4.0 that uses SQL databases. This means it can access most existing database management systems, including word processing, spreadsheets, and multimedia. A user activates the STRATMESH 2.0 icon within Windows. (See Figure 2.8 on pages 62–67.) The user is then asked for an access code. This protects the environment report, strategy report, comment files, and other supporting documents within the plan from being tampered with. Limited "Planner" access allows the manager to view the meshing-matrix and print out reports. This is suitable for senior executives who wish to passively review progress from a distance and without disrupting the cross-functional team's work. "Lead Planner" access enables the manager to write comments in the matrix cells and repaint the matrix. Master or "Super Planner" access allows the manager to change all of the files in the plan, particularly the environment and strategy reports.

STAGE	PLANNING BEHAVIOR	STAGE	PLANNING BEHAVIOR
Acknowledgment	The crisis is placed in its proper context and its ramifications are understood. A consensus develops about how the marketplace has changed. There is a constructive call for new solutions from the bottom-up.	**Adaptation and Change**	New strategies are formulated, evaluated in the light of the new marketplace environment, and implemented. The company returns to its more adventurous and open team decision-making approach.

SOURCE: Stephen L. Fink, Joep Beak, and Kenneth Taddeo, "Organization Crisis and Change," *The Journal of Applied Behavioral Science* 7.1 (1971), 15–37.

The relevant plan is pulled from the BookShelf function. To select a plan off the shelf requires unselecting the currently activated plan. The master planner can then update the detail in the environment report or strategy report by using the Detailer function. The Detailer allows the inclusion of charts, figures, photos, video, and spreadsheets as detail supporting the environment report or strategy report. For example, the section on company goals might include a window button that, if activated, will call up a video clip of the CEO describing the firm's current goals. Another example is that a section in the strategy report describing the advertising campaign can include a Windows button that calls up the proposed TV advertisement. Another button can access a spreadsheet that describes the advertising budget and its expected reach and frequency compared to rival's campaigns.

The Outliner option on the top of the window's screen is used by senior management or the cross-functional team to form the heading outline of the environment report and strategy report. Being able to vary the outline makes STRATMESH 2.0 very much an all-purpose planning aid. As will be shown in Chapter 10, the choice of some very different outlines enables STRATMESH 2.0 to be used in product development planning and for tracking product development progress along the plan's blueprint using "fuzzy" milestones or stagegates (see Chapter 10). STRATMESH 2.0 also can be used by senior management to assess their portfolio of products along more than the standard two dimensions of market growth potential and profitability (see Chapter 4).

The strategy and environment details are meshed by using the MESH function or the MESHING Matrices function. The MESHING Matrices option offers three ways of viewing the painted meshing matrix. At the micro level (Detail Matrix) only a few cells are viewed at a time. The other two levels (Topic Matrix and Summary Matrix) allow a full view of the painted matrix. Activating a cell in the Detail and Topic Matrices opens up a comment file that describes the team's current perceptions of the fit between the environment issue and the planned strategy or action. Relevant sections of the environment report and strategy report can be accessed by pointing the mouse at a heading on the left of the rows or a heading at the top of a matrix column and pressing the right pad of the mouse (rather than the left pad, which is used to open files or activate buttons).

The Reporter function allows the printing of the current environment report, strategy report, or the printing of the meshing matrix the way it is currently painted in full color (using, of course, a color printer). The Helper function is available to give advice on the general use of STRATMESH 2.0, advice on how to use a particular marketing plan, and notes for future managers on how to improve their intelligence gathering and decision-making process. In effect, the Helper files, stored with the individual plans, becomes the firm's collective memory and wisdom about the firm's marketing decision making process.

Figure 2.8 **STRATMESH 2.0**

STRATMESH 2.0 is a decision support system that enables the strengths, weaknesses and prospects of a marketing plan to be assessed at a glance and then the reasons for the evaluations explored in detail. STRATMESH 2.0 can also be used to manage the implementation of a project or program and can serve as an archive of past plans and projects.

It is a Windows based software that accesses SQL databases. This means it can access most existing data base management systems including word-processing, spreadsheets, and multimedia. A user clicks on the STRATMESH 2.0 icon within Windows—point the mouse and click the *left* button on the mouse. STRATMESH 2.0's main menu will appear (see A).

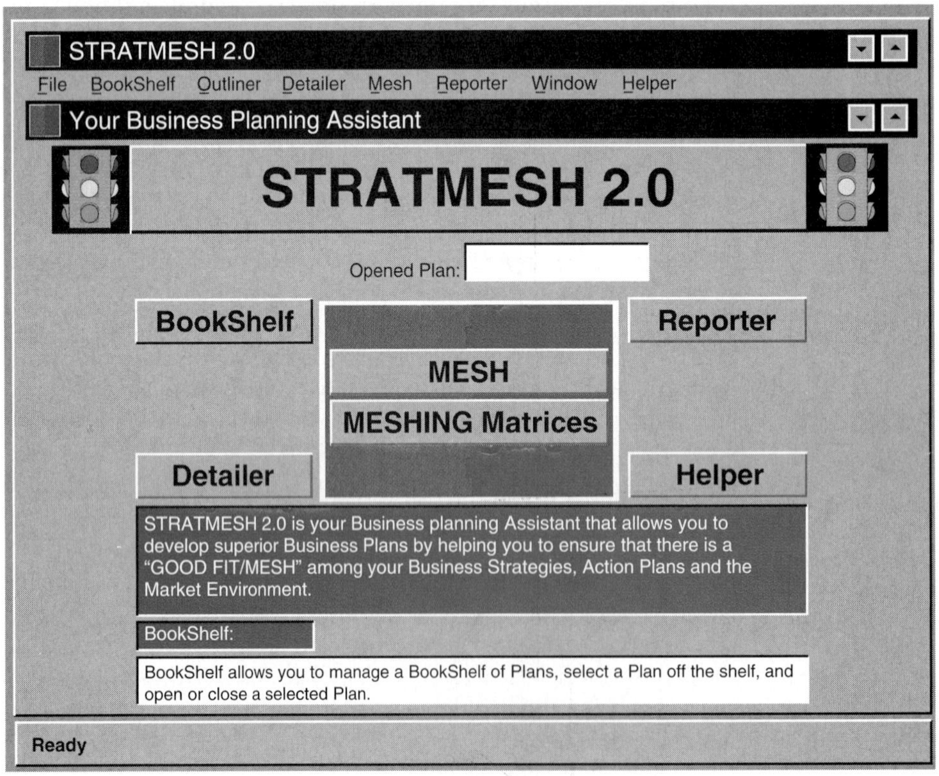

A

(continued)

Figure 2.8 (continued)

In STRATMESH 2.0's main menu, the Reporter bar opens up all of the printing options that include the printing of the current environment report, strategy report, comment report on the fit, or the printing of the meshing matrix, the way it is currently painted in full color (using, of course, a colored printer).

The Helper bar provides advice on the general use of STRATMESH 2.0, advice on how to use a particular marketing plan, and notes for future managers on how to improve their intelligence-gathering and decision-making process. In effect, the Helper files stored along with the individual plans becomes the firm's collective memory and wisdom about the firm's marketing decision making.

The Outliner option on the top of the Window's screen is used by senior management or the cross-functional team to form the heading outline of the environment report and strategy. As you will see in later chapters, being able to vary the outline makes STRATMESH 2.0 very much an all purpose decision-support aid. To explore some of the possibilities, see the sample STRATMESH 2.0 templates for a product development plan, a product-market portfolio analysis, a relationship market-share matrix, a person × situation segmentation analysis, and a quality function deployment matrix.

The "Detailer" bar accesses the environment and strategy reports. Click on the line to access the topic of interest in the report. The team can then update the detail in the environment report or strategy report. For example, a section in the strategy report describing the advertising campaign can include a file that calls up the proposed TV advertisement. Another file can access a spreadsheet that describes the advertising budget and its expected reach and frequency compared to rival's campaigns.

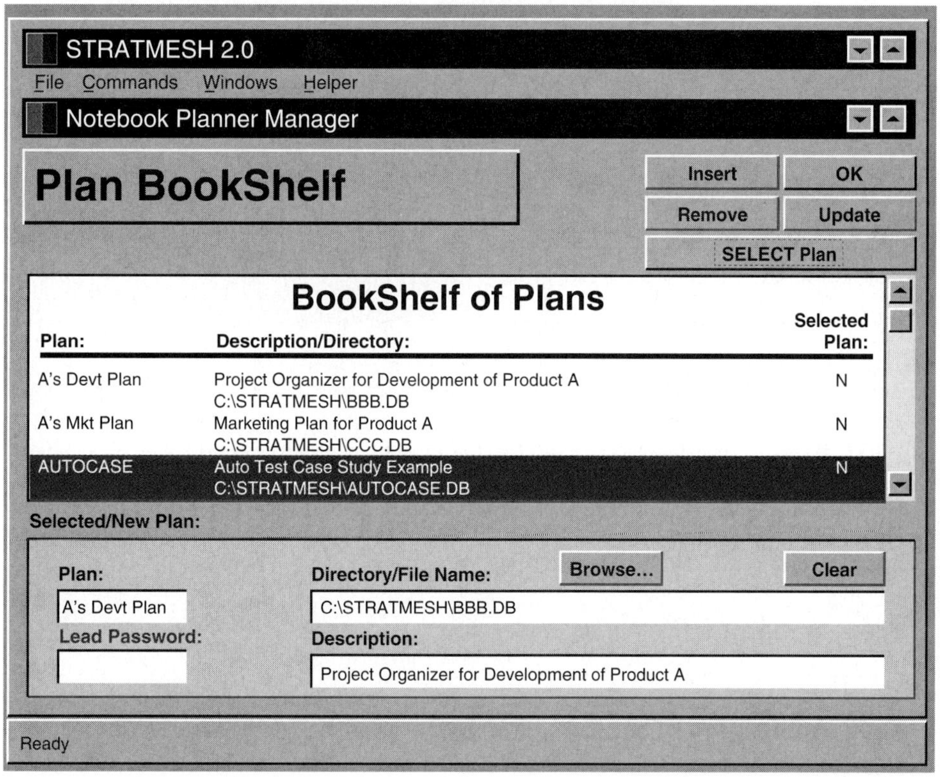

B

To select an existing plan from the bookshelf click on the Bookshelf button and select the Plan Bookshelf option. After a few seconds the Plan Bookshelf window will appear (see B). To select a plan (such as the Autotest Case) off the shelf, scroll down the bookshelf and click on the line that has the Autotest Case Study Example. The Autotest case should become highlighted in blue. Click on the selected plan and the OK box in the top right hand corner of the Plan Bookshelf window. After 2 to 3 seconds STRATMESH 2.0 returns to the main menu with the Autotest plan.

(continued)

Figure 2.8 **(continued)**

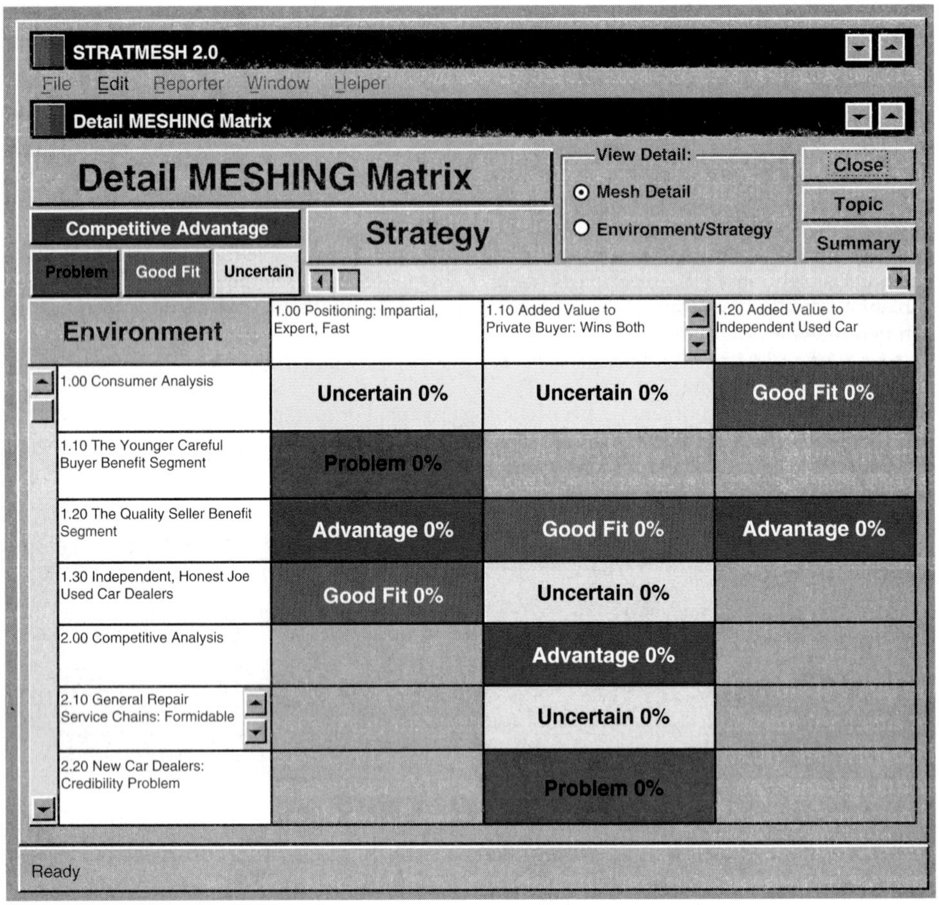

C

In the main menu, click on the Meshing Matrices bar and the Meshing Detail Matrix bar and the Autotest Detail Meshing Matrix window will be displayed (see C). Clicking on a colored cell such as the top left yellow cell reveals the explanation for the uncertain mesh of proposed positioning with the consumer analysis (see D). The evaluation and color coded mesh fit can be updated. You can also add comments and action plan information specifically related to the fit or lack of fit between the consumer facts and the positioning strategy. Click on the Close bar to return.

(continued)

Figure 2.8 (continued)

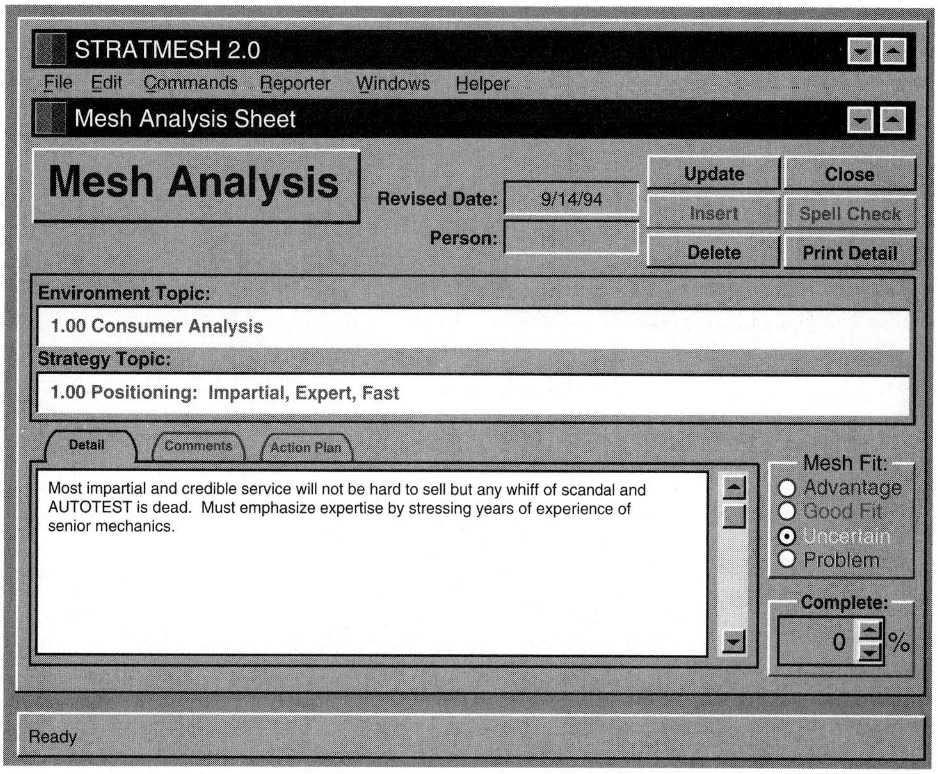

D

To scan and update the environment report point the mouse at the 1.00 Consumer Analysis cell and click the *right* mouse button, rather than the usual left mouse button. The market environment topic window is then displayed (see E). Six pages of information about the topic can be stored along with diagrams, charts, illustrations, multimedia, and spreadsheets associated with the specific environment topic, which can be accessed by clicking on the respective folder. Click the Close bar to return.

To scan and update the strategy report point the mouse at the 1.00 Positioning: Impartial, Expert, Fast cell and click the *right* hand mouse button. The market strategy topic window is then displayed (see F). Supporting comments, action plans, diagrams, and spreadsheets can be attached to each market strategy topic and accessed. Click on the Close bar to return.

(continued)

Figure 2.8 **(continued)**

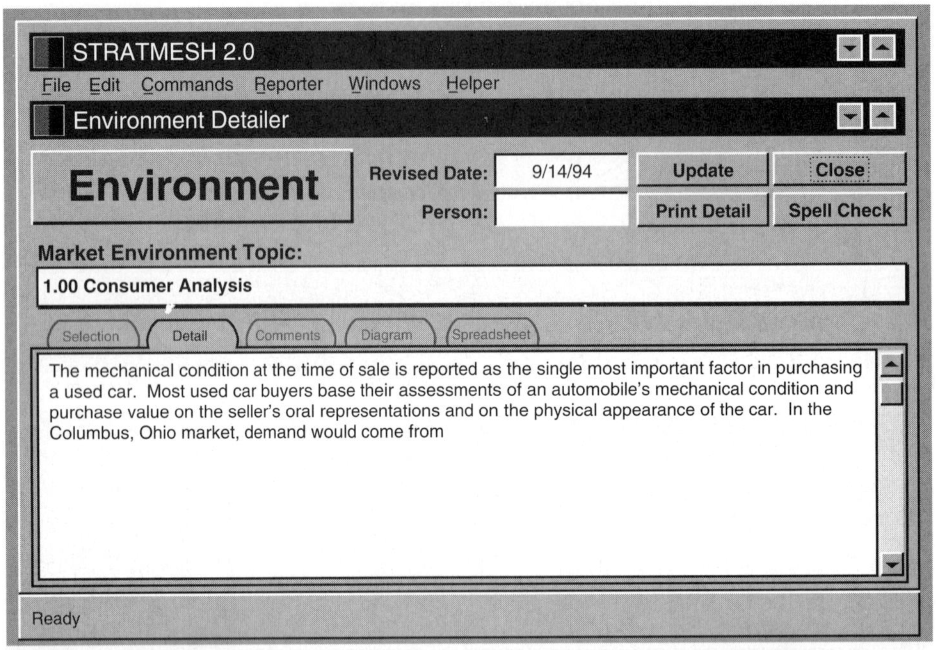

E

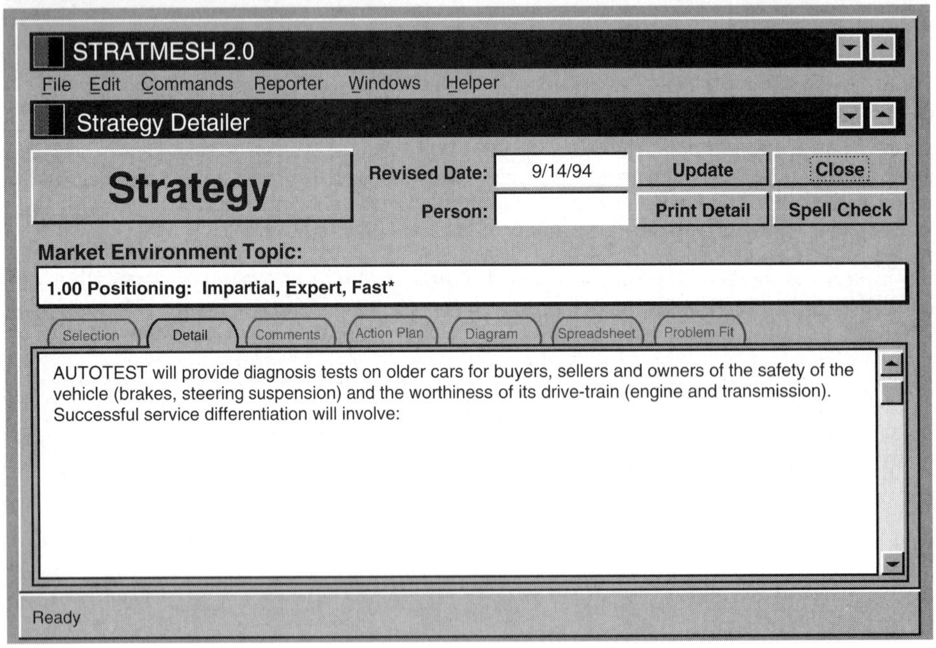

F

(continued)

Figure 2.8 **(continued)**

The Meshing Topic bar and the Meshing Summary Matrix bar within the Meshing Matrices option in the main STRATMESH 2.0 menu window display the entire meshing matrix (see G). A more appropriate name for these classes of meshing matrices is *prospect matrices* as they are a visual way of portraying and assessing the prospects of a strategy or different options, as framed by the Outliner topic headings. This is because the pattern of colors in the cells summarizes the strengths and weaknesses of the strategy and its individual programs and tactics. The more purple and green in the matrix, the brighter the prospects (assessed strengths and weaknesses of the strategy). The more red and yellow, the more negative are the prospects. *STRATMESH 2.0, is a way of visually displaying the strengths and weaknesses, and hence prospects of any decision alternative. It can also be used by senior- and middle-management teams to track the implementation of the programs and their changing prospects.*

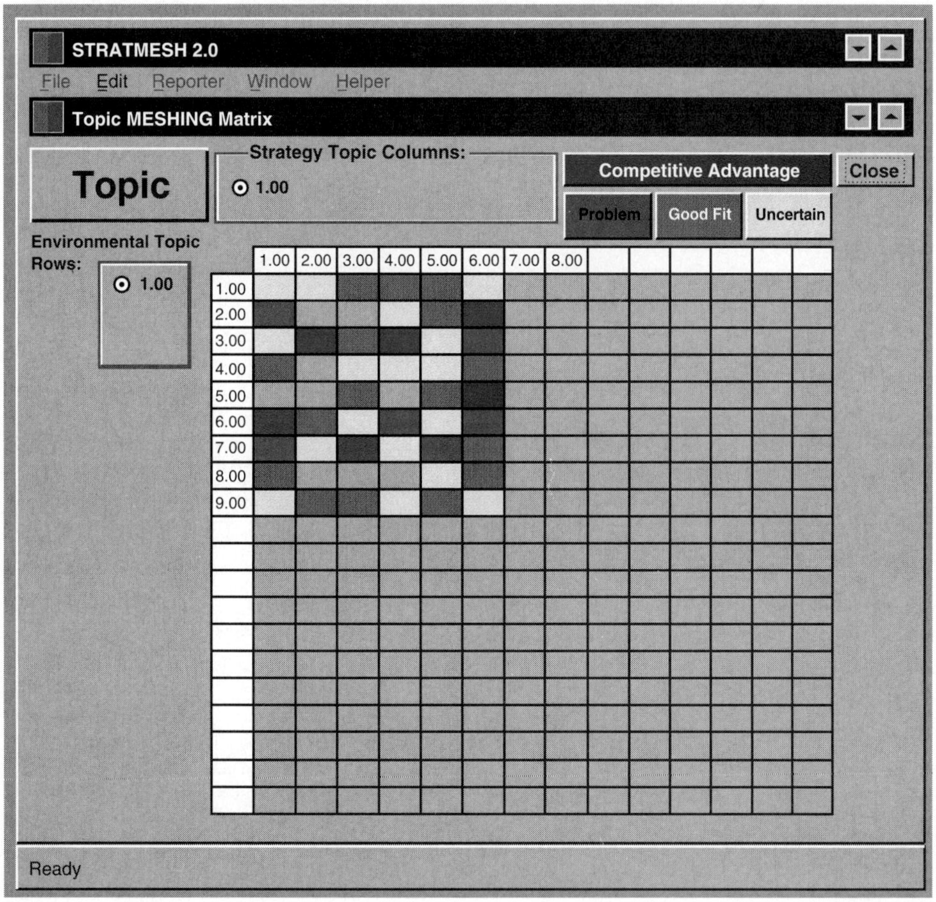

G

"Facts that are not frankly faced have a habit of stabbing us in the back."

Sir Harold Bowden

The secret of business is to know something that nobody else knows.

Aristotle Onassis

C H A P T E R   T H R E E

Market Orientation and Intelligence

"Back in 1980, Mr. Walton and I went into a Wal-Mart in Crowley, La. The first thing we saw was this older gentleman standing there. The man didn't know me, and he didn't see Sam, but he said, 'Hi, How are ya? Glad you're here. If there's anything I can tell you about our store just let me know.' Neither Sam nor I had ever seen such a thing. The store it turned out, had had trouble with shoplifting. Its manager didn't want to intimidate the honest customers by posting a guard, but he wanted to leave a clear message, that if you stole, someone was there who would see it. Well, Sam thought that was the greatest idea he'd ever heard of. We put greeters in the front of every single store. I guess his vindication was that in 1989 he walked into a Kmart in Illinois and found they had installed people greeters at their front doors." (Tom Coughlin, senior vice president, Sam's Club)

This story tells much about the market alertness of Wal-Mart and the market alertness and learning of Kmart! Sam Walton, at the time the wealthiest man in the world, was famous for doing his own market research. Indeed, he spent more time visiting stores and talking to customers than he did in his Arkansas headquarters. Many CEOs are much more remote from their markets. They and their company culture are market oriented but oriented to the wrong market—to the stock market and

wheeling and dealing, rather than staying close to their customer markets.

Market orientation is about quickly introducing new market intelligence into the cross-functional team's decision making by creating and rewarding intelligence generators (e.g., salespeople, distributors, suppliers) who send the team useful market information. It is about developing a mental model of the market (a way of observing and thinking about a market) that serves as a framework for collecting, storing, reporting, and thinking about changes in the market environment. Market research is a $9 billion worldwide business growing at 15 percent a year as competition between manufacturers and retailers intensifies the need to be alert.

This chapter discusses the gathering of and use of market research and the building of a decision support system that makes the individual, team, and firm more alert and market oriented. How hard is it to gain an advantage over your rivals by improving market intelligence gathering and use processes? Often it is not that hard. A 1990 Conference Board study of *Fortune* 1000 firms that prepare formal annual marketing plans (and not all do) found that fewer than one in eight report changes in the consumer environment, competitive environment, trading channels environment, and regulatory environment in their marketing plan. The rest are more casual and sloppy in their tracking of changes in their markets. A 1995 study found that thirty-two out of one hundred companies do not have a formal process for gathering and producing intelligence to help make decisions.[1] These "ostriches" compare with the "eagles," such as General Electric, Motorola, Microsoft, Hewlett Packard, IBM, AT&T, Intel, 3M, Xerox, Merk, Coca-Cola, and Chrysler, that are known for their market alertness, their market orientation, and their clever use of market research. ■

The generation and use of market research enables a management team to *learn* about *changes* in the market *faster* than the competition, making it a major component of competitive rationality and competitive advantage. The question is, How can a decision-making team manage market research and internal self-analysis better than its rivals? This chapter addresses this question.

Market orientation has been defined as "the organization-wide generation of market intelligence, dissemination of that intelligence among departments, and

[1] Kelly Shermach, "Much Talk, Little Action on Competitor Intelligence," *Marketing News*, August 28, 1995, 40.

organization-wide responsiveness to it."[2] This definition requires some reinterpretation when decision making and management are undertaken by a cross-functional team. In a cross-functional team, departmental dissemination of information is of minimal concern because decision making is made *within* the group rather than *among* the departments. For such a cross-functional team, market orientation is largely determined by two skills: the generation of market intelligence and the team's use of the intelligence.

The generation of market intelligence primarily involves the gathering of data: searching for secondary sources, choosing a research contractor, developing a research technique, framing samples, framing questions, and establishing the right type of analysis and presentation format. Most market research texts and courses focus on the data-gathering technology of market intelligence. How the research is presented to and *used* by the decision-making team has been largely neglected, although it is becoming recognized as crucial:

> There are two elements to information process quality. One has to do with the psychological, sociological, and other organizational dynamics affecting information use. The second has to do with the collection and treatment of data in technically sound and appropriate ways. While each element is important, it is far more likely that a problem will exist with the behavioral element. The technologies for data collection— storage, retrieval, and statistical analyses—are well developed. The technology for putting data into use, however, is in its infancy.[3]

Considerable anecdotal evidence and an increasing amount of research support the claim that market orientation increases new product success, sales growth, and profitability.[4] So how in practice does a firm become market oriented? It does so by improving its market intelligence *gathering* processes and its market intelligence *use* processes.

The first section of this chapter describes how market intelligence can be generated by using a number of techniques and processes that vary greatly in their sophistication. The end of this section discusses how market research processes change in hypercompetitive markets that often have no time for traditional techniques. Some of the misuses and limitations of market research are also explained.

The second section explains how the gathered market intelligence can be best used by creating (1) a cross-functional team, (2) a consensus mental model of the market that enables pieces of market intelligence to be fitted together in an environment report by the team to generate insights about the market, and (3) a Market Intelligence E-Mail box (MIEM™).

---

[2] Ajay K. Kohli and Bernard J. Jaworski, "Market Orientation: The Construct, Research Propositions, and Managerial Implications," *Journal of Marketing* 54 (April 1990): 1–18.

[3] Vincent P. Barabba and Gerald Zaltman, *Hearing the Voice of the Market* (Cambridge, MA: Harvard Business School Press, 1991).

[4] See Stanley F. Slater and John C. Narver, "Does Competitive Environment Moderate the Market Orientation-Performance Relationship?" *Journal of Marketing* 58 (January 1994): 46–55; Bernard J. Jaworski and Ajay K. Kohli, "Market Orientation, Antecedents and Consequences," *Journal of Marketing*, 57 (July 1993), 53–70; Stanley F. Slater and John C. Narver, "Market Orientation, Performance, and the Moderating Influence of Competitive Environment," *Journal of Marketing*, 58 (January 1994), 46–55.

Figure 3.1 illustrates how the two sections (the gathering and use of intelligence) fit together. The gathered data and information become knowledge and insight when interpreted within the framework of how the decision maker thinks about the market, or the mental model of the market.

Figure 3.1 How Gathered Market Information Is Used

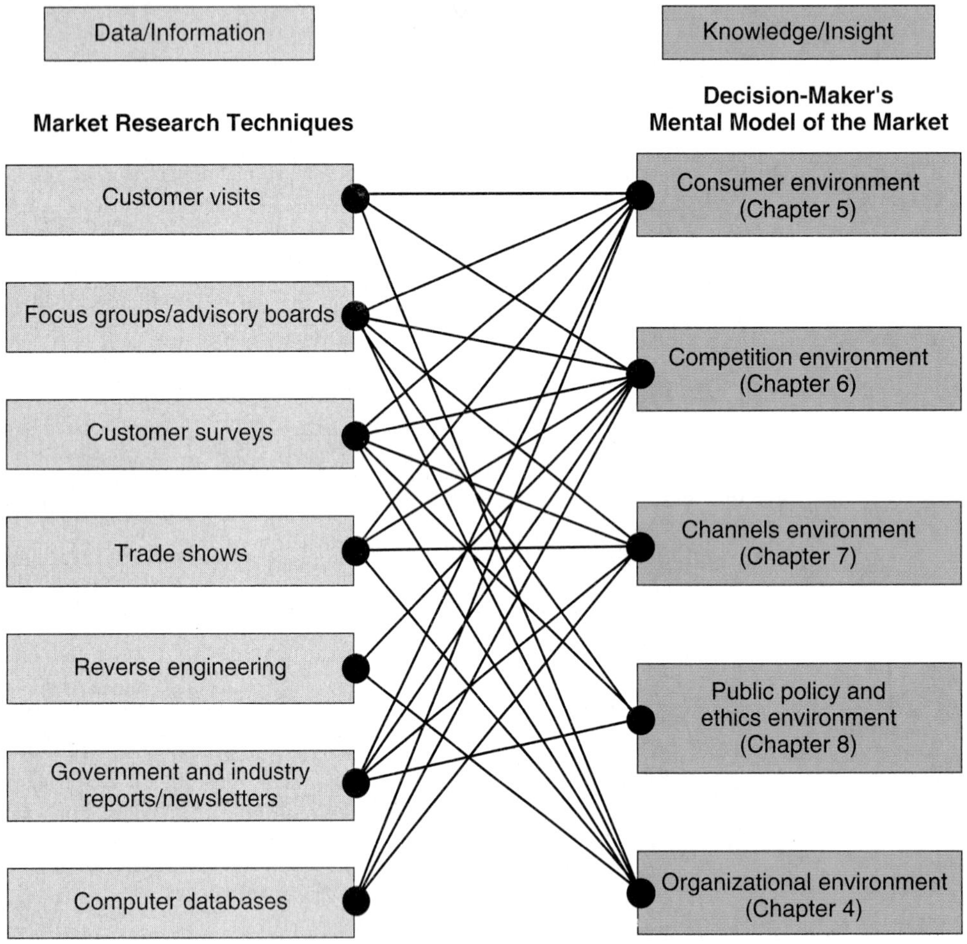

An organizational and cross-functional team gathers market intelligence by the use of many direct and indirect research techniques. It is converted into knowledge and understanding when it is interpreted by, stored in, and changes the decision makers' mental models of the market environment. The first section of this chapter discusses market intelligence-gathering techniques. The second section introduces a 5E mental model that interprets and assimilates market information; that is, it uses market intelligence. The mental submodels that can be applied to understanding consumers, competition, channels, public policy/ethics, and the firm itself are detailed in Chapters 4–8. Generally, the most common problem in organizations is the breakdown in the process of converting market data and information into marketing knowledge and insight.

Market Intelligence Gathering

Many methods of gathering market intelligence are available to the decision-making team. Although the degree of complexity among these options varies, they all offer the cross-functional team one of its most indispensable resources—information.

The Customer Visit

Having cross-functional team members visit customers has emerged as one of the most important market research activities a firm can adopt. Talking directly to customers seems so obvious, and yet some firms have lost themselves in sophisticated, arm's-length consumer research. The problem with survey research is that too many steps and interpretative judgments separate the consumer and the decision maker (see Figure 3.2). The vivid impact of listening to the customers' own words, of seeing how they use the product, is lost if the customers are not visited in their homes or, in business-to-business relationships, their production lines. Consequently, the importance of customers' concerns have less impact in decision making: "Visits allow the voice of the customer to be heard, and they make this voice audible throughout the organization."[5] Furthermore, all the richness of observing the product or service in the usage situation is lost if customers are not communicated with directly. Japanese firms such as Panasonic and Sony prefer hands-on consumer research that focuses on the way current customers use specific products and brands.[6] For example, one appliance manufacturer took two hundred photos of actual Japanese kitchens and concluded from the photos that the major problem that appliance manufacturers have to address when designing new appliances is the tremendous shortage of space in many kitchens. This observation might not have been made had executives not visited the homes in person and taken the photographs. Photos should have the time, place, and contact phone number recorded on the back of the photo and displayed on the walls of the room where the team meets. They are a constant reminder of the customers' usage situation that can be "revisited" by simply looking up from the meeting table, and, if need be, the customer can be called back. Photos and videos can be similarly used in visits to retailers.

The customer visit is particularly crucial for business-to-business marketing because a few key customers often account for 80 percent of the firm's business. Marketing's responsibility in such markets is to make sure that everyone interacts with customers instead of simply passing on secondhand information about customers. DuPont's customer-oriented culture goes beyond its cross-functional teams staying in close contact with its customers; its "Adopt a Customer" program encourages manufacturing process workers to visit a customer once a month and represent the customer's needs on the factory floor.[7]

The cross-functional team should also have firsthand experience of being a customer of competitors' products and services. For example, a team of Mariott executives spent six months on the road staying in economy hotels, learning about competitors'

---

[5] Edward F. McQuarrie and Shelby H. McIntyre, "The Customer Visit: An Emerging Practice in Business-to-Business Marketing," working paper (Cambridge, MA: Marketing Science Institute, 1992), 92–114.

[6] Johny K. Johansson and Ikujiro Nonaka, "Market Research the Japanese Way," *Harvard Business Review*, May/June 1987, 16–22; Lance Ealey and Leif Soderberg, "How Honda Cures Design Amnesia," *The McKinsey Quarterly*, Spring 1990, 3–14; and Kenichi Ohmae, *The Borderless World* (New York: Harper Business, 1990).

[7] B. Dumaine, "Creating a New Company Culture," *Fortune*, January 15, 1990, 127–31.

Figure 3.2 Getting Closer to the Customer

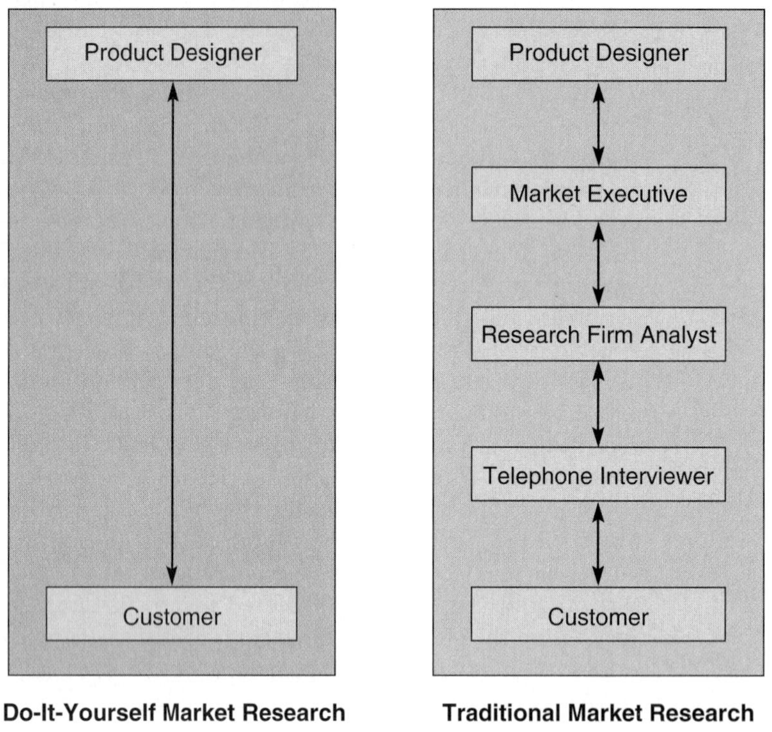

The problem with some traditional market research processes is that too many people come between the customer and the key decision maker, such as the product designer. The people in between may deliberately put their own spin on what the customer says (for internal political reasons) or may simply unwittingly filter what the customer says or does so crucial insights are lost. The solution is for the decision maker to leave the cozy office or lab and visit with customers. But such visits should involve a systematic and rigorous qualitative research process that increases the observational skills and learning of the executive. Designers, engineers, and cross-functional team members who are not eager to make such visits and prefer to obtain their information about the market third- or fourthhand, or who refuse training to become better firsthand observers, are not worthy of the trust and responsibility they have been given.

strengths and weaknesses. The result was the $500 million launch of its Fairfield Inn chain that immediately achieved an occupancy rate ten points higher than the industry average.[8] Japanese companies have been known to send up-and-coming executives to the United States for several years to do nothing but travel around and study the market for their products firsthand.

The importance of creating a company culture that encourages direct contact with the customer explains why the chief executive officer of United Airlines spends time at the ticket counter and why senior executives at 3M spend several days a month visiting customers, and not just big accounts. Some process guidelines for such visits are listed here:

[8] B. Dumaine, "Corporate Spies Snoop to Conquer," *Fortune*, November 7, 1988, 68–76.

- Have customer visits arranged by the sales force: cooperation between factory engineers and the sales force is crucial. No one likes someone else in a company doing anything behind his or her back, particularly a sales rep whose commissions depend on customer trust and goodwill. Sales reps are territorial and rightly so. Arranging the visit is a first step in improving communication and cooperation between engineering and sales.
- Visit ten to twenty randomly chosen customers, as well as important customers who are leaders in adopting new technology. This reduces the impact of an extreme, atypical opinion in later decisions.
- Only use jargon if the customer uses the same jargon. Listen carefully and note the way customers talk about the product. This gives you clues about the benefits they seek, how they think about the benefits, what problems they confront, and how to redesign the product or service to gain a competitive advantage. Rather than asking the customer to adopt your jargon, you should be adopting the customer's words and metaphors. This is how a team changes its thinking about the customer and related decisions. Do not talk in front of customers using jargon that makes them feel like you are foreign tourists.
- Learn to listen and observe the way anthropologists do so; do not treat the visit as a sales call. This is something the sales rep will find hard to accept. Do not engage in disparaging the competition when they are praised by the customer. Instead, be open to ideas that can be quickly imitated.
- Define your research objectives in advance, and use a discussion guide based on these objectives. Write a report on the visit that addresses the research objectives. Report separately on the serendipitous (unexpected) information. "Report" means informing key people within your organization about what you saw or heard.
- Observe the product in use in every usage situation. Particularly, note and photograph how an innovative customer has adapted your product, package, or service to improve its performance in a particular usage situation. This may suggest a promising new design feature to better service a market niche.
- If possible, have two or three members of the team make the visit together. The time spent talking while traveling before and after the visit is invaluable. Shared expectations, perceptions, and insights are best when made close to the customer visit. Members of the team also discover what they did not see or hear and thus learn from each other how to become better observers and listeners.

Focus Groups

A focus group is a carefully recruited group of six to twelve people who participate in a freewheeling, one- to two-hour discussion that focuses on a particular subject, such as product usage, shopping habits, warrantee experiences, and so on. A skilled, trained conversationalist called a moderator conducts the session, and members of the cross-functional decision team often watch the discussion through a one-way mirror or on closed-circuit television. Conducting focus groups is probably the most frequently used type of formal market research conducted today. Focus groups can be used successfully by following these process suggestions:

- The random calling and screening of participants for usage experience and target demographics, such as age and education, can be expensive, sometimes nearly $1,000 to find thirty to fifty willing participants. Consider spending more to create a longer list of willing, qualified participants that can be drawn from at fairly short notice. This will greatly speed up the process of running future focus groups. Take care to check how frequently they have participated in focus groups—avoid professional participants.

- Expect to pay at least $50 per participant to cover travel expenses and two to three hours of his or her time. Professionals such as doctors and architects may expect to be paid several hundred dollars for participating.
- Find a good moderator who can relate to your target group, and develop a long-term relationship with the moderator. Do not conduct focus groups yourself unless you have had professional training from a company such as Burke and you can remain emotionally detached from the subject. The marketing executive on a cross-functional team should be so trained. Be careful using someone from your advertising agency to run the focus groups because she or he may focus too much on advertising.
- Encourage the cross-functional team and senior management to watch the focus group. The attention focus and discussion that ensues has an immediacy that will have a long-term impact on decision making. It also enables questions to be passed to the moderator during a break.
- Use a videotape to record the focus group because the words and phrases recorded can be helpful in developing advertising campaigns.
- Focus-group sessions should last no more than two hours with a fifteen-minute break on the hour. When the quality of participation and insights slump, wrap up the focus group.
- Continue to run focus groups until no new, important insights are learned from the last focus group that is run. This often means only three or four focus groups need to be run.
- The concept of focus groups has been taken a step further in working with distributor and franchise advisory councils. They are permanent focus groups that regulary meet at Trade Shows to provide feedback on what is happening in the market and reactions to different ideas and programs. While focus groups are great at surfacing issues, problems, and the range of services and features desired, they are seldom representative. If there is a very strong agreement within and between focus groups on an issue then it is probably representative. Otherwise, the focus groups may have to be followed up with survey research of a representative sample of the target market.

Customer Values, Benefits, Beliefs, and Satisfaction Surveys

Survey research involves the systematic sampling of a population of consumers using a carefully prepared set of questions. Satisfaction surveys monitor customers who have recently purchased a product or service and who are contacted by telephone or return postcard.

As described in greater detail in Chapter 19, satisfaction tracking surveys are important for monitoring and controlling the quality of a product or service. If a customer is not *completely* satisfied with the performance of a product or service or with the way a distributor or retailer made the sale, then a good satisfaction survey finds out why by probing for the root of the problem. By doing this, the satisfaction survey becomes far more than a crucial quality-control device; it can suggest new product/service modifications and new marketing programs.

Major, one-time surveys of individuals or households are normally taken to segment a market by differences in buyer values, lifestyles, product usage, benefits sought, and beliefs about product performance. Table 3.1 compares the major survey research approaches. Unfortunately, low response rates are becoming a growing problem. The cooperation of households has been worn thin by telemarketing (sometimes unethically disguised as survey research), political polling, and market research. Figure

Table 3.1 Comparison of Major Survey Research Techniques

CRITERIA	DIRECT/COLD MAILING	MAIL PANELS	TELEPHONE	PERSONAL IN-HOME	MAIL INTERCEPT
Complexity and versatility	Not much	Not much	Substantial, but complex or lengthy scales difficult to use	Highly flexible	Most flexible
Quantity of data	Substantial	Substantial	Short, lasting typically between 15 and 30 minutes	Greatest quantity	Limited to 25 minutes or less
Sample control	Little	Substantial, but representativeness may be a question	Good, but nonlisted households can be a problem	In theory, provides greatest control	Can be problematic; sample representativeness may be questionable
Quality of data	Better for sensitive or embarrassing questions; however, no interviewer is present to clarify what is being asked		Positive side, interview can clear up any ambiguities; negative side, may lead to socially accepted answers	The chance of cheating arises	Unnatural testing environment can lead to bias
Response rates	In general, low, as low as 10%	70%–80%	60%–80%	Greater than 80%	As high as 80%
Speed	Several weeks; completion time will increase with follow-up mailings	Several weeks with no follow-up mailings, longer with follow-up mailings	Large studies can be completed in 3 to 4 weeks	Faster than mail but typically slower than telephone surveys	Large studies can be completed in a few days
Cost	Inexpensive; as low as $2.50 per completed interview	Lowest	Not as low as mail; depends on incidence rate and length of questionnaire	Can be relatively expensive, but considerable variability	Less expensive than in-home but higher than telephone; again, length and incidence rate will determine cost
Uses	Executive, industrial, medical, and readership studies	All areas of marketing research, particularly useful in low-incidence categories	Particularly effective in studies that require national samples	Still prevalent in product testing and other studies that require visual cues or product prototypes	Pervasive-concept tests, name tests, package tests, copy tests

SOURCE: Reproduced with permission from William Dillon, Thomas J. Madden, and Neil H. Firtle, *Marketing Research in a Marketing Environment* (Homewood, IL: Irwin, 1990), 201.

3.3 presents the conventional market research process. It indicates that intelligence gathering is often undertaken in an incremental way. The least costly source of answers to the perceived problem are first searched. Major studies are only taken if satisfactory answers cannot be found from secondary or syndicated sources, if the issue is of great importance, or if a precise answer is required.

Figure 3.3 **The Basic Market Research Process**

1. Problem Recognition:
   What happened? What is happening? Should we do it?

2. Meet and Define Problem and Determine How to Solve It:
   When is the answer needed? Limits method.
   How valuable is the answer? Limits method.
   How valuable is high accuracy? Limits method.

3. Search Secondary and Syndicated Data Sources:
   Has it happened in the past? Check archives.
   Call outside experts for answers.
   How can syndicated research suppliers help?
   Does any published research on the problem exist?
   Meet and review answers. Stop if satisfactory.

4. Undertake Quick-and-Dirty Primary Research:
   Conduct an electronic voice-mail survey of the sales force.
   Call on or fax customers/distributors.
   Run focus groups. Meet and review answers. Stop if satisfactory.

5. Undertake Thorough Primary Research:
   Select sampling frame (random-sample national panel provided by market research firm). Choose survey technique (personal visit, mall intercept, telephone, mail). Design questionnaire.

6. Analyze Information:
   Review descriptive statistics (such as percentages, means, standard deviations). Conduct relationship analyses (such as cross-tabs, Chi-square, correlational analyses, structural equations modeling, logit, ANOVA, MANOVA, Conjoint).

7. Present Findings:
   Offer progress briefings on important findings.
   Report the presentation.
   Archive findings and data.

This figure presents the conventional approach to research. Firms often undertake steps 1 through 4. If they require more formal primary research, they will likely hire a market research firm that will take a month or more to do the study at a cost of $5,000–$10,000, sometimes a lot more.

Trade Shows

Trade shows enable sellers to promote their newest products and services to customers and distributors. They are also a great source of information, not only about new products but also about how interested distributors and customers are in the new products. They provide an opportunity to network with rival salespeople and to learn about what is happening to other rivals.

Some firms still treat trade shows as two- to three-day selling parties. They sell hard and they play hard. The competitively rational firm approaches trade shows with a deadly intent to learn everything it can about the market in a disciplined way. This includes hiring market research people or using its advertising agency employees to "walk and talk" the show because it does not take many trade shows before competitors recognize their rivals' key employees.

Reverse Engineering

To understand competitors' designs and how their products are produced, most companies buy their competitors' products and put them through rigorous performance testing. The products are torn apart (reverse engineering) to see what they are made of and how they are made (see Figure 3.4). In developing the Taurus, Ford dismantled some fifty midsize cars made by its competitors in its effort to imitate and improve on the best features.[9] Basic questions were asked while studying the components, the design, and the assembly: (1) How can we do it so the target customer will like ours more? and (2) How can we do it cheaper? These two questions address the first and second competitive rationality drives.

Reverse engineering, however, requires a great deal of accumulated knowledge about the history of product design and manufacturing in the product market. Such a highly experienced engineer can quickly see a change a competitor has made to reduce costs or increase manufacturing quality. A young, inexperienced engineer might take weeks to detect the changes, if at all. Reverse engineering skills can be so important in some markets that a market research priority should be to keep the experienced engineers on the team.

[9] Russell Mitchell, "How Ford Hit the Bull's Eye with Taurus," *Business Week*, June 30, 1986, 69–70.

Figure 3.4

Xerox engineers taking apart competitors' products to better understand their design, quality, and how they were made.

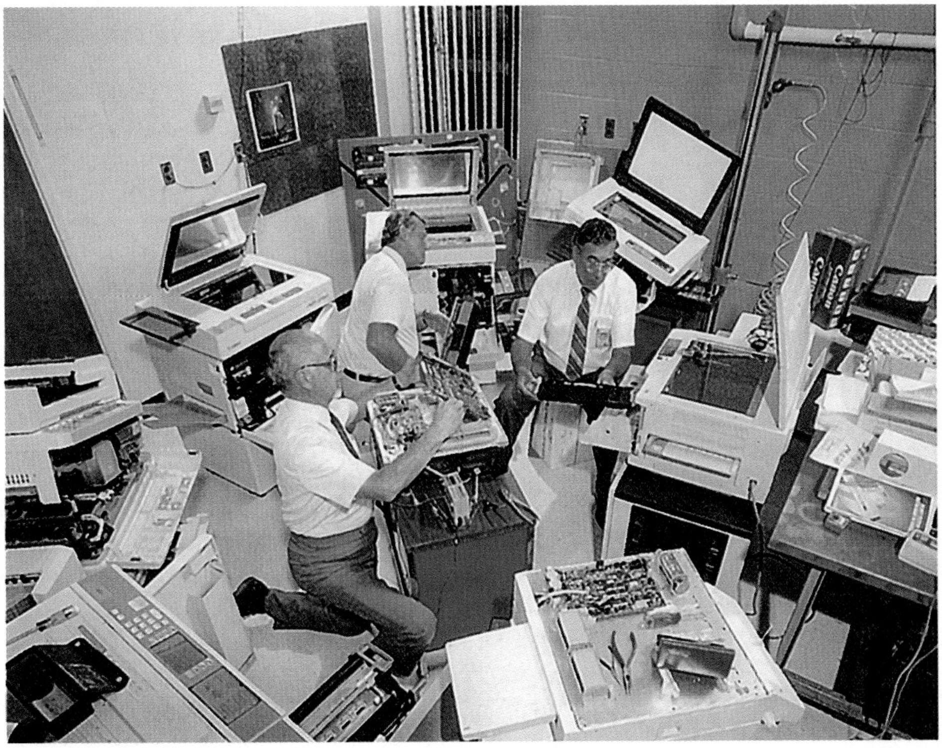

Competitor Annual Reports, 10-Ks, and 10-Qs

Although traditional annual reports appear to be glossy self-promotions to shareholders, they often contain valuable information about trends in company goals, missions, and finances that can be tracked by comparing a firm's annual reports over four or five years. Analysts often look for changes in company direction by comparing the comments of the chairperson and chief executive from year to year. The competition's newsletters to distributors and employees also often contain nuggets of information, as described by the following executive:

> Two years ago, we found an interesting article in one of our competitor's employee publications. A vice president was saying, "This is what our company is all about, and this is where we want to take the company in the next five years. We want to be this, and this, and this." There was the company's strategy, all spelled out.[10]

The following comments from the same study of competitive intelligence also indicate the value of carefully reviewing a competitor's literature:

> An electronic database is very useful when you have an identifiable question, target, or subject. But to get a sense of the trends in the industry, there's no substitute for what any junior grade intelligence officer does in the CIA: you read the literature, you follow it closely. That's what a sports writer does. . . .
>
> One of the beautiful things about competitive intelligence is that the competitor has to tell his customers what he wants them to believe. . . . If a company does a decent advertising job, the ad campaign will give you a warning signal. The ads will tell you what market segments they're emphasizing and what they're trying to do with their product line. . . . If you read their ads and their annual reports—and put them in historic perspective—it's obvious where the company is headed.

The Securities and Exchange Commission (SEC) requires public companies to file annual 10-K reports. The 10-K provides a great deal of financial and competitive information, including analysis by product line, market, and distribution channel (see Figure 3.5). It also includes valuable information on backlogs, patents, licenses granted, and franchises.

The 10-Q reports present quarterly earnings. The pressure from stock analysts has forced a further voluntary disclosure of the marketing plans of companies as chief executives attempt to sell the prospects of their firm to the marketplace each quarter. In doing this, they often reveal their hand to the alert competitor. Firms often subscribe to industry-specific newsletters issued by Wall Street research and brokerage firms to learn the latest facts or speculation about their competition, distributors, or major customers. A service such as the *Value Line Investment Survey* provides brief reports on the state of an industry and the recent moves and prospects of some two thousand companies in one hundred industries. Information about small companies is much harder to obtain; the best sources are the reference librarian in the town where the firm operates or even the local town newspapers, which will have a clippings file on the firm. The best sources of competitive intelligence and most useful

[10] Howard Sutton, *Competitive Intelligence* (New York: The Conference Board, 1988), 33.

Figure 3.5

The Form 10-K
An example of the first page of a 10-K form. Important competitive information is often buried within the form.

UNITED STATES
SECURITIES AND EXCHANGE COMMISSION
Washington, D.C. 20549

FORM 10-K

☒ **ANNUAL REPORT PURSUANT TO SECTION 13 OR 15(d) OF THE SECURITIES EXCHANGE ACT OF 1934**

For the Fiscal Year Ended June 30, 1995

☐ **TRANSITION REPORT PURSUANT TO SECTION 13 OR 15(d) OF THE SECURITIES EXCHANGE ACT OF 1934**

For the Transition Period From ___ to ___

Commission File Number: 0-14278

MICROSOFT CORPORATION
(Exact name of registrant as specified in its charter)

Washington **(State or other jurisdiction of incorporation or organization)**	**91-1144442** **(I.R.S. Employer Identification No.)**
One Microsoft Way, Redmond, Washington **(Address of principal executive office)**	**98052-6399** **(Zip Code)**

Registrant's telephone number, including area code: (206) 882-8080

Securities registered pursuant to Section 12(b) of the Act: None

Securities registered pursuant to Section 12(g) of the Act: Common Stock

Indicate by check mark whether the registrant (1) has filed all reports required to be filed by Section 13 or 15(d) of the Securities Exchange Act of 1934 during the preceding 12 months (or for such shorter period that the registrant was required to file such reports), and (2) has been subject to such filing requirements for the past 90 days. Yes ☒ No ☐

Indicate by check mark if disclosure of delinquent filers pursuant to Item 405 of Regulation S-K is not contained herein, and will not be contained, to the best of registrant's knowledge, in definitive proxy or information statements incorporated by reference in Part III of this Form 10-K or any amendment to this Form 10-K. ☐

The aggregate market value of the common stock held by non-affiliates of the registrant as of September 8, 1995 was $34,330,611,220.

The number of shares outstanding of the registrant's common stock as of September 8, 1995 was 589,952,132.

DOCUMENTS INCORPORATED BY REFERENCE

Portions of the definitive Proxy Statement dated September 25, 1995 to be delivered to shareholders in connection with the Annual Meeting of Shareholders to be held October 27, 1995 are incorporated by reference into Part III.

Table 3.2 Best Information and Sources Provided by Competitive Intelligence

	MOST USEFUL SOURCE OF INFORMATION (BY TYPE OF MARKET) PERCENT DISTRIBUTION			
	TOTAL	INDUSTRIAL PRODUCTS	CONSUMER PRODUCTS	BOTH CONSUMER AND INDUSTRIAL
Sales force	27%	35%	18%	23%
Publications, databases	16	13	15	22
Customers	14	13	11	17
Marketing research, tracking services	9	3	24	9
Financial reports	5	7	3	1
Distributors	3	4	1	1
Employees (unspecified)	2	2	6	—
Analysis of products	2	1	3	3
Other	8	6	8	13
No answer	14	16	11	11
	100%	100%	100%	100%
Number of responding companies	308	158	72	78

	MOST USEFUL TYPE OF INFORMATION (BY TYPE OF MARKET) PERCENT DISTRIBUTION			
	TOTAL	INDUSTRIAL PRODUCTS	CONSUMER PRODUCTS	BOTH CONSUMER AND INDUSTRIAL
Pricing	23%	26%	20%	19%
Strategy	19	20	15	22
Sales data	13	11	18	12
New products, product mix	11	13	8	10
Advertising/marketing activities	7	3	19	4
Costs	6	8	3	5
Key customers/markets	3	3	6	1
Research and development	2	2	1	3
Management style	2	1	3	1
Other	4	4	—	8
No answer	10	9	7	15
	100%	100%	100%	100%
Number of responding companies	308	158	72	78

SOURCE: Howard Sutton, *Competitive Intelligence* (New York: The Conference Board, 1988).

type of information collected are presented in Table 3.2.[11] Figure 3.6 is an illustration of the intelligence-gathering process of a firm that is expert in competitive analysis.

[11] Howard Sutton, *Competitive Intelligence* (New York: The Conference Board, 1988); see also Richard L. Pinkerton, "Competitive Intelligence Revisited: A History and Assessment of its Use in Marketing," *Competitive Intelligence Review* 5, no. 4 (1994): 23–31, and Bernard J. Jaworski and Liang Chee Wee, *Competitive Intelligence: Creating Value for the Organization*, (Alexandria, Virginia: The Society of Competitive Intelligence Professionals, August 1993).

Figure 3.6 **A Business Intelligence Service**

Stephen J. Bass & Partners Inc.
1335 Dublin Rd. - 200 A Columbus, OH 43215
614-481-3590 FAX 614-481-3501
1-800-323-1427

THE BUSINESS INTELLIGENCE-GATHERING PROCESS

Stephen J. Bass & Partners, Inc. (SJB&P) is a business intelligence consulting firm which gathers and analyzes information enabling executives to make timely, profitable strategic decisions. The methodology SJB&P typically utilizes in developing such intelligence for its clients is outlined below.

SJB&P has determined, based on decades of intelligence-gathering experience, that a synergistic, multi-phased process is often the most efficient approach for satisfying client intelligence needs.

Phase One

In phase one, all readily available published sources pertinent to a client's specific information needs are identified. This substantial secondary research effort encompasses, but is not limited to:

- Analysis of information and sources already contained in SJB&P and client files.
- Computer and manual literature searches of appropriate databases and hard copy indexes.
- Trade association publications and libraries.
- Federal government publications and libraries.
- Trade periodicals, and studies and special issues published by such periodicals.
- Industry/company reports published by research/consulting firms that often specialize in specific industries.
- Special libraries which focus on particular industries.
- Industry/company financial and credit performance reports.
- Industry and company directories and catalogs.
- Company financial reports, speeches, press releases, testimonies, etc.
- Wall Street analyst reports on relevant industry segments and/or companies.
- Records published or made available by relevant state/local government offices, such as state commerce departments and corporation and securities divisions, local building departments, tax assessors, and planning and development offices.
- Articles and other information available from local sources, such as regional/local business press, daily newspapers, libraries, chambers of commerce, universities, etc.
- Transcripts of studies of relevant industry segments undertaken by government agencies such as the Federal Trade Commission, U.S. Justice Department or the U.S. International Trade Administration.
- Case studies, doctoral dissertations, and other academic research published on the industry/company.

Typically, some of a client's intelligence needs will not be fully satisfied by such a comprehensive search for published information. Thus, in order to fill critical information gaps, identified in analyzing phase one's results, a second phase of the research effort is often undertaken.

Phase Two

In phase two, telephone and in-person interviews of experts on the relevant industry segments and companies are implemented to fill these key information gaps. Experts contacted in this phase often include, but are not limited to, individuals employed by government agencies, universities, brokerage houses, trade associations, advertising agencies, consulting firms, periodical/report publishers, newspapers, and industry participants, such as competitors, suppliers, sales representatives, distributors, etc. The results achieved in these interviews are enhanced by SJB&P's substantial network of industry experts covering a wide variety of diverse fields.

Other types of research often incorporated in phase two include: visits to competitors, suppliers, customers, etc; attendance at trade shows; consumer/customer interviews, etc.

To optimize the effectiveness of this phase, part of the research is sometimes carried out in the actual cities and states in which relevant firms/division/plants are located. SJB&P's network of affiliated information researchers, located in key cities in the U.S. and overseas, facilitates this effort.

Phase Three

After the phase two research, SJB&P typically completes phase three. This encompasses analysis and integration of intelligence obtained in previous phases and preparation of a report that concisely profiles the results in a format designed to effectively meet the client's specific needs.

To learn more about the techniques and uses of business intelligence, SJB&P can be contacted the following address: Stephen J. Bass & Partners, Inc., 1335 Dublin Road, Suite 200A, Columbus, Ohio 43215.

A service offered by a market research firm. Companies often prefer to use the services of such a firm. It is a way of not tipping off their competition as well as obtaining the firm's intelligence gathering process expertise.

Government Reports, Industry Reports, and Newsletters

The U.S. Census Bureau, the biggest market research organization in the world, compiles masses of information about household trends. Almost every public library has the bureau's reports, and it has offices in large cities with specialists whose job is to help businesspeople find out what they need to know. *American Demographics* magazine also presents analyses of census data, in addition to other analyses on population trends and changes in values, habits, hobbies, and entertainment. The Government Printing Office (Washington, D.C. 20402) has a *Subject Bibliography Index*, which lists free government publications on some three hundred subjects. The Library of Congress (202-707-5000) also specializes in helping people find information. The U.S. government also produces three- to thirty-page annual industry reports on more than three hundred industries that cover both national and global trends in supply and competition. These *U.S. Industrial Outlook* reports provide references, which can be followed up, and the names and phone numbers of the government researchers who prepared the report. Other important government publications are *Statistical Abstract of the United States* and the transcripts of industry studies undertaken by the Federal Trade Commission, Justice Department, and U.S. International Trade Commission. Calling and asking for information from an expert in government or industry is an important market intelligence skill. Some general contact process rules are listed here:

- The hard part is the introduction. You should politely and cheerfully introduce yourself, give your name and the name of the person who recommended you call, and state the purpose of your call. Credible compliments go a long way.
- Initially, ask specific, easy questions. Be open, enthusiastic, optimistic, humble, courteous, and grateful.
- Use a list, but do not sound as if you are following a list. An apparent lack of structure encourages spontaneous insights and allows for bond-forming casual discussions of other icebreaking topics such as sports, world events, children, or hobbies.
- Send a thank-you note (you may wish to call again), and offer to return the favor.
- Be persistent. Keep generating leads. Calling a cooperative expert is by far the best $10 value for money in market research and analysis. It may take ten such calls before you find the "true" expert who is willing to share her or his expertise.[12]

The trade associations, trade journals, and trade newsletters associated with a particular industry can be located through a local reference library or by consulting *The Directory of Directories*, *The Encyclopedia of Associations*, *The Encyclopedia of Business Information Sources*, and the *Nelson Directory*. Although trade associations spend much of their time and effort lobbying and running educational programs for their members, they are often a rich source of the history and current trends in a market. Some firms also specialize in finding relevant articles and news reports (clipping services), and other research firms sell industry or market reports, firms such as FIND/SVP. A page of its 1991 catalog is presented in Figure 3.7.

Computer Databases

An on-line INTERNET database allows users to search for articles, newsletters, or other reports on *key word* topics. Key words, such as *drink mixes* and *Europe*, can be combined to obtain information about the drink-mix market in Europe. Four examples of the many databases now available are listed here:

- DIALOG Information Services, Inc., which can access some 350 business databases, including industry directories and company financial statements.
- NEXIS, which can access four hundred major newspapers, magazines, and newsletters.
- FINDEX, a directory of industry market research reports.
- COMPUTER-READABLE Databases, the best directory of databases.

Public libraries and state university reference librarians can help locate and even access several database directories.

---

[12] This list is based in part on advice from "The Art of Obtaining Information," *Washington Researchers*, Washington, D.C.

Figure 3.7

Examples of Commercially Available Market Reports

In addition to the hundreds of industry reports prepared by the U.S. Commerce Department each year, market research firms such as FIND/SVP prepare catalogs of research reports that can be purchased. Prices range from the hundreds up to several thousand dollars.

The Market for Ice Milk & Lowfat Frozen Dairy Desserts

New gains forecast for $4.8 billion market.

Ice milk and similar products are seeing new gains due to American consumers' continued focus on health and nutrition. FIND/SVP's comprehensive new study assesses the market impact of new taste improvements, flavor additions, and other innovations that are enabling producers to position premium ice milks against premium ice creams. Aspartame and Simplesse sugar and fat substitutes are evaluated for their potential appeal to those who would not otherwise buy frozen desserts.

AA270 October, 1990 206 pages $1,700
FIND/SVP Cardholders' Price $1,530.00

The Frozen Yogurt Market

The dynamic frozen yogurt industry is currently feeling the repercussions of rapid expansion, consumer awareness, and emerging regulatory issues. Frozen yogurt's steadily increasing popularity has led ice cream giants to join existing franchises and refrigerated yogurt manufacturers in marketing a wide range of frozen yogurt products. FIND/SVP's study sizes both the current and future market for hard-packed and soft-serve, providing forecasts through 1996. It profiles leading competitors, analyzes marketing strategies, and evaluates current manufacturing practices.

AA317 February, 1992 275 pages $1,650
FIND/SVP Cardholders' Price $1,485.00

Lite Products Report 1991

The New Product News report describes, by product category, all of the reduced calorie products introduced in 1991. Brief abstracts identify manufacturers, product particulars and retail information. Compared for the segment are the number of lite products introduced in 1991 versus the total number of food products introduced by food category. The report is also available by year for each of its 28 years of publication (1964-1991).

GN16 January, 1992 c. 50 pages. $300

The Taste of Lite

Just how important is taste in these lower fat days of health, environment, and intense price competition? Consumer Network's brand-rating report addresses this and other key issues. Based on a qualitative and quantitative survey of 343 shoppers, the report contains126 verbatims on taste. In all, 41 brands spanning10 different categories are evaluated, regarding the impact of taste, price, and other factors on purchasing decisions.

CK14 1992 38 pages $280

The Light Foods Market

LA220 April, 1991 200+ pages. $1,750

The Diet Aids Market

The $450 million market for diet aids is undergoing sweeping changes. The emphasis is currently on appetite suppressants and meal replacements, but these products face competition not only from each other, but also from the many alternatives that dieters have in light foods, diet foods and special diets based on regular foods. Both past and future trends are the focus of this comprehensive Packaged Facts market study that covers, for each category of diet aids, such topics as market size and growth, projections to 1995, the competitive situation, marketing trends and new product development, advertising and promotion, retail and direct sales and consumer usage.

LA187 February, 1991 135+ pages $1,550
FIND/SVP Cardholders' Price $1,472.50

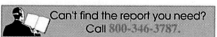

Can't find the report you need?
Call 800-346-3787.

Low-Fat & Low-Cholesterol Issues Monitor

For food and drug marketers, it is becoming crucial to keep up with the rush of medical, regulatory, and consumer information about low-fat and low-cholesterol foods. Now there's a unique resource to help you stay one step ahead of these fast-moving developments. FIND/SVP's Monitor is the only newsletter to track low-fat and low-cholesterol topics on a month-to-month basis. Each issue summarizes and reviews hundreds of published articles from food, drug, medical, marketing, business and consumer magazines. The Monitor also features a special bimonthly section containing original FIND/SVP reporting based on interviews with key FDA officials, major manufacturers/distributors and retailers.

ZA01 Subscription (12 issues) $2,700/year

The Market for Lowfat & Low-Cholesterol Frozen Dinners & Entrees

This report from FIND/SVP analyzes the market for frozen dinners and entrees that are marketed as containing low levels of fat and/or cholesterol. Marketed as "healthy" or "light," these products are expected to account for retail sales of $2.4 billion by 1996. The study discusses marketing techniques, labeling regulations, new product introductions, packaging innovations, and advertising and promotion. It analyzes the marketing strategies of leading and innovative competitors and the impact of competitive products outside of the category. The study focuses on demographic profiles of users and consumer attitudes and forecasts the size of the market by segment through 1996. Competitor profiles include the leaders ConAgra, Nestlé/Stouffer, Heinz/Weight Watchers, Campbell Soup, and Kraft General Foods.

AA322 February, 1992 282 pages $1,650
FIND/SVP Cardholders' Price $1,485.00

The Market for Low-Fat & Low-Cholesterol Foods

Sales of low-fat, low-cholesterol foods, including fat substitutes and cholesterol-lowering ingredients, are expected to soar from about $12 billion in 1991 to over $25 billion in 1996. The FIND/SVP study examines the market for these products, including frozen food, dairy and oil-based food, meat and egg products, cereals, snacks, seafood, and diet food. The competitive situation, new product trends, labeling, research, and technological advances are analyzed in detail. Government regulations and new legislation on health claims and other issues are examined. Fat substitutes such as NutraSweet's newly approved Simplesse and cholesterol-lowering products are evaluated. More than 20 leading food companies are profiled, including Campbell Soup, ConAgra, Quaker Oats, Nestlé, and Borden. Includes extensive up-to-the-minute analysis of November 1991 FDA labeling guidelines.

AA341 November, 1992 331 pages $1,650
FIND/SVP Cardholders' Price $1,485.00

Liquid Protein Diets Market

This Marketdata report investigates the liquid protein (VLCDs—very low-calorie diets) and meal replacement powders marketplace, covering prescription only and over-the-counter product programs. It analyzes market potential, the size/growth outlook (early 1980s to 1996), demographic factors and the impact of celebrity endorsements. Also examined are FDA regulation, side effects, the growing number of hospital and physicians' proprietary formulas and programs and the market for retail, nonprescription diet powders and shakes. Detailed descriptions of the top 10 medically monitored plans offered and strategic profiles of the major market competitors are provided.

RF40 July, 1991 126 pages. $495

FIND/SVP, 625 Avenue of the Americas, New York, NY 10011

Legal Information

Patent applications and awards not only provide information about a competitor's new product developments, but they often describe the technology that enables legal (and illegal) imitations to be made. Several patent databases exist, including *INPADOC*, which have information about some 15 million patents from more than two hundred countries. Other legal databases describe federal, state, and county regulations that apply to the manufacturing and marketing of products and services. They again can be identified and even searched through law school libraries at local state universities.

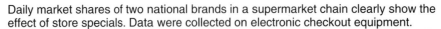

Figure 3.8 **The Use of Scanner Data to Study the Effects of Promotions**

Daily market shares of two national brands in a supermarket chain clearly show the effect of store specials. Data were collected on electronic checkout equipment.

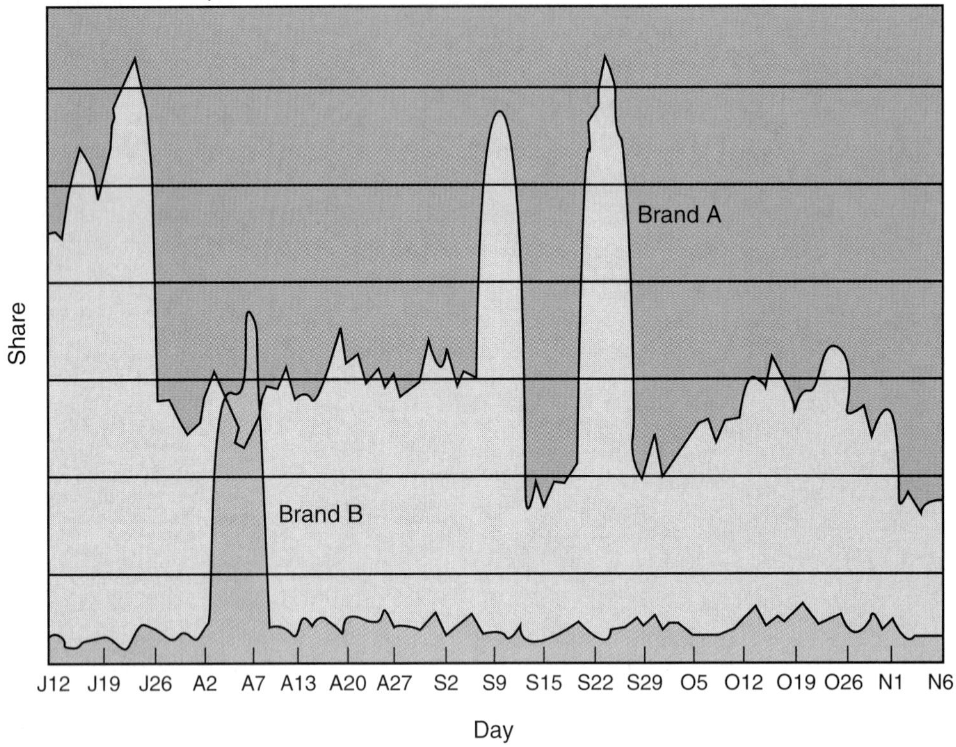

In the 1980s, supermarket scanner data were mostly used to study the effects of price and display promotions on sales. Scanner data have also been used by retailers to make their shelf-space displays more productive, increase their stock turnover, and improve inventory control. Scanner data are likely to become available for other markets during the 1990s.

SOURCE: Reproduced with permission from John D. C. Little, "Decision Support Systems for Marketing Managers," *Journal of Marketing* 43 (Summer 1979): 9–26.

Scanning Services

In the past twelve years, information on the sales of some thirty thousand grocery products have been gathered by syndicated market research companies, such as A.C. Nielsen, SAMI/Burke, and IRI, which process data provided by supermarkets or by households participating in national panels. These data are mainly used by major packaged-goods companies to monitor the behavior of their competitors and test new products, promotions, and advertising appeals. Figure 3.8 shows the effects of store price specials as tracked by scanner data. In the next twenty years, almost all products shipped through distribution channels will have UPCs (universal product codes) to be scanned to control inventory and order delivery. When this happens, there will be extensive databases on most markets about sales trends, which probably will be available in real-time, so even weekly or daily shifts in market share can be observed.

Decision Support Systems

A decision support system (DSS) is a set of computer software programs built into a user-friendly interface package such as Windows. It enables a user to answer state-of-the-market questions and market forecasting questions and to create simulations showing what might happen if tactics were changed. Behind the interactive, user-friendly icons, frameworks, prompts, and pull-down guide screens are major on-line market and accounting databases, communication networks, and powerful spreadsheets, statistical programs, and mathematical models. Figure 3.9 describes the elements and flow of information within a decision support system. The keys to a well-designed and frequently used DSS are listed here:

- It helps a team make better intuitive decisions by replacing assumptions with facts accessed by pressing a few keys or dexterously moving a mouse.
- It offers simple, decision support aids that reward novices and encourage them to move on to more complex support aids (like computer games that have novice, intermediate, and expert levels of difficulty).
- It is designed so it can be expanded to include new databases, networks, and aids.
- It self-records its use, so its designers know what is popular and what is not. Great care has to be taken to ensure that the evolution of a DSS is driven by usage and not by a compulsion to acquire the latest whiz-bang technology.
- It contains the ability to receive, send, and file market intelligence from salespeople, distributors, suppliers, and senior management.
- It can be accessed by everyone who wishes to use it (such as regional sales managers).

The initial optimism about the usefulness of decision support systems in the early 1980s has faded a little.[13] It has become clear that the tremendous investment in personal computers during the 1980s (and the associated decision support software) has significantly improved the market decision making of only a small percentage of companies.[14] In some cases, the use of a DSS has increased paralysis by analysis; in other cases the DSS has not given the firm a decisive competitive advantage over rivals because rivals are using the same or similar systems.[15] Yet other decision support systems were grafted onto creaky, outdated, and overloaded existing information systems. Finally, some of the mathematical models used to answer what-if questions have proved unreliable.[16] It is clear from some of the success stories (such as Frito-Lay's fabulous DSS) that learning to design and use a computer-based decision support system takes much longer than everyone expected. It also should take a great deal of initial conceptualization, because it will influence how generations of users think about the market (their mental models). It is hoped many more companies will have learned how to design and use a DSS by the end of the 1990s.

---

[13] For the early definitive review of DSSs, see John D.C. Little, "Decision Support Systems for Marketing Managers," *Journal of Marketing* 43 (Summer 1979): 9–26.

[14] This was reported in the responses to an open-ended question about how and why their marketing planning has improved over the past five or so years by participants in the 1990 Conference Board study; see Peter R. Dickson and Rosemary Kalapurakal, "The Theory and Reality of Environment Analysis in the Marketing Plan," working paper (Columbus: Ohio State University, 1991).

[15] Louis A. Wallis, *Decision-Support Systems for Marketing* (New York: The Conference Board, 1989).

[16] Annetta Miller and Dody Tsiantar, " A Test for Market Research," *Newsweek*, December 28, 1987, 32–33.

Figure 3.9 A Basic Decision-Support System

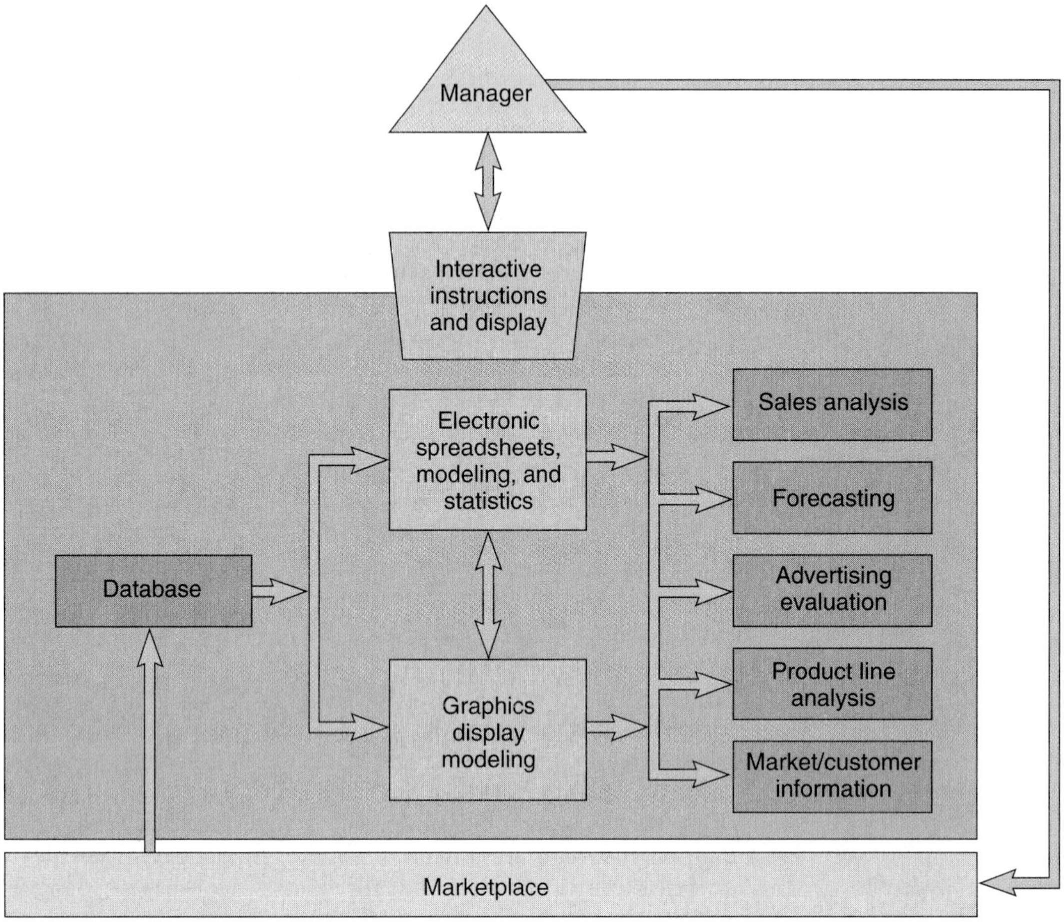

A decision support system is used for many purposes. Sales managers can look up a customer's purchase history; accountants can use it to do cost analyses, budgeting, and forecasting; managers can use it to evaluate the success of a marketing program (such as an advertising campaign) and to determine the success of positioning (who is taking a share from whom). A good DSS is improved by carefully studying who uses the old DSS most and then determining how heavy users would like to see it improved and why decision makers who were expected to use it have not.

SOURCE: Reprinted with permission of the publisher from "What the Hot Marketing Tool of the 80's Offers You," by Michael Dressler, Joquin Ives Brant, and Ronald Beall, *Industrial Marketing*, © 1983, p. 54. Copyright 1983 by Elsevier Science Publishing Co., Inc.

Transaction-Based Information Systems (TBISs)

TBISs link, communicate, and process all of the transactions between a firm's distributors/customers and its suppliers. The TBIS has evolved out of the electronic data interchange (EDI) among businesses (mainly business-to-business, just-in-time delivery relationships). As well as being used to speed quotations, bidding, order processing, and track delivery and billing, these new systems are likely to become an important part of a new generation of procurement and selling decision support systems. As discussed later in this book (Chapter 12), some of these DSSs will also include decision support systems for a firm's customers, such as McKesson's ECONOMOST system for its drugstore customers or American Airlines' SABRE reservation system for its travel agents.

Transaction-based information systems are having a dramatic effect on channel and business-to-business customer relationships. By speeding up transaction communication and increasing the monitoring and control of sales of orders, they have greatly reduced the working capital tied up in inventory and the risks of obsolete inventory. Beyond saving billions of dollars a year by reducing warehousing and inventory costs, TBISs have enabled retailers and manufacturers to become much more responsive to market demand because a TBIS provides the manufacturer with on-line information about what is "hot" and what is not. This "market research" can immediately be used to change manufacturing schedules and the procurement of supplies.

Hypercompetitive Market Research

Chapter 1 explained that hypercompetition is when several sellers are continuously innovating/imitating new products and better, lower cost, and faster processes. In such markets, firms with faster market research processes that quickly alert decision makers to important opportunities and changes in market behavior possess a sustainable competitive advantage. In a less turbulent market they can use quick alertness to heat up the pace of change, driving rivals into reactions that lead them to "shoot themselves in the foot." What are the characteristics of market research processes in hypercompetitive markets? Generally, more of the research is undertaken by the cross-functional team directly, which means that training the team members on how to talk to and visit customers is even more valuable. Team members make a constant effort to speed up research processes, to obtain preliminary results, and to undertake more frequent, small research studies rather than infrequent, major studies. Specifically, we might expect the following characteristics of intelligence gathering processes in hypercompetitive markets:

- A cross-functional team *continuously* in touch with and visiting with lead customers and suppliers.
- More use of qualitative, observational research methods from cultural anthropology by cross-functional team members. Members hope someone on their team will become the Margaret Meade of their market.
- An increased effort to find, create, and keep resident engineering experts who can quickly reverse engineer new competitor products/ services and identify changes in rivals' products and processes.
- A heightened use of sales, distributor, and foreign subsidiary market intelligence transmitted on an Intranet, more emphasis on competitive and trade intelligence, and more rewarding of generators of crucial intelligence.
- The use of Internet industry newsletters, industry gossip networks, and industry clipping services. The Internet allows the quick transmission of information that may otherwise take weeks to reach the firm.
- More use of continuous tracking of buyer behavior, trade inventories, and customer satisfaction surveys, as well as Bayesian analysis of the information (updating prior beliefs).

- The development of a customer dissatisfaction market research process that tracks and quickly follows up customer queries, complaints, returns, and warrantee claims to quickly identify and rectify problems with product design, with the service process, and with the creation of unreasonable performance expectations.
- Increased use of a small number of market research suppliers to run tracking studies, regular focus groups, and quick customer telephone or shopping mall–intercept surveys.
- The constant sharing of information across teams and benchmarking across firms on how to greatly speed up market research processes without increasing their costs and reducing their validity and reliability.

Market Intelligence Organization

In the traditional bureaucratic organization structure, getting all those involved with a product market decision closer to the market by putting the latest market intelligence in their hands is a nightmarish responsibility for a product manager. Much depends on his or her personal, boundary-spanning abilities.[17] The sharing of relevant, internally generated information among the different functions often can be an even worse problem when individual functions attempt to manage information to heighten their own political power. The situation is very different when the new information and inquiry technologies help cross-functional team decision making.[18] Internal and external information sources are interrogated by team members *for* the group, in parallel and back and forth. *This collective and consultative intelligence generation is the essence of the information-processing strength of cross-functional team decision making.*

Another feature of competitively rational team decision making is that *all* team members spend time talking to customers, distributors, and suppliers. The team has to develop a consensus mental model of how consumers use the product/service: Where do they use the product? How do they use it? What problems do they have with the product? Do differences in customer needs and benefits exist (see Chapter 5)? All of this information must be absorbed by *all* members of the cross-functional team. The new electronic decision support systems that link a firm with major customers, scanning services, or global databases can dramatically change the nature and quality of decision making, but they will never be a substitute for the direct learning that occurs when decision makers interact with suppliers and customers.

The use of a cross-functional team also greatly simplifies the concern over how information is used because not only is all important information reported to the team, but also team members are delegated to seek out further information, share it with the team, and, most important, interpret it (see Figure 3.10). This interpretation teaches other cross-functional team members new decision-making skills. The cross-functional team becomes the organizational inquiry center, where the firm "effectively and efficiently reconciles the voice of the market with the voice of the firm."[19] The following team information-processing behavior is typical:

---

[17] Some interesting research suggests that the quality of environmental analysis and effort does not depend on market turbulence and uncertainty but on the boundary-spanning efforts of product managers. See Steven Lysonski, Alan Singer, and David Wilemon, "Coping with Environmental Uncertainty and Boundary Spanning in the Product Manager's Role," *Journal of Consumer Marketing* 6.2 (Spring 1989): 33–44.

[18] Rashi Glazer, "Marketing in an Information-Intensive Environment: Strategic Implications of Knowledge As an Asset," *Journal of Marketing* 55 (October 1991): 1–19.

[19] Barabba and Zaltman, *Hearing the Voice of the Market.*

Figure 3.10 **Sources of Market Intelligence**

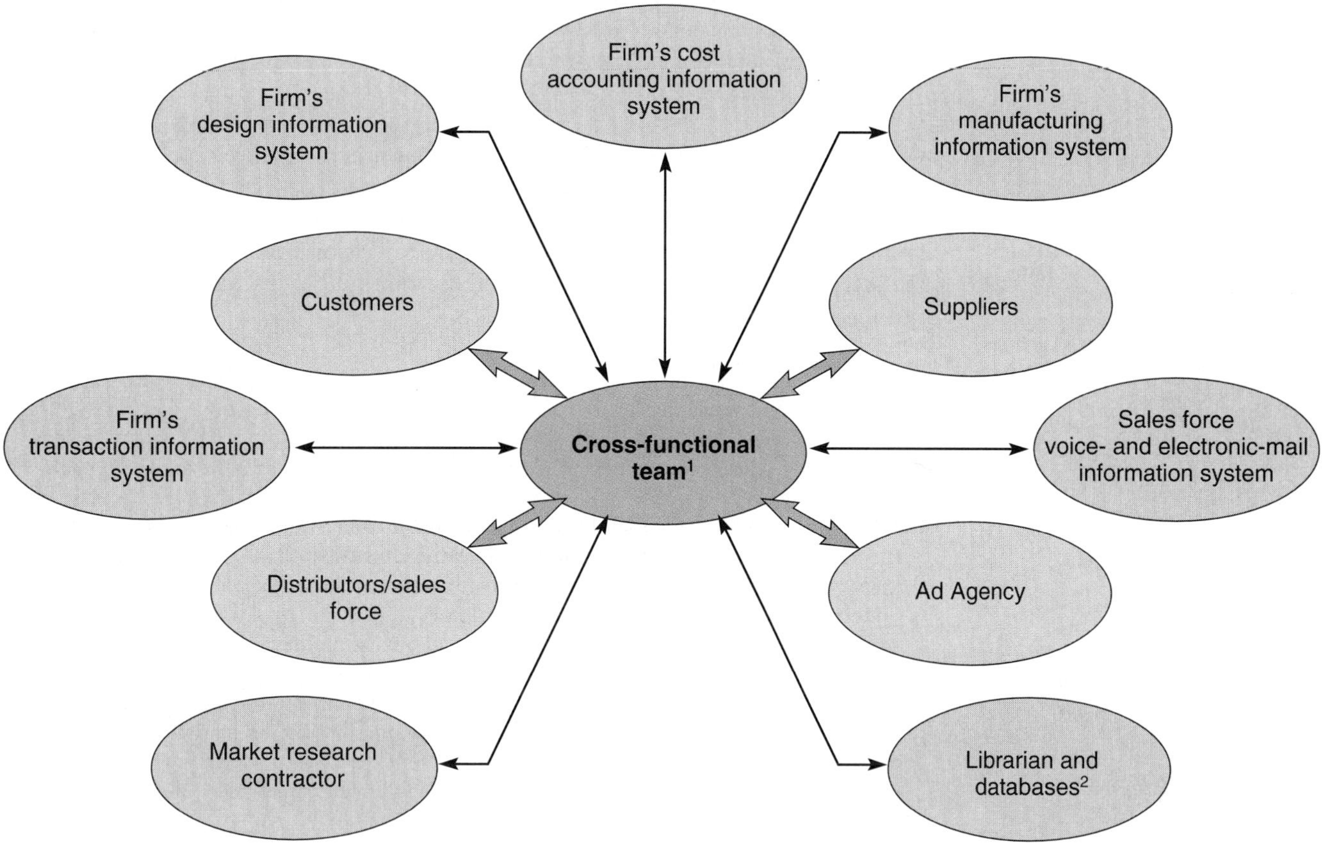

[1]Information, expert judgments, and mental models of the market environments are transmitted, stored, and assimilated within and across the membership of the cross-functional team. Group members have individual responsibilities and expertise in using and sharing different information systems, such as the transaction IS (order-processing and logistic's information system) and design IS (computer-aided design and costing information system). This occurs both concurrently and sequentially. The closer sources are sources that *all* of the cross-functional team members should interact with continuously. This is often achieved by having the suppliers, sales force, and ad agency representatives attend cross-functional team meetings.

[2]A librarian/market research analyst becomes a crucial part of a team's institutional memory, storing reports and relevant documents by cataloging them to reflect the team's agreed on mental model. The librarian also will be an expert at accessing external databases such as DIALOG, which provides access to some 350 other business databases. The duties of this analyst might also include taking the minutes of the formal cross-functional team meetings. A discussion of running such meetings is presented in Appendix 1. The role of librarian/market research analyst would be an attractive entry position for a capable new graduate. It combines the duties of an assistant brand manager and market research analyst in more traditional bureaucratic organizational structures.

> We gather about ten people in a room, twice a month, in long (think-tank) sessions—anything from three hours to a couple of days. The sessions have no formal structure. We examine and massage the latest competitor and industry information to determine where things are going and what we should be doing.[20]

[20] Howard Sutton, *Competitive Intelligence* (New York: The Conference Board, 1988), 31.

> There are a lot of people in the business unit who know something about a competitor. But it's almost like the three blind men and the elephant: Each one examines a small part of the whole. When you put them all together in a room, they are amazed about how much they know. That coalesces into one or two sheets of paper presenting all we know about a competitor's strengths and weaknesses, and our judgments with respect to a competitor's strategies and measures of success. That is the beginning of a competitor file.[21]

A new product team is likely to meet weekly; a more mature product team might meet monthly. Discussion may also be more structured, as was suggested in Figure 2.1. The essential point, however, is that the firm must invest heavily in teams, encouraging them to use market research in their decision making. Such investment is necessary because many factors, such as those that follow, discourage the best use of information.

1. Myopic, short-term perspectives discourage market research that identifies long-term competitor and consumer lifestyle trends. Most research addresses immediate, firefighting problems; longer term trends that should be researched are ignored. The firm risks being like the frog that is boiled alive in the pot because it does not notice the gradually rising temperature of the water.
2. Information that is really useful because it challenges conventional wisdom, beliefs, and mental models is ignored because it threatens the credibility of the intuition of senior managers.[22] The information may be seen as a political challenge, but it may also undermine the confidence of a decision maker who, in making risky, uncertain decisions, needs to believe in his or her existing beliefs and mental models.
3. The fear that listening to the market will mean that the firm is being led by fickle, so-called uninformed consumer tastes rather than by its own radical innovations. In this variation of paralysis-by-analysis fear, the firm becomes hooked on market research rather than managing and mastering research and development. The perceived dulling effect of market research on creativity is well stated in the following quote:

   > Enduringly successful firms focus on being creative, not reactive. . . . This will be tough for firms nurtured on reactive strategies like market research, the usual method Western firms use to find out what customers want. Car makers are among market research's biggest fans, as the dull similarity of modern cars testifies.[23]

4. Research is sometimes enacted at the eleventh hour to validate (that is, justify) the decision making. It almost invariably does so, but when later proven wrong, it undermines respect for research. Only about 20 percent of new products are reasonably successful, and the performance of new advertising and promotion programs are about equally successful.[24] Results more often fail to meet the expectations created by market research. Smoking-gun

[21] Sutton, *Competitive Intelligence*, 37.
[22] This counter-intuitive conclusion has been well documented; see R. Nisbitt and L. Ross, *Human Inference: Strategies and Shortcomings of Social Judgment* (Englewood Cliffs, NJ: Prentice-Hall, 1980); Blake E. Ashforth and Fried Yitzhak, "The Mindlessness of Organizational Behaviors," *Human Relations* 41, no. 4 (1988), 305–29; and James P. Walsh, "Knowledge Structures and the Management of Organizations: A Research Review and Agenda," working paper (Hanover, NH: Dartmouth College, June 1990).
[23] *The Economist*, December 1, 1990, 7, as quoted in George S. Day, *Learning About Markets* (Cambridge, MA: Marketing Science Institute, 1991), 91–117. To be fair to the auto industry, fuel economy and safety requirements have had much to do with the similar aerodynamic shape of many cars.
[24] Alvin Achenbaum, "How to Succeed in New Products," *Advertising Age*, June 26, 1989, 62.

research undertaken at the eleventh hour that challenges the whole project is even less appreciated. It is hard evidence of the foolhardiness of the project.

5. Information in traditional, bureaucratic decision-making situations is devalued because it is generated for its own sake (to justify unnecessary levels of middle management) or to frustrate or delay decision making rather than improve it.
6. The use of mind-numbing complexity and jargon by researchers intimidates users. Also, the third-decimal-point pretension of information creates completely false beliefs about the precision and credibility of costs, market share, or consumer preferences. Researchers often have a different value system. They seek certain types of validity and reliability that are costly in time and money. Users tend to prefer several sequential, quick-and-dirty studies.[25]

Mental Models of the Market

The competitive importance of market intelligence analysis and learning was observed in Shell Oil's study of thirty companies that had survived in business for more than 75 years.[26] What impressed the Shell planners was the ability of these companies to learn about their changing marketplaces. The cross-functional management teams in these companies were able to change their "shared mental models" of the marketplace faster than their competition did, including their views and models of consumer behavior, competitor behavior, and, perhaps most important, themselves. Such fast insight also gave them more time to innovate, imitate, and avoid crisis management. A company with such superior decision-making skills has a clear competitive advantage over its rivals. Such skills start with the right mental model framework.

Framing the Business Environment

A marketplace is a mix of many, diverse players. Some share common interests, but each also has its own distinct interests. Successful decision-making teams do not think about how *the marketplace* will react to a new product or tactic. They think about how *different players in the marketplace* will react to the firm's behavior. It is like a game—you have to anticipate how the different players will react to your move. Some will welcome your moves, others will be indifferent to them, and yet others will contest your moves.[27]

A market contains four types of players: consumers, competitors, distribution channel members and exchange facilitators, and regulators. Each of these groups can be further subdivided into segments, types, and individual entities. Consequently, it is generally recommended that the study of the external business environment be divided into four environments: the consumer, competitive, channel, and public-policy environments. If any other major players, special interest groups, or environments in the market do not fall within these categories, then a separate section of the market analysis should describe the behavior and interests of these groups. The analysis of each of these groups of players is described in detail in Chapters 5 through 8.

The "game" is further complicated by the fact a company is itself made up of different functional coalitions that represent different internal and external interests

[25] Mark Landler, "The 'Bloodbath' in Market Research," *Business Week*, February 11, 1991, 72–74; see also Gerald Zaltman, *The Use of Developmental and Evaluative Market Research* (Cambridge, MA: Marketing Science Institute, 1989), 89–107, for an excellent discussion of the lack of trust between researchers and managers.

[26] Arie P. De Geus, "Planning as Learning," *Harvard Business Review*, March/April 1988, 70–74.

[27] The problem with most game theories is that they only discuss games between two players (say, two competitors or a supplier and a distributor). Market games involve many players in different win-lose relationships with each other.

Table 3.3 **Changes in the Marketing Plan Environmental Analysis of Major U.S. Firms**

	1980			1990		
VARIABLE	IN DETAIL	BRIEF MENTION	NO MENTION	IN DETAIL	BRIEF MENTION	NO MENTION
Segmentation	60.3	29.6	4.5	75.3	13.5	2.2
Demand Forecast	76.0	19.5	2.6	64.6	23.3	4.0
Consumer Needs	57.7	36.3	3.0	58.7	30.0	3.1
Competitor Market Share	65.5	24.0	7.9	63.2	22.0	8.1
Competitor Information	65.2	28.1	4.5	48.0	39.0	5.8
Technology	41.2	43.4	9.4	43.9	35.9	9.9
Regulation	35.6	43.4	13.9	26.5	39.5	19.3
Environment	30.0	40.4	15.0	25.6	35.4	21.5
Product Portfolio Analysis[a]	22.8	23.6	37.8	20.6	25.6	27.8
Product Life Cycle Analysis	14.6	33.7	34.8	17.9	32.3	32.3
Previous Plan	19.9	43.4	29.2	14.8	38.1	36.3

[a]See Chapter 4 on Product Portfolio analysis.

(stakeholders).[28] Often, the internal coalitions are linked to different external stakeholders. Each of these internal coalitions has to be considered, consulted, and accommodated during marketing decision making. The cross-functional team enables this consultation to occur immediately, thus saving time and reducing political problems.

Surprisingly little is known about the mental models that decision makers actually use when thinking about the market. One way of understanding mental models is to study how decision makers organize information about the market in their decisions and written marketing plans. A case study of ten corporations undertaken in the 1980s found that *only* two of the ten corporations systematically structured their thinking about their markets.[29] What is even more disturbing is that all of the companies had set up special environmental analysis units in response to the growing importance of tracking changing markets!

Table 3.3 presents two Conference Board studies of the contents of the typical market analyses in the marketing plans of major U.S. companies.[30] About three-quarters of the plans describe a market segment analysis in detail, and about half analyze the competition in detail. More noteworthy is that despite all of the advances in information technology during the 1980s, the market analyses in the 1990 plans were not more thorough than they were in 1980. If anything, they were less thorough—particularly those analyzing the competition. Figure 3.11 is a Venn diagram revealing what percentage of the firms in the 1990 study presented market environment analyses in their plans that detailed changes in the consumer environment, competitive environment, channel environment, and regulatory environment. Only 12 percent

[28] Paul F. Anderson, "Marketing, Strategic Planning, and the Theory of the Firm," *Journal of Marketing* 46 (Spring 1982): 15–26.

[29] R. T. Lentz and Jack L. Engledow, "Environmental Analysis Units and Strategic Decision-Making: A Field Study of Selected 'Leading Edge' Corporations," *Strategic Management Journal* 7 (1986): 69–89.

[30] Peter R. Dickson and Rosemary Kalapurakal, "The Theory and Reality of Environment Analysis," 119.

Figure 3.11 Environmental Issues Detailed in the Marketing Plan

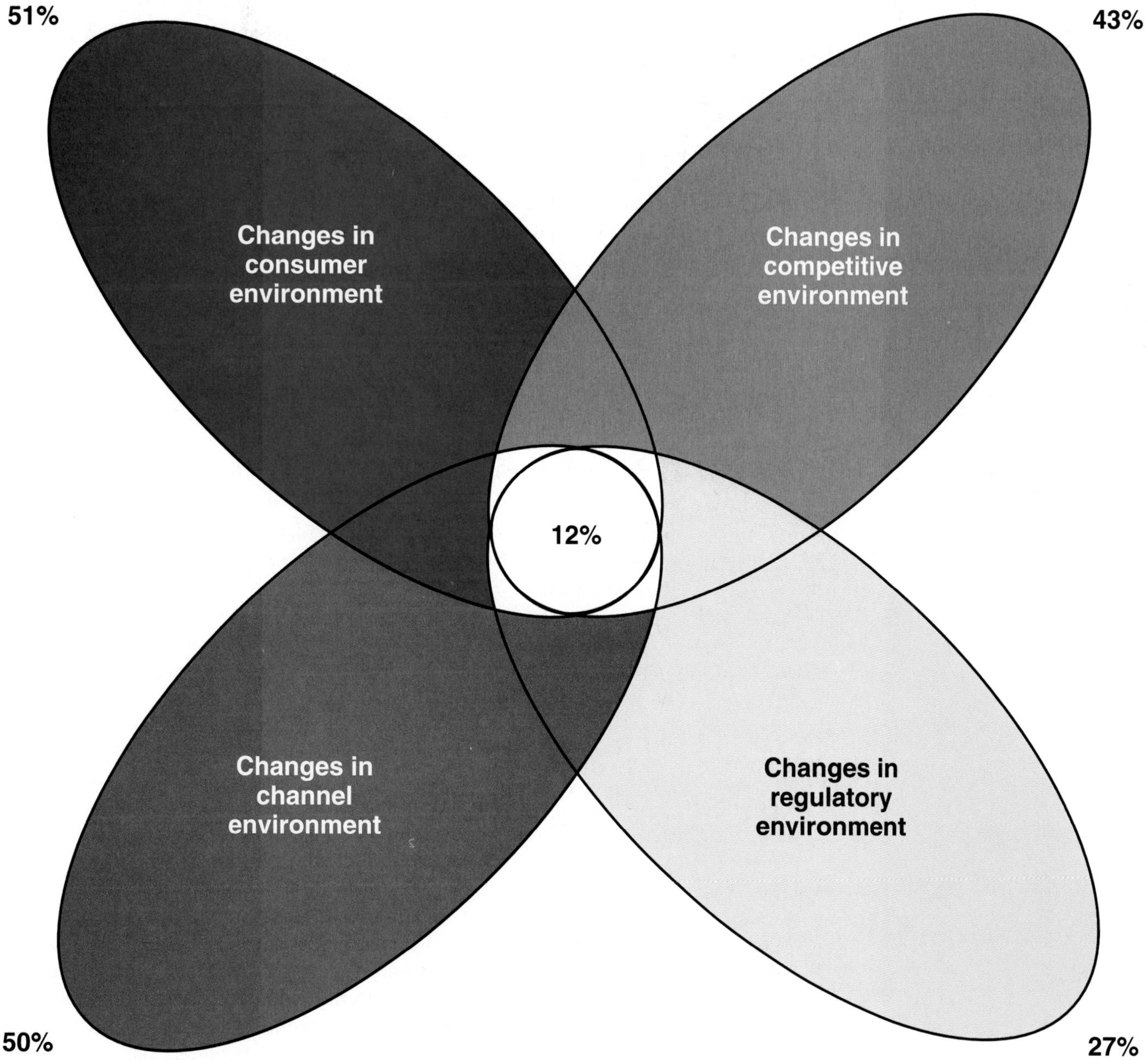

The percentages indicate the proportion of firms in the 1990 Conference Board study that include such information in their typical marketing plan. Changes in consumer environment include both a consumer needs analysis and a segmentation analysis. Changes in competitive environment include both a market share analysis and an analysis of individual competitor behavior. Changes in channel environment were only considered for companies that used distributors/dealers/retailers.

SOURCE: Adapted from *The Marketing Plan* by Howard Sutton (New York: The Conference Board, 1990).

contained such enlightened insights. It is hoped that the decision makers in the other 88.5 percent of the firms are briefed about such changes during their informal decision-making sessions; otherwise a great deal of market decision making is less informed than it could be.

A reasonable conclusion is that many firms may be able to gain a considerable competitive advantage by requiring that their marketing plans include detailed reports on changes occurring in consumer behavior, competitor behavior, channel behavior, and public policy. In the words of a marketing manager at a major consumer packaged goods company:[31]

> The most important part of our marketing plan is probably the key learning section, which is the section that outlines everything that we have learned over the past year or two about the business and the future of the business. If you don't have a sound basis there, then the rest of the plan is going to falter. . . . It's a process of going through and determining what are the key learning points. . . . Once we have reached agreement on them, we talk about how they are going to impact the business.

The importance of changing managers' mental models of the market environments was also expressed by another participant in the 1990 Conference Board study:

> A lot of people we have coming out of schools with strong MBA programs are people who are brilliant analysts, very, very skilled at understanding how to take businesses apart, but not very skilled at how to achieve market insight, how to trigger action, and most of all, how to change people's paradigm or view of the world.

Whether called a mental model, worldview, thought world, or paradigm, it is clear that many firms could benefit from rethinking how they frame their market analyses and what they learn from such analyses.[32] The next section offers such a framework for gathering and reporting market intelligence.

The Five Environments (5E) Mental Model

A great deal of uncertainty is involved in marketing planning, even when it is done well. Uncertainty occurs about whether the descriptions of the marketplace environments are accurate. Uncertainty occurs about how the marketplace will change in the future Often uncertainty occurs as to what are the real objectives of the plan and whether the objectives of the senior executives will change in the future. Uncertainty occurs as to whether the company has the resources, the will, and the cooperative political climate to implement the proposed action programs. Finally, uncertainty occurs about how the marketplace will respond to the action programs. Consequently, a decision-making team can only know a portion of the facts or truths about the marketplace. The planner has a limited knowledge of how consumers behave, how the channels of distribution operate, how competitors behave, what public policy applies

[31] These two quotations were derived during research with the Conference Board.

[32] See George S. Day and Prakash Nedungadi, "Managerial Representations of Competitive Advantage," *Journal of Marketing* 58 (April 1994): 31–44; George S. Day, *Learning about Markets* (Cambridge, MA: Marketing Science Institute, 1991) 91–117; and Jeffrey Pfeffer and Gerald R. Salancik, *The External Control of Organizations: A Resource Dependence Perspective* (New York: Harper, 1978).

to the marketplace, and the capabilities and performance of the company. Knowing more about these would provide insight and reduce decision-making uncertainty.

Figure 3.12 is a Venn diagram of a decision maker's mental model of the market. This five-environment market-orientation model extends the three market-orientation model (customer orientation, competitor orientation, and company orientation) to include channel orientation and public policy orientation.[33]

Each colored ellipse represents what the decision maker knows about each of the five environments that make up the market. If a manager knows a lot about competitors and less about the other market environments, then the manager's perspective or orientation will be colored by this bias. It is as if the manager sees the marketplace through a single colored light—say, green for competition. As a consequence, the manager is less sensitive or alert to changes in other market environments that do not show up in green light. Only by adopting a balanced mental model of the market (that is, a balanced perspective) will the manager see the market through a combination of colored lights that produces a clear white light (the overlapping center of Figure 3.12) with which to view the market. The goal of the decision maker is to increase the size of this "enlightened" circle in his or her mental model of the market. The goal of the decision-making team is to increase the size of the enlightened circle in its *collective, shared* mental model of the market. In this context, learning faster than a rival means changing the mental models or thought worlds that the cross-functional team members carry in their heads about the market faster than a rival does.[34] Figure 3.12 makes the following suggestions:

1. A cross-functional team must start with a balanced mental model of the market, which includes knowledge of each of the five business environments.
2. A cross-functional team must continuously update its mental model of the market with information about each of the five business environments.
3. The mental model is framed by the outline/headings of the environment report.

The actual size of the outer square, which represents all that could be known about the marketplace, expands as new technology or other events change the marketplace. Their unknown effects increase overall uncertainty and the size of the black box. Sometimes the size of the black box is reduced, such as when several competitors withdraw from the market and their behavior no longer has to be predicted. New, correct information about the marketplace increases planners' understanding by providing new insights or confirming and strengthening existing beliefs. It sheds new light on the marketplace and extends the boundaries of a team's knowledge. However, sometimes new information that is wrong will shrink a team's true knowledge of how the marketplace operates.

Competitive rationality is increased when the cross-functional team expands its knowledge of the marketplace. One way of achieving this is through the annual plan's analysis and report of the different marketplace environments. The sharing of such knowledge increases overall knowledge. The rationality of a firm's marketing planning is bounded or limited by its knowledge of the marketplace. The smaller the ratio of light

[33] Ajay K. Kohli and Bernard J. Jaworski, "Market Orientation: The Construct, Research Propositions, and Management Implications," *Journal of Marketing* 54 (April 1990): 1–18; and John C. Narver and S. Slater, "The Effect of Market Orientation of Business Profitability," *Journal of Marketing* 54 (October 1990): 20–35.

[34] Arie P. De Geus, "Planning As Learning," *Harvard Business Review*, 1988; and Deborah Dougherty, *Interpretive Barriers to Successful Product Innovation* (Cambridge, MA: Marketing Science Institute, 1989), 89–114.

Figure 3.12 **The Five Environments (5E) Mental Model of the Market**

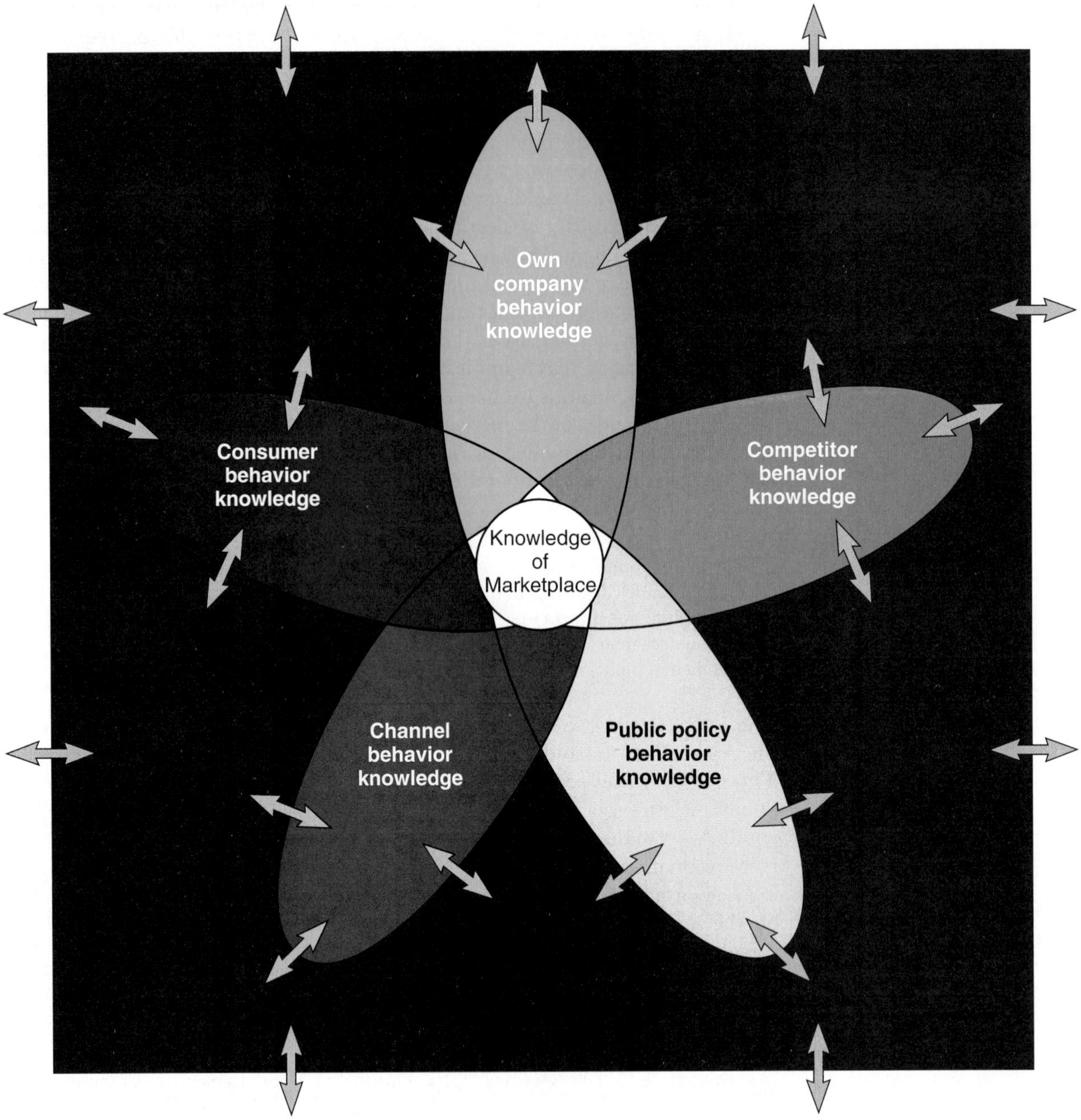

The way a decision maker thinks about a market can be described in terms of what that marketer knows about the consumer, competitor, channels, public policy, and his or her own company's behavior. The proportion of light to darkness indicates how much the decision maker knows about the market. The arrows indicate that the market is always changing, so what a decision maker needs to know is always changing. What *is* known can expand or shrink, depending on the decision maker's alertness and interpretative insight. A balanced, enlightened view of the market requires studying a strategic proposal or tactical program in the light off *all five* environments (the white circle in the middle).

to dark areas in Figure 3.12, the more limited (sometimes called "bounded")[35] is the rationality of the firm's decision making, which will become riskier and more uncertain.

A further complication exists. Figure 3.12 represents how much an individual or team knows about marketplace truth. Decision makers may have very different perceptions about how much they *think* they know about how the marketplace operates. The more confidence they have that they understand how the marketplace operates, the less uncertain they will feel, the more they will feel in control, and the more likely they will be prepared to make the necessary risky decisions and experiment. A planning process must try to minimize a team's misperceptions about the market and its misperceptions about how much its members think they know about the marketplace. This is best achieved by having them write down what they know about the marketplace in a report so it can be challenged or enriched by the knowledge of other members of the cross-functional team or by consultants. Incorrect knowledge or beliefs in the mind of a planner that are never spelled out in writing cannot be changed easily and may never be challenged and changed. It can lead to both overconfident and ineffective decision making. All other things being equal, a firm that possesses the most knowledge about a marketplace and has a *correct* perception of the knowledge it possesses will make the most rational decisions and hence possesses the highest long-term survival potential.[36]

Customary and Contemporary Analytical Frameworks

Historically, the marketing function has focused on the customer, but in the 1980s the increase in foreign competition and the influence of several best-selling books led to an increased interest in studying the competition.[37] Without exception, today's planning experts all agree that a market analysis should have sections and frameworks describing all five environments, including the company internal environment (see Chapter 4). This is because a marketing plan for a product or service must be constrained by company goals, strengths, weaknesses, cost structure, and the ability or willingness of other functional areas within the firm (such as production) to supply the inputs and activities required to execute the proposed marketing strategy.

It makes sense to first complete the external market analysis and write up the sections of the environment report describing consumers, channels, competition, and public policy. This report, or at least a summary of the report, is then passed on to senior managers to help them in their corporate planning. Senior management uses the external environmental analysis and operating performance history to develop and impose specific corporate objectives and strategies and tentative production, finance, and personnel constraints on the marketing strategy (see Chapter 4). Production, R&D, and other functional areas are also consulted at this point. The company's internal environment is then analyzed and described to include these top-down objectives and constraints. In this way, the short-term and long-term company objectives for the product or service are stated within the company section of the environment report. In essence, this section describes the voice of the firm.[38]

---

[35] Herbert A. Simon, "On the Concept of Organization Goal," *Administrative Science Quarterly* 9 (June 1964): 1–22; "Rational Decision Making in Business Organizations," *American Economic Review*, September 1979, 493–512.

[36] Of course, knowing a lot about the marketplace may not be sufficient if it is not the most important information. Hence, knowledge should be weighed by its strategic importance.

[37] Michael Porter, *Competitive Strategy* (New York: The Free Press, 1980); and Al Ries and Jack Trout, *Marketing Warfare* (New York: McGraw-Hill, 1986). See also the results reported in Table 2.1 of the 1990 Conference Board study.

[38] Barabba and Zaltman, *Hearing the Voice of the Market.*

Outlining and Writing the Environment Report

It is appropriate at this point to explain that all new environmental information should be presented in what is called an *environment report* within the marketing plan. The environment report is actually an electronic word-processor document to which new information is continuously added. A market analyst scans and abstracts new intelligence, and adds it to the appropriate sections of the environment report. This updating enables a reader to trace the history of events in the different environments of the market. The proposed strategy is presented in a *strategy report.* These two reports are major components of the written marketing plan (for an example, see Appendix 2). When the environment report is organized by the different interest groups that are likely to be impacted by the strategy or program of action, it is much easier to understand the effect on the market. It also helps to gather information about each group and to organize the facts into a sensible and meaningful framework, such as the one illustrated in Table 3.4.

Some environment reports will have much larger sections on the consumer and competition because channels in the product market are limited. Some may have minimal public policy concerns and simple company goals and constraints. Other environment reports will contain extended discussions on these later environments because preliminary analysis reveals their complexity and potential importance.

The environment report should be designed and structured to be most helpful to planners in understanding the total environment. This may mean deviating from the suggested format by creating a separate main section that deals solely with the major competitor or a major customer. The topics and headings in the environment report will depend entirely on the nature of the product being planned and the market being served. This point cannot be overemphasized. No two environment reports for different products will ever look the same, and few will approach the detail contained in Table 3.4. The initial mental model and detailed headings in the environment report that a cross-functional team adopts may prove to be not the most appropriate. However, a team and a firm with a strong drive to improve the results of its decision making will arrive at an appropriate mental structuring of the market *faster* than its competition by the way it *adapts* its structural view of the market over time. For example, as new issues surface, the headings will change. Issues are discoveries about the environment—normally about consumer, dealer, or competitor behavior—that are news and that have clear implications for future market strategy. As is revealed in the following comments of market decision makers talked to during the 1990 Conference Board study, issues have a big influence on framing the decision making:

> The first half of the process is spent in surfacing issues and the second half is spent prioritizing issues. . . . One of the issues that is common to all our businesses is the declining efficiency and effectiveness of broadcast advertising.

> The process that we have developed and used at 3M pushes for asking what's different, what's changed, what new issues do we have to address. We also push for what do we anticipate changing, to be proactive when we can.

For example, as world environment/habitat concerns become paramount, the "green" movement will become an important market constituency that changes consumer

Table 3.4 Outline of the Possible Contents of an Environment Report

Consumer Environment
- Deep benefit segmentation (unfolding causes and effects)
- Contact segmentation (media usage and retail shopping behavior)
- Analysis of key customer relationships
- Trends in values, needs, purchase, and usage behavior
- Overall demand forecast

Channel Environment
- Technology changes in logistics
- New channel-trends/channel-industry analysis
- Short-term economic effects on channels
- Key distributor relationship audit
- Facilitator audit

Competitive Environment
- Market share change analysis/ industry analysis
- Competitive trends analysis
- New technology threats
- Backward and forward integration threats
- Selected competitor audits
- Anticipated competitor behavior

Public Policy Environment
- Assistance and support programs audit
- Regulation/deregulation issues
- Environmental and other political issues
- New federal, state, and county regulations
- Relevant changes in public opinion, values, and ethics
- Emerging ethical issues

Company Environment
- Product's long-term role in corporate mission/plan
- Contribution, ROI, and cash-flow objectives
- Culture and resources and strengths and weaknesses audit
- Specific manufacturing/logistics constraints
- Specific budget constraints
- Internal political and bureaucratic constraints

behavior and public policy. It has already become a major constituency in many forest-products and agriculture markets.

Another way to improve the quality of decisions is to have senior executives, using their vast experience of the market, provide an environment report outline that the cross-functional team uses to prepare its environment report. By framing the way they want the team to gather, store, and use information and to think about the market, executives are passing on their expertise and skills. The outline they provide becomes the mental model that they, the cross-functional team, and all who gather market intelligence use to think about the market. In this way the firm develops a shared mental model of thinking about the market. The model becomes part of the organization culture, not so detailed as to constrain individual perception and creativity but structured enough to produce fast, orderly communication and advantageous use of market intelligence and insight.

Writing Style

The writing style of the environment report should be terse, to the point, and punchy. It should read more like a memo than an academic research report or a Harvard Business School case study. The report is written for the team and others who already know much about the market. Therefore, it does not need to present background information that an outsider might need in order to understand the plan. It also does not need fancy, colored pie charts and graphs to "sell" the insights. The purpose of the report is to help the cross-functional team adapt strategy to the environmental facts, and it should be written with this in mind. The detailed research, tables, and charts should be available, but it is the vital conclusions that should be summarized in the report. This avoids information overload and paralysis by analysis.

This bottom-line brevity can be disconcerting to a market research firm that is paid tens of thousands of dollars to create a one-hundred–word interpretative conclusion that is added to an environment report. Sometimes market research firms use the size of a report (often hundreds of pages of tables and charts) to increase a client's perception of the research's value, validity, and reliability.

Changing the Way We See and Think

The objective of the environmental analysis is to provide insights that enable the team and others to view the proposed strategy from the perspective of each of the major players and their latest behavior in the marketplace. To anticipate the acceptance and likely success of an element of marketing strategy, the team has to place itself in the shoes of the consumer, competitor, distributor, regulator, company production manager, and company senior executive. If the team understands their situations and objectives, then it can anticipate how they will react. Repeated use of this framework will lead to the categorization and storage of information in memory about the marketplace under these "headings." This will naturally increase the team's ability to think intuitively, like a consumer, a competitor, a channel member, a regulator, or a production manager, during its informal decision-making sessions. Another highly valued outcome will be an increase in creative ideas.[39]

Answers to Five Common Questions

Marketing decision makers who normally organize market analyses in a different way than discussed here may have a number of questions, which we will now address.

Where Are the Economy and Changes in Technology Described?

Changes in technology and the economy, along with changes in population demographics and cultural beliefs, are all vital concerns, but their total effects are best tracked by observing their *separate* effects on consumer behavior, channels, current and potential competition, government policy, and the company. Changes in technology, demographics, cultural norms, and the state of the economy can touch all five of these environments. Simply describing the likely state of the economy or new technology in a marketing plan is an incomplete analysis. It leaves it up to the planner to interpret their effects on all the different players in the market.

If such interpretations are unwritten, then an important recorded step in the process of developing strategy is missing. This increases the risk that the impact of the economy and new technology on *all* of the marketplace environments will not be considered. Given Murphy's Law ("If something can go wrong, it will"), overlooking the effect of the economy or new technology on one of the five environments will turn out to be fatal to the venture. When decision makers seek advice from experts about the economy and new technology, it makes sense to have them also forecast the impact of these forces on consumer, competitor, channel, regulator, and company behavior. This should be integrated into each of the relevant sections of the environment report.

This recommendation defies conventional practice, which is to report the state of the economy and technological change as separate topics in an environment report. Again, the reason for folding economic and technological change into changes in consumer, competitor, channel, public policy, and company behavior is that doing so explains how and why the market will change. It forces intelligent interpretation of and thus produces insight on the effects of economic and technological change on the behavior of all of the players in the market.

[39] See Robin M. Hogarth *Judgement and Choice* (New York: John Wiley, 1987); and Henry Mintzberg, "Planning on the Left Side and Managing on the Right," *Harvard Business Review*, July/August 1976, 49–60; and Appendix 1 for a discussion of the positive effect of multiple perspectives and views on creativity in problem solving.

Where Is the State of the Industry Described?

An overall analysis of the state and structure of the industry should be presented in the competitive analysis section of the environment report. This is because an industry analysis normally involves a description of major competitive trends. Michael Porter, in his best-selling book on competitive strategy, demonstrated the value of applying industrial organization theory to describe general competitive trends in an industry (as well as analyzing specific competitors).[40] Trends in the markets of business customers should be described in the consumer section of the environment report. If major industry trends are occurring in channels of distribution, then these should be described in the channel section of the report.

This raises another frequent point of confusion. Why does the proposed marketing plan have a section on channels of distribution in the environment report and a section on distribution strategy in the strategy report? The answer is that the environment report describes what is happening in all the available channels of distribution. It is not limited to the existing channels being used. The strategy report describes proposed distribution programs. Comparing it against the section describing channels in the environment report enables the team to assess what the effect of its proposed distribution programs will be on current channels and other alternative channels. This explains why this textbook has a chapter on channel analysis (Chapter 7) *and* a separate chapter on distribution relationship strategy (Chapter 11).

Where Are the Opportunities and Problems Described?

The proposed environment report organization is also different from some other recommended reports in that a summary of opportunities and problems is not prepared before developing marketing strategy. The reason is that an opportunity or a problem often can only be defined or evaluated in the context of a particular current or potential strategy. Chapter 2 demonstrates that opportunities and problems are often identified at the meshing stage of the proposed planning process, when specific strategy is being considered. Indeed, a major purpose of the meshing process is to identify problems with the fit of the firm's strategy to the market environment *and* to identify a new strategy that exploits an opportunity, creates a new opportunity, or even converts a problem into an opportunity.

This is not to suggest that the environment report will not identify possible opportunities and problems. As the environmental analysis proceeds, it is inevitable that problems, opportunities, and exciting new marketing strategies will be discovered. These should be listed in a notebook or workbook, but they must be put aside until the environment report is completed. Otherwise, they may dominate the thinking of the planner and bias the rest of the analysis.

The time to get excited about new ideas is after the environment report has been completed and the idea has been tested against all the realities of the marketplace. A related mistake of students and executives alike is to include current strategy in the environment report. An environment report should discuss and explain the environment, and only the environment. When strategy creeps into the description of the environment, it becomes viewed as a given. It discourages thinking about any alternative strategy, and its fit with the marketplace environment is not challenged.

What Should Be the Time Horizon of the Plan?

Many companies undertake an annual marketing planning exercise for each of their products or lines of products. The environment report proposed here is designed for annual marketing planning but can be used no matter what planning horizon is

[40] Porter, *Competitive Strategy.*

adopted. Once the initial investment is made in understanding the marketplace environment, the cost and effort needed to update the environment report is a lot less. However, marketing strategy often takes several months, sometimes several years, to implement and take effect. Consequently, the time horizon of the marketing plan is often longer than twelve months. For a new product launch, it may be three to five years. A marketing planner has no choice but to remain open and flexible about time horizons. If the marketing plan is updated annually, then it will build on, extend, and adapt strategy that has been implemented and continues to be implemented.

The time horizon of an environment report is frequently influenced by how often and how far senior management looks into the future. Management experts Professors Gary Hamel and C.K. Prahalad believe that only 40 percent of management time is spent looking outward, only 30 percent of this 40 percent is spent considering more than two years into the future, and only 20 percent of this 30 percent is spent with other executives developing a shared vision of the future. What this means is that on average senior executives spend less than 3 percent of their time (40 percent × 30 percent × 20 percent) developing a shared, thoroughly discussed consensus model of what the future market is likely to be. If this is true, then the firm that makes the effort to extend the horizon of its environment report beyond the immediate market events is likely to possess a sustainable competitive competence and advantage over its more myopic rivals.

The environmental analysis and report must, therefore, not only discuss the current environment but also look ahead and project how the marketplace will change over the next twelve months and beyond. This is not easy to do, but it must be attempted. Fitting proposed strategy to the current environment, when the environment will certainly change, is like planning to live in the past.

Where Is the Sales Forecast Presented?

The projected industry-wide sales forecast should be presented in the consumer analysis because it is most influenced by the effects of social and economic trends on consumer behavior. Where to present the forecast of the company's sales is a more controversial issue. The whole purpose of planning is to develop a strategy that, once implemented, will have an effect on sales and profitability. Therefore, the forecast of company sales should be made *after* the strategy and action programs have been developed.[41] It should appear in the budget and profit projections prepared at the end of the planning process (see Chapter 18). Consequently, the company's past sales and market share should appear in the company analysis; but forecasts of future sales and share, which depend on strategy, should not appear in the environment report. To do so would be like putting the cart before the horse.

Approving the Environment Report

Obtaining a consensus that the environment report represents a true and fair statement of the expected operating environment is a very important step. When executives disagree on a strategic approach, the basis for the disagreement often can be traced to different views or interpretations of environmental facts. It, therefore, makes

[41] David S. Hopkins, *The Marketing Plan* (New York: The Conference Board, 1981), 20; and David L. Hurwood, Elliott S. Grossman, and Earl L. Bailey, *Sales Forecasting* (New York: The Conference Board, 1978).

sense to settle the "What is the likely state of the operating environment?" question before the "What is the best strategy, *given* the likely operating environment?" question to avoid unnecessary conflict and frustration. This may require further market research or expert opinions.

Often, strategy will need to be tested against several likely environmental scenarios, rather than just the most likely scenario. This happens when an aspect of the environment is so uncertain (perhaps, for example, because of the expected entry of new competition or the passage of new legislation) that a strategy must be able to accommodate each possible environmental circumstance. It is desirable that the alternative environmental scenarios be described and understood at an early stage in the process, rather than lurk as a hidden agenda that may or may not be disclosed by participants late in the process (particularly senior executives privy to information about company constraints). Initial acceptance by everyone of the soundness of the market analysis (even one containing multiple scenarios) reduces the opportunity to challenge a strategy later in the planning process. In Chapters 4 through 8, we develop further frameworks and models for thinking about each of the five environments that make up the 5E mental model of the market.

Using MIEMs to Gather and Store Intelligence

How can a firm increase its competitive rationality by using technology that enables it to put the data it collects to better use? How can firms in hypercompetitive markets speed up their use of the information they gather? How can cross-functional teams best capture all the intelligence that flows into the team, as illustrated in Figure 3.13? How can some of the problems of gathering and using information just described be avoided or reduced? How can the firm best use the electronic communication offered by E-mail and the Internet to speed up its gathering and use of market intelligence? The answer to all of these questions is simple but requires a creative shift in thinking about E-mailboxes. What a firm needs to invent is its own MIEMs—its own Market Intelligence E-Mailboxes.

People have come to think that E-Mailboxes are associated with a firm or a person. Why not give a product market or a project its own mailbox where information can be sent about changes in the project's market environment? Why not go further and develop a directory of topics within such an E-mailbox into which relevant intelligence can be dropped? An example of a MIEM is given in Figure 3.13. The full benefit of the MIEM is achieved when its subdirectory headings are the major headings of the environment report. When this is done, all the intelligence gatherers scan the environment with these headings in mind and provide the first level of analysis and insight by interpreting the intelligence as applying to a particular environment report heading. Of equal importance is that intelligence gatherers and the cross-functional team be trained to use the MIEMs. The use of a MIEM increases the competitive rationality of a firm in the following ways:

1. Its universal use by all intelligence generators—from chief executive to shipping clerk, from market research contractor to advertising agency, from key customers to key suppliers—develops a consensus way of thinking about the market within the firm and across crucial trading relationships.
2. It informs all intelligence generators as to what intelligence is being sought.

Figure 3.13 Market Intelligence E-Mailbox

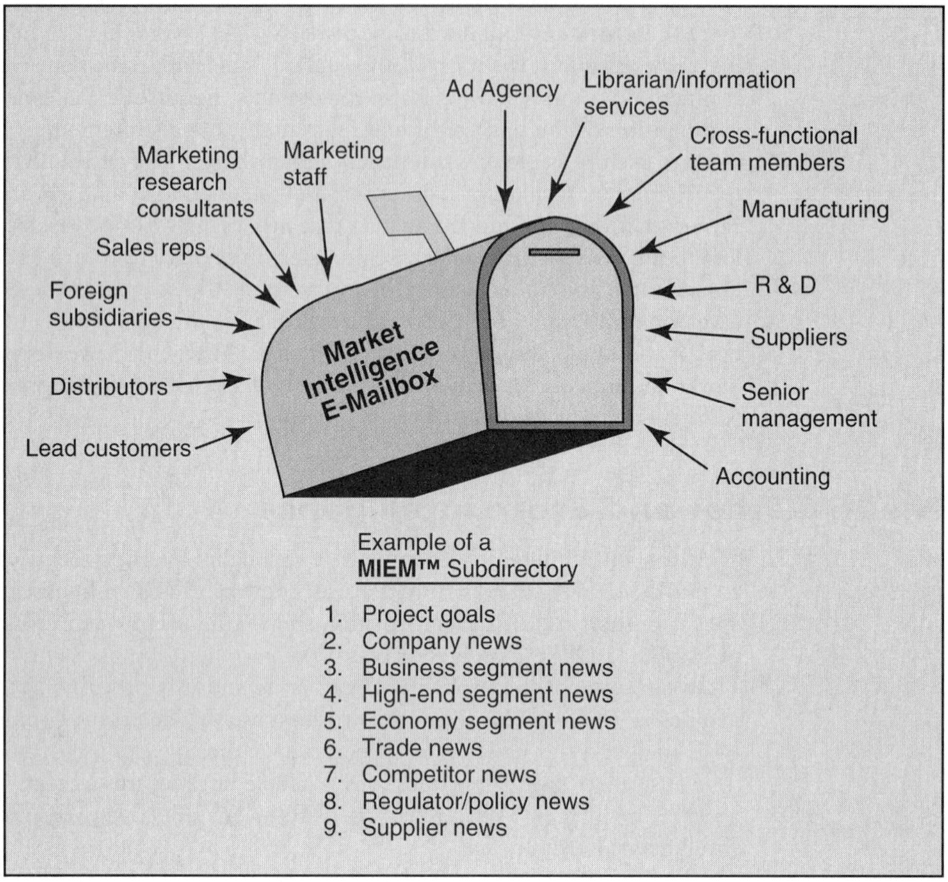

3. It enables intelligence to reach the cross-functional team within hours, if not minutes, rather than weeks. if not months.
4. It enables the market analyst within the cross-functional team to scan the MIEM several times a day, to edit and abstract the latest intelligence, and to add it to the environment report. Alternatively, different members of the cross-functional team may be assigned responsibility for scanning, editing, and posting particular information from the MIEM into the section of the environment report they are responsible for maintaining.
5. It enables management to quickly inform the team of changes in company goals, budgets, and details such as manufacturing schedules or logistic processes.
6. It enables senior management and select implementers to scan the mailbox.
7. The MIEM subdirectory provides immediate insight by organizing the intelligence so evolving changes in the behavior of customers, competitors, and the trade can be immediately seen by scanning the appropriate subdirectory file.

Figure 3.14 **Color Printer/Scanner Project**

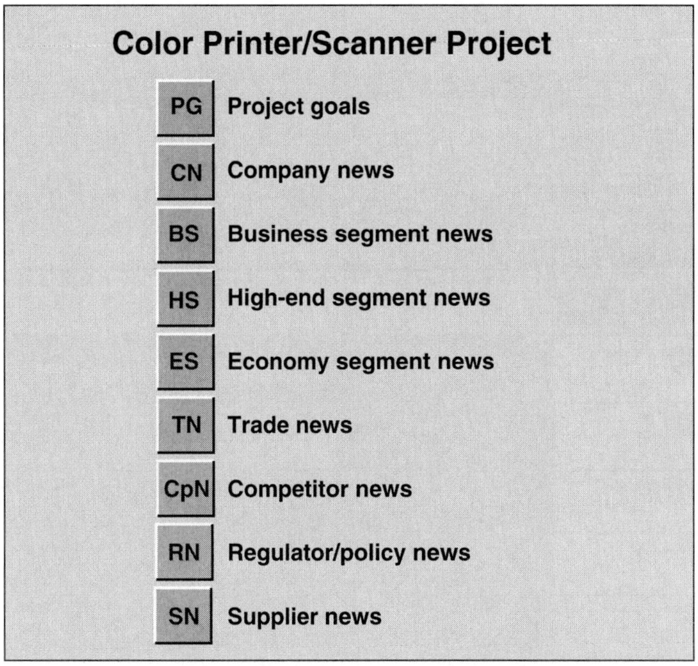

A MIEM window as seen through an Internet or E-mail connection.

Figure 3.15 **Business Segment News**

An intelligence gatherer with information about the economy segment would click on the economy segment news and this would access a memo window as illustrated in Figure 3.15.

Figure 3.16 **Detail MESHING Matrix Screen**

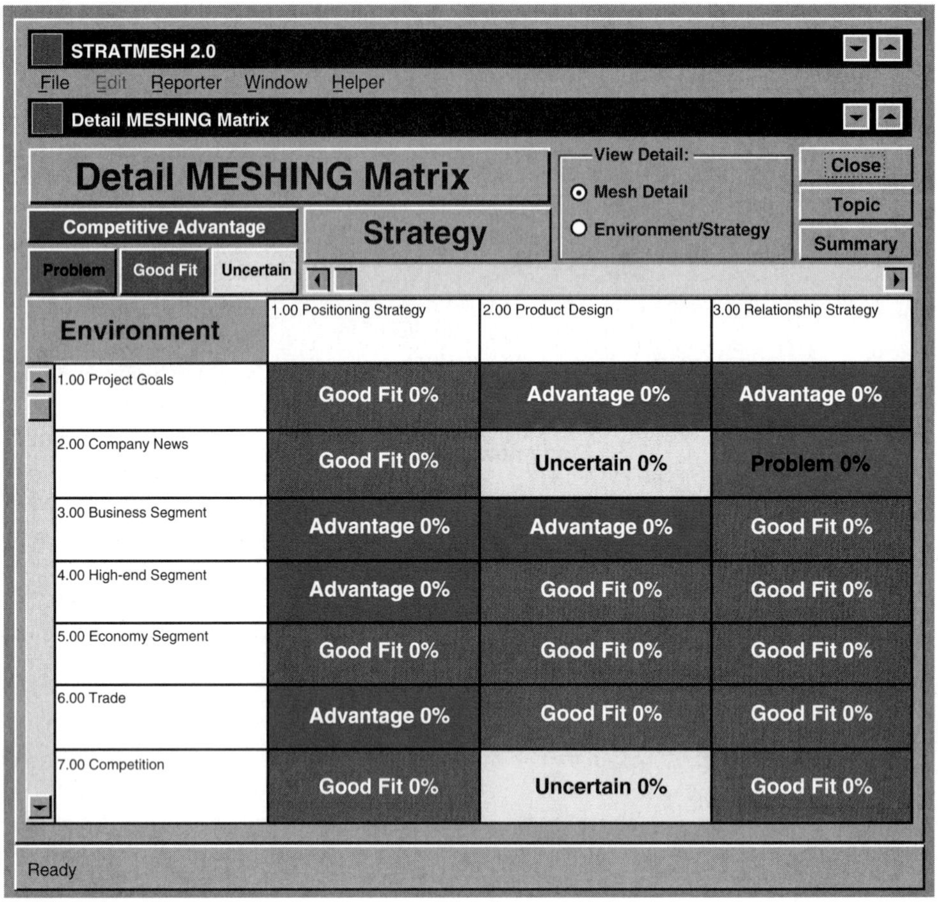

As explained in the previous chapter, a market analyst sifts through, edits, abstracts, and posts this new intelligence into the economy segment section of the STRATMESH 2.0 environment report. This new information would then be used to update the product market meshing matrix as seen in Figure 3.16.

Apart from the obvious details of access address and security codes, intelligence generators need to be taught how to write intelligent memos rather than dump hundreds of pages of data into the MIEM. They also have to be taught the mental model of the market that defines the MIEM directory and must learn to use it to frame their thinking about that market.

This last issue of framing thoughts is very important because, in recent years, some creative research in economic psychology and marketing has revealed important biases in the use of information and decision making.[42] For example, decision makers tend to frame problems as either threats *or* opportunities, and they overweigh certain information and underweigh other information.

A Quick-Response Decision Support System

The decision making processes described in Chapter 2 and the intelligence gathering and use processes described above can be combined to create a quick-response decision support system.

Intelligence generators gather information, call up the product's MIEM and leave a memo. The marketing analyst (called the product manager, business analyst, or cross-functional team executive assistant) scans the E-mailbox sometimes up to several times a day. He or she sifts through the information, edits, abstracts, dates, and posts the new intelligence under the relevant heading of the marketing plan's environment report stored in STRATMESH 2.0. The cross-functional team then meshes the new intelligence with the strategy, programs, action plans, sales forecasts, and budgets and repaints the meshing matrix. This involves adding new, dated commentary to a meshing cell and changing the color of the matrix cell when deemed appropriate. A message could be sent to the original intelligence generator's E-mailbox thanking the person for his or her altertness and insight. If the generator is a sales rep or employee not associated with the project, then the bonus account of the individual could be credited. At the end of the year, individuals might be paid bonuses based on the intelligence they generated that made a difference; that is, led to the repainting of the meshing-matrix.

According to de Geus, the only competitive advantage firms will have in the future is their managers' ability to learn faster than their competitors.[43] Learning faster depends much on the mental adaptive skills of the management team (see Appendix 1) and the company's business planning process. The use of MIEMs and STRATMESH 2.0 in a quick-response decision support process speeds up the collective learning of the key decision makers about changes in the marketplace. It also gives management more time to implement a planned and well-considered reaction and thus to avoid panicky crisis management. Executives who closely monitor *real-time* information from intelligence generators develop a much deeper understanding of the market environment and their firm's situation which allows them to react to change better.[44] The MIEM and STRATMESH 2.0 software is designed to deliver real-time intelligence to the team and make it easy to mesh the new information with the implementation of their strategy and programs so they can react to change better and faster.

---

[42] Appendix 1; also J. H. Barnes, "Cognitive Biases and Their Impact on Strategic Planning," *Strategic Management Journal* 5 (April/June 1984): 129–38; Amos Tversky and Daniel Kahneman, "Rational Choice and the Framing of Decisions," *Journal of Business* 59, no. 4 (1986): s251–78; Robin M. Hogarth, *Judgement and Choice* (New York: John Wiley, 1987); William Samuelson and Richard Zeckhauser, "Status Quo Bias in Decision Making," *Journal of Risk and Uncertainty* 1 (1988): 7-59; and J. E. Russo and P. J. H. Schoemaker, *Decision Traps: Ten Barriers to Brilliant Decision Making and How to Overcome Them* (New York: Doubleday, 1989).

[43] Arie P. de Geus, "Planning as Learning," *Harvard Business Review*, 1988, 70–74.

[44] Henry Mintzberg and J.A. Waters, "Tracking Strategy in an Entrepreneurial Firm," *Academy of Management Journal*, 25, 1982, 465–499; Kathleen M. Eisenhardt, "Making Fast Strategic Decisions in High-Velocity Environments," *Academy of Management Journal*, 32, 543–576; Shona L. Brown and Kathleen M. Eisenhardt, "Product Innovation as Core Capability; The Art of Dynamic Adaptation," Working Paper, Stanford University Computer Industry Project, March 1995.

Figure 3.17 The Most Extensive Library

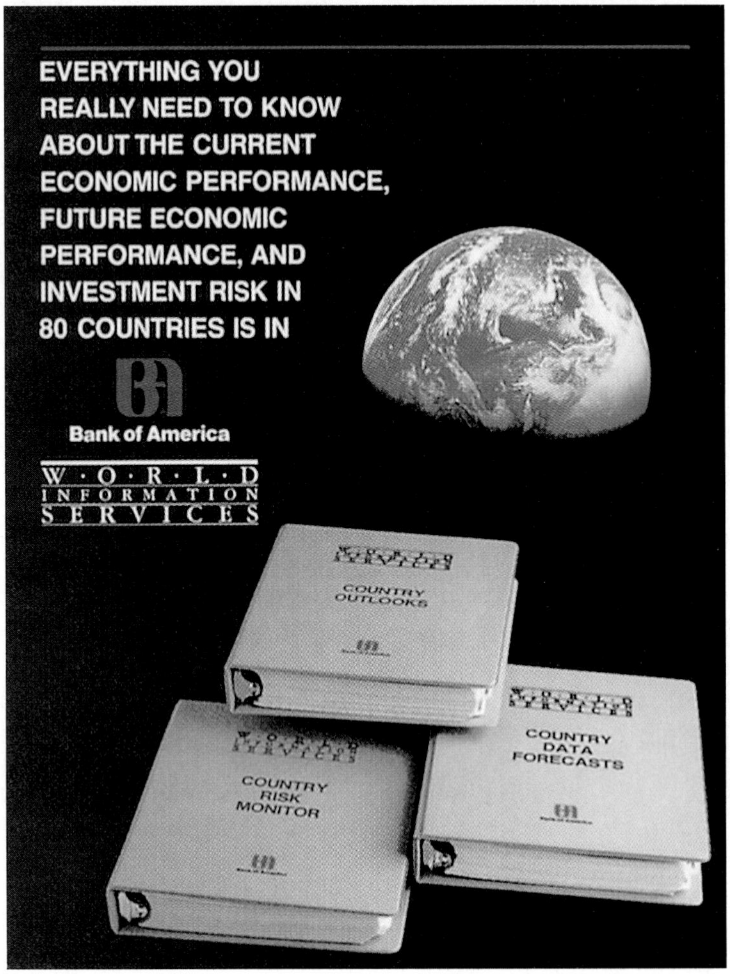

Many banks market economic analysis products and services to customers. If they had read their own reports, they might have avoided huge losses on third-world loans in the 1980s.

Global Market Research

This discussion on the gathering of intelligence about foreign markets is built on the following assumptions. It is assumed that a great deal of the decision making about the marketing programs in foreign markets is decentralized, that is, in the hands of an executive team in charge of regional or national markets. For firms new to exporting, such decision-making activity will be in the hands of local agents or distributors. Thus, much of the previously stated advice on how to gather market intelligence is directed at these executives or agents.

This is not to suggest that market intelligence on foreign markets is hard to find in the United States. The U.S. Department of Commerce publishes two invaluable, brief reports on marketing in more than one hundred countries: *Foreign Economic Trends and Their Implications for the United States* (semiannual) and *Overseas Business Reports* (annual). Not only are these reports a great buy, but they also provide a foundation for seeking further expert advice from the U.S. Department of Commerce and U.S. embassies. If such trade specialists cannot help, they are likely to know and be able to recommend experts in the foreign market who can be called. Thus, the first step in global market intelligence gathering is to use the market intelligence gathered by the U.S. government or by banks (see Figure 3.17). A free guide detailing government information and counseling services can be obtained by calling (800) USA-TRADE.

Whatever the geographical market, be it global, regional, national, or a specific city, it is assumed that the 5E mental model of thinking about a market will hold. Having all markets in a multinational enterprise analyzed using the same (5E) mental model makes supervision and oversight a great deal easier. The commonalities and differences among markets, and the trends over time in such commonalities and differences, is much easier to detect. Thus, the standardization also contributes to the development of major strategic decisions on grouping markets, on transcultural market segmentation, and on the standardization of various product lines and marketing programs in the global market. A further advantage is that when a foreign market is analyzed using such a framework, the market will be perceived to be much less exotic, perplexing, and mysterious. The systematic gathering and use of market intelligence using a familiar mental model takes much of the "foreignness" out of a foreign market.

However, the standardization can be taken too far. For some developing markets still under the control of political and economic autocracies (rather than free market forces), a special section of the environmental analysis must be devoted to considering the changing objectives and behavior of those in authority and the changing relationship that the firm or its agents have with such a powerful market constituency. Such concerns are discussed in greater detail in Chapter 6 on the public policy and ethical environment.

The final issue in global market intelligence gathering and use is the value of site visits by senior American executives. Such visits allow executives to make initial contacts with distributors and agents (often during trade delegation tours led by politicians). They are also symbols of concern and respect for the foreign market and the efforts of local employees. However, they are no substitute for informed briefings on the culture, on the purchasing power of target consumers, on the existing distribution system, on import regulations, and on taxes provided by expert nationals or expatriots. If senior executives do not have the time to be so briefed by expert distributors, economists, historians, and cultural anthropologists *before* making the next site visit or *during* the visit, then local management is likely to conclude that the American managers really have neither the time not the respect to be making the visit.

In short, overseas trips should *not* be spent on emergency negotiations or used as scouting breaks from the turbulent domestic market. It is not a coincidence that much of the success of Japanese firms in the U.S. market can be traced to their practice of being excellently briefed before and during visits to the United States. Unlike some U.S. firms, who do not listen and take to heart the advice received from Japanese distributors, Japanese companies squeeze all of the market intelligence they can out of the distributors they visit in a foreign market, and they use the information. Consequently, their mental models of the U.S. market are often much closer to the truth than some U.S. firms' mental models of the Japanese market.

Discussion Questions and Minicases

1. What two negative effects does a recession have on a firm's use of market research?
2. If decision makers prefer market research that confirms their current beliefs, then how do they learn to adapt to changes in the market?
3. All told, do you think it is better for firms employing many brilliant, creative inventors to do market research? Justify your answer. If they should do market research, when should they do it, and what sort of research should they do?
4. Imagine you were part of the cross-functional team developing the Depend's adult disposable diaper. Several members of the team seem to be having a problem understanding consumer complaints about the existing product in the market. What market intelligence-gathering activity might you suggest to raise their understanding?
5. The following figure suggests that the most learning occurs with the first focus group or in-depth customer interview and that learning new things almost ceases by about the fifth or sixth focus group or in-depth interview. What else does the figure tell us that is very interesting?

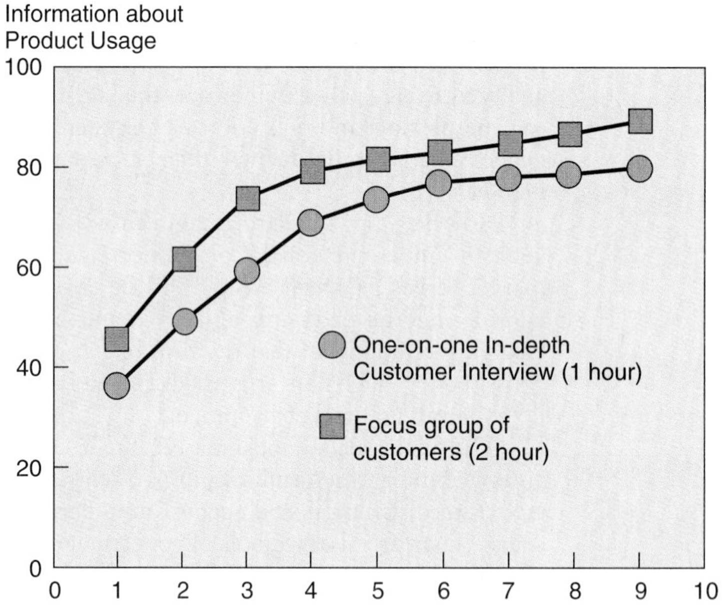

6 When researching customer needs, would it be better for a product designer to visit customers personally or to read a survey research report on customer needs, beliefs, and behaviors? What biases are inherent in each approach that will reduce the designer's rationality?
7. The Rationality in Practice box on page 114 discusses the effect of information technology on an organization. What lessons does it contain about DSSs? (Hint: For information technology to increase productivity, what has to change?) Do you think the use of DSSs is improving? If so, why?
8. The following table presents an interesting analysis of changes in the cost of living prepared by *Consumer Reports* magazine. The data are based on U.S. Bureau of Labor statistics hourly wage rates and the prices of goods and services in ninety-one urban areas. The data collectors visited twenty-five thousand stores and service firms to obtain

This table shows how long the average American had to work, before taxes, to earn enough to purchase the goods and services listed. Calculations are based on the actual prices of items in 1962, 1972, 1982, and 1992 and the average hourly wages in each of those years. For simplicity's sake, the inexpensive items in the top third of the list are given in minutes of work, the more costly goods and services are given in hours, and the big-ticket items at the bottom are given in days.

	1962	1972	1982	1992
Small items	MINUTES OF WORK			
Postage (first class, 1 oz.)	1.1	1.6	1.7	1.6
Newspaper (*New York Times*, daily)	1.4	2.4	2.3	2.8
Long-distance phone call (3 min., N.Y. to L.A.)	60.8	23.5	13.4	4.3
Apples (Red Delicious, 1 lb.)	3.1	2.9	3.3	4.7
Gasoline (1 gal.)	7.5	5.2	9.1	6.4
Chicken (whole, cut, 1 lb.)	13.5	8.7	7.4	7.4
Milk ($\frac{1}{2}$ gal.)	12.5	9.6	8.8	7.8
Ground beef (chuck, 1 lb.)	15.3	13.9	13.0	11.1
Film (Kodak, 35 mm, color prints)	60.0	37.9	27.7	27.2
Barbie doll	81.1	60.8	33.2	31.3
Medium items	HOURS OF WORK			
Record album	1.8	2.2	1.2	1.6[a]
Consumer Reports (1-yr. subscription)	2.7	2.2	1.8	2.1
Timex watch (men's Mercury model)	3.1	2.1	2.2	2.4
Electricity (500 kwh)	4.6	3.3	4.2	3.9
Theater ticket (Broadway, best seat)	3.4	4.1	5.2	5.7
Television (RCA, 19-in.)	85.1	121.6	42.6	21.7
Dishwasher (GE, midpriced model)	112.2	64.9	55.3	35.5
Washing machine (Sears, midpriced model)	92.3	52.7	58.3	37.8
Refrigerator (Frigidaire, top-freezer)	168.0	99.2	83.7	59.8
Mattress (Simmons, with box spring)	71.6	59.5	44.0	60.7
Large items	DAYS OF WORK			
Auto insurance[b]	7.1	7.8	7.3	11.3
Income taxes (federal)[c]	50.0	48.3	63.8	49.0
Child delivery[d]	15.5	37.2	33.3	62.2
College (public)[e]	61.7	64.1	68.9	99.2
Car (average, new)	203.1	131.0	161.0	197.8
College (private)[f]	129.5	140.4	144.0	251.4
House (3-bedroom ranch, Matawan, NJ)	1125.5	1330.7	1530.0	1777.3

[a]Compact disc.
[b]National average.
[c]Includes Social Security.
[d]Normal delivery (hospital and doctor fees).
[e]University of Michigan (room, board, tuition; 1 yr.).
[f]Colgate (room, board, tuition; 1 yr.).

SOURCE: *Consumer Reports*, June 1992, 393.

Rationality in Practice

Parkinson's Law, Continued

Or why computers and faxes demand more, not fewer, bureaucrats to feed and comfort them

"It is a commonplace observation that work expands to fill the time available for its completion." With those words this newspaper coined Parkinson's Law in 1955, naming it after the (anonymous) author of the article, Professor C. Northcote Parkinson. Since then, wonderful to report, technology has entirely rescued us from the bureaucratic suffocation envisaged by Mr. Parkinson. The world of administrators has been so transformed by computers, faxes and cheap telephones that their productivity grows ever more prodigious, their numbers ever leaner. Governments have shrunk to mere skeleton staffs of irreplaceable paragons. Obstructive bureaucracy has gone the way of wick-trimmers.

Would it were so. This year, for the first time, more Americans work in government than in manufacturing. Mr. Parkinson's observation that bureaucracies grow inexorably, independent of their workload, is as true today as on the day it was first made. Between 1980 and 1991 the number of officers in the American army grew by 7%, while the total number of soldiers shrank by 3½%. In 1965–85 the number of non-teaching staff in school administration in the United States grew by 102% while the number of students shrank by 8%.

No doubt there are more laws and rules to enforce. But there are also more computers to share the work. Robots have reduced the number of people it takes to make a car. Why have computers—white-collar robots—not reduced the number of people it takes to run a government?

The Hard Disk Effect

Parkinson's Law consisted of two maxims: an official wants to multiply subordinates, not rivals; and officials make work for each other. Or, as explained in *The Economist*, "In any public administrative department not actually at war the staff increase may be expected to follow this formula: $x = (2k^m + p)/n$," with the resulting x then shown to be 5¾% a year. In the 1950s the trouble started with the real, or imagined, overwork of an offi-

the prices. What does it tell us about the standard of living in America? What does it tell us about changes in price sensitivity over time? Marketers of which products should be most interested in the results?

9. In terms of intelligence gathering and use, what does the Sam Walton story at the beginning of the chapter teach us? What does it teach us in terms of competitive rationality?
10. The customer survey (on page 116) is included with every purchase of Rockport shoes. How could Rockport use this information? What other questions might have been included? What questions would you eliminate to make room for the questions you would add?
11. A survey of 149 major U.S. firms taken in 1989 by the Conference Board asked which research techniques they used to identify the benefits and outcome performance requirements customers sought from using a product or service. The answers follow on the table on page 115. What do they tell us about the perceived net value (benefit/cost) of different research techniques? Using the theory of competitive rationality, what techniques do you think should be used more often?

cial whom Mr. Parkinson called A, who came to be the master (and slave) of his proliferating subordinates, C–H. A's successor achieves the same alphabetical explosion by new means.

The trouble began a few years ago when A first installed a computer in his office. The new computer required A to hire C and D to help him, partly because he was so busy with the computer that he had less time for his other duties, and partly because it was immediately evident that the computer would enable somebody to analyse the information passing through his department in an entirely fresh way.

Nor was A the only one to get a computer. B's group was also technified at the same time, and its overall boss thought it wise that A should see B's memos and vice versa, because there might be—he was rather proud of the word—synergy between them. There was, indeed, synergy. That is to say, C and D found that criticising B's absurd proposals took up more and more of their time. Synergy was soon increasing at an alarming rate, because C had hired two technical wizards, E and F, who plugged the department into adMinNET, the new public administrator's electronic mail service. A was then in no position to refuse D's demand for a new computer since the hard disk of the first one was entirely full of junk mail from Omaha about forthcoming conferences on improving productivity in administration.

This is not to imply that computers reduce productivity. On the contrary, the output of A's department is vastly greater than it was before he got the computer. He could never, in the old days, have generated 80 megabytes of data in a year, even if most of it was repetitious. Nor is it fair to describe this workaholism as make-work. Much of the output is worthy stuff. But running a country, or a school district, is more like digging a hole than cutting down a tree—there is no end to it. The work that could be done is infinite and the capacity for expansion of productive, diligent staff is Malthusian. As Mr. Parkinson put it, 38 years ago, "the number of the officials and the quantity of the work to be done are not related to each other at all."

Let us therefore add a coda to Parkinson's Law. Because data expands to fill the hard disks available, and officials proliferate to process the data available, technology is the ally of bureaucratic expansion, not its foe.

SOURCE: *The Economist*, August 8, 1992, 16.

12. A leading supermarket chain surveyed its senior managers to obtain their estimates of consumer price search behavior. The first column of the table on page 117 presents the results of a major consumer survey, the second column presents the average estimate of

TECHNIQUE	NUMBER OF TIMES MENTIONED
Focus groups	40
Surveys of customers' needs, expectations, attitudes, and perceptions by mail and/or telephone. Includes surveys by consultants and in-flight surveys by airlines	22
Direct contacts with individual customers, including visits by senior executives and technical personnel	14
Customer and user group councils, forums, panels, advisory groups, and awareness meetings	12
Teams and teamwork between customers and companies	7
Shopping mall studies, intercepts (exit pools), and interviews	5
Benchmarking (comparison of a company's performance with that of competitors whose performance is known to be excellent)	4
Analysis of complaints	4

SOURCE: Francis J. Walsh, *Current Practices in Measuring Quality* (New York: The Conference Board, 1989).

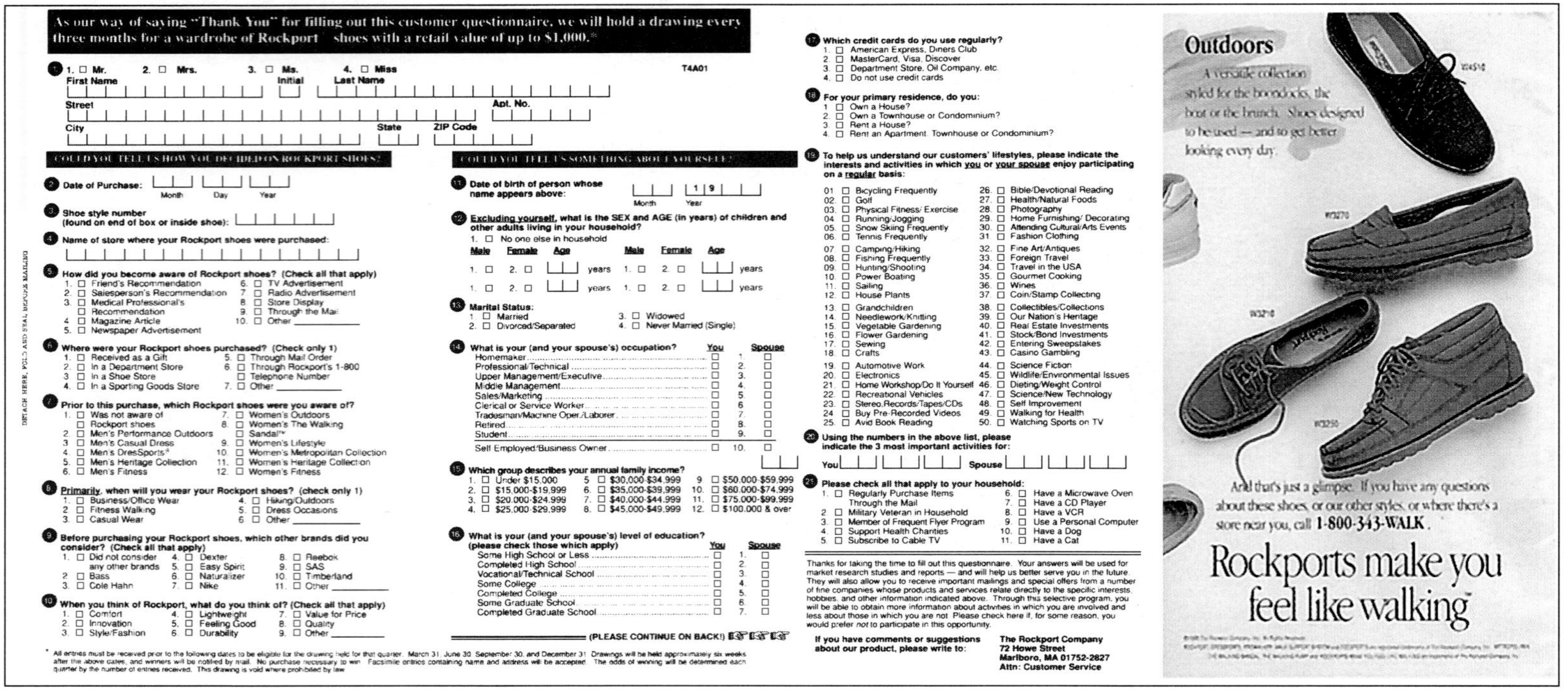

As our way of saying "Thank You" for filling out this customer questionnaire, we will hold a drawing every three months for a wardrobe of Rockport shoes with a retail value of up to $1,000.*

T4A01

1. 1. ☐ Mr. 2. ☐ Mrs. 3. ☐ Ms. 4. ☐ Miss
First Name / Initial / Last Name
Street / Apt. No.
City / State / ZIP Code

COULD YOU TELL US HOW YOU DECIDED ON ROCKPORT SHOES?

2. Date of Purchase: Month Day Year

3. Shoe style number (found on end of box or inside shoe):

4. Name of store where your Rockport shoes were purchased:

5. How did you become aware of Rockport shoes? (Check all that apply)
1. ☐ Friend's Recommendation 6. ☐ TV Advertisement
2. ☐ Salesperson's Recommendation 7. ☐ Radio Advertisement
3. ☐ Medical Professional's Recommendation 8. ☐ Store Display
9. ☐ Through the Mail
4. ☐ Magazine Article 10. ☐ Other
5. ☐ Newspaper Advertisement

6. Where were your Rockport shoes purchased? (Check only 1)
1. ☐ Received as a Gift 5. ☐ Through Mail Order
2. ☐ In a Department Store 6. ☐ Through Rockport's 1-800 Telephone Number
3. ☐ In a Shoe Store
4. ☐ In a Sporting Goods Store 7. ☐ Other

7. Prior to this purchase, which Rockport shoes were you aware of?
1. ☐ Was not aware of Rockport shoes 7. ☐ Women's Outdoors
8. ☐ Women's The Walking Sandal™
2. ☐ Men's Performance Outdoors
3. ☐ Men's Casual Dress 9. ☐ Women's Lifestyle
4. ☐ Men's DresSports® 10. ☐ Women's Metropolitan Collection
5. ☐ Men's Heritage Collection 11. ☐ Women's Heritage Collection
6. ☐ Men's Fitness 12. ☐ Women's Fitness

8. Primarily, when will you wear your Rockport shoes? (check only 1)
1. ☐ Business/Office Wear 4. ☐ Hiking/Outdoors
2. ☐ Fitness Walking 5. ☐ Dress Occasions
3. ☐ Casual Wear 6. ☐ Other

9. Before purchasing your Rockport shoes, which other brands did you consider? (Check all that apply)
1. ☐ Did not consider any other brands 4. ☐ Dexter 8. ☐ Reebok
5. ☐ Easy Spirit 9. ☐ SAS
2. ☐ Bass 6. ☐ Naturalizer 10. ☐ Timberland
3. ☐ Cole Hahn 7. ☐ Nike 11. ☐ Other

10. When you think of Rockport, what do you think of? (Check all that apply)
1. ☐ Comfort 4. ☐ Lightweight 7. ☐ Value for Price
2. ☐ Innovation 5. ☐ Feeling Good 8. ☐ Quality
3. ☐ Style/Fashion 6. ☐ Durability 9. ☐ Other

COULD YOU TELL US SOMETHING ABOUT YOURSELF?

11. Date of birth of person whose name appears above: Month Year 1 9

12. Excluding yourself, what is the SEX and AGE (in years) of children and other adults living in your household?
1. ☐ No one else in household
Male Female Age — 1. ☐ 2. ☐ years 1. ☐ 2. ☐ years
1. ☐ 2. ☐ years 1. ☐ 2. ☐ years

13. Marital Status:
1. ☐ Married 3. ☐ Widowed
2. ☐ Divorced/Separated 4. ☐ Never Married (Single)

14. What is your (and your spouse's) occupation? You / Spouse
Homemaker 1.
Professional/Technical 2.
Upper Management/Executive 3.
Middle Management 4.
Sales/Marketing 5.
Clerical or Service Worker 6.
Tradesman/Machine Oper./Laborer 7.
Retired 8.
Student 9.
Self Employed/Business Owner 10.

15. Which group describes your annual family income?
1. ☐ Under $15,000 5. ☐ $30,000-$34,999 9. ☐ $50,000-$59,999
2. ☐ $15,000-$19,999 6. ☐ $35,000-$39,999 10. ☐ $60,000-$74,999
3. ☐ $20,000-$24,999 7. ☐ $40,000-$44,999 11. ☐ $75,000-$99,999
4. ☐ $25,000-$29,999 8. ☐ $45,000-$49,999 12. ☐ $100,000 & over

16. What is your (and your spouse's) level of education? (please check those which apply) You / Spouse
Some High School or Less 1.
Completed High School 2.
Vocational/Technical School 3.
Some College 4.
Completed College 5.
Some Graduate School 6.
Completed Graduate School 7.

(PLEASE CONTINUE ON BACK!)

17. Which credit cards do you use regularly?
1. ☐ American Express, Diners Club
2. ☐ MasterCard, Visa, Discover
3. ☐ Department Store, Oil Company, etc.
4. ☐ Do not use credit cards

18. For your primary residence, do you:
1. ☐ Own a House?
2. ☐ Own a Townhouse or Condominium?
3. ☐ Rent a House?
4. ☐ Rent an Apartment, Townhouse or Condominium?

19. To help us understand our customers' lifestyles, please indicate the interests and activities in which you or your spouse enjoy participating on a regular basis:
01. ☐ Bicycling Frequently 26. ☐ Bible/Devotional Reading
02. ☐ Golf 27. ☐ Health/Natural Foods
03. ☐ Physical Fitness/Exercise 28. ☐ Photography
04. ☐ Running/Jogging 29. ☐ Home Furnishing/Decorating
05. ☐ Snow Skiing Frequently 30. ☐ Attending Cultural/Arts Events
06. ☐ Tennis Frequently 31. ☐ Fashion Clothing
07. ☐ Camping/Hiking 32. ☐ Fine Art/Antiques
08. ☐ Fishing Frequently 33. ☐ Foreign Travel
09. ☐ Hunting/Shooting 34. ☐ Travel in the USA
10. ☐ Power Boating 35. ☐ Gourmet Cooking
11. ☐ Sailing 36. ☐ Wines
12. ☐ House Plants 37. ☐ Coin/Stamp Collecting
13. ☐ Grandchildren 38. ☐ Collectibles/Collections
14. ☐ Needlework/Knitting 39. ☐ Our Nation's Heritage
15. ☐ Vegetable Gardening 40. ☐ Real Estate Investments
16. ☐ Flower Gardening 41. ☐ Stock/Bond Investments
17. ☐ Sewing 42. ☐ Entering Sweepstakes
18. ☐ Crafts 43. ☐ Casino Gambling
19. ☐ Automotive Work 44. ☐ Science Fiction
20. ☐ Electronics 45. ☐ Wildlife/Environmental Issues
21. ☐ Home Workshop/Do It Yourself 46. ☐ Dieting/Weight Control
22. ☐ Recreational Vehicles 47. ☐ Science/New Technology
23. ☐ Stereo, Records/Tapes/CDs 48. ☐ Self Improvement
24. ☐ Buy Pre-Recorded Videos 49. ☐ Walking for Health
25. ☐ Avid Book Reading 50. ☐ Watching Sports on TV

20. Using the numbers in the above list, please indicate the 3 most important activities for:
You / Spouse

21. Please check all that apply to your household:
1. ☐ Regularly Purchase Items Through the Mail 6. ☐ Have a Microwave Oven
7. ☐ Have a CD Player
2. ☐ Military Veteran in Household 8. ☐ Have a VCR
3. ☐ Member of Frequent Flyer Program 9. ☐ Use a Personal Computer
4. ☐ Support Health Charities 10. ☐ Have a Dog
5. ☐ Subscribe to Cable TV 11. ☐ Have a Cat

Thanks for taking the time to fill out this questionnaire. Your answers will be used for market research studies and reports — and will help us better serve you in the future. They will also allow you to receive important mailings and special offers from a number of fine companies whose products and services relate directly to the specific interests, hobbies, and other information indicated above. Through this selective program, you will be able to obtain more information about activities in which you are involved and less about those in which you are not. Please check here if, for some reason, you would prefer *not* to participate in this opportunity.

If you have comments or suggestions about our product, please write to:
The Rockport Company
72 Howe Street
Marlboro, MA 01752-2827
Attn: Customer Service

* All entries must be received prior to the following dates to be eligible for the drawing held for that quarter: March 31, June 30, September 30, and December 31. Drawings will be held approximately six weeks after the above dates, and winners will be notified by mail. No purchase necessary to win. Facsimile entries containing name and address will be accepted. The odds of winning will be determined each quarter by the number of entries received. This drawing is void where prohibited by law.

MEASURE	CONSUMERS (% OF SAMPLE)	MANAGERS' ESTIMATE	STANDARD DEVIATION	RANGE
Shop stores' specials regularly	18.6%	33.9%	20.3	5–90
Compare prices weekly	29.6	36.0	22.3	1–90
Never compare prices	36.0	22.7	20.5	0–98
Scan shelves for specials	78.0	49.9	22.6	10–90
Buy larger quantities on special	67.3	42.8	22.1	0–100

the managers, and the third column presents the variation in the managers' answers. What does this tell us about the chain's use of market intelligence, the managers' mental models of consumer behavior, and the firm's shared mental model of consumer behavior?

13. Table 3.2 presents information about the usefulness of competitive intelligence and the most useful sources of competitive intelligence. Why is price information more important than strategy information? List several reasons. What do the results of the most useful sources tell us about how we should set up an intelligence gathering operation?

14. The Secret Service and CIA are likely to become increasingly involved in preserving U.S. company trade secrets and in gathering economic intelligence. Do you think it is a good thing for government secret services to be employed in economic intelligence gathering? Should they be involved in industrial espionage? What if their involvement is needed for the United States to maintain its economic leadership of the world economy? What tactics should the CIA be allowed to employ to obtain crucial intelligence? Should they be allowed to pay for it? To pay bribes? To blackmail? To silence people involved in major scandals that would bring disrespect to the United States and threaten its economic future and, hence, national security? Does your answer change if other nations are already employing their security services in such activities?

15. The State Department is in charge of more than one hundred U.S. embassies and consulates scattered around the world. How is the U.S. diplomatic service and State Department likely to change if the predominant conflict among countries in the twenty-first century will be economic rather than ideological?

The rate at which individuals and organizations learn may become the only sustainable competitive advantage.

Ray Strata
President, Analog Devices

True leadership must be for the benefit of the followers, not the enrichment of the leaders.

Robert Townsend

CHAPTER FOUR

Analyzing the Organization

To implement their vision of the company future, senior executives must be relentless drivers of change, continuously motivating innovations, imitation, and improvised adaptations to achieve their goals. It is not hard to motivate fearful employees when the company is drowning in red ink, but how do you generate continuous learning and change before you are up to your armpits in red ink?

Managers often do so by pointing out to employees the harsh consequences of not continuously improving. Facing declining demand in the late 1980s, Boeing embarked on a dramatic process reengineering project to reduce costs, shorten product development time, and increase customer perceived quality. Employees were shown a video in which an actor played the role of a reporter describing the death of a company. Workers were depicted handing in their badges in empty plants. This alternative option helped convince all employees to support management's goals. Hallmark Cards shocked its senior executives into improving their product development processes by showing them chilling videos of Hallmark outlets that were dying and a high-level Wal-Mart executive questioning whether Wal-Mart could continue to do business with Hallmark. Ameritech went through several generations of

executives who "talked" the right "change line" but did not "walk" it—they were frustrating footdraggers. CEO William Weis then shocked everyone by firing them and promoting junior-level people to run his divisions and head the change effort. Although these are seemingly negative approaches to gaining cooperation, the harsh lesson learned by many firms is that positive exhortations and incentives often do not work. Organizations may have to be frightened into accepting change and ever more change.

This Chapter explains how senior management lead and direct product-market teams (see Figure 4.1). First, they must focus the learning toward particular markets, processes, and technologies. Second, they must set financial goals that make it very clear what the priorities are among strategies and action plans. The alternatives are short-term profits versus long-term growth; tried-and-true strategies and action plans that generate safe, certain sales and profits (sure "singles") versus high-risk, innovative strategies and action plans that can generate very high returns (a "home run") but also may strike out. Third, senior management must create and sustain a learning and change culture using both carrots and sticks. The team also needs to be informed about other developments within the company that impact marketing strategies and action plans. Examples are a candid assessment of manufacturing scheduling problems that will effect on-time delivery, an update on the success of a quality-improvement program undertaken with suppliers that will increase product quality, and a report from the sales vice president on the successful introduction of a new software package that enables the sales force to service customer inquiries about order status and delivery dates on new orders on the spot. This is what a company analysis is all about. It guides the decision making of the team by informing members about the current situation within the company. ■

Leadership Vision and the Company Mission

Any marketing plan, strategy, program, or decision naturally must be consistent with the overall competitive strategy of the firm as expressed in the corporate mission statement and by senior management. But a state-of-the-company analysis needs to go beyond top-down strategic and financial direction. It needs to realistically identify the competitive competencies and culture of the firm that may either limit or boost the likely success of a marketing program. The company situation often can be described more readily than external market environment issues relating to consumers,

Figure 4.1 **Chapter Organization**

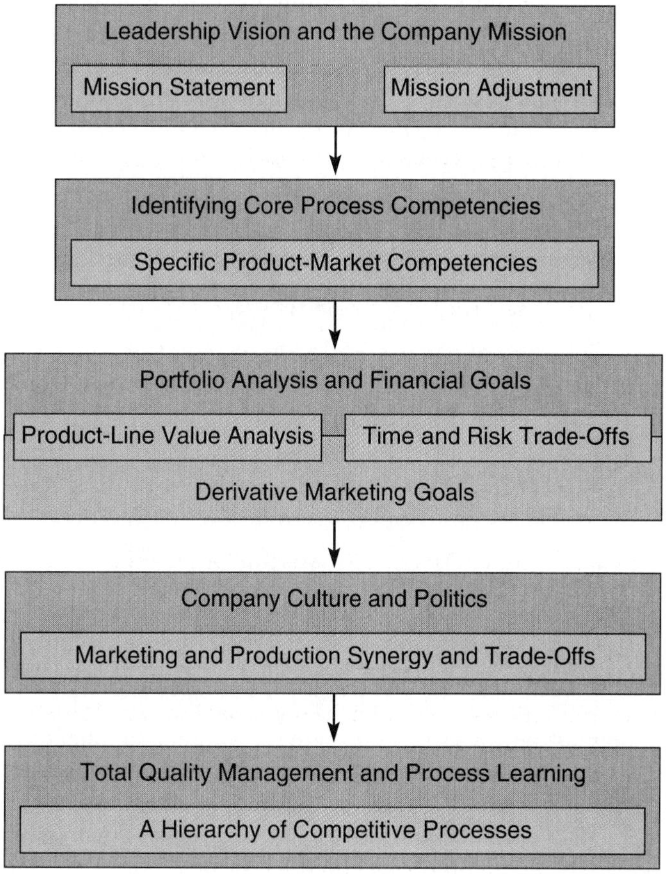

In this chapter the internal (company) environment is analyzed. It starts with a discussion of the importance of leadership vision and a clear corporate mission that identifies the markets the company intends to serve, the technologies, products, services, and processes to be mastered. This leads into a discussion of core process competencies and specific product-market competencies that can be identified using a competitive analysis template. This analysis is then used to compare the prospects of the company's portfolio of product-lines, make capital-budgeting decisions, and set specific financial goals for a product-line. The chapter then discusses the importance of considering company culture and politics in product-market decision making and the need to appreciate how total quality management and process learning affect the current and future competitiveness of the company.

competitors, channels, and public policy. Company issues are also usually more controllable than aspects of the external environment. This chapter discusses the sort of information that needs to be gathered for the company section of an environment report.

Corporate planning texts and articles emphasize the important role of the corporate mission statement.[1] Without its direction, marketing managers will use their

[1] Derek Abel, *Defining the Business: The Starting Point of Strategic Planning* (Englewood Cliffs, NJ: Prentice-Hall, 1980); and John A. Pearce, "The Company Mission As a Strategic Tool," *Sloan Management Review* (Spring 1982), 15–24.

personal beliefs about the corporate management's company vision, or corporate mythology, to guide their planning. This will result in unnecessary internal uncertainty and conflict and a waste of resources on tangential projects.

The purpose of the corporate mission statement is to direct planning and strategy by broadly describing how the organization intends to fulfill its basic responsibilities to its owners. In doing so, it should help resolve the competing and contradictory demands made on the company's resources. No corporate mission, even if written by Solomon, can resolve all of the inherently conflicting interests of shareholders, customers, management, employees, suppliers, and government. However, a corporate mission statement can go a long way toward expressing and achieving a consensus.

Thus, the company analysis should start with a visionary statement that gives direction to the product positioning, target marketing, marketing action plans, and all other efforts at reengineering the products, processes, and systems within the firm. This vision is far more than a rudder that steers the company. It does more than require that the company be shipshape—that every process and function in the company work efficiently. The mission statement defines the very design of the company. A battleship, no matter how shipshape and where it is steered, cannot fulfill the mission of a submarine or an aircraft carrier. This explains why AT&T has split itself in three.

As mentioned previously, management experts Professors Gary Hamel and C.K. Prahalad believe that senior executives spend less than 3 percent of their time developing a shared, thoroughly discussed consensus model of what the future market is likely to be.[2] But this is only the first step. Senior executives must then develop a shared vision of how to be the leader in such a future market. This requires identifying the key customer needs that must be satisfied better than the competition, the firm's process competencies that must be developed, the technology standards that must be advanced and shared with other suppliers to lead the industry along the desired path, and the new distribution relationships that must be created.

These tasks can be risky and challenging. For example, Bill Gates, the founder and CEO of Microsoft, wants to provide a whole range of multimedia information services to tomorrow's homes. But he is not sure yet which delivery standard to adopt and promote. Should it be through telephone lines or through TV cables, or will these be quickly superseded by wireless communication? His vision of the future entertainment, education, and home production needs of tomorrow's household is important because he has the resources to make his vision happen. But if he is wrong and leads his company down the wrong technology path, then any number of media, telephone, or computer companies with a superior vision could take his company's "future" away from him. He is only one of many CEOs racing to develop the required competencies internally or through alliances to compete with their different visions of the future. Each no doubt imagines that his or her company will play a crucial role in the home entertainment/management/education market. Only a few of them will make their future happen.

Chairperson Bob Allen has a vision of AT&T as an "anytime, anywhere" communication company.[3] In 1993 he spent $12.6 billion to make this happen by buying McCaw Cellular Communications, and in 1995 he spun off the telecoms-equipment business and the business built around the former National Cash Register (NCR)

---

[2] Gary Hamel and C. K. Prahalad, *Competing for the Future* (Cambridge, MA: Harvard Business School Press, 1994).
[3] Bart Ziegler, "AT&T's Bold Bet," *Business Week*, August 30, 1993, 26–30.

computer company. Now AT&T will be focused on wireless communication technology linked to its long-distance and credit-card services. Ironically, AT&T's Bell Labs invented cellular technology, and AT&T sold cellular transmission gear but missed the boat by not pioneering the market itself. The integration of AT&T's long-distance service and local wireless service enables AT&T to offer an integrated service to lucrative business customers, to bypass the $14 billion yearly long-distance connect charges it pays to local phone systems, and to enter developing-country markets where it is easier to establish modern phone services with wireless rather than wired systems. Allen's vision and bold strategy, if a little belated and expensive to achieve, looks like a winner—at least much more promising than AT&T's venture into computing, including its acquisition of NCR.

The common problem with company vision and leadership is that they overreach. In 1982 Xerox decided it was not a copier company but an "information" company. Its R&D group at Palo Alto was superb and actually invented the mouse and icon menus made familiar by the Macintosh and Windows computer programs, but the company could not convert the R&D into marketable products. Meanwhile, it allowed Canon and Sharp to steal away the low-end copier market, and Kodak trumped Xerox at the high end with its superior copier. Under new leadership the mistake was rectified. Now Xerox is a "document" company, expert in the market and technologies of input copying and output printing documents.[4] It has won the Deming quality prize in Japan, the Baldridge quality award in the United States, the European quality award, and, more important, it has steadily regained market share over the past ten years. Eastman Kodak was also led down the wrong path in recent decades. In the early 1970s senior management decided that the future of silver halide photographic technology was bleak and, as a result, the company galloped off in all directions, including stealing Polaroid's technology and acquiring a pharmaceutical company.[5] Now it is back building its core competencies around photography, current silver halide technology, and future digital imaging technology. Other examples abound, such as Fisher-Price, market leaders in toys for one to five year olds, making a disastrous foray into the toy market for older children and McGraw-Hill, helped by management guru Michael Porter, trying to become an "information turbine" rather than sticking to its "knitting," which was publishing.

The Corporate Mission Statement

The company mission statement results from senior management taking a long look at what business it wants to be in and how it intends to be competitive and profitable. Companies build their competencies around their mission, processes, and people and not around a bureaucratic management structure.[6]

The generally accepted opinion of experts is that the corporate mission should describe the target markets, the basic product or service, the principal technologies to be mastered, and the competitive competencies that will be employed. Figure 4.2 illustrates such a statement for Federal Express. Statements like "Providing energy for a better America," "Maximizing profits through consumer satisfaction," "Making

---

[4] Subrata N. Chakravarty, "Back in Focus," *Forbes*, June 6, 1994, 72–76.

[5] Subrata N. Chacravarty and Amy Feldman, "The Road Not Taken," *Forbes*, August 30, 1993, 40–41.

[6] See Sumantra Ghoshal and Christopher A. Bartlett, "Changing the Role of Top Management: Beyond Structure to Processes," *Harvard Business Review*, January–February 1995, 86–96.

Figure 4.2 **The Business Definition of Federal Express**

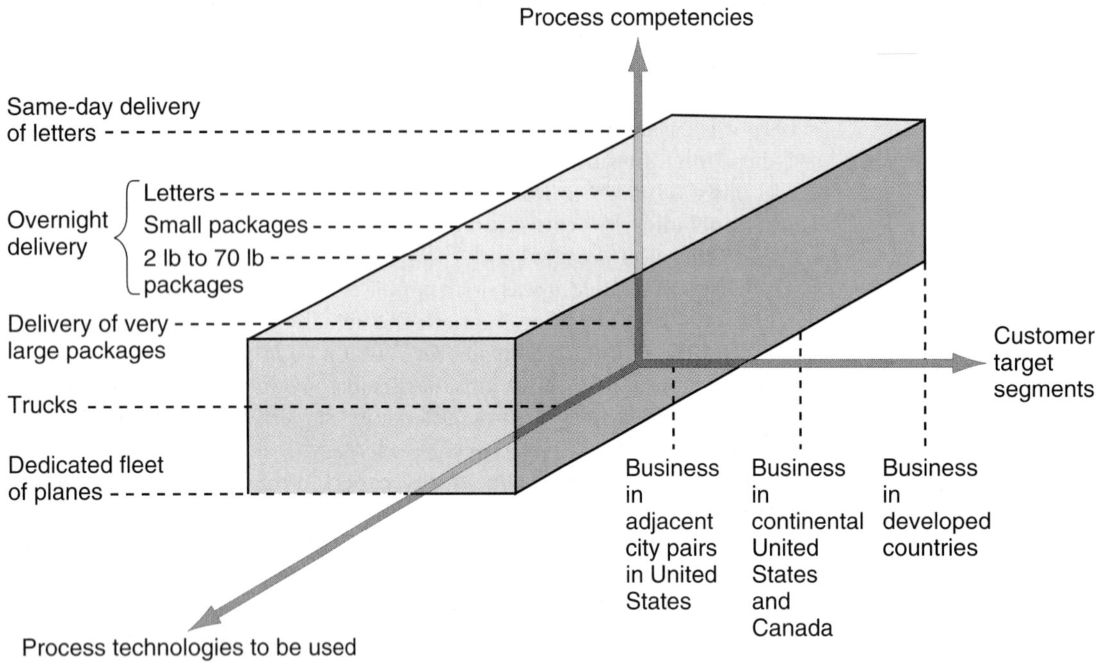

The three-dimensional framework here defines the corporate mission of Federal Express in terms of target market segments process competence and benefits delivered, and process technologies used to deliver such benefits to the segments. Federal Express also pioneered the hub-and-spoke logistics process strategy (later imitated by the passenger airlines) and a superb computerized tracking process. Both of these management technologies and processes enable it to deliver, as promised, "Absolutely, positively, overnight."

SOURCE: Reprinted by permission from George Day, *Analysis for Strategic Marketing Decisions* (New York: West Publishing Company, 1984).

tomorrow happen," "Preserving and improving human life," or "Making people happy" are too vague and sound more like public relations statements. They are not corporate mission statements for the simple reason that they do not provide explicit direction. A great example of a goal statement was that given to NASA by President Kennedy: "achieving the goal, before this decade is out, of landing a man on the moon and returning him safely to earth." The goal was ambitious, yet achievable and had a clear objective and deadline. Its vision inspired not only NASA but a nation. A less profound but equally clear goal was that of Home Depot: "To go national with $10 billion in sales and 350 locations by 1995."[7]

Although the mission statements of NASA and Home Depot are clear and inspiring, both are somewhat lacking in that they do not describe the competencies or technologies needed to be employed to achieve the goals. Jack Welch, the CEO of General

[7] C. Hawkins, "Will Home Depot Be the Wal-Mart of the '90s?" *Business Week*, March 19, 1990, 124.

Electric, outlines the sort of competence he seeks by describing how he plans to change his company's culture: "As we succeed in ridding the company of ritual and bureaucracy, we are now better able to attack the final, and perhaps most difficult challenge of all. And that is the empowering of our 300,000 people, and the releasing of their creativity and ambition; the direct coupling of their jobs with some positive effect on the quality of a product or service."[8]

The choice of product or service depends on the identification of target markets. The target product markets are the market segments you intend to serve with your product or service offering. The competitively rational way is to define target product markets after you have undertaken your customer analysis (see Chapter 5) and segmented the market into groups of customers with common usage situations and usage needs. During the development of competitive positioning strategy (see Chapter 9), a cross-functional team aligns the product line so each model caters to the needs of a different segment. Consequently, the mission statement section that identifies the target market needs to be broad enough to allow the cross-functional teams to identify the most attractive target segments, but not so broad that it provides no direction.[9] For example, defining the industry (e.g., the air-conditioning industry) is too broad. One air-conditioning company's mission statement may direct product development toward the commercial rooftop market. Another air-conditioning company's mission may be to focus on selling room air-conditioners to Wal-Mart and Sam's Club. A third air-conditioning company may target the automobile or pleasure-boat air-conditioning markets. Within each of these broad target markets are many market segments that each firm must decide whether or not to serve. Each of the three companies also will use different product designs, technologies, and distribution channels that they must master.

Three complete mission statements are presented in the Rationality in Practice box. They all provide a vision, delineate company values and ethics, and describe the nature of the target markets and products. They also outline the strengths that will empower the competitiveness of the enterprise, and they place constraints on management decision making.

Mission Adjustment

While a company mission must be enduring enough to provide stable direction, even it must change from time to time in response to changes in technology and the competitive marketplace. In such times of corporate transition and repositioning, the senior executives really exercise their vision and earn their salaries.

Often organizational leadership is not up to the task:

> We have seen that the winners are often the ones that are most experimental and flexible in matching the early forms of the product with unexpected demands and opportunities and that think through the development of their innovation in the most thorough and systematic way. As we have seen, firms that stay the course must be prepared to shift their strategic and competitive postures at several points along the way. . . . It is a great irony that wisdom for many firms that derive current good fortune from

---

[8] *General Electric Company* (Schenectady, NY: The General Electric Company, 1989), 128.

[9] George S. Day, "Strategic Market Analysis and Definition: An Integrated Approach," *Strategic Management Journal* 2 (1981): 281–99.

Rationality in Practice

Corporate Mission Statements

The Prudential Mission Statement

The Prudential is, and will remain, the No. 1 insurance company in America. Leading with this strength, we will become the No. 1 financial services company in this market and a leader in global financial markets. We will achieve this goal by enhancing our core businesses and by entering related businesses that either reinforce our core businesses or provide superior returns. We will actively explore global markets and will enter those where we can leverage our strengths. We serve our clients through four core businesses:

- Individual Insurance
- Individual Investments
- Institutional Asset Management
- Institutional Employee Benefits

Our strategies will build on the competitive strengths that distinguish The Prudential:

1. Our name and reputation, based on public recognition of our integrity and rock-solid foundation;
2. Multiple distribution channels, including the largest full-time sales force in financial services;
3. Financial size and the skills to capitalize on it; and
4. A range of products and services that gives our clients the advantages of choice and our company the benefits of diversification.

We will be aggressive and market driven. We will operate through distinct business units, targeting specific market segments with coordinated strategies. We will emphasize accountability and reward accomplishment while stressing ethical behavior. We will continue Prudential's tradition of social responsibility.

As a mutual company, we will act always in the long-term interests of our policyholders. We will measure our performance by balanced growth among earnings, revenue, and market share, and by our competitive ranking on these measures.

SOURCE: "The Prudential Mission Statement" is reproduced from John C. Shaw, *The Service Focus* (Homewood, IL: Dow Jones Irwin, 1990), 55.

Extracts from Hewlett-Packard's Corporate Mission Statement

1. **Profit.** To achieve sufficient profit to finance our company growth and to provide the resources we need to achieve our other corporate objectives. . . . Our objective is to rely on reinvested profits as our main source of capital. . . . This can be achieved if our return on net worth is roughly equal to our sales growth.
2. **Customers.** To provide products and service of the greatest possible value to our customers, thereby gaining and holding their respect and loyalty. . . . Products must be designed to provide superior performance and long, trouble-free service. . . . A prime objective of our marketing department is to see that the finished product is backed by prompt, efficient service. . . . Our customers must feel that

> radical innovations of the past lies in erecting barriers to these same types of innovations. Indeed, for some, the development projects that made them wealthy would be rejected if presented to current corporate staffers.[10]

Firms that have the visionary technological foresight to make a jump into a new technology and new markets tend to grow and prosper. In the late 1950s, IBM's Thomas Watson Jr. boldly mandated that all new developments must be based on solid-state electronics. This led the way to the System 360 but left behind decades of electrical-valve technology expertise. Motorola has moved from vacuum-tube radios to cellular

[10] James M. Utterback, *Mastering the Dynamics of Innovation* (Cambridge, MA: Harvard Business School Press, 1994), 216, 224.

they are dealing with one company with common policies and services, and that our company is genuinely interested in arriving at proper, effective solutions to their problems. Confusion and competition among sales teams must be avoided.

3. **Fields of interest.** To enter new fields only when the ideas we have, together with our technical manufacturing, and marketing skills, assure that we can make a needed and profitable contribution to the field.
4. **Growth.** To let our growth be limited only by our profits and our ability to develop and produce technical products that satisfy real customer needs.
5. **Our people.** To help HP people share in the company's success, which they make possible; to provide job security based on their performance; to recognize their individual achievements; and to ensure the personal satisfaction that comes from a sense of accomplishment in their work. . . . The objective of job security is illustrated by our policy of avoiding large ups and downs in our production schedules, which would require hiring people for short periods of time and laying them off later.
6. **Management.** To foster initiative and creativity by allowing the individual great freedom of action in attaining well-defined objectives.
7. **Citizenship.** To honor our obligations to society by being an economic, intellectual, and social asset to each nation and each community in which we operate.

SOURCE: Extracts from Hewlett-Packard's company mission statement are reproduced from William G. Ouchi, *Theory Z* (New York: Avon Books, 1981), 193–99.

Giro Sport Design Vision Statement

Values and Beliefs

- Customer satisfaction is first and foremost.
- It takes great products to be a great company.
- Integrity is not be compromised; be honest, consistent, and fair.
- Commitments made are to be fulfilled.
- Never cut corners; get the details right.
- The golden rule applies to peers, customers, and employees.
- Teamwork should prevail; think "we," not "I."
- There is no reason to make any product that is not innovative and high quality.
- Style is important; all of our products should look great.

Mission Our mission is to become a great company by the year 2000—to become to the bicycling industry what Nike is to athletic shoes and Apple is to computers.

The best riders in the world will be using our products in world-class competition. Winners of the Tour de France, the World Championships, and the Olympic Gold Medal will win while wearing Giro helmets. We will receive unsolicited phone calls and letters from customers who say, "Thank you for being in business; one of your helmets saved my life." When you ask people to name the top company in the cycling business, the vast majority will say "Giro." Our employees will feel that this is the best place they've ever worked.

SOURCE: "The Giro Sport Design Corporate Vision Statement, 1991," quoted in James C. Collins and Jerry I. Porras, "Organizational Vision and Visionary Organizations," *California Management Review* (Fall 1991).

phones to computer chips, Hewlett-Packard from video oscillators to calculators to laser printers, Kodak from emulsion film photography to digital imaging, and Canon from cameras to photo copiers. Recently, Procter & Gamble made a number of acquisitions that clearly indicated that much of its future growth will come from marketing over-the-counter health care products to an aging population. Ryder International was quick to recognize that deregulation led many airline companies to search for ways of trimming costs and financial risk. The truck rental company is now a major player in aircraft leasing, aircraft engine overhaul and maintenance, and aircraft spare-parts supply.

Top-down predetermination of the markets to be served and how to serve them is not without its critics. If such direction includes specific marketing strategies or focuses on a specific market or technology, it can reduce the peripheral vision of lower level planners.[11] They only look for opportunities under the "light" provided by senior management. This reduces the organization's foresight and adaptability. A McKinsey and Company study suggests that competitively successful companies have the ability to pool the environmental insights of their intelligence gathering employees, such as salespeople, engineers, and shop floor workers (as described at the end of Chapter 3). Successful companies often seem to make strategic accommodations to numerous environmental changes rather than executing the grand strategy of senior management imposed from the top down. They pursue new technologies and markets in step-by-step adjustments (sometimes large but often small) without overreaching. What may be preferred is a combination of bottom-up adaptation and top-down integration.

Whatever the process, senior executives must work with lower-level cross-functional teams to create the most accurate future vision of the market (see Chapter 17). The goal is to answer questions such as: How can consumer demand be changed by innovations in technology and distribution? How are population demographics, lifestyles, and values changing? Senior executives have a better understanding of the strengths and the weaknesses of the enterprise and can see the forest rather than just the trees. They understand and are concerned about production constraints, working capital, cash flow, costs, and contribution control. Experienced senior managers are also better at crisis management.

The challenge is to find a way to make senior executives aware of changes in product market environments that may have company-wide strategic implications before they develop corporate objectives and strategy. One solution is to decentralize all decision making to divisions and then combine marketing and all functional planning into divisional planning, as described in Chapter 2. Another solution is to introduce a company-wide information system, in which new information about the marketplace is cataloged and constantly disseminated on-line (such as the decision support system described at the end of Chapter 3) or in reports that are specially designed for different levels of management.

Identifying Core Process Competencies

Corporate missions that describe target markets and technologies may successfully guide plans and strategy. However, they still may provide insufficient direction because they do not explicitly state the unique competitive competencies to be developed by the organization. A company should search for a common thread in its activities and acquisitions.[12] This thread should be its process competencies. Such process competencies, be they involved in purchasing, production, technology, human resources, materials, logistics, or marketing, should be identified in the corporate mission statement. During the first and great diversification period of modern management in the 1920s, chemical companies such as Du Pont, Union Carbide, Allied Chemical, Hercules, and Monsanto all diversified from a common specific technological base. General Electric and Westinghouse also diversified around production and technological process strengths.

---

[11] Richard Pascale, "Our Curious Addiction to Corporate Grand Strategy," *Fortune*, November 2, 1982, 148–56.
[12] H. Igor Ansoff, *Corporate Strategy* (New York: McGraw-Hill, 1965). This is the classic work on the subject.

One of the most basic decisions senior management must make is whether to develop expertise in a particular process or whether to form an alliance with an independent entity that has world-class expertise in that process.[13] This "make" or "buy" decision is becoming an important part of company vision and mission statements because the ability to manage networks of such alliances has advanced greatly in recent years. Chapter 17 on implementation and organization further discusses this issue. However, two distinctive process competencies a firm cannot "farm out" or "buy" are its product-development and decision-making skills in particular markets. Everything else, from arranging finance to production, from accounting systems to distribution, can be provided by partners in an alliance.

The further a company gets from its current products and markets, the less likely it is to make a profit.[14] This is a logical consequence of the firm's inability to use its existing competitive process competencies. In the 1970s and 1980s, a number of companies rediscovered the importance of such product-market synergy. Johnson Wax diversified from packaged goods into recreational equipment in the early 1970s by acquiring fifteen different companies. In the process, it lost momentum in its mature markets for furniture polish (Pledge), insect repellent (Raid), and shaving cream (Edge) by overpricing (up to 25 percent higher than its competitors) and underpromoting.[15] It later returned to what it knew and did best and regained lost market share in its core product markets by launching new products. Efforts by Gillette, Coca-Cola, Philip Morris, Mobil, Beatrice, and General Foods to diversify into very different markets have failed, despite these companies' undisputed marketing skills.

For many years, IBM's corporate mission was to be the best service organization in the world. This process competence, when applied to the information-processing market, provided the company with an outstanding early competitive advantage. Many other companies, such as UNIVAC and RCA, had competitive products but did not appreciate the importance of service. Marriott determined that its special competence was in hospitality management and food-service processes. It sold its cruise-ship, travel-agency, and theme-park businesses and even sold its hotels to investor groups. It found that its most profitable niche was managing hotels rather than owning them.[16] Service is not one of the competencies of the highly successful BIC Pen Company ("What BIC proposes, the world disposes"). This is because the company seeks to manufacture and sell products that are cheap, used relatively briefly, and then discarded. Instead, the company's process competencies lie in quickly adopting and improving on competitors' innovations and then efficiently mass producing, distributing, and promoting such products.

Specific Product-Market Competencies

When a company already has a presence in a specific product market, then an audit similar to that made of competitors should be taken to identify its product market's specific competencies. The possible dimensions of such a self-audit are suggested in the company analysis template in Table 4.1. It is the same as the competitive analysis template which is discussed in detail in Chapter 6. Because of the sensitivity of some

---

[13] Frederick E. Webster Jr., "The Changing Role of Marketing in the Corporation," *Journal of Marketing* 56 (October): 1–17.

[14] Thomas J. Peters and Robert H. Waterman, *In Search of Excellence* (New York: Harper and Row, 1982).

[15] *Business Week*, June 8, 1987, 130.

[16] Walter Kiechel, "Corporate Strategy for the 1990s," *Fortune*, February 29, 1988, 34–42.

Table 4.1 A Company Analysis Template

Competitor ______________________ Analyst ______________________ Data ______________________

SUMMARY OF COMPANY'S POSITION

- Goals ______________________
- New product development strategy ______________________
- Decision-making skills ______________________
- Product and process R&D ______________________
- Innovation/imitation skills ______________________
- Implementation skills ______________________
- Current success story ______________________
- Current mistakes ______________________
- Advantage with buyers ______________________
- Disadvantage with buyers ______________________
- Cost advantages ______________________
- Cost disadvantages ______________________

COMMENTS AND RATING OF COMPANY'S MARKET POSITIONS

Financial Position ______________________
- Importance of this profit center ______________________
- Short-term liquidity ______________________
- Access to working capital ______________________
- Access to capital for major expansion ______________________
- Contribution margin ______________________
- Fixed cost/breakeven ______________________
- Marginal cost structure ______________________

Market Position ______________________
- Major geographical markets ______________________
- Major target markets ______________________
- Way market segmented ______________________
- Current expansion efforts ______________________
- Current holding efforts ______________________
- Overall strength ______________________

Product Position ______________________
- Raw material quality ______________________
- Workmanship quality ______________________
- Design quality ______________________
- Design efficiency ______________________
- Durability ______________________
- Ease of servicing ______________________
- Feature innovations ______________________
- Appearance ______________________
- Brand strength ______________________
- Product range ______________________
- Fit to segments ______________________
- Packaging effectiveness ______________________
- Overall strength ______________________

Pricing ______________________
- How much above/below average ______________________
- % increase in last year ______________________
- Increases in last two years ______________________
- Margin to trade ______________________
- Volume discounts ______________________
- Payment terms ______________________
- Promotional discounts ______________________
- Leasing terms ______________________

(continued)

RATING OF ADDED-VALUE PROCESSES BENCHMARKED AGAINST INDUSTRY BEST

- Buyback allowance ____
- Overall strength ____

Inbound Logistics Processes ____
- Sources of supply ____
- Purchasing skills ____
- Raw materials inventory control and efficiency ____
- Overall competitive driver ____

Production ____
- Production capacity (long-term and seasonal) ____
- Production efficiency ____
- Labor relations ____
- Labor turnover ____
- Ability to retool/adapt ____
- Quality control ____
- Production costs ____
- Overall competitive driver ____

Outbound Logistics Processes ____
- Finished product stock control and efficiency ____
- Warehouse/storage method ____
- Transportation method ____
- Order-delivery lag ____
- Back-order lost sales ____
- Longistics service features ____
- Overall competitive driver ____

Trade Relations Processes ____
- Major channels used ____
- Image of channels ____
- Trade loyalty ____
- Trade promotions ____
- Trade advertising ____
- Overall competitive driver ____

Advertising and Promotion Processes ____
- Message theme ____
- Past message themes ____
- Media used ____
- Schedule/seasonality ____
- Effectiveness ____
- Close efficiency ____
- Consumer promotions ____
- Overall competitive driver ____

Sales Force Processes ____
- Selling strategy ____
- Sales-force management ____
- Sales-force morale ____
- Sales-force turnover ____
- Sales-force selection ____
- Sales-force training ____
- Sales-force discipline ____
- Territory allocation ____
- Sales-force calling cycle and patterns ____
- Use of new technology (telemarketing, etc.) ____
- Service reputation ____
- Overall competitive driver ____

Table 4.2 **Seeing Ourselves As Others See Us**

PROCESS/PRODUCT CHARACTERISTIC	DISTRIBUTOR'S EVALUATION OF SELF	COMPETITOR'S EVALUATION OF DISTRIBUTOR	SUPPLIER'S EVALUATION OF DISTRIBUTOR	CUSTOMER'S EVALUATION OF DISTRIBUTOR
Minimal back ordering	10.0	8.0	7.4	8.2
Timely payment of invoices	8.8	8.5	8.5	NA[a]
Purchasing expertise	9.0	7.9	7.3	8.3
Managerial competence	9.6	7.9	7.5	8.1
Flexibility/adaptability	9.6	8.0	7.9	8.5
Overall profitability	9.6	8.3	7.3	7.5
Inventory management	7.3	7.5	7.3	8.2
Off-the-shelf availability	9.7	8.0	7.3	8.3
Quality of products	10.0	8.7	8.1	8.7
Wide range of products available	8.7	7.5	7.9	8.6
Large number of options for each product	7.0	7.0	7.2	7.8
Competitive pricing	7.7	7.8	7.5	7.6
Convenient ordering system	9.3	8.3	8.1	8.6
Timely notification of order status	9.0	8.0	6.9	7.6
Consistent, timely delivery of regular orders	10.0	8.1	8.0	8.5
Responsive to special handling requests	9.3	8.1	7.5	8.6
Rapid delivery of rush orders	9.3	8.1	7.5	7.9
Territory coverage	8.0	7.0	6.7	NA[a]
Technical knowledge of sales force	9.0	7.9	6.7	7.7
Assertive sales personnel	7.7	7.6	7.1	7.0
Appropriate frequency of contact with veterinarians	8.7	7.9	6.9	6.6
Detailing and demonstration skills	8.7	7.9	6.6	7.4
Flexible return policy	8.3	8.0	7.1	7.9
Professional ethics	10.0	8.8	7.6	8.3

[a]NA = Not Asked

When a company evaluates its own competitiveness, it often does not view its own strengths and weaknesses the way its suppliers, customers, or competitors do. The above 1–10 ratings report on the competitiveness of a distributor of veterinary supplies as seen by a survey of the company senior managers, suppliers, competitors, and end consumers (veterinarians).

of the evaluations, this audit should preferably be under the supervision of senior management and perhaps involve outside consultants to provide objectivity and perspective. A company with a market orientation should also incorporate suppliers' and distributors' perceptions of the company's strengths and weaknesses. Table 4.2 presents the results of an audit taken for a distributor of veterinary supplies. It shows that on some performance characteristics, customers and suppliers had a less positive view of the company products and processes than the company had of itself.[17]

A new approach to studying a company's skills in particular functional areas is called *benchmarking.* It involves going beyond competitors and even the industry to find companies that are excellent at a particular function to use as a benchmark. Companies such as Ford and Xerox have used this approach to improve their production processes, customer service, and logistics functions. Benchmarking, which will be discussed in

[17] Murray Young, "The Company Audit," Ph.D. dissertation, Ohio State University, 1988.

detail later, is an imitative learning process that a firm uses to improve its operational processes.

Portfolio Analysis and Financial Goals

Almost all of the contemporary corporate planning and marketing management texts describe various product portfolio models designed to assist the senior executive and board of directors in evaluating changing market conditions, the company's overall strategic position across all of its product-markets and to guide the allocation of the enterprise's resources (capital-budgeting) across the competing demands of divisions or product groups. Serious questions have been raised in the marketing, management and finance literature about the adequacy of information presented to senior management and the due dilligence of boards of directors in demanding such information to help improve the firm's capital-budgeting decision making, particularly pulling the plug on projects and exiting product-markets.[18]

Portfolio models generally evaluate product-lines or groups using a two-dimensional graph whose dimensions for measuring changes in market conditions are:

1. The attractiveness of the industry/market
2. The competitive position of the company within the industry/market

The Boston Consulting Group uses specific measures of market growth and market share. General Electric and Shell Oil have used composite measures of industry attractiveness and competitive advantage (see Figure 4.3). Much of the criticism of the portfolio technique is not that a company makes comparisons between the prospects of different product-lines but the appropriateness of the evaluative dimensions. Prospect comparisons based on specific dimensions are criticized for ignoring many other important environmental facts relative to niche market opportunities, competition, channels and public policy. An experimental study of capital-budgeting found that the use of the Boston Consulting Group portfolio matrix led to fewer subjects using all of the information presented and selecting the most profitable investment. On the other hand, analyses that are composite evaluations of market prospects are considered to be too general and abstract.

About 20 percent of the companies participating in the 1990 Conference Board study of marketing planning reported using product portfolio analysis in their planning but when asked to identify how their planning had improved over the last decade, very few mentioned such an analysis. Indeed, some mentioned they had abandoned product portfolio analysis in favor of obtaining better, more timely information about the markets; better and faster communication within the company; and faster, more cooperative decision making.

If senior management have to assign different financial goals to product-lines, and in particular transer cash flow from one product-line to another that offers better prospects it seems that this might be best achieved by asking for a bottom-up summary market environment analysis from the team managing each product-line. A portfolio of these summaries would then be used by the board of directors or senior

[18] See Michael C. Jensen, "The Modern Industrial Revolution, Exit, and the Failure of Internal Control Systems," *The Journal of Finance*, 68 (July 1993), 831–880.

Figure 4.3 **Product Portfolio Analyses**

The first figure presents an example of the share/growth matrix developed by the Boston Consulting Group in which seven product-lines (A–G) make up the portfolio. The empty circle represents the current position, the dark circle the forecast future position. The area of the circle is proportional to the product-line's contribution to company sales volume.

SOURCE: George S. Day, "Diagnosing the Product Portfolio," *Journal of Marketing*, 41 (April 1977), 29–38.

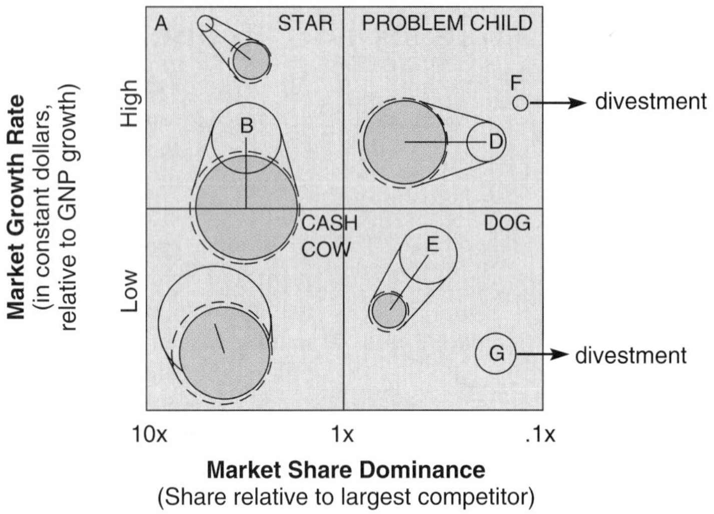

The second figure presents a business strength/industry attractiveness matrix where the ratings of a product-line on the two dimensions is a composite of many determinants of business strength and industry attractiveness. The pie slice within the circle represents the gross profit contribution of the product-line.

SOURCE: Roger A. Kerin, Vijay Mahajan and P. Rajan Varadarajan *Strategic Market Planning*, Boston: Allyn and Bacon, 1990, p. 74.

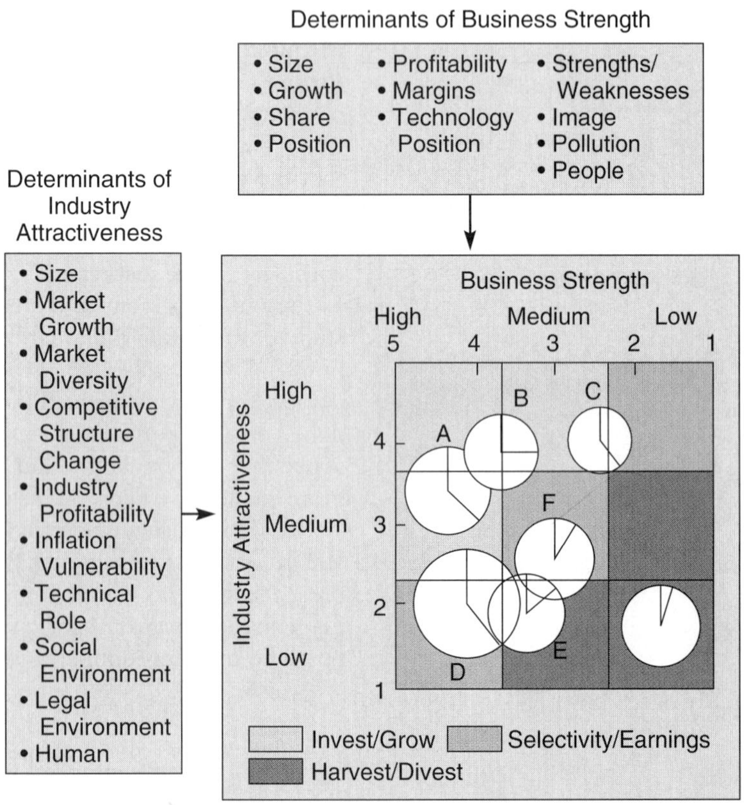

Figure 4.4 A STRATMESH 2.0 Product-Market Portfolio Matrix

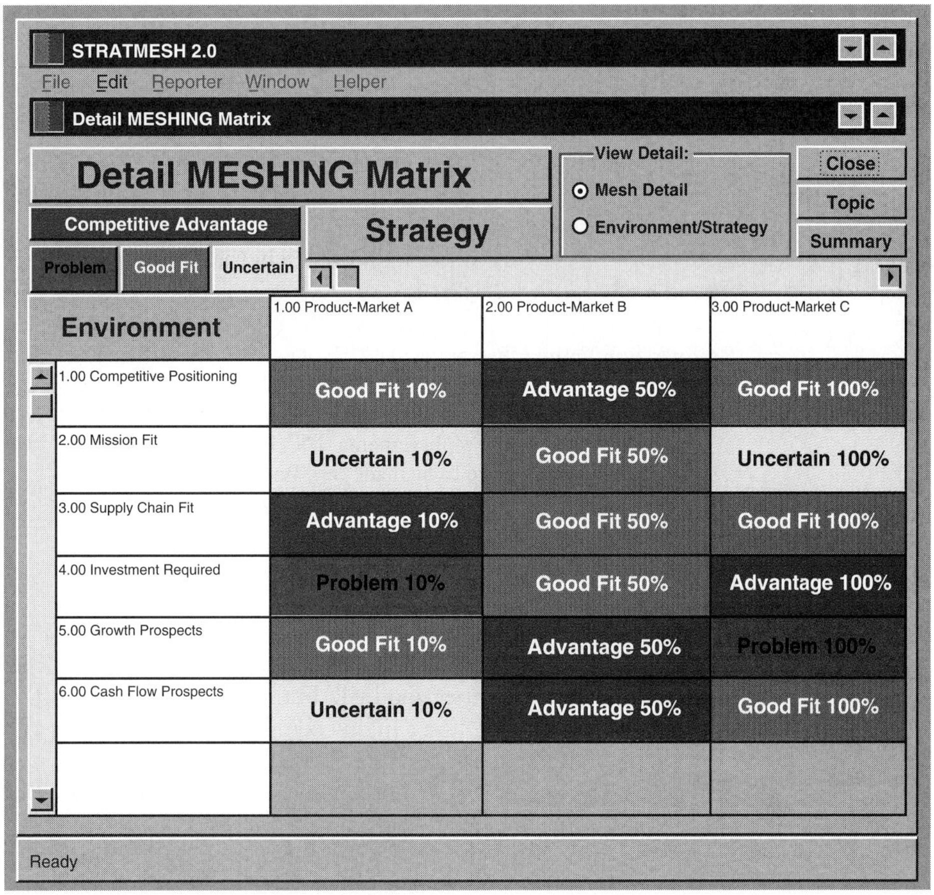

The above STRATMESH 2.0 template displays evaluations of three of a company's product-markets. The percentage indicates how far product development has progressed. The company has an established position in Product-market C (indicated by the 100 percent), it is about 50 percent along the product development process for Product-market B and it is basically only at the product concept stage for Product-market A. For this potential market, the company is rated to have a competitive advantage with the supply chain fit but a problem with the investment required. Clicking on the cell with the mouse provides further explanation of the evaluation. Clicking on the product-market cell and criteria cells provide background information on the product-markets and criteria.

executives to decide the future role and financial objectives of each product-line and to allocate resources. But this portfolio analysis should be based on strategy-driven performance forecasts and product-line value analysis. The performance forecasts should be made after the environment has been analyzed and the new positioning strategy and market development programs proposed, not before such activities (see Chapter 18). Figure 4.4 illustrates a STRATMESH 2.0 portfolio analysis matrix that does this and summarizes the prospects of each product-market at a glance. The details about the criteria, projects and evaluations can be accessed by pointing and clicking. Even more usefully, this framework can be used to evaluate the changing prospects of a product-market as it progresses from concept development (10 percent developed) to initial prototype (50 percent development) to launched (100 percent development). The next section presents product-line value analysis and is followed by a discussion of risk and how it needs to be managed in the short- and long-term.

Product-Line Shareholder Value

A recent trend has been the growing effort by managers of diversified companies to search for ways of increasing the value of shareholders' stock in the company.[19] This effort has made an impact on marketing planning by creating a new measure of bottom-line performance called *shareholder value.* It is measured by evaluating an overall product-line marketing strategy, plan, or project in terms of its ability to generate cash flow and the initial additional debt that must be incurred to pursue the plan. The formula follows:

Product-line Value = Present value (PV) of net after-tax **CASH FLOWS** over estimated life
+ PV of **DEPRECIATION** of the assets employed over life
+ PV of the **RESIDUAL VALUE** of the venture at the end of its life
– PV of incremental **INVESTMENT** in fixed and working capital that have to be made over its life
– Any other initial project **DEBT** incurred

While complicated, this formula directly connects a product-line's performance to the shareholders' interests. As with estimating all future performances, severe problems are inherent in forecasting cash flow, future costs, and the final residual value of the venture. Predicting residual value is particularly difficult to do if the venture plans to create or enhance customer goodwill. Future customer goodwill is an important asset or equity, but estimating it in a highly competitive market is often very difficult. However, simply understanding how this formula is calculated does provide the marketing planner with very useful guidelines on what financials are of greatest concern. Such an approach also may be useful in making decisions as to which product markets appear to offer the most attractive investment prospects. But, again, everything is dependent on the quality of the forecasts (see Chapter 18).

Investing or Directing?

The issue of how to allocate resources across a portfolio of products begs a fundamental question: To what extent should an enterprise spread risk and resources across a range of products? The advice to "stick to your knitting" runs counter to investment portfolio theory, which suggests that the larger and more diversified the portfolio, the lower the risk. Risk can also be reduced by the insightful combination of product markets. Take, for example, the South Seas island trader who invests in ice cream and umbrellas. Whether it rains or shines, one of his investments will profit, and he is not so vulnerable to major fluctuations in weather. The island trader's business portfolio, however, may benefit from some further shrewd environmental insight and strategy. Perhaps the rainfall and sunshine vary over time or among islands, suggesting locational advantages. The umbrellas also may be designed so they can be

[19] George Day and Liam Fahey, "Valuing Market Strategies," *Journal of Marketing* 52 (July 1988): 45–57; and Kerin et al., *Strategic Market Planning,* Chapter 9.

used as sunshades. Strategy is being driven no longer by simple risk reduction but by recognizing environmental issues and technological competencies that can be turned into competitive advantages.

This example demonstrates an important difference between a product and an investment portfolio. An investor has little control over the destiny of his or her portfolio. A marketing planner has considerable influence on the performance of the products in his or her portfolio. Indeed, planners are paid to exercise such influence. Senior executives who allocate resources across a portfolio of ventures as if they were just investments are denying the influence they can have on outcomes. They are either taking little advantage of the unique competencies, economies of scope, and experience of the firm, or they are, in effect, admitting that the firm, under their stewardship, has no such competitive advantages. If, in fact, senior executives approach their product market planning from an investment perspective, then a provocative question is whether they should exercise any strategic influence on marketing strategy at all. It might be better to allow the individual product groups to market their products the best way they can and to allow those at corporate headquarters to pursue their real interest in investment banking, mergers, and acquisitions. The downfall and takeover of AMF (a 1970s prototype of the successful conglomerate) was blamed, in part, on its senior management, which ran its divisions like a financial portfolio rather than understanding and playing to each divisions' individual strengths and needs.[20]

Another difference between a portfolio of products and a portfolio of investments is the consideration of synergies among products in the portfolio. A poor-performing, mature product market may still be a vital support for another high-growth product market because its sales open the door for the new business. Product markets also may share plant, R&D, and other costs, which makes it hard to determine the profitability and hence attractiveness of the market. In the abstract, let PV (A) be the present value of the earnings stream from product A and PV (B) be the present value of the earnings stream from product B. Synergistic interdependency exists if the present value of making and marketing A and B together is greater than the present value of making and marketing A and B separately [i.e., PV (A+B) > PV (A) + PV (B)].[21] A practical test of synergy is to ask the question: Would the performance of our products be just as good if they were produced by independent small firms? If the answer is "yes," then no synergies from the firm producing the portfolio of products exist, and it may be better if the firm were split up into a set of independent, smaller companies, as happened with the leveraged buyouts during the 1980s.

A higher order learning synergy also can occur among product markets. The battery company Rayovac is a supplier of batteries for notepad computers. The notepad computer market is so hypercompetitive that the companies that manufacture and market notepads put tremendous, continuous pressure on Rayovac as a supplier to continue to add quality and reduce the cost of its batteries. They also suggest innovations in battery design themselves. Rayovac does not make much profit on this business, but what it learns from being driven to innovate and imitate it has applied (transferred) to increasing sales and profits in other product markets. This suggests that one way a company can develop and sustain a driven learning culture is to deliberately

---

[20] *Business Week*, August 12, 1985, 25.

[21] Timothy M. Devinney and David W. Stewart, "Rethinking the Product Portfolio: A Generalized Investment Model," *Management Science* 34.9 (September 1987): 1080–95.

compete in hypercompetitive markets and to manage its sales so 20 percent of them are made in such markets. Its profits would come from its sales in other markets, but most of its learning and its improvement drive would come from competing in the hypercompetitive markets.

Important Time and Risk Trade-Offs

When a company operates several divisions or profit centers in different product markets, the financial performance objectives for each of the product groups are not likely to be the same. In this sense, every diversified company has a portfolio of products with different financial objectives. Consequently, marketing planners often have to accept the roles their products must play. One of the least desirable roles is as a source of cash flow and funds for another product group pursuing a growth strategy. However, an even worse situation than your product being treated as a so-called cash cow can occur. It is when corporate management demands high performance across conflicting objectives. The result is confused divisional or product market management, planning, and strategy. Clear top-down financial directives are a must. The corporate mission statement is often open to interpretation, resource constraints can be bent, and compromises with manufacturing can be made; but at the end of the year, the financial targets always come back to haunt, if not hang, the marketing planner or team. That is why it is so important to seek clarification and realism at the time the directives are given. The alternative is to search for excuses later or to have to explain why concerns were not raised about the impossibility of the objectives at the outset.

Simply put, two critical trade-offs occur in financial goal setting: a trade-off between long-term growth and short-term profit taking and a trade-off between assured, stable financial performance and the high-risk, adventurous strategy that may either strike oil or fail disastrously. The challenge is to have senior executives accept the responsibility for the financial goals they set for the marketing planner by answering the two basic questions presented in Figure 4.5. The answers to these two questions should be constantly in the back of the minds of marketing planners when developing their marketing strategy. Marketing decision makers may find that senior management will resist providing such explicit direction because it forces them to reveal their priorities and to take responsibility for their leadership and direction.

As Figure 4.5 illustrates, the goals of a division or a product group are defined by the following basic questions that need to be answered by senior management:

1. When faced with a choice, should the marketing plan aim to reinvest for growth and develop marketing strategies and tactics that build goodwill and sales, or should its goal be to generate short-terms cash and profits that enable the company to siphon off the cash and profits?
2. When faced with a choice, should the marketing plan aim for assured but modest financial performance, or should it attempt to achieve uncertain but possibly spectacular performance?

In short, senior management must choose a goal from one of the figure's quadrants that then defines the financial role of the product or product group in the company plan. Professor R. G. Cooper, an expert on product development, has observed that two principal dimensions drive product innovation strategies: market orientation and

Figure 4.5 **Alternative Financial Performance Goals**

Emphasis on?		Emphasis on?	
		Short-term cash and profits	Short-term growth, long-term profits
Emphasis on?	Conservative, assured performance	**Safe cow:** short-term, low-risk profits	**Safe calf:** long-term, low-risk profits
	High but uncertain performance	**Wild cow:** short-term, high-risk profits	**Wild calf:** long-term, high-risk profits

Senior management must define the financial role of the product or product group by placing it in one of the above quadrants.

technical orientation.[22] The most successful strategy is one in which market orientation and technological orientation are balanced. The firm puts effort into learning about its existing and potential customers and makes incremental improvements. These are safe-cow projects. Meanwhile, it also expends effort in riskier but potentially high pay-off R&D, developing a strong technical base and gaining abilities in adapting to and advancing new technology paths. These are wild-calf projects.

Ten years ago Emerson Electric seemed to face a bleak future. The markets it was in, such as compressors for refrigerators, in-sink garbage disposals, and electrical motors of all sizes, were low-growth markets and under attack from new suppliers from less developed countries such as Korea and Brazil that possessed both low labor costs and state-of-the-art equipment. Chief Executive Officer Chuck Knight launched a "best-cost producer" that placed squeezing the costs out of production and distribution processes as the number-one financial priority. Out went businesses such as Weed Eater gardening tools and defense contracting where the prospects of increasing profitability were weak. In came extensive employee consultation and feedback. By 1994 profits and cash flow were up 50 percent on the same volume of business done six years before.[23] But now the priority has shifted from growing margins and profits to growing sales by taking risks. The growth in demand for appliances in emerging economies has taken off, and Emerson wants to be a dominant player in supplying the components. Planning sessions now focus on growing sales, overseas expansion, and

[22] R. G. Cooper, *Winning at New Products: Accelerating the Process from Idea to Launch*, Reading, MA: Addison-Wesley, 1993: "The Performance Impact of Product Innovation Strategies," *European Journal of Marketing*, (18.5, 1984), 5–54.

[23] Seth Lubove, "It Ain't Broke, but Fix It Anyway," *Forbes*, August 1, 56–60.

new product development. Management compensation now rewards long-term sales growth rather than short-term profit growth. Emerson Electric is an example of a company that has clear financial priorities for its dozens of business units. It has changed over time, but every product development team has understood clearly what was the financial priority.

Derivative Marketing Goals

The financial goal setting just described can be reduced to derivative goals. For example, a company might seek to increase, by a particular percentage, the number of a particular type of customer account, the size of particular customer accounts, sales of a particular product item, sales in a market segment, or the number of inquiries. One of the best ways of encouraging growth through innovation is for senior management to set challenging marketing goals such as 30 percent of company sales must come from products fewer than four years old. Other marketing goals could be to increase customer satisfaction, increase product awareness in the market, decrease complaints, decrease average service time, and achieve numerous sales-force performance and cost-control goals (see Chapter 19).

The mistake that some marketing planning approaches make is to prescribe these marketing goals at the outset in great detail and to search for a strategy that bridges the gap between current performance and target performance. Planners sometimes forget that strategy and performance expectations drive each other. Rather than being fettered by a hundred lilliputian marketing performance and cost-control goals, it seems to make more sense to step back and develop strategy that meshes with all of the environmental issues and the overall performance goals. If it does, then the implementation of the strategy has to be monitored and controlled using marketing performance indicators related to the bottom-line target. In summary, although it sounds like a radical proposition, detailed marketing goals and performance targets may be best used to control and monitor marketing's effectiveness rather than to derive strategy. These issues are further explored in the discussion of budgeting and control in Chapter 18 and Chapter 19.

Company Culture and Politics

No internal audit is complete without an assessment of a company's unique organizational culture and its likely impact on marketing strategy. *Company culture* is defined as the shared values and beliefs that help individuals understand how an organization functions and thus provide norms for behavior within the organization.[24] It is primarily the responsibility of senior management to develop and nurture the right company culture. Figure 4.6 lists some characteristics of excellent corporate cultures. These characteristics have been identified by a number of consultants and researchers.[25]

[24] Rohit Deshpande and Frederick E. Webster Jr., "Organizational Culture and Marketing: Defining the Research Agenda," *Journal of Marketing* 53 (January 1989), 3–15.

[25] This list of excellent cultural characteristics is based on the work of William G. Ouchi, *Theory Z* (New York: Avon Books, 1981); Thomas J. Peters and Robert H. Waterman, *In Search of Excellence* (New York: Harper and Row, 1982); Carol J. Loomis, "Secrets of the Superstars," *Fortune*, April 24, 1989, 50–62; Carol J. Loomis, "Stars of the Service 500," *Fortune*, June 5, 1989, 54–62; and Modesto A. Maidique and Robert H. Hayes, "The Art of High Technology Management," *Sloan Management Review* 26 (Winter 1984): 1–31. See also Roger A. Kerin, Vijay Mahajan, and P. Rajan Varadarajan, *Strategic Market Planning* (Boston: Allyn and Bacon, 1990), Chapter 11.

Figure 4.6 **The Characteristics of Excellent Company Cultures**

1. They are able to introduce change and adapt to change in the marketplace very quickly. This involves the ability to make decisions quickly and implement the decisions faster than their competition. They have a do-it, fix-it, try-it culture.
2. They are market driven. They are close to their customers, whom they listen to and respond to with relevant product features and service.
3. They are market leaders in specific product markets and in the use of specific technologies. They have become expert at doing something very well, and they find other uses for such process skills.
4. They have few layers of management and have a lot of informal contact up, down, and across the organization.
5. They decentralize decision making and encourage autonomy and entrepreneurship.
6. Everyone in the organization is very cost conscious.
7. Senior managers take a hands-on approach. They manage by walking around the production plants, visiting customers, and talking informally with the managers and other employees. They are active managers and are experts on their product markets.
8. The organization is more like a clan than a bureaucracy.
9. Special venture teams of marketing, engineer, and production specialists are informally and formally formed to find innovative or imitative solutions to quality and cost problems.

Marketing planners must evaluate how their division or company performs based on these characteristics in determining whether the strategy they propose will be acceptable to the rest of the company and can be implemented. The impact of company culture on implementation is further discussed in Chapter 17, "Organization and Implementation."

Company politics also often play a major role in determining whether something can be done. Company politics, which are an outgrowth of a company's culture, involve conflict and cooperation among various members and factions of the organization. The most important internal politics involved in marketing planning are the politics between the marketing function and production, which will be discussed next.

Marketing and Production Synergy

In recent years, as many companies have evaluated their strengths and weaknesses and strategic posture, the classic confrontation between marketing and manufacturing has reemerged. What marketing planners need to recognize, however, is that a production-oriented culture can provide important competitive advantages, including a special type of peripheral vision.[26] Engineers not only can answer the question, "Are we doing the job right?" but can and should also address the question, "Are we doing the right job?" At times a change in technology or process confers significant competitive

[26] Robert H. Hayes and Steven C. Wheelwright, *Restoring Our Competitive Edge: Competing through Manufacturing* (New York: John Wiley & Sons, 1984); and Alan M. Kanthrow, "The Strategy-Technology Connection," *Harvard Business Review*, July/August 1980, 6–21.

advantages to the innovator. The use of the continuous-process cigarette manufacturing machine in the 1880s reduced the cost of manufacturing a cigarette to one-sixth of its previous cost. The first two users of this technology, James B. Duke in the United States and the Wills brothers in the United Kingdom, very quickly dominated their product markets. The Japanese became fierce competitors in the automobile and home electronic markets in large part because of innovations in operations: inventory management, work flow, quality control, and automation.[27]

The Growth-Choke and Adaptation-Efficiency Trade-Offs

Inevitably, a strategic accommodation must be made between marketing and production. The two commonly occurring situations that create conflict are the growth-choke and the adaptation-efficiency trade-offs.

In a growth market, marketing activity can often overheat demand. Order backlogs build up, supply is worked to capacity and then overcapacity, costs rise, and quality drops. For these reasons, competitors are able to gain a toehold with copycat entries. Marketing effort often has to be turned down or even turned off, and the market momentum is lost while expansions in the manufacturing process and materials management are made. Such changes then produce rapid increases in capacity and a tendency to oversupply. Marketing is then asked to raise demand again. Such swings can happen several times in a rapid growth market and can create enduring tensions between marketing and production. Turning market demand off and on is just as frustrating to the sales force, the channel, and the advertising agency as asking production to first overstretch itself (growth-choke) and then operate at below capacity and optimum efficiency. Both marketing and production are also expected to control costs to produce profits and cash flow to fund further market or production expansion. This often leads to finger pointing, as one functional area accuses another of inefficiency. Ironically, such inefficiencies often can be traced to accommodating the demands or constraints of the finger pointer.

For example, in recent years Harley-Davidson has faced growing demand for its "image" bikes that greatly exceeds supply. Having once been driven almost into bankruptcy over its products' poor quality, senior management refuses to risk sacrificing a now high-quality reputation by expanding production quickly. Marketing managers may be upset that distributors have no bikes to display, let alone sell, but it was they who demanded the initial turnaround in quality. Fortunately, Harley-Davidson's unique brand image means that competitors cannot take advantage—there is no substitute for a "hog." In fact, scarcity has added to the Harley mystique and increased, rather than decreased, demand.[28]

In any market, cost efficiencies and high-quality conformance (few rejects) come from bedding down a production process; cranking it up in long, uninterrupted production runs; and stretching the life of the plant by creative maintenance. New products involve investment in retooling, changing work flow, adding downstream and upstream inventory during the transition, retraining staff, start-up operating inefficiencies, numerous quality control problems, and extra marketing expenses.

[27] Steven C. Wheelwright, "Japan—Where Operations Really Are Strategic," *Harvard Business Review*, July/August 1981, 67–74; and Robert H. Hayes, "Why Japanese Factories Work," *Harvard Business Review*, July/August 1981, 57–66.
[28] Gary Slutsky, "Hog Wild," *Forbes*, May 24, 1993, 45–46.

But product change may be needed to increase competitive product differentiation or to match a competitor's new product features. Traditionally, this resulted in an adaptation-efficiency trade-off that often had to be resolved by senior management.

Recently, however, a new manufacturing strategy has emerged that bridges production's demands for low costs with marketing's demands for product innovations. Termed *flexible manufacturing*, this strategy emphasizes manufacturing many different products on the same line and switching from one product to another without set-up time and at a low cost. The objective is to make as much profit on short runs as ordinarily would have been obtained only on long, uninterrupted runs while gaining the ability to adapt quickly to market demands. The National Bicycle Company of Japan can make and deliver a bike to an individual customer within ten days with more than 11 million configurations of model, color, frame size, and other features. Dell Computers can assemble and deliver a notepad computer with hundreds of speed, memory, screen, and other feature combinations within five working days. To make this strategy work, however, a culture must promote close cooperation between manufacturing and marketing. Marketing and production can work together to each other's mutual advantage in two additional areas: improving quality and decreasing the sluggishness of all company routines.

One approach to improving relations and cooperation is to change functional areas' perceptions of interfunctional relationships by promoting the idea that they are customers of each other's processes. The internal customers of marketing's research processes are R&D, design, and manufacturing. The internal customers of manufacturing's processes are distribution and sales. From this perspective, an internal-customer orientation means providing quality output and service support and delivering on promises made. Performance guarantees can be developed that involve extra services if performance fails to meet the promises.[29] The total-quality-management approach is to redesign products and manufacturing processes so costs are reduced and, at the same time, quality is increased.

Total Quality Management and Process Learning

American manufacturers have only recently recognized that as production quality goes up, costs can come down. It has been claimed that 20 to 25 percent of the operating budgets, 25 percent of the labor costs, and up to 30 percent of the final production costs of U.S. manufacturers are spent on finding, fixing, and compensating for production mistakes.[30] Companies can learn to remove the causes of variation in the production process through statistical process control (SPC), which spots defects where and when they are made rather than after the fact. Statistical process control is a feedback process that improves the manufacturing and distribution processes of a firm (see Chapter 19).

A drive for improved quality requires a change in the whole company culture. Quality improvement must become a major focus of the business plan, must be part of each manager's annual review, and must involve all workers in job and production process design. It requires increased quality control from suppliers and that everyone

[29] "The ABCs of Internal Guarantees," *Inc.*, March 1993, 29.
[30] "The Push for Quality," *Business Week*, June 8, 1987, 130–43.

on the production line understand that the person operating the next added-value process is the customer they must satisfy. Computer programs are now being developed that enable engineers to evaluate how they can manufacture a rough design and determine its production costs. Such computer assistance allows engineers to make clear the trade-offs among form, function, cost, and the likelihood of zero-defect production of the component. The input-output matrices used in quality function deployment (QFD) and described in Chapters 9 and 10 also increase interfunction communication and the employee's understanding of how to create customer perceived quality and reduce costs.[31] Such frameworks enable marketing, engineering, and manufacturing to see all the facets of design, manufacturing, and marketing in one big picture that they can all review and agree on. This increases communication and suggests ways of resolving disagreements. It is claimed that Toyota has used QFD successfully to increase quality, lower costs, and bring products to market much faster. American companies have had mixed success using the approach, but the problems appear to stem less from QFD and more from the organization's commitment to change and making QFD work.

While it may take several years for a company to benefit from making quality a major corporate goal, the long-term benefits can be considerable. Ford started a quality drive in 1981. Five years later, the company's cost were down, quality was up, customer satisfaction was up, and profits were even greater than those of General Motors, which had almost twice the market share of Ford. Who can object to investing in quality when it helps sell the product, makes production more efficient , *and* reduces costs? The discussion now turns to how a firm invests in quality by learning to improve its processes.

Competitive Rationality and Process Learning

Microcompetitive rationality, discussed in Chapter 1, describes how competition develops an experimentation drive within the firm, but a drive to experiment with what? The theory of competitive rationality also emphasizes alertness to environmental change and imitating rivals. But what must the firm be alert to, and what must it be imitating? Finally, the theory describes the importance of implementation of innovations and imitations, but innovations and imitations of what? The answer to all of these questions, as noted earlier, is *processes.*

The drive to experiment with new processes enhances the quality, reduces the cost, and increases the speed of delivery of new products and services to the market. Measure and improve the process, and a superior product will result from the new superior process. Alertness to changes in processes in the market and in the product of these new processes is most important. Learning about, imitating, and improving on rivals' processes is a major goal of market alertness and learning. Finally, a firm must be able to implement (install) the new processes within the firm and across its trading relationships, quickly adapting them to the unique culture, human capital, and trading networks of the firm. Fundamentally, competitive rationality is about being driven to learn about and implement new processes.

---

[31] Abbie Griffin, *Evaluating Development Processes: QFD as an Example*, 91–121 (Cambridge, MA: Marketing Science Institute, 1991), 91–121; and John R. Hauser and Don Clausing, "The House of Quality," *Harvard Business Review*, May/June 1988, 63–73.

Figure 4.7 **The Evolution of Organization Learning and Competitive Advantage**

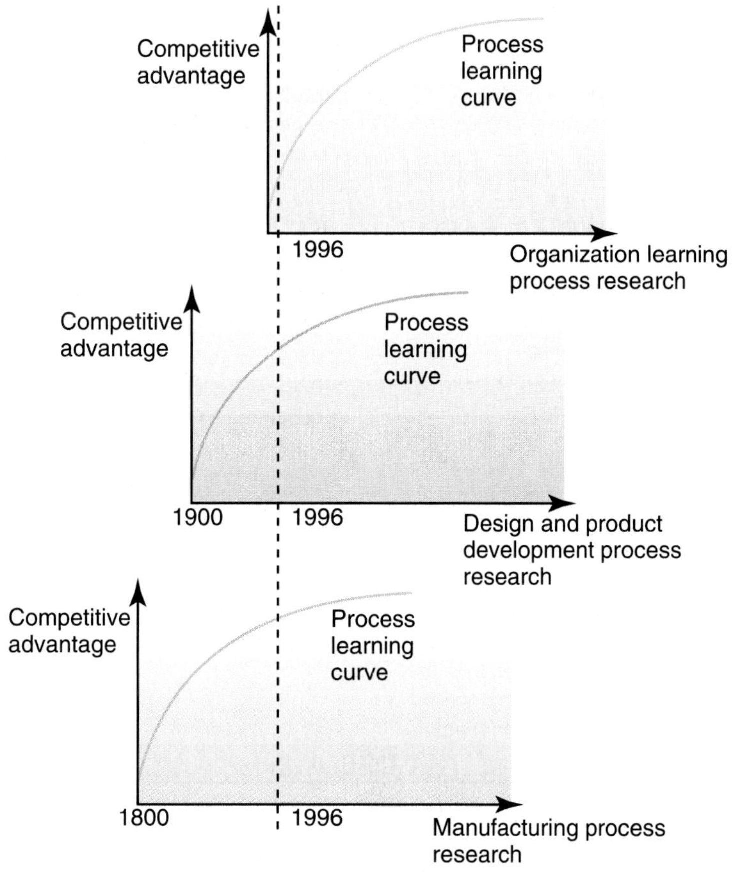

Manufacturing process experimentation and research has been advancing rapidly since the 1800s. The rate of improvement, and hence potential competitive advantage, has slowed in the late 1900s compared to the early advances. But in the past fifty years innovation in product development processes has accelerated. Only recently have firms started to innovate with organization learning processes, and, hence, the process learning and competitive-advantage curve for organization learning processes is generally steeper than for design and product development processes, which is generally steeper than for manufacturing processes.

Developing the Process Learning Competence

What happens when the rate of improvement in manufacturing processes and product development processes slows down in a market (see Figure 4.7)? As manufacturing process conformance, quality, and costs become standardized across competitors in an industry through the diffusion of innovative manufacturing processes and process controls, it becomes increasingly hard to compete by introducing lower cost production processes or by squeezing costs out of existing processes with methods such as downsizing.[32]

[32] "When Slimming Is Not Enough," *The Economist*, September 3, 1994, 59–60.

Rationality in Practice

Implementation Speed: A Sustainable Competitive Advantage

If a company can accelerate the pace of change in the marketplace, then it makes it more difficult for competitors to keep up with its moves. If a company can move faster than its competition, then this speed creates a sustainable competitive advantage. Sometimes a company will make mistakes, but its ability to rectify such mistakes quickly and regain momentum will put it out in front again. Implementation speed enables a company to be more aggressive, to stay out front, and to defend itself better in highly turbulent markets. Implementation speed reduces costs by eliminating wasted time and effort. It also increases cooperation within the organization because greater cooperation is needed to get things done quickly. Finally, it lifts the overall image of the company's service and innovativeness. Increasing the overall pace of operations in a company results in faster response to leads, faster fulfillment of orders, faster design and manufacture of special orders, faster delivery, and faster repair services. Speed kills the competition.[1]

As pointed out in Chapter 2, action or reaction time first involves seeing change in the marketplace before others do and understanding its implications faster. The second component involves adapting and implementing faster. When the CEO of Hewlett-Packard, John Young, introduced the company-wide program called BET (break-even time), which was the time it took to move a product from concept development to its break-even position in the marketplace, he recognized two important trends: (1) The company that gets new technology to the market first can charge a premium until competitors catch up and (2) manufacturing typically takes up only 10 percent of the time between when an order is placed and when the new product reaches the customer. The rest of the time is consumed by administrative duties; this time can be greatly reduced. A McKinsey & Company consulting study found that it is more profitable to get high-tech products out on time but over budget than to get them out on budget but late.[2] Figure 4.8 presents a benchmarking process designed to improve an organization's responsiveness.

[1]This is one of the key propositions of competitive rationality theory. See also Derek F. Abell, "Strategic Windows," *Journal of Marketing* (July 1987): 21–26; Tom Peters, *Thriving on Chaos* (New York: Harper & Row, 1987); Walter Kiechel, "Corporate Strategy for the 1990s," *Fortune*, February 29, 1988, 34–42; Amar Bhide, "Hustle as Strategy," *Harvard Business Review*, September/October 1986, 59–65; and George Stalk Jr., "Time—The Next Source of Competitive Advantage," *Harvard Business Review*, July/August 1988, 41–50.

[2]Brian Dumaine, "How Managers Can Succeed through Speed," *Fortune*, February 13, 1989, 54–59.

In such markets, competitive success depends on the invention of an even higher order process skill. The skill of introducing learning processes into a family business or a larger firm enables the enterprise to be continuously, incrementally improving its current product design and manufacturing processes. These higher order learning processes are the most fundamental core competencies and competitive thinking skills of the technologically advanced firm and direct its quality management.[33] Some argue that these learning processes are the only sustainable competitive advantages a firm can achieve.[34] Examples of such core learning processes are benchmarking (see Rationality in Practice box and Figure 4.8), reward processes for individuals and teams that reinforce desired behaviors (see Chapter 19), and activity-based cost-accounting processes (see Chapter 19). They can be applied to *all* processes within a firm and will increase their efficiency. Many consulting firms have shifted their focus to teaching firms how to learn (see Figure 4.9 on page 148).

[33] H. Itami, *Mobilizing Invisible Assets* (Cambridge, MA: Harvard University Press, 1987); C. K. Prahalad and G. Hamel, "The Core Competence of Corporation," *Harvard Business Review* 68 (1990): 79–91; and Peter R. Dickson, "Process Capital," working paper, A.C. Nielsen Center for Marketing Research, University of Wisconsin—Madison, 1995.

[34] See A.P. deGeus, "Planning as Learning," *Harvard Business Review*, March–April 1988, 70–74; Ray Stata, "Organizational Learning—The Key to Management Innovation," *Sloan Management Review*, spring 1989, 63–74; and Peter R. Dickson, "Competitive Rationality," *Journal of Marketing*, January 1992, 69–83.

Figure 4.8 **Implementation Speed Benchmarking**

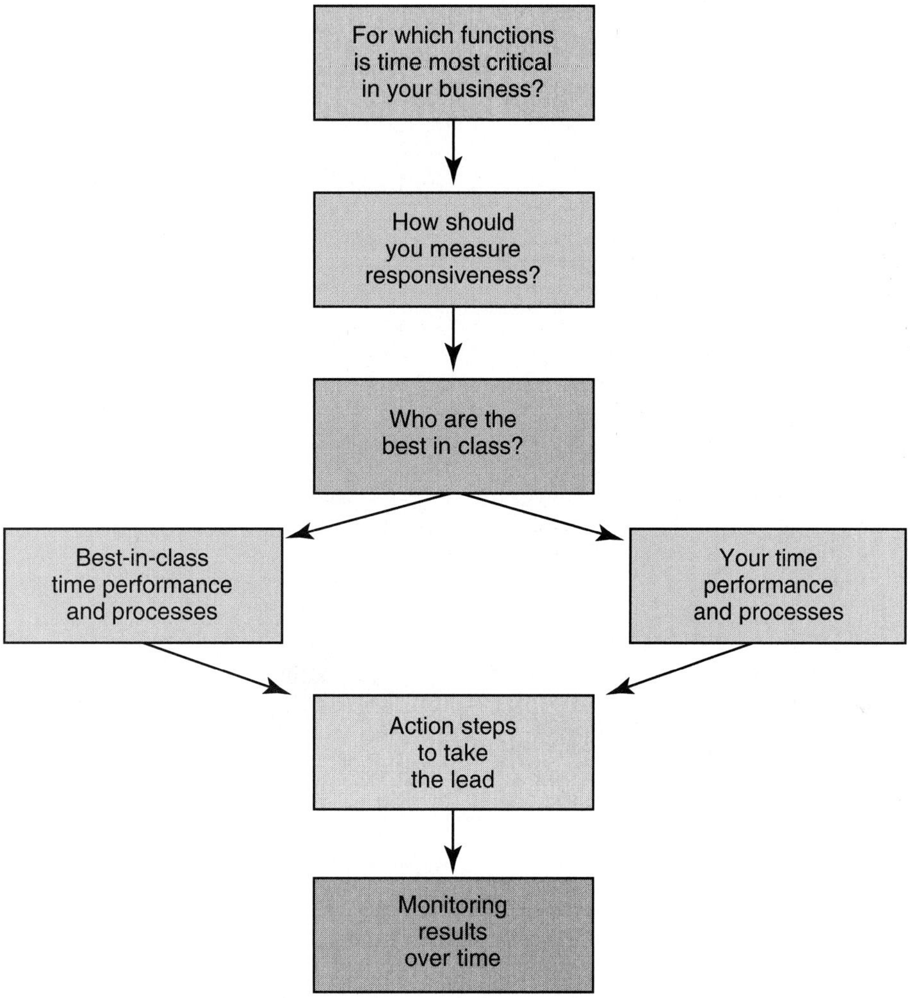

This flowchart, developed by Kaiser Associates, Inc., describes seven steps involved in improving the action and reaction speed of a firm. The "best in class" need not be in the firm's industry. For example, companies such as Xerox have turned to the catalog company L.L. Bean to learn how to improve the responsiveness of their customer service operations.

Because of their general applicability, core learning processes can be more readily transferred (imitated) across technologies, industries, and economies than can specific design or manufacturing process innovations. However, the *implementation* of such learning still depends very much on company leadership and culture, as described above. An organization's ability to learn is tested when a good product concept that is poorly designed fails: Does the organization learn from the failure and keep trying? Apple had such learning ability when its Lisa failed in 1983. A year later it launched a

Figure 4.9 **Consulting Advice on Process Learning**

Before you can succeed, you need to learn what direction to take.
Today, sharing a common direction and vision for a company's future is critical. It's a key principle used in "organizational learning"—one that can increase employee commitment, energy and performance. By applying these revolutionary principles, companies can learn and profit from change.
The journey to organizational learning can be a long one. However, Arthur Andersen can help companies turn lofty principles into tangible, measurable performance improvement.
Using the proprietary Global Best Practices℠ knowledge base, Arthur Andersen professionals will offer insights into how the world's finest companies have managed change. They'll work with you to help you implement what you've learned. With wisdom gained from thousands of engagements in implementing change, and the experience of applying learning principles internally, you can trust Arthur Andersen.
Find out how you can develop a shared vision. To learn how Arthur Andersen can help you turn learning theory into successful reality, call 1-800-257-2915.
Global Best Practices℠
Putting insight into practice.℠
ARTHUR ANDERSEN
©1995 Arthur Andersen, Arthur Andersen & Co, SC. All rights reserved.
ARTHUR ANDERSEN & CO, SC

SOURCE: *Forbes*, May 22, 1995.

Table 4.3 Organization Learning Principles[a]

1. Learning must be led from the top.
2. Superior process thinking leads to superior process learning.
3. Superior process learning leads to superior organizational processes.
4. The use of sound learning principles leads to superior learning processes.
5. Learning is learning how to improve processes, not just products.
6. Learning should improve all organizational processes, not just production or marketing processes.
7. Learning is for everyone.
8. Learning is for all teams and groups, not just individuals.
9. Learning is continuous.
10. Learning must be *used* to be learning.
11. Repetitive practice makes routine execution perfect.
12. Learning involves experimentation with processes.
13. The benefits of experimentation must be balanced against the benefits of repetitive practice.
14. Learning comes from outside, not just from inside, the organization.
15. Learning involves both success and failure.
16. Learning must be measured.
17. Use a plan-do-assess-act process to change all processes, including learning processes themselves.
18. Increasing process feedback quality increases all process learning.
19. Process feedback includes feedback about process output quality, process input costs, and process dynamics such as time.
20. Process mapping identifies the drivers of output quality, input costs, and process dynamics.

[a]Adapted from Edwin C. Nevis, Anthony J. DiBella and Janet M. Gould, "Understanding Organizations as Learning Systems," *Sloan Management Review*, winter 1995, pp. 73–85; and Peter R. Dickson, "Process Capital," working paper, University of Wisconsin, 1996.

lower priced, faster version of Lisa called Macintosh. At about the same time, IBM launched PC Jr. It, too, failed, but IBM went into something akin to an innovation sulk and did not come out with another innovation in the PC market for almost five years. The difference was that Apple was more driven to experiment, learn, and ultimately succeed in the market. Another organization with a severe learning disability is the U.S. Mint. In the twenty years since it made its Susan B. Anthony $1 coin-size mistake, it has yet to try again. The Mint's inability to apply what it learned from failure, and try again, has cost the U.S. taxpayer billions of dollars in the savings that would have been made in switching twenty years ago to a dollar coin.

A Hierarchy of Competitive Processes

Figure 4.10 outlines a hierarchy of competitive process skills. At the very top are the personal process thinking skills of entrepreneurs, managers, and engineers contained in their activity schedule memory (see Chapter 17). Without such individual process thinking and implementation skills, firms cannot develop organizational learning process skills that build their competitive competencies. These key decision makers use process learning principles in their thinking to develop the firm's informal and formal learning processes. Some of the higher order learning principles that should be applied in constructing higher order learning processes are described in Table 4.3. Be it small or large, a family business or a multinational, a firm uses its core learning

Figure 4.10 **A Process Skills Hierarchy**

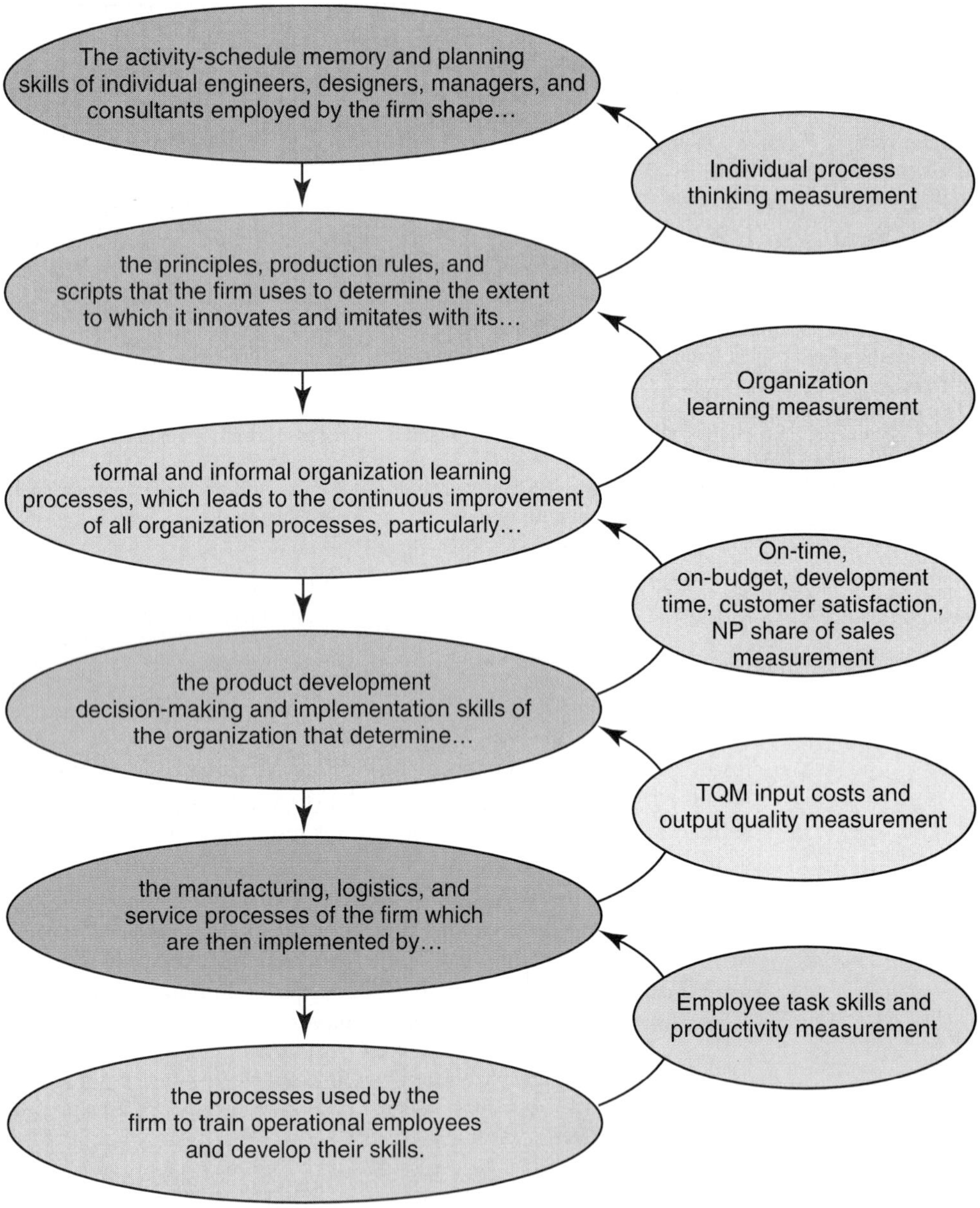
The activity-schedule memory and planning skills of individual engineers, designers, managers, and consultants employed by the firm shape...
the principles, production rules, and scripts that the firm uses to determine the extent to which it innovates and imitates with its...
formal and informal organization learning processes, which leads to the continuous improvement of all organization processes, particularly...
the product development decision-making and implementation skills of the organization that determine...
the manufacturing, logistics, and service processes of the firm which are then implemented by...
the processes used by the firm to train operational employees and develop their skills.
Individual process thinking measurement
Organization learning measurement
On-time, on-budget, development time, customer satisfaction, NP share of sales measurement
TQM input costs and output quality measurement
Employee task skills and productivity measurement

The process skills of an organization create competitive advantages and are a form of capital in that they generate future profit streams. Assuming a firm's organization should facilitate process learning and improvement, the above process hierarchy should be transparently evident in a firm's management structure. The figure also demonstrates the importance of measurement in the feedback control loop of the learning process at each process level. Such measurement controls (discussed in Chapter 19) should be used to continuously improve processes rather than simply assure conformance to a rigid work-to-rule process.

processes, such as benchmarking, reward processes, and activity cost-accounting processes, to constantly improve all of its decision-making and operational processes. These learning processes are called higher order processes and are at the top of the process hierarchy because they create all other organization processes.

Such higher order, formal and informal learning processes of the firm should be foremost applied to improving the firm's product development processes. Why? Because the product development processes of a firm determine all other manufacturing, distribution, and operational processes. One of the key product development processes is the process that senior management use to develop the vision and mission of the firm because it defines the types of products to be developed. The target markets and technological process skills defined in the mission statement directly influence the product development and operational processes of the firm. The intelligence-gathering and decision-making processes described in Chapters 2 and 3 are also key product development processes.

Below the product development processes in Figure 4.10 come all of the firm's operational processes. The operational processes are where the core technological expertise and competencies of the firm are often stored. The mission statement and product development decisions direct these operational processes along particular technological paths. For example, with its acquisition of McCaw, AT&T's mission is now to lead in the innovation of wireless technology and service processes, including wireless computer modem services.

Finally come all of the firm's processes used to train, retrain, and cross-train all of the production and service workers to execute the manufacturing and operations processes and to contribute to product and process innovation. Companies such as Charles Schwab, Hewlett-Packard, Apple, AT&T, Intel, and Andersen Consulting have used their superior higher order learning processes to create innovative, new training processes for their employees. This has enabled these firms to successfully implement their product and service innovations. Chapter 17 further discusses how a firm can design its organization and develop its culture around the nested process learning hierarchy described in Figure 4.10.

Discussion Questions and Minicases

1. What are Black & Decker's core markets, and what technology has it mastered? (Hint: Name some of its major products, and then think of what technology they have in common.)
2. What problems arise when setting performance objectives for a product group? In answering this question, consider what is wrong with the use of portfolio analysis to allocate resources and provide strategic direction.
3. Your boss refuses to give clear direction as to whether or not a project should be given short- or long-term attention, but your boss wants high, assured profits. Your boss promises to make the tough decisions, but you know that if you keep running to your boss, he or she will soon lose confidence in your leadership and management skills. What should you do in this situation?
4. Which of the goals in Figure 4.5 is likely to end up being a "bum steer"? When the S&Ls got into more and more desperate trouble, which of the four goal quadrants did they end up in, and why did these decisions seal their fate?
5. A number of years ago, corporate planners in the General Electric Company appliance division looked at the demographics and assumed that the demand for smaller appliances would increase because family size was shrinking. Because they were not in touch with home builders and retailers, they did not understand that kitchens and bathrooms were

the two rooms in the house that were not shrinking and that buyers wanted bigger refrigerators to cut down supermarket trips. Senior management listened to the planners but then discovered that the demand for smaller appliances was not there. What lessons can you learn from GE's experience?

6. In the 1980s, Pan Am proposed to sell its New York headquarters to save the company from a cash-flow crisis. This evoked angry protests from shareholders who, at the annual meeting, insisted that the board was made up of a "bunch of dummies" who should have kept the building and sold the airline. How was selling the building a right decision? How was selling the airline a right decision?
7. Why is an ounce of prevention worth a pound of cure when it comes to quality control? What is the recommended recipe for prevention?
8. Explain in detail what can happen when there is not a strategic accommodation between marketing and production.
9. Why do you think it so difficult for marketers, engineers, and production people to work together in teams? Suggest solutions to the problems you identify.
10. On what performance characteristics in Table 4.2 is the distributor perceiving itself to be doing better than reality? What impact is this likely to have on the firm's competitiveness?
11. A chief executive of an operating division of a small company is paid a lot because of his or her leadership and thinking skills. How should such a CEO explain how she or he thinks about the dynamics of the competitive market to subordinates? Do you think that this is an important function of a CEO over and above providing the mission statement and setting objectives?
12. Marc Isambard Brunel, the father of the engineering genius Isambard Kingdom Brunel, designed 45 machine tools (with interchangeable parts for simple maintenance) that started producing rigging blocks (pulleys) for the Royal Navy in 1803. The British Admiralty undertook the manufacturing at Portsmouth Dockyard paying Brunel the costs saved in a year's production, which in today's dollars made him a millionaire.[35] The capital that he created and earned came from his design of a mass production line process. Over 100,000 rigging blocks were needed because the Royal Navy, under Lord Horatio Nelson, was engaged in a crucial standoff with the French as to who would rule the waves. An assured supply of quality rigging blocks was a vital national defense priority as they tended to be shot to pieces along with the rest of the ship's rigging in battle.

    The process was operated by ten unskilled hands. These ten unskilled hands produced as many blocks in a day as 110 skilled craftsmen working for the established contractor Fox & Taylor, who was offered and refused to buy the new manufacturing process and machinery. Samuel Taylor was convinced that the existing process employed by his skilled craftsmen could not be improved on, "I have no hope of anything ever better being discovered, and I am convinced there cannot." Two years later Fox & Taylor were out of the block making business. The Brunel production line helped Nelson win the war and was still producing rigging blocks up until 1967. What really made Brunel a millionaire? What lessons are there in this story for marketing managers?
13. As described in Chapter 1, great companies are founded by successful entrepreneurs who grow their proprietory enterprise through creative innovations in their manufacturing and product development processes. As the original proprietor they are often the heart and soul of their organization's learning processes. The nested learning hierarchy (Figure 4.10) provides a new perspective of the problem of transition from the original entrepreneurs creative leadership to a leadership that must find a new source of process innovation and learning other than that provided by the entrepreneurial founder's human capital. When the entrepreneur leaves, the firm often stagnates and decays and leads to a

[35] K. G. Gilbert, Brunel's Block-Making Machinery at Portsmouth, HM Stationery Office: London, 1965.

clogs-to-clogs rise and fall of family prosperity over three generations. The gifted entrepreneur has not created a gifted, learning organization. British industry declined because 10,000 gifted entrepreneurs did not create 10,000 gifted learning organizations. So what should happen when the entrepreneurial leaders of family businesses start to approach retirement? The preeminent desire of most entrepreneurs who have dedicated their lives to building their own business is to keep the business flourishing long after their departure. In this way, their families are supported, and part of their genius lives on. With this goal in mind, how might such an entrepreneur best spend his or her time in the last few years of actively running their business. They often become preoccupied, and rightly so, with their personal finances and management succession. Sometimes this can lead to feuding between families and within families causing much of their time to be spent on trying to minimize such discord now and in the future.

"Why?" and "how?" are words so important that they cannot be too often used.

Napoleon Bonaparte

There is only one boss: the customer. And he can fire everybody in the company, from the chairman on down, simply by spending his money somewhere else.

Sam Walton

CHAPTER FIVE

Analyzing Customers

The development of the disposable camera market is a nice example of usage-situation/benefit segmentation. Fuji pioneered the disposable camera in Japan in 1986, and Kodak launched its disposable in the United States in 1987. Sales grew from 4 million units in 1988 to 25 million units in 1993 and 50 million units in 1994. The cameras are sold close to national, state, and entertainment parks, resorts, sporting events, and shows. People who forget to bring their cameras snap up the disposable. Now they are placed on tables at weddings, and their use has greatly expanded because the product line has grown to include ultrafast film for stadiums, wide-angle-lens cameras for the Grand Canyon, short-focal-length-lens cameras for baby photos, waterproof cameras for under water, fish-eye-lens cameras for fun, and foggy-lens cameras for a romantic, rosy glow. Each of the models is designed to include a specific feature that meets a desired need and delivers a desired benefit in a usage situation. Kodak and Fuji identified the most common usage situations or desired usage situations and designed a disposable camera for each usage situation.

The growth in sales of disposable cameras has invigorated the camera/film market, which had been only quietly growing at about 5 percent a year. The competition between Fuji and Kodak led to further

experimentation with new models targeted to specific usage situations and further growth. Ironically, the disposable camera is a return to Kodak's roots. In 1888 George Eastman invented the Kodak box Brownie and sold it with film installed for $25 ($400 today). The marketing slogan was "You push the button and we do the rest." Customers mailed their cameras back to Eastman, and he developed the one hundred-shot film, installed a new film, and returned the camera.

This chapter analyzes consumer behavior from an applied perspective. The *who, where, what, how,* and *why* questions about consumer behavior are answered in active terms: What groups or segments of consumers use the product in which particular situations? Do they seek similar benefits from using the product, use the product a particular way, and buy the product in similar ways? Are these groups different from each other in their needs, attitudes, interests, and behavior? How are the preferences and behaviors of these different segments changing? Chapter 5 discusses these questions and their importance to customer analysis (see Figure 5.1). ■

For thousands of years most of the world's products were custom designed and manufactured for particular consumers. The first automobiles were made this way—beautiful, expensive works of art. Pioneers of manufacturing processes recognized that standardization and production lines greatly reduced the cost and price of an automobile, opening up the market to middle-income and low-income consumers. The product would no longer fit the unique needs of each buyer, but that was the price of lowering the cost. The Ford Model T only came in five models and one color, but in 1916 its economy model cost only $360. Specialist automobile companies who found they could not compete with the cost advantages of Ford either became exclusive, were taken over, or went out of business. Ford's compromise between making the crafted product and mass production of a single model was the marketing of a line of several models, each designed to target and meet the needs of different groups of consumers, called market segments (see Table 5.1). General Motors did not invent automobile market segmentation, but in the late 1920s and 1930s General Motors did develop a *better* segmentation framework than Ford and gained a consequential strategic advantage over Ford that it held for several decades. For fifty years, American auto companies segmented the market primarily by making cars for low-, medium-, and high-income households. What a household could afford dominated their mental models of consumer demand. Today, the industry mental models of consumer demand also consider lifestyle and the benefits consumers seek from product features.[1]

---

[1] Peter Drucker, "The Big Three Miss Japan's Crucial Lesson," *The Wall Street Journal,* June 18, 1991, A18. Japanese auto manufacturers were able to break into the U.S. market by segmenting the market more by lifestyle than by socioeconomics.

Figure 5.1 **Chapter Organization**

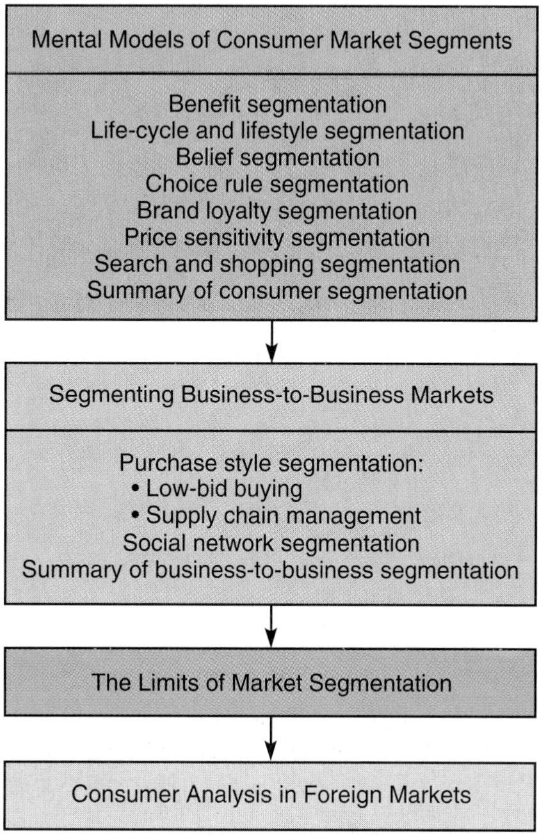

Answering the who, when, where, how, and why of consumer behavior is best organized by thinking about groups of potential users who share common motivations, beliefs, and behaviors. These are groups called market segments. In this chapter we first analyze consumer/household market segments and then business-to-business segmentation. The chapter closes with a discussion of the limits of market segmentation and consumer analysis in foreign markets.

A market segment is a group of consumers with distinct needs (demand) or behaviors (both usage and shopping behaviors). The mental model that a cross-functional team uses to identify groups of consumers with distinct needs or behaviors is called a *market segmentation framework* or *model.* The firm that chooses a consensus mental segmentation model that best explains how and why consumers differ in their attitudes and behavior toward a product market has a clear competitive advantage over its rivals. *Market segment analysis* is the search for and understanding of variability in demand (that, in turn, determines customer satisfaction). It is therefore as important a part of a firm's competitive rationality as understanding cost structure. The way a firm thinks about and segments buyers will determine how the firm designs and positions the items in its product line. This positioning will, in turn, determine sales and profits. The firm with a superior mental segmentation model can be competitive, even if it is not a

Table 5.1 **Models and Prices of the Model T**

	TOURING	RUNABOUT	COUPE	TOWN	SEDAN	2-DOOR	4-DOOR
1909	$850	$825	$ 950	$1,000			
1910	950	900	1,050	1,200			
1911	750	680	1,050	1,200			
1912	690	590		900			
1913	690	590		900			
1914	490	440	750	690	$975		
1915	440	390	590	640	750		
1916	360	365	505	595	640		
1917	360	345	505	595	646		
1918	425	500	650		775		
1919	525	500	650		775		
1920	575	550	850		975		
1921	415	370	695		760		
1922	348	319	580		645		
1923	393	364	530			$595	$725
1924	295	265	525			590	685
1925	290	260	520			580	660
1926	380	360	485			495	545
1927	380	360	485			495	545

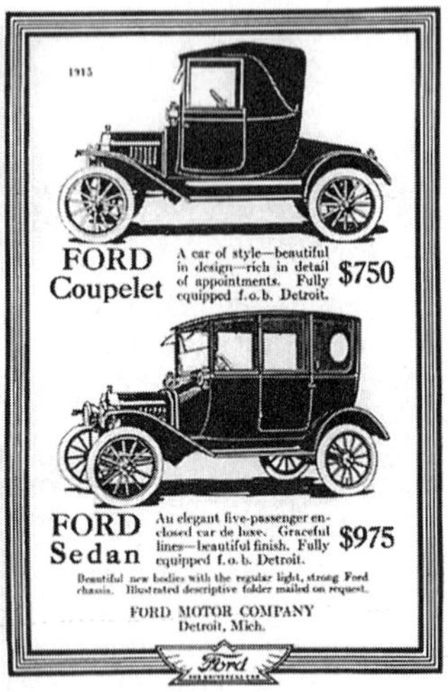

A 1914 Ford ad for the Coupe and Sedan.

The basic 1915 touring Model T.

The 1917 Town Car or Landaulet for buyers who had a chauffeur do the driving.

The above table and illustrations reveal that, contrary to legend, Ford made and sold more than one type of Model T that was based on a segmentation of the market by usage situation and income. As indicated by its prices and designs, Ford made an economy model, a sports model, a middle-of-the-road model, and a luxury model. Ford also made Tourster, Topedo, and Fore [sic] Door models between 1909 and 1913. Extracted from Gordon Schindler, *Ford Model T Catalog of Accessories* (Osceola, WI: Motorbooks International, 1991).

pioneer or low-cost producer. Ultimately, a better segmentation model may enable a firm to dominate the market. Casio segmented the LCD watch market much better than did Texas Instruments, which pioneered the watches but lost the market to Casio. The specific consensus market segmentation model used in market decision making crucially determines the competitiveness of a firm's thinking (its competitive rationality).

Consumer analysis must track how consumer preferences and behavior are changing in reaction to changes in supplier behavior. These changes are the result of the introduction of new products/services, new distribution channels, or something as simple as a short-term price reduction. For example, the introduction and mass marketing of fairly inexpensive ink-jet color printers is changing consumer preferences for home personal-computer printers. In addition, the consumer analysis must consider the impact of economic, social, and political events and trends on consumer behavior. As explained in the theory of competitive rationality, changes in consumer behavior are best understood by studying changes in the behavior of groups of consumers (segments) who behave similarly but differently from other groups of consumers (see Figure 1.3 on page 19). Are new segments being created as a result of new market offerings or changes in the economy? If so, what is unique about each segment's behavior, and how can the firm serve the segments better than the competition? How are the preferences and behavior of existing market segments changing? Price-sensitive shoppers are likely to have similar reactions to a change in the economy. Performance- or quality-sensitive consumers may respond similarly to technological improvements.[2] These factors are crucial to a customer orientation and hence market segmentation.

Mental Models of Consumer Market Segments

Numerous articles have been written about how consumer markets can be segmented by demographic classifications such as income, class, age, or geographical region, and almost all marketing texts list a large number of segmentation variables. Historically, firms have chosen a simple framework for segmenting the market, such as sex, age, ethnic group, or income. It makes common sense to use income to identify the shoppers who are most likely to buy higher quality goods and services. Similarly, age is often used these days to segment the market for movies and clothing. But if all of the suppliers are using the same common-sense, competitive thinking to identify and target prospective market segments, then, maybe, there is an opportunity for an innovator to gain an advantage by using a more insightful way of thinking about segmenting consumers. Rather than assume that income and age are the best way of segmenting the market, do market research by tracking and identifying who the heavy users are of your product. The following is an example of a company that bested its competition by rethinking the way it segmented the market.

Up until recently, Taco Bell, like many fast food chains, segmented the market by age. Leaving the young children and family market to McDonald's, Taco Bell had targeted its product and service to people ages 13 through 24. In the late 1980s, corpo-

[2] Frederick W. Winter and Howard Thomas, "An Extension of Market Segmentation: Strategic Segmentation," in *Strategic Marketing and Management*, ed. H. Thomas and D. Gardner (New York: John Wiley & Sons, 1995), 260.

rate executives of Taco Bell studied its actual market and determined this market's wants. The segmentation study identified two high-potential segments: *penny pinchers* and *speed freaks*. The penny pinchers were 18 to 24 year old frequent users who purchased three to four items from the low end of the menu. Speed freaks, who were typically harried, two-income families that visited less frequently, wanted quick, easy service, and wanted higher quality and taste regardless of price. These two groups were less than 30 percent of Taco Bell's customer base but accounted for 70 percent of sales. This new segmentation model led to a major rethinking of the product offering and service. To attract and service penny pinchers, prices were reduced in 1988 by shifting its core menu offerings down to 25 percent lower than they were in 1982 to 59-cent, 79-cent and 99-cent items. To attract and service the speed freaks, Taco Bell opened outlets in malls, gas stations, and airports. It also supplemented its on-demand production process for periods of peak demand with a process that built up an inventory of popular items. In effect, Taco Bell repositioned and redesigned its entire organization, its locations, its products, and its core processes based on this new customer segmentation. Between 1988 and 1994 sales rose from $1.6 billion to $4.5 billion and profits rose from $82 million to $273 million.[3]

What can be learned from this is that rather than use a simple, single segmentation criteria, firms can increase their competitiveness and profits by *combining* the variables they use to segment consumer demand. Taco Bell used in conjunction age, life-stage, income, price-sensitivity, and benefits sought to segment the market. Today, many packaged-goods companies segment demand by using a *combination* of demographics, values, and interests called psychographics.[4] This makes sense because segmentation variables such as personal differences, usage situation differences, benefits sought, beliefs about products, and behavior are *theoretically* related, as shown in Figure 5.2. Unique behavior, beliefs, benefits sought, and lifestyle should all be described in identifying a segment because they are *related* to each other. This deep segmentation creates a richer mental model of consumer behavior in the market compared to the single-variable segmentation of a simplistic mental model.

Figure 5.2 also suggests an ordered deep-segmentation process that a decision-making team can use to create a mental model of consumers and their behavior. The first step is to start with benefit segmentation by deciding whether groups of buyers have different needs and, hence, seek different product benefits and value different product features.[5] The second step is to determine whether differences in lifestyle or usage *cause* the distinct benefit segments. Such information may suggest new features and innovations that might be appealing to a buyer segment.

As explained by Geraldine Fennell, an expert in person × situation segmentation, a firm needs to understand why distinct benefits are desired: for example, why power

---

[3] Alan W. H. Grant and Leonard A. Schlesinger, "Realize Your Customers' Full Profit Potential," *Harvard Business Review* (September–October, 1995): 59–72.

[4] According to Russell Haley, in 1965 an advertising executive studying the demographics, lifestyle, benefits sought, and behavior of a market segment provided by a survey research study, said, "Boy, this stuff goes way beyond standard demographics. Why, you're showing us people's psychologies! These are psychographics." Psychographic questions measure buyer and nonbuyer interests, lifestyles, hobbies, self-images, and values. Unlike standard personality measures or measures of social class, sets of psychographic questions are usually designed and assembled to study buyers in a particular product market. The study of psychographics was one of the first major advances in measuring differences in consumer demand and behavior in a product market.

[5] As shown later, establishing the benefits that different consumer segments seek is a crucial first step to designing quality into a product or service using QFD (see Chapter 10).

and ease of handling benefits are desired in a car and why complexion care benefits are desired in facial cleansers:[6]

> Three motorists may say power is important to them. But consumer A may want power because his habitual driving pattern makes it necessary to be able to enter fast moving traffic; B, because owning a powerful car is associated with his masculine self-image; C, because he enjoys the sensory experience of driving a powerful machine. . . . Three facial cleanser consumers may rate complexion care as important. But consumer A may want complexion care because she believes sun and central heating dry her skin; B, because taking good care of her skin is part of her feminine self-expression; C, because she enjoys the appearance and feel of lovely skin. (P. 39)

Understanding the causes behind the desired benefits better specifies the benefit and enables product and service designers to deliver the appropriate features and engineering specifications (see Chapters 9 and 10).

The third step is to explore whether the benefit segments hold different beliefs about the product and competitive brands. Most important, this analysis needs to determine whether the benefit segments differ in their buying loyalties, shopping behaviors, media usage, and sensitivity to various marketing tactics. If they do not, then it will be very difficult to reach a broad range of benefit segments with a targeted and specially designed marketing campaign.

Some marketers prefer to begin the segmenting process by categorizing consumers by their usage behavior (for example, heavy, moderate, light, or nonuser) or brand loyalty and work backward to see if beliefs, benefits sought, and general lifestyle measures explain the difference in behavior. In such an analysis the behavior is treated as a symptom, and the analysis searches for causal explanations. These analysis processes are very similar to what some advertising people do when they construct means-end chains as a way of organizing and understanding consumer behavior.

Linking different segmentation variables does not need to be as complex as the process described in Figure 5.2. Many firms simply focus on the connections between heavy usage or brand loyalty (see the bottom of Figure 5.2) *and* the buyers' responses to different products, distribution channels, media, advertising message strategies, or price promotions (such as coupons). The steps and elements of the deep segmentation process will be described in detail now.

Consumer Benefit Segmentation

Benefit segmentation was originally used to identify groups of consumers who were particularly responsive to specific advertising messages.[7] However, benefit segmentation also can be used to design a product. For example, a group of former Hewlett-Packard executives formed Tandem computers in 1974 to satisfy the needs

---

[6] Geraldine Fennell, "Consumer's Perceptions of the Product-Use Situation," *Journal of Marketing* vol. 42 (April 1978): 38–47.

[7] Russell I. Haley, "Benefit Segmentation: A Decision-Oriented Research Tool," *Journal of Marketing* 32 (July 1968): 30–35. To measure how different buyers value the different benefits and features of a product offering, see Paul E. Green and Yoram Wind, "New Way to Measure Consumers' Judgments," *Harvard Business Review*, July–August 1975, 107–17.

Figure 5.2 **A Model of Consumer Behavior for Deep Benefit Segmentation**

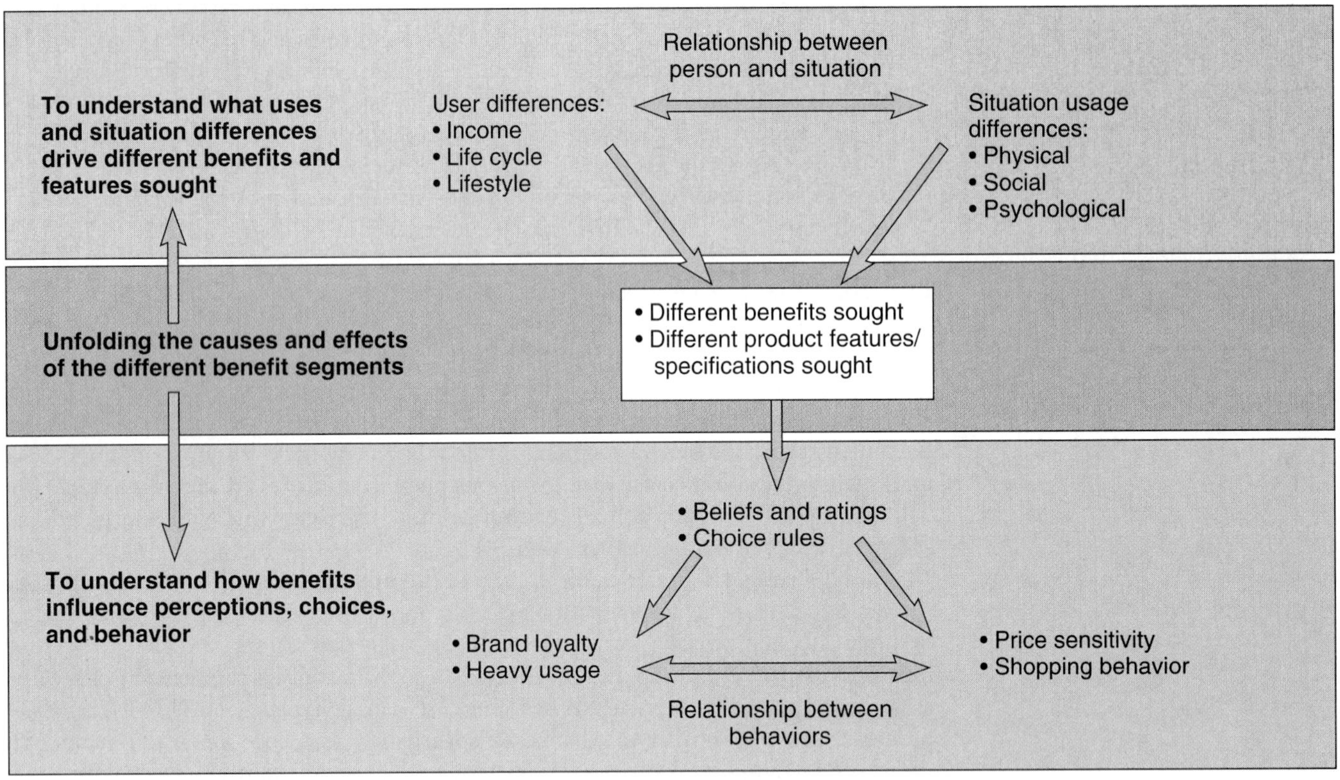

This model explains that user and usage situation differences combine to determine behavior [behavior is a function of personal differences interacting with situation usage differences: $B = F(P \times S)$]. In between are benefits sought from using the product. The benefits sought determine how the product alternatives are perceived and rated. These perceptions determine product choice and use. Deep segmentation starts with benefits and works forward and back or starts with behavior and works back. Each segment is then described in terms of its behavior, preferences, benefits sought, usage situations, user demographics, geographics, and user lifestyle. This can be an intuitive process that uses managerial experience and judgment, or it can be a process that uses sophisticated statistical analysis. Whatever the tools used, the fundamental deep segmentation process is the same.

SOURCE: Peter Dickson, "Person × Situation: Market Segmentation's Missing Link," *Journal of Marketing* 45, (Fall 1992), 56–64.

of computer buyers who desired an ultrareliable computer. Hospitals, banks, and airline reservation systems cannot afford to have their computers crash. To service this need, Tandem linked two central processing units together. If one went down, the other automatically took over the processing until the first unit was repaired. In 1986, sales of Tandem's "crash-free" computers reached $800 million. The company profited greatly from identifying a need and then creating a product that serviced the need.

Table 5.2 Student Preferences for Beverages by Benefit Sought

Which of the following would you choose to meet each benefit/need?

	COFFEE	TEA	MILK	BEER	COLA	NONCOLA	OTHER
To relieve throat irritation	5%	30%	11%	2%	16%	6%	30%
To help your digestion	6	13	46	0	12	8	18
To provide energy and pep you up	32	5	5	1	42	3	11
To help you unwind and mentally relax	3	5	2	38	11	3	39
To settle an upset stomach	0	14	33	0	20	23	10
To provide nutrition and vitamins	0	0	63	2	0	5	31
To stimulate your taste buds	3	5	7	13	32	12	27
To relieve a headache	4	24	9	5	10	10	38
To quench your thirst	0	5	3	8	35	11	38

Most product markets can be segmented by the benefits sought. Table 5.2 reports the different beverage preferences of students. It reveals that each beverage satisfies a specific physical need. The reason why the colas dominate the young-adult beverage market, rather than, say, milk, is because the students surveyed needed to pep themselves up, stimulate their taste buds, or quench their thirst much more often than they needed a sleep aid or to obtain nutrients and vitamins.

In 1993 CNS, a company that makes diagnostic equipment for sleep disorders, began making a stiff, butterfly-shaped adhesive strip that pulls open the sides of the nose. Its target benefit segment was those with nasal congestion caused by a cold (cold sufferers in bed) and chronic snorers (snorers in bed). In 1995 the product was approved by the Federal Drug Administration as an "aid" to reduce snoring. Dan Cohen, the founder of the company, sent strips to all twenty-eight National Football League trainers in 1994. Herschel Walker and Jerry Rice started to wear them on television, the announcers talked about them, and a public relations campaign gave the new product a tremendous boost, doubling sales in a few months. A single 30-second advertisement for Breathe Right was aired during the 1996 Superbowl showing numerous football players wearing the product. The newest person × situation benefit segment became exhausted athletes on the playing field, and the benefit is 30 percent improved breathing.[8] This is an example of the same product (Breathe Right) first targeted at one person-times-situation benefit segment (cold sufferers and snorers in bed) and then, with the help of athletes seeking a competitive advantage, targeted at another distinctive person × situation benefit segment.

The Four Basic Human Needs

Consumers purchase or rent a product or service to satisfy one or more of four basic human needs: physical, emotional, mental, and spiritual needs. Within each of these

[8] Ann Marsh, "Nose Job," *Forbes*, March 13, 1995, 140.

Table 5.3 Basic Benefits, Specific Benefits, and Sample Products

FUNDAMENTAL BENEFITS	SPECIFIC BENEFITS SOUGHT	COMMERCIAL MEANS OR PATHS USED TO ACHIEVE THE BENEFIT
Physical/bodily benefits	Health	HMOs, vitamins, new drugs
	Physical fitness	Jogging shoes, spas
	Beauty	Cosmetics, Nautilus machines
	Procreation	Artificial insemination
	Sex	Spouses, X-rated movies
	Safety	Seat belts, security systems
	Thirst	Nonalcoholic beverages
	Hunger	Food
	Mobility	Automobiles, airplanes
	Sleep	Bedding, drugs
Emotional benefits	Love	Flowers, gifts
	Friendship	Social clubs, cards
	Pleasure	Music, drugs, food
	Humor	Joke books, comedy clubs, television
	Aggression	Professional boxing, football
	Power	Investments, career schools
Mental/intellectual benefits	Curiosity	Tourism, books
	Problem solving	Games, detective stories
	Education	College, TV documentaries
	Control	Yoga classes, religious items, media
	Creativity	Artwork, gardening tools
	Truth	Nonfiction books
Spiritual benefits	Peace	Meditation tapes, vacations
	Communality	Club memberships, trendy items
	Philosophy	Books, Internet
	Patriotism	Flags, political items
	Ritual	Christmas decorations, engagement rings
	Guilt	Gifts, religious items

categories are many subcategories (see Table 5.3). However, consumers tend to be extremely goal directed, and once they have fully or partially satisfied one need, they promptly turn their attention to another need or goal. In our day-to-day and year-to-year lives, we normally use a multitude of products and services to satisfy a wide range of short- and long-term needs.

The perceived quality of a product or a service depends on its effectiveness and efficiency in achieving the benefits desired.[9] One new market research technique, *conjoint analysis*, has been effectively used to identify segments that seek different benefits. In the Rationality in Practice box titled "Benefit Segmenting the Food-Processor Market," conjoint analysis was employed in a study to identify benefit segments and position new product models; each model was specially designed to offer the qualities desired by a specific benefit segment.

[9] The words *quality*, *utility*, and *instrumentality* (as in an instrument used as a means to an end) all have the same general meaning, although some scholars argue about the differences.

Figure 5.3 **Different Lifestyle Vehicles**

These vehicles are all priced in the $25,000 range (depending on options). While similarly priced, they are clearly designed to provide different benefits to families and individuals with various lifestyles and usage situations.

Often products are purchased to achieve several benefits. For example, going to a restaurant with friends may satisfy hunger, a need for friendship, a need to be seen in the right places with the right faces (the status benefit), and a need to do something different (the novelty benefit). An automobile provides physical mobility that earlier civilizations would have envied. However, it also can be seen as a thing of beauty or used to confer status, power, and sex appeal. Some people use cars as an outlet for aggression (speeding and racing) or as an outlet for curiosity and problem solving (a restoration or tinkering hobby). Different cars are designed to provide different benefits, and these benefits are, as already mentioned (see Figure 5.3), often related to an individual's life cycle and lifestyle. A discussion of life cycles and lifestyles follows.

Consumer Life-Cycle and Lifestyle Segmentation

If consumer needs are to be served, they must be anticipated. The major, long-term driver of many predictable trends in the American economy is the changing distribution of ages in the population. These trends in the size of age categories and associated life-cycle stages are important to the marketer for two reasons:

Rationality in Practice

Benefit Segmenting the Food-Processor Market

In June 1983 the Sunbeam Corporation undertook a study using conjoint analysis to identify the benefit segments in the food-processor market. More than five hundred women were interviewed in four different sites around the country. The interviews took place in high-traffic shopping malls and produced a complete preference ranking for twenty-seven different model designs. The preference rankings of five hundred women were then clustered into the benefit segments. This produced four clusters of consumers. Within each cluster the consumers shared similar preferences for different design features in a food processor; that is, they sought similar feature benefits.

The differences in benefits sought among clusters can be illustrated by comparing which features the "Cheap" segment wanted in a food processor with which features the "Multi-speed" segment wanted. It is clear that a new $49.99 product designed with a four-quart bowl and very little else would appeal to one segment, and a new $99.99 blender/mixer model with seven speeds and a two-quart cylindrical bowl would appeal to the other. Sunbeam launched two such models in 1984 that appear to have been successes. Note that Sunbeam also used lifestyle and brand loyalty information to develop a deep understanding of each segment, as suggested by the procedure in Figure 5.3.

SOURCE: For the full case study, see Albert L. Page and Harold F. Rosenbaum, "Redesigning Product Lines with Conjoint Analysis: How Sunbeam Does It," *Journal of Product Innovation Management* 4 (1987): 120–37.

	THE CHEAP AND LARGE SEGMENT	THE MULTI-SPEEDS AND USES SEGMENT
Very Important Features	$49.99 price Four-quart bowl	Seven speeds Can be used as a blender and a mixer
Moderately Important Features	Two speeds Seven processing blades Heavy-duty or professional power motor Cylindrical bowl Pouring spout	$99.99 price Two-quart bowl Cylindrical bowl Regular discharge bowl
Other Demographic, Psychographic, and Brand-Loyalty Features of the Segment	Least likely segment to already own a food processor Higher than average ownership of Oster and Sears brands Most likely segment to give a food processor as a gift Older in age Midrange incomes Comprise 22% of the food-processor market	Most likely to own a GE brand food processor Younger in age Lower than average incomes Comprise 28% of the food-processor market

1. Age categories can be predicted with reasonable reliability. If marketers know how many five-year-olds existed in 1990, they can use current mortality rates to accurately forecast the number of fifteen-year-olds in the year 2000.
2. Both the needs and wealth of individuals and households change as they progress through the family life cycle (see Table 5.4).

Psychographics is a type of lifestyle segmentation. It groups customers not by demographics but by psychological and personality differences. Recently, Porsche hired a team of anthropologists to get to know its customers better. The demographics of the typical owner is a college graduate over age forty and earning $200,000 plus a year. The psychographic segments of Porsche buyers revealed by the anthropologists were more interesting (see Figure 5.4). Now Porsche advertising and its salespeople are using different sales pitches targeted at the various personality segments.[10]

[10] Alex Taylor, "Porsche Slices up Its Buyers," *Fortune*, January 16, 1995, 11.

Conjoint analysis led to the evolution of Oskar Models 14181 and 14201. The Oskar Junior, Model 14131, came later.

The best known of the commercial lifestyle classification techniques is called VALS, introduced in 1978. It was later discovered that shifting values and lifestyles created problems with the original classification.[11] The VALS2 segmentation framework was offered in 1989. Its segment sizes are roughly equal, and its creators claim that VALS2 will be more stable over time. The new framework is also more directly linked to age and income. The VALS2 psychographic analysis works best for products that are ego involving and important to consumers in achieving their desired lifestyle (such as automobiles and clothing), but it is less useful for small, "invisible" items such as toilet paper.[12] Another basic problem with general lifestyle profiles such as VALS or VALS2 is that they suffer from the same limitation that affects general personality inventories—they do not apply to all life situations. A "grizzly bear" at work may turn

[11] See Martha Farnsworth Riche, "Psychographics for the 1990s," *American Demographics*, July 1989, 24–31.
[12] Riche, "Psychographics for the 1990s," 24–31.

Table 5.4 Changing Priorities and Purchases in the Family Life Cycle

STAGE	PRIORITIES	MAJOR PURCHASES
Fledgling: teens and early 20s	Self, socializing, education	Appearance products, clothing, automobiles, recreation, hobbies, travel
Courting: 20s	Self and other, pair bonding, career	Furniture and furnishings, entertainment and entertaining, clothing
Nest building: 20s and early 30s	Babies and career	Home, garden, do-it-yourself items; baby-care products; insurance
Full nest: 30–50s	Children and others, career, midlife crisis	Children's food, clothing, education, transportation, orthodontics, career and life counseling
Empty nest: 50–75	Self and others, relaxation	Furniture and furnishings, entertainment, travel, hobbies, luxury automobiles, boats, investments
Sole survivor: 70–90	Self, health, loneliness	Health-care services; diet, security, and comfort products; television and books; long-distance telephone services

into a "teddy bear" at home. One of the latest commercial segmentation research services, PRIZM, can locate lifestyle segments by zip code, even down to the city block. Although it is very expensive, it is possible to obtain a map of the U.S. market that identifies concentrations of households by their lifestyle, values, and demand for various products and services. This is obviously useful for targeting mailings and locating attractive retail outlets. One of the most effective ways of segmenting by lifestyle is to segment by existing activity or interest groups and then add a feature to the product or service that caters to the common affinity of the group. MBNA Corporation offers Visa and MasterCard "affinity" credit cards through some 3,500 organizations, such as more than three hundred alumni associations, professional associations, scout groups, the Sierra Club, and Chicago Bulls fans. The organization gets a share of the commissions, which for the Sierra Club amounted to almost $500,000 in 1994. Such "interest" niching has created close to 15 million affluent affinity credit card customers who are less likely to default and who desire more of a premium (higher profit for the business) service.

Lifestyle segmentation has been greatly affected by the changing roles of women in American life. World War II, the birth control pill, the high divorce rate, laws against sex discrimination, and the writings of the feminist movement have created nothing less than a cultural revolution. Contemporary women often choose to work or have to work *and* maintain their homes at the same time. The increasing opportunities for women have created many stresses on professional and social relationships, in large part because some men have been very slow to adapt to the new roles women play in pursuing a career or helping earn enough money to put bread on the table.

This trend has greatly affected product innovation and marketing strategies. In 1990, more than 36 million women (more than half of all women between the ages of eighteen and sixty-four) spent approximately nine hours a day at work or commuting. This is time they no longer had for teaching their children to read, cleaning, waxing, polishing, mending, weeding, writing, delivering, cooking, shopping, and socializing. As a result, convenience-food sales have soared (see Figure 5.5), the telephone call and

Figure 5.4 A Taxonomy of Porsche Buyers

TYPE	% OF ALL OWNERS	DESCRIPTION
TOP GUNS	27%	Driven, ambitious types. Power and control matter. They expect to be noticed.
ELITISTS	24%	Old-money blue bloods. A car is just a car, no matter how expensive. It is not an extension of personality.
PROUD PATRONS	23%	Ownership is an end in itself. Their car is a trophy earned for hard work, and who cares if anyone sees them in it?
BON VIVANTS	17%	Worldly jet-setters and thrill seekers. Their car heightens the excitement in their already passionate lives.
FANTASISTS	9%	Walter Mitty types. Their car is an escape. Not only are they uninterested in impressing others with it, but they also feel a little guilty about owning one.

SOURCE: *Fortune*, January 16, 1995, 11.

Figure 5.5

An early competitor in the gourmet prepared-meal market aimed at the time-poor consumer. A primitive ancestor was the TV dinner. Today, the products must also be low in both calories and fat.

electronic mail have replaced the letter, refrigerator-freezers have grown in size, dishwashers have become more efficient, and microwave ovens have become standard appliances in households throughout the country. Supermarkets stay open late at night and have become one-stop shopping centers for busy women. Catalog shopping has increased in popularity because of the convenience it offers. Other important lifestyle trends, such as Hispanic immigration, the flight to the suburbs, and the decline of public education, have created new, distinct lifestyle segments based on subculture, literacy, employment, and income.[13]

Consumer Product Usage-Situation Segmentation

One of the most ignored aspects of segmentation has been the importance of a product's usage situation. Usage situation is an important determinant of benefits sought and features desired (see Figure 5.3). In this form of segmentation, analysts identify and study how a product or service is used in different situations and then market it accordingly. For example, drinks are *packaged* for their usage situation (lunches, picnics, and so on), and many products are *designed* for a specific usage situation (for instance, Sony Walkmans, bicycles, and lawn mowers). Richardson-Vicks Inc. entered the very competitive cold-remedy market by focusing on nighttime cold relief with its brand Nyquil. Congestion and discomfort from a cold usually increase at night because nasal passages do not drain as well when people are sleeping. Cold symptoms also become more of an irritant when people are relaxing. Nyquil was specially designed for nighttime use and was effectively advertised to appeal to such problems. Once Nyquil was strongly established in this usage segment, the company then rolled out Dayquil for daytime use. Although the drowsiness side effect was an advantage for a nighttime cold remedy, Dayquil was designed to minimize such side effects—for obvious reasons.

At Steelcase Inc., the largest office-furniture maker, a $1.6 million noise lab studies office noise situations.[14] The most distracting noise was found to be the human voice, and the problem is likely to get worse as people start to talk to their computers. The task Steelcase faces is to design furniture that better absorbs the human voice in different work situations. But it should not be absorbed too much, because research has shown that workers prefer some background noise to total silence and are more productive as a result.

An interesting variation of person-situation segmentation is that drug companies and hospitals are starting to segment their markets by illness or condition and then target a particular illness or condition. For example, a number of leading cancer clinics exist, and Quantum Health Resources has specialist clinics for treating hemophiliacs.[15] By such specializations, Quantum has reduced its costs by 20 percent compared to its rivals' costs. Paradigm, a California firm, treats catastrophic injuries such as brain damage or serious burns from car crashes. One of the advantages of such condition segmentation is that in surgical processes it has been clearly demonstrated that "practice makes perfect." The more a hospital does a surgical procedure, the higher is the quality of the service. Thus condition segmentation and targeting in health care produces a TQM result—lower cost *and* higher quality processes.

[13] The magazine *American Demographics* provides excellent articles and statistics on how changing life cycles and lifestyles influence demand.
[14] John Bigness, "Scientists Study Secrets of a Quiet Office," *The Wall Street Journal*, August 18, 1995, B1, B3.
[15] "Case Histories," *The Economist*, July 15, 1995, 46.

The usage-situation factor has many obvious dimensions, such as the way temperature and weather might affect how, when, and where a product is marketed. However, the following section discusses the not-so-obvious effects of situation-induced time pressure on the benefits sought from products and services and on buying behavior.

The Effect of Time Pressure on Consumption

In leisurely paced societies, a lot of free time is allowed for play, a midday siesta, and recreational pursuits such as fishing, hunting, and sports. Time is not of great importance, no one is punctual, and what can be postponed may as well be. In North America, the situation is very different for most adults and households. Punctuality is important, scheduling is a must, and whatever leisure time available is often spent recovering from the rat race.[16] Time is a highly valued commodity for two groups in particular: high-income couples who are pursuing dual careers and low-income couples and single parents who are struggling to pay the rent and raise children so they, too, can survive in the rat race. Many marketers have yet to fully appreciate this fact. Income and time pressure have the following important interaction effects on consumption.

Income and Household Behavior

As a household's income and the hourly wage of its members rise, families buy homes, then larger homes, a second home, a swimming pool, more cars, recreational vehicles, boats, vacations, skis, and so on. However, most of these goods take up more personal time to buy, enjoy, and maintain. As income rises, more activities can be or have to be squeezed into leisure time. The result is that the perceived value of free time increases and produces what has been called the harried leisure class. Leisure time management has some significant effects on decision making, particularly on each of the following:

Risk Taking If consumers are more harried in their work and family life, then they may not be novelty seekers and innovators when they make purchases. They already have enough stimulation and excitement in their lives. What the wealthy often want are not the latest products but high-quality, low-maintenance, high-reliability products. They do not want to waste time returning goods or waiting for a new innovation to be repaired. Further, many of the working wealthy do not have time to invest in a hobby or to become an expert, enthusiastic do-it-yourselfer. The real innovators are likely to be the consumers who have more leisure time to devote to their interests. What this suggests is that new innovations should be first marketed to interest groups—perhaps through clubs, newsletters, or the Internet—rather than through expensive department stores or catalogs to the wealthy.

Searching and Shopping Consumers have developed a series of informal buying rules to save time but still ensure satisfactory purchases. For example, consumers tend to buy quality brand-name products, follow the advice of friends, buy from quality catalogs, and remain loyal to high-service stores. The latter not only reduces shopping time and effort but also increases personal service at restaurants, dry cleaning services, florists, and so on. Two of the biggest pet peeves of American shoppers are waiting in line while other windows or registers are closed and waiting at

---

[16] See Staffan B. Linder, *The Harried Leisure Class* (New York: Columbia University Press, 1970).

home for a no-show delivery or a service call.[17] Seventy-five percent of consumers who earn $50,000 or more a year boycott stores because of such poor service. In an era of fierce competition between retailers, reducing costs by reducing personal service may be the wrong way to go. The more competitive strategy could be to develop a reputation for excellent in-store customer service and expertise.

Product Expertise

One of the ironies of the wealth time trap is that some higher income consumers may not get the most out of their purchases because they do not have the time to learn to use the products properly. They do not learn how to adjust an expensive camera or use all the features on their sound system, answering phone, or VCR. As a consequence, some of the advantages they gain from buying quality products are lost by their not learning to use the products for maximum effect. In an interesting role reversal, teenagers often teach their parents how to use some luxury products, particularly electronic equipment. What this suggests is that manufacturers need to place a very high priority on design simplicity that makes their products easy to use and easy to learn to use. This includes design of more user-friendly instruction manuals for the equipment. In the 1970s and 1980s numerous companies thought that increasing quality meant adding complex features and providing 30-page instruction guides. They lost share to competitors who increased the design quality and performance of the core features while providing all of the instructions on a concise laminated sheet.

Demand for Quality

Although members of the harried leisure class pay top dollar for time-saving, high-quality devices and services, they do so not just because they can afford to, wish to conspicuously display their wealth, or want very reliable performance. When time is very scarce, consumers try to squeeze the very most out of their free time. They therefore demand goods that increase the enjoyment and quality of their leisure. A large-screen television with a super sound system increases the quality of television viewing time. A high-quality tennis racquet enriches exercise time. A sports or luxury car enhances the time spent in recreational driving. Higher incomes enable consumers to buy higher quality items, but it is the perceived *value* of leisure time that often motivates the demand for high-quality products.[18] This is one of the reasons why higher quality products and services have increased in value and will continue to appreciate as leisure time becomes scarcer for families, whether they are wealthy or struggling to make ends-meet.

Consumer Belief Segmentation

Returning to the mental model illustrated in Figure 5.3, note that the benefits consumers seek from a product or service determine their beliefs and choices. Belief segmentation uses consumers' beliefs about a product to segment demand. Beliefs are usually measured to explain heavy usage or brand loyalty. However, if all sellers target

[17] David Wessel, "Sure Ways to Annoy Consumers," *The Wall Street Journal*, November 6, 1989; and Francine Schwadel, "Shoppers' Blues: The Thrill Is Gone," *The Wall Street Journal*, October 13, 1989.

[18] In effect, this is the pleasure productivity of leisure time. A leisure good is more productive when it produces more pleasure per minute in use.

the heavy user, it may be worthwhile to look for opportunities among current nonusers. Such a strategy is particularly appropriate for the market leader interested in expanding the market or for a smaller company interested in finding a new market segment that is separate from the rest of the competition.

Figure 5.6 presents a potential segment categorization framework of nonusers of a product category or brand. It compares nonusers who are simply unaware of a product or service with potential consumers who do not know where to buy the product, who are in a state of inertia about the product, or who have negative opinions about the product. These different market segments suggest very different marketing tactics. It may be possible to develop a new product and image that overcomes the objections of the consumers who have even the most negative beliefs, particularly if the beliefs are wrong. A campaign that raises the awareness of the segment that is unaware of a particular brand would be very different from a campaign targeted at the segment that has specific negative beliefs about a particular brand.

In the mid-1980s the leading lawn care service company was facing slowing growth and a lot of price competition from local, upstart imitators. About 16 percent of households used a lawn care service. A belief segmentation study was undertaken to identify growth opportunities among nonusers. Facing much adverse publicity about the serious health hazards caused by spraying chemicals on lawns, senior management were considering offering a granule service that would cater to the nonuser segment

Figure 5.6 **A Nonusage Belief Segmentation Framework**

Nonuser of Product Category
- Unaware of product/service
- Aware but has never seriously considered purchase
- Aware but product/service is unavailable in channels
- Aware but habit and inertia prevent trial
- Aware but a perceived risk prevents trial
- Aware but rejected because of believed poor performance
- Aware but rejected because of high price
- Tried and rejected because of poor performance
- Tried and rejected because of low value for money
- Previously used but no longer needed

Product User but Non-brand User
- Unaware of brand
- Aware but has never seriously considered purchase
- Aware but brand is unavailable in channels
- Aware but habit and inertia prevent trial
- Aware but a perceived risk prevents trial
- Aware but rejected because of believed poor performance
- Aware but rejected because of high price
- Tried and rejected because of poor performance
- Tried and rejected because of low value for money

concerned about the spray's danger to pets and runoff environment pollution. Management were also planning a price promotion campaign to cater to the segment who believed that lawn care services were too expensive. The results of the national study were eye-opening. The size of the environment/safety-concerned segment was only 5 percent of nonusers. Thirty-five percent of the nonusers believed they could do a better job caring for their own lawn's unique needs and enjoyed doing so. Twenty percent of nonusers believed the service was too expensive. The real opportunities for the company were the segment that had never really thought about it (30 percent of nonusers) and the segment that was quite favorably disposed toward a lawn care service and would use one if approached (10 percent of nonusers).

The belief segmentation results suggested a new strategy of expanding advertising early in the spring (particularly in the South) to get more households to think about a lawn care service and a better telemarketing campaign to reach the 10 percent of nonusers who were customers for the picking. Unfortunately, the company and its advertising agency pursued its original strategy, and this contributed to its continuing problems that led to it ultimately being taken over by a smaller rival whose marketing better fitted the beliefs and behavior of the market.

The tactics used to change specific beliefs also depend on the ways consumers choose among alternatives. Three ways consumers make purchase decisions will be discussed. The first is based on logic, the second on emotions, and the third on habit. Different benefit segments may predominantly use one of these decision methods for making specific purchases; for example, subcompact cars purchased for commuting are most likely to be bought on logic, sports cars on emotion, while older consumers choose cars more often based on habitual brand loyalty.

Consumer Choice Rule Segmentation

Logical Choice Behavior

An information-processing choice model assumes that human decision making and problem solving is more or less rational.[19] It suggests that we use reason and logic to carefully evaluate alternatives. Many choice models and rules have been developed to describe such decision making. Generally, the information-processing choice model is based on the type of decision logic that appears in computer programs. It suggests that consumers do the following:

1. Identify and evaluate the choice options (brands and models within brands) on several abstract dimensions. For example, the consumer may rate several automobile models on such characteristics as fuel efficiency, acceleration, top speed, braking and cornering performance, interior noise, mechanical reliability, comfort and convenience features, price, and financial terms.
2. Add up the ratings to create an overall quality score or use some other algebraic rule to decide which alternative is most preferred. For example, the consumer may assess an

[19] James R. Bettman, *An Information Processing Theory of Consumer Choice* (Reading MA: Addison-Wesley, 1979); and Brian Sternthal and C. Samuel Craig, *Consumer Behavior: An Information Processing Perspective* (Englewood Cliffs, NJ: Prentice-Hall, 1982).

automobile's overall quality by adding up its scores on each of the choice dimensions, weighted by the importance of each dimension.

Choice rules may be applied in a priority sequence. Consumers often know what they definitely do *not* want in a product. This "no way" elimination process quickly whittles down the set of choices. A more complex preference rule then may be used to identify the best of the acceptable alternatives.[20]

Experiential Choice Behavior

Experiential choice behavior occurs when the benefits we seek from a product are driven by our fantasies and emotions. Fantasies are our wishful thoughts about who and where we would like to be and what we would like to own. Emotions are our feelings of pleasure, pain, excitement, relaxation, fear, and stress, among many others. People, pets, and our physical environment (such as a warm bakery or a steamy sauna) create such reactions. Many products and services are designed to arouse pleasure, excitement, and relaxation. For example, rock music might make us feel energized, woodsy fragrances might make us feel romantic, or the latest fashions might make us feel confident. The function of these products is to create feelings, imagery, or fantasies that give pleasure and lift the user to a higher experiential plane. Brands are also often given personality associations and images whose congruence with the ideal or actual self can motivate users to purchase one brand over another.[21]

Fantasizing creates and enhances emotional experience. Sometimes fantasies recreate the past. Nostalgia products are often popular at times of heightened emotion, such as during the Christmas holidays. For example, favorite holiday movies and television dramas are shown each Christmas. They become part of the symbolism of the season. Particular products in our home can become almost sacred, because they express and celebrate treasured memories, connections with ancestors, or associations with a loved one, a special group, or an exceptional time in our life. The value of the symbolism and meaning of these products far exceeds their replacement cost or the value of their more functional uses.[22] Other products allow users to fantasize about a world where they are much more powerful, beautiful, or wise than they are in reality. Young children spend a good deal of their play acting out such fantasies with their toys. Many adults also act out such fantasies using cosmetics, fashion, and exotic vacations. When we cannot afford to play with the toys or they do not have the desired effect, we may escape through projection, that is, by reading romantic novels or watching the adventures of others at the movies or on television. Figure 5.7 shows two automobile ads, one aimed at the car buyer that uses a logical choice rule and the other aimed at an "experiential" car buying segment.

[20] Dennis A. Lussier and Richard W. Olshavsky, "Task Complexity and Contingent Processing in Brand Choice," *Journal of Consumer Research* 6 (September 1979): 154–65.

[21] Elizabeth Hirschman and Morris B. Holbrook, "Hedonic Consumption: Emerging Concepts, Methods and Propositions," *Journal of Marketing* 46 (summer 1982): 92–101. Russell Haley, the father of benefit segmentation, has pointed out, however, that it is much more difficult to segment the market for products that involve sensory or emotional benefits because so much depends on the execution of the advertising appeals. See Russell I. Haley, "Benefit Segmentation—20 Years Later," *The Journal of Consumer Marketing* 11 (1986).

[22] Sidney J. Levy, "Symbols for Sale," *Harvard Business Review* 37 (July/August 1959): 117–24; "Interpreting Consumer Mythology: A Structural Approach to Consumer Behavior," *Journal of Marketing* 45 (summer 1981): 49–61; Dennis W. Rook, "The Ritual Dimensions of Consumer Behavior," *Journal of Consumer Research* 12 (December 1985): 251–64; and Russell W. Belk, "Possessions and the Extended Self," *Journal of Consumer Research* 15.2 (September 1988): 139–68.

Figure 5.7 **Ads Targeting Different Choice Rule Segments**

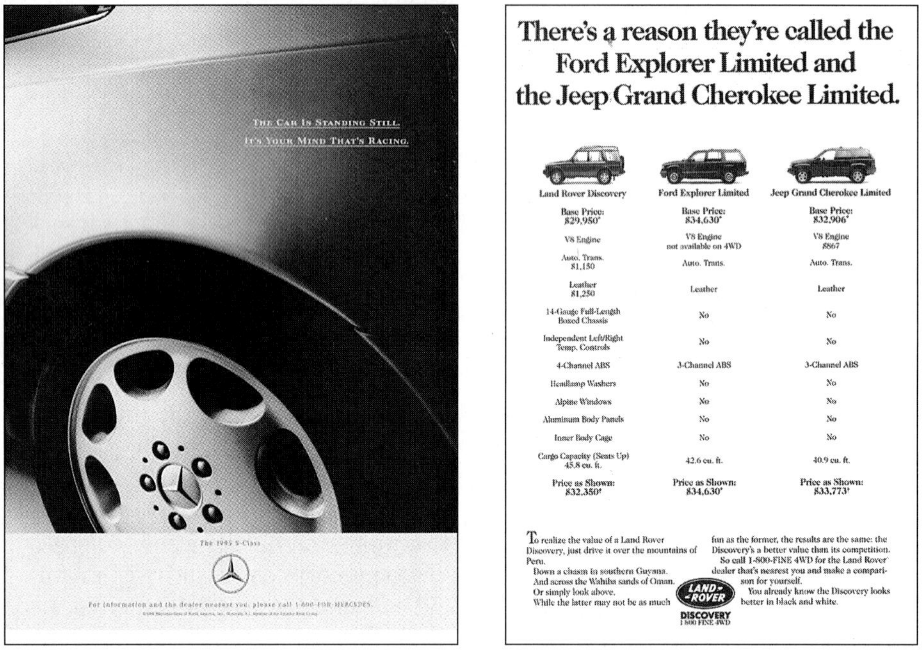

Which ad targets consumers who buy an automobile using a logical choice rule, and which ad targets consumers who will make an "experiential" choice?

Habitual Choice

Reptiles are slaves to routine. They do the same basic thing at the same time every day and they cannot help it. They behave this way instinctively. To a certain extent, so do we. A bit of the crocodile is in all of us. As a result, a good deal of consumer behavior is habitual. Many of us do the same thing at the same time every day. We have many routines and rituals, and we give many of these activities about as much thought as a reptile does mindlessly mooching around its swamp. This is not all bad. Consumption habits have survival value for several reasons:

1. What has worked in the past is likely to work again in the future.
2. Habits allow us to save time making decisions.
3. Routines can be executed more efficiently than new behaviors.
4. Habitual behavior frees the mind to think about other things while executing the behavior.
5. Habits bring a sense of discipline, order, and control to a person's life and self-perception.

Evolution also helps us understand when many of our habits are formed. Most of the behavior patterns of primitive man and woman were learned before the individual reached maturity. In ancient times, people seldom lived beyond the age of thirty, so continuing to develop thinking skills that kept people learning through old age (thirty plus!) had little evolutionary value. Unfortunately, our memories are still "designed" to learn that way today. Of course, we can keep learning, but curiosity and learning are greatest when we are young. The best time to influence human consumption behavior, such as diet, sports, and artistic interests, is before the age of about fifteen. This helps explain why debates over cigarette advertising aimed at teenagers, over unhealthy fast food, and over the influence of recreational reading versus MTV have raged for more than a decade.

How We Learn Habits

Habitual behavior is common in the frequent buying and usage of products and services ranging from groceries to dry cleaning. It normally starts with a trial, experiential purchase. If the product is not liked, it is never tried again; new products and services seldom get a second chance, which is why a new consumer product must get it right the first time. A successful new product is likely to produce a very enthusiastic reception, such as the "Yumm, this is really good" reaction to a new food product. If consumers actually say this to themselves, this positive verbal reaction is clearly remembered the next time the consumer is in the market for a product in that category. When consumers volunteer such a remark out loud in a product test, the marketing team really knows it has a winner. By about the fifth trial, the habit of buying will be firmly in place, and much of the initial reinforcing buzz will have faded.[23] But not all buying routines and loyalties are "mindlessly" created. Sometimes we deliberately plan a course of action through information gathering and alternative comparison. We then execute this consumption or production process over and over again, for instance, when choosing where we eat lunch during the work week. In such cases, consumers may be able to explain rationally what appears to be "mindless" routines and loyalties.

Consumer Brand Loyalty Segmentation

The creation of consumer loyalty to a brand or service is akin to domesticating the consumer. The buyer's behavior becomes routinized and, in that sense, tamed or controlled by the seller.[24] This is achieved through a stream of marketing activities and exchanges that results in an enduring *relationship* between the seller and the consumer. Some buyers can be so domesticated that they will allow themselves to be "branded." For example, they will pay extra to have the firm's brand advertising on a T-shirt, hat, or other article of clothing (notice how often you see the logo for Nike or Panama Jack T-shirts). A common way to target heavy users is to attempt to make them loyal to a brand or service by giving them volume discounts through "frequent flyer" types of promotions.

Brand loyalty and repeat purchasing do not always involve a high involvement relationship with the brand. Table 5.5 describes different brand loyalty segments and the marketing implications of each. It is important for a firm to understand the different loyalty segments in the market, because the *type* of loyalty as well as the size of the

[23] For a review of learning theories, see Michael L. Rothschild and William C. Gaidis, "Behavioral Learning Theory: Its Relevance to Marketing and Promotions," *Journal of Marketing* 45 (spring 1981): 70–81; and Walter R. Nord and J. Paul Peter, "A Behavior Modification Perspective on Marketing," *Journal of Marketing* 44 (spring 1980): 36–47.

[24] The concept of market domestication has been discussed by Johan Arndt, "Toward a Concept of Domesticated Markets," *Journal of Marketing* 43 (fall 1979): 69–75. His focus was on imperfectly competitive seller-reseller markets and did not connect brand loyalty to domestication of demand as suggested here.

Table 5.5 Types of Brand Loyalty/Relationship Segments

NATURE OF LOYALTY/RELATIONSHIP	MARKETING IMPLICATIONS
Emotional loyalty: Unique, memorable, reinforcing experiences create a strong emotional bond with brand. Examples: hospital that saves child's life, fragrance given by future husband.	Goodwill is immune from attack by competitors or company mismanagement. Positive word of mouth is likely to be very high.
Identity loyalty: The brand is used as an expression of self, to bolster self-esteem and manage impressions. It becomes part of the extended self. Examples: Porsche cars, L.L. Bean clothes, Chicago Bears caps.	This loyalty resists attack, but a firm can hurt itself by brand mismanagement over a long time. Brand extension prospects into related product categories are good.
Differentiated loyalty: Brand loyalty is based on perceived superior features and attributes. This perception may be outdated because of a lack of recent research. Example: appliances.	Goodwill can be undermined if competitor proves superior performance. Demonstrations and trials are very important tactics.
Contract loyalty: Consumer believes that continued loyalty earns him or her special treatment or that the seller is trying very hard to keep customer loyalty. Such an "I'll stay loyal if you keep trying hard" social contract applies in retailing and service markets.	Competitor can question whether the consumer's trust is being exploited. However, loyalty is most likely to be lost by a single or series of experiences that expose the seller's efforts or claims as insincere.
Switching cost loyalty: Consumer is loyal because effort involved in considering alternatives and adapting to a new alternative is not worth the expected return. Example: loyalty to the Apple Macintosh operating system. Sometimes the consumer even may be dissatisfied but will remain loyal because competition is perceived to be the same. Example: slow bank service.	Competitors can undermine loyalty by making it easy to switch through product design, training, and terms. If loyalty is based on both attitudes and behavior, it can be used in product extensions (for example, the Macintosh power notebook).
Familiarity loyalty: Loyalty is the result of top-of-mind brand awareness. Brands are perceived to be similar. Example: colas.	Loyalty is defended and attacked by constant attention-getting advertising that builds top-of-mind brand awareness. This loyalty is very vulnerable to promotions.
Convenience loyalty: Loyalty is based on buying convenience. Examples: cola sold by favored food outlet. Frito-Lay snacks are available at most convenience stores.	Loyalty is attacked by expansion of competitor into convenience channels.

segments determine not only a firm's marketing tactics but also the potential value of its brand name (called brand equity; see Chapter 10). Some habits and loyalties are relatively easy to change because the habit is only superficial, sustained by buying convenience or the fact the brand is the first to come to mind (top-of-mind brand familiarity). While apparently loyal, buyers may be very open to trying a new product. This raises a related issue of the buyers' price sensitivity and how this can vary across market segments.

Consumer Price Sensitivity Segmentation

When segmenting market demand by price sensitivity, a seller has to recognize that price sensitivity has many determinants, a number of which are described here.

Expenditure Importance

The higher an item's price relative to the buyer's income, the greater the buyer's price sensitivity. Housing sales are very sensitive to interest rates for this reason. With each percentage point decrease in the prime rate, thousands of home buyers enter the market. In contrast, the typical consumer is not very price sensitive to the cost of a can of oil. However, the lube service business segment is very sensitive to the price of oil because it greatly affects its cost of doing business.

Sensitivity of the Buyers' Market

This sensitivity only applies when buyers use the items purchased as inputs to the items they make or resell. If their marketplace is price sensitive, then buyers will also be price sensitive when purchasing their input products. For this reason, the discount store-chain segment is likely to be more price sensitive in its buying habits than the prestigious department store-chain segment. This suggests that sellers design and market economy models for the discount chain segment and higher quality, higher priced models for the specialty and department stores.

Economic Circumstances

Consumer expectations of future wealth can influence price sensitivity. The stock market crash of October 1987 severely affected Christmas sales of luxury goods and other nonnecessity items. The anticipation of hard times makes market segments more conscious of spending habits and hence more price sensitive. On the other hand, when a market segment experiences windfall profits (for instance, a greater-than-expected tax refund because of a change in the law that favors a profession or property owners), the segment is likely to be less price sensitive in the expenditure of the windfall profits.[25] This suggests that indulgent luxuries such as holiday cruises and the latest high-technology golf clubs should be advertised in March when higher income individuals are likely to receive their tax refund and are tired of winter. The anticipation of inflation also may reduce sensitivity to current prices, because differences among current competitive prices are not as important as differences between current prices and future (higher) prices.

Product Differentiation

The more distinct the image positioning and performance of a product or service on dimensions desired by the segment, the lower the price sensitivity of the segment will be. Because such product differentiation (unique positioning) is more common in growth markets than in mature markets, growth markets are likely to be less price sensitive. This explains why high-performance notepad computers, loaded with differentiating features, are more expensive than similar desktop personal computers that compete in a much more undifferentiated market.

[25] Richard R. Thaler, "Toward a Positive Theory of Consumer Choice," *Journal of Economic Behavior and Organization* 1 (March 1980): 39–60.

Awareness of Substitutes

Shoppers may believe a product has unique features or is of high quality simply because they are unaware of alternatives. In general, less-informed segments are less price sensitive. When it is easy and inexpensive to try alternatives, price sensitivity is likely to be low for truly differentiated products and high for similar ("me-too") products.

Ease of Access to Substitutes

Price sensitivity, therefore, can change dramatically if potential buyers can easily find substitutes in different retail outlets. The reason why generic fruit cans are not usually sold alongside name-brand fruit cans is because sales of all branded fruit cans (including the store's private labels) would become much more price sensitive. The harder it is for a segment to find substitutes, the less price sensitive the segment will be. One of the reasons why mail-order companies that sell cameras in photography magazines have lower prices than camera shops for the same brand and model is that it is much easier to compare prices among mail-order advertisements than across camera stores.

Ease of Substitution

Substitutability depends on more than just quality differentiation. If the switching costs of using the substitute are high (that is, the user has to change his or her behavior too drastically in order to switch, or the switch involves financial costs), then price sensitivity is less in the short term. For example, if a consumer has to modify existing equipment in order to use the alternate product (such as switching from a gas furnace to an electric one), or if he or she has to learn new operating procedures (such as special microwave cooking directions for a new brand of rice), then the switching costs may be too high, and the consumer will be less likely to switch to the alternate product. Market segments that do not have the skills or time to invest in the switching costs will be less price sensitive.

Ease of Storage and Postponability

The demand for products that can be stored easily will be more price sensitive. This is because an item's current price is compared with and competing against its expected future price as well as any current price substitutes. The same product purchased in the future can be a perfect substitute for a product purchased today and stored for the future. For similar reasons, the market segment that can postpone the purchase is more price sensitive than the segment that cannot. This explains why products such as snow shovels are promoted at a sale price in the fall but are sold at full price when they are needed immediately, such as in the middle of winter.

Price/Quality Signaling

When a product is purchased to signal power, prestige, or quality, a higher price helps position the product. The higher priced product is a signal to the target market that greater value comes at a higher price. In order to buy a product with high quality, the buyer has to spend more. The more a segment believes that a higher price signals greater value or quality, the less that segment's price sensitivity will be (see Chapter 16 on pricing tactics).

Consumer Search Behavior and Shopping Segmentation

Most market segmentation practices emphasize isolating the differences in product demand among buyers. However, the market can be usefully segmented even if consumer demand for a product and its price do not vary. Buyers sometimes differ in their *search* behavior: They use different retail outlets, they use various shopping styles, they are exposed to diverse media, and their sensitivity to advertising campaigns varies.

It is important to study what types of retail stores buyers patronize and are loyal to.[26] Buyers may evaluate the services, convenience, and pricing of retail stores differently. It is also possible to segment buyers by the way they shop, such as reviewing how much comparison shopping they do or determining whether they shop for price, value, or service or use catalogs and other sources of written information.[27] Shopping behavior may be a more enduring personality characteristic than other lifestyle or psychographic measures. If differences in retail store or catalog loyalty are evident, then it is important for the marketer to pursue several distribution strategies; even if offering the same product to each distribution channel. Otherwise, all of the market cannot be reached (see Chapter 11). When both demand and shopping behavior vary, then the marketer may offer different product forms or promote different product features in different distribution channels and advertising media. In retail stores where buyers are concerned with quality and reliability, an extended warranty could be emphasized. In retail stores where patrons are more price sensitive, value could be stressed in point-of-purchase displays and economy packages could be offered.

In mature markets it may be more effective not to segment by demand sensitivity at all but instead to segment by shopping behavior. Much depends on the variability of buyer search and shopping behavior. Shopping behavior segmentation also may be less obvious to competitors and hence will be more difficult to imitate. But to segment the market by shopping behavior, a firm needs to develop a better understanding of how consumers shop. A firm with a better understanding of this than its rivals is more competitive.

Complex Search and Shopping Behavior

Inexperienced consumers may not be able or willing to make time to undertake complex analyses of product information, but that does not mean they make foolish or wasteful purchase choices. For one thing, consumers know that many experts in the marketplace can help them make decisions. Such experts were used to help solve problems long before the computer was invented. Realtors, stockbrokers, accountants, travel agents, interior designers, wardrobe consultants, and car and appliance salespeople are used by people who are short of time, lack confidence in their choice ability, or lack knowledge of what is available and where it is available. The success of professional advice agents depends on their expert knowledge of the product or market and their ability to

---

[26] Fitting the product and marketing campaign to the shoppers loyal to a particular specialty store is discussed in greater detail in Chapter 11, "Relationship Strategy."

[27] Jack A. Lesser and Marie Adele Hughes, "The Generalizability of Psychographic Market Segments across Geographic Locations," *Journal of Marketing* 50 (January 1986): 18–27.

The shopper for a major investment, such as a house, automobile, or major appliance, will often spend several days actively shopping and may find the experience stressful because of the expense involved and the shopper's lack of current knowledge about the market. General Motors' Saturn dealers have recognized this and worked very hard to provide a pleasant shopping experience. It has proven to be an important competitive advantage, creating very satisfied and loyal buyers (see section on complex search and shopping).

1. Understand what benefits the consumer really wants
2. Help define the features wanted and *not* wanted
3. Show and explain the alternatives
4. Find or make the consumer a deal that makes it unnecessary for the consumer to look any further

Figure 5.8 is a model of the search and shopping behavior of buyers that recognizes the important role of professional advice.[28] Some event arouses the buyer to start actively shopping. Shopping activity may be prompted by a product failure, a change in family circumstances, the purchase behavior or recommendation of a friend, a magazine article, a television program, or an advertisement. Naturally, shoppers use their past direct and vicarious experiences to help decide what to do next. This normally involves first deciding what is wanted or where to look for what is wanted. Brand and store loyalty has its greatest influence at this stage. Friends, advocate sources such as *Consumer Reports,* and catalogs may give helpful advice on how to choose and identify the options. The store visit comes next (see photos of shoppers), perhaps triggered by a sales advertisement (see Figure 5.8).

The good salesperson helps the buyer to define the purchase requirements precisely, explains features, and suggests what may be best for the consumer. Folklore often portrays the salesperson as an adversary of dubious integrity. It is true that most of us have been deceived at some time by a dishonest sales pitch, but what we tend to forget is that the great majority of exchanges we have with sales clerks are helpful and rewarding. We are often unaware of the obstacles they have piloted us past in order to help us make good purchase choices! The bottom line is that a decision-making team

[28] William L. Wilkie and Peter R. Dickson, "Shopping for Appliances: Consumers' Strategies and Patterns of Information Search," working paper, Marketing Science Institute, Cambridge, Mass., 1985.

Figure 5.8 **An Adaptive Model of Shopping and Decision Making**

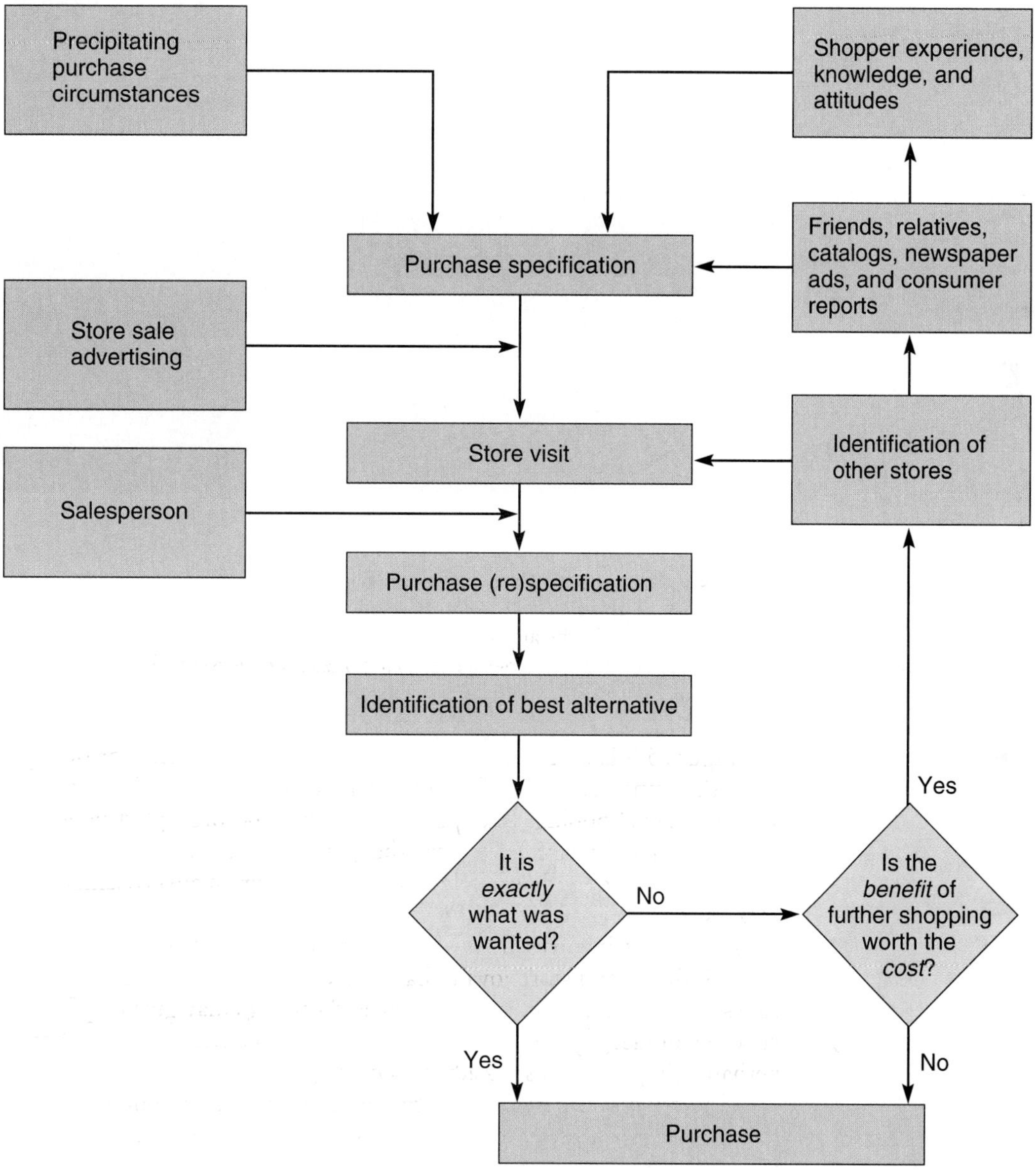

The first store visit leads to interaction with a salesperson, which frequently leads to a respecification of what is wanted (this often occurs with appliances, automobiles, furniture, furnishings, fashion clothing, and cosmetics). The salesperson helps identify satisfactory alternatives. If one of them is not exactly what was wanted, the shopper has to decide whether shopping elsewhere will be worth the effort. The process is adaptive because decision making and behavior intentions change as new information is learned.

After a shopper learns the layout of a supermarket, grocery shopping becomes a habitual activity. It's done with little thought and is consequently hard to change. It means that some aisles are never walked down. This makes end of aisle displays very valuable (see section on habitual shopping).

should not assume a salesperson's role is to hard sell. Instead, the salesperson should be viewed as playing a partnership role in a joint purchase decision. The successful salesperson soft sells by discussing the pros and cons of the options, by indicating which models are popular and why, by explaining how to judge quality, and by sharing personal experiences and insights with the prospective buyer.

If the salesperson cannot convince the buyer that he or she has exactly what the buyer is looking for or that no one else has a better deal, then the salesperson often does not get paid for the effort. This is a strong incentive for the salesperson to gain the buyer's confidence and make the sale. The more a salesperson expects the chance of repeat business, the greater is the incentive to give honest, helpful advice. This economic survival incentive explains why the salesperson often plays a major role in the purchase and why shoppers lean fairly heavily on the salesperson's expert advice. It is important that the shopper know just enough to decide whether the salesperson is expert, sincere, and well meaning. The consumer who cannot confidently spot the salesperson who is a sham or a shark will often shop with a relative or friend who has such skills. Alternatively, such a consumer will go to a quality store where such expertise is known to exist and either purchase there or use the advice obtained there to shop the discount stores.

Recreational Shopping

A major limitation of the model in Figure 5.8 is that it does not pay enough heed to shop-till-you-drop recreational shopping. It is human nature to develop recreational interests and hobbies, including shopping. They provide a sense of competence and mastery over a small part of an extremely complex and uncertain world. As children, teenagers, and adults, we become experts through reading about, using, and buying

Shopping is often a recreational activity associated with a particular hobby or interest, such as interior decorating, fashions, or collecting particular objects. Such a shopper will often spend several days a month enjoying such activities. Unlike habitual shoppers, recreational shoppers are interested in shopping in new stores and finding out about new products and services. Recreational shopping often occurs on vacations which explains the popularity of antique stores and hobby shops at tourist resorts (see section on recreational shopping).

products associated with our hobbies. Such hobbies include many types of arts and crafts, antiques, photography, gardening, cooking, fishing, or activities that involve computers, cars, and boats, to name a few. An important recreational aspect of such hobbies is going shopping for supplies and new equipment. Such shopping is frequently done at specialty stores, and personal relationships often develop with store owners and their salespeople. A two-way learning process takes place in which customers and salespeople exchange information about what is going on in the marketplace, new trends, and what works and what does not.

This product-enthusiast market segment is important because hobbyists are heavy users, are important influence agents, and can be targeted. They often gather together in clubs where information about new products, new distribution channels, and special deals offered by retailers is exchanged and discussed. But their influence extends well beyond the immediate group of heavy users. Product enthusiasts are consulted by friends, relatives, and work associates.[29] They often give advice and even help others shop, because enthusiasts derive some of their self-esteem from their expertise. The skilled marketer can harness the tremendous pool of knowledge and product involvement among enthusiasts by offering workshops and lectures, special credit terms, and even part-time employment to the enthusiast.

[29] Lawrence F. Feick and Linda L. Price, "The Market Maven: A Diffuser of Marketplace Information," *Journal of Consumer Research* 13 (June 1987): 119–26. For insights into the different decision-making practices of experts, see also Joseph W. Alba and J. Wesley Hutchinson, "Dimensions of Consumer Expertise," *Journal of Consumer Research* 13 (March 1987): 411–54.

Media Use

Buyers also may be segmented by the media they use heavily. To make sure they are reached, different media schedules may have to be developed to advertise to buyers who have been segmented by their media habits. Both heavy users of products and heavy users of particular media exist. According to the advertising agency Needham, Harper and Steers, the regular (heavy) readers of magazines use more ideas from magazines, spend significantly more time reading magazines, and record higher ad-page exposure levels and significantly higher verified recall of ads than do less active readers.[30] Regular television viewers are also more likely to recall advertising than casual viewers. If these heavy media users are *also* heavy product users, then a firm can target them effectively with repeated advertising in the magazine and newspaper sections, television programs, and radio shows that are popular with the heavy product user. Some advertisers have a long history of doing this by associating themselves with specific television programs; for example, Mutual of Omaha has been associated with "Wild Kingdom" and Prudential Assurance with the "College Football Scoreboard." In summary, it may be worthwhile to segment the market by its regular and heavy contact with different media (see also Chapter 15 on media advertising).

Another possibility is that buyers may not differ in their evaluation of the product, their buying behavior, or their media use, but they may respond differently to features of specific advertising pitches. For example, when marketing to both men and women and a range of age groups, it may make sense to use spokespeople or models that specific segments of buyers can relate to; young men will respond more to young male models in the advertising campaign, young women to young female models, and older buyers to older models. This way marketers can segment the market by applying buyer sensitivity to features of the advertising campaign. A frequent question in advertising is whether the basic message theme should be logical or emotional. A "This is how we are better than them" message will be more effective if the market segment prefers to use a logical choice rule and process a lot of factual information when making a decision. A market segment that is more "right-brain" dominant and experiential will be more persuaded by a campaign that expresses "Wow! What an experience!" message themes (see Figure 5.7).

Summary of Consumer Segmentation

This completes the review of the mental segmentation model of consumer behavior described in Figure 5.3. To summarize, market segmentation is undertaken for a purpose: to profit by targeting the product and marketing to particular groups of buyers. Table 5.6 summarizes the active relevance of different segmentation variables in consumer markets. Recall, however, that all these variables are related to each other, and deep segmentation analysis describes *each* segment in terms of its level of consumption, brand loyalty, shopping behavior, media use, sensitivity to different message themes, price sensitivity, choice rules, beliefs, features preferred, benefits sought, usage situations, lifestyle, life cycle, income, and geographical concentrations. The use of the mental model of consumer behavior shown in Figure 5.3 helps sellers really get to know their different consumers and satisfy them more efficiently than the com-

[30] Needham, Harper, and Steers, *The Core Audience Concept: A Media Position*, white paper, New York, February 1983.

Table 5.6 The Frequency of Use of Consumer Segmentation Bases

SEGMENTATION BASIS	ACTIVE FREQUENTLY USED IN
Demographics	■ Choice of sales regions ■ Estimating segment size ■ Choice of local distribution channels or channels that cater to different age, income, and education groups ■ Choice of media that serve different age, income, and education groups
Usage situation	■ Product performance specifications ■ Delivery service ■ Advertising themes ■ Brochure design ■ Written and video usage instructions
Benefits sought	■ Different models with different features ■ Different advertising messages that emphasize different benefits ■ Sales training
Beliefs	■ New offerings that solve a previous problem ■ Campaigns that raise awareness ■ Campaigns that change image and positioning
Heavy product usage	■ Special products (sizes and quality) ■ Special services ■ Special frequent-user promotional programs ■ Special financial terms
Channel loyalty	■ Choice of distributors ■ Different product mix for different distribution channels
Heavy media usage	■ Promotion tailored to media ■ Media buying ■ Message tailored to media

petition. Such a superior thinking framework gives a firm a competitive rationality advantage over its competition.

Segmenting Business-to-Business Markets

In markets where buyers are other businesses (often called accounts), the first two natural segmentation variables are the size of the account and the growth potential of the account. In Chapter 13 a spreadsheet is described that categorizes business-to-business customers into A, B, C, and D account segments, depending on their size, growth potential, and the service they receive from competitors. This segmentation is often used to determine the annual number of sales calls on a customer and other relationship services. Figure 5.9 presents a heavy usage/benefit segmentation analysis undertaken for a shipping service.[31] Customers were first segmented by amount of usage, and then within each segment the most important service features and benefits were identified. Note that heavy users want to negotiate special terms and are most

[31] Steven Hokanson, "The Deeper You Analyze, the More You Satisfy Customers," *Marketing News*, January 2, 1995, 16.

Figure 5.9 **Resource Allocation List Comparison: Segments by Volume**

High Volume (Top 10%)	Moderate Volume (Next 30%)	Low Volume (Bottom 60%)
Good value	Handle claims fairly	Sales reps know business
Handle claims fairly	Accurate billing	Accurate billing
Accurate billing	Timely service	Willing to negotiate
Willing to negotiate	Sales reps know business	Good value
Timely service	Good value	Availability
Reliability	Willing to negotiate	Timely service
Availability	Trustworthiness	Support services
Concerned about customer	Overall satisfaction	Helpful employees
Trustworthiness	Availability	Handle claims fairly
Overall satisfaction	Concerned about customer	Easy to deal with when problems arise
Respond quickly to questions	Reliability	Respond quickly to questions
Support services	Helpful employees	Trustworthiness
Sales reps know business	Support services	Overall satisfaction
Easy to deal with when problems arise	Easy to deal with when problems arise	Concerned about customer
Courteous employees	Respond quickly to questions	Courteous employees
Helpful employees	Courteous employees	Reliability

High Priority   Medium Priority   Low Priority

cost conscious because they spend so much on shipping and it is a major budget item. Low-volume users are concerned that the shipping service understands their business—a classic problem in managing a sales force's servicing of small accounts. The analysis reveals that a competitive opportunity would be to increase the business of small accounts by having the sales force get to know the customers' business, shipping needs, and current distribution processes.

When a firm does 80 percent of its business with three or four accounts, it cannot help but adopt a special-relationship marketing approach that actually goes well beyond traditional segmentation. Moreover, business-to-business buyers are directly and constantly in contact with the seller. The seller can tailor the marketing campaign to the buyer by promoting the items in the line that will be of most interest to the buyer

Figure 5.10 **SIC Code Outline**

Standard Industrial Classification Index

The first two digits of the SIC number show the major industrial group into which the company is classified. There are 11 divisions, which have a code range as follows:

01 to 09	Agriculture, Forestry, and Fishing
10 to 14	Mining
15 to 17	Construction
20 to 39	Manufacturing
40 to 49	Transportation, Communications, Electric, Gas, and Sanitary Services
50 to 51	Wholesale Trade
52 to 59	Retail Trade
60 to 67	Finance, Insurance, and Real Estate
70 to 89	Services
91 to 97	Public Administration
99	Nonclassifiable Establishments

Retail Trade (52 to 59)
General Merchandise Stores

5311	Department Stores
5331	Variety Stores
5399	Miscellaneous General Merchandise Stores

Eating and Drinking Places

5812	Eating Places
5813	Drinking Places (Alcoholic Beverages)

by providing the relevant brochures, and by adapting to the unique aspects of the buying firm's purchasing processes. Each account is likely to be provided with special products and services that fit its unique requirements. Today, the business-to-business buyer is likely to ask the selling firm if it can be involved in helping design the product. An ordering process that minimizes the transportation and inventory holding costs also can be especially designed for the customer (see Chapter 12 on distribution logistics). This sort of unique relationship marketing makes talking about broader segment strategies somewhat irrelevant.

Usage situation segmentation is often used to target particular industries or groups of accounts within industries where hundreds of businesses exist. One helpful approach is to study the different uses of the product or service by the industry and to rate each usage situation in terms of long-term growth potential and the competitiveness of substitutes. One manufacturer, 3M, has dominated the industrial adhesive market for several decades by adopting such an approach.

The Standard Industrial Classification (SIC) coding system (see Figure 5.11) is used by the government to describe the line of business of a specific firm. In a way, having access to SIC data that the Commerce Department provides is equivalent to knowing the demographics, lifestyles, and product usage situations of consumers or households, all rolled into one. SIC information also can be used to determine how many potential buyers exist in a region. However, a full understanding of the different usage situations, production processes, and benefits sought by the different industrial markets requires a close working relationship with several companies in each SIC-created segment.

Purchasing Style Segmentation

The cross-functional decision-making team should find it relatively easy to view the business buyer's purchase decision from two cross-functional perspectives: the engineering-user view and the purchasing view. This is because both perspectives are likely to be encountered in the different individuals the team has to deal with and satisfy in the buying organization. The segmentation of a business-to-business market by usage and purchase behavior is similar to the distinction between demand and shopping behavior segmentation in consumer markets. The end users in a buying firm are more sensitive about product performance and hence can be segmented by demand sensitivity. The purchasing agents in a buying firm may vary in their sensitivity to selling approaches and use of trade media and, hence, can be segmented by their readership of different trade magazines and newsletters (i.e., shopping behavior segmentation).

Often wide variations occur in the way firms make the purchase decision and in their standard purchasing procedures. The short- and long-term financial positions of customers within such a submarket also may influence the way they respond, as will the unique personalities and sociopolitical climates that exist within a buying firm at any time. Indeed, it may be difficult to generalize and aggregate industrial buyers based on their purchasing characteristics because each of them uses a different bidding and buying process. This again emphasizes why an adaptive sales force is needed to spearhead the marketing effort.

To handle such complexity, a systematic analysis of a key buying account should proceed through a step-by-step description of the people involved, the organization's use of the product or service, the major players' perceptions of the benefits sought, and perceptions of the competitive offerings. The firm's standard buying behavior can even be mapped out in a flowchart (see Figure 5.11). If the seller is lucky, such a buying guide may even be provided by the buying firm.

Low-Bid Buying

Much of the literature on organizational buying suggests that buyers play a rather passive, receptive role in the purchasing process by responding to the seller's marketing efforts. In fact, this is far from the truth. Business buyers generally search for information more actively than do households or individuals. They go out and solicit bids. Competition has forced many companies to search for new, economical sources of supply. Purchasing agents and entrepreneurs from the United States have carried samples of parts and finished products to Pacific Rim countries to be copied by Asian manufacturers. The growth in off-shore sourcing of high-tech components came about by economic necessity for many American manufacturers.

Figure 5.11 Developing Requests for Bids

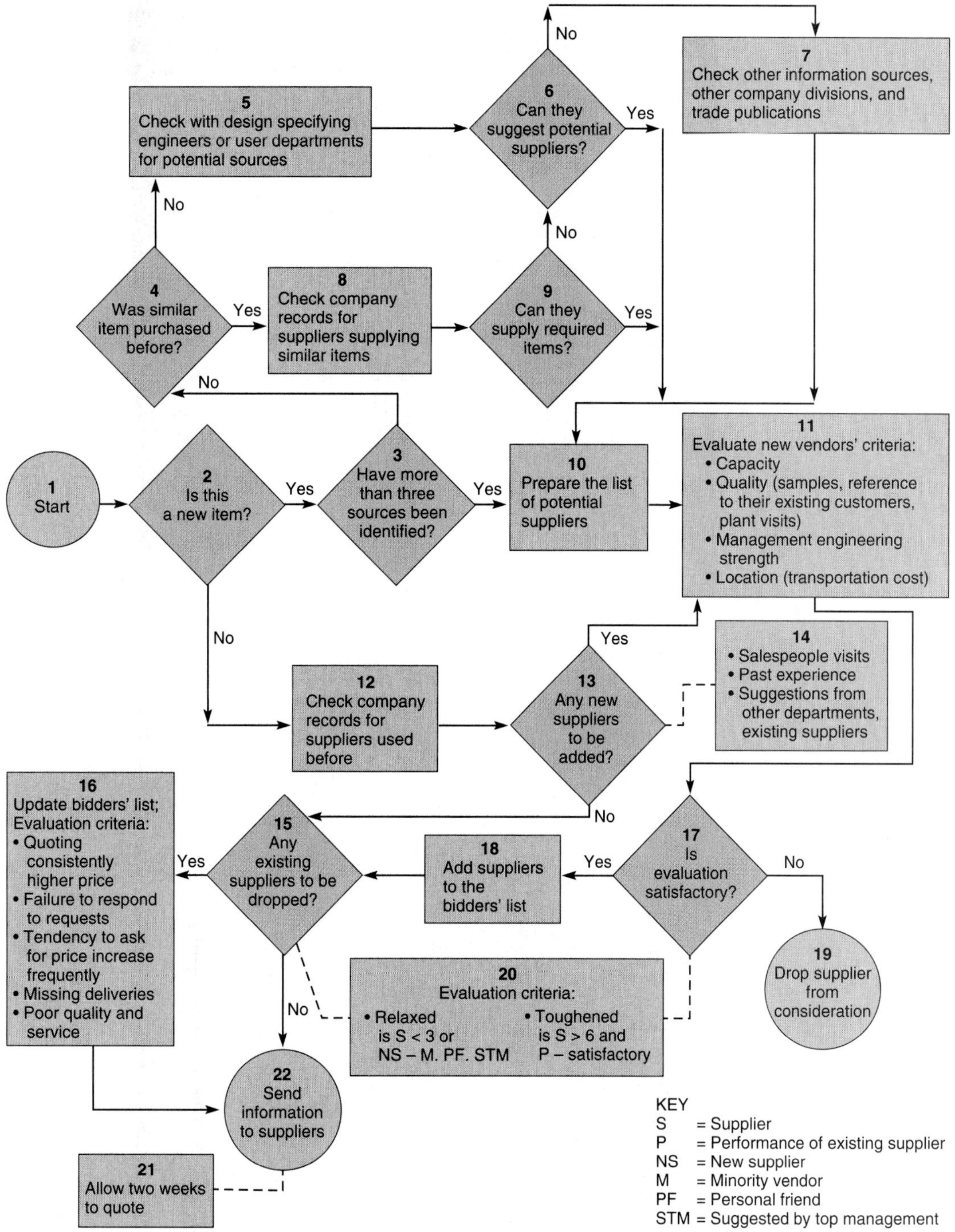

This flowchart is an activity sequence script (AS script) which describes the actions it takes to solicit bids. It reveals just how complex organization buying can get. The shortest path is 1-2-12-13-15-22. What is the longest path? Reproduced with permission from Niren Vyas and Arch G. Woodside, "An Inductive Model of Supplier Choice Processes," *Journal of Marketing* 48 (Winter 1984): 30–45.

The typical process of seeking and then evaluating bids can initially appear *very* complicated (see Figure 5.11). However, after a purchasing agent has learned the ropes, the process becomes routine, depending on the yes or no answers to a series of questions presented in the different sections of the flowchart. The process is an application of a series of activities and rules that make the decision making much more systematic and predictable. Such purchasing process activities and rules include the following:

1. Actively seek new sources when the number of suppliers on the bid list is less than three.
2. Keep using current suppliers when their performance is satisfactory and the number of suppliers on the list is greater than three.
3. Toughen acceptable performance standards when the number of suppliers on the list is greater than three.
4. Drop the existing vendor with the worst performance when new vendors are included on the bid list.

Such product performance specifications and rules are likely to have evolved from past group decision-making sessions that involved technical experts and senior management. For some purchases undertaken by very large companies or governments, it is even possible to develop computer-based expert systems that guide a purchasing officer through a purchase decision, according to rules set up by expert buyers and the original design and production engineers.[32] Future expert systems are likely to integrate information from production that rates a supplier within the supply chain in terms of defect rates within individual order batches, on-time delivery, and other performance criteria. This will make buying a much more objective process and will identify problems that can be eliminated by improving specific processes within the trading relationship (see Chapters 11 and 12).

A striking characteristic of most bidding processes is their emphasis on encouraging competition among suppliers by seeking bids from three or more vendors (see Figure 5.11). The explanation is simple: a bidding competition among suppliers is in the interests of the buyer. It is not a coincidence that a bias exists toward always accepting the lowest bid, rather than the bid that offers the most value for price. This bias is often encouraged by company audit procedures that require purchasing agents to file a written justification if they do not accept the lowest bid. However, powerful arguments may exist for choosing superior quality and service rather than the lowest price. Furthermore, the whole process of bid buying has started to be questioned by many organizations, as discussed in the next section.

Supply Chain Management

In an attempt to become more competitive in their markets, many manufacturers are now reaching back up the supply channel to help their suppliers develop more innovative materials and components, establish more efficient production processes, and produce a product that exceeds the buyers' desired quality and performance specifications. Such behavior is called *supply chain management.*

[32] Mary Kay Allen, *The Development of an Artificial Intelligence System for Inventory Management Using Multiple Experts* (Oak Brook, IL: Council of Logistics Management, 1986).

As described in later chapters, it makes a great deal of sense to involve suppliers in the development of new products. Rather than taking over their key suppliers, firms set up joint ventures that give them exclusive rights to any product or process innovations developed in cooperation with the supplier. The logic behind the idea of the supplier and buyer working together is that two independent, innovative, and entrepreneurial firms are better than a single, vertically integrated firm. The continued independence between the supplier and buyer enhances innovation and keeps the *entrepreneurial* leadership in both the selling and buying firms happy.

Joint venturing also can produce major cost savings for both parties. Ongoing selling and purchasing costs are reduced to a minimum, and cooperation on product design can significantly reduce costs. Perhaps the most publicized advantage is that the inventory holding costs of both the supplier and buyer can be dramatically reduced by developing a just-in-time (JIT) delivery system. JIT is a supply system where the seller delivers its product as it is needed to the production line of the buyer. JIT offers the following features:

1. Items and subcomponents (i.e., assembled modules of items such as hard drives, transformers, or keyboards for a personal computer) are designed and produced according to buyer specifications.
2. All delivered items are inspected by the supplier before delivery, reducing the defect rate to zero for the buyer.
3. Delivery is frequent and absolutely reliable. Suppliers often relocate close to an account to provide such service.
4. Initial negotiation of terms and operating procedures among senior executives is extensive. Prices are often based on supplier costs revealed to the buyer, and both parties work together to reduce these costs.
5. Likelihood of repeated contract renewal is very high.

The power of advances in information technology to create close working relationships between vendor and customer is demonstrated in Ryder's Fast Track Maintenance Service for its 162,000 trucks.[33] An on-board computer in each truck records the history of its performance, which can be obtained by connecting a handheld computer to a coin-sized disk in the truck's cab. The information quickly detects performance problems, thus speeding up repairs and reducing truck downtime. But the information has even greater strategic value. It enables Ryder to focus on parts' defects with its suppliers and to demand higher quality and longer warranties. It also enables Ryder and its suppliers to identify what situation usages (e.g., city versus highway use) wear out which parts faster and to redesign Ryder trucks and parts for such hard-wearing usage. The $33 million system is expected to pay for itself in two years. The vendors most responsive to analyzing the information and responding with suggested design changes will be clearly preferred over suppliers who want to do business the old-fashioned way—low bidding on a standard part.

An example of such a vendor that has become expert in serving its customers who wish to develop a close, long-term trading relationship is automaker supplier Prince Corp. It designs and manufactures car interior trims and works with its automaker customers using computer-aided design and manufacturing and three-dimensional prototypes. It prides itself on beating deadlines and also stays close to the ultimate

[33] Ira Sager, "The Great Equalizer," *Business Week/The Information Revolution*, 1994, 100–07.

customer—the car buyer.[34] To keep its costs down, it runs its factories up to twenty-four hours a day, six days a week.

The aim of business-to-business marketers like Prince is to become members of the actual cross-functional platform teams that Chrysler and Ford use to develop new models. Twenty-four such "guest engineers" are working at Honda's product development center in Ohio. In such a situation, the trusted supplier-partner works (with the team) backward from the target selling price of the car to determine the target price for each part. The supplier is then expected to deliver a zero-defect part on time and at or below the target price for the part. In the 1980s such supplier partnering gave Japanese auto companies a $300 to $600 per-car cost advantage over U.S. automakers in addition to superior designs and features and fewer defects. Such partnering where the supplier becomes a subcontractor allows the automaker to focus on its core competitive processes (see Chapter 4 and Chapter 17). For example, in setting up its new manufacturing plant in South Carolina, BMW concentrates on designing and manufacturing its cars' power train, suspension, and cockpit—the processes that create the differentiated BMW driving experience. The rest of the car is made by suppliers, each world-class experts in the design and manufacturing of the rest of the BMW car parts. Most have built plants right beside the BMW factory.

The development of such supply-chain relationships involves a different sort of selling to organizations that wish to buy this way. The emphasis is on the long-term relationship rather than the immediate transaction (see Chapter 13 for more on such team selling). Sellers who have developed this relationship skill, and already have a track record of being able to smoothly implement such relationships, have a clear advantage over sellers who are novices. This advantage will be particularly important when selling to buyers who are new to joint-venture buying. A further point is that switching costs from one supplier to another can be very high in such joint-venture buying. Seller joint-venturing experience therefore becomes particularly valuable because the sellers who are the first to develop such relationships with buyers often get to keep the business for a long time. It is safe to predict that the sellers who serve multiple industrial markets and who are first to offer buyers joint ventures in product development and JIT delivery will end up with a very important and sustainable long-term competitive advantage.[35]

Social Network Segmentation of Business-to-Business Markets

Within a business-to-business market there often exists powerful social networks that can become the basis for purchasing segmentation. Although word of mouth is important in the selling of any product or service, the following sociological characteristics of the business-to-business marketplace make it critical:

[34] Alex Taylor, "The Auto Industry Meets the New Economy," *Fortune*, September 5, 1994, 52–60.

[35] The significance of the long-term rewards that will be achieved from being a pioneer in offering such supply-chain management service to buyers and transferring this managerial and technological skill across to other markets may not be fully appreciated by marketers and Wall Street investors. On the other hand, situations arise in which a buyer who develops close relationships with several suppliers can play them against each other even more than the buyer could before the close relationships were established. This will be discussed further in the context of the retailer's global sourcing of supply (see Chapter 7).

1. Generally, the most influential members of the buying firms received comparable training in engineering or trade schools. They think in similar ways, which enables them to communicate more readily with each other. Their similar training also instills like values, as well as parallel skills and mental models.
2. Industry trade associations encourage the exchange of ideas and learning within an industry (even among competitors) through conferences, trade shows, seminars, and annual meetings.
3. Executives who move on to a position with a competitor, supplier, or major customer often maintain personal friendships with their previous coworkers.
4. Engineering consultants act as word-of-mouth megaphones; they often pass on what they have learned to others. A consultant's advice to one company is also often noted and copied by other companies.
5. Sellers often use testimonials and encourage prospects to contact satisfied customers. Finding and talking to dissatisfied customers is harder, but the competition will often find them and encourage them to talk to other buyers about their dissatisfaction.
6. Keeping up with what the competitors are buying is a necessity because the survival of the firm may depend on the early adoption of new technology. The buyer also knows that even if the purchase is not a success, the rival whose purchase behavior was imitated is likely to be in the same sinking boat.

The reasons listed explain why a letter of introduction or an open endorsement from an opinion leader in an industry can be a powerful marketing tool. Conversely, in a close-knit industry that has strong personal networks, a supplier and its sales force cannot afford to make any major blunders. The word will get around. Well-established social networks may be important enough and stable enough in a market for a supplier to invest the time and effort necessary to map them out. A social network then can be divided into niches based on influential individuals and organizations that become the targets of a coordinated selling effort. In fact, experienced salespeople already know these social networks and use them constantly. When they exist, they should become a formal basis for purchase behavior segmentation because they are powerful in the diffusion of new ideas and products in an industrial market.

Summary of Business-to-Business Segmentation

Table 5.7 presents other potential business-to-business market segmentation criteria and the elements of marketing management most shaped by each criterion. Segmenting by whether a major account's purchasing is decentralized or centralized will influence whether the account is serviced by a regional sales force or treated as a national account. An industrial sales force is often regionally structured and managed. Region or geographical location is therefore another natural way of segmenting the market and may indeed also reflect different usage situations based on concentrations of particular types of industry in different regions and sales territories. Also, distinct, regionally based management subcultures (styles, etiquette, and protocol) can make doing business in New York very different from doing business in Los Angeles, Atlanta, or Houston. The sales and marketing campaign must be sensitive to such business subcultural differences. Accounts can be further rated in terms of their sensitivity to personal relations and service or price promotions and managed accordingly. Ultimately, the credit ratings of buyers also must be integrated into any segmentation strategy because slow or no payers will have to receive special attention (or nonattention).

Table 5.7 The Frequency of Use of Industrial Segmentation Bases

SEGMENTATION BASIS	FREQUENTLY USED IN
Account size and growth potential (A,B,C, or D)[a]	■ Account and relationship management
SIC usage code	■ Geographical sales territory allocation ■ Product design ■ Choice of trade journal to carry advertising ■ Choice of trade show attendance
Usage situation	■ Product design ■ Sales force training ■ JIT delivery service ■ Advertising theme/brochure design
Purchasing process is centralized/decentralized	■ Organization of sales force
Location	■ Organization of sales force
Low-bid buying versus joint venturing	■ Involvement of senior management ■ Emphasis on design versus low price
Automation of buying	■ Timing of selling ■ Electronic linkage

[a]In a mental segmentation model of a business-to-business market, each account may be given a code such as A6P, where *A* stands for an A account, in terms of size and growth potential; *6* is a code for the SIC/usage situation; and *P* stands for a low-bid price orientation, rather than a joint venturing on innovation orientation.

An important feature of business-to-business segmentation is the instability of the segment structure. Industrial markets are usually more volatile than consumer markets. First, industrial markets are often based on derived demand from other markets. If the economy hesitates or new competitors enter the served markets, then demand in an industrial market can collapse and radically change a firm's segment framework. Second, important new product, service, or process innovations in technology occur more frequently in industrial production than in household production. Such innovations are likely to radically change the usage situation of a product or service, perhaps eliminating its use altogether in one industry sector and opening up a new use for the product or service in another industry sector. This instability leads to a more general discussion of some other limitations to using mental segmentation models in decision making.

The Limits of Market Segmentation

If a firm's product or service positioning and marketing tactics are not directly influenced by the way it segments the market, then its segmentation approach is useless. But a mental model of how a market is segmented must do more than influence strategy and tactics. It must increase sales and profits.[36] Offering a single product and un-

[36] Frederick W. Winter, "A Cost-Benefit Approach to Market Segmentation," *Journal of Marketing* (fall 1979): 103–11; Shirley Young, Leland Ott, and Barbara Feigin, "Some Practical Considerations in Market Segmentation," *Journal of Marketing Research* 15 (August 1978): 405–12; and Peter Resnick, B. Turney, and J. Barry Mason, "Marketers Turn to 'Counter-Segmentation,'" *Harvard Business Review* (October 1979): 100–06.

dertaking a single marketing strategy enables economies of scale. Design costs, start-up production costs, production variable costs, administration costs, inventory handling costs, and advertising and promotion costs all will be lower per unit sale than when multiple products are offered and multiple marketing strategies are implemented to serve several market segments.

One way to solve the higher cost of serving multiple segments is to keep the cost of serving particular multiple segments down. This can be achieved by the following product and process design tactics:

1. Use standardized or modularized components that can be used by several models in the line. This is called *product-line* or *robust* design.
2. Delay assembly to reduce inventory of the shared modules (see Chapter 12).
3. Favor low fixed-cost production processes.
4. Use low fixed-cost marketing, such as manufacturer representatives (see Chapter 13).
5. Develop an umbrella ad campaign shared by all models.
6. Develop brochures and promotional materials that are expandable by adding inserts on the specific model for a specific segment.[37]

A firm that pursues such a design and cost-structure strategy is able to profit more from targeting several segments in its product line, compared to its rivals.

In addition to the higher costs of targeting several market segments, things also can get out of control rapidly if marketers in a company are asked to juggle too many balls in the air at once.

The profitability of identifying and pursuing market segments also may be here today but gone tomorrow because of changes in input costs and new competition. Changes in consumer values, demographics, and lifestyles add to the uncertainty and instability. For example, during a recession, consumers may become more price sensitive and may want to trade product features or quality for a more standard product with a lower price. After the recession is over, they become less price sensitive and return to their old behavior. What this means is that the market segment mental model has to be updated often, leading to the merging of old segments and the creation of new segments.

At what stage in the life of a product market is market segmentation most important? The best time to segment a market is at the rapid market growth stage when other competitors have yet to segment the market. When growth slows down, most market segments are already being well served by a competitor and are too expensive to attack. The rapid growth stage is also when new types of buyers are entering the market in large numbers. Often they are entering the market for the first time precisely because an innovative seller has designed a new model that nullifies their previous objections to purchasing or offers a feature or price that tips the scales. The seller also may have discovered a previously unused distribution or media channel to reach a virgin market segment. Markets often expand precisely because such new market segments are developed. In summary, a growth market often meets all the requirements for profitable segmentation: different segments are responsive to different benefits and product characteristics, vary in their price sensitivity, and use different buying channels.

[37] Winter and Thomas, "An Extension of Market Segmentation: Strategic Segmentation," 259–60.

Consumer Analysis in Foreign Markets

Foreign consumers often differ from American consumers in conspicuous ways. They speak diverse languages, and, when the listener is unfamiliar with the language, they seem *very different.* They dress in different ways, eat different foods, and have different customs. However, foreigners do *not* all behave the same way. Some are rich; many are very poor. Some are highly educated and live in industrialized environments; many are illiterate and lead very simple lives. The segmentation mental model described in Figure 5.3 can be applied just as well to a foreign market as it can to a U.S. market. In fact, a case can be made that deep segmentation is more applicable to foreign markets because it provides structure and discipline to a decision-making team's thinking that reduces its nationalistic prejudices.

The problem lies in obtaining insightful information that results in a segmentation of consumer behavior that leads to superior competitive strategy. The greatest danger is that, like the early missionaries and sociologists, the decision-making team imposes its own values, beliefs, and behavior on the analysis. Executives who find it impossible to empathize with consumers who have "foreign" ways should be kept well away from global marketing decisions. On the other hand, sellers also need to beware of nationalists and expatriots whose romantic or idealistic views can be just as dangerously biased.

Every foreign market has its own unique demand and distribution characteristics. When IKEA, the Swedish furniture-retailing firm, entered the United States, its advertising stressed its blue-and-yellow Swedishness and clean Scandinavian designs. But what had worked in its expansion across Europe ran into problems. Americans complained that the beds were too narrow, IKEA did not sell matching bedroom suites, the bedroom chests needed to be deeper to store sweaters, the kitchen cupboards were too narrow for the large dinner plates sold in the United States, and the glasses were too small for a society that fills them full of ice.[38] After making the necessary design adjustments and decentralizing more of the decision making to local management, the firm has done well. As it opens stores in China, it has decided to moderate its standardized global marketing approach. The basic modern design is still there, but the furniture has had to be redesigned to fit the realities of local usage situations.

Although firms need to recognize that they may have to redesign their products and use different distribution and selling approaches in foreign markets, the basic benefit sought by the consumer is often the same. For example, P&G has a 57 percent share of the shampoo market in the three major Chinese cities where market-share studies have been undertaken, even though it is three times as expensive as local brands.[39] The reason is that dandruff is a problem in a nation of black-haired people, and P&G's Head and Shoulders, introduced in China in 1988, is the most effective antidandruff shampoo. P&G's Pert, with an added antidandruff additive (called Rejoice in China), also has sold well and has the most popular ads on Chinese television. P&G used tens of millions of free samples in launching its shampoos (because shampoo is an "experience" product, it needs trials to establish its superior performance). The company also cleverly ran a cooperative promotion program with washing-

[38] "Furnishing the World," *The Economist*, November 19, 1994, 79–80.
[39] Joseph Kahn, "P&G Viewed China as a National Market and Is Conquering It," *The Wall Street Journal*, September 12, 1995, 1, A6.

Table 5.8 Earth's Three Socioecological Classes

OVERCONSUMERS 1.1 BILLION >US $7,500 PER CAPITA (CARS; MEAT; DISPOSABLES)	SUSTAINERS 3.3 BILLION US $700–$7,500 PER CAPITA (LIVING LIGHTLY)	MARGINALS 1.1 BILLION <US $700 PER CAPITA (ABSOLUTE DEPRIVATION)
Travel by car and air	Travel by bicycle and public surface transport	Travel by foot, maybe donkey
Eat high-fat, high-calorie, meat-based diets	Eat healthy diets of grains, vegetables, and some meat	Eat nutritionally inadequate diets
Drink bottled water and soft drinks	Drink clean water, plus some tea and coffee	Drink contaminated water
Use throwaway products and discard substantial wastes	Use unpackaged goods and durables and recycle wastes	Use local biomass and produce negligible wastes
Live in spacious, climate-controlled, single-family residences	Live in modest, naturally ventilated residences with extended/multiple families	Live in rudimentary shelters or in the open; usually lack secure tenure
Maintain image-conscious wardrobe	Wear functional clothing	Wear secondhand clothing or scraps

SOURCE: Based on Alan Durning, *How Much Is Enough*, Worldwatch Institute, 1993.

machine manufacturers, giving away free boxes of its Tide laundry detergent to buyers of washing machines (laundry detergent is also an "experience" product that needs trials to penetrate a market).

An example of cross-cultural global segmentation is presented in Table 5.8. Environmentalists use this to demonstrate the consequences of rising standards of living that move more "sustainers" into the "overconsumer" segment. It will lead to an increase in global warming and a rapid depletion of crucial scarce resources such as timber and oil.[40]

Perhaps one of the more unique problems facing American firms in dealing with global consumer behavior is the reaction of distinctly different cultures to the encroachment of American culture. For example, the Islamic religion has dominated and enriched civilizations for centuries. But some factions of Islam are going through a period of hatred and violence directed at the United States. The global appeal of American products is a threat to some:

> It should by now be clear that we are facing a mood and a movement far transcending the level of issues and policies and the governments that pursue them. This is no less than a clash of civilizations—the perhaps irrational but surely historic reaction of an ancient rival against our Judeo-Christian heritage, our secular present, and the worldwide expansion of both. . . . From constitutions to Coca-Cola, from tanks and

[40] Alan Durning, *How Much is Enough*, Worldwatch Institute, 1993.

> television to T-shirts, the symbols and artifacts, and through them the ideas, of the West have retained—even strengthened—their appeal.[41]

Companies and their global marketing decision-making teams are becoming increasingly aware that while segments of foreign cultures, particularly the young in Asia, South America, and the Middle East, are enthusiastic consumers of American culture, other segments, particularly the elderly or deeply religious, are quite antagonistic toward the effects of American influences on their culture. This creates special marketing segmentation problems in such countries.

Discussion Questions and Minicases

1. Imagine that your first assignment on your new job is to create a segmentation model for your firm's major service market. You spend four weeks working through piles of secondary data and old market research and talking to industry experts, sales managers, and distributors. Halfway through your presentation to the senior executive team and other junior marketing and operation's executives, it is evident that you have lost control of the presentation. A vigorous, sometimes heated discussion about market segmentation ensues among the executives in your audience. You have a sinking feeling in your stomach, but it is quickly replaced by exaltation. Why did you have the sinking feeling, and why is it replaced by a feeling of exaltation?
2. Figure 5.2 illustrates several very different lifestyle vehicles. Imagine you are working for an auto company and you decide that one way to really make your point about lifestyle segmentation is to ask your colleagues to imagine what sort of music would be played on the sound systems in each of the cars. What would be your guess? How might such judgments be used to gain a competitive advantage?
3. What evidence is there in Table 5.1 that the Ford Motor company used a socioeconomic market segmentation model to developing its Model T product line? Can you see any evidence of lifestyle segmentation as well?
4. The basic psychological theory used in Figure 5.3 to analyze demand structure is that behavior results from the interactions between individuals and the different situations they face. Buying behavior is a function of the person times the situation [$B = F(P \times S)$]. This is called Lewinian Field theory. Individual differences that we are born with (nature) or are the result of our unique life experiences (nurture) determine how we view our physical and social situations and how we behave in each situation. We do things for a purpose, and it is our values and beliefs that give direction to our buying behavior. Thus differences in beliefs and values explain why consumers behave differently. What are the implications of this theory for market segmentation?
5. Market researchers undertook a test to determine how different variables affected the explanation and segmentation of demand.[42] Of the 37 product-markets studied, the benefits consumers wanted from a product was the most important purchasing factor in 19 of the markets, product beliefs were most important in 15 of the markets, and the consumer's lifestyle was most important in only 3 of the markets. How do these results support the mental model presented in Figure 5.3? What is fundamentally wrong with the test?
6. In the box on benefit segmenting, why do you think lower than average income users preferred the more expensive food processor?
7. The twentieth century has seen a radical change in home economics brought about not just by the many laborsaving appliances but also by numerous food-preparation and cleaning innovations. Many older people alive today can still remember their

[41] Bernard Lewis, "The Roots of Muslim Rage," *The Atlantic Monthly*, September 1990, 47–60.
[42] Russell I. Haley, "Benefit Segmentation—20 Years Later," *Journal of Consumer Marketing* (1986): 5–13.

grandmothers hand-washing clothes, making home preserves, and even stoking a wood-burning stove and buying ice. Why is it safe to predict that the changes in household products and consumption over the next few decades will not be nearly as great? What impact will this slowdown have on brand loyalty?

8. At what market segment is the *Reader's Digest* advertisement above aimed? Do you think it is effective?
9. Some futurists are paid large fees to give speeches about how technology will change transportation, housing, leisure, food, and health care over the next twenty years. Make your predictions (in less than two hundred words) for each of these markets.
10. An association of peach growers in Georgia has requested your help with a marketing campaign aimed at increasing the consumption of peaches among young, upscale adults, particularly university students. The association figures that fruit consumption habits, once established, tend to continue for life. How might you segment the students' consumption of fruit into three usage situations? How would you guess the following fruits would be ranked in terms of popularity in each of the usage situations: apples, bananas, grapes, kiwifruit, oranges, peaches, plums, and strawberries? Would you agree

that fruit preferences, once established in early adulthood, do not change very much? Think of your parents' or grandparents' tastes.

11. The advertisement above is for a line of multivitamins targeted to different users. Identify the unique benefits each formula is meant to satisfy. Is there a user segment that is missing? Why might it be difficult to sell such a line to a family?

12. The household cleaner market has been segmented into distinct usage situations, with different brands and products serving each situation. List all of the uses. Why has such niche marketing worked? Why do households now have four to five bottles under the sink when they once only had one? What trend helps explain this phenomenon?

13. The following is a rather simple example that illustrates a typical information processing choice rule. Let us imagine that two consumers are interested in buying a pair of running shoes. A is an overweight yuppie who has been told to exercise. B is a lean, serious runner. They consequently rate the importance of the choice attributes of running shoes differently (see table on page 203). Buyer A emphasizes comfort and appearance while buyer B emphasizes comfort and functional performance characteristics.

Three alternative shoes, X, Y, and Z, and their ratings on each of the attributes by the magazine *Runner's World* are also presented in the following table:
Predict which shoes A and B would choose. What if they chose based on value for their money? What if B would not buy a shoe that did not rate high on comfort? What if A could only afford a $30 shoe?

14. Some experts believe that benefit segmentation does not work with fantasy feeling goods. What segmentation approach might you use for a women's fragrance?

	IMPORTANCE WEIGHT (LOW 1 ⟵⟶ 10 HIGH)		RATED PERFORMANCE OF SHOE (LOW = 1, AVG. = 2, HIGH = 3)		
FEATURES	BUYER A	BUYER B	X	Y	Z
Comfort	10	10	Avg.	High	Avg.
Appearance	10	2	Avg.	High	High
Durability	7	5	High	Avg.	Low
Shock absorbency	5	10	High	Avg.	Low
Arch support	5	10	High	Avg.	Low
Price			$50	$50	$25

15. How might you use the belief measures in Figure 5.6 to segment retail store patronage? Construct potential segments.

16. What are the implications of the shopping model in Figure 5.8 for retailers and manufacturers?

17. Why might it be a good idea for Ford to buy a toy company and make and market toy models of its cars?

18. How good are you at intuitively matching food preference with demographics? On the left of the table on page 204 are the demographic descriptors of five segments in comparison to each other. On the right are the food preferences of the segments. Match up the food preferences (1–5) with the demographics (A–E) and name each segment.

19. From a market segmentation perspective, which is more effective and efficient: to offer advertising coupons to reduce the price of a product or to give a trade discount that results in a "sale" price? Hint: Review the definition of market segmentation, and think about who benefits from a sale price and how different buyers react to a sale price.

20. Executives involved in major equipment and material purchases often see things differently. Why should these different perspectives be expected? What motives and biases are frequently present in design engineers, production engineers, finance and accounting executives, senior management, and purchasing agents?

21. Computers and expert systems are automating routine buying. Orders are automatically placed with approved suppliers when buyer inventory levels drop to a minimum order level. Such automatic ordering systems have been operating successfully for a number of years in the hospital supplies, pharmaceutical, and book markets. Their ability to collect and analyze information, such as reject rates and on-time delivery, is incredible. Over the long term, how is such automation likely to affect marketing?

22. Often influential people within an organization have conflicting objectives and amicably disagree over the following questions:
a) Whose product, if any, is really superior?
b) Can a supplier's claims and promises be believed?
c) What is the added performance really worth to the organization?
d) What is wrong with accepting the low bid?
How do you think such uncertainty and disagreement influences how the organization makes its choice? What implications does this have for marketing?

23. Northern Telecom has developed single-sourcing partnerships that have resulted in a reduction of its previous order-delivery cycle by half, a 49 percent reduction in its

DEMOGRAPHIC DESCRIPTORS	FOOD PREFERENCES
A. Larger households More blue-collar workers From smaller towns More high school graduates Female head less likely to be employed	**1.** Fresh fruit Rice Natural cold cereal Wheat germ Yogurt Granola bars Bran/fiber bread
B. Below-average income More likely to be retired More nonwhite Older Fewer children More two-person households	**2.** Wine Mixed drinks Beer Butter Rye/pumpernickel bread Bagels Swiss cheese
C. More upper income More younger people More one-person households More college graduates More professionals More people from West Coast	**3.** Whole milk Pork Roast beef Boiled potatoes Gravy Pies
D. Below-average income Above-average age Fewer professionals More nonurban More nonwhite	**4.** Skim milk Diet margarine Salads Fresh fruit Sugar substitutes
E. Upper income More one-person households Fewer children under eighteen Female heads employed full time More college graduates More professionals and white-collar workers Larger cities	**5.** Lunchmeat sandwiches Hot dogs Soda pop Fruit drinks Spaghetti Pizza

inspection staff due to a higher quality incoming product, and a 97 percent reduction in shop floor problems caused by defective material.[43] Hearing about this, you decide to approach one of your major customers, Hewlett-Packard, with the notion of developing a similar sole sourcing relationship. You, however, will have to make H-P a deal it cannot refuse. What might it be?

24. Some companies have abandoned the centralized buying approach and have returned the purchasing responsibility to the line production managers who are responsible for quality and cost control. What are the advantages and disadvantages of such a move? What implications does it have for a seller?

25. A seller of computer software has had difficulty selling to a large company in an industry that is very close and traditional and in which everyone knows everyone else. It has sold its software to one of the major companies and is making good progress with several other accounts. How might the seller creatively use the social network in this market to make a breakthrough with this difficult customer?

[43] Roy Merrills, "How Northern Telecom Competes on Time," *Harvard Business Review* 67 (July/August 1989): 108–14.

26. When can market segmentation hurt a firm's competitive advantage? How must you consider competitors' behavior in segmenting a market?
27. International marketers are often concerned that the executives who are making decisions about what to sell and how to sell do not really understand consumer behavior in foreign markets. How might you test to see if this problem exists?

Don't worry because a rival imitates you. As long as he follows in your tracks he cannot overtake you.

Anonymous

"When you've got good, strong competition, you drive harder."

Roger Maris

CHAPTER SIX

Analyzing the Competition

In many markets today the focus of competition is among new manufacturing and distribution technologies. Short-term price competition often occurs, but the fierceness of the price competition is often driven by longer term technology trends in the market. In the television industry the high stakes competition is among High Definition Television (HDTV) technologies. Japanese and European high-tech firms have pursued one path, and they are now ahead, but it seems their path has a dead end. They have developed the existing analog technology to the point that the television picture is two-to-four-times sharper than current televisions. Japanese manufacturers are already making HDTV sets that cost several thousand dollars and are trying to sell the broadcast equipment. Thompson, the French firm that bought RCA from General Electric has received billions of dollars (yes, billions!) in grants from the French government to help it develop and market the analog technology.

The problem with the analog path is that in the late 1980s some U.S. high-tech companies were correct in assuming that digital technology would advance so rapidly that it would quickly surpass any analog HDTV in signal and definition quality (like digital tapes and discs compared to traditional tapes and records). But digital's added advantage is that it is also used to communicate among

computers, so digital HDTV is the future means for multimedia integration of sound, film, games, computing, systems controls, and two-way communication. Analog HDTV cannot compete against the versatility of digital signals. Fortunately, American technologists were confident enough to convince the Federal Communication Commission (FCC) not to approve a new analog HDTV standard (particularly, neither the Japanese nor European) for the domestic television market. With the rapid advances occurring in digital HDTV (particularly overcoming the amount of information that needs to be sent to create each picture), it is now clear that analog HDTV's time has come and gone, before it ever really became commercial. The losses of the Japanese and European companies that refused to see that digital technology was rapidly catching up can be put in the tens of billions. Included in this cost is their having to play catch-up to stay a player in the multimedia, electronic, global information transmission market. This market, incidentally, includes AT&T, MCI, Microsoft, IBM, Apple, and Sony—some tough competitors in converging technologies and markets.

The example demonstrates how U.S. high-technology leadership can still deliver. The rest of the world made the mistake of not betting on U.S. engineering ability to make the innovations in digital transmission and storage technology that would make digital HDTV possible. They underestimated the competitive rationality skills of U.S. high-technology enterprise and entrepreneurship. They may, however, soon exhibit their superior imitation skills, catch up quickly, and, in fact, surpass U.S. rivals in the quality and cost of their products and services. If they do, they will end up "winning," because most economic rent (higher-than-average profits) comes from serving the consumer best and having the lowest cost structures at the *peak* of market demand for a technology and its associated lines of products and not at the *early growth* stage of the technology's market. This chapter discusses how to analyze the competitive situation in a market, particularly the dynamics of technology trends and how and why the competitiveness of rivals' products, services, and processes is changing. ■

Competitiveness is how effective and efficient a firm is, relative to its rivals, at serving customers and resellers. Effectiveness has to do with the quality of products, market share, and profitability; efficiency has to do with response speed and low costs. Both effectiveness and efficiency ultimately depend on competitive rationality—the strength of the firm's competitive drives and its decision-making skills.

American firms have been exhorted by almost everyone—government agencies, associates overseas, and industry insiders, among others—to become more competitive. But becoming more competitive is like losing weight or converting fat to muscle. It is easy to talk about but not that easy to do. The task is almost impossible if it is not based on a thorough competitive analysis. The analysis should start with a general overview of the competitive structure and dynamics of the product market (see Figure 6.1). This includes a market-share analysis, a review of the history of the market, and a search for new competitors that threaten to drive existing firms and their products into extinction. The analysis should then zoom in on major rivals and their likely behavior.

It is surprising how often companies, even the best-run companies, take their eyes off the competition. Throughout the late 1970s and early 1980s, the DEC Vax computer architecture made major inroads to the mid-range computer market previously dominated by IBM. It took until 1986 for IBM to set up a task force (with its own war room) to really respond to DEC. By then it was too late: The new unrecognized threat was networkable PCs, a threat that both IBM and DEC did not respond to sufficiently.

One problem with talking about competitiveness is that Americans have ambivalent attitudes toward it. We admire competitiveness in sport but often disparage it in the classroom. American executives often expend all their energy fiercely competing with each other for promotions (see Figure 6.2). Another problem is that management can sometimes become more fixated on the competition than on staying close to their customers. A competitive orientation involves understanding the competition and gaining advantage from exploiting their weaknesses. It does *not* mean attacking the competition at every opportunity, no matter what the cost.

Market Structure

The first question almost every company asks in its decision-making process is who are the major players in the market; that is, who has what share of the market? Market share is measured as a percentage of total industry sales over a specified time period. About 70 percent of the companies in the *1990 Conference Board* study tracked their competitors' market shares. The reasons are fairly obvious. Because market share identifies who the major players are, changes in market share identify who has become more or less competitive in the marketplace, that is, who has gained share from whom.

But first the meaning of "the market" must be decided. Clearly, problems in defining the market exist. A company's market share can change dramatically depending on whether the market is defined as global, a particular export market, the U.S. market, a region of the United States, a city, or a segment of users or usage. The scope of the market is normally specified by a realistic assessment of company resources and by company growth objectives. Operationally, the market is often specified by the way market researchers are able to collect sales and market-share information.

Some of the different types of markets a product competes in are illustrated in Figure 6.3. The closest and most immediate competition comes from rivals' products targeted at the same segment that share similar, specific design features (e.g., a twelve-ounce can of diet cola). The cross-price elasticity is going to be greatest among almost identical substitutes. Cross-price elasticity is high between A and B when a change in the price of A has a significant effect on sales of B. The next level of product category competition comes from products that share some similar features (e.g., soft drinks).

Figure 6.1 **Chapter Organization**

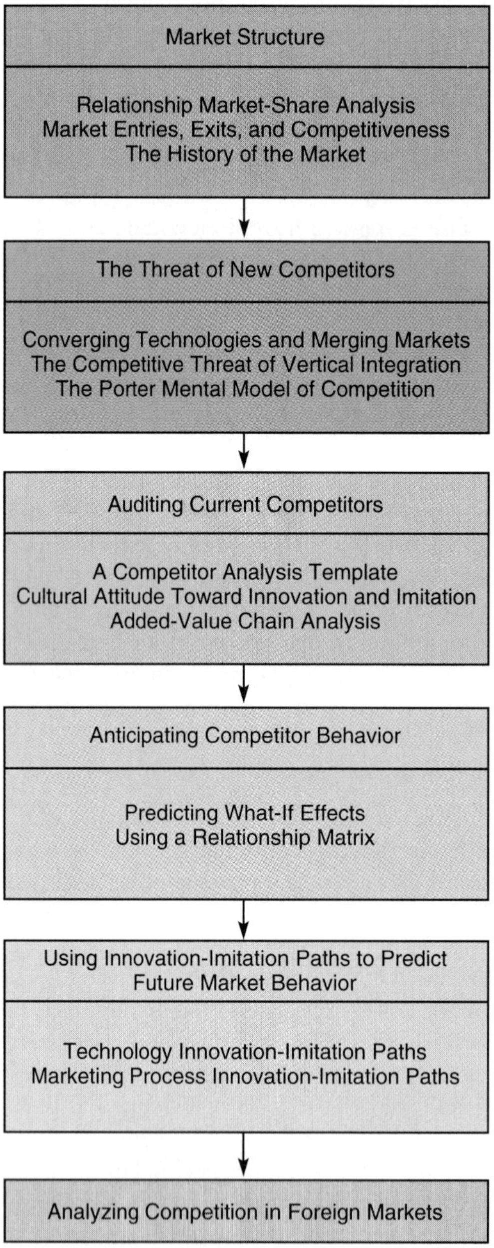

This chapter starts by defining what is a market, how to measure some aspects of the structure of the market and describe its history. Discussion then turns to identifying and analyzing new and current competitors. The second half of the chapter focuses on understanding how these competitors are likely to behave in the future and, by studying path dependencies, how to determine what are likely to be the competitive drivers of the market in the future. The chapter closes with a brief discussion of some of the unique problems of analyzing competition in foreign markets.

Figure 6.2 **The Wrong Sort of Competitive Outlook**

Chapter 9 introduces product positioning maps that identify similar brands and product forms by the specific usage benefits they provide. More general competition comes from products that satisfy a core benefit (e.g., thirst quenching or pick-me-up drinks). The most distant competition is for consumers' discretionary spending. At this level a new car may compete against a new deck for the house or an overseas trip.

The historical problem with analyses of market structure has been too much reliance on market statistics, such as number of current competitors, concentration of market share (the combined market share of the largest three competitors), and current balance-sheet assets of major competitors. The emphasis needs to be on market dynamics, such as who is introducing new manufacturing, distribution, and product development processes into the market? Competitive insight comes from explaining such drivers of success in the market and not from knowing who has the largest market share. The acid test for such insight is whether an executive wants to know what company has the largest market share (he or she is a static thinker) or what company has experienced the largest charge in market share (he or she is a dynamic thinker). Does the firm study the history of change in the industry to identify the regularities in changing supply to further identify which paths the market will take in the future (i.e., production and distribution technological paths)? A dynamic analyst is thus able to identify what and who are the drivers of change in the market. Recall the propositions from the theory of competitive rationality. Changes in the economic process change the economic structure. Study the changes in the economic processes in the market to understand what the drivers of competition are, which competitors will survive, which companies will die, and which companies will dominate.

In short, do not spend time working out to the last share point (1 percent of market share) what the market share is because defining the exact bounds of the market is seldom that precise. Instead, spend the funds finding out which established competitor

Figure 6.3 **Examples of Levels of Competition**

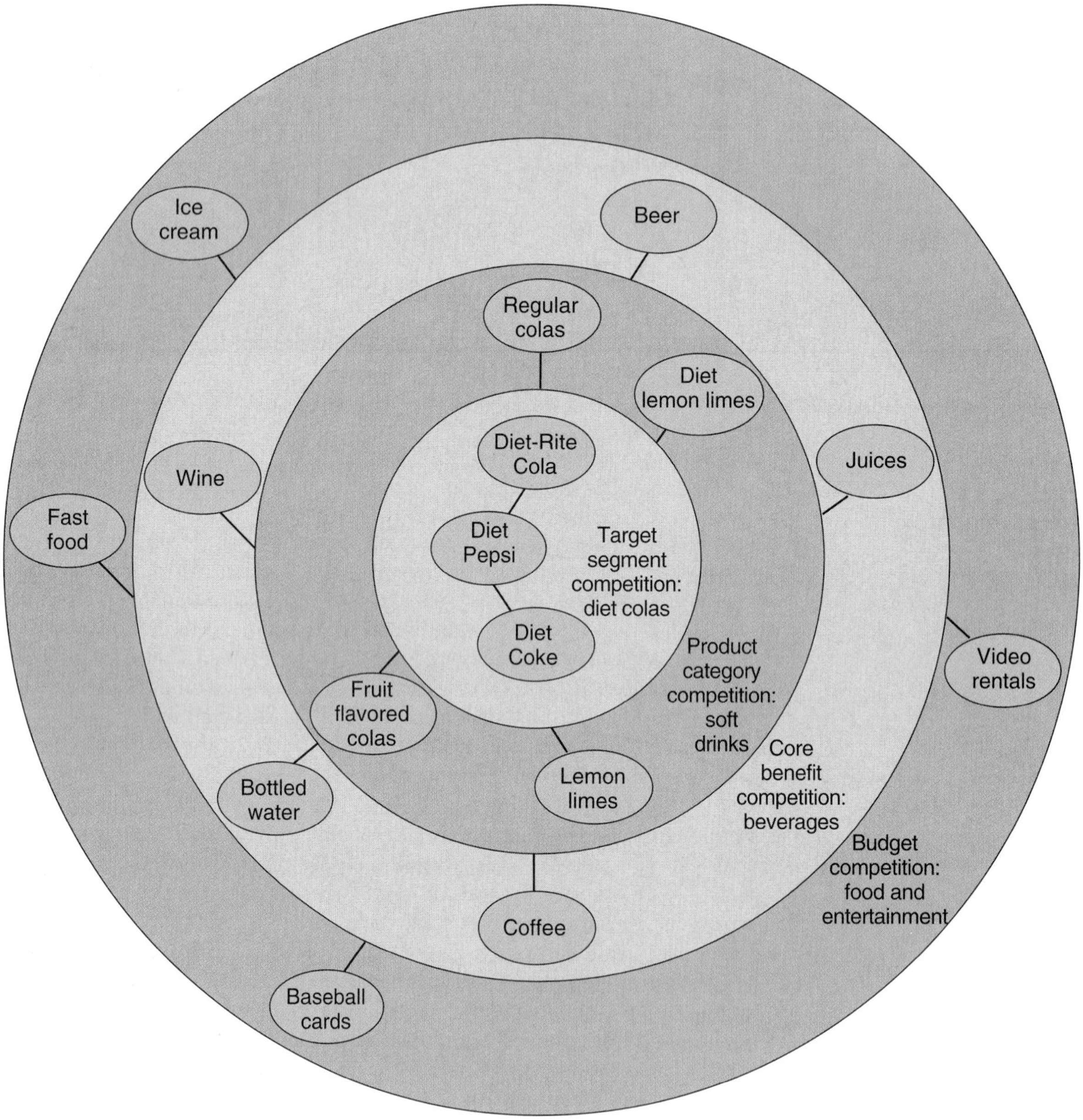

Adapted from Donald R. Lehmann and Russell S. Winer, *Analysis for Marketing Planning* (Homewood, IL; Irwin, 1991), p. 22. Most managers just consider their segment or product category competition and are sometimes blindsided by the success of less direct competition (e.g., bottled water and iced tea's effect on diet cola sales).

or new start-up is using radical new product or process technology to increase customer satisfaction and reduce costs. The history of technology suggests that such small companies often revolutionalize a market:[1]

> Mueller and Tilton . . . contend that a new industry is created by the occurrence of a major process or product innovation and develops technologically as less radical innovations are introduced. They further argue that the large corporation seldom provides its people with incentives to introduce a development of radical importance: thus these changes tend to be developed by new entrants without an established stake in a product market segment. In their words, neither large absolute size nor market power is a necessary condition for successful competitive development of most major innovations. (P. 88) . . . We have seen that most firms look in exactly the wrong places for vital signs of technological change: namely their universe of traditional rivals. Large and similar competitors are the focus today of vigorous benchmarking efforts by many firms. Benchmarking is an excellent source of information to guide evolutionary change and continuous improvement, but probably a poor source for signals of discontinuities. Looking toward more obscure new entrants and unconventional sources of competition is more fruitful. (P. 220)

For example, the typewriter was invented by Christopher Sholes, working in Milwaukee as a civil servant and not for a printing or publishing company. The electric typewriter was developed and enhanced by IBM and not by Remington or Underwood, the market leaders in manual typewriters. In turn, it was Wang and Apple, rather than IBM, who developed the computer word processing and desktop publishing market.

The change in market share over time is a vital indicator of competitive dynamics during the growth stage of a product market. It indicates whether a firm is ahead, abreast, or behind the market's total growth rate. Part of the reason Japanese companies are concerned about gaining market share is that they often compete in high-growth markets, and they understand that the growth stage is the crucial time to develop brand loyalty. For example, Japanese production of calculators grew two hundred times during the 1970s. A firm had to expand its sales by this multiple just to keep its market share—Casio raced ahead of its rivals and grew its market share from 10 percent to 35 percent.[2]

During a market growth stage, market share competitiveness really pays off. Having a large percentage of an infant market means having a lot of very little. In a mature market, it is often too expensive for firms to go after market share because every move draws fierce retaliation. The activity among firms during a growth stage is akin to the behavior of competing species when a new habitat has been discovered. The firm that "wins" multiples the fastest and establishes a dominant hold through new models that command different niches. In evolutionary theory this is called adaptive radiation.

However, market share dynamics are not the only measures of competitiveness. The following measures are often used as leading indicators of a likely change in future sales and profits.

---

[1] James M. Utterback, *Mastering the Dynamics of Innovation* (Cambridge, MA: Harvard Business School Press, 1994).

[2] Subrata N. Chakravarty, "Economic Darwinism," *Forbes*, October 6, 1986, 52–56; and J. W. Brittain and D. R. Wholey, "Competition Coexistence in Organizational Communities: Population Dynamics in Electronics Components Manufacturing," in *Ecological Models of Organizations*, ed. Glenn R. Carrol (Cambridge, MA: Ballinger, 1988).

1. *Mind share:* The percentage of customers who name the brand when asked to name the first brand that comes to mind when they think about buying a particular type of product. This indicates the consumer's top-of-mind brand awareness and preferences. How is it changing among different segments?
2. *Voice share:* The percentage of media space or time a brand has of the total media share for that industry, often measured simply as dollars spent on advertising. This is likely to lead to a change in mind share (but not always, if the messages are weak). How and why is it changing?
3. *R&D share:* A company's research and development expenditure as a percentage of the total industry R&D expenditure. This is a long-term predictor of new product developments, improvements in quality, cost reductions, and, hence, market share. It is an important measure of future competitiveness in many high-technology markets. How is it changing, and what is it being spent on?

Relationship Market-Share Analysis

Developing trading relationships and alliances have become an increasingly important marketing management activity. A new type of market share analysis measures the competitive importance and influence of *relationships* in a market. An example of a relationship matrix is presented in Table 6.1a.[3] Assume there are three major manufacturers: X, Y, and Z. Manufacturer X has a market share of 50 percent, Y has 30 percent, and Z has 20 percent of the sales in the product category. There are also five major resellers/distributors/retailers: A, B, C, D, and E. The resellers, in their sales of the product to the end user, have the following market shares: A has 50 percent, B has 20 percent, C has 10 percent, D has 10 percent, and E has 10 percent.

One way of appreciating the competitiveness of the relationships between the manufacturers and resellers is to estimate each relationship's market share. For example, the business that A and X do together (that is, A's sales of X's products) constitutes 20 percent of total market sales. Firm A might be the giant retailer Wal-Mart; X might be the giant laundry detergent manufacturer Procter & Gamble. X-A's market share would then be the estimated share of total laundry detergent sales that the Wal-Mart/P&G relationship has achieved. According to conventional economic theory, in Table 6.1a, X and A exercise countervailing power on each other and consequently make the market more competitive. The X-A relationship has a 20 percent market share, and this is matched by the equally large Y-A and X-B relationships. The remainder of the relationships are much smaller, and five potential relationships do not even exist.

The competitive situation, however, could be very different, even though the market shares of the manufacturers and retailers stay the same; that is, the market shares at the end of the rows and bottom of the columns are the same. What if 40 percent of the total market share was generated by the X-A relationship? In the situation illustrated in Table 6.1b, it is clear that rather than counterbalancing each other, seller X and reseller A are now in a position to work together to dominate the market with their pricing and marketing practices. This illustrates the importance of estimating the market share of relationships, rather than just measuring market share at the seller or reseller level.

[3] This discussion develops and extends the channel dependence matrix concept presented in Peter R. Dickson, "Distributor Portfolio Analysis and the Channel Dependence Matrix: New Techniques for Understanding and Managing the Channel," *Journal of Marketing* 47 (summer 1983): 35–44.

Table 6.1 Measuring Relationship Market Share Using the Relationship Matrix

Table 6.1a

Major Sellers		MAJOR RESELLERS A	B	C	D	E	SELLER'S SHARE
	X	20%[a]	20%	5%	0	5%	50%
	Y	20	0	5	5%	0	30
	Z	10	0	0	5	5	20
Reseller's Share		50%	20%	10%	10%	10%	100%

Table 6.1b

Major Sellers		MAJOR RESELLERS A	B	C	D	E	SELLER'S SHARE
	X	40%[a]	0	5%	0	5%	50%
	Y	10	10%	5	5%	0	30
	Z	0	10	0	5	5	20
Reseller's Share		50%	20%	10%	10%	10%	100%

[a] The term seller is used to describe a manufacturer or importer selling to a reseller who is a distributor, wholesaler, or retailer. The trading relationship X-A has a 20 percent share of the market. The business X does with A, and A with X, constitutes 20 percent of all of the sales of the product category. In some cases, it may be useful to group sellers and resellers into types rather than treat them as individual entities. The individual relationships are then aggregated into a set of relationships with some common characteristic.

A relationship matrix provides a foundation for developing a deeper understanding of competitive market structure. For example, in Table 6.1a, the trading relationship X-B, with a 20 percent market share, has presumably flourished because X and B have worked together to generate such sales. It may be relatively easy for B to switch to new sources of supply, but it is more likely B has built its reputation by selling manufacturer X's line exclusively. It would be expensive, in both effort and goodwill, to switch suppliers or to add another line. Distributor B is clearly very important to X, but X does have some alternative trading relationship options. Hence, it appears that B is relatively more dependent on X than X is on B. Of course, other issues may change this diagnosis, including sales of other product lines. Reseller B also may serve a special segment that cannot be reached any other way. Consequently, the competitive advantage provided by B to X is not readily substitutable. Further, X may highly value the exclusivity of B's buying, and hence X may be very responsive to any move B makes to introduce a competitive line. It also is important to look beyond market share and examine the profitability of the trading relationship for each party.

Despite these limitations, estimating the relationship matrix can be a good starting point for assessing the competitiveness of trading relationships. The relationship market share provides a lot more information than conventional seller and reseller market share data used to measure conventional market structures. It is also more important in determining long-term sales because the market share of a seller is the sum of its relationship market shares with resellers. Similarly, the market share of a reseller is the sum of its relationship market shares with sellers. It is therefore very important to understand how such relationships are changing. An example of a STRATMESH

2.0 Relationship Share Matrix that enables consideration of such issues is illustrated in Figure 6.4.

Market Entries, Exits, and Competitiveness

The dynamic effects of the entry of a new supplier or a new reseller also can be tracked in the relationship matrix just described to determine who is going to be hurt and who is going to be helped. This raises an important fact in the balance of power between suppliers and resellers: The entry of a new seller increases the power of resellers. First, it allows resellers to negotiate better terms as part of the price that the new supplier has to pay to enter an established distribution channel and to cover the increased effort and cost of adding the new line. Alternatively, resellers can discuss the situation with their current suppliers to explore ways to sweeten current trading relations to reduce the incentive for resellers to add the new supplier—a move that would clearly threaten the existing suppliers' sales to resellers.

The flood of manufacturing imports in recent years (particularly in the clothing industry) has not only taken market share away from domestic suppliers but also has enabled resellers to extract better terms. The net effect is that domestic suppliers are selling less and making even less on what they sell. A similar power shift can occur when the number of resellers shrinks because of mergers or failures. On the other hand, when the number of resellers increases or the number of independent suppliers is reduced, power will shift in favor of suppliers. For example, when Heinz finally gave up and pretty much turned over the canned soup market to the Campbell's Soup Company, power shifted dramatically in favor of Campbell's Soup.

The relative incidence of entries and exits over time at various trading levels of a supply chain (particularly between manufacturers and retailers) directly determines long-term shifts in power among levels in a channel. It leads to the renegotiation of contracts and terms that reflect the new power change. This power-shift theory of competitive dynamics makes the following arguments:

1. When a sellers' market becomes more competitive, the resellers, who are free to choose who to do business with, become more powerful. A sellers' market becomes more competitive with the entrance of new sellers or an increase in the production and distribution capacity of existing sellers.
2. When a sellers' market becomes less competitive, the resellers become less powerful. A sellers' market becomes less competitive by the exit of sellers, a reduction in production and distribution capacity, or the merger of current sellers, thus reducing the number of buyers.
3. Power is most effectively exercised at the time of a structural shift in the amount of competition in the sellers' or resellers' market.
4. The first three propositions also apply to changing competition among suppliers and manufacturers.

The History of the Market

A study of the recent history of the product market identifies the dimensions on which sellers have competed most strongly to serve the interests of the resellers and consumers. In some markets, this competition may have resulted in a price war. In others, sellers have competed with each other to improve product and service quality. Often, a technological improvement made by an innovator forces every competitor to respond. This occurred when Duracell introduced the alkaline battery. All of its competitors were forced to match the new technology.

Figure 6.4 **STRATMESH 2.0 Relationship Market Share Matrix**

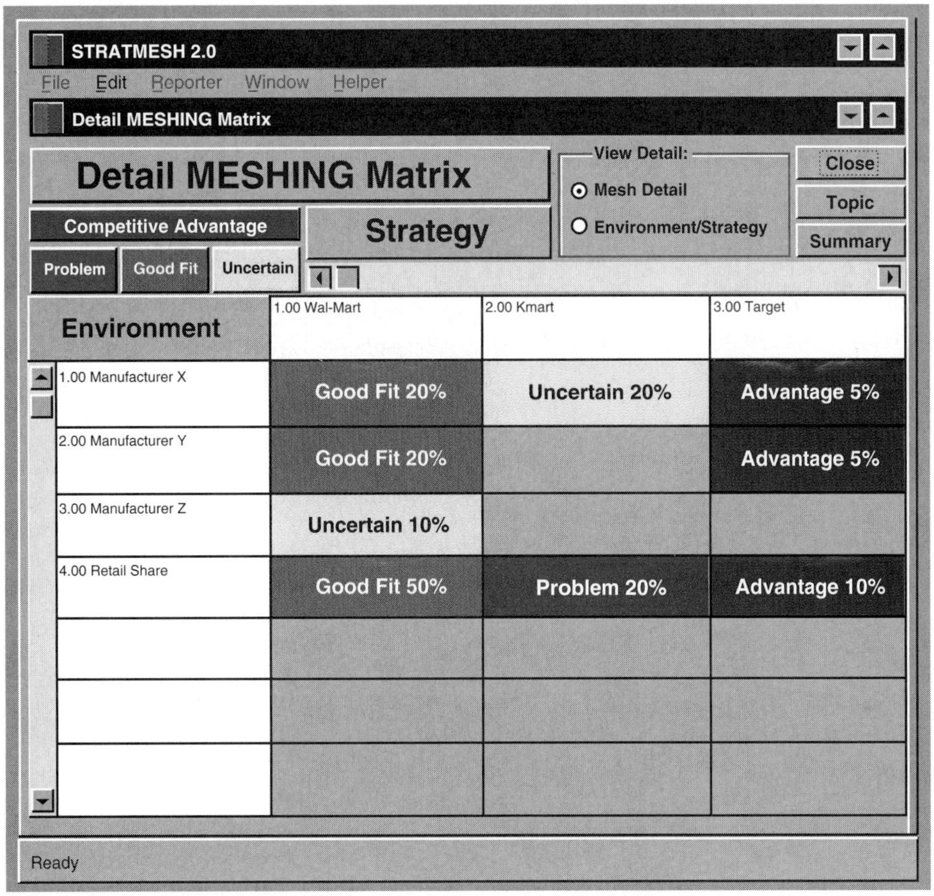

The above STRATMESH 2.0 template reproduces Table 4-1a. In the matrix the color stands for the direction that the relationship is going in and the percentage the current estimated market share of the relationship. For example, the trading relationship between Manufacturer X and Kmart has 20 percent of the market but the state of the relationship is somewhat uncertain. Clicking on the cell with the mouse will provide the explanation for this evaluation. The overall situation for Kmart is rated a problem because it does not have established trading relationships with Y and Z, and is, hence, in a precarious competitive situation in this market. This template allows the team to play what-ifs as discussed later in the chapter.

The study of competition as a process, a series of events over time, tells a lot more about the dynamics of the marketplace than a single here-and-now snapshot view that is assumed, often incorrectly, to describe the market in equilibrium.[4] The Rationality in Practice box titled "Waking up a Sleeping Giant" describes such a process. The history of the product market is seldom recorded. It is often carried around in the heads of experienced executives, and the invaluable insights they can provide are lost when they retire.

[4] Richard N. Langlois, ed., *Economics as a Process* (Cambridge: Cambridge University Press, 1986). This view of competition is more consistent with the theory of competitive rationality than conventional economic static-equilibrium theory.

Rationality in Practice

Waking up a Sleeping Giant

When Philip Morris bought the Miller Brewing Company, it intended to shake down what it saw as a sleepy product market. It did change the rules of competition in the industry, but it did so in ways that it did not and could not have anticipated. In the end, it was Anheuser-Busch who proved to have the better marketing plan.

Behind the beguiling appeal of the television beer advertisements, a knock-down-drag-out fight for market share and profits has been going on for more than a decade. Beer prices have fallen, and advertising agencies have been changed frequently. The big winner by far has been Anheuser-Busch, whose market share rose from 25 percent in 1978 to 40 percent in 1988. Miller Brewing Company, which started the new marketing era with its intensive advertising of Miller Lite, went from a 19 percent to a 21 percent market share over the decade. Schlitz, Stroh's, G. Heileman, and dozens of regional breweries have been the big losers.

Beer is a mature market, and the changing demographics are against it. The postwar baby boomers have grown out of the heavy beer-drinking stage. Wine coolers have cut into beer's summer sales. Fitness and nutritional awareness has resulted in a reduction in beer bellies. Tougher drinking and driving laws and an increase in the legal drinking age to twenty-one in most states (in part from a federal threat to withhold highway construction subsidies) have also taken their toll. In 1972, Miller got a jump on the competition by launching its very successful Lite beer and later its classic TV-sports advertising campaign. Until that time, Schlitz had been the most profitable brewery, with its emphasis on cost control, but it had become too greedy and had begun reformulating its beer using cheaper ingredients. The consumer noticed the change about the time Miller launched its marketing offensive.

Anheuser, crippled by a ninety-day strike, was also temporarily stopped in its tracks. But over the next five years the Budweiser ad budget was tripled, and the company sponsored, and dominated, every sporting niche it could. The strategy worked brilliantly. The slogan "This Bud's for You" matched the appeal of the "Miller Time" and the humorous old jocks claiming "Great taste, less filling" in the Miller Lite ads. A network of efficient refrigerated warehouses also gave Bud the best distribution system in the country, and a new generation of management, led by August Busch III, has had a lot to do with Anheuser's current success. The new managers have proven to be excellent hands-on marketing planners and implementers. They face a new challenge, however, in combating the Microbrews with their unique and fresh tastes.

SOURCES: G. Bruce Knecht, "How Bud Won the Battle," *Dun's Review*, February 1982, 83–85; "A Shrinking Market Has Beermakers Brawling," *Business Week*, August 20, 1984, 59, 63; and William Dunn, "Where the Beer Industry is Heading," *American Demographics*, February 1986, 37–39.

An industry often has standard marketing tactics and rules that are universally adopted. Examples are certain formulas for cost-plus pricing and spending a certain percentage of the previous year's sales on advertising in the next year. Sales force commissions and incentives are also often standardized in an industry. These rules of doing business make the market more predictable and stable. If the market "learns" and has over time been moved by competitive innovation toward more efficient ways of making and marketing its products, then these rules and processes should reflect such learning and, hence, make sense.

Knowing how and why standard industry practices and decision rules came about enables a firm to better understand whether the rules are based on competitive logic or whether they have simply become "established" practice to keep from rocking the boat.[5] If they are based on logic, then a competitor can better understand what works and what does not in the marketplace and why. However, if the rules are based on old-fashioned agreements to restrain competition, then violating them represents an opportunity for the aggressive firm.

[5] Gloria P. Thomas and Gary F. Soldow, "A Rules-Based Approach to Competitive Interaction," *Journal of Marketing* 52 (April 1988): 63–74.

Figure 6.5 **The Technological S-Curve**

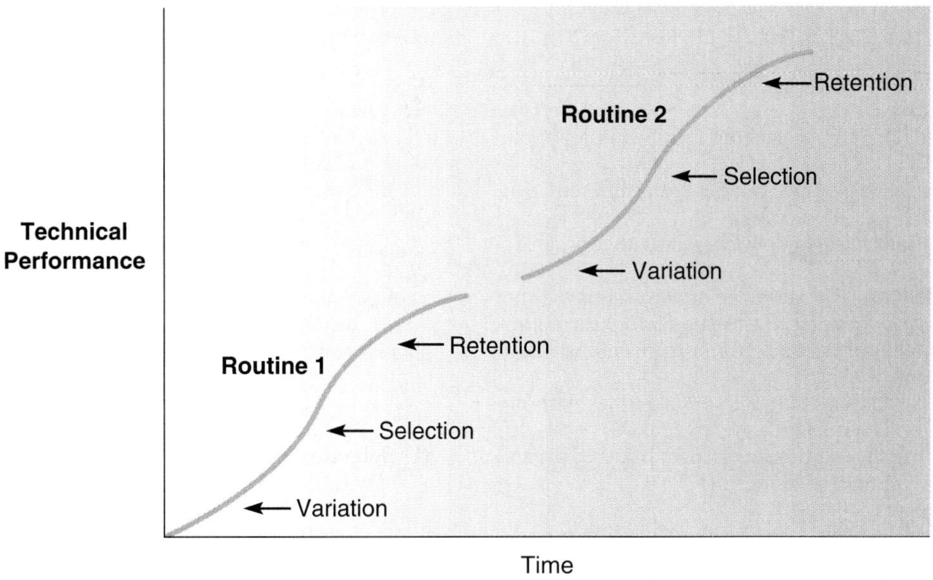

A market advances over time by several firms testing different innovation in products and processes (variation). The firms then learn which products and processes are best (selection); imitate and refine them, and the product or process becomes standardized (retention). Some time later another burst of innovation in some other product or process leads to another population learning cycle. In reality such innovation/imitation cycles will often overlap or occur in parallel.

In many of the examples of innovative marketing tactics described later in this textbook, the innovator often profits from breaking the established rules of doing business. These risk-taking, new entrants often have little regard for the old rules of the game.

The change in nature and mix of organizational processes among suppliers that results from innovation/imitation is called *population-level learning*.[6] As illustrated in Figure 6.5, organizational processes such as that the airlines use to reward frequent flyers (frequent-flyer promotion programs) follow a path called a *technological S-curve.* In the beginning a variety of programs were offered to frequent-flyer business customers. Different airlines used different programs (processes), which were advanced with innovations such as the issuing of a plastic card, more attractive incentive programs, and targeted mailings based on analysis of customer data that identify key customers. Over time, the different airlines learned from each other more efficient operational and marketing processes and abandoned their less-effective frequent-flyer program processes for better ones. After this selection phase, airlines are now trapped. None have a significant competitive advantage in their frequent-flyer programs, yet

[6] Anne S. Miner and Pamela R. Haunschild, "Population Level Learning," *Research in Organizational Behavior* 17 (1995): 115–66.

Table 6.2 Examples of Variation, Selection, and Retention Processes in Population Learning

POPULATION-LEVEL LEARNING THROUGH ORGANIZATIONAL INTERACTION

I. Variation Processes
- A. Organizations recombine existing routines in a population
  - 1. Organizations combine routines from different consultants
  - 2. Organizations miscopy routines from other organizations
- B. Organizations copy routines from organizations in other populations (routines new to this population) through
  - 1. Blind copying of routines from organizations in different populations
  - 2. Selective imitation—copying only routines with apparent "good" outcomes
  - 3. Making inferences from experiences of other organizations to generate new routines

II. Selection Processes
- A. Multiple organizations copy routines already in a population, resulting in increased prevalence (selection) of those routines. Copying occurs through
  - 1. Blind copying of routines from organizations in same population
  - 2. Selective imitation—copying only routines with apparent "good" outcomes
  - 3. Making common inferences from experiences of others
- B. Broadcast transmission
  - 1. Single organization disseminates routines to others
- C. Competition among firms
  - 1. Market impact of routines leads many firms to drop or add them
- D. Collaboration among firms
  - 1. Collaboration produces market impact, leading to selection of routine
- E. Definitional processes
  - 1. Case law develops over time, defining permissible/nonpermissible routines in specific context
- F. Exogeneous shocks permit some routines to survive
  - 1. Marxist revolution enhances presence of collective routines

III. Retention Processes
- A. Individual organizations depend on others that demand certain routines
  - 1. Supplier/buyer relationship where buyer demands supplier conform to ISO9000 standards
- B. Interdependent nature of technology generates high switching costs
- C. Routines become part of "take-for-granted" norms

POPULATION-LEVEL LEARNING THROUGH POPULATION-LEVEL PHENOMENA

I. Variation Processes
- A. Collective deliberate experiments to produce new organizational routines
- B. Creation of new population-level routines
  - 1. Group of firms creates new collective action like a standards board, a trade association, a research consortia, or collusive pricing
- C. Populations copy routines from other populations through
  - 1. Copying population-level routines from other populations
  - 2. Making inferences from experiences of other populations to generate new routines (not just copying)

II. Selection Processes
- A. Trial-and-error learning by populations
  - 1. Established firms acquire, copy, or raid personnel after observing period of start-up efforts
- B. Competition among populations
  - 1. Populations and their routines systematically fail or thrive as a result of competition
- C. Cooperation among populations
  - 1. Populations and their routines systematically fail or thrive due to cooperation
- D. Deliberate adoption of standards
  - 1. Industry adopts technical standards
  - 2. Industry adopts quality standards
- E. Exogenous shocks yield new mix of routines
  - 1. Marxist revolution enhances collective organizations, extinguishing capitalist routines through selective retention of organizations

III. Retention Processes (apply to organization-level or population-level routines)
- A. Deliberate collective enforcement of previously adopted technological or quality standards
  - 1. Industry enforcement of technological standards such as ISO9000
- B. Deliberate collective enforcement of administrative routines
  - 1. Industry enforcement of routines such as safety standards
- C. Routines become part of "take-for-granted" norms
  - 1. Routines become part of standard industry practice assumed by banks, lenders, clients
- D. High switching costs
  - 1. Established coordination methods continued across firms, such as distribution relationships and organizational processes

SOURCE: Anne S. Miner and Pamela R. Haunschild, "Population Level Learning," *Research in Organizational Behavior* 17 (1995), 115–66.

they dare not discard them. The potential loss of goodwill among their heavy users forces them to retain the programs. The newest innovation is cross-promotion with other services and businesses. Currently, much variation and experimentation with the ways airlines will reward consumers with "earned miles" is occurring. Over time this is likely to settle down as airlines discover which cross-promotions actually achieve their goals of attracting new customers or increasing existing customer loyalty and which cross-promotions are not worth the effort. Some of the many ways population-level learning occurs in a market are presented in Table 6.2. The use of learning paths to understand the history of the market can also be used to predict the future of the market as discussed at the end of the chapter.

The Threat of New Competitors

Once established in an industry, a firm must extend its vigilance beyond its current competitors and identify potential competitive threats. The first question the established firm must ask is How difficult is it to enter this product market? Economists have analyzed this difficulty in terms of barriers to entry. Barriers to entry are created by the existing advantages of established competitors. Table 6.3 lists twelve barriers to entry and examples of individual firms whose strengths (sustainable competitive advantages) create such barriers.

In a sense a barrier to a market entry is a driver of competition in that market because it confers a major competitive advantage to the firm or firms that hold one of the barriers/advantages listed in Table 6.3. The way such firms use their advantage drives their competitiveness. Furthermore, a new competitor must find another driver of competition that will more than compensate for the existing supplier advantages.

Sometimes *entry* barriers appear to be overwhelming, until newcomers recognize that a barrier has two sides. Huge investments in particular raw-material resources,

Table 6.3 **Different Types of Barriers to Product Market Entry**

These barriers to entry are often the core competencies of the leading firms that are seemingly sustainable competitive advantages.

1. Economies of scale and scope in research—Boeing (aerospace and defense contracts).
2. Economies of scale and scope in production—General Electric (lightbulbs).
3. Economies of scale and scope in distribution logistics—Anheuser-Busch (beer).
4. Locked in distribution channels—General Motors (car dealerships).
5. Advertising expenditure—Procter & Gamble (laundry).
6. Proprietary patents—Polaroid (instant photography); proprietary processes—Bausch & Lomb (contact lenses).
7. Ownership of raw materials—Exxon (oil reserves).
8. Location advantages—McDonald's (fast food).
9. Government regulation—utilities and television cable companies.
10. Management expertise—Merck (pharmaceutical).
11. Customer switching costs—General Dynamics (nuclear submarines).
12. Brand franchises (customer loyalty)—IBM (computers).

processes, distributors, and consumer goodwill also can become barriers to an existing competitor's *mobility*—that is, its ability to change and adapt. The company is locked into a technology, a resource, or a brand image (for example, assets) that can only be used in a specific product market. The great nineteenth-century railway companies often have been criticized as myopic, as too production oriented, and for not noticing the threats posed by new technologies. They were constrained by the very resources that made them great—the thousands of miles of track and rail and their rolling stock and expertise in running a railway. How could they readily dispose of such assets and invest in trucking or aircraft? A forest products company that owns thousands of acres of forest must similarly grow and market forest products.

Consumer attitudes and habits also may pose a barrier to mobility. Banks have found it more difficult than expected to sell products such as insurance and airline tickets to their customers. Consumers see banks as banks. They want their bank to stick to providing safe investment returns, loans, and check-cashing services—not economy travel packages. Some other less-obvious barriers to mobility exist. For many years oil companies have possessed powerful franchised dealer networks, but this competitive advantage has constrained their ability to supply independents, who are often neighborhood competitors with their franchised dealers. AT&T faced a similar problem when it launched into the personal computer market. Not wanting to offend its telecommunications sales forces, AT&T was far too tentative in developing exclusive dealer relationships with computer and office equipment retailers. Some companies find their product differentiation and brand franchise both a tremendous advantage and a straitjacket. McDonald's will be forever constrained by its Ronald McDonald image. Billions of dollars of advertising spread over twenty years has firmly established McDonald's positioning in the American psyche. Other companies are constrained by fears that others will cannibalize their established products. IBM was so protective of its PC that it launched a PCjr that threatened neither its PC nor, for that matter, any rival's product.

While history has shown that some markets are very difficult to break into (for instance, the pharmaceutical and automobile markets) without considerable resources, this perceived difficulty can lead to dangerous complacency. These days, an aggressive new entrant can turn to many sources for resource assistance. Global suppliers and venture capitalists can assist overcoming any financial and production barriers. Even powerful distribution channels can sometimes be circumvented. Many small manufacturers are finding that specialist mail-order catalogs provide one way to launch a new product that department and chain stores will not touch until it has a proven sales record. New companies also can supply private-label and generic brands to retailers, thereby sidestepping the need to invest in a brand image and opening channels and shelf space that otherwise would be closed. Even regulations prohibiting entry can be outmaneuvered. Stockbrokers were able to offer a mutual fund with checking services by contracting banks to run the customer accounts while they operated the investment portfolio.

Also, increasing evidence shows a competitive trend that can be summed up by the phrase "marketing muscle in search of product markets." Consumer marketing firms such as R.J. Reynolds, Procter & Gamble, Gillette, and Campbell's Soup are stalking the marketplace looking for small companies with new products. They have superb distribution and marketing organizations, massive R&D resources, and access to enough funds to take a small company's product or service and roll it out nationally.

Figure 6.6

Federal Express's ill-fated ZapMail service never really caught on.

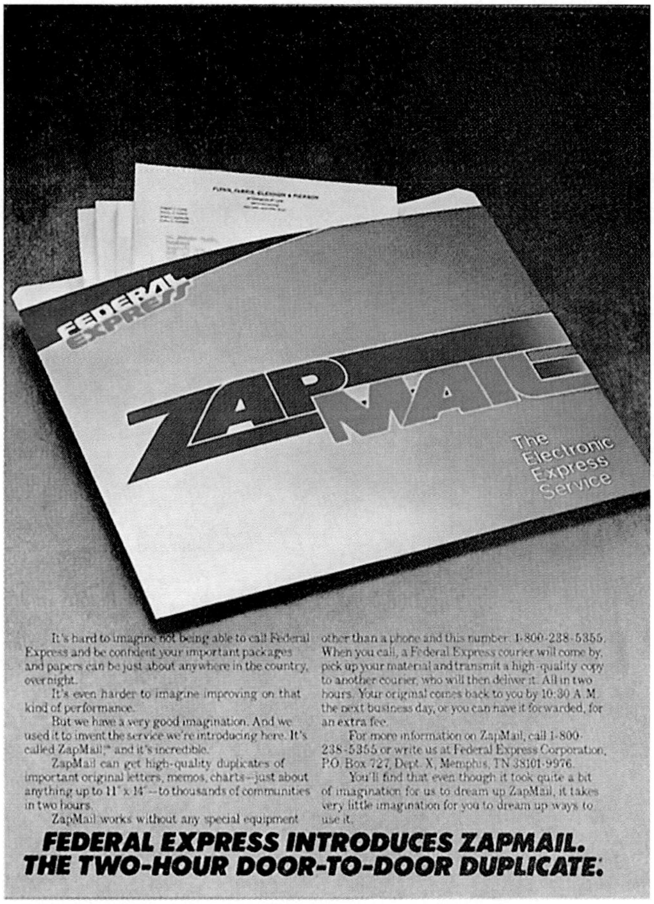

Converging Technologies and Merging Markets

In many markets today, new entries are often established companies with new technology that has expanded the boundaries of their traditional market.[7] The express-mail market is experiencing a clash among converting technologies. In 1974, Federal Express launched its overnight letter and package delivery service, which is now a $5 billion-plus market. Beyond its direct competition, such as the U.S. Postal Service, Federal Express faced threats from several other technologies. Western Union, the original telegraph company, launched an Easylink electronic mail service that could also converse with Telex, the long-established, conventional business-to-business electronic mail system. Easylink failed, but really serious threats were posed by the fax machine and the integration of telephone and computer systems that enabled organizations and individuals to create and operate their own electronic mail services. MCI has attempted to foster such networks. Ironically, Federal Express indirectly encouraged fax competition by developing a ZapMail service based on facsimile machines (see Figure 6.6). Although this service failed, it was meant to protect Federal Express

[7] This is akin to a species (firm) mutating (innovating) in such a way that it can flourish in a new habitat (market).

Figure 6.7

A Potential Supplier Becomes a Competitor

Federal Express's ZapMail faced a severe threat from the very fax machines that were used to provide the ZapMail service. Internet and Intranet electronic mail now challenges fax machines and Federal Express–type services.

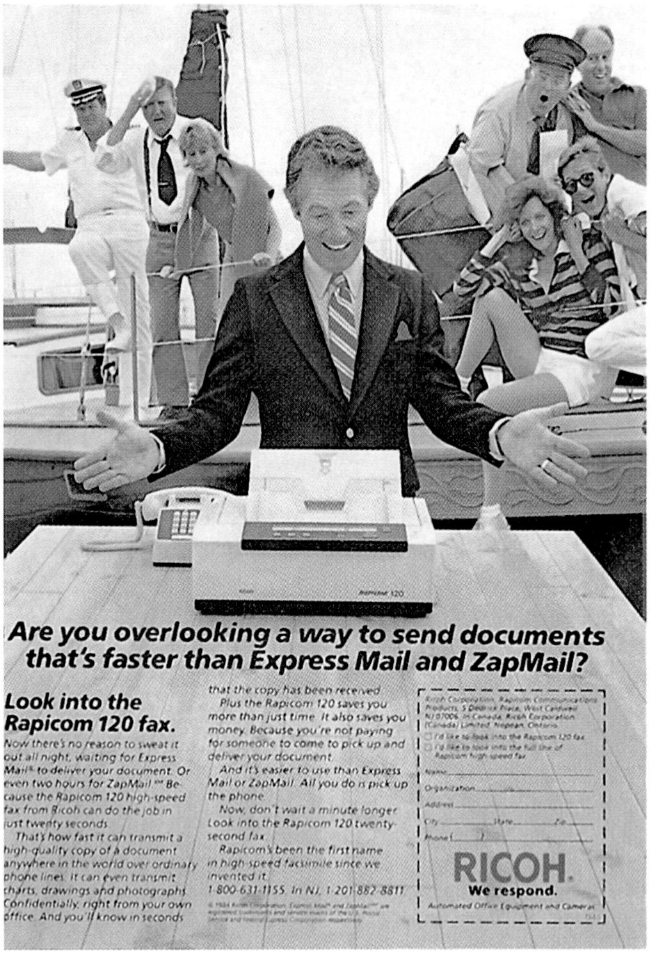

from the long-term threat of customers owning their own fax machines.[8] Instead, it helped manufacturers of facsimiles sell their product (see Figure 6.7).

The Competitive Threat of Vertical Integration

Sears Roebuck offers several case studies of how to enter markets by backward vertical integration. Its Craftsman tools, Kenmore appliances, DieHard batteries, and Roadhandler tires are leading national brands. It does not own any factories outright, but it has owned large shares of some of its suppliers. Sears's product development and testing labs have also produced more than one thousand patents since 1930.

Even distributors who do not undertake R&D or product development are often in a position to take advantage of the new ideas of small domestic or foreign manufacturers

[8] "The Zapping of Federal Express," *Newsweek*, October 13, 1986, 57; and John P. Tarpey, "Federal Express Tries to Put More Zip in ZapMail," *Business Week*, December 17, 1984, 110–11.

who are not adequately protected by patents or binding nondisclosure agreements. It is not unusual for even quite respectable retail chains or mail-order companies to take samples (requested for "testing" purposes) to another company and have it manufacture a "me-too" copy under the reseller's own private label.

Sears's startling aggressive move into the financial services industry was an example of innovative vertical integration.[9] Although considered a risky move by many, it was a natural extension of a long-established financial service. Sears has for decades been one of the biggest consumer credit-granting, and hence personal-financing, institutions in the United States. It was also one of the biggest insurance companies through its Allstate company, founded in 1931. The purchase of Dean Witter in 1981 and other financial-service acquisitions finally woke up the complacent banking industry. Sears became a major competitor in a new market that is merging banking, insurance, and investing: full-service personal finance management. Other players are the deregulated national and regional banks such as Citicorp and Ohio's Banc One, stockbrokers Merrill Lynch, and the credit card company American Express. This is another example of traditional boundaries collapsing and markets blending as the result of (1) deregulation, (2) breakthroughs in electronic banking and financial-services technology, (3) innovative products, and (4) vertical integration. This new financial market will produce a number of new and highly volatile competitive interfaces. One significant result may have already occurred. The new competition has hastened the extinction of the traditional savings and loan as an economic species.

Suppliers also may become competitors when they see opportunities for making higher returns by adding value themselves or when they become frustrated with distributor or customer behavior. An obvious example was the cloning of IBM personal computers by offshore component suppliers. Another example occurred in 1978, when Cuisinart launched its $140 food processor in the United States, a product actually made by French supplier Robot-Coupe. The Cuisinart was so successful that it attracted dozens of competitors who flooded the market with cheaper imitations. Cuisinart extended its product line by turning to a Japanese supplier who provided an even more competitive new product that was less expensive and offered more features. By 1980, the new Japanese model was outselling the original Robot-Coupe model. Unhappy with such sales cannibalization, Robot-Coupe launched its own distribution network and advertising campaign. The result was a nasty war of words in their advertising and a messy court case. Cuisinart's U.S. operation went bankrupt under Chapter 11 in 1992.

These examples clearly illustrate that a company must be on its guard against the new entrants from merging markets and from others up and down the channel. This concern is best addressed in the marketing plan by asking and answering the questions presented in Table 6.4. Such questions force a company to look beyond its traditional competitors. They also require the marketing decision maker to test the traditional assumptions about entry barriers, ask how they might be overcome, and determine who might do it.

---

[9] Steve Weiner, "The Rise of Discover," *Forbes*, May 4, 1987, 46–48; and John Heins, "Name Recognition," *Forbes*, November 30, 1987, 137.

Table 6.4 New Competitive-Threats Audit

The skill in identifying potential new competition is to ask a series of questions that narrows in on the most likely competitor and its situation.

NEW TECHNOLOGY—CONVERGING MARKETS THREAT

- What price changes in other technology markets appear to influence our sales? Is this effect changing?
- Which new technology or service is starting to be considered as a substitute for our product or service by consumers? Is this occurring in any particular usage situation or by any particular group of buyers? Are our existing channels encouraging such substitution?
- What is our closest new technological or service competition?
- Who is the major mover and shaker in this new industry?
- What appears to be its current objective and strategy?
- What is its growth rate?
- What has been its effect on our sales?
- What further threat does it pose?
- What constraints does it face?

CHANNEL INTEGRATION THREAT

- Which supplier is most likely to become a downstream direct competitor in the near future? Why? How would it do it? Is there any evidence of this occurring?
- Which customers are most likely to become upstream, do-it-themselves competitors in the near future? Why? How would they do it? Does any evidence of such plans exist?

COMPETITOR TAKEOVER—MERGER THREAT

- Which mergers, takeovers, or trading coalitions among competitors or from inside pose the greatest threat to our position? What evidence exists that this is likely to occur?

The Porter Mental Model of Competition

Michael Porter's pioneering text on competitive strategy changed the way many companies think about their competition.[10] Porter identified five forces that shape competition: current competitors, the threat of new entrants, the threat of new substitutes, the bargaining power of distributors (or business-to-business customers), and the bargaining power of suppliers. This structure can be reduced further to include simply *current* competitors and *potential* competitors and substitutes. This is because, as will be shown, the bargaining power of distributors depends very much on the extent to which rivals are competing to supply these distributors. The bargaining power of suppliers also depends on how actively rivals are bidding for their supplies. Hence, the bargaining power of suppliers and distributors depends on the rivalry among firms in a market. What Porter overlooks is that this is not a one-way process. The bargaining power of a firm over its suppliers and distributors also depends on the rivalry among suppliers in the supply market and the rivalry among distributors in their markets.

The way distributors and suppliers behave determines the threat posed by immediate and potential competition. Distributors and suppliers are therefore not separate competitive elements but moderators or amplifiers of competition (see Figure 6.8). Generally, suppliers and distributors are used to gain competitive advantage and

[10] Michael E. Porter, *Competitive Strategy* (New York: The Free Press, 1980). Porter's work is largely based on industrial organization economics. He merged it with marketing literature on competitive analysis and the product life cycle. His work is a clear presentation of these frameworks with many excellent examples.

Figure 6.8 **Current and Potential Competition**

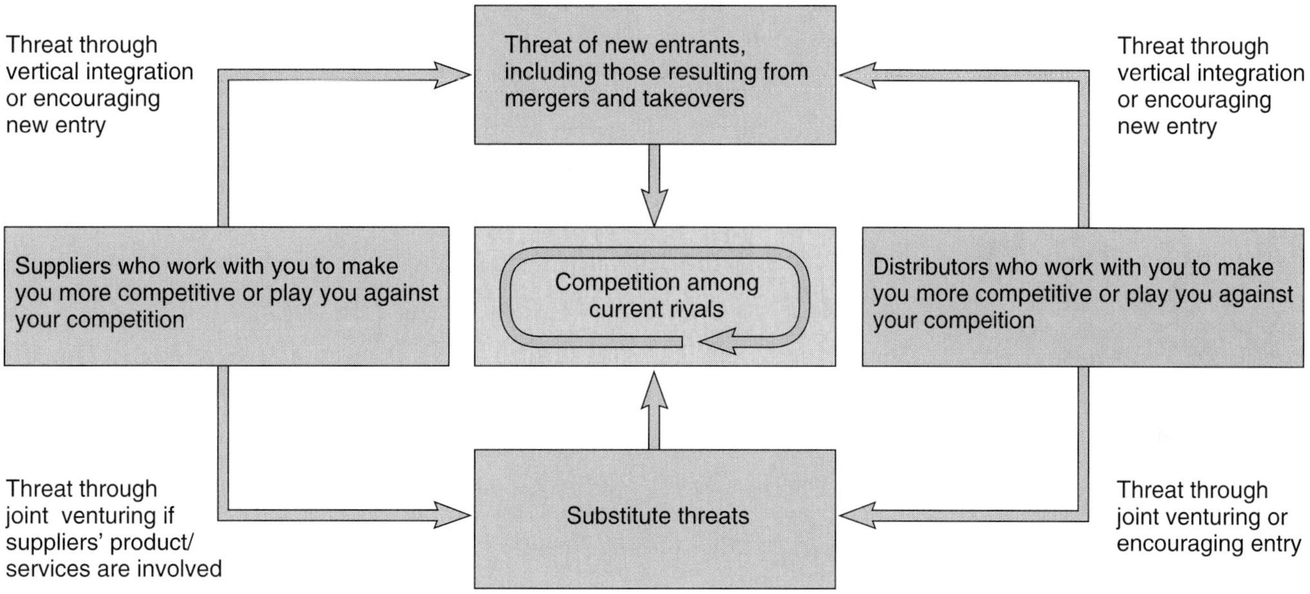

Competition occurs among current rivals. Distributors and suppliers can help or hinder a firm's efforts to become more competitive (see Chapter 7). Sometimes, they even encourage a new entrant or the development of a new substitute. They seldom, if ever, discourage such entry or the development of a new technological substitute. However, distributors and suppliers are not competitors. In fact, as shown in Table 6.1, the trading relationship a firm has with a supplier or a distributor is a cooperative effort that competes with other trading relationships in the market.

should be seen in this light. That is why the distributor and marketing channel environments are separately analyzed (see Chapter 7) and given much more attention than Porter's framework suggests. Furthermore, as noted earlier in the discussion about trading-relationship market share, distributors and suppliers cooperate with each other to compete against other distributor-supplier trading relationships.

It is true that at times distributors and suppliers have to be directly considered in a competitive analysis, but *only* when they threaten to become a new, direct competitor by supplier forward integration or distributor backward integration. This is not to belittle Porter's considerable contribution, which encouraged firms to analyze both the current and potential competitive environment.

Auditing Current Competitors

For most companies it is not possible to put all current competitors under the microscope and undertake an in-depth analysis of their competitive strengths and weaknesses. However, particular competitors are always worthy of such attention, either because they are attacking with a new product or because the company has decided, in a previous plan, to attack them. The isolation of aggressors or targets usually requires a preliminary analysis that identifies from which rivals you are gaining business and to which competitors you are losing business. This is the way you identify your immediate current competition, which may or may not be using similar technology.[11]

Many major U.S. cities now only have one daily newspaper, yet such monopolies have not created super profits for the publisher. The reason is simple. Although other newspapers may have died, competition for advertising has increased from the suburban weeklies, direct marketing, and other media. Television, radio, and local magazines also have become more competitive with their news and features. The mistake the newspaper publishers made was not identifying these competitors early on when they could have been countered.[12]

In a new venture it is useful to study the position of a typical, apparently successful, major company and the position of a small, but high-growth, company. The analysis may reveal that an established company is not as successful as initially assumed, and some of the reasons for its less-than-impressive position and performance also will emerge. The initial investment in time, effort, and expense necessary to audit competitors may be very high (amounting to several weeks or even months of an executive's or consultant's time), but it should be treated as an investment. The results will produce a file and a word-processed report that can be built on from year to year with constantly expanding details and insights. This file then becomes part of the collective memory of your organization to be passed on to successive managers.

A Competitor Analysis Template

Table 6.5 on page 230 (discussed throughout this section) presents a comprehensive competitor analysis form that is still not exhaustive. It is better characterized as a template that a company can use as a basis for developing its own unique competitor analysis form. The analysis should start with a general assessment of the competitor's product positioning, current objectives, strategy, major strengths and weaknesses, and likely next moves. The specific vulnerabilities of the competitor during the planning time horizon and what is going to be the competitor's major growth and response constraints also should be highlighted. A very important part of this summary will be an assessment of the rival's goals and basic innovation/imitation competitive strategy. This information will enable predictions to be made about the competitor's future behavior and reactions. It is not sufficient to describe how the competitor is performing in terms of market share and profits. A competitive analysis must diagnose how the competitor has managed to generate such performance outcomes, be they good or bad.[13] The research discussed next suggests that firms adopt a general competitive strategy that is reflected in their new product development behavior.

---

[11] Thomas W. Dunfee, Louis Stern, and Frederick D. Sturdivant, "Bounding Markets in Merger Cases: Identifying Relevant Competitors," *Northwestern University Law Review* 78 (November 1983): 733–73.

[12] Subrata N. Chakravarty and Carolyn Torcellini, "Citizen Kane Meets Adam Smith," *Forbes*, February 20, 1989, 82–85.

[13] George S. Day and Robin Wensley, "Assessing Advantage: A Framework for Diagnosing Competitive Superiority," *Journal of Marketing* 52 (April 1988): 1–20.

New Product Strategy: Cultural Attitude toward Innovation and Imitation

The direction and tone established by top-level management shapes the way the firm will pursue new product opportunities. A company can pursue two general strategies with its product development activity.[14] In the first approach, the firm attempts to achieve a continuous stream of modestly successful new product introductions. Each of these new products builds on the firm's knowledge of its customers and its technology—the firm never strays far from its core competencies. Individually, these new products do not remake the market or the organization itself. However, in sum, they add up to a consistently successful company. This approach requires a modest, but continuous, investment of resources to sustain it.

The second strategy is to search for a revolutionary product that changes the market and the company. Such an approach often requires a substantial commitment of resources and a relatively long development period. The result, though, is a discontinuity in the performance of the firm. This is probably accompanied by the reshaping of the product market, or even the creation of a new one. A hybrid or portfolio approach can also be pursued, in which the firm attempts to produce the occasional discontinuous innovation while generally pursuing a series of incremental ones (see Chapter 4 on financial goals). The hybrid approach may take even greater resources than the "big hit" approach.

The amount of innovation and new product development that a firm undertakes will depend largely on the organization's financial goals, overall strategy, its entrepreneurial aggressiveness, and its focus. Miles and Snow have categorized companies by their willingness to launch into new markets with new technologies and products.[15] The categories are:

1. *Prospectors:* Companies that follow the prospector strategy are aggressive innovators prepared to risk failure. Prospectors respond quickly to new ideas and seek them out from every possible source. They place high value on being first in the marketplace with new products or first into new markets. They emphasize the *innovation* component of innovation/imitation.
2. *Analyzers:* Firms that emphasize the analyzer strategy monitor the prospectors and adopt their ideas by coming out with their own products, which may have additional superior features, may be lower priced, or may be offered through a superior marketing program. Analyzers often make a commercial success out of a prospector's idea. They may well end up being perceived as the pioneering entrepreneur because they "made the market" for a product that an innovating prospector invented. They emphasize the *imitation* component of innovation/imitation.
3. *Defenders:* Firms that can be described as defenders stick to a market or market segment they know, and they defend it by raising quality and lowering price. Their distinctive characteristic is their single-minded focus on meeting the needs of their existing customers and potential customers who are like their existing customers. They know these people very well and make the most of that knowledge. They innovate and imitate narrowly.

[14] Robert G. Cooper, "The Impact of New Product Strategies," *Industrial Marketing Management* 12 (1983): 243–56; and Robert G. Cooper, "Predevelopment Activities Determine New Product Success," *Industrial Marketing Management* 17 (1988): 237–47.

[15] R. E. Miles and C. C. Snow, *Organization Strategy, Structure, and Process* (New York: McGraw-Hill, 1978); also see Daryl O. McKee, P. Rajan Varadarajan, and William M. Pride, "Strategic Adaptability and Firm Performance: A Market-Contingent Perspective," *Journal of Marketing* 53 (July 1989): 21–35; and Carolyne Smart and Ilan Vertinsky, "Strategy and the Environment: A Study of Corporate Responses to Crisis," *Strategic Management Journal* 10 (summer 1984): 149–71.

Table 6.5 A Competitor Analysis Template

Competitor ______________ Analyst ______________ Date ______________

SUMMARY OF COMPETITOR'S POSITION

- Goals ______________
- New product development strategy ______________
- Decision-making skills ______________
- Product and process R&D ______________
- Innovation/imitation skills ______________
- Implementation skills ______________
- Current success story ______________
- Current mistakes ______________
- Advantage with buyers ______________
- Disadvantage with buyers ______________
- Cost advantages ______________
- Cost disadvantages ______________

COMMENTS AND RATING OF COMPETITOR'S MARKET POSITIONS

Financial Position ______________
- Importance of this profit center to rival ______________
- Short-term liquidity ______________
- Access to working capital ______________
- Access to capital for major expansion ______________
- Contribution margin ______________
- Fixed cost/breakeven ______________
- Marginal cost structure ______________

Market Position ______________
- Major geographical markets ______________
- Major target markets ______________
- Way market segmented ______________
- Current expansion efforts ______________
- Current holding efforts ______________
- Overall strength ______________

Product Position ______________
- Raw material quality ______________
- Workmanship quality ______________
- Design quality ______________
- Design efficiency ______________
- Durability ______________
- Ease of servicing ______________
- Feature innovations ______________
- Appearance ______________
- Brand strength ______________
- Product range ______________
- Fit to segments ______________
- Packaging effectiveness ______________
- Overall strength ______________

Pricing ______________
- How much above/below average ______________
- % increase in last year ______________
- Increases in last two years ______________
- Margin to trade ______________
- Volume discounts ______________
- Payments terms ______________
- Promotional discounts ______________
- Leasing terms ______________

(continued)

RATING OF ADDED-VALUE PROCESSES BENCHMARKED AGAINST INDUSTRY BEST

- Buyback allowance
- Overall strength

Inbound Logistics Processes

- Sources of supply
- Purchasing skills
- Raw materials inventory control and efficiency
- Overall competitive driver

Production Processes

- Production capacity (long-term and seasonal)
- Production efficiency
- Labor relations
- Labor turnover
- Ability to retool/adapt
- Quality control
- Production costs
- Overall competitive driver

Outbound Logistics Processes

- Finished product stock control and efficiency
- Warehouse/storage method
- Transportation method
- Order-delivery lag
- Back-order lost sales
- Longistics service features
- Overall competitive driver

Trade Relations Processes

- Major channels used
- Image of channels
- Trade loyalty
- Trade promotions
- Trade advertising
- Overall competitive driver

Advertising and Promotion Processes

- Message theme
- Past message themes
- Media used
- Schedule/seasonality
- Effectiveness
- Close efficiency
- Consumer promotions
- Overall competitive driver

Sales Force Processes

- Selling strategy
- Sales-force management
- Sales-force morale
- Sales-force turnover
- Sales-force selection
- Sales-force training
- Sales-force discipline
- Territory allocation
- Sales-force calling cycle and patterns
- Use of new technology (telemarketing, etc.)
- Service reputation
- Overall competitive driver

4. *Reactors:* Reactor companies are complacent. They only respond to competitive innovations when they absolutely must, which is often too late.

The first three types of companies are active scanners of the marketplace for information about new product ideas, although they tend to scan different types of information. Prospectors look everywhere, analyzers focus on what the competition is doing, and defenders focus on their specific markets. Reactors do very little environmental scanning. The central lesson from the ideas of Miles and Snow is that top management creates the internal environment for the pursuit of new opportunities.

However, much still depends on the quality of the individuals or teams making the current decisions. If they are fixed in their ways, then their thinking may be rigid and old-fashioned and their vision myopic. On the other hand, if they are young and inexperienced, then they may be too impulsive and trigger happy. Assessing decision-making skills involves identifying the skills of the "old hands" and of any new executives who may have been recently hired. When a company is taken over or merges with a strong marketing-oriented company, this often results in an injection of managerial strength (this occurred when Philip Morris took over the Miller Brewing Company). Sometimes, however, it can lead to the disillusionment of current quality managers who may then resign, leaving an experience vacuum during the transition and the competitor vulnerable. It is important to base the evaluation of a company's experience and knowledge on the reputation of the managers *currently* making the decisions rather than any general reputation the firm has earned over the years. The firm's current decision-making *processes* also need to be assessed; for example, has it recently moved to decentralized, cross-functional team decision making?

The quality of a firm's intelligence gathering and R&D is not necessarily related to years of experience in the market. By investing shrewdly, a new entrant in these areas can quickly acquire much knowledge and experience, and through the right combination of imitation and innovation, it can leapfrog ahead of established firms. Consequently, a competitor's current market research and R&D projects are often early warning signals of a major new strategic effort or change of direction.

Added-Value Chain Competitive Analysis

Michael Porter has argued that competitive advantage in product and service quality and costs can come from one or more of the following stages in the added-value chain:[16]

1. Inbound logistics processes
2. Operations processes
3. Outbound logistics processes
4. Marketing and sales processes
5. Service processes

The implication is that a rival's competitive standing at all stages of the added-value chain from inbound logistics to after-sales service must be studied. The analysis form presented in Table 6.5 addresses characteristics of these processes.

[16] Michael E. Porter, *Competitive Advantage* (New York: The Free Press, 1985).

Before proceeding to discuss the headings in Table 6.5, the comments and ratings used to evaluate the competitor need to be explained. The comments should be as specific and concrete as possible, stating facts and, when considered necessary, referencing the source. This will help establish the validity and reliability of important conclusions and will enable the interested reader to follow up and obtain more information. Assumptions and rumor should be stated as such so as to avoid confusion with fact. Rating the added-value processes is proposed as a tool to make comparisons between competitors and your own enterprise. This relative rating (say on a scale of 1 to 10 with 5 being average) highlights both the direction and the extent of the difference on each of the dimensions of added value. Finally, the reality is that few competitive analyses will be as detailed as suggested in Table 6.5. Often, not enough information is even available to make a good assumption about a competitor's particular skill. In reality, comments on the template are likely to focus on aspects of a rival's competence or behavior that has recently changed.

Financial Position

The financial importance of the product market to the competitor tells how aggressively it is likely to respond. In hindsight, Procter & Gamble may have regretted taking on General Foods in the coffee market because Maxwell House was a very important profit earner for General Foods. General Foods fought tooth and nail against the market expansion efforts of P&G's Folgers brand.

Cash-flow problems may increase the possibility that the competitor will slash prices or using trade deals to pump inventory down the channel. But it also may mean the competitor will not be able to maintain its voice share and mind share against an aggressive advertising or promotional assault on its market share. A competitor's potential access to long-term capital through its parent company—by borrowing (as indicated by its debt-to-assets ratio) or by issuing more shares (indicated by its share earnings ratio and change in stock price)—enables some predictions to be made about whether it can keep investing in an expanding market or new production and distribution technology. The leveraged buyout frenzy of the 1980s left more than a few major companies up to their necks in debt. A rival's estimated average contribution margin, marginal costs, fixed costs, and capacity utilization all indicate its ability to sustain a price war and expand its market share.

Marketing Positioning

What is the competitor's targeting/positioning strategy? How well is this executed, in the sense that the competitor's positioning really appeals to the target segment or segments? These truly fundamental questions must be answered at the time a firm decides on its own positioning and are discussed at length in the positioning strategy chapter (Chapter 9). Apart from talking to distributors and suppliers, much can be deduced about a rival's target audience from the advertising media it chooses. What it says in its advertising claims tells a lot about how it is positioning and differentiating its products and services. A study of a competitor's entire product line or service offering will help anticipate a competitor's reactions and in particular its blind spots.

The operating performance and durability of the competitor's product can be established in the laboratory, by market research user trials, or by surveys of distributors and independent service outlets. Consumer testing organizations such as *Consumer Reports* also can provide some free and independent evaluations of a competitor's products.

Pricing

List prices often have little relevance because of promotions and special discounts. Consequently, it is important to establish what are the lowest, typical, and highest billed prices of each item in the competitor's product line. This variation tells something about its choice of loss leaders, the problem items in its line, and its high demand items (these will be the least discounted). Price trends over time may suggest a deliberate repositioning of the line. It also may simply reflect cost-control problems. An understanding of how the competitor sets its prices (for instance, cost-plus or competitive parity) may enable further interpretation of changes in price. Information on the recency of price changes, particularly during periods of price inflation created by cost increases, may facilitate anticipation of a competitor's price increase in the planning period and development of contingency plans.

Analysis of pricing often must go beyond purchase price to a consideration of the life-cycle cost to the consumer of the competitor's product. A rival may be very competitive on the purchase price, but, because of service charges or running costs, the product may be an expensive buy over its life compared to others' products (or vice versa). This is a particularly telling analysis in industrial marketing and is often the basis of the competitive advantage for the seller producing the highest quality, most reliable product.

Production Processes

In recent years, production and operations have become a major strategic concern in many markets. Automation and work-flow innovations have dramatically lowered costs, boosted productivity, and reduced reject rates and wastage. Production performance characteristics are leading indicators of changes in the quality image of a competitor's product and pricing.

Knowledge of short-term production capacity enables some estimates to be made of constraints on a competitor's likely behavior. If a competitor is working at or near its production capacity, it is not in a position to capture new business in an expanding market or to threaten a rival's market share if the competitor raises prices. On the other hand, if a competitor has slack capacity, the competitor may be tempted to lower its prices.

The period during which a company is in the process of retooling or renovating is a good time to make an assault on its market. General Motors was given its golden opportunity by Henry Ford when he closed his factories down for a good part of 1928 to retool his plant to produce the Model A rather than the Model T. Many of Ford's loyal customers who wanted to buy a new car that year turned to GM and never returned to Ford. The impact on Ford's distribution network and channel goodwill was serious.

A competitor's labor relations and labor turnover may have a number of implications for the short term. High labor turnover may indicate low morale, low average worker skills, and a consequent decline in product quality and productivity. Poor labor relations also may have a creeping, debilitating effect on quality and service. The influence of labor relations also can be sudden and dramatic in a unionized industry when a union picks on a particular competitor and the result is a strike or a lockout. To the extent that such events can be anticipated in the short term, preparations can be made to serve that competitor's customers. A further serious effect is that labor unrest can so preoccupy management that they neglect the interests of resellers and customers. When management become less alert and less responsive to changes in the market, then the company is always more vulnerable to attack.

Distribution and Logistics Processes

Inventory levels and the stock control methods of a competitor give clues to its vulnerability and problems. High inventory levels may suggest problems with product acceptance, but they also could mean that the competitor is about to launch a special promotion campaign. The efficiency of the competitor's stock control system indicates the likelihood that the competitor will ultimately hurt itself by either tying up too much working capital in stock or investing too little in finished stock, which results in poor service and stock-outs. Some competitors will operate a chronically overstocked or understocked system. Other competitors will fluctuate between the two extremes by constantly overreacting to overstocking or stockout crises.

Sources of supply should be looked at because the price and quality of raw materials are often the basis for product differentiation and cost competitiveness. Skilled purchasing for competitive advantage has been a neglected area of business policy and marketing management and will become even more important with the globalization of supply sources. When a rival changes its source of supply, it is particularly important to find out why (perhaps from the old sources) because it may suggest a change in product design, a technological breakthrough, a significant raw-materials price advantage, or the possibility the competitor knows more about long-term reserves of raw material.

The competitor's transportation and storage system says a lot about that competitor's service tactics, which will be reflected in its order-delivery reliability and its spare-parts service. The geographical positioning and size of new warehouse facilities give clear leading indicators of a firm's long-term logistics strategy. What is often overlooked is that a firm's logistics and distribution system may face undercapacity and overcapacity problems that are just as important to costs and service as a firm's production under- or overcapacity. A firm's distribution/logistics system also can be less adaptive than its production system because it involves agreements and contractual arrangements with third parties who, in their own self-interest, may become inflexible.

Advertising and Promotion

The reasons for studying a competitor's advertising and promotions are obvious. Of particular interest is how its product positioning has changed over time. Changes may suggest (1) problems with previous product positioning, (2) new insights resulting from market research, or (3) simply a new advertising agency that has suggested a new campaign theme. The agency may have designed a campaign that, while creative and attention grabbing, is not well integrated with the competitor's overall marketing tactics and product positioning. The creativity and attention-grabbing appeal of a competitor's advertising is obvious and often intimidating. What is not so clear is whether its positioning is really getting through to the customer. Consequently, it is just as important and useful to ask target customers to explain and give their reactions to a competitor's advertising and promotions as it is to ask the same target customers to react to the firm's own advertising and promotions.

The competitor's media tactics, measured in terms of volume and size (extent of campaign), choice of media (indicating its target market), and seasonality, need to be studied, so the company can plan its own purchase of media space and the timing of its campaigns in the next planning period. Much of this part of the competitor analysis should be prepared, as a matter of course, by the advertising agency.

Trade Relations and Sales Management Processes

This area, along with promotion, is probably the easiest part of a competitor analysis to undertake because information is so readily obtainable from trade sources. The problem lies in getting information that has not been filtered or deliberately distorted by resellers intent on playing one supplier against another. The first aspect in this area to be identified is the overall nature of the competitor's distribution system (for instance, is its emphasis on franchising, particular types of retailers, image, or location?) and how it is changing. This often requires an understanding of how the distribution system evolved historically. Monitoring trade loyalty may reveal a sharp difference in goodwill among different types of resellers toward the rival or problems in a particular region or at a particular time, such as after a bungled promotion or product introduction.

It is important to establish whether the competitor's loss of loyalty and channel cooperation is the result of a weak positioning strategy or poor execution before any attempt is made to exploit the competitor's misfortune. The idea may have had merit, and with a little modification and much better execution, a company could benefit from the competitor's learning experience. Trade advertising, promotions, and shows; in-store or warehouse promotions; displays; and new competitor shelf-space management programs need to be watched carefully to spot new competitive thrusts and product repositioning before it is too late to react effectively.

Sales-force selection criteria and training indicate the importance the competitor places on sales management in its long-term competitive strategy. Changes in the reward system (particularly the basis for bonuses) and the sales control system are indicators of likely changes in the resourcefulness and aggressiveness of the competitor's sales force. The reward system, calling cycles, and sales territories often give away the competitor's target segments, selling priorities, and overall marketing objectives.

Anticipating Competitor Behavior

An analysis of the competitive environment can reveal what likely initiatives rivals can and will mount and their ability to respond. What it cannot reveal is what the final outcome will be of the interaction among the company's initiatives, competitors' initiatives, and the sequence of counter-responses.

Thus, the competitively rational firm attempts to assess rival behavior and reactions in deciding what to do. Many firms study what rivals are likely to do in the next period ($t + 1$) but fail to conjecture their future reactions at time $t + 2$. An example of such rational reasoning is presented in Figure 6.9. Perhaps Hewlett-Packard used such a process in August 1995 when it launched a new, low-priced line of home personal computers. Later, in the same week, Compaq, now the largest seller of PCs, cut its prices in a range of 13 percent to 25 percent. The next day IBM responded by cutting its prices in a range of 9 percent to 26 percent. Hewlett-Packard then announced that it planned to cut the prices of its other PCs very soon. With such regular rounds of price cuts, occurring along with the improvements in performance, it is easy to understand why PCs have become much better buys. It is also easy to understand that it only takes three or four competitors to create both fierce price competition and fierce improved-performance competition in a market.

The basic reasons why most firms do not undertake such conjectures about a competitor's behavior are that it is too hard to do and the results are too uncertain to be worth the effort. But even when a firm tries, the common mistakes made are to downgrade the capabilities or determination of the competitor or to assume the rival thinks like the firm and will behave the same way.[17] One approach to correcting such

[17] Marian Chapman Moore and Joel E. Urbany, "Blinders, Fuzzy Lenses, and the Wrong Shoes: Pitfalls in Competitive Conjecture," *Marketing Letters* 5, no. 3 (1994): 247–58.

Figure 6.9 **Rational Reasoning When Considering a Price Cut**

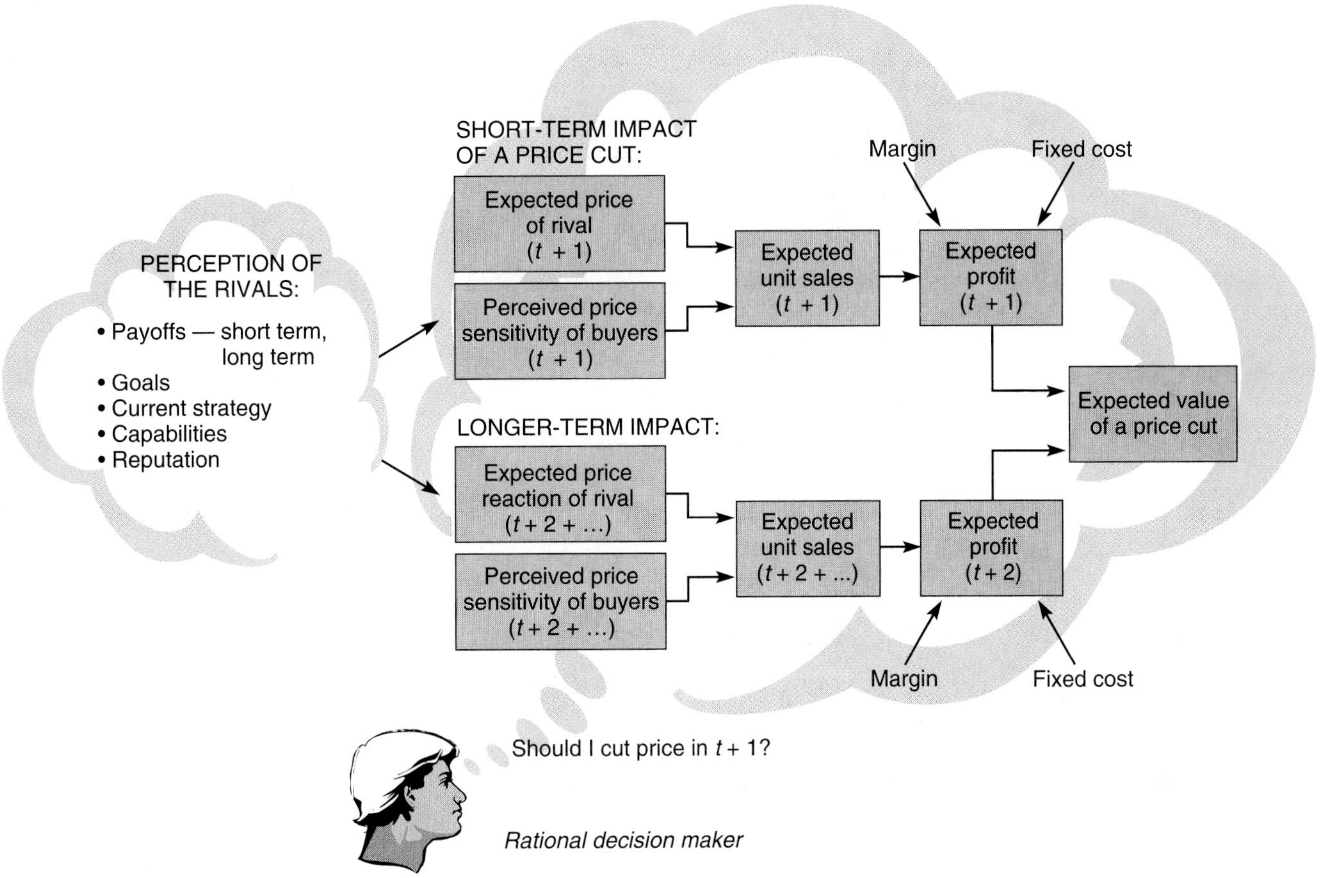

SOURCE: Marian Chapman Moore and Joel E. Urbany, "Blinders, Fuzzy Lenses, and the Wrong Shoes: Pitfalls in Competitive Conjecture," *Marketing Letters*, 5.3 (1994), 247–58.

biases is to study the history of competitor reactions to the firm's changes in strategy and price cuts to determine how they will retaliate.[18] Two problems with such an analysis are that it may not produce clear response patterns and that competitors' past reactions may not be a good predictor of their future behavior. Given these difficulties, it is still worthwhile for a firm to think through the implications of its behavior on competitors' and trade behavior.

The first step in anticipating a competitor's likely behavior is, as explained earlier, to understand its current objectives, its self-perceptions, and how it thinks about the product market, that is, its competitive thinking. A second step is to study the

[18] See Venkatram Ramaswamy, Hubert Gatignon, and David J. Reibstein, "Competitive Marketing Behavior in Industrial Markets," *Journal of Marketing* 58 (April 1994): 45–55.

Rationality in Practice

Swept Along and Swept Away by the VCR Boom

In 1984, some 7 million videocassette recorders (VCRs) were sold in the United States, raising the proportion of U.S. households that own a VCR to about 20 percent. Market penetration had hit 40 percent by 1986, and by 1995 more than 80 percent of U.S. households had a VCR. Over a period of about ten years, the evolution of the VCR product market had a dramatic effect on complementary and substitute products, such as the sales of color televisions sets and blank videotapes, video movie rentals, library usage, and network television viewing. It also helped revive the sagging audio-TV retail sector.

The videodisc product market was the big loser. RCA took a $580 million loss on its disc player, which it doggedly marketed from 1981 through 1984. RCA chose to develop disc rather than tape technology because it (1) did not believe the consumer really wanted a recorder/player and (2) did not believe that a mass-produced tape pickup head could be manufactured that would record and reproduce a quality picture. Sony and JVC proved them wrong. Despite the fact that for two decades Japanese ingenuity often demonstrated its ability to halve, and halve again, the production costs of electronic equipment, RCA also did not expect the VCR to drop in price so rapidly (from more than $1,000 in 1979 to less than $300 in 1984 and $200 in 1988). All is not lost for the videodisc, however; the product has found a new market niche, changed its appearance, and developed new organs. It has mutated into a splendid computer data-storage device.

Sony also made its biggest marketing mistake with VCRs (according to founder Akio Morita) by sticking with its Beta format, which it had hoped to make the industry standard. The switch in standard from Beta to VHS caused only a hesitation in the development of the product market. For too long Sony fought the new standard. Pride dominated pragmatics and profits.

The VCR software business boomed in the 1980s. By 1984 some 120 million videocassettes were being sold annually at a market value of $700 million. But the industry was heading toward a major price war and shakeout among such daunting competitors as Polaroid, Kodak, 3M, Fuji, Sony, Memorex, Maxell, and Basf. As distribution moved from the appliance store to the already crowded shelves of the drugstore, supermarket, and discount store, some manufacturers were beginning to sell solely on price. Others were desperately attempting to establish a brand image before it was too late by marketing heavily promoted high-grade, high-margin tapes. This turned out to be unsuccessful because buyers were not able to perceive any difference among the tapes. Blank VCR tapes have become a commodity product. In 1987, 300 million blank VHS tapes were sold at a market value of just more than $1 billion.

In 1984, the Video Software Dealers Association's annual convention attracted two thousand people, triple the 1983 attendance. Some twelve thousand specialty video outlets were selling and renting videocassettes, but they were facing increasing competition from thousands of bookstores, grocery stores, movie theaters, and even U-Haul rental agencies moonlighting as videocassette rental outlets! Many of the nonconventional

past decision-making and general personal style of the competitor's key decision makers. Have they sent signals in the past indicating how they would respond to having their market share and brand image attacked? Are such threats credible, in that they have always followed through, or do they frequently blow smoke? Do they respond rationally or emotionally? If the competitor's marketing planners are fixed in their thinking and ways, as many executives are, then studying their past behavior and reactions (even if they occurred in different product markets) will probably be the best predictor of how they are likely to behave in the future. Senior executives are often good intuitive judges of the mindsets of rivals because they have played against them for years.

A third step is to become fully acquainted with any "game playing" rules that may exist in the industry and will enable you to predict competitor responses. Regrettably, few, if any, analytical tools are available to predict a competitor's response. Such a predictor would require a computer-based simulation that accurately anticipates all of

Blockbuster Video was the big winner in the shakedown of the video rental market.

outlets were charging as low as $2 for a one-night rental, half the fee the video stores were charging, but they did not offer the same selection. Start-up costs were low and profits were high. Everything looked rosy.

In 1985, some 50 million videos were sold and 1.2 billion were rented, more than the 1.1 billion books checked out from public libraries. Sales of color television sets were up 40 percent in 1983 and up another 25 percent in 1984. More than 100 million movie videos were sold in 1987 as prices of box-office hits were slashed from $89.95 to $29.95 to encourage buying rather than renting. Sales did not stop the renting, however, which experienced similar growth. Major chains such as Kmart and 7-Eleven were now renting for as low as 99 cents a night.

The writing was on the wall for most of the 25,000 rental outlets. Sales started to level off. Most households had seen *Top Gun, Gone with the Wind,* and every other movie they had wanted to see as many times as they could stand. The pool of software was running out. Worse, by 1989 some discount stores were renting three tapes for $1. The video rental business had boomed and busted in five years, leaving Blockbuster Video the big winner.

The growth of the VCR product market resulted in the near extinction of the videodisc product and laid the foundation for the dynamic growth of the video movie-rental market. The evolution of the VCR product market created a wave that washed into several other new and mature markets. Even the marketing experts did not anticipate the rapid rise and fall of the videotape rental industry. An emerging problem is that home computers are competing for family recreational time, and this contributed to a 20 percent decline in video rentals over the summer of 1995. Another factor is the lack of new blockbuster movies. The industry solution to the shortfall in expected income is to raise prices for the most popular new releases by up to a $1, which is likely to drive away even more consumers from the rental stores.

SOURCES: "The Anatomy of RCA's Videodisc Failure," *Business Week,* April 23, 1984, 89–90; "The VCR Boom Puts Blank Tapes in Fast Forward," *Business Week,* August 6, 1984, 92–93; Susan Spillman, "Videocassette Rental Sites in Darndest Spots," *Advertising Age,* August 30, 1984, 1–5; Alex Ben Block, "Hard Dollars in Video Software," *Forbes,* June 17, 1985, 128–32; Stephen Kindel, "Goodbye, TV Hello, Video," *Forbes,* July 1, 1985, 100–101; Randy Pitman, "A Tale of Two Cultures: The Video Business and Libraries," *Wilson Library Bulletin,* May 1988, 27–28; and Peter M. Nichols, "Home Video," *New York Times,* October 10, 1995, B10.

the moves of players in the marketplace, which is impossible. One of the ironies of economic theory is that so many of the models assume that the marketplace will quickly settle into a steady-state equilibrium.[19] It is ironic because the theory of competitive rationality asserts that a marketing planner's mission in life is to constantly find ways of profiting from disturbing such economic equilibrium. If a new marketing strategy does not disturb competitive equilibrium, then it is not having any impact on the market. The Rationality in Practice box titled "Swept Along and Swept Away by the VCR Boom" demonstrates the dynamic and complex interplay among competitors in a market.

Although trying to predict competitor behavior by using analytical models does not seem feasible, it is still sensible to attempt to anticipate and play through the most likely

[19] K. Sridhar Moorthy, "Using Game Theory to Model Competition," *Journal of Marketing Research* 12 (August 1985): 262–82.

consequences of your planned strategy. This can be done by asking and answering the following questions:

1. What will be the competitive responses to our new strategy?
2. What impact will this have on the market?
3. How will we respond?
4. What will be the repercussion of our response on *(a)* the marketplace and *(b)* our financial performance goals?
5. Return to number 1.

It is often useful for members of a marketing team to role play as competitors in such an exercise. A sufficient number of such iterations often leads one to conclude, "I think I'd better think it through again." For example, Pepperidge Farm certainly wished it had thought its plan through once more after launching its branded, high-quality, premium-priced, blended apple juice. Other juice manufacturers slashed retail prices by more than 40 percent, reducing their price to ninety-nine cents a gallon. This particularly hurt Pepperidge Farm because it had invested up front to make the juice on its own rather than contract it to outside producers and packers. In 1981, Honda and Yamaha each had a 35 percent share of the motorcycle market. That same year, Yamaha announced its intentions to become number one and introduced 60 new models. Honda launched 63 new or modified models and announced that Yamaha had stepped on the tiger's tail. Over the next eighteen months, Honda introduced 81 new models and Yamaha 37. The market was flooded, and prices were slashed. In 1983, Honda introduced 110 more models. Yamaha introduced only 23 models in 1983 and in 1984 had to sell assets and cut salaries.[20] If Yamaha had understood how fiercely Honda would react, it probably would have pursued a less aggressive and outspoken strategy.

Predicting What-If Effects Using a Relationship Matrix

If changes in a trading relationship are planned, then a relationship matrix also can be used to study competitive repercussions. Table 6.6 presents one likely scenario that often occurs in a market. In this hypothetical market, distributor B, feeling it is not getting the service it should get from X, given that it only stocks X's products, decides to approach supplier Y with a view to developing a trading relationship. If trading relationship Y-B does develop, what is likely to happen? In the scenario presented in the table, what happens is that B's total sales do not increase. Instead, 25 percent of its sales (5%/20%) are now of Y's product line, and they are made at the expense of X's sales. Naturally, X is likely to be upset that it has lost five percentage points of market share from its X-B relationship and is likely to attempt to regain its share by increasing its relationship share with another distributor—probably A. If it cooperates with A on a new marketing campaign to counter the Y-B marketing campaign, then it is likely to regain its share by growing the X-A trading relationship up from 20 percent to 25 percent market share. But for distributor A, all such a campaign may do is to cannibalize its sales of Y's line, so the net effect on its overall sales is a wash. A's X-A trading relationship jumps to 25 percent but at the expense of its Y-A relationship share, which

[20] R. B. Kennard, "From Experience: Japanese Product Development Process," *Journal of Product Innovation Management* 8 (1991): 184–88.

Table 6.6

	DISTRIBUTOR'S/RETAILER'S MARKET SHARE					
MANUFACTURER'S MARKET SHARE	A	B	C	D	E	
X	20%	20% ↑	5%	0	5%	50%
Y	20	←0→ ↓	5	5%	0	30
Z	10	0	0	5	5	20
	50%	20%	10%	10%	10%	100%

What happens when Y-B channel is activated?

	DISTRIBUTOR'S/RETAILER'S MARKET SHARE					
MANUFACTURER'S MARKET SHARE	A	B	C	D	E	
X	25% ~~20~~ +↑ (+ ←)	~~20~~ 15% ↑−	5%	0	5%	50%
Y	15 ~~20~~ (← −)	~~0~~ 5	5	5%	0	30
Z	10	0	0	5	5	20
	50%	20%	10%	10%	10%	100%

shrinks to 15 percent. So, facing such a likely scenario, B has to ask whether it really wants to drive X and A into an even bigger trading relationship, the price it has to pay for becoming a distributor of Y's products. It may be more profitable in the long term, or it may not be, but, whatever, the relationship matrix can serve as a useful mental model of playing through the consequences of competitive strategy on channel trading relationships.

Using Innovation-Imitation Paths to Predict Future Market Behavior

A competitive path-dependency, as defined in Chapter 1, is a discernible pattern in the way that demand (buyer behavior) and supply (seller behavior) evolve.[21] In simple terms it is a market trend. Understanding such innovation-imitation paths in a market is key to successful competitive conjecture about what will happen in the market in the future. While it may be hard to predict individual rival's behavior, it is a lot easier to identify supply and demand trends that are driving the competitive evolution of a market.

A process innovation that confers a competitive advantage is often quickly imitated across the market, particularly by very driven and alert competitors. As it is imitated it

[21] W. Brian Arthur, "Self-Reinforcing Mechanisms in Economics," in *The Economy as an Evolving Complex Systems*, ed. P. Anderson, K. Arrow and D. Pines (New York: Addison Wesley, 1988); "Positive Feedbacks in the Economy," *Scientific American*, 263 (February 1990), 80–85; *Increasing Returns and Path Dependency in the Economy*, (Ann Arbor: The University of Michigan Press), 1994.

is incrementally improved. Meanwhile the initial innovator has advanced further along the experience learning curve and is itself making innovative refinements.

This innovation adoption path is driven by an amplifying feedback effect—the more that rivals have adopted the process that gives them a competitive advantage, the greater is the need for the remaining suppliers to imitate or answer with a different process innovation.[22] The more that the amplification effect imparts competitive momentum to the trend, the greater the competitive force is applied to the remaining suppliers to adopt too (that is, imitate).[23] This force becomes a competitive driver of the late adopter's behavior.

A market is full of such process innovation-imitation paths at different stages of adoption and adaption (diffusion) across the population. Some are short, sharp paths that lead to universal adoption because of the appeal of the innovation and its ease of adoption. For example, when a microwavable shrinkwrap was innovated, all of the competition had to quickly imitate. Fortunately for them they were able to quickly imitate. Some paths are slow to develop because they are difficult to implement. For example, just-in-time distribution processes and activity-based cost accounting processes give their users a major advantage over their competition. But they are often slow to be imitated in a market because they require extensive changes in a firm's core operational and control processes.

Other innovation-imitation paths meander along and sometimes fizzle out as many management fads do. It could be said that a management fad is a management process trend that fizzled out. They do not become part of the history of process evolution in a market or industry. Rather they turned out to be a process evolutionary branch whose genes were defective and died out. The management literature on population learning studies all of these different types of diffusion paths (see Figure 6.5, The Technological S-Curve). In the following sections we discuss the tracking of product technology paths and the impact of marketing process innovation-imitation paths.

Technology Innovation-Imitation Paths

The following is a classic example of the domination of one technology innovation-imitation path over another technology path, and a firm's inability to see the inevitability of the trend. Professional video cassette recording equipment was first made and marketed by an American company. In the early 1970s the Japanese company Sony made and marketed a VCR for advertising agencies and schools but it was too expensive and too large for home use. Several years later Sony had developed its Beta technology into a VCR for home use. About the same time another Japanese company, JVC, using a technology invented in Europe, launched a VCR that used a competing VHS technology. The VHS tape was a little larger but by sacrificing some of the recording quality, the initial VHS tapes were able to record for two hours compared with Beta's one hour. This made VHS more appealing for recording and watching movies. Sony took too long to respond to consumer and video rental stores' complaints about Beta's limited recording time. By the time Sony had developed a two hour tape, VHS had gained an initial preference advantage in the market. JVC was

[22] Economists call a force that drives a trend a positive feedback effect.

[23] For an example of such a force in the domain of price-cutting see Joel E. Urbany and Peter R. Dickson (1991), "The Effects of Price-Cutting Momentum and Consumer Search on Price Setting in the Grocery Market," *Marketing Letters*, 2:4, 393–402.

also able to quickly imitate Sony's process of effectively doubling recording time and came out with a four-hour tape.

JVC also quickly licensed its technology to other manufacturers and soon, for every Beta model in the consumer electronic's stores there were five VHS models made by different manufacturers to choose from. This is an example of how a particular technology can gain a dominant promotional advantage in the leading trading channels which reinforces and sustains its innovation-imitation path—it is a form of channel goodwill or channel equity that the new technology possesses.[24]

As sales of VHS recorders soared past Sony's Beta recorders a transformation occurred on the shelves of the video stores that was very obvious to consumers. Where at first the stores stocked more Beta rental tapes, soon they were stocking the same number of VHS tapes, then twice as many VHS tapes, and soon there were five times as many movie choices in VHS format than in Beta format at the rental store. This gave VHS a distinctive advantage during the crucial stage when the bulk of households purchased its first VCR between 1980 and 1985.

The suppliers of the movies noticed the emerging dominance of VHS and soon stopped supplying Beta versions of their product. This ensured the complete dominance of VHS over Beta. As friends and family wished to share prerecorded, recorded, or camcorded tapes, this consumer networking and need for compatibility further drove the emerging dominance of VHS.

Sony, the world class developer of the Walkman and other very successful electronic products, was competitively irrational in stubbornly sticking to its Beta technology. It finally admitted defeat and switched over to making VHS VCRs in the early 1990s. The possibility that Sony is not very good at tracking and understanding the implications of innovation-imitation paths in a market has been recently reinforced by its launch of a new portable compact disc player that uses much smaller CDs. Yes, the product is much smaller and convenient for usage situations such as exercising but the problem is that it is competing hopelessly against the dominance of the larger CD technology. Consumers have invested billions in buying the larger CDs and multiple players in the home and car. The cost of switching to the new technology is way too high for most consumers. Music retailers, facing their own survival problems, were not prepared to carry extensive selections of the new mini-CDs. This could also have been predicted by Sony. There are many other examples of firms using (or not using) the realities of competitive innovation-imitation paths in their markets to drive their decision making.

The risks of staying on an obsolete technological path are well illustrated by Amdahl's behavior. Over 20 years Amdahl built mighty main-frame computers out of ultrafast computer chips. The chips consume a lot of electricity and emit intense heat—so much so that Amdahl computers require very expensive climate-controlled rooms. But the real problem was that for every million dollars Amdahl was spending on hot chip research and development, the rest of the computer industry was spending a billion dollars on advancing cool PC chip technology.[25] By 1998 Amdahl predicted the speed of the fastest cool chip will exceed the speed of the fastest hot chip. Such a cool chip computer will be one-tenth the size and have one-tenth the number of parts. No

[24] Paul W. Farris, Willem J. Verbeke and Peter R. Dickson, "Modeling the Evolutionary Effects of Path Dependencies in Markets," *Working Paper*, The Darden School of Business, University of Virginia, 1995.

[25] Thomas Petzinger Jr. "A Tale of Two Chips: Amdahl Decides It's Better to be Cool," *The Wall Street Journal*, August 18, 1995, B1.

contest. Which is why in 1995 Amdahl abandoned an investment of $100 million in the next generation of hot chip computers and switched to developing a new line of cool chip computers with Fujitso of Japan, a low-cost manufacturing partner. Amdahl had no choice but to abandon the technological path it had taken and all of the process skills it had developed in designing and producing hot chips. Technology was marching down another path much faster. Looking into the future, Amdahl saw that it had become dependent on the wrong technology path for its success.

Prodigy, American On-Line (AOL), and Compuserve are companies that deliver information, entertainment, and communication services to PC owners. Their common problem is that the technology drivers and paths in their service is threatened by the new Internet technology path that may provide unlimited free access to a number of the services they provide. The initial response of Prodigy and AOL is to try to surf the Internet wave by making it very easy for its subscribers to use the Internet. But within five years, new connect software sold by long-distance telephone companies and start-ups will provide much the same services as these companies at much lower prices. Unless Prodigy and AOL can come up with exclusive information, communication, and entertainment services that justify their monthly access charges, they face a bleak future. The Internet has cut off their growth path. Compuserve has been able to shift its positioning strategy toward developing within firm and between firm "Intranet" communication services where the volume of data and data security makes the Internet unattractive. Shifting its focus and target markets away from the Internet was easier for Compuserve because it was founded as a service for businesses rather than home PC users. Its process competencies at serving business information and communication needs are so much more advanced than Prodigy and AOL that this expertise and continued learning constitutes a sustainable competitive advantage.

In its development of the wireless phone market, AT&T is racing down two alternative and competing technology paths to avoid such risks. By acquiring McCaw, it has the lead in Cellular market penetration, but it has also spent $1.68 billion on licenses for the new personal communication services (PCS) radio spectrums.[26] PCS handheld phones are lighter, cheaper, and have longer battery life. PCS transmitters can also handle more calls, lowering operating costs. By spending a further $4 billion on building PCS networks and linking it with McCaw's cellular system, AT&T will be able to double its wireless coverage to reach 200 million Americans. Just as importantly, it will be better positioned to ultimately switch its entire system over to PCS technology (if it proves superior) compared to any of its wireless competitors. By contrast MCI is betting that advances in compression technology will create an over-supply of wireless capacity that greatly reduces the value of the "bandwidths."[27] If the compression technology does follow the path of a geometric improvement in performance, MCI will be in a buyers market and will be able to lease all of the channel capacity it needs. If the compression improvement path runs into a roadblock, MCI could be in trouble.

Marketing Process Innovation-Imitation Paths

We have been talking about high-stake technology trends, but similar trends also occur in marketing processes. Indeed, much of the rest of this book is about describing

[26] Mark Lewyn, "Catching the Next Technology Wave," *Business Week*, August 30, 1993, 31–32; John J. Keller, "AT&T Eagerly Plots A Strategy to Gobble Local Phone Business," *The Wall Street Journal*, August 21, 1995, A1.
[27] Fleming Meeks, "Betting on Moore's Law," *Forbes*, September 25, 1995, 42–45.

such trends. For example, many markets are still learning how to use telemarketing, the Internet, and much more segmented cable television in the most competitive way. Innovative companies are innovating more efficient ways of controlling the flow of goods and services along the supply (value-added) chain. This technology and process skill is being rapidly diffused across many product markets, because when such processes are imitated (learned and implemented), the results are spectacular. Costs can often be cut by half, and service to distributors and consumers increased at the same time. Equally radical innovations and trends in product-development processes, team-selling processes, and benchmarking-control processes are shortening process times and improving within and between firm coordination. The next chapter discusses how innovations in distribution technology and organization have shaped the learning and evolution of marketing processes at the marcoeconomic level. Chapter 8 explains how regulation and deregulation have created evolutionary (population learning) market paths.

Sometimes a trend in a particular genre of marketing process dominates other trends in a product market. In the 1980s consumer price promotions became the dominant innovation-imitation path in some packaged goods' markets at the expense of distribution innovations and product innovations (see Chapter 16).

A market path dependency can also occur from repeated use of marketing decision and resource allocation rules such as expenditure on marketing efforts. One of the most famous market path dependency effects produced by the repeated application of a marketing decision rule occurred during the Great Depression of the 1930s. The rigid application of a cost-plus pricing rule led to the raising of prices as demand declined and average costs rose. This led to a further decline in demand, and the cost-plus pricing response drove prices further up and demand further down.

An example of a resource allocation rule path occurs when marketing expenditure in the next year is tied to sales in the previous year. If marketing expenditure increases sales, then sales will increase market expenditure, which, in turn, increases sales. Thus the routinized application of a percentage of sales advertising expenditure rule by manufacturers and their distributors can create path dependencies in an evolving market.[28]

The bottom-line conclusion of the above section on competitive conjecture is that a firm may not be able to predict the quirky short-term behavior of a competitor, but longer-term path dependency trends, such as performance improvement in different technologies, can be predicted. Thus a firm should direct its competitive conjectures to understanding the innovation-imitation paths an industry is taking in improving product or service quality and improving the competitiveness of key operational and support processes. Such market trend analysis and forecasts are the first step in predicting what is likely to happen down the road (or path) in a market. Figure 6.10 presents the growth in use of e-mail and fax communication processes and how they seem to be related to the growth in work-at-home telecommuting. Such growth paths have clear path dependency implications for a number of product and service markets.

The second step is to recognize that marketing plays an important role in giving momentum to technology trends. Investment in marketing campaigns such as consumer education campaigns about how to use a new technology have been identified as the initial source of a major innovation-imitation path. For example, the dominance

[28] Paul W. Farris, Willem J. Verbeke, and Peter R. Dickson, "Modeling the Evolutionary Effects of Path Dependencies in Markets," *Working Paper*, The Darden School of Business, University of Virginia, 1995.

Figure 6.10 **Effects of Increased Communication on Telecommuting**

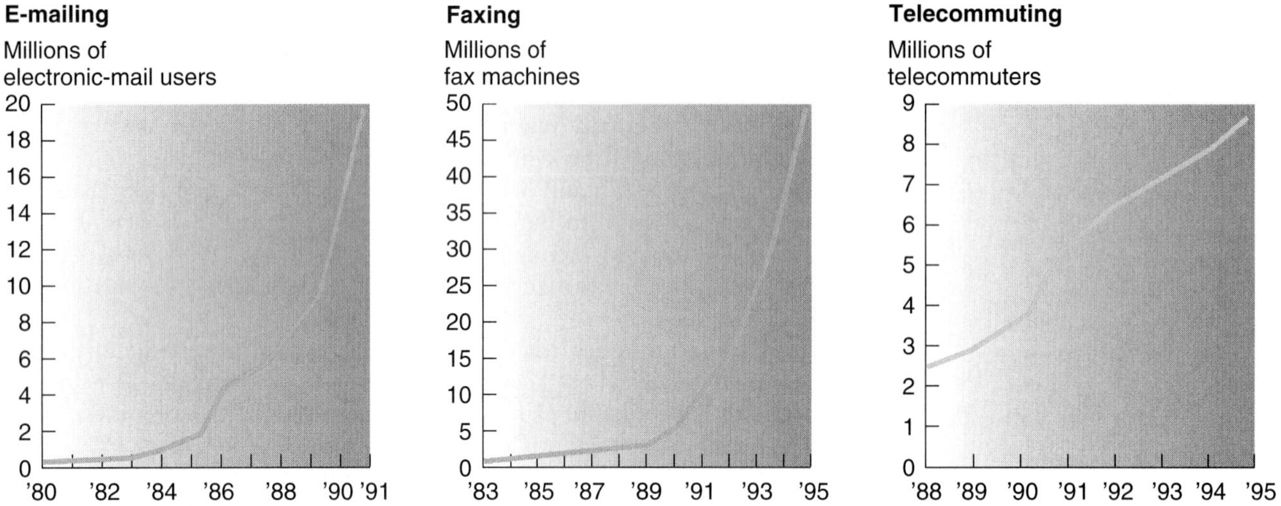

The growth in the use of E-mail and fax communication is clearly related to the growth in work-at-home telecommuting.
SOURCE: *Forbes*, November 23, 1992, p. 190.

of the QUERTY typewriter keyboard and FORTRAN over their claimed superior technological rivals was, in part, due to the superiority of the consumer education programs in the market that taught consumers how to use these technologies in the touch typing process and the computer-programming process.

The third step is to then assess what impact such trends are likely to have on rivals' competitiveness and behavior. Will they lead, follow, struggle, or drop out of the race down such paths? This should include an analysis of likely trends in channel relationship market shares. Computer market simulations might even be set up to predict the likely winners and losers.

Analyzing Competition in Foreign Markets

Much has been written about global competitiveness, but few generalizations or conclusions can be made. Each foreign market differs in its competitive structure, as analyzed using Figure 6.8. What we do know is that fierce domestic rivalry produces firms that are superbly conditioned to compete in foreign markets and the general global market. This is the major argument against government policy that protects long-established domestic firms.

In foreign markets such as Southeast Asia, the labor cost has been low, and the labor productivity has been high. In other foreign markets, such as Japan, the cost of capital has been low, and hence the cost of investing in new plant and equipment has been low. The basic theory of production functions in economics tells us that output is determined by labor and capital inputs. The empowering coefficients associated with labor and capital reflect the efficient and effective use of labor and capital (that is, competitive rationality). As long as the United States is prosperous, its semiskilled and unskilled labor force will never be price competitive with the labor forces available in emerging countries. As long as its saving rate is low (a cultural characteristic) compared to Japan and Germany, the U.S. cost of capital will never be lower. The solution is clear. U.S. firms must employ superior technology and management to overcome their labor and capital cost disadvantages. American scientists, engineers, and managers must be more insightful, innovative, and adaptable, particularly when it comes to working together on product design and flexible manufacturing. U.S. manufacturing skills fell far behind those in other countries in many industries from the mid-1960s to the mid-1980s.[29] For example, GM senior management was stunned when Toyota managers (in a joint venture) made a mothballed California assembly plant with old equipment into GM's most efficient factory; in fact, it was twice as productive as a typical GM plant.

American firms also must be prepared to become global enterprises by using cheap labor and cheap capital where they can be obtained. The global market has a larger and more diverse group of players, but competitiveness in the global market is no different in theory or in practice than competitiveness in the domestic market—it still comes down to outthinking, outrunning, and outlasting rivals.

Discussion Questions and Minicases

1. Researchers at the Wharton Business School presented students with a simple problem involving a choice between the following:[30]
   a) Keeping the price of a product low, causing competition to suffer substantial losses
   b) Maintaining a higher price that would produce higher long-term profits but would also allow the competition to prosper

   The results of more than thirty experiments were very disturbing. Some 40 percent of the students preferred to hurt the competition rather than maximize profits for their owners. Why do you think the students were so aggressive?
2. Given the following shares, analyze the competitive position of A.

	1989 (%)				1990 (%)				1991 (%)			
	A	B	C	D	A	B	C	D	A	B	C	D
R&D share	30	20	25	25	25	25	25	25	20	30	25	25
Voice share	30	25	25	20	40	25	15	20	40	20	20	20
Mind share	40	30	20	10	50	25	15	10	50	30	10	10
Market share	40	25	20	15	40	25	20	15	30	30	20	20

3. A relationship matrix would not provide any useful information if each seller's market share of each reseller's sales were equal to the seller's overall market share and vice versa. Such a balanced relationship structure is an extremely unlikely event. Please change Table 6.1a so all of the relationships are so balanced, and contrast it with the original Table 6.1a and Table 6.1b.
4. How might the types of consumer loyalty identified in Chapter 5 be used to assess the competitive position of rivals? What questions does this raise about market share?

[29] "Can America Compete?" *Business Week*, April 20, 1987, 44–69.

[30] J. Scott Armstrong, Robert H. Colgrove, and Fred Collopy, "Competitor-Oriented Objectives and Their Effects on Long-term Profitability," working paper, Wharton Business School, University of Pennsylvania, January 1993.

5. Name two different technologies that are competing with the greeting card business. What do you think is going to happen in the long term as these product markets converge?
6. The local "baby Bell" telephone companies and the cable TV companies appear to be converging on the broadband, fiber-optic communication and entertainment market. In 1992 Congress was trying to decide whether to allow telephone companies to offer cable TV services. What strengths and weaknesses do the two types of companies bring to the impending clash in the marketplace?
7. In 1984, American Express Merchandise sold more than $200 million in products through its mail-order business. Its best-selling items were VCRs, Gucci watches, grandfather clocks, and IBM typewriters. About 6 million cardholders got billing inserts, and 2 million hot prospects got solo mailings, including catalogs. By 1989, Amexco's direct marketing sales were higher than L.L. Bean's mail-order sales. What sort of competitive move has Amexco made? What is its big advantage?
8. Give two examples of industries or specific corporations that generally present formidable barriers to entry but also tend to be trapped by their resources. Why is this so? When does it matter?
9. A competitor-threat audit reveals a possible threat from a new entrant firm into a product market. What is likely to be its motive? If you were in the competitor's shoes, what would be your major reason for entering the market? What implications does it have for existing competitors, and what dilemma does this create for public companies compared to private companies?
10. General Motors purchased Electronic Data Systems (EDS) for $2.5 billion. GM is EDS's biggest customer as it streamlines and integrates its own morass of computer systems, including its linkages with suppliers and dealers.[31] This variant of backward integration (of a service rather than a raw material or component's supplier) into the $20 billion computer services industry will inevitably bring GM into competition with the hardware/software systems giants. In another transaction, Exxon invested more than $1 billion in venture capital in office automation ideas for more than a decade. In 1980 the objective of its information systems division was to become a major supplier of advanced office systems and communication systems to large companies within three to five years. But in late 1984 Exxon sold the business.[32] What is your theory on why General Motors purchased Electronic Data Systems? What opportunities for GM might emerge from this transaction? On the other hand, what might GM learn from Exxon in this particular market?
11. Managers of mutual funds often talk about investing in companies with superior management. Use the theory of competitive rationality to develop a list of criteria to evaluate the superior management of a rival or of an investment opportunity. Does it matter whether the superior management is the result of superior systems, processes, or people?
12. What might changes in a competitor's advertising message themes over time reveal? What might an analysis of its media strategy reveal?
13. Some product markets maintain rules of behavior called industry or professional practices. List some examples. How and why do you think they have come about?
14. The two boxed cases in this chapter present a brief history of two markets: the mature beer market that experienced the Lite beer innovation and the relatively new VCR and videotape markets. These examples demonstrate the importance of being able to anticipate competitor behavior. Using library reference sources, write a one-page report that brings these two case studies up to date. Do you think that what happened in these two markets could have been anticipated? How?

[31] Stephen Koepp, "Driving into the Computer Age," *Time*, July 9, 1984, 65.
[32] Marilyn Harris, "Exxon Wants out of the Automated Office," *Business Week*, December 17, 1984, 39; and "Exxon's Next Prey: IBM and Xerox," *Business Week*, April 28, 1980, 92–103.

15. Use the section on anticipating competitors' behavior to explain why competition is much more intense when a company has two or more competitors rather than just one competitor. Why are the drive to innovate with new products and the drive to reduce costs so much stronger and more constant when a company has more than one competitor? What does this suggest about the number of sellers it takes to make a market competitive and keep it competitive?
16. Will computer software kill the $2 billion school textbook business? Over the last five years, school spending on textbooks has declined 7 percent a year (adjusted for inflation).[33] Meanwhile annual dollar spending on computer software is increasing more than textbook annual dollar spending is decreasing. In your answer describe some of the path dependency limits to software replacing textbooks. (Hint: revisit the Sony CD example in the text.)
17. The problems of predicting what path a technology takes are illustrated by predictions being made by experts in 1995 as to what effect the Internet will have on computing.[34] Scott McNealy the chief executive officer of Sun Microsystems predicts that network accessed, disposable (rented) software will kill the market for the purchase of operating systems and software for personal computers. The operating system will be in the network rather than in the computer. The president of MCI agrees that computing will follow this path. The chief executive officer of the PC chip maker Intel, Andy Grove, believes that progress along this path will be slow because most personal computers will still be dependent on phone lines to talk to each other. This limits access to network-accessed software. People also prefer to carry their own software around with them in their computers. The 100 million plus users of Microsoft Word and PowerPoint software are likely to continue to use upgraded versions of these software packages because high switching costs keep them on the Microsoft path-dependency. In giving your assessment as to how quickly Internet-rented software will replace software installed on personal computers, describe what sort of software is likely to be rented and what impact the renting of software will have on the design of personal computers.

[33] Damon Darlin, "Reprieve," *Forbes,* July 17, 1995, 62–64.
[34] "George Gilder and His Critics," *Forbes ASAP,* October 9, 1995, 165–181.

You must be in tune with the times and prepared to break with tradition.

William M. Agee

You on the cutting edge of technology have already made yesterday's impossibilities the commonplace realities of today.

Ronald Reagan

CHAPTER SEVEN

Analyzing Market Channels

Within our lifetime one hundred or more cable TV channels will target different market segments selling computers, books, hiking boots, compact discs, bedding, and fashion. Now about seven such marketing channels exist; by far the biggest are QVC, which reaches 50 million households, and Home Shopping Network (HSN), which reaches 69 million television households. But the futurists prediction of a revolution in direct marketing and retailing will not happen quickly. Home shopping constitutes a fraction of 1 percent of all retail shopping in the United States, and 50 percent of QVC and HSN's sales are still high-margin rings, bracelets, necklaces, pins, and other baubles.[1] QVC's breakneck growth in sales through the 1980s has slowed in the 1990s, and its "Can We Shop?" show with Joan Rivers lost a bundle. So, what is the future of TV and interactive home-computer shopping as a marketing channel?

For a start, forget grocery shopping as a large market. Only the very wealthy living in big cities where groceries are expensive and grocery shopping is difficult will use such services, and they come expensive—about $30 a month above the cost of the groceries. People like to squeeze the produce and see the meat they are buying. And while they are there, they may as well pick up the diapers, soft drinks, and pet food that they

need. But prospects for CUC International look very good. It provides a "Shopper Advantage" information service on thousands of products such as refrigerators, sound systems, and holidays and where to find the cheapest prices to millions of members. CommerceNet, a joint venture between forty Silicon Valley companies and the government, is inventing new shopping systems, including specialized shopping directories. But major technological limitations still exist that have to be overcome. For example, it takes several minutes to transmit a high-resolution photograph, and most shoppers will not buy unless they can see what they are buying. However, the Internet is bad news for travel agents. By the year 2000, 20 to 30 percent of airline, rental car, and holiday reservations will be made using the Internet.[2]

What should a retailer do facing the future threat of electronic shopping competition and the current fact of an oversupply of retailing space? Do you go high-tech such as Macy's, Spiegel, Eddie Bauer, Nordstom, and JCPenney, or do you wait until this new type of distribution channel really progresses farther down its development path and learn from the mistakes of the pioneers?

Meanwhile, the electronic data interchange (EDI) revolution has already occurred in business-to-business marketing and retailer supply-chain management, and the savings have been enormous. Over the past decade, the percentage of Gross National Product (GNP) spent on physical distribution has dropped from around 15 percent to less than 10 percent. The innovations in technology and processes in distribution channels are marketing's true contribution to increasing the competitiveness of the American economy over the past twenty years. Compared to this trading relationship revolution, the reality and potential of home shopping may be just a blip on the screen. ■

The majority of marketplace exchanges made today involve the use of a trading channel—third-party entities that are separate from the original seller and the final buyer. The trading channels that marketers use play a critical role in determining competitive advantage. The obvious channels are resellers, such as wholesalers, importers,

[1] David Whitford, "TV or Not TV," *Inc.*, June 1994, 63–68; and Laura Zinn, "Why Barry Needs Larry," *Business Week*, July 18, 1994, 30–32.

[2] "Net Profits," *The Economist*, July 9, 1994, 83–85; John Verity, "Planet Internet," *Business Week*, April 3, 1995, 118–24; and David C. Churbuck, "Dial-a-Catalog," *Forbes*, October 10, 1994, 126–30.

retailers, commission agents, and brokers, but any entity that is employed to facilitate the exchange process can serve as a trading channel. Banks and shipping agents help the payment process, advertising agents and trade show organizers facilitate the flow of information, and common carriers and the public warehouses facilitate the flow of goods.

In a marketplace, where the players are free to choose what to sell and what to buy, channels survive and flourish because both buyers and sellers pay them to perform particular functions. The services of the many and varied organizations that can make up a marketing channel are not just important to the individual seller. Economic history demonstrates that channel intermediaries have played, through their entrepreneurial marketing innovations, a crucial role in creating and shaping the modern U.S. economy. Many of the significant differences among today's international economies can be traced to the evolution of different trading channels in their economy.

Because the choice of channel partners, be it up or down the channel, has a profound effect on the profitability of a business, a marketing plan for a venture in a market that uses trading channels should include an analysis of current and potential channel members and exchange facilitators. This analysis can prove to be as important as an audit of the consumer or the competition.

In order to address the economic and political problems that may arise from trading channel relationships, marketers must maintain the following:

1. A macroeconomic understanding of how and why the different types of channel services and participants evolved.
2. An understanding of the major changes occurring today in distribution channels.

The first section of this chapter traces the origins of some of the major marketing intermediaries in the United States (see Figure 7.1). Understanding how channels evolved helps to explain how and why they are likely to change in the future. The development of trading channels is also an excellent demonstration of evolutionary economics. Much of the change in the organization of marketing channels can be traced to the ways entrepreneurs have used technological inventions to increase the effectiveness and efficiency of the flow of money, information, goods, and services. Social and political events also have created entrepreneurial opportunities.

The second section discusses how some of the technological and institutional changes occurring today are likely to reshape distribution channel relationships. The third section describes the basic functions of intermediaries. The fourth section presents a general audit template that can be adapted to evaluate suppliers and distributors. The fifth section discusses global channel analysis and sourcing.

Marketing Channels That Created the Modern Economy

The folklore of marketing has held that mass marketing came about as a result of mass production. In truth, it was the other way around. In his Pulitzer Prize–winning book, *The Visible Hand*, Alfred Chandler convincingly argues that the evolution of distribution channels in the United States can be traced to changes in the transportation and communication infrastructure, largely caused by the huge investment made in developing the national railway system.[3] The improvements in physical distribution

[3] Alfred D. Chandler, *The Visible Hand* (Cambridge, MA: University Press, 1977). Chandler presents an excellent history of the development of modern management.

Figure 7.1 **Chapter Organization**

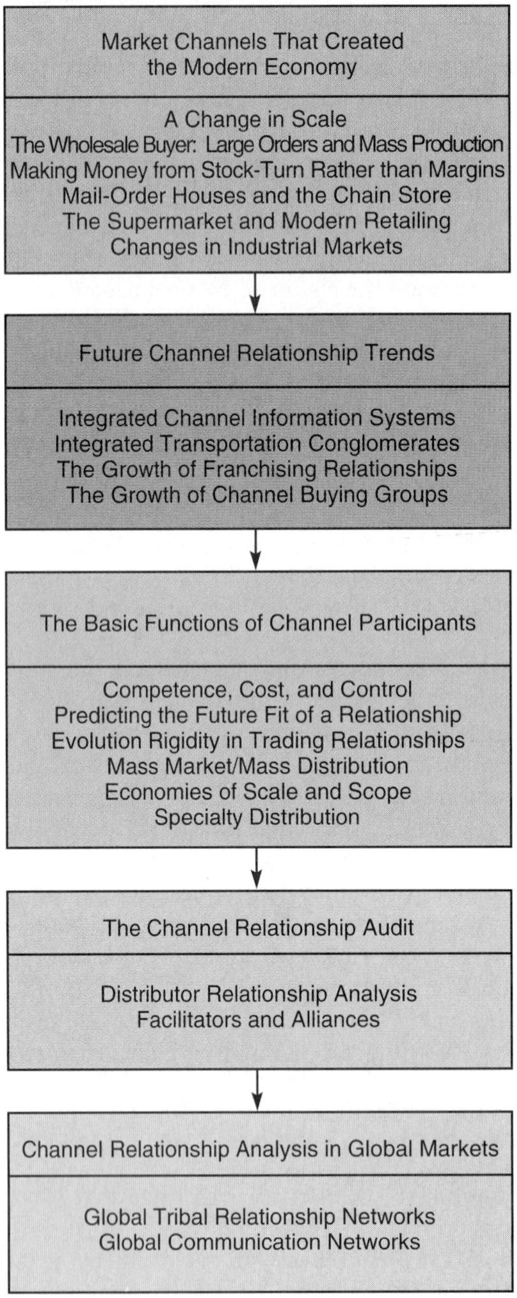

The chapter starts off describing how innovations in distribution have been a major driver of the development of markets and continue to be so. The basic functions of channel participants are explained, and a method of auditing current channel trading relationships is presented. The chapter closes with a discussion of channel relationship analysis in global markets.

provided by the railway and steamship over the sailing ship, canal barge, and wagon, and the improved communication provided by the telegraph over the primitive mail service, enabled the creation and growth of large, centralized wholesaling companies (see Figure 7.2). These institutions, in turn, created mass production.

A sudden change in scale of operations occurred between 1840 and 1870. The largest importers in the 1840s had annual sales of around $250,000 and employed fewer than twenty employees. By 1870, Alexander T. Stewart, the largest dry-goods wholesaler/importer, had annual sales in excess of $40 million and employed a buying and selling organization of two thousand persons.[4] Prior to the transportation revolution, merchants sold the products of local manufacturers, local agriculture industries, and imported goods to storekeepers, some of whom had to trek hundreds of miles every six months to buy their supplies. Having purchased the goods, the storekeepers then had to arrange a complicated and risky delivery chain involving numerous regional carriers and storehouses so goods could be unloaded and await the next barge or wagon. Much spoilage, damage, theft, and delay occurred.

By the 1860s, a new form of merchant, the wholesale jobber, had evolved. Wholesalers did not sell on a commission of 2 percent to 5 percent but instead took title to the goods. The sellers were happy because they now received prompt payment. The buyers were happy because the railway brought the wholesaler's traveling salesperson to the buyer's door with samples, catalogs, and a more reliable and less expensive delivery service. The wholesaler system also resulted in further cost savings because extra inventories needed to avoid the stock-outs caused by delivery uncertainty could be reduced. Of even greater significance, the wholesaler could now define its markets in national terms and gain huge economies of scale from bulk purchasing and buying expertise.

The Wholesale Buyer: Large Orders and Mass Production

The wholesaler's traveling sales forces spearheaded the mass marketing revolution. They introduced new products, spread merchandising innovations, and taught local retailers the rudiments of bookkeeping and retail management. The sales forces also reported back on regional economic conditions, new products and ideas, changes in demand, and retailer credit ratings.

It is interesting to note that at the very time these economic pioneers were helping to build a new industrial state, Karl Marx was characterizing this new class of "bourgeois" traders as economic leeches in *Das Kapital* and quoting no less than Thomas Jefferson in support of his argument that channel intermediaries only make their money from lying and thieving. The characterization of manufacturing as more honorable and productive than distribution has its roots in such ill-informed, if well-intentioned, slanders.

The large sales force was a new phenomenon, but just as important was the emergence of a new breed of buyer who had developed expert knowledge of a particular product group. These buyers were given total autonomy and were often involved in profit-sharing plans. The fortunes of the wholesalers depended on their skills. The buyer's expertise, built over years of experience, became greater than that of either the manufacturer (who often maintained a limited, parochial, local vision) or the end user and was, consequently, worth paying for. Many wholesalers set up buying offices in Europe where they searched for better buys or new products. Separate traffic departments

---

[4] Chandler, *The Visible Hand.*

Figure 7.2 **Technology That Revolutionized Distribution**

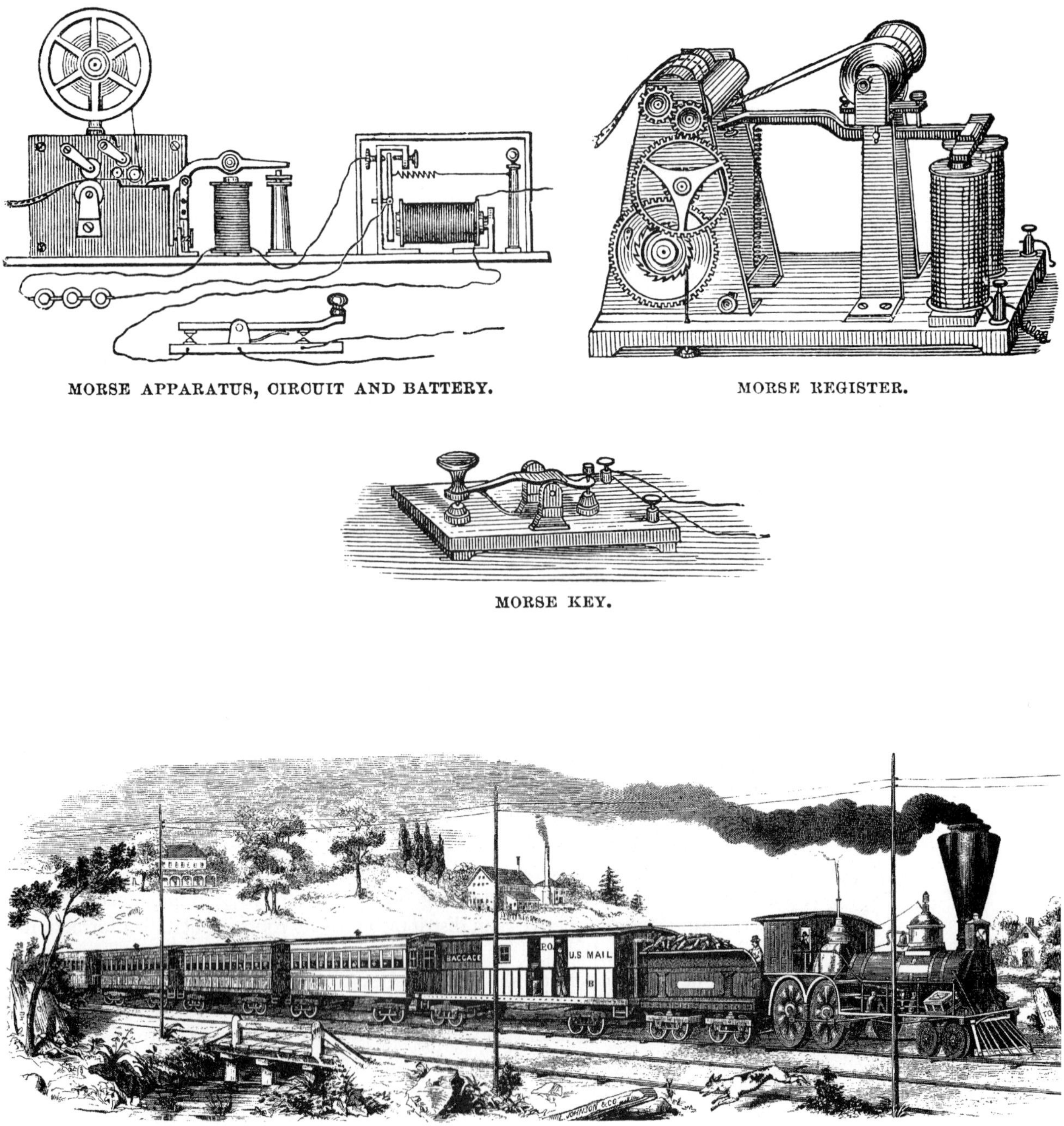

A hundred years ago the telegraph and competitive railway created national distribution and a national market. Now the modem equivalent technologies, the networked PC and the jumbo jet have created global distribution and a global competitive market.

(continued)

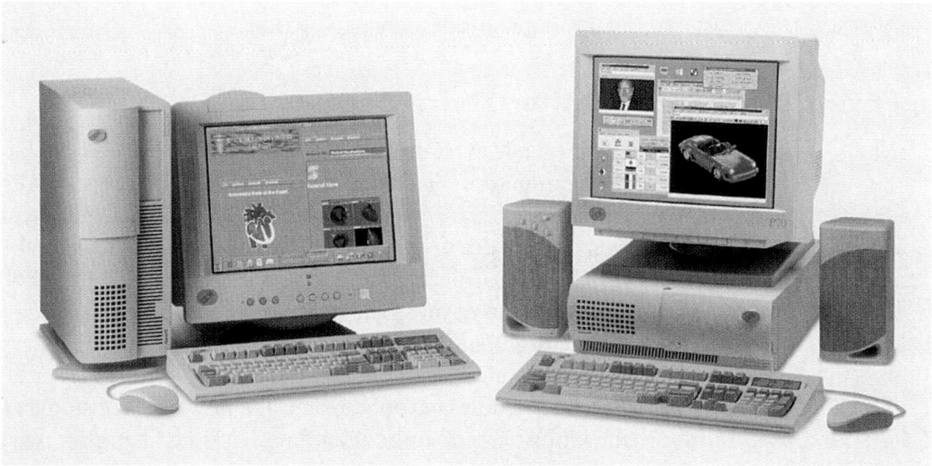

handled the shipping and negotiated special bulk rates with the railway and steamship companies. Credit and collection departments were set up that introduced standardized payment terms. The sheer scale of the wholesalers' operations gave them not only great buying power but also the opportunity to encourage manufacturers to expand to fill the wholesalers' large orders. In this sense, it is clear that mass distribution led and fostered the development of mass production.

Making Money from Stock-Turn Rather Than Margins

The wholesalers made even more money when they learned the basic law of retailing: Profits come from margin *and* stock-turn. *Margin* is price minus direct manufacturing and marketing costs. *Stock-turn* is the number of times a firm's inventory turns over in a year (annual dollar sales divided by the dollar value of the annual average inventory). These new measures of performance were introduced in the 1860s, and the wholesalers particularly focused on stock-turn.

By 1880 the dominance of the wholesaler had peaked as enterprising local retailers vertically integrated up the channel by buying or merging with wholesalers or setting up their own wholesale operations. By now the consumer was also becoming more urban, sophisticated, and demanding. In such changing market conditions, the retailer benefited by being closest to the consumer.

Consistent with the theory of competitive rationality, when the market environment changes, the players who are first to notice such changes and adapt gain an initial, and perhaps permanent, advantage. The first department stores were set up in New York and quickly spread to the major urban centers. Profits were made on sales volume and stock-turn rather than on margins. In 1887, Macy's recorded an average stock-turn of six over six months—double the typical stock-turn of today's department stores, even with their computerization. The department stores' lower prices wiped out many small retailers. The merchandising practices of the department store were little different from what they are today: extensive local advertising (that itself spawned the formation of advertising agencies), money-back guarantees, and markdown sales of slow-turning and seasonal items.

Mail-Order Houses and the Chain Store

Mail-order companies evolved to serve rural buyers who found it difficult to shop locally, let alone visit the big-city department stores. Sears & Roebuck was able to take advantage of the rapid improvement in postage and railway service in the 1890s. Its revenues increased geometrically from $745,000 in 1895 to $37,789,000 in 1905.[5] The mail-order houses were such a threat that the extension of the parcel-post service introduced in 1912 was vigorously opposed by traditional wholesalers and retailers.

As the small towns and suburbs grew in the early decades of this century, other entrepreneurs saw the opportunity and expanded their wholesaling or regional retailing operations into national chains of stores. The first chain stores were grocers, drug stores, and furniture stores in urban markets where the department stores concentrated on clothing and furnishings. For example, in 1865 the Great American Tea

[5] In fact, Sears's sales increased so rapidly that during the Christmas season of 1905 the company almost collapsed from within because it started to lose control of all of the orders and its shipping department became impossibly overloaded and chaotic. Great success can threaten a firm by overwhelming its logistics system.

Company (later A&P) sold only tea in 26 stores in downtown New York. The Great Western Tea Company (later Kroger) and the Jewel Tea Company started from a similar base of operation. Woolworth started the first five-and-dime variety store, in which all items were priced at either five or ten cents. By 1913, 680 such stores had sales of $66 million.[6] Other specialty chain stores flourished, such as the United Cigar Stores Company with 900 stores nationwide in 1914.

The chain stores operated in a way similar to the department store except that they required greater control over operations and logistics. The newly invented telephone and truck greatly assisted the management of these two activities. Many of the chains were also innovative in their management style. They gave managers a minority ownership of their store, and they operated the businesses in a manner similar to today's retail franchises. The competitive advantage of the chains came from their buying power, lower margins but higher stock-turn, scientific selection of store locations, standardized advertising, standardized store arrangement, window displays, sales training, and inventory control.[7] By the 1920s, the growth of the chain store had become so threatening that the two major mail-order houses, Montgomery Ward and Sears & Roebuck, responded by opening their own chain stores. Other merchants attempted to have tax and price control legislation passed to combat the enterprise and initiatives of the chain stores.[8]

The Supermarket and Modern Retailing

The spread of the suburbs during the prosperity of the 1920s, coupled with increased automobile ownership, led to the development of the first suburban shopping centers (anchored by a supermarket) and shopping malls (anchored by major department and chain stores). During the Great Depression of the 1930s, which killed off a lot of small merchants, the lower priced supermarket flourished. For the first time, a single store sold meat, produce, and dry foods. Previously, the consumer had to shop at the butcher shop, the bakery, the dairy, the drugstore, and the grocery store. Now they were all combined in a one-stop location that provided parking. The new refrigerator technology that provided in-home, in-store, and in-transit storage of perishables was also essential to the success of the supermarket.

Another innovation, self-service—in which most of the inventory was stored on the display shelves rather than in a back storeroom—reduced labor and inventory holding costs, encouraged consumers to experiment with new products, and paved the way for brand-image marketing by manufacturers such as Pillsbury and General Mill's Betty Crocker. This, coupled with the introduction of new advertising media (radio, magazines with superior graphics, and finally television), launched the golden era of household brands marketing (1950–1990).

In the 1950s, suburban shopping started to overshadow downtown shopping. Inner-city congestion and decay diminished the entertainment value of what had once been a special family event (dressing up to go shopping downtown on Friday night). By the mid-1960s, the shopping mall had evolved into its current form—anchor stores

---

[6] Ralph S. Butler, *Marketing Methods and Salesmanship* (New York: Alexander Hamilton Institute, 1914), 47. This book was one of the first marketing management texts ever published.

[7] Butler, *Marketing Methods.*

[8] The Robinson-Patman Fair Pricing Law was the result. It required a manufacturer to administer its prices so it sold its products at much the same price to all retailers. This law, which obviously runs counter to the spirit of the Sherman Act's *price-fixing* clauses, protected the interests of economically inefficient but politically powerful local merchants.

surrounded by specialty boutiques and service stores. Self-service discount stores, furniture warehouses, and catalog showrooms were launched by entrepreneurs who took advantage of improvements in mass distribution and computerization. Other forms of discount shopping have since evolved such as hardware superstores (Home Depot), off-price clothing outlets, and, of course, the most successful of all, Wal-Mart. Most of these forms of discount stores have succeeded because an increasing number of knowledgeable and skilled shoppers prefer price discounts and a wide selection of choices over a convenient location—especially when they don't have to sacrifice good service.

During the 1970s and 1980s, the major changes in consumer marketing channels largely resulted from the new channels of distribution being created by existing retailers, not from new forms of retailing. Pharmaceutical and health care products are now sold in convenience stores, discount drug chains, supermarkets, and department stores, as well as family-owned pharmacies. Soft goods and fast food are increasingly being sold in supermarkets. Department stores were being squeezed by discount and off-price clothing stores on one side and the premium fashion chains, such as The Limited and Lands-End, on the other side. This explains why many ended up in bankruptcy in the 1990s.[9] Warehouse clubs have made some inroads into the sales of more traditional supermarkets, drugstores, and discount stores. According to the Food Marketing Institute, because of their lower labor and facility costs, the operating expenses for warehouse clubs are about 7 to 9 percent of sales, compared to 19 to 21 percent for traditional grocers.[10] This is a considerable advantage. However, the growth in sales of warehouse clubs in the past few years has slowed considerably; it appears that for many shoppers warehouse clubs' locations and bulk packaging are too inconvenient.

Changes in Business-to-Business Channels

The discussion so far has focused on evolutions in consumer product channels. Changes in business-to-business marketing channel entities have not been as dramatic. The wholesaler may have faded in importance in the marketing of consumer goods over the last one hundred years, but this is certainly not so in many industrial markets. Wholesaler distributors are still personally responsible for much of the customer service and introduction of new products to businesses.

In many firms that competed in business-to-business markets prior to the 1970s, distribution was fragmented, and the responsibility was divided among several functional departments, such as accounting, manufacturing, and marketing. However, over the past two decades the distribution function has been integrated, leading to major changes in order processing, transportation, and warehousing. Business-to-business marketers have only recently made advances in distribution and channel management for several reasons.[11]

First, compared with manufacturing and promotion, distribution has been neglected. Marketers gradually realized that the cost reduction or service differentiation that might result from paying more attention to distribution could create a considerable competitive advantage. Second, large increases in gas prices in the 1970s and high interest rates in the early 1980s also focused attention on distribution management.

[9] The polarization of large retailers into general low-cost merchants and specialized, high-service retailers is predicted by Management Horizons (a prominent retail consulting firm) to continue.

[10] Linda L. Hyde, "Catalysts for Change in Retail Strategy," *1992 Strategic Outlook Conference* (Columbus, OH: Management Horizons, 1992).

[11] Bernard J. LaLonde, John Grabner, and James F. Robeson, "Integrated Distribution Systems: Past, Present, and Future," *The Distribution Handbook* (New York: The Free Press, 1985), 15–27.

Third, as increasing competition made it difficult to increase sales, managers started to really appreciate the profit leverage that came from reducing distribution costs instead. Fourth, the computerized integration of order-processing, warehousing, and dispatching functions did not become common until the early 1980s. Fifth, global marketing places a premium on logistic efficiencies.

Future Channel Relationship Trends

Several major forces are likely to change market channel relationships in the future. Technological changes in communications and third-party transportation services will influence who is involved in distribution. The political economy of channels is also likely to change as a result of the continued growth in franchising and the formation of channel buying groups. Each of these is discussed in the following sections.

Integrated Channel Information Systems

Electronic information technology has greatly increased distribution efficiency in business-to-business markets. For example, P&G is linked to Wal-Mart by computers, and orders for its personal care and cleaning products are received, processed, and dispatched automatically. This relationship is similar to the just-in-time management of raw materials by a manufacturer whose production process computers are linked to its suppliers' order-processing and dispatch computers. The advantages for market forecasting, inventory management, and production scheduling are obvious. The savings in time, documentation, and paperwork are profound. At a strategic level technology also has shifted the balance of power in the channel (see the Rationality in Practice box: Information Is Power).

The availability of electronic information has affected marketing channels in other ways. For example, industrial buyers can consult electronic catalogs, which are constantly updated with information about new lines, availability, delivery, volume price breaks, and innovative payment terms. The use of UPC-type coding also allows a firm to track the progress of an order through the channel in real time.

Integrated channel information systems (channel intranets) enable a company to assess the performance of channel members, the profitability of doing business with them, and the success of promotional programs and new, more efficient operating processes. Not being a part of such an information system may become a real barrier to entering some markets. On the other hand, being part of the system also may limit the managerial options of the participant by limiting the company's ability to switch to alternative distribution options. These and other inter- versus intrachannel competition antitrust issues have yet to be adequately addressed by managers and legislators. The outcome of such judgments will profoundly shape the way business-to-business relationships are conducted. For instance, the electronic revolution in channel relationship marketing has allowed retailers and distributors to greatly reduce their *number* of supplier relationships. For example, Federated, a major department-store chain, reduced its number of suppliers from fourteen thousand to two hundred in the late 1980s.[12] Ford has reduced the number of its global supplies from several thousand to several hundred. The effect on suppliers can be imagined.

---

[12] Linda L. Hyde, "Catalysts for Change in Retail Strategy," *1992 Strategic Outlook Conference* (Columbus, OH: Management Horizons, 1992), 14.

Rationality in Practice

Information Is Power

Point-of-sale electronic technology and supply-chain management processes that use it enable stores such as Wal-Mart to tell manufacturers such as Manco (who supplies Wal-Mart and Target with a range of duct-tape products—a $500 million business) what they want and exactly when and where they need it. This information is driving the product-development and manufacturing scheduling processes of such vendors. Retailers' real-time awareness of "what is hot, where, and what is not" has shifted the balance of power in the distribution channel because consumer-goods manufacturers have had to become much more responsive order takers and order makers.[13]

An excellent example of the power of point-of-sale information is the way it has changed the competitiveness of record stores. Traditional record stores have continued to target the MTV crowd, and between 1990 and 1992 their market share of prerecorded music dropped from 72 percent to 62 percent.[14] Their competitors, the mail-order clubs and discounters such as Wal-Mart, were tracking the boom in sales of country music and shifting their offering to meet this demand.

Twenty years ago, consumer-goods manufacturers managed the distribution channel with advertising campaigns that pulled new products through the channel and with trade promotions used by a sales force that pushed the product down the channel. Such a *push/pull* strategy often does not work today, and the reason has to do with not only faster and more accurate *ordering processes* and cycles but also faster and more reliable quick-response *delivery processes* that now use tracking information to move bar-coded products down the distribution channel. The combination of these new computer-driven order and delivery processes such as those used by Wal-Mart, Home Depot, and Office Depot moves products at speeds tentimes faster than in the past to where and when customers want them. It is called "efficient consumer response." In the past, the presence of many slow-moving finished goods held in inventory by wholesalers and retailers helped manufacturers "own" the distribution channels because channel members had to move these mountains of manufacturers' goods to make a living. Now distribution channels carry small inventories of particular manufacturers' products, making the wholesalers and retailers less dependent on manufacturers. Conversely, with so little stock in distribution channels, what income manufacturers make next week almost literally depends on what they sell today. As a result, a problem with a major distribution channel has immediate effects on manufacturing and cash flow. A manufacturer has a short time to negotiate, to react, and at worst to switch some of its business to another distribution channel.

Transportation Efficiencies

Continued innovations in transportation technology and regulation also are likely to have a major impact on channel structures and relationships (see Figure 7.3). Containerization has changed the competitive dynamics in the marketing channel. The redesigning of international and domestic transportation infrastructure around the container has reduced costs for the original shipper and the final buyer. Not only has intermediate handling been reduced, but also containers have reduced losses due to spoilage and theft. They also serve as useful short-term miniwarehouses for storing inventory. Perhaps most important, the integration of competing modes of transportation around the container has introduced much more competition among these modes (rather than just within each mode). Before the container, it was labor intensive, expensive, and time consuming to switch from one transportation mode to another (for example, truck to rail or rail to truck).

Containerization has forced the different transportation modes (ship, rail, air, and truck) to focus on the haulage activities they undertake most efficiently and to introduce

[13] Peter Burrows, "The Great Equalizer," *Business Week/The Information Revolution*, 1994, 102.
[14] Nina Munk, "Shopping in Peace," *Forbes*, March 14, 1994, 94.

Figure 7.3 **The Declining Cost of Physical Distribution**

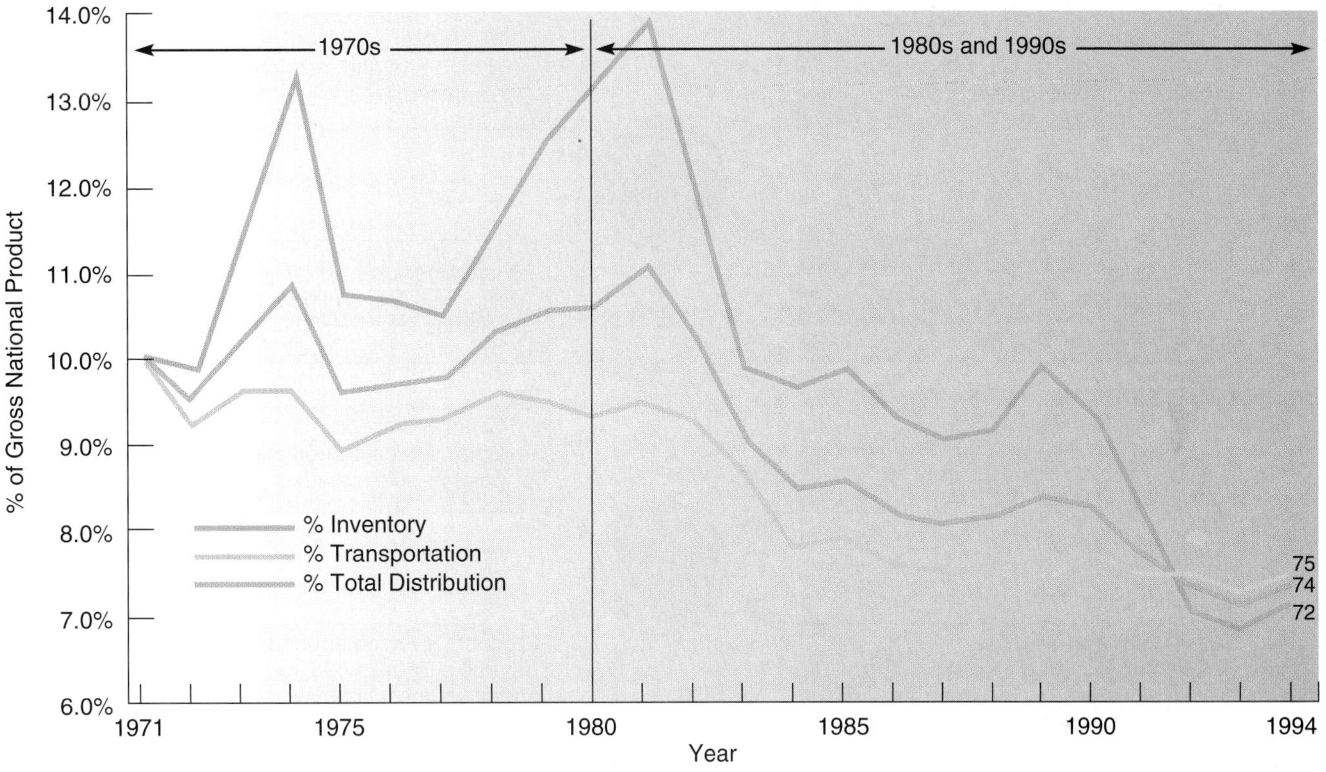

Physical distribution costs have declined from 13.2 percent of the Gross National Product in 1971 to 9.8 percent in 1994. In between, costs rose in 1974 and 1981 as a result of high interest rates. The decline in transportation costs in the early 1980s was the result of deregulation, which increased competition in trucking and among railroads. Throughout this period innovations in communication, containerization, and warehousing processes also have contributed to this extraordinary increase in distribution efficiency.

SOURCE: Robert V. Delaney, *Is Logistics Productivity at a Crossroad? Simple Facts, Plain Arguments and Common Sense*, St. Louis Information Systems and Cass Information Systems.

and adapt new technologies. Freight forwarders (transportation specialists) now mix and match the modes to offer a greater variation in service and price to customers than was previously available. All of these changes have occurred somewhat at the expense of the intermediate public warehouse and most certainly at the expense of the domestic supplier. Technology has now made it much easier and cheaper for importers and manufacturers to physically move their goods and offshore-assembled components into and around the United States. In short, innovations in physical distribution have decreased the global marketplace by making it much more accessible.

The Growth of Franchising Relationships

A *franchise* is a trading relationship in which the franchisor (the seller or supplier) gives a franchisee (a reseller) the rights to sell its product, often including exclusive

Figure 7.4 **Typical Services Franchisors Provide Franchisees**

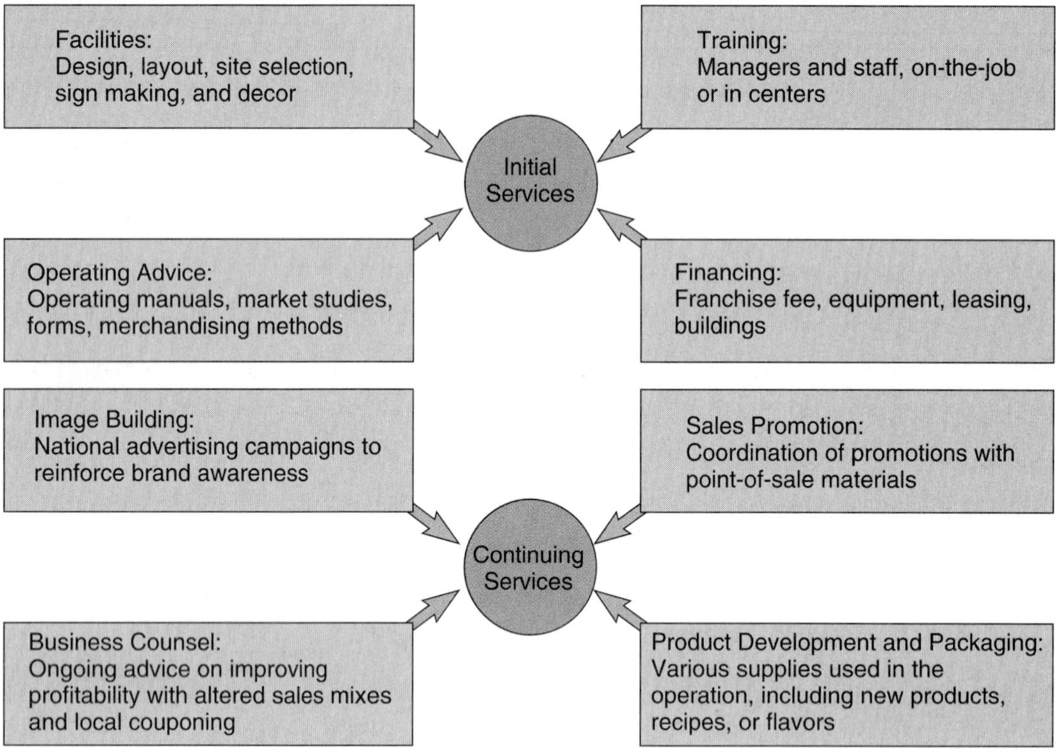
Facilities:
Design, layout, site selection, sign making, and decor
Training:
Managers and staff, on-the-job or in centers
Initial Services
Operating Advice:
Operating manuals, market studies, forms, merchandising methods
Financing:
Franchise fee, equipment, leasing, buildings
Image Building:
National advertising campaigns to reinforce brand awareness
Sales Promotion:
Coordination of promotions with point-of-sale materials
Continuing Services
Business Counsel:
Ongoing advice on improving profitability with altered sales mixes and local couponing
Product Development and Packaging:
Various supplies used in the operation, including new products, recipes, or flavors

SOURCE: From Kenneth G. Hardy and Allan J. Magrath, *Marketing Channel Management: Strategic Planning and Tactics*. Copyright © 1988 by Scott, Foresman and Company. Reprinted by permission of HarperCollins Publishers.

rights to a particular geographical territory. The franchisor also supplies the services described in Figure 7.4. In return, the franchisee agrees to buy exclusively from the franchisor. In addition to paying for the supplies, the franchisee pays the franchisor a commission on all of its sales and an initial franchise fee.

About $800 million (40 percent) of all retail sales are made by franchise organizations, and their sales grew 10 percent in 1994, twice the retailing sector's average. For the past ten years *Fortune* 500 companies have shrunk by 1 million jobs, and franchises have added 2 million jobs to the economy.[15] Typical of the growth in franchising is the development of the realtor Century 21. It began conversion franchising (converting an existing independent real estate business with one or more offices into a franchisee) in 1971 and by 1979 had 7,500 franchise offices worldwide and a $10 million-plus annual advertising budget to build the brand name, making it by far the dominant voice-share and mind-share realtor in the market. Other highly visible franchise oper-

[15] Montgomery Garrett, "The Twenty-First Century Franchise," *Inc.*, January 1995, 79–88; and Gregory Matusky, "The Franchise Hall of Fame," *Inc.*, April 1994, 86–89.

ations are McDonald's, H&R Block (10,000 offices worldwide), and Blockbuster videos (3,000 plus stores). Franchising is the major channel that industries such as pest control use to deliver their services. Service franchisees are required to follow prescribed service delivery scripts and train their employees to follow such scripts (see Chapters 9, 10, and 17).

Franchising enables entrepreneurs to quickly, economically, and efficiently launch their ideas into many other local markets. The advantage to a franchisee is that franchising provides a way to profit from the innovative creativity and early risk taking of the franchisor. The franchisee is, in a sense, paying an up-front fee and continuing royalty for a sure thing. Franchising is a way of quickly spreading a good idea and accelerating change across an economy and society. It is one of the most efficient mechanisms of the free market and capitalism.

Franchising effectively places the entrepreneurial decision making and marketing planning for many separately owned enterprises in the hands of a few. The franchisor had better continue to be very good at marketing decision making, for its own sake and the sake of all its franchisees. When the franchisor's marketing planning loses its competitive edge, as happened with General Motors in auto sales and Burger King in fast food, the franchisees feel very uncomfortable about their lack of control over their destiny. The marketing and production planning systems introduced must compensate for the loss of the personal creative flair (competitive rationality) that the original franchisor entrepreneurs and their management teams provided. Another solution is for the franchisor to reward franchisees richly for suggesting new operational and marketing ideas that can be adopted generally by the franchise network.

The Growth of Channel Buying Groups

The growth of buying groups such as Tru Value Hardware stores is another excellent example of evolutionary competitive economics. Buying groups are formed when a major chain threatens to dominate a market through economies of scale. Individual businesses that could not survive on their own combine to form an economic "herd" that initially seeks and obtains volume buying discounts from sellers. The group then develops cooperative management, merchandising, and marketing programs.

The market share of the top twenty-five home-improvement chains increased from 25 percent of hardware sales in 1990 to 33 percent in 1993.[16] Purchasing collectives such as Ace and True Value are surviving by buying at wholesale almost as cheaply as the big chains, by feature pricing the most price-sensitive items shoppers use to judge overall store prices, by sharing in the cost of national advertising campaigns, and by developing expertise in specific areas such as plumbing, garden supplies, woodworking tools, or rental equipment. Small, independent office-supply companies are also finally getting together in buying cooperatives to compete against the discounters (Wal-Mart, Kmart) and category killers (Staples, Office Depot, Office-Max) that have driven seven thousand small office suppliers out of business between 1986 and 1995. Figure 7.5 not only highlights the advantages gained from such buying groups but also describes how they evolve. When fully evolved, a buying group has many of the buying, management, and marketing strengths of the competitor that brought it into being. A buying group requires cooperation and some conformity, but its integrated organization increases the chances of survival of its individual members.

[16] Tom Ehrenfeld, "The Demise of Mom and Pop?" *Inc.*, January 1995, 46–48.

Figure 7.5 The Evolution of the Intermediary Buying Groups

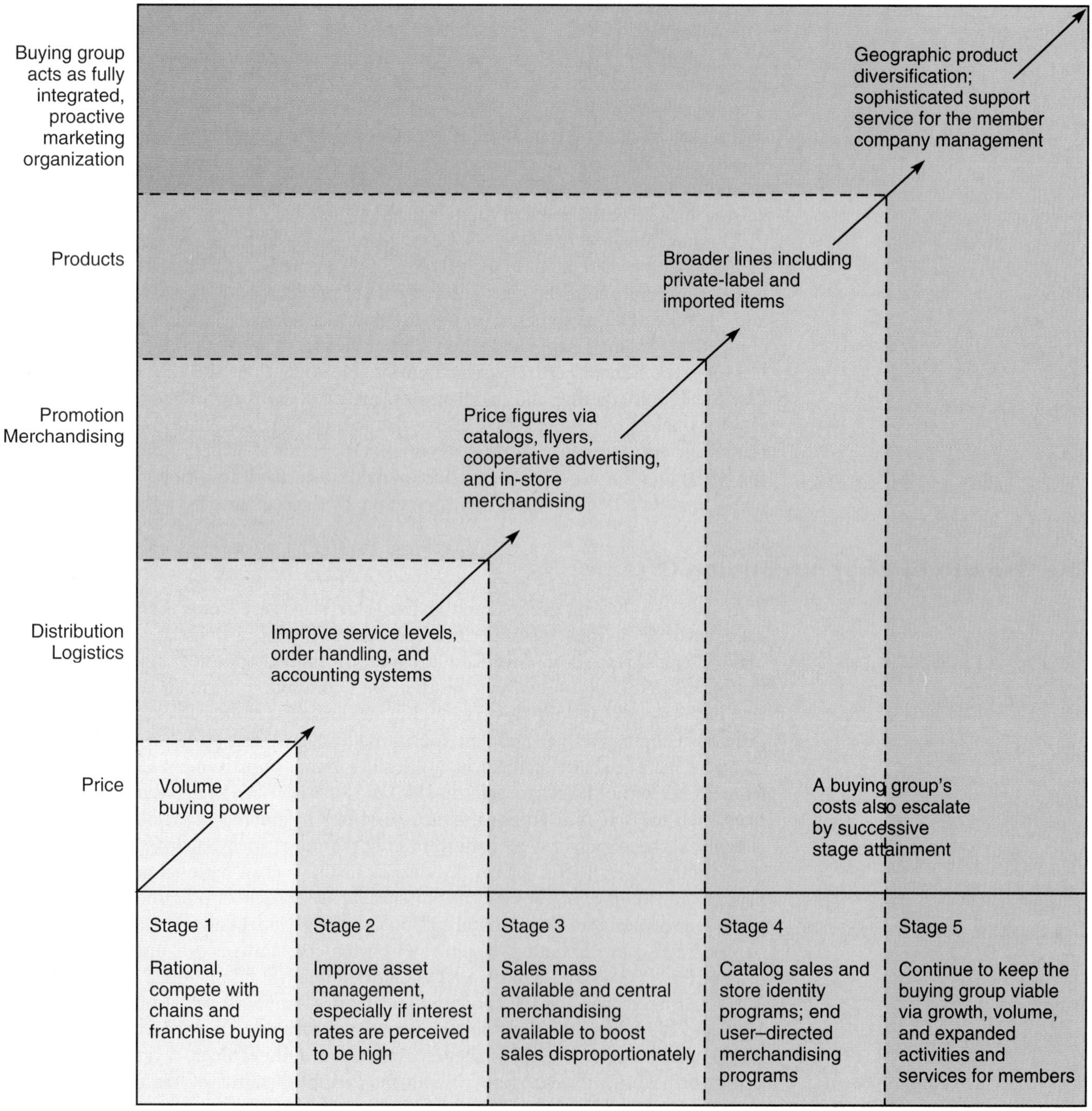

SOURCE: From Kenneth G. Hardy and Allan J. Magrath, *Marketing Channel Management: Strategic Planning and Tactics.* Copyright © 1988 by Scott, Foresman and Company. Reprinted by permission of HarperCollins Publishers.

The Basic Functions of Channel Participants

Because of the increasing competition among channels and the ever present possibility of technological or economic change, it is imperative for an enterprise to be prepared to adapt its distribution system. This requires a sound understanding of the basic functions of a channel.[17] The players may change, the technology may change, and where and how the functions are undertaken may change, but the fundamental activities of a marketing channel and the economic principles governing a channel do not change. Sometimes this truth is lost in the adaptation process.

The most common function of a marketing channel member is to resell the product into a market that could not be reached as efficiently or effectively by the original seller. Intermediaries have already established goodwill with their customers, and those customers trust the intermediary's buying judgments. Retailers often have multiple selling outlets that are both in prime geographical locations and have the right image. This gives the manufacturer both *physical* and *psychological* market positioning.

Intermediaries play a major role in bringing the product or service to the end user at the right place and right time by *transportation* and *storage*. Many intermediaries also work with the manufacturer to provide customer *training*, *education*, and after-sales *maintenance and repair services*. The *risk-taking* and *financing* activities of channel intermediaries have been greatly reduced over the last one hundred years. Nowadays, many new products are sold to retailers on consignment (retailers pay for what they sell and return the rest) or purchased with buyback deals in the contract. Some retailers are even demanding up-front cash payments (shelf-slotting allowances) to compensate for the cost and the risk of placing a new product on their shelves. With established products, the credit allowances given to the wholesaler or retailer are such that a high-turn product is often sold by the retailer before the wholesaler or retailer pays the manufacturer for the product.

Sometimes merchants do take risks with seasonal products and are caught with stock at the end of a season that has to be sold at a loss or carried over to the next year. Many retailers also offer their shoppers no-questions-asked, money-back guarantees. On the other hand, the manufacturer usually provides a product performance warranty even though the retailer or wholesaler is the new legal owner of the product. Channel members are able to provide valuable customer feedback, but often the manufacturer also provides information down the channel to retailers that creates interest and support for its product. Hence, *market research* and information flows form a two-way street with findings and data often being interpreted in different ways by the various parties.

Competence, Cost, and Control

Just who should undertake these distribution and marketing activities depends essentially on three factors: competence, cost, and control. Each of these criteria has to be considered before deciding whether a particular function should be done in-house or undertaken by a channel partner. Marketing expertise and competence can be provided immediately by an intermediary, but this often results in a higher cost and a loss of some control over the marketing of the product. Determining whether it is less expensive to subcontract marketing responsibilities to channel partners is similar to

[17] For an excellent discussion of channel functions, see Louis Stern and Adel El-Ansary, Marketing *Channels*, 3rd ed. (Englewood Cliffs, NJ: Prentice-Hall, 1988).

deciding whether to subcontract or manufacture a product in-house. A channel member may, through economies of scale or scope, be able to provide service at a lower cost. But whether these cost savings are passed on to the manufacturer or are retained as profits by the channel participant depends largely on the competition among channel members to serve the supplier.

Competence and control have to be evaluated from two perspectives: the fit between the fundamental competitive strategies of channel partners and the channel members' ability to execute the planned joint-marketing strategy. Each alternative channel participant can be evaluated on the competence, cost, and control dimensions for each of the different functions described. The problem is that often the channel functions cannot be unbundled. They are offered in a take-it-or-leave-it package by a channel intermediary (reseller). This makes channel selection very difficult because a reseller may be strong on one function but weak on another function compared with other resellers. Figure 7.6 illustrates the variety of channel intermediaries that exist, their functions, and typical gross margins earned.

Evolutionary Rigidity in Trading Relationships

In distribution channels, traditional trading practices, rituals, and trappings often frustrate the introduction of innovations. This is called *channel evolutionary rigidity.* Such cautious change can be seen best in the recent, but long-delayed, computerization of stock trading. Almost all product markets mix archaic trading practices with modern innovations. Cultural change generally lags behind technological or economic change. The stronger the trading traditions in a market, the less adaptable the market will be to change. But because others in the market will be slow to adopt and adapt, the innovator can reap tremendous rewards. Hence, a strong incentive to innovate in nonadaptive markets exists. Such innovations will ultimately "break" the evolutionary rigidity of these markets.

Over the past decade, advances in physical distribution, communications, and information processing technologies also have radically reduced the need for some of the customary activities undertaken by channel intermediaries such as brokers and wholesalers. As markets mature, the pioneer personal-selling and order-taking efforts of the channel are no longer needed and are replaced by direct selling and billing. Less inventory is carried in the channel because sales stabilize, and orders are often drop shipped (bypassing the intermediary). The problem is that margins, payment terms, and other traditional trading practices are sticky. The renegotiation of terms often puts considerable strain on relationships. A relationship that does not have enough give and take ultimately results in a channel fracture, and the manufacturer or retailer breaks out of its traditional relationship only to face the internal and external adjustment problems of breaking into different levels of the channel or breaking into a completely new channel. Another serious consequence of evolutionary rigidity is that a channel member's failure to move with the times drags down its suppliers and resellers, whose loyalty may prevent them from keeping up with the competition. The reverse can happen when an innovative retailer is slowed by suppliers who are reluctant to change their products and trading practices. It often takes a new generation of executives to fully adapt to the new trading channel realities and relationships.

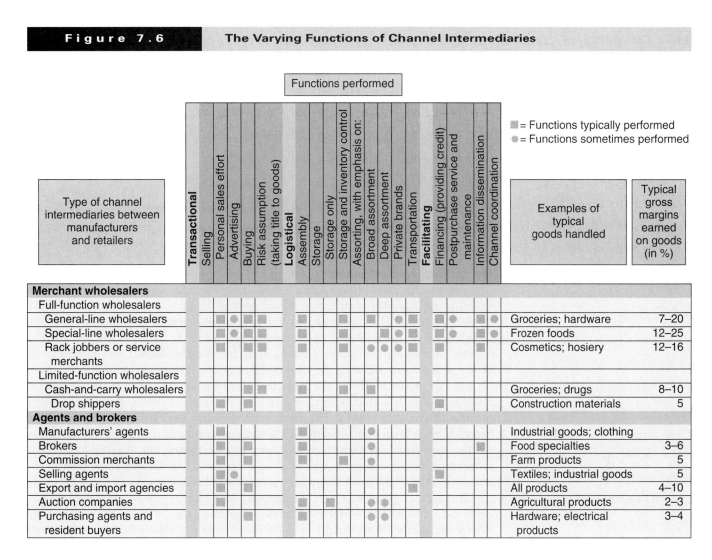

Figure 7.6 **The Varying Functions of Channel Intermediaries**

Functions performed

■ = Functions typically performed
● = Functions sometimes performed

Type of channel intermediaries between manufacturers and retailers	**Transactional**	Selling	Personal sales effort	Advertising	Buying	Risk assumption (taking title to goods)	**Logistical**	Assembly	Storage	Storage only	Storage and inventory control	Assorting, with emphasis on:	Broad assortment	Deep assortment	Private brands	Transportation	**Facilitating**	Financing (providing credit)	Postpurchase service and maintenance	Information dissemination	Channel coordination	Examples of typical goods handled	Typical gross margins earned on goods (in %)
Merchant wholesalers																							
Full-function wholesalers																							
General-line wholesalers			■	●	■	■		■			■		■		●	■		■	●	■	●	Groceries; hardware	7–20
Special-line wholesalers			■	●	■	■		■			■			■	●	■		■	●	■	●	Frozen foods	12–25
Rack jobbers or service merchants			■		■	■		■			■		●	●	●	■		■		■		Cosmetics; hosiery	12–16
Limited-function wholesalers																							
Cash-and-carry wholesalers					■	■		■			■		■									Groceries; drugs	8–10
Drop shippers			■		■													■				Construction materials	5
Agents and brokers																							
Manufacturers' agents			■					■					●									Industrial goods; clothing	
Brokers			■		■			■					●							■		Food specialties	3–6
Commission merchants			■		■			■			■		●									Farm products	5
Selling agents			■	●														■				Textiles; industrial goods	5
Export and import agencies			■		■											■						All products	4–10
Auction companies			■					■		■			●	●								Agricultural products	2–3
Purchasing agents and resident buyers					■			■					●	●								Hardware; electrical products	3–4

These diverse types of intermediaries have arisen because different sellers and buyers had a need for their various services. Their long-term survival and competitiveness depend on a continuing need for their bundle of services. This need may be threatened by technological innovations that change the added value of channel intermediaries.

SOURCE: Reprinted with the permission of Macmillan Publishing Company from *Marketing*, by James Heskett. Copyright © 1976 by Macmillan Publishing Company.

Mass Market/Mass Distribution

In discussing the functions of a distribution channel, it is important to recognize that different products require different distribution systems. The distribution strategy for many convenience products, such as batteries and soft drinks, is very simple: Make the product as convenient to buy as possible by getting it into as many channel outlets as possible. Convenience products are called that because shoppers will not go out of their way to buy the preferred alternative. When that product or service is not available, then the next most preferred alternative will do. Consequently, the best distribution for a convenience product is to be everywhere the competitors are and are not. Mass distribution is best suited for products with the following characteristics:

- Inexpensive
- Easy to try
- Frequently purchased
- Nondurable
- Low risk

The distributor adds little to the product except low cost and access convenience. Product knowledge and purchase preferences are cultivated through the manufacturer's advertising and product trial. The benefits of shopping at and buying through a select channel are minimal for convenience products because reseller image, services, and marketing add little value.

Mass distribution often means several levels of channel intermediaries are required in the channel to reach, service, and control the merchandising and sales of the ultimate resellers. This means giving away added margin (trade discounts) to distributor wholesalers, manufacturer representatives, brokers, or rack jobbers to have the product delivered to the retailer. Consequently, in mass distribution, much of the focus of competition is on reducing the costs of distribution and keeping the shelves stocked.

One of the strengths of the large packaged-goods companies is the significant economies of scale and scope in their own mass distribution system that reaches down to the individual retail outlet. Their new products share the fixed and variable costs of operating this distribution system with established products. Systems and procedures are also well established (through past learning) for rolling out new products. Such distribution system competences have been recognized as an undervalued asset in recent years and are the justification for a number of major mergers and acquisitions.

At the other extreme, a start-up company with a new convenience product must either cut a deal with the centralized buying organizations of a major chain store, piggyback on another manufacturer's distribution system, or saturate a very localized market. In the latter case, the initial success can be used to roll out the product progressively, first regionally and then nationally. All of this is much easier said than done. Many entrepreneurs and naive marketers have prematurely licked their lips at the prospect of gaining one half of 1 percent of the U.S. market in a particular product category. The reality is that a particular distributor, in a specific market, needs much better sales performance (probably a 5 percent to 10 percent market share) in its local market before it will push the new entry. Even when a new product is able to pass such a test, its troubles are really only beginning. As mentioned in Chapter 1, the manufacturer of the new product can do little to prevent a major company from analyzing the situation and slipstreaming, that is, entering the market behind the innovator and using its own well-oiled, superior distribution-channel machinery to roll out nationally and earn most of the "entrepreneurial" profits.

Specialty Distribution

The concept of *consumer franchise* is critical when thinking about how to distribute products. Every culture, whether primitive or advanced, ancient or modern, has cus-

The Limited is a specialty clothing store that has spawned several new store concepts (The Limited Express and Limited Too) that cater to the children of its original customers.

tomary ways of obtaining its products and services. In most economies, information about where products or services can be purchased or leased is passed from one generation to the next (either from parent to child or from senior to junior executive). In this way, distributors and retailers develop a consumer franchise that is created as a result of both cultural influences and individual enterprise. A consumer franchise is measured in terms of the *number* and *type* of existing customers and their *loyalty* to the reseller. The more the consumer believes a retailer contributes to a product's ultimate performance (through the retailer's assistance in problem recognition, solution specification, recommendations and endorsements, tangible services, warranties, and an intangible image), the more the consumer is likely to seek out and be loyal to this retailer. This is the essence of its consumer franchise.

For mass market products, a reseller's consumer franchise is based on convenience and price image. In specialty markets, expertise, service, and image also shape the nature and loyalties of a reseller's consumer franchise. A specialty reseller, be it a distributor or a retailer, opens a door for a supplier into a unique submarket: the reseller's consumer franchise. Each retail store's assortment of customers has varying degrees of uniqueness measured in terms of individual differences (such as age or income), product usage, needs, perceptions of the competitive offerings, sensitivity to different promotional strategies, and loyalty to the store.

Specialty distributors are generally used for expensive specialty products where design, choice of technology, and after-sales service are important. For a supplier of a mass distribution product, the basic problem is how to get into the mass distribution channels. For the marketer of a specialty product aimed at a specialty market, the problem is more complex. The choice of distributor can make or break the ultimate competitiveness of its offering. As discussed in Chapter 11, a match must exist between the supplier's strengths and weaknesses and the reseller's strengths and weaknesses. A

The Sharper Image has expanded from a catalog selling expensive toys to yuppies to a successful modern chain store.

match also must exist between the supplier's target markets and the reseller's loyal customers.

The Channel Audit

The suggested procedure for auditing the channel is first to address a number of questions about general changes in the channel and then to zero in on a detailed audit of key resellers. Table 7.1 lists several questions that address the impact on the channel of (1) changes in technology, (2) new entrants, (3) changes in established channel relations, and (4) changes in the way existing channel members do business. The first three types of change were described earlier. The recorded music market provides an excellent example of how the way channel members do business impacts manufacturers.

In the 1950s and early 1960s, record retailers allowed consumers to play new records in the store. This was an important way of exposing a new artist or title to the public, because the enthusiasts and opinion leaders did most of this in-store sampling. But as popular music took off with rock 'n' roll and the spending power of the baby boomers increased, chain stores opened record bars that did not provide the sound booths for sampling but undercut the record stores on prices. Consumers would often listen to the music in the record store and buy at the chain store. To compete, the record stores dropped the sound booths but offered a generous return policy. Eventually, the return policy was dropped.

As a result of the termination of in-store sampling, popular radio stations became critical in marketing records. But radio was also going through a transition. Increased competition was forcing the stations into Top 20 or Top 40 formats where the hit-parade music was played continuously at the expense of new artists and songs. This program format kept the audiences and advertisers happy, but it forced the recording

Table 7.1 Channel Change Audit

Answering these questions will reveal the dynamic path dependencies that are occurring in the available distribution and reseller channels.

- *Who are the latest new entrants in the reseller market?*
  What is their competitive advantage?
  Which existing resellers are being most affected?
  How has it affected us?
- *What new trading coalitions among resellers are occurring?*
  What will be their competitive advantage?
  How will it affect us?
- *What changes in order-processing technology are now occurring?*
  What impact will they have on the way business is done?
  What competitive advantage do they provide?
- *What changes in transportation technology are now occurring?*
  What impact will they have on the way business is done?
  What competitive advantage do they provide?
- *What changes in warehousing technology are now occurring?*
  What impact will they have on the way business is done?
  What competitive advantage do they provide?
- *What changes in payment technology are now occurring?*
  What impact will they have on the way business is done?
  What competitive advantage do they provide?

companies to buy airtime in order to advertise their new releases (where previously such exposure was free). This increased the cost of launching a new release, thus giving a major competitive advantage to the larger recording studios and distributors. MTV pulled the recording industry out of the doldrums in the early 1980s, but this new channel has forced the studios into a whole new marketing activity—video production. The music video component has become an important new competitive element in selling compact discs and tapes and a further entrance barrier for new competition.

Many channels of distribution have changed dramatically in recent years. Figure 7.7 illustrates how cut-flower distribution changed between 1970 and 1984. Importers from around the world entered the market and now produce more than 40 percent of the cut flowers sold in the United States. At the other end of the channel, mass marketers, such as supermarkets, have expanded their market share from 2 percent to 20 percent (and that percentage is still growing). Caught in between, wholesale florists are facing a radically changing supplier and reseller market and all sorts of new competitive channel mutations, including ship-it-direct companies such as 1-800-FLOWERS.

Auditing Individual Resellers

Once the channel change audit has been undertaken, the important resellers and suppliers will have been identified for further study. Clearly, not all resellers and suppliers can be studied, and some good managerial judgment is needed to make sure greater attention is paid to the major players and innovators. When a manufacturer's sales force uses an account management approach for its major retail trade accounts, it should be relatively easy to complete audits of such resellers. However, care must be taken that day-to-day operating relations do not drive the valuations of those who are in constant contact with representatives of suppliers and resellers. The reseller audits require the auditor to stand back to assess the changes that have occurred over the past trading year and explain some of the basic reasons for predicting longer term changes.

Figure 7.7 **Changes in the Cut-Flower Distribution Channel, 1970–1984**

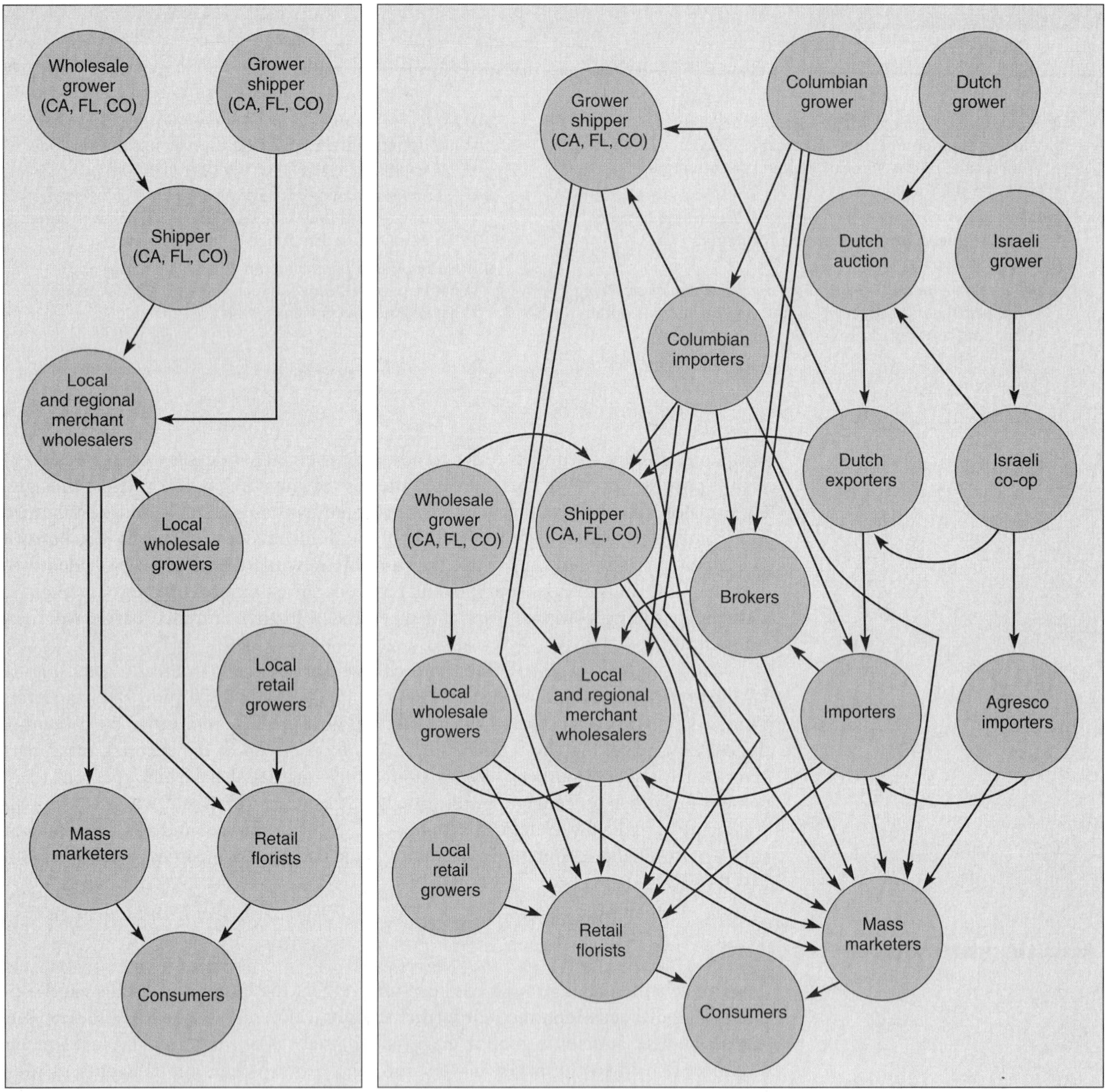

The entry of supermarkets and other retail chains into cut-flower retailing and the growth in size of some of the wholesale florists opened up the market for bulk contracts with foreign suppliers. Without the Boeing 747, the globalization of this market would not have occurred.

SOURCE: Thomas L. Prince, *An Empirical Investigation of Market Power and Channel Conflict in the Cut-Flower Distribution Channel* (unpublished master's thesis, The Ohio State University, n.d.).

The reseller audit in Table 7.2 starts with a summary evaluation that can also be used as a short-form audit when the product team does not have the time or interest to fully evaluate particular resellers. A paragraph can be written to provide responses to the concerns listed. The evaluation can be updated on a regular basis (normally annually), so the major investment is in preparing the initial evaluation. The detailed evaluation questions have been categorized into those dealing with the reseller's trading performance, marketing positioning, competitive effort, and purchasing behavior. Understanding what is going right or wrong in a channel relationship almost always involves taking information and putting it together like a jigsaw puzzle. That is why it is important to add depth to the audit by answering as many questions as possible using facts, good judgment, and best guesses. Trying to understand the reasons for a channel member's change in performance or behavior often means tracing back from its buying behavior, through trading and operating indicators, to its competitive effort and market position. The reseller audit also must forecast the reseller's future competitive strengths and weaknesses.

Distributor Relationship Analysis

Some of the audit information should automatically be compared across resellers. An example of such a visual comparison is provided in Figure 7.8.[18] A distributor portfolio analysis can be undertaken by reviewing the information on a reseller's growth rate (the y axis), the company's share of the reseller's sales in the particular product market (the x axis), and the percentage of the company's total sales made through the reseller. The latter is represented by the area of the circle, best visualized as a cross-sectional view of trading channel "pipes" down which the company's sales "flow."

The deals and discounts the company has given a distributor are three sections of the pie chart. The remaining two slices of the pie are the manufacturing costs and the gross profit (overhead recovery) the company earns on sales to that distributor. These calculations depend on the mix in sales to the distributor and require use of internal management accounting information.

The purpose of such an analysis is to visualize the actual trading *relationships* that exist between a firm and its major distribution channels. Often a firm discovers that its current dealings with a distributor are outdated. They are based on its past performance and long-established personal relationships and loyalties rather than on current trading realities. The real advantage of such comparative analyses emerges over time. The dynamic changes that have occurred can be tracked, and future performance can be projected based on the trends that emerge.

As shown in the following two examples, distributor portfolio analyses are becoming increasingly important, given the shifting competitiveness of different distribution channels and the overall shift in power toward the distributor discussed earlier in this chapter.

Hallmark Cards Inc. for decades has been a standout company. Privately held, it has a reputation for caring for its employees, and it has expanded and developed the greeting card business with its many product innovations. But beginning in the

[18] Peter R. Dickson, "Distributor Portfolio Analysis and Channel Dependence Matrix: New Techniques for Understanding and Managing the Channel," *Journal of Marketing* 47 (summer 1982): 35–44. See also Patrick M. Dunne and Harry I. Wolk, "Marketing Cost Analysis: A Modularized Contribution Approach," *Journal of Marketing* 41 (July 1977): 83–94.

Table 7.2 **Reseller Audit**

RESELLER AUDIT

COMPANY NAME: ______________________ DATE: ______________

Summary Evaluation

- Major strength, unique value, and importance of this reseller ______
- Major weakness and failure of reseller ______
- Change in reseller's dependency on us as a supplier ______
- Change in our dependency on reseller ______
- Reseller's perceptions of its dependency on us ______
- Reseller's perceptions of our dependency on it ______
- Special personal relations with supplier ______

Detailed Evaluation

Trading Performance

- Current annual sales ______
- Current annual sales of our products ______
- Current contribution earned from sales to this reseller ______
- Recent growth in sales ______
- Growth in sales of our products ______
- Previous 12-month contribution earned from sales to this reseller ______
- Changes in product mix sold ______
- Current average stock-turn of our products ______
- Past average stock-turn of our products ______
- Most recent profit performance ______
- Credit rating ______

Marketing Positioning and Served Marketing

- Years in business ______
- Current image and reputation ______
- Past image and reputation ______
- Geographical markets served ______
- Customer segments served ______

Competitive Selling Effort

- Recent investment in new plant, premises, and technology ______
- Product customization ______
- Recent marketing strategy ______
- Quality of locations ______
- Quality of advertising ______
- Quality of premises ______
- Quality of reseller's buying staff ______
- Quality of sales staff ______
- Sales-staff knowledge of our products ______
- Standard pricing strategy ______
- Price promotion selling of our products ______
- Inventory management ______
- Order-delivery service to reseller's customers ______
- Extent we are treated as a preferred supplier ______
- Special marketing efforts and cooperation ______

Purchasing Behavior

- Recent ordering history (frequency ad size) ______
- Recent payment history ______
- Volume deals/discounts sought and given ______
- Other allowances and considerations sought and given: ______
  - Freight ______
  - Cooperative advertising ______
  - Promotions ______
  - Returns ______
  - Push money and sales contests ______
  - Special credit terms ______

Figure 7.8 **A Distributor Relationship Analysis**

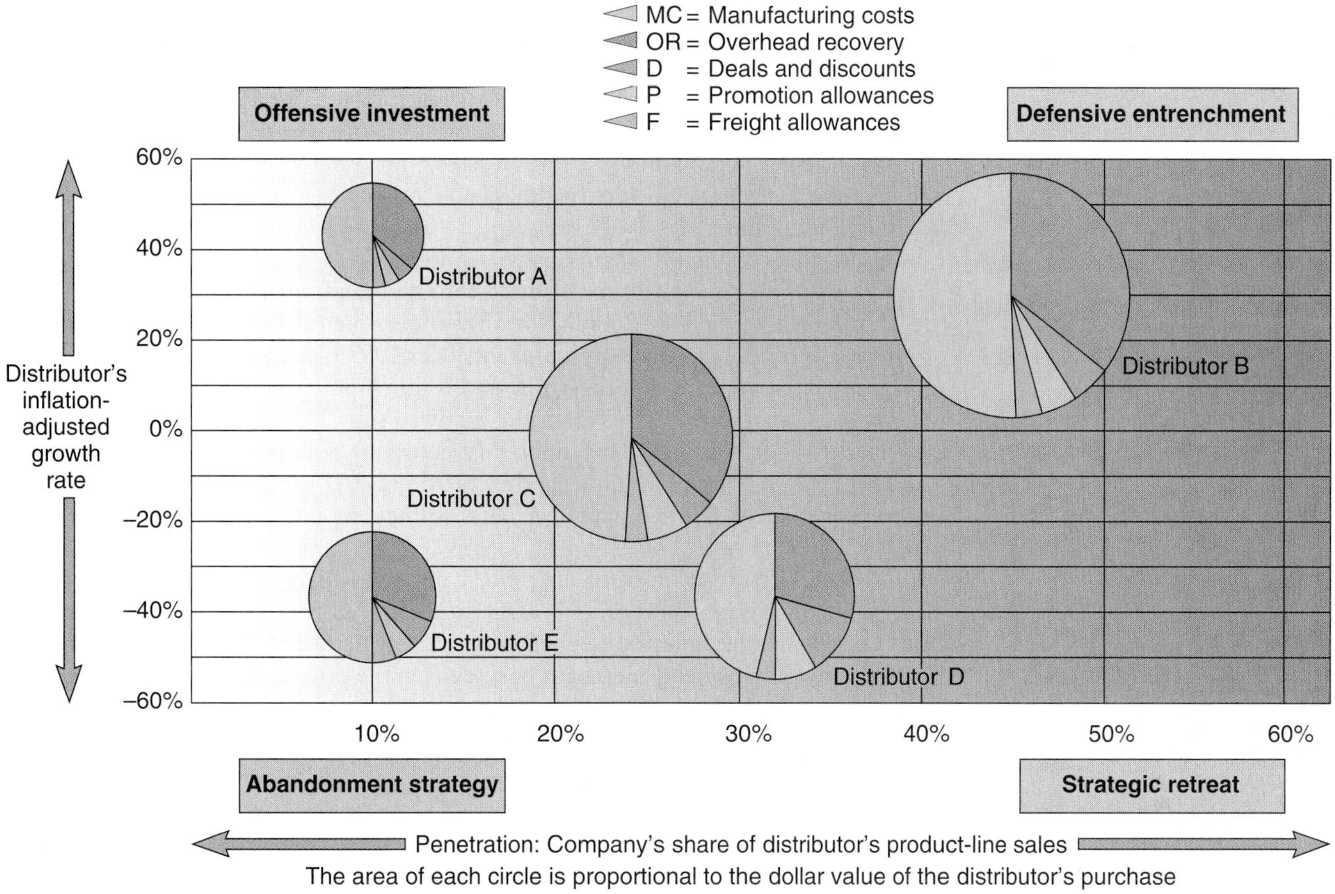

This figure presents a great deal of information about channel trading relationships. It indicates which distributors are thriving, which distributors are giving a lot of their business to the company, and which distributors the company depends on most for sales and profits. It also indicates how the distributors are being rewarded differentially in terms of the extra discounts/allowances they received as a percentage of sales.

1970s, with women (who buy 90 percent of the cards) working more and wanting more one-stop shopping and with cards creeping up in cost, discounters, supermarkets, and drugstores started selling more cards. Twenty years ago 50 percent of cards were sold through specialty shops such as the ten thousand franchised Hallmark card shops that now exist.[19] Today, the percentage is 30 percent and shrinking. Hallmark's competition, American Greetings, Gibson, and a number of recent start-up brands featuring "Farside"-type humor are more flexible and mobile in their choice

[19] William M. Stern, "Loyal to a Fault," *Forbes*, March 14, 1994, 58–59.

of channels. Hallmark does have a separate brand called Ambassador that it launched in 1959 to serve the mass-merchant channels. But now it faces some terribly hard choices. With franchisee card stores going out of business every day, should it remain loyal to its existing dominant channel, through which it does the bulk of its business, within which it faces little competition (i.e., it has more than 90 percent of the card business in its franchised outlets), but whose business is in long-term decline? Or should it offer Hallmark cards to mass merchants such as Wal-Mart and, by doing so, contribute to putting even more of its franchised Hallmark card stores out of business? The win-win solution is to find other products for its Hallmark stores to sell, such as flowers, candies, and other-occasion gifts—a strategy that Hallmark is pursuing.

Whirlpool corporation also learned a similar lesson by tying itself too closely to the success of Sears as a retailer of the Kenmore brand, made by Whirlpool. When Sears stumbled, so did Whirlpool. Now discounters such as Best Buy and Circuit City dominate the appliance distribution channel. In 1992 General Electric stopped supplying its major appliances to Best Buy and is developing its local and regional chain channels. In November 1994 Whirlpool followed suit. The advantages of developing the smaller retailers is that they tend to do a better job selling the new technology and the features of the premium models, they provide better service, and their business is more profitable to the manufacturer because they do not push so aggressively for lower wholesale prices.

The important lesson from distributor portfolio analyses and these examples is that no supplier wants to become hostage to a single distribution channel. Hallmark, for example, has become too dependent on its own stores and wishes to expand its share of the growing mass-merchant business. On the other hand, appliance manufacturers have become leery of the big mass merchants and are attempting to develop the smaller, specialized appliance retailer channel.

Facilitators and Alliances

Finally, a thorough channel audit should also give status reports on all other marketing facilitators vital to sustaining sales. For example, often a service company relies on the assistance of other enterprises or individuals to provide introductions and recommendations and to help deliver and market its line of services. Two services (for example, a law firm and an accounting firm) develop a relationship in which they cross-sell each other's services. The marketplace, standing, and situation of such facilitators are consequently very important and should be investigated and detailed in the environmental report. The list of such facilitators includes brokers; bankers; insurers; lawyers; accountants; senior executives and directors of other companies; the Chamber of Commerce; federal, state, and local government officials; advertising agencies; shipping agents; and common carriers.

It is also worthwhile to explore the possibility of developing a business alliance with another company that sells a complementary product (products used with each other). Microsoft used IBM as a facilitator to launch its MS-DOS operating system. Apple Computer worked with Adobe Systems to develop its desktop publishing. Now Apple and IBM are working together to develop new networking software. The key to the success of such alliances is to take full advantage of the skills and resources each party brings to the alliance, to overcome cultural differences between organizations, and to protect joint investments and trade secrets with legal contracts that anticipate

Table 7.3 Potential Facilitator/Alliance Audit

Answering these questions is a rational way of choosing an alliance partner to help a company market its goods or services.

- What is its relationship with the target market? __________
- What is its reputation with the target market? __________
- What are its key skills and resources? __________
- What is our short-term reason for seeking this alliance? __________
- What is our long-term reason for seeking this alliance? __________
- How will working with this facilitator affect other relationships? __________
- What is its decision-making culture? __________
- What type of legal contract will the target market want? What type will we want? __________

future problems.[20] Alliances that facilitate trade and increase the competitiveness of the joint offering are likely to increase with the globalization of markets. Table 7.3 lists questions that need to be answered when evaluating the potential of various parties who, although not part of a standard or conventional channel, may be able to play a critical role in planned marketing and selling efforts.

Channel Relationship Analysis in Global Markets

Suspicion is increasing and some evidence indicates that the hidebound tradition and inertia of the distribution channels in Japan, Europe, and emerging less-developed economies have been turned into a barrier against foreign competition. Trading loyalties and practices are often used to protect the domestic market from the rapid entry of foreign competition. As a result, exporters often have to enter foreign markets through a back door, such as Schick using Seiko's distribution network to sell its razors in Japan, Olivetti distributing typewriters directly to retailers, and Melitta selling coffee makers through coffee bean channels. In the latter case, the traditional appliance channels were controlled by Japanese manufacturers.

For many years, international marketing textbooks have stressed the need to understand foreign distribution channels and how they operate. The failure of export initiatives is frequently attributed to the arrogant, ignorant attitudes and behavior of U.S. exporters toward foreign distributors and markets. While sometimes this is so, in reality it is often quite the reverse. U.S. companies and regulators often have been exploited by foreign distributors and governments. Publicly, the exporter receives endless excuses, condolences, advice, and exhortations to try harder. Privately, the foreign distributors and governments are working to launch or boost domestic, low-cost, me-too competition. Such opportunistic behavior not only reduces the U.S. imports

[20] Louis P. Bucklin and Sanjit Sengupta, *Balancing Co-Marketing Alliances for Effectiveness*, working paper, Cambridge, Massachusetts, Marketing Science Institute, 1992, 92–120. See also Chapter 17.

(hence saving foreign exchange), but it also offers the possibility for foreign distributors to enter the U.S. marketing channels and attack the home base of U.S. companies.

Ironically, U.S. distribution channels have been very accommodating to foreign suppliers. Indeed, a number of foreign manufacturers of consumer and industrial electronics may have benefited from being foreign. Their radical suggestions and innovations in distribution may be forgiven and even considered more favorably by distributors, mass merchandisers, and retailers looking for new sources of supply. As outsiders, these foreign manufacturers were not breaking any rules they had previously accepted. A domestic supplier, who should "know better," would be perceived to be arrogant, pushy, and breaking the rules if it made the same suggestions.

In the current global marketplace, the most effective strategic, defensive initiatives are not being built on the geographical borders between countries. They are already in place in the distribution channels of an economy. Channel barriers are much less obvious than border barriers and less likely to provoke political retaliation. Everyone studying macroeconomics follows the daily, weekly, or monthly trade statistics to make predictions about the health of different national economies and their competitiveness. But such statistics reflect the consequences of decisions made in trading channels months, even years, before. The buyers and sellers in these channels can tell you precisely who is winning and losing the latest skirmish in their channel because they are *deciding* who will win and lose in the battle between imports and domestic suppliers. That is why international trade should be studied by observing what is going on in the channels of distribution and not just by belatedly tracking trade statistics or analyzing a country's import quotas and tariffs.

Global Tribal Relationship Networks

Global tribes have played immensely important roles in developing the global economy. *Global tribes* are transnational ethnic groups that possess strong group identification, group values, loyalties, and interpersonal global networks. They are slow to assimilate into the local cultures. Home is their country of origin or ancestral origin, be they New Zealand farmers whose grandparents migrated from Scotland or Japanese managers of a Honda plant in Ohio. Examples of the great trading tribes of modern times are discussed next.[21]

The Jewish Tribal Network

Their forced dispersion around the "old world" made Jews the classic global trade intermediaries and merchants. Their common culture and shared estrangement and alienation led to a shared trust and deal-making rules that were necessary for survival. Such trust and trading conventions settled on a handshake and led to low transaction costs and low risks when trading with merchants within and across borders who shared their culture and trading conventions. The Jewish merchants also emphasized education (human capital) because they were often not allowed to own land or were frequently dispossessed of their property. Ironically, this gave them greater mobility, enabling them, as traders and financiers, to follow and expand the flow of international commerce and to become wise about the world and intensely skilled and competitive in their trading.

[21] The following summaries are mostly abstracted from Joel Kotkin, *Tribes* (New York: Random House, 1993); and Philip D. Curtin, *Cross-Cultural Trade in World History* (Cambridge: Cambridge University Press, 1984).

The British Tribal Network

The British Empire spawned and spread much of the modern global culture, such as its common trading and scientific language and its law, science, and arts. Britain's advantage over its larger European rivals (France and Germany) was its emphasis on international trade and its ever restless search for new resources, new markets, new lands to colonize, and new technologies. Britain gained a first-mover advantage into new markets through an aggressive colonial policy between 1600 and 1900 that expanded its empire into India, North America, the Caribbean, Africa, Southeast Asia, and Australasia. The more unruly, maverick, and adventurous sons of the aristocracy sought their fortunes abroad, and they exhibited a Calvinist acceptance of the merchant profits in their competitive rationality and concern over idleness expressed best by Benjamin Franklin: "Remember, that time is money."[22] Britain did more than spread new technology, such as steam engines and railways, around the globe. It also once led in competitive-rationality skills, such as cost accounting, financial accounting, and all types of management and marketing decision-making activities.

The Japanese Tribal Network

The Japanese used the manufacturing and distribution innovations of its Anglo-American conquerors to help forge the greatest modern global, tribal network. Japanese trading companies send scouts out on global wanderings and management assignments of two to five years, supported by a network of Japanese-owned hotels, spas, bars, restaurants, schools, and golfing clubs. The modern Japanese tribe has its basis in the corporate family clans that were formed three hundred years ago during the period of Japan's great isolationism from the world. These clans are linked by a tribal ethos of mutual self-help that has transcended international borders. Another important value was the emphasis on reinvesting almost all profits back into expanding the family business, into new markets, or into new technologies. This resulted in large networks of extraordinarily adaptive, efficient, and aggressive small firms.

The Chinese Tribal Network

Close to 60 million Chinese live overseas, more than 80 percent of them in Asia. The annual entrepreneurial productivity of this global tribe (more than $500 billion) is extraordinary, as much as the Gross National Product of mainland China itself.[23] Not only do they trust, help, and support each other, but also the same skills are used to build personal relationships with those in power in foreign countries. The drive to glorify ancestors and accumulate wealth for descendants is deeply ingrained in the Chinese culture. A haunting desire to develop links with the homeland that manifests itself in an extraordinarily energetic global trading network also exists. Overseas Chinese have created more than one-hundred thousand export joint ventures in China. Led by Chinese merchants from Taiwan, Hong Kong, Malaysia, and Singapore, the new Chinese traders have expanded the already existing Chinese community networks around the world. Coupled with their extraordinary energy and enterprise is a great willingness to cooperate with local business partners. Like many Asian immigrants, they focus on building family businesses and investing in children's education. An extended-family "clan" system that emphasizes discipline, self-control, a work ethic, and frugality pervades the network of Chinese communities around the world.

On a much smaller scale, such trading diaspora also have developed in ethnic communities within the United States, particularly in retailing sectors, such as Vietnamese ownership of grocery stores in the inner city. Starting about 1970, Cambodians now

---

[22] Max Weber, *The Protestant Ethic and the Spirit of Capitalism*, tran. Talcott Parsons (New York: Scribners, 1958).
[23] Andrew Tanzer, "The Bamboo Network," *Forbes*, July 18, 1994, 138–44.

own about 80 percent of the doughnut shops in California, driving out the existing competition. Some of the original entrepreneurs now supply other Cambodians; for example, one of them distributes doughnut-making equipment to 2,400 Cambodian doughnut shops.[24]

Politicians, social scientists, and business scholars have consistently underestimated the importance of trading tribes. The European aristocracy vilified the Jews. France and Germany dismissed the British as a nation of shopkeepers. The British, in turn, did not see the emerging Asian trading networks as a threat. Even more recently, East African nations, such as Kenya and Tanzania, learned a bitter lesson about the importance of global tribal trading networks when they expelled their Indian communities and their export trade promptly collapsed.

The importance of global tribal trading networks is hardly ever discussed in books on international marketing or economics, even though one of the biggest problems faced by emerging nations such as Russia, Poland, India, Pakistan, Egypt, and Brazil is that they have to build such networks. The alternatives are to develop a close facilitating relationship with one of the existing global tribal networks or to operate at a severe and sustained competitive disadvantage.

Global Communication Networks

The problem with global distribution is that in some product markets it takes a major, long-term investment, and installing a competitive distribution system can take even longer than building manufacturing plants. General Motors' Cadillac division faces such a problem.[25] It has won the Malcolm Baldridge award for its product and service quality but it still faces a major competitive disadvantage compared to its foreign rivals, such as Mercedes Benz, BMW, Jaguar, and Infiniti. It lacks a worldwide distribution system for selling Cadillacs. As a result, all of its rivals have economies of scale and learning advantages over Cadillac from their global distribution. To survive, the Cadillac division therefore must be better than its foreign rivals at something else—not an easy task.

Operationally, success in global distribution comes from communicating electronically and finding ways of shipping goods in containers as quickly as possible. The tremendous improvements in communication and transportation have opened up the world as a source of supply for the American distribution system. Hence the number of potential global suppliers for retailers such as Wal-Mart, Kmart, Sears, The Limited, and Toys Я Us has increased much faster than the number of new retailers in the United States. The natural consequence of this, as illustrated in Figure 7.9, is a shift in power and potential long-term profits to the existing successful distribution channels that have strong consumer franchises.[26] The same power-shift effect in favor of an economy's existing distribution channels is occurring in every major economy. This power shift is producing an extensive restructuring of the U.S. economy as investment leaves sectors facing fierce global competition. U.S. manufacturers have responded by developing close working relationships with retailers and distributors, and by moving manufacturing offshore. They have also developed their own new distribution channels,

---

[24] Seth Mydans, "Doughnut Shops Put New Twist on Immigrants' Success Stories: Cambodian Entrepreneurs Take Over California Market," *Miami Herald*, June 4, 1995, 7A.

[25] Jerry Flint, "A German Cadillac," *Forbes*, July 31, 1995, 60.

[26] Peter R. Dickson and Carl Steidtmann, *Globalization 2000* (Columbus, OH: Management Horizons, 1992).

Figure 7.9 **The Dynamics of Globalization**

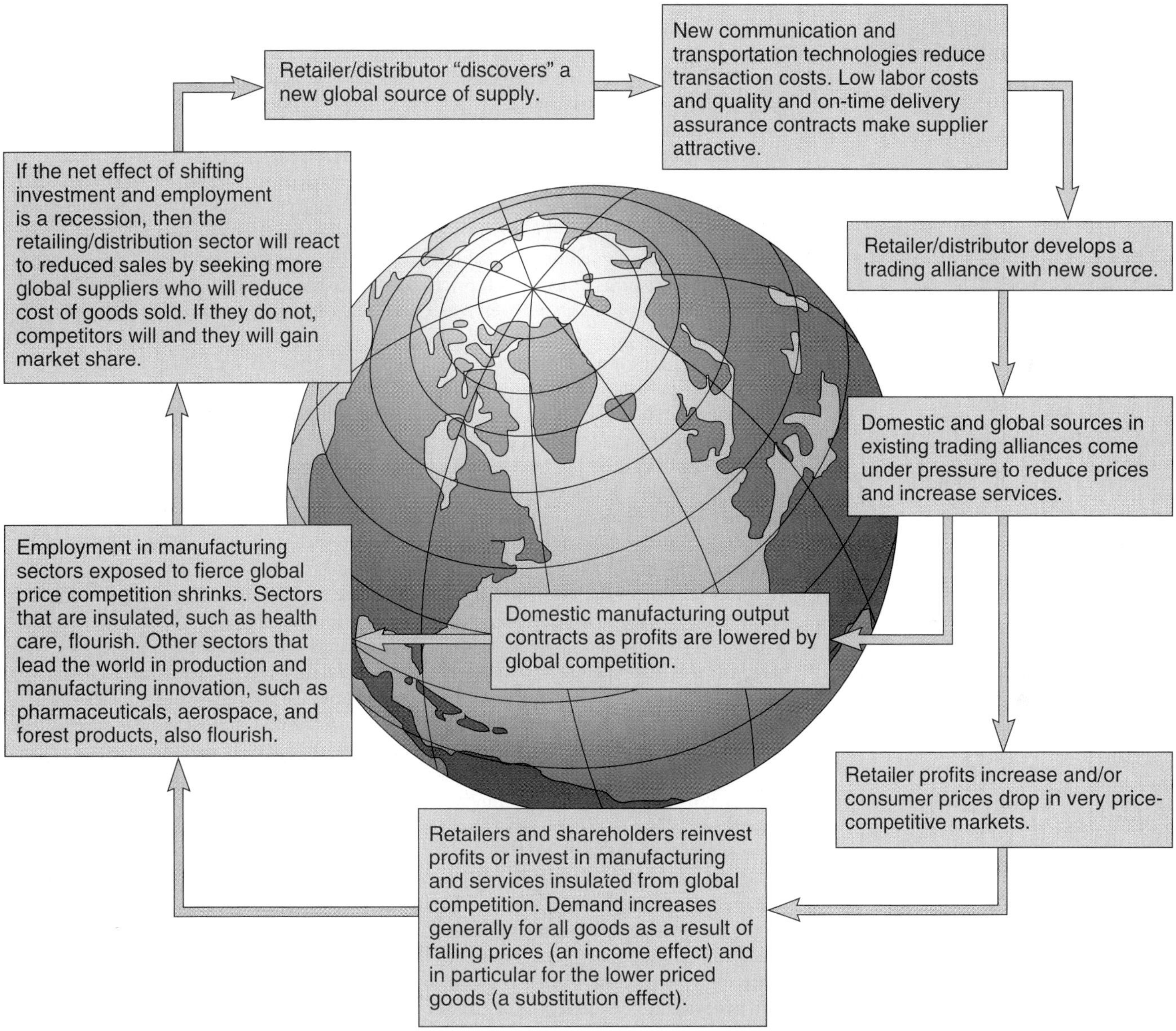

This figure explains why investment and employment are constantly shifting away from markets where retailers and distributors are discovering new global sources of supply.

such as was the case when Van Heusen, the shirt manufacturer, developed a very successful chain of outlet stores. If the 1960s was the decade of focusing on the consumer, the 1970s the decade of focusing on new public policy, and the 1980s the decade of focusing on the competition, then this power shift has made the 1990s the decade in which businesses focus on their marketing channel relationships.

Discussion Questions and Minicases

1. Why was it so important for the Russian Communists to wipe out the bourgeois intermediaries and traders soon after the 1917 revolution?
2. A decade ago, a wheel-of-retailing theory was in vogue. It argued that as forms of retailing mature, they become less cost efficient and trade up by increasing services and by positioning themselves to service the less price-sensitive consumers. New forms of lower cost retailing enter the market and, in time, they move upscale in their positioning, and so the wheel rotates. What might be the real explanation for what appears to be a wheel effect? Can you think of any successful retailers who are exceptions to the wheel theory?
3. A large part of the success of Wal-Mart can be explained by the orthodox economic theory of competition. What is it? (Hint: Think about small-town rural markets.)
4. A retailer is currently selling disposable diapers at 30 percent margin for $10 a box and has twelve stock-turns a year. What price could it charge for the diapers if it received a delivery of diapers to its stores every week and it increased its stock-turn to thirty-six a year?
5. In 1976, 6.8 percent of convenience-store sales came from gas. By 1981, that share had grown to 23 percent, and it is still climbing. The reasons for this dramatic swing in line of business can be traced to changes in the economy, technology, demographics, and traditional gasoline marketing. In the 1950s and 1960s the major gasoline companies heavily promoted their branded gasoline, often making somewhat dubious product superiority claims. The credibility of such product differentiation was wearing thin by the early 1970s, when the price of gas doubled. Consumers, scrambling to stretch their budgets, economized by first using less gas and then turning to self-service and independent, unbranded gas.

   The erosion of their brand franchises and margins and the doubling of the cost of holding gas in their underground tanks hit the major dealerships very hard. Many had to extend their opening hours to increase revenues and match the service of the independents. A desperate survival search began for new ways of paying the increased bills. New chains, such as Sears and Midas, had eliminated the opportunity for gas dealerships to profit from auto maintenance. The aftermarket in tires and batteries also had been lost to discount merchants. The most promising new line of business was the sale of convenience products such as tobacco, soft drinks, beer, candy, and snack foods—products that the traveler would buy or the local consumer would purchase late at night when many of the conventional outlets for these products were closed. What effect did these events have on competing channels?
6. What new technologies gave the mail-order business a big boost in the 1970s and 1980s?
7. What effect do direct electronic funds transfers among businesses have on banks? What might the banking industry's response be?
8. Electronic shopping has been forecast as the future wave of retailing for the past twenty years. Why has the wave never come in, and what cautionary lesson does this story have?
9. Two major economic drivers of distribution logistics costs are very volatile. What are they, and how do they affect costs and innovations?
10. What might be discussed in the channel section of an environmental analysis for a service company that does not use conventional distribution channels?
11. What determines seller dependency on a channel reseller? Is it true that if a seller is very dependent on an intermediary, then the seller lacks power?
12. Investment will move from low return on investment markets to high return on investment markets. What implications does this have for channel profitability and power given what is known about the relative ability of retailers and manufacturers to switch product markets?
13. Explain, using the theory of competitive rationality, why franchising is so successful.

14. What advantage does the UPC information that retailers gather from their checkout scanning systems give them over their suppliers?

15. Study the growth of the cut-flower market in Figure 7.6. How do you think this market evolved? What impact do you think its evolution has had on the channel power of the different players over time? Why do you think supermarkets like Kroger entered the market?

16. What are two reasons governments protect the interests of the distribution channels in their economies against foreign threats?

17. Many experts suggest that developing a close trading relationship with a distributor or retailer through automatic ordering, electronic information links, and new product-development joint ventures is a way of building a sustainable competitive advantage. But most of the time it is assumed that the supplier will be the sole supplier. What do you think happens when a distributor or retailer develops such close working relationships with several suppliers? How can a supplier prevent this from happening?

18. Blockbuster Video dominates the video rental market with its many locations, large selection, and convenient hours. It has millions of customers, whose purchase history can be tracked. Blockbuster's problem has been maintaining demand by finding a way to effectively promote its latest releases. How might it develop a facilitating relationship with national magazines? What might the magazine, in turn, get out of the relationship/alliance that would make the magazine even more competitive?

To see what is right and not to do it is a lack of courage.

Confucius

Those who stand for nothing fall for anything.

Alexander Hamilton

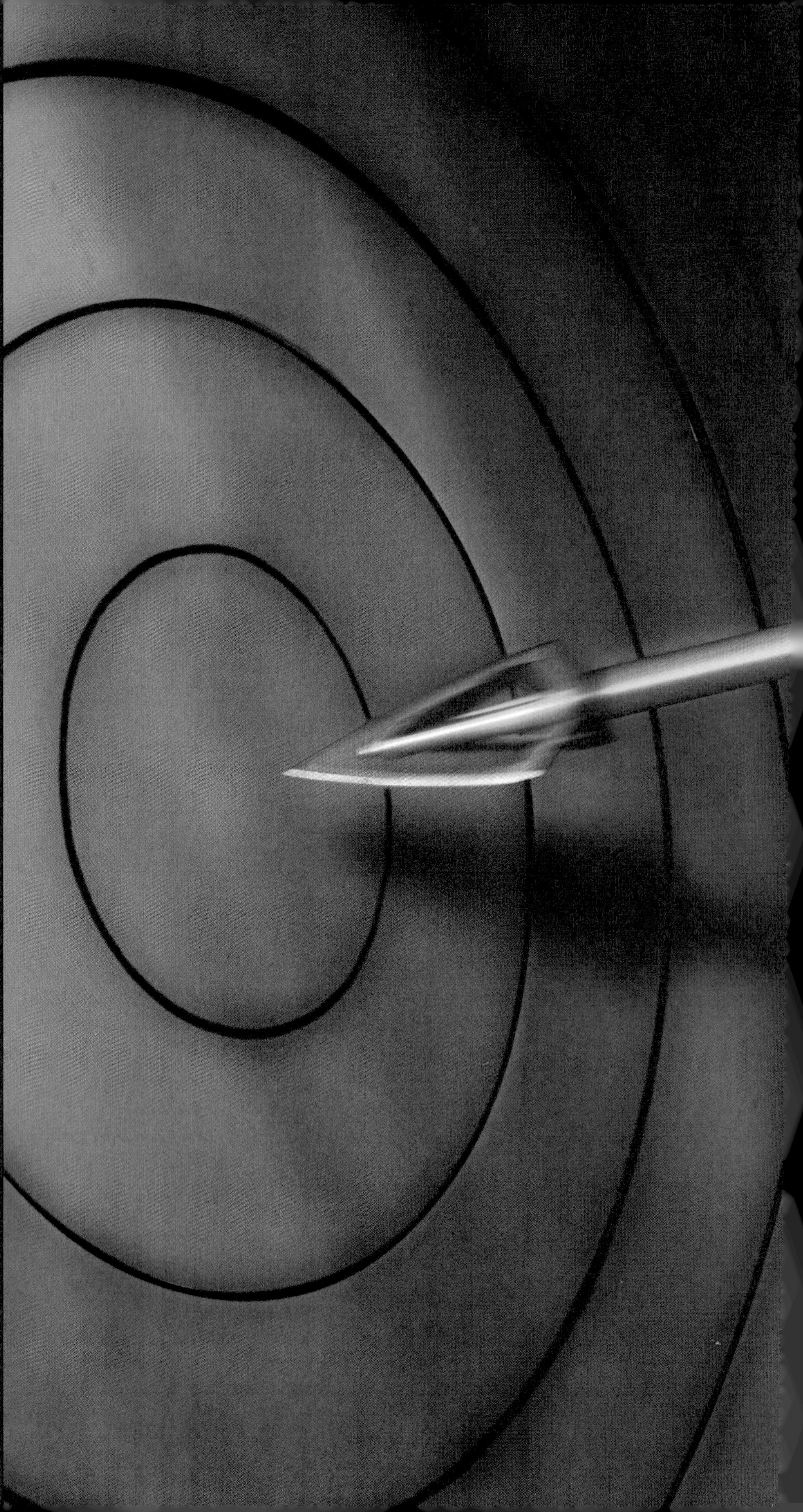

CHAPTER EIGHT

Analyzing Regulation and Market Ethics

Dagonet, a diversified U.S. manufacturer, undertook a major effort to introduce its products in Latin American markets but ran into an ethical dilemma. The company was asked by several potential distributors to overbill and then, when paid, to send the overpayment to the foreign distributors' accounts in Switzerland and the Cayman Islands. In this way, the distributors' profits are understated and they avoid taxation. The practice is customary in these countries because local taxes on company profits are considered by the distributors to be unreasonably high. Should Dagonet help its foreign trade customers cheat on their taxes?

This case is particularly interesting because it was posed to a sample of some 264 senior executives (CEOs, legal counsels, etc.) in companies in the United States, Europe, and Canada.[1] Ninety percent reported they would deny the request, and 82 percent indicated that this should be a general global policy. A typical explanation was "Local customs and practices should be considered, but not if the action would be in conflict with basic company beliefs. Dagonet's leadership will have to live with this decision." When faced with such a choice, the executives chose to follow the firm's own moral compass: "A company should be consistent;

its managers should not rely on 'situation ethics.'" "Without trying to pass judgment on others, ethics decisions must be based on the company's standards." However, a few cautioned that a "one size fits all" policy is simply unrealistic if the firm intends to market globally. "I'm not sure we can force our view of right and wrong on the whole world." "Sometimes multinationals must play by local rules provided local rules do not migrate home." One honest response was "I have no overseas experience. I might be less high minded if I had."

Global marketing and trading relationships are requiring U.S. companies to consider the laws and ethics of marketing both in the United States and in numerous other countries. This places a premium on marketing teams' and managers' ability to sensibly analyze and understand market regulations and ethics. Firms also need to develop a decision-making process that addresses these issues—that is, based on consistent moral principles but adapts to situational contexts. ■

As individual citizens, our behavior is constrained by the law and our considerations of right and wrong, our personal ethics. It is no different for firms and marketing decision makers. The marketplace is full of rules. Many are written into law, some are stated in professional codes of ethics, and others are stated in company ethical guidelines. Finally, we all have some sense of what is honest, decent, and fair. The interpretation of morality may vary greatly among individuals, but it still exists. In business, what is made and how it is marketed are also constrained by perceptions of the law and mental models of what is right and wrong—that is, codes of ethics.

Marketing plans seldom feature legal concerns and almost never raise ethical issues. But the law and ethics still influence marketing decision making. It is usually assumed that marketing planners are familiar with marketing law and that their decision making is ethical. In particular, any new law or potential litigation that must be paid attention to because of recent events in the marketplace needs to be singled out and described in the environment sections of plans. This might include the recent actions of a government agency, a consumer lawsuit against a competitor, or impending legislation. Plans should also note current ethical issues that have been raised by public-interest groups or consumers and demand consideration.

Foundations for a Policy and Ethical Mental Model

This chapter does not list all of the possible laws and ethics that might apply to a marketing decision. That would be impossible and impossibly dull to read. Instead, it asks

[1] See Ronald E. Berenbeim, *Corporate Ethics Practices* (New York: The Conference Board, 1992), 25–27.

students to think about the legal issues that affect marketers in certain ways in order to lay a foundation of framework for understanding marketing law.[2] Such considerations may seldom be revealed in actual written marketing plans or decisions, but they are important in team decision making.

Despite the fact the U.S. marketplace is one of the most open and free in the world, federal and state laws and agencies impose numerous constraints. The great surge in public policy activity that occurred in the 1970s resulted in several new agencies (for example, the Product Safety Commission) and numerous new laws. More regulation means more restrictions, and more crusading regulators means higher legal expenses and the risk of a company losing its reputation if it is tried by the press. The Library of Congress has calculated that the annual cost of completing, filing, and handling an estimated 15,000 different government forms is $40 billion, well over the national expenditure for *all* research and development. Clearly, some of this paperwork is worth the cost, but much of it is not. Note that much of this red tape resulted from requests made by businesses themselves.

Although the law and paperwork can frustrate initiative, public policy, in general, is positive for business. The exhibit outlines some ways government benefits the marketplace. For example, in the late 1940s the Japanese government Electro Communications Laboratory (ECL) diffused information about the transistor (invented in 1948), undertook pathbreaking research, and in June 1953 demonstrated prototype transistor radios, phonographs, and hearing aids in a major Ginza department store. Texas Instruments introduced the first commercial transistor radio in late 1954, eight months ahead of Sony, but by the end of the decade the Japanese dominated the technology. The Japanese Ministry of International Trade and Industry (MITI) helped Japanese firms purchase favorable patent rights, renegotiated terms of existing agreements, and guaranteed royalty payments. The Japanese government created an innovation community by using government organizations to work with universities, professional societies, trade associations, and individual firms to develop new products.[3] This model has been used around the world to help develop the competitiveness of countries and their firms. Such innovation communities often help set technology standards that further foster the growth of domestic industry. More generally, government higher-education policies and programs have the goal of fostering domestic expertise in various technologies and processes (e.g., training high-quality electrical and chemical engineers). Germany's economic growth in the 1870s and Korea's growth in the 1970s had a great deal to do with the government creation and funding of several excellent engineering schools.

The point is that marketers can be just as shortsighted about the role played by public policy in the marketplace as they can about changing consumer needs or technological innovations in production. A hostile attitude toward regulation that is generalized into a hostile attitude toward public policy is unreasonable (competitively irrational), and if it encourages a marketing strategy that willfully frustrates the letter or intent of the law, it can be disastrous.

This discussion begins with why some markets are heavily regulated. This is followed by an analysis of what happens when these markets are deregulated. The remaining sections describe regulations that apply to all markets. These regulations

[2] For details, see Robert J. Posch Jr., *The Complete Guide to Marketing Law* (Englewood Cliffs, NJ: Prentice-Hall, 1990).
[3] Leonard H. Lynn, "The Commercialization of the Transistor Radio in Japan: The Functioning of an Innovation Community," working paper, Weatherhead School of Management, Case Western Reserve University, Cleveland, Ohio, 1995.

EXHIBIT

Examples of Public Policy Designed to Help Business

1. *Protective tariffs, subsidies, and tax breaks.* Although Americans take pride in having a free-market system, some 25 percent of U.S. product markets are protected by tariffs and import quotas. Even more are protected by threats of action, which result in voluntary constraints by overseas competitors (such as the Japanese auto manufacturers). Prices in some markets are subsidized (such as the agricultural product market). Our tax laws are such that many billion-dollar companies pay little or no taxes. Unfortunately, some of the tax breaks have grossly distorted the investment and marketplace behavior of companies.
2. *Contract laws and fair-trade practices.* The law and the courts provided by the U.S. government are essential to maintain the integrity of legal contracts. The importance of this legal infrastructure is often taken for granted until a business faces inept or corrupt courts of law, as can exist in some less developed countries such as Nigeria. Nothing discourages investment and closes down a marketplace faster.

cover product, price, distribution, advertising, and selling and help determine the evolutionary paths that markets follow. Each subsection can be matched with later chapters that discuss these elements of marketing strategy. The organization of this chapter and an explanation of the organization is further described in Figure 8.1.

Industry Regulation and Deregulation

In a completely regulated market, the number of sellers is controlled, and any marketing strategy must be approved by a controlling authority. Many of the widely accepted reasons for completely regulating a product market are primarily economic. In some markets, it does not make sense to have competition. Imagine several local phone companies, each with its own lines. Everyone would need a telephone line for each phone company. Instead, it makes sense to operate the telephone hardware as a monopoly that rents out the use of its lines to a competitive market of telephone service companies. In effect, this is what AT&T, MCI, and Sprint do. They pay a service connect fee to the local telephone company every time someone makes a long-distance call.

When a monopoly results in lower costs, it is called a natural monopoly. Monopolies are often associated with but do not always result in higher prices. Whenever the fixed costs of a service are high and large economies of scale in production or distribution processes exist, a monopoly service can result in lower prices than if competition existed. Most utility product markets fall into this category. They allow a single seller, but they regulate its prices and other marketing and production strategies. Other markets allow competition but are heavily regulated to assure orderly competition and to maintain adequate safety standards. The broadcast media (television and radio) are regulated. Each station is allocated a band of radio wave that it uses to transmit its signal. Without such control, the airwaves would be congested. The airline industry was initially regulated to help it get started. Its later regulation was justified on the grounds of public safety. Recent events appear to justify such regulation.

3. *Government agencies.* The services of government agencies range from setting standards to checking for accurate measure at the gas pumps (in both volume and rated octane) to ensure that advertising claims made about competitors' products can be substantiated. Such accurate information makes the market fairer and more competitive. The law also protects extremely valuable patents, trademarks, and brand names.
4. *Government as a source of market research.* Through its Census Bureau and Department of Commerce, the U.S. government provides invaluable free information to marketers about consumers, suppliers, distributors, competitors, technology, and economic trends. In addition, the government subsidizes higher education and research establishments that provide technological research and development, market research, and career and occupational training. This encouragement and support of research and development of products and processes is a key driver of the United States economy's long-term competitive advantage.

The problem with government-protected monopolies is that the enterprise, vitality, and change provided by the forces of competition are no longer present. The absence or limitation of competition discourages innovation, risk taking, and efficiency. For several decades it seemed that some industries could not resist convincing legislators to pass laws that effectively restricted new competition, even competition among existing firms. In recent years, public policymakers have taken a hard look at the industries listed in Table 8.1 and have decided to rejuvenate them by allowing free-market forces to operate again.

The Chaos of Industry Deregulation

In a typical competitive marketplace, it is possible to determine the impact that might occur if one firm makes a change in strategy while the competition is conducting business as usual. Imagine the opposite extreme, however: Suppose *everyone* in the market changes strategy. To make the situation even worse, what if no past history could be used to forecast the impact of any of the players' new strategies? Some completely new and unpredictable players might also be introduced into the market. This is the sort of extreme shock a decision-making team faces when a market is deregulated.

A regulated market, by definition, restrains and controls competition; it imposes order. When a market is deregulated, the players are allowed to attack each other's market share, change pricing strategies, and undertake competitive product differentiation and advertising. Deregulation introduces a state of chaos into the market.

- Many of the players take new competitive positions and launch new strategies. These moves intersect and interact with each other, creating an unpredictable and volatile market. Based on the initial performance of their new moves, some participants have second thoughts and change their positioning and strategy. This creates new disturbances in the market.
- Everyone in the deregulated market is inexperienced. The players, including the consumers and distribution channels, must adjust to new competitive realities. As they learn to cope, their behavior and loyalties change, creating new market dynamics.

Figure 8.1 **Chapter Organization**

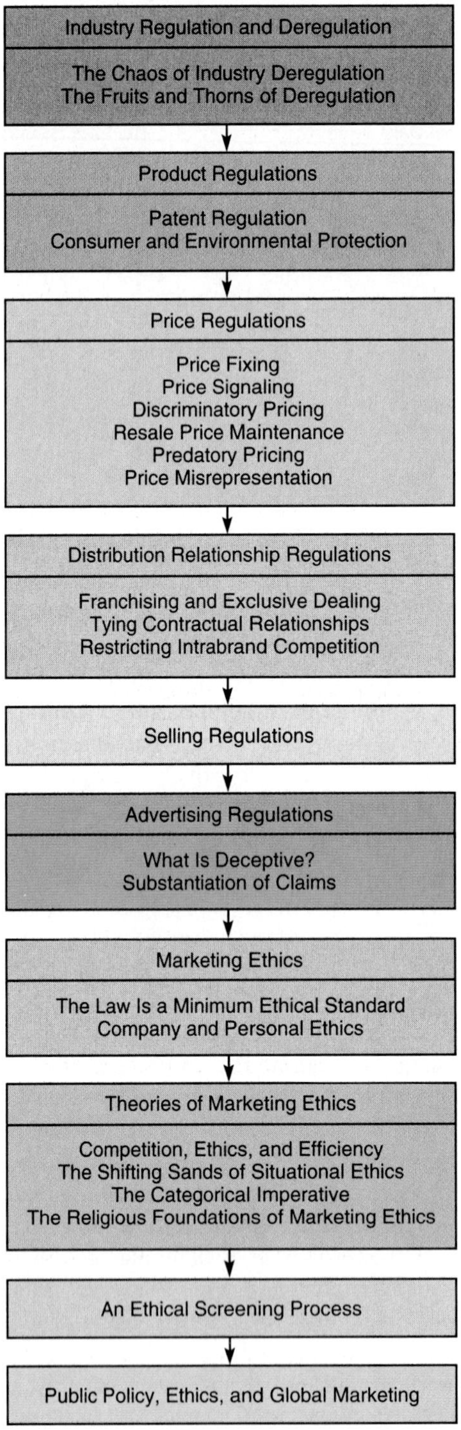

This chapter starts with an initial general discussion about the effects of market regulation and deregulation. It then proceeds to a discussion of specific marketing regulations from product regulations through to advertising regulations. The chapter then turns to a discussion of marketing ethics, what are they, why are they important, and how they can come into play in marketing decision making and implementation processes.

Table 8.1 The Effects of Deregulation on Selected Product Markets

Banking

- The number of banks fell from 12,000 to 6,000.
- Allowing across-state mergers created several "national" banks.
- The freeing of interest rates led to the introduction of interest-bearing checking accounts, a greater variety of savings accounts, and generally higher rates of interest.
- Direct costs were raised, and charges for checkbooks and bounced checks were raised.
- Banks initially lengthened the holding period for checks and used the extra "float" as a no-cost source of funds.
- A shocking failure rate in the savings and loans industry was caused by competition for funds, risky investments, foolish tax and accounting policy, lax regulation of bank solvency, and fraud. Customers were not selective and vigilant because the security of their deposits was still assured by the government. Thus, an important determinant of competitive efficiency was not present.
- Labor costs were trimmed. Fewer full-service branches and more automated teller machines were provided.
- Enterprising banks focused on market niches; for example BancOne in Columbus, Ohio, specialized in processing cash management accounts for brokerage firms that by law could not issue and process checks themselves.

Telephone Services

- Long-distance rates fell by at least 20 percent and are still dropping.
- The local cost of calls increased by more than 30 percent, but so did the volume; therefore, the cost per call increased less.
- The number of telephone suppliers increased from 25 to more than 200. Innovations and variety greatly increased.
- Introduction of fiber optics in long-distance networks accelerated, led by Sprint as a point of differentiation.
- Service complaints increased. Many consumers were confused and unhappy with the AT&T breakup—"If it works, why fix it?"
- A new round of deregulation is opening up the local telephone markets to AT&T again and to cable companies. The "Baby Bells," in return, will be allowed to offer their own long-distance services.
- AT&T kept more than 70 percent of the long-distance market. MCI and Sprint, having invested the necessary billions in new networks, are now creating global alliances.

Railroads

- The industry continues to restructure into several national railroad systems with regional feeder carriers.
- Concentration increased from 25 major companies in 1978 to 12 in 1994 that carried 91 percent of the freight revenue.
- Investment in new rolling stock and profitability increased. Railroads invested in other transportation modes to offer integrated services.
- The reliability and on-time quality of service increased with automation and superior tracking information systems.
- Railroad costs per ton-mile fell by 30 percent after deregulation.

Trucking

- Since 1980, 20,000 new trucking companies (mainly small fleets of one to three vehicles) have been launched; about half have failed.
- Services were broadened, new terminals were built, and rates were lowered.
- Concentration in the less-than-truckload (LTL) market increased, with about five companies dominating.
- Highway accidents increased per haulage mile, caused by desperate operators driving dangerous vehicles.
- Trucking prices fell by 20 percent to 30 percent after deregulation.

Air Carriers

- Between 1978 and 1988, 215 new air carriers entered the market. The number of airlines authorized to fly planes with more than 60 seats rose from 36 in 1978 to 123 in 1984 and then decreased to 74 in 1987 and 61 in 1994.
- Tickets were estimated to be 40 percent cheaper in 1987 than they would have been under regulation. However, fares were much cheaper on major competitive routes and much higher on other routes. Continued price wars and promotions drove three major airlines into bankruptcy in 1991, and between 1990 and 1994 industry profits were slim to nonexistent.
- The number of domestic passengers increased from 418 million in 1986 to 628 million in 1994.
- Low airfares forced a merger between the two major bus companies, Greyhound and Trailways, creating a monopoly.
- More than 900 previously monopolized routes were made competitive.
- Airlines restructured around hubs, with commuter airlines expanding to serve abandoned routes and to feed the hubs.
- Airline labor costs were reduced significantly.
- Service deteriorated as industry infrastructure (that is, airports and air traffic control) did not expand to cope with increased demand. Reduction in service personnel also reduced service.
- Travel agents became more powerful as airlines competed on routes. Agents increased their commission percentages.
- Frequent-flier programs were introduced to encourage loyalty among heavy users.
- Air safety per mile flown initially decreased but then increased.

SOURCES: Lewis M. Schneider, "New Era in Transportation Strategy," *Harvard Business Review*, March/April 1985, 118–26; Chris Welles, et al., "Is Deregulation Working," *Business Week*, December 22, 1986, 50–55; Stephen Koepp, "Rolling Back Regulation" *Time*, July 6, 1987, 50–52; Joel A. Bleeke, "Strategic Choices for Newly Opened Markets," *Harvard Business Review*, September/October 1990, 158–65; Richard J. Herring, and Ashish C. Shah, eds., *Reforming the American Banking System* (Philadelphia, PA: The Wharton Financial Institutions Center, 1991); Robert V. Delaney, Cass Sixth Annual State of Logistics Report, St. Louis, Missouri, 1995; Association of American Railroads; and the Air Transport Association of America, Washington, D.C.

Observing the impact of a risk taker, for example, an initially conservative competitor may then throw caution to the wind and quickly mimic the innovator or pursue a different but equally extreme strategy. In the process, it may bump heads with another company pursuing the same target market with a similar strategy. Both may recoil and back off, or both may dig their heels in, expecting the other to withdraw. Meanwhile, another competitor that elected to pursue a different target market with a different strategy may reap the greatest benefits, partly because it also may have had time to gain a dominant presence in this market segment.

The competitive inexperience of the marketing strategists also may lead to major mistakes in strategy. Certain environmental constraints may be overlooked simply because they never had to be considered in the good old days when the market was regulated. For example, when the airlines were initially deregulated, the ability of each airline to compete on price became constrained by fuel efficiency, the suitability of its fleet for the new markets (routes), and labor costs. Continental was the first major carrier to fail because its pricing strategy was unrealistic, given its cost structure. Its bankruptcy, however, may have been a blessing in disguise because its initial failure to adapt to the new competitive realities gave it the opportunity and courage to (1) restructure its debt and fleet and (2) renegotiate its labor contracts with its pilots and other labor unions. The new company that emerged was better adapted to the new market realities, even if it was taken over by another company (Texas Air). Southwest is a low-cost airline that has adapted very well to the deregulated environment.

The Fruits and Thorns of Deregulation

The initial purpose of regulation was to ensure adequate service for *all* at a reasonable cost in industries where economists believed competition would not lead to such an outcome. However, the price of regulation was often bad management, inefficient operations, poor customer service, inhibited innovation, and inflated franchise values because of restricted entry to the industry's supply sector. Deregulation was meant to produce more competition, to lower prices, to increase efficiency, and to provide more choices for the consumer. As described in Table 8.1 deregulation appears to have achieved most of its goals, but some of its effects have been unexpected.

In several of the deregulated industries, major competitors have quickly reorganized and created networks that tend to monopolize certain geographical markets. For example, Northwest Airlines, with its hub in Minneapolis; TWA in St. Louis; and USAir in Pittsburgh control more than 80 percent of the business through these airports. The major airline hubs are fed by minor players. In these symbiotic relationships, the small airlines feed the larger carrier, and the larger carrier provides reservation and check-in services, ground and baggage handling, and advertising.

Public policymakers worry most that the networks formed in the restructuring of several deregulated markets will create formidable barriers to entry, mobility, and innovativeness—the very barriers deregulation attempted to remove from the market. However, even if these barriers occur, the major competitors will still compete on the boundaries of their niches, keeping the market more competitive than it was under regulation. New technologies also will disturb any contrived equilibrium. It is not at all clear that an oligopoly market (one with a few large competitors) can maintain a stable equilibrium anyway. Differences in the ambitions and competitiveness of the participants in an oligopoly market are inherently and ultimately destabilizing, as described in Chapters 1 and 6.

Finally, some policymakers believe that new regulations may be necessary in the trucking and airline markets to protect consumer and public safety. It is possible that competition can become too desperate in markets and thus lead to lower maintenance on equipment and overworked employccs, both of which can endanger public safety. Other policymakers are unhappy that the advantages of deregulation are not distributed equitably. The faster, smarter, and wealthier consumers have reaped most of the benefits, but this is to be expected in any free and competitive market. Survival of the fittest affects both sellers and buyers. The hard facts are that not all sellers benefit the same from their selling practices and not all buyers benefit the same from their buying practices. The discussion now turns to specific regulations and policies.

Product Regulations

The specific laws applying to products cover packaging requirements, information labeling, instructions labeling, usage warnings, minimum quality or performance standards, mandatory warranties, product ratings, and production and marketing licenses and permits. Industry associations, often active in shaping such laws, can be of great help in providing information on relevant laws and recommended compliance procedures. This section focuses on two of the most important product policy issues: patent regulation and product safety.

Patent Regulation

The U.S. patent system is the result of a balance achieved between competing economic forces and the judiciary in order to maximize what is judged to be the most benefit to society. Much of the intent, legal prescription, and interpretation of marketing law involves the evaluation of several different arguments, each with merit. Marketers have to become familiar with these arguments in order to adapt to the law. Patents also provide a nice example of the problems inherent in implementing marketing law. Before this discussion expands on these points, note an important concept in marketing law: The law itself adapts to changes in the economy and specific markets.

The Rule of Reason

The rule of reason, first applied in the early 1900s by the Supreme Court, says that the law should be interpreted to fit the prevailing competitive, political, and social situations. It should not be interpreted rigidly (called *per se* judgment). Instead, the interpretation should be flexible so the original intent of the law can be achieved, even if the new precedent conflicts with the letter of the law. Reason and reasonableness are used to judge whether the law has been broken. The rule of reason permits the law to keep up with technological and social innovations and to be progressive in its fostering of competition and protecting consumers. The disadvantage is that it may be difficult to predict how a law will be interpreted by the courts. Old precedents may not apply. The rule of reason increases uncertainty and risk for a company thinking about a groundbreaking marketing strategy. The rule of reason has been exercised in the following debate.

Innovation Competition versus Price Competition

A patent allows the holder to extract monopoly profits for an invention or design for up to seventeen years. No one else is allowed to design a product or service using the patent without the inventor's permission. A patent rewards creative genius. It is meant to encourage the development of new processes and product innovation that will ultimately benefit society. By protecting a good idea from immediate imitation by competition, patent law encourages an important type of competition. New inventions create obsolescence and force competitors to upgrade their technology, service, and marketing. Without patents, the incentive to invest in risky R&D that leads to new and improved products would be greatly reduced. The number of new products would decline, ultimately reducing competition. In other words, weak patent protection encourages imitative price competition and discourages innovation competition. On the other hand, patents restrict imitative competition in the sense that only the holder of the patent or companies that pay royalties to the patent holder can manufacture and market the invention. This results in higher prices and possibly slower further innovation that advances the original invention.

The conflict between long-term new-product competition and short-term price competition has been debated and partially resolved in the pharmaceutical market. Many patented drugs now have a much shorter patent protection of only seven years. This is to enable imitative price competition, particularly with generic substitutes, much sooner than was possible in the past. On the other hand, legislators accepted the argument that the United States would lose its international leadership in pharmaceuticals if some reasonable patent protection was not in place to recover the huge costs and risks involved in developing, effectively testing, and marketing not only successful new drugs but also less successful innovations that never make it to the market.

The evidence suggests that the initial patent protection from competition continues after the expiration of the patent (see Figure 8.2). The medical profession tends to remain loyal to the pioneering brand of a drug, and a pioneering brand's price remains higher than the generic substitute. This is a nice example of a brand reputation's positive effect on margins and cash flow (see Chapter 10). Although some may argue that the original brand dissolves faster or provides some other minor advantage, the Federal Drug Administration (FDA) believes that many of the superiority claims are false. As a consequence, all fifty states have passed laws that give pharmacists the discretion of substituting a less expensive generic unless the doctor specifically forbids it. In Florida, pharmacists are *required* to inform consumers about how much they can save if they purchase the generic equivalent.

But the more fundamental problem in the drug market is that the buying expert consulted (the doctor) has no financial incentive to recommend the cheaper, generic substitute. In fact, due to the extent that the drug industry provides conference expenses and other promotions to the medical profession, the incentive is quite the opposite. The consumer often does not pay directly for the medication, further reducing the price sensitivity of the competition. Price is also not a very salient concern when life-and-death health is at stake. The lesson that can be learned is that patent protection gives a company a chance to establish strong consumer and channel loyalty. If the patent holder markets its product well, this loyalty will carry on past the period of legal monopoly into the free market. The way to make the drug market more price competitive is not to reduce the patent time period but to encourage the consumer, doctor, health maintenance organization (HMO), and pharmacist to become more price sensitive.

Figure 8.2 **Comparing Drug Prices**

Name of Drug	AARP Pharmacy Service (by mail)	America's Pharmacy (by mail)	Walgreens (chain store)	OSCO (chain store)	Independent Pharmacy
Apresoline 25mg/100 tablets	$25.90	$25.14	$29.99	$27.99	$25.92
Generic hydralazine	4.25	4.55	6.99	7.93	3.71
Calon 80mg/100 tablets	37.40	40.66	43.99	43.39	41.92
Generic verapamil	15.95	4.64	15.99	16.39	19.98
Diabinese 100mg/100 tablets	29.60	30.58	34.95	32.99	29.95
Generic chloropropamide	8.90	1.49	8.99	8.39	8.66
Dyazide 100 capsules	28.95	34.14	31.99	28.99	36.20
Generic triamterene & hydrochlorothiazide	16.75	16.82	19.99	19.99	19.98
Elavil 50mg/100 tablets	54.50	59.44	63.99	60.99	46.97
Generic amitriptyline	6.90	4.10	9.99	8.39	13.06
Lasix 40mg/100 tablets	16.95	17.70	16.99	16.99	23.00
Generic furosemide	5.95	4.50	7.99	6.99	9.45
Motrin 400mg/100 tablets	12.95	18.07	15.99	19.99	29.11
Generic ibuprofen	8.45	5.20	9.99	10.99	15.45
Nuprosyn 375mg/100 tablets	79.90	82.76	88.99	84.39	99.80
Generic—none available	—	—	—	—	—
Procardia 20mg/100 tablets	82.45	94.01	87.99	88.99	100.00
Generic nifedipine	45.95	43.66	54.99	55.99	70.00
Valium 5mg/15 tablets	8.75	7.78	11.79	11.39	14.52
Generic diazepam	2.50	.74	5.29	5.39	7.71

The originally patented drug still often sells at a huge premium over the generic competition. Prices vary less among stores than between the brand and generic drug. This suggests that doctor loyalty to the original drug explains the huge price premium and not the fact consumers have little incentive to search because they do not pay for the medicine directly. Health maintenance organizations (HMOs) are changing such doctor loyalty. Under tremendous pressure from health insurance companies to reduce their costs, HMOs are now directing their doctors to prescribe cheaper drugs or generic versions.

SOURCE: Elliott H. McCleary, "How and Where You Can Save Over 50% on Prescription Drugs," *Consumer's Digest*, November/December, 1992.

Patent Piracy and Weak Policing

Unfortunately, United States patent law often does not function the way it should. Firms get away with patent infringement by pleading ignorance or by claiming that the damage to the patent holder is minimal. Larger enterprises sometimes steal patents and then wear down the patent holder in the courts. A small company or individual who holds a patent hardly stands a chance against a big domestic or foreign company in court.

Come critics argue that the patent law hurts, rather than helps, the protection of inventions. The required disclosure of working drawings is helpful to competitors. Because the courts have been so weak in upholding the rights of the holder, some

Rationality in Practice

An On-line Patent Office

Given that the U.S. economy depends on innovation to keep it competitive, what could be done with the patent law to encourage more American invention and innovation? Several changes might be made. First, the patent infringement trials could be speeded up by appointing special patent infringement judges with some background expertise in particular markets (e.g., software) to respond quickly to cases. Second, the courts could be made more informal with fewer expensive lawyers tying up procedures. Third, the judge should be able to call expert scientists and engineers, as "friends of the court," to help in making judgments. Fourth, the law could be changed so that if the defendant in a patent infringement is found guilty, the defendant pays all plaintiff and court expenses and triple damages, as with any other anticompetitive litigation. Fifth, foreign companies that are found guilty could be barred from supplying any finished products or components to the U.S. market for five years (not just the product markets that the cases were about but all products the companies make).

The patent service itself needs a complete overhaul. The Japanese patent office is years ahead of the U.S. Patent Office in its computerization. The U.S. office needs to be computerized, so

companies would rather keep certain processes a secret than "protect" them with a patent. Today, many people believe economic survival depends on maintaining a lead in technological inventiveness and initiative. This means that public policy is likely to shift in the direction of making patent law much tougher, particularly on low-cost, offshore patent pirates in countries such as China. The courts are likely to take a much harder line on patent infringements by all competitors, whether foreign or domestic, leading to an increase in returns from innovations that can be patent protected. This will produce an increase in R&D investment and innovation, which must be the goal of all modern economies. The patent service itself could also benefit from some innovation of its processes (see the Rationality in Practice Box).

Consumer and Environmental Protection

Much of U.S. consumer and environmental protection legislation has come about as the result of horrific cases in which companies marketed dangerous foods, medications, cosmetics, or machines that eventually killed or maimed users or polluted the environment. We all need to be protected against dangerous products, but how much protection do we need?

A further problem with consumer and environmental safety is that sometimes the long-term consequences of product use cannot be determined beforehand. The discoverer of DDT won a Nobel prize for his invention. The insecticide saved hundreds of thousands of lives by killing the malaria-carrying mosquito. However, the product was so successful that excessive and possibly irresponsible agricultural use led to a buildup of DDT in the food chain of birds, particularly the bald eagle (the American national symbol). DDT was banned, and pesticides now require much more testing before being allowed on the market. Companies cannot anticipate all of the consequences of product use (and misuse), but they do have a responsibility to remain vigilant in their effort to sniff out emerging problems. They should be open and responsive to questions about product safety and environmental pollution raised by users and the public. Table 8.2 presents an example of a positive approach to environmental protection by one of the leading waste-disposal service companies.

patent searches can be undertaken by citizens and companies at any public library. Such an expert system available in libraries could offer many services, but, primarily, it would allow a patent search to make sure an idea has not been patented already. It also would provide templates and guides to filling out the patent application. A huge amount of time is wasted because the current forms are not filled out correctly. Such waste keeps plenty of patent lawyers and patent office employees employed, but it is an extraordinary inefficient process.

The computerized system would enable citizens to print copies of the search results and forms off their own printers and also would log when citizens did their search and filled out the forms. In fact, the whole system could work off the electronic record rather than off the paper trail. The largest expense would be in computerizing the millions of existing patents, but, even if that cost $100 a patent and the whole exercise cost $1 billion, it would be worth it in that it would encourage invention by making it less costly and laborious to patent ideas. Currently, Congress siphons off some $25 million a year of patent office revenues to spend on other programs, rather than reinvesting the money in developing an on-line patent service. This seems to be a competitively irrational government policy, given the benefits to the economy of faster, cheaper, and better patent protection.

Using Competition to Improve Product Regulation

It took from 1967 to 1976 for the Federal Drug Administration to approve beta-blockers that treat cardiovascular disease and hypertension. It has been estimated that each year of this delay ten thousand lives could have been saved by their use.[4] Whatever the true number, the problem this illustrates is how to have regulation that protects the consumer from criminally negligent poisonings or accidents and yet does not delay the introduction of lifesaving medications to the market. One factor is that establishing the long-term safety of a drug takes long-term tests. Sometimes such tests can be compressed in time by innovations in laboratory and computer simulation, but field trials take time.

One regulatory innovation would be to allow several certifying agencies to compete to provide safe and fast approval. Such agencies could be leading medical schools and foundation-sponsored testing laboratories. Their services would be closely monitored by an independent authority that was not offering its own testing services. This would encourage innovation in the supply of testing and approval services and total-quality, continuous improvement in such services. The current FDA does not operate under such competitive pressure to improve its service to all of its constituencies.

It also has been argued that environmental regulation needs to follow a new path that encourages competitive innovation. Rather than a pollution-control model of regulation, agencies should switch to a resource-productivity model.[5] Regulation should encourage innovation in design, manufacturing, and distribution processes (see the next Rationality in Practice box). The goal would be to make greater use of input resources and reduce pollution at its source, rather than to require the addition of specific pollution disposal processes to the processes that produce the pollution. Just as prevention of quality defects is more efficient than screening and repairing them, identifying and eliminating pollutants at their source in the production process is more efficient. Such changes in the production process often also produce other substantial competitive benefits that offset the initial cost of meeting the new regulations.

[4] Peter Brimelow and Leslie Spencer, "Food and Drugs and Politics," *Forbes*, November 22, 1993, 115–19.

[5] Michel E. Porter and Claas van der Linde, "Green and Competitive: Ending the Stalemate," *Harvard Business Review*, (September/October 1995): 120–34.

Table 8.2 Environmental Principles of Waste Management, Inc.

1. **Environmental Protection and Enhancement**
The company is committed to improving the environment through the services that we offer and to providing our services in a manner demonstrably protective of human health and the environment, even if not required by law. We will minimize and strive not to allow any releases to the atmosphere, land, or water in amounts that may harm human health and the environment. We will train employees to enhance understanding of environmental policies and to promote excellence in job performance on all environmental matters.
2. **Waste Reduction, Recycling, Treatment and Disposal**
The company will work to minimize the volume and toxicity of waste generated by us and others. We will operate internal recycling programs. We will vigorously pursue opportunities to recycle waste before other management practices are applied. The company will use and provide environmentally safe treatment and disposal services for waste that is not eliminated at the source or recycled.
3. **Biodiversity**
The company is committed to the conservation of nature. We will implement a policy of "no net loss" of wetlands or other biological diversity on the company's property.
4. **Sustainable Use of Natural Resources**
The company will use renewable natural resources, such as water, soils, and forests, in a sustainable manner and will offer services to make degraded resources once again usable. We will conserve nonrenewable natural resources through efficient use and careful planning.
5. **Wise Use of Energy**
The company will make every reasonable effort to use environmentally safe and sustainable energy sources to meet our needs. We will seek opportunities to improve energy efficiency and conservation in our operations.
6. **Compliance**
The company is committed to comply with all legal requirements and to implement programs and procedures to ensure compliance. These efforts will include training and testing of employees, rewarding employees who excel in compliance, and disciplining employees who violate legal requirements.
7. **Risk Reduction**
The company will operate in a manner designed to minimize environmental, health, or safety hazards. We will minimize risk and protect our employees and others in the vicinity of our operations by employing safe technologies and operating procedures and by being prepared for emergencies. The company will make available to our employees and to the public information related to any of our operations that we believe cause environmental harm or pose health or safety hazards. The company will encourage employees to report any condition that creates a danger to the environment or poses health or safety hazards, and will provide confidential means for them to do so.
8. **Damage Compensation**
The company will take responsibility for any harm we cause to the environment and will make every reasonable effort to remedy the damage caused to people or ecosystems.
9. **Research and Development**
The company will research, develop, and implement technologies for integrated waste management.
10. **Public Policy**
The company will provide information to and will assist the public in understanding the environmental impacts of our activities. We will conduct public tours of facilities, consistent with safety requirements, and will work with communities near our facilities to encourage dialogue and exchange of information on facility activities.
11. **Public Education**
The company will support and participate in development of public policy and in educational initiatives that will protect human health and improve the environment. We will seek cooperation on this work with government, environmental groups, schools, universities, and other public organizations.
12. **Participation in Environmental Organizations**
The company will encourage its employees to participate in and to support the work of environmental organizations, and we will provide support to environmental organizations for the advancement of environmental protection.
13. **Monitor and Report Environmental Matters**
The Board of Directors of the company will evaluate and will address the environmental implications of its decisions. The Executive Environmental Committee of the company will report directly to the CEO of the company and will monitor and report upon implementation of this policy and other environmental matters. The company will commit the resources needed to implement these principles.
14. **Annual Report**
The company will prepare and make public an annual report on its environmental activities. The report will include a self-evaluation of the company's performance in complying with all applicable environmental laws and regulations throughout its worldwide operations.

This progressive approach to protecting the environment might be expected from a leading waste-disposal company.

SOURCE: Reproduced with permission from Joan V. Bernstein, "Environmental Policy and Strategic Planning," in *Corporate Stewardship and the Environment*, ed. Barbara H. Peters and James L. Peters (New York: The Conference Board, 1991), 20.

For example, in Japan a 1991 law set new standards to increase the ease of recycling home appliances. In response, Hitachi made it easier to take apart washing machines and vacuum cleaners by reducing the number of parts in a washing machine by 16 percent and in a vacuum cleaner by 30 percent. This redesign also made it easier to assemble the product, which increased assembly quality and reduced cost. This effect more than offset the costs of product redesign to meet the new standard. In another case, the 1992 U.S. Energy Policy Act officially recognized an industry standard for rating electric motor efficiency. This testing standard now can be used to sell "low lifetime" energy costs to buyers and will help drive innovation in variable-speed motors that can reduce energy consumption by up to 50 percent.

The new nutritional labeling standards in the United States are also encouraging supplier nutritional innovations. By helping teach consumers which high-fat products to avoid, the regulation changes buyer demand. This change in demand is leading to new food product or process innovations (e.g., baked versus fried potato chips). The marketing of these new products will increase the importance of nutrition in consumer preferences. Such dynamic market effects are likely to lead to a continuous supply of healthier, new products that could not have been achieved by regulations prescribing recipes and production processes. Good product regulation encourages suppliers and consumers to constantly experiment with ways of reducing pollution or of increasing product safety and leads to other competitive benefits. Product regulation that locks compliers into a particular technology or compliance process and discourages creative, new solutions to safety and pollution problems is bad regulation.

Price Regulations

The laws that apply to pricing are primarily aimed at preventing unfair and deceptive practices. Avoiding price competition and charging different buyers different prices for the same products are considered unfair practices. Price deception occurs when an actual selling price turns out to be more than was claimed.

Price-Fixing

Price-fixing among suppliers is the best-known illegal marketing tactic. It is an obvious conspiracy against the free market, unless of course the government does it in its regulation of a market. Price-fixing, the setting of prices artificially, has occurred in many and varied markets from giant electricity-generating turbines to school milk programs to Ivy League colleges. Price-fixing can have dire consequences for the firm and individual executive. In ancient Rome, price-fixers were put to death. Today, they may go to jail. The real economic threat is that if a company is found liable, it can be forced to pay triple damages to the aggrieved party to cover not only the consequences of its own actions but even the consequences of the actions of all of its coconspirators. Price-fixing has resulted in huge fines (in the hundreds of millions of dollars).

Price Signaling

Some industries fix prices less blatantly by having the market leader report its intended future prices to the other suppliers, who then set their prices only after they know what the leader's price will be. Illegal price signaling can be hard to determine.

Rationality in Practice

Sponsored Design Contests

An enlightened example of public policy is the efforts of the Environmental Protection Agency (EPA) to increase the energy efficiency of refrigerators that do not use chlorofluorocarbons (CFCs), which destroy the ozone layer. New energy efficiency standards and a ban on CFCs are pending, but the EPA decided also to use a "carrot" rather than a "stick," called The Super Efficient Refrigerator Program (SERP).

Refrigerators can account for up to 20 percent of a household's energy use, so the EPA got twenty-four utility companies to fund a $30 million prize for the refrigerator manufacturer who promised to design, manufacture, and sell the most refrigerators with the highest energy-saving running costs (i.e, save the most total kilowatt hours). The new refrigerator had to be CFC free and at least 25 percent more efficient than the 1993 federal standards, and at least 250,000 had to be sold between January 1994 and July 1997. The prize came in the form of a rebate of about $100 for each of the newly designed refrigerators sold. This reward mechanism ensured that the winner got paid not just for designing a better refrigerator but also for selling it. The winner, Whirlpool, received the bragging rights plus a $100 subsidy on the price of its new generation of refrigerators, which enabled it to lower its price. The buyer of the refrigerator benefits from this more competitive price. The utilities saved on their limited capacity—they were paying large customers to save electricity, anyway—and the EPA will see a new generation of refrigerators that are even more efficient than the new standard and are CFC free.

Most important, SERP has redirected the R&D focus of the manufacturers to energy saving, and now all the competitors will have to try to match Whirlpool's award-winning leaner, greener machine.[6] The contest deadlines also encouraged the firms to speed up and improve the quality of their product development processes, thus increasing the long-term competitiveness and efficiency of the market. Better product development processes produce higher quality, low-cost products. The SERP policy innovation was very effective because everyone benefited from its results. It was a win-win policy.

Everyone agrees that a market is more efficient and competitive when suppliers and consumers have information about market prices. Advertising prices helps achieve this, and some critics argue that suppliers should be required to make public their actual selling prices, not just their list prices. A rule of reason is therefore applied to judging whether any potential price signaling is illegal. The private exchange of price information among suppliers (with or without the assistance of a trade association) is illegal if it results in a period of stable or rising prices. However, when prices are signaled in public and a price war results, such price signaling among competitors is judged not only legal but also desirable.

Discriminatory Pricing

A supplier is allowed to respond to changes in demand by charging various prices for a product or service in different situations and at different times. Charging two customers different prices for exactly the same type and amount of goods in the same situation and time period is not allowed. The Robinson-Patman Act, passed in 1936, is the major law banning price discrimination. It prevents manufacturers from selling their goods at lower prices to major chain stores unless the company can prove proportionate cost savings in trading with such large customers. The act was passed to protect smaller, inefficient, but possibly more service-oriented family stores.

[6] See James B. Treece, "The Great Refrigerator Race," *Business Week*, July 15, 1993, 78–81.

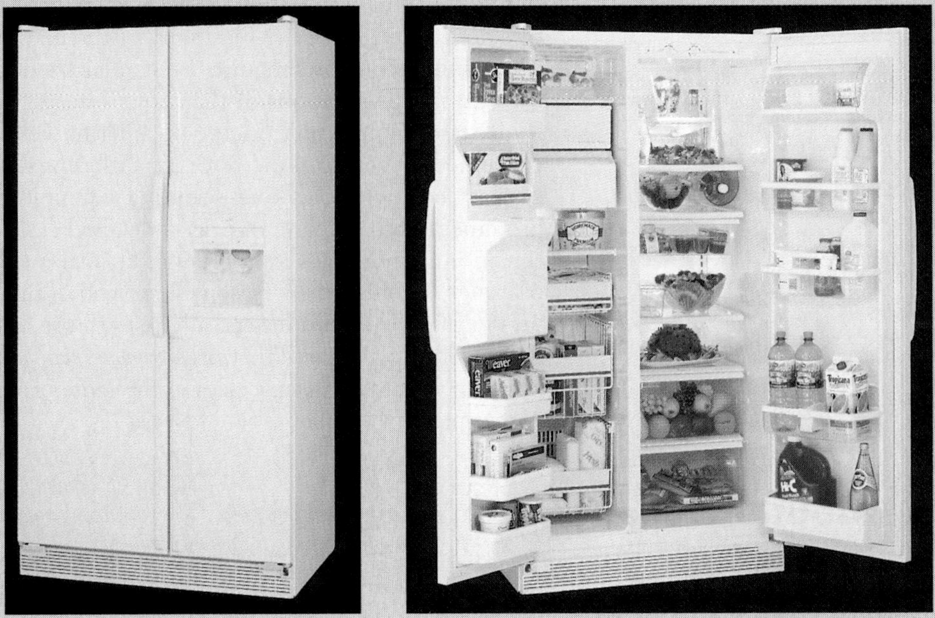

Examples of Whirlpool's new, more efficient refrigerators

Resale Price Maintenance

Although manufacturers are required to sell their products at the *same* wholesale prices to different retailers, they are not allowed to enforce *standard* resale prices. Attempts to enforce a minimum retail price may encourage a retailer (often a discounter) to sue. Any pressure in the form of threats or acts, such as the withdrawal of service or delivery tardiness, can be damning. A manufacturer, however, can print its manufacturer recommended selling price on its packaging.

Predatory Pricing

In order to drive fledgling competition out of the market, the classic tactic is for a market leader to cut its prices to the bone. When a monopoly is achieved, the predator, faced with no competition, raises prices. Such a predator must have deep pockets or a lower cost structure. It also must have a good deal of confidence that other entrepreneurs with superior products or production processes will not enter the market in the future. The standard evidence of predatory pricing (which is very hard to obtain) is that the price is below marginal or average cost, whichever is the lower. Such a price is clearly unprofitable, and the obvious inference is that it has been applied solely to hurt the competition more than it hurts the predator. However, a seller can match (but not undercut) the prices of competitors even if the price is below cost. Size and success also have a lot to do with establishing a predatory pricing case. It is difficult to accuse a company with a small market share of predatory pricing.

Price Misrepresentation

Public policymakers have been long aware of the competitive practice of quoting or stating prices in ways that make price comparisons among options difficult. Competitors do this to reduce the sensitivity of the market to price and hence price competition. A number of laws require the standardized presentation of price. Lenders are required to state the terms of their loan offerings in annual simple-interest rates, and some states require unit pricing of supermarket packaged goods to make it easier for consumers to compare the prices of different sizes. With the advent of the universal product code and checkout scanning equipment, many state laws also require the prominent shelf labeling of prices, detailed cash-register receipts, and even the continuation of individual item pricing. Special introductory pricing offers must be new offerings and must last a reasonable period of time. They also must offer genuine savings in that the final price actually rises to the level that will substantiate the claim of the introductory offer. The words *economy*, *budget* or *bargain* can be used to describe a price only if other package sizes in the same product line are priced at least 5 percent higher per unit volume.

Distribution Relationship Regulations

The laws that apply to distribution relationships cover franchising and exclusive dealing. These practices restrict competition among outlets selling the same brand (intrabrand competition). The regulations also address the tricky situation of trading with distributors or customers who are also competitors.

Franchising and Exclusive Relationships

Franchising is a long-term trading contract or partnership with another party. The fundamental legal issue is whether a franchising arrangement substantially reduces competition in the relevant market. In part, this is determined by the relative strength of the competitors and the market share involved. As in other areas of marketing law, judgments have been inconsistent.

The Brown Shoe Company, for example, arranged with its dealers (who made up about 1 percent of all shoe retailers) to provide group insurance, assistance with shop design, and other marketing help. In return, the distributors agreed to concentrate on purchasing Brown shoes. Even though the agreement was not binding and could be terminated by the dealers at any time, the Supreme Court supported the Federal Trade Commission's claim that this arrangement potentially injured competition. Thousands of franchise contracts are more binding. The difference is that normally they are made between a supplier and an entrepreneur who is setting up in business. Consequently, the arrangement does not affect other suppliers' sales to the franchise.

A Shift in Legal Power

The general view is that franchise contracts greatly favor the franchisor or supplier. This no longer may be true. In early 1984, Porsche AG attempted to break from its Volkswagen of America franchised dealers so it could sell through factory-owned outlets. It hoped to be able to better control its marketing, service, and pricing. However, a dealer group representing about 80 percent of Porsche cars sold in the United States sued, claiming $1 billion in damages. Porsche quickly backed down.

Franchisee gas stations won a major settlement with the oil companies, allowing them to shop for the cheapest gasoline available. For example, a Texaco dealer can now buy Mobil gas, but it must inform its customers that the gas comes from a different company. Evidence indicates that unhappy franchisees are now joining together and using the threat of an antitrust suit to obtain what they want from the franchisor. This trend is another indication of thc growing influence of retailers and distributors over suppliers.

Tying Contractual Relationships

You cannot use demand for one product to sell another. For example, motion picture distributors once required television stations to buy films such as *Gorilla Man* if they wanted to purchase popular features such as *Casablanca.* This tying arrangement was deemed a violation of the Sherman Antitrust Act. However, companies are allowed to offer cheap financing tied to a purchase. Forced reciprocity, in which a business is forced to sell its product to a supplier on particular terms as part of the price of obtaining a desired product, is also regarded as illegal tying. Tying arrangements are illegal when monopolistic or economic power is used to force a buyer to purchase an otherwise unattractive product or service.

Restricting Intrabrand Competition

Although the courts may frown on the exclusive franchising of existing distributors, they have allowed manufacturers to deliberately restrict their number of product resellers in a particular market, be it a regional territory or a group of customers. Refusal to supply other resellers is acceptable if such a tactic increases or is likely to increase competition *among* manufacturers' brands— that is, if it increases interbrand competition.

Although the purpose of antitrust regulation is to promote competition, the law is unclear when *intrabrand* competition (competition among retailers selling the same product and brand) should be traded off against *interbrand* competition (competition among manufacturers' brands). Applying the rule of reason, the Supreme Court objected to the refusal of Schwinn Bicycles to deal with new distributors wanting its bikes. The court ruled that increasing the number of Schwinn outlets in the market would increase service and reduce the retail prices of the then leading brand. Expanding the outlets would increase intrabrand competition without materially hurting the interbrand competitiveness of Schwinn.

On the other hand, in a case involving Sylvania, the television manufacturer was allowed to restrict distribution of its product. At the time, RCA, along with Zenith and Magnavox, dominated the market. Sylvania argued that it could improve its distribution efficiency and competitiveness in the market by restricting its outlets to only two per metropolitan center. The court agreed that in this case interbrand competition very likely would be increased, even if at the expense of intrabrand competition.

Other acceptable grounds for restricting sales to resellers include when the product is highly perishable, is inherently dangerous to handle, or requires considerable investment on the part of a reseller to service the product. Distributors who sell the product and send their customers to a competitor's authorized service outlet are unfairly taking a free ride on the competitor's investment in customer service. When a distributor has to make a similar considerable investment to handle a product's perishability or risk of handling, it expects to recover such investments by being offered a larger, exclusive sales territory. One way a manufacturer or supplier cannot restrict intrabrand competition is by setting a recommended reselling price and not selling to trade customers who undercut the price. Not allowing a manufacturer to do this encourages intrabrand price competition between a manufacturer's resellers and distribution channels. Note that it is often a manufacturer's existing distribution channels that object strongly to any increase in intrabrand competition. They are often furious when a manufacturer starts supplying another retailer in their market, particularly a retailer who is an aggressive price cutter (see Chapter 11).

Selling Regulations

Apart from the laws of contract that apply to business-to-business marketing, the major laws affecting personal selling apply to door-to-door, or in-home, selling. Once very common, this type of marketing has declined because of its high cost and the dramatic increase in the numbers of women working outside the home. Over the years, it has fallen into disrepute because of hard-selling tactics involving harassment and misrepresentation and the frequent occurrence of pyramid schemes involving a management hierarchy that does nothing but skim profits off the sale.

The law now requires door-to-door salespeople to immediately make clear the true purpose of the sales call. Market researchers report that misrepresentation has become so wide spread that many people asked to participate in surveys are suspicious that the real intent is to make a sale, not conduct a survey. The unscrupulous behavior of a few has hurt the ability of all marketers to study consumers.

The law also requires a cooling-off period of three days during which the consumer can withdraw from a signed agreement or contract. This regulation also applies to dance studios and health clubs, some of which have been accused of being too successful at talking potential customers into long-term contracts. The greatest problems with personal selling, however, are caused by the thieves who prey on the elderly or feebleminded. A typical ruse is to inspect victims' chimneys (for free) and declare them a safety hazard. The victims are then charged thousands of dollars for so-called repairs that can never be inspected and amount to nothing more than cleaning the chimney. The best protection for such vulnerable consumers may not be federal or state law but a friendly, caring, old-timer banker who flags major withdrawals from these consumers' savings, discreetly determines their purpose, and reports anything suspicious to the police. This example serves to remind us that the law often has great difficulty preventing the behavior of those with clear criminal intent. To be more effective, it requires a great deal of public cooperation.

In the case of in-home telephone selling, new Federal Trade Commission (FTC) regulations taking effect in 1996 require telemarketers to disclose both what they are selling and the full price at the outset of a call. Estimates of annual telemarketing fraud vary from $4 billion to $40 billion.

Advertising Regulations

The major concern of the government regulation of advertising is the control of deceptive practices. Initially, such regulation was justified on the grounds that advertising deception was unfair to competitors and, hence, came under the jurisdiction of anticompetition laws (for example the Wheeler-Lea Amendment). Not until the

1930s was deception declared illegal because it was unfair to consumers.

The Federal Trade Commission was set up in 1914, but it did not become an advertising regulatory agency until the 1960s. This commission investigates complaints and is empowered to make rules that advertisers must follow. Most advertising deception cases are settled out of court by withdrawal of the offending advertisement, but occasionally advertisers are required to make restitution to consumers or to undertake corrective advertising to change false consumer perceptions.

What Is Deceptive?

The definition of a deceptive advertising claim has been argued in the courts and academic journals for a number of years. Initially, advertising was considered deceptive if the claim was related to an important product characteristic and was not literally true. The question of its honesty was answered by consulting dictionaries. Today, however, with television and magazine advertising involving few words and much imagery, deception is more often judged by measuring the impact of the advertising on consumer beliefs and attitudes. If the advertising creates product performance beliefs that cannot be substantiated by the advertiser (using market research or product testing), then the ad may be judged as making false representations.

False representation can include not telling all, as well as telling lies. For example, a television advertisement for an acne remedy was considered deceptive on two counts. First, the endorsers, singer Pat Boone and his daughters, had not actually used the formulation (as some viewers inferred). By law, an endorser must have used the product and must continue to use the product. Second, the advertisement did not disclose that Pat Boone was president of the company marketing the product. The advertisement must disclose whether the endorser has been paid to endorse the product or is receiving a commission on sales. When such deception occurs, the Federal Trade Commission may require the offender to place corrective advertising that changes any lingering false beliefs created by the initial deceptive advertising.

"Expert" endorsers must possess expertise relevant to the product claims and must have legitimately evaluated the product and its competitive substitutes. Advertising deception applies to product characteristics, price claims, information about product availability, and any promotional contests and sweepstakes. For example, sweepstakes advertising must disclose the number of prizes and the odds of winning.

Substantiation of Claims

The long era of using superlatives in advertising, such as "the best," "the cheapest," and "the easiest to use," may be drawing to a close. Such general, positive claims (called *puffery* in advertising) were long considered acceptable, because advertisers were expected to praise their product. Most of us learned at an early age to be suspicious of advertising claims. Our parents taught us, and we learned from experience. Even so, increasingly, advertisers are asked either to provide substantiation for their claims or to stop making them. For example, comparison advertising must be based on valid laboratory tests, market research, or other objective information. The advertising agencies creating the deceptive advertising are now also liable.

Deceptive advertising by sellers also needs to be put in perspective. How many of us strenuously object to deceptive advertising but do not think twice about using enticing words to attract buyers when we are selling our own cars that have become, for one undisclosed reason or another, too expensive to maintain? Honesty in advertising presumably applies across the board, whether you are the buyer or the seller.

Marketing Ethics

Ethics are our beliefs about what is right and what is wrong. The marketing planning process recognizes responsibilities to consumers, channel members, and the company. This responsibility is accomplished by designing a marketing strategy to satisfy the needs of each of these groups. The law and general public-policy issues also come into play. However, personal beliefs about what is right and what is wrong also should constrain our decision making. It is called exercising ethical standards.

Ultimately, marketing planners must live with their professional behavior and decisions in the same way that they must live with their personal behavior and decisions. Why are these ethics and values of marketing planners so important? Because supplier behavior shapes consumer behavior, the values of marketing planners expressed in what they make and how they sell set a moral tone in and beyond the marketplace. The resulting ethical dilemmas can be complex.

The Law Is a *Minimum* Ethical Standard

Why do we need ethics when we have the law, which tells us what we can and cannot do? One answer is that the letter of the law is generally considered to be only a minimum ethical standard. Another answer is that the law often does not work the way it should. As aptly stated in the code of ethics of Caterpillar Tractor, the law is a floor and must not serve as the *only* basis for individual and corporate ethics.[7]

Company and Personal Ethics

Despite the general public image, many companies are moral enterprises, led by men and women of impeccable character. Such enterprises have written codes of ethics and unwritten company cultures that influence marketing decision making. A company code of ethics is actually a type of company constraint on marketing decision making similar to a production constraint or a financial goal.

Table 8.3 presents a summary of the business conduct guidelines of IBM and P&G. Figure 8.3 summarizes the content of some two hundred company ethics statements. About 60 percent of American companies have formal codes of ethics and about one in three have ethics offices or ombudspersons.[8] Such ethical codes are assumed to be applied to all decisions made, so they may go unstated in marketing plans and reports. The narrower and more prescriptive the code of ethics of a company, the less the ethical discretion of the marketing strategist and planner. However, many ethical dilemmas are situational, involving trade-offs among different interest groups or between the means and the end, so company codes of ethics are often general. Specific interpretation is left to the individual executive. Ethical dilemmas also arise in the implementation of strategy. Decisions often must be made without an opportunity to consult superiors. Such situations throw heavy responsibility on the cross-functional team, marketing manager, product manager, and salesperson.

---

[7] Gene R. Laczniak and Patrick E. Murphy, *Marketing Ethics* (Lexington, MA: Lexington Books, 1985).
[8] "Good Grief," *The Economist*, April 8, 1995, 57.

Table 8.3 **Business Conduct Guidelines for IBM and Goals for P&G**

IBM
- Do not make misrepresentations to anyone you deal with.
- Do not use IBM's size unfairly to intimidate or threaten.
- Treat all buyers and sellers equitably.
- Do not engage in reciprocal dealing.
- Do not disparage competitors.
- Do not prematurely disclose an unannounced offering.
- Do no further selling after competitor has the firm order.
- Keep contact with the competition minimal.
- Do not illegally use confidential information.
- Do not steal or obtain information by willful deceit.
- Do not violate patents or copyrights.
- Do not give or accept bribes, gifts, or entertainment that might be seen as creating an obligation.

P&G
- To provide customers with superior benefits.
- To listen and respond to customer opinions.
- To ensure products are safe for intended use and anticipate accidental misuse.
- To strive for fair and open business relationships with suppliers and retailers.
- To help business partners improve performance.
- To reject illegal or deceptive activities anywhere in the world.
- To safeguard the environment.
- To encourage employees to participate in community activities.
- To be a good neighbor in communities in which business is done.
- To provide employees a safe work place.
- To show concern for the well-being of all employees.
- To create opportunities for employee achievement, creativity, and personal reward.
- To provide a fair annual return to the owners.
- To build for the future to maintain growth.

SOURCES: Gene R. Laczniak and Patrick E. Murphy, *Marketing Ethics* (Lexington, MA: Lexington Books, 1985), 117–23; and Jan Willem Bol, Charles T. Crespy, James M. Stearns, and John R. Walton, *The Integration of Ethics into the Marketing Curriculum* (Needham Heights, MA: Ginn Press, 1991), 27.

Ethical stress on the marketing executive can be greatly heightened by the presence of a double standard. Executives must meet performance goals. A company must make clear what action it will take against unethical behavior and establish credibility by following through. If actions are taken *only* when a company's behavior is publicly challenged, then the company sends the wrong signals to its marketing executives. What it says is that the company does not really mind what an executive does to achieve financial goals, as long as someone from outside does not raise hell. If this happens, the firm will piously stick it to the executive. Unfortunately, many marketing decision makers face this conflict to varying degrees. It places great demands on their personal codes of ethics.

Junior marketing executives also need to have strong personal codes of ethics. Subordinates are responsible for their own behavior even if following orders or under the threat of dismissal. Ignorance is also no excuse. No one gets an easy way out. To take a stand may put at risk a promotion or even the job. To not take a stand is to sell out one's values, self-respect, and soul. To pass the responsibility on to senior executives may be construed as weakness or, worse, setting up the boss. When orders and ethics collide, a trusted mentor in an organization can be invaluable.

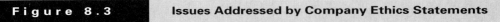

Figure 8.3 **Issues Addressed by Company Ethics Statements**

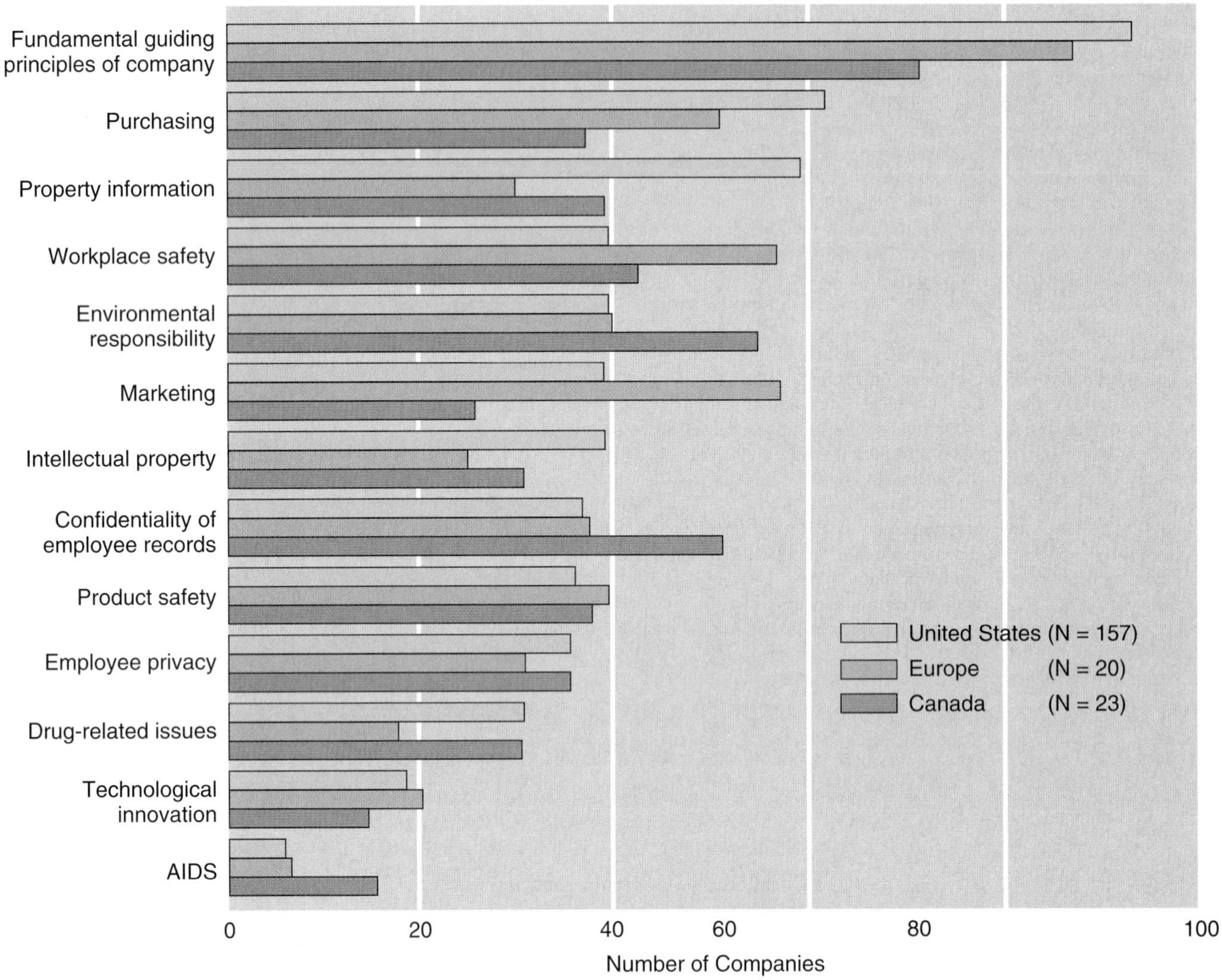

It seems that companies are more concerned that their purchasing is ethical than that their marketing is ethical. In the cross-cultural comparison, U.S. firms are more frequently concerned about proprietary information, Canadian firms are more frequently concerned about environmental responsibility, and European firms are more frequently concerned about workplace safety.

SOURCE: Reproduced with permission from Ronald E. Berenbeim, *Corporate Ethics Practices* (New York: The Conference Board, 1992).

On a more positive note, many companies' mission statements and ethical codes contain core ethical values that have become part of the enduring corporate culture. The values have become so ingrained in the corporate cultures that they are automatically applied to the evaluation and implementation of strategy. They do not have to be stated in the marketing plan, as they are accepted by all concerned as a given.[9] Where do such values and rules come from? The next section discusses some of the issues and moral philosophy that underlie personal and organizational ethics.

Theories of Marketing Ethics

This section discusses models of business ethics. One model argues that humans do not really need ethics, and another argues that no tried-and-true code of ethics can exist. The discussion then turns for guidance to the underlying religious values of American society. Yet even this approach has problems. As explained in the next section, it seems that the best we can do is to confront ourselves honestly with a series of questions to challenge our thinking. Such an approach will at least stop us from avoiding or shelving the questions of ethics. We also may come away from the experience with a better understanding of who we are and why and how we made our choices.

Competition, Ethics, and Efficiency

Social Darwinism is the idea that the laws of natural selection and survival of the fittest apply to the marketplace. It is a dog-eat-dog world, and just as the competitive behavior of beasts of prey cannot be considered unethical, so the competitive behavior of firms cannot ever be considered unethical. Social Darwinism was used to excuse the sharp trading practices of the so-called robber barons who dominated American business at the turn of the century. These industrialists, financiers, and entrepreneurs helped make the United States a superpower. They left endowments that built some of the finest universities in the world. But they were also quite unscrupulous at times. On a similar theme, some marketers and economists have used Adam Smith's economic philosophy to argue that it is right to pursue self-interest (read selfish interests) in the marketplace, using any means within or around the law. It is true, as explained by the theory of competitive rationality, that competition makes the market efficient, but the point that is often missed is that it works only in an *ethical* environment. For example, if suppliers conspire to reduce competition, then competition ceases to exist. Competition is also reduced if suppliers are not honest in their product or service claims. If advertising is deceptive or contractual promises are not kept, then the competitive pursuit of self-interest will no longer be efficient and serve the interests of consumers and society. When ethics do not exist, markets fail and the visible hand of government regulation must be present to ensure that competition works honestly and openly.[10]

The Shifting Sands of Situational Ethics

The famous philosophers David Hume, Jeremy Bentham, and John Stuart Mill developed the *principle of utility:* The right action is that which produces the most good for the most people in a specific situation. This is a very useful guide because ethical problems often arise when a trade-off occurs between rights and interests. The guiding

[9] Donald P. Robin and R. Eric Reidenbach, "Social Responsibility, Ethics, and Marketing Strategy: Closing the Gap between Concept and Application," *Journal of Marketing* 51 (January 1987): 44–58.

[10] This argument is based on the philosophies of Thomas Hobbes and Jean-Jacques Rousseau, which state that society needs sets of rules (morality) accepted by all (the social contract) for it to function effectively.

principle is relativistic and *situational*, in that one action is judged against another instead of by an absolute standard. This relativism raises a number of problems.

First, how does one calculate the most good for the most people? A problem with the principle of utility is that it does not help in measuring good or bad. Obviously, a decision maker cannot assess the total good of an action if the total good and bad cannot be measured. A second concern is whether people can measure good by adding up all the positive outcomes and then subtracting all the negative outcomes. For example, is it allowable to have 1 out of 10,000,000 consumers die from the side effects of a new drug if the drug is twice as effective at relieving the headache pain of the other 9,999,999? Third, how do people avoid mixing what is good for others with what is good for themselves? How does a decision maker avoid overweighing the benefit that he or she is likely to receive personally from pursuing one strategic option over another? It is not easy to separate one's desires and goals from the judgment of what is right.

Situational ethics can also result in sinking to the lowest ethical standards among a group of competitors, when each rationalizes that it is at least as ethical as the competition. "If we were to be any more ethical," a company might argue, "we, as a good guy, would go out of business, and what good would be gained from that? We did not start it, so what has occurred is also not our fault." This kind of thinking can become moral quicksand. Another harsh reality is that the more desperate the company or personal situation, the lower the applied ethical standards will be and the more the decision maker will be fixated with how his or her company will benefit. Sometimes it seems that only successful companies and executives can afford a conscience. In practice, it can mean being dragged down to the ethics of the most desperate competitor.

The Categorical Imperative

Immanuel Kant's famous *categorical imperative* offers an alternative to situational ethics. The categorical imperative asks whether the proposed action would be right if everyone did it. What would happen to the social fabric? What would happen if you were constantly on the receiving end of such ethics? This approach takes most of the situation or context out of the ethical evaluation and, in that sense, is more explicit than the utilitarian principle. But the categorical imperative still requires the decision maker to *see* the universal wrong or evil in the act if everyone did it. Immoral or amoral individuals, caring nothing for society, may answer that, yes, it would be fine for society and that others are welcome to act in the same way toward them. Both situational ethics and the categorical imperative still require a basic set of values. Such values are often based on religious beliefs.

The Religious Foundations of Marketing Ethics

It is no accident that both primitive and advanced civilizations have ethical and moral codes that constrain group and individual behavior. The enlightenment of a civilization is often measured by its underlying ethics. When ethical codes break down, societies cease to function and ultimately collapse from within (for example, the decline and fall of the Roman Empire) or under external pressures (for example, the defeat of the Third Reich in World War II). How do such ethical codes come about? The history of civilization reveals that they are based on a society's predominant religious creed. Because the obvious source of a marketing decision maker's code of ethics is the society's general code of ethics, this suggests that marketplace ethics have a religious basis. For example, the predominant religion of the United States is Christianity. The Judeo-Christian creed has greatly influenced the Constitution, common law, and the system of justice in the United States. Thus, it can be argued that marketers in the United States should adopt a code of marketing ethics based on Judeo-Christian religious beliefs.[11]

But what happens to freedom of worship and thought? It is to be expected, and appropriate, in a free society that a believer of another religion will apply his or her religious ethics to all situations, including marketing decision making. This exercise of different religious beliefs and values increases the variability in ethics that we are likely to observe in the marketplace. One economic reason we should use the predominant religion's values as the common core for our society's ethics, even if we are not followers of that religion, is that the universal acceptance of its code enables us to anticipate the likely behavior of other parties in the market. This anticipation leads to an increase in trust and a sense of confidence and control that the market is orderly and fair and thus reduces the costs of doing business. If the clearly dominant and underlying religious creed in our society is *not* to be used as the foundation for a generally accepted code of business ethics, then what should be used? It would be extraordinarily difficult to argue that some other religious or moral philosophy should be substituted. All of these issues make it very difficult to prescribe answers to the common ethical questions and dilemmas that executives wrestle with.

An Ethical Screening Process

Aristotle described ethics as a way of thinking about and acting on ethical dilemmas. For market decision making and behavior, an individual's mental model is used to ethically screen suggested product market goals, strategy ideas, and implementation programs. An example of such a mental model is the set of screening questions presented in Table 8.4. This mental model is first used to perceive and recognize an ethical issue involved with a goal, a strategy, or program details. The ethical issue is then added to the environment report and becomes an environment issue to be meshed, along with other new environment information issues, with proposed positioning strategy and marketing programs—particularly how the ethical issue meshes with building long-term, caring relationships with distributors and customers.

The cross-functional team uses cultural, professional, and company ethical codes and the interaction of these with team-member ethical codes and beliefs to make the decision of whether to proceed with the goal, strategy, or program. Ideally, the team creates a consensus way of thinking (mental model) that is traded off with effects on customers, shareholders, suppliers, alliance partners, distributors, other employees, other specific stakeholders, and the team itself and its members. This process, detailed in Figure 8.4, combines the use of some universal moral principles, consideration of other situational issues, and the practical trading off of caring for and loyalty to different communities of interest, values, and principles that produced the ethical dilemma. Like the rule of reason applied to competitive regulation, such a process determines

[11] That the moral norms in a democracy are determined by the community standards of the majority (the social contract) has been argued by Lawrence Kohlberg, "The Just Community Approach to Moral Education in Theory and Practice," in *Moral Education: Theory and Application*, ed. Marvin W. Berkowitz and Fritz Oser (New York: Lawrence Erlbaum, 1985).

Table 8.4 **A Personal Ethics Checklist for Marketers**

1. Am I violating the law? If yes, why?
2. Are the values and ethics that I am applying in business lower than those I use to guide my personal life? If yes, why?
3. Am I doing to others as I would have them do to me? If not, why not?
4. Would it be wrong if everyone did what I propose to do? Why?
5. Am I willfully risking the life and limb of consumers and others by my actions? If yes, why?
6. Am I willfully exploiting or putting at risk children, the elderly, the illiterate, the mentally incompetent, the naive, the poor, or the environment? If yes, why?
7. Am I keeping my promises? If not, why not?
8. Am I telling the truth, all the truth? If not, why not?
9. Am I exploiting a confidence or a trust? If yes, why?
10. Am I misrepresenting my true intentions to others? If yes, why?
11. Am I loyal to those who have been loyal to me? If not, why not?
12. Have I set up others to take responsibility for any negative consequences of my actions? If yes, why?
13. Am I prepared to redress wrongs and fairly compensate for damages? If not, why not?
14. Are my values and ethics as expressed in my strategy offensive to certain groups? If yes, why?
15. Am I being as efficient in my use of scarce resources as I can be? If not, why not?

This set of questions can be used as the basis for a team's or an individual's mental model to perceive and recognize an ethical issue associated with a proposed goal, strategy, program, or tactic.

what is reasonable and decent behavior *within* the current market and culture.

The creation of a team-consensus code of ethics is ideal but is likely to be very hard to achieve in practice. The team leader and members must be careful not to needlessly endanger the unity and productivity of the team but at the same time to protect the individual's right and responsibility to challenge the consensus ethical code. If a company has an ethics ombudsperson or an office of ethics, then their expertise and wisdom may help a team resolve any internal conflicts.

Perceiving and Recognizing Ethical Issues

The set of general questions in Table 8.4 can be asked by the decision maker or decision-making team seeking to develop its own ethical standards or ethical mental model. Although most questions are self-explanatory, others need some brief justification or raise issues worth exploring.[12] It seems that the least society should require of marketing executives is that they *ask* such questions. Sometimes not asking a question can be as wrong as asking and giving a poor answer. For example, not considering the safety of a toy being marketed is as irresponsible as considering the safety and deciding to sell the toy anyway. The effects are the same. One of the most common situations in which marketing executives suffer a lapse of ethics is when they have to make a quick decision and are preoccupied with other concerns. The ethical sufficiency of the decision is simply not examined.

Unfortunately, relaxing ethical vigilance can have as serious a consequence as relaxing competitive vigilance. Ethical vigilance means, in practice, asking hard questions. It is important to confront excuses and reasons for violating personal ethics. Avoiding or

[12] Some of the questions are based on the thinking of Gene R. Laczniak, "Framework for Analyzing Marketing Ethics," *Journal of Macromarketing* (spring 1983): 7–18; and William David Ross, *The Right and the Good* (Oxford: Clarendon Press, 1930).

Figure 8.4 An Ethical Screening Process

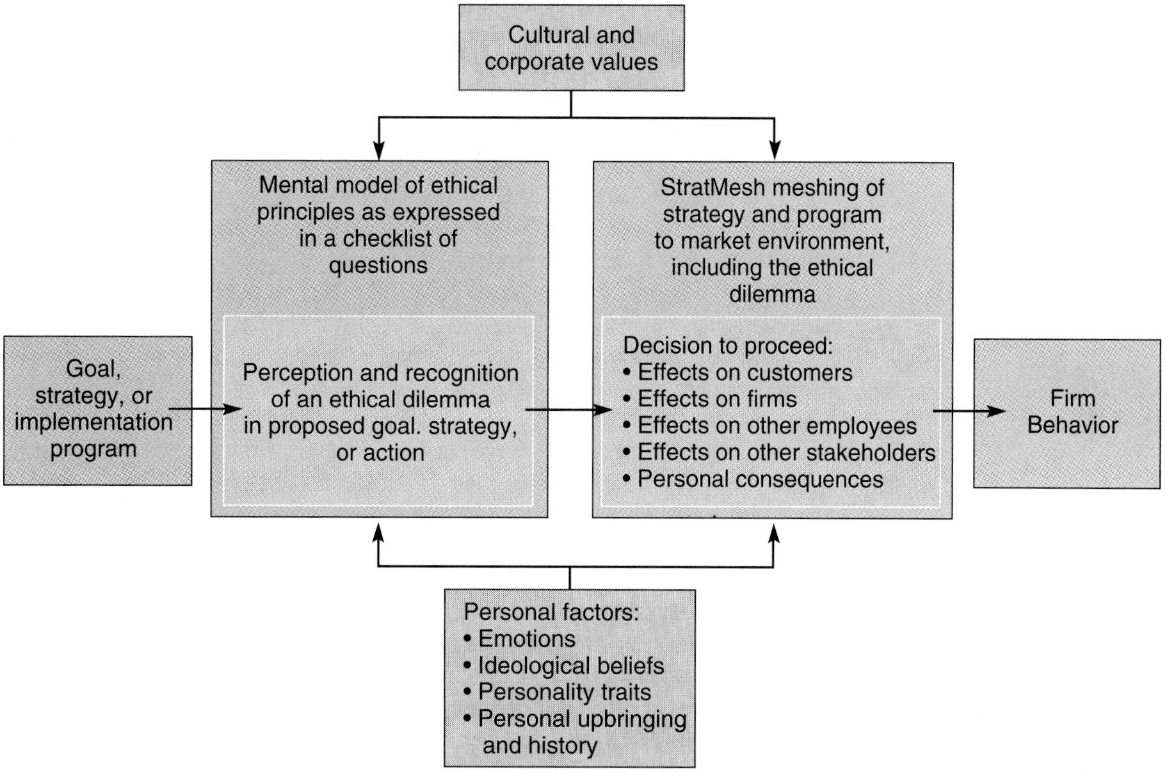

Aristotle described ethics as a way of thinking about and acting on ethical dilemmas. For market decision making and behavior, a mental model is used to ethically screen suggested product market goals, strategy ideas, and implementation programs. The ethical issue is then added to the environment report and becomes an environment issue to be meshed, along with other new environment information issues, with proposed positioning strategy and marketing programs—particularly how the ethical issue meshes with building long-term, caring relationships with distributors and customers. This process combines the use of some universal moral principles, consideration of other situational issues, and the practical trading off of caring for and loyalty to different communities of interest, values, and principles that produced the ethical dilemma.

SOURCE: The above model is based on a combination of ethics models developed by Craig J. Thompson, "A Contextualist Proposal for the Conceptualization and Study of Marketing Ethics," *Journal of Public Policy and Marketing* 14, no. 2 (fall 1995): 177–91.

shelving the answers to such questions is no solution. Decision makers who ask why they do or do not behave in certain ways are more honest with themselves about their true intentions. This is the essence of executive responsibility, and it also can be the first step down the path of change. Such questions lead people to recognize that most of us have at least two codes of ethics: (1) the set we espouse and want others to apply in their behavior toward us and (2) the code of ethics that, for whatever rationalizations, we actually live up to. The more we recognize the differences between them, the closer we come to understanding how easy it is to talk about ethics in black and white while practicing them in tones of gray.

The list of questions in Table 8.4 is organized in approximate order of importance and by the nature of the ethical or moral principle involved. The first question in the table is the first and last question the ethical minimalist will ask. The second question addresses the application of a double standard and the basis for such a double standard. The third question addresses the extent to which marketers apply the Golden Rule: "Do unto others as you will have them do unto you." A prominent British chief executive officer has suggested that a better way of posing the question is to look at oneself and ask "What would I think of someone who has my business ethics or took the action that I propose to take?"[13] The fourth question argues that if it would be wrong for everyone to do it, it is wrong for anyone to do it. Why is one marketer the exception that makes it right? For example, if a marketer were considering paying a bribe to a foreign businessperson, would it be right if, from now on, everyone had to pay bribes to do any sort of business? Would this change one's view of the ethics of the single action?

Marketing planners have to decide whether they live in a society where they are expected to care about the welfare of others. It has been called the social contract by philosophers. A "free market" does not mean suppliers and consumers are free to do what they like. Competition forces sellers to serve the interests of consumers. Also, competition benefits from laws that enforce contracts and at times needs to be constrained by codes of conduct. The interests of society at large and future generations also have to be promoted and protected by informal ethics and formal laws. Today, so many complex laws exist that it pays to have an expert lawyer screen any proposed strategy that is questionable. It is in the interest of both the firm and society at large that the firm sensibly constrains its planned competitive behavior rather than have to defend it later in overloaded courts involving expensive litigation.

As noted earlier, the ethical standards of morality that constrain marketing decision making should be a product of the combination of personal conscience and the morality of the company as stated in its code of ethics. Figure 8.5 illustrates the several layers of ethical standards that apply to marketing decision making. Ethical behavior is required to make the market work efficiently and to keep it free and open. Marketing planners must therefore respond to the almost universal ethical codes involved in trading: to be honest and not conspire to cheat and steal. But their decisions as to what to offer the marketplace and how to offer it also have an impact on the prevailing values and ethics of a society. Some products and marketing practices are ethically questionable. This heavy responsibility cannot be simply shrugged off. The enlightened leadership that marketing planners are expected to display is most put to the test when they are faced with ethical dilemmas created by conflicts of interests among customers, employees, and owners. How they choose to resolve such dilemmas tells them a lot about themselves.

Public Policy, Ethics, and Global Marketing

Into the foreseeable future, the world will be engaged in fairly friendly global competition that will lead to new types of public policy. In theory, an open, free-trade, global market works to the advantage of all nations if each nation trades goods that it is best

[13] Sir Adrian Cadbury, "Ethical Managers Make Their Own Rules," *Harvard Business Review* 87, no. 5 (September/October 1987): 69–75.

Figure 8.5 **The Legal and Ethical Constraints on Marketing**

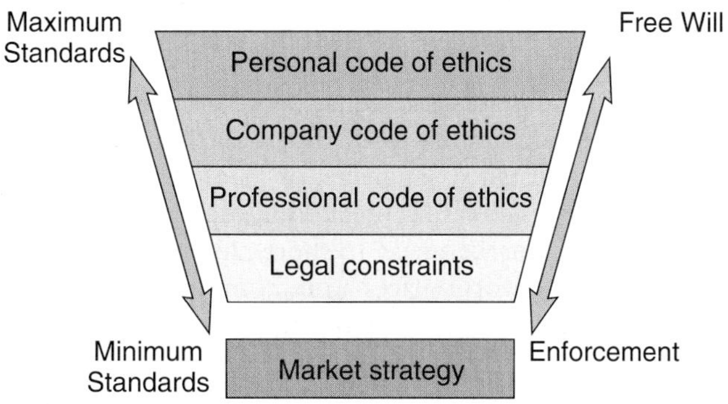

The marketing decision should be constrained by the law, professional, company, and personal codes of ethics. Unfortunately, the marketing profession has been inactive in policing its code of ethics, in removing violators from membership in its professional association, and in encouraging new laws that police and punish highly unethical marketing practices. An inverse relationship often exists between the standards and enforcement. The law is the floor in ethics, but it can be enforced. The personal code of the enlightened citizen, in theory, should be the most demanding but is only enforced by personal values and conscience.

at producing and marketing. Even if one nation erects trade barriers, it is still best if other nations do not. But in practice, what happens if some nations make some parts of the product and other nations market the product to the rest of the world and make most of the profits? What happens if nations erect barriers to protect special-interest groups out of spite and frustration? What we would have is the world we do live in. As large, new, free-trading blocks emerge and the global economy develops, politicians will experiment with new types of interventionist policies to save their jobs by saving their citizens' jobs. This is because the innovative/imitative competitiveness of firms increasingly will be judged by global, rather than national, standards. Firms that are superior to their global competition will flourish; firms that are inferior will perish. This will lead to large shifts in investment from uncompetitive sectors of a national economy to globally competitive sectors. Financial and human capital will flee from economies that lack globally competitive sectors. Such economic restructuring will lead to the rapid growth of some economies and the stagnation and decline of other economies. Responding to public pressure, politicians will resort to four basic strategies:

1. Investment in research, education, and infrastructure with the goal of boosting the innovative/imitative competitiveness of national industry (a competitive rationality strategy)
2. Financial management that results in an economy that is trim and fit (low inflation, low interest rates, near-balanced budget) rather than bloated with election-promised giveaways
3. The creation of taxes on imports (tariffs) and less obvious and more discreet trade barriers that protect domestic products, services, and jobs. Tariffs are better than import quotas because they raise money for governments, whereas quotas raise prices, and the excess profits then go to the foreign seller. Quantity quotas on automobiles and clothing also encourage foreign competition to sell high-quality, high-profit items rather than economy, low-profit items. Thus, U.S. quantity quotas on autos and clothing encouraged foreign competition to compete in the most attractive market segments, an unintended outcome

that reveals that the policy was not well thought through. This demonstrates that the success of a nation in the global trade war depends on the competitive rationality of its trade policy as well as the competitive rationality of its firms

4. Direct support for export enterprise in the form of tax subsidies and geopolitical arm-twisting

In the worst-case scenario, the overprotection of industries will lead to major barriers among trading blocs. Today the international marketplace barriers are no longer as much distance, language, or ideology. The major barriers are often economic and political, erected to protect domestic products and services that are not competitive in the global marketplace. In short, this age of great free-market economic development around the world places a premium on understanding the current and future trading policies of nations and the thinking (competitive rationality/irrationality) of their leaders.

The need to understand the commercial law of foreign markets, as it is practiced, is also critical. For example, foreign competitors, suppliers, and distributors are often able to infringe patents with immunity. Some less-developed and emerging economies have attractive labor costs and are responsive and cooperative. But if anything goes wrong with the relationship, it is often very difficult to get legal redress from their justice systems, which are often corrupt, very political, or very slow.

More generally, a serious and unresolved situational ethics problem often occurs in global marketing. No international code of business ethics exists, because each society's ethics vary—some slightly and others greatly. Fortunately, most of the world's major religions and cultures share common norms and ethics and would answer the questions in the ethical checklist similarly. But in some countries bribery, kickbacks, and dishonesty in advertising, selling, and dealing are much more acceptable than in others. How should American firms behave in such markets? If they do not tolerate such standard practices, they risk not doing business and may be further hated for arrogantly imposing their values where they are not wanted. For example, should American garment manufacturers be concerned about the working conditions in the offshore factories that produce many of their clothing lines? Liz Claiborne makes unscheduled visits to its suppliers to ensure they meet the company's standards and attempts to work with suppliers that provide the best working conditions. Presumably, other companies are less particular, only caring about price and output quality. But just how much American companies should be responsible for the human rights of their suppliers' low-paid employees is very unclear, particularly if caring puts the American company at a competitive cost disadvantage.

The quick and easy answer, "When in Rome, do as the Romans do," is no real answer for at least two reasons. First, international business is carried out in two places at once, between a seller in New York and a buyer in Rome. What is the social contract in this situation? Is it determined by the accepted norms of the American or the Italian trading partner's political economy? Second, this philosophy suggests abandoning one's own "moral compass" and replacing it with the ethical standards of the party with whom one is dealing. With the increase in global marketing comes a pressing need to adopt an international code of ethics. Unethical behavior will always exist, but it can be defined the same way and condemned by every society. Even if this occurs some time in the future, international marketing decision makers still will have to reconcile their personal moral compass with situational issues and trade-offs among interest groups and stakeholders they are paid to serve.

Discussion Questions and Minicases

1. Canada Dry launched a caffeine-free cola in 1967. The product was ordered off the market by the Food and Drug Administration because Coca-Cola and PepsiCo convinced the regulators that a cola without caffeine was technically no longer a cola drink. Coke and Pepsi later launched their own noncaffeine colas, but they had the clout to change the FDA's mind. What problems does this incident reveal, and how might it be redressed?
2. What predictions would the theory of competitive rationality make about the consequences of the deregulation of an industry?
3. In a move that they perhaps now regret, the airlines strategically withdrew from the ticket-booking business several years before deregulation. By default, they passed on much of the business to travel agencies, whose offices grew in number from 12,000 to 26,000 between 1975 and 1985. The travel agencies have loved deregulation because, along with competing with other airlines in the air on most routes, the airlines have had to compete on the ground for the agents' attention and favors. The travel agents also have become more important to the consumer, who simply cannot keep up with the changes in airfares and route services. In their attempt to sew up the loyalty of the agents, airline companies such as United and American have provided free use of their computerized booking systems (Apollo and Sabre) for up to three years, free training, and even initial adoption bonuses. Despite protestations to the contrary, it is clear from their actions that these airlines believed that the use of their system would give them *some* competitive advantage. It appears they were right. Overall, the commissions airlines have paid to travel agents have risen from an official 10 percent to an average of 14 percent. What lessons can we learn from this case about deregulation?
4. A competitor's disgruntled employee has just mailed you plans for what looks like a promising new product. Should you throw the plans away? Send them to your R&D people for analysis? Notify your competitor about what is going on? Call the Federal Bureau of Investigation?
5. Late in the nineteenth century, acetylsalicylic acid was a new medicine. Its discoverer, Hermann Dreser, claimed that it relieved headaches, reduced fever, and alleviated the aches and pains of arthritis. Typical of the period, the claimed effects were not scientifically proven. It was then discovered that acetylsalicylic acid produced severe reactions in some users. Even moderate overdoses were likely to produce dizziness, vision problems, severe gastric irritation, nausea, vomiting, and psychological confusion. Larger overdoses were fatal. How does modern-day regulation protect the consumer from such drugs? Do you agree with the regulation?
6. Cigarette manufacturers add a chemical to cigarettes to make them burn faster and to make them easier to smoke. Fire prevention offices around the country have convincingly demonstrated that the use of this chemical also results in more bedding and upholstery fires, which kill or injure hundreds of Americans each year, because cigarettes treated with the chemical continue to burn longer and hotter when dropped. Some manufacturers have reacted to potential lawsuits by running advertising campaigns that discourage smoking in bed. Such advertisements are meant, in part, to signal the companies' good intentions to the courts and to help reduce any settlements against manufacturers if they are found liable. Should manufacturers remove the ingredient? What should they do about the advertising?
7. After almost a decade of sales, the Dalkon intrauterine device (IUD) was found to be defective and unreasonably dangerous to use. On the other hand, the medical community considered the Searle IUD a safe, quality product. This distinction was lost on a number of lawyers who hounded Searle with lawsuits. In one case, Searle spent $1 million defending itself—successfully. Many women who cannot use other forms of contraception would like to use the Searle IUD. Should Searle stay in this business?
8. All-terrain vehicles were involved in 1,500 deaths and 400,000 serious injuries during the 1980s—20 percent affecting children age twelve and under. The automobile industry stopped selling the three-wheeled version and notified dealers to instruct buyers that the

vehicles should not be driven by children under age sixteen. However, many dealers have ignored the direction. The industry view is that because state laws allow children to use the vehicle, it is the parents' responsibility to supervise their children's use. Should the product be banned?

9. Punitive damages were introduced in order to punish firms for deliberately and knowingly breaking the law and causing harm to consumers and employees. However, in recent years, huge punitive damages above assessed compensatory damages (those that compensate the injured party for loss of income, pain and suffering, and so on) have been awarded by juries. As a result, litigation in this area has increased, casting a paralytic effect on many enterprises. How might the law be changed to discourage the unscrupulous behavior of lawyers and firms that knowingly and calculatingly endanger consumers?

10. Figure 8.6 indicates how consumers perceive the risks of different activities. Based on your own intuition and what you know about the activities that are high for each characteristic, please label the ends of all four dimensions by identifying characteristics 1 and 2. What does the figure tell us about how the public views safety risks?

11. In some high-income, highly educated segments of American society, consumers are prepared to pay more for products and services that are "earth friendly." The problem is that it is difficult for consumers to understand terms such as biodegradable, photodegradable, or organically recyclable and to understand the environmental impact of different production processes. Many companies are exploiting this lack of understanding

Figure 8.6

A Perceptual Map of the Public's Perception of Risks

SOURCE: Based on Paul Slovic, "Perception of Risk," *Science* 236 (April 17, 1987): 280–85.

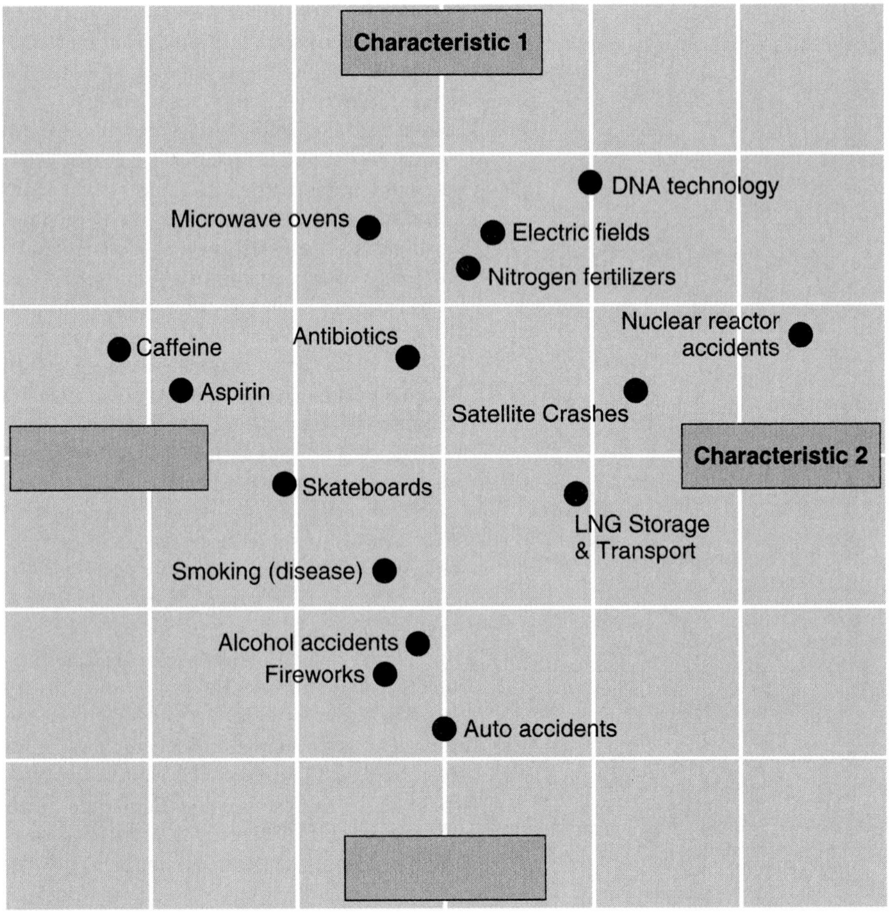

by making exaggerated claims about the earth friendliness of their products. What free-market solution might help (not including government regulation)?

12. American Can Company invented rolled-steel beverage cans in the late 1960s. They take at least 20 percent less energy to produce than aluminum cans, and they are cheaper and biodegradable. But although recycling rolled-steel cans is not cost effective, recycling aluminum cans is. Recycling also produces important income for "street people" and social organizations such as the Boy Scouts. Many Coke bottlers were using steel cans in the mid-1970s but, reacting to pressure from vocal critics, switched back to aluminum. What would you have done? How would you respond if Americans were facing a landfill crisis? What if Americans were facing another energy crisis?
13. The only way for many less-developed countries to develop their economies is to exploit their natural resources (such as cutting down the rain forests) or to use dirty energy sources (such as high-sulphur coal in China). Do you think it is hypocritical for advanced economies to complain about such environmental crimes when each went through a similar stage in its own history? What is the long-term solution, assuming that unless some solution is found, we will all run out of air to breathe?
14. What is the intrabrand versus interbrand issue in distribution law really all about? How is it an example of the rule of reason? What sort of experts do judges have to become to make such judgments?
15. In the late 1970s, credit-card interest rates rose to between 18 percent and 20 percent because of inflation. Through the 1980s, many credit-card interest rates remained about the same long after inflation had cooled and the cost of money had dropped to less than 10 percent. Many banks have argued that the cost of servicing credit-card debt is high, but some banks charge only 13 percent on their cards. The merchant is charged a fee (2 percent to 5 percent) for each purchase made on a card. This covers the cost of the transaction and some of the risk of card theft and bad debt. Is still charging the consumer 18 percent to 20 percent ethical?
16. A manufacturer of tables and chairs always increases its prices when the cost of timber increases. It does not lower its prices when the cost of timber decreases. Is this pricing rule ethical? Is it fair? What other rule might the manufacturer use?
17. A supermarket serving a low-income, African American market charges higher prices for its staples (such as bread and milk) than do supermarkets in the suburbs. Consumer groups have complained that this practice exploits the poor. The store argues that suburban shoppers buy more profitable luxuries, allowing suburban stores to lower their prices on staples. The store's management also can prove that more incidents of shoplifting and vandalism occur in its store, resulting in hardly any profit, even at the higher prices. Should the store lower its prices? Should it simply close down if it would lose money by lowering its prices? What other creative options does the store have?
18. Why do you think services such as airlines and movie theaters are allowed to price discriminate based on customer age (such as offering lower rates to seniors and students) but when hiring are not allowed to discriminate based on age? Do you think it would be acceptable to price discriminate based on race? Why is age different from race?
19. Consumer product-testing research undertaken for a major lawn-care company revealed that putting two parallel rows of holes on a lawn sprinkler increased consumer perceptions of the product's performance and quality. However, tests show that performance actually is not improved. Should the company produce a sprinkler with one or two rows of holes? If it uses two holes, should it feature them in the advertising as a point of product differentiation? Research shows that if the company charges a higher price for a product, the consumer will believe it is of higher quality. Should the company charge a higher price?
20. The cartoon on page 322 presents an ethical dilemma. Please answer the questions listed. In addition, why do you think that using cartoons to present dilemmas is effective in ethics training?

SOURCE: Reproduced with permission of Armstrong World Industries from Ronald E. Berenbeim, *Corporate Ethics Practices* (New York: The Conference Board, 1992), 40.

1. **How is Armstrong's reputation affected by a retailer's misrepresentation? How could Armstrong be affected by Jenny taking action? not taking action?**

2. **If you were Jenny, what would you do and why: talk or write again to the retailer? raise your concerns with the Division staff in Lancaster? ignore it?**

21. To make used cars safer and shopping more efficient, the Federal Trade Commission proposed a rule in 1981 that would require dealers to disclose a used car's known defects on a window sticker. The dealers argued that any prospective buyer could have the vehicle mechanically checked at his or her own expense. They argued that since few buyers actually have the vehicles checked, then the information is not really needed. The dealers gave millions of dollars to the election campaigns of numerous senators and congresspeople who overwhelmingly, and with very little explanation, voted down the rule. Was what the dealers did ethical?

22. A marketer of orange juice added the world "fresh" in its brand name and the following phrases on its cartons: "Pure, squeezed, 100% orange juice . . . We pick our oranges at the peak of ripeness. Then we hurry to squeeze them before they lose their freshness." The juice is made by adding water to concentrated orange juice, pulp, and "orange essence." Do you think the behavior was lawful? Do you think it was ethical?
23. A Save the Children Fund (SCF) ad features little Pedro with the sad eyes and Joanne Woodward saying, "Imagine, the cost of a cup of coffee, 52 cents a day, can help save a child." But SCF has not been in the business of directly sponsoring children for many years. It is involved in community development work, such as building playgrounds and providing start-up loans for small businesses. The problem is that community development does not pull cash donations the way that little Pedro does. Only about 35 percent of the funds raised are actually spent on charitable projects—the rest is spent on marketing and overhead. Was SCF's behavior ethical? Should SCF be held to a higher or lower standard than would be applied to a profit organization?
24. What double standard seems evident in Figure 8.3, which illustrates the contents of companies' ethical guidelines?
25. You are in a foreign country where bribing government officials and businesspeople is essential to do business, and bribery is not outlawed as it is in the United States. Officials from the country approach you, saying they have many buyers for your products and you could make good profits in their country. Would you do business and pay the bribes? Would you hide the practice, hoping that no one in the United States would find out? Would you pay a distributor in the country a set fee to take care of everything for you, pretending not to know what taking care of everything means?
26. A major U.S. bank in Chicago has been approached by an oil sheik who wishes to make a large investment in its New Ventures Mutual Fund that has been brilliantly managed by a thirty-five-year-old female executive. The bank is keen to make the sale, but the sheik will only do business with men. Normally, the female mutual-funds manager would travel to meet such a client. What should the bank do? What if a major commission is involved in making the sale? Would it make any difference if the sheik were visiting the United States and refused to meet the female executive?
27. Now that the cold war is over and a global trade war in some markets is heating up (American jobs versus "their" jobs), do you think it is appropriate that the Central Intelligence Agency (CIA) change its mission and recruit economists and market researchers to help gather economic intelligence? What should be the limits to the CIA's involvement in industrial espionage? What agency should be responsible for making sure that international environmental protection laws and free-trade laws are obeyed? Why is any United Nations agency likely to be ineffective?

The pessimist sees the difficulty in every opportunity, the optimist sees the opportunity in every difficulty.

Winston Churchill

Chance favors the prepared mind.

Louis Pasteur

CHAPTER NINE

Positioning Strategy

Launched in 1959, Tylenol (acetaminophen) was marketed only to physicians and hospitals as a painkiller for patients who could not take aspirin (because aspirin caused gastrointestinal irritation and bleeding). Between 1969 and 1974 Tylenol spent $200,000 on consumer advertising, and its market share jumped from 2.5 percent to 10 percent of the analgesic market.[1] In comparison, Bayer spent $83 million on advertising its aspirin products to the consumer, but its market share slipped from 16 percent to 12 percent. In mid-1975 Bristol-Myers tried for the second time to launch its brand of acetaminophen called Datril. Its first attempt in 1967 was called Neotrend, but it failed, in part because it was promoted directly to consumers and did not have the physicians' support. Datril was positioned as the same as Tylenol but cost a dollar a bottle less. On June 3, 1975, Tylenol's price was cut by 30 percent, and Datril had to retreat from its lower price claim. In May 1976 Extra-Strength Tylenol (500mg-strength Tylenol) was launched and promoted as "You can't buy a more potent pain reliever without a prescription." By 1977 Datril had gained a 2 percent share, but Tylenol's share grew to 20 percent and 30 percent by 1981. In May of 1984 Advil (ibuprofen) was approved as an over-the-counter pain killer and in its first year gained 4 percent of the market, mainly from aspirin

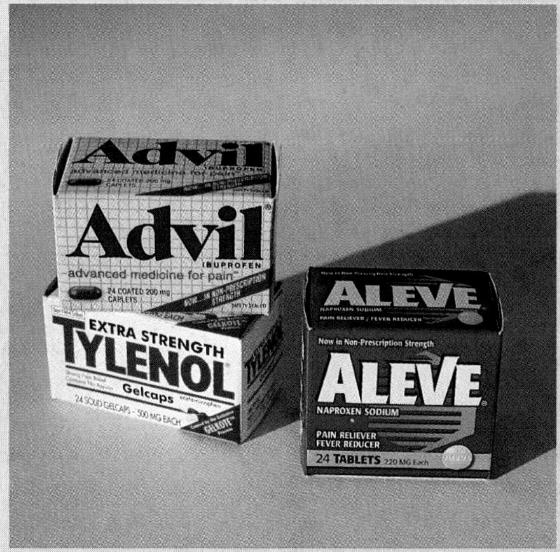

brands. During this year the Federal Drug Administration required that aspirin products warn about the risk to children of developing Reyes Syndrome, and as a result Tylenol increased its share of the children's analgesic market to close to 70 percent.

Through the late 1980s and early 1990s, ibuprofen products gained about 25 percent of the analgesic market, Tylenol and other acetaminophen brands 45 percent, and aspirin 30 percent. The only good news for aspirin was its new positioning as a product that reduces blood clots and fights heart attacks. Tylenol attempted to strengthen its position as a treatment for the pain of arthritis, a huge analgesic benefit segment. In June 1994 it faced a challenge from Aleve, a version of a prescription drug for arthritis. Its advantage was its strength and that it lasted eight to twelve hours. A month later Tylenol Extended Relief was launched that lasted eight hours and was priced lower than Aleve. Aleve was positioned as softer on the stomach than aspirin. Tylenol Extended Relief was promoted as softer on the stomach than aspirin, Advil, *and* Aleve. Tylenol also continued to extend its product line with Tylenol Allergy Sinus Nighttime and Tylenol Flu Nighttime in gel-cap and a powder form that could be added to a hot liquid. Its in-store "Tylenol Store" displays feature more than two-dozen versions of Tylenol aimed at different person × situation benefit segments with supporting consumer information and education brochures. Meanwhile, Aleve gained about 7 percent of the market, again mainly at the expense of aspirin; Advil focused its positioning on being best at relieving headaches; and private-label painkillers increased their share to 15 percent. Tylenol is a case study in brilliant positioning. First, it gained tremendous credibility through hospital and doctor endorsements. Second, it has defended its positioning by implementing rapid counter-offenses that have stymied the success of new, powerful analgesics. Third, it has extended its product line and product form to target specific illnesses and conditions and to boost its brand reputation for being customer oriented. ■

After studying and understanding the market environment, the first and most critical strategic decision to be made is the choice of the target benefit segment. Once this

[1] The sources for this Tylenol story are Charles C. Mann and Mark L. Plummer, *The Aspirin Wars* (New York: Alfred A. Knopf, 1991); Joseph Weber and Zachary Schiller, "Painkillers are about to O.D.," *Business Week*, April 11, 1994, 54–55; and "The Tan Sheets: Nonprescription Pharmaceuticals and Nutritionals" (Maryland: F-D-C Reports Inc., 1993–1995). Thanks to Anandi V. Lau for her help in preparing this chapter introduction.

segment has been chosen, the market management team must determine its product's competitive positioning. These two strategic decisions are pivotal, in that they influence all of the marketing decisions that follow them.

How did a small start-up company such as Apple succeed in an industry dominated by hugely successful computer manufacturers? The answer is positioning. The first Apples were distinctively positioned as stand-alone personal computers. During the time of Apple's rise, the rest of the manufacturers were in a race to build ever larger, faster computers. Although other start-up companies such as Osborne came and went, Apple flourished by targeting the education market, which it later dominated. The entry of IBM opened up another segment—the business market for personal computers. Even though its operating system and software were totally incompatible with IBM and MS-DOS, Apple was able to compete in that segment. Why? Because it targeted a business segment that demanded graphics applications, report preparation, and desktop publishing. Apple's mouse, pointers, software, and early laser printers ideally positioned its computer to serve these usage segments. Later the company added a further positioning advantage—the Apple was user-friendly, and it was marketed as the system that was easy to learn. The success of Apple, first in the education market and then in the business market, had a lot to do with its focus on distinct usage-benefit segments and the positioning of its product to deliver the desired benefits.

The task of spotting a positioning opportunity in a market tests the true genius of an entrepreneurial marketer. Positioning skill can make entrepreneurs into millionaires and chief executives out of middle managers because clever positioning can produce above-average profits. The first section of this chapter discusses the targeting decision because at some point every company must ask itself: Which consumers do we want to target, and what benefits do they expect from the product or service? The second section discusses positioning and differentiating: What benefits do we want to deliver to the consumer, and how will our product deliver better benefits compared to the competition? The third section explains how a positioning concept on a competitive map is converted into an actual differentiated product or service: How will our product or service be designed to deliver the desired quality? The fourth section explains how to estimate a price using quality-added analysis: How much are our target consumers prepared to pay for the superior quality of our product? The process concludes with a method of assessing the financial feasibility of the proposed positioning: Will the proposed positioning, design, and price produce sales forecasts that are attainable and that will meet company financial goals? In the second major section of the chapter, the dynamics of competitive positioning are discussed. It includes product-line positioning strategy, attacking and defending a position, and flanking and price-point brands. Finally, a number of positioning issues that arise in global marketing are discussed. The recommended approach to developing a positioning strategy is detailed in Figure 9.1, which also describes the basic organization of the chapter.

Targeting Benefit Segments

The competitively rational positioning process summarized in Figure 9.1 starts with identifying the nature and potential of benefit segments, as described in Chapter 5. Customers are grouped together (clustered) by the benefits they seek from using the product or service. This includes the features and other specifications that are required or are highly desired in the product and service. In this way, the initial benefit

Figure 9.1 **Chapter Organization**

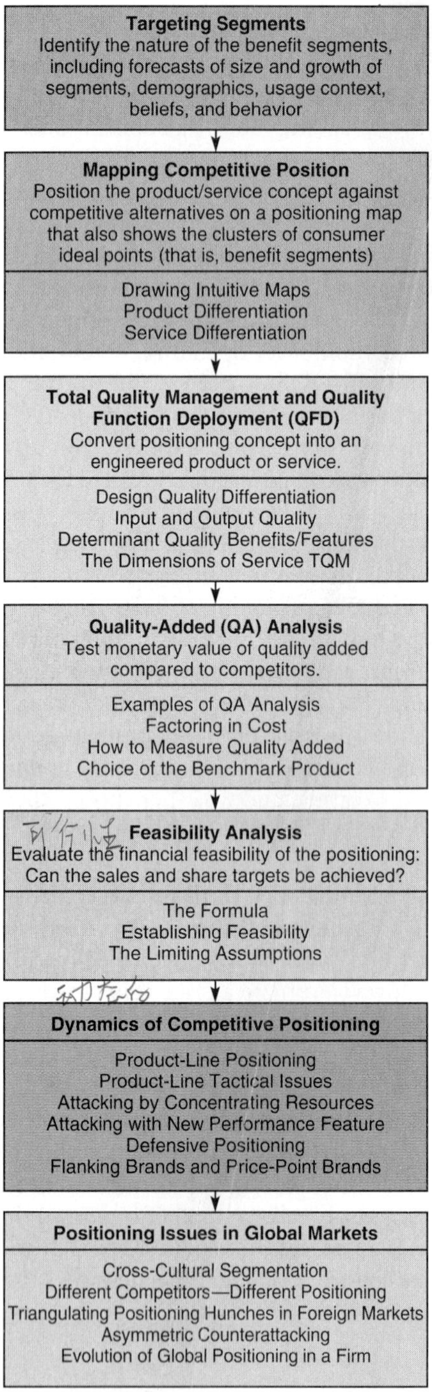
Targeting Segments
Identify the nature of the benefit segments, including forecasts of size and growth of segments, demographics, usage context, beliefs, and behavior
Mapping Competitive Position
Position the product/service concept against competitive alternatives on a positioning map that also shows the clusters of consumer ideal points (that is, benefit segments)
Drawing Intuitive Maps
Product Differentiation
Service Differentiation
Total Quality Management and Quality Function Deployment (QFD)
Convert positioning concept into an engineered product or service.
Design Quality Differentiation
Input and Output Quality
Determinant Quality Benefits/Features
The Dimensions of Service TQM
Quality-Added (QA) Analysis
Test monetary value of quality added compared to competitors.
Examples of QA Analysis
Factoring in Cost
How to Measure Quality Added
Choice of the Benchmark Product
Feasibility Analysis
Evaluate the financial feasibility of the positioning: Can the sales and share targets be achieved?
The Formula
Establishing Feasibility
The Limiting Assumptions
Dynamics of Competitive Positioning
Product-Line Positioning
Product-Line Tactical Issues
Attacking by Concentrating Resources
Attacking with New Performance Feature
Defensive Positioning
Flanking Brands and Price-Point Brands
Positioning Issues in Global Markets
Cross-Cultural Segmentation
Different Competitors—Different Positioning
Triangulating Positioning Hunches in Foreign Markets
Asymmetric Counterattacking
Evolution of Global Positioning in a Firm

The differentiated positioning concept is developed after the benefit market segments are identified. This concept is then converted into a product or service blueprint using quality function deployment (QFD). The QFD blueprint is then quality added (QA) tested to establish its price differential superiority. Finally, the feasibility of the strategy is tested by estimating the sales and market-share goals and assessing whether the goals are achievable.

Figure 9.2 **Benefit Segmentation and Quality Functional Deployment**

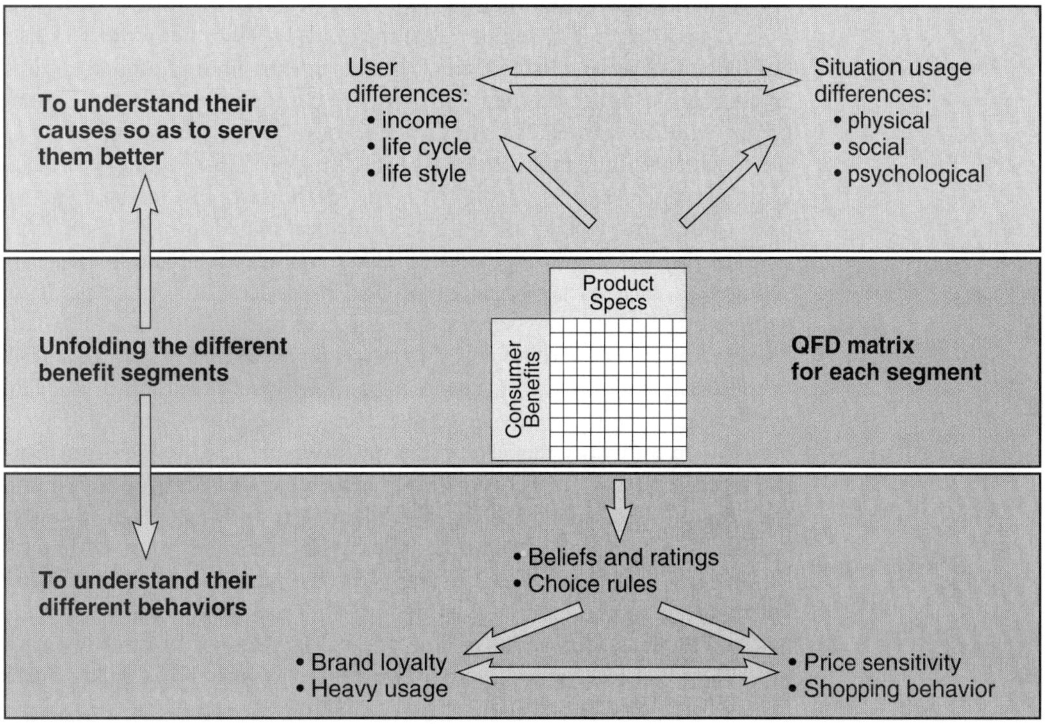

Chapter 5 discussed how to segment the market starting with the different benefits and levels of outcome performance that consumers seek from using a product or service. The QFD matrix shows the relationships (correlations) between consumer benefits and product design and engineering specifications. A product or service is then designed, engineered, and manufactured to the specifications most related to a specific segment's desired benefits and levels of performance. This is called positioning a product to satisfy the needs of a target segment or market niche.

segments are created. Deep segmentation then uses individual differences and usage contexts to explain why different customers belong in a particular benefit segment. It also studies the beliefs, choice behavior, brand loyalty, and shopping behavior of each benefit segment (see Figure 9.2).

Having identified and developed a deep understanding of each benefit segment, a cross-functional team then must decide which, if any, segment or segments the company should attempt to serve. This involves more than estimating the size and growth potential of each segment. It requires an understanding of how well the existing competitive products and services are positioned to serve the benefit segments. How well are competitors' products and services fitted to the needs of each benefit segment? Are the existing products and services in the market designed and engineered to specifications that will deliver the desired benefits to the target segment? If they are not well designed and engineered, then an opportunity exists to introduce a new product model or service that is positioned to serve the needs of the target benefit segment better than the existing competition. The question then is whether such a target segment can be profitably served and the positioning defended over the long term. This question cannot be answered with certainty, but it is best answered by evaluating the environmental factors, as described in the Stratmesh process in Chapter 2.

A market niche is another name for a segment of the market. The word *niche* means a state of nature that is well suited to the holder ("With her writing skills, she has found her niche as a journalist"). Market niching means finding, understanding, developing, and serving a target segment that *fits* the competitive strengths or objectives of the company. Ideally, the niche should allow room for only one supplier or significant barriers to entry should exist, as described in Chapter 6. For example, the National Hole in One insurance company, run by a golf enthusiast, insures sponsors of hole-in-one prizes and earns a profit of a million dollars a year doing so.[2] Lee, the number-three manufacturer of jeans, targeted the female market niche and became the number-one supplier to this market segment. A health service clinic in a major city focuses on women by offering many service conveniences to its ten thousand patients, including a free lending library with books on women's physical, psychological, and social concerns.

Chrysler's revival from near death and recent profitability has had much to do with its targeting strategy. President Bob Lutz talks about "focus . . . focus . . . focus"—on minivans, jeeps, and now pickup trucks.[3] Chrysler's positioning is to have the highest quality, highest performance vehicles in these product markets. This is at the cost of abandoning the big V-8 luxury car to the foreign imports and to GM's Cadillac and Ford's Lincoln and Jaguar. The sensible point is that Chrysler established early on a positioning advantage in the minivan and sports-utility markets and has maintained and extended its quality-added advantages in these markets over the past fifteen years. It was never able to establish similar positioning advantages in the luxury-car market, but it sees an opportunity to do so in the pickup truck market.

Mapping Competitive Positions

The easiest way to visualize the positioning of competitive products is to use a two-dimensional map to compare the consumer's image of competing products on two critical performance features.[4] These product positions can then be compared to where a consumer's ideal product would be positioned on the map. An *ideal point* indicates the combination of the two features the consumer would like most, if they were available. If some consumers' ideal points cluster together, then they form a potential target benefit segment. Figure 9.3 illustrates and explains such a map. The reason why Tylenol has about 30 percent of the total analgesic market is obvious. It is the best known brand of acetaminophen, a powerful painkiller with very few bad side effects. Evidence shows that ibuprofens, such as Advil, are as effective but do have some side effects. Aspirins are not as effective and are not as gentle, particularly on the lining of the stomach of young children and heavy-user adults. Also as noted previously, a chance exists that aspirin can produce Reyes Syndrome in children.

Figure 9.4 presents a competitive map of bathroom tissues, which reveals that two brands have unique positions in the two-dimensional space. What is interesting about this map is that it is not based on perceptions but it is based on the actual cross-price

[2] Rita Koselka, "The Best of Both Possible Worlds," *Forbes*, July 23, 1990, 52–74.
[3] Jerry Flint, "The Big Profits Will Be Back," *Forbes*, September 25, 1995, 90–92.
[4] The competitive map can be based on consumer ratings of each brand's performance on each dimension. It can also be derived from consumer judgments of brand similarity, brand preferences, or brand switching behavior.

Figure 9.3 **An Intuitive Competitive Map of the Analgesic Market**

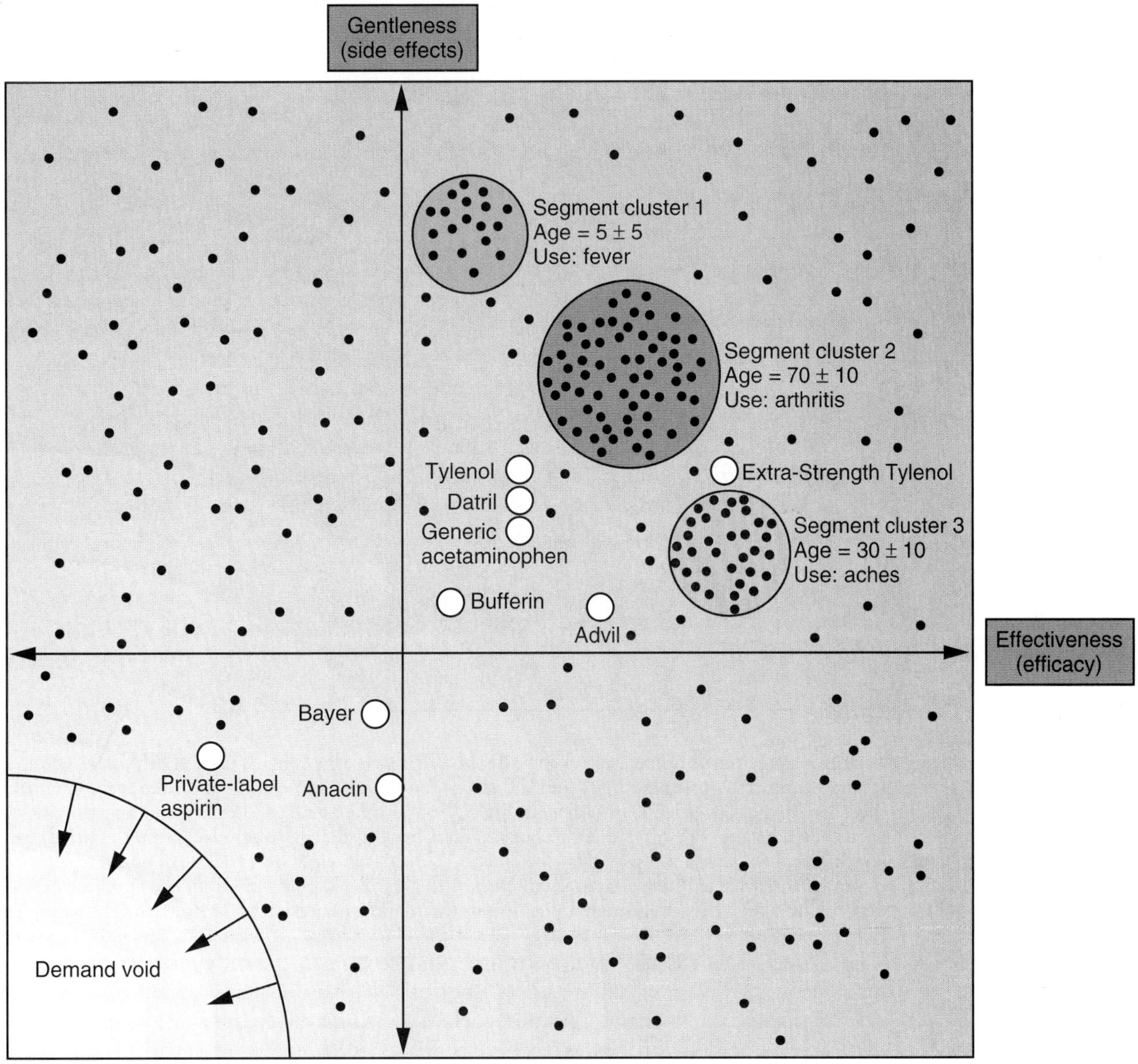

This map shows three major benefit segments: children, for whom gentleness is a priority; the elderly, who seek to reduce the aches of old age and need medication that is gentle to the stomach (which aspirin is not); and a younger segment of the population that seeks relief for occasional sharp pain. Tylenol's positioning explains why it gained such a large share of the analgesic (painkiller) market. This intuitive map illustrates the value of using competitive maps to decide which benefit segments to target.

elasticities among the brands. The greater the distance among the brands, the less a change in price of one affects the sales of the other. Thus, this map truly represents how well a brand has distanced itself from the price competition of other brands. It

Figure 9.4 **A Competitive Map of Bathroom Tissues**

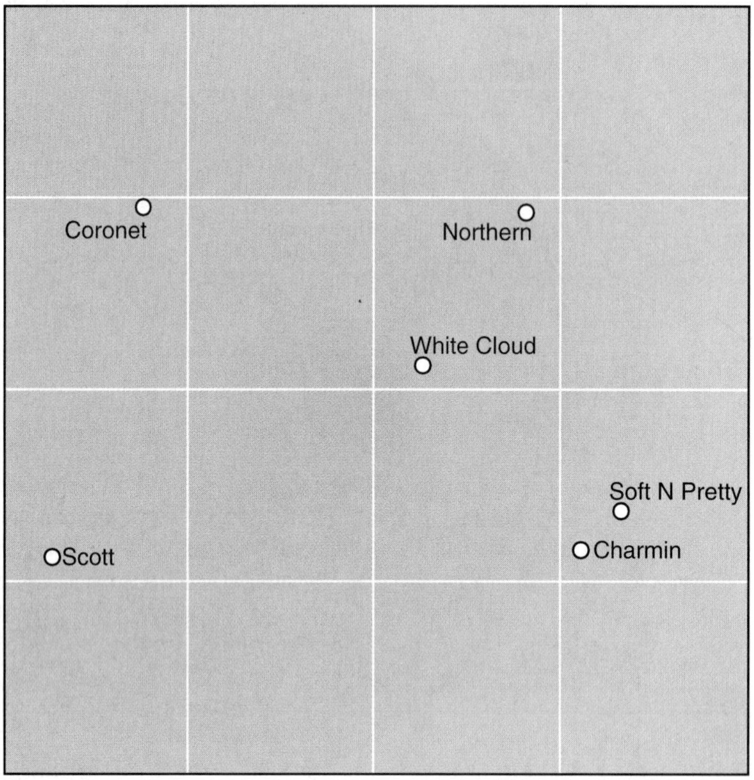

In this map, the distance among brands is determined by measuring the effect of changing one brand's price on the sales of the other brands. The greater the effect, the higher the cross-price elasticity and the closer the brands are positioned on the map. Charmin and Soft N Pretty are close together because their cross-price elasticities are high. On the other hand, Coronet's and Scott's sales do not change very much at all when the prices of Charmin or Soft N Pretty change. They have distanced themselves from the price competition of their rival brands. The major difference is that Scott is sold by the roll and Coronet in eight-roll packs. All of the rest are sold in four-roll packs. It seems that Scott and Coronet have differentiated themselves with their packaging. Charmin has emphasized softness in its promotion, but it has not been able to achieve a differentiated position in the market because Soft N Pretty has also emphasized softness.

SOURCE: Greg M. Allenby, "A Unified Approach to Identifying, Estimating and Testing Demand Structures with Aggregate Scanner Data," *Marketing Science* 8, no. 3 (summer 1989): 265–80.

reveals that some brands of bathroom tissue have used the number of rolls in a pack to successfully differentiate themselves from competition. Two brands that have promoted their softness quality are positioned closely together but are differentiated from the others.

Drawing Intuitive Maps

Complex statistical techniques can be used to identify opportunities and to position products competitively, but most positioning is based on intuition—an important competitive rationality component of decision makers. Although analytic methods of drawing competitive maps can be very useful in the real world of marketing decision making, they are only used by a fraction of marketing planners. Most positioning decisions are largely based on intuition. Unfortunately, this intuition is often not spelled out or mapped out on paper. It can be very useful for a cross-functional team to create its own intuitive map of the major benefit segments and the positioning of the competition. For instance, a cross-functional team might gain a great deal of insight by taking the two most critical buyer-choice dimensions and positioning the competitive products in the resulting two-dimensional map. The position and size of the market segments could then be estimated and drawn in on the map. The result is a competitive positioning map similar to that in Figure 9.3. The chosen dimensions and map prepared before a meeting by different executives involved in the decision making will make interesting comparisons, reflecting different ways of thinking about the market. The resulting consensus map is a very important mental model that can form a basis for product development and other marketing decisions.

Product Differentiation

When a firm positions its offering to serve a target segment or niche, this positioning may either be unique or, at the other extreme, be exactly the same as a competitor's offering. Two products may be positioned to serve the same segment and be very similar in design and in the image they attempt to present. They are positioned, but because they are not *uniquely* positioned they lack product differentiation. *Product differentiation* is the act of distinguishing a product from its competitors on one or more basic performance or image features.

The objective of a differentiation strategy is to convince the target market that your product or service is clearly the best choice to achieve the target buyer's particular end or ends. Differentiation requires that your positioning be unique. This is because if any alternative is positioned close to your image, then your product will no longer be perceived as clearly the best choice. Note that such differentiation provides an important way for a firm to gain competitive advantage and make extra profits by distancing its products from the price competition of less well positioned substitutes.

But it is not the only way to compete and make profits. If a firm has a lower cost structure than its rivals, it might find it profitable to offer a product or service with exactly the same performance positioning as the competition but at a significantly lower price. If it can sustain its cost structure advantage, it can continue to differentiate and compete purely on price. For example, McKee Foods makes Little Debbie, the number-one snack cake with a 54 percent market share. It mostly sells its cakes and cookies to children under age fifteen for a price that is at least 50 percent less than its competition. Its cost advantage comes, in part, from using natural preservatives that give its products a shelf life of thirty days, three times longer than Hostess Twinkies.[5] This means that McKee does not need to employ its own expensive sales force and logistics system to make weekly deliveries. Instead, it uses low-cost, independent distributors. McKee Foods also employs nonunion, low-cost labor; has low management overheads; and enjoys other economy-of-scale advantages over its competition (the next largest being Hostess, with 18 percent of the market). The low-price positioning fits

[5] William Stern, "Mom and Dad Knew Every Name," *Forbes*, December 7, 1992, 172–74.

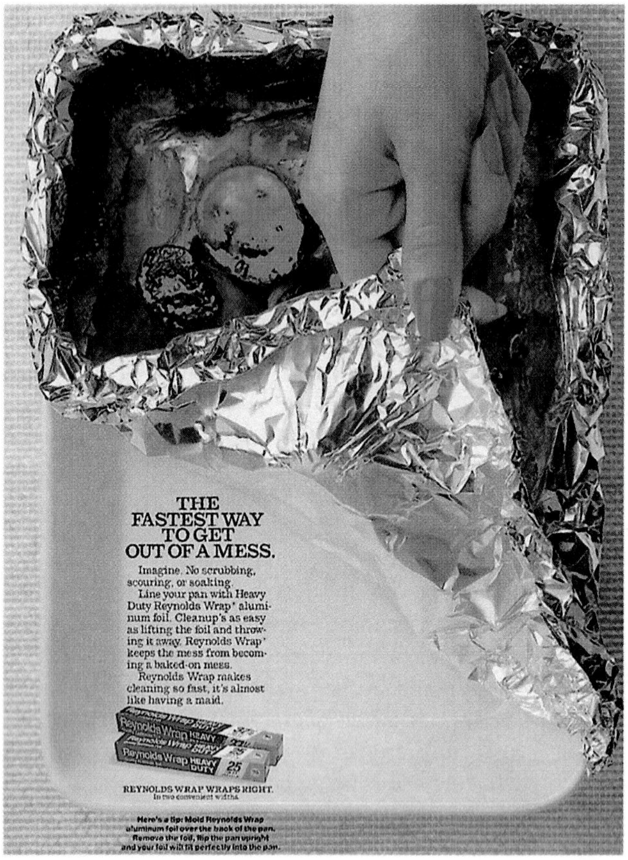
THE FASTEST WAY TO GET OUT OF A MESS.
Imagine. No scrubbing, scouring, or soaking.
Line your pan with Heavy Duty Reynolds Wrap* aluminum foil. Cleanup's as easy as lifting the foil and throwing it away. Reynolds Wrap* keeps the mess from becoming a baked-on mess.
Reynolds Wrap makes cleaning so fast, it's almost like having a maid.
Reynolds Wrap HEAVY DUTY
25
REYNOLDS WRAP WRAPS RIGHT.
Here's a tip: Mold Reynolds Wrap aluminum foil over the back of the pan. Remove the foil, flip the pan upright and your foil will fit perfectly into the pan.

A clever way to expand the demand for aluminum wrap is to *position* it as a product that goes *in* the dish as well as *over* the dish.

with the benefit that most children and parents seek from such snacks—economy rather than gourmet flavor and quality.

Product Differentiation in a Competitive Positioning Map

Product differentiation implies that a firm has unique positioning, that it has come up with a design or image innovation that has successfully differentiated it from the competition in the eyes of the target market. A differentiated strategy is therefore a more subtle and complicated type of positioning strategy, which, if it works as planned, is highly desirable.

To be successful, a product must be differentiated on a dimension that is important to at least one segment of the market. Importance without differentiation is not sufficient; neither is differentiation without importance. Manufacturers of telephones found this out in 1977 when it became possible to buy, rather than rent, phones from AT&T. Phones with multiple features and functions did not sell nearly as well as expected. The features that differentiated them were only desirable and important to a small usage segment. In the late 1980s, a quarter of the phones sold to the public were still the basic dial models, and a further 20 percent were the basic push-button models. Also, although AT&T's prices were comparatively high, 40 percent of homes still rented from AT&T, and 25 percent of the phones sold were marketed by AT&T.[6]

[6] Nicholas Shrady, "When More Is Not Better," *Forbes*, May 6, 1985, 94–95.

One of the dangers of competitive positioning maps produced by intuitive judgment or various multivariate statistical techniques is that an unoccupied space may or may not represent a new positioning opportunity. It can also indicate a combination of features that nobody wants (a "demand sinkhole"). A company that designs and markets a product into such a sinkhole can lose a great deal of money. Product positioning often boils down to determining whether or not enough actual or potential demand for a product with such a new positioning exists. Sometimes it is easy to avoid such risks. For example, in Figure 9.3 no analgesic is positioned in the bottom left quadrant because no one demands a painkiller that does not kill pain and has unpleasant side effects! At other times it is more difficult to recognize a demand void or sinkhole. For example, a number of major news media companies spent hundreds of millions of dollars attempting to market various computer-based information and shopping videotext systems. However, the demand for the product they offered did not exist, even after the companies gave months of free trials to potential customers. Existing alternatives were at least, often more convenient to use.

New Combinations of Benefits

Sometimes an area of a competitive positioning map shows little demand because buyers believe it is not possible to obtain such a combination of benefits. The task of the positioning strategy is to convince the dubious consumer that the new brand does indeed successfully combine these features. The Miller Lite beer "less filling, great taste" campaign was an example of such successful positioning. Attempts by breakfast cereal companies to convince a suspicious market that high-fiber cereals can also taste good (with the addition of fruit) is another example. If successful, such differentiation will be particularly powerful because what was previously believed to be a trade-off between two desired but contradictory features then becomes a combination of the two desired attributes. Whereas once a plus on one important choice dimension meant a minus on another, now the brand that positively links the two attributes receives a double plus in positioning.

Service Differentiation

Differentiation of a service rather than a product depends on understanding customer needs and attempting to meet such needs on a one-to-one level with genuine consideration and caring. A new service can quickly be copied by competitors, but the first company to introduce such new services conveys a genuine concern for customers. Continuous innovation in customer service creates an image that is not easily copied.

The necessity to provide consideration and caring in the delivery of the service poses a tricky problem for a substantial portion of service providers. As the service market has expanded, providers have had to choose between the customization of their service to suit individual consumer needs and the trend toward standardization and lower prices. When service positioning involves offering a standardized service or a reduced level of service for a lower competitive price, success hinges on the service provider's ability to provide a satisfactory level of service for the target market segment. But even at lower levels of service, the provider must pay attention to the personal interaction aspects of service if he or she is to maintain customer satisfaction.

Charles Schwabb is a good example of a company that offers a reduced set of services (securities brokerage, without the investment advice) appropriate for its target customers (people who follow their own investment strategies and pick their own securities to buy). Meanwhile, Schwabb still offers a number of service features, such as

Figure 9.5 **The Development of Standardized Services**

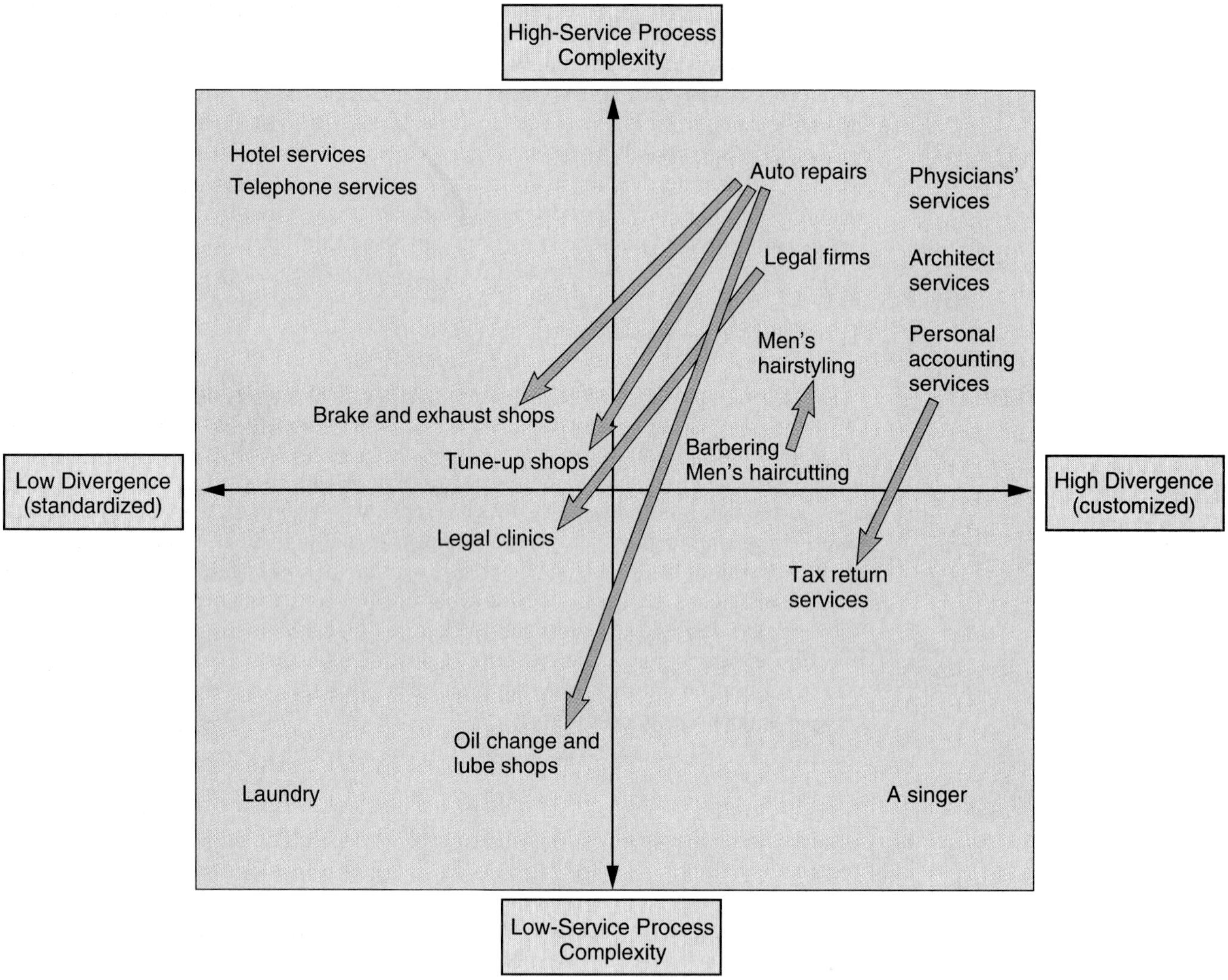

This competitive positioning map shows how a number of services have evolved from being complex and highly customized to being less complex and more standardized. An exception to the trend is men's haircutting services, which moved in the other direction.

SOURCE: This figure is based on a framework developed by G. Lynn Shostack, "Service Positioning through Structural Changes," *Journal of Marketing* 51 (January 1987): 34–43.

twenty-four-hour access, that contribute to its customers' total satisfaction. Figure 9.5 illustrates how some mass-delivered services have catered to the market by becoming more standardized and, hence, more affordable.

Service Quality, Expectations, and Satisfaction

The central goal of service quality is meeting or exceeding the expectations of customers, particularly on the determinant positioning dimensions.[7] However, viewing quality positioning from such an expectations perspective raises an interesting issue. Customers develop service expectations based on past service experiences, the price they are paying, and other factors. Service satisfaction, then, depends on the difference between the service customers expected to receive and the service they actually received. A service is judged to be very good if it exceeds such expectations. But a service with a high-quality reputation (that is, achieved positioning) may not generate high satisfaction, even though it is perceived to be very high quality.

Therein lies the rub. With each positive experience, expectations of even better performance in the future build up, bit by bit. The service or product's quality positioning increases. Consequently, the ability to pleasantly surprise and satisfy customers reduces as these expectations build, and the chances of unpleasantly surprising and dissatisfying customers increase. If service then slips badly, it can create such dissatisfaction that the customer is lost forever. That is why restaurants lose business when a favorite waitress or waiter leaves. It also explains why stockbrokers are constantly hustling to improve the timeliness and quality of their advice and why a sudden collapse of the stock market after a sustained and prosperous climb (that is, a long period of "good advice") creates panic among brokers. Along with a long climb in the stock market goes a long climb in customers' expectations and trust that the advice they receive will continue to make them money. This tricky expectation/performance relationship poses a problem. Should a service company set high service expectations with its marketing and just meet such expectations with its performance, or should it be more modest in its marketing claims and then offer a service that greatly exceeds expectations? The first marketing strategy will attract more business immediately, but the second marketing strategy will lead to stronger loyalty and sustained growth through customer referrals. Whichever long-term strategy is pursued, conformance (consistent delivery of quality service) becomes much more important as overall quality expectations rise. This is because a downside deviation (a negative decline in service quality) can be very serious. It may be better for a service provider to *meet* expectations rather than continually exceed ever-increasing expectations, because to do the latter is to raise expectations eventually to a level that is hard to attain and maintain.

Total Quality Management and Quality Function Deployment (QFD)

A product or service is an instrument or means used in a production or consumption process to achieve a buyer's particular end or ends. This was explained in Chapter 5. The product positioning strategy should convince the targeted consumers that the offering has the product features, characteristics, or specifications necessary to satisfy their desires. To create and sustain such a positioning image, the product or service must be designed and manufactured to quality specifications that live up to its intended positioning concept and promotional image.

Developing a differentiated positioning *concept* is one thing; converting the concept into a competitive differentiation in the *design* of the final product or service is quite another. Quality function deployment (QFD) was developed by Yoji Akao, a

[7] Valarie A. Zeithhaml, A. Parasuraman, and Leonard L. Berry, *Delivering Quality Service: Balancing Customer Perceptions and Expectations* (New York: Free Press, 1990).

Japanese professor, in the late 1960s and was being used by more than half of the 135 largest Japanese manufacturing companies by the mid-1980s.[8] QFD is the deployment of quality, reliability, technology, and cost so the design features of a product or service deliver the desired customer benefits and satisfaction. QFD takes a positioning concept and converts it into an engineered product or service that is competitively superior in performance on the desired differentiation dimensions. Japan's competitive technological edge has been identified as precisely this process skill, "the ability to convert demand from a vague set of distant wants into well defined products."[9] QFD also involves seamlessly connecting such product specifications to the appropriate manufacturing and production process. (This aspect of QFD is explained in the new-product development section in Chapter 10.)

Designing Quality Differentiation

It is said that beauty is in the eye of the beholder. In terms of marketing decision making, quality is in the eye of the target benefit segment. Buyers will choose a product based on quality (or quality and price) when they perceive that a product's quality is higher than a competitor's quality in product benefits, characteristics, features, and specifications important to them. It is therefore essential that target customers be constantly consulted about what they want, and their answers, in their own words, must be always in the minds of the marketing decision makers.

The reputation of Japanese products over the past thirty years may help explain what it means to make a quality product. In the 1950s and early 1960s, most Japanese exports were of a trinket nature sold in discount stores. They were poorly designed and soon broke. However, in the 1960s, Americans started to become aware of a change. Japanese electronic products, such as transistor radios, began to flood the market. Everything about the radios was quality in comparison to American radios. They came in higher quality packaging. They came with batteries that often lasted longer than the replacement American batteries. They had more features, more range, and a superior tone. The Japanese radios also looked more impressive and were better assembled. In summary, the radio was better constructed and offered superior performance. This was achieved by caring about design details and assembly quality control. The same brand reputations developed for Japanese motorcycles, cars, and almost everything else.

Input and Output Quality

Quality should be defined in terms of inputs and outputs. Superior design, superior materials, superior assembly, and quality control are all inputs used to contribute to quality output, which is the bundle of benefits the product or service provides the consumer. However, these inputs may not contribute additively. The development of an image of quality requires all input to be of a high standard. If just *one* of these elements is weak, then the overall quality rating may be weak. For example, the design may be excellent and high-quality materials may be used, but if assembly is poor, then the product will *not* develop a quality reputation. Making a quality product demands

[8] John R. Hartley, *Concurrent Engineering* (Cambridge, MA: Productivity Press, 1992).
[9] Fumio Kodama, *Emerging Patterns of Innovation: Sources of Japan's Technological Edge*, (Boston, MA: Harvard Business School, 1995), 8.

extensive cooperation and coordination through the value chain of activities within an organization to produce value for buyers.[10] QFD is an unforgiving and very demanding process. One weak link and the whole effort can be wasted.

Consumers also use various cues to judge quality that may be different from an engineering or design view of quality. Most consumers are not aware of the quality of the inputs, as judged from an engineering or technical perspective. For example, consumers judge pencil's quality from its output: its ease of holding, lack of smudging, and time lapse between sharpening. Note that children may evaluate pencil quality differently from adults. An engineer, however, evaluates input quality in terms of product specifications (see Figure 9.6). The relationships between benefits and the engineering specifications described in the QFD product specification matrix will be the same for all benefit segments, but the importance of the relationships will change because the importance of the benefits changes among the segments. The product specification matrix is key to designing a product to deliver the desired positioning benefits, and that is why it is placed at the *core* of the deep segmentation process presented in Figure 9.2. Benefit segmentation is not based on segmenting by benefits sought *and* product features, characteristics, and specifications desired. It is based on benefits or outcomes desired. A QFD product specification matrix then converts the benefits desired into the engineering specifications desired. In this way, benefit segmentation can be seamlessly linked to the QFD process.

A product will develop a consumer image of quality if it excels on the cues used to judge output quality. The task of market research is to provide R&D and product designers with information on how consumers judge such quality so it can be engineered into the offering. For example, the quality of jeans may be judged by the number of brass studs used, the weight and thickness of the denim, and whether double or even triple stitching is used at the seams. For fashion knitwear, even the label may be an important cue of quality. The buyer often reads the label to find out what the garment is made of. If such information is presented on a very high quality label, it will enhance the image of the clothing. Quality foods and beverages are often packaged in glass, rather than plastic or cans, because the glass container conveys a quality image.

The question is not merely what makes a quality product but which inputs produce the most quality outputs for the cost. For example, the best way to enhance the quality image of a sports car may be to fit it with the highest quality tires, gauges, steering wheel, and shift knob. The best way to enhance the quality image of a family sedan may be to equip it with a quality sound system and interior carpeting. The makers of minivans found that customers used the number of cup holders as an important indicator of the quality of the product. It is not good enough to bury quality in a product. It must be *seen* and *experienced* to be recognized and believed. Quality also has something intangible about it. It resides in the feel, the look, and the sound of an item. We may not be able to explain it, but we know it when we see it.

Performance, whether functional or symbolic, is an important component of quality. Table 9.1 lists some of the other dimensions used to measure quality. If the conceptual positioning of a product emphasizes durability and reliability, then quality must be related to long-term performance. If the positioning of a product emphasizes a particular benefit, then QFD should be used to emphasize the feature or attribute quality that provides the benefit.

---

[10] John R. Hauser and Don Clausing, "The House of Quality," *Harvard Business Review*, May/June, 1988, 63–73.

Figure 9.6 **Positioning Using Quality Functional Deployment (QFD)**

▲ Strong correlation
● Some correlation

		Product Specifications: Pencil length (inches)	Time between sharpenings	Lead dust (particles/line)	Hexagonality (%)	Quality Added: Importance rating	Writesharp (now)	Competitor X (now)	Competitor Y (now)	Writesharp (new)
Consumer Benefits	Easy to hold	●			●	3	4	3	3	4
	Does not smear		●	▲		4	5	4	5	5
	Point lasts		▲	●		5	4	5	3	5
	Does not roll				▲	2	3	3	3	4
Benchmarks	Writesharp (now)	5	56	10	70					
	Competitor X (now)	5	84	12	80					
	Competitor Y (now)	4	41	10	60					
	Writesharp (new)	5.5	100	6	80					

Engineering Ratings

Consumer Perception Ratings
Quality-Added
Scale: 1 to 5
(5 = highest quality)

This figure was constructed by a staged process called quality function deployment (QFD) that involves (1) finding out the benefits and outcomes the customer wants, (2) identifying what engineering specifications are most related to the benefits and levels of outcome the customer most desires, (3) determining which product features, characteristics, and attributes (product specifications) are most important to the target segment, (4) measuring consumer perceptions of relative competitive performance, and (5) measuring the tested relative competitive product specifications (benchmarking). The figure presents three matrices: a QFD product specification matrix, a quality-added matrix on the right, and a benchmarking matrix at the bottom. This enables the new Writesharp product to be positioned against the competition in terms of consumer perceptions and engineering specifications.

SOURCE: Based on an example presented in Robert Neff, "No. 1—And Trying Harder," Business Week, October 25, 1991, 23.

Determinant Quality Benefits/Features

Determinant performance benefits/features are what a consumer uses to choose among alternatives.[11] If feature A (delivering benefit X) does not vary across all of the

[11] Mark I. Alpert, "Identification of Determinant Attributes: A Comparison of Methods," *Journal of Marketing Research* 8 (May 1971): 184–91; and James H. Myers and Mark I. Alpert, "Determinant Buying Attitudes: Meaning and Measurement," *Journal of Marketing* 32 (October 1968): 13–20.

Table 9.1 **Eight Ways of Defining Quality**

1. *Performance:* Whether the product or service meets specified design and operating standards measured on specific dimensions, such as the quietness of an automobile's ride. Measurement depends on the primary benefit sought from using the product.
2. *Features:* The ancillary features that provide secondary benefits—the bells and whistles.
3. *Reliability:* Normally measured as the mean time to the first failure, the mean time between failures, and the failure rate per unit of time.
4. *Durability:* A measure of product life and robustness under stress.
5. *Serviceability:* The speed, courtesy, competence, and ease of repair.
6. *Aesthetics:* The sensory appeal of the product—how it looks, sounds, feels, tastes, and smells.
7. *Reputation:* The reputation inferred from company name or brand image.
8. *Conformance:* How often and how much the product or service diverges from the target standards.

It should be noted that a number of these dimensions overlap. For example, durability, serviceability, reliability, and features are often associated with performance. Perceived quality might be viewed as covering perceptions of all of these dimensions. The last dimension, conformance, is the most distinct because it deals with production consistency and product uniformity instead of a perceived or average performance characteristic.

SOURCE: These eight dimensions of quality are based on David A. Garvin, "Competing on the Eight Dimensions of Quality," *Harvard Business Review,* November/December 1987, 101–9.

alternatives, then feature A will not be a determinant feature and benefit X will not be a determinant benefit. For example, the first digital watch with a lithium battery made the lithium battery a determinant feature and battery life a determinant benefit. The lithium battery lasted five times longer than its alternatives and reduced the inconvenience of the watch stopping and having to have its battery replaced. It became such an important choice feature that all of the watch manufacturers had to incorporate lithium batteries into their models. Now that they all have imitated the innovator, battery life is no longer a determinant benefit and a lithium battery is no longer a determinant feature. Determinance can be detected in the QFD matrix by observing the variance in consumer perceived performance of the product alternatives for each benefit and the rated importance of the benefit to the consumer. In Figure 9.6, the most determinant consumer benefit is having the pencil point last because the quality-added ratings varies greatest on this benefit (varying from a 3 for Competitor Y to a 5 for Competitor X and for the new Writesharp) and because this benefit scores an importance rating of 5. Thus, Writesharp is an excellent name for the new model because this is the benefit that will most determine choice and because the new Writesharp scores best on possessing a lasting point.

But notice that for children the pencil's most determinant benefit may well be identification and involvement with the cartoon character imprinted on the eraser and shaft. A popular cartoon character is a distinctive feature, and personalizing children's possessions in this way is perceived by children to be a very important benefit. Put simply, different generations of children have "died" to have Snoopy, Big Bird, and Barney on their pencils. Thus, determinant usage benefits will vary across benefit segments. In a related example, Professor Mark Alpert found in his 1971 study of determinant benefits/features that "smoothness while writing" was the most important determinant benefit/feature in choosing a pen. But these days, for the segment that seeks to use a pen that conveys status, wealth, or a person with discriminating taste, the determinant benefit will be the appearance of the pen and the status of the brand. In recent years, antique pens from the 1920s to 1940s have become popular as expensive gifts. They are often refurbished with modern refill and writing mechanisms that ensure unsurpassed writing smoothness and refill convenience, and they are repackaged in attractive gift boxes. But their distinctive, determinant feature/benefit that adds hundreds of dollars in quality-added value is their "antiqueness." Their beauty can be imitated but not their age.

The Symbolic, Intangible Dimensions of Quality Management

Some market segments buy quality as a *symbol:* Quality merchandise says something about the owner. Just as most humans take pride in a job well done, we also take pride in owning someone else's job well done. It suggests we have standards and are discriminating. That is why we treasure ancient works of art. In fact, part of the national concern over becoming competitive on quality has to do with national pride. All of us feel some residual satisfaction in knowing that we have the best universities and make the best computers in the world. We are not happy when the quality of our automobiles suffers in comparison with foreign competition. We take pride in the output of our culture, which we believe produces much more than great sports teams or smart weapons. The quality of many of our culturally significant products and services—such as automobiles, clothing, art, music, films, high-technology items, and education—is an important symbol of national self-esteem.

However, as discussed in Chapter 5, the main reason we prefer quality products is that we get more satisfaction from using them and have to spend less time repairing them. The more valuable our time, the more we will value quality in a product or service. From the marketer's perspective, quality means less customer service, more customer goodwill, and an important basis for building brand equity.

A quality pen or watch often makes its owner feel like a higher quality person. It also raises the quality reputation of the retailer selling the brand.

Mercedes has always connected satisfaction and quality to engineering, as is recommended by the QFD process.

A product is often endowed with *intangible* characteristics, such as performance guarantees, delivery, before- and after-sales service, finance terms, status, style, or some other image associated with its brand name and price. Often such seemingly peripheral features are keys to successful product positioning. This occurs when little difference exists among competitors' products on the core benefits and features.

Almost any product, including commodities, can be differentiated on service dimensions such as delivery, terms, training, and usage advice.[12] De Havilland built the first passenger jet to provide faster travel, but did not design the jet's capacity and range for routes on which the airlines wanted to use a fast aircraft (a basic targeting/positioning mistake). Furthermore, the company did not offer attractive financing terms and ultimately lost to Boeing and Douglas, which entered the market with more competitive purchase packages.[13] Boeing and Douglas matched De Havilland with their planes and then differentiated their payment terms.

The Dimensions of Service Total Quality Management

Services vary in quality on *performance* dimensions, such as dependability, speed, competence, courtesy, caring, customization, and accompanying products (for example,

[12] Theodore Levitt, "Marketing Success through Differentiation—Of Anything," *Harvard Business Review*, January/February 1980, 83–91. This article argues that even in a commodity market, a seller can differentiate its product.
[13] Peter F. Drucker, "The Discipline of Innovation," *Harvard Business Review*, May/June 1985, 67–72.

Figure 9.7 A Model of Service Quality

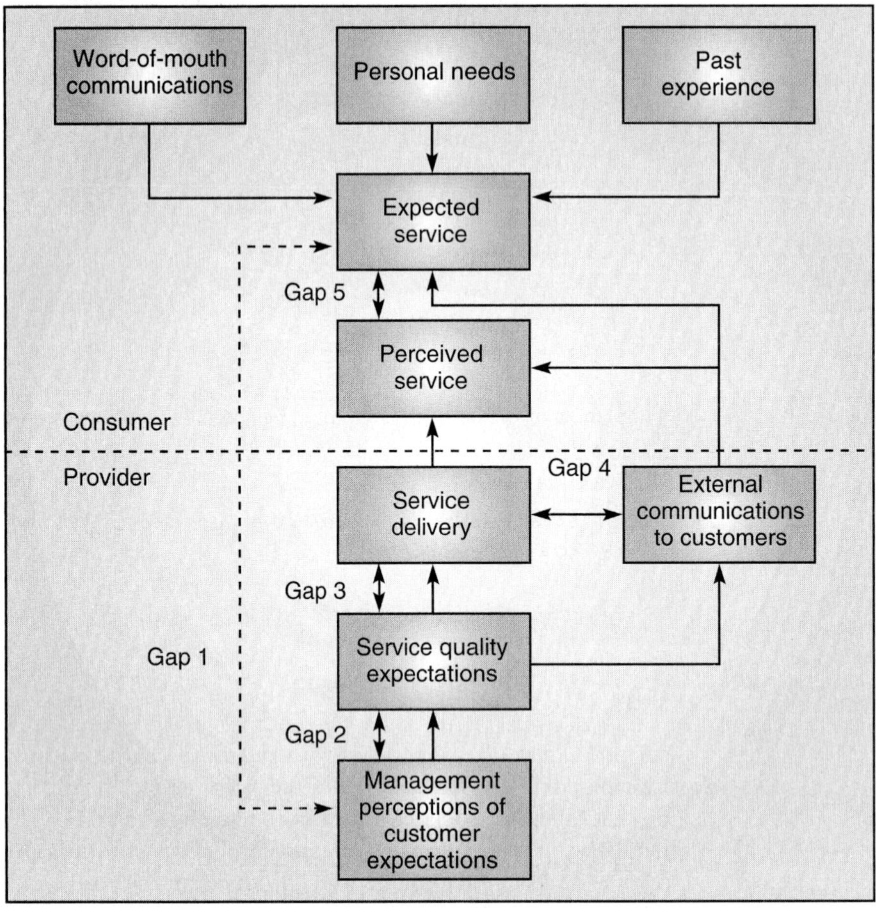

The top of the model describes the factors that determine service expectations and demand. The bottom of the model describes how a company generates the service it provides. Gap 1 indicates a benefit segmentation problem; Gap 2 indicates a positioning problem; Gap 3 indicates a QFD problem; Gap 4 indicates a promotion positioning problem; and Gap 5 indicates a satisfaction problem.

SOURCE: For details see Valarie A. Zeithaml, A. Parasuraman, and Leonard L. Berry, "A Conceptual Model of Service Quality and Its Implications for Future Research," *Journal of Marketing* 49 no. 4, (fall 1985): 41–50.

the shampoo and conditioning a hairdresser uses).[14] *Conformance*, which is delivering the same dependable service consistently over time to the same customer and to different customers (for a standardized service), is also very important. However, service conformance is particularly hard to manage compared to manufacturing conformance.

[14] For a more complete description of quality service features, see A. Parasuraman, Valarie A. Zeithaml, and Leonard L. Berry, "A Conceptual Model of Service Quality and Its Implications for Future Research," *Journal of Marketing* 49 (fall 1985): 41–50. More recent work by Joseph J. Cronin and Steven A. Taylor, "Measuring Service Quality: A Reexamination and Extension," *Journal of Marketing* (1992), suggests that the importance of different quality features varies among different services, such as banking, pest control, dry cleaning, and fast food.

This is because services are produced by people, who are much harder to control and regulate than machines.

Service quality can be measured as an input process involving the functional deployment of resources and activities. The output is the delivered service benefits. Consequently, a QFD-type input/output framework also can be used to study services. Such a service quality framework has been developed and is presented in Figure 9.7. It employs a gap analysis, which has close parallels with positioning and QFD. The task is for the service provider to identify and reduce the following gaps that have been identified by researchers as significant barriers to delivering a quality service:

Gap 1: *Management beliefs about consumer expectations are wrong.* Management's benefit segmentation analysis is flawed.

Gap 2: *Management operational specifications of the desired service do not match management perceptions of the target consumer's desired benefits and expectations.* Management's positioning of the service is wrong.

Gap 3: *The delivered service does not meet management operational specifications.* The QFD implementation and control of the service production script is basically flawed.

Gap 4: *Promises do not match performance.* The *promoted* positioning does not match the delivered service.

Gap 5: *Consumer perceptions of the delivered service do not meet consumer expectations.* Consumers are dissatisfied.

Because a service is often made up of a sequence of distinct activities (a production script), Gaps 2 and 3 can be reduced by studying the correlations between the actual operational performance of each service activity and the quality ratings of the overall service by the customer. Figure 9.8 is a service quality process map for credit card processing that indicates the relationship between the customer's perceived service performance and operational performance on four activities that make up the credit card service. Service process maps are equivalent to the QFD product specification matrix. They indicate which feature or activity performance are most crucial to delivering perceived quality to the customer, as well as specifying the flow of activities that constitute the service production script.

Maintaining Service Quality

The meeting of customer service expectations depends on the design of the service, employee training, employee rewards, and control. Because service is personally delivered, its implementation depends on the performance of many people in an organization. It is therefore particularly important that a service company create a company-wide culture that encourages all employees to present a quality service image during their personal interaction with customers and to conform to the expected standards of service behavior. An airline does not help its service image by keeping callers on hold waiting for information on flight arrivals. It conspicuously improves its service image by helping young families and the elderly get their luggage to and from their ground transportation, free of charge.

Interestingly, service companies often direct their advertising at both their customers and their service employees. Such advertising positions the product not only in the minds of consumers but also in the minds of the service providers out in the field. It spells out what the service provider promises to deliver and reminds the field service staff of what they are expected to deliver to the customer. In this way, service advertising acts as an employee motivator and a control program (encouraging service quality conformance to the service production script), as well as a selling device.

Figure 9.8 **An Input/Output Process Map of a Service**

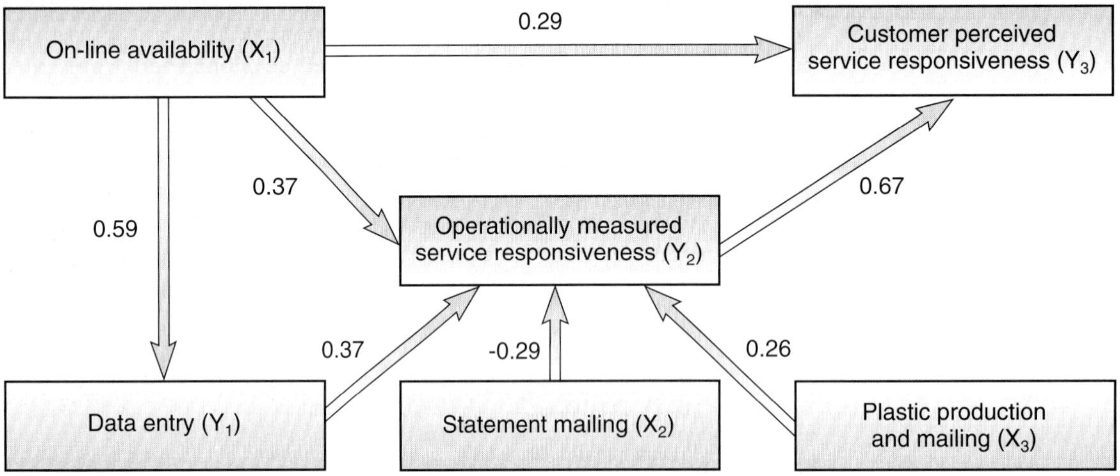

Four operationally distinct activities make up the service process: on-line service, data entry, statement mailing, and plastic production. The error rate and other operational performance measures (X1, Y1, X2, X3) can be used to assess the month-by-month quality of the execution of each of these activities. These ratings can then be connected to an overall operational measure of service responsiveness (Y2) and surveys of customer perceptions (Y3). The size of the weightings indicate the relationship between activity performance and operational quality and the perceived quality of service. The actual relationships are as follows:

$$Y_1 = 0.59X_1$$

$$Y_2 = 0.37X_1 - 0.29X_2 + 0.26X_3 + 0.37Y_1$$

$$Y_3 = 0.29X_1 + 0.67Y_2$$

SOURCE: For further details, see David A. Collier, "A Service Quality Process Map for Credit Card Processing," *Decision Sciences* 22 (1991): 406–16.

Service Worker Morale and Performance/ Conformance Slippage

Maintaining service quality conformance is particularly important when a service organization faces a financial squeeze.[15] When a company cares for and looks after its employees, it sets an example for its employees to follow in servicing customers. The opposite also can occur. Cutting back on staff, raises, benefits, expenses, and general overhead support can lead to a deterioration in morale, which quickly shows up in a deterioration in customer service quality. As morale drops, employees are less likely to go the extra mile or do things right the first time. Customers then become dissatisfied because service is not what they had come to expect, and this results in lost sales. The lost sales then lead to further belt-tightening and a further decrease in morale and service. This downward spiral is called a negative reinforcement path dependency.

[15] Christian Gronroos, *Strategic Management and Marketing in the Service Sector* (Cambridge, MA: Marketing Science Institute, 1984).

It is imperative that service firms think carefully about how decisions made in other aspects of the business may affect employee service performance.[16] For example, efficiencies in the productivity of service employees can be achieved through extensive practice training and productivity incentives. Employees can be taught from a production script where they mechanically execute a routinized service step by step. This training increases quality control and standardization but may do so at the expense of servicing the unique needs of particular customers. A service company has to decide on its service positioning and be very careful to keep all of its operations and marketing strategies consistent with this positioning.

Quality-Added Analysis

A product's price is justified based on its perceived quality to the target market segment. Products offering more quality than alternative products can be sold at higher prices. Having developed a positioning concept and used benefit segmentation and QFD to design quality into the product or service, a marketing executive must then assess whether the new or modified product is economically feasible. This feasibility analysis involves two steps. The first is to price the product against the competition; the second is to estimate what sales levels will have to be achieved at the proposed price to meet financial targets.

Quality-added (QA) analysis attempts to estimate the extra price the target market segment is prepared to pay to obtain the added quality (benefits and performance outcomes) that a product offers over its competitive alternatives. Sometimes it is called economic value analysis. The quality added can be measured in engineering terms, such as output, reliability, and durability, or it can be symbolic and intangible. It is easier to undertake a QA analysis when the quality output can be measured in engineering terms because it can be computed based on objective performance tests. However, the difference in quality between two brands can still be measured using a simple test that asks target buyers to state how much more they would be willing to pay for the quality added compared to other brands. It becomes more difficult to measure QA when the target buyers are not familiar with the alternatives.

The consideration of quality added at the concept stage would seem to be an obvious, rational step for an enterprise to take, but sometimes it does not happen then or the initially planned value for money disappears as the cost of the product or service increases greatly through development and production. For example, the Chunnel (the tunnel underneath the English Channel that connects England to France) is an engineering marvel. The problem is that it costs from $250 to $460 for a round trip on the train that carries cars through the tunnel. The price varies by the tourist season.[17] This compares to $90–$150 for the equivalent round trip on the ferries that leave from many different ports on the English and French coasts. The Chunnel shuttle service takes thirty-five minutes, a ferry trip around ninety minutes. But ferry goers can party on the ferry (they spend an average of $18 on duty-free drinks on the ferry), which they cannot do in the Chunnel. The ferries also offer greater location convenience, which reduces the time advantage of the Chunnel. If the Chunnel had

---

[16] Leonard A. Schlesinger and James L. Heskett, "The Service-Driven Service Company," *Harvard Business Review*, September/October 1991, 71–81.

[17] Joshua Lekvine, "Chunnel Vision," *Forbes*, February 14, 1994, 146.

not cost more than twice as much to build as expected (more than $15 billion), it might have been competitive, but, as it stands, apart from its novelty it has major problems promoting the service quality it adds to justify its much higher price.

American Express (AmEx) does not have quite the same problem with its Optima True Grace card. Introduced in 1994 as the first new AmEx card in seven years, it does not charge consumers interest on new purchases for twenty-five days, even if the account has a balance. All other major cards give such a grace period only when no outstanding balance exists. The annual cost savings for a typical Visa consumer who averages a $1,700 balance, who makes $2,500 per year in purchases, and who is charged an interest rate of 17.38 percent is $45.[18] But for higher income card users who buy more and carry a higher balance, the savings can be much higher. Thus, the Optima True Grace card particularly targets the most attractive market segment—the high-income, heavy-user consumer. The problem for AmEx is twofold. First, other cards offer more tangible quality-added benefits, such as airline frequent-flier miles or discounts on new cars. Card users who prefer such added value to cost savings may not view the Optima card as offering higher quality benefits to the cards they are earning miles or discounts on, or they may be slow to switch until they can cash in their mileage or discount benefits. Second, Visa and MasterCard have a quality benefit that American Express cards cannot match: They are accepted by three times as many merchants worldwide.

If the quality added is symbolic or intangible, then consumer research should be undertaken to assess the average dollar value the target market places on the differentiation. The difference in price between the QA product and the standard product is then set so the majority of the target buyers gain a noticeable and significant net value (benefit-cost) advantage from buying the new product. QA analysis is most successful for pricing capital equipment, raw materials, components, or supplies to be sold to original equipment manufacturers, farmers, or the government.

Examples of QA Analysis

The QFD analysis of pencils in Figure 9.6 includes a simple but effective quality-added analysis. On the right of the product specification matrix is a QA matrix. It presents the results of target consumer test ratings of the new pencil and the competition on important quality dimensions. Underneath the product specification matrix is a benchmarking comparison of the prototype's performance on objective tests. These engineering benchmarking tests would be made *before* the consumer tests because there would be little point in testing consumer perceptions of the new pencil's added quality if the pencil did not outperform its rivals on key technical specifications known to be correlated with the performance benefits and outcomes that the target segment desires.

Added output quality can come from superior product performance or from cost savings in the use and disposal of the product. Table 9.2 compares the performance of a new product with that of the current standard product (the benchmark product). The choice of the benchmark is important. For now, assume it is the best-selling product in the target market. The price of both products is $500, but the new product costs 50 percent less to install and 20 percent less to operate. The new product also

[18] Leah Spiro, "Is This AmEx's Trump Card?" *Business Week*, October 24, 1994, 32–33.

Table 9.2 An Example of Quality-Added Analysis

PRICE, COST, AND QUALITY ADDED	BENCHMARK PRODUCT	NEW PRODUCT PRICE A PLAN	NEW PRODUCT PRICE B PLAN	NEW PRODUCT PRICE C PLAN
Purchase Price	$ 500	$500	$600	$ 700
+ Start-up cost	100	50	50	50
+ Post-purchase costs (maintenance and operations)	500	400	400	400
– Net disposal value (disposal sale price less disposal cost)	100	150	150	150
Life-cycle cost	$1,000	$800	$900	$1,000
Added dollar value of superior performance over lifetime compared to benchmark product		$200	$200	$ 200
Net gain to buyer from choosing new product over benchmark product		$400	$300	$ 200

uses more advanced technology that results in lower operating costs. Therefore, its disposal value is $50 more. The total cost savings for installation, operation, and disposal amounts to $200 over the life of the product. The new product is also more productive than the standard product, thus increasing productivity by $200. Under price plan A, buyers stand to gain an extra $400 in value added by buying the new product instead of the standard product. They pay the same purchase price, $500, but receive $200 in cost savings and $200 in added productivity.

Factoring in Cost

Until now we have assumed that the new product and the standard product cost the same to make. Suppose the new product costs $50 more to manufacture than the standard product. Price plan B covers such extra costs and also gives an extra $50 in contribution margin. A salesperson can still sell the new product on its life-cycle cost advantages of $100 and extra performance utility of $200.

Under price plan C, the salesperson is likely to have more difficulty. At a purchase price of $700, the new product is 40 percent more expensive than the standard product. The new product also can no longer be sold on its total life-cycle cost savings against the benchmark. The salesperson must try to convince the customer that the added quality (performance utility) of the new product is worth its price. This is a difficult task for several reasons. First, the cost savings and performance superiority are future benefits that may be discounted because of their uncertainty. What is certain is that the new product costs $200 more than the standard product. Second, future dollars earned from future benefits are worth less than current dollars because current dollars can be invested today to earn profits for tomorrow. Third, people naturally tend to stick with the status quo if the status quo is adequate (a psychological switching cost).

For these reasons, plan B is likely to be the best choice of the three alternative price plans. It offers two selling points—life-cycle cost savings and superior performance—and adds a healthy extra margin for the seller. Both buyer and seller share the added benefits and value of the new innovation. At a price above $600 and below $700, the product would be targeted at and sold to only the buying segment who value the product's differentiation most (its superior performance and life-cycle cost savings). Such a price would mean the buyer has to pay for much of the added quality.

How to Measure Quality Added

Quality added should be measured by target consumers and not company engineers, designers, or accountants. This may well be the most common and biggest competitive rationality mistake made by marketing decision makers. They convince themselves that a product or service has a quality advantage over its competitors that in the minds of consumers, simply is not true. Alternatively, a product may have a quality advantage that is not needed by the target market (for example, a buyer neither needs the added productivity nor considers the whole life-cycle cost of the product).

Market researchers have developed a method of establishing the buyer's perceived worth of extra features, performance, and lifetime cost savings. The method, called conjoint or trade-off analysis (see "Segmenting the Food Processor Market" in Chapter 5), is based on customer ratings of product alternatives described in terms of their selling features. From these ratings, incremental utility of improvements in performance, quality, or cost savings can be calculated and different benefit segments identified.[19]

Sometimes marketers can provide independent confirmation to back up their claims of superior product performance. For example, marketers of herbicides, insecticides, fertilizers, and hybrid grains often have universities run tests that compare under different field conditions the performance of their products to alternatives. They can use this information to support their claims, thus increasing buyer confidence. In fact, agricultural scientists first used conjoint analysis more than fifty years ago to test for differences in actual test performance rather than differences in farmer perceptions of performance.

Choice of the Benchmark Product/Service

In QA everything hinges on the choice of the benchmark product or service. Common sense suggests it should be the most competitive current offering. What, exactly, does "most competitive" mean? Does it mean the product with the largest market share? This makes sense, because the added-value price would then appeal to the largest number of current buyers. However, if an aggressive competitor launches a new product offering superior value for the money over the current market leader, a QA analysis also may have to be applied to the new entry to set a price that heads it off at the pass.

It makes no sense to compare the new product against a clearly weaker product. The comparison will have no meaning to buyers of more competitive products and, in fact, may lead customers to question the firm's integrity. Thorough marketers may undertake QA analyses against all of the major competitors' offerings. This will help

[19] The Japanese use a variation of conjoint analysis called *Taguchi* methods; see *Taguchi Methods: Applications in World Industry* ed. A. Bendell, J. Disney, and W. A. Pridmore (Kempstone, England: IFS Publications, 1989).

to ensure that the quality for price is superior to any major competitor. Alternatively, such analyses may lead to a change in targeting toward the loyal customers of the competitors whose products or services are discovered to be the least competitive, using QA analysis.

Feasibility Analysis

At this stage of decision making, the manager has done initial positioning, QFD, and QA competitive analyses of the product or service. These analyses will suggest a competitive market price that, along with relevant cost information, can be used in a target return analysis to determine the number of units that must be sold to either break even or achieve a specified profit target. This is the point at which bottom-line considerations play an important part in assessing the attractiveness of the proposed positioning. A *feasible position* is a differentiation position that can be made into a product (using QFD) and sold at a price (using QA analysis) such that the required sales to meet the financial goals are feasible.

If the financial feasibility of a new or modified product or service is to be established before it is launched, then some sort of profitability analysis must be taken. Without it, how can a company decide whether or not to proceed? Some sort of financial feasibility analysis, however rough, should be made before developing detailed tactics. The analysis can be repeated again when all the details have been developed and the cost estimates are much better. Fortunately, personal-computer spreadsheet programs are ideally suited to do such analyses. They are a variation of old-fashioned break-even analyses (see Figure 9.9 on page 353).

The Formula

Break-even volume (Q_{pBE}) is the sales volume needed at selling price p that generates a contribution equal to estimated fixed costs. At Q_{pBE} all fixed and variable costs are covered.

$$\text{Break-even sales} = Q_{pBE} = FC/CM = FC/(\text{Price} - AVC)$$

where

$$CM = \text{Contribution margin from each unit sold}$$

$$FC = \text{Fixed costs}$$

$$AVC = \text{Average variable cost}$$

If a specific target return on assets employed is desired, then

$$\text{Target return sales} = Q_{pTR} = (FC + ROA \times AE)/(\text{Price} - AVC),$$

where

$$ROA = \text{Percent target return desired on assets employed}$$

$$AE = \text{Value of assets employed}$$

These formulas can be converted into a visual graph called a break-even chart or target sales chart (see Figure 9.9). It can also be used in a spreadsheet. The TARGET spreadsheet presented in Figure 9.9 allows a decision maker to test a price by computing the target sales and market share required to cover costs and meet return on assets (ROA) goals.

Establishing Feasibility

Having determined the target sales volume for a given price, the pricing decision maker must now answer the following questions:

1. Given the target market, competitive positioning, sales effort, likely distribution coverage of the market, advertising reach, and estimated share of industry advertising spending ("voice" share), what is the likelihood of achieving the required market share and unit sales at the proposed price?
2. Is the chance of achieving the required sales good, given the results of the QA analyses?
3. How long would it take to reach the target sales and market share? Is this time reasonable?

If the answers to these questions are positive, then the positioning is feasible. The QA analysis helps establish the credibility of the sales and, particularly, the share targets, because the sales must come at the expense of the current popular substitutes. Estimates about where the sales will realistically come from (an expanded market or a competitor's market share) also will help establish the credibility of achieving the sales and share goals. This suggests that when assessing the feasibility of achieving the sales needed, decision makers should identify where the sales will come from—what percentage of the sales will come from which competitors, including the firm's existing products or services? Feasibility assessments that do not detail where the majority of the sales will come from are less realistic and credible. When executives start to predict where the sales are going to come from, they start to think about how the competitors will react (see Chapter 6), and this will temper their estimates and optimism.

Other elements of marketing strategy also must be considered. For example, the planned distribution strategy may not reach sufficient potential customers to attain the sales goal. The planned advertising budget may not produce the unique mind share needed to generate the market share required to break even or reach the desired ROA. The plausibility of achieving the target sales and market share required depends on much more than price. An executive must test the overall feasibility of the sales goal, given the proposed marketing strategy and everything known about the size of the market, consumer behavior, competition, and channels of distribution. In effect, the fit of the required sales goal is tested against every marketing fact the marketing planner possesses. The problem is that at the positioning stage, the rest of the logistics and marketing tactics have yet to be developed. This means their effectiveness and costs have to be roughly estimated and fine-tuned at a later date.

If the required sales and market share goals are clearly not attainable, then marketers must reevaluate the offering. If a feasible positioning/price/sales target combination cannot be found, then the project must be considered a doubtful venture. A thorough QFD reanalysis must be done to determine ways that new features can be added to increase the QA competitiveness of the offering. Alternatively, efforts can be made to change the design so variable and fixed costs are reduced and the product can be sold at a target price suitable to generate the required sales. This is possible—P&G

Figure 9.9 Using TARGET to Test the Feasibility of a Price

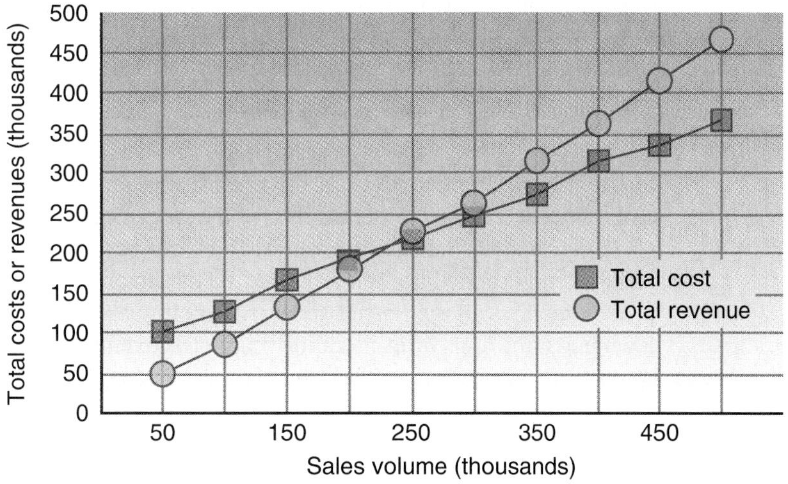

Target Return for a Given Price
(units in 000s)

Fixed Costs		
Manufacturing		
• R & D	$10,000	
• patent	10,000	
• other	10,000	
Total Fixed Manufacturing		$30,000
Marketing		
• advertising	$10,000	
• sales expense	5,000	
• distribution	5,000	
• other	0	
Total Fixed Marketing		$20,000
Administrative Overhead		10,000
Other Fixed Costs		0
Total Fixed Costs		**$60,000**
Target Return on Assets Employed		20.0%
Value of Total Assets Employed		**$60,000**
Enter target selling price		*$1.00*
Estimated variable cost per unit		*$0.60*
Size of total target market		*1,000*
Target break-even volume		*180*
Market share at break-even volume		*18.0%*

did it with Pampers. Some Japanese companies start with price in their positioning strategy (see Chapter 2). They set a target price that they know will be value-for-the-money competitive, and then they use QFD to design a product at a cost that will achieve the desired financial goals. Price is often one of the *first* considerations in positioning a product or service.

The Limiting Assumptions

Feasible positioning analysis is the most useful and sound procedure a company can employ to determine the feasibility of a new positioning or repositioning strategy. It also offers an excellent basis for marketers, designers, engineers, and financial officers to work together. The analysis may result in only approximate numbers, but the process enables all the parties to learn a great deal from each other. However, the following assumptions limit its validity and effectiveness:

- As the volume of production and sales increase, fixed costs do not stay fixed. Ultimately, a new plant and more management are needed. Fixed costs may therefore increase in very large steps as production and sales increase.
- It is unlikely that variable costs will increase in a straight line as the volume of production and sales increases. Cost economies will create a curve that also may have steps in it, such as at points where suppliers give volume discounts.
- Price does not stay constant as sales volume increases because sellers give sales volume discounts to major buyers.
- Inventory holding costs and costs of receivables (which finance buyers' payment tardiness) are not easily incorporated into break-even analyses.

Most of these problems can be addressed by making the formula and spreadsheet more complicated. However, the incremental advantage of adding such extra requirements to the decision-making model may not be worthwhile, particularly if they complicate the understanding of what is going on so much that users give up on the technique.

The Dynamics of Competitive Position

Repositioning involves changing the perceived and actual characteristics of a service to better fit a changing marketplace environment. It can be gradual, such as when Pepsi-Cola Co. repositioned itself from the second-class soft drink defined by its slogan "Twice as much for a nickel" in the 1950s to its more contemporary "Take the Taste Test" image of the 1980s. Or it can be moderately fast, such as the Gap's repositioning from "the denim store in the mall" in the early 1980s to a seller of high-quality sportswear and casual wear in the late 1980s. Repositioning can be dramatic, such as when Ronald Reagan, a longtime Democrat, switched parties and became a Republican. Or it can be constant, such as the Japanese Kaizen approach, in which everyone in the enterprise is constantly thinking of ways to make minor improvements in a product or service. When four or five Japanese companies compete using Kaizen in any market, anywhere in the world, one can assume that their efforts will completely change the product designs over the next two to three years.

Sometimes, changing technology forces an entire product market to shift positions. Computer manufacturers now position their products on their software compatibility, software availability, and connectability. Previously, they had emphasized speed and capacity, which are no longer as important because all companies offer satisfactory speed and capacity for almost all users, at an even lower cost.

The objective of positioning is to find an attractive niche, occupy it with a distinctive innovation, and then use innovation/imitation to defend it against all competition. As will become apparent in the following discussion, an attack on a position is often very focused, and defense often involves a counterattack. First the traditional defensive strategy will be discussed, and then how it can be attacked and counterattacked will be described. However, since attack and defense is often initiated by adding new models to the product line, the strategy behind positioning a line of products must first be understood.

Product-Line Positioning

A product line is a group of specific product models marketed by one company that are in the same product category (in terms of basic design and function). They vary in price, quality, and features and are targeted at different market segments. The items in the line also vary in competitiveness and profitability with each other and with rival models. The questions that propel product-line strategy are simple: Should the company expand or contract the product line or reposition items in the line? Answering these questions is much more difficult.

A brilliant target and product-line extension has been executed by Kinkos. Kinkos was launched in 1971 at the University of California—Santa Barbara (UCSB) by student Paul Orfalea as a cheaper and more convenient copy service to that provided by university libraries.[20] He charged four cents a page, while the university library charged ten cents a page (enough said about the "enterprise" of universities). Having saturated the student service market, Kinkos is now targeting the small business as a twenty-four-hour "branch office" that offers all of the *newest* computer, copying, printing, and videoconferencing services a small firm might want. Orfalea, worth several hundred million dollars from his clever, opportunistic service-positioning strategies, now teaches a course on entrepreneurial marketing at UCSB.

Whether a company is on the offensive (going after more market share or expanding the total market size) or defensive (responding to a competitor's recent or current offensive), a change in product-line strategy usually involves a decision to add or remove an item. Success in expanding or contracting the product line consequently depends on the positioning of the item relative to

1. Consumer needs
2. Specific competing products
3. Existing items in the current product line

The profitability of adding or repositioning an item depends on what happens to overall market size, and what happens to the sales of existing items.

Expanding Market Size

Consumers who are currently outside the existing product market may be drawn into the market by a new offering. This will expand the market size, increase the company's overall market share, and generate higher earnings that will contribute to fixed-costs and overhead recovery. When diet colas were introduced, the cola market grew because diet colas attracted adults back into the soda market.

[20] Zina Moukheiber, "I'm Just a Peddler," *Forbes*, July 17, 1995, 42–43.

Forecasting how much a market will grow in size or how much market share will be gained from competition is not easy. It depends very much on the success of the marketing campaign and the response of the competition. In some markets, the competitors do not respond at all to the loss of market share. In other markets, the reaction of competitors is swift and effective. This uncertainty highlights the importance of analyzing the competitive environment.

Cannibalizing Existing Sales

It is also likely that a new item or repositioned item will cannibalize the market share of existing items in your line. Every time Gillette introduces a new wet shaving system it takes most of its sales from existing Gillette products. Why? First, Gillette dominates the market. It has more than 40 percent of existing sales, so naturally it is likely to be most affected by its own innovation. Second, a new Gillette product will appeal more to Gillette's loyal users than to consumers who are loyal to Schick, BIC, or another manufacturer. The new product is almost certain to increase administration fixed costs and involve expensive advertising and trade promotions (to obtain more shelf space and change buyer perceptions and attitudes). However, the new item is presumably being introduced because it has particularly attractive features. This may enable the company to charge a premium price that compensates for the added expenses and the cannibalization of existing sales. It also may fill a gap in a product line that, if left unfilled, may enable a competitor to gain a foothold in the market.

At first, the introduction of Miller Lite beer in 1973 seemed to be a great marketing success. However, over time it became clear that much of the market share Miller gained was cannibalized from the brewer's premium beer, Miller High Life. It was still a good decision, however, because the introduction of light beers by the competition was inevitable. In summary, the potential advantages and disadvantages of product-line expansion follow:

POTENTIAL ADVANTAGES	POTENTIAL DISADVANTAGES
■ Expands total market size	■ Cannibalizes market share of existing items in the product line
■ Takes market share from competitors	■ Increases operating overheads
■ Blocks competitor entry	■ Requires extra management time and skill
■ Preempts competition	■ Involves major launch expenses
■ Increases gross margin on each dollar sale	

Most new product failures in the market are due to unsuccessful product-line extensions. They generate very little extra revenue and cost a great deal in management effort and costs. Many of these failures could be prevented by the adoption of a more hard-nosed approach when considering the introduction of a new item in the line.

Product-Line Tactical Issues

In highly competitive markets, particularly those driven by continual technological innovations, product-line repositioning, expansion, and pruning are constant. It is a fact of life, a consequence of continual innovation/imitation. Repositioning is the sign of healthy competition and a healthy marketplace. The question, therefore, is not whether to change the product line but how to change it to remain competitive and best meet overall company objectives. In doing so, it pays to consider the following issues and tactics.

Differentiation Shrinkage

Technological innovations in product features coupled with production process cost reductions can quickly shrink the differentiation of the models in a line and the justification for price differences. For example, consider the dilemma faced by companies that marketed both dot-matrix and laser computer printers. Between 1991 and 1993 the cost of making the engines for laser printers halved. This led to laser printers competing with ink-jet printers and ink-jet printers in turn competing with and driving the older dot-matrix printers out of the market.[21]

Economy Substitutes

Although the decision to add an item to a product line should generally focus on the items in the line closest to the new model in the competitive-feature map, such a narrow perspective can be a mistake. If the consumer uses value for the money to decide which item in a line to choose, then the model or service package closest to the planned new model may not be the most competitive substitute. Instead, a very competitively priced option much lower down or higher up the product line may be what the buyer would otherwise buy. This implies that best-selling items in the product line may dominate other models because they are underpriced in terms of value for the money. They are economy substitutes, in that they may not be as close to the new item as others, but they are more price competitive. For example, low-priced, low-octane gas poses more of a threat than medium-priced, medium-octane gas to high-priced, high-octane gas. The solution may be to eliminate the dominated items or to adjust the relative prices of the items.

Image Anchors

Very low and very high priced items in the line can be used as general image anchors. The objective is to drag the perceptions of the whole line in a desired direction. Bottom-of-the-line specials are often advertised to attract customers into a store with the intention of having them trade up to a more expensive model. This "bait and switch" is illegal only when the bait item is not available for purchase, either immediately or by a rain check. At the other end of the line, some brands advertise an extreme high-quality, high-priced item with the hope of enhancing the quality image of their biggest-selling models. Fisher electronics had a $2,500 audio-video system, which it advertised in *Time* and *Newsweek*. While sales of such a top-end system might barely pay for the campaign, the incremental enhancement of the entire Fisher brand name and line of audio-video equipment by such an image anchor may well have made it a very worthwhile product-line strategy. Exclusive department stores such as Neiman-Marcus and Saks Fifth Avenue use expensive display porcelain, jewelry, and perfumes to enhance the image of a thousand more modest items of merchandise throughout their stores.

New Items That Merge Market Segments

An attractive feature in a new model may actually lead to a merging of several previously distinct segments. The minivan, which offered maneuverability without sacrificing capacity, had such an effect. It drew together the two respective target segments of the traditional family station wagon and the full-size van. Now they are largely one segment. A new item in a line can have unexpected effects on other long-standing positioning relationships.

[21] "Laser Printers Reproducible," *The Economist*, October 30, 1993, 98–99.

Attacking by Concentrating Resources

Now that some of the important aspects of product-line tactics have been covered, it is time to return to the question of how an existing market might be entered. Rather than embarking on an all-out assault, the entrant may prefer to target an attractive segment of the market where the competition is weak. This is often a growth segment, because the major competition does not yet have a strong image in the minds of the new users.

The new users of a product or new uses for a product also may change what is valued in the product or service, opening up an important new positioning or differentiation opportunity. Pepsi started its major assault on Coca-Cola's brand loyalty in the 1950s by concentrating its push in specific regions and, with creative packaging, targeting the take-home market, a market that, up to then, Coke had largely overlooked. Once such a positioning weakness in the market is found, the attacker must position itself as superior on a consumer choice dimension that the competition will find difficult to counter. The objective of the new entrant should be to become number one on quality, economy, style, or some other important choice dimension in the minds of consumers.[22] This will require new product design and a saturated advertising campaign directed at the heavy users in the target market. Such a resource concentration strategy is most evident in the behavior of small companies that focus on a regional market. They develop a local consumer franchise and often use the local media and distribution channels more effectively than large competitors whose marketing tactics are devised at national headquarters and applied nationwide.

Attacking with a New Performance Feature

One leading economist has argued that most markets can be entered successfully only by a massive launch of a whole new product line.[23] The history of marketing campaigns suggests otherwise. An existing market is most vulnerable to the introduction of an important new feature. Such a competitive move can have an effect equivalent to undermining a fortress by crumbling the walls around the rival's competitive positioning. It fractures and transforms the current competitive positioning map. The defender has to scramble, often at great cost, to cope with the upheaval and repair the damage.

Cuisinart, the innovator of the food processor, had a decision to make in 1985 when Sunbeam launched Oskar, a compact food processor/blender, for $60. Cuisinart had taken the high road in the late 1970s with its large, powerful, feature-laden processors that caught the gourmet cooking fad. The company successfully gambled that it could expand its product line to unheard-of price points of $200 plus for a glorified chopper/blender. Cuisinart became chic among gourmet cooks. But in the early 1980s, as the economy recovered, eating out increased by 50 percent, and although gourmet cooking was still in, the Cuisinart was increasingly in the kitchen cupboard. It was too bulky and too difficult to clean. Enter Sunbeam with its compact, convenient, and low-priced Oskar. Cuisinart chose not to respond, fearing the damage to

[22] Al Ries and Jack Trout, *Marketing Warfare* (New York: McGraw-Hill, 1986). Some might argue that if you have more than one differentiation advantage you should promote them all. Ries and Trout point out that you must be superior on at least one important choice dimension, and this must be clearly and effectively promoted.

[23] Kelvin Lancaster, *Variety, Equity and Efficiency* (New York: Columbia University Press, 1979).

sales of its large processors would not be offset by increased sales of a smaller item. The company badly underestimated the demand for convenience and compactness. Sunbeam sold 700,000 Oskars, 25 percent of all food processors sold in 1985. Cuisinart's volume share dropped from 20 percent to 10 percent. In the fall of 1986, Cuisinart responded belatedly with the $40 Cuisinart Mini-Mate chopper/grinder. But the damage had already been done to both market share and the company's image—consumers no longer saw Cuisinart as a cutting-edge innovator and, just as important, neither did retailers.[24]

A number of stomach acid-blockers, such as Tagamet HB and Pepcid AC, have entered the billion-dollar, over-the-counter-drug heartburn market. When Pepcid AC was launched in June 1995, by August it had 22 percent of the antacid market.[25] Tagamet HB ads claimed that the drug was based on research that won the Nobel Prize for medicine. The British acid-blocker Zantac has yet to enter this market, and it is the best-selling prescription drug in the world. The performance advantage of the acid-blockers over Tums and other existing medications is that a dose of an acid-blocker lasts eight to twelve hours, thus enabling a heartburn sufferer to have a good night's sleep. The current antacids last only two or three hours, so users are likely to wake with indigestion several times during the night. The acid-blockers are positioned as not only more effective, with less side effects, but also as lasting a lot longer, therefore an important positioning differentiation in nighttime usage. This enables the acid-blockers to sell at twice the price of Tums and the other antacids. But, in turn, the curing of stomach ulcers by the use of antibiotics that kill the bacteria that create common types of ulcers and chronic heartburn is a performance feature innovation that is sweeping the world and likely to seriously challenge several acid-blocker market segments, leading to a new round of performance feature repositioning.

If a new feature innovation can quickly be adopted by established competitors, the successful assault of the new entrant may be short-lived. The best the attacker can hope for is that it gets a toehold into the market channels and included in consideration sets (the set of brands a consumer will choose from) that it can build on. In the financial services market, competitors are constantly hustling to develop innovative offerings and services to investors because new service competitive advantages are usually impossible to sustain. For example, the Reserve Fund of New York invented money-market mutual funds in 1972, but by 1986 it had over three hundred competitors and only 0.8 percent of the market for such funds. Competing in the marketplace, particularly service markets where product imitation is relatively quick and easy, requires relentless innovation/imitation repositioning and cost control.

Defensive Positioning

A defensive "island fortress" strategy is one in which a firm protects its most profitable line items by surrounding them with a wall of flanking models that stave off competitive threats. Such a strategy will work best if the line is positioned on top of a demand concentration: a benefit cluster in a market map (see Figure 9.3 for examples of benefit clusters). A company so positioned on top of such a demand peak then occupies the high ground. It can develop a coordinated image directed at its captive market segment and may realize production, R&D, and marketing economies of scale and scope.

[24] A. Pomice, "Losing the Cutting Edge," *Forbes*, October 6, 1986, 162. Cuisinart declared bankruptcy in 1992.
[25] Leon Jaroff, "Fire in the Belly, Money in the Bank," *Time*, November 6, 1995, 56–58.

Kellogg, the eight-hundred-pound gorilla in the breakfast cereal market, pursued an island fortress strategy. In 1983, Kellogg was being written off as a company past its prime, even though it had 36.7 percent of a $3.7 billion market. By 1988, it had 41.7 percent of a market it had helped grow to $5.4 billion. What did Kellogg do? First, it focused on the 80 million baby boomers who were looking for a convenient and nutritious breakfast. In five years, consumption of cold cereal by twenty-five-year olds to forty-nine-year olds increased by 26 percent. In 1987, Kellogg introduced forty-seven new cereals worldwide, spending $40 million on R&D and $600 million on advertising. Kellogg is so dominant in its category that it does not have to pay shelf-slotting allowances (shelf-space rent) to get retailers to stock its new products. This gives the company a considerable advantage over competitors, who may have to spend up to one-third of a new product's first-year budget on such allowances. But Kellogg's cost advantages do not stop there. Its gross margin rose from 41 percent to 49 percent through automation and relentless cost control. The rest of the industry averaged 35 percent. The other competitors are no slouches (for example, General Mills, Ralston Purina, RJR Nabisco, and Quaker Oats). Kellogg dominated a fiercely competitive market by being the complete competitor. It targeted, it positioned, and it controlled its costs.[26] But even the eight-hundred-pound gorilla with a fortress strategy can be brought to its knees by rival product innovations such as Ralston Purina's fad Batman and Ninja Turtle cereals and the oat-bran craze that Kellogg was slow to serve.[27] Kellogg's market share has recently fallen back from 42 percent to 35 percent. Much cheaper private-label cereals have also undercut Kellogg's prices, which were raised six times between 1991 and 1994. A major rival, General Mills, also lowered its prices.

Flanking Brands and Price-Point Brands

A flanking brand is often used to protect a premium brand from price competition. It is launched as an economy brand to pick up the price-sensitive consumer and to offer distributors an alternative (and hence blocking competitors out of the channel). Sometimes the threat of a low-priced competitive entry can be deterred by a company announcing its willingness to launch a price flanker that undercuts the competitor's price. For example, in 1990 Chrysler was very worried about rivals creating a price war in its highly profitable minivan market niche. So the president announced that Chrysler had a plan in its desk drawer if it needed to build a very low-priced minivan.[28] The implication, not lost on the competition, was that if competitors created a price war, then Chrysler would create a low-price flanker model and would win the war. Offering a flanking brand is considered a better option than extending the product line of the premium brand down to lower price points. It is possible that such a move would undermine the quality image of the premium brand. Even private branders such as Kroger have recognized this in its marketing of a premium Kroger brand of coffee and a separate Cost-Cutter flanking brand of coffee.

Sometimes price-point brands can be mismanaged. The original intent of General Motors was to sell Chevrolet, Pontiac, Oldsmobile, and Cadillac at increasing price

[26] Patricia Sellers, "How King Kellogg Beat the Blahs," *Forbes*, August 29, 1988, 54–64.
[27] James B. Treece, "The Nervous Faces around Kellogg's Breakfast Table," *Business Week*, July 18, 1994, 33.
[28] "Chrysler Mulls Cut-Rate Minivan," *USA Today*, April 26, 1990, 6B.

points, so the buyer would graduate up the brand/status ladder as his or her income increased. The plan went astray when these divisions became too independent. It led to Chevrolet offering economy cars, sports cars, luxury sports cars, and family sedans. The GM brands, designed to flank each other, ended up tearing each other's markets apart and opening opportunities for new foreign brands that had distinct and focused images.

In an industry where costs have been skyrocketing, DeVry, with its Keller Graduate School of Management, has price positioned its product. Its bachelor of science (BS) degree costs $24,000, half the cost of a major state university BS and one-third the cost of a private university BS.[29] DeVry's degree programs were accredited in 1977 and 1981, thus assuring a minimum quality standard. In addition, companies such as Hewlett-Packard, U.S. Robotics, Price Waterhouse, and Deloitte & Touche helped design the curriculum, and their association with DeVry adds to the perceived quality of the DeVry degrees. Finally, by DeVry operating year-round its degree takes three rather than four years, and the job placement of DeVry graduates is excellent: 90 percent within six months of graduation. When benchmarked against its competition, DeVry is so competitive on price for the quality of service provided that the New York State Department of Education is questioning DeVry's application to set up its university in Manhattan and Long Island. The state's concern is that DeVry is too competitive against existing state-subsidized universities!

Perhaps the best method of defending a market position is with an adaptive counterattack. This places a premium on the defender's ability to marshall its reserves (resources) and counterattack quickly. Following this strategy, the defender does not build island fortresses. Instead, it introduces new counterattacking products and brands when and if needed. This strategy depends on superior alertness and imitation-implementation speed. The way Tylenol defended itself against the entry of Datril into the over-the-counter painkiller market as described in the chapter introduction is a classic example of such a defense.

An example of how *not* to defend a market position is the behavior of the dominant players in the coffee market, Folgers, Maxwell House, and Hills Brothers. The gourmet coffee market innovated by Seattle-based Starbucks Corp. and imitated by others taught consumers that freshly ground coffee (ground in the store or at home) is to the big-brand ground coffee what fresh orange juice is to frozen concentrate—it has much more desirable taste.[30] Taste, rather than price and convenience, has become the determinant differentiating choice dimension. The major coffee makers did not recognize this until it was too late. Instead of launching their own wide variety of exotic, gourmet bean mixes, they spent their time and money promoting their brand names and reducing their prices.

Positioning Issues in Global Markets

The global marketplace can be viewed in many ways. The traditional way was to view each country as a separate market with separate import regulations, tariff regulations, distribution systems, and communication and transportation systems. The likely first venture into export marketing for a U.S. company is to an English-speaking country,

[29] Leslie Spencer, "Competition? Heaven Forbid," *Forbes*, January 2, 1995, 46–48.

[30] Kathleen Deviney, "For Coffee's Big Three, a Gourmet-Brew Boom Proves Embarrassing Bust," *The Wall Street Journal*, November 4, 1993, B4.

such as Canada or the United Kingdom, with very similar consumption cultures and competitive behavior.

Cross-Cultural Segmentation

The modern global marketing view is to see market segments first and countries second.[31] The question is not so much what is the market potential in Norway, but what is the sales potential among all the college-educated nineteen-year olds to twenty-nine-year olds in Europe or among those who support the strong environmental movement in Europe? Major companies are now describing and targeting global market segments and niches that transcend national boundaries. They may be reached physically using very different communication and distribution channels, but they are psychologically targeted the same way. They are assumed or identified by testing to share similar ideal product concepts. This allows a firm to design the same product line for such segments, and the product line is sold to the same targeted benefit segments in numerous countries.

The Americanization of world culture through science, entertainment, and business has helped to reduce the cultural differences, particularly among countries with highly educated populations.[32] This opens up the possibility for global segmentation and positioning, where the segmentation spreads across cultures rather than within cultures. In a way, even the word *culture* is inappropriate because the very process is premised on the assumption that cross-cultural differences are no longer as strong as within-culture differences. In short, cultures no longer follow national, political, or cultural borders as much as they did even one hundred years ago.

However, through and beyond the year 2000, many countries will still vary in their consumer wealth, buying power, price elasticity, experience with the product category, and competitive behavior. Consequently, relatively few products can be positioned exactly the same way across the global marketplace. Those that *can* normally have a strong symbolic or intangible image that transcends cultural, technological, and economic differences (for example, Coca-Cola has such an image). A special set of products are made in the United States whose positioning should be the same in all global markets. These products symbolize and embody the American culture. They include movies, rock music, television programs, clothing, outdoor equipment, motor bikes, and automobiles. These brands should maintain their American image positioning but also match their foreign competition on other performance dimensions.

Different Competitors—Different Positioning

Global marketing often requires the same product be positioned somewhat differently in each of its foreign markets, reflecting the positioning of the different competition in each market. So even though a global segmentation approach is used, the positioning and design of the product may have to be different because of competitive pressures and the higher consumer quality standards in some cultures. For example, U.S. products sold in Japan must be of the very highest quality because the Japanese market

---

[31] For an even more provocative view of the collapse of borders and the development of interlinked economies, see Kenichi Ohmae, *The Borderless World* (New York: Harper Perennial, 1990).

[32] Benjamin R. Barber, "Jihad vs. McWorld," *The Atlantic*, March 1992, 53–65.

demands higher quality in many product markets than do other global markets. This is true even if the determinant differentiation feature is the trendy American brand name (that is, a cultural symbol).

Triangulating Positioning Hunches in Foreign Markets

In global marketing, the most desirable positioning decision process is one in which the potential of the tentative strategy is confirmed from several different sources (such as experts, channels, suppliers, and consumers). It is called *triangulation* and helps increase the validity of the hunch. Triangulation is very important when deciding how to position a product or service in an unfamiliar foreign market. A cross-functional team must spend a great deal of its available time and effort arriving at a consensus on the fundamental choice of target segment (market niche) and basic positioning. The options will emerge as the environmental analyses are being undertaken in each foreign market, but the final choice should not be made until the planning environment reports are completed and thoroughly understood. This is because the planning team needs information about consumers and competition to identify the opportunities. Information about distribution channels may reveal whether a new product can reach and supply such new market niches.

Asymmetric Counterattacking

A standard counterattack to the entry of a new competitor from a foreign market (that is positioned close to a firm's established products) is for the firm to launch its own products in the foreign rival's home market. If it cannot, then it is at a severe positioning and competitive disadvantage.[33] The foreign competition can position, QFD, and lower prices in the new U.S. or other market, knowing that the great percentage of its sales are not at risk. In fact, it can subsidize the cost of entering the new market, because the major players in the new market cannot strike back at the entrant's major home market. This is why restricted access to the Japanese market has effectively given Japanese companies an unfair advantage in the United States—the U.S. manufacturers did not find it at all easy to strike back at the Japanese market. The major presence that Japanese companies have established in newly industrializing countries provides another uncontested profit source for these companies to use when attacking Western markets.[34]

Companies must understand and account for such asymmetries in the ease of counterattacking when responding to foreign competitors and when entering foreign markets. These asymmetries result, in part, from the fact that trade is freer in some political economies than it is in others.

Repositioning Skills in Global Markets

The entry of foreign clones into the United States PC market in the 1980s was somewhat predictable because foreign manufacturers had been supplying the parts for U.S.-branded computers for several years. What was surprising was their ability to launch

[33] Gary Hamel and C. K. Prahalad, "Do You Really Have a Global Strategy?" *Harvard Business Review*, July/August 1985, 139–48.

[34] Hamel and Prahalad, "Do You Really Have a Global Strategy?" 139–48.

sophisticated notepad PCs into the U.S. market in the early 1990s. Whereas previously they had been making lower cost, me-too imitations, now they were marketing uniquely positioned and differentiated portable PCs. The major U.S. brands of PCs were very slow to react to this repositioning of foreign competition—a serious mistake.

This repositioning example illustrates a competitive law developed by Charles Darwin. Native species (products) are never so perfectly adapted to their domestic ecology (market) that foreign species (products) cannot find a foothold. Indeed foreign products often take hold and come to dominate.[35] For example, Japanese TV manufacturers entered the U.S. market focusing on portability and designing small, high-quality, black-and-white and color televisions. They were able to use private-label distributors, such as Sears, who were very keen to help them sell their sets. Now they also own the big-screen television market.

Darwin's law of competitive positioning places a premium on reacting quickly to the entry of new foreign products and services. It should also encourage U.S. manufacturers to enter new global markets. As global competition increases, new, differentiated products are entering markets at an increasing rate. Often, strong positions in foreign markets are lost because senior executives neglect to pay attention to competitive threats in the specific market. This is an argument for decentralized decision making, which allows the local management to make major strategic repositioning decisions.

Evolution of Global Positioning in a Firm

As mentioned, a U.S. firm often starts to export to foreign markets that have (1) segments that desire the firm's current offering and (2) weak competition. As it gains international experience, the U.S. firm recruits local managers and expands its product line with products uniquely developed (positioned and QFD designed) for the foreign market.[36] Ultimately, a global positioning strategy evolves where the same positioning concepts and products are used to target similar segments that exists in all countries, domestic and foreign. Some foreign markets will still have uniquely positioned products in the product line catering to a unique culture-specific or climate-specific benefit segment or competitive situation. But when the benefit segment transcends culture and geography, then standardized positioning and design and the same differentiation theme can be used to promote to the target benefit segment. Such a global positioning strategy requires a commanding understanding of consumer behavior and the benefit segments in the many countries and cultures around the world.

Discussion Questions and Minicases

1. Many packaged-goods markets are mature, and executives bemoan the fact that their market has become a *commodity market*, meaning that the rival products are all close substitutes for one another. When price becomes the major factor that drives consumer choice among alternatives, then the product and image differentiation of competitive offerings has been reduced or lost altogether. In a commodity market, price is all-important, and the lowest cost producer is most competitive. It is called a Walrasian price-competition market. What can a seller do in such a market?
2. An enterprising manufacturer of filing-cabinet hanging folders makes them in several bright, modern colors rather than the standard, dull, cardboard green. Why was this a very successful and very profitable differentiation strategy?

[35] Philip Appleman, *Darwin* (New York: W. W. Norton, 1979).

[36] Susan P. Douglas and C. Samuel Craig, "Evolution of Global Marketing Strategy: Scale, Scope and Synergy," *Columbia Journal of World Business* (fall 1989): 47–59.

3. Please describe the unique positioning of each of the following brands.

BRAND	POSITIONING
Polaroid cameras	
Honda cars	
Apple computers	
Perrier mineral water	
Harvard Business School	
VISA credit card	

4. In the 1950s, Rayovac had a 35 percent market share of the consumer battery market, but later it missed the alkaline boat and slumped to a 6 percent share. New owners in the 1980s introduced six-to-eight-battery packages. Rayovac also designed new types of flashlights with superbright krypton lights and lithium power. These flashlights stay functional for up to ten years.[37] What usage segments did Rayovac target?
5. The advertisements below present samples of successful and unsuccessful differentiation. Identify which is which and explain why.

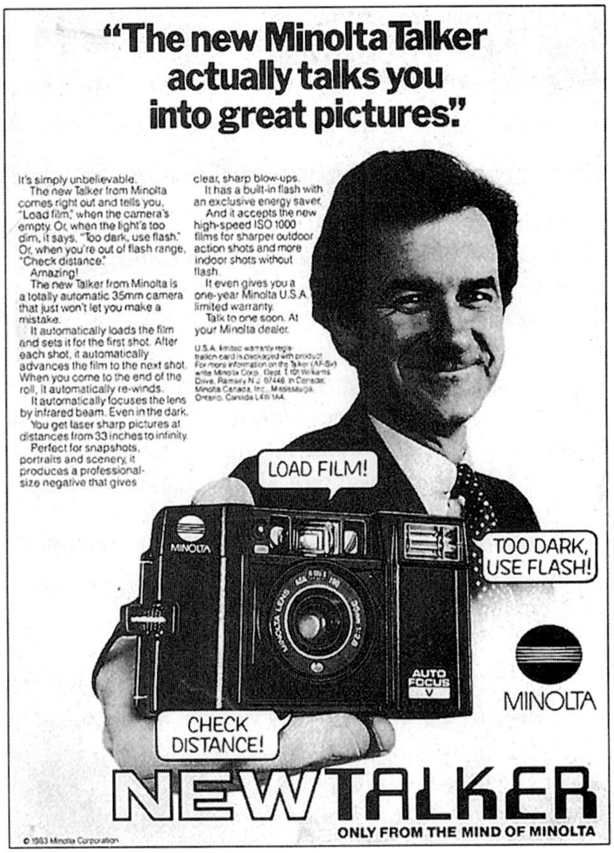

[37] Steve Weiner, "Electrifying," *Forbes*, November 30, 1987, 196–98.

SOURCE: Adapted from John W. Keon, "Product Positioning: TRINODAL Mapping of Brand Images, Ad Images, and Consumer Preference," *Journal of Marketing Research* 20 (November 1983): 380–92.

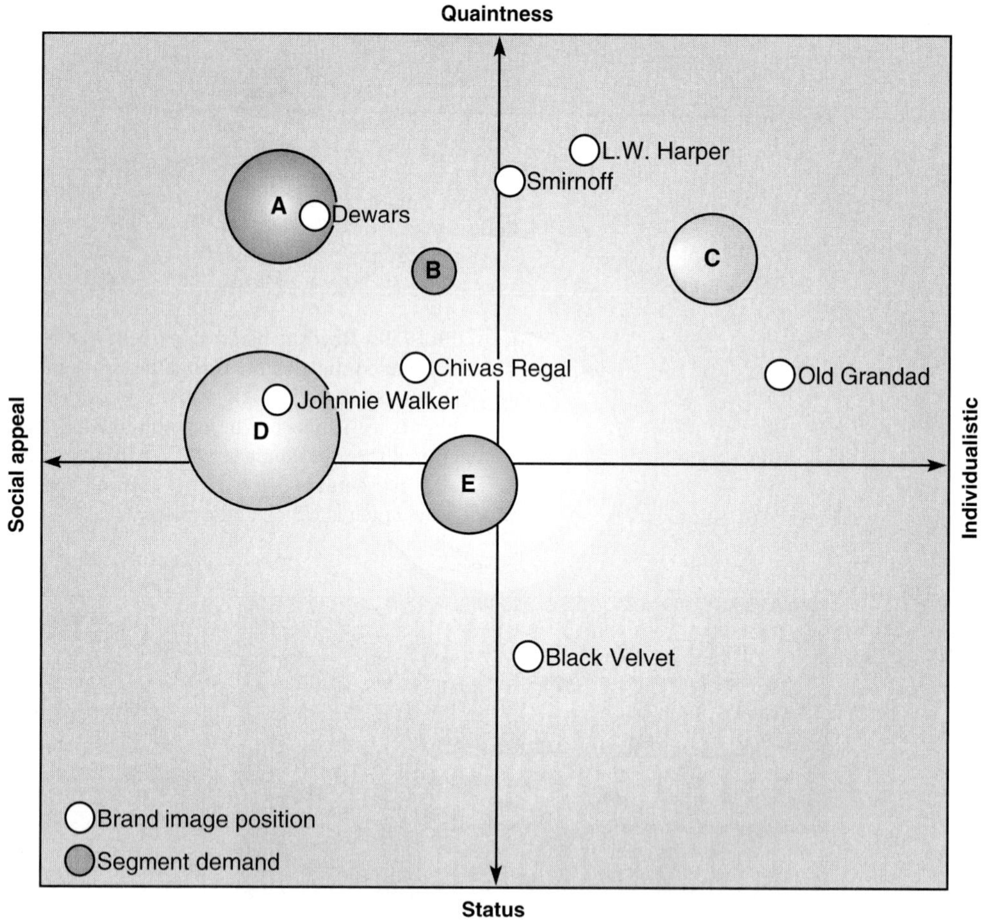

6. Segmentation analysis should reveal the user and usage segments that seek different benefits from a product. A seller can then position its offering differently to such segments. To segment A it will position its product as delivering the benefit most desired by segment A, and to segment B it will describe the way its product delivers the benefit most desired by segment B. Consider a manufacturer of buffered aspirin. How might it take the same product and position it differently to two separate segments? (Hint: Think about a recently discovered new benefit of aspirin.)
7. *Consumer Reports* evaluates brands and models of products. How might a market planner use such information to develop a positioning strategy? What are the risks of using this information?
8. Using the above figure, describe what each segment wants. Evaluate the positioning of each of the brands. In particular, how would you rate the positioning of Chivas Regal? Do you think it is profitable? Do you think it is vulnerable?
9. How might you apply QA analysis to a drug developed to help prevent infections in cancer sufferers whose immune systems have been weakened by chemotherapy? What statistical data would you need and how would you use the data? (Hint: How do you measure quality added in this case?)
10. Managers working for a developer building houses for professional couples in the $95,000–$125,000 price range could not agree on whether to build houses with three

SOURCE: Adapted from Richard R. Batsell and John B. Elmer, "How to Use Market-based Pricing to Forecast Consumer Purchase Decisions," *Journal of Pricing Management* 1, no. 2 (spring 1990): 5–15.

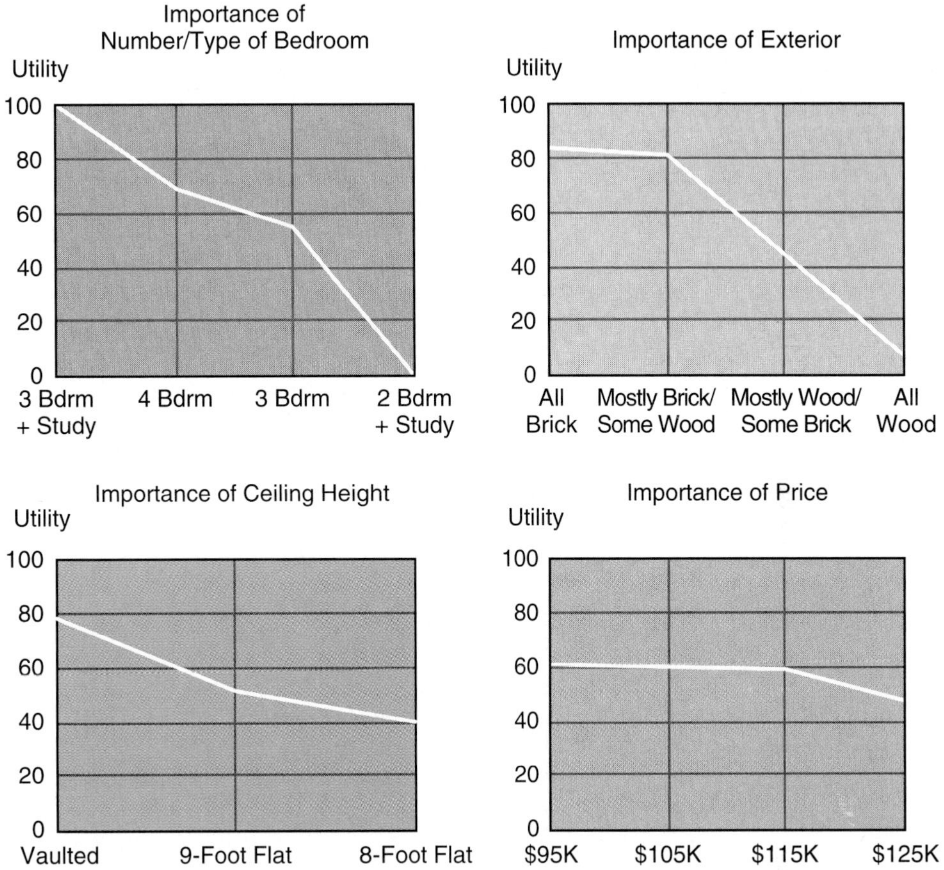

bedrooms, four bedrooms, or three bedrooms plus a study. How important was the exterior finish, the ceiling height, and the price? Seventy-one prospective buyers were recruited and divided into groups where they discussed drawings and details and then ranked, in order of preference, thirty-two cards describing hypothetical homes. The resulting conjoint analysis of their answers produced the added utility ratings of each feature (on a 100-point utility scale) presented in the graphs above. What type of house should the developers build? (Hint: Use your commonsense knowledge of building costs.) Do any of the features interact with each other?

11. Can you think of a positioning approach that is the opposite of quality-added analysis? Who uses it, and what does the company say in its promotion?

12. What are some of the basic reasons a positioning strategy fails?

13. Think of any new product positioning that combines benefits and features that previously were considered incompatible. Explain why the two features seemed implausible in the minds of some consumers.

14. Interpret the following breakfast-food competitive map on page 368 using the ideal-points information as well as the positioning of the different foods.

15. The demand equation for segment A is

$$Q_a = F_a(p_a, X_{1a}, X_{2a}, X_{3a}, \ldots X_{na})$$

SOURCE: Paul E. Green and Abba M. Krieger, "Recent Contributions to Optimal Product Positioning and Buyer Segmentation," working paper, Wharton School, University of Pennsylvania, 1989.

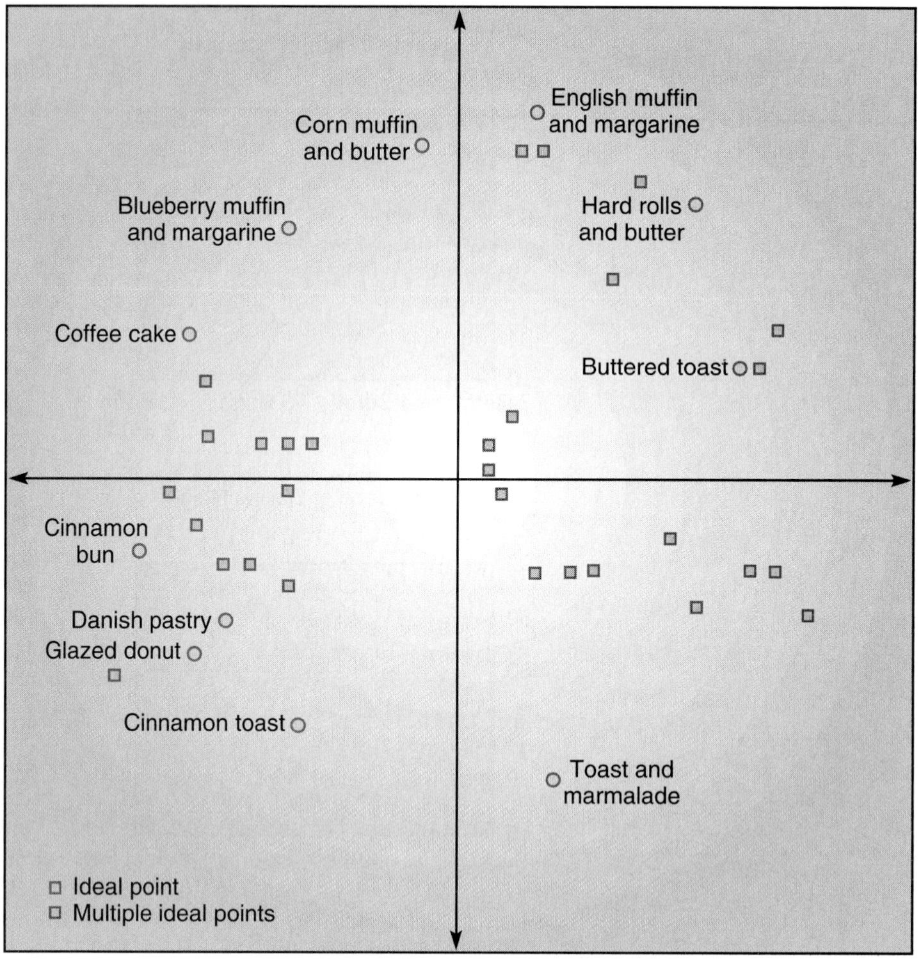

where Q_a is quantity demanded, F_a is the demand function unique to segment A, and p_a, $X_{1a}, X_{2a}, X_{3a}, \ldots, X_{na}$ are segment A's perceptions of price and the n features of the product. These perceptions determine demand through their influence via the F_a function.

When a seller modifies the demand of segment A by changing segment A's appreciation of specific features, what would change in the equation? When a seller changes its product design and product differentiation, what would change in the equation? If a seller changes its target to segment B, what would change in the equation? Illustrate your answer by describing a market where marketers have pursued these strategies (e.g., the personal computer market).

16. Trace the history of product positioning in the analgesic market described in the chapter opener by creating several adaptions of Figure 9.3 that present the competitive positioning in 1970, 1976, 1985, and 1994. Think about how the size of the benefit segments may have also changed.

17. For decades, Coca-Cola promoted its drink as "The Real Thing" and claimed that "Coke Is It"; both were intangible appeals to being genuine and traditional. In the 1980s, Pepsi made its first big differentiation move by claiming that it outperformed Coke on the core benefit: taste. The sustained taste-test attack was so successful that Coke changed its formula. Was Coke's repositioning a mistake?

18. Clorox, the major bleach marketer, entered the laundry detergent market with Clorox Super Detergent. It had previously been very successful with its niche marketing of Tilex mildew stain remover and Pre-wash stain remover. How should Clorox position its laundry detergent, and how should Procter & Gamble respond?

19. Do firms attack each other the way that armies do?

20. A cooperative dairy company in the Northeast developed a premium nutritional additive for cows. When administered according to a careful schedule, this Super Cowchow increases milkfat by 5 percent compared to using the standard Cowchow supplements currently available on the market. Quality-added tests at several major universities demonstrate that if a farmer now earns $500,000 in milk sales, using Super Cowchow could increase earnings to $525,000. The average farmer is currently spending $50,000 a year on one thousand sacks of Cowchow ($50 a sack). Super Cowchow costs an extra $5 a sack to manufacture.

What should be the price of Super Cowchow? What are likely to be the long-term economic effects of the use of Super Cowchow? In the light of the long-term effects, which farmers benefit most from using Super Cowchow? What influence will the special Super Cowchow feeding schedule have on dairy farmer behavior, and how should this influence marketing strategy?

21. The exhaust venting fans above the grills in most fast-food restaurants are on full speed all of the time, even when no cooking is going on. How would you establish the value to potential customers (such as Wendys or McDonald's) of an automatic device that switches the fans on only when they are needed? Where are the savings from using such a device? (Hint: Think carefully about what costs are really being controlled by this device.)

22. The feasible positioning analysis computes the cost of making and marketing the QFD positioning concept. It then includes these costs and the competitive price suggested by the QA analysis and inputs them into a TARGET spreadsheet. This spreadsheet computes what sales and market-share goals will have to be achieved to meet the input financial goals.

How is the realistic achievability of the required sales and market share then assessed? What is to stop an executive from lowering the required sales and market share by simply plugging in a higher price? How are costs likely to be fudged to make the project look more feasible? (Hint: Read the section on cost analysis in Chapter 18.)

23. Several market research techniques and visual frameworks are available to help make the positioning decision. One approach is to use a person-situation usage segmentation matrix (see following figure on page 370). The cells in the matrix represent potential target market niches. The potential depends on the uniqueness of the benefits sought by the users in the situation, how much of the product category is used by the particular group of users, and whether competitors are already serving the niche.

a) Consider the upper-left segment cell. Develop a new suntan lotion for the children/beach/boat market segment that has a new attractive benefit and feature.

b) Position the product lines of several brands in the matrix by studying their packaging and advertising. Where are the gaps in their positioning and product lines?

PERSON/SITUATION SEGMENTATION PROCEDURE

Step 1 Use observational studies, focus group discussions, and secondary data to discover whether different usage situations exist and whether they are determinant, in the sense that they appear to affect the importance of various product features and benefits sought.

Step 2 If Step 1 produces promising results, undertake a benefit, product perception, and reported market behavior segmentation survey of consumers. Measure benefits

(continued)

and perceptions by usage situation as well as by individual difference characteristics. Assess situation usage frequency by recall estimates or usage situation diaries .

Step 3 Construct a person/situation segmentation matrix using a StratMesh 2.0 template.. The rows are the major usage situations, and the columns are groups of users identified by a single characteristic or combination of characteristics.

Step 4 Score the cells in the matrix in terms of their submarket sales volume. The situation/person combination that results in the greatest consumption of the generic product would be scored 100.

Step 5 State the major benefits sought, important product dimensions, and unique market behavior for each nonempty cell of the matrix (some person types will never consume the product in certain usage situations).

Step 6 Position your competitors' offerings within the matrix. The person/situation segments they currently serve can be determined by the product feature they promote and other marketing strategies.

Step 7 Position your offering within the matrix on the same criteria.

Step 8 Assess how well your current offering and marketing strategy meet the needs of the submarkets compared to the competitors.

Step 9 Identify market opportunities based on submarket size, needs, and competitive advantage. Color code the cells accordingly.

Speculative Person/Situation Segmentation Matrix for Suntan Lotion

	Persons								
	Young Children		Teenagers		Adult Women		Adult Men		
Situations	Fair Skin	Dark Skin	Fair Skin	Dark Skin	Fair Skin	Dark Skin	Fair Skin	Dark Skin	Situation Benefits/Features
beach/boat sunbathing					summer fragrance				a. windburn protection b. formula and container can stand heat c. container floats and is distinctive (not easily lost)
home/ poolside sunbathing					combined moisturizer				a. large pump dispenser b. won't stain wood, concrete, or furnishings
sunlamp bathing					combined moisturizer and massage oil				a. designed specifically for type of lamp b. artificial tanning ingredient
snow skiing					winter fragrance				a. special protection from special light rays and weather b. antifreeze formula
person benefit/ features	special protection a. protection critical b. non-poisonous		special protection a. fit in jean pocket b. used by opinion leaders		special protection female fragrance		special protection male fragrance		

24. The following table presents a CANNIBAL spreadsheet, which can help a single-product company estimate the effect of introducing a second product. The first column estimates what will happen to annual sales and ROI if the new product is *not* introduced. It assumes that the firm will gain one whole percentage point of market share from its rivals, that the market will grow by 10 percent, and that the firm will gain 10 percent of the growth. The second column estimates what will happen to the old or existing product if the new product is introduced. It will gain half of a share point from rivals but will lose a whole share point to the new product (a quarter of its existing sales will be cannibalized). The market will grow by 15 percent (an extra growth because the new product and countering efforts of competitors will expand the size of the entire market), but the old product will only get 5 percent of this growth. The third column presents the expected performance of the new product. It is forecast to take two share points away from competitors, one share point from the old product, and a fat 50 percent of the entire market's growth. The fourth column adds columns two and three together to present the overall results.

a) The Marginal Analysis column presents the marginal effect of adding the new product. Describe the effects in a memo. In the memo, indicate which estimates or forecasts of the new product's performance you think the profit and ROI increase projections are most sensitive to (that is, what affects bottom-line income forecasts most?).

Product Line Extension Analysis: The Effect of Cannibalism

	SINGLE PRODUCT	EXTENDED LINE			MARGINAL ANALYSIS
		OLD	NEW	COMBINED	
Current market (000)	14.000			14,000	
Current share	4.0%	4.0%	0.0%	4.0%	
Forecast change in share:					
Share points gain/loss over competitors	1.0%	0.5%	2.0%	2.5%	1.5%
Share points gain/loss to own cannibalism		–1.0%	1.0%		
Forecast market growth	10.0%	15.0%	15.0%	15.0%	5.0%
Share of growth	10.0%	5.0%	50.0%	55.0%	45.0%
New market size (000)	15,400	16,100	16,100	16.100	700
New market share	5.5%	3.7%	9.1%	12.8%	7.4%
Sales volume (000)	840	595	1,470	2,065	1,225
Unit price	$2.00	$2.00	$1.75		
Total revenue (000)	$1,680	$1,190	$2,573	$3,763	$2,083
Gross margin/unit	$1.00	$1.00	$0.75		
Gross margin (000)	$840	$595	$1,103	$1.698	$857
Marketing costs (000)	$200	$200	$350	$550	$350
Allocated overhead (000)	$100	$100	$100	$200	$100
Profit before tax (000)	$540	$295	$653	$948	$407
Investment (000)	$4,500	$4,500	$1,000	$5,500	$1,000
Return on investment	12.00%	6.56%	62.25%	17.23%	40.75%

SOURCE: The above spreadsheet is an extension of a method discussed in Roger A. Kerin, Michael G. Harvey, and James T. Rothe, "Cannibalism and New Product Development," *Business Horizons*, October 1978, 25–31.

b) Use the spreadsheet to test the assumptions by changing each of the following estimates of the effect of adding a new item (reducing each one at a time, leaving the others the same) by 20 percent in an unfavorable direction: that is, the gain in share points from competitors would drop to 1.6 percent, the cannibalization would increase to 1.2 percent, market growth would be only 12 percent, share of growth would be 40 percent, and marketing costs would be $420,000. In the light of these "what-ifs," what forecasts have to be most accurate?

25. QFD analysis of a service requires the mapping of the service process script (activity sequence) and the identification of activities that most determine customer perceptions of service quality. This can be done using survey research and structural equations analysis, but most of the time the determinant quality activities are identified using executive experience and judgment. The following diagram is the activity sequence for a bank's installment lending service process:

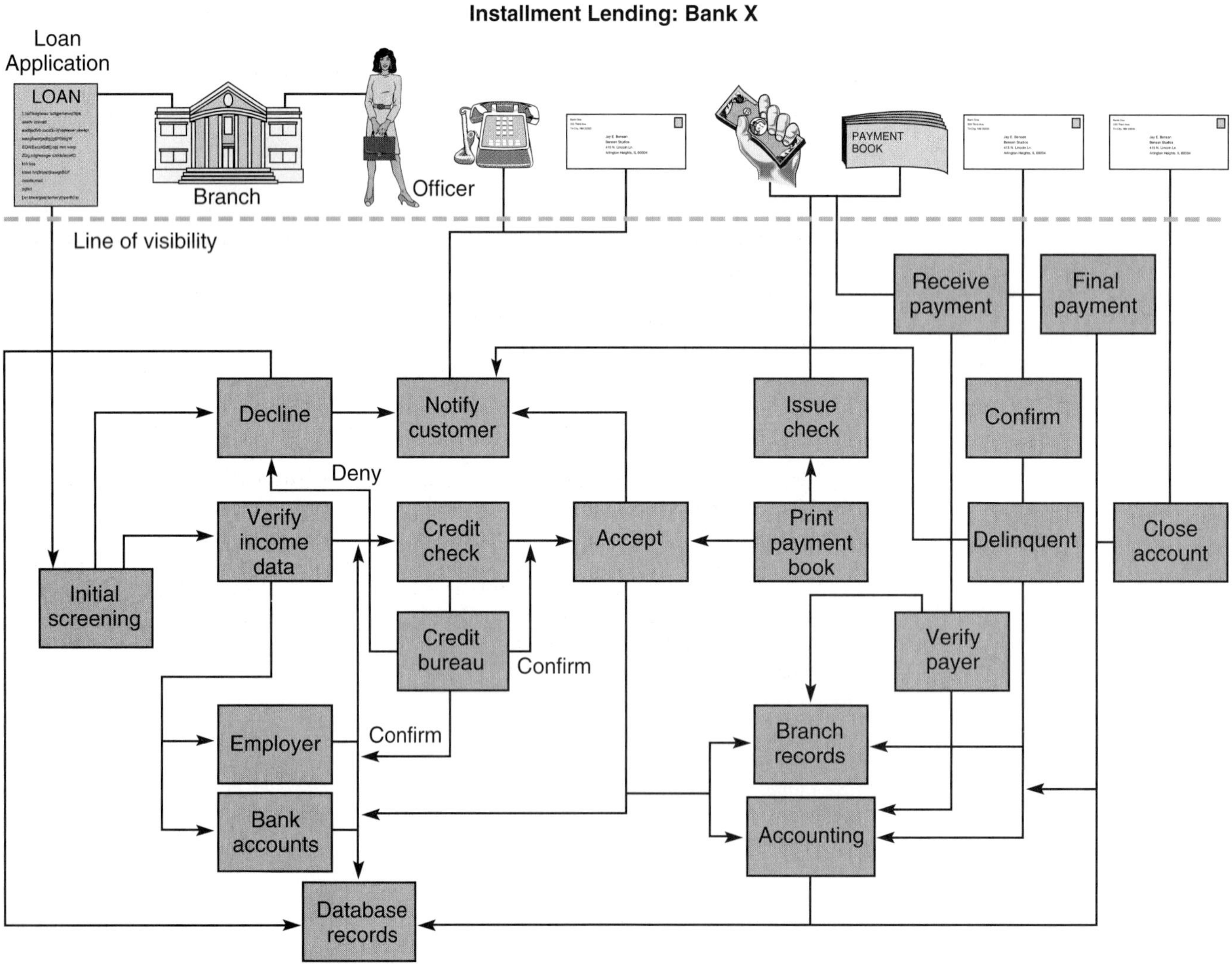

SOURCE: Adapted from *Automotive News*, September 15, 1986.

a) Which activities do you think most determine customer perceptions of overall service quality?

b) In recent years, some banks have attempted to speed loan approval. How could the activity sequence be modified to speed up approval?

26. In 1991, the Goodyear tire company introduced the Aquatred brand (see above advertisement). What is the target market and why is it such a clever, differentiated positioning? (Hint: Successful differentiation is in the minds of the consumer.) Which brand do you think will be most hurt by Aquatred? (Hint: Think of the different positioning appeals of brands.) The Aquatred actually works best with ABS braking systems. How might you use this information in future product-line positioning and branding strategies?

27. On page 374 are two competitive positioning maps of auto brands. The first also has segment ideal points identified. Give a name to each of the segments. Where would you place Acura? Where would you place Lexus and Infiniti? In the second map, what is the problem with Pontiac's ("we build excitement") efforts at repositioning? Do you think Oldsmobile's ("not your father's car anymore") campaign was a good one in the light of these maps?

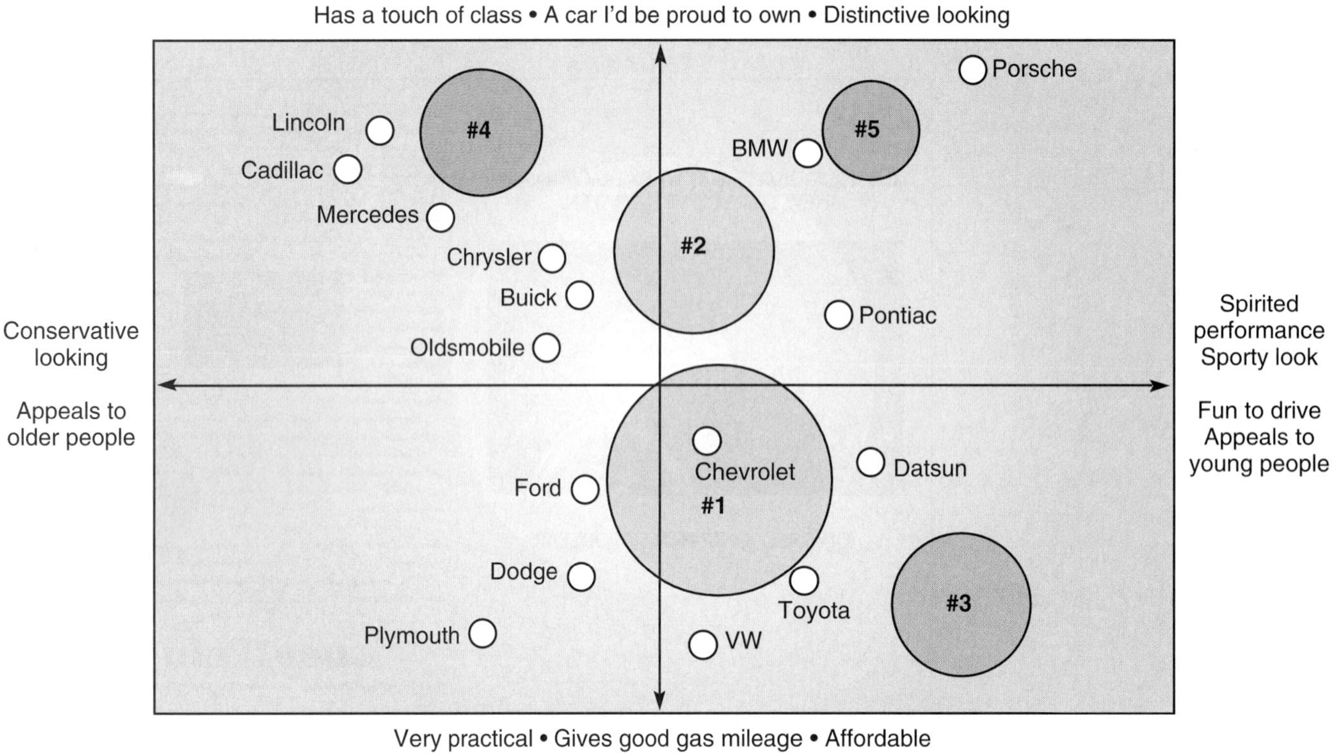

The Planned Repositioning of Pontiac

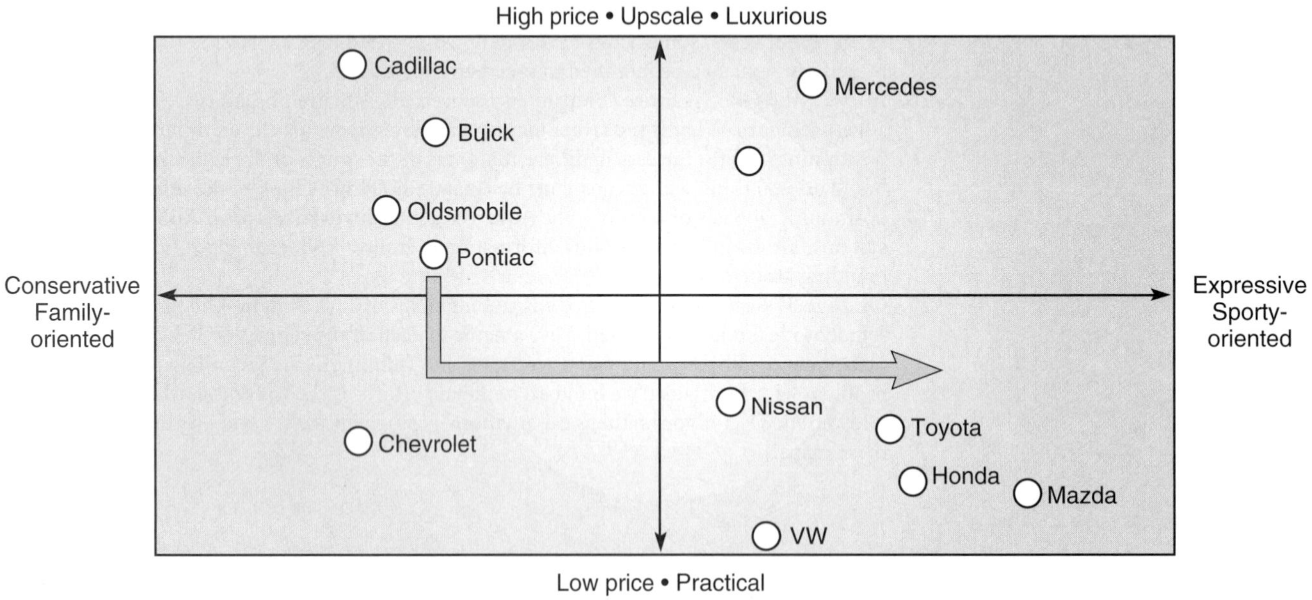

SOURCE: Adapted from John Koten, "Car Makers Use 'Image' Map as Tool to Position Products," *The Wall Street Journal*, March 22, 1984, 31.

When the product is right, you don't have to be a great marketer.

Lee Iacocca

The reason a lot of people do not recognize opportunity is because it usually goes around wearing overalls looking like hard work.

Thomas A. Edison

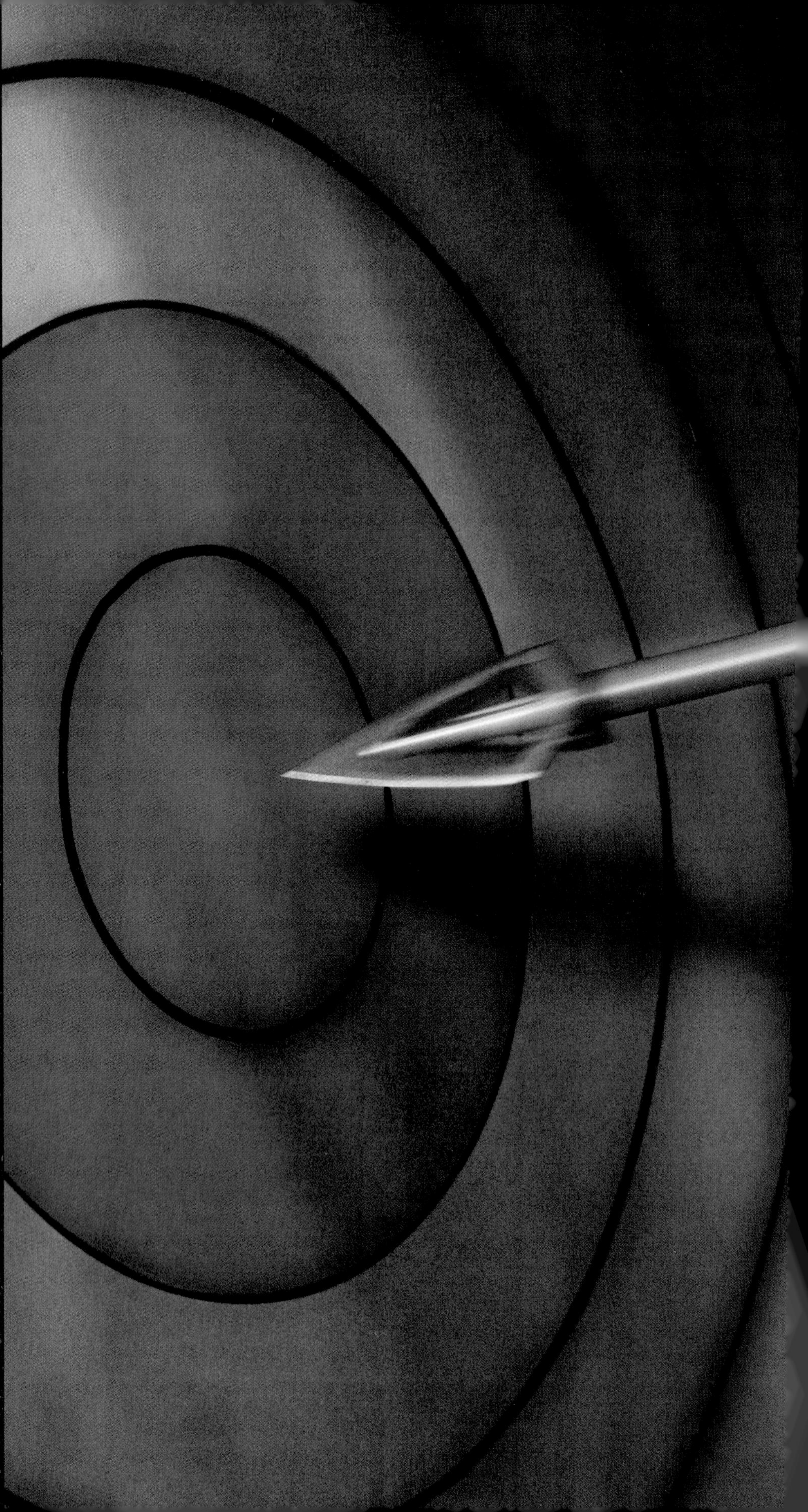

CHAPTER TEN

Product Development

Despite all of its quality improvements over the past decade and the tremendous success of the Taurus and Explorer, Ford Motor Co.'s product development process apparently still can be improved. By better pacing new product development that bunched up in 1995, by sharing the same chassis and basic parts across models, by reducing the number of parts, and by speeding up the boardroom to drawing-board to showroom development process from thirty-seven months to Toyota's twenty-four months, Ford expects to shave 30 percent off its annual $8 billion product development costs.[1] This extraordinary goal means that many firms can, like Ford, make huge improvements in their product development process.

The most important change in Ford's product development is the creation of five global development centers whose cross-functional teams will stay with their projects as long as the vehicles they design are in the market. Keeping the same team together and having them "own" the models through several redesigns has major learning benefits. The team learning that occurs in the initial design and development will mean much faster and smoother development processes in the future. When designing a new model, the team also can be planning design improvements for its future models, knowing that such plans will be implemented. This

future planning will help resolve disputes over whether to design an improvement into the current model or not at all. Such planning also will enable the team to experiment with some design issues and will give flow, consistency, coherence, and integrity to the design and development over several generations of models, which builds the competitive positioning of the model in the market and brand equity.

The advantages of centralizing Ford design is that the great majority of parts will be standardized to meet the most demanding of international safety and pollution standards. In many countries Ford vehicles will be higher quality than the law requires, but such quality will be a selling point and will come at no cost. Why? Because the adoption of a worldwide standard for major components of cars will mean savings in development cost and time and major savings in production costs. Suppliers working with the teams will receive larger orders but will be expected to also significantly reduce their prices.

Moreover, Ford and its suppliers will develop a company-wide core competence in learning about how to cost-effectively design and manufacture safety and environmentally friendly features into its vehicles. Its learning also should be faster than its competition because its goals will be more demanding, and its learning experience curve will be steeper because it will be producing more vehicles that meet such standards.

However, Ford's firing of thousands of development engineers and worldwide relocation of more than ten thousand employees around the new, centralized product development groups does have its risks. Will the greater centralization produce cheaper, higher quality cars faster but generate a stifling bureaucracy that produces blander "McFords"? Much depends on whether the new product development process produces performance and styling that truly does cater to local tastes and usage situations better and more inexpensively than the competition. Ford's international quality-tracking service will enable the tailoring of performance and styling to local needs. The question is Will the new development process listen to and respond to such information? Many firms will be watching Ford, hoping to learn how to design and develop in the global marketplace. ■

A major theme of this textbook is the constant development of new technology such as television into viable new products that make their own market segments and the continual modification and adaptation of existing products, which already are advances on

[1] Keith Naughton, "Ford's Global Gladiator," *Business Week*, December 11, 1995, 116–18.

previous products. Fast, efficient, effective product development has become the top priority of senior management over the past decade. The reason is that in increasingly competitive global markets where innovation/imitation cycles are speeding up, product development process improvement is a key, sustainable competitive advantage.

The theory of competitive rationality emphasizes continuous improvement of a firm's innovation/imitation processes, of the quality of its output, of the cost of its inputs, and particularly of learning how to speed up the process. Senior executives of highly successful growth companies agree with this theory. In a recent study, three-fourths of the CEOs of *Inc.* 100 or *Inc.* 500 manufacturers reported that adopting fast-track approaches to new product development would most improve their firms' competitiveness, compared to improving their manufacturing processes or making new plant and equipment purchases.[2]

These days the innovation process, from environment analysis to targeting/positioning to the launching of new products and services, not only needs to be fast but also needs to be a *continuous* business planning activity.[3] Management guru Tom Peters has suggested that a company should be producing at least a dozen ideas each month on how each of its product lines should be improved. The process in which everyone in the enterprise is constantly thinking of ways to make minor improvements to the product, service, or the production process is called *kaizen* in Japan, and it works. This chapter discusses the product development process and product development issues that are constantly being updated and reviewed using the informal *kaizen* approach and more structured activities.

Chapter Organization

The organization of this chapter is presented in Figure 10.1. How senior management create the product development culture is first described. This builds on the discussion in Chapter 4, which explained how a mission statement, financial goals, and the corporate culture direct product market planning. A product development blueprint is then presented that contains five stages. This recommended process also builds on previous chapters. The product market-environment analysis is initiated at the idea-generation stage, expanded in the concept development stage, and continually updated throughout the development process. The target market and competitive positioning defines the concept and leads to product/service specifications. It has been argued that a large part of the brilliant success of Japanese companies has been due to their skill at this step in the product development process. They possess "the ability to convert demand from a vague set of distant wants into well-defined products."[4] If the product concept, specifications, and financial feasibility are approved, then the development team carefully plans how to proceed with the design of the product and making and testing prototypes.

---

[2] Peter R. Dickson, Wendy Schneier, Peter Lawrence, and Renee Hytry, "Managing Design in Small High-Growth Companies," *Journal of Product Innovation Management* 12, no. 5 (1995): 406–14.

[3] Tom Peters, *Thriving on Chaos* (New York: Alfred A. Knopf, 1987); and "Strategy Follows Structure: Developing Distinctive Skills," *California Management Review* 26 (spring 1984): 111–25. See also George S. Day and Robin Wensley, "Assessing Competitive Advantage: A Framework for Diagnosing Competitive Superiority, *Journal of Marketing* 52 (April 1988): 1–20.

[4] See Fumio Kodama, *Emerging Patterns of Innovation: Sources of Japan's Technological Edge* (Boston, MA: Harvard Business School Press), the product/service specifications, 8. It is called *demand articulation* in Japan, and it actually involves a two-step process from market data to product concept (in this book's terms, fitting product positioning to market environment facts in Chapter 2) and from product concept to developmental project (in this book's terms, QFD analysis in Chapter 8).

Figure 10.1 Chapter Organization

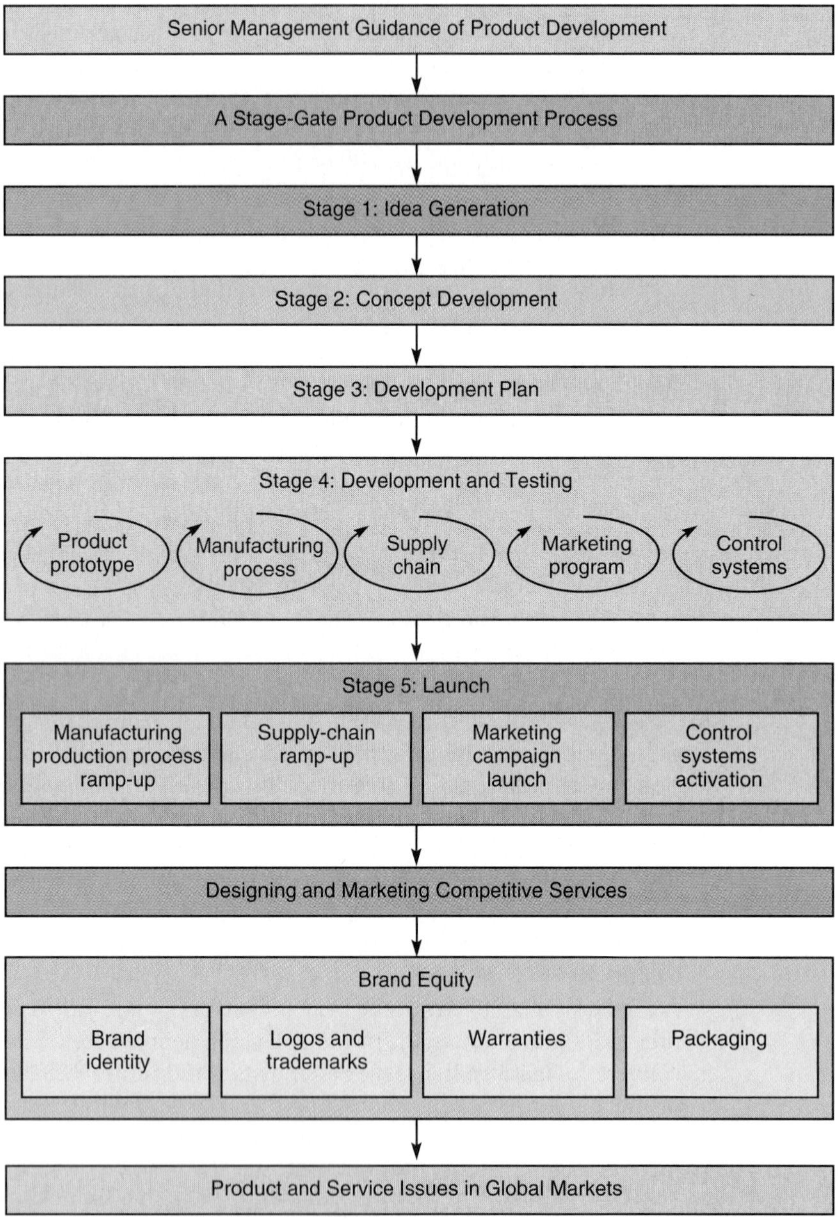

How senior management create the product development culture is first described. A product development process blueprint is then presented which contains five stages. A section on the unique issues associated with service design and development follows the presentation of the product development process. As a team moves through the product/service development process it has to make decisions about naming and branding the product/service and dressing the product/service (designing packages and labels which include warranties). Sections discussing such marketing programs wrap up the chapter which concludes with a discussion of product and service issues in global markets.

At the same time, other subteams work on designing the manufacturing process, the marketing plan and programs, designing control systems, and updating costs, sales, and profitability forecasts. Such concurrent engineering of the product and processes is far superior to a sequential product development process, but it takes careful, up-front planning and coordination to make it work. The next stage in the development process is the actual development of a series of product or service prototypes that are tested in the lab and in the field. Finally, the production and marketing campaigns are started, and the product is launched. After the launch, the cycle starts again with new ideas for the next generation of products or services being screened.

As will be shown, for some products that are very new or risk being eclipsed by competitors' new products, it may be a smarter development strategy to launch the product quickly (rather than go through several more prototype testing cycles), make the early market, learn what design features can be improved, and quickly launch several new models that incorporate the desired features and benefits (see the Rationality in Practice box). This design-on-the-fly approach enables a firm to create a path dependency in consumer demand that competitors have to follow.

A section on the unique issues associated with service design and development follows the presentation of the product development process. Although much of the recommended product development process can be applied to designing and developing services, special problems occur that a service development team has to consider. A great deal has been written about the shift in the U.S. economy away from traditional manufacturing and toward services. Services such as medical care, entertainment, education, travel, accommodation, home repairs, communication, information processing, investment, and business and legal consulting have greatly expanded in the past two decades. The marketing of services has come under the spotlight, because demand for services has grown and the development and marketing of services in the past was primitive compared to major and packaged goods. Many Americans remain dissatisfied with the service they get not only from service companies but also from manufacturers of products they buy and the retailers that sell them.[5] In addition, worker productivity in the service sector has increased very little over the past fifteen years compared to that in manufacturing, wages are low, and career prospects are limited. In short, the service sector has much room for improvement through the development of existing and new services.

As a team moves through the product/service development process, it has to make decisions about naming or branding the product/service and dressing the product/service (designing packages and labels that include warranties). Sections discussing such marketing programs wrap up the chapter, which concludes with a discussion of product and service issues in global markets.

Senior Management Guidance of Product Development

Success in product development requires a complex interaction of all a firm's functions. Accordingly, it is senior management's responsibility to direct this activity if the product development process is to produce successful products and services both

---

[5] Jeffrey A. Trachtenberg, "Shake, Rattle and Clonk," *Forbes*, July 14, 1986, 71–74; Stephen Koepp, "Will Somebody Help Me?" *Time*, February 2, 1987, 48–57; and "Making Service a Potent Marketing Tool," *Business Week*, June 11, 1984, 164–70.

Rationality in Practice

Necessity Is the Mother of *Invention*

Sometimes it is not possible for a formal, sequential stage-gate process to produce information about customer needs and product benefits early in a product development process. If the market is not yet well defined or the technology is still in its infancy, it may not be possible for consumers to know what they want and what they think of particular features. This makes it difficult to develop a competitive position and product/service specifications. The cross-functional team may wish to pursue an alternative approach, called an *exploratory approach*, which allows learning about customers in an emerging market.

Interviews with marketing managers and founders of technical companies suggest that several approaches are used to develop marketing strategies for new products:

1. *Exploratory.* With this approach, the company gets a product to market quickly, so it can receive feedback from customers. The company revises the strategy rapidly and gets a new version of the product launched, usually to a somewhat different and larger market. The company may go through several iterations of the product and positioning strategy. This approach involves informal customer contact while the strategy is being developed initially and also after the product is offered.
2. *Experimental.* With this approach, all portions of the marketing strategy are developed and experimentally tested before the launch, using both formal and informal market research. The company launches the product with the idea that it is the right product for the market and does not expect to make major adjustments to the strategy after the launch.
3. *Incremental.* This approach is often used in markets where a company has an established technology and a built-in relationship with an existing group of customers. The approach builds on the established base to offer this customer group more and more value. New products are designed based on extensive customer contact. The product is offered and little adjustment is needed after the launch.
4. *Over-the-wall.* This is the direct antithesis of the experimental approach. The company develops a product with little or no input from customers. The product is still believed to be the right product for the market, but this is often a matter of speculation until customers in the market either buy the product or not.*

Under conditions of high uncertainty about consumer acceptance and how the market may evolve, it is better to maintain

efficiently and quickly. Senior management have to back up the direction they provide in mission statements and goals with resources and their own timely participation in the key go/stop and spending decisions. But, most important, they must create informal and formal cross-functional development teams that behave as if they are entrepreneurs (i. e., running their own business). Note that senior management's role is to guide, support, and champion the team's efforts (as discussed further in Chapter 17, on marketing organization and implementation) but *not* to direct the specific design solutions.

An example of such guidance is for senior management to encourage and reward striving for simple solutions—simpler products produced by a simpler development process. The belief in and pursuit of the *simplicity principle* (good design is simple design) may be otherwise known as *KISS* (keep it simple stupid!). It can produce quite remarkable achievements. IBM's new Selectric typewriter has fewer than one-twentieth the number of parts the old Selectric model had, primarily because all of the screws, nuts, and bolts were replaced by clips and fasteners built into the plastic casings. Many products are now assembled from a few modules that can be much more simply assembled, repaired, upgraded, and recycled. Designing simplicity into products not only flexibility and learn quickly through improvisation and experience.[†] Hence, the exploratory approach is recommended in such a case.

The exploratory approach involves the rapid development of an initial prototype using considerable customer contact during the initial concept development and design stage, several prototype testing cycles, and the quick launching of a first version of the product to a relatively small initial market. In a sense, the repeated prototype testing continues on into the marketplace. Market feedback is used immediately ("real-time" information) to redesign the product in order to launch a revised version in a form that customers have indicated has a high level of value to them.

This rapid succession of new generations of products in the market creates and shapes demand along a new path dependency. Each incremental model improvement brings more consumers into the market, and new market segments start to emerge that can be further developed by product-line extensions. The rapid development and launch of new models also generates a positive cash flow faster and teaches the firm how to develop products faster. But most important, although such rapid product development seems very risky, it is usually less risky than the more traditional approach, which tries to "create" the market for the product with one big bang.

An extreme example of the use of this approach was the Apple Macintosh computer. Apple can argue legitimately, with only minimal exaggeration, that the Macintosh changed the world. It did so by producing an initial product (the "Lisa"), by listening to the market (thumbs down—way too expensive), and by producing subsequent revisions (much cheaper and more powerful) as fast as possible to rectify shortcomings identified by customers.[‡] Although the use of the exploratory approach for the Macintosh computer was apparently not entirely intentional, it still illustrates the capability this approach has to establish a product or product line with great impact. Smaller companies complete the same sort of process all the time with less dramatic but certainly successful results. However, some products, such as drugs and the Boeing 777, cannot be developed using the exploratory approach for obvious safety reasons.

[*] Joseph J. Giglieranco and M. Jeffery Kallis, "Marketing Strategy Development in New Products and New Companies in Technical Industries," *Proceedings*, American Marketing Association Summer Educators Conference, 1991, 504–11.

[†] Shona L. Brown and Kathleen M. Eisenhardt, "Product Development: Past Research, Present Findings, and Future Directions," *Academy of Management Review*, (20, no. 2 1995): 343–78; Kathleen M. Eisenhardt and Behnam N. Tabrizi, "Accelerating Adaptive Processes: Product Innovation in the Global Computer Industry," *Administrative Science Quarterly* 40 (1995): 84–110; and Christine Moorman and Anne S. Miner, "Walking the Tightrope: Improvisation and Information Use in New Product Development," Report No. 95-101, Marketing Science Institute, Cambridge, Massachusetts, 1995.

[‡] Guy Kawasaki described this exploratory approach as "Lead, take a shot, listen, respond, then lead again." Kawasaki, *The Macintosh Way* (Glenview, IL: Scott, Foresman, 1990), 54–56.

reduces costs and defects but also reduces product development time.[6] In short, design simplicity produces what competitive rationality and TQM strive to achieve: higher quality, lower cost design, and manufacturing processes that are completed faster. The simplicity principle is now also extended into product-line design, where the same part or module is used across all products in the line.

Simplicity is also the key to improving the speed and quality of the product development process by eliminating or simplifying cumbersome and overelaborate activities.[7] Why prepare hard-copy blueprints of computer designs? Why prepare and circulate hardcopies of electronic progress reports? Have the development team talk continuously to a few lead users, and watch focus groups discuss concepts and evaluate

[6] Abbie Griffen, "Modeling and Measuring Product Development Cycle Time Across Industries," Report No. 95–117, Marketing Science Institute, Cambridge, Massachusetts 1995.

[7] See Murray R. Millson, S. P. Raj, and David Weilemon, "A Survey of Major Approaches for Accelerating New Product Development," *Journal of Product Innovation Management* 9 (1992): 53–69; Necmi Karagozoglu and Warren B. Brown, "Time-Based Management of the New Product Development Process," *Journal of Product Innovation Management* 10 (1993): 204–15; and E.F. McDonough III and F. C. Spital, "Quick-Response New Product Development," *Harvard Business Review* 62 (1984): 52–53.

prototypes, rather than have a market research contractor undertake the studies and prepare elaborate reports. Give senior management continuous access to electronic progress reports (such as those contained in decision support software such as StratMesh 2.0), rather than stage elaborate approval presentations that take weeks to prepare and schedule.

In some firms senior management have found that simplicity is achieved by setting very high expectations that force the abandonment of standard operating procedures or conventional ways of thinking about design. For example, one of the reasons why the Canon AE-1 single-lens-reflex camera was such a success was that senior management asked the team to design a lightweight, easy-to-use, compact, automatic-exposure camera that had to be priced 30 percent lower than the prevailing price for such a camera! This led to the design of an electronic brain made by Texas Instruments, to modularized production, and to a 30 percent reduction in parts compared to the competition.[8] Similarly, a goal of halving the product development time often forces a radical rethinking of the entire process, rather than incremental changes in the existing development process. Very demanding goals break mind-sets. They also force a rate of continuous improvement and simplification that otherwise might be achieved by the organization only if it had its back to the wall.

In Chapter 4 the learning-process hierarchy theory emphasized that the focus of senior management and organization learning should be on continual improvement of the product development process. A benchmarking study of the critical success factors in new product development support this priority.[9] Designing and implementing the right development process is more important than any other factor in determining the success of a product in the market. It has been tried and proven in the marketplace that a version of the following product development process is more likely to produce success than any other process.

A Stage-Gate Product Development Process

The recommended "stage-gate" product development process is illustrated in Figure 10.2a. A stage-gate process involves progressive stages where the outcomes at the end of each stage are compared against preestablished criteria. When the deliverables for that particular stage meet or surpass the minimum levels for the criteria, the project gets the "green light" to pass through the stage gate to the next stage.

The Rationality in Practice box, "Necessity Is the Mother of Invention," points out a major problem with overplanning the product development process in very new product markets. Another potential drawback to a stage-gate system can be that the system is perceived to be rigid and inflexible. An alternative to the stage-gate method is the introduction of "fuzzy" stage gates (Figure 10.2b), in which the project is allowed to conditionally pass on to the next stage, even though all of the criteria for passage have not yet been met. Sometimes it is difficult to meet all of the prespecified criteria at a stage gate, such as the environment or safety regulations and codes. Rather than make a project wait two months for such a report, the project is given a conditional "go," with the condition being something like "the incomplete tasks must

[8] Hirotaka Takeuchi and Ikujiro Nonaka, "The New Product Development Game," *Harvard Business Review*, (January-February, 1986), 137-146.

[9] Robert G. Cooper and Elko J. Kleinschmidt, "Benchmarking the Firm's Critical Success Factors in New Product Development," *Journal of Product Innovation Management* 12 (1995): 374–91.

Figure 10.2 **The Stage-Gate Development Process**

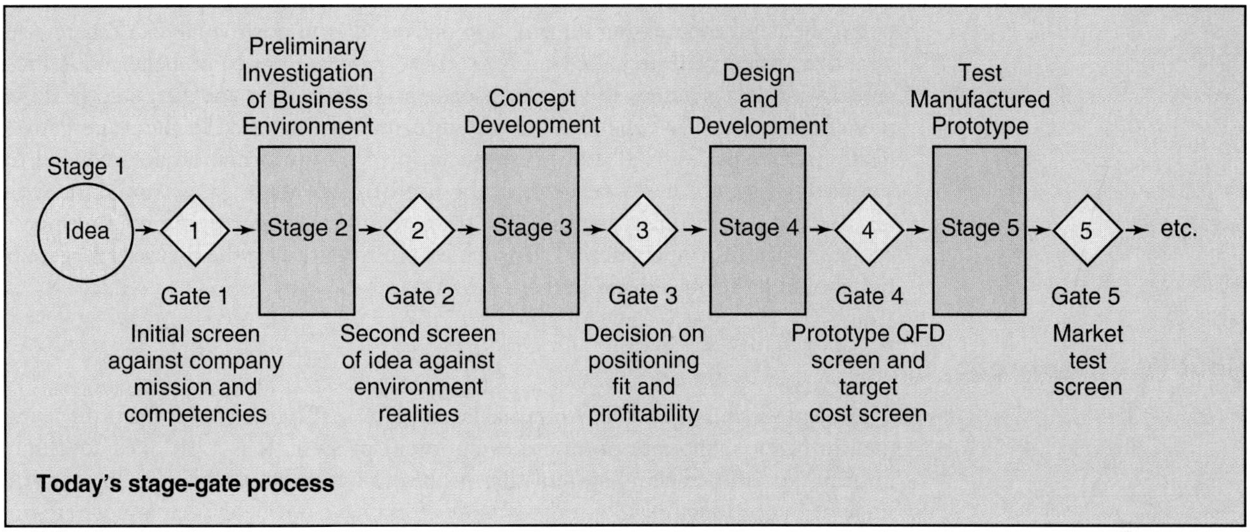

(a)

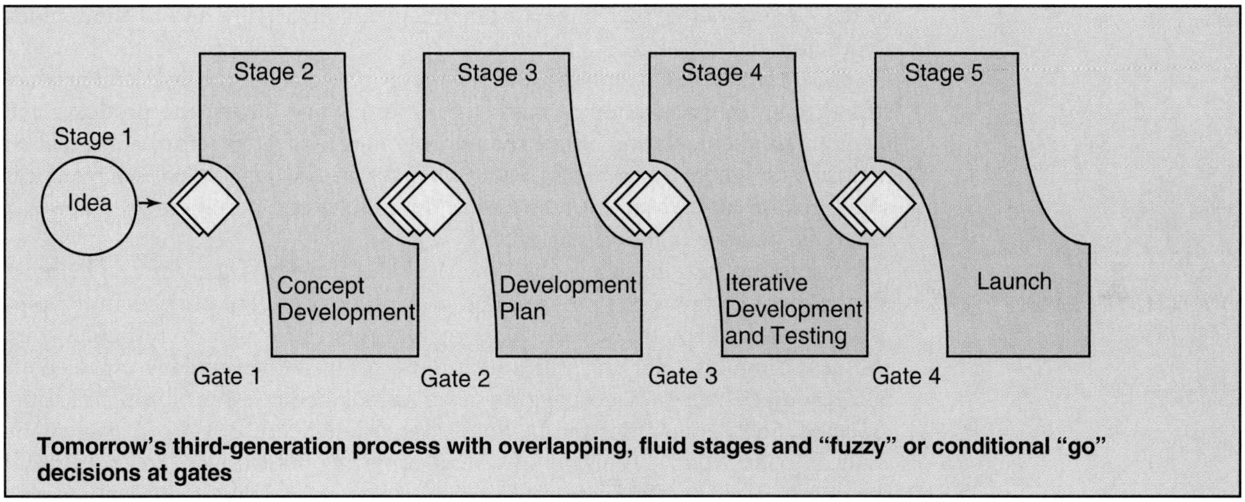

(b)

According to the product development expert Robert Cooper, the stage-gate process used by many firms today follows the process at the top of this figure. Tomorrow's stage-gate process will be more flexible, allowing the project to partially pass through a gate. This speeds up the whole project's progress. This next-generation stage-gate process also incorporates concurrent development of the product prototype, manufacturing process, supply chain, marketing program, and systems controls during Stage 4. In addition much iterative development and testing/retesting of prototypes, prospective supplier components, manufacturing processes, marketing programs, and control systems is likely.

Although most of the "development" occurs in Stage 4, it is preceded by careful targeting/positioning of the concept, market feasibility analysis, and Stage 3, where the cross-functional team plans how to proceed. This involves the breaking down of the project into subtasks that can be undertaken in parallel by subteams and agreement on coordination, consultation, and cooperation processes among the subtasks and subteams. Often the actual subtask cannot be planned out in detail because much depends on what is learned from the first prototype development-testing cycle and so on. In more general terms, specific improvisation cannot, by definition, be planned.

SOURCE: Adapted from Robert G. Cooper, "Third-Generation New Product Processes," *Journal of Product Innovation Management* 11 (1994): 3–14.

be finished and the missing information delivered (and positive) by XYZ date. Otherwise the project will be halted on XYZ date."[10] What has to be balanced is the cost and risk of delays versus the risk of proceeding. As long as the next step in development is not crucially dependent on the information reviewed at the stage gate, such flexibility makes sense. If, however, crucial pieces of information are reduced to assumptions that are never rechecked, the use of fuzzy stage gates should be avoided. Similarly, if conditional passage to the next stage becomes creeping commitment to a project, without proper support for such commitment, then the fuzzy stage-gate practice should be reviewed and perhaps curtailed.

Project Management

The StratMesh 2.0 Project Organizer template in Figure 10.3 helps a firm implement a fuzzy stage-gate product development process. It is a product development information and tracking system that monitors what criteria have been met at each stage of the product development, what criteria have not been met, and where uncertainty exists as to whether the criteria has been met or not. The template also captures the explanation for the color-coded status revealed by "mousing" the cell of interest. This matrix also visually helps the team and its leader to cognitively "mesh a variety of factors together to create an effective, holistic view and to communicate it to others."[11]

The development team also has to be prepared to adapt the tasks and product design through improvisation as market realities change during the product development and implementation of marketing programs. The latest information that comes in from intelligence generators about changes in the market environment can be added to the StratMesh 2.0 template. This enables the development team to react faster and better to a moving market.[12]

A tracking system such as the StratMesh 2.0 Project Organizer also helps senior management compare the progress and potential of different projects in the pipeline using a standardized framework. This enables them to reallocate resources to teams and new products emerging with much more promise than initially expected and to take resources from projects bogging down or looking far less promising than initially expected. Such evaluations can be done at any time because senior management can study the StratMesh 2.0 matrix of several projects unobtrusively and read the latest progress reports and evaluations on each project at any time in real time:—that is, while a team is using StratMesh 2.0 to exchange more information and make further decisions. Each of the stages in the fuzzy stage-gate process now will be discussed in detail (Figure 10.2b).

---

[10] Robert G. Cooper, "Third-Generation New Product Processes," *Journal of Product Innovation Management* 11, no. 1 (1994): 3-14.

[11] Shona L. Brown and Kathleen M. Eisenhardt, "Product Development: Past Research, Present Findings, and Future Directions," *Academy of Management Review*, 20, no. 2 (1995), 370. This quote actually defines what Brown and Eisenhardt call product development leadership vision, but such a StratMesh 2.0 product development template would enhance this cognitive ability whether the user is a senior manager, the product champion, team leader, or team member.

[12] Henry Mintzberg and J. A. Waters, "Tracking Strategy in an Entrepreneurial Firm," *Academy of Management Journal* 25 (1982): 465–99; Kathleen M. Eisenhardt, "Making Fast Strategic Decisions in High-Velocity Environments," *Academy of Management Journal* 32 (1989) 543–76; and Shona L. Brown and Kathleen M. Eisenhardt, "Product Innovation as Core Capability; The Art of Dynamic Adaptation," working paper, Stanford University Computer Industry Project, March 1995.

Figure 10.3 The StratMesh 2.0 Project Organizer

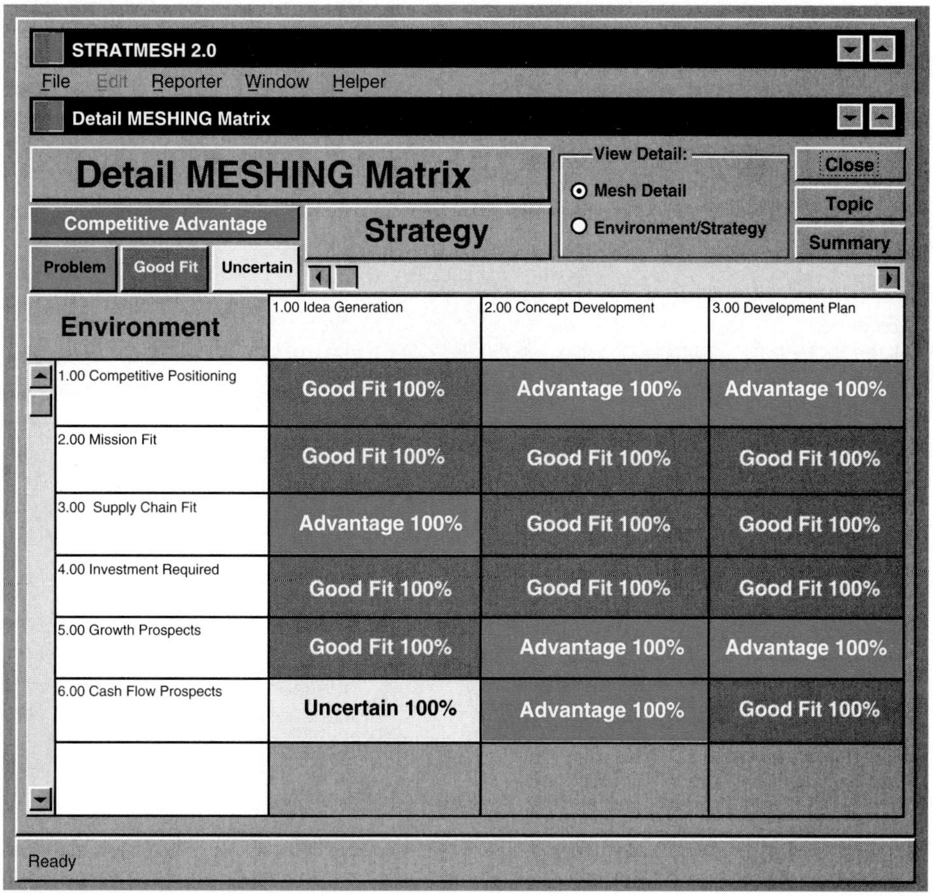

The StratMesh 2.0 software can be used to track progress through the various stages and stage-gates developed for a project. The rows in Figure 10.3 reflect the issues that have to be considered throughout the project and the sign-on and sign-off responsibilities of functional groups. In Figure 10.3 only a portion of a progress matrix is presented. Notice that the development and testing stage has been subdivided into prototype development and testing, manufacturing-process development and testing, marketing-program development and testing, and so on. This reflects the concurrent development of these activities. The subteam working on manufacturing-process development reports on its progress, and the other subteams are expected to report their progress and cross-check each other's progress, specifically what the current issues are behind the changes in cell color. Senior management can be similarly passively monitoring progress and stepping in when they think they can help.

A StratMesh 2.0 product-market portfolio template also can be created for senior management to review progress on different product development projects (see the portfolio analysis section in Chapter 4). This will assist senior management in making resource reallocation decisions when the development of some projects becomes more promising than expected and the development of others becomes mired in problems.

Stage 1: Idea Generation

At the idea-generation stage, and throughout the product development process, it is essential that any "not-invented-here" attitudes in the organization are eliminated. A

Figure 10.4 **Sources of Innovation/Imitation Ideas**

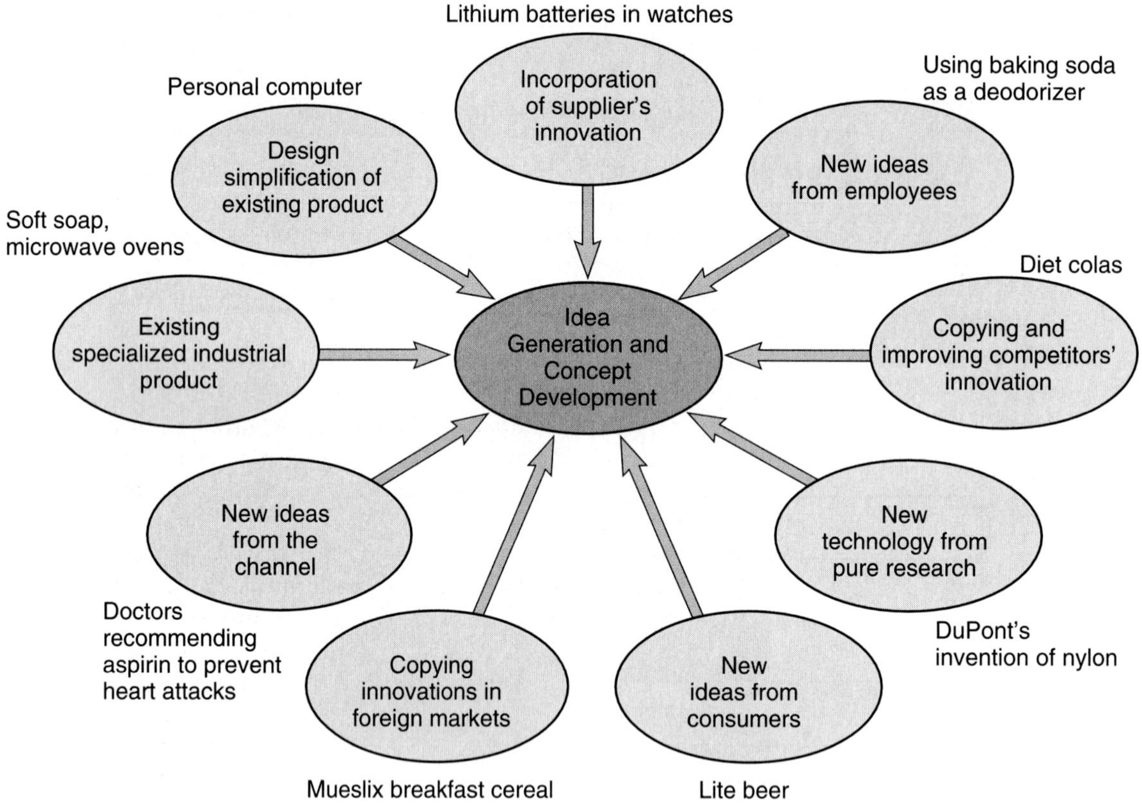

Some companies only develop new products from in-house R&D. They do not even seek out the suggestions of all of their employees. As can be seen from this figure, those firms are at considerable risk of losing their markets to competitors who seek new ideas from all possible sources.

not-invented-here attitude is that any idea not originating within the R&D group is not even considered. It must be replaced with a "beg, borrow, and steal" attitude by rewarding a team (and all employees) for creatively using a wide range of sources for ideas (see Figure 10.4) on designing and developing the product. Particularly, the firm must take the best ideas of competitors' new products and advance them, if only because consumers will expect it. This is the very essence of the innovation process and why *innovation* as used colloquially is actually a double word. It means both innovation and imitation or innovation/imitation.

Screening Ideas

Somehow these new product ideas must be screened to determine which ones will receive the green light to go to the next stage of development. Two idea-screening stage-gate processes have been proposed. A firm may choose to screen batches of ideas all at once at given intervals, or it may choose to screen ideas on an ad hoc basis when one or more ideas has been developed enough for consideration. Both approaches have their strengths and drawbacks. Screening at periodic intervals allows better comparison of the relative merits of the various ideas. It also allows a somewhat more rational allocation of the available resources. Problems arise, though, from the variability in rates of progress on the development of new ideas. Some new ideas may wait several months before they are reviewed, and others actually may be killed prematurely because they were prepared too quickly for idea-screening review simply because the review date was fast approaching. Such behavior is competitively irrational.

Ad hoc reviews make sense when it is important to move new ideas quickly from the idea stage to business planning stage. In competitive environments where time to market is important, a quick decision to move ahead may be crucial. On the other hand, the project's budgeting and personnel assignments can become a nightmare. It also may become difficult to maintain a semblance of a rational strategy when the project pipeline is forced to accommodate a mix of product types with unanticipated target markets and unforeseen project durations. The daunting logistics of getting together busy managers on an ad hoc basis to screen ideas may exacerbate these problems. Accordingly, firms may use some hybrid of the two types of screening approaches, solving their own particular problems by emphasizing one approach or the other and by setting aside slack resources to accommodate ad hoc projects when they arise.

Experts suggest that senior management use a fairly rigorous set of criteria that involves two passes when evaluating new ideas: The first pass employs "must have" criteria derived from the corporate mission and financial goals. The second pass employs "should have" criteria derived from organization manufacturing and distribution competencies, compatibility with currently served product markets, and cultural constraints.[13] Obviously, all must-have criteria must be met. For should-have criteria, a scoring system can be used to evaluate the project. The project would be scored on a scale of, say, "very high" (five points) to "very low" (zero points) for each of the criteria. The scores might be weighted by importance of the criteria, and then the scores would be added up. The score for the project would have to be above some minimum level for the project to pass to the next stage. Alternatively, a StratMesh 2.0 evaluation matrix might be created that indicates, at a glance, the prospects of a product idea.

Stage 2: Concept Development

Ironically, marketers have learned that fast, effective product development requires a careful and thorough effort at the front end of the process. In short, the advice of the experts supported by research (see Table 10.1) is that firms should spend more time than they have in the past on concept development because it will speed up the entire process, increase the quality of the product, reduce its cost, and lead to higher profits. Concept development is the development of the positioning concept and product specifications.

Figure 10.5 presents the activities two Massachusetts Institute of Technology experts in product development recommend should be undertaken for concept development. Note how similar these activities are to the targeting/positioning process described in Chapter 9. In the concept development stage, in addition to developing the competitive positioning and product specifications, marketers undertake an initial

[13] R. G. Cooper, *Winning at New Products: Accelerating the Process from Idea to Launch* (Cambridge, MA: Addison-Wesley, 1993), Chapter 6.

Table 10.1 The Competitive Advantages of Concurrent Engineering

BENEFITS FROM DESIGNING MANUFACTURABILITY, QUALITY, AND EASE OF MAINTENANCE INTO THE PRODUCT AT THE START	PERCENT	WHEN DESIGN CHANGES ARE MADE	COSTS
Development time	30%–70% less	During design	$1,000
Engineering changes	65–90 fewer	During design testing	10,000
Time to market	20–90 less	During process planning	100,000
Overall quality	200–600 higher	During test production	1,000,000
White-collar productivity	20–110 higher	During final production	10,000,000
Dollar sales	5–50 higher		
Return on assets	20–120 higher		

Concurrent engineering by a cross-functional team emphasizes a heavy investment in design at the outset of the project because the costs of changing the design late in the development process are much greater. Concurrent engineering also saves time, increases quality, and is generally a far more rational decision-making and implementation process than bureaucratic new product development processes, which require that tasks undertaken by marketing, R&D, manufacturing, and finance be addressed sequentially.

SOURCES: These charts are based on data from Dataquest, Inc., the National Institute of Standards & Technology, the Thomas Group, Inc., and the Institute for Defense Analyses. See Otis Port, Zachary Schiller, and Resa W. King, "A Smarter Way to Manufacture," *Business Week*, April 30, 1990, 110–17.

Figure 10.5 Concept Development

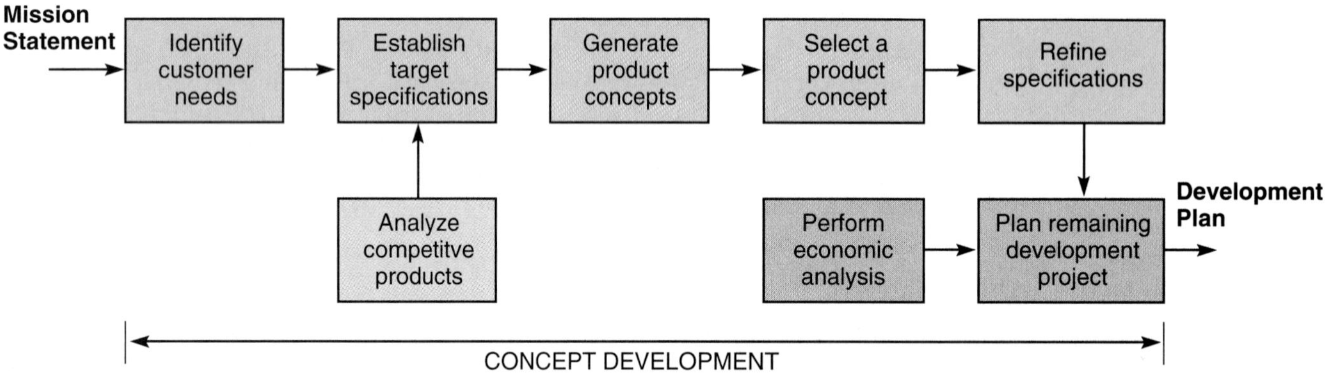

This is a suggested concept development process. It involves competitive benchmarking, benefit segmentation, and an economic feasibility study of the proposed positioning and price point. In fact, concept development seems to be synonymous with targeting/positioning.

SOURCE: Karl T. Ulrich and Steven D. Eppinger, *Product Design and Development* (New York: McGraw-Hill, 1995).

economic feasibility study. The evaluation of several different design concepts that are developed into working drawings, evaluated, and paired down to a single design also might be added to this stage.[14] At the first milestone review, the results of this initial

[14] See Karl T. Urlich and Steven D. Eppinger, *Product Design and Development* (New York: McGraw-Hill 1995), Chapter 6, for a fine example of how a design team selected several design concepts for a reusable syringe. In general this text has excellent examples and applications.

concept selection and feasibility study are discussed, and if the project is given a green light, then the rest of the development process is planned.

Stage 3: Development Plan

After the green light is given to the concept development, the next stage is to plan what to do next and how to do it. It may sound strange that a high-quality product development process has a stage where the team decides how to proceed. And why doesn't this stage occur at the very beginning?

To answer the last question first, it does not make sense to start detailed planning and implementation of the supply-chain process, manufacturing process, control system processes, and marketing programs at the idea-generation stage or concept positioning stages. This is wasted effort if the project does not pass the idea screening or the evaluation of the positioning concept. But once the green light has been given to develop the product (at the end of Stage 2), some serious, up-front planning of how to proceed with the development as fast as possible must be immediately undertaken.

This involves creating subteams to plan and manage various product development activities that, it has been proven, can be undertaken in parallel rather than in sequence. For example, in the past, planning and installing the manufacturing process often was undertaken *after* the product design was developed and approved. Designing the manufacturing process at the same time as the product not only greatly shortens development time but also forces back-and-forth communication that results in a product designed for manufacturability (low cost, low defects, and easy to adapt to future model extensions). This also benefits consumers because design for manufacturability means lower consumer prices and fewer defects.

Concurrent Engineering

This parallel product and production process design has been called *concurrent engineering* (see Table 10.1).[15] It can be taken even further. While the entire cross-functional team works on design and prototype development, a subteam of marketers, salespersons, distributors, customer service reps, and the ad agency can start planning the integrated marketing communication campaign (e.g., use instructions, sales brochures, a World Wide Web service site, and trade and consumer advertising) after the green light is given to the targeting/positioning concept. Another subteam of purchasing agents, leading suppliers, manufacturing engineers, systems engineers, and processing equipment vendors can start designing the manufacturing process. A further subteam can be updating the costs and financial plans as a result of the decisions made by the other subteams (see Chapter 18), designing the systems controls (discussed in Chapter 19), and taking responsibility for ensuring that cost targets are met.

Concurrent engineering involves open sharing and continuous discussion of information across the team and subteams about progress and problems as they occur. Figure 10.6 illustrates how an extension of the quality function deployment (QFD) process introduced in Chapter 9 can help coordinate product and process design. The QFD process flows from consumer benefits sought to product specification to parts specification to manufacturing process description to manufacturing process specifications. Whenever a product, part, or process specification is changed, its effects on the other two specifications and on the delivered consumer benefit can be tracked.

[15] John R. Hartley, *Concurrent Engineering: Shortening Lead Times, Raising Quality, and Lowering Costs* (Cambridge, MA: Productivity Press, 1992).

Figure 10.6 **The QFD Process**

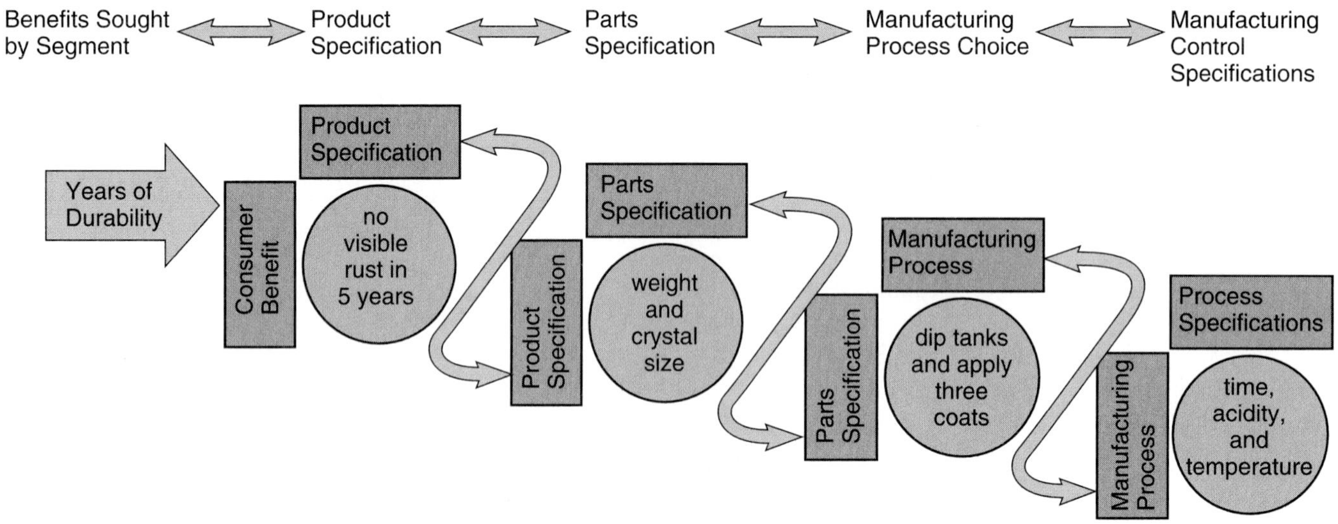

The QFD process flows from consumer benefits sought to product requirements to part or module specifications to manufacturing operations to process specifications. All of the manufacturing implementation issues surface in this QFD flow.

SOURCE: Adapted from Vincent P. Barabba and Gerald Zaltman, *Hearing the Voice of the Market* (Cambridge, MA: Harvard Business School Press, 1991), 54.

Software such as StratMesh 2.0 can be used to make available the latest information from the market or from a subteam, and its groupware capability allows a team to work on improvised solutions immediately. The decision making of the different subteams can then be adapted to each other interactively rather than in sequence. The result is a synchronization of product design, manufacturing process design, marketing campaign design, and systems controls that could never be achieved by a sequential development process, and in much less time. The information exchange catches downstream problems, such as manufacturing or distribution problems, when they can be easily and inexpensively designed out of the product. A progress tracking system also makes sure that different activities are not moved too far out of phase: For example, marketing is back on the fifty-yard line while manufacturing is ramped up, on the one-yard line, and ready to score a touchdown.

It has been proven that concurrent engineering is very effective, but it is also not easy to implement. Table 10.2 reveals that many CEOs of high-growth, high-profit companies feel they are not managing the transition from sequential to concurrent design very well. Many also admit they are not doing a good job of testing for manufacturability, of estimating costs, and of involving customers and suppliers during the design process. As indicated earlier, all of these activities can be improved by concurrent engineering. In turn, the improvement in these activities will increase the quality of the final product and, in particular, will help the firm design low cost into the product—something only half of the CEOs feel they are managing well.

Table 10.2 The Design and Development Skills of High-Growth Companies

	MANAGES POORLY (1–2)	(3)	MANAGES WELL (4–5)
Designing quality into products.	6%	19%	75%
Designing manufacturability into products.	11	25	65
Changing traditional ways of doing things.	9	26	65
Finding new design ideas—not just me-too imitations.	14	25	62
Getting new product/service ideas from customers/dealers.	10	30	60
Getting different functions in the firm to work together.	9	32	59
Quickly becoming aware of competitor innovations and imitations.	17	25	58
Designing low cost into products.	15	33	52
Designing and launching new products/services faster.	20	30	50
Involving customers/dealers in the design process.	23	28	49
Using the latest computer-aided design tools effectively.	27	25	48
Estimating the true costs of new product/services during the design process.	23	30	47
Finding people with excellent design skills.	22	31	47
Replacing sequential with concurrent design.	20	38	42
Testing manufacturability of new product/services during the design process.	27	33	40
Involving suppliers in design process.	32	28	40

More than two hundred CEOs of *Inc.* 500 and *Inc.* 100 Companies (rated as excellent, high-growth, small companies) rated how well they manage the above product design and development tasks.

SOURCE: Peter Dickson et al. "Managing Design in Small High-Growth Companies," *Journal of Product Innovation Management* 12, no. 5 (November 1995): 406–14.

The major difficulty with implementing concurrent engineering is obvious. The required across-process coordination and integrative learning is incredibly demanding and commands sixty-hour work weeks where half the time is spent talking to and informally meeting with members of other subteams. But this extra mental effort and exercise seems to have the same effect on "flabby" minds as a boot camp has on flabby bodies. It develops the information-processing capabilities of team members "such that they become more efficient in gaining and using the information being conveyed."[16] They become superfit thinkers and improvisers with enhanced self-esteem, can-do attitudes, and strong team loyalties.

Such personal expertise and confidence will be carried forward to future development projects. When is it most useful? At the beginning of Stage 3 of future product development projects when the previous learning is most needed to plan the subteams and how they will work with each other. Furthermore, because each future project poses unique design, engineering, manufacturing, and marketing problems, the concurrent engineering processes and how they are synchronized also will be unique. Thus each development process will have its own unique flow that needs to be planned by experts as early as possible, which is immediately after the concept is approved.

[16] Brown and Eisenhardt, "Product Development," 368.

Stage 4: Development and Testing

A prototype is a model of a product that attempts to embody the entire wish list of specifications created by product positioning and quality function deployment. It is developed for *four* basic purposes. As will be shown, how companies use prototypes in product development tell much about the company's competitive rationality.[17]

1. *Specification Feasibility* The first purpose is to evaluate whether the product actually can be designed so it performs to specification. "To specification" covers a multitude of performance requirements, including performance in use, cost of manufacturing, and ease of assembly and disassembly (for recycling). The specification also can involve subjective evaluations of aesthetic appearance.
2. *Design Experimentation* The second purpose is to help a cross-functional team experiment with new design ideas and answer questions about usability/user interface, appearance, maintenance, manufacturability, new materials, and cost. "Green" prototypes address disassembly, recyclability, and biodegradability. Product-line prototypes consider parts standardization and modularization.
3. *Understanding Tradeoffs and Conflicts* The third purpose of a prototype is to help enable cross-functional teams to bridge disciplinary and functional boundaries.[18] The design conflicts and trade-offs are embodied in the prototype's design and can be explained and understood by everyone, thus creating the potential for more innovative solutions.
4. *Selling to Senior Management* A fourth, more doubtful, purpose is to sell the project to senior management at a stage-gate review. IBM product developers became notorious for showing one type of prototype to senior management to procure additional funding and another type to elicit feedback from fellow technocrats. This is because provocative prototypes are only shown to senior management if they are painted, polished, and close to the ultimate production prototype. "Never show fools unfinished work" is a prototype production process rule.[19] Why? Because fools (read senior management) cannot visualize or make the required conceptual leap to see the prototype's advantage.

Drawings, Mockups, and Prototypes

Most prototypes begin on paper in two-dimensional form. Sony requires an exploded-view format, important to improve design for assembly. Computer-aided design (CAD) has enabled development teams to design and test virtual prototypes. Timex moved from expensive artwork and then three-dimensional prototypes to CAD photorealistic mock-ups used both internally and in consumer testing. Boeing designed all of the parts of its new 777 on the computer and preassembled them digitally. Customers also participated in the computer-aided design, and this led to an interior design that allows British Airways, All Nippon, United Airlines, and other future customers to move around the galleys, toilets, and seating to meet their particular needs. Boeing then undertook computer-simulated performance stress tests on what it designed to ensure it met safety, fuel efficiency, and other performance specifications. It still manufactured a prototype and had airline maintenance engineers evaluate the prototype for its ease of maintenance. The prototype also was test flown to calibrate its actual performance against its performance observed in the virtual reality of the computer. Its calibration test flight resulted in a major malfunction in one of its engines (worn out by bench testing) that led to a redesign of the engine casing around the fan blades. The lesson Boeing learned is that CAD speeds up and greatly reduces

[17] Michael Schrage, "The Culture of Prototyping," *Design Management Journal* (winter 1993): 55–65.
[18] Dorothy Leonard-Barton, "Inanimate Integrators: A Block of Wood Speaks," *Design Management Journal* 2, no. 3, 66.
[19] Schrage, "The Culture of Prototyping," 55–65.

the cost of prototyping design and testing, but it cannot replace the real-world testing of a design.

Early prototypes are often handcrafted out of cardboard, wood, or foam and are important in stimulating creativity. Rough, informal prototypes are used to further drive the experimentation/innovation process as well as products of the innovation process. Later prototypes are actually manufactured using the proposed production process to test whether the design, when mass produced, will perform to desired quality-in-use specifications (see the next Rationality in Practice box). In organization cultures with strong technical and engineering traditions, the working model that the organization has figured out how to manufacture is called the *prototype* (production prototype); all others are called *models* or *mock-ups*.

The Competitive Advantages of Fast Prototyping

Fast prototyping engineering research is funded by the National Science Foundation because it leads to faster product development, which is key to innovation/imitation. Part of the lack of competitiveness of the U.S. automobile industry can be traced to the use of intricate, expensive, full-sized sculptured clay models. Such prototypes were not able to be easily modified or used in rapid design iterations. The result was a design culture that allowed very few iterations. The lesson to be learned is that "hard" models can harden thinking. Until quite recently, the clay model was the input into the computer-aided design system. By contrast, at Toyota it is the opposite: The clay model becomes the output of the CAD process, and Toyota can go from a new idea to quarter-scale clay in less than forty days. Sony takes about one week to go from a new product concept to a rough working prototype. To encourage prototype learning, some organizations, such as Honda and Motorola, require building a new prototype periodically, such as every two weeks. This forces the development team to keep up the pace of experimentation for improving prototype user friendliness, manufacturability, and so on, and allows senior management to assess progress from prototype to prototype.

The number of prototypes developed, time between cycles, and number of modifications per cycle are metrics that can be used to assess the productivity of the development process. The nature of the modifications also says much about the focus of a firm's product development. Kodak is known for building and testing many ecoprototypes; Nissan and Toyota are known for prototyping new materials. Xerox, once obsessed with prototyping for manufacturability, now uses a lot more prototypes to improve user interface and ease of maintenance.

A common problem observed by product development experts is that organizations spend thousands of hours developing detailed specifications only to have the first prototype invalidate most of the effort. In short, they wait too long to develop their first prototype and to discover what the problems are designing a product to perform to specification. Indeed, sometimes the QFD process described in Chapter 9 can lead to too much emphasis on ideal specifications rather than on practical prototypes and improvisation.[20] Companies that have rigid review structures tend to have fewer, more elaborate, and more expensive prototypes. Thus, superior product development processes must have staged reviews and must use the power of QFD to convert competitive positioning into design specifications but also must allow a great deal

[20] This may explain why some research has found that QFD does not always improve a firm's product development process as much as expected; see Abbie Griffin, "Evaluating Development Processes: QFD as an Example," *Marketing Science Institute*, Cambridge, Massachusetts, 1991.

Rationality in Practice

The Making of the Miata

What does it take to develop and launch a car that the very first buyers in July 1989 bought for $16,000 and were able to immediately resell for $20,000? Project P729 started in late 1982 with initial sketches of the basic concept: the creation of "oneness between rider and horse." The first two clay models made in 1984 were considered too stiff and serious (although it is hard to tell from the photos), but the third clay model had the correct rounded lines and "emotion." Mazda encouraged its designers to flex their muscles. The first working prototype of the Miata was made in 1985 by International Automotive Design (IAD) in the Sussex coastal town of Worthing, England. IAD constructed a working prototype, down to the cigarette lighter from the first clay model. When it was taken for test rides, gawking bystanders chased it for a closer look.

Concurrently, the Japanese engineers used computer-aided design (CAD) to design a steel unibody and power-plant frame with all of the weight concentrated within the wheel frame to give it an extraordinarily solid feel on the road. The engineers were able to evaluate the stress and flex at 8,900 different body points. They also designed racing components into the engine, such as trumpet intakes. "Soul" was added with dozens of design details, such as a toggle gear shift with the "sweetest feel" of any car on the road and a "throaty" exhaust sound chosen from more than one hundred different tones. In April 1987 the final prototype was unveiled to driving enthusiasts, and their response was so overwhelmingly positive that the green light was immediately given to production ramp-up. In retrospect, what were the design flaws corrected in later Miata models? A trunk release button in the lockable console between the seats and a light in the rearview mirror. Miata, developed in California, England, and Japan, epitomized the best of form, feel, and function in design and demonstrates again how much all of us are willing to pay for such qualities.

An early sketch of the basic concept by Yagi-San in 1982.

The first working Miata prototype developed in England in late 1985. Drivers chased the prototype for a closer look—early confirmation of the design's appeal.

of prototype iteration where numerous prototypes are developed and tested in parallel and sequentially by the development team.

The theory is that developers learn more about what works by doing numerous laboratory trial runs with prototypes than by trying only a few well-thought-out prototypes. More forms are tried, creating more chances for a very good design to emerge. When failures occur, they will be small, and their psychological effect is also likely to

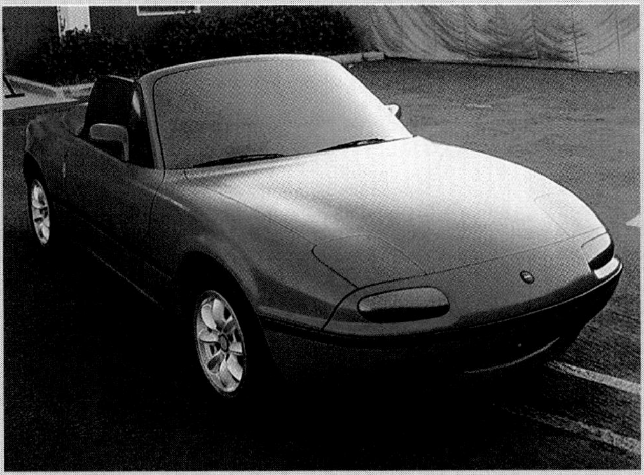

Development in 1986 of the third-stage clay model served as a basis for the preproduction prototype model. The model later was adopted for production in the Japanese factory.

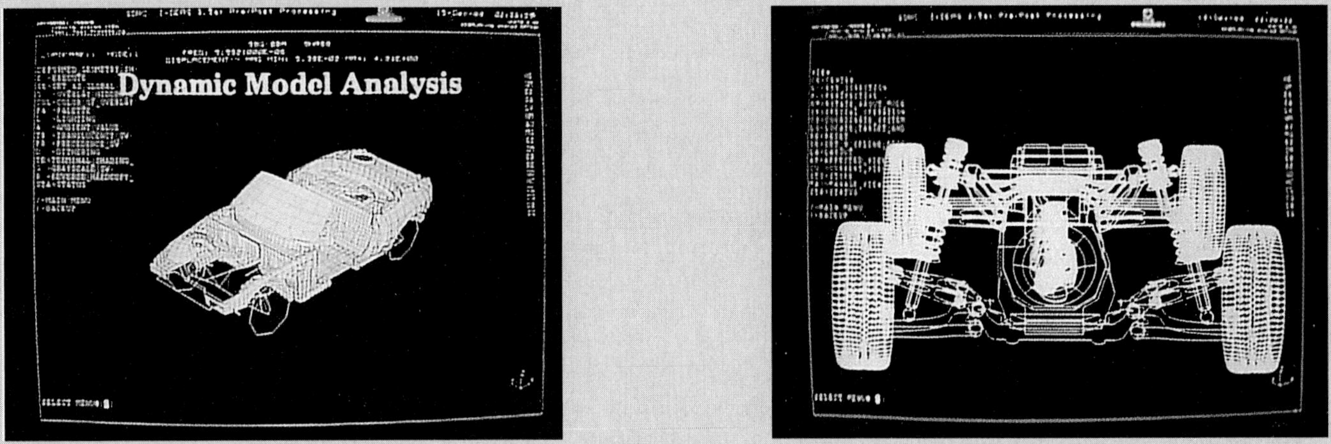

Meanwhile Japanese engineers spent hundreds of hours testing components using computer-aided design.

be small. With small failures, problems will be easier to pinpoint and solve since less can go wrong. Essentially, more trial-and-error learning occurs. If a customer is present to give feedback, prototypes will quickly converge with customer needs.

Field Testing of Prototypes

Field trials are the natural extension of the prototype testing carried out earlier in the laboratory. The recommended field testing process that involves both customers and

Figure 10.7 The Design-Testing Loop

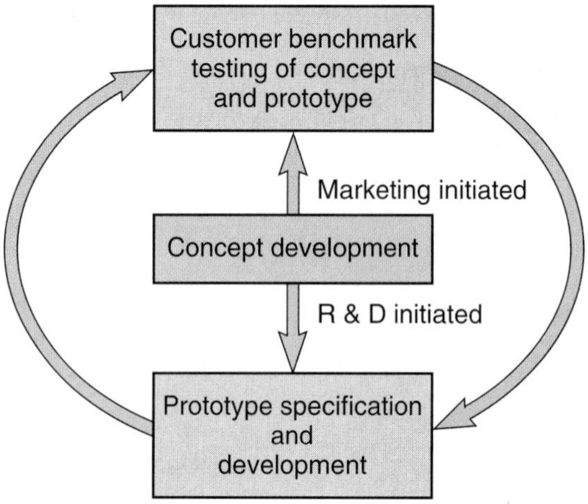

A new product idea may come from R&D or from the marketplace. A prototype must be designed, manufactured, and tested using trusted customers. The feedback from the testing modifies the design by adding features or reducing costs. Engineers also have to design for manufacturing, and this may involve working with suppliers. The result is then retested by customers and evaluated against competitive products. The loop continues until both the customer and manufacturing are satisfied. The speed of this looping is an important characteristic of competitive rationality because it determines how alert the firm is to the needs of the customer, its willingness to experiment, and its ability to implement. This looping speed becomes even more important the greater the number of loops to be completed—that is, the newer and more difficult the technology.

manufacturing is shown in Figure 10.7. This testing encourages cooperation among the R&D, manufacturing, and marketing functions.[21] The common practice is to perform what is called *beta testing* at the customer's home or business site. The idea is to place the product in a real customer usage situation for an extended period of time. The feedback from such a test can lead to significant design changes and even can suggest revisions to positioning, sales, or communications plans. For example, Apple's very successful PowerBook notepad computer went through seven prototype cycles that involved field testing each prototype and incorporating the feedback into the next prototype. This led to the design of a larger "mouse" trackball for finer control of the cursor and the addition of a hard disk drive. But both these improvements increased the size and weight over the desired specifications, so other components were reduced in size. The following two Rationality in Practice boxes describe the benefits of field testing the ergonomics (fit between the user and a product) of cordless phones and desk chairs.

Usually beta tests are simple product performance tests that determine whether or not the product works in the customer usage situation. However, firms sometimes need more information about how their product stacks up against the competition, so beta sites may become benchmark sites where the in-use performance of the prototype

[21] See Chapter 17 and also Ashok K. Gupta, S. P. Raj, and David Wilemon, "A Model for Studying R&D-Marketing Interface in the Product Innovation Process," *Journal of Marketing* 60 (April 1989): 7–17.

is evaluated against competitors' products. Finally, if the firm has gone to the trouble of setting up extensive trials, it is probably a good idea to obtain feedback from the customer on all the other aspects of the marketing mix as well. Even though customers are not placed in a real selling situation, their experience with the product can create insights that other market research cannot tap.

In summary, the *ying* and *yang* of product development is the *planning discipline* of up-front and continuous environmental analysis, targeting/positioning, product specification, judicious stage-gate reviews of the emerging products' fit, feasibility, and estimated profitability *combined* with the *creative improvisation* from a team's many iterations of prototype design and testing (sometimes called the *skunkworks* approach).

Stage 5: Launch

At this stage, manufacturing engineers assemble the production processes to mass produce the product. Long before this stage, production will have been designing and testing the machinery to make and assemble the parts and choosing suppliers and supervising their production processes. The design of the production process should start as soon as the first prototype is developed, perhaps even earlier. It occurs concurrently with product design. In the past it often occurred after the product had been designed, which made no sense at all. The manufacturing process directly determines a large part of the product's cost, the quality of its parts, and the quality of assembly. Including production engineers at the beginning of the product development process greatly increases the chances of enhancing the manufacturing quality and reducing cost by designing for manufacturability as well as to customer performance specifications. The concurrent design of the product and the manufacturing process also greatly reduces the total time taken to develop the product. By the time production ramp-up approval is given, the design and testing of the manufacturing process and its equipment has been completed. But the production ramp-up stage is often the point of no return, for at this stage major contracts are signed for plant and equipment purchases and for long-term supplier relationships.

Production ramp-up involves carefully bringing the manufacturing process to full speed. During this ramping up, production batches are constantly checked for quality conformance. Any changes in product design are extremely expensive at this stage because they have so many repercussions and often involve expensive modification of production equipment. For a service, ramping up means the mass training of service employees to deliver the service script and the spot checking of service delivery out in the field to make sure it conforms to the desired specifications. Again, discovering that the hired service workers cannot undertake particular activities is extremely costly, and it should have been discovered early in the service development process.

Purchasing often plays a major role in production ramp-up as machinery and raw materials are ordered and delivered. But for purchasing to play an effective role in product development, it, like manufacturing, must be involved in product development at a much earlier stage.[22] In many bureaucratic companies, purchasing is regarded as little more than a clerical task. This is a huge mistake. In the modern world of supply-chain management and alliances, purchasing plays a key role in product

[22] David N. Burt and William R. Soukup, "Purchasing's Role in New Product Development," *Harvard Business Review*, September–October 1985, 90–97.

Rationality in Practice

Sony's Hot Ear

Ergonomics (also called human factors) is an applied science that seeks to improve the fit between a user and a product to increase safety, comfort, and productivity. Incorporating ergonomics into design requires an understanding of human performance limitations and behavioral response patterns relative to product use. These limitations are either physical or cognitive/perceptual in nature, but all address how people respond to human-made designs. Ergonomic applications encompass a wide range of interdisciplinary areas, including concept modeling and product design, job performance analysis, work-space and equipment design, computer interfaces, and so forth.

Although cordless telephone technology has evolved at breakneck speed over the past decade, advances in design sophistication have come at great expense to human factor issues. Current cordless telephone systems offer a vast array of features and functions, but research shows few end users actually utilize them. This problem extends far beyond consumer apathy toward user manuals; too often, phone design and aesthetics actually impede proper use. To combat this problem, Sony Electronics joined forces with Metaphase Design Group, St. Louis-based design research and ergonomic specialists, for an in-depth investigation into factors that affect cordless phone usability.

Thermogram Prints used to improve fit of phone to ear and hand.

Metaphase employed a *user-centered approach* throughout this research program to gain a thorough understanding of end users' physical and behavioral wants and needs relative to cordless telephone use and operation. First, *usability analyses* were conducted with targeted end users to identify factors that affect

development by first identifying potential parts suppliers and involving them in early cross-functional prototype development. Second, purchasing's role is to be constantly up-to-date about the cost, performance, market availability, quality, and reliability of different supplier components that could be used in the design. This enables purchasing to make suggestions such as redesigning the product so it can use a low-cost component that is readily available and of proven quality, rather than having a supplier make from scratch a component that is assured to be more expensive and of questionable quality. Such recommendations can be stored in CAD software files and lead to standardization of parts across product lines, which can lead to huge savings in costs, faster product development, and less and cheaper maintenance. In turn, by listening and learning from other members of the cross-functional team, purchasing will be alert to problems and issues that arise at the ramp-up stage with suppliers and may be able to develop contingency plans such as backup sources of supply. To play such a role, purchasing must have technical expertise, and this is often achieved by rotating engineers from design and manufacturing into purchasing. This not only brings the necessary expertise to the purchasing function but also fosters an appreciation of the benefits of close cooperation between purchasing and engineering, opens up the eyes ease of use, the comprehension and learning of functions, and so on. During one-on-one-interviews, subjects interacted with seventeen cordless systems from a variety of manufacturers. Testing included both quantitative and qualitative measures—ratings and ranking of different phone characteristics (e.g., handset weight, balance, ear comfort, etc.) and preferences toward features and functions. In total, researchers conducted seventy-five interviews in three geographically diverse cities.

Based on results of the *usability analyses* and various other design analyses conducted in the early stages of concept development, four new cordless-handset concept models were developed and tested with an existing Sony model handset in a *thermographic study*.

Thermograms were used to analyze the physical interaction between a product and its user. For this form of ergonomic research, a product or concept design is treated with a proprietary heat-sensitive paint system that changes color when it comes in contact with heat from a person's body. The result is a visual imprint that maps all contact points between the user and a product. Relative to the Sony cordless phone study, color changes on the handsets allowed researchers to map the interface of phone models with test subjects, thereby providing a record of the degree of anatomical fit each design offered. Research data were useful in diagnosing potential interface problems, such as accidental activation of handset keys and pressure loads on sensitive anatomical features, such as users' ears and hands.

These ergonomic research methods provided the project team with the following benefits to aid in Sony's development of its new line of ergonomic cordless phones and subsequent marketing efforts.

- An understanding of the factors that make functions and features easy to learn, understand, and use
- An understanding of consumer behavior and psychology with respect to purchasing, installation, use, and so forth
- A profile of consumer design vocabularies as a function of socioeconomic background and phone design preferences
- Ranked lists of consumer preferences for telephone function, features, and physical design characteristics
- Design and ergonomic guidelines for the definition of new product forms and the refinement of existing products

Generally, the success of this research program stems from the interdisciplinary approach taken by the project team. By studying end users' wants and needs, and then validating research results through expert ergonomic analyses throughout the design process, designers were able to produce a new line of cordless telephones that is easy to understand and use and offers users a proper anatomical fit.

SOURCE: Bryce G. Rutter and Anne Marie Becka, Metaphase Design Group Inc., St. Louis Missouri, 1996.

of engineers to the possibilities of outsourcing, and enables engineers to develop more of a general management perspective.

Designing and Marketing Competitive Services

In the preceding sections, services have been sometimes referred to as products. Although the various concepts discussed are applicable to services as well as to tangible products, it is important to be aware of the unique nature of services and the service components of product offerings and to discuss how this uniqueness can be managed.

Service Prototypes

A service prototype is a script that describes the flow of activities to be provided to customers. A new service prototype is created when an activity in the old service is eliminated or altered or a new activity is added to the service, such as a supervisor call-back to check on customer satisfaction with a home cleaning service. Such prototype

Rationality in Practice

Steelcase's Hot Seat

Quantifiable design research methods can be employed to help product developers and marketers gain a more thorough understanding of their target customers. *End-user research* moves beyond more shallow market research methods, such as phone surveys and focus groups, by examining an end user's actual experience with a product, both physical and psychological. Such methods help marketers gain a more thorough understanding of their target customers, thereby ensuring that the final design fully meets end users' needs and expectations. End-user research identifies specific product features and functions that enhance usability, as well as unnecessary elements and characteristics that add no tangible value to a product. It serves to measure a product's overall efficacy on a wide range of design issues—crucial information to marketing professionals.

When Steelcase Seating sought to design a new ergonomic desk chair that is intuitive, easy to use, and highly accessible, it turned to Metaphase Design Group of St. Louis, product design research and ergonomic specialists, to conduct an in-depth investigation into end users' wants and needs. Throughout the program, Metaphase sought to (1) implement a *user-centered approach* to design development, whereby the chair design was directed by end-user responses to models and prototypes throughout the program; and (2) serve as a conduit of end-user feedback to designers for immediate implementation into the evolving chair design. Over the course of the study, more than 180 individuals from sixteen different companies across the United States were interviewed.

The award-winning desk chair

scripts are tested by role playing or actual field testing. A video of such role playing and field rests can be studied and discussed by the development team in much the same way as a product prototype.

Making Intangible Features Tangible

A service is *intangible*, which means a consumer cannot see, touch, and feel a service before purchase, making it harder for a sales representative to sell its quality aspects. Intangibility prevents customers from having something concrete to evaluate—they must trust the provider's word that the service was done as well as possible for the money the customer paid. In addition, if customers have little idea of how a service is performed or what costs they would incur if they attempted to do the service for themselves, then very often they will undervalue the service. For these reasons, brand image, reputation, and equity are particularly important when selling a service and

Throughout all stages of product development, the chair's design was defined by end users and purchasing decision makers who remained within the development loop from the initial stages through prototype evaluation. After each stage of research, data were fed back to designers for integration into the evolving design concept.

As part of the research program, Metaphase employed a *user needs analysis*, which served to identify and establish a hierarchy of chair design requirements as seen by end users and decision makers (architects, interior designers, facility managers, etc.). Researchers interviewed end users and decision makers from a variety of companies in order to inventory current needs/problems experienced with ergonomic seating and to gather recommendations for design. This included both quantitative and qualitative measures—ratings/ranking of different chair characteristics and preferences toward features and functions.

Based on research results from the *user needs analysis*, designers created a half-scale model of Rapport, which was then tested on end users for *design validation*. This testing yielded areas of improvement needed in the concept. Following the model testing phase of the research program, two prototypes of the evolving Rapport design were developed and tested against four leading competitors' chairs. During this competitive product analysis, which is a form of product benchmarking, users rated each chair in terms of overall impression, aesthetics, comfort, ergonomics, ease of control, chair dimensions, and various other "design excellence" criteria. To investigate the relationship between perceived and actual performance, subjects were interviewed both prior to and after contact with all chair designs. Inasmuch as perceptions of the chair drive purchasing decisions, the perceptual testing provided the design team with feedback on both positive and negative cues.

By establishing a program in which each step of the design evaluation process is dependent on research results from each preceding phase, product developers were able to move continuously from "big picture" problems to details without any major steps back. This process also allowed the design team to move faster, with a higher confidence level that the design would meet consumers' expectations.

Research results from the *benchmarking* show the Rapport chair concept was overall rated superior to similar competitors' products. Subjects gave Rapport five times as many "very positive" (the highest rating) votes as any of its competitors. Rapport received rankings of "positive" or "very positive" from nearly 70 percent of the sample—two-and-a-half times better than any competitor. In addition, more than two-thirds of the sample group rated Rapport "above average" or "excellent" in terms of overall design excellence—two-and-a-half times better than its nearest competitor.

The success of this process was also evident in the receipt of a 1994 Industrial Design Excellence award for the Best Product Design of the Year (Design Research) from the Industrial Designers Society of America and *Business Week* magazine, as well as a 1994 Gold Best of NeoCon Design Award from *Facilities Design & Management* magazine.

SOURCE: Bryce G. Rutter and Anne Marie Becka, Metaphase Design Group Inc., St. Louis, Missouri, 1996.

introducing new services. Because of their intangible natures, services try to choose brand names and logos that are rich in tangible imagery (for example, the Prudential rock). The appearance of the service provider, such as grooming and uniform, are also important tangible signals of service image and a very important component of service management because a service is more *personal* than a product.

Developing Quality Employee Behaviors

A service company also must strive to employ people-oriented staff members to undertake its services. Employees who like helping other people are ideal service providers because their interest in serving others is a fundamental feature of their characters. What they say and do conveys their genuine caring and concern. People-oriented employees will go the extra mile; they will innovate and adapt the service to the unique needs of the customer. This is important, because a service must be designed to meet the needs of the customer even more than a product. It is a little easier to excuse a product for not doing exactly what you want or expect. The product does not know any better and cannot change its form or function. It is much more difficult to excuse a service provider who is not being responsive. It makes no sense to ask a product why it is not meeting your needs, but such a question is often directly or indirectly raised with a service provider. An unsatisfactory response is both embarrassing and unprofitable. It requires excuses and rationalizations. What it reveals is either the incompetence of the service provider or the crass economic motivation of the exchange. A product will never say "lady, you got what you paid for."

Introducing New Services Can Be Too Easy

Although intangibility makes a service harder to sell, it makes it easier to introduce new services by simply varying the nature of the service, changing the service production routine, and retraining the service provider. However, if overdone, this practice can lead to a proliferation of new services that ultimately confuses the customer and hurts a service firm's positioning (for example, in 1985 British Rail created so many new types of tickets [travel services] that it ended up confusing its consumers.)[23] It also places tremendous stresses on operations and delivery, so much so that the quality of all services can suffer. Establishing the cost of a new service is also more difficult than establishing the cost of a new product because so many costs are shared with old services (for example, they share the same human delivery system). Consequently, a service firm has to study carefully the image and operational implications of a new service.

Problems with Quality and Cost Control

Services are also consumed at the same time they are produced. This *simultaneity* allows a service company to increase customer satisfaction by uniquely tailoring the service to the needs of a specific customer. The problem with such special service is that it creates tremendous quality and cost control problems for the operations managers in a service company. If a service is not standardized, then standards are difficult to set and conformance is hard to control. It seems that operations managers play an even more important role in designing new services than they do in designing new products because they are often in closer contact with the customer than their marketing managers (via their operational field forces), they know the mechanics of how a service is delivered, and they can determine whether the existing field force can deliver such a service. With services, QFD involves engineering of human behavior. In the benefits times features of the QFD matrix for service, engineering design features are replaced with specific activities undertaken by the service provider. Alternatively, a service activity map can be created and the output of each activity related to overall customer service satisfaction, as described in Chapter 9.

Combining Operations and Marketing

Operations management has to break down a service into a sequence of activities, each of which contributes, in a different way, to a separate component of customer

[23] Christopher J. Easingwood, "New Product Development for Service Companies," *Journal of Product Innovation Management* 4 (1986): 264–75. Much of this section is based on the insights gained from this excellent article.

satisfaction. Just as mechanical engineers understand the mechanics of a product, service operations managers understand the mechanics of a delivered service. But unlike mechanical engineers, they are closer to their customers ("manufacturing" occurs in the presence of the customer); therefore service operations managers have a better firsthand, intuitive understanding of the links among service activities, consumer benefits sought, and consumer satisfaction. Thus, operations people often exercise more influence in new service management than they do in new product management. Some experts have gone so far as to suggest that service companies should cut back their marketing departments and boost the size of their frontline operational team so it can manage the new service.[24] In fact, many service companies have a separate department, a permanent cross-functional team made up of marketing and operation's top guns, that develops and manages new services.[25]

Test marketing also requires that the field force execute the new service activity sequence within the desired quality and cost standards. These tests often are low key and involve exploratory, on-the-job refinements of the service. A final important difference between service and product marketing is that the service provider is the best marketer for a service company. A product can use its packaging as a sales aid. A service company's service providers are often its packaging, its product, and its sales force combined into one. Thus, a service company depends a great deal on its service providers. Service quality is also notoriously difficult to control because service organizations involve people and not machines. The quality performance tolerances of a machine can be much more readily monitored, adjusted, and maintained.

Service providers differ in the degree to which a service is customized for each client. At one end of the spectrum are professional services, such as legal or management consulting firms, that are highly adapted to the client's individual circumstances. At the other end are mostly routinized services, such as dry cleaning or mass transit (see Chapter 9). The distinction between customization and routinization is an important one. For customized services, the importance of people is emphasized. People providing the service should have strong training, be adaptable, and be thoroughly competent in the area of their expertise. Routinization can be used for some aspects of customized service, such as billing, but these aspects are not its primary focus. Routinized services, on the other hand, depend on well-designed systems and standard activity sequences that deliver the principal service. The service systems and scripts should be designed to perform the required tasks with efficiency and speed. Employees should be well trained to perform routine tasks efficiently. But equally important, someone needs to be trained to handle exceptions, problems, or breakdowns in the service system and script.

Brand Equity

For thousands of years, men and women have been putting their names on everything from cattle and pyramids to children and ideas. Product branding is a variation of these very basic ownership and self-expressive human behaviors. Product branding, though, has another important use from the standpoint of meeting customer needs.

---

[24] Christian Gronroos, "Innovative Marketing Strategies and Organization Structure for Service Firms," in Leonard L. Berry, G. Lynn Shostack, and Gregory D. Upah, eds., *Emerging Perspectives on Services Marketing* (Chicago: American Marketing Association, 1983).

[25] Easingwood, "New Product Development," 270.

Customers, whether they are individual consumers or organizational buyers, must handle an enormous amount of information in the course of their daily activities. Consequently, people develop efficient ways of processing information—including the use of selective attention, memory shortcuts, and rules of thumb—in order to make decisions.[26] With that reality in mind, potential buyers often will use symbols, such as brands, to stand for larger chunks of information and simplify information handling.

A brand is a conditioned cue that, through its long association with a product or service, comes to stand for something, be it quality, reliability, craftsmanship, exclusive styling, status, or value. Brand names assure customers they will receive the same quality with their next purchase as they did with their last. Consequently, buyers are willing to pay a premium for such quality and assurance. On an impressionist painting, the name Vincent van Gogh can add tens of millions of dollars to the price. The brand name on a mass-produced item can seldom make that much of a difference, but the principle is the same. For this reason, branding has emerged as an essential element of product strategy, whether for expensive sports gear, cars, or commodities (such as Morton's salt, Chiquita bananas, or Tyson chickens).

In fact, some brands are, in the aggregate, actually worth a great deal more than a great artist's signature. Kohlberg Kravis Roberts purchased RJR Nabisco for $25 billion—more than double its book value. Philip Morris, Inc., paid $12.9 billion for Kraft (four times book value) and $5.7 billion for General Foods (more than four times book value). Nestlé paid $4.5 billion for Rowntree (five times book value). Even under the generous assumption that the tangible assets of all these companies were undervalued by 50 percent, this still means that the goodwill and reputation of their brand names (called *brand equity*) were worth billions. The enormous value of the equity of some brands indicates that today companies are clearly disenchanted with the risks involved in spending hundreds of millions of dollars to launch completely new brands. Instead, they prefer to market new products under the umbrella of well-established brand names that have become part of our cultural heritage. The management of brand equity has many aspects, as Figure 10.8 illustrates, some of which will now be explored in more detail.

The Durability of Brand Names

Brand names can be very durable. Booz, Allen, and Hamilton, Inc., compiled a list of the twenty-four leading consumer brands of 1923. Fifty years later, nineteen were still market leaders and the others placed in the top five in their product-markets. For example, ten of the top twenty candy bars (including Snickers and Hershey's) have been around for fifty years and today account for 80 percent of all candy bar sales. The histories of four great brands are presented in Figure 10.9.

Strong brand equity is not only used to roll out new products and break into new markets. It also can serve as a formidable barrier, making it difficult for competitors to enter or expand in the market. However, some great brand names do die from neglect and mismanagement. Magic Markers, introduced in the 1950s, were the first felt-tipped markers, but later entries improved the technology and expanded the

[26] James R. Bettman, *An Information Processing Theory of Consumer Behavior* (Reading, MA: Addison-Wesley, 1979).

Figure 10.8 **The Many Aspects of Managing Brand Equity**

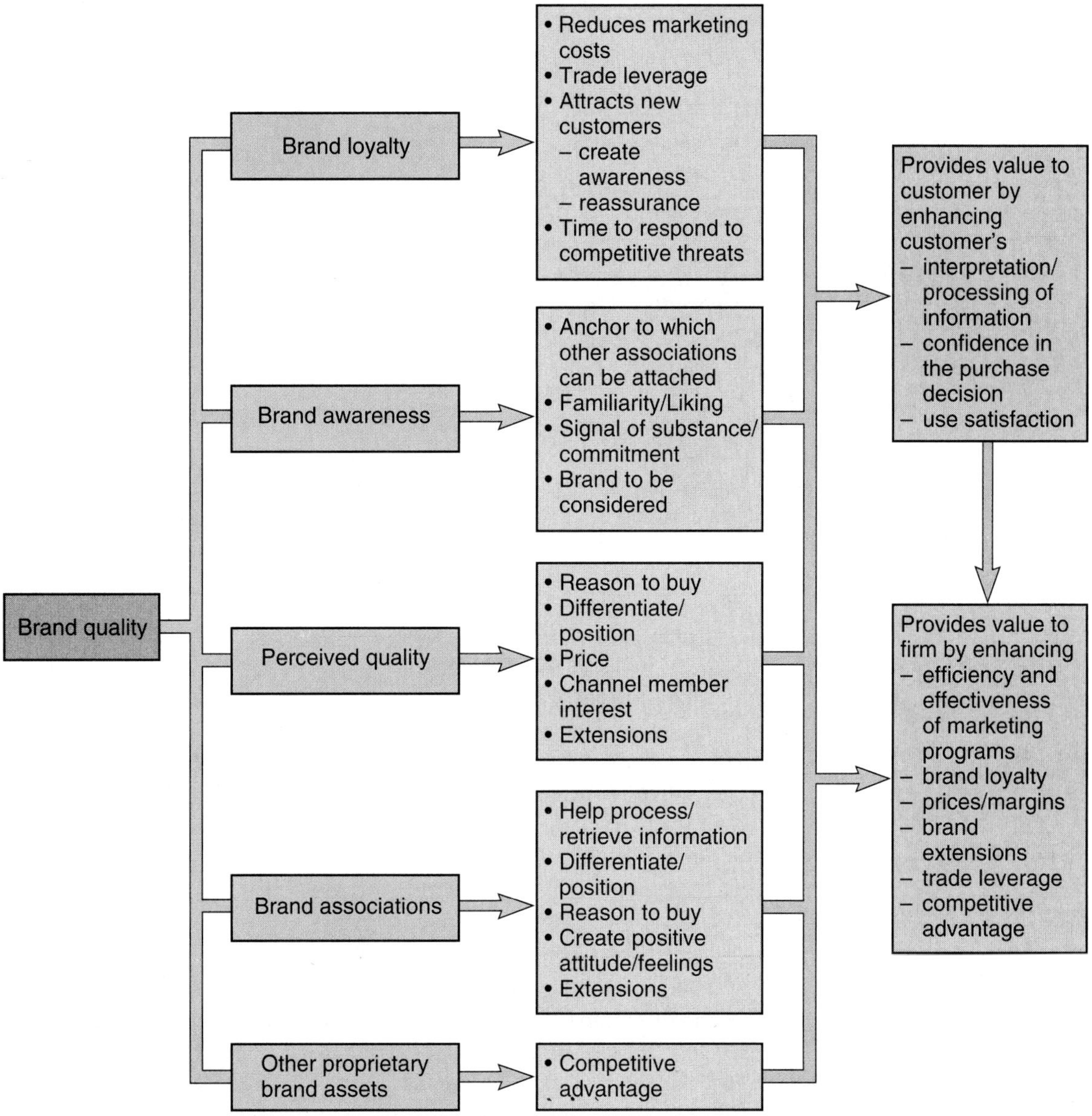

Brand equity has many aspects, including brand loyalty (discussed in Chapter 5), brand awareness, image and perceived quality, brand associations, and extensions. If managed well, these aspects add value to the product or service and create additional customer satisfaction, which, in turn, provides a number of benefits to the firm.

SOURCE: Reprinted with the permission of the Free Press, a Division of Macmillan, Inc. From *Managing Brand Inquiry: Capitalizing on the Value of a Brand Name* by David A. Aaker. Copyright © 1991 by David A. Aaker.

Figure 10.9 The Histories of Four Great Brands

IVORY SOAP

The 108-Year-Old Soap

One Sunday morning in church 108 years ago, Harley Procter wrestled with a nagging problem. At 32—determined to retire at 42—he was in charge of Procter & Gamble sales, and wanted the perfect name for the white soap his cousin Jim Gamble had just invented.

He found himself listening to the congregation reading Psalm 45, verse 8: "All thy garments smell of myrrh, and aloes, and cassia, out of the ivory palaces. . ." The word straightened Harley like a ramrod. "Ivory!" Smooth—white—hard—long-lasting. Like Jim's soap. That was it!

In October, 1879, the first bar of Ivory soap went on sale as a trademarked product. Since then Americans have bought 30 billion more.

99 44/100% Pure

Harley wanted people to know how pure Ivory was. In 1882, he commissioned laboratory analyses of Ivory and three costly Castile soaps. As he suspected, Ivory, with only 56/100% impurities, scored highest. He subtracted the fraction from 100. Ivory was "99 44/100% pure!" Ever since, Ivory's classic slogan has told why it leaves the skin so clean, so fresh.

"It Floats"

At first, Ivory *didn't* float. But it seems a workman left a batch of the soap in a mixer and somehow, the machine whipped tiny air bubbles into the mix—just enough to make the soap buoyant. People wrote in that they *liked* floating soap; when it slipped into murky river or tub water, it popped back up to the surface all by itself. Keep making it float, Harley ordered. In 1891, Ivory advertisements began telling the world, "It floats."

What happened to Harley? Just as he had planned, Harley retired at 42, and spent the rest of his life in Massachusetts. And what happened to Ivory soap? It became America's No. 1 soap. And it still is today, because Americans just can't get enough of that pure clean.

KLEENEX®

From Wisconsin to the World

People respected Charles B. Clark of Neenah, Wisconsin. So, in 1872, when the Civil War veteran talked about building a paper mill, John A. Kimberly listened. Clark, Kimberly and two other men invested $7,500 each to form Kimberly, Clark & Company. Their first product was newsprint made from rags.

The four founders of Kimberly, Clark & Company

The mill prospered on principles set by the founders: make the best possible product, serve customers well, and deal fairly with employees. In 1928, when Kimberly, the last of the four founders, died, the paper company was reorganized as the Kimberly-Clark Corporation.

Meanwhile, the company's chemists had developed CELLUCOTTON®, a revolutionary breakthrough in absorbent material, used extensively during World War I for gas mask filters and surgical dressings. After the war, Kimberly-Clark refined CELLUCOTTON and marketed the new product in 1924 as KLEENEX® Facial Tissue, the "Sanitary Cold Cream Remover." And Broadway stars, such as Helen Hayes and Gertrude Lawrence, endorsed the product.

Six years later, surveys showed that most consumers used KLEENEX Facial Tissue as disposable handkerchiefs rather than as a cold cream remover. Kimberly-Clark responded by developing such advertising slogans as, "Don't put a cold in your pocket." Sales boomed.

Today, Kimberly-Clark's annual sales are over $4 billion. KLEENEX, the most popular facial tissue in the world, is sold in more than 130 nations. Through leadership in fiber-forming, absorbency, and other technologies, Kimberly-Clark has evolved from a small Midwestern newsprint manufacturer to a highly diversified international company best known for its quality consumer products.

An elegant KLEENEX tissue box from the 1930s, and the current classic foil package design.

TYLENOL®

The trusted pain reliever

One hundred years ago, a young pharmacist opened a shop in the Kensington area of Philadelphia. The community marked the occasion with a dinner. The pharmacist was happy to celebrate. It had been a successful first day, with sales totaling $5.79.

At about the same time, across the Atlantic, a European pharmacist was in no mood to celebrate. Young and inexperienced, he had incorrectly sent an obscure drug to two doctors who had given it to a patient. The pharmacist worried what the outcome might be.

Fortunately, the new medication quickly reduced the patient's pain and fever, working better than the drug the doctors had originally prescribed. Later, it was discovered that in the body, the drug became acetaminophen, the active ingredient in TYLENOL.

Today, we do not even know the name of that European pharmacist. But the young Philadelphia pharmacist, Robert McNeil, went on to found McNeil Laboratories, the company that turned a brand of acetaminophen called TYLENOL into the country's most popular pain reliever.

In 1951, scientists at McNeil, now a member of the Johnson & Johnson family of companies, became interested in the unique benefits of acetaminophen. After four years of tests and study, they concluded that acetaminophen effectively relieved headaches, fevers, and body pains generally without the side effects commonly associated with aspirin.

In 1955, the FDA approved TYLENOL as a prescription drug, and five years later, as a nonprescription pain reliever. Success came quickly. Within a few years, TYLENOL became the pain reliever used most by hospitals. It continues to be dispensed today more than all other leading pain relievers combined.

Proof of the public's trust in TYLENOL was put to an almost impossible test during two tampering incidents of the 1980s. McNeil acted with model corporate behavior in rapidly and responsibly dealing with the problem, quickly restoring the brand to the marketplace in tamper-resistant packaging and product forms.

But it is clearly consumers', doctors', and hospitals' trust in the brand that has allowed TYLENOL to regain its place as the largest brand of pain reliever in the country.

McNEIL

McNeil's original pharmacy.

KODAK

'You Press the Button, We Do the Rest'

This year, picture-takers around the world will "press the button" almost 40 billion times. Perhaps that's astonishing, but it's also understandable. Photography fills a vital human need. It allows us to preserve a visual image of the people, places, and events in our lives; to keep a record of our family joys and our children's growth; to revisit the scenes of our travels. Without photography, the world would have only half a memory. And no one has done more to advance the art in the last century than Kodak, which in 1988 celebrates the 100th anniversary of its first camera.

George Eastman

George Eastman, founder of Eastman Kodak Company, didn't invent photography, but he made modern photography possible with several breakthrough inventions. Perhaps most significant was his development of flexible roll film, which served to bring photography to amateurs. Eastman also set about reducing cameras' weight. That first camera bearing the Kodak name, introduced in 1888, not only could be held in the hand, but delivered "snapshots" at the push of a button. "You press the button, we do the rest," was the advertising slogan. The camera came loaded with film for 100 pictures. After taking all 100, the photographer sent the camera to Rochester, New York. The pictures were developed and the camera was reloaded and returned.

But the camera that truly put photography within the financial reach of everybody was the famous box Brownie, sold for $1 in 1900. It introduced generations of people all over the world to the lasting joys of picture-taking, changing forever the way we look at ourselves.

These simple beginnings spawned a long line of spectacular photo-

How "Kodak" Came to Be

In 1888, George Eastman sought a brand name for his first camera, a short word that could be easily recognized and pronounced in any language. The letter "K" was a favorite of his, and he used it twice to coin a name that has become world-famous in photography.

SOURCE: Reader's Digest

market to include pens. Magic Marker's quality image slipped, and a decision to drop its premium positioning and compete on price hastened the slide into oblivion. In the 1980s, the Italian luxury shoe and handbag manufacturer Gucci stretched its exclusive brand name, reputation, and equity to a breaking point by indiscriminately putting its brand logo on fourteen-thousand different products, including T-shirts, key chains, sunglasses, watches, and coffee mugs. It has taken ten years for Gucci to recover its reputation, equity, sales, and profits by associating the Gucci brand with only very expensive, high-quality clothing, bags, and a few accessories. It is difficult to hurt a great brand name, but it can be done.

Apple computer has lost the premium its stock once commanded for its brand reputation and brand equity. Although it still has 20 million "die-hard" customers delighted with its easy-to-use product features, the problem is the value of its brand and customer base is declining rapidly.[27] Why? Because the path the personal computer market is taking is based on Windows technology rather than Apple's operating system, it is expected that Apple will be left behind with outdated technology and much less software. Apple blew its window of opportunity to license its operating system and software to Macintosh clones in the late 1980s. It also did not undertake a major rewrite of its software (allowing Windows to catch up), and, although it was the first to commercialize the laser printer, it gave the market away to Hewlett-Packard because it refused to make versions of its printers that worked with DOS-based PCs.[28] In short, maintaining brand equity depends on the company making the correct long-term product development decisions and backing the right technology in its markets. Harley-Davidson learned this by arrogantly assuming that the look, tremor, and rumble of a Harley compensated for the pool of oil under the motorcycle where it was parked. Having raised its quality, the company is now focusing on making sure the Harley does not lose its original look, tremor, and rumble that is so distinctive.

On the other side of the coin, while risky and expensive, new brand names can be launched successfully. Compaq computers became a billion-dollar company in three years. Reebok, with sales of $3 million in 1983, greatly expanded its line of products during the first six months of 1986, and sales have grown to $9 billion. Having acquired Rockport, the leading maker of walking shoes, Reebok faced an interesting embarrassment of riches. Should it make Rockport walking shoes, Reebok walking shoes, Rockport Reeboks, or Reebok Rockports? Much depends on who the target market is and the respective images and equities of the two brands in the target market. The company ended up making both Rockport and Reebok walking shoes.

Brand Clout in the Channel

In addition to signaling quality, a high-status brand name gives a manufacturer clout over retailers, because the presence of the brand in the store raises the reputation and status of the store. Ralph Lauren franchised his own Polo men's clothing stores that capitalize on the image of his designer label—old money, panache, and understated, waspish conspicuous consumption. Although clearly irritated at Polo's downstream integration, the major department stores continued to sell the Polo label because of customer demand. Ralph Lauren's logic was that if the exclusive stores can integrate

[27] Peter Burrows et al., "How Much for One Apple, Slightly Bruised?", *Business Week*, February 12, 1996, 35.
[28] Walter S. Mossberg, "Apple of America's Eye Falls Victim to Pride," *The Wall Street Journal*, January 24, 1996, B1.

upstream and push their own exclusive designer labels to compete with Polo, then he was perfectly entitled to retaliate by integrating downstream. Now Levi Strauss also has Levi and Dockers stores.

The success of The Limited and Gap clothing chains suggests that when retailers combine their merchandising skills with creative and competitive product design, quality control, and exclusive private brand imaging, they can beat manufacturers in the brand war. The battle between retailers and manufacturers for dominance of the channel may well be won or lost on the crucial issue of whether, in the end, consumer *store* loyalty is greater than consumer *manufacturer brand* loyalty. If manufacturers lose their brand equity and end up manufacturing retailers' brands under license, then they can say good-bye to their marketing departments and most of the profits from innovating. Such a trend may be occurring in some food categories.

The Pros and Cons of Family Brands

The first advantage of a well-known brand is that it can be used to launch new products. Table 10.3 presents a list of successful brand extensions into new product categories and a list of failed extensions. Two keys to successful brand extension follow:

1. Extend into product categories used in the same situation as or by the consumers of the original branded product.
2. Transfer the unique quality associated with the original brand (the characteristic that comes across as a strong benefit) into the new product category.

Brand extensions fail when the association between the products is not obvious, when the original brand has too unique an image, when already dominant brands exist in the product category, or when the quality of the new product is not as high as that of the existing product under the same brand name.[29]

A strong brand name will grab the consumer's attention and may lead to new product trial. It will provide a foot in the door—but that is all. A rose is a rose by any other name, and so is a ho-hum, me-too product. Brand name extension is most effective when it is applied to a product that is complementary in usage to the original, branded product, but it is still not assured. For example, Mr. Coffee, the brand name for the original automatic coffee machine and filter, was applied to a premium brand of ground-roast coffee, but the extension failed. Despite the strength of the brand and access to its excellent filter distribution system, the problem was that the $3 billion market already had very strong brand names, such as Folgers, Maxwell House, and Hills Brothers, that dominated the market (with about a 50 percent market share). The Mr. Coffee brand, unlike the successful new brand Starbucks, did not have a differentiated taste advantage over the established brands.

Often, the company name can be used as the brand name (for example, Kodak, IBM, and Xerox). The overlooked advantage of using the company name is that product advertising has a twofold impact: It promotes the corporate image to the stock market as well as the product to customers. These days, when companies are so concerned about adding shareholder value and obtaining new financing, this is an important

[29] C. Whan Park, Bernard J. Jaworski, and Deborah J. MacInnis, "Strategic Brand Concept-Image Management," *Journal of Marketing* 50 (October 1986): 135–45; Peter H. Farquar, "Managing Brand Equity," *Marketing Research*, September 1989, 24–33; and Joshua Levine, "But in the Office, No," *Forbes*, October 16, 1989, 272–73.

Table 10.3 Successful and Unsuccessful Brand Extensions

SUCCESSFUL BRAND EXTENSIONS TO NEW PRODUCT CATEGORIES	
BIC disposable shavers	BIC disposable lighters
Kodak film	Kodak cameras and batteries
Coleman camping lamps	Coleman stoves, tents, sleeping bags
Winnebago campers	Winnebago tents, sleeping bags
Ivory soap	Ivory shampoo, dishwashing liquid
Woolite detergent	Woolite carpet cleaner
Jell-O gelatin	Jell-O pudding pops
Rubbermaid housewares	Rubbermaid farm food bins
Barbie dolls	Barbie games, furniture, clothes, magazines
Odor-Eater foot pads	Odor-Eater socks
Dr. Scholl's foot pads	Dr. Scholl's shoes, socks, wart remover
Bausch & Lomb optics	Bausch & Lomb contact lenses, sunglasses
Minolta cameras	Minolta copiers
Honda bikes	Honda cars, lawnmowers, rototillers, generators
Fisher-Price toys	Fisher-Price playwear
Lipton tea	Lipton soup mixes
UNSUCCESSFUL BRAND EXTENSIONS TO NEW PRODUCT CATEGORIES	
Jack Daniel's bourbon	Jack Daniel's charcoal briquets
Dunkin' Donuts	Dunkin' Donuts cereal
Jacuzzi baths	Jacuzzi bath toiletries
Harley-Davidson bikes	Harley-Davidson cigarettes
Rubbermaid housewares	Rubbermaid computer tables
Stetson hats	Stetson shirts, umbrellas
Levi jeans	Levi business wear
Certs candy	Certs gum
Mr. Coffee coffemakers	Mr. Coffee coffee

advantage. The advertising agency Ogilvy & Mather has pointed out that if a company's strong brand images are not tied to its corporate identity (which can occur when the company name is not the brand name), then a difference will exist between the value of consumer goodwill toward the company and the way the stock market values the company.[30] A number of companies that adopted separate corporate names are now returning to original brand names as a name for their company.[31] During the 1970s and 1980s, company names were general and nonlimiting. This age of acquisition and diversification has passed, though, and new-age names such as Allegis and Amstar hold little meaning for customers, particularly when the parent company has divested itself of all the businesses except the original branded product line. Now the names that held strong brand equity, such as United Airlines (Allegis) and Domino Sugar (Amstar), have been rejuvenated.

[30] "Two Different Animals: Brand Awareness and Corporate Image," *Forbes*, March 6, 1989, 20.
[31] "Company Names Go Back to Basics," *San Jose Mercury News*, August 30, 1991, 12D.

Brand Name, Logo, or Trademark Tactics

As already discussed, brands serve important communication functions and, in so doing, establish beliefs among customers about the attributes and general image of a product. After a brand has been established, the brand name, logo, and trademark serve to reinforce the beliefs that have been formed. To arrive at this point, the firm must have made good on its promises. The case for a new brand, however, is different. A well-chosen brand name and a well-designed logo can give a new brand a real boost. A good brand name, trademark, or logo for a new product should have four important characteristics:

1. It should attract attention.
2. It should be memorable.
3. It should help communicate the positioning of the product.
4. It should distinguish the product from competing brands.

Brand names and logos can help form memory associations. Names that are short, pleasing, easy to pronounce, and distinctive are more memorable. Ideally, brands and logos should be symbolic of one or more of the most important product benefits. Many brand names in the supermarket cleverly describe the unique benefit of the brand (for example, NoDoze, Easy Off, Handy Wipes, Band-Aid, Weight Watchers, Spray-N-Wash, and Healthy Choice). This is a very good way of implementing the desired product positioning strategy. Insurance companies use very concrete images in their logos and slogans, such as umbrellas, good hands, or solid rocks, to symbolize their intangible services and their differentiation. It is important to keep in mind that buyers choose products based on their perceptions of the benefits. A brand or logo works best if the target customer understands the link between the logo and the benefit.

Changing Logos and Repositioning an Image

From time to time, a major company's brand logo is rejuvenated. (see the Rationality in Practice Box, "FedEx Gets a Face Lift"). This is undertaken at no small expense, because it requires changing everything from packaging and advertising to letterheads and vehicle decals. Many argue that some logos must remain contemporary, particularly if they are to symbolize the futuristic, high-tech image of the company. That is why, for more than fifty years, Ma Bell (AT&T) kept modernizing and, in the process, simplifying its famous logo. Other companies that want to convey a conservative,

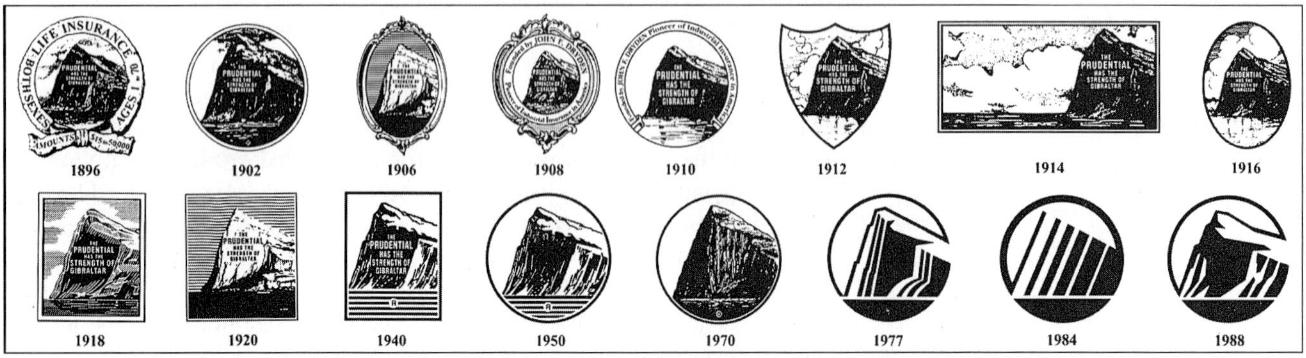

Figure 10.10

The Prudential logo has been revised many times, becoming progressively modern until it became *too* modern.

Rationality in Practice

FedEx Gets a Face Lift

Federal Express had the same purple-and-orange logo from 1973 to 1994 that had come to stand for speed, reliability, innovation, and excellent customer service. The problem came with the word "Federal." Initially, it had given the start-up legitimacy and authenticity, but by the 1990s "federal" stood for bureaucracy and slowness and in some parts of the world was associated with unpopular political parties. In some languages the word *federal* could not be easily pronounced. A worldwide brand and identity design consultancy, Landor Associates, had pitched a change to Federal Express in 1990, and in 1994 senior management decided in a hurry to revamp their logo. The urgency was that a large number of new trucks and planes were about to be purchased and painted.

The new logo, chosen from a final five out of four hundred sketches, was shortened to FedEx, the purple background to the lettering was removed, and the tag line "The World On Time" was added. Now the new message of accessibility, speed, and reliability on a global scale was captured in four words. The word "FedEx" became an action verb (to FedEx) and conveyed a much more dynamic image than the old full name. The new logo could be painted in seventy-two-inch-high letters on the side of trailers, compared to only fifty-eight inches high in the past, and it now could be seen across an entire airfield. Better yet, by cutting back the purple paint, FedEx saved millions of dollars in painting trucks and planes. The purple on the planes had increased surface temperature by 40 degrees, which added to operational and maintenance costs.

FEDERAL EXPRESS

Old logo.

FedEx
Federal Express

New logo.

SOURCE: "Why Federal Express Became FedEx," *@Issue* (Boston: Corporate Design Foundation, October 11, 1995), sponsored by the Potlatch Corporation.

traditional image (such as law firms and stockbrokerages) maintain old-fashioned names and logos. The John Hancock Mutual Life Insurance Company for a time dropped the famous signature from its logo in an overzealous spirit of modernization. The effect on attention and symbolism was very negative. Figure 10.10 shows how the Prudential Insurance logo has changed over the years. The company kept the "solid as a rock" symbolism but has modernized it to represent its innovative financial services. It is interesting that Prudential decided its logo became too modern looking, and, in the late 1980s, it reverted back to a more traditional logo.

Figure 10.11 **An Effective Warranty**

This warranty is written so the buyer understands it, and it creates an image of product quality and customer service. It is a very effective marketing and merchandising tactic. It is also a clever production tactic, because it expresses Levi's confidence in the quality of its workmanship and, hence, sends a positive signal to its suppliers and employees. Note that this warranty is used even though Levi's is a well-established and reputable brand.

Warranties: An Acid Test of Goodwill

The common law is that any good or service is automatically sold with an implied warranty of merchandisability and fitness. A product must be of merchandise quality—that is, it will do what a reasonable person would expect it to do. An oven should cook food, an oven cleaner should clean the oven, and rubber gloves should protect hands from the oven cleaner. A product must work. The basic law is quite simple. Why, then, do we have warranties? For two reasons: The first is to protect the seller, and the second is to protect the customer.

Protecting the Seller

Some firms wash their hands of responsibility for a product's nonperformance by offering a limited warranty, or *antiwarranty*. A limited warranty is for the protection of the seller, not the consumer. The following is an example of an antiwarranty.

> Opening this software package indicates your acceptance of these [following] terms and conditions. If you do not agree with them, you should promptly return the package unopened and your money will be refunded. LIMITED WARRANTY. The program is provided "as is" without warranty of any kind, either expressed or implied, including but not limited to the implied warranties of merchandisability and fitness for a particular purpose. The entire risk as to the quality and performance of the program is with you. Should the program prove defective, you (and not Standfast Software, Inc., or any authorized Standfast computer dealer) assume the entire cost of all necessary servicing, repair, or correction.

This example, with only the name of the company disguised, was used by *Consumer Reports* to demonstrate that, when it comes to warranties, buyer beware. It also demonstrates how some manufacturers refuse to stand behind their marketing claims.[32] It is understandable for a firm to protect itself against customers who have unreasonable expectations, misuse the product, or act in bad faith. However, many warranties protect the seller against the claims of consumers who are acting in *good faith*. When this happens, it is now the seller who is acting in bad faith. For this reason, at least eight states do not allow sellers to offer such limited warranties. A company pursuing this kind of a warranty policy is also behaving irrationally in a competitive sense, because it has dropped even the pretense of serving the interests of consumers.

Another criticism of warranties is that they cannot be understood by most consumers. Figure 10.11 presents an exemplary Levi Strauss warranty. It is refreshingly open, honest, and generous. Who would not have confidence and trust in a seller that offers such a warranty?

Warranties as a Point of Competitive Differentiation

On the positive side, warranties like the Levi's warranty often go well beyond protecting the consumer interest. They are used as a marketing tactic to reinforce product quality or performance claims.[33] This type of warranty strengthens a company by focusing attention on design and production-process quality control that match the warranty. Rather than constraining a warranty by engineering and production limitations, an ambitious warranty strategy acts as a spur to improve quality control and design. A significant reason for Chrysler's recovery in the early 1980s was its offer of a five-year, fifty-thousand-mile warranty on its line of K cars and other models. At the time this was significantly and noticeably better than other manufacturers' twelve-month, twelve-thousand-mile warranties. Research has shown that an outstanding warranty has an impact on consumers, particularly for a new brand.[34]

[32] "Is That Warranty Any Good?" *Consumer Reports*, July 1984, 408–10.
[33] C. L. Kendall and Frederick A. Russ, "Warranty and Complaint Policies: An Opportunity for Marketing Management," *Journal of Marketing* (April 1975), 36–43.
[34] Geoffrey Heal, "Guarantees and Risk Sharing," *Review of Economic Studies* 44 (1977), 549–60; and Rao Unnava, "The Effect of Warranties on Strong Brand Names and Unknown Brand Names," working paper, Ohio State University, Columbus, 1993.

Chrysler did more than simply offer and promote its outstanding warranty. It supported Lee Iacocca's promise to stand behind every car his company built, and many believed Chrysler could offer such a warranty because it built "the best cars made in America." The connection between the warranty and quality was spelled out. The inferior warranties of competitors also implied, whether true or not, an inferior product. The Chrysler dealers also like the warranty because the terms required maintenance and repair to be provided by an authorized dealer, which generally encourage dealer loyalty. Chrysler's big gamble achieved two important objectives: It helped differentiate Chrysler in terms of quality, and it helped its dealers combat the aggressive after-sales service competition of the emerging auto service specialists such as Sears and Firestone.

A warranty or guarantee not only raises quality expectations but also raises employee efforts and morale, so it serves as a control process as well as a point of differentiation. For example, Hampton Inns offered a refund to any customers dissatisfied with their stay. Refunds totaled $1.1 million in 1993, but revenues increased by more than $10 million.[35] Just as important, because everyone from maids to front-desk management were empowered to grant the refund, employee job satisfaction increased, and turnover fell from more than 100 percent to 50 percent. The program also helped Hampton Inns identify guests' biggest peeves—one of which was the lack of ironing boards and irons in the rooms.

Following Through on Claims

A customer whose complaint is handled promptly and graciously can become a more vocal, loyal customer. It is therefore essential to process a warranty claim quickly and efficiently. A warranty may look good on paper and still not stand for much. All the good-faith strategies in the world amount to nothing if the consumer faces an incompetent or unresponsive complaint-handling process. The consumer will interpret the nonperformance as obstructionist or antagonistic to his or her grievance. The consumer may then end up angrier than if the promised warranty had never been offered.[36]

The keys to implementation are accessibility to a sympathetic ear—not a questioning or even adversarial customer service representative—and a speedy response. An 800-number connecting users to a person trained to receive warranty claims provides the accessibility and speed of response. A problem often can be defused by a sympathetic, knowledgeable, and diplomatic customer complaints manager with the authority to rectify problems. A good customer service manager has to recognize (but does not point out) that customers often do not read the instructions, and that *product* nonperformance is often actually due to *user* nonperformance. Tracking such complaints may further reveal a problem with the product design or the readability and clarity of instruction manuals.

Packaging: Much More than Protecting

Each year, companies spend more on packaging than on advertising. As markets have matured and competitive differentiation narrowed, packaging has become a very important component of marketing strategy. Sometimes a firm forgets that the packaged product, not the product alone, is sold and purchased. A product's packaging is often

[35] David Griesing, "Quality: How to Make It Pay," *Business Week*, August 8, 1994, 54–59.
[36] William O. Bearden and Jesse E. Teel, "Selected Determinants of Consumer Satisfaction and Complaint Reports," *Journal of Marketing Research* 20 (February 1983): 21–28.

also its most distinctive marketing effort. This is not just because most consumer decisions are made at the point of purchase. The package often makes product usage easier and therefore adds to the value of the product. For instance, opening and resealing, pouring, mixing, processing, and cooking all may be enhanced or made easier by creative packaging. A package also continues to communicate on the kitchen shelf, workshop bench, and, most important, during product use. Hence instructions on the package are very important.

Instructions and Better Performance

Caring about the customer includes paying attention to details. Providing easy-to-understand instructions is such a detail. Instructions make for a more informed and skilled user. A more informed and skilled user gets the very best performance out of a product. In this way, carefully presented and written instructions lift the performance and, hence, the quality of a product. If poor package instructions lead to misuse and less-than-optimum performance, then no matter how superior a product's ingredients or material composition, the perception of its quality (and not the user) will suffer. Consequently, making a few simple improvements to usage instructions probably offers more potential return on investment than any other marketing activity. The very success or failure of a new product may turn on the clarity and quality of its usage and care instructions. To not recognize this fact is a major tactical blunder.

Packaging and Classical Conditioning

The most powerful example of classical conditioning occurs when the consumer's satisfaction with a product is transferred to its package. The next time that consumer visits a retailer or looks at a catalog, he or she will respond to that package, including its design features and shape, more positively. And each satisfactory use reinforces the learning. Consequently, the package must be distinctive, and not just to attract initial attention. It acts as a distinct after-trial cue—the package is liked because the contents are liked.

Performing at the Point of Purchase

A package also may have to be designed to fit a unique display location. For example, if a product is an impulse purchase item to be displayed at the checkout counter, then its packaging must be compact and fit the standardized display racks; otherwise, the retailer will not display it. The classic case of an eye-catching display is the L'Eggs point-of-purchase stand with its hundreds of plastic eggs in different colors. More recently, DIM, a French hosiery manufacturer (and subsidiary of the BIC Company), took the fashion hosiery market by storm with its patterned, silky-textured stockings displayed in a patented package with a hole through which a swatch of the stocking protruded. The package allowed the shopper to not just see but also feel "la difference."

Display packaging should reinforce the positioning of the product, but sometimes this does not happen. Johnson Wax, in one of its few false marketing moves, launched Clean and Clear (a cleaner) in an opaque bottle. The packaging confused both retailers and consumers, leading some to believe it was a polish. The bottle should have been sparkling clear. Cans or plastic or cardboard packages may be less expensive and easier to handle, but packaging industry research has shown that for some beverages and foods, a glass bottle or jar can significantly enhance the quality image of the brand.

Packaging to Enhance Usage

Just as distributors, retailers, and other channel intermediaries realize value from product packaging, the consumer can realize its value in the usage situation. If, for example, frequent users of eyedrops carry the product in their pockets or purses, then the consumer will receive value if the package is small and easy to open (perhaps with one hand). If jam manufacturers want their product to move from the refrigerator to the breakfast table more often, then the container should be made attractive enough to take its place on the breakfast table. But, when a product is transferred from its original package into a more attractive or convenient-to-use container, then much of the point-of-usage behavioral conditioning will be lost.

Several very innovative packages have added real convenience to product use. For example, when Beech-Nut apple juice switched from cans to bottles (onto which plastic nipples for babies could be attached), sales quadrupled. The taste improved as well. Minnetonka, Inc., was the first to introduce the soap and toothpaste pump dispensers to the U.S. market. Colgate-Palmolive, Lever Brothers, and Procter & Gamble all followed, concerned more about losing market share to each other than to the original packaging innovator, Minnetonka. Chesebrough-Ponds put nail polish in a special type of felt-tipped pen. The new convenience packaging helped increase the company's nail-polish sales by more than 20 percent, and demand for the new product was twice what was initially forecast.

Even disposal can become a dominant concern. A biodegradable or recyclable package will appeal to environmentally concerned market segments and, in fact, may be mandated by future public policy. Once upon a time, foods were sold in glass jars that could be reused by the homemaker. Today, very few packaged-goods marketers in the United States seek to add value by providing a package that has a life beyond its ingredients.

Labels: A Further Test of Customer Orientation

Whether or not a company is really customer oriented often can be determined by an examination of its product's label. If the label appears to be an afterthought, with a bare minimum of information (that is, it contains only what is legally required), then the conclusion is obvious. On the other hand, a customer-oriented label is likely to serve the following functions:

- Identify the manufacturer, country of origin, and ingredients or materials comprising the product
- Report the expiration date and the contents' grading based on a prescribed government standard (as appears on egg cartons)
- Explain how to use the product
- Warn about potential misuse
- Provide easy-to-understand care instructions

A quality label signals a quality product. Often the label also must be designed for the market segment. For example, the elderly need labels with large lettering. Furthermore, because many customers toss instructions and packaging away, the only way a customer can reach a manufacturer is through the information provided on the label. This suggests that a customer service–oriented company should always place its service 800-number on its labels.

Product and Service Issues in Global Markets

Over the past twenty years, many U.S. firms have come to rely more and more on foreign markets for a sizable portion of their revenues. When it considers a particular foreign market, a company must decide how much to adapt its product to the new market. In "The Globalization of Markets," Theodore Levitt says that basic needs are the same or very similar from country to country.[37] Accordingly, he suggests that little or no adaptation need be made for many products. This contention has raised considerable disagreement.[38] It is argued that cultures differ so much from country to country that a "one size fits all" product will tend to lose out to offerings that are more tailored to individual needs (see chapter introduction). It is also hard for a firm to argue for global standardization when it allows regions of its domestic U.S. market to offer specialized products, advertising campaigns, and promotions. In either case, the product manager considering the move into a foreign market must evaluate local needs, preferences, and buying behavior (as well as channel requirements, competition, and the regulatory environment) before deciding how much to customize the product.

While U.S. companies have expanded their operations in foreign markets, companies competing in the domestic market have discovered that the U.S. market is attracting much more foreign competition. In light of this trend, even companies that compete only domestically must pay attention to competitive trends in other countries. Many global companies launch products in their home markets first (for example, the Volkswagen Golf was first launched in Germany and then was exported to the United States as the Rabbit). After gaining domestic experience, they launch the product in attractive foreign markets, particularly the United States. Consequently, a company that watches foreign markets for developments in their product categories can anticipate that these innovations will soon appear in the U.S. market. The competitively rational choice is to become globally vigilant and to imitate overseas innovations *before* they reach the U.S. market. American companies also must rid themselves of their complacency, which is based on the belief that Japanese and other foreign competitors are able to imitate but that American firms are way ahead when it comes to real innovations. According to the National Science Foundation, in the early 1980s new U.S. patents were more likely to refer to prior patents issued to Japanese inventors than they were to refer to patents issued to U.S. citizens.[39] American companies now seem to be behind in *both* innovation and imitation and need to improve their new product development management accordingly.

The issue of global branding was discussed somewhat in Chapter 9. A cross-cultural reality is that sometimes a global brand name cannot be used because the name (or a very similar name) is already owned by another company in the foreign market, or because the name loses its positive image in the translation to a different language. This explains why Pert Plus, P&G's blockbuster shampoo in the United States, is Vidal Sassoon in the United Kingdom and Rejoy in Japan. When facing such a situation, the marketer needs to examine the perceptual and belief frameworks of target customers in the foreign country before an appropriate customized brand name is chosen.

Packaging and labeling issues are similar for domestic and international trade. Just as packaging within the United States must be functional and communicative, packaging for international markets must have the same effects. However, cultural, logistical, and regulatory differences result in packaging requirements that differ. In developing countries, for instance, packaging that can be reused by the customer is often

---

[37] Theodore Levitt, "The Globalization of Markets," *Harvard Business Review* (May/June 1983): 92–102.

[38] For a discussion of standardized versus targeted global products, see Sak Onkvisit and John J. Shaw, *International Marketing: Analysis and Strategy* (Columbus, OH: Merrill, 1989).

[39] Neil Gross, "Back to Basics," *Business Week*, special issue on Innovation, 1989, 30.

strongly preferred to disposable packaging.[40] Legal requirements may necessitate that packaging be of a specified material or meet certain size specifications. In addition, labeling may be mandated to have multilingual translations, to specify contents or ingredients, or to provide certain warnings. Regulations on packaging and labeling also may be promulgated in order to erect barriers to foreign-produced products.

International services have the same unique characteristics of domestic services. When marketing services internationally, though, the special problems of services become even greater. It is more difficult for providers to establish personal trust with their clients due to distance and cultural differences. The chances for the quality of service to vary become greater when foreign nationals, with different customs and training, are hired by an international service provider. Finally, making aspects of the service more tangible becomes difficult because the proposed tangible cues may be interpreted differently across cultures.

Finally, international marketers will face differences in regulations that affect their products beyond packaging and labeling. For example, individual countries may impose "domestic content" requirements on some products. In another example, ISO 9000 guidelines for quality management in products—published by the Swiss-based International Standards Organization (ISO) in 1979—are being adopted by the European Community as it moves toward unification.[41] Products imported or manufactured in the EC will have to be certified as meeting these standards, which may prove difficult for many foreign manufacturers. EC unification also involves new standards for product design in many product categories. This may make it easier for importers in the long run but may cause some trauma in the short term because product designs must be altered. The cross-functional development team also needs to be aware of regulations such as those recently introduced in Germany that require medical equipment suppliers, appliance companies, and automobile manufacturers to take back and recycle the products they sell when they are finally worn out. Clearly, international marketers must do their homework before entering a new foreign market. In many cases, the marketer can do this by forming a joint venture with a company in the target country.

Discussion Questions and Minicases

1. Use the theory of competitive rationality to predict what will happen as CAD/CAM (Computer-Aided Design/Computer-Aided Manufacturing) software improves.
2. The development and launch of Acuvue disposable contact lenses is a good example of what can be accomplished by a small, autonomous organizational unit. Prior to 1987, Johnson & Johnson's small Vistakon unit had concentrated on the market for contact lenses for patients with astigmatism. In 1988, Vistakon began marketing disposable contact lenses developed from technology acquired in 1983 by Johnson & Johnson. Vistakon's sales grew from $20 million in 1987 to $225 million in 1991. Much of the success of the venture would seem to stem from the autonomy that Johnson & Johnson gives its business units. Vistakon was not hindered by a lengthy and bureaucratic approval process. Consequently, Acuvue came out six months before major competitors, such as Bausch & Lomb, Inc., or Ciba-Geigy Corp., could respond.
   a) Acuvue lenses cost the consumer about $300 per year, considerably higher than the cost of other kinds of lenses. How is it that Vistakon can charge so much, particularly during what many consider is the mature stage of the contact lens market?
   b) What suggestions would you have for Vistakon to continue its high level of performance into the future?

[40] Sak Onkvisit and John J. Shaw, *International Marketing: Analysis and Strategy* (Columbus, OH: Merrill, 1989), 490.
[41] Kerry Pechter, "In Europe's Epicenter . . ." *International Business* 5, no. 8 (August 1992): 46.

3. One way to extend the life cycle of a product is to find alternative uses for it. This is exactly what Vector Group did with an unlikely product: Soviet missiles. In 1990, Vector approached the then Soviet Union's military to open talks about buying old Soviet missiles that had been obviated by the easing of tensions between the superpowers. After two years, Vector closed a deal with the Russian Defense Ministry for one hundred-fifty advanced submarine-launched missiles. The new use for the missiles was simple: target practice. After removing the warheads, Vector planned to resell the missiles to the U.S. Navy. The Russian missiles are less expensive than target missiles produced in the United States. What suggestions would you have for Vector concerning its future operations in this market? What other uses might it find for obsolete Soviet missiles?
4. Several companies are looking ahead to the next wave of personal computers, called personal information managers, (PIMs). Suppose you were a marketing manager for one of these companies and you wanted to do a quality-function-deployment analysis for this new technology.

   Discuss the problems you would encounter in doing such a QFD analysis this early in the life cycle for the PIM. How might you do a preliminary QFD analysis that would help you specify a product without getting bogged down in the problems you mentioned in the first part of your response?
5. The design for the Goodyear Aquatred tire is unique and effective. The tread design carries water away from the center of the tire so better traction is maintained. This benefit is actually communicated in part by the tire itself; the tread design makes it very clear what the tire will do. The tire also is made out of a special compound that lasts longer. This allows Goodyear to offer a sixty-thousand-mile warranty. The tire is priced about double the average price of other tires. Even so, sales for the tire have been high and the product introduction was a success.
   a) The impetus for this design came from Goodyear's advertising manager, who returned from a trade show in 1989 lamenting that tires had become boring. The company then began an effort to create something exciting. One would generally not expect a successful new product in such a utilitarian industry to come from a development goal of creating an "exciting" product. Why do you think this product was so successful?
   b) One of the interesting aspects of this tire design is that the tread design itself enhances the communication of the benefits. What might a company do in its development efforts to incorporate communications elements into its product designs.
6. Increasing customer satisfaction with the photos taken by the basic lens-shutter camera (the poor cousin of the single-lens-reflex camera) involved analyzing some eighteen-thousand photos taken by such cameras and identifying why about one in twelve were not very good.[42] The reasons were fairly evident: (1) poor focus adjustment, (2) not enough light, (3) camera not set to the correct film speed, and (4) double exposures because the film was not wound forward. How do you think the design was changed to improve the lens-shutter camera?
7. What do you think are the specific ingredient and process characteristics that create great-tasting coffee?
8. The Autotest service plan does not present a benefit times activities QFD matrix for the proposed service. Please develop such a matrix. In doing so, think of all the activities Autotest might provide to assist the target market in buying a used car.
9. McDonald's Corp. investigated the possibility of adding new offerings to its menu. One of these was pizza.[43]
   a) Why would McDonald's want to try offering such items as pizza?
   b) What problems would McDonald's have in its efforts to extend its branded product line to include pizza?
   c) What do you think McDonald's should do to address these problems?

[42] Kenichi Ohmae, *The Borderless World* (New York: Harper Business, 1990).
[43] "McRisky," *Business Week*, October 21, 1991, 114–22.

10. Below is the control-panel design for a microwave oven. Suggest how you would change the controls for a target market of older consumers (age seventy-five plus) who wish to keep cooking for themselves but are intimidated by complicated new technology.

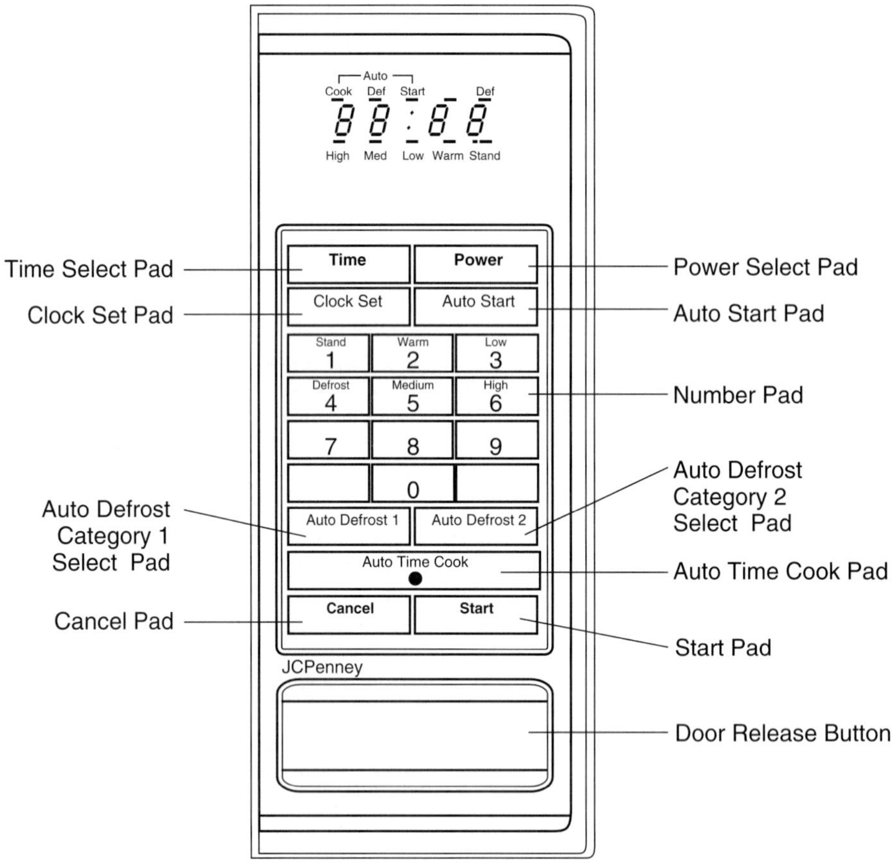

11. In 1991, Levi Strauss & Co. decided that too many counterfeit pairs of its 501 jeans were appearing, particularly in Eastern Europe. Cheap jeans of variable quality, not manufactured or licensed by Levi Strauss, were being sold with the Levi's logo. Levi's is an established brand name with an established quality image. Too many counterfeit jeans could undermine that quality image. A second problem was, of course, the loss of potential sales.

a) Should Levi Strauss be concerned about the deterioration of its image? Could it not be argued that if buyers recognize a difference between the fake jeans and the real thing, then Levi's quality image will be reinforced—not undermined?

b) One might argue that two market segments are being addressed. A cost-conscious market segment will buy the fake Levi's, and a quality conscious market segment would purchase the real Levi's at a premium price. In this case, wouldn't the loss of sales actually be negligible?

c) What might Levi Strauss do to address the problem?

12. Bruce McLaren, a New Zealander, founded the McLaren racing team that won eight Formula One world championships during the 1980s. The company has been heavily financed by corporate sponsorships, but the McLaren brand name has not been used on other product or service extensions. Suggest some licensing opportunities and explain why.

13. Comment on the strengths and weaknesses of the logo for a luxury, woolen mattress pad.

14. Why are warranties less often used in business-to-business selling and advertising? Does it mean they are less important?

15. Ford effectively responded to Chrysler's extended warranty by extending its warranties to seventy thousand miles and seven years. What did this have to do with its campaign, "Ford, where quality is number 1"? Why did the Japanese manufacturers not extend their warranties beyond twelve thousand miles and twelve months?

16. What does a service contract signal to the buyer of an appliance?

17. "We are social animals who live in families and communities. We work together, play together, and sleep together. We willingly give ourselves to those whom we love. Unselfish service to others is one of the greatest human virtues, almost deified in heroes and heroines." Does this statement describe a characteristic common to almost all religions and cultures? Many humans derive great satisfaction out of giving to other people. How does this help services marketing? How does this selfless generosity hurt services marketing?

18. TRM Copy Centers Corp. of Portland, Oregon, runs a service for small retailers. TRM installs copiers in the store for $95 and then provides repairs and supplies. Customers make their own copies for 5 cents per page. The retailer keeps about one-fourth of the proceeds.

TRM makes this business profitable by centralizing and standardizing. Supplies and repairs are centrally dispatched from one location in each of the thirty-four cities where TRM operates. The copiers are secondhand, so their cost is low. They only come in two models, so their repair service is inexpensive. Of course, TRM buys supplies in bulk, so it controls this cost as well.

a) What is it about TRM's service that makes it attractive to the retailer? The retailer can always purchase or lease its own machine and keep all the proceeds from copy sales without giving up 75 percent of the revenue. Discuss this in terms of how TRM overcomes the traditional problems of service providers.

b) What problems might TRM encounter as it expands? How would you address these problems?

19. Retail giant Sears Roebuck has had difficult times. Competition and changing consumer behavior put Sears in a position of needing drastic changes. In the early 1990s, Sears concentrated on cutting costs and improving its bottom line.

In 1992, Sears's efforts reaped unwanted results. The Consumer Affairs Department of the state of California brought charges against Sears for fraudulent activity in its auto repair business.[44] In the course of a year-long investigation, Sears was caught systematically performing unnecessary repairs. Sears made reparations and took actions to correct the organizational incentives that brought on the problems.

[44] Kevin Kelly and Eric Schine, "How Did Sears Blow This Gasket?" *Business Week*, June 29, 1992, 38.

Even with Sears's quick action to fix the problem, it suffered a loss of sales. What do you think will be the long-term effect on Sears's service businesses? Is this service snafu likely to affect Sears's other business? Please explain.

20. In the early 1990s, Apple Computer, Inc.'s efforts in overseas markets included a targeted approach to Japan.[45] Apple contracted with several Japanese companies to sell Macintosh computers to both consumer and business customers in Japan. From a product strategy standpoint, Apple initiated agreements with Japanese companies to manufacture current or future Apple products: Sony Corp. manufactured Powerbook 100s (the smallest Apple laptop computer); Sharp agreed to make Apple's Newton, the palmtop PIM; and it was anticipated that Toshiba would make a Macintosh-based multimedia product that combined computing, video, text, and sound. The overall effort was aimed at getting Apple software into multiple products offered in Japan. Macintosh sales in Japan lagged sales elsewhere in the world prior to 1990. Apple's strategy for the future, though, seems to view Japan as a leading market.

a) Why would such a shift in Apple's global strategy be attractive? What would Apple hope to accomplish with such a strategy?

b) What risks does Apple face in following such a strategy? How might these risks be mitigated?

21. Intel, the leading manufacturer of microprocessors, based in Santa Clara, California, faced increasingly tough competition in the early 1990s.[46] Other semiconductor companies began offering their own versions of Intel's 80386 microprocessor, either by winning court cases (for example, Advanced Micro Devices) or by designing "clone" 386 chips that do not violate Intel's patents (such as those designed by Cyrix Corp. and Chips and Technologies, Inc.). Apple and IBM united in a joint venture to develop their own version of a microprocessor (to be manufactured by Motorola) to handle future multimedia processing requirements. Also, RISC (reduced instruction set computing) microprocessor manufacturers, which make the chips that drive higher-end workstations, were increasingly eyeing the upper end of the personal computer market.

In response to this competition, Intel took a number of measures. On one front, the company continued to fight the patent cases in court. Internally, it revamped its product development and marketing strategies. On the product development side, Intel began to introduce products in half the time it had taken prior to these changes. Instead of beginning work on the 686 microprocessor when the 586 was introduced—a process that took about four years—Intel began work on the 686 two years into the development cycle of the 586. Thus, it hoped to introduce the 686 only two years after the 586. As the chips, and hence the development process, become more complex, new ways had to be found to speed the process, even just to keep the process under four years in duration. Toward this end, Intel has instituted more concurrent engineering, computer-aided engineering, and prototype simulation.

Perhaps the biggest cultural change for Intel's development process is a new approach to accommodating customers. Instead of providing computer manufacturers with chip specifications only near the end of the development cycle, Intel began seeking customer input from the very beginning of the process. Early on, with the help of new simulation technology, Intel was able to offer computer manufacturers virtual prototypes they could use in planning new computer designs.

a) Discuss how Intel's change in product development gave it new competitive leverage. What threats will Intel have to watch for in its competitive efforts in the future? In addition to changing the customer focus of the product development process, Intel also changed its branding strategy. In the past, Intel had focused on building brand equity among computer manufacturers and resellers. In 1992, Intel began advertising directly

[45] Neil Gross and Kathy Rebello, "Apple? Japan Can't Say No," *Business Week*, June 29, 1992, 32–33.
[46] *Business Week*, June 1, 1992, 86–94.

to consumers through television and print. Its "Intel Inside" campaign for 486 processors was the first major effort of a component manufacturer to build equity at the end-user level.

b) Why would Intel do this? What problems could potentially torpedo this effort?

22. April 2, 1993, will forever be known in the history of marketing management as "Marlboro Friday." This was the day Philip Morris slashed prices on its leading brand of cigarettes to combat the loss of share to generic no-brand competition. In one day investors reacted by wiping $13.4 billion off the stock market value of the company and many more billions off the value of major-brand companies such as RJR, P&G, Quaker Oats, Coca-Cola, PepsiCo, and Gillette.

But the writing was on the wall even at the time of the huge takeovers of the late 1980s, when the consumer-brand companies were purchased for hugely inflated prices (described in the chapter). The heavy use of price promotions undermined the brand equity by encouraging shoppers to buy based on price (see Chapter 16). Retailers were also investing heavily in their own private labels that imitated the latest major innovations. For example, Totes, Inc., launched its slipper socks in 1988, and sales of the socks peaked at 14 million a year, more than 10 percent of which were made by Wal-Mart and Kmart alone. Within two years Wal-Mart and Kmart had found suppliers to make their own brand of slipper socks, and their knockoffs were sold at a price 25 percent below Totes, which were dropped by the giant discounters. Several recent market research studies have shown that fewer consumers are shopping for a particular brand. More shoppers perceive little difference among products (perceived product parity), and the combined market share of the top three brands in many food-retailing product categories has dropped. What should the senior executives of major consumer goods companies do to rebuild their brand equity and the market value of their stock? What does the history of the above events tell you about the rationality of the stock market's behavior on April 2, 1993?[47]

[47] The above facts were drawn from "Shoot Out at the Check-Out," *The Economist,* June 5, 1993, 69–72; and, Zachary Ziller and Wendy Zellner, "Clout!" *Business Week,* December 21, 1992, 66–73.

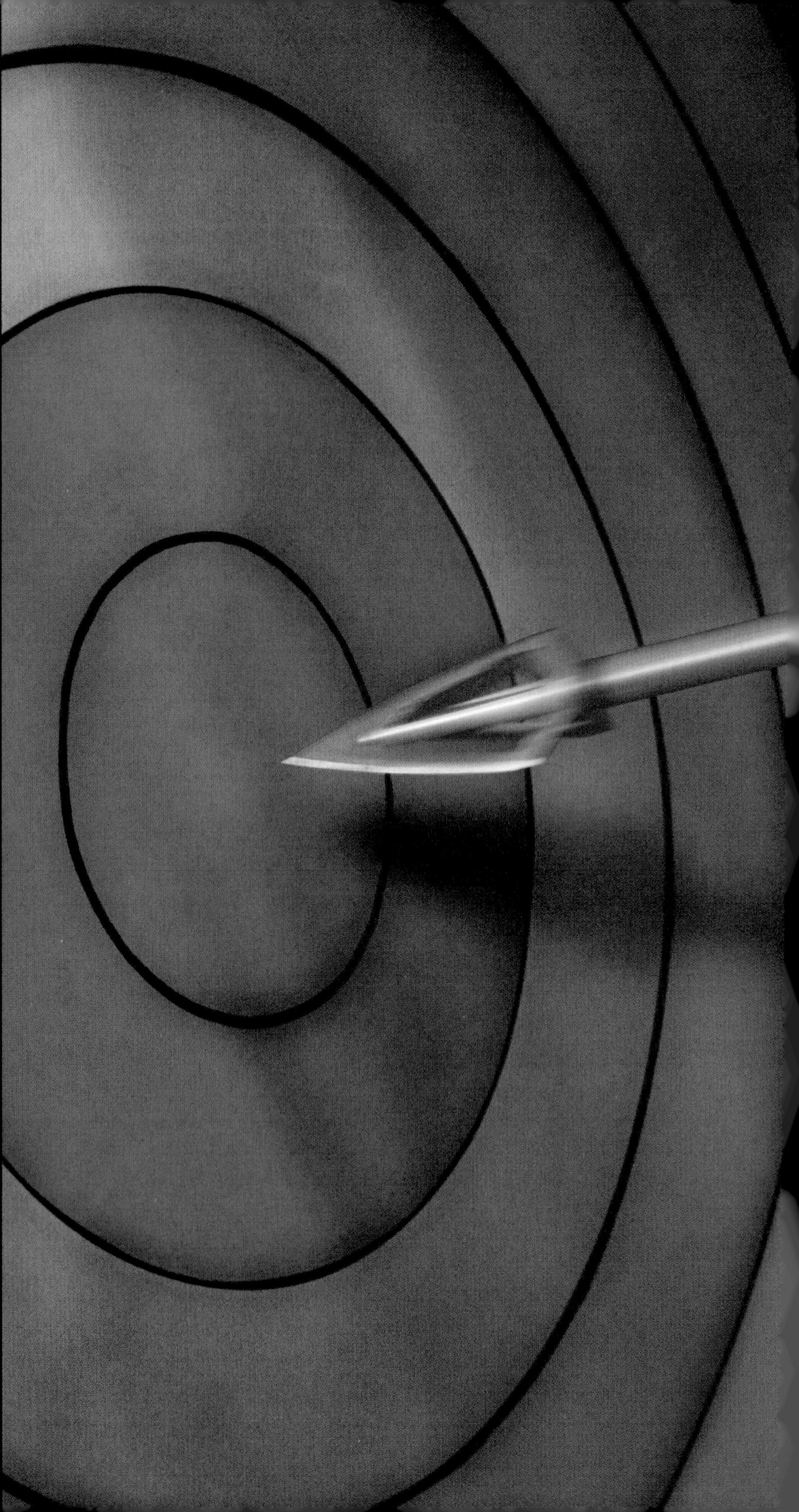

A little reciprocity goes a long way.

Malcolm Forbes

Prosperity makes friends, adversity tries them.

Publilius Syrus

CHAPTER ELEVEN

Relationship Strategy

As communication and transportation technology have shrunk the world and created a global marketplace, it has become increasingly important to develop new trading relationships with offshore suppliers of manufacturing components and then to develop further offshore trading relationships with distributors and retailers to sell the finished goods. In effect, a firm's management of its trading relationships has become as important a core competence as its targeting/positioning and product development skills. Today many firms compete by not only designing and developing more innovative products and services than their rivals but also by designing and developing more innovative trading relationships.

For example, Nike has been able to leverage its trading relationship with the retailer Foot Locker into a significant competitive advantage over its rival Reebok. In 1993, Nike's sales through Foot Locker were $300 million compared to Reebok's $228 million. By 1995, Nike's sales through Foot Locker were $750 million compared to Reebok's $172 million. The explanation is Nike's better served-market fit, strategy fit, and service.[1] Foot Locker's consumer franchise are teenagers and Generation-X customers, who are Nike's target market. Reebok appeals to older consumers and their preteen children. For several years Nike also has been making a

dozen products only sold at Foot Locker, with special marketing support that perfectly fits Foot Locker's merchandising strategy. By contrast, Reebok sold everything to everyone, including discounters down the street from Foot Locker; did not listen to Foot Locker's savvy about street-ware trends; and did not even get samples in time for Foot Locker to make its buying decisions early in the buying season. In short, Reebok was self-destructing because it is not executing the elementary ABCs of relationship management. ■

Introduction

A trading relationship is a relationship between a buyer and a seller who resells the goods and services. Trading relationships have been important since early humans began to trade. Archaeologists have discovered artifacts that indicate neolithic people traded with other tribes hundreds of miles away. The costs and risks of such trade must have led to the development of trading relationships that explored new, innovative exchanges of goods and services and the making and keeping of promises and alliances. Great wealth and empires were built on trading relationships. King Solomon's glory did not come from his gold mines. It came from a thirty-year trading relationship with the Phoenicians. He provided these legendary sailors with the timber for their boats and provisioned their voyages. The Phoenicians sailed around the coast of Africa, India, and China and developed trading relationships with local kings and queens.

Indeed, global relationship marketing is thousands of years old. As civilization made traders out of raiders, world exploration was driven by the desire to develop long-term global trading relationships among rulers. Gradually, ordinary citizens with more wit and enterprise replaced the aristocracy as the driving force behind the initiation and development of local and international trading relationships. The Dutch and British East India companies were global trading companies with vast resources and wealth greater than some of the nation states of the time. They were built by merchants who possessed great vision, creativity, and enterprise for developing trading relationships.

In principle, nothing has changed. Superior wits and enterprise win out today. At this very moment, new trading relationships are being formed among powerful companies in Europe, North America, and Japan and emerging new companies in Asia, South America, and Africa. These trading relationships will drive world trade in the twenty-first century. They are between suppliers and manufacturers and manufacturers and retailers. This chapter discusses why and how such trading relationships are formed. It focuses on manufacturer and retailer distribution-channel relationships, but the principles and processes discussed are quite generalizable to all trading relationships. Thus, while the terms *manufacturer*, *retailer*, and *manufacturer-retailer relationship* are used throughout this chapter, terms such as *seller*, *reseller*, *supplier*, and *distributor* could have been used without any loss of generality. Trading relationships are just that, whatever titles the partners give themselves. The chapter also assumes readers

[1] Joseph Pereira, "Nike's Sneaker Attack," *Miami Herald*, October 5, 1995, 1C, 3C.

understand the material presented in the channel analysis chapter (Chapter 7), particularly the sections on mass versus specialty distribution, the basic functions of channel participants, and distributor-relationship analysis.

Chapter Organization

Firms with superior ways of thinking about and making decisions about distribution relationships possess a competitive advantage as long as they can sustain their channel-relationship thinking advantage over their rivals. When they lose this advantage, some other players will, sooner or later, trump them with a more innovative trading relationship. This is particularly true in markets where innovations in products and services are so quickly imitated that little competitive product differentiation occurs among rivals. In short, the same competitive thinking skills that result in superior product/service positioning and development discussed in Chapters 9 and 10 also have to be applied to trading relationship positioning and development. The purpose of this chapter is to help develop such strategic thinking skills. The tactics of trading relationship management are discussed in the chapters that follow.

Figure 11.1 presents the organization of this chapter. The first section discusses the problem of fitting together the target markets and the competitive positioning of the parties wishing to develop a long-term trading relationship and defines relationship differentiation. The second section discusses ways of selecting specific channel relationship partners. After selecting and starting a relationship, both parties must start working at developing a superior cooperative relationship that leads to innovations that add value to the relationship and continuously increase relationship differentiation. This requires a theoretical understanding as to who initiates greater cooperation and process innovations within a trading relationship, as discussed in the third section. Naturally, when any two parties have different goals and are constantly reevaluating and trying to improve their relationship, conflict is likely to arise. In the final sections, some of the causes of conflict and solutions are discussed. It is argued that trading relationships have to be constantly under improvement and repair because constant competitive forces are trying to reduce a relationship's differentiation and unique competitive advantages. This requires an approach to trading relationship management that has become known as *relationship marketing*.

Relationship Targeting/Positioning

When choosing a type of distribution channel and a specific trading partner, a manufacturer has to look for the following:

1. A partner whose customers fit the manufacturer's target market segment
2. A partner whose service positioning and the positioning of the product mix that it sells fits with the positioning of the manufacturer's product and service
3. A partner who has superior marketing, merchandising, and physical distribution processes, systems, and skills
4. A partner who has employees who are creative thinkers and who know how to implement goals

A competitively rational retailer is looking for exactly the same characteristics in reverse. The desirable fit between the partners' served markets and their competitive

Figure 11.1 **Chapter Organization**

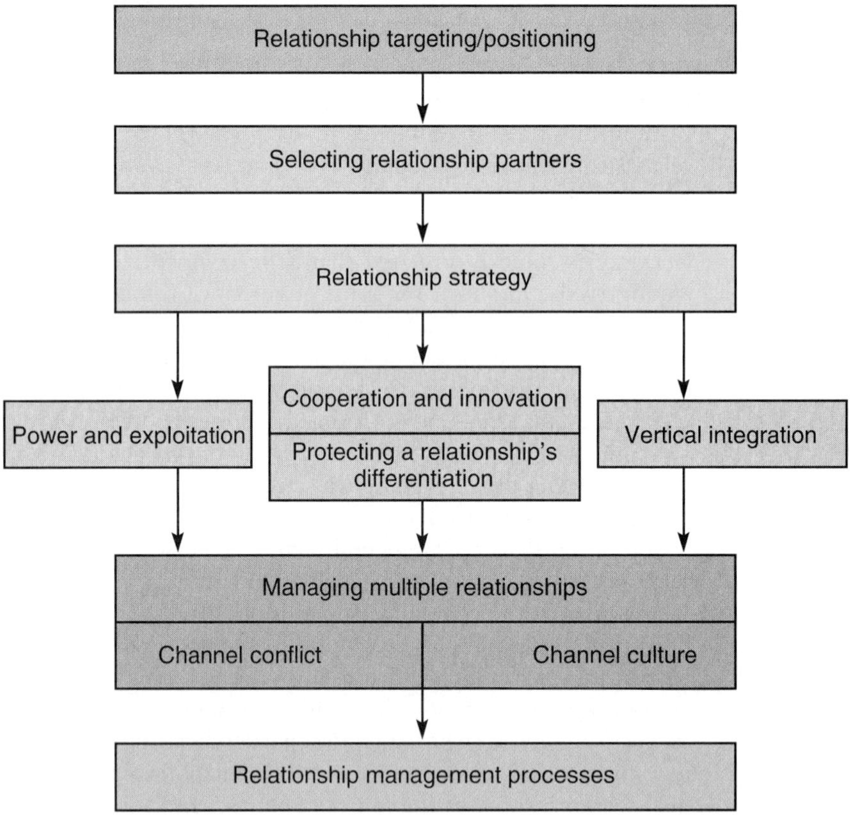

In this chapter the concept of relationship targeting/positioning, which has close parallels to product targeting/positioning, is first discussed and then followed by a process for selecting relationship partners that fit the desired targeting/positioning. The basic relationship strategy that a manufacturer pursues is next discussed. The choices are controlling and exploiting the partnership through power, managing the partnership through cooperative innovation, or complete ownership of the trading channel and partnership through vertical integration. The rest of the chapter discusses relationship management issues, particularly how to manage multiple relationships and the importance of process and people in managing a relationship.

strategies is illustrated in Figure 11.2. Bob Bennett, the CEO of Sharon, learned the hard way about served market fit. A manufacturer of a combination refrigerator-freezer and microwave oven (Microfridge) targeted for dormitory-living usage, he lined up seventeen independent appliance distributors. He reasoned that they paid quickly, had the trucks and warehouses to distribute the product to appliance retailers, and were hungry for new products because many of the major retailers were increasingly dealing directly with the large appliance manufacturers.[2] Six months after the 1989 launch, 3,500 units were backed up in the distributor warehouses, and only a few

[2] Teri Lammers Prior, "Channel Surfers," *Inc.*, February 1995, 67.

Figure 11.2 Relationship Targeting/Positioning Fit

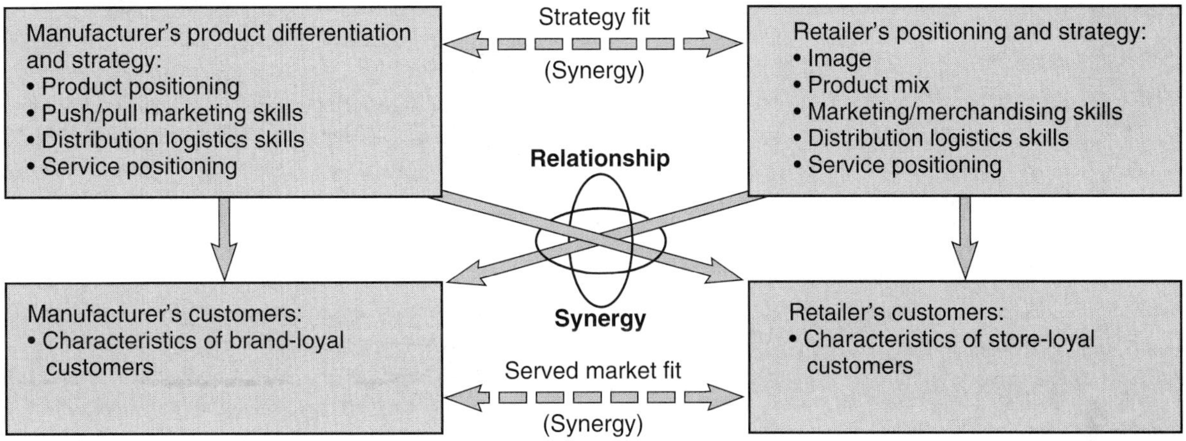

The trading relationship between the supplier and the reseller actually involves several fits and types of synergy. One is the synergy between the marketing programs and the synergy or overlap in the target markets. Another is the fit of the retailer's market and positioning to the manufacturer's target market and the fit of the manufacturer's product positioning and marketing programs to the retailer's shoppers.

hundred had been sold. Running out of cash and time, Bennett tried a very different trading relationship. He hired his own sales reps to sell directly to college-student and army-base housing directors. They sold the prospect of earning a profit of $50 to $70 a year renting each Microfridge to dorm residents over the ten-year life of the product. In 1990, 11,000 units were sold, and in 1995, 50 percent of Microfridge's $14 million in sales were made through the college channel and 25 percent through military bases. The lesson is for firms to choose a channel whose customers are their target market and whose customer service (in this case, leasing the product) fits with their product's positioning (a product for dormitory living).

Synergy occurs when the whole is more than the sum of the parts. *Relationship synergy* occurs when a high served-market fit and a fit between the marketing strategies and implementation skills of the two trading partners exists. This means that the manufacturer's positioning and strategy appeal to the retailer's served market and the retailer's positioning and strategy appeal to the manufacturer's customers. In Figure 11.2 this is illustrated by the crossed, diagonal arrows between the boxes. The resulting relationship synergy creates a unique combination of benefits to the final customer that translates into a unique competitive advantage for the relationship. The Rationality in Practice box discusses four further examples of companies that formed channel relationships in which a great deal of synergy and customer added value was created by what each party brought to the relationship and by how they worked together to add additional customer services and marketing campaigns.

In addition to trading relationships and processes that raise the perceived quality of the product and supporting services, a unique trading relationship advantage can come from both the manufacturer and retailer working together well to reduce the costs of

Rationality in Practice

Examples of Channel Synergy

The right product united with the right reseller can be a powerful combination whose effect on the customer and the competition is more than the simple sum of its parts. The combination is not additive but interactive. The incremental advantage over simply summing the parts is the unique synergy that exists between the strategies and target markets of the partners. This synergy is critical in distribution. The greater the competitive uniqueness of this combination, the greater the potential bond between the enterprises involved. The following are four examples of such relationship synergy:

- **Nexus hair-care products with hair salons:** The regular patrons of a hair salon are most likely to find premium hair-care products attractive, so the consumer franchise–target market fit is excellent. In addition, the endorsement of a trusted hairdresser combined with the proven performance of the product creates a powerful integrated strategy.
- **Swatch watches with boutiques and high-class department stores:** This successful bond, launched in 1983, resulted from Swiss product quality, trendy design, and a good pull advertising campaign perfectly fitted with the exclusivity, endorsement, and consumer franchise of the select stores.
- **Compaq with independent computer retailers:** Compaq offered a focused support system, very competitive margins, and, in its early years in the market, superior product features (such as faster processing, more memory, and more reliability). The independent stores worked with Compaq enthusiastically because Compaq's success gave the stores more clout with IBM, Wang, and DEC, whose direct sales tended to undercut the computer stores' sales and market efforts toward small and medium-sized businesses.
- **IBM with software manufacturers and value-added resellers (VARs):** IBM opened its PC architecture to software companies and VARs at a time when the personal computer market was growing rapidly. IBM gave a number of entrepreneurial software companies, such as Microsoft, credibility and access to a huge consumer franchise. In return, IBM's PC image and competitive position were greatly enhanced because its hardware was very quickly supported by a large number of software programs. This put competitive pressure on other PC manufacturers who had proprietary operating systems—and thus little software support.

doing business. If the cost-reduction drives and efforts of both parties are synchronized, as illustrated in Figure 11.3, and if this synchronization between the manufacturer and retailer is better than any other trading relationship that the manufacturer or retailer is in, then the trading relationship will have a unique competitive cost advantage.

In fact, Figure 11.3 was developed to help Procter & Gamble and Wal-Mart work together to reduce internal operating and trading costs. Wal-Mart cooperated in ways that reduced Procter & Gamble's manufacturing and shipping costs, and Procter & Gamble cooperated in ways that reduced Wal-Mart's selling costs. When both parties worked hard at taking the costs out of their internal and trading processes, the resulting trading relationship became the benchmarking standard for other manufacturers to evaluate (and imitate) their relationship marketing to retailers, and it also became the benchmarking standard for other retailers to evaluate (and imitate) their supply-chain management.

Chapter 12 details the communication, transportation, and logistical processes that can be used to increase customer service and reduce trading costs, particularly to reduce the manufacturer's cost of holding large inventories of finished goods and to reduce the costs of the retailer carrying a similar large inventory of the same finished goods. For now, the important point is that when a manufacturer and retailer work together on their trading relationship, they can achieve a total-quality outcome: increased target-customer satisfaction at a reduced cost. But total quality management of trading relationships starts with using a quality process to select trading partners.

Figure 11.3 **Manufacturer-Retailer Efficiency Loops**

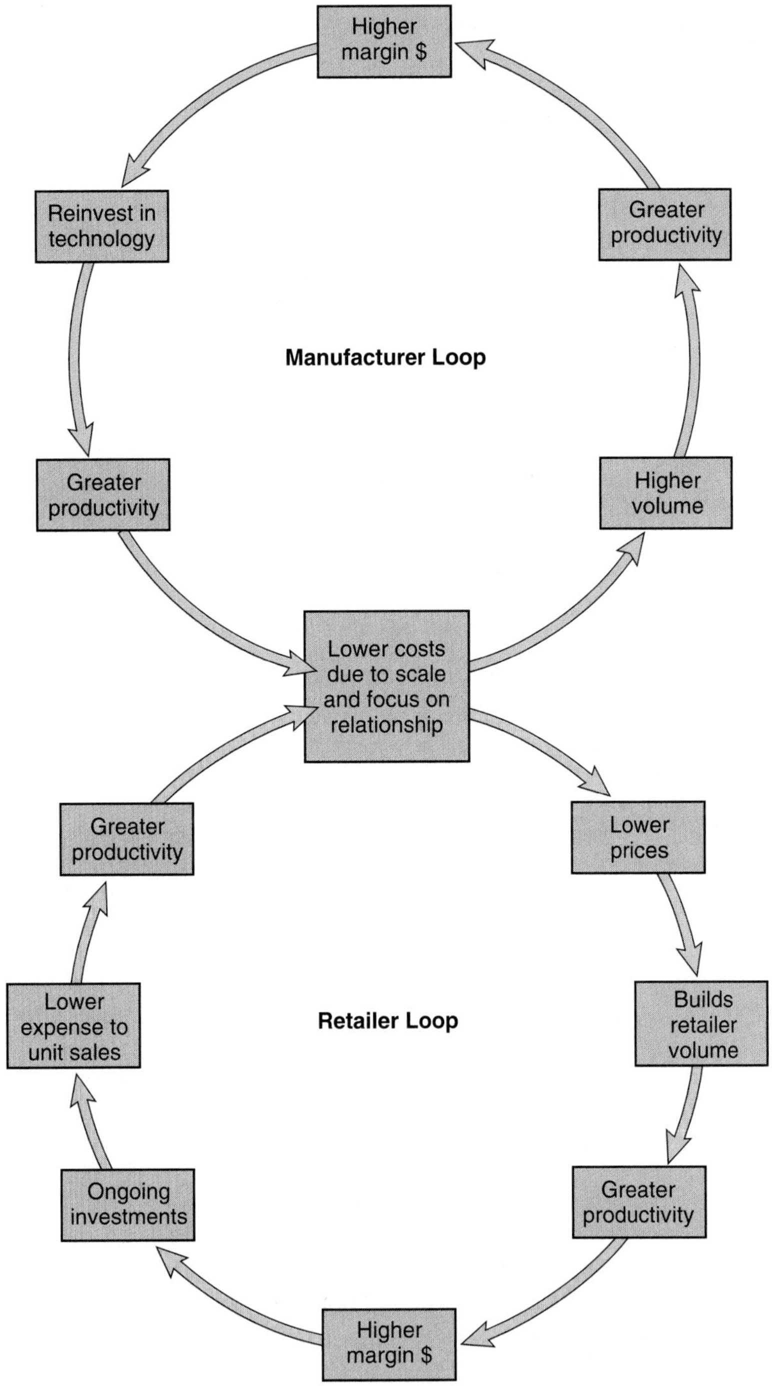

The cost-efficiency drive of the supplier helps drive the cost efficiency of the retailer, and the cost-efficiency drive of the retailer helps drive the cost efficiency of the supplier. If these two loops can be synchronized, then they will drive each other to ever higher levels of efficiency—to the benefit of both parties.

SOURCE: Reproduced with permission from Management Horizon's *Consumables Retail Review*, August 1992, 10.

Selecting Relationship Partners

Selecting trading relationship partners is truly a strategic decision because such relationships are expected to last a long time and to involve the investment of many company resources, and the most competitively driven companies expect to gain a unique competitive advantage from their trading relationships. A manufacturer has to select and manage a portfolio of distribution relationships, as described in the relationship portfolio-analysis section of the channel environment analysis chapter (Chapter 7). The following steps are involved in selecting a distribution channel to reach the target market segment:

1. Undertake a deep-segmentation analysis that identifies the needs and buying behavior of the different end-user segments (see Chapter 5). In consumer markets this involves understanding where they buy the product and what roles personal selling and after-sales service play in influencing where they shop. In business-to-business markets this involves understanding the product information needs of the customer, product customization needs, after-sales service, order frequency and size, one-stop-shopping and off-the-shelf purchase needs, and physical distribution customization needs, such as consolidation of several suppliers' orders into a truckload. Even details such as the size of the pallets the customers use to store and move their purchases have to be considered. In-depth discussions with end customers and salespeople will identify the distribution services the customer needs.
2. Identify the types of channels or combinations of distribution channels that distribute competitive products and services, defined as broadly as possible. A thorough audit of each of the alternatives then should be undertaken (see Chapter 7). The audit criteria should focus on the services the target segment needs, and then the auditor should rate the competitive capabilities and efforts of the specific or hybrid distribution channel on such criteria. In addition, consistent with the earlier discussion, the channel should be assessed in terms of its overall served-market fit and overall positioning-strategy fit.
3. The specific or hybrid distribution strategy that most cost-effectively fits the customer segment and its needs is chosen. A StratMesh 2.0 choice matrix can be created with selection criteria along the top of the matrix (the columns) and different distribution strategies down the side (the rows; see Figure 11.4). The rows with the most purple and green and least red and yellow identify the preferred strategies, and the text behind the color explains why a distribution strategy delivers a unique competitive advantage (purple light), that its fit with customer requirements is good (green light), that its fit is uncertain (yellow light), or that the strategy is flawed (red light). A summary scoring system is sometimes used to create an overall evaluation of a distribution channel, but this score can hide some real problems. Perhaps a better approach is to spend the time and effort evaluating how a red or yellow light might be turned into a green light through a trading process innovation so the relevant cell could be repainted green or purple.

For distribution networks involving hundreds or thousands of retailers, the decision to add a new reseller often lands in the laps of salespersons. If they are out beating the bushes to line up new resellers to carry the company's products, they will tend to be not quite as selective as the marketing department may want them to be. How should the firm handle this? When it is setting the channel strategy, it must establish clear policies for reseller selection, along the lines discussed in this section, to provide guidance for the salespeople. To ensure the salespeople exercise self-control and are discriminating in the trading relationships they initiate, it is important to explain to them the reasons for the selection criteria, particularly how and why being discriminating will increase the payoff and reduce their hassles down the road.

Figure 11.4a **Evaluating Alternative Distribution Strategies**

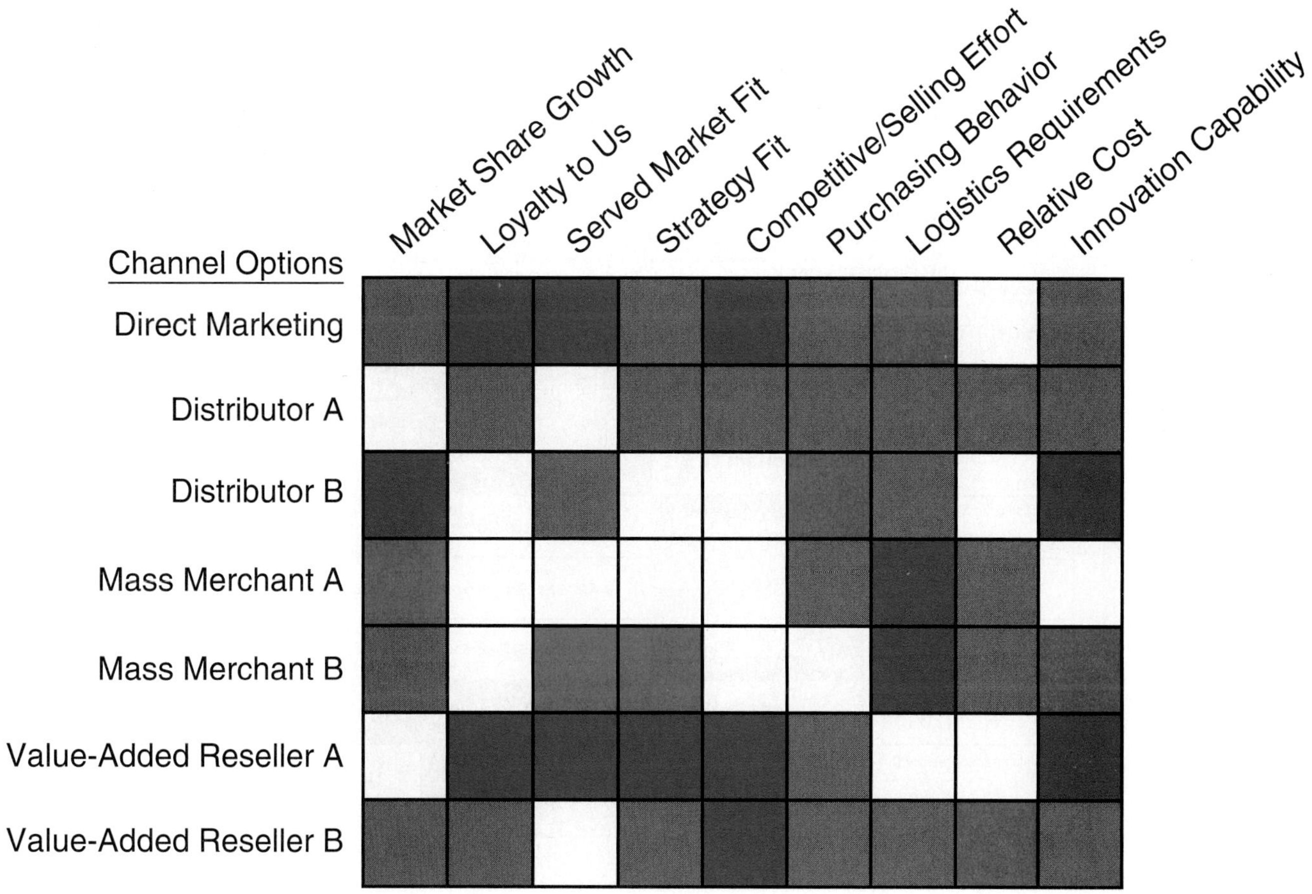

An evaluation matrix with selection criteria along the top and the different distribution options or contributions of options (a hybrid distribution strategy) down the side can help evaluate and select a distribution strategy.

SOURCES: This evaluation framework is based on V. Caster Rangan, Melvyn A. J. Menezes, and E. P. Maier, "Channel Selection for New Industrial Products: A Framework, Method, and Application," *Journal of Marketing* 56 (July 1992): 69–82; Rowland T. Moriarty and Urula Moran, "Managing Hybrid Marketing Systems," *Harvard Business Review* (November/December 1990): 146–55; and Louis W. Stern and Frederick D. Sturdivant, "Customer-Driven Distribution Systems," *Harvard Business Review* (July/August 1987): 34–41.

(continued)

Relationship Strategy

After selecting a channel, the relationship now has to be developed and managed. The next three chapters on relationship logistics, relationship selling and sales management, and integrated marketing communications discuss the programs and practices used to develop and manage trading relationships But before further exploring the tactics of relationship management in these chapters, it is useful to revisit the fundamental issue of how firms think about their trading partners. As discussed in Chapter

Figure 11.4b *(continued)*

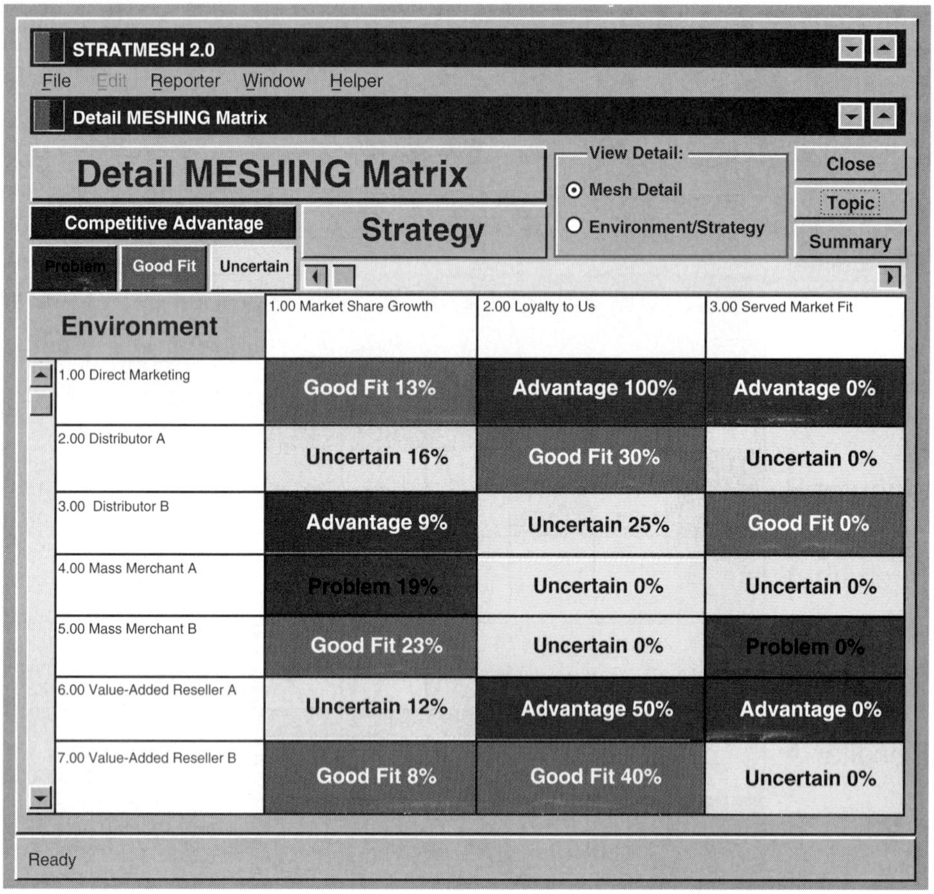

A StratMesh 2.0 matrix is created with selection criteria along the top and the different distribution options or combination of options (a hybrid distribution strategy) down the side. When in the process of rating the fit of the strategies, a new combination may suggest itself.

SOURCES: This evaluation framework is based on V. Caster Rangan, Melvyn A. J. Menezes, and E. P. Maier, "Channel Selection for New Industrial Products: A Framework, Method, and Application," *Journal of Marketing* 56 (July 1992): 69–82; Rowland T. Moriarty and Urula Moran, "Managing Hybrid Marketing Systems," *Harvard Business Review* (November/December 1990): 146–55; and Louis W. Stern and Frederick D. Sturdivant, "Customer-Driven Distribution Systems," *Harvard Business Review* (July/August 1987): 34–41.

6, one school of thought is to treat trading partners as competitors: Whatever they gain from a firm is the firm's loss and vice versa. This mental model of relationship strategy emphasizes how to exercise power and control in a trading relationship to get the most out of the relationship. This section discusses such a view of trading relationships and contrasts it with a relationship strategy that emphasizes innovation and cooperation and with a vertical integration strategy.

Relationship Power and Exploitation

Manufacturer power is the ability of a manufacturer to get a retailer to do what the manufacturer wants, and retailer power is the ability of a retailer to get a manufacturer to do what the retailer wants.[3] In practice, the *exercising of power* in a relationship means that the party subject to the power play is somewhat reluctant to cooperate in accepting the new trading terms or processes. Examples of such power plays are a manufacturer raising prices or requiring the installation of special merchandising displays and a retailer taking longer than usual to pay its bills or insisting that it be able to return all unsold merchandise for a full refund. In both cases the retailer and manufacturer, respectively, are likely to object to the behavior but comply because they really have no option: They are dependent on the relationship.

In a trading relationship, the balance of power depends on the balance of dependency. Manufacturer power is increased when a retailer perceives it has become more dependent on the manufacturer for its sales, profitability, growth, and competitiveness. Retailer power is increased when a manufacturer perceives it has become more dependent on the retailer for its sales, profitability, growth, and competitiveness. The factors that actually should determine relative dependency and, hence, relative power are listed in the following table:

THE MANUFACTURER IS LESS DEPENDENT WHEN	THE RETAILER IS LESS DEPENDENT WHEN
1. Many other retailers exist that offer a similar targeting/positioning fit.	1. Many other manufacturers exist that offer a similar targeting/positioning fit.
2. The number of such retailers has recently increased.	2. The number of such manufacturers has recently increased.
3. The number of competitive manufacturers has recently decreased.	3. The number of competitive retailers has recently decreased.
4. Sales through the retailer do not generate a large percentage of the manufacturer's profits.	4. Sales of the manufacturer's products do not generate a large percentage of the retailer's profits.
5. Costs of switching to another retailer is low.	5. Costs of switching supply from another manufacturer is low.

Basically, if either party has some attractive options and the cost of switching to the options are low, then each has quite a lot of independence. But if a manufacturer believes a retailer is more dependent on the trading relationship, then it will be tempted to try to exploit this by demanding better trading terms. If a retailer believes a manufacturer is more dependent on the trading relationship, then it will be tempted to try to exploit this by demanding better trading terms. If both are independent, then both are likely to be tempted to exploit their independence by making demands on the other party.

But notice what happens when such relationship power is exercised, even with a subtle velvet glove (rather than an iron fist).[4] If it is disputed, then interfirm communication

[3] Louis P. Bucklin, "A Theory of Channel Control," *Journal of Marketing* 37 (January 1973): 39–47.

[4] See the following for recent research on the effects of power in trading relationships: James R. Brown, Robert F. Lusch, and Carolyn Y. Nicholson, "Power and Relationship Commitment: Their Impact on Marketing Channel Member Performance," *Journal of Retailing*, 71.4, 1995, 363–92.

focuses on the perceived and actual dependency on each other, which comes down to the relative attractiveness of the alternative options. Rather than focusing on the relationship and making it mutually more productive, which increases the dependency of both parties on each other, discussion focuses on promoting the attractiveness of alternative, competing relationships to each other! With or without such discussion, the trading relationship is hurt because, even if the party that is subject to the power play passively concedes, resentment, a desire to get even, and increased efforts to find more attractive, future trading-relationship options will arise, so the "exploitation" of the relationship by the more powerful partner does not happen again. In summary, the study and strategic use of relationship power is based on the premise that an efficient trading relationship pushes the partner to the brink of abandoning the relationship: that is, the trading relationship's dependency imbalance is fully exploited. Such a heavy-handed relationship strategy is different from the following approach, which encourages trust, cooperation, and relationship innovation.

Relationship Cooperation and Innovation

The noted nineteenth-century economist Lord Alfred Marshall viewed economic progress as finding better methods for marketing at a distance. The opening up of distant markets by rapidly decreasing communication, transportation, and other transaction costs and by the removal of trade barriers (the so-called globalization of markets) obviously create tremendous dynamic changes in supply and demand in local markets, as described in Chapter 7 (channel analysis). From the previous power and control perspective, one might expect that the resulting shifts in supply capacity, in alternative sources of supply, and in relative dependency lead to numerous power plays that create anxiety, suspicion, mistrust, and exploitation in trading relationships. But, instead, what is often observed is an increase in market cooperation and innovation by both the new and the old trading relationships.

Often, the new offshore manufacturers find it difficult to get the cooperation of local retailers and have to improvise. They may develop a mail-order business, may form trading relationships with retailers who traditionally have not sold the product category, or may try to gain the cooperation of existing retailers of the product by offering special new services such as a twenty-four-hour order-delivery cycle. In addition, existing manufacturer-retailer trading relationships attempt to defend and extend their existing trading relationships by experimenting with new trading processes. How does this work?

The competitively rational response of a manufacturer to a shift of market supply/demand disequilibrium that favors the retail buyer is to seek what is called an integrative bargaining solution. *Integrative bargaining* is when the focus of discussion shifts from arguing about new contract terms that slice up the pie more in favor of the retailer (win-lose negotiation) to finding terms and solutions that make the pie bigger (cooperate-cooperate negotiation). Various forms of such negotiation are discussed in the sales management chapter (Chapter 13). The manufacturer's alternative is to allow the retailer to exploit its increased bargaining power and thus to accept less attractive trading terms (e.g., the retailer pays a lower price and/or takes longer to pay).

Before the retailer comes demanding better terms, it is in the interest of the manufacturer to react to the shift in market power by searching for new, innovative, cooperative solutions that raise the outcome prospects for both parties. This often takes the form of joint initiatives that integrate the two firms' information and logistics processes and systems or that move manufacturing and logistics processes to another party in the distribution channel. For example, Wal-Mart buys its jeans and lingerie from VF corporation, which developed ordering software for Wal-Mart that automatically adjusts the order and delivery of stock to individual Wal-Marts based on their unique sales assortment. One way to view this arrangement is that such software creates more of a mutual dependency, which leads to a long-term relationship.[5] But what really creates the mutual trust and dependency is VF's sustained efforts to develop innovative relationship processes with Wal-Mart that increase the payoff to both parties. If the innovation in the relationship process creates a sustainable relationship differentiation advantage, then this will also sustain the relationship. But even if the differentiation cannot be sustained because the innovation is quickly imitated and diffused across the market, the raised expectation of future, further relationship innovations is likely to increase mutual trust and cooperation on both sides, thus sustaining the relationship. It is the continued investment in productive relationship innovation that sustains the commitment to the relationship rather than the specific assets that result from past innovation.

Such integration of information systems and order-delivery software between supplier and retailer increases process control for both parties. This greater control also allows both parties to monitor whether the other party is sticking to its word and agreements. It thus fosters greater compliance, which increases trust, which in turn increases willingness to cooperate in the future. This leads to better identification of defective interfirm transaction processes and the diagnosis of causes. Increasing the reliability and regularity of interfirm transaction processes reduces the need for both the manufacturer and retailer to carry large inventories of the product and leads, in the extreme, to JIT delivery, discussed in the section on supply-chain management in Chapter 5. The integration of logistics processes can lead to a simplification of the added-value processes (both manufacturing and logistics processes), which speeds them up, makes them more reliable, and reduces their costs. Note that this theory takes a positive and progressive view of the effect of shifts in market power in trading relationships. It does not predict that shifts in power will lead to exploitation and resentment. It predicts that the long-term tendency of shifts in market power in trading relationships will be to build mutual trust and cooperation produced by innovations in their mechanics/logistics. A typical example of a progressive trading relationship is described in the following terms by one of the executives of a large, bureaucratic clothing catalog retailer who is talking about a partnership with a small clothing manufacturer:

> We are constantly changing things to try to improve the way we do business together. We will experiment with new ideas, test new processes, try something different. Costs are incurred on both sides but we are willing to pay them. We have learned a lot from them. They have made us a better printing company, because they are demanding, innovative and willing to try things.[6]

Just how such a progressive relationship evolves is explained by first considering manufacturer X and retailer A and the following payoff for each before a power shift if

[5] Shankar Ganesan, "Determinants of Long-Term Orientation in Buyer-Seller Relationships," *Journal of Marketing* 58 (April 1994): 1–19.

[6] Andrea Larson, "Network Dyads in the Entrepreneurial Settings: A Study of the Governance of Exchange Relationships," *Administrative Science Quarterly* 37 (1993): 94.

they choose to cooperate with the other in the relationship versus if they choose to try to exploit the relationship (i.e., take advantage of the other's relative dependence, trust, or helpful behavior).

Payoff Matrix before Power Shift

		RETAILER A BEHAVIOR	
		COOPERATE	EXPLOIT
Manufacturer X Behavior	**Cooperate**	\$800k/\$1,000k	\$500k/\$1,100k
	Exploit	\$900k/\$700k	\$700k/\$800k[a]

[a]The Nash equilibrium is the exploit-exploit cell.

The first amount in each cell is the payoff to manufacturer X, and the second amount is the payoff to retailer A. If X cooperates, it makes \$800k if A also cooperates, but if A exploits X's cooperative behavior, X gets "shafted" and makes only \$500k. On the other hand, if X adopts a somewhat exploitive approach to the trading relationship, it makes \$900k if A cooperates and \$700k if A also attempts to exploit the relationship. Thus, adopting an exploitive approach has a higher payoff for X than cooperating, no matter what A does, so X should exploit. Similarly, adopting an exploitive approach has a higher payoff for A, so in this view both should exploit the relationship, and their payoffs are indicated in the bottom-right cell. Economists call this the Nash equilibrium, and it is an inferior state of affairs compared to cooperate-cooperate, which increases the size of the total pie or the combined returns for X and A (from \$1,500k to \$1,800k). The parties do not cooperate because they fear the other party will exploit their cooperation. If they both trusted and cooperated, then manufacturer X would increase its profits by \$100,000 (\$800k – \$700k) and retailer A by \$200,000 (\$1,000k – \$800k). These amounts are the respective values of mutual trust and cooperation to manufacturer X and retailer A. Mutual trust is when both parties believe the other party will cooperate as agreed and behave according to the belief.

The difference between what economists and what marketers teach is that economists predict the Nash equilibrium will occur; that is, both supplier and retailer will exploit the relationship. Some economists are coming to understand that in a long-term relationship where repeated pay-off matrix decisions have to be made, A and X's choices may settle down to cooperate-cooperate because either player can punish non-cooperative behavior in the next round of decision making by choosing to exploit. However, this "future punishment" explanation of why cooperation is observed in long-term relationships is a much more negative explanation than the following explanation for cooperation offered by market researchers. Marketers disagree. They believe such a relationship would not survive because both manufacturer X and retailer A would be at a competitive disadvantage to their rivals who develop mutual trust with their trading partners and achieve the cooperate-cooperate state of affairs and payoffs. In other words, the presence of other competitive trading relationships (discussed in the competitive analysis chapter, Chapter 6) drives both parties to cooperate.

Moreover, changes in the number and capacity of suppliers and retailers creates market disequilibria that further encourage cooperation and innovation. Imagine power shifts in favor of the retailer because a number of new, offshore, global suppliers enter the local market, thus increasing manufacturer X's competition. The result is a shift in trading terms in favor of A, as indicated next.

Payoff Matrix after Power Shift

		RETAILER A BEHAVIOR	
		COOPERATE	EXPLOIT
Manufacturer X Behavior	**Cooperate**	\$800k/\$1,000k	*\$300k/\$1,300k*
	Exploit	*\$800k/\$800k*	*\$500k/\$900k*[a]

[a]Nash equilibrium

The payoffs in italics represent the changes in payoffs after the power shift. As before, the Nash solution is that both should exploit the trading relationship, but now retailer A gets a bigger payoff than manufacturer X, reflecting the shift in its market power. But notice that the incentive to move the trading relationship from exploit-exploit to cooperate-cooperate is much greater now for manufacturer X than for retailer A. The value of mutual trust and cooperation is now \$300k (\$800k – \$500k) to manufacturer X and \$100k (\$1,000 – \$900k) to retailer A. Before, it was \$100k for X and \$200k for A.

So what should manufacturer X's response be to the shift in market power and trading relationship terms favoring retailer A? The manufacturer should increase its efforts to create a mutually trusting and cooperative relationship by suggesting innovations in trading relationship processes such that, if both cooperate, both get much larger payoffs. In terms of the payoff matrix, assume that if retailer A cooperates with manufacturer X's supply process innovation, the cooperate-cooperate payoff increases to \$1,000k for supplier X and \$1,500k for retailer A. The important point is that the payoffs in the other cells do not change because the innovations in relationship processes can be achieved only by *both* cooperating. The new payoff matrix follows:

Payoff Matrix after Relationship Innovation

		RETAILER A BEHAVIOR	
		COOPERATE	EXPLOIT
Manufacturer X Behavior	**Cooperate**	*\$1,000k/\$1,500k*	*\$300k/\$1,300k*
	Exploit	*\$800k/\$800k*	*\$500k/\$900k*

Now the choice is clear. Both should cooperate and adopt the new innovation. Why? Because if manufacturer X cooperates, it knows that retailer A also will cooperate because the returns are now greater for A if it cooperates rather than exploits when X cooperates. Similarly, if retailer A cooperates, it knows manufacturer X will cooperate because the returns are now greater for X if it cooperates rather than exploits when A cooperates. The relationship innovation proposed by X has increased the value of mutual trust and cooperation to \$500,000 for supplier X (\$1,000k – \$500k) and \$600,000 (\$1,500k – \$900k) for retailer A.

These payoff matrices demonstrate not only the advantages of relationship cooperation that result in relationship process innovation but also who is most likely to lead such cooperation. When the market becomes more of a buyers' market, then sellers will lead such relationship innovation. When the market becomes more of a sellers' market, then buyers will lead such relationship innovation.

Protecting a Relationship's Differentiation

The competitive uniqueness of a channel relationship is the portion of joint competitive advantage that results from the partnership. This advantage would not exist for either party outside the partnership, and, if the partnership were broken, it cannot be taken by either party to another trading relationship. When the parties recognize that competitive uniqueness exists, this will result in greater mutual understanding and cooperation, as evidenced by their day-to-day interactions, cooperation on relationship innovations, and use of formal contracts. A particularly strong bond is created between a supplier and a reseller when the supplier's target niche is narrow and well fitted to a reseller's narrowly defined consumer franchise. Such a situation creates a low likelihood that either party will benefit from substituting or switching trading partners. However, sometimes executives can take such a relationship for granted, and they cease to appreciate, as much as they should, the shared competitive advantages that the relationship provides and why it needs to be protected. The next Rationality in Practice box describes what can happen when executives come to depreciate rather than appreciate the value of a unique trading relationship.

The need to foster and support a very innovative and productive trading relationship becomes clearer when both parties understand that it is often in the interests of the manufacturer and the retailer to take what they have learned in the relationship and apply it to all of their other trading relationships. This somewhat "treacherous" diffusion of the trading relationship's cooperative innovation helps the manufacturer and retailer who do it, but it undercuts the competitive advantage of their trading relationship. Several answers to this dilemma exist. One is for both parties to be honest and up-front about their intentions to apply what they have learned to other trading relationships and to commit to develop and nurture their trading relationship by investing in further process innovations that maintain the relationship's performance superiority. This is what P&G and Wal-Mart appear to have done. The innovations they have developed together they have applied to their other trading relationships, but their continued experimentation together keeps and protects the unique competitiveness of their relationship. Another strategy to protect such relationship differentiation is to either integrate vertically or to sign long-term nondisclosure agreements and binding exclusivity contracts.[7] The advantages and disadvantages of such a vertical integration strategy will be discussed next.

Vertical Integration

Developing a long-term, binding relationship with suppliers or resellers, either through investment or legal agreements, may appear to be a sensible way of protecting

[7] Oliver Williamson, *The Economic Institutions of Capitalism: Firms, Markets, Relational Contracting,* (New York: The Free Press, 1985).

Rationality in Practice

The Sweet Smell of Channel Success and Its Bitter Fruits

Once upon a time there was an innovative supplier and an enterprising reseller. The initial pioneering cooperation and joint efforts of the supplier and reseller led to a unique competitive triumph for the trading relationship in the marketplace. In combination, the supplier and reseller broke the rules and introduced many different innovations. Everything was wine and roses. Both parties handsomely profited, and the key individuals in the organization were promoted and rewarded.

As the pioneering era passed, routine set in. The personal interaction among the original executives was no longer necessary. These individuals started listening more to ingratiating subordinates telling them how smart they were (or vice versa). History started to be rewritten. New executives who were appointed to represent the buyer and seller had little or no appreciation of how much the joint venture's success was the product of the interaction of both parties' efforts. In their attempts to distinguish themselves and gain promotions within the respective firms, these new representatives increasingly attributed the success of the venture to their firms' past and current efforts and depreciated the contribution of the other party. Even worse, in renewing the contracts and adapting to market changes, the two enterprises started to believe their own posturing.

A belief that no one is indispensable, including the other party, started to take hold. Gradually it turned into a belief that other suppliers and resellers were just as good, if not better. This belief was fostered by the attempts of competitive suppliers and resellers to form relationships with the original reseller and supplier. Almost imperceptibly at first, valuable, shared information was leaked by both parties to other competitors. These other parties planted and nourished the idea that encouraging and even actively developing other alternatives would reduce dependency and increase power and profits. The inevitable disclosure of such activities precipitated a series of escalating actions and reactions. Eventually, the original relationship fractured.

The need on the part of both the supplier and the reseller to protect self-interest, powered by feelings of personal betrayal, led to an abandonment of exclusivity. The reseller began a new strategy of multiple sourcing, and the supplier began a new strategy of nonexclusive distribution. The original channel's competitive advantage was completely undermined by both partners as their manufacturing, marketing, and merchandising innovations were shared with other parties, who, in turn, shared them with their other suppliers and resellers. Not everyone lived happily ever after.

a unique relationship. It also can be a way of bypassing or changing the cultural inertia and the lack of cooperation of established channels. *Vertical integration* (owning your supplier or reseller) offers the promise of potential efficiencies gained from a reduction in management overhead, integrating information systems, reduction or elimination of selling costs within the integrated channel, and better management and control of marketing campaigns and physical distribution logistics. It is sometimes the only way to introduce new technological advances into a channel. Integration enables unilateral decisions on who is going to do what and the more direct rewarding of key personnel down the channel for responding to the changes. It also gives the integrating firm more control over training and management succession. However, competitive market forces often make the use of independent channel agents more efficient, and vertical integration should be employed only when the market fails—when gross inefficiencies result from working with independent channel participants.[8] The conditions most likely to favor vertical integration are listed in Table 11.1.

It needs to be emphasized that vertical integration and long-term, exclusive trading agreements are not the same. An exclusive, legal contract buttressed by frequent,

[8] Erin M. Anderson and Barton A Weitz, *A Framework for Analyzing Vertical Integration Issues in Marketing,* Report No. 83-110 (Cambridge, MA: Marketing Science Institute, November 1983).

Table 11.1 **Conditions That Favor Vertical Integration**

1. When the level of customer service competition in the manufacturer market decreases, thus encouraging upstream integration.
2. When it is hard to measure the output performance of the channel, and hence control is reduced.
3. When competitors can take advantage of a firm's investment in developing the channel's skills and efficiency.
4. When the environment is uncertain and a need arises for the quick adaptation of strategy.
5. When the transactions are large or frequent enough to produce economies of scope and scale that the firm should exploit rather than give away to other channel partners.
6. When unique products, trade secrets, and marketing processes need to be protected.
7. When the channel culture and norms appear to tolerate reneging on agreements, shirking duties, and the deceitful representation of competencies.

SOURCE: Reprinted by permission of Harvard Business School Press from *A Framework for Analyzing Vertical Integration Issues in Marketing*. Report No. 83-110, by Erin M. Anderson and Barton A. Weitz. Boston, 1991, p. 54. Copyright © 1991 by the president and Fellows of Harvard College.

close, interpersonal contacts often gives as much control as vertical integration at much less cost and financial risk. However, even legal contracts have their limits. Research suggests that the trust and understanding built by cooperating and innovating together over time (an implicit social contract) counts for more than clauses in a contract.[9] The unique human and financial investments that manufacturers and resellers have in a relationship, trading exclusivity, and a harmonious and cooperative trading history are likely to hold a relationship together better than a legal contract.[10] When a trading partner has to resort to the clauses of a legal contract to gain the other party's cooperation, it often means that the relationship is on the rocks.

Upstream vertical integration is a way of ensuring supply when a chance of shortages or of limiting a competitor's access to a radical innovation exists. Procter & Gamble protected the product differentiation of its new line of Ultra Pampers by helping to finance the supplier of the absorbent polymer that provided the competitive advantage. *Downstream* integration ensures access to a particularly desirable consumer segment and can choke off competitors' access to these consumers. No doubt Porsche had this in mind when it attempted to set up its own auto dealerships in the United States. Unfortunately for Porsche, current dealers, who often sell other brands of luxury cars to potential and former Porsche owners, were able to stop the move by claiming a breach of contract.

Vertical integration by acquisition or joint venture can be very risky. The company cultures and senior management styles may turn out to be incompatible. Much also depends on what is predicted to happen to the competitiveness of the supply and resale markets. If the demand in the ultimate market is uncertain, then a further investment or commitment to supply the end market (which is what downstream vertical integration means) greatly increases the stake and the risk exposure. If retailer consumer loyalty is unstable or technological innovation is changing the relative competitiveness of both suppliers and resellers, then committing to a single, long-term relationship

[9] Ian R. MacNeil, *The New Social Contract: An Inquiry into Modern Contractual Relationships* (New Haven, CT: Yale University Press, 1980).
[10] Erin Anderson and Barton Weitz, *The Use of Pledges to Build and Sustain Commitment in Distribution Channels* (Cambridge, MA: The Marketing Science Institute, 1991).

(strategic partnering) limits the integrating firm's ability to switch to the most innovative supplier or reseller. Even if the integrating firm, be it supplier or reseller, could break the relationship, the desirable new supplier or reseller is likely to take a jaundiced view of the integrator's overtures.

When integrating vertically, a firm believes it is loading the dice in its favor for the long term because the supplier or reseller it is acquiring or setting up will maintain its technological leadership, cost leadership, image, and management competence. Sustaining these may require heavy investment if market forces produce great volatility in the relative competitiveness of the players.

Managing Multiple Relationships

As a company grows in size and adds new products to its lines, it may wish to distribute through new channels. The first reason is that a different retail channel may reach a different segment of shoppers. The second is that the new channel may reach the same segment, but if the manufacturer does not supply the new retailer, then it will distribute and sell a competitor's product. Because the manufacturer far prefers intrabrand competition (several retailers selling its product) to interbrand competition (competition against its rivals' brands), it will sell into the new distribution channel. American Telephone and Telegraph (AT&T) did not get into the PC store channel until too late because it did not want to upset its sales force that sold computers directly to businesses. By the time it recognized its mistake, it was too late. The retailers were not interested in stocking and selling another premium brand; they were more interested in adding value brands to enable them to price compete with each other.

A manufacturer has to reach its target customers, and if they shift which channels they shop, then the manufacturer has to add such channels. For example, PC manufacturers had to quickly develop office-supply and mass-merchant trading relationships because a significant percentage of PC buyers (more than 30 percent) preferred to shop at these retailers rather than specialty computer stores. Basically, as PCs have become less of a mystery and more of a commodity, their suppliers are shifting from specialty to mass distribution (see Chapter 7). The PC manufacturers, such as Compaq, who first developed such office-store and mass-merchant trading relationships were able to expand their market share. Hewlett-Packard, with more than 60 percent of the printer market, absolutely had to add these new distribution channels. To not have done so would have opened up a tremendous opportunity for one of its minor competitors or for a new competitor.

Of course, such a move is likely to upset existing channel relationships. This is what happened when Levi Strauss started to sell its jeans through Sears Roebuck and Company and JC Penney. Specialty clothing stores were annoyed because they now had to compete against these mass merchandisers to sell Levis. Levi Strauss argued that if it did not sell to them, other major brands would and that selling to them enabled Levi to increase its market and invest more in marketing, which would benefit the specialty stores. The reality is that Levi Strauss is such a strong brand that specialty retailers could not afford to abandon their trading relationship with it. It was a different story for Elizabeth Arden, the manufacturer of Elizabeth Taylor's Black Pearl fragrance. It arranged to sell the fragrance in mass-merchant channels such as JC Penney. More exclusive department stores told Arden that they would dump the brand if that happened, so, after much wrangling, the manufacturer abandoned its plan and decided to stick to its more exclusive trading relationships. This example illustrates the exercise of power based on relative dependency. But it also raises questions about Arden's relationship positioning strategy. Given that it needed the more exclusive image of the upscale department stores to build and support Black Pearl's brand equity, why did it even try to expand sales into the mass-merchant channel? Creating new trading relationships is a natural source of channel conflict, and when it appears to run quite counter to the initial trading-relationship strategy of either the manufacturer or the retailer, it raises further questions about the competitive rationality of the management initiating such a move. For example, in 1992 Goodyear Tire & Rubber Company decided to start selling its tires through Sears Roebuck and Co., the biggest tire retailer, and a year later Goodyear began selling its tires through Wal-Mart. The move raised Goodyear's market share by two percentage points but alienated many exclusive Goodyear dealers. Now Goodyear is trying to recover some of its lost credibility and goodwill by offering its dealers exclusive new products and special services.

A key to operating multiple channels is to first establish, through consumer research undertaken jointly with channel members, whether the current and new channels share the same customers. Do the consumers spend much time shopping among the channels or even have the different channels in their consideration set? If not, then this fact needs to be communicated to the channel members, along with other findings they will consider credible, to heighten their acceptance that less channel conflict exists than they supposed. Second, it is important that the manufacturer sets and follows well-defined and well-understood channel performance criteria. Then, at least, the channel partners know they are being treated fairly and that special treatment depends on special performance on their part. Third, each trading relationship's uniqueness has to be recognized, both its unique strengths and problems. "Well-defined and well-understood channel performance criteria" does not mean rigidly standardized criteria. The practice of offering standardized, take-it-or-leave-it promotion programs often may be justified in terms of cost economies, control and regulations that prohibit terms and deals that discriminate. But in an age where the management of a trading relationship is no longer centralized but assigned to an account manager or account team, promotion programs that fit the unique strengths and weaknesses of the trading relationship can be designed and managed cost effectively and legally. Such tailored promotion programs may lead to claims of favoritism and unfairness, but the reality is that standardized programs often provoke the same claims. The response to conflict created by promotions tailored to a channel's needs is to provide the disgruntled trading partner its own tailored service tied to specific commitments and performance outcomes.

Resolving channel conflict over multiple relationships is more difficult when a manufacturer creates its own retail outlets, such as Ralph Lauren, Liz Claiborne, Levi Strauss, and Anne Klein have done. Their argument is that the outlets can be test labs for new product lines and merchandising innovations and that they promote the brand, which strengthens the appeal of the other retailers' lines. The reality is often that the manufacturer believes it can better retail its products and that it can earn higher profits by retailing rather than manufacturing them. But such a belief does not always drive a manufacturer's downstream entry into retailing. The growth of the manufacturer outlet stores across the country has been, in part, a repercussion of manufacturers' trying to better serve their existing channels by taking back unsold stocks. This service at first seemed to benefit the retailer by reducing its risk. But instead it has led to less discriminatory ordering by retail buyers and to the growth of the manufacturer outlets that resell the retailer returns; both of these interacting trends have hurt the competitiveness of retailers. This example demonstrates that managing multiple channels requires thinking ahead and recognizing what effects current channel policies and programs may have on future strategy and on the evolution of trading relationships (see the Chapter 6 section on competitive conjecture).

Channel Conflict within Managing Multiple Relationships

The managing of multiple channel relations is but one source of conflict that can occur in a trading relationship. Table 11.2 demonstrates how conflicting views of the trading relationship and its processes are often the source of trouble. Such conflicting views are going to occur naturally, so some disagreement is inevitable. The real issue is how the enterprising manufacturer or retailer turns such a conflict into an opportunity rather than a problem: an opportunity to create a new trading relationship that reduces the conflict.

For example, a common source of conflicts listed in Table 11.2 is not understanding the other party's viewpoint when it comes to planning and implementing joint marketing programs. Many retailers do not have the time, skill, or will to initiate and implement specific marketing programs involving the setting up of merchandise displays, demonstrating the product, and training their salespeople in every retail outlet. On the other hand, manufacturers get very upset when they run advertisements that draw prospective customers into the retail store but lose sales because the in-store marketing push was missing.

The creative solution is for the manufacturer to form and train a special task force that goes out and sets up the marketing program in large numbers of retail outlets.

Table 11.2 Opposing Views That Create Channel Conflict

MANUFACTURER'S VIEW OF DISTRIBUTOR	DISTRIBUTOR'S VIEW OF MANUFACTURER
They want all our target customers to buy from them.	They want all our customers to buy their products.
They do not provide us with information about their customers.	They do not provide us with information about their customers.
They do not understand our customers.	They do not understand our customers.
They need to improve their service to our customers.	They need to improve their service to our customers.
They do not promote our brand and lines in their advertising.	They do not promote our brand and lines in their advertising.
They do not use our promotional materials.	They do not provide the promotional materials we want.
They do not adopt our suggested price.	They want to dictate our price.
They are too price sensitive.	They are not price sensitive.
They are disorganized/uncoordinated.	They are disorganized/uncoordinated.
They never carry enough inventory to fill orders off the shelf.	They are too slow in delivering special orders.
They are constantly changing the people we have to deal with.	They are constantly changing the people we have to deal with.
They do not work with our people.	They do not work with our people.
They betray our trust to our competitors.	They betray our trust to our competitors.
They do not help us meet our goals.	They do not help us meet our goals.
They promise more than they deliver.	They promise more than they deliver.
They cannot get their act together.	They cannot get their act together.
They do not understand the meaning of cooperation.	They do not understand the meaning of cooperation.

Rationality in Practice

Innovative Retail Merchandising

Gallo Wines has a number of very strong brand names. When it delivers its cases of wine to a retailer, it delivers a consumer franchise produced by quality, targeted products, and good advertising that pulls. This gives Gallo's field force more than a foot in the door. Gallo further exploits its market strength by reaching down the channel with a merchandising program that is irresistible, sometimes even overwhelming. Gallo first requires that its distributors have the resources to employ separate, aggressive Gallo representatives. These reps build floor displays, lift cases, dust bottles, and "if you turn your back on them for a minute they will turn your store or department into a Gallo outlet."*

Gallo's field reps execute according to a three-hundred-page training and sales manual. The manual covers such topics as the sales call and maintaining shelves, and each chapter ends with a quiz. The manual contains detailed checklists and advice: Place the most highly advertised Gallo products at eye level; place impulse purchase items on shelves above the belt; the width of the display should be no more than seven feet (the largest width the eye can easily scan); and if a large-sized item offers a decided unit price advantage to the consumer, then place it to the immediate right of the smaller size. The keys to Gallo's merchandising success are its concern over details and staying on top of its distributors and retailers.

Another example, probably the most well-known textbook case of innovative retail merchandising, was the classic 1971–1972 Hanes L'eggs campaign. Again, the product and its advertising created a large pull, but this pull was matched by the push in terms of supply. Four hundred and fifty young women in red, white, and blue hot pants set up and stocked the displays in supermarkets and drugstores. They were helped by an early computerized, stock-control information system that managed warehouse inventory, sales, billings, and accounts. By 1969, pantyhose had become almost a commodity item, and the traditional sales-promotion entry would not have been enough. Hanes—with its "Our L'eggs fit your legs" slogan, its differentiation claim (based on the greater stretch and elasticity of the material used), and its eye-catching, symbolic packaging—was able to enter at a price of $1.39, compared to some private labels that were selling at 39 cents or three for $1.

A direct-mail, introductory coupon offer was made, but the real attraction to retailers was that Hanes required almost nothing of them except that they count the profits. Hanes asked for two-and-one-half square feet of display space, which was rented. The stock was sold on consignment, and the display stockers did the rest, including making every effort to have the striking display positioned in a heavy-traffic location. It should be noted that similar campaigns did not work as well for the Hanes L'aura line of cosmetics, its line of men's underwear, and its line of socks, perhaps because of entrenched, strong, brand-name competition in these markets; weaker product differentiation; and competitors whose distribution and merchandising skills were already good and got better.

*Jaclyn Fierman, "How Gallo Crushes the Competition," *Fortune*, September 1, 1986, 23–31.

They become much more efficient at implementing the program, can pass on selling tips from one outlet to another, and can improvise solutions to problems on the spot, ensuring coordination between the manufacturer's advertising that pulls customers into the store and the retailer's point-of-purchase push (see the above Rationality in Practice box for examples of such programs).

Too few manufacturers appreciate that many retailers will willingly trade margin for faster stock-turn, lower costs, and fewer hassles from a manufacturer having its people working beside the retailer's people to make a program work. A further advantage is that the relationships created by working together in the trenches are much stronger than those that result from negotiating price, delivery and return allowances across a table, or over a phone. In addition such field support people give the manufacturer a much richer understanding of day-to-day retailer operating procedures, the key people in the retailer's management, the strengths and weaknesses of the trading partner, and, finally, competitive intelligence. Often sales representatives cannot pick this information up because they are busy selling and order taking rather than implementing joint marketing programs.

Channel Convention versus Change Conflict

Another source of conflict is that what one side in the trading relationship views as an accepted, conventional practice, the other side views as an opportunity for innovation and competitive advantage. In many product-markets—particularly in emerging economies—the channel strategy seems very straightforward because trading channel traditions and customer expectations prescribe it. Managers come to view their existing supply chain systems and processes as a given that they will not even think of changing, thus presenting the classic opportunity for an innovator. Such trading practices are likely to have developed over several decades, or in some trading channels, over hundreds of years. Very often this tradition makes a lot of sense. It has produced functional specialization and reflects the cooperation, trust, and bonding that has evolved to fit the economic, political, social, and physical environment. The buyers and sellers in traditional channels have learned, from mentors and on the job, to understand the strengths and weaknesses of the companies with whom they customarily deal. Over the years, a fabric of professional and personal relationships is woven that maintains the channel relationships and customs.

The problem is that modern communication and physical logistic processes make some of the traditional practices, processes, and margins (see Chapter 7) redundant and obsolete. This can create conflict in the channel about margins and services. Competitive advantage and profits from trading relationships also comes from questioning conventional distribution practices. Thus, managing trading relationship conflict requires balancing the predictability and goodwill benefits associated with trading conventions against the benefits associated with challenging the conventions. The next section describes how this balancing depends on the personal and professional relationships that exist among individuals involved in the trading relationship and what goals (i.e., to protect or challenge the status quo) they agree they should jointly pursue and use their personal relationship to achieve.

Relationship Management Processes

Ultimately, the goal of creating a competitive advantage out of a trading relationship or of quickly settling disagreements and creating lemonade out of lemons (i.e., creating innovative solutions out of conflict) is achieved by the way the trading relationship is managed by people.

Historically, the way firms viewed the personal relationships among trading partners depended on their size. Among small firms relationships were, and still are, often among owners. Larger firms operated under the sales representative/purchasing agent mental model. This model assumed a funneling of the firms' trading relationship through primarily single agents: the personal relationship between the selling firm's salesperson (agent) and the buying firm's purchasing manager (agent). Other agency relationships were expected to develop among engineers working on supply-chain engineering specifications. But the salesperson acted somewhat as a gatekeeper to the sales firm, and the purchasing manager acted somewhat as a gatekeeper to the buying organization.

The modern relationship marketing approach to the supply chain argues that this funneling is unnecessarily restrictive.[11] It proposes that trading relationships in the supply chain should be among cross-functional teams, at least at some level of decision making (see Figure 11.5). The reality of an important trading relationship is that it is held together by relationship processes and personal relationships among agents at several levels. At the strategic level, quality relationship processes have to enable senior management to initiate, agree on, and invest in creating a unique competitive positioning for the relationship. In addition, if senior managers get on well together, it makes a big difference in obtaining subordinates' cooperation in managing operations. The development of such interfirm personal relationships is particularly valuable in hypercompetitive markets when trading relationships are stressed and have to creatively adapt to new competitive realities. Such personal relationships nurture the personal trust and commitment that enables the relationship to survive market crises through creative, cooperative improvisation.

What is "personal trust and commitment"? "Personal trust" is when the words of the individual representatives are their bond, and they are prepared to help each other to solve problems. "Commitment" is commitment to the goal of developing and nurturing the competitiveness of the relationship, compared to other competitive trading relationships. Mutual trust and commitment are determined by a history of shared values, open communication, both parties giving more to the relationship than to alternative relationships, and, particularly, not taking advantage of (exploiting) the trust.[12] The long-term return from the relationship is perceived to be higher than the return from nurturing other relationships. The driver of this long-term return is relationship process innovation: innovations in reducing process costs, increasing process speed, and increasing process output. Personal relationship goodwill and trust are needed when conflict arises and when attempts are initiated to improve systems and processes.

The new *relationship marketing* approach also emphasizes that at the heart of the trading relationship is the set of relationship processes, such as decision making and learning, that integrate the operational/implementation processes between the two firms. Here again, personal relationships are the threads that create the relationship-process fabric. Note that the greater the number of these relationships, the lesser the day-to-day relationship depends on one personal relationship between an account manager on the manufacturer's side and a purchasing manager on the buyer/retailer's side.

Finally, the idea that total-quality relationship marketing requires the continual improvement of the strategic and operational relationships is starting to be appreciated (see Figure 11.5). This is best achieved by setting up a team on each side that meets and, as a joint relationship team, undertakes the task of experimenting with new relationship innovations. Historically, distributor advisory boards have played such a role in relationship management. As well as arbitrating on fairness issues or disputes, such advisory boards propose and endorse innovations in the existing supply-chain practices. This level of cooperation is precisely what P&G is attempting to achieve in its management of relationships with retailers such as Wal-Mart. Personal relationships among the cross-functional teams create further trust and commitment

[11] Diana L. Haytko, *Advertising Agency Interpersonal, Process and Outcome Performance Management of Client Relationships*, working paper, School of Business, University of Wisconsin—Madison, 1996.

[12] Robert M. Morgan and Shelby D. Hunt, "The Commitment-Trust Theory of Relationship Marketing," *Journal of Marketing* 58 (July 1994): 20–38.

Figure 11.5 **Relationship Management Processes**

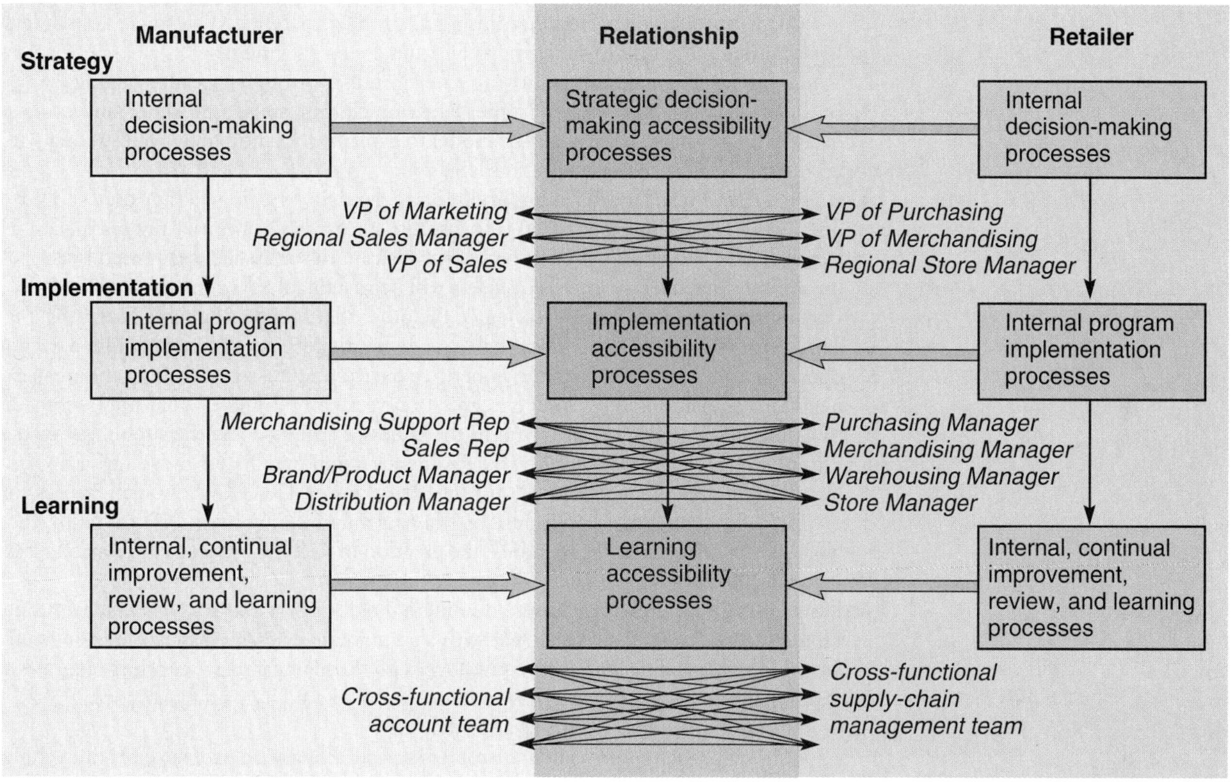

The reality of an important trading relationship is that it is held together by relationship processes and personal relationships between agents at several levels. The new *relationship marketing* approach emphasizes that at the heart of the trading relationship is the set of relationship processes that integrate the operational/implementation processes between the two firms. Finally, what is starting to be appreciated is that total-quality relationship marketing requires the continual improvement of the strategic and operational relationships. This is best achieved by setting up a team on both sides that meets and, as a joint relationship team, undertakes the task of experimenting with new relationship innovations.

SOURCE: Diana L. Haytko, *Advertising Agency Interpersonal, Process and Outcome Performance Management of Client Relationships*, working paper, School of Business, University of Wisconsin—Madison, 1997.

that encourage the inherent risk taking involved in relationship experimentation. Higher-order relationship marketing initiates programs that exchange employees to learn about a partner's internal operational processes, bring sales reps and buyers together for seminars on fashion or technology trends, and bring shipping and supply-chain management and purchasing executives together for presentations from logistics experts on innovations in physical distribution. Such relationship marketing possesses built-in, self-improvement, facilitating processes. These innovative efforts are needed to achieve and maintain the unique market *relationship differentiation* discussed at the beginning of this chapter.

Discussion Questions and Minicases

1. The Woolrest Company, an innovative manufacturer and marketer of the first luxury, woolen mattress pads, identified its target market as the over-age-fifty, traditional, upscale married woman. She was more likely to have a positive attitude toward wool as a natural fiber, to be aware of the sleeping problems the product addressed, and to be able to afford to buy the product for herself, her husband, and their parents. What types of retailers would provide the best fit for this product and contact segment?
2. What are the advantages of launching a new product through specialty catalogs?
3. In the early 1980s, a boom in designer labels on clothes, small appliances, and even cars occurred. Use the seller-reseller-fit model to explain what ultimately went wrong with the marketing of most of these designer labels.
4. A supplier and reseller are having preliminary discussions as to whether they should develop a long-term, preferential relationship. Each party's enthusiasm depends on its perception of the other's current competitive strengths or assets, discounted by its uncertainty that such strengths or assets will be sustainable over the long term. Consequently, each firm must convince the other that it has sustainable strengths if it is to extract the most from the contractual arrangement, merger, or takeover. The party that is operating in the most uncertain competitive environment is very likely in the weakest negotiating position. Why is such negotiation very complicated? What might come back to haunt the relationship? How might the issues be addressed by the supplier and reseller?
5. Often, it is the *impression* of relative dependency and power that is most important in negotiations and channel control, not the actual power. Describe how such impressions are formed. Illustrate your response by drawing a figure, if you can. (Hint: Think about what players in the market influence the creation of such impressions; i.e., who talks to whom in the channel.)
6. Home Depot has grown rapidly to dominate the do-it-yourself hardware store business. Home Depot accomplishes this feat with a combination of strong merchandising and a knowledgeable selling staff. Store employees go through extensive product and sales training. They go out of their way to help customers find items they are looking for. They even can provide demonstrations and advice.

   This approach to providing customer service, along with extensive product choice and availability, produces superior value for the customer. Not only do customers get the deep and wide merchandise of a warehouse store, but they also get a level of service uncharacteristic for such stores.

   Suppose you are a supplier of garden implements. What key issues would you face in trying to sell your products to Home Depot for resale? What sorts of things could you do to address these issues?
7. In the late 1980s, Garden Way, Inc., faced a classic case of having to manage multiple channels. Its garden-tiller business had been built by selling direct, through mail order. Tillers were shipped directly to the customers, who tended to be serious gardeners living outside urban areas. As Garden Way added new products to its lines—chippers, mulchers, snow blowers, and so forth—new target market segments also were added. The company still targets serious gardeners, but many are geographically located in suburban areas. Also, some segments, such as the segment for snow blowers, are not necessarily gardeners at all.

   To reach these new targets, Garden Way sought new channels, including independent dealers and, eventually, Sears Roebuck and Co.. Consequently, the seeds were sown for a three-way conflict because Sears Roebuck and the dealers could potentially sell to some of the same segments, and Garden Way itself still sold direct.

   If you were the vice president of marketing for Garden Way, what could you do to minimize conflict, to build relationships with all your channels, and even to get them to work synergistically?
8. An entrepreneurial manufacturer of insulated, leaded, and beveled art glass (see the following photo and figure) developed a very attractive product line for entrance doorways in residential homes that were valued at $150,000 or more. For several years, the

manufacturer had sold exclusively to door companies, and its sales were dependent on how well their doors sold. In an attempt to gain more control over its destiny, the company decided to initiate an aggressive marketing strategy. One of the first steps it took was to analyze the distribution channel for its product. The figure presents the selling prices, margins, and added value provided at each step in the channel for the most popular item in the manufacturer's line. Should the company change its distribution system?

9. Frecom is a manufacturer of low-cost fax boards for personal computers. In an effort to reach as many buyers as possible, Frecom uses multiple channels. It advertises in computer magazines and provides an 800-number for buyers to call direct. It also signs up as many independent dealers as possible. One way that Frecom finds new dealers is by asking 800-number customers what dealer is closest to them. Then the company sends the fax board to the dealer and allows the dealer to install it, charging a service fee. Frecom then approaches the dealer about carrying the Frecom line.

Frecom does a few things to provide support for its dealer channel, such as helping the dealer build its service business. On the whole, however, Frecom does not do much to maintain separation of the channels. Yet dealers do not seem to complain. Why can Frecom do this and be successful? What pitfalls could arise in Frecom's approach to the market? What would you suggest the company do about these pitfalls?

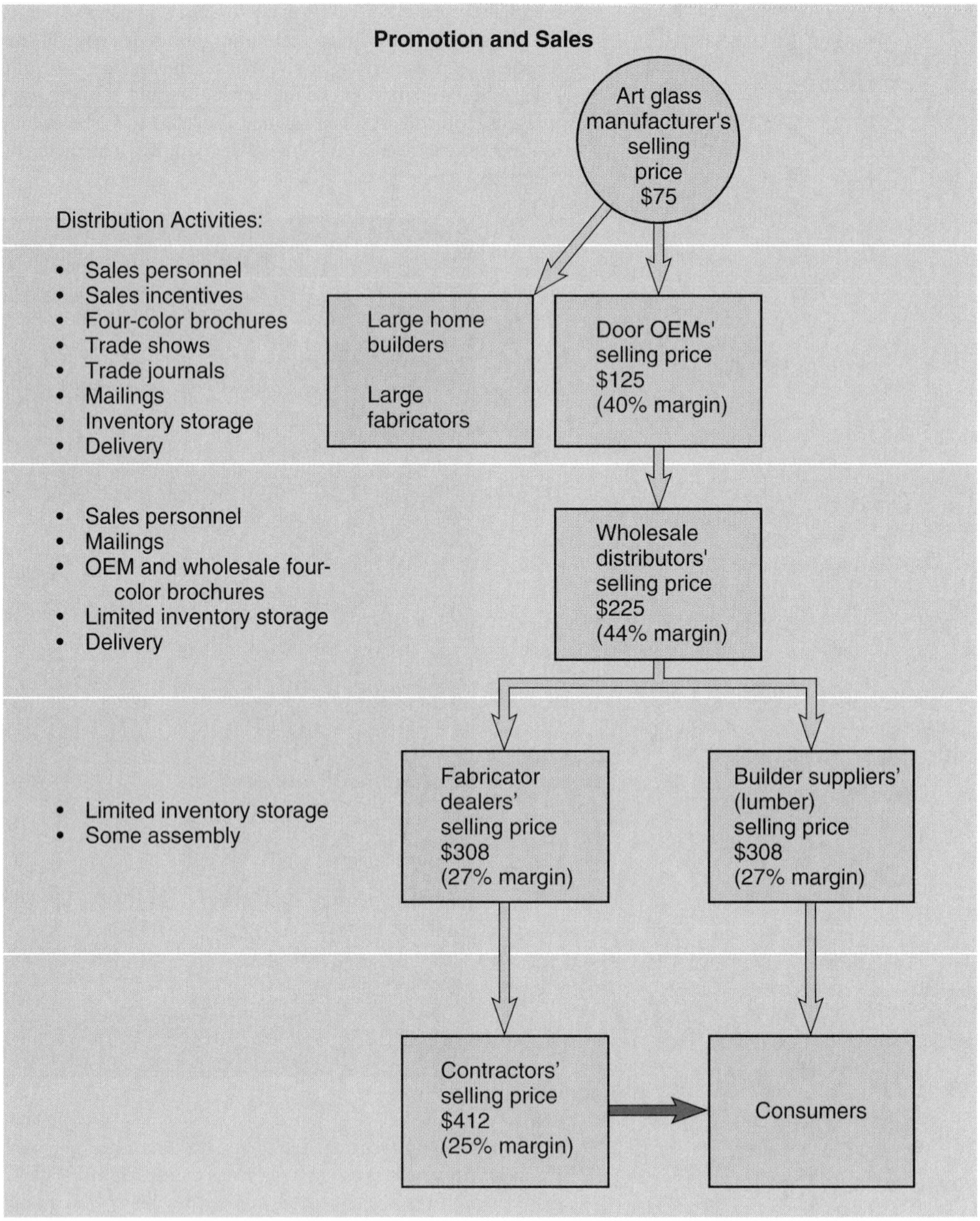

10. The Disney Store, started in 1987, is a successful effort on the part of the Walt Disney Company to sell Disney products at retail. Each of the more than 140 stores has a consistent theme and atmosphere. The main purpose of the design is to make shoppers feel they are in a Disney theme park. Service is friendly and helpful. The decor gives the feeling of being on a movie set. Merchandise is correlated with Disney movies and other promotions. Why would Disney integrate forward to sell its merchandise, instead of licensing the name and logo or selling Disney merchandise to selected resellers? What conditions do you feel have led to the success of such a venture? What factors might arise that would threaten the continued success of the Disney Store chain, and how should Disney respond?

11. A company can encounter a host of problems when it seeks a distributor or agent to sell its products overseas. Distance alone makes it difficult to meet and scout good dealers. Often, the only direct contact a fledgling exporter may have with a prospective distributor is a meeting at a trade show. Then the exporter may find itself locked into an agreement that does not result in sales. The distributor may carry competing products, or its business may go in another direction. In addition, the legal system in the distributor's country may be different from what the exporter is used to, and it will be surprised if it finds that the relationship cannot be dissolved unless an extortionist settlement is paid. What are some ways a prospective exporter might reduce the risks involved in finding a reliable distributor in a host country?

Less is more.

Ludwig Mies van der Rohe

. . . everything flows.

Heraclitus

CHAPTER TWELVE

Relationship Logistics

Logistics strategy often wins wars. Capturing the enemy's supply train almost always led to surrender. If an army raced ahead so fast it outran its supply lines, then its very success made it vulnerable. It ran out of food, fodder, ammunition, and, lately, gas. More than ever before, logistics is the key to military success. In today's brushfire wars, "getting there first with the mostest" wins with the least loss of life. This means that U.S. armed forces have had to develop rapid-deployment logistics skills and have had to learn from private industry how to do it.

It took more than five months to build up the 1991 Desert Storm force, and the order-delivery time of spare supplies from the U.S. arsenal to Saudi Arabia was twenty-six days. Half of the forty thousand containers of equipment shipped, constituting a modern baggage train, including $2.7 billion of spare parts, went unused.[1] They were idle because soldiers did not know what equipment was in what container. In 1995, it took only a month to have the Bosnia force in place, and the order-delivery time was seven days. The target goal was to provide an overnight supply service. To the military bureaucracy, this was a "mission impossible." To corporate America, it sounded like what FedEx and United Parcel Service do every day.

Indeed, the way the Pentagon is revolutionizing its $40 billion-a-year logistics system

(yes, $40 billion!) is by benchmarking against and imitating the logistics processes of the world's best businesses. A 10 million-square-foot Pentagon depot in Pennsylvania now offers a twenty-four-hour emergency service (similar to Caterpillar tractor's guaranteed parts service). Two thousand computer-controlled carts running on conveyor belts and tracks pick up bar-coded equipment and are then directed to consolidation points near loading docks where they are combined and loaded into containers for shipping to destinations around the world. All of the bar codes on the consolidated shipment of parts are scanned and stored on laser-card container tags that can be read at the destination. A radio transmitter is also attached to the container, and, when the container passes through sensors at a pier, airport, or railway yard, a location signal is sent by satellite back to the depot. In this way, computerized information control is replacing huge "safety stockpiles" once needed because of the hopeless unreliability of the old system, which sometimes took up to one hundred days to deliver supplies. It is expected that Pentagon equipment inventories will drop from $104 billion in 1990 to $76 billion in 1994 and $55 billion by 2001. But, more important, the baggage train is getting there "just-in-time." Smart bombs may win battles, but smart logistics systems win wars. Many firms can learn a lesson here about long-term competitive success in their product markets. ■

Introduction

A firm's relationship strategy, discussed in Chapter 11, describes how a firm positions itself with its trading relationships. But just as the desired product positioning has to be converted into engineering performance and cost specifications for successful product development, the desired trading-relationship positioning has to be converted into logistic service performance and cost specifications for successful trading-relationship development.

This chapter discusses quality function deployment (QFD) applied to meeting customers' delivery needs. The functions for which management has to cleverly invest in quality are order processing, warehousing and transportation. In the past two decades, innovations in order processing have made the biggest difference to increasing customer delivery-service quality, but innovations in transportation and warehousing also have raised the quality of these activities. The result is that many American companies are far more advanced in their relationship logistic skills than their foreign competition. For example, a higher percentage of North American companies have adopted new, integrated supply-chain processes with their suppliers and

[1] Stan Crock, "The Pentagon Goes to B-School," *Business Week*, December 11, 1995, 98–100.

customers than Japanese or European countries.[2] North American companies may have some catching up to do to improve their product development skills, but their logistic development skills are often the best in the world. A cross-functional team and the modern marketing executives need to appreciate, if not develop, such skills, because much of the competitive success of their projects is likely to depend on using these skills to create uniquely efficient and effective trading logistic relationships.

Chapter Organization

Figure 12.1 presents the organization of this chapter. First, a total-quality-management (TQM) approach to designing the logistics of a supply chain is discussed. The various key processes involved are then discussed: order processing, transportation, and inventory and warehouse management. The next two sections discuss the importance of integrating manufacturing, logistics, and marketing into a coherent value-added strategy. Relationship marketing emphasizes how a manufacturer and its business customers or retailers can work together to design a total-quality order-delivery service that meets the customers' supply-chain needs at the lowest cost. A feature section of this chapter explains how such a differentiated supply-chain management service can be developed by a manufacturer. At this point it is important to clarify some terms. The logistic system that connects a manufacturer to a customer has a different name depending on whether it is from the viewpoint of the supplier or the buyer. To the supplier or manufacturer, it is often its *physical distribution system*. To the customer or buyer it is its *supply chain*. The difference is not just a matter of name. A manufacturer that is truly customer oriented should think about it and really call the logistic system a supply chain. Why? Because that is how its customers think about the process. Such an orientation avoids the risk of the manufacturer designing a system of logistic processes that suits its input cost-reduction objectives but does not meet the output needs of its customers. The last two sections of the chapter discuss the logistics of delivering a service rather than a product to the customer and global logistics issues.

Quality Function Deployment in Logistics

Figure 12.2 presents the activities and processes that drive the overall quality and cost of a system of logistic processes. At the top of the system is the specified level of service quality that will be provided to target customers. The standard measure is the percent of orders that will be filled and delivered within a specified time (e.g., immediately or within twenty-four hours). A system that delivers 100 percent of orders within the time period has zero defects. The total quality of customer service then might be raised by shortening the time period (equivalent to tightening engineering tolerances for a product) and achieving 100 percent of order delivery (undamaged!) within the shorter time period.

At the same time management continuously strives to invent new order-taking, warehousing, and transportation processes that reduce the *total* costs of the service. The word *total* is stressed because a rich and complex interplay among order-processing, transportation, and warehousing costs always occurs. For example, a

[2] Lisa Harrington, "Shaping the Integrated Supply Chain," *Transportation and Distribution*, January 1995, 34.

Figure 12.1 **Chapter Organization**

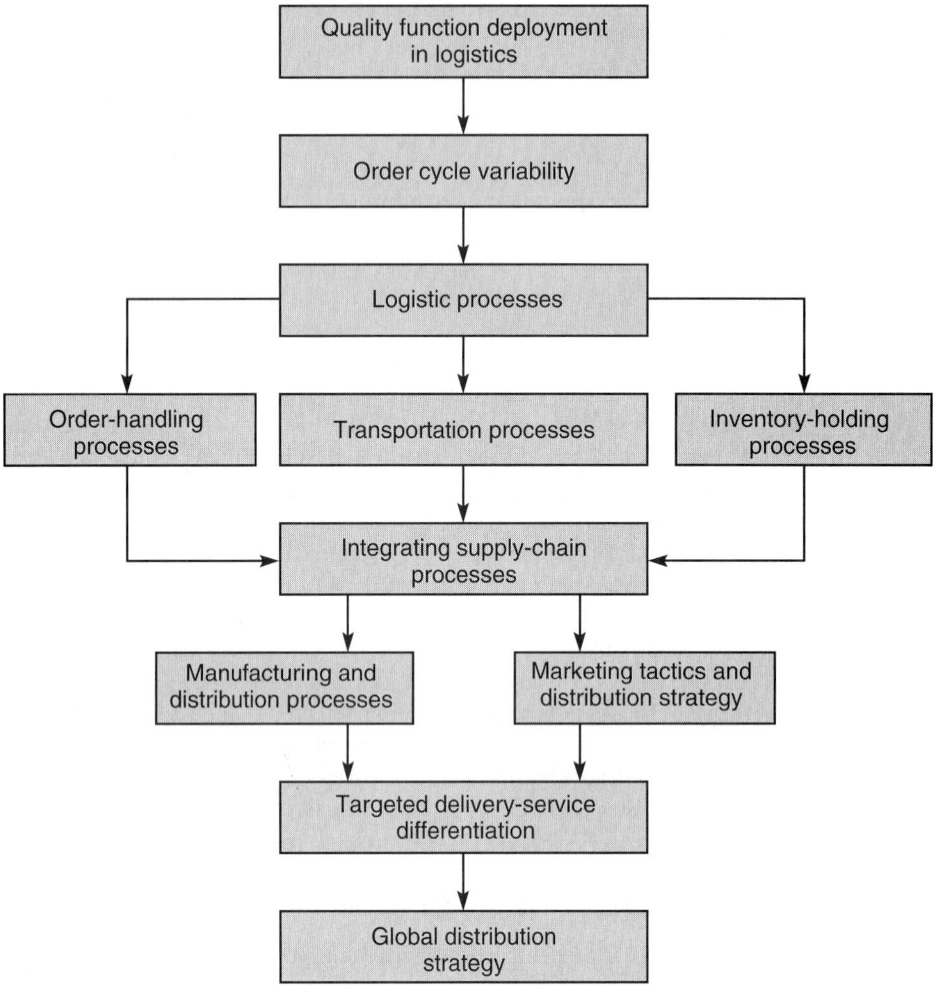

This chapter has a theme of using total-quality-management (TQM) goals and principles to integrate logistic processes in a way that provides a differentiated delivery service to target customers. The key task is managing all the processes in the order cycle that lead to a variable and hence unreliable delivery service. By introducing innovations into order handling, transportation, and inventory holding and by integrating all of the processes in the supply chain, a TQM result can be achieved: a superior delivery service that increases customer satisfaction and at a reduced cost. The chapter closes with a discussion of global distribution strategy.

reduction in transportation costs often results in increased costs somewhere else in the service supply chain. If a less expensive but also less reliable mode of transportation is used (e.g., rail rather than air), then the chance increases that the order will arrive several days or even weeks after it is needed. The only way to deal with such a possible emergency is to keep a permanent backup supply of the product, so if the order arrives late, the manufacturer or retailer will still have stock of the product on

Figure 12.2 **Total-Quality Logistic Management**

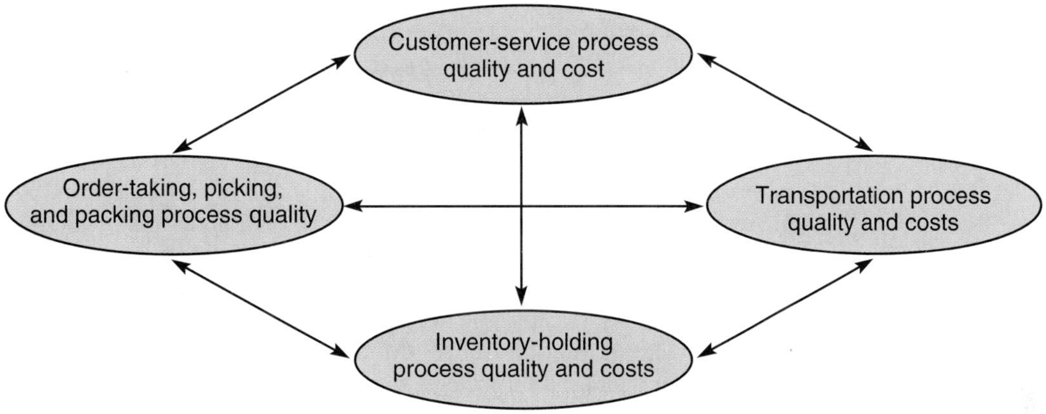

Competition to provide better customer service requires the design of a customer-service process that delivers a very high percentage of customer orders within a specific time. The costs involved are the order-taking, packing, warehousing, inventory-holding, and transportation processes that deliver the specified level of service. Total quality management of logistics involves evaluating the benefits (increased sales and customer goodwill) against the costs of increasing the service.

hand. Such an emergency supply of stock is called *safety stock.* Safety stock sits in a warehouse until it is needed to compensate for the unreliability of the time it takes a firm to process an order and ship it to its business customer, distributor, or retailer.

However, it is very expensive to have a product sitting in a warehouse waiting to be used for such an emergency. Many costs are involved: the cost of secure storage space that protects the safety stock from damage and theft, insurance against damage or theft, the cost of the investment (working capital) tied up in the safety stock (the cost of each item times the quantity judged necessary for reserve as safety stock), and taxes on the inventory (some states tax firms on the average annual value of the stock they hold in inventory). In addition, there is a risk that the safety stock may become obsolete, cannot be sold, or has to be sold at a loss because a new, more cost-effective product has been introduced into the market. The task, then, of management is to design the total supply-chain system of processes so its total cost is low and its total quality is high. Just as with product design, this is achieved by designing the order-processing, warehousing, and transportation systems concurrently rather than sequentially.

In the music business, where demand is driven by fads and the life of a product may last only a few weeks, EMI was the worst of suppliers. It took up to twenty days to deliver an order of a hot-selling compact disc (CD). Fifty percent of the distribution manager's time was spent answering angry phone calls from store managers and artists on tour who noticed their CDs were not on the racks. The savvy store managers learned how to cope with EMI's slow and unreliable replenishment service by placing massive initial orders and then returning the unsold overstock for a full refund. They ordered as if every new EMI release in the fall was going to be a hit. The returns jammed up and further slowed EMI's supply chain and were often scrapped after Christmas. For a $2.2 billion company, EMI's logistics stunk.

Applying a key TQM principle to logistics, senior EMI management decided to set ambitious improvement targets. This forced a complete redesign of EMI's whole distribution system rather than squeezing further efficiencies out of existing inefficient routines. First, a new sales tracking service based on actual store sales was used to monitor demand, and a new computer processed and tracked orders. Next, warehouses were reorganized so the five hundred CDs that made up 80 percent of the sales were stacked close to the loading bays, and state-of-the-art automation enabled an 80 percent reduction in stock pickers. Now order fill rates are up from 80 percent to 95 percent; they are delivered in two to three days directly to stores rather than to customer regional warehouses.[3] The much faster, more reliable order delivery means that retailers are now placing smaller replenishment orders related to weekly sales, the returns are much less, and the average inventory carried in the warehouses has been more than halved. In short, the TQM ideal has been achieved: an improvement of the supply-chain management process that has greatly increased the quality of customer service and, at the same time, has greatly reduced costs. However, true to the principles of TQM, a firm like EMI cannot rest on its laurels. It must continue to work on raising its fill rates and reducing its total system costs by applying the TQM experimentation testing process presented in Figure 12.3.

Order Cycle Variability

Before discussing the quality/cost trade-offs in order processing and alternative modes of transportation, it is important to clearly establish the pivotal role that order cycle variability plays by using an example. Imagine that a division of a large company uses ten boxes of photocopying paper per working day, and it has developed a routine of placing an order for ten days' supply from an office supply company every two weeks.[4]

Figure 12.4 graphs the time it takes for such an order to be prepared, mailed, and received by the supplier and the time it typically takes for the supplier to enter and process the order, to pick and pack the order of one hundred boxes off the shelf (including waiting to be resupplied when it runs out of the paper), and to transport the order. The figure also shows the time it takes for the order to be processed through the customer's centralized receiving dock and delivered to the division. The figure reveals that the time taken to prepare and transmit an order varies from 1 to 3 days, but the average is 2 days. The shortest feasible time it could take to complete the order-delivery cycle is 1 + 1 + 1 + 1 + 1 = 5 days, and the longest time an order-delivery cycle could possibly take is 3 + 2 + 5 + 3 + 2 = 15 days.

What does all of this information mean to the customer? It orders 10 days' supply, and it places this order every 10 days, but it is possible an order will take 15 days to be delivered. To guarantee that it will never run out of paper, it needs to maintain a safety stock of 5 days' worth of paper (50 boxes). Otherwise, it risks using up all of the paper from its last delivery, and it may have to wait 5 more days before it receives its most recent order. In that time it would need 10 boxes of paper a day. Now assume the office supplier introduced an order-by-telephone service that immediately enters and processes the order. The first two steps in the order cycle now take 1 day, with no

---

[3] Order fill rate is the percentage of an order that can be filled off the warehouse shelf and immediately shipped. The remaining percentage is shipped when it is found or received by the warehouse.

[4] A box of paper contains about five thousand sheets of paper.

Figure 12.3 TQM Continuous Improvement

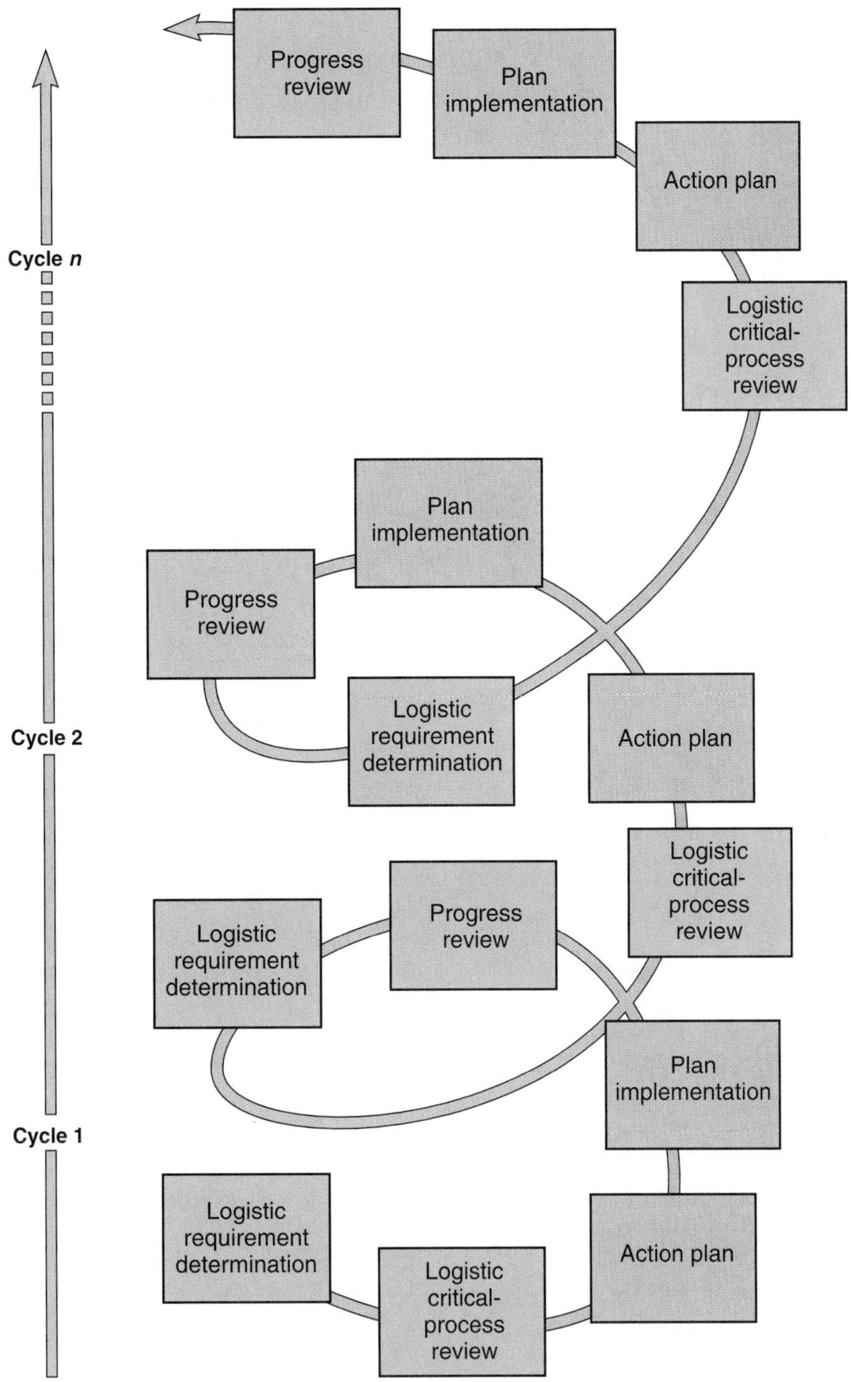

First the goals/requirements are set, and then the current system of processes is reviewed to identify the activities of subprocesses that are in greatest need of improvement and which improvement is most likely to advance the system's goals and requirements. These most-defective tasks become the focus of the action plan, which is a plan to test new ways of undertaking tasks. After appropriate experimentation (plan implementation) progress is reviewed, the basic system requirements are revisited, and new critical processes become the focus of improvement, experimentation, and innovation in the next cycle.

SOURCE: Scott A. Wagoner, "Logistics and Quality Management: Leadership and the Process Improvement Link," *Logistics Spectrum* 23, no. 4 (winter 1989): 15.

Figure 12.4 **Total Order Cycle with Variability**

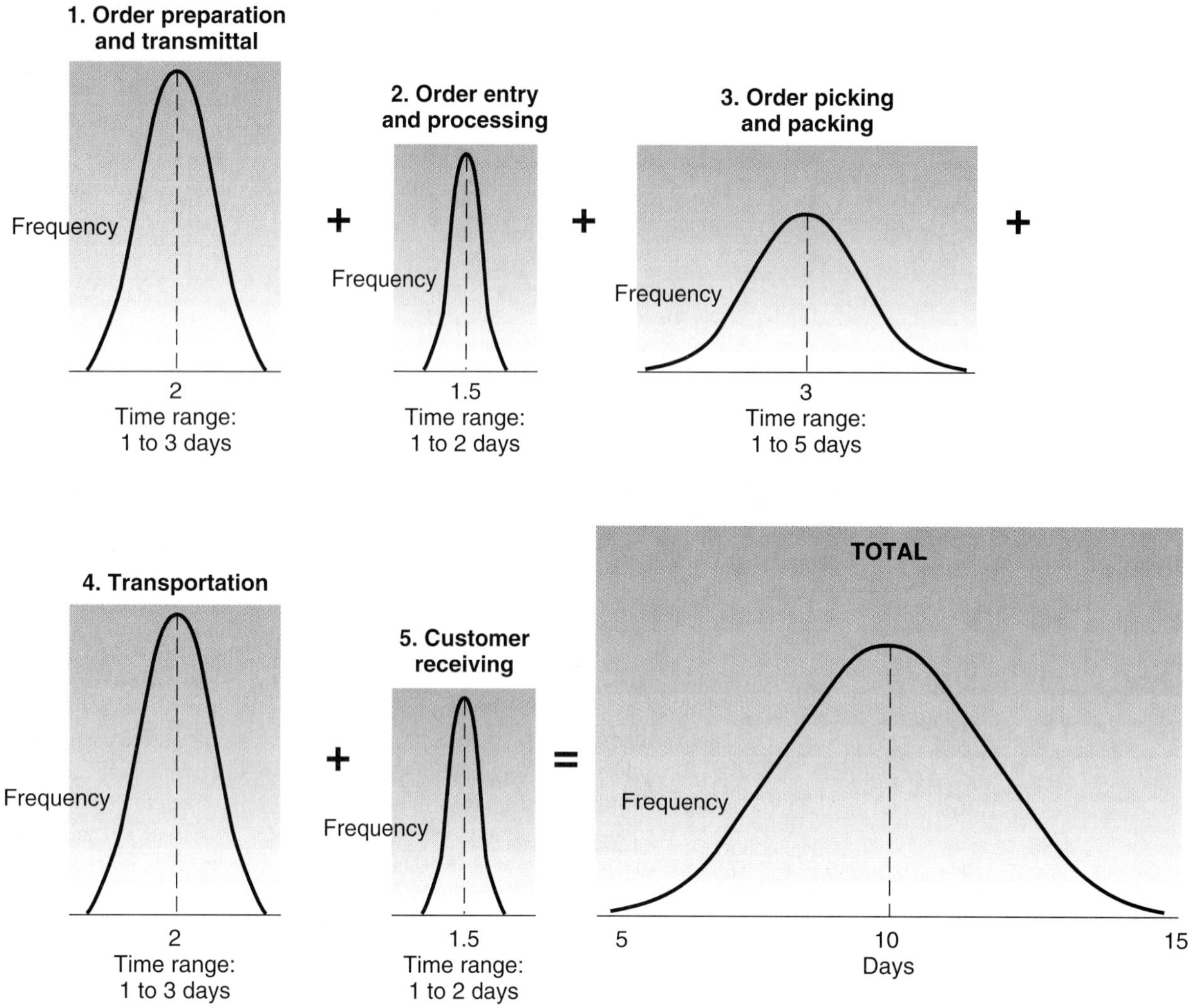

The shortest order cycle time is five days, the average is ten days, and the longest possible order cycle time is fifteen days. The focus for improvement should be order picking and packing because it is the most unreliable activity within the process. Unreliability is measured as the difference between the longest and shortest time it takes to complete the activity.

variability. Now the whole order cycle takes a minimum of 4 days, an average of 7.5 days, and at most 11 days. This means the customer now only has to carry 1 day of safety stock (10 boxes) to cover the possibility the order takes 11 days to be delivered. In addition, the customer can wait a couple of days before reordering.

This example demonstrates that a high-quality order-delivery service is not necessarily fast but does not vary in its order cycle time. Thus the goals of management are to take the variability out of the time it takes to process orders and to choose methods of transportation that arrive on time, rather than arraive sooner. For example, what if the office supplier changed its logistic system so order picking and packing always took 4 days and transportation always took 5 days, but the transport operator bypassed the customer receiving stage and delivered the order to the building where the paper is used. Should the customer prefer this slower but more reliable order-delivery service? Now the time an order takes to be delivered will be always 10 days. The service is slower on average, but, providing the customer always remembers to order 10 working days in advance, it does not need to carry any safety stock at all. Rather than requiring the customer to remember to place the order, the office supplier may suggest an automatic reorder of 100 boxes every two weeks until notified otherwise. This last customer service takes any remaining uncertainty and the risk of running out of paper out of the supply system. It further reduces the processing cost, and it is likely the office supplier's other costs will be reduced because slower (but more reliable) picking and packing and transportation is likely to cost less.

Logistic Processes

In the following sections order-taking, transportation and warehousing processes are discussed. These are the three essential subprocesses that make up the logistic system of a firm that manufactures and markets products. A great deal of innovation in these processes has occurred over the past decade, often initiated by firms that offer expertise in these services to manufacturers and retailers. They are called third-party logistic firms, the first party being the manufacturer and the second party its customer, another manufacturer or a distributor or retailer. Examples of such third-party logistic firms are companies that sell, lease, and operate electronic order-processing systems or even more advanced electronic networks of buyers and sellers; companies that offer electronic, custom clearance services with their global shipping service; integrated freight-forwarders that mix and match transportation modes to offer the most reliable and inexpensive transportation to their customers; and public warehouses that store and distribute a firm's inventories. The market for logistic services is an excellent example of the theory of competitive rationality in action: a lot of experimentation and innovation quickly imitated within and across industries.

Order-Handling Processes

Computerization has dramatically reduced the cost of order processing. It has also greatly reduced the variability in order-processing time. Electronic order entry often allows immediate notification of item availability and potential substitutes that may be on special (see Figure 12.5). Orders can be checked against master files to prevent mistakes in item codes and the size of the order. The computer also can produce courtesy confirmation letters that are automatically sent to buyers. Examples of such electronic systems are listed here:

- Federal Express provides heavy users with terminals and software that enable them to also track the movement of orders sent to customers via Federal Express.
- American Airlines provides corporate travel departments access to its Sabre reservation system.

Figure 12.5 **An Automated Ordering Inventory System Provided by Suppliers**

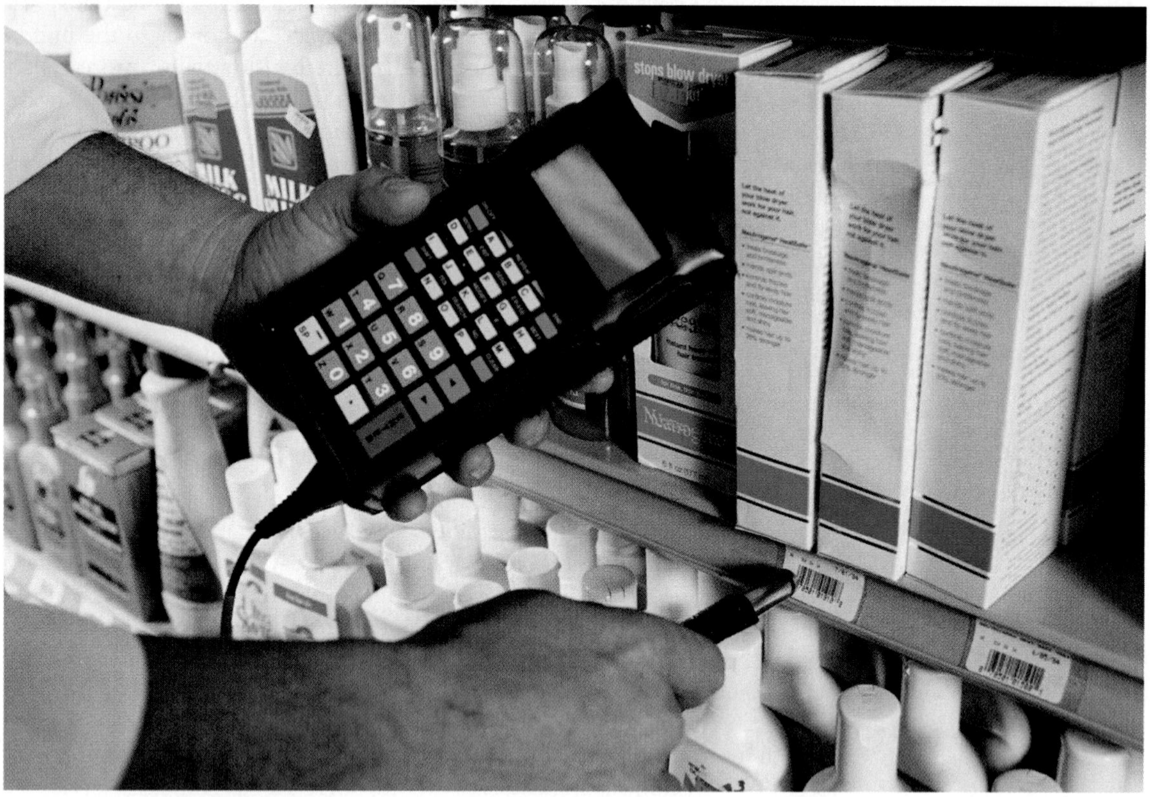

Automated systems have greatly reduced the cost of order processing and have improved stock control. They have also reduced the amount of stock that needs to be carried by increasing the reliability of the order cycle process.

- Drug wholesaler McKesson provides terminals and software used to manage stocking and almost all other operational tasks in a drugstore.
- Kodak provides terminals and software that allow for photo-finishing training and manage other aspects of a photographic retailer's business.
- Inland Steel developed a computer network that keeps customers informed of order status and provides other value-added services such as electronic billing, funds transfer, and technical advice.
- The Norton Company supplies its distributors with information on order status, pricing, and products.
- The 3M Company provides a videotext system describing existing and new products.[5]

[5] Rashi Glazer, *Marketing and the Changing Information Environment: Implications for Strategy, Structure, and the Marketing Mix*, Report No. 89-108 (Cambridge, MA: Marketing Science Institute, 1989); and Louis A. Wallis, *Computers and the Sales Effort*, Report No. 844 (New York: The Conference Board, 1985), 13.

In some trading relationships the customer's process of raising a purchase order and the supplier's process of receiving and entering the order are combined, eliminating the need for salespeople and buyers. Bose Corp., for example, has created an in-plant vendor program in which representatives from suppliers reside in Bose's purchasing departments. These representatives manage the inventory of component parts on-site, ordering new supplies when needed. This system cuts inventory costs and eliminates much of the cost of selling and order processing.[6]

The Internet will increase the amount of electronic order processing in many markets, but it will not have the revolutionary effect on buying and selling many commentators have predicted. This is because many such electronic buying and selling networks already have been established. For example, in the 1980s Orion Network enterprises created an electronic buy/sell network among six hundred junkyards across the country. It has greatly increased the availability of spare parts for older vehicles.

Applying TQM to Telephone Order Processing

Electronic order-entry systems are highly productive, but even low-tech order-processing systems such as Touch-Tone routing of customer calls (depending on their needs) can make a big difference. For example, a major airline's 800-number center handles 80 million calls a year and, up until a few years ago, cost $250 million to run; that is an average cost of $3 per call. Only 7 percent of the calls resulted in a sale that averaged around $200. The problem was that more than half the calls were inquiries about food, seat assignments, and flight delays or cancellations. They were service rather than sales calls. The introduction of a Touch-Tone call-routing system enabled the airline to have trained service agents and even a computer answer questions about flights. This enabled more salespeople to be hired and trained to answer booking inquiries. Potential customers did not have to wait as long to reach an agent, and, by giving the order-processing people more time and improved sales scripts, the result was a 100 percent increase in revenue-generating calls, and the average sale rose to around $400. Clearly, the previous system had been frustrating the most important customers—those who wished to make bigger purchases. At the same time the productivity of each call increased, the average cost per call to the center was reduced by 35 percent. This is another example of how process redesign can raise service quality and revenues and reduce costs at the same time. The net result in this case was a 400 percent improvement in profit contribution. However, it would be a mistake to attribute such success to simply the Touch-Tone routing technology. All of us have had experiences with Touch-Tone routing systems that are a hopeless, endless maze that sometimes bring us back to where we started. The trick is to design the customer interface process so the technology is used most effectively and to use well-trained people where they are needed most in the process.

Transportation Processes

Table 12.1 compares the service characteristics of the five major transportation modes. The major concern with transportation management (managing inventory on the move) is the value received for the money spent. The most valued characteristic of all modes of transportation from air freight to pipeline is reliability of delivery time. Air

[6] Walter P. Wilson, "High-Tech Firms Need Basic Business Sense," *San Jose Mercury News*, November 4, 1991.

Table 12.1 Comparison of Domestic Transportation Modes

	MOTOR	RAIL	AIR	WATER	PIPELINE
Cost	Moderate	Low	High	Low	Low
Market coverage	Point-to-point	Terminal-to-terminal	Terminal-to-terminal	Terminal-to-terminal	Terminal-to-terminal
Degree of competition (number of competitors)	Many	Moderate	Moderate	Few	Few
Predominant traffic	All types	Low-moderate value, moderate-high density	High value, low-moderate density	Low value, high density	Low value, high density
Average length of haul (miles)	515	617	885	376–1,367	276–343
Equipment capacity (tons)	10–25	50–12,000	5–125	1,000–60,000	30,000–2,500,000
Speed (time-in-transit)	Moderate	Slow	Fast	Slow	Slow
Availability	High	Moderate	Moderate	Low	Low
Consistency (delivery-time variability)	High consistency	Moderate consistency	High consistency	Low-moderate consistency	High consistency
Loss and damage	Low	Moderate-high	Low	Low-moderate	Low
Flexibility (adjustment to shipper's needs)	High	Moderate	Low-moderate	Low	Low

SOURCE: Douglas M. Lambert and James R. Stock, *Strategic Logistics Management* (Boston, MA: Irwin, 1993), 175.

travel and trucking are faster, thus reducing in-transit inventory carrying costs (which can become large when goods travel by rail or water) and enabling express or expedited delivery. Air and road transportation are also more reliable, more convenient, and more flexible. Air transportation also has the lowest incidence of pilferage and damage. Transportation by rail or water is inexpensive, and the volume discounts can be great. The transit time and reliability of these services are less attractive but improving. The deregulation of rail, air transportation, and trucking has led to the introduction of new services, price competition, and the possibility of negotiating better deals.

Full-Service Freight-Forwarders

The emergence of integrated shippers and full-service freight-forwarders has enabled these new channel entities to offer multimode transportation service packages (for example, truck to rail to truck) that combine the advantages of the modes without the disadvantages. It also has made the different modes more substitutable and hence more price and service competitive (see Figure 12.6). Containerization also has contributed to the ease of switching modes, as well as to reducing handling, damage, and pilferage. A further advantage of containers is that they often can serve as temporary warehouses. Consolidation warehouses have evolved to take advantage of full truckload or container efficiencies. Located strategically close to the buyers, the warehouse receives goods from a number of suppliers, consolidates them, and ships full truckloads to the buyers. Some innovative companies are using the information systems of their shippers to keep track of goods in transit, to identify sources of delay and unreliability, and to control the performance of the transport supplier. The future extension

Figure 12.6 Growth of Intermodal Transportation

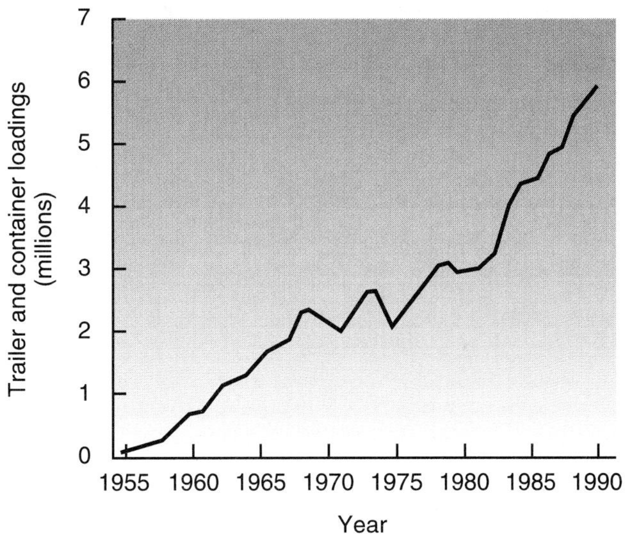

Intermodal trailer and container loadings grew rapidly between 1980 and 1990, almost twice the pace of the period from 1960 to 1980. Much of this increased growth has to do with deregulation of trucking and rail transportation at the end of the 1970s. Such intermodel transportation has increased competition between trucking and railways, because loads move to the most efficient mode for a particular part of a route.

SOURCE: "TM News Capsule," *Traffic Management* 29, no. 7 (July 1990): 19.

of the universal product code (UPC) into industrial goods will enable a supplier to know exactly where an order is (and where it is not!) in the distribution channel and to monitor its distribution system's overall reliability. The introduction of such scanning technology also will greatly increase the automation of warehousing. For example, Helene Curtis' new distribution warehouse in Chicago cut distribution costs by 40 percent, enabling the company to reduce the price of Suave Shampoo by 5 percent and still increase company profits and improve on-time order delivery.[7]

Inventory-Holding Processes

In the earlier copier paper example, the most inventory the customer carried at any time was one hundred boxes of paper, as illustrated in Figure 12.7, plus any safety stock it needed to carry. Order-cycle reliability eliminates the need for safety stock. But notice what happens if the same customer decides to place an order of fifty boxes each week. Its average inventory is halved. If it placed an order for ten boxes to be delivered daily, its average inventory carry expense would be only 10 percent of what it

[7] Rita Koselka, "Distribution Revolution," *Forbes*, May 25, 1992, 54–62.

Figure 12.7 **Order Frequency and Average Inventory**

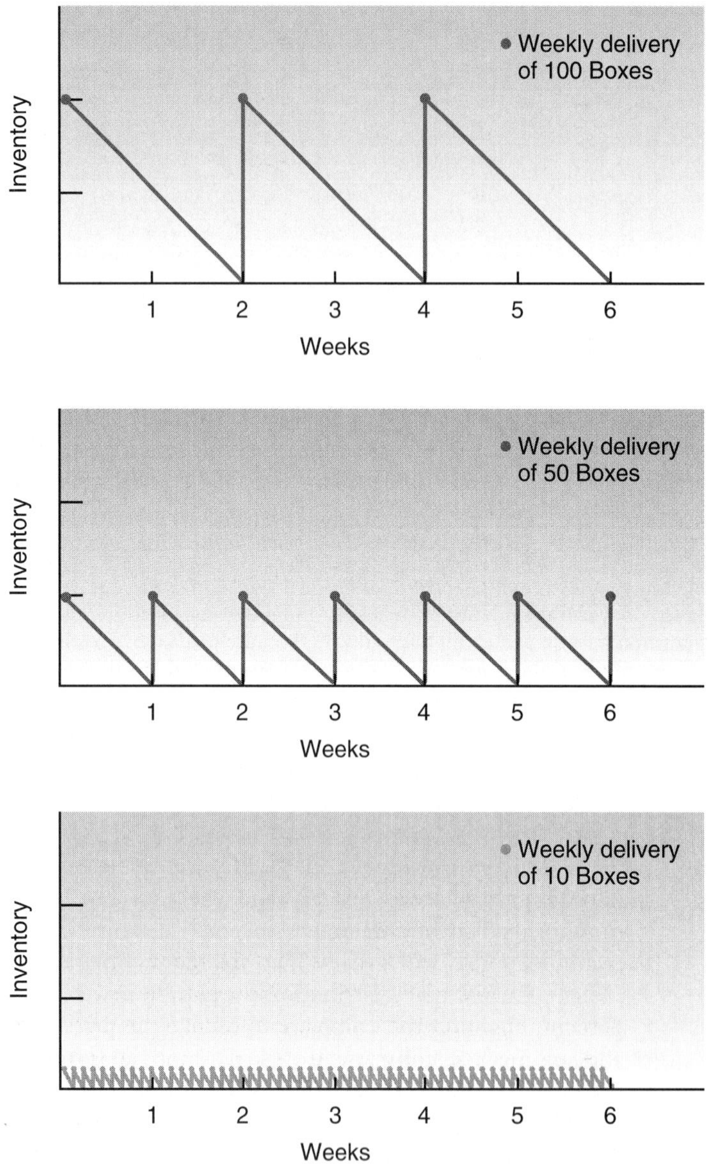

A two-week order of 100 boxes is consumed at a rate of 10 boxes a day. The average inventory held is 50 boxes. A weekly order of 50 boxes results in an average inventory of 25 boxes. A daily order of 10 boxes results in an average inventory of 5 boxes. The implication is that delivery of small, frequent orders minimizes inventory carrying costs. The extreme case is just-in-time delivery. The problem is that the cost of delivering the small orders may become prohibitive.

currently is (assuming no safety stock). Providing the office supplier is prepared to make the daily supply runs at no extra charge, the customer should prefer this almost just-in-time service. Notice that although the number of deliveries increases, the order cycle does not need to be speeded up. The automatic delivery of ten boxes is made each day, whether the original order was placed ten days before or five days before. Speed of the order cycle is only important in an emergency when a special supply is needed as soon as possible, such as a special part to repair an aircraft.

The ultimate extension of this logistic strategy is obtaining a continuous supply of parts to a manufacturer such as achieved with just-in-time service. For example, suppliers of automobile parts have built manufacturing plants next door to Honda's large manufacturing operation in central Ohio. Hourly, parts come off their assembly line and are immediately trucked over to the Honda assembly lines. More generally, an ideal supply chain has a constant flow of small deliveries that occur with great reliability and an optional rapid order-delivery cycle for special orders. This model of logistics efficiency can be made even more efficient by creating inventory pools.

Inventory Pools

Ryder Systems Inc. has become expert over the past twenty years in managing other companies' spare-parts and finished-goods inventories. The Miami-based company started with aircraft parts. Having airline customers (even competitors) pool their spare parts in a single warehouse run by Ryder allowed considerable savings. The skill Ryder developed in warehousing and truck fleet operation was then extended into other product markets. For example, Ryder now operates a Cadillac customer rapid-delivery system in Florida. Before Ryder's Cadillac service customers had to wait eight weeks for a custom order, and research showed that 40 percent would not even wait two weeks. The problem was that each of the forty-two Florida Cadillac dealers could not afford to carry hundreds of cars with different options in their yards. The solution was a distribution center in Orlando with fourteen hundred cars of every color and option package. Ryder now offers twenty-four-hour delivery from this selection pool to every dealer in the state. General Electric runs a similar service for its independent appliance dealers. The GE dealers stock display models, and when a customer wants a refrigerator with different features or in a different color, then the dealer can log into the GE order-processing system at any time and have the desired model delivered the next day. In return, the dealer has to carry the entire line of GE appliances, and more than 50 percent of the dealer's sales must be GE appliances.

Warehousing Tactics

Warehousing technology also has changed much over the past decade, as indicated by the several examples presented earlier in the chapter. The major advance has been in support software that tracks the movement of goods into the warehouse, tracks where they are stored, and tracks them out of the warehouse (see Figure 12.8). This has reduced the frequency that goods are lost in a warehouse down to almost zero. Automated stacking, picking, and packing technology also has increased efficiency, but some other changes in warehousing efficiency have less to do with technology and more to do with coordination, such as coordination of inbound and outbound shipping. In a major warehousing center serving several major retail stores daily, it would be ideal if inbound supplies could be unloaded, immediately loaded onto trucks with other inbound supplies that arrived that day, and then shipped to the stores. This process is called cross-docking. Goods are moved from a truck at an inbound dock immediately to trucks at a number of outbound docks. This is a very efficient way of supplying stores with high-volume, high-turn goods because the goods spend no time sitting in warehouses and are not handled twice. It does, however, demand a high level of reliability and regularity of inbound and outbound transportation services.

Figure 12.8 **High Technology Warehousing**

Wal-Mart used its high-tech, low-cost distribution centers as a major competitive advantage during the 1980s and is continuing to do so in the 1990s.

Integrating Supply-Chain Processes

Innovations in logistics have not been confined to the elemental subprocesses described so far. Managers also have thought "outside the box," which means they have not been bound by conventional ways of thinking about logistics (see Appendix 1). They have explored ways other manufacturing and marketing programs and processes might be changed and integrated with logistic processes so the total result would be a reduction in costs and an increase in customer satisfaction with the final product and delivery services. Such expansive thinking about the whole value-added supply chain has led to some important changes in processes and conventional wisdom.

Integrating Manufacturing and Distribution Processes

Recent innovations in integrating manufacturing and distribution processes have significantly reduced the overall costs of the entire system and, simultaneously, increased customer service and system adaptability. They are just another example of how applying total-quality-management principles can reduce input costs and increase output quality while decreasing process time and increasing process adaptability—a result that a few years ago was considered impossible. Such innovations have forced everyone in particular industries to imitate and become more skilled themselves at integrating manufacturing and distribution processes so the whole is more than the sum of the parts. In short, the core competence of process and systems integration has become a competitive driver in the market—a managerial path dependency. The following are examples of such innovations.

Postponing Manufacturing Processes

Think about how expensive it must have been to offer a range of paint colors in different sized cans before the "tint, mix, and shake" process of postponing final product assembly to the point of purchase was innovated (see Figure 12.9). A hundred times more cans of paints had to be stocked by hardware and decorating stores, and many became obsolete as color tints and hues went out of fashion. Considerable savings resulted from only having to ship and carry a base white paint to which color was added by the shop assistant. Consequently, many more colors were able to be mixed up and lower costs reduced prices for the consumer, thus increasing consumer choice and satisfaction. What is more, the whole process was much more adaptable to changes in fashion tastes, and inventory velocity (the speed with which cans of paint flow through the value-added chain) was increased, thus reducing the overall value-added process time.

Appliance manufacturers also have benefited from rethinking how to integrate manufacturing and distribution processes by moving specific processes closer to the point of purchase. Some dishwasher manufacturers have their colored panel facings added at a warehouse when the order is received. Refrigerator doors are similarly added at a warehouse when the order is received. The Italian clothing manufacturer Benetton has redesigned its manufacturing process for some clothing items by cutting and sewing white garments and then dying them when orders are received for specific colors. This is an excellent example of the transfer of a process innovation from one industry (paint) to another (fashion wear). The market environment issue they faced in common was high uncertainty about the popularity of particular fashion colors. This process strategy copes with this uncertainty and gains an advantage over rivals by moving final assembly into the distribution channel and thus integrating the manufacturing and logistic processes.

Manufacturers increasingly ship furniture, particularly imported furniture, unassembled for the retailer or even the consumer to assemble. For several decades now, consumers have been battling with assembly instructions for bicycles, lawn mowers, deck furniture, children's swing sets, exercise equipment, gas barbecue grills, and light fixtures. The savings for the manufacturer are reduced manufacturing, shipping, and storage costs. The retailer can stock more options at lower cost. In competitive markets, the consumer benefits because most of these cost savings are passed on in lower prices. The down side is that the performance quality-in-use of the product may be

Figure 12.9 **Manufacturing Postponement**

By abandoning conventional thinking that paint is made only in a paint manufacturing plant, executives in the paint industry came up with the idea of mixing the color into the paint at the point of purchase. This manufacturing-logistics innovation, introduced in the 1950s, revolutionized paint selection and lowered costs.

lower and definitely more variable because the quality of the final assembly process is likely, in some cases, to be very low! Overall, this innovation, called *assembly postponement*, often increases consumer choice; reduces the inventory, transportation, and obsolescence costs; and, by requiring the channel to learn to add value, increases channel cooperation. Harking back to the Chapter 11 discussion of relationship strategy, this greater cooperation through innovation is likely to lead to further experiments in supply-chain management integration. But, from the more cynical power-exploitation perspective, a manufacturer has to be careful how much it "shares" its manufacturing processes with a distributor.

Manufacturing-logistic integration innovation is not always achieved by shifting manufacturing further along the value-added supply chain. Some merchandising processes have been moved back up the value-added channel because they can be done more efficiently and accurately at that point. For example, the Wal-Mart price tags are put on the products when they are packaged in manufacturing rather than later in the Wal-Mart warehouse. This saves the products from sitting somewhere in the distribution channel waiting to be price labeled by someone who must sort through and find the right price tag for a specific stock-taking unit (sku) or stamp the right price on the package or hangtag. Both the cost and the mispricing defect rate are much higher when the pricing is done in the warehouse or in the store.

Shrinking Inventories and Working-Capital Expense

Flexible manufacturing is another process innovation that has arisen from total systems thinking rather than thinking about the logistic process as separate from the manufacturing process. The driver of this innovation has been the goal of reducing working-capital costs. *Working capital* is the capital a firm has tied up in average inventories of raw materials, partly finished goods, and average net receivables. *Average net receivables* is the difference between average receivables (what customers owe the firm in unpaid bills) and average payables (what the firm owes its suppliers in unpaid bills). The cost of this working capital is the interest the firm must pay a bank to borrow the capital tied up in inventory and net receivables.

Some companies are very good at the modern logistic goal of reducing working capital. American Standard's plant in Leeds, England, makes vacuum pumps for truck brakes. The product is not very innovative, but the way the plant manufactures and distributes it is quite remarkable. In 1994 sales jumped to $163 million, twice what they were five years before, and working capital dropped from $13 million to a negative $154,000.[8] This was achieved because annual average raw materials, finished parts, and finished goods inventories were only $2.2 million, and annual average net receivables was a negative $2.35 million. How was this remarkable level of competitive performance achieved? In 1989 the plant took one week to process an order and three weeks to manufacture the order. After switching from a large, cumbersome production line to small manufacturing cells that can manufacture a complete pump, the plant could manufacture small quantities of each of its six models of pumps each day. This enabled the plant to deliver small orders more regularly, which reduced raw materials inventory. The elimination of large production runs also reduced the finished parts and goods inventory. By introducing this flexible manufacturing and a faster order process, customer orders were made and shipped in three days rather than three weeks. More frequently, reliable delivery meant that customers did not have to hold as large a parts inventory. This saved them money, so in exchange for the better service, customers paid faster, which reduced receivables. The money saved was invested in product development and new equipment that further boosted the bottom line.

Across the company American Standard has reduced working capital from $725 million (25 cents per sale) to $525 million (14 cents per sale). No less than Jack Welch, the CEO of General Electric, has used American Standard as a benchmark for GE

[8] Shawn Tully, "Raiding a Company's Hidden Cash," *Fortune*, August 22, 1994, 82–87.

to learn how to reduce its inventory, which has been lowered from $9 billion to $6 billion since 1990. The shorter-production-runs lesson also has been learned by Quaker Oats, which now makes all nine of its instant oatmeal cereals each week (based on what retailers sold the week before) rather than manufacturing one recipe a week. The extra cost in 1993 of twenty-seven more hours resetting machines for the different production runs was $20,000 in lost production. But the savings in lowering inventory from $11.7 million to $5.8 million amounted to $500,000. Overall, since 1990 Quaker Oats has reduced working capital from 13 percent to 7 percent of sales, freeing $200 million in cash for reinvesting in product and process innovation. Some argue that the best measure of a well-run company is its working capital per dollar of sales and how much that ratio is reduced each year. This is achieved through innovative integration of manufacturing and logistic processes.

Integrating Marketing Tactics and Distribution Strategy

Better integration of marketing and logistic strategies and processes can also deliver major cost savings. For example, packaging should be designed for storage and transportation efficiency as well as for usage convenience and to attract attention at the point of purchase (see the Chapter 10 section on packaging). Fruit juices are increasingly being packaged in cardboard boxes, which saves space, and a trend toward concentrated liquid detergents and fabric softeners, saves weight as well as space. *Cubic efficiency* is a term that describes how efficiently a package occupies storage, transportation, and display space. Boxes are more cubic efficient than cans, and cans are more efficient than bottles. When shipping and storage space are expensive, the cubic efficiency of a package can become very important. New shipping and warehousing handling technology also may require standard package dimensions that neatly fit into a container and product code information on the package for scanners to keep track of inventory in transit and in storage.

Another huge innovation in marketing-distribution process cooperation is the effort to reduce promotion pricing. It may sound strange that backing off a common marketing tactic is a breakthrough innovation, but the promotion-price path dependency has been a very expensive, almost addictive habit for many companies (see the pricing chapter, Chapter 16). If most of a product's sales are made when it is sold at a sale price, then large spikes occur in demand. This means that the retailer and manufacturer have wildly swinging inventories of the product. They have to build up inventory for the sale and then get it down as quickly as possible after the sale. Managing such a supply chain can increase the cost of manufacturing and distributing the product from 10 percent to 20 percent. Put another way, if such swings in demand can be eliminated, then the cost savings for both manufacturer and retailer can be significant. For this very reason, companies such as P&G have attempted to greatly reduce their use of promotion pricing tactics in marketing their packaged goods. They had discovered that the use of promotion-price tactics was driving the company's whole distribution strategy. The tail was wagging the dog, rather than the other way around. On the other hand, price cuts are often part of a sensible logistics strategy. For example, seasonal sales are used to move items such as Christmas ornaments, skis, and sailboats that otherwise would have to be carried over to the next season at the risk of becoming out of fashion. Price discount promotions are also often developed to encourage pallet-sized orders that reduce shipping costs or to use an electronic ordering system that reduces order-processing costs.

A growing trend that will require the careful coordination of marketing programs and logistic processes is the disposal and recycling of products. In Germany, automobile, appliance, and computer companies are required to take back their products when they finally wear out. It can be expected that new regulations in the United States will encourage such disposal and recycling processes. An innovative company may even initiate such a marketing program as a service to its customers and as a way of reducing its costs by using recycled components. Called *reverse logistics*, such a program will require the storage and transportation of products to recycling centers, where they are reconstituted into blocks of aluminum, steel, plastic, and glass. It is likely third-party service companies will become expert at such reverse logistic recycling and that they will encourage manufacturers to redesign their appliances and automobiles so it is easier to disassemble them and recycle the parts.

Targeted Delivery-Service Differentiation

An aggressive, customer-oriented approach to logistics, consistent with a relationship innovation strategy discussed in Chapter 11, is to help design a customer's supply chain. This is a value-added service to the customer and requires a deep understanding of the customer's use of the product and current purchasing and supply-chain processes.

Helping a retailer manage its inventory is one of the more important services a supplier can provide to gain the retailer's cooperation and performance.[9] Creative logistics differentiation can be seen in the following examples:

- A supplier of cartons developed a unique competitive relationship with a manufacturing customer based on a joint feasibility study. The manufacturer eliminated its nineteen annual auction bids and consolidated its buying with the supplier, who was able to introduce savings in freight, warehousing, and order systems efficiencies. The supplier immediately reduced prices by 7 percent and guaranteed additional price reductions of at least 10 percent over the next three years. A tracking system and steering committee were created to look for ways to introduce further savings and to monitor the resulting benefits. The supplier increased its margins by more than 10 percent and increased its sales to the customer by 267 percent.[10]
- For four years, the medical supplier Baxter worked with a hospital to reduce inventory levels by $200,000 and logistic costs by $1.9 million. The working relationship involved overhauling the ordering system, standardizing supplies, improving storage systems, and even introducing a delivery system for homebound patients.[11]

One of the first steps toward developing such a customer relationship is to sit down with the customer and attempt to tailor a service that is most efficient and effective given the customer's objectives. This requires considering the customer's purchasing, transportation, inventory-carrying and stock-out problems, and costs. It is not an easy task, because these factors must not be considered separately but treated as

---

[9] John F. Gaski and John R. Nevin, "The Differential Effects of Exercised and Unexercised Power Sources in a Marketing Channel," *Journal of Marketing Research* 22 (May 1985): 130–42.

[10] Harry Strachan, "Partnership Innovation," in *Creating Customer Satisfaction*, ed. Earl E. Bailey (New York: The Conference Board, 1990), 19.

[11] Terrence J. Mulligan, "Customer Alliances—1," in *Creating Customer Satisfaction*, ed. Earl E. Bailey (New York: The Conference Board, 1990), 21.

Table 12.2 Customizing a Delivery Schedule Using a DELIVERY Spreadsheet

	Time in Working Days		
SUPPLIER ORDER PROCESSING	MINIMUM	AVERAGE	MAXIMUM
Order preparation and communication	1.00	2.00	3.00
Order entry and processing	1.00	2.00	3.00
Warehouse picking and packing	1.00	2.00	3.00

	Customer Packing, Shipping, and Delivery Costs				
ORDER QUANTITY	METHOD A	METHOD B	METHOD C	METHOD D	METHOD E
100	$ 20	$ 30	$ 20	$ 25	$ 30
200	$ 40	$ 40	$ 35	$ 50	$ 60
300	$ 60	$ 50	$ 50	$ 75	$ 80
400	$ 80	$ 60	$ 65	$100	$100
500	$100	$ 70	$ 80	$120	$120
600	$110	$ 80	$ 95	$130	$140
700	$120	$ 90	$110	$140	$160
800	$130	$100	$125	$150	$180
900	$140	$110	$140	$160	$200
1000	$150	$120	$155	$170	$220
Delivery time:					
Minimum working days	2	2	1	1	1
Average working days	3	4	3	2	2
Maximum working days	7	7	7	5	3

Customer Information			
Consumption per working day (average, maximum)	20, 26	Do you want to include in-transit inventory cost in the model? (No = 0, Yes = 1)	0
Number of working days in year	250		
Cost per unit (customer valuation)	$32	Concern over a supply-created stock-out (No concern = 0, Moderate = 2, High = 4)	4
Administration cost of placing each order	$20		
Annual inventory cost as a percentage of unit cost	25%	Concern over a consumption-created stock-out (No concern = 0, Moderate = 1, High = 4)	4
Annual in-transit inventory cost as a percentage	20%		

an interacting set of functions. Sometimes the customer may not appreciate the extent of the trade-offs involved in improving one of these delivery features at the expense of another. Such trade-offs are often unique to a particular supplier-customer relationship and must be treated as such. The development of such a new logistics relationship requires the following:

1. The development of new attitudes that change old habits.
2. Enough trust to work together to develop competitive added value.
3. A willingness not to try to exploit the new relationship at the expense of long-run cooperation.
4. Patience—payoff often takes time.
5. The supplier must be willing to adapt and change more than the customer.[12]

[12] Mulligan, "Customer Alliances—1," 22.

(continued)

Table 1

ORDER QUANTITY	AVERAGE INVENTORY REQUIRED BY CUSTOMER					
	METHOD A	METHOD B	METHOD C	METHOD D	METHOD E	# ORDERS
100	193	167	193	167	125	50.0
200	248	223	248	223	182	25.0
300	303	278	303	278	237	16.7
400	357	332	357	332	291	12.5
500	411	386	411	386	345	10.0
600	464	439	464	439	399	8.3
700	517	493	517	493	452	7.1
800	570	546	570	546	506	6.3
900	623	599	623	599	559	5.6
1000	676	651	676	651	611	5.0
Order-delivery lag (number of working days)	9	10	9	8	8	

Table 2

ORDER QUANTITY	CUSTOMER'S TOTAL ANNUAL TRANSPORTATION AND INVENTORY CARRYING COSTS				
	METHOD A	METHOD B	METHOD C	METHOD D	METHOD E
100	$3,540	$3,837	$3,540	$3,587	$3,504
200	$3,484	$3,284	$3,359	$3,534	$3,454
300	$3,755	$3,389	$3,589	$3,806	$3,562
400	$4,105	$3,657	$3,918	$4,157	$3,831
500	$4,485	$3,987	$4,285	$4,487	$4,163
600	$4,796	$4,349	$4,671	$4,766	$4,526
700	$5,139	$4,728	$5,067	$5,085	$4,905
800	$5,501	$5,117	$5,469	$5,429	$5,295
900	$5,875	$5,512	$5,875	$5,790	$5,691
1000	$6,258	$5,912	$6,283	$6,162	$6,091

The computer spreadsheet DELIVERY, presented in Table 12.2, can be used to explore ways to improve the delivery service of a product purchased regularly by an individual customer. Basically, it identifies the optimal order quantity and transportation method that minimizes the customer's annual delivery and inventory costs. It allows the supplier to identify the advantages to its customers of (1) reducing or increasing its standard order quantity, (2) using a new order-processing system, and (3) using a new method of transportation. The model considers the effect of a number of customer consumption statistics and cost estimates and the customer's risk aversion to stock-outs. DELIVERY then produces a table that identifies the customer's annual combined transportation and inventory-holding costs for different order-processing systems, transportation alternatives, and standard order quantities.

Figure 12.10 **The FedEx Overnight or Second-Day Distribution Network**

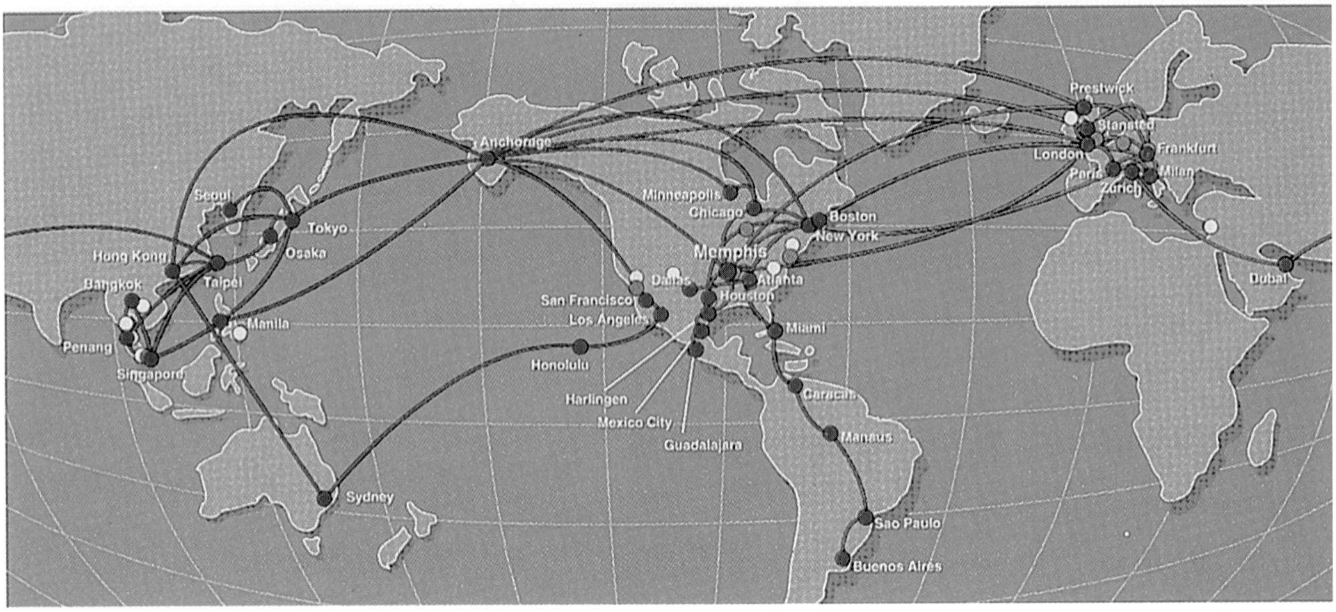

Global Distribution

Global distribution management is one of the most important issues facing a firm in the global marketplace. It involves special-information, transportation, and inventory management. The more that global distribution can be managed through superior electronic communications, the less of a problem transportation and inventory management will be. Thus, developing a superior communications system with foreign subsidiaries, resellers, and customers is the first imperative. Freight companies such as Federal Express are able to supply such an information system, along with its global overnight or second-day service (see Figure 12.10). Federal Express expects to have some one hundred thousand "powership" computer terminals installed in its customers' offices by the year 2000.[13] These terminals enable the supplier to keep control over a shipment, reducing the need for a global warehousing network. FedEx also has developed a computerized system that speeds custom clearance. Other freight companies, such as United Parcel Service and integrated freight-forwarders, are developing similar tracking systems (see Figure 12.11).[14]

[13] Seth Lubove, "Vindicated," *Forbes*, December 9, 1991, 197–202.
[14] See the discussion of channel analysis in Chapter 7.

Figure 12.11 **A Seamless, Worldwide EDI Communication System**

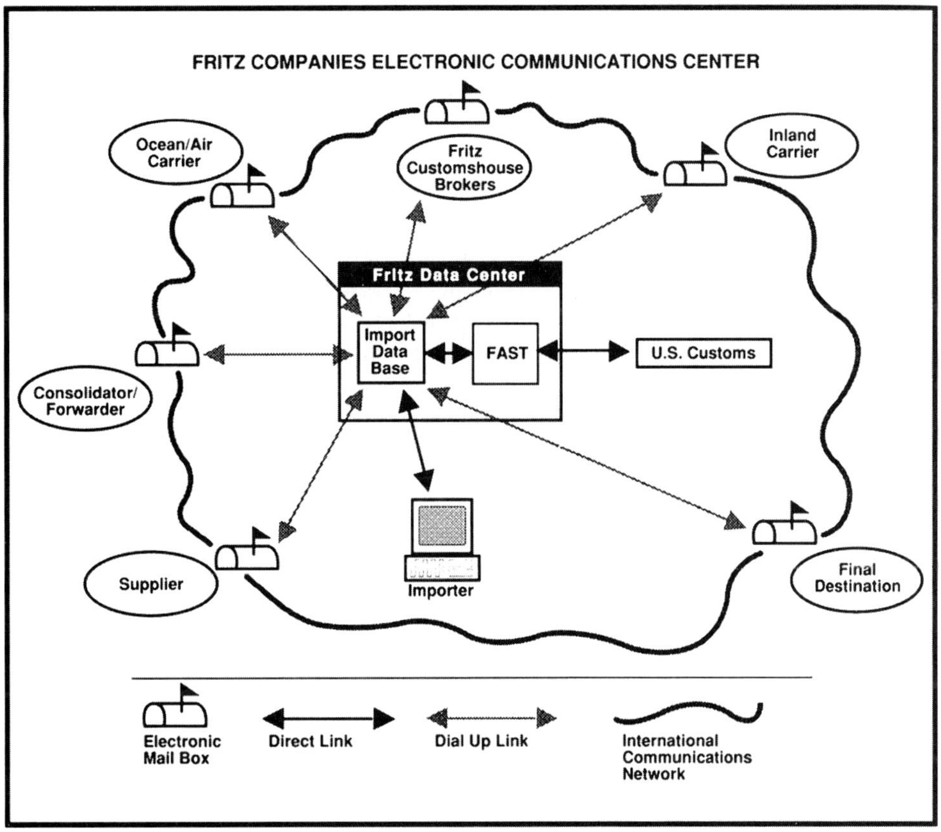

Fritz Companies has developed an EDI system that gives it the ability to see and control the entire international transaction process in a seamless service, including paperless customs processing and clearance, before the goods land in the United States. Companies such as Boeing, Dow, Sears Roebuck, and many of the Fortune 1000 importers and exporters use Fritz as a "third-party" partner to reduce their investment in channel logistics, to reduce overall costs, to simplify and speed up the international order-delivery cycle, to track orders, and to increase their choice of offshore suppliers. Soon these companies could have access to each others' electronic sales catalogs and price lists through the Fritz system. When this happens, companies will be able to sell, buy, and ship through this electronic global marketplace.

SOURCE: Fritz Companies, Inc., San Francisco.

International air freight increased from 1 billion kilometer-tonnes a year in 1960 to 25 billion kilometer-tonnes in 1983.[15] Since then it has grown at an even faster rate. Clearly, air freight has become the preferred mode of transportation for small, high-value-added products from computers to cut flowers. But international shipping

[15] Gunnar K. Sletmo and Jacques Picard, "International Distribution Policies and the Role of Air Freight," *Journal of Business Logistics* 6, no. 1 (1984): 37.

has also increased and become much more efficient as the result of globalization of port container facilities. It has reduced spoilage, waste, and theft; sped up shipment delivery; and increased the regularity and reliability of delivery times and schedules. Containers also have become important as emergency warehousing facilities, particularly in markets that lack an adequate warehousing infrastructure. Warehousing is a problem in many markets, including, most surprisingly, Japan, where warehousing is very expensive and requires long-term contracts.[16]

Chapter 11 discussed the unique cultures and conventional trading practices of trading channels. Nowhere is this more important than in global marketing. First, a channel analysis, as described in Chapter 7, should be taken in the foreign market. This analysis should involve the extensive participation of consultants who are very familiar with the distribution infrastructure of the target economy, its culture, and its trading practices. Only then should a firm make the decision to use independent agents or to build its own distribution system. Some risk is involved in either case, more so if its own distribution is pursued rather than the use of sales agents. One way to reduce the risk is to sell to a reseller at first and then, if the relationship seems to work, make an offer to buy the reseller. A study of the global distribution practices of U.S. firms found that once a firm sets up a distribution system, it tends to build on this system, no matter how shaky the initial foundations and the current inappropriateness of the supplier-reseller fit.[17] This suggests that the initial distribution-system decision making in a foreign market should be made from a long-term perspective. The study also found that

- Firms tend to rely on local resellers in cultures that are very foreign, and this is generally a good strategy. It is often encouraged, even mandated, by the foreign government. Such a trading relationship has the potential to grow into a production joint venture if protectionist government policies are introduced, such as in the European Community.
- Firms will consider building or buying their own distribution systems when their competitive advantage depends on confidential marketing processes, unique patents, product differentiation, or secret production processes that they do not want to have disclosed to the market. Treacherous diffusion and other types of opportunistic behavior are often serious risks in foreign markets because the distribution system does not have enough competition to keep the players honest.
- Distribution decision making is also not very systematic and is often based on a weak channel analysis.[18]

All of this suggests that distribution management in the global market is particularly difficult, involving long-term commitments, conflicting guidelines (such as when introducing a differentiated product in a very foreign market), and investment in high-technology control systems. However, it is in precisely such complex, uncertain, high-stakes decision-making situations that the firm with superior competitive rationality excels. All competitors are moderately good at distribution management

[16] Michael R. Czinkota and Jon Woronoff, *Japan's Market: The Distribution System* (New York: Praeger, 1986), 86.
[17] Erin Anderson and Anne T. Coughlan, "International Market Entry and Expansion via Independent or Integrated Channels of Distribution," *Journal of Marketing* 51 (January 1987), 71–82.
[18] Stephen J. Kobrin, John Basek, Stephen Blank, and Joseph La Palombara, "The Assessment and Evaluation of Noneconomic Environments by American Firms: A Preliminary Report," *Journal of International Business Studies* 11 (Spring/Summer 1980), 32–46.

in a familiar economy with stable and rigid trading practices and systems. The superior firm does well in uncertain and volatile environments, such as in international markets. Global distribution presents tremendous opportunities for the astute, alert competitor who is able to adapt and implement quickly, particularly in using the new communication technologies.

Discussion Questions and Minicases

1. What is the annual cost saving to a retailer when a manufacturer improves the reliability of its service by *reducing* order cycle variability by two days, given the following:
   a) The retailer's average sales is 100 cases a business day. The year has 250 business days.
   b) The retailer's purchase price per case is $50.
   c) The transportation cost per case is $5.
   d) The average order cycle is 10 days.
   e) The inventory carrying cost is 40 percent of the cost of inventory.
   f) The retailer places an order every 4 weeks.
2. What is the annual cost saving to the retailer in number 1 if the average order cycle time is reduced by 2 days, with no change in order cycle variability?
3. The same retailer wants to be supplied every 2 weeks rather than 4 weeks. The manufacturer says it is willing to supply more frequently, but the transportation cost it charges the retailer will have to increase by 10 percent. Should the retailer go ahead?
4. The same manufacturer offers an alternative arrangement. It will deliver 4,000 cases every 8 weeks rather than 2,000 cases every 4 weeks, and, because of transport economies resulting from a full truckload, it will reduce its transportation charge to the retailer by 20 percent. Should the retailer accept this deal?
5. A distributor has discovered that when it is out of stock, 6 out of 10 customers buy from a competitor. Two out of 10 simply order later, and 2 out of 10 request a back order. The manufacturer that supplies the distributor prepares a special expediting service where it will deliver an order overnight to the distributor. Distributors in other parts of the country have found that 9 out of 10 customers use the special service and only 1 out of 10 buys from a competitor. Given the following information, how much more should the distributor be prepared to pay for the expediting service than what it normally pays for transportation?

Average order size	$500
Distributor's gross margin	$ 30
Back-order cost per order	$ 5
Transportaion cost per average order	$ 50

6. What is the expediting service worth to the distributor in number 5 if each customer who goes to a competitor stays with the competitor for the next two years and places a $500 order every three months? Assume the cost of capital is 20 percent, which means the quarterly discount rate on future revenues is 5 percent.
7. The benefits of information technology (IT) for logistic systems are not always obvious, and this creates barriers for the implementation of an IT system. While Federal Express was successfully developing computerized tracking systems in the late 1970s and early 1980s, United Parcel Service (UPS) was having difficulties making investment in information technology pay off. It was only through a ten-year investment period, in which UPS methodically improved its information handling, that it was able to reap rewards. By 1992, UPS had in place a global data tracking system that included centralized processing, hand-held input devices for truck drivers, and a label code system that carried more information than current bar code systems. At that time, UPS was able to compete with Federal Express on delivery time and customer information.

Why might UPS have had such a difficult time implementing IT systems before it began its successful effort in 1983? If you were a systems integrator, how would you now attempt to sell information systems to companies that have been "burned" in the past by systems that never paid off?

8. Please explain the significance of the chapter opener quotes as applied to logistics and supply chain management.

Sales representatives are the heroes of an organization.

Tom Peters

Eight percent of adults in graduate management programs or intending to enter an MBA program rate the honesty of people in sales as very high or high.

Gallup Poll, 1994

CHAPTER THIRTEEN

Managing Personal Selling

From the perspective of the theory of competitive rationality, the strategic function of the sales force is to help develop the emerging new usage/benefit segments through pioneer selling to new customers or developing new business with existing relationships. As the "scouts" of the firm, salespersons also play a crucial role in quickly feeding back information into a Market Intelligence E-Mailbox (MIEM) about customer reactions to new product and service innovations and about what features hit customers' "hot buttons." The personal sales force are the front-line troops in making and shaping customer demand and in understanding how market dynamics are changing the firm's mental model of the marketplace. In hypercompetitive markets the demands on the sales force are considerable. They have to have a deep understanding of the competitive advantages and quality-added values of the firm's new products and services and rivals' new products and services that are constantly being introduced into the market. This requires close communication between the most successful salespeople and the product development teams. Such salespeople can then go back and brief their colleagues. New support technologies, such as account management software and firm-to-firm electronic data interchange and order processing, have helped improve the productivity

of sales forces. They have created more time for the sales force to spend on relationship building and "hard" selling—convincing customers to change their buying behavior. But as salespeople spend more time on such demanding tasks and less time on easier repeat-order taking, their job has become much more taxing.

Furthermore, with the increasing emphasis on building closer, cooperative ties with customers through joint product development or collaborative efforts to increase interfirm distribution efficiencies, as discussed extensively in previous chapters, the role of the salesperson in such team selling has become more ambiguous, and the salesperson's control over the management of the account has become more uncertain. The implications are that the roles of salespeople have become more important as markets have become more turbulent, more demanding, and yet the precise role salespeople will play in long-term trading relationships has become less clear. In particular many salespeople feel they have less control over their accounts because other employees interact more often with their customers.

The challenge for today's marketing management is to recognize these added stresses on the sales force and to provide all of the support and appropriate incentives to ensure that the firm's sales force is more effective and efficient than the competition. As will be discussed in this chapter, this requires rethinking some of the traditional sales management processes, such as how salespeople have been taught to think about their accounts and how they are trained and rewarded. ■

In many business-to-business markets, the heart and soul of the organization's marketing is its sales force and selling strategy. In such markets, competitors such as Du Pont (chemicals) or Merck (pharmaceuticals) have put together inspired, disciplined sales forces that are respected, even feared. But even the very best sales forces cannot afford to rest on their laurels. Changing market conditions have made some sales management strategies and tactics obsolete. IBM, which once possessed a sales force without peer in the pioneer selling of computers, has reorganized its sales force three times in the past dozen years. Meanwhile, an upstart, Dell Computer, has taught the industry that personal computers can be sold very successfully by a well-trained telemarketing sales force. Now, every major computer player is seeking to expand its telemarketing operations. Sales management may not be the most popular course in business schools, but it can be argued that more exciting innovations, technologies, and ideas are being introduced in sales than in advertising or other marketing functions. Table 13.1 lists some of these innovations.

Table 13.1 The Continuing Evolution of Personal Selling

CHANGE	SALES MANAGEMENT RESPONSE
Intensified competition	More emphasis on developing and maintaining trust-based, long-term customer relationships.
Greater emphasis on productivity	Increased use of technology (for example, portable computers, electronic mail, cellular phones, fax machines, telemarketing, the Internet/Intranet, and sales support systems).
Fragmentation of traditional customer bases	Sales specialists or support staff for specific customer types. Multiple selling approaches (such as national accounts programs, traditional territory sales force, manufacturers' representatives, and telemarketing). Globalization of sales effort.
Customers dictating vendor quality and delivery standards	Team selling. Compensation partly based on team performance and customer satisfaction.
Demand for specialized knowledge as an input to purchase decisions	Team selling. More emphasis on up-to-date product knowledge and customer-oriented sales training. More highly educated sales recruits.

SOURCE: Based on Thomas N. Ingram and Raymond W. LaForge, *Sales Management* (Fort Worth, TX: The Dryden Press, 1992), Exhibit 2.1.

This chapter discusses sales strategy, sales organization, sales management, and personal selling (see Figure 13.1). The overall message is simple. If a company does not hire people with excellent personal selling skills and cannot organize and lead such people, it cannot win in the marketplace. A new product or service will not sell itself no matter how good it is. In fact, a new product or service must always go through several selling efforts. First, it must be personally sold to investors or senior executives. Then it has to be personally sold to production and the sales force. Only then does the sales force get the chance to personally sell the product to distributors, retailers, or end users. Distributors and retailers, in turn, have to sell the idea of buying the product to their customers. Often buyers even have to sell the idea of buying the product or service to their immediate superiors! So moving a new product or service from idea to production and final usage involves a lot of personal selling.

Personal selling is the most expensive and powerful communication strategy a marketer can employ. Several basic objectives of personal selling follow:

1. To persuade a potential customer to try a new product or service.
2. To keep current customers happy and loyal.
3. To persuade a current customer to buy more.
4. To feed back ideas on customer needs, improved product positioning, and the success of company and competitor marketing tactics.

Personal selling involves much more than making a sale. Salespeople know more about their slice of the marketplace than anyone else in the company. They know customers and distributors on a personal level and are constantly crossing paths with the competition. Their livelihood often depends, more than anyone else in the firm, on their personal ability to change the way both the marketplace and their firm think about the products and services they must sell. During the selling process, the customers questions or objections may suggest changes that will greatly improve the

Figure 13.1 **Chapter Organization**

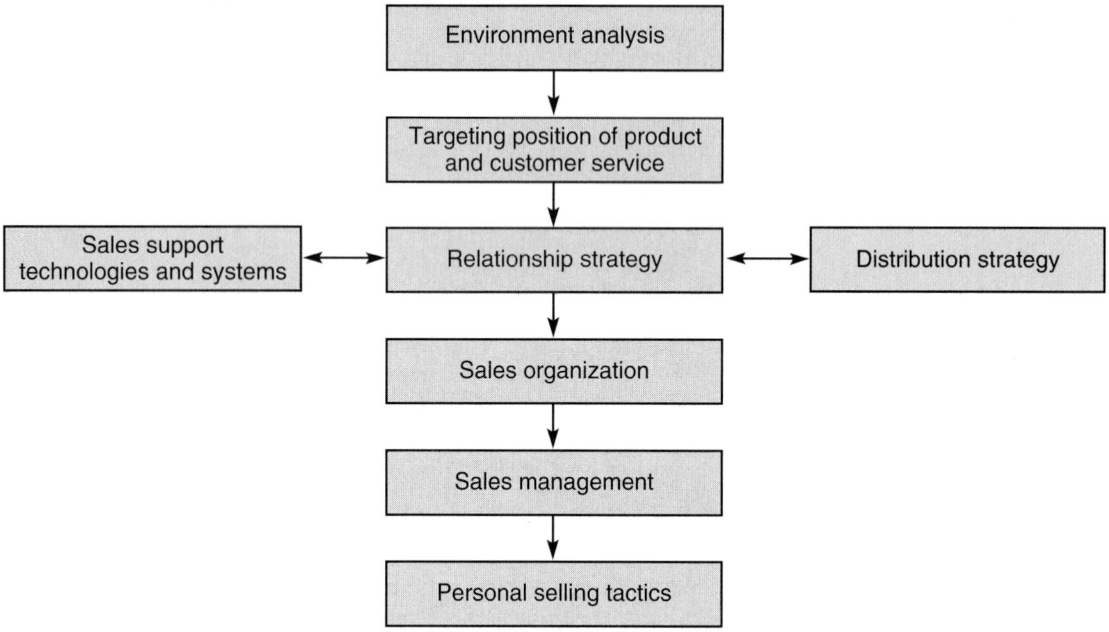

As with all marketing management programs, sales management programs are based on the market environment analysis and targeting/positioning. At the core of sales management is the firm's strategy in developing and enhancing its customer relationships. These relationships must be integrated with sales support technologies and systems and distribution strategy and service. Out of the relationship strategy evolves the firm's key selling processes that shape and determine sales organization, sales management, and, finally, personal selling tactics.

competitiveness of the offering. Salespeople also may recognize design problems not anticipated by the inventor or producer. Thus, a key role of salespeople is to be intelligence generators (see Chapter 3). In short, salespeople are often the change agents in the marketplace. They hasten the adoption of new innovations and the adaptation of their company to environmental realities. They are a key element of the competitive rationality of a firm. They also often have to unravel the marketing mistakes made by others. They are pioneering sellers and problem solvers.

Relationship Strategy

The most important objective of the sales force is to help achieve the financial and marketing goals discussed in Chapter 4. For example, if the firm's primary goal and strategy is to build market share, then the primary sales tasks will be prospecting, supplying high levels of service, and providing feedback from the market.[1] If the objective

[1] For a more complete discussion of how market-share strategies are related to selling objectives and tasks, see William Strahle and Rosann L. Spiro, "Linking Market Share Strategies to Salesforce Objectives, Activities, and Compensation Policies," *Journal of Personal Selling and Sales Management* (August 1984): 14–15.

is to protect and develop existing business, salespeople should spend more time with existing accounts, particularly those that appear to have been targeted by competitors. When a company has the dual objectives of developing new business and expanding its existing business, it often employs separate, highly skilled developmental salespersons to achieve its first objective and a regular sales force to achieve its second objective. Advertising agencies, for instance, often use a new-business sales force to identify and develop clients and then assign an account team to service the client and maintain a productive relationship between the client and the agency.

Some sales forces spend much of their time selling to distributors. An important objective of such a sales force is to motivate the distributor, implement various selling programs, and maintain service levels. On important accounts, these trade salespeople often make calls on a distributor's customer to help develop new business or handle specific usage and service problems. A sales force that calls on retail accounts often have the multiple objectives of introducing new product lines, making sure merchandising displays are put in place, attempting to increase the amount and quality of shelf space given to their product, and encouraging the account to cooperate with promotion programs. As will be discussed, these are increasingly becoming team activities.

Typical Functions of a Field Sales Force

A list of some of the varied activities salespeople who are out in the field may undertake in a day is given in Table 13.2. Note that much of a salesperson's time is spent away from the customer. A company considers sales force efficiency to be very high if salespeople spend 50 percent or more of their time actually selling.[2] Additionally, high-performing salespeople often go beyond the typical functions in ways that increase their sales and their efficiency. For instance, the list does not include creative activities such as buying a gift for a customer's secretary who has been very helpful or writing a computer spreadsheet program to monitor expenses. Yet these types of activities can help a good salesperson become a super salesperson.

Each industry has a set of expectations about which functions in Table 13.2 field salespeople should perform and how they should interact with customers. For example, a computer salesperson is likely to take an audit of customer needs, suggest and sell a system, install it, train users, upgrade the system, and handle any service problems. In other industries, technical-service specialists may undertake these functions, if they are performed at all. This is not to suggest that an enterprising firm cannot buck industry conventions and change the roles and responsibilities of its sales force to give it a new competitive edge. In fact, in many markets the established mental models of selling simply do not fit any longer with the new realities of what drives competition.

Old Selling Mental Models Do Not Fit with New Competitive Drivers

The importance of developing special new trading relationships with critical accounts has led to placing a premium on the personal selling skill of formulating new win-win, creative solutions to improving trading relationships and processes. Such skill is a driver of competition in many markets these days and was discussed in Chapters 5, 6, 11,

---

[2] William A. O'Connell and William Keenan, "The Shape of Things to Come," *Sales & Marketing Management*, January 1990, 36–41. The average salesperson spends only 33 percent of his or her time selling face-to-face; 16 percent of a salesperson's time is spent selling by phone.

Table 13.2 **Typical Functions and Activities of a Salesperson**

Selling Function
- Searching for leads
- Call planning
- Setting up appointments
- Developing a call schedule and organizing time
- Reading customer account histories
- Writing proposals
- Making sales presentations
- Overcoming objections

Working with Orders
- Handling shipping problems
- Handling back orders

Customer Service
- Problem solving, designing solutions
- Writing product or systems specifications
- Installing equipment
- Ordering accessories
- Demonstrating and training
- Undertaking minor maintenance
- Providing market intelligence on customers' competitors
- Taking customers on tours of company production and service facilities

Working with Distributors
- Establishing relationships with customers
- Collecting past-due accounts

Servicing Retail Accounts
- Setting up displays
- Stocking shelves

Administration
- Completing call reports
- Documenting and filing expense reports
- Meeting with sales manager
- Receiving feedback

Conferences/Meetings
- Attending sales meetings
- Attending exhibitions/trade shows

Training/Recruiting
- Traveling with trainees
- Planning sales activities
- Attending special training seminars
- Listening to tapes
- Reading product manuals

Entertaining
- Dining with clients
- Arranging parties

Travel

SOURCE: Based on William C. Moncrief, "Selling Activity and Sales Position Taxonomies for Industrial Salesforces," *Journal of Marketing Research* 23 (August 1986): 261–70.

and 12. Creative, win-win process improvements give the relationship a differentiation that benefits both the buyer and the seller. The seller in particular has the possibility of earning economic rents similar to the economic rents earned from a product or service differentiation advantage. The buyer's supply-chain management processes are also likely to be improved, perhaps by giving it an advantage over its competition (see previous chapter). Thus, creative relationship innovations should be highly valued, although they are seldom discussed in the sales literature.

For example, as will be shown, the sales training literature in particular still stresses the importance of teaching standard operating procedures that were developed in the 1920s, such as "how to give razzle dazzle sales pitches," "101 ways to close a sale," and "power techniques to overcome objections."[3] One hopes that the first three "ways" or processes are to (1) listen carefully to the objections, concerns, problems, and points of view of key decision makers within the buying organization, (2) develop a deep understanding of the issues and the drivers of the issues, and (3) create clever ways to improve the terms and service processes that overcome objections. Both the buyer and the seller can gain from using one of the following four relationship selling approaches.[4] The metaphor of the buyer and seller slicing a pie is used. The size of the pie is actually the added value of the exchange or the economic surplus created by the exchange, and how it is cut determines the buyer's share and the seller's share.

Four Approaches to Relationship Selling

1. *Expanding the size of the pie:* The first approach is to simply expand the size of the current deal and by doing so reduce the costs to the seller and buyer of both selling and buying. This also reduces the price to the buyer of the product or service.
2. *Giving back parts of the pie:* The second tactic is for both the buyer and seller to frankly talk about which parts of the trading terms are most important to each. This opens up the possibility of one party conceding on a dimension of the deal that is not so important to that party or that is easy to do but that is particularly important to the other party. For example, a buyer may be very interested in paying a lower price. The seller, on the other hand, may have problems getting prompt payments and faces a short-term cash flow problem that also limits the availability of discretionary working capital for initiating new innovation/imitation ideas. A deal could be struck where the buyer gets an extra discount for an order provided payment is immediate. The buyer benefits on the dimension that is most important to it, which is the price, and the seller benefits on the dimension that is most important to it, which is a prompt infusion of cash. This practice of giving on different dimensions to make a deal is called *logrolling.*
3. *Adding a new ingredient to the pie:* The third approach is to expand the terms of trade by adding another dimension, such as offering an extended after-sales service and consumables supply contract that opens up a long-term relationship possibility. This added dimension to the relationship can benefit both the seller and buyer. In this case a preservative has been added that makes the pie last longer.
4. *Reengineering the whole pie-making process:* The fourth strategy is to create a completely different trading relationship by changing the existing relationship processes. This is called *bridging.* Just as when building a bridge, bridging in negotiation involves understanding the geography and geology of both sides of the river very well. When such an understanding is achieved, novel new bridges (actually, relational exchange processes) can be created. For

[3] A. Alexandra and P. Wexler, "The Professionalisation of Selling," *Sales and Marketing Training,* February 1988, 37–43; and Kevin Wilson, "Managing the Industrial Sales Force in the 1990s," *Journal of Marketing Management* 9 (1993): 123–39, both articles comment on how out of date sales training can be in helping to develop long-term trading relationships.

[4] The four types of creative relationship selling strategies were drawn from the following sources: Peter J. Carnevale and Dean G. Pruitt, "Negotiation and Mediation," *Annual Review of Psychology* 43 (1992), 531–82; and Ellen B. Pullins, Peter R. Dickson, and Roy J. Lewicki, "Negotiation in Selling Relationships: Integration and Innovation," working paper, Fisher College of Business, The Ohio State University, Columbus, (1995).

example, another seller's reaction to the buyer's wish for a lower price may be to suggest that, as a trusted and respected, high-quality supplier, the seller be given a chance to do some subassembly work because the buyer has capacity problems, anyway. That way the price can be lowered for the overall assembled component, and the seller gets the short-term cash it needs to develop the subassembly capacity and increase its general discretionary working capital. Again, the outcome is a much closer trading relationship, but the new process has actually changed the trading relationship logistics quite dramatically.

In bridging, not just a new trading dimension is added, but also the fundamental, long-term trading processes are changed to both parties' advantage. This has happened between Wal-Mart and Procter & Gamble. The fundamental communication processes, logistics processes, and supply-chain management processes between P&G and Wal-Mart were changed. They continue to be improved by P&G's team relationship selling approach to Wal-Mart. Such selling requires process thinking skills associated with "working smarter," "learning from experience," and "adapting to different sales situations."[5] But it also requires understanding the technical operations, logistics, and communication processes of the two firms to create such innovative solutions. This means engineers must talk to engineers and explains why the customer account-service teams created by companies such as P&G and Kraft contain members with information systems, logistics, and financial expertise.

For a seller to embark on any of the four relationship selling approaches, a foundational relationship must exist based on mutual respect, trust, and performance. Otherwise, all of the strategies are "pies in the sky." In short, before a relationship can be changed, it first must be established. Thus the onus is on the selling firm to establish this foundational relationship by understanding its customers and in particular its current buying behavior and decision processes.

Fitting the Sales Function to Customer Buying Behavior

The first step in determining the role of personal selling and the basic selling strategy for a product or service is to study the way customers make their decisions. The customers' buying behavior (as described in Chapter 5) will define the selling role of top management, the salespersons, technical specialists, and office staff. Managers must also know how the competitors' sales forces are organized and managed. Does evidence show that the competitors' sales forces are not well adapted to the way their customers now make purchasing decisions? Does this suggest an opportunity for the firm? Management must ever be alert for a new angle that increases the effectiveness and the efficiency of its sales force.

The selling function will also differ depending on the nature of a customer's buying task.[6] The customer's needs dictate the salesperson's job, and the salesperson must do each job effectively to maintain customer loyalty. For instance, when dealing with a customer who is buying a product or service for the first time (a new task), the salesperson must serve a missionary function. He or she must establish a relationship with the customer to understand the customer's needs. If the customer is planning a simple reorder (rebuy), the salesperson serves an order-taking function and must make sure that the order is correct, is handled efficiently, and is delivered when promised. Years of hard selling effort can be wasted when a salesperson neglects to complete paperwork

[5] See Harish Sujan, Barton A. Weitz, and Nirmalya Kumar, "Learning Orientation, Working Smart, and Effective Selling," *Journal of Marketing* 58 (July 1994): 39–52.

[6] For a discussion of how salespeople view the customer's buying task, see Erin Anderson, Wujin Chu, and Barton Weitz, "Industrial Purchasing: An Empirical Exploration of the Buyclass Framework," *Journal of Marketing* 51 (1987): 71–86.

Figure 13.2 **The Six-Way Relationship Model of Organization Buying**

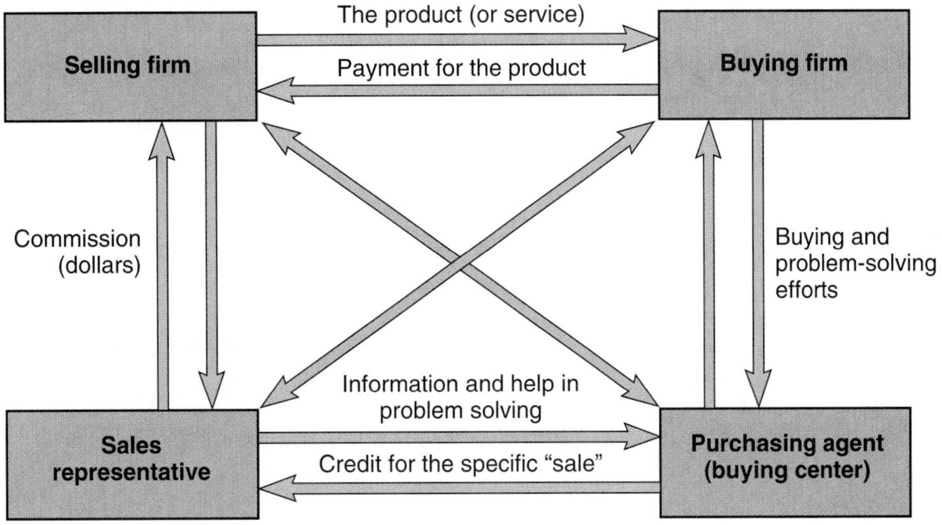

In addition to the dyadic relationship between the sales rep and purchasing agent (SR-PA), five other relationships exist that may influence the sale. The politics of selling are complicated because they involve the internal politics within both organizations and the politics between the organizations.

with the same care and energy devoted to selling. For example, a shipment that reaches the customer a week late because the salesperson did not carefully check shipping schedules can cost the customer dearly in terms of upsetting production schedules or working overtime to meet a deadline.

Fitting the sales function to buyer behavior means that the whole company adapts to the way a customer makes his or her buying decision. When every employee in the selling firm recognizes the importance of the customer, the entire company becomes a sales team. For example, a truly marketing-oriented company recognizes that whenever a customer calls for information, he or she talks to a sales representative, even if the person who answers the phone is actually an accountant or an after-hours maintenance worker. All the salesperson's efforts to win new customers can be squandered by sloppy support that costs very little to attain and maintain. The importance of handling customers must become part of the company culture, bred into the firm and nurtured from the top to the bottom. No one from the selling firm should be allowed to be rude to a customer, and every person must consider himself or herself a salesperson. Many individuals in the modern customer-oriented firm will be involved in personal selling at some time or other, and sometimes even special sales teams will be formed with employees who are not formally part of the selling function.

The relationships among the sales representative, the selling firm, the buying firm, and the purchasing agent are shown in Figure 13.2, which depicts the multitude of communications (sources of influence and tension) among these entities. It is clear that selling is more than just the interaction between a salesperson and a purchasing

Figure 13.3 The Axle Model of Competitive Relationships

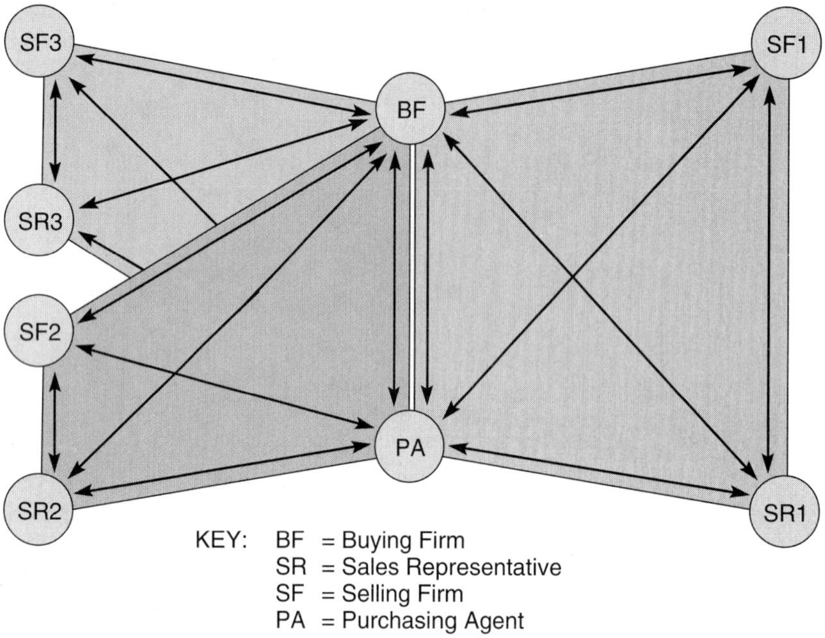

This model places the SR-PA relationship within the context of a whole set of seller relationships, tensions, torsions, and forces revolving around the buying firm–purchasing agent axle. This figure explains why simplifying the number of relationships can give a selling firm a major competitive advantage over its rivals.

agent.[7] Figure 13.3 shows how complex the situation becomes because competing sellers are also communicating with the buying firm. Figure 13.3 can be used to identify sources of conflict, such as when the purchasing agent (PA) and sales representative in firm number 1 (SR1) have a strong relationship, but selling firm number 3 also has a strong relationship with the buying firm. This creates tension between the purchasing agent and SR1, because they must deal with the pressure from the buying firm to interact with selling firm number 3.

Having emphasized that a competitive firm must view its whole organization as a sales organization, this discussion now turns to strategic sales issues.

Major Account and High-Growth Account Management

Any sensible marketing plan will give special service to the few major customers who constitute most of the business (often called house accounts).[8] It is a truism of selling

[7] T. V. Bonama, G. Zaltman, and W. J. Johnston, *Industrial Buying Behavior* (Cambridge, MA: Marketing Science Institute, 1978).

[8] Jerome A. Colletti and Gary S. Turbidy, "Effective Major Account Management," *Journal of Personal Selling and Sales Management* (August 1987): 1–10; and Benson P. Shapiro and Rowland T. Moriarty, *Organizing the National Account Force* (Cambridge, MA: The Marketing Science Institute, 1984).

that 80 percent of a firm's business comes from the top 20 percent of its customers. This top 20 percent is the firm's bread and butter. The level of support and the caliber of the selling team must be comparable with the importance of these largest customers. Senior executives often will be expected to develop personal relationships with their equals in these buying firms and to take care of the day-to-day relations for such key accounts. When a major key account is lost, then the blame often rests squarely on the shoulders of senior management.

The development of special sales teams for the largest, most complex customers is called *national account management* (NAM). NAM programs assign special sales teams to coordinate major accounts at the national (or global) level. The NAM team works closely with buyer corporate-level personnel to develop corporate-wide customer purchasing policies (and the accompanying significant quantity discounts) but communicates through local salespeople to sell and service at the customer's individual locations. Special national account management may go so far as to place a salesperson on site in the buying organization to be available on a day-to-day basis to help with designing, installing, and servicing.

The importance of a salesperson having a clear perception what his or her personal role is in the trading relationship between buyer and seller firms has been established in research.[9] Clear roles lead to higher job satisfaction. So what happens when a team of new people from the selling firm, including design and manufacturing engineers, logistics executives, and MIS (Management information systems) experts, start interacting with their appropriate contact people in the buying firm (see the Rationality in Practice box on the effect of EDI and CF teams on sellers)? It sounds like potential chaos and a huge clouding of the salesperson's role. Firms that do not handle the redefining of the salesperson's role in the new age of relationship team selling will lose key salespeople and also may lose accounts. Thus, competitive thinking has to be directed at the new role of the salesperson in the ongoing trade relationship. It seems likely that the role will be akin to that of the marketing product manager, but it will be called sales account manager. In fact, such a salesperson will play a role very similar to account managers in advertising agencies whose job it is to keep the client-agency relationship on track and expanding. A major difference is that the salesperson will have more accounts to manage than the advertising account manager, who is often full-time on a single account.

Problems with key or national account management occur when several suppliers take an on-site approach with a single customer. An account representative is then under constant pressure to jostle the competition aside to get the attention of the important customer. The customer is in a position of power—multiple sellers are rushing to meet the customer's every need, and the customer knows that the sellers cannot afford to lose his or her business. These types of NAM or house customers are often called "lost for good" customers, because once some or all of their business is lost to the competition, it is difficult or impossible to win it back.[10]

---

[9] Steven P. Brown and Robert A. Peterson, "Antecedents and Consequences of Salesperson Job Satisfaction: Meta-Analysis and Assessment of Causal Effects," *Journal of Marketing Research* 30 (February 1993), 63–77.

[10] Barbara Bund Jackson, "Build Customer Relationships That Last," *Harvard Business Review*, November/December 1985, 120–28.

Rationality in Practice

Effect of EDI and CF Teams on Sellers

What effect will the joint venturing between two businesses that were previously in a traditional supplier-buyer relationship have on sales management? As discussed in earlier chapters, electronic data interchange (EDI) enables automated just-in-time delivery and the close monitoring of quality conformance. It greatly reduces the need for a salesperson to serve an account, because much of the communication and order-delivery problems are eliminated or dealt with by other executives. Thus, the order-taking, customer-service, and quality-selling components of a salesperson's job are greatly reduced or even eliminated in business-to-business or vendor-to-retailer markets. The up-front negotiation, however, required to set up the EDI configuration, software, expediting procedures, and quality conformance assurance and monitoring must be undertaken by more senior executives. In their interactions, the talks often expand in scope, and what starts as a discussion on how to link EDI systems becomes much more of a joint venture. For example, at one time, Procter & Gamble was selling to Wal-Mart and talking about how to develop an EDI order-delivery logistics system; now P&G and Wal-Mart are talking about developing new products and working together to reduce both of their costs (see previous chapter). Essentially, the traditional salesperson may not play an important role in such relationship discussions, except as a good-natured and credible facilitator.
Cross-functional (CF) team management is also having a dramatic effect on the sales management of key accounts. A cross-functional team in Motorola or Apple almost always invites a representative of a selling firm, such as a chip maker (a major component supplier), to attend a special or occasional meeting with the cross-functional team. Some cross-functional teams even invite a JIT supplier to *become* a permanent member of the cross-functional team (see Chapter 3). The person chosen immediately becomes the primary account manager, and often the person is an engineer, rather than a salesperson. A traditional, pioneering salesperson may make the relationship break-

High-Growth Account Management

Most of the literature on key account management has assumed it is used in a relationship with a very large buyer. But a good case also can be made for developing a key account relationship with a small company with great prospects. Indeed, many companies have earned great success by working and growing with customers who were treated as a special account from their start-up. Microsoft took this approach with IBM as IBM "started up" in the personal computer market.

The loyalties established with the entrepreneurial executives in such growth companies are likely to be much more enduring than those developed with professional executives in large companies who often move up or out, leaving an account representative stranded. Some entrepreneurial risks may have to be taken to give heavy support and service to high-growth prospects that may become large customers in the future. Once the key house accounts have been identified and personnel selected to service and sell to this segment, salespeople can be assigned to the rest of the firm's customers, who will be categorized as A, B, or C accounts and serviced accordingly.

High-Growth Stresses on Sales Force Structure

A seller in a high-growth market faces particular problems because it constantly has to adjust its organization as its sales expand.[11] However, when it responds by reorganizing and subdividing its initial territories or industry segments, a company has to be

[11] David W. Cravens, William C. Moncrief, Charles W. Lamb Jr., and Terry Dielman, "Sequential Modeling Approach for Redeploying Selling Effort in Field Sales Forces," *Journal of Business Research* 20 (1990): 217–33.

through, but once the relationship moves to close cooperation on product development and reducing joint costs, the engineers and senior management take over account management.

Likewise, the same cross-functional team may include executives from major buyers of the product or service that the cross-functional team is responsible for marketing. The whole cross-functional team then becomes a selling team, selling to and servicing the major buyer representatives from companies such as General Electric or Boeing. This occurs in business-to-business markets involving the supply of complex plant, equipment, and construction where the delivered product package is uniquely designed and customized for a special buyer (for instance, a shopping mall, an oil refinery, a weapons system, or a large computer system) or in markets that require a special component designed to be a part of another product (for instance, auto parts suppliers to Ford, Chrysler, GM, or Honda). If a separate salesperson is responsible for selling to such a customer, and that customer has a representative as a member of a cross-functional team, then presumably the salesperson would be very keen to sit in on all such meetings. This is particularly so if the account is a large one (which is a safe assumption, given the importance of the buyer to the cross-functional team). Otherwise the salesperson risks losing control of a relationship on whose success his or her commission and livelihood depend (see Figure 13.2).

The alternative is for the cross-functional team to become the sales team for the account, responsible for all account selling and servicing. This would appear to be a more efficient solution. Thus, across the American and global economy, any increase in EDI and cross-functional teams that include major supplier representatives and major buyer representatives immediately impacts the nature of the players' key account sales management and incrementally changes the overall nature of selling in the economy. Two such interesting aggregate effects may be that traditional sales forces will be reduced in size, and engineers or logisticians will be preferred over MBAs and marketing graduates for many of the positions in the organization relationships just described. These effects also explain why it is difficult, but not impossible, to have independent sales reps continue to play a role in such changing relationships.

very careful not to alienate its experienced sales force. Yet if it does not adjust quickly, it leaves itself vulnerable to aggressive, small competitors who focus on a region or industry and do a much better job in their pioneer selling of new accounts. It is also vulnerable to the entry of a large company with a well-organized sales force already calling on potential customers. In a high-growth market, a company is often not sure how many potential customers exist out there. An aggressive approach to determining sales force size in such a situation is to keep adding salespeople until they no longer generate enough contribution to justify their employment. This way the true potential of the market is tested and pushed to the limit. On the down-side it takes some time for a salesperson to reach their performance potential.

The Politics of Multiple Sales Forces

Although sound arguments exist for a single territorial-based sales force supported by customer and product specialists, the reality is that many companies operate parallel sales forces. The most valid reason for operating two or more separate sales forces is that the products are so specialized or so different that they need different experts to sell them. The need for expertise overrides the increased cost and control problems. In 1994 IBM announced it was reorganizing its sales force around fourteen industry segments. Previously it had been organized by geographical region. The importance of keeping up with the specialized needs of customers in rapidly changing markets dictated the change.

In practice, a parallel sales force organization is often created as the result of a takeover or merger. The companies may still operate as separate divisions and keep their own sales forces rather than face the organizational problems that might occur if an attempt at integration were made. An even more cynical view is that many large companies prefer to maintain the separate sales forces they inherited in the acquisitions because of organizational politics. With a risk-averse view of the future, management also may prefer to maintain the separate sales forces until they are sure the merger or acquisition has worked. It is easier to sell off a division as a self-contained enterprise with its own sales force if the acquisition or merger goes bad.[12] For awhile Kraft had four different sales forces calling on individual supermarkets, representing Kraft, General Foods, Oscar Meyer Foods, and Maxwell House. Now the sales force has been arranged around three hundred customer-service teams, each devoted to one supermarket chain.[13] The advantage is greater sales-call efficiency and much more creative and made-to-measure servicing of each chain's business through integrated ordering, billing, delivery, point-of-purchase (POP) displays, and promotional campaigns. The disadvantages are the initial difficulties in integrating not just the sales forces but also the different divisions' information systems and an ongoing concern that a single salesperson cannot be as knowledgeable about Kraft's small brands and new line extensions, so they will not get the merchandising and POP stocking attention they once did.

The Strategic Use of Selling Technologies

Telemarketing is a systematic and continuous program of communicating with customers and prospects via telephone or Internet and interactive computer software connected to a database.[14] For example, automated fax-back PC systems costing about $10,000 with annual operating costs of $3,000 can handle up to 2,000 requests a day. Each request is guided by voice mail to select product information by Touch-Tone telephone. A California supplier of telephone headsets sent out 3,100 documents using the system in its first three months, and 200 of the callers left their names and addresses on the voice mail. The system saves four person-hours a day in sorting, paper shuffling, and faxing, which means it pays for itself within one hundred days.[15] It is just one example of a new generation of *electronic agents*—hardware/software systems that perform a task on behalf of a person. Future electronic agents will make travel and hotel bookings for sales reps on the Internet and will generate market intelligence by browsing the Internet using key words and "subscription lists."

Telemarketing can be used to identify prospects and qualify leads, to take orders for active accounts and reactivate inactive accounts, to promote special offerings, to provide information services, and to take customer surveys.[16] The two basic advantages of telemarketing are its tremendous cost advantages over a field sales force and the control it offers. The problems arise when integrating telemarketing with the in-the-field sales force and when too many telemarketing programs end up harassing the

---

[12] The difficulties of managing multiple sales forces are further discussed in Richard H. Cardozo and Shannon Shipp, "How New Selling Methods Are Affecting Industrial Sales Management," *Business Horizons* 30 (September/October 1987): 23–28.

[13] Greg Burns, "Will So Many Ingredients Work Together?" *Business Week*, March 27, 1995, 188–91.

[14] See Cardozo and Shipp, "New Selling Methods."

[15] Robert L. Scheier, "The Big Fax Payback," *Inc. Technology*, 1994, 70.

[16] The role of telemarketing in selling is examined in depth in William C. Moncrief, Shannon Shipp, Charles W. Lamb Jr., and David W. Cravens, "Examining the Roles of Telemarketing in Selling Strategy," *Journal of Personal Selling and Sales Management* 9 (Fall 1989): 1–12.

Table 13.3 **Advantages and Disadvantages of Telemarketing**

Advantages
1. Increased speed and accuracy of order taking (by flagging inappropriate responses).
2. Increased service image (customer orientation).
3. Much greater control over customer interaction.
4. Much less expensive than outside selling.
5. Allows salesperson to specialize in customer field service and pioneer selling.
6. Tremendous source of leads.
7. Clever selling/service approaches can be quickly adopted by all members of the telemarketing sales force.

Disadvantages
1. Coordination breakdown with field sales force.
2. Can result in harassing customers with too much teleselling results in: "Don't call us; we will call you."
3. Can really hurt if primarily seen as a cost-cutting substitute for an outside sales force. Firm is vulnerable to the personal selling skills of the competition.
4. Can be abused when selling to households: It is estimated some 10 percent of telemarketing to households (particularly the lonely elderly) is fraudulent.

customer or cut too many corners off the overall sales effort. Table 13.3 spells out the advantages and disadvantages of telemarketing.[17]

Telemarketing grew out of telephone order taking, when customers placed an order from a supplier's catalog. The operator entered the order into a computer and was able to give the customer immediate information on the order's status, such as the shipping date. Rather than waiting for orders from customers, some enterprising marketers started to initiate calls to customers on a regular, arranged basis. The development of software that described each customer's purchase history enabled the operator to run down a checklist of items the customer regularly ordered.[18] Table 13.4 presents the typical evolution of teleservicing and teleselling in a firm.

Many companies use their field sales force to undertake telemarketing programs. A study by McGraw-Hill revealed that in 1986 salespeople spent 25 percent of their time in face-to-face selling and 17 percent of their time prospecting and selling by telephone.[19] A similar survey taken back in 1977 reported that salespeople spent 39 percent of their time in face-to-face selling and minimal time selling by telephone. A good telemarketing operation is positioned to support the pioneering sales efforts of an outside sales force. It is seldom capable of totally replacing the personal contact and service of a field rep. In fact, what telemarketing does is *increase* the importance of the personal interaction and problem-solving skills of the field sales force. If the telemarketing operation is high tech, then the field sales force should provide the human interaction balance by becoming high "touch." (Note that this type of telemarketing is quite different from the telemarketing calls consumers receive at home offering aluminum siding or carpet cleaning.) As a company adjusts to this new sales technology,

[17] For several case studies on the advantages of telemarketing, see Howard Sutton, *Rethinking the Company's Selling and Distribution Channels* (New York: The Conference Board, 1986); and Denise Herman, "Telemarketing Success: A Tough Act to Follow," *Telemarketing*, March 1987, 25–28.

[18] William C. Moncrief, Charles W. Lamb Jr., and Terry Dielman, "Developing Telemarketing Support Systems," *The Journal of Personal Selling and Sales Management* (August 1986): 43–49.

[19] "Are Salespeople Gaining More Selling Time?" *Sales & Marketing Management*, July 1986, 29.

Table 13.4 Stages in the Evolution of Teleservicing and Teleselling

Teleservicing

The evolution of the use of the telephone to service customers.

1. Direct input of order into computer.
2. Immediate notification of stock availability and shipment date.
3. Real-time information on status of order.
4. Information on possible substitutes.
5. Information on related sales specials.
6. Trouble-shooting advice from manuals stored on computer.
7. Advice on equipment purchase, improved maintenance, and product utilization from Artificial Intelligence (AI) expert system software.
8. Integrated faxing service to send diagrams and other documents.

Teleselling

1. Call, screen, and code prospects.
2. Refer hot leads to salespeople.
3. Call low-grade prospects with sales promotion offer.
4. Call particular customer segments with a preferred-clients special offer, based on recent sales history.
5. Develop an Expert System software program that prompts responses to objections (provides selling scripts based on responses to previous questions).

it will produce major changes in the functions undertaken by the field sales force, which may ultimately lead to their radical reorganization.

Telemarketing in Control

Telemarketing provides excellent control in terms of the sales presentation content, the accuracy of order taking, and the generation of new leads for salespeople. An interactive set of software programs can prompt the operator with the actual words he or she should use in various selling situations so mistakes are avoided. The astute company will place its most knowledgeable and expert salespeople in telemarketing for several weeks to record their conversations with customers. From this database and related group discussions over what the salesperson could have done better, a whole set of scripts can be developed and integrated into the selling software. In this way, operators who are paid $5 to $10 per hour will bootstrap their perceived competence and selling effectiveness and increase their sales by several hundred percentage points. Unfortunately, the introduction of innovations in selling approaches to improve the company's telephone techniques can be quickly adopted by all of the operators. The result is that the telephone selling learning curve is much steeper (faster) than the outside-selling learning curve.

The introduction of artificial intelligence into order taking and customer service software programs will introduce even greater power and control into telemarketing. The basic advantage of using the computer and its prompting power is that it can make telephone selling almost as adaptive to the purchase situation as face-to-face selling. Operators can be prompted to offer special price deals on complementary products that the customer is currently not buying from the supplier. These price deals will be set according to account potential and current company pricing strategy.

A typical telemarketing workstation.

Programs can also suggest express delivery services, inquire about deviations from usual order sizes, and suggest novel solutions to out-of-stock problems. They also may point out volume price discounts available to the customer if it increases its order size.

Not only does telemarketing provide more control over the selling process, it also increases the accuracy of order taking (by having exception routines that query any unusual entries and insist that all information is entered before accepting the order), increases the speed of order processing, and reduces the order-delivery cycle time. It also can provide end-of-the-day, end-of-the-week, and end-of-the-month feedback control over the implementation of a selling program.

Telemarketing's most important benefit may be that it can revitalize a field salesperson. Specialized telemarketing prospectors are capable of making one hundred calls a day by identifying prospects from the Yellow Pages, directories, or mailing lists. Telemarketing prospecting is low cost and provides a boost to salespeople. A morning of unsuccessful prospecting will kill a salesperson's enthusiasm for selling, but a list of fresh leads from the telemarketing center is bound to create excitement. A company has greater control over its field sales force when it hands a rep a list of positive prospects and says "go get 'em." The field salesperson can no longer claim the leads are not there and will have to produce call reports that measure his or her sales conversion ability.

Telemarketing out of Control

Despite its current and potential power, telemarketing has been so mismanaged or abused by some companies that it has become a competitive disadvantage. These firms view telemarketing as an opportunity to drastically cut back the field sales force, which makes the company vulnerable to the personal selling skills of the competition.

A second common problem with telemarketing is that it is so inexpensive that some companies are tempted to implement too many special telemarketing sales promotions to customers. Telemarketing then changes from customer service to the hassle of a hard sell. Once a company's telemarketing operation becomes overbearing, it is very difficult to recover from the negative image. The "don't call us; we will call you" customer attitude is a sure signal that telemarketing is out of control and can mean death to a telemarketing operation. Telemarketing must attempt to maintain its image as a customer service by orchestrating and sticking to customer calling schedules in the same way personal sales calls are scheduled.

A major disadvantage of having telemarketing separate from the field sales force is the problem of coordinating customer selling and service. One organizational solution is to have the field salesperson do the telemarketing to his or her major accounts and have separate telemarketing salespeople handle all the small accounts. In fact, many companies are pleasantly surprised by the growth in their business that comes from telemarketing to small accounts that the field sales force often ignore. After all, a friendly telephone call is better than no call at all.

Strategic Use of Selling Decision Support Systems

Just as the introduction of computers has increased the span of a senior manager's control, the introduction of a decision support system connected to notebook computers used by the sales force has increased the sales manager's span of control over a number of salespeople. It also can reduce selling costs dramatically and increase customer service and satisfaction (see the Rationality in Practice box, "Applying TQM to Sales").

Table 13.5 Effects of Computer Information Systems on Selling

Percent of Companies Reporting Favorable Effects of Support Systems	
Information such as customer account status, sales or order summaries, sales in process, and bids outstanding provided to salesperson	80%
Individual time and territory management	58
Faster order-to-shipment time	56
Sales volume per salesperson	51
Increased calls per salesperson	36
Control of sales expenses	31

Typical Information Contained in Computer-Prepared Sales-Call Reports

- Name, address, and key contact at prospect or customer visited
- Purpose of call—prospecting, qualifying, closing
- Outcome of call—more information needed from whom and when, business lost and why, business won (order details), business on hold (why, details on recontacting, waiting)
- Competitive information obtained
- Date of next scheduled call

Illustrative Effect of Honeywell's Introduction of Its Focus 7 System

- In the first year, overall sales force productivity rose 31%
- Shipments rose 33%
- Sales force turnover dropped 40% (it cost $50,000–$75,000 to train a salesperson)

SOURCE: Louis A. Wallis, *Computers and the Sales Effort*, Report No. 884 (New York: The Conference Board, 1986).

Figure 13.4 A Sophisticated Sales Support System

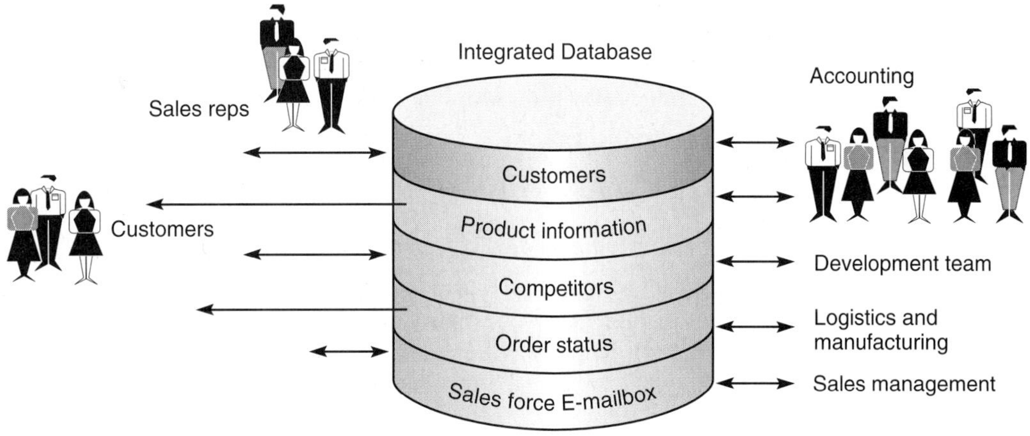

The apparent simplicity of the above integrated database is deceptive. The design of a system that everyone can use by "pointing and clicking" is very sophisticated. Notice that users enter and access the information themselves, thus making such a system much less expensive to operate because everyone is both a supplier and customer of the system. This ensures its support and generates much less paper and paperwork. Customers can be given access to product information and order status.

Sales decision support systems also have increased a salesperson's servicing of diverse customer types and products. Customer account profiles can describe the unique needs and buying approach of a customer and enable the salesperson to stay current on changes in product lines and the availability of individual items (see Table 13.5). A sophisticated sales support system such as that illustrated in Figure 13.4 should be used by both the telemarketing sales force and the field sales force, who would download the customer file into their notebook computers, including the latest information on a customer's telemarketing interactions with the firm. Parts of such a system also can be directly accessed by customers or distributors via their computers and the Internet.

Field Sales Force Organization

The field sales force can be organized in several different ways: by product, geographic region, customer, or stage in the selling process. Regardless of the approach used, the selling firm must recognize several important environmental realities. Some customers deserve (and must get) better sales service than other customers. The nature of the market and the competition in the market must be considered. In a growth market, the firm must be able to hire and train new salespeople to keep up with demand. In a market where the competition has a stranglehold, less selling effort might be used than would be used in markets where more opportunity to gain market share existed. The territories also must be large enough, in terms of sales potential, to motivate the salesperson to work hard but small enough so potentially important customers are not

Rationality in Practice

Applying TQM to Sales Management

Is it possible that Total Quality Management (TQM) reengineering of processes can be applied to sales and produce the same benefits as in manufacturing—higher quality output at less cost? The answer seems to be yes. In the 1980s, when Compaq computers was starting up, it thought it was doing the right thing by imitating IBM's sales force strategy of selling to businesses from large branch offices in big cities. In 1991, the economy faltered, and the sales force was not able to deliver when it was needed. Sales fell by 10 percent and profits by 70 percent. The new CEO, Eckhard Pfeiffer, initiated a study of Compaq customers to find out what was going wrong. The answer was that they could never get hold of a salesperson, some of whom were building up a backlog of forty voice-mail messages a day. The obvious answer was to increase the size of the sales force, but Compaq instead chose to review its sales systems and processes and then decided to overhaul its sales strategy by investing heavily in sales support technology.

Rather than increasing his sales force, Pfeiffer shrunk it from 359 to 224 and closed down three of eight regional offices. To handle the backlog of service inquiries, an 800-number was set up to answer questions about products and pricing. The remaining sales force work mostly from home, and every morning they log onto a client/server network with a point-and-click, integrated customer-account file where anyone from any function within Compaq records their latest contact with a lead or a current customer. The salesperson also can call up marketing material and technical reports that the sales rep can make into a tailor-made brochure for a prospect. Other promotional material can be downloaded onto a Compaq notebook computer, which includes presentation, spreadsheet, and time management software.

After four or five sales calls a day, the sales rep returns home, updates the common database with the latest news, sends E-mail

ignored. Finally, all salespeople are *not* equal, and the skill and experience of each must be considered when deployment decisions are made.

Keeping these issues in mind, the old-fashioned geographical territory is often still preferred over organizational structures designed around customers or products because it offers the firm the greatest control at the lowest cost.[20] Creating a specialized customer or product-based sales force drastically decreases the efficient time utilization of the sales force unless types of customers or product sales already cluster together by territory. This often can occur when a particular industry is concentrated in a region (such as computers in Silicon Valley or automobiles in Detroit). Whatever the structure, management must determine the size and range of a territory and must assign salespeople to territories.

Determining Sales Force and Territory Size: A Workload Approach

Territory design decisions must be made when starting a new firm or new division, when adding a new product line that increases the workload of the existing sales force, or when reorganizing a sales force because of major market changes. A common procedure for designing territories is illustrated in Table 13.6 on page 508. It starts with the assessment of the type and number of present and potential accounts in the firm's target market. First, customers are categorized by their importance (the most important

[20] Gilbert A. Churchill Jr., Neil M. Ford, and Orville C. Walker Jr., *Sales Force Management* (Homewood, IL: Irwin, 1990), 36–44, 132–34.

messages to systems engineers and other sales colleagues, and writes and prints correspondence. In the evening clients are faxed technical papers or press releases off the system. In a year or so they will be sending most of these messages on the World Wide Web. Already, more than one-third of small businesses are using commercial on-line services to correspond with customers.

The downside to the change is that the sales force do not get to personally interact as much, but sales reps and technical service reps are constantly in touch with each other about how to solve customer problems. The all-important bottom line is that Compaq's general and administrative expenses fell from 22 percent of revenues in 1991 to 12 percent in 1993, and they are continuing to fall. More important, the sales force has tripled its revenues per person, and customer satisfaction is up. Now IBM is imitating Compaq's home-office, high-technology selling systems and strategy.

Not all reengineered sales support systems work as effectively as Compaq's, and some experts estimate that up to 80 percent fail to perform up to expectations. In the late 1980s the information technology department of Hewlett-Packard started work on such a project. The result was a gold-plated, overengineered sales tool that far exceeded the projected budget and time and had software that crashed the sales force's laptops. The lesson from HP's experience is to get users to design a system that works the way they need it, to do several iterations of prototype field testing with lead users (as for a new product), and to train the sales force to not simply use the new technology but to change their work processes. All of these experiences show that new selling technologies can deliver a major strategic advantage but only if introduced as part of a TQM reengineering of sales management and selling processes.

SOURCES: R. Lee Sullivan, "The Office that Never Closes," *Forbes*, May 23, 1994, 212–13; Jeffrey Young, "Hit the Road, Jack: IBM's Wandering Tribe," *Forbes ASAP*, August 28, 1995, 93; Jennifer deJong and Robert L. Scheier, "Virtual Selling," *Inc. Technology*, 1994, 61–71; and "Not on the Net? You're Not Alone," *Inc.*, August 1995, 98.

are AA; the next, A; and so on through D).[21] The size of a current account will always be an important determinant of customer service. The theory of competitive rationality argues that the growth potential also should determine the extent of sales force customer service. Any other criteria for categorizing accounts should be related to increasing the targeted market segments' size (consistent with Chapter 5 and Chapter 9).

Table 13.6 presents an example of a set of criteria that can be used to rank customers. In this case, the firm has a corporate strategy of rapid growth. Therefore, the most important accounts (AA) are large, with high growth potential and an opportunity for increased sales (low penetration of the account's current purchases). Other important accounts (A) are those with high growth rates and opportunity for growth and medium accounts with opportunity for growth and increased sales. The number of each type of customer in the firm's target market is then estimated. Typically, a firm will have fewer AA, A, and B customers and more C and D accounts (the 80/20 rule again!). The next step is to establish a company norm for the average call frequency on each type of account in a year and the average time that should be spent on each call. These norms should be based on past experience and the current selling objectives. More time will be spent with AA, A, and B accounts, but C and D accounts should not be ignored because, with effort, they could become more important (they could also become high-growth accounts, discussed previously). AA accounts might,

[21] For other criteria, see Henry Porter, "The Important Few—The Unimportant Many," *1980 Portfolio of Sales and Marketing Plans* (New York: Sales and Marketing Management, 1980), 34–37; and Rosann L. Spiro and William D. Perrault Jr., "Factors Influencing Sales Call Frequency of Industrial Salespersons," *Journal of Business Research* 6 (January 1974): 1–15.

Table 13.6 Determining Sales Territory Workload[a]

1. Categorize all current and potential accounts using a table such as the following:

		Current Size: Large		Current Size: Medium		Current Size: Small	
		GROWTH		GROWTH		GROWTH	
CURRENT PENETRATION	COMPETITOR ACTIVITY	HIGH	LOW	HIGH	LOW	HIGH	LOW
High	High	A	A	A	B	B	C
	Low	A	B	B	C	C	D
Low	High	A	B	B	C	C	D
	Low	AA	A	A	B	B	C

2. Identify the number of minutes spent per call and the total number of calls per year for each account.
3. Calculate the total time, total number of accounts, and total hours per year for each account type.
4. From this information, determine the number of salespeople needed to service these accounts each year.

How to grade accounts from AA to D:

- On size (how much they contribute to gross profit)
- On growth (how fast are they growing) and whether they are a member of a targeted market segment
- On penetration (how much of their business do we have)
- On competitor activity (level of calling/service, etc.)
- Highly innovative customers should receive special attention from R&D and service people to facilitate improvements in user training, maintenance, and product design.

[a]The WORKLOAD spreadsheet executes the following process.

for example, receive thirty minutes every other week, while A accounts receive thirty minutes every three weeks.

Next, the total amount of time required in a year to service all accounts should be calculated by multiplying the number in each account category by the minutes per year to service that category and summing the totals for AA, A, B, C, and D accounts. This will result in the total amount of selling time needed to reach corporate objectives. At this point, the number of salespeople required is determined by dividing the total time required to service accounts by the selling time available to the average salesperson (remember that many salespeople spend less than 50 percent of their time actually selling). For example, suppose a firm has a total of 1,500 of all types of customers, and the time required to service those customers totals 13,000 hours per year. The firm's salespeople have 25 hours of selling time a week multiplied by 48 weeks (remember to subtract vacations, holidays, and sick days) for a total of 720 hours of selling time a year. Thus, 13,000 divided by 720 equals 18.1, or 18 salespeople needed to cover the market.

The number of salespeople may or may not be the same as the final number of territories. Territories are units of control for which objectives are set and results evaluated. Management may combine several individual workloads into a territory for reasons of product usage, customer similarity, geographical proximity, or competitive factors. The customers within one territory must be similar on an important characteristic (such as geographic location or type of business) so a cohesive set of sales goals can be set for each territory. Continuing the previous example, the firm's 18 salespeople may be divided into five territories based on five geographic areas of the state (for example, northwest, northeast, central, southwest, and southeast). Once the number of salespeople needed and the number of territories has been determined, the next task is to assign salespeople to territories.

Assigning Salespeople to Territories

The important job of assigning individual reps to territories must focus on the needs of the territory and the abilities of the sales representatives. Not all salespeople have equal abilities, experience, preferences, or backgrounds. An attempt should be made to match salespeople with territories so as to assure maximum customer service and the use of the salesperson's best skills. For instance, a salesperson with a highly technical background should be assigned to a territory with the most technically sophisticated customers. An inexperienced rep should not be placed in a territory with large accounts that demand high levels of expertise. Increasing a salesperson's efficiency should be the constant goal of management and is a major consideration in territory design. However, a fundamental limit to the efficiency of a salesperson is the distance between sales calls. If customers are geographically close, then a salesperson can make two, four, or more sales calls per day; but if customers are distant, then the salesperson's productive selling time is greatly reduced.

Many companies have well-established sales territories. These have historically evolved based on concentrations of customers, geography, and transportation services. Some companies employ consultants who use sophisticated computer programs to create territories that minimize travel, balance workload, and maximize profit.[22] Changing a sales territory is a significant event because it disturbs established customer relations and has repercussions on other territories. However, technology innovations sometimes necessitate even a complete restructuring of sales force territories. The introduction of convenient and faster air travel in the 1960s led many companies to reconsider their sales territory strategy. In the 1980s, the growth of telemarketing again forced many companies to reevaluate how they should define their sales territories.

Field Staff Support

Field staff support (which is often made up of engineers) can greatly increase the efficiency and productivity of the sales force. The expertise of corporate customer and product specialists can be used on an as-needed basis by all salespeople. The specialists are always available to the customer or the salesperson by telephone or e-mail. The field staff can make calls with the local salesperson, particularly when selling to new accounts. A serendipitous advantage of having such customer or product service specialists is that they are the ideal people to interact with R&D and production on the development of new products, quality control, or service problems. Their role in developing new business keeps them on the edge of product advances and discovering new customer applications. Most of a company's new product and service innovations are likely to be suggested by such boundary-spanning product specialists. They

[22] Arthur Median, "Optimizing the Number of Industrial Salespersons," *Industrial Marketing Management* 11 (1982): 63–74; and Andris A. Zoltners and Prabhakant Sinha, "Sales Territory Alignment: A Review and Model," *Management Science*, November 1982, 1237–56.

should be particularly rewarded for developing with customers, on new products and product modifications.

Deploying and Managing an Independent Manufacturers' Rep Sales Force

All firms must decide whether they are going to develop and fully support their own field sales force, use manufacturers' reps, or employ a combination of the two. Some fifty thousand manufacturer representative businesses or partnerships service hundreds of industries and thousands of markets in the United States and Canada. *Manufacturers' reps* are family businesses that sell ten to twelve product lines manufactured and marketed by several different producers. Usually they operate as exclusive commission agents who have been granted exclusive rights to sell to their territory (typically a few states). They do not carry competing lines but often will sell the complementary lines of other manufacturers. Their typical sales commission is around 7 percent, but this varies by product line.[23]

The advantages and disadvantages of employing a sales force made up of manufacturers' reps are listed in Table 13.7. Some small companies must use reps because they do not have the start-up resources or the breadth of products to build and support their own field sales force, particularly in distant markets. Even large companies see cost advantages in employing a rep sales force (see the next Rationality in Practice box).[24] The major risk of hiring a rep firm to cover a territory is that the rep firm may not perform. This risk can be minimized by running a credit check, calling the other companies whose products the manufacturer's rep sells, and talking to some of its major customers. A day's work will establish the credentials of a rep organization. Another form of insurance is to sign a short-term, three-month contract that can be terminated for nonperformance. If it takes a rep longer than three months to start moving the product, then the rep is not selling it to his or her existing customers but is instead trying to use the product to break into new markets. When this happens, much of the advantage of using a manufacturer's rep is lost.

The Fit of the Rep's Existing Customer Franchise

In an earlier chapter we discussed the importance of the fit between the supplier's target market and the channel intermediary's consumer franchise. The same concerns apply to manufacturers' reps. Reps should be screened in terms of the amount of business they currently do in the target industry and with important major accounts in that industry. If the distributor or rep is selling leading brands of complementary products to the industry, it is evidence that the rep has a legitimate, desirable consumer franchise (strong credibility and deep ties with the desired target market).

A supplier should never lose sight of the rep organization's basic strategic objective, which is to represent well-known, very strong suppliers' brands. The smart thing for the rep to do is to build a stable of well-known, noncompeting lines that are all

[23] Henry Lavin, "When and How to Use Manufacturers' Representatives," *The Handbook of Modern Marketing*, 2nd ed. (New York: McGraw-Hill, 1986).

[24] Thayer C. Taylor, "The Raging 'Rep'idemic," *Sales & Marketing Management*, June 8, 1981, 33–35; and Erin Anderson, "Strategic Implications of Darwinian Economics for Selling Efficiency and Choice of Integrated or Independent Sales Forces," *Management Science* 4 (Summer 1988): 234–54.

Table 13.7 Advantages and Disadvantages of Employing Manufacturers' Reps

ADVANTAGES OVER A COMPANY SALES FORCE	DISADVANTAGES OVER A COMPANY SALES FORCE
■ Fast way of building consumer franchise—reps open doors.	■ Some customers prefer to deal directly with the company.
■ Low start-up investment costs	■ Diseconomies of scale—relatively expensive to use with major customers (high commission payments)
■ Low risk—reps get paid for what they sell.	■ More difficult to manage and control
■ Improved cash flow—you pay when you get paid.	■ Harder to train on product knowledge
■ Higher average selling skills and lower turnover of salespeople	■ Difficult to fire—may lead to loss of customers and betrayal of confidences and trade secrets
■ Good advice from reps on product design and marketing for a new venture	■ Less continuous feedback
■ Easier to establish proven performance	■ Current customers may not fit the rep's consumer franchise.
■ The halo effect—the company benefits from the other brands the rep sells.	■ Reps paid on commission so will push products easiest to sell
■ Sales territories with fewer customers are covered more efficiently.	■ Selling time split among several lines
■ Lower average selling costs	

sold to the same buyers. A little of the brand loyalty of each line then rubs off on the rep. The rep also builds loyalty directly through service and personal friendships. The rep firm's security is its confidence that if the trading relationship with a major principal supplier fractures, most buyers will adopt the rep's new replacement line rather than continue to buy the original supplier's line through a new sales channel. In other words, the initial positional power of the buyer and supplier that was clearly so in favor of the original supplier may, in time, become quite uncertain.[25] This risk of losing buyer loyalty, plus the trust and relationships that develop over time, is likely to lead a manufacturer to stick with its manufacturers' reps rather than replace them with its own field sales force.[26]

Reps and Customer Service Problems

Difficulties between reps and customers arise from two sources. The first arises when a customer wants to deal directly with the supplier. The supplier has no choice but to respond to the customer's desires. However, the supplier is still bound to pay the rep his or her commission on the sale unless it was specified in the original agreement that this business was to be treated as a house account. Recently, some "power" retailers, such as Wal-Mart, have decided that they will no longer deal with manufacturers' reps because they feel they are a large enough customer to deserve direct sales service from a supplier. In such cases, the contracts with the rep who previously handled the account must be renegotiated.

[25] In fact, it has been argued that independent agents may ultimately exploit this transfer of buyer goodwill at the expense of the supplier. This risk of being exploited is an argument for a supplier creating and supporting its own sales force. See Oliver E. Williamson, *Markets and Hierarchies: Analysis and Antitrust Implications* (New York: The Free Press, 1975); and Jan Hiede and George John, "The Role of Dependence Balancing in Safeguarding Transaction-Specific Assets in Conventional Channels," *Journal of Marketing* 52 (January 1988): 20–35.

[26] Allen M. Weiss and Erin Anderson, *The Effects of Switching Costs on the Termination of Distribution Channel Relationships* (Cambridge, MA: The Marketing Science Institute, 1991).

Rationality in Practice

Choosing between Direct Reps and Independent Manufacturers' Reps

How might a firm make the fundamental strategic decision to create its own field sales force or use an independent manufacturers' rep sales force? The competitively rational approach is to estimate which course will be most effective and will make the most contribution to operating margin (COM). Effectiveness can be predicted by estimating the penetration of the two approaches. Penetration is the percentage of an account's business the firm can expect to get, using either its own direct sales force or reps. A direct force would be expected to achieve higher penetration because its selling efforts are not divided across several different manufacturers' product lines. Penetration also depends on the number of sales calls and service efforts. The number and size of potential accounts (customers), the average cost of each sales call, and the commission paid to independent reps also need to be estimated.

When provided with all of these estimates, the OWNVREP spreadsheet presented here does the appropriate analysis. In this spreadsheet the cost of each call and the commission paid to reps can be varied to see what impact they have on the decision. Based on the information in the tables, an all-rep sales force will earn $623,500 in contribution and a direct sales force will earn $591,300. An even better option is to use a direct sales force to serve accounts above $100,000 in potential and let independent reps serve the smaller accounts. This generates $785,000 in contribution. However, this combination can be achieved only if the firm started with a field sales force serving all accounts. A firm that started with reps serving all accounts can hardly take the big accounts away from reps once they have developed the business. Several firms have tried this tactic, and it so upset their reps that the reps went to work for the competition, taking many of their large and high-growth accounts with them. A firm also has to be concerned about the rep's ability to add accounts (increase penetration). The spreadsheet can be used to forecast penetration and COM five to ten years out.

Owner versus Rep Sales Force

CONTRIBUTION TO OPERATING MARGIN (COM) OF A DIRECT SALES FORCE
(ASSUMING A COST PER PERSONAL SALES CALL OF $110)

ACCOUNT POTENTIAL (IN THOUSANDS OF DOLLARS)	NUMBER OF ACCOUNTS	AVERAGE PENETRATION	ESTIMATED SALES (IN THOUSANDS OF DOLLARS)	AVERAGE GROSS MARGIN	AVERAGE GROSS MARGIN (IN THOUSANDS OF DOLLARS)	ACCT. CALLS PER YEAR	SALES FORCE COST (IN DOLLARS)	COM (IN THOUSANDS OF DOLLARS)	COM/ACCOUNT (IN THOUSANDS OF DOLLARS)
800–1,200	1	40%	400	39%	156	50	5,500	150.5	150.50
500–800	1	40	260	39	101	50	5,500	95.9	95.90
300–500	3	40	480	39	187	50	16,500	170.7	56.90
100–300	6	40	480	39	187	45	29,700	157.5	26.25
50–100	7	35	184	41	75	35	26,950	48.4	6.91
25–50	22	35	289	41	118	35	84,700	33.7	1.53
12–25	14	35	91	41	37	20	30,800	6.4	0.45
6–12	18	30	49	43	21	10	19,800	1.1	0.06
3–6	28	30	38	43	16	6	18,480	−2.2	−0.08
1.5–3	25	30	17	43	7	6	16,500	−9.2	−0.37
0.5–1.5	21	30	6	43	3	6	13,860	−11.2	−0.53
0–0.5	80	30	6	43	3	6	52,800	−50.2	−0.63
			2,299		912			591.3	

CONTRIBUTION TO OPERATING MARGIN (COM) OF AN ALL-REP SALES FORCE
(ASSUMING A MANUFACTURER'S REP COMMISSION OF 5%)

ACCOUNT POTENTIAL (IN THOUSANDS OF DOLLARS)	NUMBER OF ACCOUNTS	AVERAGE PENETRATION	ESTIMATED SALES (IN THOUSANDS OF DOLLARS)	AVERAGE GROSS MARGIN	AVERAGE GROSS MARGIN (IN THOUSANDS OF DOLLARS)	SALES FORCE COST (IN DOLLARS)	COM (IN THOUSANDS OF DOLLARS)	COM/ ACCOUNT (IN THOUSANDS OF DOLLARS)
800–1,200	1	30%	300	39%	117	15,000	102.0	102.00
500–800	1	30	195	39	76	9,750	66.3	66.30
300–500	3	30	360	39	140	18,000	122.4	40.80
100–300	6	30	360	39	140	18,000	122.4	20.40
50–100	7	30	158	41	65	7,875	56.7	8.10
25–50	22	30	248	41	101	12,375	89.1	4.05
12–25	14	30	78	41	32	3,885	28.0	2.00
6–12	18	25	41	43	17	2,025	15.4	0.86
3–6	28	25	32	43	14	1,575	12.0	0.43
1.5–3	25	25	14	43	6	703	5.3	0.21
0.5–1.5	21	25	5	43	2	263	2.0	0.10
0–0.5	80	25	5	43	2	250	1.9	0.02
			1,794		713		623.5	

CONTRIBUTION TO OPERATING MARGIN (COM) OF A MIXED SALES FORCE
(ASSUMING THAT A COST PER PERSONAL SALES CALL IS $110, THE MANUFACTURER'S REP COMMISSION IS 5%, AND THE REPS ARE GIVEN ACCOUNTS WITH POTENTIAL LESS THAN OR EQUAL TO [IN THOUSANDS OF DOLLARS] 100)

ACCOUNT POTENTIAL (IN THOUSANDS OF DOLLARS)	NUMBER OF ACCOUNTS	AVERAGE PENETRATION	ESTIMATED SALES (IN THOUSANDS OF DOLLARS)	AVERAGE GROSS MARGIN	AVERAGE GROSS MARGIN (IN THOUSANDS OF DOLLARS)	SALES FORCE COST (IN DOLLARS)	COM (IN THOUSANDS OF DOLLARS)	COM/ ACCOUNT (IN THOUSANDS OF DOLLARS)
800–1,200	1	40%	400	39%	156	5,500	150.5	150.50
500–800	1	40	260	39	101	5,500	95.9	95.90
300–500	3	40	480	39	187	16,500	170.7	56.90
100–300	6	40	480	39	187	29,700	157.5	26.25
50–100	7	30	158	41	65	7,875	56.7	8.10
25–50	22	30	248	41	101	12,375	89.1	4.05
12–25	14	30	78	41	32	3,885	28.0	2.00
6–12	18	25	41	43	17	2,025	15.4	0.86
3–6	28	25	32	43	14	1,575	12.0	0.43
1.5–3	25	25	14	43	6	703	5.3	0.21
0.5–1.5	21	25	5	43	2	263	2.0	0.10
0–0.5	80	25	5	43	2	250	1.9	0.02
			2,199		871		785.0	

SOURCE: C. Davis Fogg and Josef W. Rokus, "A Quantitative Method for Structuring a Profitable Sales Force," *Journal of Marketing* 37 (July 1973): 8–17.

The second difficulty occurs when the reps do not follow up on leads. One way that a firm supports its rep sales force is by passing on referrals and leads from advertising, trade shows, publicity, and other marketing activities. However, hot leads are not always followed up by the manufacturers' rep. Manufacturers' reps are good at responding to their regular customers but sometimes do not like having to go out of their way to chase inquiries.

A firm needs to check on the status of such leads on a regular basis, and managers are also often frustrated when reps do not report their progress.[27] Out of sheer exasperation, some companies start to follow up on leads themselves, chase down the sale, and bypass the rep. It may keep the rep on the trail of the leads, but it also undermines the relationship. The fair and honorable way of handling nonperformance is for the firm to inform the rep that it will chase down any leads on which it does not receive call reports within a specified time. When potential customers are left waiting, their image of the company's service diminishes.

Managing the Sales Force

Managing the sales force involves recruiting, selecting, training, rewarding, and leading. The purpose of this section is to only acquaint the reader with such management functions, because entire chapters of sales management texts and scores of trade books are devoted to each of these topics.

Recruiting

Recruiting is very important because hiring and training a salesperson is a considerable investment in human capital. In high-technology and pharmaceutical markets, a company is likely to spend more than $100,000 in the salary and direct expenses involved in training. Three basic costs are involved in hiring ineffective salespeople. The first is the wasted cost of spending a great deal of time and effort training such a person. The second is the cost of exposing the customer to a poor salesperson. This is largely the opportunity cost of lost sales that would have been made by a more competent employee. The third cost, which is related to the second, is the strain on the enterprise and its management because the ineffective salesperson does not cover his or her compensation and expenses.

The first step in recruiting is to develop a sales representative's job description. A good job description details the specific responsibilities of the position, the skills required, and the person to whom the new hire will report (see Table 13.8). Job descriptions are not only used for recruiting and selecting; they also are often used to set objectives and to evaluate performance. Recruiting is an area that is fraught with legal difficulties for the sales manager (see the Rationality in Practice box on page 516). Anyone who will be involved in the interviewing process has to be aware of what legally can be asked of a job applicant.[28] For instance, interviewers cannot ask about a job applicant's age, marital status, or religion. In addition, during recruiting the candidate must

[27] The problem is that reps often resent close supervision and controls. See Jayashree Mahajan et al., "A Comparison of the Impact of Organizational Climate on the Job Satisfaction of Manufacturers' Agents and Company Salespeople: An Exploratory Study," *Journal of Personal Selling and Sales Management* (May 1984): 1–10.

[28] C. David Shepherd and James Heartfield, "Discrimination Issues in the Selection of Salespeople: A Review and Managerial Suggestions," *Journal of Personal Selling and Sales Management* 4 (Fall 1991): 67–75.

Table 13.8 Example of a Salesperson's Job Description

JOB DESCRIPTION

Position Territory sales person, Southern California	**Division** Office equipment

Summary
Sell office staplers, paper shredders, and mail room supplies to office equipment dealers and major account end users in Southern California territory.
Specific Responsibilities
Cover Orange, Los Angeles, and Riverside counties. Call on dealers and important end users. Meet quota projections. Check dealer inventory. Discuss promotions/incentives. Help train dealer sales staff. Product-train dealer, supply dealer literature. Work with dealer on store displays and advertising. Work product shows. Enter orders and follow through with order entry system. Call on major accounts. Make demos, surveys, and proposals. Report on competitive activity. Report calls and sales activity. Suggest new products.
Reporting Structure
Report to district sales manager.
Knowledge, Skills, and Experience
Requires two years college, some mechanical aptitude, good verbal and writing skills, and four years outside sales experience, preferably in office equipment industry. Experience calling on dealers mandatory. Experience calling on end users highly desirable.

SOURCE: Gene Garofalo, *Sales Manager's Desk Book* (Englewood Cliffs, NJ: Prentice-Hall, 1989).

be fully informed about company procedures and expectations. Important topics include the term of employment (it may be a trial period or a year-long contract), the compensation plan, company policies, and steps taken in the termination process. Both the prospective salesperson and the employer should try to eliminate all uncertainties about expectations before the job offer is extended and accepted.

Selecting Salespeople

It is clearly worth making the very best attempt to increase the effectiveness of sales force selection, but a company must realize that the screening and selection process merely increases the odds of making a good decision and reduces the odds of making a bad decision. The following vignette helps capture what makes a successful salesperson:

> Like any successful salesperson, no matter what the product is, Ohlson remembers names, returns phone calls, smiles a lot, is sensitive to pecking orders, takes office politics very seriously, and knows when you are having a bad day without having to be told.
>
> All of that still matters, of course, but maybe not as much as it used to, not in the new world of selling. What makes Ohlson a *special* salesman is the depth of his *business* empathy. That means drawing on a deep reservoir of technical knowledge. It means talking less and listening more. It means making his customers' problems—the cash-flow crises, the order backlogs, the inventory-management issues—his own and finding sales opportunities in problem solving. It means, essentially, becoming a consultant, the kind Ohlson's sales manager, Tom Griffies, would describe as "a sustaining resource to the customer."[29]

[29] David Whitford, "This Year's Model," *Inc.*, February 1995, 45–46.

Rationality in Practice

Avoiding Discrimination by Sticking to the Job Description

"I don't want to hire any salesperson who's been arrested." Sales managers or recruiters who ask about a potential employee's arrest record may be in for legal trouble themselves. Such a question may be discriminatory, because the American legal system assumes innocence until guilt is proven, and an arrest is not considered evidence of guilt. Questions about arrests (without a conviction) are never appropriate in the recruiting and selection process.

Seeking other types of information during the recruiting process can also lead to charges of discrimination. A series of legal decisions from the Civil Rights Act (1866 and 1964) to the Americans with Disabilities Act (1992) prevents employers from discriminating against persons on the basis of race, color, religion, national origin, sex, physical or mental disabilities, Vietnam-era veteran status, or disabled veteran status. Questions that might lead to discrimination against any of these groups should be avoided.

While most employers do not knowingly discriminate, some typical job interview questions may be considered discriminatory. For example, questions about height and weight may discriminate against females or Americans of Asian or Spanish descent. Courts have ruled that qualifications such as race, gender, or age (or other physical characteristics) can only be justified if "no person of a particular sex, race, color or religion can adequately perform the given job." This has become known as the Bona Fide Occupational Qualifications criterion, or BFOQ. The sales manager or recruiter is safest if all job qualifications are derived from written job descriptions that define the specific tasks, duties, and responsibilities involved in the sales positions to be filled. Although totally avoiding discrimination is difficult, managers should take a proactive approach to nondiscrimination in selection.

SOURCE: C. David Shepherd and James C. Heartfield, "Discrimination Issues in the Selection of Salespeople: A Review and Managerial Suggestions," *Journal of Personal Selling and Sales Management* 11, no. 4 (fall 1991): 67–75.

Psychologists and personnel specialists have earned hundreds of millions of dollars over the past one hundred years attempting to help companies identify successful salespeople such as Graig Ohlson. They have not had a lot of success. It does not take much skill to recognize the very bad and the very good candidate. The problem is to discriminate among the bulk of applications in the middle of the range.

Because the environment in which most firms operate is rapidly changing, it is important to conduct a job analysis at regular intervals to identify the typical salesperson's actual day-to-day activities. An outside consultant will often observe and analyze salespeople at work and will develop a list of the tasks that must be completed to succeed on the job. These tasks then become part of the job description. Sales managers can work with the consultant to develop this list of necessary skills. The more a firm's selection procedures mimic the realities of the work environment, the greater the probability that the salespeople will have the skills to succeed. The investment in the job analysis and job description will pay off in the quality of the recruits and in the larger percentage of recruits who succeed at the job.

Many sales managers have gut-level feelings about what makes a good salesperson. A résumé may tell a lot about an individual's experience, but the personal interview is probably more important when selecting salespeople than any other criteria. If candidates cannot demonstrate confidence when selling themselves, then they are unlikely to be able to sell other products and services. Another important characteristic is adaptability.[30] Confrontational interviews that incorporate role playing are often

[30] For further information on salesperson adaptability, see Rosann L. Spiro and Barton Weitz, "Adaptive Selling: Conceptualization, Measurement and Nomological Validity," *Journal of Marketing Research* 27 (February 1990): 61–69.

used in the later rounds of the selection process to see how adaptable and enterprising the potential salespeople are under fire. Some companies, such as Ford, also test the activity schedule skills of potential recruits using problem-solving exercises.[31]

Training the Sales Force

As the cost of making a personal sales call rises, many companies are trying to find ways of increasing the return from each call. Training is an investment in human capital that can produce a highly profitable return. It increases the day-to-day efficiency and effectiveness of a sales force. Some companies look at the high turnover of their sales force and regard the investment in up-front training costs as a waste. This can become a self-fulfilling prophecy as turnover increases because of inadequate training. If a company hires a salesperson in good faith to service its customers, then it must, in good faith, follow through by giving the sales recruit the training to do the job. Moreover, on-the-job specific training may be a more important determinant of sales performance than any personal characteristics.[32] Some companies might be better off spending more on training and less on selecting and buying raw talent.

Two types of training occur: basic behavioral sales training that is common to many markets and company-specific sales training. Basic sales training increases the general competence of salespeople, making them generally more valuable to any enterprise. Company-specific training increases human capital or skills that only can be applied in the current employment situation. Both types of training are needed to increase a sales rep's effectiveness, but the second type of training has an added advantage—it increases the loyalty of the salesperson and reduces turnover.

A good sales training program should encourage curiosity and the desire to learn on the job and to share such learning. Many sales training programs do not succeed because they are so concentrated in time that they produce a mental meltdown. On the other hand, another common problem with sales training is that much of it is made up of entertainment with far too little on-the-job follow-up.[33]

Basic Behavioral Sales Training

The universally important skills needed for basic selling can be obtained from sources outside the organization. These sources are expensive, but through them the trainee realizes that he or she is not the only salesperson working hard to develop skills. The competition is learning them, too. A much less expensive approach would be to combine a package of books, audiotapes, and videotapes on selling with roundtable discussions with the sales manager and some of the successful salespeople. Many firms overlook the fact that much of sales training is inspirational. All salespeople need to hear "you can do it, too." The inspirational part of training should be continued throughout the salesperson's career, and new inspirational audiotapes are often the most cost-effective way to provide it because the salesperson can listen to the tapes while driving.

Specific Content Training

Table 13.9 lists possible training topics and recommended training methods. They are organized in terms of company specificity, starting with the general and progressing

---

[31] For a comprehensive guide, see *Selection and Evaluation of Salespersons* (Princeton, NJ: Educational Testing Service, February 1985).

[32] Gilbert A. Churchill Jr., Neil M. Ford, Steven W. Hardly, and Orville C. Walker Jr., "The Determinants of Salesperson Performance; A Meta-Analysis," *Journal of Marketing Research* 22 (May 1985): 103–18.

[33] Jack R. Sander, "Why Most Sales Training Doesn't Work . . . And What You Can Do about It," *Business Marketing*, May 1984, 90–96.

Table 13.9 Sales Training Needs and Recommended Methods

1. **Goal:** Basic selling and presentation skills that increase self-confidence, poise under fire, manners, and dress.
   Solution: Special how-to courses, books, and tapes such as Xerox's *Planned Selling Skills.* Role playing can be videotaped to identify mannerisms and mistakes.
2. **Goal:** Time and territory management.
   Solution: Game-playing exercises. On-the-job advice from successful salespeople and mentor. Read company *Standard Operating Procedures Manual.*
3. **Goal:** How to train others.
   Solution: A lecture-type course that explains learning and teaching techniques. Vicarious learning from mentor.
4. **Goal:** Customer knowledge.
   Solution: Read marketing plan environmental analysis on consumers, market segmentation analysis, history of customer industry from trade magazines, books on customer, customer account profiles on computer. Most important, learn from a mentor about the rituals and legends in the industry—the who's who in the customer industry. Read sales territory account book that reports number of calls each customer should receive, personal contacts, products purchased, and so on.
5. **Goal:** Competitor knowledge.
   Solution: Read marketing plan environmental analysis on competition. Study company market research reports. Learn from mentor and on-the-job monitoring. Read and become familiar with trade press.
6. **Goal:** Company knowledge.
   Solution: Annual reports, in-house magazines/newsletters. Discussions with sales manager and mentor.
7. **Goal:** Product knowledge.
   Solution: Marketing literature, product use manuals, packaging, videos, production plant tours, and tours of the service department. The latter reveals what is not in the marketing literature.
8. **Goal:** Systems training.
   Solution: Built into reporting software, sales manuals. A boot-camp-style, two-day course in following instructions down to the very last details. Discussions with sales manager.
9. **Goal:** Specific short-term product sales programs.
   Solution: The teaching of standard scripts, strategies for coping with common objections through videotaped role playing. On-the-job mentor observation.
10. **Goal:** Adaptive selling techniques.
    Solution: Videotaped role playing. On-the-job mentoring.

to the very specific. Perhaps the most controversial topic is the proposal to teach the trainees how to train others. There is method to such madness. The best way of preparing people for training and learning is to place them in the shoes of the teacher. They are then forced to confront themselves and the problem in a nonthreatening way. By learning how to teach, they learn better how to learn. They also will be better able to teach other salespeople, to teach customers, and to become mentors. Knowledge about an emerging usage market segment should be taught by experienced, successful salespeople because they are most likely to be able to identify the sales "hooks" based on the superiority of product and service design. They also must be rewarded for identifying such sales approaches and for training the rest of the sales force in a series of iterative sales conferences—like the approach the product development team takes to iterative prototype development and testing. These leaders also should be working closely with the development team, particularly on positioning and quality-added analysis (competitive benchmarking), which will give them a deep product knowledge that they can pass on to their other sales colleagues.

Mentoring

The company culture must encourage salespeople to help each other. A variation on this theme is the development of a mentoring program to supplement on-the-job coaching. It is difficult for sales managers to be good mentors because they are also

Some innovative companies are using instructional software to increase the product knowledge of salespeople. In time, firms will build libraries of information that the salesperson will be able to access during sales calls by using a notepad computer. This information will also be available to telemarketing salespeople to answer service questions.

the boss, nipping at the heels of the salespeople to make sure they do their jobs. Ideally, a new recruit should be paired with an experienced mentor, who can make calls with the new salesperson, observe the newcomer's selling style, and provide valuable advice formally and informally.[34] The chemistry cannot be forced, so such a mentoring program will always have varying success. A mentoring program also addresses a classic social group problem in sales force management—the polarization between the old guard and the new recruits. The old guard may view the new salespeople as hopelessly ignorant about the specific market, arrogant, and opportunistic. The recruits may view the old guard as dead-end stick-in-the-muds. A mentoring system forces members of both parties to see the others as interesting and capable individuals. The mentor has a great deal of wisdom to share, and the protégé can provide enthusiasm and respect that helps fire up the mentor. Furthermore, the best way of teaching an old dog new tricks is to use a young dog to do the teaching. The salespeople fresh out of college are likely to be more computer literate and, hence, will be able to teach their mentors how to use high-technology products, while their mentors can teach the recruits the soft touch of selling. A mentor also can teach the new salesperson about the firm's culture and values and the roles played by key people. The standards, norms, and expectations of the company culture are also often established at this time through example and through the legends and stories that make up the firm's folklore. In sales, real learning often comes from improvisation told through stories and legends and not from formal training.[35]

---

[34] David Marshall Hunt and Carol Michael, "Mentorship: A Career Training and Development Tool," *Academy of Management Review* 8, no. 3 (1983): 475–85.

[35] Alan J. Dubinsky, Roy D. Howell, Thomas N. Ingram, and Danny N. Bellinger, "Salesforce Socialization," *Journal of Marketing* (October 1986): 192–207; Richard Pascale, "Fitting New Employees into the Company Culture," *Fortune*, May 28, 1984, 28–40; and John S. Brown, vice president of Xerox, "Seeing Differently," *Seeing Differently: Improving the Ability of Organizations to Anticipate and Respond to the Constantly Changing Needs of Customers and Markets*, Report No. 93–103, Marketing Science Institute, May 1993, 2.

Rewarding the Sales Force

Basically, motivation is how hard a salesperson wants to work to accomplish a task or achieve a goal. Salespeople often strike out when they go to the plate, but motivation is what makes them continue to swing. Many theories and explanations for what motivates people are based on the idea that people want to work hard when outcomes are valued and when effort is linked to performance. For one salesperson, money may be the strongest motivator, while, for another, receiving an award at a banquet is the best incentive. Motivation always has been of interest to sales managers because it is the link between the rewards offered by the sales compensation system and the salesperson's performance.

Sales Compensation

Salespeople are motivated to work by the reward system they are offered. No other dimension of sales management directs, controls, and encourages the initiative of a sales force more than the way a sales force is rewarded. The starting point for the compensation package must be the market rate in the industry, including the customary incentive schemes used by the industry, if they exist. If a company pays less, then it will not attract talent from competitors. If it pays more, then it is potentially placing itself at a competitive cost disadvantage. The trick is to carefully design a compensation scheme that matches the competition and, more important, achieves specific objectives.

The Advantages of Clarity and Simplicity Perhaps the most fundamental rule of sales compensation is to keep it as clear and simple as possible. If a scheme becomes too complicated or is changed too often, then confusion and uncertainty about the reward schedule will increase. A scheme can become too complicated when it has multiple objectives and rewards the salesperson for performance on several different dimensions (obtaining new accounts, running special customer training programs, increasing sales on existing accounts, controlling expenses, and so forth). A company may desire to change its incentive schedule to adapt to the new competitive realities of the marketplace or company constraints, but changing the scheme has two negative effects. First, it is likely to confuse the more experienced salespeople who have worked under several different schemes. Having adapted to them, they may find it difficult to break their behavioral adaptation and to distinguish among the schemes in their memory. Second, a history of such changes increases the expectations that the scheme will be changed again in the future, thus reducing commitment to the new scheme.

The Salary versus Commission Debate Should a sales force be paid a salary or a commission? Much depends on the realities of the marketplace environment. Most companies pay a base salary with bonuses for exceeding quota or a commission on all sales. For the first year, a salesperson may be paid a much higher base salary to compensate for time in training and the time needed to build commission sales. From the salesperson's perspective, salary provides the security that comes with a regular income to pay the bills. It signals the company's belief in and support of the salesperson, whether sales are good or bad. But it also is attractive to insecure or lazy salespeople who see it as a way of maintaining a comfortable income, no matter what they do. Also, a salary is unattractive to the motivated and capable salesperson who views the salary as an unfair ceiling or cap on rewarding his or her efforts. When an organization does not recognize differences in skill and drive in its compensation scheme, it places itself in a position of devaluing and losing the most competent salespeople.

From an organizational perspective, a salary compensation scheme is simple to administer. By disconnecting compensation from selling performance, it also encourages salespeople to perform important but nonincome-generating tasks, such as service and administrative duties. When these tasks are important, salary should make up a larger percentage of the compensation package.[36] Industry studies have shown that in markets where personal selling is not so important in making the sale, a sales force is more likely to be paid a salary.[37]

The general advantages of a commission approach are obvious. It focuses the attention and behavior of a sales force on selling, perhaps even to the detriment of other activities the company would like the salesperson to undertake. The company only pays for performance, so, in a sense, all of the compensation risk is shifted from the company to the individual. The more that personal selling is needed to move the product, the greater a firm's enthusiasm for a commission reward system will be. A commission plan is cost/performance efficient—it encourages greater selling effort from all of the sales force and will automatically screen out the poor performers.

The importance of personal selling is likely to change as a market matures, and this affects the compensation plan. During the product or service's introductory period, a salesperson is likely to have spent a lot of time learning and prospecting—necessary functions but financially unprofitable in the short run. Unless the salesperson is one of the entrepreneurial founders of the company, it is unfair to ask him or her to bear a lot of risk by working solely on commission. But as the market enters its growth period, it is particularly important that an enterprise sells as fast and hard as it can. To gain a larger slice of a rapidly expanding sales cake, a company must grow faster than the industry average. It is not good enough for sales to keep growing; the *rate* of growth must increase. This suggests that tying commissions and bonuses to not just sales growth but *increases* in the *rate* of sales growth will help to increase market share. In a mature market, competitors jealously protect their major customer accounts, so it is very unlikely that an extra sales push will not have much effect. It then may be appropriate to return to a mostly salary-based compensation scheme with large one-time bonuses for stealing an account from a competitor.

The Effort-Performance Connection The more rewards are tied to performance, the more a sales force will perform. However, for a reward-for-performance compensation scheme to be really effective, the salesperson's effort and skill must determine performance. In markets where a company's sales are highly volatile because of frequent and dramatic changes in the trading environment or in the company's marketing strategy, a straight commission approach may not work because an uncertain link exists between effort and results (see Figure 13.5).

For example, in emerging target market segments with high growth potential, increased uncertainty about competitor entry, reactions, trade acceptance and behavior, and customer acceptance is likely. The uncertainty about these external determinants

[36] George John and Barton Weitz, "Salesforce Compensation: An Empirical Investigation of Factors Related to Use of Salary versus Incentive Compensation," *Journal of Marketing Research* 26 (February 1989): 1–14.

[37] Charles A. Peck, *Compensating Field Sales Representatives,* Report No. 828 (New York: The Conference Board, 1982); and Lesley Barnes, "Finding the Best Compensation Plan," *Sales & Marketing Management,* August 1986, 46–49.

Figure 13.5 The Effort-Success Compensation Connection

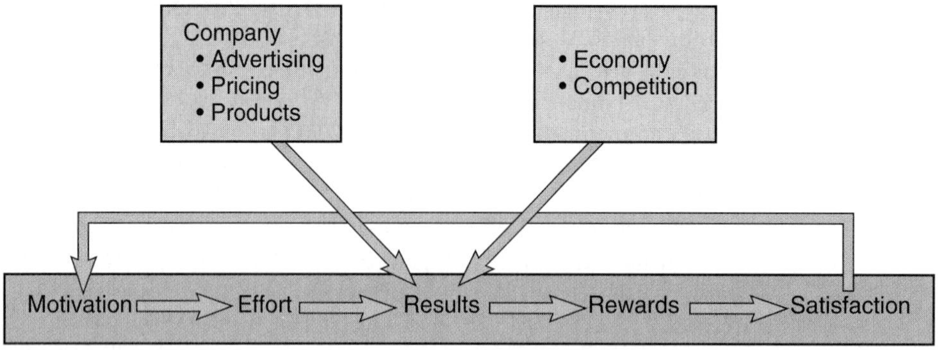

It is fair to link compensation directly to dollar sales or measures of customer satisfaction, providing factors beyond the control of the salesperson do not greatly affect sales or customer satisfaction. However, when changes in the economy or a change in the competitiveness of the firm's products or services have a major effect on outcomes, then no matter how hard the salesperson tries, he or she has little influence on the final result of those efforts. In such circumstances, linking rewards to outcomes is unfair and competitively irrational.

of success makes it less fair and reasonable to tie sales force rewards directly to sales force sales success.[38] In such cases it is better to tie rewards more directly to effort (generation of leads, calling on leads, leads conversion) and to initiatives such as tactical selling-approach suggestions, product redesign or customer service suggestions, and intelligence generation bonuses, as described in Chapter 3.[39]

Another example of a doubtful link is when the economy booms and then busts. During the boom period, even the salespeople who are cruising will be rewarded; but when the economy busts, even the superseller may not be fairly rewarded. Such market volatility has a net negative effect on the salespeople because it creates the correct perception (particularly among the most aware and capable salespeople) that their compensation is no longer under their own control. Finally, if specific actions taken by the company, such as an increase in the production of inferior products, weaken the link between effort and performance, then the sales force is likely to become very upset. In summary, a company cannot expect its sales force to carry all of the risk in the compensation scheme when the marketplace and the company's marketing strategy are uncertain.

Commission on What?

The standard approach is to base the commission or bonus on sales. This encourages a sales force to sell more and to increase market share. However, this approach may be appropriate only in special circumstances, such as during times of rapid growth. Generally, the overall objective of an enterprise is to

[38] David W. Cravens, Thomas N. Ingram, Raymond W. LaForge, and Clifford E. Young, "Behavior-Based and Outcome-Based Salesforce Control Systems," *Journal of Marketing* 57 (October 1993): 47–59.

[39] Amiya K. Basu, Rijiv Lal, V. Srinivasan, and Richard Staelin, "Optimal Compensation Plans: A Theory," working paper, Graduate School of Business, Stanford University, 1984.

increase profitability. This suggests that the sales force's compensation scheme perhaps should be connected to the gross margin earned on sales or contribution to operating margin rather than dollar sales.[40] Basing compensation on gross margin requires that salespeople be informed of the relative profitability of the items in the product line in order to focus attention on high-margin products. Salespeople also should get regular feedback on their performance, which can be provided by notebook computer software linked to the firm's accounting system (see Figure 13.4). Other issues of sales force control are discussed in the final chapter on marketing control processes.

When the potential of sales territories varies, it is clearly unfair to use the same commission or bonus plan for every territory. One way of handling this is to set a different base quota (sales performance target) for each territory determined by its potential and sales history. Any sales above quota are then rewarded using the same commission or bonus schedule. However, even under this scheme some territories are likely to be more financially attractive than others. The dilemma for the sales manager is how to assign unequal territories among salespeople. If the goal is to keep turnover low, then the most senior salespeople should receive the best territories. If the goal is to maximize performance, then the sales manager should assign the best territory to the best salesperson, whatever that person's seniority. Longevity may be rewarded best by giving special bonuses to salespeople at the end of every second year. In many industries, salespeople only last three or four years, so few such bonuses will be paid. But bonuses may encourage a salesperson to stay that extra year.

When team selling is a common practice in a particular industrial market, the company must determine whether to pay a separate commission to each member of the group. It may be better to pay salaries and a group bonus that is divided up equally among the group members or based on the judgment of the group leader. At a more fundamental level, incorporating the sales force's incentive scheme into a general company-wide bonus system has a lot of merit, as discussed in Chapter 19. A general bonus scheme encourages overall cooperation and creates a company culture where everyone is aware that the company's competitiveness depends on everyone's performance and risk is shared by all employees.

A final problem with commission compensation schemes is that they tend to encourage a short-term and selfish perspective. They motivate salespeople to sell rather than service accounts. Some firms have overcome this problem by giving a salesperson part of the commission on all sales made in the future to a new account that they develop. This encourages the salesperson to view obtaining new business as an investment activity. The compensation scheme also should be flexible enough to allow the payment of split commissions to two or more salespeople who worked together to obtain a sale that otherwise would not have been made. Finally, the compensation scheme must attract and keep the superstar (see the next Rationality in Practice box).

Sales Force Leadership

A sales force must be led from the front.[41] What this means is that salespeople should not be asked to do things that the sales manager and senior management would not

[40] Douglas Dalrymple, P. Ronald Stephenson, and William Cron, "Gross Margin Sales Compensation Plan," *Industrial Marketing Management* 10 (July 1981): 219–24; and Alan J. Dubinsky and Thomas E. Barry, "A Survey of Sales Management Practices," *Industrial Marketing Management* 11 (April 1982): 133–41.

[41] Sales force budgeting and sales force leadership, are further discussed in Chapter 18.

Rationality in Practice

Attracting and Keeping the Superstar

Most compensation schemes are designed to reward mediocre to average performers because they make up a large part of any sales force. What such schemes tend to overlook is that some companies owe their existence to the efforts of one or two super salespeople who developed major business. As markets concentrate into fewer but bigger buyers seeking to develop a more long-term trading relationship with single suppliers, the importance of the stellar salesperson may increase.

The firm's compensation scheme can encourage the emergence and continued presence of selling superstars. Any company, particularly a start-up operation, can offer its sales force an attractive stock-option bonus scheme for extraordinary performance. A scheme that kicks in at a certain level of performance and is graduated to provide even higher rewards for higher performance offers several advantages. The rewards to the salesperson do not come off the current bottom line. Stock-option bonuses encourage the salesperson to take a more long-term perspective and, hence, service accounts as well as sell. Also, it differentially recognizes the superior competence of such a salesperson over his or her peers. Because peer recognition has been found to be an extremely important motivator of salespeople, this last advantage is probably the most important in this type of bonus scheme.

Instead of supporting and nurturing its super salespeople, some firms make the mistake of leaning in the opposite direction—and they pay dearly for it. In the early years of a new product line or during the company's start-up days, firms are very grateful for the selling success of the superstars. But over time, the firm's financial officers or senior executives, who often personally resent the annual commission of the major salespeople compared with their own salaries, may be tempted to change the sales commission scheme to rectify the situation. They may argue that the reps no longer earn their compensation, even though they created much of the wealth for the owners of the company that is being divided out among senior management in stock options. What sometimes happens is that the salesperson who found and nurtured the key accounts takes his or her case to the customers, who then, along with the salesperson, switch their loyalties to a competitor. A good salesperson hired by a good competitor will take as much as a third of his or her accounts over to the competition. On top of this, the firm has to hire and train a replacement. (The reverse applies when a firm steals a good salesperson from a rival.) When these kinds of situations arise, the company has made the mistake of viewing the salesperson as an unnecessary *expense*, when in fact he or she was a highly valued and irreplaceable *asset*.

do. One of the reasons that CEOs have been so successful as spokespeople in advertising is because they are able to convey the same enthusiasm to the public that they use to inspire their sales forces. Most senior managers wine and dine the executives of major accounts at country clubs and in stadium skyboxes, but the inspired senior manager joins the sales force on the hot and dirty shop floors and the cramped back offices of the smaller accounts. Requiring the senior executive team to spend time out on the road with salespeople calling on small accounts has three major benefits. First, it gives executives a firsthand sense of the market. Second, it helps senior executives understand the effects of their decision making on the salesperson. Third, it fosters a belief in the sales force that senior management really cares. Salespeople will feel more comfortable talking to a senior executive after a day on the road than they ever would on the executive's corner-office turf. The benefits to manufacturing efficiency of a "walkabout" leadership style has been well established. It can be equally applied to sales management.

Sensible marketing planners also involve salespeople in their planning from the outset. They often test the implementation of proposed selling tactics in several high-potential territories or in a sales region. The trick, then, is to work with sales to closely monitor the implementation and success of the program without getting in the way of the routine functioning of the sales force. The goal is to have salespeople 100 percent behind the marketing plan. Anything less reflects badly on the quality of the planning effort.

Ultimately, it is the responsibility of the sales manager to motivate the sales force. It is not an easy job because sales managers have three major responsibilities that can often conflict: (1) They are involved in the marketing planning for key product markets; (2) they execute the different selling strategies for different products as directed by senior management or cross-functional teams; and (3) they maintain the general enthusiasm of the sales force, all of whom are individuals with different needs. Since most sales managers are former salespeople, their natural tendency is to be very loyal to their sales force. However, when sales managers share their frustrations with the sales force, the contagious dissatisfaction that can result hurts both morale and cooperation with other functional areas. Instead of taking such risks, sales managers often blow off steam with trusted senior salespeople who they know will not spread the dissatisfaction.

Characteristics of a Good Sales Manager

Not all sales managers are born inspirational leaders, but they should compensate for it by building a personal library of inspirational audio- and videotapes that can be loaned to their reps. What they must have is the ability to understand the unique personalities they manage. Everyone has a button that will motivate them if pushed. The major job of the sales manager is to find the right button.[42] To do this, a good sales manager gets to know his or her salespeople. Accompanying the salesperson on sales calls and discussing sales objectives provide opportunities for the manager to find out what the salesperson needs and values.

As the managerial link between the organization's objectives and the implementation of those objectives through the sales force, the good sales manager must have both a macro and a micro perspective. He or she must be able to deal with the economy's effect on corporate strategies one minute and bungled paperwork the next minute. In addition to being good at one-on-one interactions, a manager also must be good at conducting weekly sales meetings. Table 13.10 lists some suggestions made by salespeople as to how sales managers can improve such meetings.

Annual Sales Conferences

Annual sales conferences are important venues for managing and leading a sales force. The objectives of these conferences are to boost morale, build camaraderie, educate, and brief the sales force on plans for the year ahead. These objectives are achieved in varying ways. Holding the annual conference in an exotic setting is a signal of appreciation to both the salesperson and the spouse or family. An annual trip to a resort location is an additional compensation that the salesperson and the family can enjoy. Similarly, paying $10,000 to $20,000 to have President Ford talk about the current situation in the Middle East to five hundred salespeople who sell industrial adhesives signals that the company thinks its sales force is important. Salespeople can take photos and shake the man's hand. The annual conference is also the time to give out lots of awards. The more applause the better. It feeds the competitive and status drive of all, from the super rep to the novice. The

---

[42] For discussions on the use of contests as incentives, see William C. Moncrief, Sandra H. Hart, and Dan H. Robertson, "Sales Contests: A New Look at an Old Management Tool," *Journal of Personal Selling and Sales Management* (November 1988): 55–61; and for how motivation changes as a salesperson's career progresses, see William L. Cron, Alan J. Dubinsky, and Ronald E. Michaels, "The Influence of Career Stages on Components of Salesperson Motivation," *Journal of Marketing* (January 1988): 78–92.

Table 13.10 **Sales Force Suggestions as to How Sales Managers Can Improve Sales Meetings**

1. Make brief technical presentations using visual aids and then break out into discussion groups to maintain interest and get quality feedback.
2. Keep the sales force informed of changes in corporate, marketing, and sales strategies and plans.
3. Have key members of cross-functional teams, such as advertising and customer service executives, make brief presentations on issues of direct relevance to sales.
4. Don't try to squeeze too much into a meeting. Allow salespeople to share experiences, so they learn from each other.
5. Circulate the agenda beforehand, so salespeople know the purpose and content of the meeting.
6. Ask salespeople to add their own items to the agenda and to suggest speakers.

SOURCE: Rayna Skolnik, "Salespeople Sound Off on Meetings," *Sales and Marketing Management*, November 1987, 108.

ceremonies, initiations, rites of passage, and knighting of the superstars that occurs at sales conferences all contribute to the growth of the company culture.[43]

Personal Selling Skills and Relationship Management

A company will spend up to several hundred dollars on a personal sales call for two basic reasons. The first is to enable the salesperson to get a better understanding of the needs of the customer. No other type of contact with the firm offers the same opportunity. However, to take full advantage of customer contact, the salesperson must carefully question, listen, and interact with the potential client. We often view successful salespeople as smooth talkers, but they are more likely to be excellent listeners and acute observers of human behavior. The second advantage of personal sales calls is that they enable the salesperson to exercise his or her most effective persuasion skills. The salesperson must convince the customer that what the firm has to offer meets the needs of the customer better than any other competitive alternative. The mechanics of personal selling can be reduced to the following steps: prospecting, qualifying, presentation, negotiation, closing, and service. Each of these steps are now discussed.

Sales Prospecting

Prospecting for potential customers involves searching yellow pages, trade listings, government reports, and .magazines. It also involves relying on word-of-mouth networks to pass on information about new prospects. Prospects are often categorized as A, B, or C leads according to criteria such as presented in Table 13.6. A leads are immediately sent literature and called by a sales rep. B leads are likely to be sent literature and called by a telemarketing salesperson. A C lead is likely to be sent literature only. As the global marketplace opens up, the art and science of prospecting, particularly how to work trade shows, a major source of customer leads, has taken on new significance.

[43] Mark Thalenberg, "Rituals and Rewards," *Sales and Marketing Management*, June 3, 1986, 72.

The trade show has ancient and honorable roots that go back to the medieval fairs where buyers and sellers gathered together to create an annual marketplace. With booths, demonstrations, and hawkers, trade shows are a modern version of the medieval fair. Thousands occur each year, and they occur in every country. At their best, they can be an opportunity for a new company to break into a market by providing access to new customers and a chance to generate leads. In some specialized markets, the annual trade show is "an absolute must attend."

A successful trade show strategy starts with a list of goals. These will determine who will attend, the nature of the display, the appropriate sales approach, and the development and implementation of postshow follow-up activities.[44] Apart from the development of a traveling exhibit, the major expense in trade show marketing is the rental of the space and the cost of salespeople's time. As early as possible, a list of trade show attendees should be obtained from the trade show organizers. A friendly "see you at the show" letter with accompanying trade literature should be sent to prospective buyers.

A good trade show team employs at least two people: a screener and a good closer. The screener is at the front of the exhibit to meet people and to sort out the serious prospect from the inquisitive competitor and the general public. The closer spends his or her time at the back of the booth or in a hotel suite with serious prospects. Such selling efforts, followed up by a telephone call, often result in orders. The companies that take a very hard-nosed selling approach to trade shows may gain the reputation of being party poopers, but they will differentiate themselves in terms of their professionalism and efficiency.

Many companies dilute the effectiveness of their trade show efforts by not promptly following up on leads. Follow-up personal letters should be sent and dated the day after the end of the trade show. The period after a major trade show is a time when customers and distributors judge the service of a company against the efforts of competitors who also will be following up on leads. That is why it pays to be the first to follow up. If a trade show does not draw new business, then it should be dropped. In general, trade shows are much more important selling tools in high-growth industries such as computer software and hardware that are attracting new customers and new competitors.

Qualifying the Customer

Qualifying is a term used in personal selling to describe the process of learning to understand a customer's needs. The keys to personal selling are being able to put oneself in the shoes of the customer and to convince the customer you are trustworthy. If you succeed, then customers will open up and start talking honestly about their concerns about the product and, particularly, your offering. When this happens, the salesperson can take the most advantage of interpersonal communication by answering the questions that really need to be answered and giving advice that the customer wants. The salesperson then becomes a problem solver on the buyer's side, rather than an adversary engaging in a verbal and intellectual wrestling match. As the dialogue continues, the buyer's confidence in the expertise and sincerity of the salesperson will increase.

[44] It has been argued that trade show selling requires a selling approach that says, "Thanks for coming in. What prompted your interest in our product?" However, this approach is unfamiliar to most salespeople. See Betsy Wiesendanger, "Are Your Salespeople Trade Show Duds?" *Sales and Marketing Management*, August 1990, 40–46.

At some point, the customer will start disclosing preferences, the reasons for those preferences, and the true objections. The following is an excellent example of a master salesperson at work:

> A major research laboratory wished to purchase 200 potentiometers from Honeywell to measure temperatures, pressures, and speeds. Denzil Plomer, a 36-year veteran salesperson, recommended the company not buy Honeywell potentiometers but instead buy a data acquisition and analysis system that Honeywell could not even supply! Six months later, Honeywell had developed a data acquisition and analysis system, but the research lab only wanted to buy the potentiometers. Plomer convinced the lab to allow him to bid on both the potentiometers and the system. The competitors only bid on supplying the potentiometers. After a careful review, the lab opted for the Honeywell system and potentiometers that offered a superior solution. Plomer believes that integrity, listening, and creativity enabled him to serve his customers rather than simply make the quick sale. He seeks to build long-term relationships.[45]

The best way to establish customer needs is to ask questions and *listen* very carefully. A salesperson who does not listen will not fully understand a customer's needs. Asking questions is an art.[46] A study conducted by Xerox learning systems established that successful salespeople use words such as *what*, *where*, *why*, *how*, and *tell me*, which allow the customer to respond more freely. Such questions are called open probes. Closed probes, the use of words such as *is*, *are*, *do*, *does*, *have*, *has*, and *which*, often limit answers to *yes* or *no* or a choice of alternatives. They do not get to the reasons behind the answers.

Qualifying the Selling Situation

Salespeople also need to learn to correctly categorize the selling situation, which includes the personality and competence of the buyer, the nature of the buying task (new or rebuy), how close the buyer is to making a purchase, and the organizational culture within which the buyer operates. They then must have the experience to choose the selling strategy that best fits the situation.[47] Experienced salespeople can help by holding group training sessions where they discuss how they deal with different types of customers when selling the company's products. This exchange of knowledge can be tape-recorded and circulated among the sales force, so salespeople can listen to the tape when traveling to sales calls.

A simpler way of sharing knowledge with other salespeople is to use a desktop system to write and publish a selling guide full of advice and anecdotes from successful salespeople. Such a book will help the novice and enhance the status of the quoted experts. This book might even form the foundation for a computer-based expert advice system that helps all salespeople to adapt their selling techniques on a continual basis.

---

[45] This example comes from Christopher Harvey, *Secrets of the World's Top Sales Performers* (Holbrook, MA: Bob Adams Inc., 1990): 99–106.

[46] Camille P. Schuster and Jeffrey E. Danes, "Asking Questions: Some Characteristics of Successful Sales Encounters," *The Journal of Personal Selling and Sales Management* (May 1986): 17–27; see also Jeremy Main, "How to Sell by Listening," *Fortune*, February 1985, 52–54.

[47] Barton A. Weitz, Harish Sujan, and Mita Sujan, "Knowledge, Motivation, and Adaptive Behavior: A Framework for Improving Selling Effectiveness: The Importance of Declarative Knowledge to the Personal Selling Concept," *Journal of Marketing* 52 (January 1988): 64–77.

Presentation

Videotapes, full-color brochures, and flip charts can greatly improve the quality of sales presentations. Many firms have no sense of proportion when it comes to investing in presentation aids for their sales force. After spending $200 or more to place the salesperson in the office of a buyer, they are reluctant to spend a few additional dollars to improve the quality of the presentation. It bears repeating that a quality sales presentation will increase direct communication and persuasion and also will act as an indirect cue to the overall quality of the selling company and its products.

A salesperson must have superior quality overheads or slides to use during a sales presentation to a buying group. It is probably better to invest in this sort of high-impact presentation tool, which a rep can adapt to his or her audience, than to present the sales pitch on a sales video. A sales video is unchangeable, difficult to update, and expensive to produce to the quality expected by the audience. Modern movies and TV commercials have set presentation and communications standards that few industrial selling videos can match.

Instead, a video is best used to demonstrate the on-site applications of the product or service and to explain how and why the product is used by other buyers. In short, it presents credible endorsements that also demonstrate the product in use. Such videos can be taped on-site, inexpensively, and with little editing (which will add to their credibility). Again, a sales rep must learn to adapt the use of sales presentation aids to the unique selling situation. There is a right and a wrong time to introduce them. Forcing a canned sales presentation may alienate the customer and indicate the salesperson's lack of composure and command of the selling situation. The skilled sales presenter orchestrates the interaction so the customer requests such a presentation.

A good sales presentation leaves a strong, concrete visual image in the customer's memory around which abstract information and arguments for buying the product or service can be stored and built up over time. It is better to leave one very strong visual image of the product's superior performance on a particular dimension than to overwhelm the customer with a multimedia song and dance show. The literature that is left behind should reinforce the key product differentiation advantages.

Adapting Presentation Pitch to Personality

The personal approach used to gain the confidence and trust of a buyer must be built on the natural personality and interpersonal skills of the salesperson. This is one of the reasons why it is so hard to identify the successful salesperson from personality tests.[48] The successful salesperson makes the most of his or her personality by adapting it to the selling situation.[49] As humans, we are more comfortable being ourselves than trying to be someone we are not. However, some basic rules apply to all personal selling situations. For example, salespeople who do their homework and who can display detailed knowledge of their customer's business will create the impression that they really want to understand the buyer's needs. If a customer account profile is not available, then the salesperson should prepare by consulting the company's annual

---

[48] Another reason is that the duties of a salesperson vary greatly among industries and firms; see William C. Moncrief, "Selling Activity and Sales Position Taxonomies for Industrial Salesforces," *Journal of Marketing Research* 23 (August 1986): 261–70.

[49] Barton A. Weitz, Harish Sujan, and Mita Sujan, "Knowledge, Motivation, and Adaptive Behavior: A Framework for Improving Selling Effectiveness," *Journal of Marketing* (October 1986): 174–91.

report or articles about the company in trade magazines. Ideally, the salesperson also should have access to the product plan's environmental analysis, which describes the customer, the competition, and other market trends.[50]

Furthermore, it is important to recognize that the perceived expertise of a salesperson is judged relative to the buyer's own expertise. Hence, sales calls to expert buyers require greater-than-normal preparation. This explains why Merck and other leading drug companies spend more than a year training their college-educated sales recruits and why they often prefer to hire pharmacy majors. Merck's sales force is interacting with doctors who must be expert in the judgments they make about what to prescribe to a patient. Another rule is that good manners, politeness, courtesy, and old-fashioned charm are universal keys to creating an impression of competence and trust.

Negotiating and Bargaining with Customers

When the customer is satisfied that the supplier has a viable product or service, the important process of negotiating often begins. It most often occurs at the closing stage of the selling process, but negotiating tactics can occur at other stages as well. A good salesperson must be a good negotiator, even if the negotiating involves the most minor details.

All salespeople should be assigned to read several of the popular paperbacks on negotiation strategies as part of their general training.[51] However, a number of simple rules and tactics often can be successfully applied during negotiations with customers or distributors. Most of the following suggestions can be used by either party involved in any trading negotiation. It therefore pays to assume, until proven wrong, that an adversary has read the same books on negotiation the sales force have read.

1. Trading relationships are built on personal commitment, enthusiasm, communication, and trust. Threats to discontinue dealings or not renew a contract are a poor way of managing a relationship and should be made only as a last resort. Reaching for the fine print in the contract is often the same as reaching for the exit door. Contracts are used as insurance and protection against flagrant fraud and scoundrels. Unfortunately, they also can be misused, which occurs when one party unscrupulously uses a contract to take advantage of the other. Most executives, particularly senior executives, pride themselves on their word and woe to the junior executive who misunderstands this ethical code. Such unwritten understandings are, in fact, necessary for the U.S. and world economies to continue functioning. Most commercial trading relationships operate on informal quid pro quos (favors done and owed), which are called up from time to time, rather than on the letter of the law.
2. However, a seller should protect its products, processes, and trade secrets with all the power of the law it can muster before negotiating with distributors and customers. Such actions signal that the company is being managed with an iron hand, even though it is extended in the velvet glove of friendship. It also signals that the supplier has an important competitive advantage that is worth protecting, the benefits of which will be shared with cooperating customers or distributors. Patents, copyrights, trademarks, and nondisclosure agreements arouse interest, discourage temptation, and engender respect.

[50] In presentations, purchasing executives are most critical of salespeople who are poorly informed about their business, who are poorly informed about competitors' products and services, who run down competitors, who are too aggressive, and who deliver poor presentations. See Milt Grassell, "What Purchasing Managers Like in a Salesperson . . . And What Drives Them up the Wall," *Business Marketing*, June 1986, 72–77.

[51] Roy J. Lewicki and Joseph Litterer, *Negotiation* (Homewood, IL: Richard D. Irwin, 1985); and Roger Fisher and Scott Brown, *Getting Together: Building a Relationship That Gets to Yes* (Boston: Houghton Mifflin, 1988).

3. Increasingly, what is negotiated is not a single sale, but a customer-supplier joint venture whose terms involve much more than price. Such negotiations can be handled best in a way similar to negotiations between superpowers. Senior executives meet and reach an accord or understanding on win-win trading innovations such as discussed earlier in the section on relationship selling. They then withdraw from the negotiation, leaving it up to their subordinates to work out the details. Their accord forces the subordinates to make settlements they would otherwise not make because they will face sanctions if they fail. As a last resort, senior executives can get together again and work out any final impasses.
4. Sellers should always enter negotiations knowing their minimum acceptable terms (their "reservation" point), below which they will walk away from the negotiations. When such terms are not offered, they must walk away. Sellers should know the rival's options and decide beforehand when and if they are going to reveal such knowledge and attempt to back the customer against the wall. If the negotiator declares what he or she believes are the customer's options and is right, then the seller is in a very powerful position. However, if wrong, the negotiator will lose credibility and will be in a weaker situation. When an industrial buyer calls for bids or tenders for supplying a product or service, the accepted bid is often the starting point for negotiations: "We will award you the bid, if you change these areas." The response is, "We will accept if you address the following issues not contained in the initial Request for Proposal."
5. It often pays to let the other party make the initial offer and to justify it. If it is absurdly low, the seller should politely explain why, using marketplace facts, and then ask the other party, in the light of the facts, to consider making a more realistic starting offer. If the other party does so, then it is conceding that the seller is in command of the facts. A negotiator should not counter absurdity with absurdity. Doing so loses some control by implicitly agreeing to play by the other party's games and by disconnecting the negotiation from reality. Questionable bargaining tactics that inconvenience or embarrass the negotiator should be challenged and confronted. Not doing this admits a lack of bargaining power. The negotiator should always maintain his or her cool and take a time out if things appear to be getting heated.
6. Some disagree as to how much the initial offer should deviate from the reservation price or terms (the minimum acceptable). Some experts claim sellers end up with a better deal if they start high. However, this tactic does not work when an opponent knows the seller's alternatives.
7. In complex negotiations with an unfamiliar party, a seller should make an initial attempt to establish whether a settlement is possible on the most important issues. Each party makes a positional statement that describes the type of product and services it is seeking from the other party. A detailed negotiating agenda should then be discussed and followed. When an issue cannot be agreed on immediately, then it should be left and returned to later. By doing this, both parties then know what is up for trade. The next topic for discussion should be how to proceed with these remaining contested issues. At this stage, items are often coupled together to help produce a compromise. Sometimes, each party alternates in making concessions. The last issue is normally price or margin, because each party then knows the exact nature of the bundle of products and services it will be delivering and receiving. Each also has developed an understanding of the negotiating skills and style of the other party, which is information that each will prefer to have before settling the most negotiated issue—price.
8. It is best to try to find new solutions that satisfy the basic objectives of both parties when a block is reached. The more negotiators explore each other's fundamental objectives, the more they are likely to come up with new win-win solutions.
9. It is a gesture of courtesy and an acid test of good faith to invite the other party to draw up the first draft of the final contract based on his or her understanding of the agreements reached in the discussions. It also reduces the supplier's legal costs. If the other party is going to attempt to exploit the relationship, he or she will use the fine print in the contract

to do so. With the help of notes from the negotiations and a lawyer who can translate legalese into English, such booby traps can be defused or sometimes made to explode in the face of the perpetrator. More than likely the contract will pass the test and confirm the goodwill and trust developed in the negotiations.

Handling Objections and Closing the Sale

The art of handling objections is to anticipate all or most of the objections in the sales presentation. A skilled salesperson can turn an unanticipated objection into a problem that the salesperson and the customer can solve together ("How can we find a way through or around this problem?").[52] A salesperson should never dismiss an objection immediately ("Don't worry, that's not a problem."). To do so might cause the buyer to counterargue or simply politely clam up. Such outcomes have to be avoided at all costs because they change the negotiating parties from joint problem solvers to potential adversaries. At the least, the customer becomes embarrassed and defensive over voicing such an easily dismissed objection. It is much better to respect the concerns of the buyer by going over the issues step by step to let the buyer discover, with a little prompting, how they can be handled.

The fear of being unable to close the sale can give inexperienced salespeople nightmares. However, closing can be easier if the following suggestions are used. The key is to make a request to which the customer responds positively. For example, if a buyer quickly dismisses the salesperson's request for a trial order, the salesperson must work with the customer to determine the most useful next step. It is a human tendency to want to make some other concession to someone to whom you have just refused a request, particularly when social rapport exists between the negotiators.[53] Even if the salesperson only elicits an interest in receiving further information or bringing another person into future discussions, it is important to end the meeting on a positive note. A definite and committed negative response closes the door to any future positive advances.

Building Relationships through Service

The relationship between a customer and a salesperson is like a marriage. It starts with a courtship period, when both parties begin to get to know each other. Next a ceremony, or contract to do business, binds both parties to certain terms. The relationship is then maintained by developing high levels of trust and service norms that guide future interactions. If the relationship becomes unsatisfactory for either party, they divorce.

Developing strong relationships with customers gives a salesperson a sustainable competitive advantage in the marketplace. If a customer feels a certain level of commitment to the relationship, which has been fostered by the salesperson's attention to detail and willingness to go the extra mile in after-sales service, then, when a problem does occur, the customer will not immediately seek another supplier. Even though the marketplace may have many attractive potential partners, the customer will be loyal to a salesperson who has shown commitment and dedication over the long term.

---

[52] Paul H. Schurr, Louis H. Stone, and Lee Ann Beller, "Effective Selling Approaches to Buyers' Objections," *Industrial Marketing Management* 14 (1985): 195–202.

[53] Robert B. Cialdini, *Influence* (Glenview, IL: Scott, Foresman and Company, 1988).

To develop a long-term relationship, it is important for the salesperson to first understand the customer's needs and then to adapt selling techniques to those needs. However, the relationship has to be sustained, and it is sustained through attention to service, such as promptly returning calls, making special deliveries quickly and personally, seeking out answers to technical questions, and working with the customer to design the next generation of products and services.

Global Sales Management

Global selling is no different, in principle, from selling in the U.S. market. In practice, however, much greater care has to be taken in selecting selling agents. The compensation scheme should fit the local market conditions and be competitive with local salaries and commissions. The expense allowance structure also is likely to be very different in categories such as travel and entertainment. Whatever the stage of a country's economic development, if electricity and telephone are available, a computerized sales support system can be introduced. Such a system provides tremendous communications and control advantages. Training is likely to be expensive, because it is best to use training facilities at the universities and engineering institutes within the foreign market rather than to train in the United States. Local training ensures a cultural fit and also is geared to the competitive expectations of the foreign market, not the U.S. market. Finally, it is very important to have a technical advisor in the market as soon as possible who can troubleshoot and keep a close watch on the selling programs, pricing practices, and after-sales service programs of the local manufacturers' reps or distributors. Preferably, such a sales manager should be a national or someone who is, at the least, fluent in the language and culture of the foreign market.[54]

Selling skills that work in the home market might not be effective in the foreign market. Training salespeople in the market in which they will be selling is helpful because salespeople must become very familiar with local selling customs. In cultures that are quite different, it is imperative to hire nationals to do the selling because they understand the culture and selling customs. Salespeople cannot impose their own standards on a customer from a different culture. For instance, many typical Ameri\can selling customs, such as asking for the sale when it looks as though a customer is ready to do business, are perceived as too aggressive in Japan. Just as a good salesperson will work hard to gear a sales presentation to suit the specific customer in the home market, a good salesperson should work even harder to gear the presentation to suit the customer in the foreign market.

Discussion Questions and Minicases

1. What problems may arise if senior management believes that their field sales force is made up of "impression managers" of somewhat questionable honesty?
2. How can the two quotes at the beginning of the chapter be reconciled? Does the first mean that salespeople are heroes because they are dishonest a lot of the time? What problems and opportunities are associated with the Gallup Poll statistic?
3. Why might it be argued that sales is the area where a firm will be able to gain the biggest advantage over its competition during the 1990s?
4. Please redraw Figure 13.3 to demonstrate (1) the advantage a small family firm (in which the head of the firm is the salesperson) has over a large rival in selling to a large company

[54] For additional insight, see John S. Hill and Richard R. Hill, "Organizing the Overseas Sales Force: How Multinationals Do It," *Journal of Personal Selling and Sales Management* 100 (spring 1990): 57–66.

and (2) the mutual advantage a small family firm has in selling to another small firm, compared to two very large firms trading with each other. What implications do these have for the practice of relationship marketing?

5. How can a salesperson directly and indirectly influence the quality and economy images of the product he or she sells?
6. In addition to providing information about a product or service, a sales presentation includes two persuasive elements. The first is an attempt to ingratiate the buyer by praising the buyer's skills, personal appearance, good taste, personality, and so on. The second is a salesperson's subtle attempts at self-promotion through emphasizing his or her experience, success, and so forth. Little is known about how these two elements of persuasion should be combined in a presentation. Do you think a sales presentation should involve self-promotion first and ingratiation second or the other way around? Should they be mixed together throughout the presentation? Justify your answer. Would your suggested tactic change if you were dealing with buyers who were excellent at impression management themselves?
7. Role playing during sales training, where salespeople are videotaped while taking turns playing the role of buyer or seller in a simulated sales call, has recently become a very important way of training recruits and providing refresher training of experienced salespeople. Whole books have been written on the subject. Explain all of the reasons why role playing is so effective.
8. Mentoring is a great idea if it can be done well, but its success depends very much on the fit of personalities between the mentor and the rookie. Make a practical suggestion as to how a sales manager might make such pairings. (Hint: Do not suggest the use of personality tests.)
9. In developing an objective method of categorizing an account as AA, A, B, C, and D, such as described in Table 13.6, what should determine whether size, growth, current penetration, or competitive activity is more important in ascertaining the rating? Explain your answer by changing the table in the text to reflect company X's emphasis on growth. How would you change the table for a company Y whose emphasis is on attacking competition?
10. How might a learning-oriented sales manager handle imbalances in sales territory workloads in the short term?
11. The text presents a list of bargaining rules or tactics. Describe the one you most disagree with and explain why.
12. In major negotiations with a foreign buyer, it often may help to play the "simple Jim"—that is, behave in a way that leads the other party in a negotiation to underestimate your ability. Why?
13. Some companies use very complicated compensation schemes to achieve multiple objectives, and they change them frequently. What problems can this create?
14. What perverse incentive might be created by keeping a sales commission reward system for sales of old products to established customers and switching to a salary compensation for a salesperson to pioneer sell new products to uncertain new customer segments?
15. Why should a commission schedule be progressive (increasing as a salesperson's sales increase) rather than regressive? That is, rather than sticking with a straight-line (constant) commission, why increase commission from, say, 8 percent to 10 percent of gross margin at a point where a certain level of sales has been achieved?
16. Why does stealing a super salesperson from a rival result in a great triple play (that is, what are three competitive rationality advantages from making such a steal)?
17. How might a firm increase the sharing of good ideas and the competitive rationality of its sales force and the firm in general?

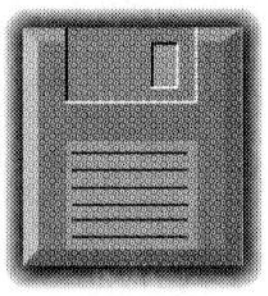

18. Why do annual sales conferences often make or break aspiring young marketing executives?
19. By analyzing the costs and returns from serving the different-sized accounts described in the OWNVREP spreadsheet in the box on pages 512–513, explain the inherent advantages and disadvantages of using the company's own salespeople versus using manufacturers' reps.

20. Some people have argued that the most important recent technological revolution in sales has been the widespread use of the cellular/mobile telephone. Detail all of the ways that mobile telephones have been used by salespeople to increase the effectiveness and efficiency of their performance.

21. How should the notebook computer be introduced to enhance its use by a sales force? (Hint: Take a customer-orientation approach in your answer.)

22. The following statement presents the advocacy position of a lobbying group representing the interests of independent reps. From what you have read in this and earlier chapters, argue the merits of the reps' case, the power buyers' case, and the case of the supplier who seems to be caught in between.

Power buyers are large-volume purchasers who use their buying power to obtain unfair competitive advantages. A recent survey conducted by the Council of Manufacturers Representatives Associations estimated that 101 companies are power buyers.[55]

- *Issue:* These power buyers use their market power to force suppliers to sell direct, denying suppliers the benefit of independent sales representatives in order to obtain a discount in price in lieu of brokerage.
- *Manufacturers are harmed:* Suppliers and manufacturers who have chosen to market and sell their products through independent sales representatives are being required by power buyers to sell direct in order to continue to sell to such buyers. Suppliers and manufacturers who continue to service the power buyer accounts by redeploying or hiring personnel face increased costs of doing business. Thus, power buyers obtain discriminatory price reductions, which other buyers do not receive, and force increased costs on suppliers.
- *U.S. economy is harmed:* Power buyer actions harm the U.S. economy. Small and medium-sized businesses who compete with the power buyer face higher costs for products as suppliers' marketing costs increase. These businesses find it more difficult to compete with the power buyers, reducing consumer choices and increasing consumer prices. Power buyers fail to return their savings to consumers, often raising prices in areas where competition has been driven out. Lastly, independent-sales-representative companies face the loss of their highest volume accounts and often must lay off employees or go out of business completely.
- *How abuse occurs:* Power buyers abuse their market power in several ways. For example, a large discount chain that has refused to deal with independent sales representatives has unilaterally increased its new store discount from 5 percent to 10 percent. The same chain also requested a price discount of 2 percent to 3 percent on all orders it placed during June and July with the understanding that noncomplying manufacturers will no longer do business with the chain. A large supermarket chain demanded that a supplier eliminate its sales representative and reduce its prices by 10 percent, the commission the chain claimed the representative was earning, or lose the account.
- *Violations of law:* These practices of the power buyers force the suppliers and the manufacturers to violate Sections 2(a), (c), and (f) of the Robinson-Patman Act, which prohibits price discrimination and discounts in lieu of brokerage received by a buyer from a seller. The practices also violate Section 2 of the Sherman Act, which prohibits the abuse of market power.

23. Review the questionnaire appearing on the next two pages that was developed to select manufacturers' reps. How would you improve it?

---

[55] Coalition of Americans to Save the Economy, 1100 Connecticut Avenue NW, Suite 1200, Washington, D.C. 20036, (800) 752-4111.

FANMISER CORP.
MANUFACTURING REPRESENTATIVE EVALUATION FORM

Company Name ______
Street Address (no P.O. Box numbers) ______
City ______ State/Province ______ Country ______
Zip Code ______ Telephone ______ Fax ______
Contact Person ______ Position ______

For Prospective Canadian Distributors:
Federal Sales Tax Exemption Number (if applicable) ______
Provincial Sales Tax Exemption Number (if applicable) ______

For Prospective U.S. Distributors:
Employer Identifier Number (I.R.S. Tax Number): ______

If you wish to register more than one office, please provide on a separate typewritten sheet a summary of all locations for which you would like authorization. For each location provide the name of the office, its address, phone number(s), and key personnel.

Company Information

History

1. Are you a . . . ______ A) Corporation ______ B) Partnership ______ C) Sole Proprietorship
2. How long have you been in the business? ______
3. What was your gross sales volume last year? ______
4. Have you ever been terminated by a manufacturer for violation of a reseller agreement? ______
   If yes, by what manufacturer? ______
5. What professional company organizations does your company belong to? ______

Territory

6. What territory do you cover? ______
7. Will you accept deviations from this territory? ______
8. Who are your major accounts? ______
9. Will you provide references from some of your key accounts, if requested by FANMISER? ______

Office Facilities

10. What are your normal business hours of operation? ______
    What percentage (%) of time, in a typical business day, are your office telephone lines presently covered by:
    ______ Trained sales staff ______ Trained technical support staff
    ______ Secretary or Office Personnel ______ Outside Answering Service
    ______ Answering Machine ______ Nobody or nothing
    ______ Other
    Do you expect these %'s to change if you are appointed as a FANMISER manufacturing representative? ______
    (if Yes, write in the revised percentages to the right of the ones noted above.)
11. Do you have a fax machine? ______
    If not, do you plan on getting one in the near future? ______

Personnel

12. How many full-time salespeople does your company have? ______
13. Will you provide resumes of your salespeople upon request of FANMISER? ______
14. How do you compensate your salespeople? ______
    How are commissions paid? ______
    How often? ______
15. Do you have incentive programs or profit sharing for employees? ______

Product Lines

16. Please furnish a list of your principals and product lines you currently represent including the territories covered with each principal and the number of years you have represented them. Attach this information to this evaluation form.
17. Please describe any of the products you manufacture for distribution ______
18. How well do you understand the FANMISER product? What type of information or training would help make you more comfortable in presenting it? ______

MARKETING AND SALES

1. Which industries do you sell to?
   ______ HVAC ______ Food Service ______ Other, please list
2. How well do you know FANMISER's market and customer? ______
3. How does FANMISER fit into your core business? ______
4. What do you feel is the average call cycle needed to make a FANMISER sale in your territory? ______
5. Which of your current or future contacts could benefit from FANMISER? ______

6. What type of support will you require from FANMISER? ______
7. What do you see as your sales potential for FANMISER? ______
   ______ Year 1 ______ Year 2 ______ Year 3 ______ Year 4 ______ Year 5
8. How would you sell our product? Distributors or direct? ______
9. Where do you plan to be in five years? ______
10. How will you handle sales leads from the factory? ______
11. Would you agree to send monthly sales activity and/or booking report to FANMISER? ______

PROMOTIONAL EFFORTS

12. Do you have a direct mail program? ______
13. How many people are on your mailing list? ______
14. Do you participate in any local trade shows? ______
15. Do you have your own catalog? ______

SERVICE AND TRAINING

16. Do your salespeople perform minor service or customer education? ______

ADDITIONAL INFORMATION

1. Please provide any additional information on your company (resume, brochures, etc.) that may assist us in the evaluation process and attach along with this application.
2. Summarize your business plan, including special market focus, capabilities, facilities, or other value-added features offered by your organization. Attach this information to this evaluation form.
3. Please complete page 6.

Credit References

Please provide one Bank Reference.
Bank Name ______
Address ______
City ______ State/Province ______ Country ______
Account Number ______ Telephone ______

Please provide three Supplier references (companies you currently purchase from an open account basis).

1. Company Name ______
   Address ______
   City ______ State/Province ______ Zip ______
   Contact Person ______ Position ______
   Telephone ______
2. Company Name ______
   Address ______
   City ______ State/Province ______ Zip ______
   Contact Person ______ Position ______
   Telephone ______
3. Company Name ______
   Address ______
   City ______ State/Province ______ Zip ______
   Contact Person ______ Position ______
   Telephone ______

I HEREBY CERTIFY THAT ALL INFORMATION CONTAINED ON THIS FORM IS CORRECT AND I REALIZE THAT ANY FALSIFICATION MAY RESULT IN THE IMMEDIATE CANCELLATION OF ANY RESULTING AGREEMENT.

Signature ______ Date ______

For consideration on an authorized FANMISER manuf. rep., please complete and return this form to:

FANMISER CORP.
1053 E. Fifth Ave.
Columbus, OH 43201-3099

In order for FANMISER to process this application, it must be accompanied by a cover letter and a business card.

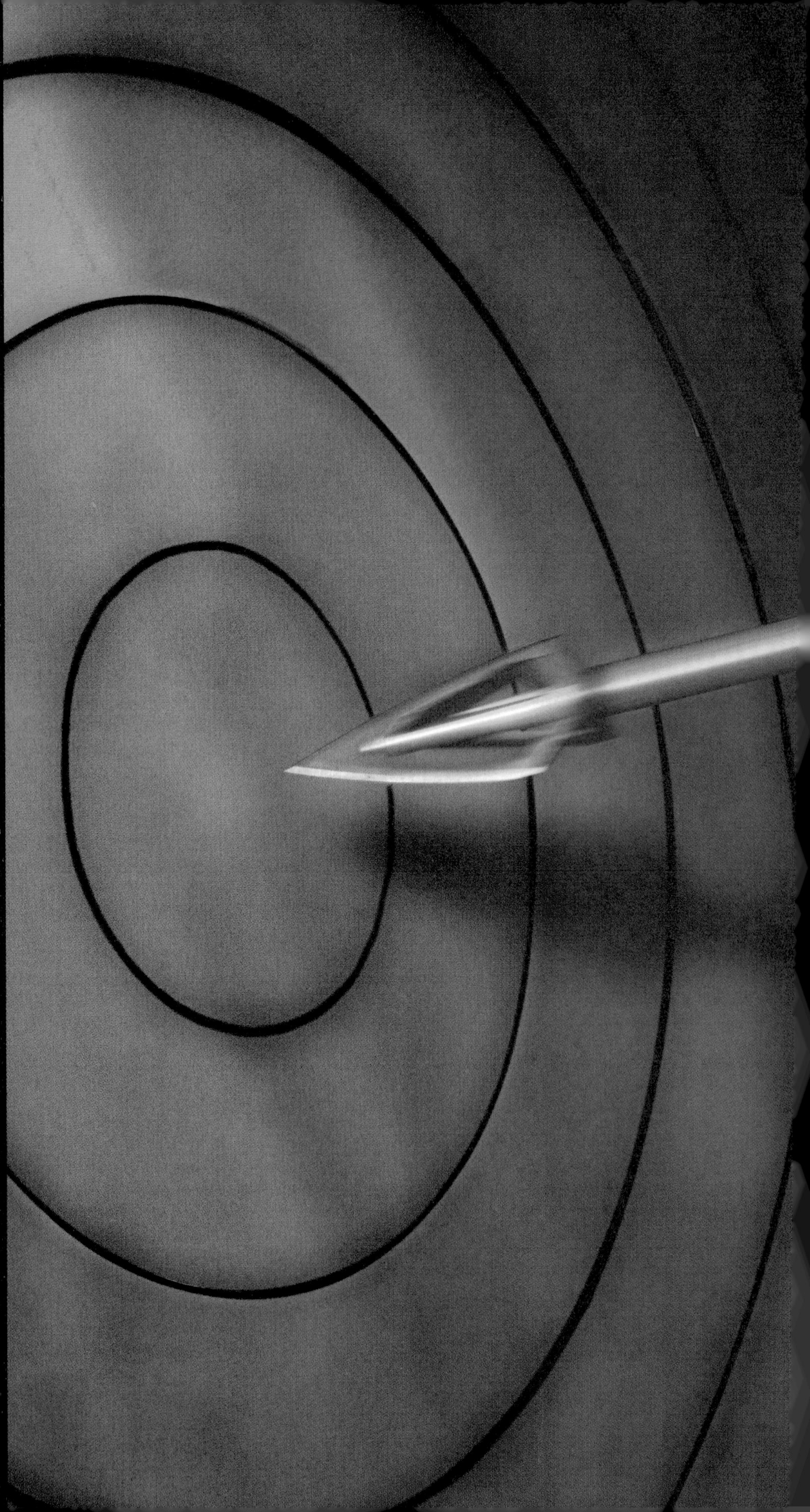

Many small thing has been made large by the right kind of advertising.

Mark Twain

If you think advertising doesn't pay—we understand there are 25 mountains in Colorado higher than Pikes Peak. Can you name one?

Anonymous

CHAPTER FOURTEEN

Integrated Marketing Communications

It seems everyone knows about the Energizer Bunny who just keeps going and going.[1] The advertising campaign for Eveready Battery Company began in 1989 and is one of the most successful campaigns in recent years. The commercials used parody, with the Energizer bunny marching across the screen, interrupting spoofs of clichéd pitches for products such as flavored instant coffee, wines, deodorant soap, and nasal spray. Most recently, the bunny has been featured in commercials with a slightly modified theme, such as one featuring the Darth Vader character from the movie *Star Wars,* who is intent on terminating the bunny. Another spot features Boris and Natasha from the Bullwinkle cartoon trying to capture the pink bunny. Over the past several years, the bunny has been featured in more than twenty-five spots, entertaining consumers and helping to deliver the key advertising message: Energizer batteries are long lasting and, like the bunny, "keep going and going."

The Energizer bunny commercials have been among the most popular on television and have received numerous creative awards. More important for Eveready, the bunny campaign helped stop Energizer's decline in market share and significantly increased sales. However, the campaign is more than just great advertising.

Eveready has expanded the entire concept into a very effective *integrated marketing communications (IMC)* program. An IMC program requires the advertiser to communicate synergistically through a variety of media vehicles. Eveready has used the popularity of the bunny campaign to generate support from retailers in the form of shelf space, promotional displays, and other merchandising activities. Consumer promotions include in-store displays, premium offers (such as stuffed pink bunnies), and several sweepstakes. Pictures of the bunny appear on Energizer packages to ensure brand identification and to extend the campaign's impact to the point of purchase. Eveready also extended the integrated approach to tie-ins with sports marketing and sponsorships. For example, the Energizer bunny threw out the first pitch of the 1992 season at the home opener for all twenty-four major-league baseball clubs. As part of the deal, Energizer sponsored the season-long radio broadcasts for all of the clubs. The popularity of the advertising campaign has led to enormous publicity that has contributed to awareness of the Energizer brand name and helped make the bunny a pop-culture icon.

In order to keep the campaign fresh and fun and to guard against wearout, Eveready has its advertising agency, Chiat/Day, continuously develop new creative executions for the bunny commercials. Commercials that began airing in the fall of 1993 feature the evil Supervolt Battery Co. employing the wicked witch from the *Wizard of Oz* and King Kong to snare its nemesis, the Energizer bunny. For several years consumers are likely to see many different foes, powered by Supervolt batteries (which, of course, die just prior to zapping the bunny), try in vain to stop the bunny. The ads, along with Eveready's successful integrated marketing communications program, will probably keep Energizer sales going and going and going. ■

Communication management is the process of developing and supervising strategies that keep targeted consumers informed about a product's competitive superiority. Promotion emphasizes the *communication* of benefits already contained in the product, including images that symbolize the product's quality. Thus, while product management might decide to package toothpaste in a pump for convenient dispensing,

[1] The sources for this story are George E. Belch and Michael A. Belch, *Introduction to Advertising and Promotion: An Integrated Marketing Communications Perspective,* 3rd ed. (Chicago: Irwin, 1995); Julie Liesse, "How Bunny Charged Eveready," *Advertising Age,* April 4, 1991, 20, 55; "Opening Day and the Bunny Goes Up to Bat," *Advertising Age,* April 6, 1992, 1, 37; and "Charged-Up Foes for Bunny," *Advertising Age,* October 11, 1993, 3.

communication management has the responsibility of making consumers aware of this benefit and persuading them to buy the target brand. Marketers not only communicate product positioning through advertising but also through their product, price, and distribution decisions. For example, as described in Chapter 11, selling a product at a prestigious store communicates the product's prestige value to the target market. This chapter separates a marketer's decisions about product, price, and distribution from the strategies and programs adopted to communicate those decisions to the market. The discussion will be confined to what a marketer's communication options are and how they should be managed profitably.

In the North American market, consumers are exposed to hundreds of commercial messages every day. These messages may come from commercials we hear on the radio as we drive to and from work, billboards we see along the way, a coupon given out by a nearby cafe owner as we enter the office building, or the telemarketer who calls us in the evening to see if we are interested in buying a water purifier system. The tools and techniques used to achieve an organization's communication objectives are called the *promotion mix*. Promotion has been defined as "the coordination of all seller-initiated efforts to set up channels of information and persuasion to sell goods and services or promote an idea."[2] Most of an organization's communications with the marketplace occur through a carefully planned and controlled promotional program. The basic elements of the promotion mix include advertising, point of purchase, personal selling, public relations/publicity, and direct marketing. Each of these promotion-mix variables is discussed here.

Advertising is the dominant method marketers use to reach consumers. It is defined as "paid nonpersonal communication from an identified sponsor using mass media to persuade or influence an audience."[3] Through advertising, marketers attempt to make consumers aware of their product's positioning (unique benefits or low price) in the hope that this information will lead the consumers to choose their product.

Point of Purchase refers to materials beyond the usual media vehicles used to promote products in supermarkets and other types of stores, such as displays, banners, and shelf signs. A wide variety of options are now available to organizations, including video displays on shopping carts, kiosks that provide recipes and coupons at the ends of counters and at cash registers, LED (light-emitting diode) boards, and ads that broadcast over in-store screens.

Personal selling, discussed in Chapter 13, is used to promote a product that is complicated and that demands a substantial information exchange between customers and sellers. Some companies (such as Avon or Tupperware) use this form of communication even for relatively simple products, because they wish to develop a long-term, personal relationship with the customer.

Public Relations is defined as "the management function which evaluates public attitudes, identifies the policies and procedures of an individual or organization with the public interest, and executes a program of action to earn public understanding and acceptance."[4] Public relations uses publicity and a variety of other techniques, such as newsletters, community activities, and sponsorships to manage the organization's

---

[2] George E. Belch and Michael A. Belch, *Introduction to Advertising and Promotion: An Integrated Marketing Communications Perspective*, 3rd ed. (Chicago: Irwin, 1995).

[3] William Wells, John Burnett, and Sandra Moriarty, *Advertising Principles and Practice*, 3rd ed. (Englewood Cliffs, NJ: Prentice-Hall, 1995).

[4] George E. Belch and Michael A. Belch, *Introduction to Advertising and Promotion: An Integrated Marketing Communications Perspective*, 3rd ed. (Chicago: Irwin, 1995).

image. Publicity refers to nonpersonal communications regarding an organization, product, service, or idea that is not directly paid for under identified sponsorship. It is usually disseminated through the news media in the form of a news story, editorial, or press release about an organization or its products. Although publicity cannot be purchased, it may be managed carefully to the advantage of a marketer. Publicity is not always under the organization's control and is sometimes quite negative.

Direct Marketing involves direct communication between organizations and target customers to elicit a response or transaction. Direct mail and mail-order catalogs are only a small component of direct marketing, which also includes direct selling, telemarketing, and direct-response ads through direct mail, print, and broadcast (e.g., infomercials) media.

Integrated Marketing Communications (IMC)

In the past, many organizations viewed the elements of the promotion mix as separate, distinct units, each with its own strategies and tactics to influence the target consumer. Thus, the advertising function was managed separately from the sales promotion, public relations, and direct-marketing functions. Each area had its own budgets, view of the market, and goals and objectives. With the increasing sophistication of the information available on consumers and the fragmentation of media options available to marketers, companies began to realize that the wide range of communication choices must be coordinated to communicate effectively and present a consistent image to target markets (see Figure 14.1). The biggest trend in communications management in the 1990s is the continued growth in *integrated marketing communications (IMC)*, which, as noted in the introduction, involves coordinating the various promotion mix elements with other marketing activities to communicate *synergistically* with a firm's customers.[5] The American Association of Advertising Agencies defines integrated marketing communications as

> a concept of marketing communications planning that recognizes the added value of a comprehensive plan that evaluates the strategic role of a variety of communication disciplines—for example, general advertising, direct response, sales promotion, and public relations—and combines these disciplines to provide clarity, consistency, and maximum communications impact.[6]

IMC calls for companies to take a broad perspective of the communications function. It requires firms to develop a total marketing communication strategy that recognizes how all of their marketing activities communicate with their customers. Consumers' perceptions of a company and its various brands are a synthesis of the complete package of messages they receive (such as media advertisements, price, direct-marketing efforts, packaging, publicity, sales promotion, and the type of store in which a product is sold). Advocates of the IMC approach argue that it is one of the easiest ways a company can maximize the return on its investment in marketing and

[5] Adrienne Ward Fawcett, "Integrated Marketing—Marketers Convinced: Its Time Has Arrived," *Advertising Age*, November 6, 1993, S1–2.

[6] Don E. Schultz, "Integrated Marketing Communications: Maybe Definition Is in the Point of View," *Marketing News*, January 18, 1993, 17.

promotion.[7] Although it is simply putting snyergy into practice, the IMC revolution is affecting everyone involved in the marketing and promotional processes. Companies are realizing they must change the ways they market their products and services. For example, in mature markets, companies are selling to customers who are increasingly price sensitive and less likely to respond to mass-media advertising. Thus, companies such as Nestlé, IBM, Sprint, Microsoft, and Nike, have adopted an IMC approach to determine new ways to communicate with price-sensitive customers.[8]

Figure 14.1a **Kodak's Web Site**

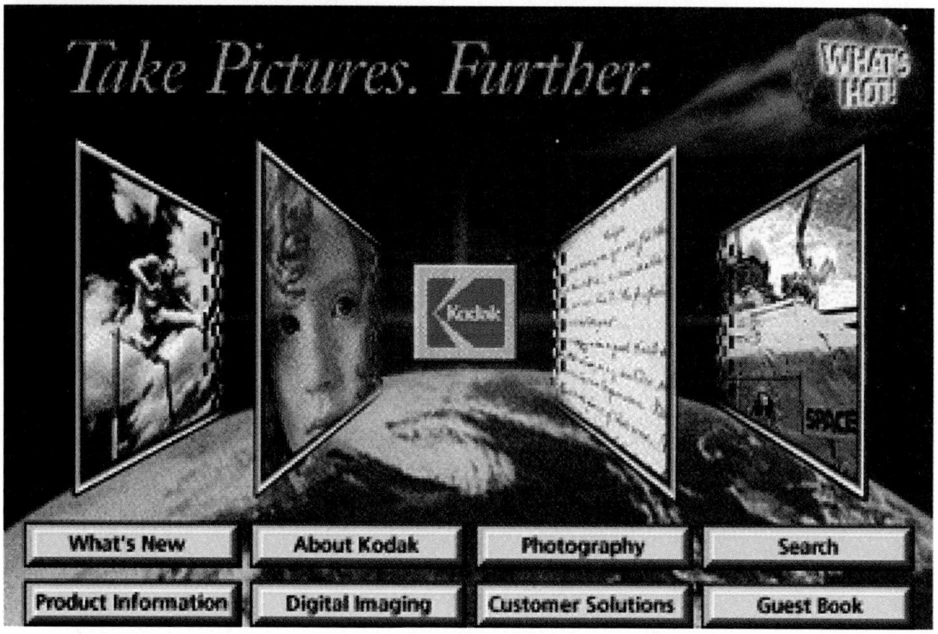

Much hype has been created about the use of the World Wide Web (www.) to market products and services. In reality, it is likely the companies that do the best job of integrating their traditional advertising campaigns with their Web "home page" will pioneer the effective use of Web marketing. Kodak is likely to be on the forefront of such experimentation, for, as the magazine advertisement indicates, its digital science products are positioned and designed to help small businesses create their home page on the Internet. It is therefore essential that Kodak's own home page demonstrates the effectiveness of integrating it with other communication efforts! How a prospective customer is directed by an "intelligent" home page to the information he or she wants, thus reducing the information overload and making the interaction fast and enjoyable, will be a determinant competitive advantage. "Dumb" home pages that present hundreds of pages of instructions and options will, more than anything else, simply communicate a lack of customer-service orientation, that is, the "dumbness" of the company.

(continued)

[7] Anthony J. Tortorici, "Maximizing Marketing Communications through Horizontal and Vertical Orchestration," *Public Relations Quarterly* 36, no. 1 (1991): 20–22.
[8] Thomas R. Duncan and Stephan E. Everett, "Client Perception of Integrated Marketing Communications," *Journal of Advertising Research* (May/June 1993): 30–39.

Figure 14.1b **Integrating Advertising with Web Marketing**

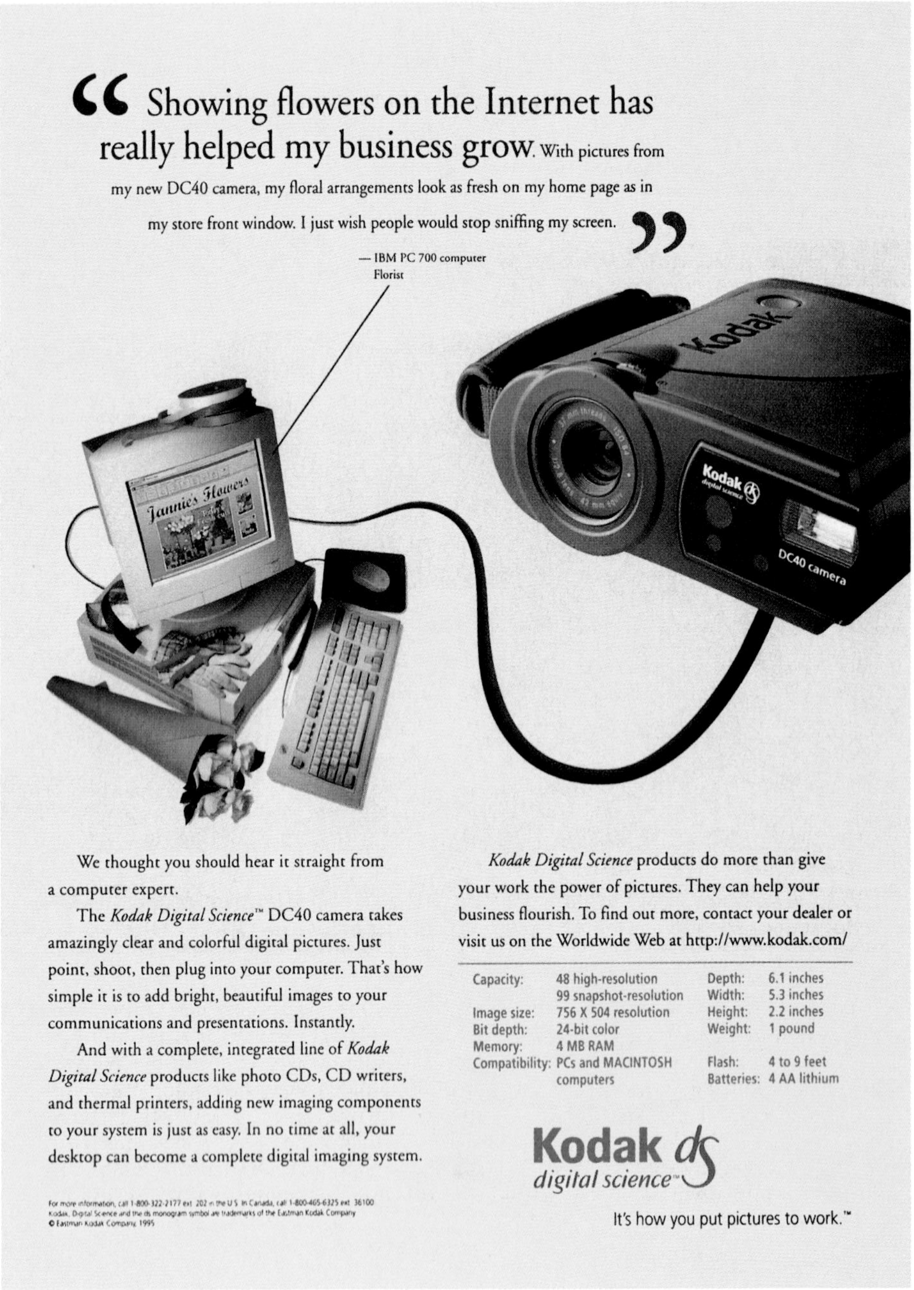
"Showing flowers on the Internet has really helped my business grow. With pictures from my new DC40 camera, my floral arrangements look as fresh on my home page as in my store front window. I just wish people would stop sniffing my screen."
— IBM PC 700 computer
Florist
Jannie's Flowers
Kodak
Kodak digital science
DC40 camera
We thought you should hear it straight from a computer expert.
The Kodak Digital Science™ DC40 camera takes amazingly clear and colorful digital pictures. Just point, shoot, then plug into your computer. That's how simple it is to add bright, beautiful images to your communications and presentations. Instantly.
And with a complete, integrated line of Kodak Digital Science products like photo CDs, CD writers, and thermal printers, adding new imaging components to your system is just as easy. In no time at all, your desktop can become a complete digital imaging system.
Kodak Digital Science products do more than give your work the power of pictures. They can help your business flourish. To find out more, contact your dealer or visit us on the Worldwide Web at http://www.kodak.com/
Capacity: 48 high-resolution, 99 snapshot-resolution
Image size: 756 X 504 resolution
Bit depth: 24-bit color
Memory: 4 MB RAM
Compatibility: PCs and MACINTOSH computers
Depth: 6.1 inches
Width: 5.3 inches
Height: 2.2 inches
Weight: 1 pound
Flash: 4 to 9 feet
Batteries: 4 AA lithium
Kodak digital science™
It's how you put pictures to work.™
For more information, call 1-800-322-2177 ext. 202 in the U.S. In Canada, call 1-800-465-6325 ext. 36100
Kodak, Digital Science and the ds monogram symbol are trademarks of the Eastman Kodak Company
© Eastman Kodak Company, 1995

Figure 14.2 Chapter Organization

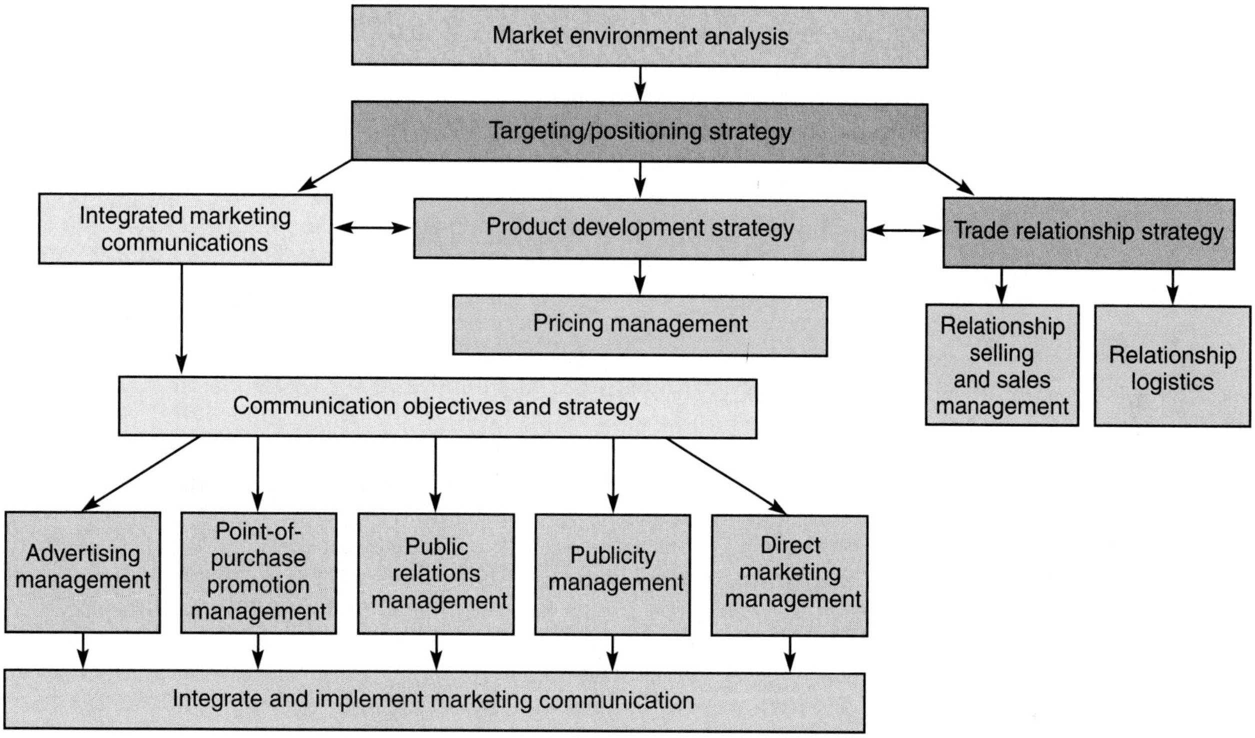

The goal of integrated marketing communication is to use all of the different ways of communicating with the target market to describe and promote the positioning of the product or service. This chapter discusses advertising, point-of-purchase (POP) promotion, public relations, publicity, and direct marketing. Each of these activities has to be integrated together in a way that produces synergy: The whole effect of the communication campaign is more than the sum of its parts. Note that integrated marketing communications, as a whole, has to be also integrated with the product development strategy and trade relationship strategy.

The IMC Planning Process

Planning plays a fundamental role in the creation and execution of an effective IMC program. IMC campaign planning begins with the development of the communication objectives and strategy. This strategy should be based on the cross-functional team's overall marketing strategy and plan. A model of the IMC planning process is shown in Figure 14.2.[9] Planners also must decide the role and function of each of the elements of the promotional mix, develop strategies for each element, and implement the plan. Prior to developing the communication objectives, planners must complete several tasks.

[9] The discussion of integrated marketing communication and the model of the IMC planning process are adapted from George E. Belch and Michael A. Belch, *Introduction to Advertising and Promotion: An Integrated Marketing Communications Perspective*, 3rd ed. (Chicago: Irwin, 1995).

First, the marketing plan must be reviewed. It is important to understand the company (or the brand) in terms of its past, present (positions in the market), and future (goals and how it plans to achieve them). Next, the planners must review the parts of the environment report that focus on the factors that influence or are relevant to promotional strategy. This promotion analysis includes an internal and an external component. The internal analysis examines the capabilities of the firm itself and its ability to develop and implement a successful promotional program, the organization of the promotional function, and the success or failure of past efforts. This analysis also includes the classic "make or buy" decision regarding promotion mix elements and the choice of outside suppliers (such as advertising agencies, public relations firms, or direct marketing experts). A final goal of the internal analysis is to examine the strengths and weaknesses of the brand from an image perspective and from a true product performance perspective. The information gleaned from both of these analyses will be crucial to the creative personnel who must develop the advertising message for the brand.

The external analysis of the environment report focuses on the target market (demographic and psychographic analysis) and the competition. When evaluating competitors, attention is given to the entire communication program. Focus is on the firm's primary competitors: their specific strengths and weaknesses, segmentation, targeting and positioning strategies, and promotional strategies. The size and allocation of their promotional budgets, their media strategies, and the messages they are sending to the marketplace should all be considered.

Once the marketing plan has been reviewed and the promotion analysis completed, the promotion planner can move on to the analysis of the communication process and the setting of communication objectives. The planner must consider the process consumers will go through in responding to messages and the decisions consumers will make at each stage. The differences between low-involvement and high-involvement consumer segments must be determined because these differences will influence promotional strategy (see Chapter 5). Specific issues regarding these processes are discussed in Chapter 15. After the communication objectives have been developed, the promotional budget is determined (see Chapter 18 on budgeting).

Developing the IMC program is the most involved and detailed step in the promotion planning process. Each promotion-mix element has strengths and weaknesses as well as its own objectives, and tactics. Decisions have to be made regarding the role and importance of each element and its coordination with every other element in the mix. Once the plan is implemented, procedures must be developed for evaluating the performance of each element and the entire IMC plan and making any necessary adjustments based on results. This relates to the final stage of the process, which includes monitoring, evaluating and controlling the promotion program. This stage is also referred to as the learning stage of the promotional planning process and provides managers with continual feedback concerning the effectiveness of the plan, which in turn can be used as input into the planning process.

Now that the IMC planning process has been reviewed, the remainder of the chapter focuses on the strengths and weaknesses of several communication tools in an IMC campaign: advertising, point of purchase, public relations/publicity, and direct marketing. Sales promotion (discussed in Chapter 16) and personal selling (discussed in Chapter 13) are not covered here, though it is important to remember that tactics and processes relating to these communication techniques must be integrated with the other promotion mix elements for an IMC program to succeed.

Advertising

Advertising is so pervasive in American culture that most consumers passively accept it in all its myriad forms. The competition among advertisers to get attention is far from passive. Television and radio stations, magazines, and newspapers fiercely compete to serve as an advertiser's communication channel. The reason the broadcast media focuses on ratings and the print media focuses on circulation is because their advertising rates are dependent on the number and types of consumers who patronize their product. In 1995, total advertising expenditures in the United States was projected to be $234.5 billion.[10] The cost of a thirty-second television commercial on Super Bowl XXX in 1996 reached an all-time high of $1.2 million. Thus the advertising business is at times very big business.

From 1950 to 1980, U.S. companies increased their advertising to an extent never seen before in any economy. The Depression and World War II had dramatically reduced consumer spending, and a great deal of pent-up demand existed. Consumers cashed in their war-bond savings and increased their consumption of durable goods, such as new cars and appliances. Along with this new age of consumer affluence came the population increase now known as the baby boom. Sellers responded accordingly, and the growth in new magazines, radio, and, most important, television encouraged and catered to the soaring demand. No other culture in history had ever been exposed to so many new products or so much advertising.

In the 1960s, known as the golden age of advertising, new persuasion theories and tactics were developed by legendary advertising executives such as Rosser Reeves, David Ogilvy, and Bill Bernbach. Some myths about advertising's effectiveness were also created, such as the power of subliminal advertising. However, in the 1980s, attitudes toward advertising started to change. The major problem with advertising was not that it was dangerously and insidiously persuasive. The problem was that it too often had little to say and became lost in the clutter of other advertisements. Recognizing this, marketers shifted spending from brand- and corporate-image advertising to short-term sales promotions. But this too often led to price wars, higher costs, and lower profits.

A more productive solution to the problems with general, mass media advertising has been the evolution of advertising into IMC. IMC has had a significant impact on the advertising industry and traditional advertising agencies. Many agencies have responded to the call for synergy among communication tools by acquiring public-relations, sales-promotion, and direct-marketing companies and touting themselves as IMC agencies that offer one-stop shopping for all their clients' communication needs. Some agencies have struggled with this option because of the costs involved and lack of corporate competencies in these areas. However, most agencies recognize that their future success depends on their ability to understand all the communication options and help their clients design and implement integrated marketing communication programs. The key relationship in IMC planning occurs between the advertiser (or client) and the advertising agency and other promotion suppliers. The next sections examine these participants and the interaction between them.

---

[10] R. Craig Endicott, "Direct Ads Spur 12 Percent of Consumer Sales," *Advertising Age*, October 9, 1995, 34.

Table 14.1 **Leading National Advertisers**

			TOTAL U.S. AD SPENDING (MILLIONS)		
RANK	COMPANY	HEADQUARTERS	1994	1993	% CHANGE
1.	Proctor and Gamble Co.	Cincinnati	$2,689.8	$2,391.4	12.5%
2.	Philip Morris Co.	New York	2,413.3	1,882.1	28.2
3.	General Motors Corp.	Detroit	1,929.4	1,539.7	25.3
4.	Ford Motor Company	Dearborn, MI	1,186.0	1,015.5	16.8
5.	Sears, Roebuck & Co.	Chicago	1,134.1	1,013.3	11.9
6.	AT&T Corp.	New York	1,102.7	812.1	35.8
7.	PepsiCo	Purchase, NY	1,097.8	1,038.8	5.7
8.	Chrysler Corp.	Highland Park, MI	971.6	761.6	27.6
9.	Walt Disney Co.	Burbank, CA	934.8	777.3	20.3
10.	Johnson & Johnson	New Brunswick, NJ	933.7	835.0	11.8
11.	Nestlé SA	Vevey, Switzerland	894.2	793.8	12.6
12.	Time Warner	New York	860.0	697.0	23.4
13.	Warner-Lambert Co.	Morris Plains, NJ	831.2	900.1	–7.7
14.	Toyota Motor Corp.	Toyota City, Japan	766.1	690.4	11.0
15.	Grand Metropolitan	London	764.3	656.1	16.5
16.	McDonald's Corp.	Oak Brook, IL	763.7	736.5	3.7
17.	Kellogg Co.	Battle Creek, MI	732.9	621.6	17.9
18.	Unilever NV	London/Rotterdam	654.7	731.8	–10.5
19.	J.C. Penney Co.	Dallas	621.7	585.2	6.2
20.	Federated Department Stores	Cincinnati	614.0	646.0	–5.0

SOURCE: *Advertising Age*, September 27, 1995, 16.

Advertisers

The advertisers, or clients, are the key participants in the promotion planning process for obvious reasons. They have the products, services, or causes to be marketed, and they provide the funds that pay for advertising and promotion. The major responsibility for developing the marketing program and the final decisions relating to the advertising and promotion program are the advertiser's (though agencies are playing a greater role in this process). It is difficult to imagine the amount of money spent by client companies each year on advertising. Each of the top seven advertisers in 1994 spent more than $1 billion in the United States alone (see Table 14.1).

Although nearly every organization uses some form of marketing communications, there is no right way to organize the function. The way a firm organizes these activities depends on several factors, such as the size of the company, the number of products it markets, the role of advertising and promotion in the marketing mix, the budget, and the organization of the marketing function within the firm. Direct responsibility for administering the advertising and promotion program always falls to someone within the firm. Organizations have three options for promotion management: the centralized system, the decentralized system, and an in-house agency. In a *centralized system*, the firm has an advertising department headed by an advertising or communications manager operating under a marketing director. The advertising manager is responsible for all promotion activities except sales. The most common example of the centralized approach has the advertising manager controlling the entire promotions operation, including budgeting, coordinating the creation and production of the advertisements, planning media schedules, and monitoring and administering the sales promotion programs for all the company's products or services.

Although the centralized system was the standard operating system for many years, as companies grew, problems with coordination and responsibility arose. Marketing decisions were made by several functional managers and had to be coordinated by someone in the marketing department. No single department had specific responsibility for individual products or brands. These problems led to the development of the decentralized system of promotion organization. The *decentralized system* is referred to as the *product* or *brand manager organization*, and it is the most common organization in use today. In this system, the product manager and cross-functional team are responsible for planning, implementing, and controlling the marketing program for a product, product line, or brand. The product manager is responsible for sales projections and profit performance and must develop and coordinate the budget. Companies with this form of organization generally support product managers with a number of additional marketing services, including sales, marketing research, and advertising departments. In a product management system, the responsibilities and functions associated with advertising and promotions are supervised by the product manager, who becomes the liaison with the outside service agencies as they develop the promotional program. Companies that have moved to decentralized, cross-functional-team management make the product manager a key member of the team, responsible for implementing the integrated marketing communication program.

The third option available to firms for organizing the promotion process involves setting up their own agency internally. Companies may do this in an effort to reduce costs and maintain greater control over agency activities. An *in-house agency* is an advertising agency that is set up, owned, and operated by the advertiser. Some in-house agencies are simple advertising departments while others are given a separate identity and control the entire advertising budget. Large advertisers that use in-house agencies include Calvin Klein, Radio Shack, and Benetton.

Advertising Agencies

Many corporations utilize advertising agencies to assist them in developing, preparing, and executing their communication programs. Although a firm might choose to keep the advertising function in-house, most companies outsource this function. An ad agency is a service supplier made up of highly skilled individuals who are specialists in their chosen fields. More than seven thousand agencies are listed in the *Standard Directory of Advertising Agencies;* however, the majority of these companies are individually owned, small businesses employing fewer than five people. Thirty-seven agencies, the number with gross income above \$50 million (about \$350 million in billings) account for \$4.89 billion or 52 percent of the top five hundred's total gross income. Table 14.2 lists the top twenty agencies, ranked by their U.S. gross income. The table shows that the agency business is also geographically concentrated in New York City (on Madison Avenue).

Many companies work with what is known as a full-service agency, which offers its clients a wide range of marketing communications and other services, including planning, creating, and producing the advertising; performing research; and planning/buying media space and time. A full-service agency also may offer additional services

Table 14.2 **Leading U.S. Advertising Agencies**

			GROSS INCOME		BILLINGS
RANK	AGENCY	HEADQUARTERS	1994	% CHANGE	1994
1.	Leo Burnett Co.	Chicago	$322.1	5.7%	$2,226.3
2.	J. Walter Thompson Co.	New York	317.4	6.6	2,218.8
3.	Grey Advertising	New York	302.2	6.9	2,015.7
4.	McCann-Erickson Worldwide	New York	261.4	3.3	1,743.9
5.	BBDO Worldwide	New York	245.9	7.1	2,423.2
6.	Saatchi & Saatchi Advertising	New York	241.5	6.3	1,932.2
7.	True North Communications (FCB)	Chicago	236.8	8.4	2,589.2
8.	DDB Needham Worldwide	New York	228.2	1.6	1,919.1
9.	D'Arcy Masius Benton & Bowles	New York	219.3	11.3	2,247.2
10.	Young & Rubicam	New York	184.7	7.1	1,885.6
11.	Ogilvy & Mather Worldwide	New York	173.7	6.5	1,776.2
12.	Bozell Worldwide	New York	164.5	32.8	1,315.0
13.	Bates Worldwide	New York	135.4	6.4	1,083.3
14.	TMP Worldwide	New York	117.7	37.3	784.8
15.	Ammirati & Puris/Lintas	New York	112.9	−9.0	753.3
16.	Chiat/Day	Venice, CA	106.6	4.0	820.0
17.	Campbell Mithun Esty	Minneapolis, MN	106.3	2.4	850.6
18.	Lintas Campbell-Ewald	Warren, MI	99.4	10.9	663.0
19.	DIMAC Direct	Bridgeton, MO	99.3	56.4	271.4
20.	N W Ayer & Partners	New York	98.8	15.2	861.2

Note: Dollars are in millions and reflect returns from the U.S. only.

SOURCE: *Advertising Age*, April 10, 1995, S-8.

tied to the IMC perspective. Generally, the agency consists of the following departments that perform the various functions:

- *Account Service* Account service, or account management, is the link between the client firm and the agency. The account executive acts as the liaison by understanding the client's goals and strategies and communicating them to the agency's personnel. He or she coordinates the agency efforts in planning, creating, and producing the campaign. The account executive also presents agency recommendations and obtains client approval on each step of campaign planning.
- *Creative Department* The creative department is responsible for the creation and production of the campaign. The department is composed of teams of art directors and copywriters. The art directors prepare layouts, which are drawings that specify visuals from which the final artwork will be produced. Copywriters are responsible for communicating the message; they create the headlines, subheads, and body copy (the words constituting the message). Art directors and copywriters generally work under the supervision of a creative director, who oversees all advertising produced by the agency. Another function of the creative department is the production group. Most agencies outsource the actual production; however, agency producers are responsible for hiring directors/photographers, casting, and completing the project.

- *Media Department* The media group is split into two key functions: planning and buying. The planning group analyzes and selects the best options to deliver the client's message to the target market. Media specialists must know the audience-reach levels of media vehicles, their rates, and how well they match the client's target market. Media planners review information on demographics, psychographics, magazine and newspaper readership, radio listenership, and TV viewing patterns to develop an effective media plan. The media buying department takes the approved media plan and purchases the actual time and space.
- *Research Department* Most full-service agencies maintain a research department whose function is to gather, analyze, and interpret information that will be useful in developing and executing advertising plans and programs. Research as a function has declined in recent years, because clients have moved toward utilizing their own internal departments to conduct advertising research.
- *Other Departments* Agencies also might have additional specialty departments, such as direct marketing, public relations, sales promotions, and so forth. Of course, like any other business, they also have finance, accounting, personnel, and office management departments to coordinate agency billing.

Choosing an Advertising Agency

Advertising agencies are responsible for the majority of decisions regarding their client's advertising strategy and tactics. Choosing an advertising agency with a good team is central to the success of the campaign. Agencies that are creative and energetic and that implement projects even faster than deadlines constitute a very important and too rarely acknowledged competitive advantage. Choosing an advertising agency with a weak management team can be disastrous to a company's marketing efforts and competitive rationality.

Clients select advertising agencies based on what is termed the "new-business pitch." Agencies gain access to potential clients through referrals from current clients and solicitation of new clients. Often, clients will put their accounts up for review. This means the client is actively considering new agency options. As with any service provider, competition brings out the best in the agency. The driving force is not just the profit motive. Pride and rivalry are also at stake when agencies compete for accounts. The standard new-business pitch gives the agency an opportunity to present information about itself, including its experience, personnel, capabilities, and operating philosophies, as well as its previous work. Part of the presentation may include a "spec" creative presentation, in which the agency evaluates the client's marketing environment and proposes a tentative communications campaign. These presentations require a significant amount of time, effort, and expense, without a guarantee of gaining the business. Nevertheless, most agencies do participate in this type of selection process. The client may choose an agency based on the new presentation or may choose to have additional meetings and presentations before selecting an agency. The agency chosen to handle the client's account is termed the "agency of record."

Campaign Development

Now that we have reviewed the departments that exist within an advertising agency and how one is selected by a client, this section discusses how the advertising campaign is developed (strategy stage), executed (implementation stage), and evaluated (learning stage). The campaign is developed through the interaction between the client (advertiser) and the advertising agency. Figure 14.3 depicts each of the stages.

Strategy Stage

Advertising campaigns begin with the development of an advertising strategy. The advertising strategy document is based on the client's overall

Figure 14.3 Campaign Development

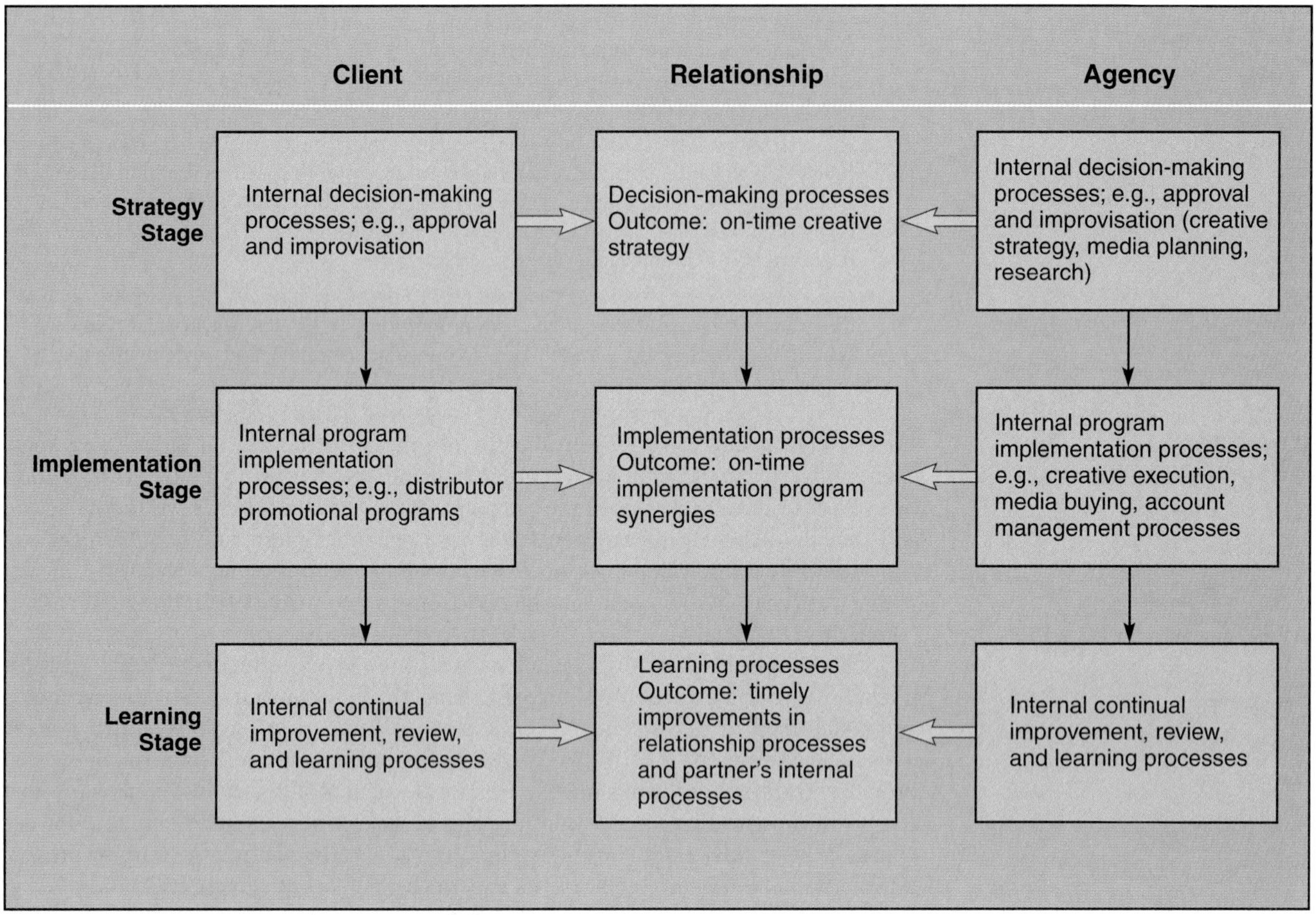

An IMC campaign requires the development of a close working relationship between an advertising agency and its client. It starts with coordinating the strategic decision making through relationship processes that produce a creative strategy. This strategy may have to be revised and improvised in response to market dynamics. Implementation requires relationship processes that produce program synergies and programs that are executed on time. Finally, for the working relationship to grow more productive, not just the campaign but also the working relationships and processes that produced the campaign need to be reviewed. When the campaign requires the agency to orchestrate several communication programs and to ensure they synchronize and synergize with the client's internal action programs, the agency has much to learn and often has a great deal of room for future improvement of the working relationship. Personal relationships, particularly between the brand manager and account manager at the implementation stage, hold together and improve the client-agency relationship.

product-positioning strategy and includes several sections. Clients and agencies work closely together in the development and approval of the entire document. Although the account management department is most often central to the process, several other agency departments are consulted and involved. One of the advertising strategy documents is the "creative brief" or "creative strategy." This document includes the campaign objectives, target market, product positioning, message strategy, executional factors, and so forth. It is designed to guide creative development and is developed with input from the creative department. The other major section of the advertising strategy document relates to the media planning and buying function. This document includes the campaign objectives from a media perspective, target market, negotiation factors, and so on. It is designed to guide both the planners and buyers in reaching the campaign objectives. This section is developed based on input from the media department. A final section relates to the research function of the agency. Many advertising strategy documents include guidelines about testing the campaign development at various stages of completion, from the initial test of the creative concepts to storyboard testing to final-version theater tests (see Chapter 19). This section of the strategy document is developed with input from the client and agency's research department. The implementation process does not begin until both the client and the agency sign the final advertising strategy document.

Implementation Stage Within the agency, the implementation stage begins with the dissemination of the advertising strategy document to the agency departments involved in execution. A timetable for completion of tasks is developed and approved. The creative department begins concept development, which proceeds to storyboard development (or print layouts for magazines), to animatic (or photomatic) representations of the spot (ad), and finally to production. Concurrently, the media planning group begins analyzing programming to determine which purchases would deliver the appropriate levels of target audiences or readers most efficiently and within budget. Once the plan is final and approved both internally and by the client, the buying department takes over, and the negotiations for commercial spots on various shows or magazines begins. The research department is involved with the creative department in testing the various stages of creative work. The account management department is overseeing the other departments' functions and coordinating client approval processes to maintain both the implementation schedule and budget.

Within the client organization, the implementation stage involves working closely with the agency to approve the various stages of creative and media planning development. In addition, the client personnel and cross-functional team are heavily involved in implementing programs related to the overall marketing strategy (beyond the advertising strategy), which may include specialized consumer or trade promotions, price deals, public relations efforts, distribution and logistics planning, and so forth. As a result, while the agency is focused on the implementation of the client's advertising program, the client may be focused on implementing many other related marketing programs.

Learning Stage The learning stage of the advertising agency–client relationship has most often been based on analyzing the outcomes of campaign execution, such as recall and recognition tests for creative executions and actual (delivered) target audiences from a media buy. Through the process of analyzing results, the success or failure of the campaign is determined. From the client's perspective, analysis of the success or failure of internal programs, such as direct-mail response rate, cooperative advertising results, distributor price cuts, and retailer specials, also provide insight into the campaign's success. This evaluation process provides input to both the client and agency that is used for future campaign planning and improving integrated marketing communication processes.[11]

[11] Diana L. Haytko, "Advertising Agency Interpersonal, Process, and Outcome Performance Management of Client Relationships," working paper, University of Wisconsin, Madison, 1996.

The Advantages and Disadvantages of Advertising

The use of advertising in a firm's promotional mix has several advantages. Because advertising is paid for by the company, it can *control* what it says, when it's said, and, to some extent, to whom the message is sent. Advertising also can be cost effective for reaching large audiences. It can be used to portray images and symbolic appeals for products and services, something difficult for companies selling products not easily differentiated from competitors. For example, many consumers cannot differentiate one brand of soda or beer from another on the basis of taste. Thus, the image or psychological associations consumers have of the brand become an important part of their purchase decisions.

Another advantage of advertising is its value in creating and maintaining *brand equity* (see Chapter 10). This equity allows a brand to capture higher sales, market share, and margins than it could without the name and also provides the company or brand with a competitive advantage.[12] Quite often, the strong equity position a company and its brand enjoys is established and reinforced through advertising that focuses on the image, product attributes, service, or other features. For example, companies such as McDonald's, Nike, and Maytag, as well as brands like Jello, Ivory Soap, Wheaties, and Campbell's Soup, enjoy strong brand equity that has been established and maintained, at least in part, through advertising.

Although advertising can be quite effective, it also has a number of disadvantages. The costs of producing and placing advertising can be very high. Consider that each thirty-second spot on the 1996 Super Bowl cost more than $1 million dollars, not including production (some companies spent up to $4 million on celebrity talent and completion). Measuring the results of advertising is also very difficult. Lack of direct feedback makes it nearly impossible for the advertiser to determine how well the message was received and whether it was effective.

Other problems with advertising include its credibility and the ease with which it can be ignored (see Chapter 15). In addition, the advertising industry and the ads themselves are often viewed with cynicism and skepticism by consumers, many of whom perceive them as biased and focused on persuasion. As such, most consumers say they ignore most advertising. With so many messages competing for attention every day, it is relatively easy for consumers to selectively process only those messages of personal interest. The high level of advertising message "clutter" is a major problem in advertising. The sheer number of ads make it difficult for any one message to be noticed and attended to by consumers. In addition, new technologies exist that enable consumers to block out commercials completely. For example, a new videocassette recorder automatically shuts down when it detects a commercial break.

Point of Purchase: The Last Word in Advertising

An often-neglected aspect of advertising occurs at the point of purchase (POP), which might be better described as the point of choice. In some product categories (such as candy), up to 85 percent of shoppers' purchases are made on impulse.[13] The decision

[12] Peter H. Farquar, "Managing Brand Equity," *Journal of Advertising Research* (August/September 1990): 7–11.

[13] "P-O-P Spending Increases 10%," *Marketing News*, October 10, 1988, 22. POP spending increased 12 percent a year between 1983 and 1985. John A. Quelch and Kristina Cannon-Bonventre, "Better Marketing at the Point of Purchase," *Harvard Business Review* (November/December 1983): 162–69.

Figure 14.4 **Point of Purchase (POP) Communication Effectiveness**

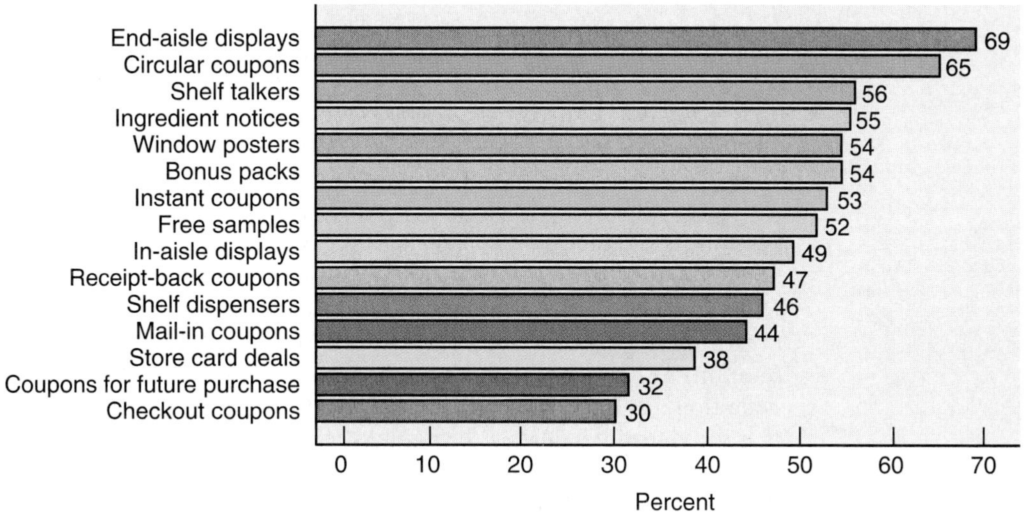

The percentage of supermarket shoppers whose attention is frequently attracted to different POP communication tools varies from high attention paid to end-of-aisle displays down to low attention paid to checkout coupons (partly because they are not offered by all supermarkets). Notice that in-aisle displays are much less effective in attracting attention. This is because shoppers are often too busy to shop all the aisles.

SOURCE: "Impact in the Aisles," *Promo: The Magazine of Promotion Marketing*, January 1996, 25–28.

to purchase from a product category and the choice of brand within the product category are frequently made at the POP by today's busy shopper. The impulse shopper tends to be exposed to less media advertising and is not very impressed with the quality of advice and service offered by today's low-skilled retail salespeople. Consequently, POP advertising is often the first and last chance to influence the consumer.

How effective is point-of-purchase advertising? For a start, it is much more cost-effective per thousand target *shopper* exposures than any other media. Second, the advertising exposure often occurs only moments before purchase, so it is much more timely than any other advertising. Actmedia, the company that hangs ads on shopping carts, promises average sales increases of 8 percent or more for the four weeks a product is advertised in the store. Sales increases on impulse items such as ice cream can be 20 percent. The store gets 25 percent of the ad revenues and sells more products.[14] By contrast, a retailer often has to give away margin on a price promotion to get the increased volume in sales. POP advertising also often has the effect of a billboard: It prompts the consumer to recall a television or a magazine ad. In combination with media advertising and packaging, POP advertising can be doubly effective. Figure 14.4 presents a study undertaken in 1995 of shoppers' use of POP advertising and promotions. End-of-aisle displays, followed by coupons in store circulars/fliers, shelf talkers, ingredient notices, and window posters are most frequently used by today's supermarket shoppers.

---

[14] Russell Mitchell, "An Upstart is Upsetting Actmedia's Shopping Carts," *Business Week*, September 7, 1987, 28–29.

Public Relations Management

When consumers buy products, they are essentially saying they trust the products to satisfy their needs. This trust can result from their past experiences with products and the companies that make those products. In other words, what consumers think of a company or its brand name should have a significant influence on their buying habits. For example, although other reasons existed, consumers' positive attitudes toward IBM must have contributed to the success of IBM PC in the early 1980s, even though IBM entered late into the PC market. Realizing the value of creating positive images for their companies in people's minds, businesses often undertake coordinated public relations campaigns targeted at various constituencies of importance to them, such as employees, stakeholders, the media, and the general public.

According to *Public Relations News*, public relations (PR) is "the management function which evaluates public attitudes, identifies the policies and procedures of an organization with the public interest, and executes a program of action (and communication) to earn public understanding and acceptance."[15] As can be seen from this definition, PR is a conscious and targeted attempt to mold a company's image. Notice that the company's image is being marketed, not any of its products. The expectation is that positive feelings about the company will translate into increased patronage of its products. More important, if the company makes mistakes that could upset consumers, good public relations are expected to soften the negative impact of such mistakes. Public relations efforts are targeted at various groups of people. Although the ultimate objective is to give people a positive feeling about the company, the feelings of various audiences will have different kinds of influences on the company's success. Therefore, the content of PR programs varies with the targeted audience.

The employees of a firm often may not be aware of key decisions made at the top management level. Similarly, they may be so focused on their jobs that they are oblivious to the changes taking place in other company divisions. Employees may be unable to appreciate the vast and complex competitive environment within which the firm operates and the firm's successful positioning in the industry. Communication, in the form of internal memos from the top management or announcements during informal company get-togethers, helps provide valuable information to employees, boosts their morale, and makes them feel like a valuable part of the company. Such public relations communication should strive not just to present the company in a positive light but also to make the employees feel like an important part of it. Informed employees will stand behind their company, a strength that becomes especially critical during times of trouble or transition, such as General Motors experienced in the early 1990s.

Public relations are also managed to convey an impression of financial soundness and well-being to stockholders and investors. The trust that develops with these constituencies will serve to insulate the firm from the vagaries of the stock market. The public relations management surrounding the departure of longtime CEO Ken Olsen from Digital Equipment Corporation, for example, might be one of the reasons the market reacted favorably to Olsen's departure and raised the stock price. Similarly, General Motors issued more than $5 billion' worth of stock that was quickly purchased by investors, even when the company was posting colossal losses in 1991 and 1992.

[15] Raymond Simon, *Public Relations, Concept and Practices*, 2nd ed. (Columbus, OH: Grid Publishing, 1980): 8.

The public relations team that kept assuring people everything was fine at GM must be credited for the automaker's success in drawing people's savings into the company.

Finally, the general public is addressed through corporate advertising. Although the value of such advertising is controversial and unproven, intuition tells us that when consumers are positively predisposed to a company, they are more likely to pardon its mistakes and purchase its products. Dow Chemical Company, according to several newswriters, contributes to environmental pollution through the release of industrial effluents into the atmosphere. In this age of environmentalism, such negative information might hurt the company. While working hard, and successfully, to reduce industrial effluents released by its factories, Dow also has launched advertising campaigns that show how the company cares about the environment. This type of a campaign should aid in the development of positive public opinion that may help innoculate against the effects of future negative information.

Generating Publicity

Publicity is advertising's Cinderella. More than one hundred thousand media editors in the United States and Canada are constantly searching for news and public-interest stories, including stories about interesting new products, new product uses, and new services. The explicit or implicit endorsement given by the independent media when they publicize a new product can give a marketing campaign a powerful boost. Americans love to read or hear about Horatio Alger–type success stories. Consequently, nothing succeeds like success when it comes to publicity.

Coleco's publicity campaign for its Cabbage Patch dolls is a classic example of the power of publicity.[16] Planned almost a year before production, the publicity campaign was carefully orchestrated with the advertising and promotion campaign to peak in December 1983. The campaign started with the American Toy Fair in New York early in the year. In the fall, First Lady Nancy Reagan gave Cabbage Patch dolls to two South Korean children flown to the United States to undergo heart surgery. Jane Pauley gave the dolls much enthusiastic coverage on the *Today* show on November 18, and other media rushed to pick up the story about the 1983 "must have" Christmas present. This complemented the extensive coverage given in the Christmas-gift-ideas features of numerous November women's magazines. Coleco representatives appeared on TV talk shows, the dolls were featured on NBC's *Tonight Show* several times, and a Cabbage Patch Kid's sketch was presented in Bob Hope's Christmas show. Meanwhile, dolls were being given away to children in hospitals, and radio stations were distributing the dolls as contest prizes. The whole promotion actually got somewhat out of hand when frantic buyers started to make the news because of their wild attempts to buy a doll. Coleco then had to request that the news media cool the story—demand had exceeded supply.

The Advantages and Disadvantages of Publicity

The advantages of publicity over advertising are its greater credibility, the independent endorsements of media celebrities such as Bryant Gumbel on NBC's *Today* show,

[16] Jerry Adler, "Oh, You Beautiful Dolls!" *Newsweek*, December 12, 1983, 78–81; and Lynn Langway, "Harvesting the Cabbage," *Newsweek*, December 12, 1983, 81–85.

the speed of coverage, the creation of public interest, word of mouth, momentum, and excitement few advertising campaigns can match. In fact, often such media publicity stories are reproduced or mentioned in a company's advertising because as news they are so much more credible (see Figure 15.2b). All of this can be achieved at a quite modest expense if the story is newsworthy.[17]

The disadvantages of publicity is that it is often an all-or-nothing proposition, and control over the process and execution is lacking. If no editor takes the bait, then the plan is sunk. However, if one editor thinks a message is newsworthy, then others are likely to follow. If the wire services then pick it up, and other local media scramble to cover the story and extend it, then extraordinary reach and frequency can be obtained in a short period of time. Several sources carrying the story also increases credibility. The problem in terms of control is that the media are likely to change the angle of the story, particularly for news releases. Photos and videotapes provide more control because they cannot be edited so readily. The skill of a good publicist depends, in part, on his or her friendly contact with the media. Because they are often ex-journalists or ex-editors themselves, many publicists have a network of contacts in the media.

The Importance of Implementation and Follow-Through

Publicists have to walk a fine line with the media. They must package the message as conveniently as possible without removing the possibility for the media to create their own angle on the story. Some media will publish press releases as they are. Others have a policy never to do this because they see it as surrendering editorial policy to thinly disguised advertising. In practice, firms often provide a company or, even better, an independent spokesperson the press can call to build a story around. Publicity also can be generated through publicity stunts or media events or by giving the product or service away to prominent celebrities, to charities, or for use as contest prizes. Rather than asking the media to approach company spokespeople, it is often better to put such people on the road, so they can appear on local or national talk shows.

The media are very sensitive about the legitimacy of claims of performance superiority because they know that repeating them through the media will give such claims further credibility. Media professionals also know they are likely to be besieged by complaints of editorial bias and demands that the story be retracted (tantamount to an apology and a lack of professionalism) from competitors if the claims are not watertight. This is why test performance results from independent researchers or testing labs are often more useful for obtaining publicity than for adding credibility to advertising.

Publicity in Industrial Markets

Publicity is often even more important in industrial markets because of the power of word of mouth. In industrial markets, the objective is to be featured in the new-products sections of trade, technical, and industry-specific magazines and newsletters. This kind of publicity is likely to draw far more inquiries from potential users and interested

[17] Another type of advertising-as-publicity that emerged in the 1980s made use of popular movies. Firms bought their way into movie scripts in order to have their products featured prominently and positively. In a sense, the stars are seen to be endorsing the product.

distributors or reps than any advertising (which, incidentally, the company may have had to purchase in the same magazine issue). Sometimes such publicity may be all that is needed to launch a new product or service into an industrial market.

Relationship Marketing and Integrated Marketing Communication

The impact of an advertising or publicity campaign on the attitudes and behavior of channel members is rarely researched formally. This is surprising, because many retailers will not sell a new packaged or durable good unless it is supported by an advertising campaign. If the trade wants such a campaign, then most likely it is interested in the excitement to be generated by the campaign's ads. Car dealers have been known to force automakers to return to old advertising campaigns by refusing to use new campaigns in their local advertising. In fact, whether key channel players are consulted about a proposed IMC campaign is perhaps a defining issue as to whether a firm is both relationship marketing and undertaking an integrated marketing communication campaign. To frame it in the negative, what sort of relationship exists if the relationship partner is not consulted about an integrated marketing campaign and their cooperation solicited? Likewise, how integrated could a marketing communication campaign be if it is not integrated with the marketing communication campaign of relationship partners?

The effect of an ad campaign on channels has a personal side. Buyers, merchandising managers, and sales associates who are employed within the channel and like the campaign ads will become more knowledgeable and enthusiastic about a product's advantages and positioning. They then will be able to sell it more enthusiastically. This in itself can be an important secondary effect of an advertising campaign. The ad campaign can create its own synergy with distribution tactics. It clearly pays to pretest ads on small groups of channel representatives or on the firm's own sales force.[18]

Direct Marketing

In the past decade, the practice of contacting consumers directly has experienced substantial growth. You very likely have received offers for books, tapes, or compact discs from the people who produce them. What is interesting is that the scope of this type of direct marketing has grown to an extent that a Direct Marketing Association now exists, which helps companies involved in direct marketing to standardize their practices and have a collective voice in dealing with legislation. Direct-marketing advertising, at $134 billion in 1995, will account for 57.1 percent of the total U.S. media advertising spending of $234.5 billion. Direct-marketing advertising will generate 7.1 percent of combined U.S. consumer and business-to-business sales. It will spark 12 percent of consumer sales—$594.4 billion out of $4.9 trillion. Direct advertising will generate 5 percent of total business-to-business sales, or $498.1 billion of $10.6 trillion.[19] The Direct Marketing Association defines direct marketing as "an interactive use of advertising media which stimulates (immediate) behavior modification in such a

---

[18] A surprising finding is that most *Fortune* 500 companies do not plan advertising campaigns with sales managers. See A. J. Dubinsky, T. E. Barry, and R. A. Kerin, "The Sales-Advertising Interface in Promotion Planning," *Journal of Advertising* 10, no. 3 (1981): 35–41.

[19] R. Craig Endicott, "Direct Ads Spur 12 Percent of Consumer Sales," *Advertising Age*, October 9, 1995, 34.

Figure 14.5 Direct-Database Marketing

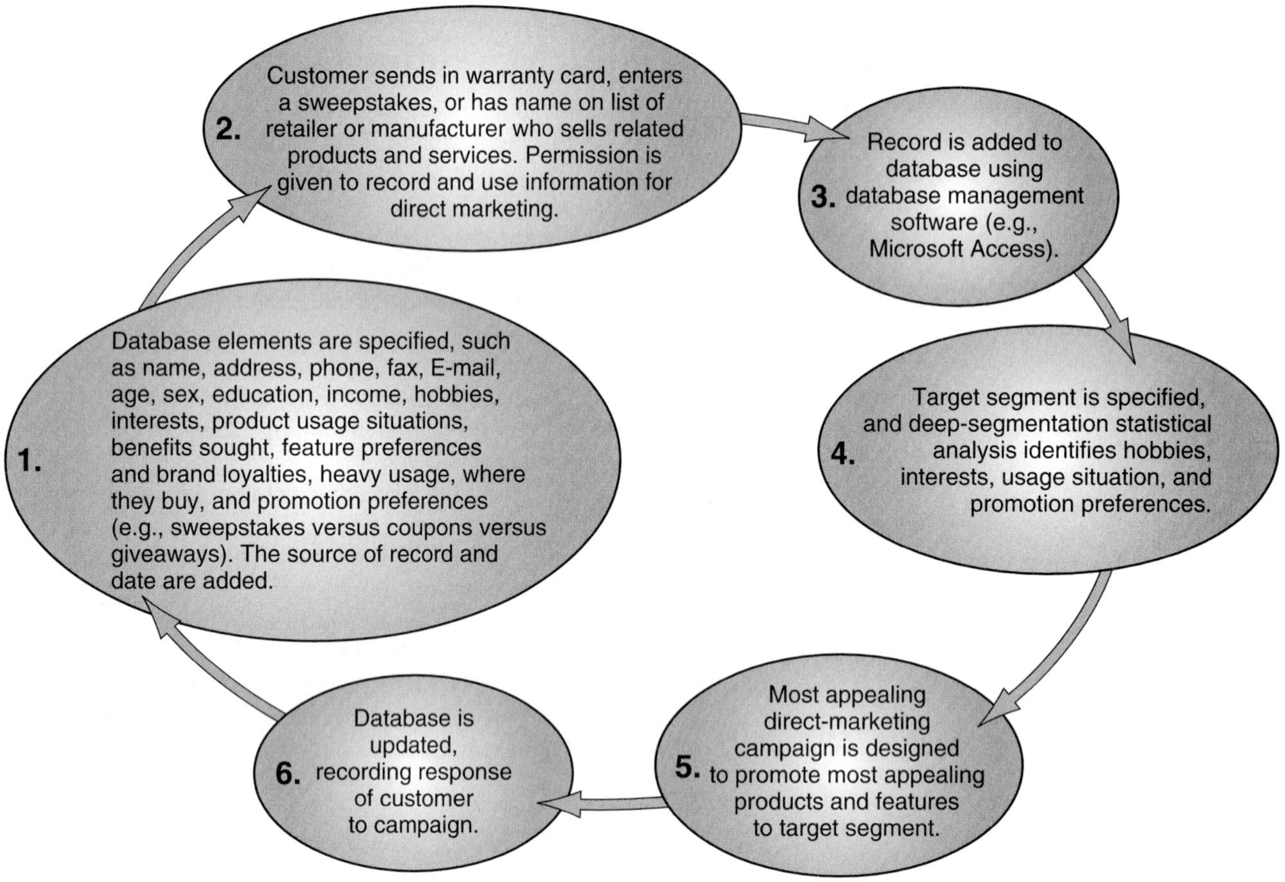

Direct-database marketing is a tool for direct communication with target customers of a special product and promotion offer that has a high chance of appealing to customers. It combines the fundamentals of deep market segmentation (see Chapter 5) with modern database technology and the implementation of microcommunication promotions offered to thousands of hot prospects rather than millions of mostly indifferent consumers. As the database records the history of interactions with each customer, customer segmentation can go beyond a deep understanding of heavy users and identify the sort of marketing interactions and trading relationships that groups of customers wish to have with the company.

way that this behavior can be tracked, recorded, and analyzed, then stored in a database for future retrieval and use." The steps involved in direct-database marketing are described in Figure 14.5.

Direct marketing has become so popular today for many reasons. The most important one, of course, is the availability of computer hardware and software, which has enhanced its contact efficiency. For example, the manufacturer of a water purifier system may want to reach only new-home buyers. An ad on a popular prime-time television show would be a waste of dollars because it reaches many people who do not form part of the target market, yet the advertiser is required to pay for it. A direct phone call or a mailer to current or recent home buyers is more efficient because it targets the market precisely.

The availability of computerized databases today allows sellers to choose their prospective buyers. Manufacturers increasingly rely on direct marketing for other reasons as well, including time pressures on consumers (especially in two-income households) that preclude them from allocating precious hours for shopping, thereby forcing them to shop from home; the increased use of 800- and 900-numbers that allow easy ordering; an explosion in the issue and use of credit cards, which facilitate purchases by phone; and, importantly, the growth of quality sellers (such as L.L. Bean and Dell Computers) who provide impressive guarantees and deliver quality merchandise.

The heart of any direct-marketing system is the "list." The list consists of the names, addresses, and telephone numbers of people in whom a manufacturer may be interested. In some instances, lists contain psychographic information obtained through surveys (for instance, a magazine may conduct a lifestyle survey of its subscribers and store it in a database). Public information, such as tax records and home-buying activity, are also included on some of the lists. Recent estimates indicate that more than thirty thousand lists are available for rent. These lists have been prepared by various parties involved in business activities. For example, when you send in your warranty registration card for a new product you just bought (say, a humidifier for the winter), you may have provided information about yourself as you answered some questions on the registration card. This information will be stored by the company and very likely sold to other sellers who might be interested in it. A host of other manufacturers (perhaps, of dehumidifiers) would be very interested in getting those names and addresses so they can reach customers like you directly. Similarly, your credit history contains information on your purchases and even brand choices. The few companies that monitor your credit history have access to substantial amounts of information about you, which they sell to outside parties. Of course, certain rules prevent them from selling highly private information, but they can still sell plenty of information that many people are interested in buying. Also, some companies prepare lists as part of their business.

When choosing a list, two criteria are often viewed as critical. First, how old is the list? That is, does the list contain names of individuals whose records have been updated with their most recent purchase activities? If the list is old, it may not be a good predictor of market potential because list users will not know how the consumers have been making their purchases in recent months. Second, the amount of money spent on direct buying by each individual on a list is a critical piece of information. The more money an individual has spent on direct buying, the greater the likelihood she or he will spend more when approached with an interesting product. List sellers know this and often charge higher prices for the names and addresses of individuals who have spent large amounts of money buying directly from manufacturers. Increasingly, companies are creating their own lists from company records and by running contests or sweepstakes.

Advantages and Disadvantages of Direct Marketing

Direct marketing seems to be most beneficial for selling specialized products. The low costs of printing and distributing catalogs and of advertising on a specialized cable channel (to predominantly reach only the members of the target market) enable sellers to realize higher margins on their products. When Dell Computer Company started selling computers by catalogs, it was scoffed at by analysts because consumers were not expected to make such expensive purchases by catalog. However, by offering low prices and proven technology, Dell has managed to become one of the most profitable personal-computer sellers in a low-margin, cutthroat market. Thus, no limit really exists on what type of a product can be sold directly to the customer—including services. In fact, direct marketing is often used by dentists, doctors, veterinarians, eye doctors, tax preparers, pest control companies, and many other services to remind their clients that it is that time of year again. It is a crucial element of maintaining the relationship.

On the other hand, not everyone prefers to buy directly from manufacturers. Many consumers enjoy shopping, and direct buying would deprive them of the pleasure of browsing (see Chapter 5). This is one of the reasons why catalog sales have grown rapidly but plateaued over the past few years. The growth potential for direct marketing is limited not so much by the type of merchandise but by the type of people who patronize direct sellers.

Finally, two problems face direct marketers that need immediate attention. As with any high-growth industry, direct marketing has grown faster than its supporting systems could be implemented. Too many lists are available, too much duplication exists among lists, and too many manufacturers are jumping into the game without much market analysis. The excess competition causes clutter that is difficult to break through and attract consumer attention. Weak competition, by its inefficient and ineffective methods, also will upset consumers, who may be pushed into avoiding all direct-marketing attempts. The Direct Marketing Association plays a significant role in reducing damage to the industry by these processes.

Second, anytime a list has been accessed and used, the issue of privacy is raised. Consumers may not appreciate getting letters that refer to recent purchases because they may feel that the manufacturer from whom they bought the product has betrayed them. Direct marketers have to exercise a great deal of caution in this regard. Even when knowledge exists about a consumer's recent purchases, the consumer should be approached with suppressed enthusiasm, only referring to the purchase tangentially. Any consumer feelings of privacy violation can propel consumer advocates into pushing for legislation that might ban the use of lists. The Direct Marketing Association, once again, has acted proactively in this regard and provides consumers with options to remove their names from various lists.

In conclusion, much like the way scanner technology has provided important point-of-purchase sales information, computer technology has made selling directly to a choice group of consumers easier and cheaper. As long as the efficiencies of the process are maintained and consumers continue to buy directly from manufacturers, this type of marketing is here to stay.

Global Communication

The major issue in global communication is whether a single message theme and the same IMC tactics should be used in all foreign markets or whether separate messages and tactics should be developed. Because the availability and cost of media vary among markets, the media schedule will have to be clearly different. Some scholars have argued that the appeal of some products is cross-cultural and so generic that a single campaign theme can be used in many markets.[20] This has cost and positioning consistency advantages. Other marketers believe a firm should always be very sensitive to differences in cultural values and the competitive environment, which demand different themes and IMC tactics in different markets. The advertising agency chosen to buy the media in the foreign market will be able to help in judging the appropriateness of the appeal. This is a hard test, because it is in the agency's interest to work on preparing new ads. Consequently, independent copy testing in foreign markets is very important. It is essential in non-English-speaking markets where the message has to be translated into a foreign language.

Publicity and public relations also have to be handled with great sensitivity if the product poses a threat to domestic competition. Patriotic appeals to buy domestically occur in all world markets. It is here that distributors and retailers play an important role in advising a company on how to conduct such campaigns. In fact, in some cases it may be best to let the distributor or retailer develop the ads and choose the media. Two advantages of such an initiative are that many new approaches may be tested and it encourages channel ownership of the marketing campaign. The very successful campaigns may be able to be modified and used with equal success in other markets around the world.

Discussion Questions and Minicases

1. Inspect and then suggest three improvements that could be made in Kodak's Internet home page.
2. The fundamental purpose of an IMC campaign is to communicate what? What is another name for integration of marketing communication programs and tactics?
3. Make up a terse list of do's and don'ts that an ad agency might use as a guideline when bidding for an account.
4. The following figure presents the market test results of a special newspaper advertising campaign, an in-store coupon campaign, and a combined campaign where the availability of the in-store coupon was also promoted in the newspaper advertising. What does the table demonstrate? What does it tell about managing communications?

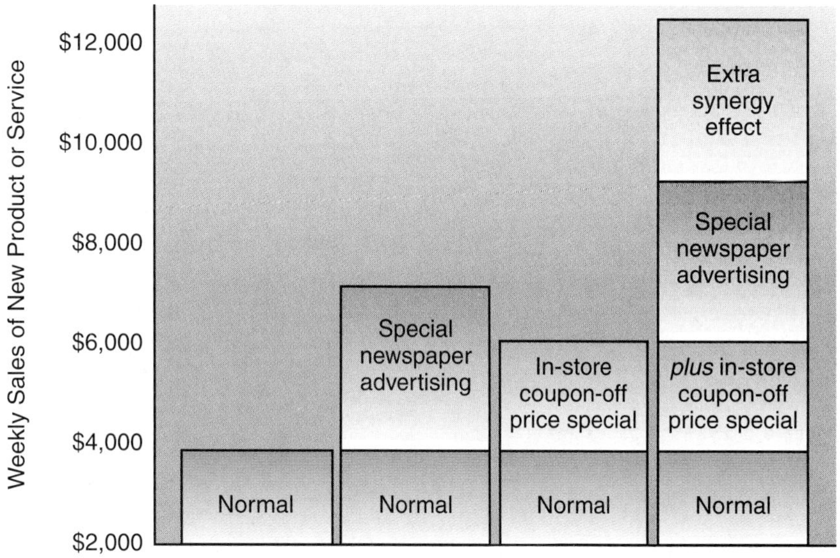

[20] Theodore Levitt, "The Globalization of Markets," *Harvard Business Review* (May/June 1983): 92–102.

5. In the early 1960s, the pioneering ad agency Doyle Dane Bernbach began teaming up the copywriter with the artist or art director. Previously, they had worked separately on a campaign. What advantages come from such a team? Who else might be added to an IMC team?
6. Service providers, such as dentists, eye doctors, tax accountants, pest controllers, carpet cleaners, lawn-care services, and hair salons, do a lot of local advertising in newspapers and on door hangers. However, this normally should be only a minor part of their marketing communication program. What communication programs should they spend most of their marketing/advertising dollars on?
7. What does the fact that sales are seldom consulted about advertising campaigns say about the relationship between the company and its sales force? What might be some reasons why sales managers are not consulted about proposed advertising campaigns?
8. Publicity is often credited with being very effective, when, in fact, the credit should go to another element of the firm's competitive strategy. What is that element?
9. How might a company's permanent point-of-purchase cabinet in supermarkets be redesigned so that the advertising on the cabinet is not simply taken for granted and constantly overlooked by shoppers?
10. What other marketing management program/tactic should always be integrated with a firm's advertising, point-of-purchase, personal selling, public relations, and direct marketing so as to ensure an integrated marketing communication campaign?
11. Why are direct database marketing campaigns still targeted to segments rather than the individual consumer in the database?
12. Which promotion program in an IMC campaign is most helped by relationship marketing? (Hint: See Chapter 11).
13. When promoting a service, which elements of an IMC campaign most need to be integrated?
14. What impact will the development of the World Wide Web have on direct marketing?
15. What are some of the best ways that an IMC can be coordinated effectively so as to increase communication synergy?

The meek shall inherit the world, but they'll never increase market share.

William G. McGowan

Nothing but the mint can make money without advertising.

Thomas B. Macauley

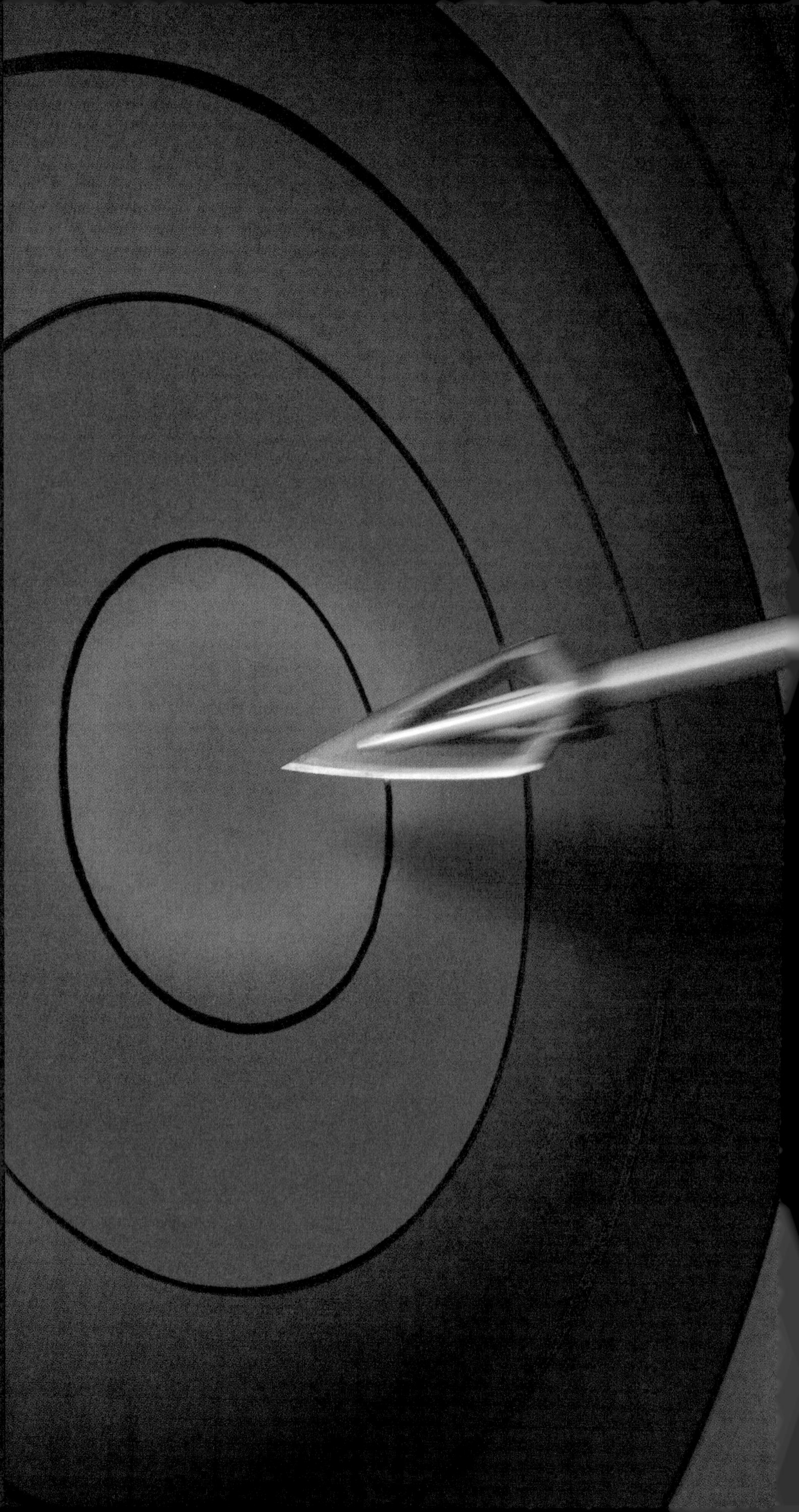

CHAPTER FIFTEEN

Advertising Management

Infomercials are the most important innovation in television advertising since the introduction of color advertisements in the 1960s. Initially, they were sneered at by the advertising establishment, who were trying to squeeze thirty seconds of persuasion into fifteen seconds rather than stretch them out into thirty minutes. Three emerging realities are proving that infomercials will produce most of the future growth in television advertising revenues. The first reality is that network television advertising has become too expensive, beyond the reach of most companies. Second, multichannel television has created channels designed to target very specific segments. Infomercials first appeared during the dead time (1 A.M.–6 A.M.) on these channels but has spread to prime time on the Lifetime channel and even to the major networks. Marketers have discovered that many special-interest audiences are willing to watch infomercials for products and services that match their special interest. The third reality is that hundreds of carefully controlled experiments have established that television advertising has almost no effect on sales of established brands and products but is effective in advertising new products and services. Infomercials are particularly effective in launching new products and services because they can present detailed explanations of product superiority

supported by numerous endorsements and can teach consumers how to use a product or service. When coupled with an 800-number, they can be the entire marketing campaign for a small company.

The 1995 top-grossing infomercials in the United States were, in order, the HealthRider exercise machine, the Psychic Friends Network, the Fast Track exercise machine, the Abflex exercise machine, Jake's Hip & Thigh machine, Murad Skin Care, and Kenny Kingston's Psychic Line.[1] Products or services that make people look or feel better seem to be most suited for infomercials.

Particularly exciting for both the advertising industry and marketers is that infomercials are just as popular in Japan, China, and one hundred other countries as they are in the United States, and the emerging global cable networks soon will reach billions of consumers around the world. What is encouraging for small entrepreneurial companies is that these global networks are often eager to become marketing partners, sharing revenues rather than charging a fixed fee upfront. Infomercials may be the most effective way of launching new products and services in the global marketplace and of pulling the products and services through established distribution channels or bypassing channels completely by the use of an 800-telephone number and a global postal service company such as FedEx. TV infomercials may be a much more important tool in the twenty-first century than accessing the World Wide Web by personal computer for a very simple reason: Hundreds of millions more households have television sets. ■

Advertising is the most conspicuous marketing activity and, consequently, is probably given too much emphasis and credit in marketing campaigns. Strategically speaking, product/service positioning and development and relationship strategy and logistics are much more important than advertising. A cross-functional team must place the importance of advertising in perspective, but it also should understand the fundamentals of message strategy, creative tactics, and media planning. Taking the mystery out of creating advertising campaigns is an important first step in making them much more focused and effective. In addition, the principles underlying advertising apply to all elements of an integrated marketing communication campaign. These principles are straightforward: understand how the target audience make their choices, create message themes that play to such choice processes, execute the message theme using

[1] Kim Cleland, "Infomercial Audience Crosses Over Cultures," *Advertising Age International*, January 15, 1996, i8.

appropriate creative tactics, and communicate using media that reach as many as possible of the target segment frequently enough for the ads to be effective.

Chapter Organization

The organization of Chapter 15 is presented in Figure 15.1. It starts with a discussion of three different ways advertising can be effective. These form the basis for thinking about different types of message themes for achieving the integrated marketing communication goals. The next section describes how various creative tactics are used by copywriters and art directors in advertising agencies to execute message themes. The only role the cross-functional team should play here is to make sure a message theme and positioning strategy do not get lost in the cleverness of the creative tactics. The second half of the chapter discusses media planning. First, some of the advantages and disadvantages of the major media are presented along with some media trends. The basics of media buying are then described in terms of achieving low costs per thousand exposures to a target audience, and technical terms such as *reach* and *frequency* are discussed. The chapter closes with a discussion of the advantages of regional advertising campaigns and the importance of campaign timing.

Advertising Effects Models

Almost every advertising agency has its own mental model of how advertising works and uses it to train its employees and sell its skills to clients (i.e., in its pitches, discussed in Chapter 14). It is consequently very difficult to develop a consensus model of how advertising practitioners and experts think about advertising. About the only thing they all agree on is the obvious point that advertising must gain the attention of its target audience. In practice, this can be extraordinarily difficult to achieve because, just as families living near an airport or a railway line learn to screen out most of the noise, from a very young age Americans learn not to pay attention to a great deal of advertising to which they are exposed. Hence a great deal of effort and dollars are spent simply to gain attention.

Current thinking about what happens after attention has been gained is that it depends a great deal on consumer choice in the product market, but advertising research and practice suggest three general *hierarchy-of-effects* ways of thinking about how consumers react to advertising. The oldest model proposes that an advertisement attempts to teach consumers about the product. The learning goal simply may be awareness of the brand or product's existence, but often it is to teach consumers much more so they form specific beliefs about the product. For example, the Pork Council found that most consumers thought pork was red meat and tried to convince them it was actually white meat. This resulted in the "Pork, the other white meat" campaign. According to this hierarchy-of-effects model, such new beliefs will in turn lead to new attitudes toward the product; favorable attitudes lead to purchase intentions and purchase intentions to purchase. It is a hierarchy of effects because consumer *learning* about the product leads to *feelings* toward the product that lead to *buying* the product. It is a *learn-feel-buy (LFB)* model of consumer reaction to advertising. This LFB model assumes consumers make thoughtful decisions about buying products such as major appliances, automobiles, and computers and fits the logical-choice process discussed in Chapter 5. Infomercials are almost always based on the LFB model because

Figure 15.1 **Chapter Organization**

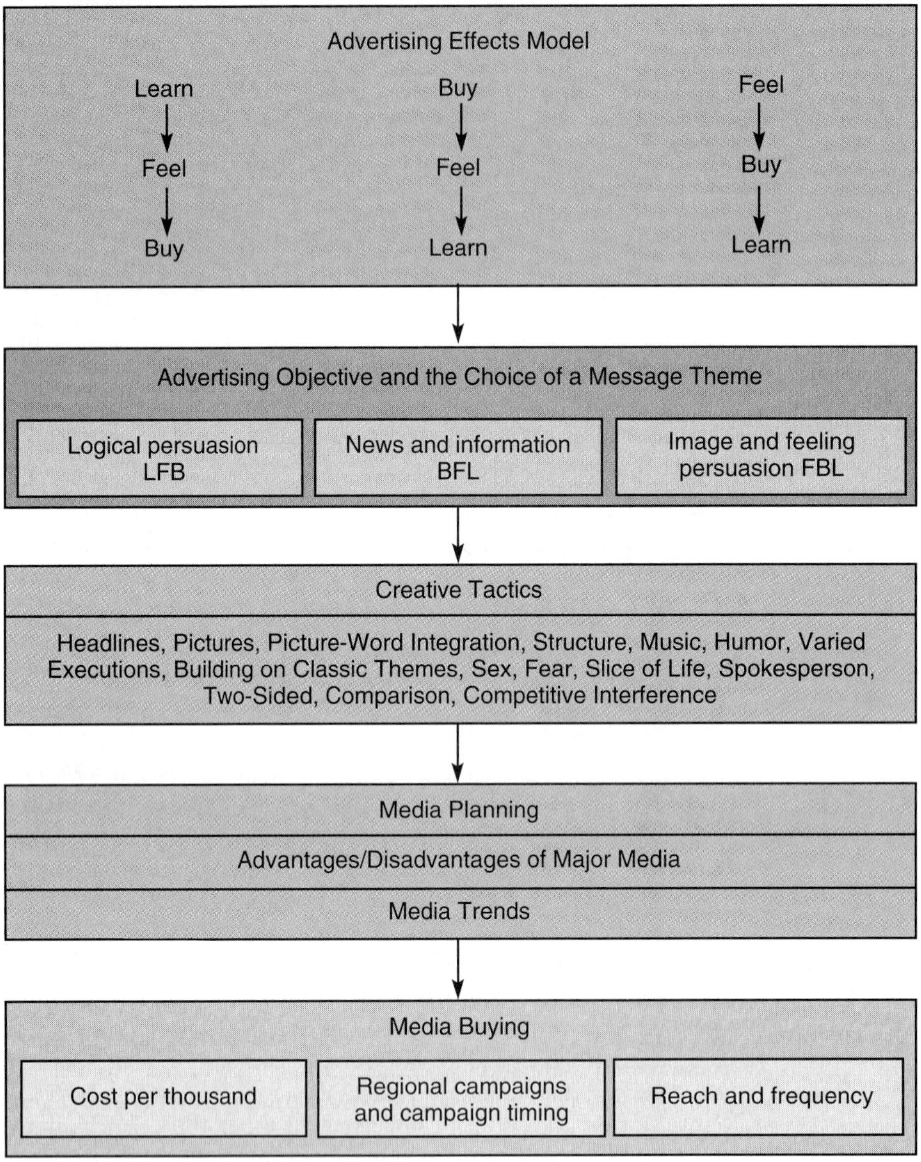

This chapter starts with a discussion of three different models of advertising effectiveness. The next section describes how various creative tactics are used by copywriters and art directors in advertising agencies to "execute" the message theme/strategy. The second half of the chapter discusses media planning. First, some of the advantages and disadvantages of the major media are presented along with some media trends. The basics of media buying are then discussed and the chapter closes with a discussion of the advantages of regional advertising campaigns and the importance of campaign timing and flighting.

they have the time to change beliefs, develop favorable attitudes and can initiate a purchase with just a single exposure.

The problem with this very logical persuasion model is that it does not seem to explain many advertising effects. For example, what about advertising that announces a new flavor of supercreamy ice cream and exhorts you to try it simply "because you will love it"? The message seems to be based on a *buy-feel-learn (BFL)* model of consumer reaction to advertising. This model proposes a different hierarchy of effects. The advertisement encourages consumers to buy the product and try it; the trial results in feelings (e.g., "yummy" or "yuck") that lead consumers to form beliefs about the product's attributes. This BFL model recognizes that consumers often buy things they do not know much about, so the purchase is not very involving and is often impulsive. They simply try it to see if they like it. Some experts and advertisers also use this mental model to create advertisements that remind consumers of their feelings of satisfaction toward the products they have previously purchased. The idea is that the advertisement reinforces the buying habit. This latter variation of the buy-feel-learn model seems to fit the habitual-choice process discussed in Chapter 5.

Yet again another type of advertising seems to have evolved that uses humor or popular spokespeople and cultural icons (e.g., the bald eagle) to evoke positive feelings that will transfer to the product or service. Learning about the attributes of the product or service occurs after trial. A more sophisticated version of this advertising, often used for fragrances and vacations, combines few words with powerful images to create strong positive feelings in consumers. Marketers hope that the feelings lead to purchases and purchases lead to consumers forming beliefs about the product's attributes. This is a *feel-buy-learn (FBL)* model of consumer reaction to advertising and fits the experiential-choice process discussed in Chapter 5.

Undoubtedly, the three models can be complicated by adding or substituting different terms in different orders, but the analysis in the next section suggests that the great majority of message themes are based on these process models of how advertising works. It is consequently reasonable for a cross-functional team to ask its advertising agency which of the models is being used to motivate the advertising campaign.

Advertising Objective and the Choice of a Message Theme

Message strategy addresses the problem of what to say about the product and how to say it. Generally speaking, an advertisement for any product should promote the unique differentiation or selling proposition of the product. This is where the links among segmentation, product positioning, and message strategy become clear. When a marketer segments a market, a segment is identified that is either currently unoccupied or is not being served well. The segment that becomes the focal point for future marketing attention is first described by the required benefits and outcomes sought from the product. The product that is developed, engineered, and manufactured based on such research is expected to contain the attributes necessary to provide the desired benefits to the segment. For example, if consumers in the sensitive-teeth segment are looking for a toothpaste that tones their gum lines, then the marketer addressing that segment should have a product that contains ingredients that will provide this attribute, and it should be positioned based on its ability to help fight weak gum lines.

Table 15.1 **Message Themes: Repetition, Reach, and Media**

THEMES	REPETITION NEEDED	REACH NEEDED	BEST MEDIA[a]
1. News, Informational Themes (BFL)			
"I'm for sale."	Low	High	N,R,TV
"I have arrived."	Low	High	N,R,TV
"I'm a bargain right now."	Low	High	N,R,TV
"Time to use me now."	Medium	High	D,N,R,TV
"Try me; like me."	High	High	TV, M
2. Logical-Persuasion Themes (LFB)			
"Have you got this problem? I have the solution."	Medium	Medium	TV, M
"This is more of a problem than you think."	Medium	Medium	TV, M
"This is how I work."	Low	Medium	TV, M
"I am . . . I have . . ."	Medium	Medium	TV, M
"I'm better than they are because . . ."	Medium	Medium	TV, M
"I'm better than they are in this usage situation."	Medium	Medium	TV, M
"Don't believe what they say."	Low	Medium	M,TV
3. Image and Feeling Persuasion Themes (FBL)			
"Remember me."	High	High	B
"Look at me; like me."	High	High	TV, M
"Smile; like me."	High	High	TV,R
"Think X; think me."	High	High	B,TV, M
"I'm chic; you can be too."	Medium	Medium	M,TV
"I'm a dream, a mood, a good-time product."	Medium	Medium	TV, M

[a]These recommendations are only general and would depend on the creative approach employed and cost-per-one thousand exposures to the target audience. B = Billboards, M = Magazines, R = Radio, TV = Television, N = Newspaper, and D = Direct mail.

The message conveyed to a targeted consumer should automatically emphasize the unique benefit(s) the promoted product provides. In the example, any advertisement should necessarily inform the consumer that the advertised brand of toothpaste will help him or her fight sensitive gum lines. The repetitive education provided by advertisements is expected to create a unique position in the minds of consumers for the advertised brand—in this case characterized by the problem situation (having sensitive teeth) and the available solution (the advertised brand).

The advertiser and its advertising agency share the responsibility for developing the message theme. It should evolve naturally from the positioning strategy and persuasion model that seem best, given the likely choice behavior of the target segment. If the message theme is not based on such foundations, it can result in campaigns that are irrelevant to the product or service's competitive positioning or, even worse, that damage it.

The agency should participate in all marketing planning meetings so it understands the desired positioning strategy. It also will come to appreciate the need to fit the creative execution, media choice, and media scheduling to the market facts. If the agency ignores the environmental analysis, which the marketing strategy is meant to fit, then it has demonstrated it cannot work within the decision-making process, and it should be replaced. The primary role of any agency is to develop a message theme and creative tactics that execute the positioning strategy. To help the agency complete this mission, a marketing planner or cross-functional team needs to realize that the majority of advertisements fall into one of three basic message categories, listed with examples in Table 15.1, which are discussed and illustrated throughout the chapter. In fact, Table 15.1 is a general framework or mental model for thinking about advertising.[2]

Newsworthy—BFL Themes

The first and most basic message theme presents the advertisement as a newsworthy announcement. This theme succeeds as long as the ad's message is "news." This type of message strategy is most commonly found in "For Sale" display advertisements in newspapers (see Figure 15.2), classified advertisements, advertisements announcing a new product or service, and advertisements announcing visiting entertainment shows (such as where to get tickets for a Smashing Pumpkins concert).

Another type of news message reminds consumers that this is the time to use the product or buy the product (such as lawn-care company advertising in the spring). The advertisements present basic facts with minimal persuasive elements. The description of the product's characteristics is considered sufficient, because the target audience is moderately involved and the behavior is habitual.

A news theme does not try to create new feelings because the audience already has well-established feelings about the subject (for instance, the announcement of a rock concert date or a department store sale is not expected to create *new* fans of the band or new shoppers). Little attempt is made at elaborate product differentiation because brand differentiation has been established from the consumer's previous experience with the product or because the differentiation is clearly newsworthy and does not need elaboration ("50% off!"). Consumers learn of the news, understand it, and react to it. They react either positively (by buying the product) or negatively (by not buying the product). Advertisements using this type of message strategy need to reach a high percentage of the target audience. Most of their news is in the headlines, and the audience takes only one or two exposures to get the message. The message speaks for itself and does not require much elaboration or attention-grabbing gimmicks. Consequently, newsworthy advertisements do not need a high frequency of exposure in order to be effective. Radio, newspapers, and television carry much of this newsworthy advertising.

Finally, a simple message theme whose intent is to get the consumer to try the product ("Try me; like me"; see Figure 15.3) is often empowered by a free sample or by the words or images of a satisfied user (one example is the Alka-Seltzer classic "Try it, you'll like it" message). This theme is often used by new, low-involvement, experience goods. Experience goods are products and services whose performance really can be judged only through trial (see Chapter 5). The advertising neither informs nor creates lasting feelings. It simply prompts trial.

A pertinent example for this type of strategy is the California raisins ad. For six years, raisin growers experienced flat sales. The raisin market appeared to be in the last stages of maturity and nearing decline. Then came the California raisins television

[2] Another interesting dichotomy exists between the advertising theme that promises the removal of a problem (LFB) and the theme that promises more satisfaction (FBL). See John R. Rossiter and Larry Percy, *Advertising and Promotion Management* (New York: McGraw-Hill, 1987), Chapter 7.

Figure 15.2 **Example of an "I'm for sale" News (BFL) Theme**

ads created by Foote, Cone & Belding, which added excitement to a previously dull product. The ads did not promote raisins as a convenient, nutritious snack. They simply encouraged kids and adults to try raisins again—and it worked. The ads won awards and were the most popular advertisements among viewers in 1987. More important, industry sources estimated the campaign increased raisin sales by 14 percent.[3]

[3] Edward F. Cone, "Terrific! I Hate It," *Forbes*, June 27, 1988, 130–32. The California raisins ads were also rated number one in popularity in 1988 and 1989 and number three in 1990.

Figure 15.3 **Example of a Simple Message Theme**

Left: A BFL "Try me; like me" message theme. *Right:* An FBL "Like me" message theme. This print ad was supported by a humorous television advertising campaign.

Logical—LFB Themes

The second major category of advertising message strategies uses a similar influence path, but it is a much harder sell. It relies on logical arguments, expert evidence, and test demonstrations—similar to the way a lawyer or scientist attempts to argue his or her case by the use of facts (see Table 15.1). Words and language are more prominent in this type of advertising. Examples of such advertisements are presented in Figure 15.4. These strategies generally assume a high level of interest and involvement from the target audience.

If the product category is new, the message strategy often attempts to raise interest and involvement by teaching consumers about the problem the product solves (see the Listerine ad). If consumers are familiar with the product category, then the message strategy must credibly explain why the promoted brand provides superior performance or value for the money.

Figure 15.4 **Examples of the Logical-Persuasion (LFB) Theme**

(a)

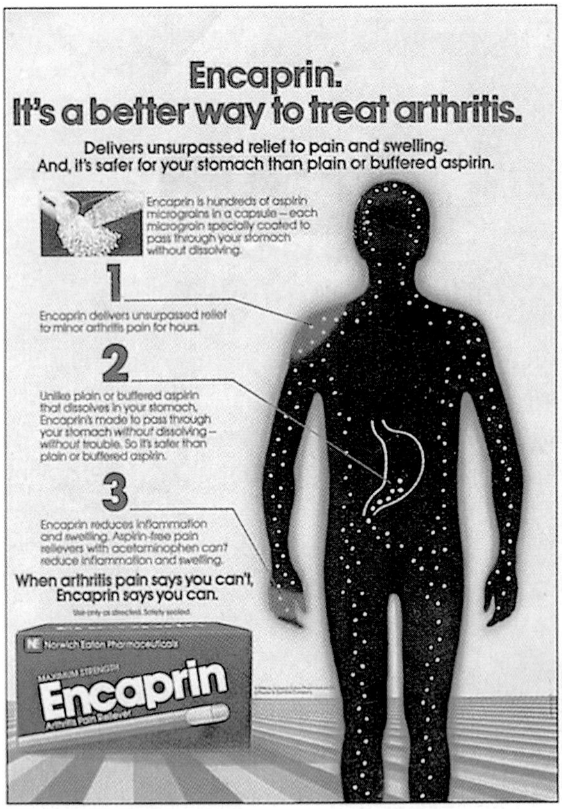

(b)

(a) Example of a "Have you got this problem?" theme. (b) Example of a "This is how I work" theme. (c) Example of an "I'm better than they are . . . " theme.

Some evidence suggests that the trend has moved away from the use of mood and emotion in creative executions and back to the bread-and-butter techniques of selling superior performance. For example, Procter & Gamble changed its Bounce fabric-softener ad from the commercial featuring the hit song "Jump" (which was a finalist for the 1986 Clio Award for best ad) to an ad that discussed how and why its brand made clothes feel, smell, and wear better.[4] The advertisement shifted from explaining how Bounce makes you "feel" to a promise of "softness with no static cling," a functional, logical message strategy.

The first subcategory of this message strategy attempts to increase consumer demand for the product or service by amplifying the importance of the problem it solves or by highlighting a problem that to date had not been solved (see Figure 15.5). Arm & Hammer did this with its brilliant "Have you got this problem? I have the solution"

[4] Edward F. Cone, "Image and Reality," *Business Week*, December 14, 1987, 226–28.

(continued)

(c)

campaign that raised household awareness of the use of baking soda as a refrigerator deodorant from 1 percent to 57 percent. Over three years, the company's baking soda sales increased by 72 percent.[5]

A second subcategory of logical persuasion attempts to increase the attractiveness of the brand by explaining the uniqueness or superiority of its features and performance ("I am . . . I have . . ."). Another type of message strategy spells out the competitive product differentiation ("I'm better than they are because . . ."—see the microwavable Saran Wrap ad on page 365 in Chapter 9).

The most argumentative and combative type of logical message strategy attacks a competitor's advertising claims or product weaknesses either explicitly or implicitly (such as the "Bring your Visa card . . . because they don't take American Express"

[5] Jack J. Honomichi, "The Ongoing Saga of 'Mother Baking Soda,'" *Advertising Age*, September 20, 1982, M-2, M-3, M-22.

Figure 15.5 **Problem-Identification Advertising**

This advertisement using the LFB "Have you got this problem?" message theme attempts to increase demand by educating consumers about both the problem and the solution.

advertisements). The final and most ambitious ad is the direct-marketing ad that attempts to take the consumer from attention to action (ordering) in one advertisement, although not necessarily in one exposure.

Image—FBL Themes

The third general type of message theme connects or associates an image, feeling, or mood to a brand (see Table 15.1). In its most basic form, image persuasion can be seen in the billboard that simply states the brand name and illustrates the product attractively (it is a "Remember me" or "Look at me; like me" theme). The theory is that repeated exposure to an attractive presentation of the brand will build familiarity, top-of-mind brand awareness (mind share), product appeal, and trial among nonusers and will bolster the product's appeal with current users. Rather than using information to persuade consumers, it uses emotions and feelings to change opinions and attitudes.[6]

In reality, most feeling or mood advertising is probably best at maintaining current market share by maintaining top-of-mind awareness for the brand but does not do much more. The idea is that familiarity and recency of exposure to brand names will increase the probability of purchase. This tactic is likely to be pursued in a mature market with little product differentiation. In a sense, it is an alternative to price competition. The brand with the highest top-of-mind familiarity is most likely to be chosen. Consequently, continuous advertising is needed to maintain "remember me" brand familiarity and loyalty, and it can become boring.

A more complex type of feeling advertisement attempts to evoke memory of past usage experiences that are positive and reinforcing. The effect is to remind consumers of positive feelings associated with the brand that may prompt consumers to buy it. The Hallmark greeting card ads often use this technique.

Association through Repetition

A classical-conditioning persuasion strategy is the basis for "Think X; think me" message strategy.[7] Advertisers hope that by constantly associating their product with X, the ads will encourage the target audience to associate X with their product (see Figure 15.6). Advertisers who want their products to possess a glamorous, exciting image pair themselves with glamorous, exciting celebrities or sports events (such as Wimbledon). The frequency of repetition needed to establish the connection depends on the target audience's level of involvement. In high-fashion women's clothing advertisements, the chic looks, arrogant posturing, and pouting of the model are associated with the outfit, and one exposure to a fashion-conscious New Yorker will do the trick. On the other hand, it may take many repetitions for a brand of fabric softener to convince consumers of its snuggle softness by associating itself with a snuggly soft teddy bear (see Figure 15.6).

A "Smile; like me" strategy is meant to work in a similar way. The internal feeling of amusement and external smile or even laughter created by a cute or humorous ad is designed to transfer to the advertised product.[8] The result should be an increase in warm, fuzzy feelings toward the product. In this case, advertisers are attempting to connect the product with positive feelings rather than an image or performance attribute. The qualifier is that many very humorous advertisements create emotions and feelings for the ad itself that never do transfer to the product.

Bringing the Dream World into the Real World

The most complicated form of the learning-reinforcement message strategy uses a feeling-transfer persuasion theory. In this type of ad, product use is shown to create highly desirable feelings, moods, or outcomes. For example, perfume advertisements often present dreamy, high-imagery scenes. The connections between products and

---

[6] W. R. Nord and J. P. Peter, "A Behavior Modification Perspective on Marketing," *Journal of Marketing* 44, no. 2 (1980): 36–47.

[7] M. L. Rothschild and W. C. Gaidis, "Behavioral Learning Theory: Its Relevance to Marketing and Promotions," *Journal of Marketing* 45, no. 2 (1981): 70–78; and J. P. Peter and W. R. Nord, "A Clarification and Extension of Operant Conditioning Principles in Marketing," *Journal of Marketing* 46, no. 3 (1982): 102–7.

[8] B. Sternthal and C. S. Craig, "Humor in Advertising," *Journal of Marketing* 37, no. 4 (1973): 12–18.

Figure 15.6 **Example of the Image and Feeling (FBL) Theme**

Example of a "Think X (softness); think me" theme. By repeatedly associating teddy bear softness with the brand, the advertiser hopes to increase the belief that using Snuggle will make clothes, towels, and sheets softer.

feelings or images in such advertisements can be so powerful that not only do such promises lead to purchase, but also when the product is used (be it perfume or a Porsche), the actual moods and emotions portrayed in the ad are re-created in the user's mind and learned. The product user role plays what he or she saw in the ad, and the feelings created by the ad reemerge in acting out the fantasy. Because the user feels, through fantasizing, more confident, assured, cool, attractive, sensual, hot, or macho, the dream becomes the reality. Such advertising does not need much exposure if it is connected to powerful needs, such as the needs for social power and sexual attraction (see the ad on page 584).

Creative Tactics

Once a company has chosen its basic message theme, it begins the often difficult process of translating its theme into a creative concept and final advertisement. Like many artists, the creative people in advertising agencies sometimes dislike direction. The dilemma is making sure the product's desired positioning and message direct their artistic skill without crushing their enthusiasm and creativity. The critical test is the creative execution. If the message comes through loud and clear, then the theme has been executed successfully. If it does not, then the creative execution has failed. Although almost all the decisions regarding creative tactics should be made by the advertising agency, an advertiser can influence the creative process in important ways. One way is by ensuring that the creative elements do not eclipse the product positioning message. This particularly can happen when humor or celebrity endorsers are used. The advertiser also can make certain the advertisement does not attempt to achieve so many communications objectives that in the process it achieves none. A commonly believed creative principle is that successful advertisements convey a single message, a single image, a single claim of superiority, or a single reason to buy.

Describing the elements of a successful creative execution is like trying to describe a work of art. The use of the elements or techniques can be identified, the process of how they are put together can be explained, but exactly how the artist derives the right combination of pieces remains part of the mystery of creativity. Consequently, all marketers can and should try to understand the strengths and weaknesses of the following creative elements used in advertising.

Headlines

Headlines should promise a benefit through product use, identify the target audience, name the brand, and be newsworthy and dramatic (see Figure 15.7). They can pose questions to an involved audience that will arouse curiosity and thought. They can be humorous, such as the directive "Go to Elle" from the women's fashion magazine called *Elle*. Computer graphics are opening up exciting new opportunities for enhancing headlines, copy, and logos.

Pictures

Seeing and hearing come naturally. We have to learn to read and listen to words.[9] Natural pictures and sound are therefore easier to process than words and are powerful communicators. A picture *is* often worth a thousand words, particularly when it makes a hero out of the product. Although visuals and sound can arouse attention, they work best when they execute the message strategy. Otherwise, attention-grabbing sight and sound images may distract consumers from the actual product message.

[9] J. R. Rossiter and L. Percy, "Visual Communication in Advertising," in *Information Processing Research in Advertising*, ed. R. J. Harris, (Hillsdale, NJ: Lawrence Erlbaum Associates, 1983), 83–125.

Figure 15.7

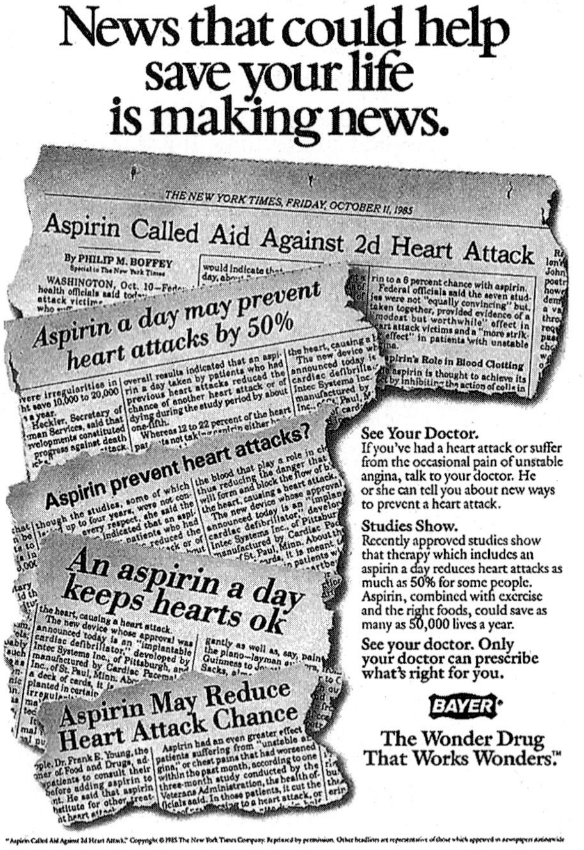

The clever use of publicity in advertising adds credibility and helps execute a LFB logical persuation theme. This is also an excellent example of integrated marketing communication.

Picture-Word Integration

The integration of images with a written message has been shown to increase consumer memory for brand names and themes.[10] For example, an ad for the Rocket messenger service that includes a logo showing a flying messenger with a rocket tied to his back results in greater recall on the part of consumers than presenting the same information as words alone. Similarly, the campaign by Nationwide Insurance, in which its tag line "Nationwide is on your side" is depicted by the movement of the word "Nationwide" to one side on the TV screen, is another example of how pictures

[10] Kathy A. Lutz and Richard J. Lutz, "The Effects of Interactive Imagery on Learning: Application to Advertising," *Journal of Applied Psychology* 62 (August 1977): 493–98.

and words can interact to produce a memorable effect on the viewer. Federal Express launched its fast delivery service by using a fast-talking spokesperson (Mr. Spleen) who described the benefits of using Federal Express. Many remember this ad for its humor, and the theme of speed is conveyed effectively at the same time.

Structure

The most important messages are generally placed at the beginning of an ad and repeated at the end. The layout and flow should be designed so the audience processes the ad in the intended order. Advertisers should beware of creative distractors that interfere with this flow.

Music

Familiar tunes can grab attention and induce a mood.[11] They are even better if their lyrics reinforce the message strategy. Sprint's "I just called to say I love you" ad produced an immediate 25 percent increase in inquiries to the new long-distance phone company. It is possible for an advertising jingle to become so popular that it is fleshed out and released as a song. For example, Coca-Cola's 1972 ode to brotherhood, "I'd like to teach the world to sing," became a top-forty hit. Coca-Cola now airs the singing ad every Christmas as a nostalgic masterpiece. The "I want to be like Mike" song was originally a Nike advertisement.

Humor

Humor can attract attention, create a good mood, or be passed on by word of mouth (who can forget the slogan "Where's the beef?"). Humor can be very powerful if it reinforces the basic message strategy, but that is difficult to do. One successful example was the Federal Express ad mentioned earlier, "Fast-Paced World," which featured the fast-talking Mr. Spleen as a symbol of the need for speed and Federal Express's ability to meet a demanding executive's standards. Another example is Miller Lite's "Tastes great, less filling" shouting matches. The downside is that humor can overwhelm and distract.[12] Many people can remember an ad by its punch line but not the brand. Jokes also wear out very quickly.

Varied Executions

Brand-name memory has been shown to increase when advertising executions are varied. For example, each Dewar's whiskey ad portrays a different person who consumes that brand of whiskey.[13] In the bunny-drummer Energizer ads, the pink bunny interrupted more than two dozen different fictitious commercials and in this way maintained high audience interest.

---

[11] Gerald J. Gorn, "The Effects of Music in Advertising on Choice Behavior: A Classical Conditioning Approach," *Journal of Marketing* 46 (winter 1982): 94–101; P. Sherrid, "Emotional Shorthand," *Forbes*, November 4, 1985, 214–15; and Gordon C. Bruner II, "Music, Mood and Marketing," *Journal of Marketing* 54, no. 4 (October 1990): 94–104.

[12] B. Sternthal and C. S. Craig, "Humor in Advertising," *Journal of Marketing* 37, no. 4 (1973): 12–18.

[13] Robert E. Burnkrant and H. Rao Unnava, "Effects of Variation in Message Execution on the Learning of Repeated Brand Information," in *Advances in Consumer Research*, vol. 14, Provo: Utah; Association for Consumer Research, ed. M. Wallendorf and P. Anderson, 1987, 173–76.

Rationality in Practice

Old Is Gold

As the competitive clutter around ads increases, advertisers are struggling to find creative executions that will stand out from the rest. Although modern graphics and loud sounds cease to attract audience interest, advertisers have found truth in the adage "Old is gold."

AdvantEdge Television Advertising in New York sells old award-winning television advertisements that can be customized to a new client's product. Often, all the client needs to do is change the logo at the end of the commercial, and she or he is ready to air it within a week. What is the price? It is often as low as 10 percent of what it cost to produce the commercial originally. Buyers like True Quality Pharmacy of Texas agree that old wine in a new bottle does taste good, especially at these prices.

Meanwhile, Coca-Cola has made a splash with Paula Abdul, who is shown pitching Diet Coke as she dances with old, and now dead, celebrities like Louis Armstrong and Humphrey Bogart. It appears as though the old and forgotten are not as old and forgotten as one might assume. If consumers truly are turned off by the new and turned on by the old, maybe this is an avenue creative directors should start thinking about.

SOURCE: Excerpted from Stuart Elliott, "More Scenes from the Past Sell Products in the Present," *New York Times*, April 24, 1992; and Melanie Wells, "Old Ads Get Recycled by Different Retailers," *Advertising Age*, February 15, 1993, 12.

Building on Classic Themes

An old campaign's familiarity to customers often can be an excellent way to launch a new creative approach and help integrate past usage with present usage. Creative directors also have discovered that, in general, nostalgia sells (see the Rationality in Practice box, "Old is Gold") or at least appeals to some market segments.

Young and Rubicam (Y&R) cleverly built on Ogilvy and Mather's "Merrill Lynch is Bullish on America" theme, which had been used for seven years. They created the slogan "Merrill Lynch, a breed apart" using one bull (symbolizing a sustained stock market rally) in a china shop (symbolizing the need to be careful and cautious) instead of a herd of bulls thundering out of the TV screen. The bull was put out to pasture prematurely (dropped) in 1985 by Y&R, which may have been the reason why the agency lost the account the following year.[14] The bull has since returned to Merrill Lynch's advertising.

Sex

The steamy ménage-à-trois scene in Figure 15.8 helped sell Calvin Klein's Obsession (it at least fulfilled some fantasies; within a year Obsession became one of the top three fragrances). Sexual cues are great attention grabbers. However, they must be used in a setting relevant to the product, or else they can backfire. If an ad is viewed as crass, cheap, exploitive, and tasteless by the target audience, than all of these characteristics may become attached to the advertiser and its brands, such as happened with Calvin Klein's recent underwear advertising.

Fear

Fear can be turned into a powerful tactic for drawing attention to a problem, but only if a credible solution is offered, such as smoke detectors to prevent house fire deaths.

[14] Christine Dugas and Paul B. Brown, "How Five Advertising Agencies Ran for the Bull," *Business Week*, April 14, 1986, 90–91.

Figure 15.8 Sex in Advertising

An FBL "I'm a dream, a mood, a good-time product" message. While attention grabbing, is such sex in advertising appropriate for this product?

If the message is too strong, people will avoid future exposure to the ad, and the effect of repetition will be reduced. It also may create negative emotions and feelings that become associated with the brand. Normally, the media will not accept ads that create fear about using a competitor's product.[15]

Slice of Life

The slice-of-life creative approach is more readily integrated into personal experiences of product use and can help teach consumers how to use the product. It also can increase use (for example, AT&T's successful "Reach out and touch someone" campaign) and reinforce the user's later experiences with the product. Slice-of-life creative executions rely on vicarious learning strategies (learning by watching), which everyone employs from birth.

Slice-of-life ads can be very powerful if they ring true in the same way a great movie rings true. In fact, product placement in movies or television shows is an ideal

[15] Peter Wright, "Concrete Action Plans in TV Messages to Increase Reading of Drug Warnings," *Journal of Consumer Research* 6 (December 1973): 256–69; and J. J. Burnett and R. E. Wilkes, "Fear Appeals to Segments Only," *Journal of Advertising Research* 20, no. 5 (1980): 21–24.

way to execute a slice-of-life creative approach. When Snapple is featured on *Seinfeld* or KitchenAid on *Mad about You* and *Friends*, it is only fleeting, but it is highly credible and is about one-hundredth the cost of producing and airing a thirty-second TV commercial.[16]

Spokesperson

More than half of Japanese TV ads use a spokesperson who is immediately recognizable to the public.[17] The most successful ads use Western pop stars and actors. Using a spokesperson draws attention and transfers the celebrity's image to the brand. It is best if the spokesperson's image complements and reinforces the desired brand image and the audience's perceptions of the product category. Spokespeople also can establish claim credibility, providing they are not exposed as being ingenuine. The problem is they are very expensive and can overwhelm the basic message.[18]

Two-Sided Ads

Ads that are not all positive provide credibility with more highly involved audiences; negative admissions can enhance the positive claims made about the product or service.[19] This approach can be used by new entrants to inoculate against a competitor's arguments. A classic example is Avis's "We are #2, but we try harder."

Comparison Ads

Comparisons should be used only when competing against a market leader or when a product has compelling advantages over a competitive brand. They are good to use when the target audience is involved and it is easy to compare the benefits of one product against others (see Figures 15.9 and 15.10).[20] About 30 percent of TV ads are comparative. This tactic carries the risk of identifying worthy competitors and raising their top-of-mind recall ratings by identifying them as alternatives.

Competitive Interference

Interestingly, advertising also can be used to make consumers forget competitors' brand names. When consumers see advertising information for a brand, they appear to forget some competitive brand names.[21] This suggests that attention-getting, point-of-purchase materials can make a consumer think about that brand to the

[16] "Starring Role," *Entrepreneur*, December 1995, 30.

[17] See Andrew Tanzer, "The Celebrity Is the Message," *Forbes*, July 14, 1986, 88–89.

[18] See D. Ogilvy and J. Raphaelson, "Research on Advertising Techniques That Work—And Don't Work," *Harvard Business Review* 60 (1982): 14–18. Their evidence suggests that a spokesperson can distract attention and reduce learning. Another study suggests that audiences are becoming bored with celebrity spokespeople. See Joanne Lipman "When It's Commercial Time, TV Viewers Prefer Cartoons to Celebrities Any Day," *The Wall Street Journal*, February 16, 1990, B1, B4.

[19] Micheal Etgar and Stephen A. Goodwin, "One-Sided versus Two-Sided Comparative Message Appeals for New Brand Introduction," *Journals of Consumer Research* 8 (March 1982): 460–65; and Edward Giltenan, "Confronting the Negatives," *Forbes*, April 27, 1987, 83–84.

[20] Chow-Hou Wee, "Comparative Advertising: A Review with Implications for Further Research," *Advances in Consumer Research*, vol. 10, ed. R. R. Bagozzi and A. M. Tybout, (Ann Arbor, MI: Association for Consumer Research, 1983); and "Red in Tooth and Claw," *The Economist*, May 18, 1991, 79–80.

[21] Joseph W. Alba and Amitava Chattopadhay "Salience Effects in Brand Recall," *Journal of Marketing Research* (November 1986): 363–69.

Figure 15.9 **Comparison Ads**

Left: An LFB "I'm better than they are in this usage situation" message theme combined with a "Try me" coupon campaign. *Right:* An LFB "I'm better than they are because . . ." message theme, combined with a "Try me" promotion.

detriment of competitive brands. This point-of-purchase idea is especially appealing because advertising has become cluttered with competition: 42 percent of the products advertised during a regular prime-time hour of programming have a competitive ad present in the same hour.[22]

Media Planning

For some new products, the choice of communication channels can be as important as the choice of distribution channels. This section discusses the media in terms of its

[22] Joe Mandese, "Rival Spots Cluttering TV," *Advertising Age*, November 18, 1991.

Figure 15.10 **Factual Comparisons**

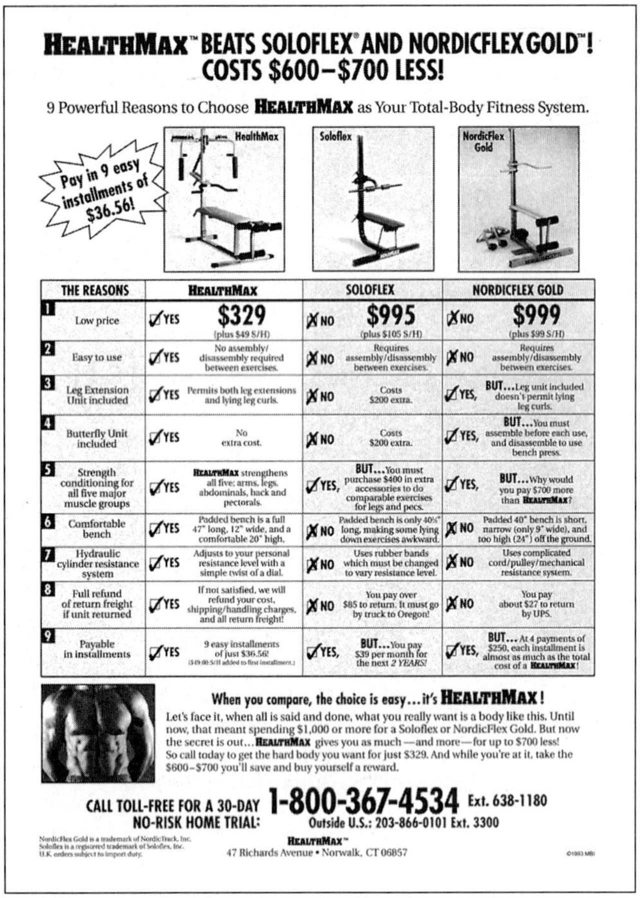

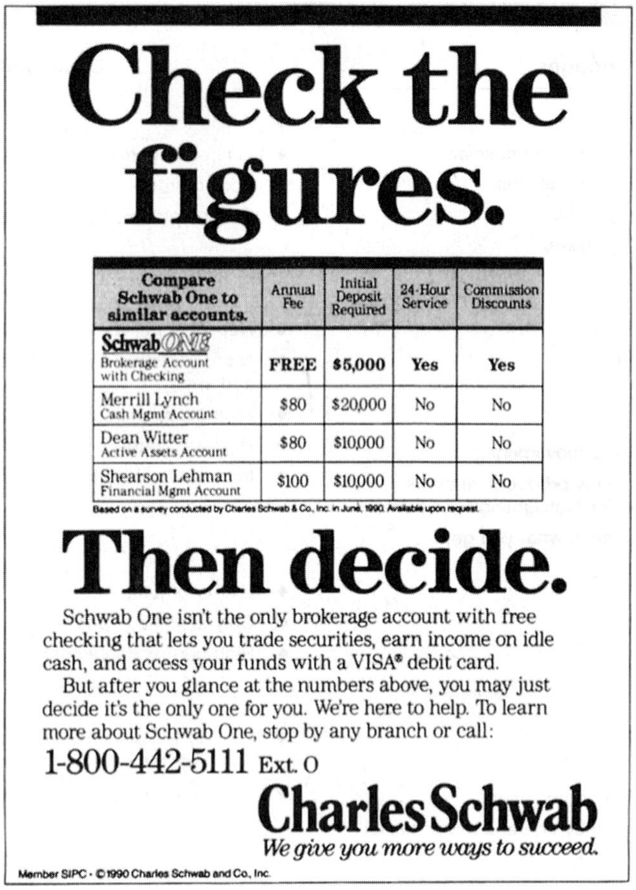

Two very detailed, factual LFB "I'm better than they are because . . ." advertisements.

suitability for carrying various creative messages as well as its ability to reach specific market segments at different levels of message repetition. This information is needed to assess the effectiveness of a media schedule and to execute a target segmentation strategy.

Each media type possesses unique strengths, weaknesses, and cost structures (see the next Rationality in Practice box). Potential advertisers receive a great deal of information from each advertising medium stating why it is the ideal communication vehicle, all supported by detailed and often contradictory audience and impact research. The problem centers on identifying the shortfalls of each media type. Table 15.2 summarizes the generally accepted advantages and disadvantages of each major media type. These assessments should be qualified by the unique circumstances of the

Rationality in Practice

Something in the Air

Something about a blimp fascinates us all. Children and even adults will point out one of these floating billboards in the distance, and it will remain the center of attention in the car or stadium or even on the television like no other advertisement can. For companies that simply seek top-of-mind brand awareness and brand reinforcement through association with a fun object that creates extreme attention, the advertising blimp is unbeatable and cost effective. Sea World's whale blimp *Shamu* costs about $3 million a year to run, but its free exposure time on television each year would cost $10 million to buy as advertising.* In addition, it has the traveling-billboard added value and the goodwill of giving important trade customers free rides and of giving free rides as incentives to employees and their families.

More than seventy years ago, the Goodyear Tire & Rubber Company first used a blimp as a marketing tool, but it was not until the early 1990s that blimps really caught on. In 1996 twenty blimps will hover over sports events around the country, and several smaller "lightships" (only 120 feet long compared to their larger 200-foot cousins) will be able to change their banners in a day. The bigger ships are expensive to paint and must be leased for a year. The innovative lightships are illuminated from the inside with bulbs that shine through the skin, which gives them the added advantage of being a beacon in the sky at night. Companies such as Blockbuster, the Family Channel, and Met Life have leased lightships. And if you were wondering whether you will ever see one of these dream machines go down in flames, do not worry. They are filled with inert helium, and the worst that can happen to them, as happened to one on Long Island in 1994, is that they land in an undignified flop as a result of a loss of pressure. But even then such an event makes the evening news and another million dollars' worth of free publicity.

*Joshua Levine, "Lighter than Air," *Forbes*, October 10, 1994, 120–21.

advertiser. Media suitability depends on the target market, the basic message strategy, and the creative tactics used to execute the message strategy (see Table 15.1).

Minor competitors are often advised to bypass the medium dominated by a major competitor unless their differentiation and message theme are very strong. Otherwise, the company's media voice share (its percentage of industry advertising seen on the medium) will be too small to register a significant impact.

Media Trends

What is the future of broadcast advertising? Some academics are predicting the death of all advertising. The argument is that some evidence shows that advertising expenditures are declining, and "The information superhighway will become the global electronic supermarket of the 90s, uniting producers and consumers directly, instantly and interactively."[23] Advertising will be completely transformed into information that is sought

[23] Roland T. Rust and Richard W. Oliver, "The Death of Advertising," *Journal of Advertising* 23, no. 4 (December 1994): 73.

Table 15.2 Advantages and Disadvantages of Major Advertising Media

MEDIA	ADVANTAGES	DISADVANTAGES
Newspapers	Creates greater urgency Excellent for local retail sales and specials Major private-ads media (classifieds) Short ad-placement lead time Co-op advertising with retailers High credibility	Limited reach Limited targeting (can use suburban papers) Poor reproduction Section readership varies greatly High cost per thousand
Television	Intrusive, attention getting Most persuasive media High reach High frequency Offers visuals, sound, and movement Best for demonstrating new products, features, and problem/solutions and for highlighting zany humor Believable—what you see is what you get	Networks deliver a mass audience Narrow casting limited to cable television, specific programs, and local television High production and placement costs High ad clutter Information limitations Only seems to work for new products and services
Direct mail	Highly targeted from lists Personalized message Enables direct selling Very important in industrial marketing	Clutter of junk mail Only a single exposure High per-exposure cost
Radio	High intimacy Can reinforce TV ads Can use announcer disc jockey endorsements Highly targeted audiences by age and music tastes Low production and running costs Short ad-placement lead time	Lack of visuals limits learning and linking to point-of-purchase displays Difficult to buy national coverage
Magazines	Very specific targeting, particularly for industrial markets Credible source effects of some magazines Allow detailed information for new products and comparison ads Extended life of magazine and readership over time Can direct market and include coupons in ad	Needs high involvement Long ad-placement lead time Difficult to get high frequency within purchase cycle time For some magazines, placement costs of full-color ads high Location of ad in the magazine critical
Outdoor (billboards)	High frequency Less clutter Primarily for image and brand awareness Low running costs Moving parts create attention	Limited attention span Limited reach Limited targeting Quite high production costs
Point of purchase	Closest to purchase Can be powerfully integrated with TV and magazine ads Useful for both high- and low-involvement products Three-dimensional effects	Depends on retail cooperation Poor frequency Occurs too late in choice cycle Quite high production costs

out, provided by rating services, or in the form of electronic catalogs, or product brochures. Home personal-computer expert software will scan and select information of interest to its human "masters" and help select "customized" products and services on the superhighway.

Other futurists look at long-term advertising trends and see a brighter future.[24] The argument is that, in the long term, the information superhighway may reduce the buying of media time and space but will create increased demand for advertising. The trend is already evident. Niche cable channels such as The Nashville Network, The Travel Channel, and The History Channel already need specific creative executions targeted at their different audiences. The number of consumer magazines tripled between 1963 and 1988, and the number of business publications increased by 50 percent.[25] This magazine fragmentation also increases the number of creative executions designed for specific magazines. Thus advertising spending will shift: More will be spent on unique creative executions targeting special segments and even specific individuals, and less will be spent on time and space in mass media. The next Rationality in Practice box also critically examines the future "revolutionary" impact of the Internet on advertising.

Television

Television has been the medium preferred by national advertisers. It is the most expensive communication medium but is also potentially the most persuasive for new products and services. However, much of television advertising may be a waste of time and money, which explains why P&G decided to cut back its television advertising in Britain in 1996 by 10 percent. A systematic and rigorous study of television advertising-campaign effectiveness has shown that television advertising only works for new products (See Figure 15.11). Many advertisers spend most of their budget on television in spite of the cold, hard facts that it does not work, that the rates charged by television companies keep increasing, and that television audiences are shrinking. The major television networks are under siege by cable television and videocassette recorders. During the 1980s, the three major networks' share of the prime-time audience dropped from 92 percent to 67 percent, while the cost of a thirty-second commercial in a choice spot rose 85 percent to $185,000.[26] Many advertisers have since recognized niche marketing advantages by advertising on cable channels such as MTV and ESPN.

A major trend in television commercials during the 1980s was the advent of the fifteen-second commercial. About 35 percent of all television commercials are fifteen seconds long. Some advertisers claim that a fifteen-second news or logical-persuasion advertisement has 80 percent of the effect of a thirty-second commercial, at about half the cost.[27] They are much less effective for emotion/feeling themes. This increase in shorter advertisements has led to increased clutter that over the long term may reduce the effectiveness of all television advertising. As described in the chapter opener, television's saviour may be the 30-minute infomercial.

---

[24] Richard J. Fox and Gary L. Geissler, "Crisis in Advertising?" *Journal of Advertising* 23, no. 4 (December 1994): 79–83.
[25] James B. Kodak, "25 Years of Change," *Folio* 19, no. 3 (March 1990): 83–89; and "The Life Cycles of Business Magazines," *Folio* 21, no. 1 (January 1994): 68–69.
[26] Zachary Schiller, "Stalking the New Consumer," *Business Week*, August 28, 1989, 54–62; and Jeffrey A. Trachtenberg, "The Revolt of the Couch Potatoes," *Forbes*, January 11, 1988, 260–61.
[27] Jill Andresky, "Time and Emotion Studies," *Forbes*, November 18, 1985, 254.

Figure 15.11 **The Ineffectiveness of Advertising Established Products on Television**

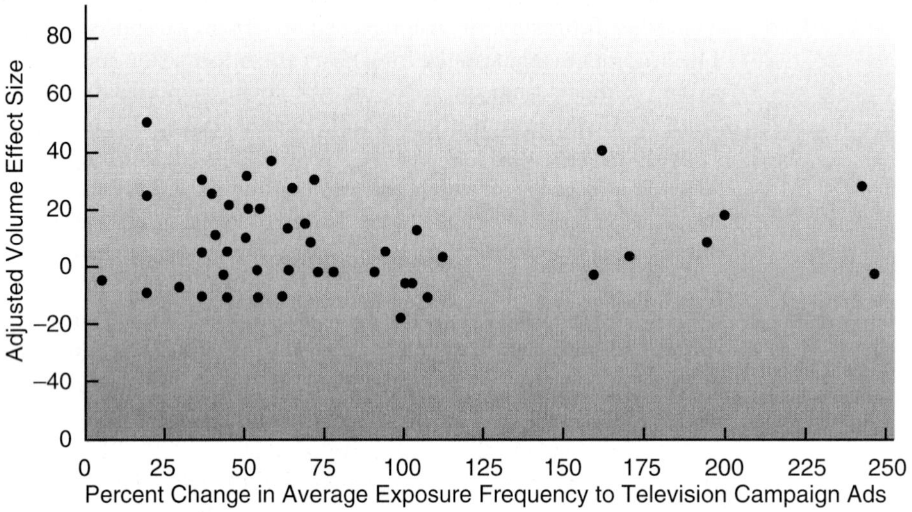

This graph shows the relationship between the average frequency of target-audience exposure to television advertisements and sales volume increases. No relationship exists. According to these results, advertising an established product on television does not increase sales and is a waste of money. The study found that the effectiveness of advertising new products on television was also much weaker than expected. The results were obtained from controlled experiments using the BehaviorScan process that tests the real-world effectiveness of TV advertising using a split-cable system and a panel of matched households. The only differences among the matched households is their controlled exposure to different TV advertisements. This study also was sponsored by a number of major advertising agencies, advertisers, and major TV networks ABC, CBS, and NBC.

SOURCE: Leonard M. Lodish et al., "How TV Advertising Works: A Meta-Analysis of 389 Real World Split Cable TV Advertising Experiments," *Journal of Marketing Research* (May 1995): 125–39.

Radio

The major trend in radio has been the increasing domination of stereo FM technology and the specialization of radio stations by the type of music played (hard rock, light rock, alternative rock, easy listening, country, and so on). Radio advertising directed at commuters can be very effective.[28] The impact car phones have on the listening habits of upscale commuters has not been determined, but it is likely to be negative, unless radio advertisements encourage listeners to call in for further information or to make a purchase. More generally, radio is a secondary advertising medium that supports advertising in primary media such as television and newspapers. Labeling it "secondary" does not mean the dollar effectiveness of radio advertising is lower. Often it is higher because it inexpensively boosts the effectiveness of more expensive television and newspaper advertising.

[28] Joshua Levine, "Drive Time," *Forbes*, March 19, 1990, 144–46. A major advantage of radio is its low cost per thousand exposures of $2, compared to a television's cost per thousand of $14 and a surprisingly high $23 cost per thousand for newspapers.

Newspapers

High technology is affecting the production and delivery of newspapers, although it is not so obvious to readers. The launching and surprising success of *USA Today* would not have been possible without the use of satellite technology and computerized printing. This newspaper poses a long-term, legitimate challenge to other newspapers and other media because it offers advertisers national coverage with a heavy predominance of readership among traveling businesspeople. Newspapers will remain dominant in local classified advertising and retail display advertising, but they are losing national-brand advertising because they have limited reach and limited reproduction quality in terms of their graphics. *USA Today* addresses some of these problems and targets itself to a very attractive market segment.

Magazines

The trend in magazines is toward focused topics. Color television killed many general-interest magazines, but sports, recreational, business, and highbrow magazines continue to flourish. The more narrow a magazine's focus and the more in-depth its coverage for a particular recreation or sport, the more likely its subscribers will be real enthusiasts, early adopters of related products, and opinion leaders. Such media should be used first when launching a new product or service that the real enthusiasts are expected to initially adopt and then spread the word about. The characteristics of the media having been discussed, the next section considers how to buy media space and time.

Media Buying

The greatest percentage of advertising expenditures (80 percent to 90 percent) are for media time or space. This suggests that the productivity of advertising expenditure can be improved by one or more of the following approaches: (1) finding the media that delivers the lowest cost per thousand members of the target audience, (2) achieving the most effective mix of reach and exposure frequency, (3) switching from national to regional campaigns, and (4) improving the timing of the campaign. Each of these media scheduling issues is now discussed.

Minimizing Cost Per Thousand of the Target Audience (CP[TA]M)

Media costs are generally measured in cost per thousand of delivered audience (CPM). The problem with this industry standard is that it does not reflect audience discrimination. A nonuser of an advertised product category is weighed the same as a heavy user of the product category. Anheuser-Busch has publicly admitted that in the mid-1970s it misjudged the attractiveness of the *ABC Monday Night Football* package.[29] Anheuser looked at the cost of the package on a total dollar basis rather than on a cost-per-thousand-beer-drinkers' basis and decided to forego the advertising opportunity. Miller, on the other hand, recognized the program's attractiveness based on a cost per thousand of *target* audience. Also, special advertising context effects were operating. Not only was a large portion of the audience made up of heavy beer drinkers, but also many were drinking beer while watching football and the Miller Lite Beer ads. They were primed to respond.

[29] Anheuser reacted by becoming the nation's top event sponsor. By 1987 it sponsored 80 percent of all professional sports teams in the country. See Michael Oneal, "Anheuser-Busch: The Scandal May Be Small Beer After All," *Business Week*, May 11, 1992, 72–73. In 1992 Miller hired away Anheuser's top marketing executive to be its new CEO.

Rationality in Practice

Technology Path Dependencies in Advertising

Two realities have to be considered in evaluating the impact of information technology on the future of advertising. The first reality is that as consumers spend less time exposed to television, newspapers, and magazines and spend more time on their home-computer entertainment systems connected to the information superhighway, advertising on the blockbuster TV programs or most popular media will become even more valuable and priced at a premium. Companies, politicians, and nonprofit organizations will be competing to buy a dwindling supply of a truly mass audience that is "involuntarily exposed" to their persuasive bombardments. The programs and media most hurt by the information superhighway will be those caught in between: They do not attract a truly mass audience sought by big national advertisers, nor do they have enough narrowcasting to an enthusiast niche audience sought by the specialist advertiser.

The second reality is that the integration of traditional advertising and detailed information on the Internet will increase dramatically. Already, advertisements on television, on billboards, and in magazines provide the World Wide Web (WWW) addresses (See Figure 12.1). The Web connection will provide multimedia sales brochures, individualized information, where-to-buy details (including comparative prices), and direct buying capabilities. All of these will be designed by the new generation of advertising creative artists. In short, traditional advertising will increase the effectiveness of WWW marketing and will continue to drive its evolving use. In the same way newspaper and magazine advertising evolved with the introduction of radio advertising, and all three evolved with the introduction of TV advertising, all four will evolve with the

Increasingly, more sophisticated advertisers and agencies are measuring the cost per thousand of a specific target audience (TA) that the media delivers—abbreviated CP(TA)M. This refined statistic indicates the cost efficiency of the media vehicle's reach of the desired target market segment. This requires knowing customers' media usage and evaluating the cost effectiveness of different media based on this information (see Chapter 5 on buying behavior segmentation). For advertisers who purchase millions of dollars of advertising space per year, such a study is worth the cost.

Achieving Effective Reach and Frequency

Advertising campaigns often are measured by their reach and frequency. *Net reach (NR)* refers to the percentage of the target audience exposed to an ad message one or more times during a given time, usually four weeks. NR is a useful measure when only one exposure is needed to relay a message and when the goal is to have as many people as possible hear it. This applies to newsworthy advertisements, such as special clearance sales, with a simple, compelling message that generates further word of mouth. But what happens when experts say consumers need to be exposed more than once to an ad for it to be effective? Marketers then should use a measure of *effective reach*. The effective reach of a proposed media schedule is the percentage of the target audience exposed to an ad the minimum number of times (frequency) that is judged necessary for the ad to be effective.

Frequency measures the total number of times a person or household is exposed to an advertising message. The necessary frequency of exposure required for an ad to be effective depends on the brand's competitive position, consumer behavior, and the basic message strategy. Dominant, established brands with high brand loyalty need development of WWW marketing. Thus they will evolve rather than die.

Just how else the superhighway will be used to buy and convey information is still quite unclear. Pizza still will be ordered by the telephone, and paper catalogs still will be used for twenty to thirty years. The problem with Web marketing is that the only way firms will be able to contact consumers is if the consumer contacts them first. A ten-minute barrage of unsolicited advertising (that cannot be bypassed) when you hook up to the Web will be about as well received as unsolicited advertising jamming up your fax machine. In addition, the infiltration of WWW interest groups by marketing and public relations communications is also likely to be poorly received. For example, what happens when telemarketing organizations become WWW marketing organizations? Hundreds of operators will choke up interest-group bulletins with their constant stream of contrived commercial or political-interest-group messages masquerading as coming from individual citizens. Very quickly limits on such WWW marketing will be set. The reality is that the Web will be a much improved, multimedia, 800-number service that in some product and service markets will threaten traditional distribution channels more than it will threaten traditional advertising.

less frequency. A number of researchers have argued that three exposures within a purchase cycle (time between purchases) is optimal.[30] But this advice applies mainly to ads using a logical-persuasion approach. Ads that attempt to imprint associations and feelings are likely to require many more repetitions. Figure 15.12 explains what factors drive the need for higher exposure frequency.

The average frequency of an ad's exposure to the target audience is often used as a measure of a campaign's effectiveness or potency.[31] It is usually measured in GRPs (Gross Rating Points = Average Frequency × 100). Note, however, that this measure includes potential buyers who were exposed to the ad only once or twice, which may have been not enough to have any effect. As a measure of effectiveness, average frequency weighs ten exposures as twice as potent as five exposures and ten times as potent as one exposure. This is a very unrealistic assumption. It assumes that each exposure is equally valuable; that is, the tenth has the same impact as the first (see the Rationality in Practice box, "Choosing the Best Campaign").

Advertising Objectives and Media Choice

Simple awareness building implies reaching as many people as possible. Not many exposures to the ad would be required because all the advertiser needs to tell consumers

[30] Michael J. Naples, *Effective Frequency: The Relationship between Frequency and Advertising Effectiveness*, Association of National Advertisers, 1979.

[31] Peter R. Dickson, "Gross Rating Points: A Case of a Mistaken Identity," *Journal of Advertising Research* 31, no. 1 (1991): 55–59; and "Simplicity and Parsimony versus the Status Quo Definition of GRP," *Journal of Advertising Research* (June 1992). These articles explain that how the industry defines GRP as Net Reach × Frequency is actually Average Frequency × 100.

Figure 15.12 **When Higher Advertising Frequency Is Needed**

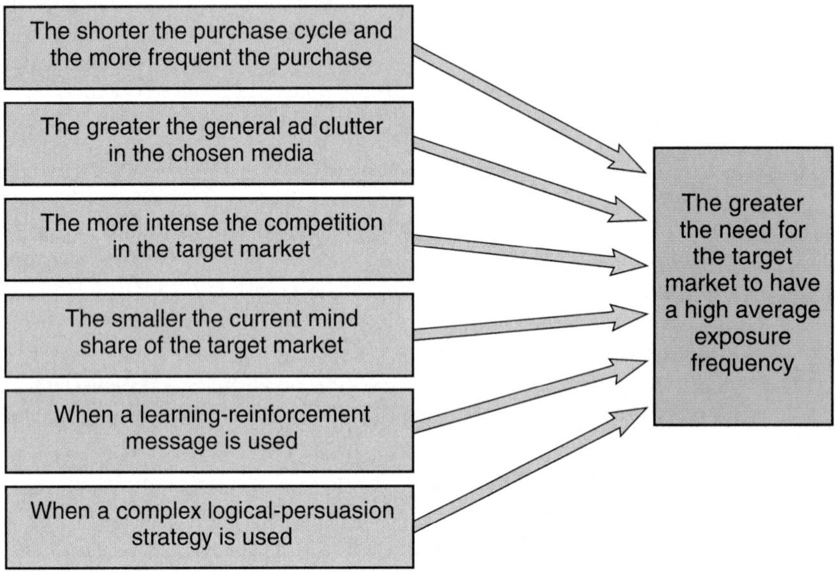
The shorter the purchase cycle and the more frequent the purchase
The greater the general ad clutter in the chosen media
The more intense the competition in the target market
The smaller the current mind share of the target market
When a learning-reinforcement message is used
When a complex logical-persuasion strategy is used
The greater the need for the target market to have a high average exposure frequency

is that a given brand exists. The medium (or media) that is chosen, then, will be based on the overlap its target audience provides with the target market for the brand. For example, if the manufacturer of a gift item for graduation wants to reach many families and inform them of their product's availability, the *Reader's Digest* may be an appropriate magazine because it reaches a large proportion of American families.

In contrast, persuasive campaigns not only require that the target market be reached but also that they be reached repeatedly to convince them of the product's superiority. In the example, if the manufacturer of the gift item has to convince people to buy the item through repetitive advertising, then *Reader's Digest* may not be an appropriate vehicle because it is issued only once every month and graduation gifts are seasonal items bought during May. The manufacturer then might opt for a medium that reaches families more frequently (e.g., weekly, in family-oriented television shows) or to combine advertising in March and April's *Reader's Digest* with advertising in other magazines that reach families about the same time.

Another variable that impacts media choice is a brand's position within a market. To understand how this happens, first realize that a brand that is a market leader nationally does not necessarily have to be a leader in every regional market (think of how a president can get elected in America!). Also realize that various regions within the country have different sales patterns for the same product. For example, bottled water is consumed in large quantities in the West and in the northeastern parts of the United States. However, although image, taste, and avoiding alcohol may be the main reasons why Californians consume bottled water, northeastern residents consume it to avoid contaminated tap water. Thus, although Evian may lead the market in the West, it may not do so in the Northeast.

Finally, the market size within a region also will impact media choice. For example, BMW realized that its major markets were ten metropolitan areas in the United States and invested in spot television in those areas rather than in advertising on national television. This leads to a discussion of the concepts of regional advertising and campaign timing.

Regional Advertising Campaigns

Increasingly, campaigns are being regionalized. Small, local companies have always used regional advertising, but even bigger companies such as Campbell's Soup are finding it more cost effective to control and manage regional campaigns than a national campaign.[32] Managing market-specific campaigns also allows the use of ads and media tailored to a particular regional market's tastes and lifestyles.

As the marketing efforts of many companies become more focused, the decision of which markets to develop next can make or break a firm's growth. The market potential of a city or region is an important factor. A number of market research companies can provide sales data of a product category by city or county. When a firm is dealing with a new product category, census data can provide information on the markets with the highest concentration of the target audience as measured by various demographic characteristics. However, the costs of reaching the target audience also can vary considerably among cities, and other factors such as retail support and climate may have to be considered when making the choice (see the Rationality in Practice box, "Choosing Regional Markets"). Increasingly, national advertisers are using local advertising agencies to buy their media space, even if they use a national agency to produce the creative executions. The logic is that local agencies are better buyers because of their knowledge of the local media.

Improving Campaign Timing

Media decision making is more than CPMs, reach, frequency, and going regional. Over the planning period, marketers must decide whether to concentrate advertising seasonally or to give it greater continuity. Much depends on the nature of consumer demand and whether selling seasons exist. Many consumer products have their major selling season in the three months before Christmas. For these products, most advertising is concentrated in the last quarter of the year. Other advertisers have several peak selling seasons. For instance, plant stores and their associated products have major spring and fall selling seasons. Advertising campaigns often are concentrated in two seasonal "flights" lasting six to eight weeks. They are likely to be intensive and to use several media at the same time. The company's tactical objective is to dominate its voice share (the total ad dollars spent by the individual company as a proportion of the dollars spent by the industry as a whole) without producing "wearout" (consumer boredom).

Low-involvement products that sell as much on their brand names as on their features, and that have short repurchase cycles (for instance, sodas that are repurchased weekly), need to have a constant advertising voice share to maintain their mind and market shares.[33] Advertising continuity is therefore very important to sustain the

---

[32] Christine Dugas "Marketing's New Look," *Business Week*, January 26, 1987, 64–69; and Glen L. Urban, "Allocating Ad Budgets Geographically," *Journal of Advertising Research* (December 1975): 7–16.

[33] Erwin Ephran, "More Weeks, Less Weight: The Shelf-Space Model of Advertising," *Journal of Advertising Research* 35 (May/June 1995), 18–23.

Rationality in Practice

Choosing the Best Campaign

An advertising campaign has two major components, a creative execution of the theme and a media schedule. Often advertisers will choose among two or three creative executions, and sometimes they will choose between two different media schedules (for instance, between a short, intense campaign or a longer, drawn out campaign). Almost never does a firm choose among advertising campaigns with different ads and different media schedules. A firm normally chooses the creative (the ad) and then chooses the best media schedule for the creative. A more competitively rational approach would be to choose the best combinations of creatives and media schedules; that is, to choose among alternative campaigns that sensibly and synergistically combine the creative execution and the media schedule.

For example, what if a company decides it should spend $5 million on TV advertising? Campaign option A is to buy twenty fifteen-second prime-time slots at $200,000 per repetition and spend $1 million on ad execution, including paying a spokesperson. Campaign option B is to spend $2 million on a thirty-second ad execution featuring a better-known spokesperson who is more attention grabbing and credible and to buy only ten thirty-second prime-time slots at $300,000 per repetition. To determine which campaign should be chosen, the firm needs to know what *percentage* of the audience will notice or see ads A and B once, twice, five times, and so on. Media schedulers or even the medium itself can provide such exposure frequency estimates. The advertiser also needs to know the relative *impact* on the target audience of seeing ad A and B once, twice, five times, or more.

The firm and its advertising agency then can use this *ADIMPACT* spreadsheet to compute the overall effectiveness of campaign A and campaign B. For example, given the exposure frequency estimates and impact estimates presented in the table, campaign A is only 83 percent as effective as campaign B, using an impact-weighted GRP score (the sum of each percentage of target audience that sees an ad *n* times weighted by the estimated impact of seeing the ad *n* times). However, using the standard GRP measure, campaign A is more than twice as effective as campaign B. The source of the difference is the assumption that the standard GRP measure makes about the impact of repeated exposures of an advertisement on the average viewer.

The impact index is scored from 1 to 20. An impact score of 20 for one of the ads that the target audience is exposed to a certain number of times (vehicle exposure frequency) means that it is twenty times as effective in its general impact (from attention to behavior) than an ad-vehicle exposure frequency with an impact score of only 1.

The impact scores are derived from the two impact curves estimated by the planning group or the ad agency of the two ads (A and B).

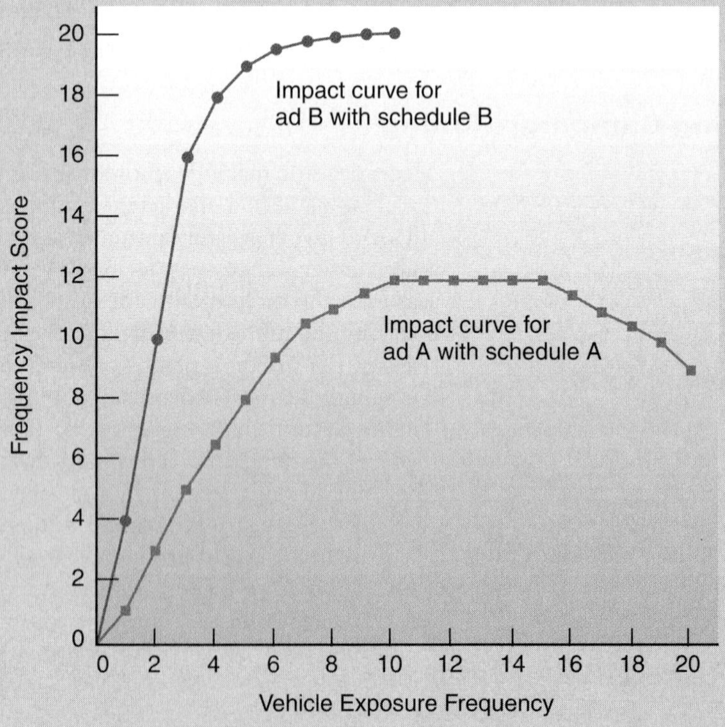

The ADIMPACT Spreadsheet

Comparison of Two Ad Campaigns Based on Reach, Frequency, and Impact
The percentage of the target audience exposed to the number of ads is estimated from audience statistics. The exposure frequency impact is an educated estimate of the cumulative impact of exposure on attention, beliefs, attitudes, and behavior.

VEHICLE EXPOSURE FREQUENCY	PERCENTAGE OF AUDIENCE REACHED: SCHEDULE A	EXPOSURE FREQUENCY IMPACT FOR AD A	PERCENTAGE OF AUDIENCE REACHED: SCHEDULE B	EXPOSURE FREQUENCY IMPACT FOR AD B
1	16.3%	1.0	9.0%	4.0
2	13.8%	3.0	6.7%	10.0
3	9.9%	5.0	5.6%	16.0
4	8.9%	6.5	4.8%	18.0
5	6.7%	8.0	4.2%	19.5
6	5.1%	9.5	3.7%	20.0
7	4.1%	10.5	2.7%	20.0
8	3.3%	11.0	2.3%	20.0
9	2.7%	11.5	1.8%	20.0
10	2.2%	11.8	1.4%	20.0
11	1.7%	12.0	0.0%	0.0
12	1.4%	12.0	0.0%	0.0
13	1.1%	12.0	0.0%	0.0
14	0.9%	12.0	0.0%	0.0
15	0.7%	12.0	0.0%	0.0
16	0.6%	11.6	0.0%	0.0
17	0.5%	11.0	0.0%	0.0
18	0.4%	10.5	0.0%	0.0
19	0.3%	10.0	0.0%	0.0
20	0.2%	9.0	0.0%	0.0
Net reach	80.8%		42.2%	
2 + Exposure Reach	64.5%		33.2%	
3 + Exposure Reach	50.7%		26.5%	
4 + Exposure Reach	40.8%		20.9%	
5 + Exposure Reach	31.9%		16.1%	
6 + Exposure Reach	25.2%		11.9%	
8 + Exposure Reach	16.0%		5.5%	
12 + Exposure Reach	6.1%		.0%	
Average frequency	3.83		1.69	

			CRITICAL RATIO (CAMPAIGN A TO B)
GRP	383	169	2.26
Impact-weighted GRP	495	599	0.83

Step 1: Insert reach at each level of vehicle exposure frequency for campaign A and campaign B (in columns 2 and 4).
Step 2: Estimate impact curves and insert impact weights (in columns 3 and 5). Press F10 to see curves.
Step 3: Play "what if" with the estimates of reach and impact.

desired awareness and brand preference levels. This may require the company to rotate its ads frequently (using several variations on a theme) to avoid creative wearout.

Smaller companies that cannot afford a continued high-advertising presence often adopt a pulsed approach. They keep a low level of advertising, often in a single medium (for instance, in a magazine read by heavy users), and then they use pulsed bursts of increased television or radio advertising to bring them up to the level of the market leader. These pulses are normally timed around peak demand periods or special promotions. The higher level of advertising is primarily aimed at gaining market share, while the lower level of advertising is aimed at the company's core of loyal, heavy users.

Another problem faced by advertisers is how to sequence and schedule the different media. As previously discussed, television and radio advertising often are designed to create interest and excitement and must precede the print advertisement that provides the detailed, persuasive message. Timing is critical because the powerful boost that advertising in the hot broadcast media can have on the effectiveness of advertising in the cool print media is often short-lived.

Discussion Questions and Minicases

1. Over the years children and adults learn to screen out intrusive advertising in newspapers, in magazines, and on billboards, radios, and television. Over the same years advertising agencies have become more creative, worked harder, and spent more money on gaining children and adults' attention. What impact have these two trends had on advertising? What is the implication for global marketing campaigns?
2. Which advertising effects model is likely to have the most certain effects, the least certain effects and which is the least expensive to execute in an advertisement?
3. Some researchers and practitioners believe in the *buy-feel-learn* model and that a major role of advertising is to reinforce feelings of satisfaction with brands already bought.[34] The idea is that when you see the brand name in an advertisement, it reminds you of your past satisfaction and serves as a form of reinforcement, although not as direct as the satisfaction you get from actually using the product. Still it creates positive feelings toward the brand and thus reinforces the buying habit. The model has a great deal of merit, but what do you think happens to the effectiveness of advertising based on this model when a major, new innovation comes along that the consumer tries and clearly prefers?
4. Identify from Table 15.1 the message subtheme employed in the "Pork, the other white meat" campaign.
5. In which type of message themes and subthemes is the order of reading or flow of the ad most important?
6. In which type of themes and subthemes do you think peripheral cues (cues in the ad unrelated to the product) will be most influential?
7. Do you think people sometimes imagine they are the person in the ad when they use a brand? What sorts of people do this with what sorts of products not mentioned in the text?
8. Since 1886, Coca-Cola company has used the following slogans: "Drink Coca-Cola," "Coca-Cola revives and sustains," "The pause that refreshes," "It's the real thing," "Look up America," "I'd like to buy the world a Coke," "Have a Coke and smile," and "Coke is it!" Categorize these themes, and relate them to the product's life cycle.

9. Describe the results of the ADIMPACT spreadsheet in the box on page 599, and explain why one advertiser might choose A and another might choose B. What is the unrealistic assumption of GRP? Construct an impact graph that demonstrates this assumption. What is the shape of the resulting curve?

10. What is the underlying model used in the Woolrest spreadsheet in the box on page 603? Interpret the results. Boston was also chosen for political reasons (the American vice

[34] Andrew S.C. Ehrenberg, "Repetitive Advertising and the Consumer," *Journal of Advertising Research*, 14.2 (April 1974): 25–34.

president of Woolrest lived there). Given the judgments in this spreadsheet, what were some of the reasons why the Boston market sales and profits were rather disappointing?

11. In an ad in *Vanity Fair*, a casually dressed, young blonde slung over a young man's shoulder struggles as she is carried to a garage. In the next scene, her jeans are off, and she is dazed, tousled, and partially nude. The advertisement is selling Guess? jeans. What do you think was the ad's message? What do you think Guess? wanted the message to be? Do you think *Vanity Fair* would have accepted an interview with a rapist promoting the pleasure of sexual assault? Who is responsible for this advertisement's effects?
12. Advertising is often criticized for its intrusive and formative influence on our culture, particularly on the values and ambitions of the young. Outside the business world, very few people consider that advertising has a positive influence on our culture. Placing the effects of advertising in the context of the effects of parents, schools, pop music, films, soap operas, and popular magazines on the young, what should be done about the cumulative negative effects of advertising?
13. The Lincoln brand of Ford automobile runs an advertisement with an accompanying picture of President Lincoln. What persuasion theory is Ford using in its advertising? Do you think it works?
14. In the past fifty years, sports heroes have made hundreds of millions of dollars from endorsing products. Do you think this will continue to happen, will increase, or will decrease over the next fifty years? Why?
15. Why is the "Just add Barcardi to everything. Except driving" advertisement so efficient and effective? What cardinal rule of communication objectives and creative principle does it break? Why can it break the rule?

16. Why might a firm tend to undertake too many regional or country specific advertising campaigns instead of running very similar ads in each country. In whose interests is it to have very distinct campaigns?

Rationality in Practice

Choosing Regional Markets

If a firm cannot afford a national advertising campaign, how does it choose the cities or regions on which to focus its campaign, and which cities should be the rollouts (that is, the cities that will follow the initial launch city)? A firm making luxury, woolen mattress pads called Woolrest launched a very successful ten-week fall campaign in Seattle, Washington, in 1984. It wanted to know what new markets it should enter (roll out in) for fall 1985. To improve the quality of its decision making, the spreadsheet on the right was developed.

A number of cities were compared to Seattle in terms of campaign cost for a standard media schedule (estimated by seeking advice from local ad agencies), of media reach and fit with the target market (provided by local ad agencies), of the quality rating of the distribution channel fit (mainly department stores) in each city, of the suitability of the climate and attitude of the region toward wool, and of the number of households with a head of household more than fifty-five years old and with an income more than $15,000 (from the 1976 census data). The latter was as close to the target market as could be measured. Some of these ratings were quite objective; others were very subjective.

The simple cost-effectiveness rating (target market size/cost) was computed by dividing the number of target households by the media cost and by standardizing the rating so the Seattle score would be one hundred (the known standard). By this calculation, Baltimore, Pittsburgh, and Philadelphia all looked as attractive, if not more attractive, as Seattle. However, when all the other attractiveness factors were considered (by multiplying the size/cost rating by each of the attractiveness ratings), then only Philadelphia looked about as attractive as the known standard, Seattle. The company used this spreadsheet to choose some of the cities for its fall 1985 campaign.

Woolrest Market Potential: U.S. 1985 Fall Season

STANDARD METROPOLITAN STATISTICAL AREA	TARGET 55+ AND $15,000 +	WOOL-AWARE AND RIGHT CLIMATE	RATING OF RETAIL DISTRICT	TV REACH	NEWSPAPER REACH	RADIO FIT	TEN-WEEK MEDIA COST INDEX
Seattle	81,228	100	100	92.0%	47.0%	100	100
Baltimore	92,610	90	100	81.0	39.0	90	110
Boston	129,634	85	70	81.0	50.0	90	216
Cleveland	97,345	90	110	91.0	39.0	80	140
Denver	64,397	95	60	91.0	58.0	90	122
Hartford	36,495	90	100	65.0	40.0	90	128
Milwaukee	63,665	90	80	93.0	46.0	80	107
Minneapolis/St. Paul	85,138	90	100	93.0	46.0	100	158
Providence	35,391	90	50	67.0	49.0	80	76
Pittsburgh	112,087	85	85	82.0	44.0	100	126
Philadelphia	214,253	85	100	90.0	40.0	100	199
Portland	54,570	100	85	89.0	45.0	90	72

STANDARD METROPOLITAN STATISTICAL AREA	SIZE/COST RATING	SIZE/COST (DIST. ADJ.) RATING	SIZE/COST (MEDIA ADJ.) RATING	SIZE/COST (CLIM. ADJ.) RATING	SIZE/COST (DIST. AND MEDIA ADJ.) RATING	SIZE/COST (ALL ADJ.) RATING
Seattle	100.0	100.0	100.0	100.0	100.0	100.0
Baltimore	103.6	103.6	68.2	93.3	68.2	61.3
Boston	73.9	51.7	62.3	62.8	43.6	37.1
Cleveland	85.6	94.2	56.2	77.0	61.8	55.6
Denver	65.0	39.0	71.4	61.7	42.8	40.7
Hartford	35.1	35.1	19.0	31.6	19.0	17.1
Milwaukee	73.3	58.6	58.0	65.9	46.4	41.7
Minneapolis/St. Paul	66.3	66.3	65.6	59.7	65.6	59.1
Providence	57.3	28.7	34.8	51.6	17.4	15.7
Pittsburgh	109.5	93.1	91.4	93.1	77.7	66.0
Philadelphia	132.5	132.5	110.4	112.7	110.4	93.8
Portland	93.3	79.3	77.8	93.3	66.1	66.1

Courageous managers raise prices, desperate managers cut them.

Anonymous

There are two fools in every market; one asks too little, one asks too much.

Russian proverb

CHAPTER SIXTEEN

Managing Pricing

During the Great Depression of the 1930s, it was observed that prices rose in markets where demand was down and business inventories had risen. This seemed inexplicable to economists and politicians because, according to the orthodox theory of changing supply and demand, prices should drop when demand decreases and an oversupply exists. Suspecting a widespread conspiracy by the captains of industry to rig prices, special congressional investigators studied why a basic mechanism of the free-market capitalist system had failed to work. What did they learn about price setting that explained the competitive irrationality they observed?

They discovered that many sellers regularly used what is called a "cost plus" process to set their prices. First, they used management accounting to estimate the average cost of a service or product, and, second, they added a percentage (e.g., 20 percent) for profit, and that was the price they set—cost plus 20 percent of cost. In the Great Depression, when demand fell, two things happened. Fewer units were sold, and thus the average cost of goods sold increased because the fixed costs of production and marketing were spread over fewer sales. Also, as the oversupply of goods increased manufacturers' inventories, storage costs increased, and thus variable costs also increased. If both fixed costs and variable costs per unit

sold increase, then average cost increases. When manufacturers applied the same cost-plus-20 percent rule during the depression as they had in the past to the higher average costs their prices rose.

In several markets during the early 1930s, sellers kept raising their prices, demand decreased, average costs of the goods sold increased, and the sellers responded by increasing their prices even more. This is an example of how the application of a habitual pricing routine is competitively irrational. Yes, the price of a good must be sufficiently greater than the cost of the good so it makes a contribution to profit. But rather than raise prices, why not lower manufacturing costs, and not by simply reducing fixed costs by closing factories and putting more consumers out of work? Instead, work with employees to redesign the product in ways that reduce the costs of its manufacturing and inventory holding processes.

This brief history is an example of how firms become slaves to naive decision routines that create a very unfortunate path dependency. Pricing intelligently involves thinking like Cadillac did in designing to target market price points, thinking like Nintendo and Netscape did in almost giving part of their products away to establish a relationship with many customers quickly, thinking like Compaq and Southwest Airlines did about costs and how they can be designed away, and, finally, thinking like P&G did in using (or not using) several different competitive pricing tactics. In the modern marketplace, pricing should never be as simple as charging cost plus a percentage or matching the market leader's price. Like all other marketing decisions, the firm with the more competitively rational pricing process is more competitive in the marketplace, and such a process is likely to involve a lot of thinking about different pricing issues. ■

Despite decades of study by economists and market researchers, price setting is still determined by a best-guess decision that is often quickly revised when the guess turns out to be wrong. For example, each year the giant automakers proudly roll out their new "price-to-sell" models. If dealership waiting lists develop, then the manufacturers know they have priced the new models too low. To raise prices, they begin to manufacture and sell cars loaded with high-price options. If, on the other hand, a model moves off the lot slowly, such as the 1996 Taurus, then manufacturers devise various price promotions to make their offerings more attractive to buyers. The effect is lower prices.[1] The auto manufacturers use very sophisticated design and manufacturing techniques. However, when it comes to setting price, they ultimately use simple trial and error.

When the great packaged-goods manufacturer and marketer Procter & Gamble first market-tested Pampers, it priced the diapers at ten cents apiece. The product bombed, because parents perceived disposable diapers to cost more than buying and washing cloth diapers. The convenience advantage of disposable diapers did not compensate for their higher cost. P&G returned to the drawing board and developed a new design for its product and package. It cut material costs and lowered production time. As a result, production costs decreased, as did profit objectives. P&G relaunched the product at a price of six cents per unit, and Pampers became a great success and hugely profitable.

How can companies reduce the uncertainty associated with finding the "right" price for either a new product or a product modification? Most marketing texts offer various price-setting methods but suggest that the appropriateness of each method depends on the company's individual pricing objectives. In this chapter, we present a procedure and mental model that build on the positioning-price technique described in Chapter 9 and link *all* of the major pricing methods and objectives.

Pricing Objectives and Decision Making

Pricing decisions are very important means of achieving the firm's overall goals and, therefore, should be made with specific objectives in mind. At the very least, the firm's pricing process should

1. Support a product's positioning strategy (e.g., high end quality versus low end economy)
2. Achieve the financial goals of the enterprise (e.g., market share, profitability, capacity usage, cost reduction)
3. Fit the realities of the marketplace (e.g., not provoke price wars)

Figure 16.1 describes a price-setting framework designed to satisfy these objectives. In addition, it provides an organization for this chapter. A product's positioning strategy attempts to differentiate the product from its competition on at least one desirable feature. It specifies the product's target segment, desired benefits, and value delivered. These characteristics in turn determine the product's quality, cost, and price. The figure reiterates the competitively rational approach to setting price described in Chapter 9, where added-value analysis and careful comparison to competitors' quality and prices are the core elements in the process; a quality function deployment (QFD) and quality-added analyses produce an initial price that is tested in a feasibility analysis. This analysis determines the level of sales and market share needed to meet company profit goals. The feasibility of achieving such sales and market share is assessed in light of the overall environmental analysis and the anticipated effectiveness of the rest

[1] When demand is uncertain, the tactic of pricing high and then reducing prices if sales are slow is not new but only recently has been developed into a formal economic theory. See Edward P. Lazear, "Retail Pricing and Clearance Sales," *The American Economic Review* 76 (March 1986): 14–32. The model describes a type of market clearance pricing that lowers the price to raise demand to the level of supply. The airlines have incorporated such a pricing approach into their revenue management system. If bookings come in quickly for a flight, the number of low fares offered is reduced. If bookings are slow, the number of low fares is increased.

Figure 16.1 **A Systematic Approach to Setting Price**

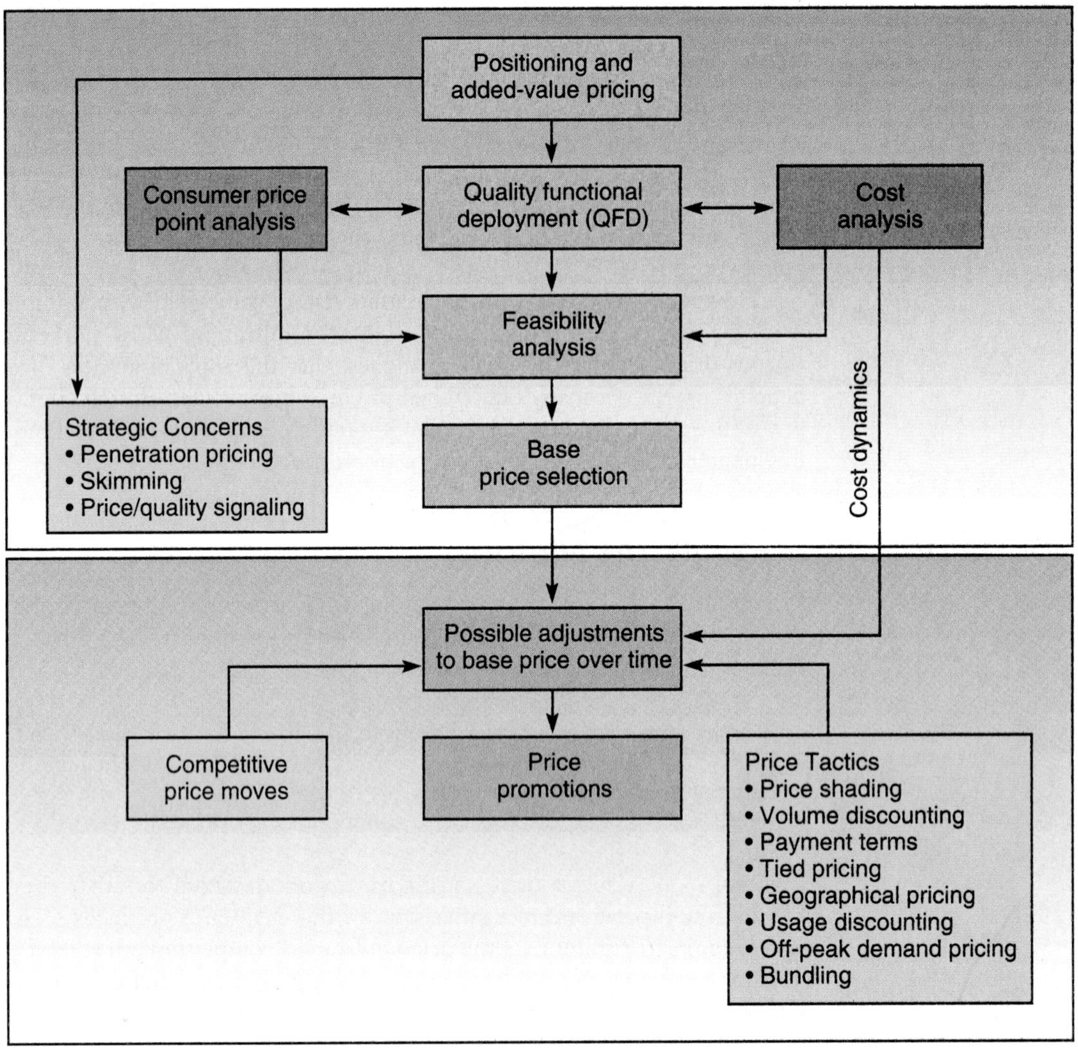

This figure presents a mental model that integrates several methods of pricing, which are usually discussed separately. In this textbook, cost analysis is discussed in Chapter 18. Positioning added-value pricing, QFD, and feasibility analysis are discussed in Chapter 9 (positioning).

of the proposed marketing strategy, such as distribution, advertising, and personal selling. If the sales goals at the initial price are infeasible, then the decision-making team must go back to the drawing board. An alternative price may be tested in the target return analysis. If no price/sales combination is feasible, then something more fundamental has to change. Either the positioning, product design, or profit goals will have to be revised.

At the same time, the firm may consider other strategic issues in helping to determine the new product's base price. These include whether price should be set strategically high to "skim" profitability early on or set low to penetrate the market and maximize early sales. Further, the issue of price/quality signaling arises in some product categories; if consumers use price as an indicator of perceived quality, then firms must be careful to make sure prices are high enough to signal high quality.

As Figure 16.1 indicates, all of these factors are critical determinants of the selected price point (or base price) for the new product. Once a price is set, however, a need for adjustment caused by competitive moves, by the desire to boost sales via price promotion, and by price schedule tactics (the lower three boxes in the figure) will occur over time.

This chapter walks the reader through the process described in Figure 16.1 (save the issues of positioning, QFD, and feasibility analysis, which already are covered in Chapter 9). Cost-based pricing is addressed first and then demand-based pricing, and customer price points, followed by a discussion of strategic pricing concerns including penetration pricing, price skimming, and price/quality signaling. The last sections of the chapter discuss factors that lead to a change in the base or list price of a product over time.

Cost-Based Pricing

Although many pricing experts say that costs should never determine price, the fact is costs determine the great majority of prices. Examples of real-world, cost-based pricing rules are listed here:

- A department store sets its prices based on a rule that states the selling price should be twice the purchase cost. Retailers call this *turnkey* pricing.
- Defense contractors are required by law to detail their costs in each bid and apply a set profit margin to those costs. This is called *cost-plus* pricing.

One of the most widely known formulas for pricing professional services is to bill clients at an hourly rate of three times the hourly wage of the individuals performing the service. Payments then break down this way: one-third goes to salary, one-third goes to overhead, and one-third becomes profit. This is called the rule-of-three.[2]

Table 16.1 lists the advantages and disadvantages of using cost rules to specify price. Good arguments exist on both sides of the issue. Although it may not be wise to use a cost-based formula to set price, costs must be known and cost structure understood to ensure that the product can be manufactured and sold at the proposed price for a profit; if profits are not made immediately, they should at least be anticipated down the road. Anything less than a thorough analysis of the present and future cost structure is folly, which is why a good deal of Chapter 18 is devoted to understanding costs.

[2] Victoria Arnold, "Believe It or Not, Most Professionals Don't Charge Enough," *Journal of Pricing Management* 1, no. 2 (spring 1990): 57–59. This article points out the problem of applying pricing rules that may have worked in the past but are no longer appropriate because cost structures have changed and are always changing.

Table 16.1 **The Advantages and Disadvantages of Cost-Based Rules**

ADVANTAGES OF COST-BASED PRICING RULES

1. A firm is in business to make a profit. Profit depends on the difference between unit price and unit cost. If this difference is negative, then profits are impossible. Hence, price must be set higher than unit cost.
2. It is fair to base price on costs. The Roman emperor Justinian, Saint Thomas Aquinas, Karl Marx, and Adam Smith all proposed that the just or normal price of a product should be related to its costs. Modern economic theory and public opinion also agree that the fair long-term price is related to cost plus a fair, risk-adjusted profit.
3. Costs are both measurable and known. Modern purchasing, production, and marketing information systems can compute the past and current unit costs of producing and marketing products down to a "claimed" fraction of a cent.
4. Cost rules are easy to administer. Once a rule is specified, pricing can be delegated to lower management or even to a computer.
5. Cost rules stabilize prices in a market. If everyone uses cost rules (perhaps even the same cost rule), price increases can be predictable when input costs increase. No seller is going to upset the apple cart by doing anything crazy with its prices.

DISADVANTAGES OF COST-BASED PRICING RULES

1. All costs cannot be known at the time prices are set. Most costs can be known only after they have been incurred. When future costs are uncertain, a cost-based rule does not assure a positive difference between unit price and unit cost. A firm's cost structure may change in such a way that the old pricing rule based on specific costs no longer works.
2. In some situations, a product can be sold at less than its average cost and still contribute to profits. This occurs when price exceeds the marginal cost of production and marketing.
3. Cost-based rules are economically inefficient. The forces of both demand and supply must be allowed to determine price for the marketplace to work efficiently. Charging a price the market will bear (rather than cost-plus pricing) may be considered unfair, but, according to long-standing economic theory, it is the best way to ensure the efficient allocation of resources.
4. Costs are often managed. Many costs are shared between product lines and items within a product line (see Chapter 18). The apportioning of these costs to a particular product line or item involves a judgment made by cost accountants. The decision may be affected by noneconomic motives such as company politics that want the costs of a product to appear high or low.
5. A cost rule is based on a wrong perspective. It implies the product should be considered first (that is, product, then cost, price, and consumer), rather than starting with the consumer (that is, consumer, then price, cost, and product). The latter is the Japanese approach to pricing and product design and is discussed in Chapters 3 and 9.

Consumer Price-Point Analysis

Demand analysis uses positioning strategy to address the following questions:

1. Given the product's positioning, how sensitive is the target market to variations in price?
2. Do price points exist around which the target market is particularly price sensitive?

If a broad enough price range exists, then every market will be price sensitive. For example, no one will pay $100 for a can of Coke (unless of course it is the last can on the lifeboat), and almost everyone will pay a nickel (except those who hate the taste). However, when setting price, firms are constrained at the low end by their own cost structure and at the high end by the competition's prices. It is the price sensitivity of shoppers *within* these constraints that is important. Many of the issues that determine buyer price sensitivity are presented in Chapter 5, which analyzes consumer price sensitivity market segments.

In theory, the overall sensitivity of a product's sales to price is described by its demand curve. The *demand curve* specifies the quantity of goods sold at various price levels and the sensitivity of purchases to fluctuations in price. Demand curves, however, are very difficult to estimate. The only way to systematically derive a demand curve is to test the product at different prices in markets that have similar promotion campaigns, distributors, and consumers. The competition also must be similar across test markets and not change between measuring demand and making the final pricing decision. Very few marketers are able to estimate their product's demand curve this way because such price tests are extremely expensive, and many factors that influence sales besides price cannot be controlled.[3]

What alternatives are left if the demand curve cannot be estimated successfully? At the very least, the key price points on the demand curve can be estimated. Key price points are those points around which many consumers enter (buy) and exit the market (no longer will buy), thus increasing or decreasing sales sharply. Marketing a product to a key price point can be a very successful positioning strategy. How did Henry Ford manage to sell so many Model T runabouts at $380 to $400 and still make a profit? Simple. He gambled that a huge unmet market existed for the automobile—the middle-class consumer. He thought he could have a profitable venture if he could sell a car that was affordable to the middle class. In 1916, without using any fancy market research techniques, he lowered the price of the Tourer from $440 to $360. He then worked on improving product design and reducing costs in the production process so he could sell the car at the lower price (see Table 5.1 in Chapter 5) and increase his profits. The car was spartan, simple, rugged, and, most important, its price was right. The original Ford Mustang also was built to a specific price point of $2,500 and was very successful. Price is seldom the last marketing decision made in launching a new product. Rather than determining a price for a product, a product is often designed for a price—a price that, based on executive judgment and consumer research, will be attractive to the product model or service package's target segment (see Chapter 9).

Kinked Demand Curve

Economists usually represent the functional relationship between sales and price [$Q = f(p)$] as a continuous, smooth curve where the responsiveness of sales to changes in price is expressed as a mathematical function called *price elasticity*. However, the demand curve that the marketer actually faces has sharp kinks in it, as the figure in the Rationality in Practice box illustrates. For decades, retailers and manufacturers have been talking about the price points that kink the demand curve. Market research supports the anecdotal experience of many executives.[4] A good reason for identifying a product's price points is also illustrated in the box. It can be mathematically shown that the highest profits are earned at the price point kinks on a demand curve, because

[3] For examples of experiments that test demand at various price levels, see Alan G. Sawyer, Parker M. Worthing, and Paul E. Sendak, "The Role of Laboratory Experiments to Test Marketing Strategies," *Journal of Marketing* 43 (summer 1979): 60–67; Gerald Eskin, "A Case for Test Market Experiments," *Journal of Advertising Research* 15 (April 1975): 27–33; John R. Nevin, "Laboratory Experiments for Estimating Consumer Demand," *Journal of Marketing* 11 (August 1974): 261–68; and Sidney Bennet and J. B. Wilkinson, "Price-Quantity Relationship and Price Elasticity Under In-Store Experimentation," *Journal of Business Research* 2 (January 1974): 27–38.

[4] In the jargon of economics, if buyer reservation prices (the most a buyer will pay) are not distributed evenly along the price dimension but instead cluster at various prices, then such prices will be price points and the aggregate demand curve will kink at these points. Therefore, a price point is a discontinuity in the demand function $Q = f(p)$.

Rationality in Practice

Adapt-A-Jug and Eco-Spout Demand Pricing

An entrepreneur in Columbus, Ohio, invented a brightly colored pouring funnel that attached to small jugs and other plastic containers. Compared to conventional plastic watering cans, this funnel gives superior reach when watering house plants, and it can be used to pour higher viscosity liquids, such as motor oil, into hard-to-reach tanks. A further advantage is that when attached to a plastic container, the unit protects and stores liquid better than conventional plastic pouring cans.

The demand curve for Adapt-A-Jug was estimated by asking several hundred shoppers outside of a Kmart store what was the most they would pay for such a product.* The demand curve thus applies only to Kmart, the type of store where the product would be sold. Each shopper was first shown the alternative watering cans available in the Kmart store. Those cans were priced from $2.99 to $4.99. As can be seen, a kinked demand curve was found with critical price points for the watering spout of $0.99, $1.49, and $1.99. The price point that will earn maximum profits for the seller of the Adapt-A-Jug is $1.99. It should be noted that some caution must be taken in interpreting consumers' self-reports of how much they are willing to pay for products (e.g., they are likely to overestimate their true willingness to pay). Quality-added analysis (see Chapter 9) also can be used effectively to assess price sensitivity.

*For a method of measuring demand by asking buyers about the most they would pay, see Peter R. Dickson and Alan G. Sawyer, "Entry/Exit Demand Analysis," in *Advances in Consumer Research*, ed. Thomas C. Kinnear, vol. 11 (Ann Arbor, MI: Association for Consumer Research, 1984), 161–70.

The Adapt-A-Jug Demand Curve

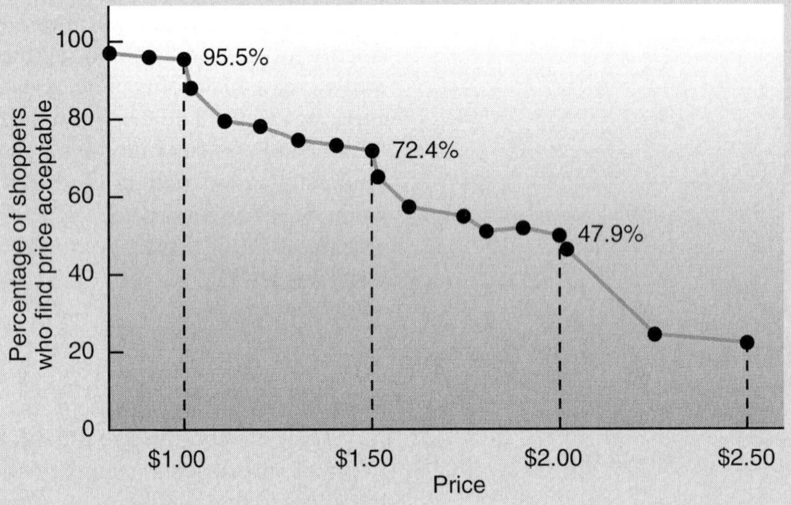

sales fall sharply above the price point, thereby hurting profits. Below a price point, sales stay about the same; but because the price is lower, the profits are lower. Identifying price points can therefore narrow down the choice of various prices to charge. These hot price points in demand occur for the three main reasons described next.

The adaptor-jug with an earth-friendly positioning as a watering can.

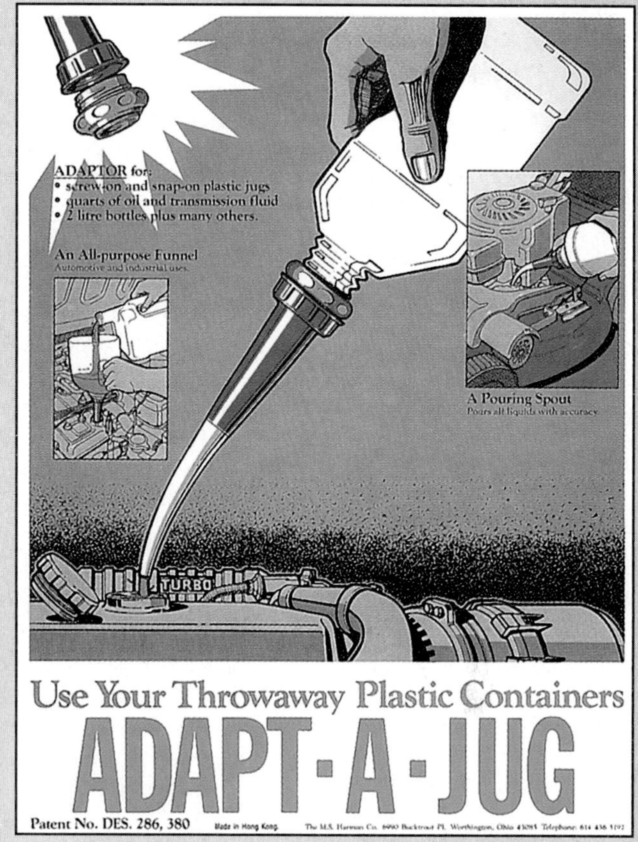

The adaptor-jug positioned as a useful pouring spout.

Perceptual Price Points

Perceptual price points are points that, if exceeded, simply make the price look larger because the actual expression of the price is larger. For example, \$10.00 is a larger expression than \$9.99. It is a four-figure number rather than a three-figure number. Likewise, \$10,000 is a larger expression than \$9,999. Consumers are therefore more sensitive to a $200 increase in a car initially priced at $9,900 than they are to a car initially priced at $9,700. For the first car, the increase pushes the price over the psychological $10,000 barrier. For example, a 1991 Ford Taurus was priced at about $13,000; the 1996 Taurus started at $19,150 and fully loaded with options was priced at $24,850. For many potential buyers, the latest Taurus price exceeded their perceptual price point for a family sedan.[5] Evidence reveals that prices ending in a nine (just below a round figure) are hot price points. In a study done at the University of Chicago, researchers showed that reducing the price of Imperial margarine from 89 cents to 71 cents increased sales 65 percent. Reducing the price to 69 cents increased sales 222 percent.[6]

Customary Price Points

Customary prices are those that shoppers have become accustomed to paying, perhaps because the price has remained the same for years (such as a 25-cent local telephone call). The price could be related to the convenience of using coins to pay for the product. Not long ago candy bars were priced at 25 cents or 50 cents. They used to cost 5 cents or 10 cents. The marketers of these products faced a problem when cost increases required them to raise the price of the 5-cent candy bar. Did they raise it to 6 or 7 cents? No, because customers would resist paying 6 or 7 cents for a 5-cent candy bar. Instead, they shrunk the candy bar's size, and then they later raised its price to 10 cents and once more increased the size of the candy bar. They increased its price again after people adjusted to the fact that the price of all candy bars had risen. The vending-machine distribution channel also required any recommended price changes in its channel to move in steps of 5 cents.

Substitute Price Points

The third and probably most common explanation for the existence of price points is that they occur at or close to the price of competitive substitutes. When an item's price is raised above the competition's price, many buyers switch to the competitor's product, thus producing a sharp kink in the demand curve for the item. The extent of the kink depends on the perceived differentiation in image and performance between the two alternatives, which can be established by quality-added analysis (discussed in Chapter 9). If the item's differentiation on important quality-added features is significant, then no noticeable substitute price points will exist. On the other hand, if the item is perceived as almost identical to a competitor's product, then demand for the item will change dramatically depending on whether it is priced above, at, or below the competitor's price; that is, a major substitute price point will exist in the item's demand curve.

Strategic Pricing Concerns

Knowing and understanding costs and price point "hot spots" provide a significant advantage to a manager who is setting prices. This section examines the strategic pricing approaches of skimming and penetration pricing, along with a number of important concerns about when consumers use price as a cue for quality.

[5] Keith Naughton, "Prices Like These Can't Last," *Business Week*, November 20, 1995, 46–47. The problem appeared to be twofold. First, for many target consumers, the new styling was not worth the added dollars compared to the old design (a quality-added problem); and, second, for many car buyers, a price above $20,000 signals a luxury car, which the Taurus is not (a perceptual price-point and positioning problem).

[6] See Thomas Nagle, *The Strategy and Tactics of Pricing* (Englewood Cliffs, NJ: Prentice-Hall, 1987), 249. Nagle quotes Kenneth Wisniewski and Robert Blattberg, Center for Research in Marketing, University of Chicago.

Penetration Pricing

The feasibility pricing analysis described in Chapter 9 assumes that the major pricing objective is to earn revenues that at least achieve a target return on assets employed. Marketers need to determine the time horizon for the break-even analysis. With many new products and services (for example, Federal Express's overnight delivery service), it takes several years before sales reach the break-even point and even longer before profit targets are achieved. When this happens, a marketing planner has to work backward from a long-term target return price that is based on future expected volume and costs. Until the desired sales volume is achieved, major losses must be accepted.

The goals of *penetration pricing* are to build market share and earn profits from future repeat sales and word of mouth (see next Rationality in Practice box). The effect on the target sales analysis is to require a much greater volume of sales and market share to achieve long-term profit goals. A firm can offer a penetration price in several ways. At the extreme, for example, a company selling new pharmaceuticals will often introduce them at a zero price through free sampling. Computer software is also often given away to opinion leaders. The first adopter of a new aircraft is often given a special discount. Tactically speaking, setting a high base price and using an introductory price discount has two advantages. First, it allows the high base price to signal the quality of the product. Otherwise, a low penetration price may lead some buyers to suspect the quality of the product. Second, the expiration of a special early-adopter discount also will produce less resistance than raising the price. Penetration pricing can be a very effective pricing strategy for the following reasons:

1. It results in faster adoption and market penetration. This can take the competition by surprise. While scrambling to react, they may make major mistakes in their pricing and channel relationships.
2. It creates an early adopter goodwill, which results in more word-of-mouth adoptions. Early adopters are often the most interested buyers and are more prepared to pay a higher price. The lower price can create a great value-for-money image (providing price is not used by consumers as a signal of quality). It should be noted, however, that the new product priced to penetrate must be free of defects. Defects could lead to negative publicity and an expensive recall. Sellers have little opportunity to adjust quality when a high-volume strategy is pursued.
3. It creates tremendous cost-reduction and cost-control pressures from the very outset. It is much easier to tighten costs and increase productivity from the start. Costs will also reduce faster with improved economies, higher volume, and a cost-concern orientation. Penetration pricing is most attractive to a firm that believes it can become and remain the low-cost producer and seller.
4. It discourages the entry of competitors. Penetration pricing can be very intimidating and demoralizing to existing competitors because it signals that the new competitor is in for the long haul and will not be easily discouraged. It also signals that the firm believes it has a sustainable, cost-competitive advantage over the competition.
5. The resulting higher stock-turn in the channel creates more channel support. A problem with penetration pricing is that it is difficult to keep the channel's dollar margin the same or more than the distribution channel usually receives from competitors selling their product at a higher price. A penetration pricing strategy may require giving a higher percentage margin on the retail price to the channel so as to keep the dollar margin the same and the distribution channel happy.
6. Penetration pricing of a secondary or export market is often based on marginal costing. However, it is not viewed as predatory or illegal until it has demonstrated its effectiveness.

Rationality in Practice

The Art of Penetration Pricing

It has often been said that Japanese companies used penetration pricing to gain their initial foothold in the North American consumer electronics markets. In reality, their targeting position strategy was much more complex than simply producing an economically priced model. For example, with the portable transistor radio, one of Japan's first manufacturing triumphs in the global market, Japanese firms introduced new features that added value and differentiated their radios in terms of sound quality and convenience. At the same time, Japanese firms continued to reduce costs and maintained their penetration pricing strategy. Very quickly, consumer goodwill toward the Japanese brands began to grow. This consumer goodwill toward the retailer who sold Japanese brands increased the Japanese manufacturers' influence and power in the channel. Japanese firms have repeatedly demonstrated how a market can be penetrated and then dominated when product and cost innovation/imitation techniques are used to build brand equity and sustain the penetration pricing strategy. However, it is clear from the figure that Japanese automobile manufacturers learned, or could have learned, from Mercedes-Benz how to use penetration pricing in the U.S. market.

> It is hard for an established competitor with a 20 percent or more market share to credibly complain about the unfair penetration pricing of a new competitor that starts with no market share.

A penetration pricing strategy is attractive if a company can sell an initial part of the product cheaply, creating the necessary long-term relationship with a customer that generates profitable future sales. For example, Nintendo often sells its game consoles at below cost but makes a handsome profit on the game software. Penetration pricing is a particularly attractive strategy if it not only generates future sales but also creates an industry platform or standard to which all other rivals must use or conform (that is, a technological path dependency). In 1995 the chairman of Netscape, Jim Clark, became a paper multibillionaire on his $4 million investment made in 1993. The strategic process that generated this fabulous increase in capital was to sell Netscape's Mozaic (now Navigator) software to 10 million consumers for browsing the Internet at no price—yes, the entrepreneurs became billionaires by giving the product away! The hook is that the software encrypts credit-card-order messages that only can be read by Netscape server software, which costs about $5,000 for a merchant to buy. The giveaway enabled Netscape to secure a long-term user relationship with 80 percent of the Internet browser market, a dominant foothold in the Internet shopping market that even a company as mighty as Microsoft is finding difficult to compete against.

Price Skimming

Price skimming is an alternative strategy to price penetration. A seller price skims by launching a high-priced product targeted to the segment who most values the product. After the initial sales boom to this segment levels off, the company launches a

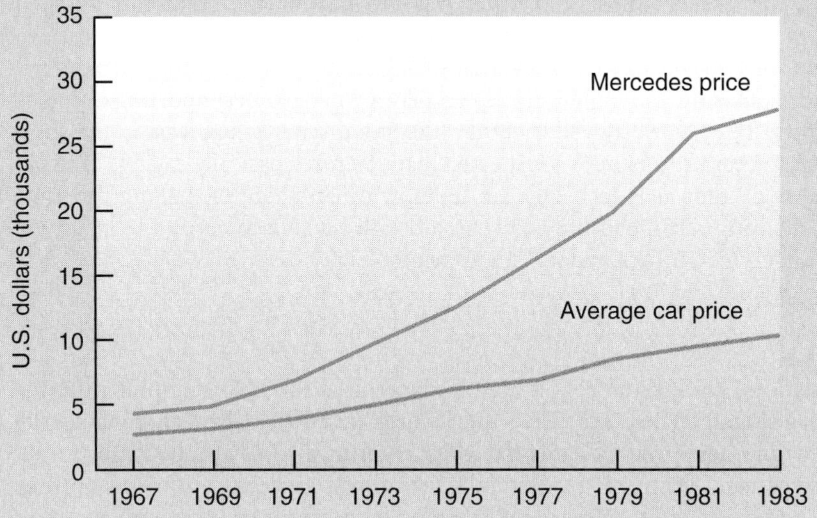

Mercedes-Benz's Price Penetration of the U.S. Market

Although a counter-intuitive example, given its current premium price position, Mercedes-Benz initially priced low to penetrate the high-end automobile market. In 1967, the Mercedes-Benz models were priced close to the average car price. This enabled the company to penetrate the consumer market segments that sought luxury, reliability, performance, and status from owning and using a car. Having penetrated the market, Mercedes-Benz proceeded to raise its prices at a faster rate than the average car price increases throughout the 1980s.

SOURCE: Reprinted from Hermann Simon, "Pricing Opportunities and How to Exploit Them," *Sloan Management Review* (winter 1992), 55–65, Figure 5, by permission of the publisher.

lower priced model targeted to the segment who also values the differentiation but who is not willing to pay as much for it as the first segment did. Once sales to this segment level off, the company introduces an even lower priced model. With such sequential targeting, product positioning, and price skimming, a firm can convert more of the added value of its differentiation into profit. This clever strategy prevents the seller from giving away profits by selling at too low an initial price to those who most value the product, and it enables the seller to later sell to those who want the product but who do not value the differentiation enough to pay the initial high price. Many new technologies are priced this way.

For example, between 1963 and 1977, Polaroid came out with six successive camera models beginning with Model 100 priced at $164.95 and ending with the Super Shooter priced at $25. With each model it reduced some incidental features, and new design and production innovations greatly reduced production costs. The basic patented differentiation feature—the instant color photograph—was still offered. In constant dollar terms, the last model was less than one-tenth the price of the initial model. Polaroid was able to control market price because its differentiation was protected by patents. Kodak did enter the market in the mid-1970s, but it was later judged to have violated Polaroid's patents. Polaroid was able to earn extra profits from its patented differentiation, and its sequential targeting/positioning strategy combined with its price skimming earned it even greater profits.[7]

[7] See *The First Thirty Years, 1948–78: A Chronology of Polaroid Photographic Products* (Cambridge, MA: Polaroid Corporation, 1979).

Price/Quality Signaling

If a claim of superior performance cannot be verified objectively by credible independent sources, then sellers must find other ways to bolster the credibility of their claims. One way is to associate their products with high-quality brand images. Another way is to use higher prices as a signal of higher quality. When used together, trusted brand reputation and higher prices can play a vital role in supporting claims of superior quality. They work so well together (i.e., good synergy), at least in the short term, because it is easier to believe a respected manufacturer basically saying, "You get what you pay for," than it is to believe an unknown manufacturer making the same claim. Over the long term, consumers eventually will be able to verify the quality of most goods or services, independent of their prices.

Quality Assurance Pricing

In many instances, price reinforces a brand image of quality (as exemplified by the Curtis Mathes slogan "More expensive—but worth it"). Price also can enhance the quality of a whole new product category when compared to established substitutes. Elegant, battery-run, electronic clocks and watches were priced too low when they first appeared on the market. Sales soared when prices were raised comparable to their mechanical substitutes. In actuality, they were not only less expensive to make but they also performed better than the spring-run timepieces they superseded. The problem created by the initial low price was that consumers did not believe they were getting more than they were used to paying for, largely because the cost and quality innovations were so radical and not visibly apparent to the shopper.

Price is a signal that extra effort has been put forth to produce a superior product that will perform to the buyer's satisfaction. A high-priced brand provides assurance that an acceptable consumption outcome will result. Thus quality-assurance pricing is most likely in product markets in which the following circumstances exist:

1. Product performance varies.
2. Search and inspection do not provide adequate certainty regarding product performance.
3. The cost of search and shopping is high compared to the cost of the product.
4. The product's true performance cannot be clearly tested through trial.
5. The cost of product malfunction is high (including direct consequences and the cost of wasted repair time).
6. The cost of remedying poor performance is high.

In these situations, many shoppers will be willing to pay more to get higher quality. They believe the risk of nonperformance far outweighs the risk of paying too much. The greater their uncertainty about the product's performance, the higher the price premium they will be willing to pay compared to economy offerings. For example, Pathmark Premium, priced at 89 cents, was a household cleaner with the same cleaning formula as Fantastik, the market leader, priced at $1.79. Despite vigorous point-of-purchase promotions, including Day-Glo labels on the Premium packing stating, "If you like Fantastik, try me," the product did not move off the shelf and was finally withdrawn. In the household-cleaner market, the cost of the cleaner is small compared to the labor input. If it smears or does not clean, then the labor has to be repeated. Consumers believe they are avoiding such a risk by paying a few cents more per use for a high-quality cleaner. Of course, how much extra money consumers will pay for the quality of a well-known brand name has a limit.[8]

Prestige Pricing

When buyers want the *very best* quality money can buy, their sensitivity to product performance increases more than their sensitivity to price. They believe you get what you pay for, and therefore they will pay more with the expectation of getting more. Owning top-quality goods gives people confidence in their purchases and security in themselves. High-priced products are more exclusive to own and, hence, become more desirable to those who want *only* the best.

When Viking Studio Books evaluated the proposal to publish *Blue Dog*, painter George Rodrigues's obsession with yellow-eyed blue dogs, the proposed list target price was $19.95.[9] But Peter Mayer, CEO of Viking's parent company (Penguin USA), disagreed. His positioning vision was a beautifully designed book sold expensively, rather than a mutt of a book sold cheaply. He was right. Viking sold two thousand special-edition copies at a price of $250 and sixty thousand copies of a $45 hardcover book. In a market where best-seller-list books are discounted from day one, Viking was able to use price to signal quality and generate demand.

The average consumer must live within budgetary constraints that limit the expression of individuality (or conformity) through the purchase of prestige goods. For wealthier individuals, prestige permeates their entire living environment. The products and services they buy authenticate their success or economic power. These products also may serve as signals of membership to an exclusive group. Wealthy people want exclusivity in their purchases of homes, cars, clothing, accessories, and vacations. High price assures such exclusivity.

Legend has it that several years ago Porsche made an attempt to price its aging 911 model out of the U.S. market as it introduced the new 928 model and planned for the 944 model. But something unexpected happened. As the 911's price rose, demand strengthened rather than weakened. At the higher price, the 911 became more exclusive and desirable among yuppie sports-car aficionados. Whether true or not, the underlying logic helps to explain why exclusive clothes and perfumes are often very expensive. Joy is advertised as the costliest perfume in the world (see Figure 16.2). It would not be nearly as "desirable" at half the price.

Possible Adjustments to Base Price Over Time

Pricing tactics and promotions convert a product's base price into a range or spread of prices called a price schedule. A price schedule enables a seller to cater to the different needs and price sensitivities of different customers. It also recognizes the varying costs of doing business with individual customers. Figure 16.1 indicates how the consideration of price tactics builds on a firm's basic pricing strategy. However, before these tactics are discussed, a method of fine-tuning a target price will be explained.

---

[8] Quality-assurance pricing is important in some consumer markets but not in others. For example, Barbasol shaving cream sold very well as a low-price brand, but Barbasol deodorant did not. Consumers wanted to pay more for the peace of mind offered by a high-quality deodorant. See *Forbes*, February 24, 1986, 114.

[9] Mary B.W. Taylor, "A Lesson on Selling a Book by Its Cover," *New York Times*, September 4, 1995, 21.

Figure 16.2 Joy Makes High Price a Selling Feature

How many products advertise that they have the highest price in the world? Note that by using the word *costliest,* the ad also suggests that Joy uses the most expensive ingredients. That is, it is the costliest to make and, hence, is the highest quality perfume.

Up to this point, price setting for new or improved products has been discussed. However, many pricing decisions involve an adjustment to the price of an existing product. They are prompted by disappointing sales caused by unexpectedly tough competition, a short-term economic downturn, or some other reason. In this section, a technique for testing whether such a price change should be initiated is presented. Price changes also can be used to fine-tune a proposed base price. Fine-tuning involves increasing and decreasing the proposed or existing price and examining the advantages and disadvantages of the change. It involves calculating the percentage contribution margin at the current price and estimating price elasticity, how much sales volume will change with a change in price. These two pieces of information are combined to determine the potential gain from raising or lowering the price.

The Relationship between Price and Contribution

A company that is in business to make a profit is always concerned about profits. A change in price, therefore, should be judged in terms of its effect on company profits.

A company is often prepared to forgo short-term profits to earn more profits over the long term. However, bottom-line profit must always be a concern at some point in time. *Contribution* is the difference between the price and average variable cost multiplied by unit sales—$(P - AVC) \times Q$ (see Chapter 18). Profit is contribution minus fixed costs. Therefore, in order to increase profit, contribution must increase. This means that when thinking about changing a price, a seller is most interested in its effect on contribution.

Changing a price affects contribution in two ways that almost always work against each other. First, lowering a price decreases the contribution margin (the difference between the price and average variable cost) by the amount of the price decrease. Second, in a price-sensitive market, a price decrease increases unit sales. Combining these two effects, a price decrease increases contribution if the percentage of the sales increase is large enough to compensate for the percentage of the decrease in the contribution margin. Similarly, a price increase increases contribution if the percentage of the increase in the contribution margin is large enough to compensate for the percentage of the decrease in sales.

The Formula

The marketing planner should examine two formulas when considering a price change. A price decrease increases contribution when

$$\%\Delta Q > [\%\Delta p/(\%CM - \%\Delta p)] \times 100\%$$

where

$$\%\Delta Q = \text{Percentage increase in quantity sold}$$

$$\%\Delta p = \text{Percentage decrease in price}$$

$$\%CM = \text{Current percentage contribution margin}$$

For example, if $\%CM = 30\%$ and a 10 percent price reduction is being considered, then such a price reduction would have to result in a 50 percent increase in sales just to match the previous contribution $\{[10\%/(30\% - 10\%)] \times 100\% = 50\%\}$. For help with this method, see The Rationality in Practice box, "The FINETUNE Spreadsheet." In many markets, a 10 percent reduction in price will boost sales by less than 20 percent, so, in this situation, such a price reduction is not a good idea.[10]

A price increase increases contribution when

$$\%\Delta Q < [\%\Delta p/(\%CM + \%\Delta p)] \times 100\%$$

[10] A survey of the price elasticity of 367 brands from 1961 to 1985 computed the average price elasticity to be –1.8. That means that, on average, a 10 percent reduction in price will lead to an 18 percent increase in sales volume. See Gerard J. Tellis, "The Price Elasticity of Selective Demand: A Meta Analysis of Econometric Models of Sales," *Journal of Marketing Research* 25 (November 1988): 331–41. The price elasticity of markets varies greatly depending on the similarity and availability of substitutes and the amount of innovation and imitation in the market.

where

$$\%\Delta Q = \text{Percentage decrease in quantity sold}$$

$$\%\Delta p = \text{Percentage increase in price}$$

$$\%CM = \text{Current percentage contribution margin}$$

For example, if $\%CM = 30\%$ and a 10 percent price increase is being considered, then contribution increases if the estimated price increase reduces unit sales by less than 25 percent $\{[10\%/(30\% + 10\%)] \times 100\% = 25\%\}$. The critical question, then, is what percentage of sales volume will be lost if the price is increased by 10 percent? If the percentage is less than 25 percent, then the price can be increased without hurting short-term profits. The FINETUNE spreadsheet also explains how this decision can be made easily.

The evaluation of price changes in this manner is made somewhat more complex when planners account for "experience effects"—that is, the tendency for unit costs to drop as the firm gains experience in producing the product. This is a complexity that can be accounted for. However, even if such subtle issues cannot be accommodated in the price analysis (due to time and information constraints), it is still essential for managers to evaluate break-even sales changes for price changes. If they do not, they put substantial profit dollars at significant risk![11]

Competitive Price Moves

In this section, the focus shifts from initiating a price change to responding to a price change. Just as marketers should not initiate price changes impulsively, response to a competitor's price change also should be carefully considered and measured. Very few markets exist in which consumers react immediately to price changes. Commodity markets and the stock market are notable exceptions. Usually customers exhibit a great deal of inertia, caused by ignorance or loyalty, which allows time for sellers to think carefully about what their next move should be. Sellers can learn a great deal from watching and waiting. Impulsive reactions can lead to price wars, which severely decrease all sellers' contribution margins and profits.[12]

The Price-Increase Case

A competitor may initiate a price increase for several reasons. Demand may have suddenly increased. Past price wars may have lowered the price to such a level that no seller is making a profit. The most frequent reason for price increases are cost increases. In this case, if the market leader and others initiate an increase, then all sellers in the market can raise prices. No change in market share will occur, but dollar contribution will increase, and that money then can be spent on a future competitive advantage or

[11] Stephen J. Hoch, Xavier Dreze, and Mary E. Purk, "EDLP, Hi-Lo, and Margin Arithmetic," *Journal of Marketing* 58 (October 1994), and Thomas F. Schuster, "A Breeze in the Face," *Harvard Business Review* 87 (November/December 1987) 36–43.

[12] For a discussion on price wars and price-cutting momentum, see Joel E. Urbany and Peter R. Dickson, "The Effects of Price-Cutting Momentum and Consumer Search on Price Setting in the Grocery Market," *Marketing Letters* 2, no. 4 (1991), 393–402; and Joel E. Urbany and Peter R. Dickson, "Reactions to a Competitive Pricing Move," *Journal of Retailing* (summer 1995): 1–16.

distributed to shareholders. Sales will only decrease if buyers switch right out of the product market to other substitutes. The major risk is that buyers will consider the price increase unfair, resulting in a loss of brand loyalty as well as a loss in sales.

A more competitive tactic is to wait before raising prices in response. This will allow the firm to take market share from the competition by appealing to the price-sensitive market. If competitors pull back their price increases, a company still may keep some of its newly acquired customers. If the competition does not pull back, then when the increase in sales from new customers levels off, the company can raise prices. This price response tactic is called *price shadowing*. Often prices are not raised all the way up to the competitor's new higher level in order to retain most of the new business. Using this pricing tactic results in both a sales volume increase and an increase in contribution margin.

Another reason to wait is that the price increase initiator is vulnerable and will often signal its intention to raise prices with a preannouncement. If the competitors do not send signals back that they intend to follow suit, then the initiator will be less likely to follow through its announced price increase. This has often happened with air-travel price competition among U.S. domestic airlines.

The Price-Decrease Case

In a price-decrease situation, a firm can end up losing contribution margin, sales volume, or both. Dealing with a competitor's price decrease is an acid test of a seller's confidence in its target/positioning strategy. If a firm responds immediately to a competitor's price cut, it may not lose any business and may, in fact, gain business from other competitors who have not yet dropped their prices. If a price decrease is delayed, then marginal customers will be lost. Much depends on which firm has initiated the price cut and the reasons for its move. If the initiator is a major competitor with long-term cost advantages, then the best strategy is to hold the current price and lose price-sensitive customers but work harder to create a market niche through improvements in quality, service, and differentiation. This strategy does not play to the cost-advantage strength of the competition. If the price reduction is the result of a design or production innovation that has reduced costs, and if this innovation can be imitated, then obviously a seller must do so and lower its prices as well. Many firms react to a competitor's price decrease by lowering prices but not to the level of their competitors' prices. This tactic, called *price covering*, is based on the belief that the remaining price difference will be unimportant to loyal customers.

Price Tactics That Create a Price Schedule

This section covers a number of pricing tactics used to change the base price. They are mostly either price discrimination tactics or ways of adapting to the varying costs of doing business with different customers. In applying them, a seller creates a complex price range around the base price (see Figure 16.3 on page 626). The following are some of the more common price tactics used.[13]

[13] For excellent descriptions of various pricing tactics, see Thomas T. Nagle, *The Strategy and Tactics of Pricing* (Englewood Cliffs, NJ: Prentice-Hall, 1986); Gerard J. Tellis, "Beyond the Many Faces of Price: An Integration of Pricing Strategies," *Journal of Marketing* 50 (October 1986): 146–60; Andrew A. Stern, "The Strategic Value of Price Structure," *Journal of Business Strategy* (fall 1986): 22–31; and Joel Dean, "Pricing Policies for New Products," *Harvard Business Review* 54 (November/December 1976).

Rationality in Practice

The FINETUNE Spreadsheet

The FINETUNE spreadsheet presented in this table makes fine-tuning price a very simple process. First of all, the price elasticity of the market must be estimated. *Price elasticity* is the percentage change in volume expected from a 1 percent change in price. All the executives involved in the pricing decision should estimate the percentage increase in sales volume ($\%\Delta Q$) for various percentage *decreases* in price ($\%\Delta p$) and the percentage decrease in sales volume ($\%\Delta Q$) as a result of various percentage *increases* in price ($\%\Delta p$). The highest, average, and lowest estimates then can be tested for different percentage changes in price. It is also very important to discuss the credibility of these estimates. For example, if the sales manager is advocating a 10 percent reduction in price, then at the very outset of the discussion the manager should provide his or her best guess of how a 10 percent reduction will affect sales. This must be justified in terms of where the sales will come from (from which competitor's market share or from which growth segment). Value-added analysis and general assessments of price sensitivity based on past price changes made by the seller or competitors should form the basis of these judgments.

The second step in using FINETUNE is to estimate the current percentage contribution margin ($\%CM$) of the product. This figure is inserted into the spreadsheet. The spreadsheet then computes the minimum percentage sales increase needed for a price decrease to be worthwhile. It also computes the maximum percentage sales decrease needed for a price increase *not* to be worthwhile. The best estimates of the effect of a price change are compared against the FINETUNE increase and decrease in sales needed to match or exceed current performance. If the estimates of the effect of a price decrease do not exceed the minimum percentage sales increase needed, then the price should not be decreased. If the estimates of the effect of a price increase exceed the maximum percentage sales decrease allowable, then the price should not be increased.

Fine-tuning with FINETUNE increases competitive rationality. As the example shows, if a product has a 30 percent margin, then a modest 10 percent price reduction would have to increase sales by more than 50 percent for it to be worthwhile. A 10 percent increase in price would have to produce a loss in sales greater than 25 percent for it not to be worthwhile. The reason for the high price elasticity needed to make a price reduction profitable is fairly straightforward. A 10 percent price reduction on a \$10 item with a 30 percent contribution margin comes right off the bottom line. It drops the contribution by 33.3 percent, from \$3 to \$2 per unit. To generate the previous contribution requires a fifty percent increase in sales. A 10 percent increase in price raises the per-unit contribution from \$3 to \$4 and therefore requires a twenty-five percent loss in sales to wipe out the advantage. If the current average contribution margin is uncertain, then more conservative and liberal percentages can be tested to see whether they materially change the decision.

The FINETUNE spreadsheet draws attention to the importance of understanding competitor reactions (see Chapter 6 section on anticipating competitor behavior). In the case of a price reduction, the competition is likely to match or even undercut it. This should result in more conservative estimates of likely sales volume gains from a price reduction. In the case of a planned price increase it is also possible competitors will match it, and hence the loss in sales estimate will be too pessimistic. Consequently, long-term competitive reactions should make marketers even more reluctant to drop prices and less reluctant to raise them. The behavior of competitors depends greatly on their perception of how sensitive their loyal customers are to price and on their own concerns over losing any market share.

Price Shading

Price shading occurs when a salesperson reduces the list price during a sales negotiation. It is price discrimination based on buyer knowledge and negotiating aggressiveness. Buyers who are aware of the lowest prices offered in the market and who are tough negotiators pay less. Common in industrial markets, it also occurs in some consumer product markets such as the automobile market. Shading off the list price occurs for several reasons:

Using FINETUNE to Evaluate a Price Change

How sales must change to match the effect of a price change on dollar contribution to overhead recovery and profit

CURRENT CONTRIBUTION MARGIN: 30.0%

PRICE REDUCTION	INCREASE IN SALES NEEDED TO MATCH THE CURRENT DOLLAR CONTRIBUTION	PRICE INCREASE	DECREASE IN SALES THAT WIPES OUT THE CONTRIBUTION GAIN OF THE INCREASE
1%	3.4%	1%	3.2%
2	7.1	2	6.3
3	11.1	3	9.1
4	15.4	4	11.8
5	20.0	5	14.3
6	25.0	6	16.7
7	30.4	7	18.9
8	36.4	8	21.1
9	42.9	9	23.1
10	50.0	10	25.0
11	57.9	11	26.8
12	66.7	12	28.6
13	76.5	13	30.2
14	87.5	14	31.8
15	100.0	15	33.3
16	114.3	16	34.8
17	130.8	17	36.2
18	150.0	18	37.5
19	172.7	19	38.8
20	200.0	20	40.0
21	233.3	21	41.2
22	275.0	22	42.3
23	328.6	23	43.4
24	400.0	24	44.4
25	500.0	25	45.5
26	650.0	26	46.4
27	900.0	27	47.4
28	1400.0	28	48.3
29	2900.0	29	49.2
30	∞	30	50.0

1. It allows sellers to give more favorable terms to attract the large buyer or important customer. The more such favorable terms are unexpected, the greater the effectiveness of price shading.
2. The list price can be adjusted up and down to adjust to seasonal fluctuations in supply and demand.
3. It allows the salesperson to adapt to each customer's level of market knowledge. The buyer who is well informed about competitive suppliers will have to be offered a competitive price.

Figure 16.3 **How Pricing Tactics Create a Price Range**

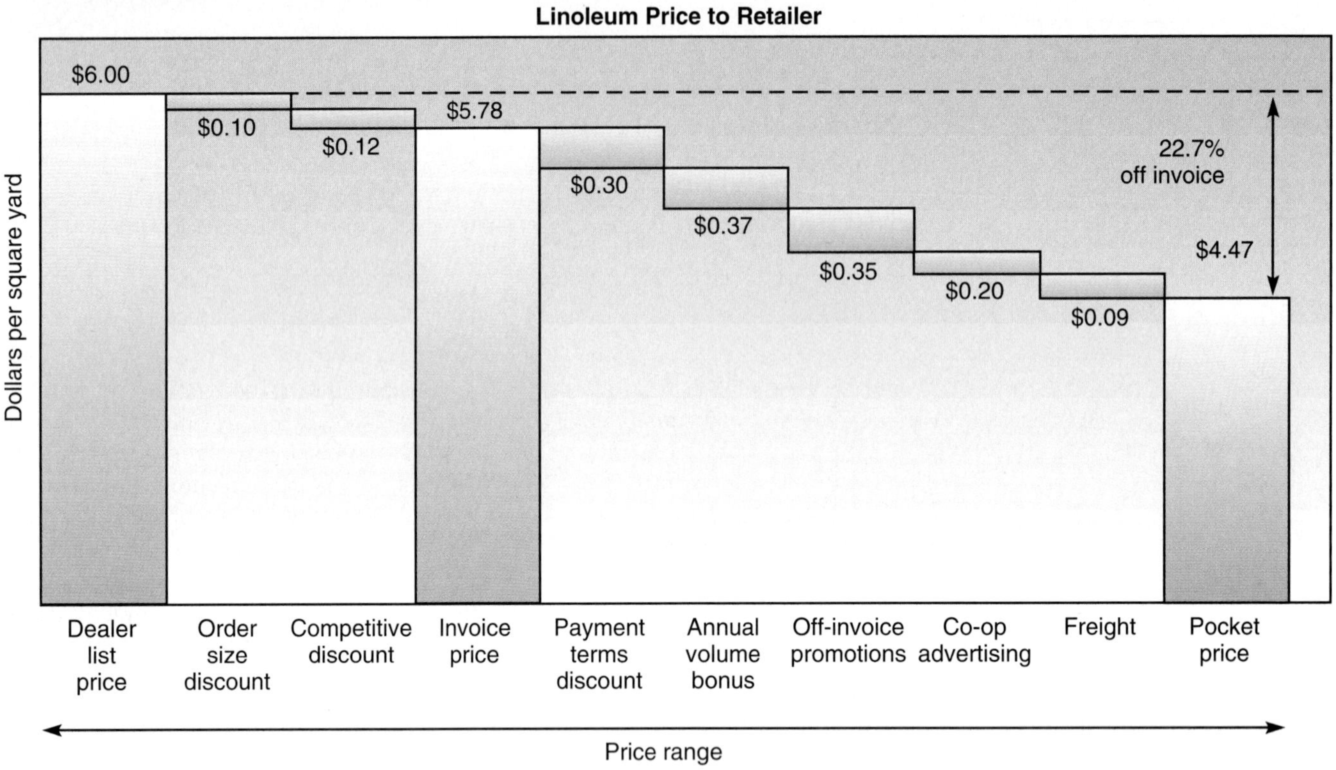

The granting of each of the above price discounts or marketing allowances to a retail account reduces the list wholesale price down to the final selling price—the revenue left in the seller's pocket. The difference between the list price and the list price with all of the possible discounts and allowances given to the buyer is the price range or band. Managers are often surprised by the width of this range and also which customers are getting which allowances and discounts and who is paying the highest and lowest prices at the end of the range. Some customers are also more sensitive to certain types of discounts than other customers, and this knowledge should influence pricing tactics and negotiations.

SOURCE: The figure is adapted from Robert L. Rosielli, "Managing Price, Gaining Profit," *Harvard Business Review*, September/October 1992, 86.

4. It is customary business practice for buyers to haggle with sales reps in an attempt to extract better buys. A buyer's sense of control, self-esteem, and job satisfaction are all directly related to the buyer's perceived success in such price shading negotiations. Some firms actually pay bonuses to their buyers based on how much they can shave off a seller's list price.

Sellers who do not shade their list prices may be perceived as uncooperative and unreasonable. They risk alienating buyers who have become accustomed to receiving such discounts. Buyers might not believe that a firm simply does not deal. Instead, they assume the seller chooses not to deal with them. To avoid such problems and allow the sales force some discretion over price, a firm should determine the average discount to be granted across all sales and add it back onto the base price to set the list price. This new list price is then no longer the true base price because it includes a shading allowance to be given at the salesperson's discretion, provided the average final price does not end up lower than the target base price.

Although price shading is a very useful pricing and selling tactic, it must be controlled. Giving the sales force too much price shading discretion may result in lower sales and profits.[14] Many salespeople overestimate customer price sensitivity. Rather than overcoming price objections by emphasizing product or service differentiation, such a salesperson often takes the path of least resistance and reduces the list price too much. If sales personnel are given discretion, it should be within strict guidelines and perhaps take the form of more generous payment terms or volume discounts.

Payment Terms

Payment terms price discriminate against slow-paying customers. Buyers who pay promptly pay less. It is a standard practice in most industrial markets to give a discount for prompt payment. The money owed by customers for their purchases (called debtors or receivables in accounting terminology) can become an important working capital cost. In their efforts to reduce such costs, sellers give incentives for prompt payment. Many product markets use the standard term "two-ten, net thirty," which means that a 2 percent discount will be given if the account is paid within ten days; otherwise the full price must be paid within thirty days. What happens after thirty days is not made clear—in fact, very few sellers feel they are in a strong enough position to impose and extract interest penalties on delinquent customer debt. They are often happy enough to finally get paid. Aggressive buyers also sometimes deduct the 2 percent for prompt payment, even when they settle the account after ten days.

Rather than accept the customary prompt payment terms (that have often eroded in effectiveness), can a seller develop a more effective, competitive way of rewarding prompt payment? One approach is to offer graduated terms based on the time it takes the buyer to pay. The tactic works this way: A customer is required to pay the full invoice price. On its next invoice, the customer is notified that it has earned a credit by promptly paying its last account. The terms are carried forward and applied to the next purchase. This pricing tactic is based on three behavior modification principles: increased reward for greater compliance, positive feedback based on actual performance, and reinforcement conditional on future positive behavior.

Volume Discounting

Giving quantity discounts is a standard practice in many markets. It is price discrimination, in that buyers who place large orders pay less. Sellers can afford to initiate such discount schedules because larger orders result in lower per-unit selling, processing, and production costs.[15] Quantity discounts also help increase or maintain the loyalty of heavy users. On the down side, buyers may exploit volume discounts by placing large orders and reselling surplus units to smaller accounts. A variation of this buying

[14] P. Ronald Stephenson, William L. Cron, and Gary L. Frazier, "Delegating Pricing Authority to the Sales Force: The Effects on Sales and Profit Performance," *Journal of Marketing* 43 (spring 1979): 21–28.

[15] James B. Wilcox, Roy D. Howell, Paul Kuzdrall, and Robert Britney, "Price Quantity Discounts: Some Implications for Buyers and Sellers," *Journal of Marketing* 51 (July 1987): 60–70.

tactic is achieved by groups of small customers who form buying groups to take advantage of volume discounts. A common problem with applying standard industry discount schedules is that no competitive advantage can be gained by offering them.

Volume discounting has become much more complicated with the introduction of just-in-time open contracts, in which products are supplied continuously. In such situations, a special price can be arranged that will apply to all products delivered for a three-, six-, or twelve-month period. Various clauses may allow for certain price increases related to input cost increases and price decreases based on volume economies or the introduction of cost-saving innovations. Pricing can become particularly complicated when the arrangement extends to a joint investment in the plant. In this case, the buyer-partner often agrees to a contractual cost-plus price.[16]

Tied Pricing

Tied pricing is a price discrimination tactic based on captive markets created by the purchase of complementary products (see discussion on illegal tying contacts in Chapter 8). It is normally applied to the pricing of accessories or supplies, and some companies make more money through tied pricing than they make selling the original equipment. Kodak film, IBM punch cards, and Xerox paper all had higher percentage profits than did Kodak camera, the IBM card-punch machine, and the Xerox copier. Attempts to contractually require buyers of particular pieces of equipment to buy the operating consumable is called a tied pricing contract, and it is illegal. However, in practice tied pricing often occurs informally. Either out of respect for the manufacturer, concern over compatibility between equipment and supplies, or lax purchasing management, billions of dollars of tied sales are made each year. A strategy of selling the original equipment at a very low price and profit margin and then making the profits on complementary products is actually a form of cost allocation where the aftermarket sales are subsidizing the original equipment sales. It is economically sound in that it enables an initial penetration price and the creation of a captive customer market, which then can be exploited by the monopoly pricing of supplies and accessories.

Another variation of tied pricing occurs when suppliers use the price to entice buyers into usage situations and then charge high prices for complementary products or services that are also commonly purchased and consumed in the usage situation. Movie theaters often advertise attractive, competitive prices in the local newspapers. However, the sales of high-priced soft drinks, popcorn, and candy made to captive customers account for a large percentage of a moving theater's profits.[17] Naturally, these prices are not advertised. The loss-leader specials run by supermarkets work on a similar principle. The losses on advertised specials are made up on the other purchases shoppers make.

[16] Nagle, *The Strategy and Tactics of Pricing*, 233.

[17] Snacks and beverages sales account for 75 percent of movie theater profits. A Coke that costs 10 cents sells for 75 cents; candy that costs 35 cents sells for $1; popcorn that costs 30 cents sells for $2. See "Those Peculiar Candies That Star at the Movies," *Forbes*, May 19, 1986, 174–76.

Segment Pricing

Some pricing tactics are blatant forms of price discrimination. Senior citizens receive transportation and entertainment discounts; children's seats on planes cost less than adult seats. Family-recreational air travel is much more price sensitive than business travel. Because of this, airlines charge less for children and offer early booking discounts that effectively exclude businesspeople from purchasing such tickets. As with all forms of price discrimination, segment pricing works best when buyers in the high-priced target segment cannot buy the product or service directly or indirectly (through resale) at the lower price. The following are more subtle types of price discrimination directed at different customer/usage segments.

Geographical Market Pricing

Differential pricing among regional markets (location segments) is a long-standing form of price discrimination. Free on board (FOB) pricing requires customers to assume the cost and responsibility of transportation. It is equitable in that the buyers pay according to their distance from suppliers. The disadvantage to suppliers is that their product becomes incrementally more expensive and less price competitive as the geographical distance between themselves and the buyer increases.

The opposite of FOB is uniform delivery pricing. Here, the costs of transportation are averaged among all customers (the U.S. Post Office's domestic first-class postage charges, for example). It enables a marketer to be more competitive in distant markets at the expense of its competitiveness in local markets. Various zone pricing schemes, which are compromises between the first two approaches, are often adopted. Such delivery pricing schedules often are based on considerations of both transportation costs and the competitiveness of different regional markets. For example, a company entering a secondary geographical market where price competition is greater than in its primary market may use the profits in its local market to subsidize the extra transportation costs to the secondary market. The problem is that competitors are likely to retaliate in kind.

Usage Segment Discounting

Another form of price discrimination is based on product or service usage. How can a seller encourage new uses of a product or service without reducing the price of the product or service for existing uses? Electric utilities have developed usage segment discounting to compete in the home-heating market segment. Electricity provides light and runs home appliances, but alternative fuels, such as gas and oil, can heat water and homes, and these alternative fuels are price competitive. How can utilities discriminate prices between these two uses in the same home? They charge a higher rate for the first one hundred or so kilowatt-hours used each month (presumably for lighting and running appliances) and a much lower rate for the remaining kilowatt-hours used. This makes electricity competitive for heating. Research can establish how many kilowatt-hours the typical target household consumes per month on lighting and appliances. This information is then used to set the discount point, which might only apply in the winter. Otherwise, the heavy consumption of electricity for air conditioning during the summer would be priced at the discount rate. Giving such a summer discount has no competitive advantage unless an increase in consumption is desired during the summer. This is unlikely because most utilities operate at their highest capacity levels at this time.

Off-Peak Demand Pricing

The most common form of usage segmentation pricing is based on the time of usage. Long-distance phone companies, electricity utilities, hotels, bars, restaurants, amusement parks, and movie theaters all use off-peak demand pricing. For firms like these, demand for their products and services fluctuates over time, and they cannot store their production. Consequently, they have periods of underutilization and often low incremental variable costs. At off-peak time, such companies welcome any additional revenue, as long as it makes some contribution toward their high fixed costs. Off-peak demand pricing also occurs with items that can be inventoried, but the cost of inventorying the product to the next season is high (it includes storage cost, handling, working capital costs, and the risk of obsolescence). Off-peak demand pricing explains after-Christmas sales and end-of-season fashion sales. Unfortunately, some price-sensitive shoppers learn when these sales occur and wait for them. This has the effect of reducing the overall average selling price and contribution margin.

Price Bundling

A number of pricing experts have suggested that a clever way to maximize revenues is to bundle products rather than sell them separately. However, unlike the previous pricing tactics, which vary price according to variations in individual demand, this tactic reduces variability in individual demand, thus increasing the economic efficiency of a single price.[18]

The following example illustrates the approach.[19] Assume that 75 percent of the one thousand patrons of a city's symphony orchestra prefer traditional orchestral pieces and 25 percent prefer avant-garde works. Each segment naturally would rather attend concerts whose programs are made up entirely of the type of compositions they prefer. Few are happy at the way program directors adopt an antisegmentation approach by offering programs that mix traditional with avant-garde. However, such product bundling allows the symphony to charge higher prices and fill more seats.

Consider the traditional patrons. They are prepared to pay $6 for each classic piece played but only $3 to listen to avant-garde music. On the other hand, the "Moderns" (avant-garde patrons) are prepared to pay $9 for each modern piece played but only $3 for each classic piece (see Table 16.2). A $9 ticket to a concert featuring three classic pieces or three avant-garde pieces sells out the 1,000-seat performing arts center and brings in $9,000. An $18 ticket to a concert featuring three classic works sells 750 seats and earns $13,500, while a $27 price tag to a three-piece avant-garde evening sells 250 seats and brings in only $6,750 in revenue. However, because both segments will purchase a concert package, a bundled program of two classic works and one avant-garde piece priced at $15 a ticket sells out and earns $15,000. The symphony, however, cannot do this if it faces a competitor who caters to the traditional

[18] An efficient price is one that is very close to the most a customer is prepared to pay for the product (reservation price). High variability in individual demand means that buyers' reservation prices vary a lot and many are well above the price paid. Thus, the price is not very efficient.

[19] This example comes from Thomas T. Nagle, "Economic Foundations for Pricing," *Journal of Business* 57 (1984): s3–s26.

Table 16.2 Willingness to Pay for Different Music Pieces

SEGMENT	CLASSIC PIECE	AVANT-GARDE PIECE
Traditionals	$6	$3
Moderns	3	9

segment and another competitor who caters to the avant-garde segment. The logic of such bundling also fails if one segment hates the other's music—that is, each segment must have at least some interest for the other's music.

Managing Price Promotions

Price promotions can be a very effective way of encouraging consumers to try a product, of reaching price-sensitive segments, and of moving inventory quickly.[20] They also now form one of the most common marketing tactics employed by companies. Sales promotion budgets are, on average, 50 percent greater than advertising expenditures. This trend toward greater price competition simply reflects the maturing of many consumer goods markets.[21] In mature, low-innovation markets, sales growth can be achieved only by gaining market share from competition, and price is the tactic usually used to achieve this goal.

Promoting a New Brand

Two basic learning-theory principles have been used to explain how introductory promotions work. The first is that a reinforced behavior will persist. A price promotion is a form of behavior reinforcement, as well as an inducement to buy. The second is that repeated associations between a new product and its price promotions lead to a transfer to the product of the positive feelings felt toward the promotions.[22]

When it comes to launching a new packaged good and building a brand franchise, a free-sample promotion is clearly superior to both coupons and introductory discounts. Both the number of trials and the speed of responses to a free trial are greater than the responses to coupons. The problem with a free-trial promotion is the expense of providing and delivering the product. Direct mail ceases to be economical for large items, but companies exist in all urban areas that can deliver samples to the front door with the weekly package of advertising fliers. If a national campaign is too expensive, more limited local campaigns can give punch to a regional rollout. Niche markets can be reached by dispensing giveaways at special events that attract the potential users (for example, giving away MTV T-shirts at rock concerts) or through

[20] For a guide to sales promotions, see Robert C. Blattberg and Scott A. Neslin, *Sales Promotion* (Englewood Cliffs, NJ: Prentice-Hall, 1990). This is an excellent and comprehensive reference text on the topic.

[21] In 1967, 45 of 50 consumer goods markets were still growing. By 1982, only 8 were still growing. See John Phillip Jones, "The Double Jeopardy of Sales Promotions," *Harvard Business Review*, September/October 1990, 145–52. This article presents an excellent discussion of the advantages and disadvantages of price promotions.

[22] Blattberg and Neslin, *Sales Promotion* Chapters 2,3, and 5. Whether these positive feelings are permanent is debatable.

radio stations with distinct consumer franchises. Another focused approach is to give a free sample away with a complementary product (even one produced by another company) that is purchased by the target market. This promotion helps both products (see Figure 16.4) and is difficult for a competitor to imitate.

Promoting a Mature Brand

Few experts dispute the effectiveness of using price promotions to launch new products. Their effectiveness in mature markets, where category sales increase very little when price is reduced, can be questioned. Category sales refer to the primary demand, that is, sales of all brands in the category. Price promotions in mature markets are a form of price discrimination across time. The theory is that with random reductions in price, a consumer must continue to search the market (because past experience cannot be used) or frequently pay a higher price. Thus, price promotions attract the price-sensitive shopper with low search costs.[23] The promotion price attracts deal-prone switchers, as well as current buyers who want to stock up. The problem is that since promotions encourage switching, they can break down loyalty in a mature market.[24] If all competitors run promotions, then over time more promotions encourage consumers to switch than to stay loyal. Thus, switching will increase (loyalty will decrease) in a market that uses high/low promotion pricing compared to a market that has stable prices set somewhere between the high/low prices of a promotion market. Promotions can further damage brand loyalty if previously loyal and price-insensitive shoppers start anticipating the yo-yo promotions (Tide $1.99 one week and $2.99 the next week) and adjust their buying and consumption schedule to the promotion schedule. They are not deal-prone switchers, but deal-prone loyals; they buy only one brand (say Diet Pepsi) but only when it is on promotion. In effect, promotions can increase both the secondary demand elasticity of consumers (by increasing brand switching) and the primary demand elasticity of consumers (consumers only entering the market when a favored brand is on promotion).

The Timing of Promotions

The timing of promotions is an important tactical decision.[25] Promotions running late in the season are designed to reduce inventory carrying costs and the risk of fashion obsolescence. A promotion run at the beginning of a season has a very different objective. It extends the selling season by starting the season early. The sensitivity of the market to an early promotion also will be greatest, since it is the first price promotion of the season. On the other hand, it also may attract buyers who would otherwise buy later at the usual price.

---

[23] See Hal R. Varian, "A Model of Sales," *The American Economic Review* 70, no. 4 (September 1980): 651–59; and Blattberg and Neslin, *Sales Promotion*, 95.

[24] See William Boulding, Eunkyu Lee, and Richard Staelin, "The Long-Term Differentiation Value of Marketing Communication Actions" (Cambridge, MA: Marketing Science Institute, 1992), Report no. 92-133. They found that advertising and sales force activities "increased a firm's ability to insulate itself from future price competition." Price promotion *decreased* a firm's ability to insulate itself from price competition, that is, it reduced its product's competitive differentiation (see Chapter 9).

[25] For excellent reviews on promotion tactics, see Dudley M. Ruch, *Effective Sales Promotion Lessons for Today: A Review of Twenty Years of Marketing Science Institute-Sponsored Research* (Cambridge, MA: Marketing Science Institute, 1987), Report no. 87-108. Kenneth G. Hardy, "Key Success Factors for Manufacturers' Sales Promotions in Package Goods," *Journal of Marketing* 50 (July 1986): 13–23; John A. Quelch, "It's Time to Make Trade Promotion More Productive," *Harvard Business Review*, May/June 1983, 130–36; and Michel Chevalier and Ronald C. Curhan, "Retail Promotions as a Function of Trade Promotions: A Descriptive Analysis," *Sloan Management Review* (fall 1976): 19–32.

Figure 16.4 A Cross-Promotion That Is Difficult to Copy

Combined price promotions are difficult for a competitor to imitate quickly, because they involve cooperation with another division or another firm.

In markets where all manufacturers offer trade promotions, retailers often manage the promotions by scheduling them. For example, Coke may be on special one week and Pepsi on special the next week. This ensures that the retailer always has at least one brand at a sale price all of the time, thus maintaining its low-price image. But it also makes it easier for consumers to schedule their buying around the promotions of their preferred brand or brands; that is, it encourages deal-to-deal buying.

The Advantages of Coupons and Rebates

Close to 80 percent of coupons directed at households are inserted into Sunday newspapers or flyers hung on doorknobs. They are used primarily to attract new triers and price-sensitive brand switchers, to increase product category sales, and to enable manufacturers to control the final price more directly.[26] As illustrated in Table 16.3, the number of coupons distributed has increased dramatically in recent years. In 1991, consumers redeemed 7.5 billion coupons with an average face value of fifty-four cents. This amounts to an overall savings of $4 billion. Retailers received about $600 million in fees according to NCH Promotional Services, the nation's largest coupon processor.

[26] Blattberg and Neslin, *Sales Promotion.*

Table 16.3 **Coupon Trends (1984–1990)**

YEAR	NUMBER OF COUPONS DISTRIBUTED (BILLIONS)	PERCENTAGE CHANGE OF COUPONS DISTRIBUTED	NUMBER OF COUPONS REDEEMED (BILLIONS)	PERCENTAGE OF COUPONS REDEEMED
1984	163.2	—	6.25	3.8%
1985	179.8	+10%	6.49	3.6
1986	202.6	+13	7.12	3.5
1987	215.2	+ 6	7.15	3.3
1988	221.7	+ 3	7.05	3.2
1989	267.7	+21	7.13	2.7
1990	279.4	+ 4	7.09	2.5

SOURCE: Donnelley Marketing Inc., "13th Annual Survey of Promotional Practices," 1991.

On the other hand, only about 3 percent of all coupons are redeemed, leading manufacturers to experiment with new ways of dispensing coupons (see Figure 16.5).

Coupons and rebates should be used instead of simple price discounts for several reasons.[27] Retailers may not pass on a price discount to the consumer. They may engage in a common practice called *forward buying*, whereby they make the purchase at the trade discounted price and then hold much of the merchandise in inventory only to sell it later at the full price. They also may sell what they buy at a discount price to other retailers around the country (called *diverting*). However, retailers have to accept a coupon, and to gain any unique competitive advantage from a coupon promotion over the competition, an individual retailer must double or triple its value.

Coupons are also more efficient to offer than discounts passed on to consumers, because price-sensitive consumers, to whom the promotion is targeted, are the ones most likely to redeem coupons. Coupon and rebate redeemers select themselves as being highly promotion responsive. Coupons and rebates are not wasted on shoppers who do not use them. Experimental research also suggests that consumers may have a more positive feeling about coupons and rebates than about an equivalent price reduction.[28] This is in part because they feel using coupons and rebates makes them smarter shoppers. Everyone gains the benefit of a general price reduction, but only the shoppers with initiative gain from clipping coupons or mailing in a rebate.

On the other hand, many price discounts are wasted because (1) about 50 percent are not supported by special point-of-purchase displays, (2) about 30 percent are not even passed on to consumers, (3) many are not noticed by buyers, and (4) they are

[27] Coupons are redeemed at a retail outlet. Rebates are redeemed by returning proof of purchase to a redemption center. Manufacturers often make the redemption task difficult to reduce the redemption rate. This enables rebates to have a much higher face value than coupons, making them a more powerful purchase inducement in advertising or point-of-purchase merchandising.

[28] Robert Schindler, "How Cents-Off Coupons Motivate the Consumer," in *Research on Sales Promotion: Collected Papers*, ed. Katherine E. Jocz, (Cambridge, MA: Marketing Science Institute, 1984), Report no. 84-104, 47–62.

Figure 16.5 **An In-Store Coupon Dispensing Machine**

Manufacturers are seeking ways to make it easier for price-sensitive consumers to gain access to coupons. One approach is the use of coupon dispensing machines. Another is to issue coupons at the checkout stand, based on what has been purchased (this procedure allows many manufacturers to target their rivals' customers).

automatically given to all buyers, including the price-insensitive shoppers who would have purchased anyway.[29] At the least, it makes sense to consider reducing the amounts of consumer and trade discounts and using the savings to increase the point-of-purchase promotion of the price reduction.

One trend that marketers should make note of is that, although the number of coupons distributed has been increasing continually, the percentage of those coupons redeemed dropped from 3.8 in 1984 to 2.5 in 1990 (see Table 16.3). This suggests that marketers need to continually search for new means of emerging from the clutter of current coupon inserts with creative new approaches for distributing them (e.g., in-aisle dispensers).

[29] Peter R. Dickson and Alan G. Sawyer, "The Price Knowledge and Search of Supermarket Shoppers," *Journal of Marketing* 54 (July 1990): 42–53.

Promotional Differentiation

The best promotions are those a competitor cannot copy quickly.[30] A tie-in price promotion with another product cannot be copied or countered quickly (see Figure 16.4). It also makes sense to build a promotion on a unique competitive advantage. GM, Ford, and Chrysler all have strong finance divisions. The Big Three use this strength to attack foreign competitors' market share—but not each other's—by offering low promotional financing, which is something the foreign competition cannot readily match. Toro, the snowblower manufacturer, designed a preseason trade-in promotion program with its dealers that competitors were not able to counteract effectively until the start of the next season. MCI's Friends & Family promotion launched in 1991 offered a 20 percent discount on long-distance telephone calls among friends and family. Its market share jumped from 13 percent to 17 percent. AT&T found it difficult to respond in kind because it lacked the sophisticated billing system needed to link customer accounts.[31] A promotion should, if at all possible, market the product's competitive differentiation. Coupons should be placed in advertisements to attract attention to the product differentiation claims, and point-of-purchase displays should promote the item's basic points of competitive differentiation.

Sales Promotion Problems

As described previously, when price promotions become the dominant tactic in a market, they increase the price sensitivity of the market, reduce loyalty, and increase the cost and difficulty of doing business. Some promotion campaigns will be extremely successful, others will not be effective at all, but over the long term they will somewhat average out. When all sellers are using the same price promotion (and achieving the same average performance), then the promotion no longer confers any sustainable competitive advantage. So why do sellers keep promoting? They fear that if they stop price promoting, then competitors' continued promotions will have a devastating effect on their market share and cash flow.

Also, the only viable alternative marketing strategy, once a seller is trapped in an endless cycle of price promotions, is a back-to-basics product-differentiation strategy that rebuilds customer loyalty. This strategy depends on technological innovation, which is slow and risky. Additionally, the firm may not have the financial or management resources to put into the needed R&D because the discretionary financial and management resources are being spent on price promotions.

The marketing history of Procter & Gamble's Pert shampoo nicely illustrates the advantage of genuine differentiation over price promotions (see Figure 16.6). Pert was languishing with a market share of less than 2 percent, and price promotions were having no effect on long-term sales—even when combining the manufacturer's rebate with the retail discount meant that the shampoo was, in effect, being given away. The company shifted its strategy and concentrated on the product rather than its promotions. Pert's formula was changed so it combined a shampoo and conditioner in one. This patented innovation gave Pert Plus an outstanding performance advantage over the several hundred competitive brands, and it was recognized in the *Consumer Reports*

---

[30] John A. Quelch, Scott A. Neslin, and Lois B. Olson, "Opportunities and Risks of Durable Goods Promotion," *Sloan Management Review* 28, no. 2 (winter 1987): 27–38.

[31] Mark Lewyn, "MCI Is Coming through Loud and Clear," *Business Week*, January 25, 1993, 84–88.

Figure 16.6 **Product Innovation Is the Answer to Costly Price Promotions**

The example here is a costly price promotion. Procter & Gamble offered a $2.50 rebate, and the supermarket reduced the price of the product to $2.99. In effect, the shampoo was almost being given away to shoppers who redeemed the rebate. An effective alternative to such costly price promotions is shown on the right: the introduction of a new shampoo innovation. Pert Plus was the first shampoo to successfully combine a shampoo with a conditioner. It was very well received in the market, and its unique selling proposition (differentiation) was so strong that it did not need price promotions in order to compete.

product testing. The brand's market share shot up to a market-leading 12 percent. Product extensions, such as an antidandruff version, also helped increase sales. Pert could never have achieved such success and profitability with promotions. Gillette's Sensor shaving system is another example of a firm using product differentiation and superior quality to rise above the hurly-burly of price-promotion selling.

Another stark example of the superiority of product innovation over price cutting is the success of grind-your-own gourmet coffee beans. While the big brands such as Maxwell House and Folgers fought a price war among their run-of-the-mill, canned ground coffees, a number of entrepreneurial firms have prospered by offering seventy-five different varieties of gourmet flavors sold at twice the price.[32] In this case, innovators had to enter the market to teach the established big players that many consumers buy coffee, first and foremost, for its taste and not for its price.

Changing Goals and Incentives

A careful analysis of a promotion's likely profitability can have a sobering effect and strengthen the backbone of a company or an executive who was once hooked on promotions but is now experiencing promotion "withdrawal." The FINETUNE spreadsheet can be used to assess the profitability of short-term trade promotions or consumer price discounts. Another way of discouraging price promotions is to operate close to production capacity. This reduces the seductive appeal of the marginal, incremental promotional sale, which is most attractive when fixed costs are high and there is excess capacity. Sales force incentives also should be based on contribution rather than sales. Toughing it out requires everyone from the top down and bottom up to cut back on their use of promotions. A gradual, rather than precipitous, withdrawal from promotions is more likely to be successful. It gives everyone time to adjust.

Changing Channel Behavior

A problem with many trade promotions is that they are not linked to any specific behavior such as extra selling efforts, merchandising programs, or advertising. One solution is for manufacturers to pay special allowances to retailers for participating in a price promotion program after evidence of performance is provided, instead of unconditionally deducting the allowances off the initial invoice. The trade should be rewarded for proven performance rather than expected performance. Another even more positive approach is for the manufacturer to work with major retailers on the type of merchandising promotions they would prefer to offer. This flexible approach is based on the reasonable assumption that the retailer knows best what sells in its stores. Implementing unique price promotion programs with individual retailers will not only ensure they are implemented but will likely make those promotions more effective for both the manufacturer and the retailer.

To discourage deal-to-deal buying, manufacturers can place restrictions on the quantity of goods that retailers and wholesalers can purchase on the deal by tying deal purchasing to normal purchase quantities. However, cracking down on the resale and diversion of promotionally priced products to other geographical markets is not easy. The problems of an out-of-control promotion strategy and out-of-control channel partners go together because they both have the same root cause—weak product differentiation and brand equity. Procter & Gamble put its considerable brand equity (P&G controlled the number-one and number-two brands in some thirty product categories) to the test in 1992 when it announced its intentions to move away from promotion pricing, starting with its Luvs and Pampers disposable diapers.[33] The new program reduced the list wholesale price and provided retailers with brand-development rebate incentives based on six monthly sales increases. Thus the incentives were based

[32] Zina Moukheiber, "Oversleeping," *Forbes*, June 5, 78–82.

[33] Zachary Schiller, "Not Everyone Loves a Supermarket Special," *Business Week*, February 17, 1992, 64–68; Eben Shapiro, "P&G Takes On the Supermarkets with Uniform Pricing," *The Wall Street Journal*, June 26, 1992; and Bradley Johnson and Jennifer Lawrence, "P&G Tests New Retail Plan, Cuts Diaper Price," *Advertising Age*, June 22, 1992.

on the recent sales performance of the brand. In this way, retailers are rewarded for past performance, rather than given trade promotion discounts, no matter how they had used such discounts in the past. But the real key to P&G's success was to couple its value pricing to a comprehensive and continuous drive to reduce its costs and its retailer's costs, as described in Chapter 11. This is in addition to saving all the costs involved in managing wildly swinging demand, in reducing the erosion of brand loyalty, and in reducing retailers' pocketing of the promotion allowances. Since 1991 P&G has closed 25 percent of its most inefficient factories; trimmed its product lines by a quarter, eliminating poor-selling brands, sizes, and flavors. It reorganized its sales force around customer teams that provide data analysis and financing to customers; introduced a simple single-invoice computer to its computer billing system; and organized its order deliveries to be delivered by a single truck to each retailer.[34] The result has been reduced list prices for consumers of up to 20 percent and increased profits for P&G and cooperating retailers. P&G's approach was risky because some retailers, upset at losing the profits from frequent promotions, favored other major brands or promoted their own private labels. However, the bottom line is that P&G has decided that price promotions are not worth the cost, particularly the cost of managing wildly swinging demand and inventories.

Changing Competitor Behavior

Once competition among promotions has begun, it is difficult to convince competitors to cease the promotion war. Only a market leader such as P&G, be it in a national, regional, or niche market, might feasibly implement the following strategy. First, the manufacturer publicly announces it intends to switch to a lower everyday list price and gradually reduce the size and frequency of its promotions. However, retaliatory promotions will be run if rivals do not follow the lead.[35] Such tit-for-tat promotions will attack any competitor in the major markets who continues to promote prices heavily. The term *tit* × two stands for a response that is twice as strong and effective as the initiator's promotional initiative. The success of such a tactic depends on targeting the rival's customers with a heavy comparative advertising campaign by doubling the face value of coupons, moving inventory quickly into the channel, and squeezing shelf space. The seller even can use direct marketing with special promotional offers to pinpoint customers.[36] If a seller is intent on ridding itself of the promotion yoke, then it must spare no expense and be ready to strike fast and very hard at a competitor. Establishing itself as such a credible threat is a sound investment.[37] But this strategy is only effective for market leaders with plenty of courage and funds. It is not the best competitive strategy for others. The best competitive strategy, once again, is for a seller to develop product and service differentiation, which builds the kind of consumer loyalty that is immune to the promotional assaults of competitors (see Figure 16.6), and to develop trade cooperation through cost-saving service innovations. This is not an easy task in many markets, but it is *the* task.

---

[34] Zachary Schiller, "Ed Artzt's Elbow Grease Has P&G Shining," *Business Week*, October 10, 1994, 84–86.

[35] Game theory research has shown that the best way of eliciting cooperation from a competitor is to make an initial conciliatory offer ("we will run no more price promotions") and then respond tit-for-tat to any aggressive responses. See Douglas R. Hofstadter, "Metamagical Themas," *Scientific American* 248, no. 5 (1983): 16–26. Tit × two ups the ante.

[36] Aimee L. Stern, "New Marketing Game: Stealing Customers," *Dun's Business Month*, February 1985, 48–50.

[37] Research has demonstrated the value of a reputation for fierce combativeness in a market. See Paul Milgrom and John Roberts, "Predation, Reputation and Entry Deterrence," *Journal of Economic Theory* 27 (1982): 280–312.

Pricing Tactics in the Global Marketplace

Export pricing requires paying special attention to all of the issues discussed in this chapter. As far as costs are concerned, export pricing is often marginal pricing that uses the direct variable costs of producing, shipping, and selling the product in the export market. Some of the unique export costs are export tariffs, "consultants commissions" that end up as bribes paid to government officials, and special climate and transport packaging. The advantage of marginal pricing is that it enables penetration pricing. The disadvantage is that, as the export market grows, domestic sales will lose some of their competitiveness because they are increasingly burdened by their subsidizing of the increased export sales' overhead costs.

This problem is often brought to a head when current production capacity is reached. If capacity is to be expanded to meet export demand, then the cost of the expansion must be borne by the export prices. Export prices will have to rise unless production efficiencies at the new plant compensate for moving from marginal to full-cost pricing. Otherwise, the domestic price will be loaded with an even greater burden of subsidizing export sales.

The more conservative approach is to adopt a rigid cost-plus pricing to exports from the outset, with an added profit margin to compensate for the risk or frustrations involved in export marketing. Such a conservative, take-it-or-leave-it pricing approach is hardly conducive to developing global market sales. Once upon a time, American companies escaped the price competitiveness of the U.S. market by finding cozy export markets. Today, export markets are often more price competitive than the U.S. market because large companies from the United States, Japan, and Europe are all behaving in the same way, which is to use marginal pricing in export markets.

Controlling distributors' pricing practices is difficult in any market, but in some export markets it is particularly difficult because of the lack of on-site control. The most cost-effective way of keeping tabs on the pricing practices of distributors is to keep in direct contact with end users. Marketers of consumer goods may have to employ a local market research firm to undertake occasional price checks without the "help" of the distributor. A further problem with channel pricing is that export channels have a tendency to become very long, with many intermediaries adding their margins and very little value. The increasingly common, "value-added" taxes (usually a tax on the selling price at each point in the channel) makes the problem even worse.

Financial terms are particularly important in export marketing because of the greater risk of bad debt (nonpayment) and currency fluctuations.[38] Payment risk is normally covered by asking for a *letter of credit* from a respected bank. The letter establishes creditworthiness and serves as a legal claim on funds. As far as terms are concerned, instead of the seller offering terms to the buyer or distributor in a distant market, it is often better for the seller to help the buyer obtain financing from the buyer's local banks or financial markets. They are in a better position to assess the risk of buyer default or changes in exchange rates—and to deal with the consequences.

The problem of foreign exchange fluctuations is most often handled by quoting all prices in U.S. dollars (the international exchange currency) and hedging. *Hedging* is when a firm uses a financial service that buys foreign currency futures in the same way that pork-belly futures are bought and sold. Through a complex formula, a firm can

[38] Fred Cohen and Rhonda Price, "Competitive Pricing Strategies for Exporters," *Journal of Pricing Management* 2, no. 2 (spring 1991): 37–39.

purchase a mix of such futures that reduces the effects of future foreign exchange fluctuations. If it does not hedge, then a firm inevitably winds up speculating on exchange rates. Because that is not its business—nor should it be—such unskilled speculation adds a dangerous uncertainty to the profitability of a firm's export activity. Investing in hedging is like paying an insurance premium to protect against unfavorable currency fluctuations (such as a stronger U.S. dollar that effectively increases export prices). It is an added cost of global marketing.

Other ways of handling an exchange fluctuation that strengthens the U.S. dollar is to seek countertrade deals and keep earnings in the host country for the short term. A more long-term solution is to invest the earnings in expansions of host-country assembly, service, and distribution facilities. Such investments are best made when the dollar is strong. Some global companies are able to shift their sourcing of supply, depending on currency fluctuations. For example, Cummins Engine supplies the Latin American market from either the United States or the United Kingdom, depending on whether the dollar or the pound is weaker. It is hoped that as international financial markets merge into a single global financial market, currency fluctuations will be less of a problem. Global marketers then will be able to focus on making and selling better products instead of being distracted by the lure of making profits from outsmarting the foreign-exchange market.

Discussion Questions and Minicases

1. One price skimming tactic is to charge early adopters, who value the product most, a high price and then to lower the price later. This tactic can have some very negative consequences. What are they?
2. In 1984, Noumenon Corp., a California software company, launched Intuit, priced at $395, to compete against Lotus's Symphony and Ashton-Tate's Framework, which both sold for $695. Despite a major ad campaign, Intuit failed to sell. The price was then dropped to only $50 and raised each week by $20 to test demand. At $90 sales peaked and fell off completely at $210. The company decided to relaunch Intuit at $89.95. What mistakes did this company make both before and after its initial launch?
3. Apple Computer launched its Macintosh computer at $2,500 in January 1984 (with the infamous Super Bowl ad). It was designed to sell at $1,000, but production cost increases raised it to $2,000, and John Sculley (the legendary PepsiCo brand manager) added $500 for a lavish marketing campaign. Mac's mouse/windows technology was child's play to use and made the Mac accessible to the general public. A more powerful, faster Mac with a color monitor was launched in 1987, again at a premium price. From 1986 to 1991, Apple's share of the world personal computer market was from 6 percent to 8 percent with a gross margin of 50 percent. In 1990, Microsoft launched Windows, which makes a cheap IBM clone as easy to use as a Mac. Did Apple make a mistake with its pricing approach? What was its alternative, and how might the alternative have been more profitable?
4. Videotaped movies were initially sold to the public in the early 1980s at a price of around $79.95. In the mid-1990s, they are being sold as low as $9.95. What do you think would have happened if the distributors had used a penetration price at the outset? Who benefited from the price approach that was adopted?
5. Along with consumer price sensitivity, how does the current contribution margin affect any future decision to price skim or price penetrate the market? (Hint: the FINETUNE spreadsheet can be used effectively to answer the question by playing "what if" with the %*CM* variable.)
6. Sellers sometimes match competitors' price reductions, particularly the market leader's price reductions, when all the information indicates buyers are not very price sensitive. Give some of the reasons why this happens.
7. Is it a good idea to reduce your price during a recession? What if you sell to businesses and they are pressuring you to reduce prices?

8. Most volume discount schedules are standard within an industry. All competitors follow the same schedule, which suggests an opportunity for an innovator to break in with lower volume discounts. Can a firm develop a more competitive volume discounting schedule that attracts growth business and does not hurt overall profitability? Develop such a proposal. (Hint: First draw a declining cost/volume curve, and then impose the industry discount schedule as a step function on top of the curve; now draw your alternative step function.)
9. Create a spreadsheet that computes a graduated percentage discount that is equivalent to paying the net amount thirty days after the invoice date and depends on the seller's cost of working capital (expressed as an interest rate) and the days between invoice date and payment. How could such a discount be assessed automatically by the seller's billing software?
10. The challenge for every business-to-business seller is to find a pricing tactic that attracts the business of start-up firms who may grow to be multimillion-dollar accounts without risking devastating bad debts. Extending credit is particularly dangerous in the U.S. economy, which regularly cycles from boom to bust. It is especially risky in global markets, where the chances of recovering bad debts are much lower. Propose a prepayment scheme that is friendlier than simply putting up the money and that price discriminates based on the buyer's creditworthiness (Hint: escrow accounts).
11. How can a shrewd buyer extract more concessions from a seller who uses price shading? Do you think price shading is economically efficient for the firm and for the economy as a whole? Do you think it is fair?
12. A ferry runs between Martha's Vineyard and Cape Cod in Massachusetts. It is a popular mode of transportation for wealthy people who maintain summer homes on Cape Cod and for tourists. The ferry had developed quite a complex rate structure:

    The regular fare is $4 each way, but travelers can buy a ten-ride card for $30. The name of the passenger is written on the card, so only one person can use the ticket. The ferry also carries autos at a rate of $25 each way. Discount rates for round trips that originate on the island are available. A return trip on the same day costs $25 for a car and a return trip within five days of departure costs $40.

    Why has the company developed such a scheme? How do you think it could improve the scheme by offering different discounts?
13. In 1991, Transmedia Network sold its charge card for $50 a year. The card offered a 25 percent saving on meals in some one thousand restaurants in Florida, New Jersey, and New York. The deduction was made off the VISA or MasterCard bill. Transmedia actually advanced the restaurant $5,000 in exchange for credits worth $10,000 in tabs. It rebated $2,500 to the patrons and kept $2,500 for itself. Restaurants liked it because they still cleared $1,000 because the cost of food and beverages usually amounted to only 40 percent of the gross tab. Transmedia expected its membership to grow to one-hundred thousand by the end of 1993. What is the long-term problem with this deal for the restaurants?
14. Why does the off-peak pricing of some services, such as long-distance telephone calling, have to be carefully set? What can go wrong?
15. Product/service bundled pricing (antisegmentation pricing) has many advocates, but it does not work well in some situations. What firms in what markets can best apply price bundling?
16. The metered pricing of the typical Xerox copier in 1974 was as follows:

1–3	4.6 cents per copy
4–10	3 cents per copy
11 plus	2 cents per copy

    What type of price segmentation and discrimination is this, and what competitive facts do you think led Xerox to adopt such a pricing strategy?

17. The proprietor of a small Mexican restaurant has come to you with the audacious idea of allowing customers to decide how much they will pay for their meals. He thinks it will be a great marketing gimmick and probably just as profitable as having to set prices. He offers the following menu: 8-inch Mexican Pizza (\$3.00), Smothered Burrito (\$3.00), Plato de Sopapilla (\$4.50), El Bandito (\$4.40), Fried Clam Dinner (\$4.50), El Puerco (\$10). The prices in parentheses are the minimum prices he would charge if he were to fix his prices. Prepare a "Choosing Your Own Price" handout to customers that implements his idea. How would customers feel about the price they end up paying?

18. In 1982, the Windmere Corp. sold 670,000 hair dryers to retailers such as Eckerd drugstores for \$6.50 each. In 1983, the company raised its price to retailers to \$8.00 but offered a \$5.00 rebate on each dryer provided the buyer got the rebate coupon, filled it out, saved the purchase receipt, ripped the proof-of-purchase mark off the box, and mailed them all to Windmere. Windmere paid an 80-cent processing fee to a company that ran the rebate promotion. Normally priced at \$12.99, the VIP Pro hair dryer was often featured in store advertising at a sale price of less than \$10, which meant that the price was less than \$5 with the rebate. The rebate campaign was a smashing success. How could this be? What was the critical statistic that determined its success?

19. Which of the following full-page newspaper advertisements do you think would be most effective? Do they appeal to different market segments? What do you think will be competitors' responses to each ad?

The best executive is the one who has the sense enough to pick good men to do what he wants done, and self-restraint enough to keep from meddling with them while they do it.

Theodore Roosevelt

We take eagles and teach them to fly in formation.

D. Wayne Calloway

CHAPTER SEVENTEEN

Organizing and Implementing

Organization culture is the pattern of role-related beliefs, values, and expectations shared by the members of an organization.[1] These in turn produce the rules and norms for behavior, which have a powerful influence on the ways teams, and individuals experiment, cooperate, and work. According to theorists, two extreme forms of organization exist: bureaucracies and clans. A bureaucratic organization relies on a formal structural hierarchy, top-down commands, meeting rules, procedural rules, and close personal supervision. Lower management work to rules, and upper management rule. Some experts have argued that such marketing bureaucracies are appropriate when the implementation tasks are repetitive, routine, and unchanging in stable, competitive markets.[2] But a stable, competitive market is an oxymoron. Competitive markets are not stable. At times they may move quite slowly along their innovation/imitation paths, but inevitably they will experience turbulent stages, and it is then when bureaucracies fail. Bureaucracies are bad at noticing change. This is because when employees look up to the next layer of management for direction, they turn their backs on their customers and the market. Bureaucracies are also bad at adapting to change and, in fact, often strongly resist change because it provokes conflict among functions and factions. They are even worse

at initiating change through market experimentation. For example, many universities are giant bureaucracies; they are very slow to change their teaching methods and the way they hire, promote, and fire faculty. Some experts claim that formalizing procedures and centralizing processes can lead to higher effectiveness and efficiency in implementation. But how does such an organization first discover or invent better ways of doing things that then would be formalized throughout the organization by centralized authority when their management processes discourage experimentation and when individual innovators are "burned as heretics"?

A clan organization manages through socialization of individuals into an informal social system that, like a search-and-rescue organization, stresses teamwork and cooperation with internal customers and a common interest in creating a high level of external customer satisfaction. Extremely adaptive and responsive clan cultures can create, through their sustained innovation, enough market turbulence to drive their large, bureaucratically organized rivals into self-destructive modes of decision making and market behavior. Rivals' competitive rationality crumble under the sustained pressure of change. ■

Implementing marketing decisions requires many skills, two of which are featured in this chapter. The first skill is the ability to structure the organization in a way that increases competitive rationality. The second skill is the individual ability to schedule activities, allocate resources, assign responsibility, and monitor progress. Marketing strategy, organization, and implementation are closely linked issues. Good strategy with poor organizational structure and implementation, poor strategy with good organizational structure and implementation, or poor strategy with poor organizational structure and implementation can all result in failure.[3] Consequently, determining the cause of failure, learning from it, and correcting it can be very difficult.

Moreover, as a planned strategy is implemented, it often is changed by creative managers into a new strategy better adapted to the changing marketplace.[4] At other times, organizational structure and politics change the implementation of strategy in less desirable ways. In today's extremely competitive, global environment, the ability to adapt to change, reduce costs, and maintain competitive levels of quality and service, all at the same time, are extremely important. Also, the ingenuity used to deploy

---

[1] Rohit Deshpande and Frederick E. Webster, "Organization Culture and Marketing: Defining the Research Agenda," *Journal of Marketing* 53 (January 1989): 3–15.

[2] Robert W. Ruekert, Orville C. Walker Jr., and Kenneth J. Roering, "The Organization of Marketing Activities: A Contingency Theory of Structure and Performance," *Journal of Marketing* (winter 1985): 13–25.

[3] Thomas V. Bonoma, "Making Your Marketing Strategy Work," *Harvard Business School*, March/April 1984, 69–76.

[4] See the discussion on marketing management practice in Chapter 2, particularly J. B. Quinn's work on how strategy incrementally evolves from implementation decisions.

organizational human resources and a network of working relationships with other organizations contributes to the successful implementation of new strategies. A firm must be nimble. Often profits and success come from the ability to react opportunistically to changes in the marketplace rather than from long-term product differentiation or other so-called sustainable competitive advantages.[5] In this chapter the evolution of marketing is first discussed, followed by the organization of external networks of relationships and the internal organization of the company (see Figure 17.1). The major section of the chapter discusses individual organization and implementation skills.

The Evolution of Marketing Organization

The marketing organization in many established companies developed as a separate function because of the traditional, narrow focus of the sales organization. Exasperated by the inability of the sales force to adopt a long-term customer perspective, senior executives during the 1960s created a separate marketing function and organization to manage sales forecasting, market research, product development, advertising, promotions, and pricing. Product managers, who reported to a marketing vice president or marketing director, were responsible for coordinating the marketing and selling in particular product markets. In theory, they increased coordination, planned and implemented more effective and efficient marketing campaigns, and were able to react faster than a committee. In practice, product managers' lack of authority limited their effectiveness and reduced them to the role of communication facilitators who sometimes created unnecessary reports, memos, and other paperwork. What is more, product managers' lack of specific functional skills (such as engineering, design, accounting, or sales) and their high turnover rates (and hence low product market experience) raised questions of what they added to the competitive rationality of firms and, hence, of their value for the money.

Rethinking Marketing Management

In recent years three important organization developments are changing the way marketing is managed and implemented. First, the arguments for creating a marketing organization separate from sales are being questioned. Today's sales forces are trained and managed to develop and are rewarded for developing long-term relationships with customers, often working within customer service teams (see Chapter 12). Sales managers often have college degrees in marketing or have been sent to executive development courses in marketing management. If a company has made the large investment in creating its own sales force, then presumably it considers the unique selling and service skills of such a sales force, very important for developing and sustaining the firm's competitive advantage. Otherwise, why not outsource selling to independent manufacturers' reps and telemarketing operations? So a firm that has its own sales force but a separate marketing function is saying that its sales force is good enough to own but not good enough to manage the firm's marketing. What competitive advantage can be gained from creating such a separation of sales and marketing

[5] See Chapter 2 and also Amar Bhide, "Hustle as Strategy," *Harvard Business Review* (September/October 1986): 59–65; George Stalk Jr., "Time—The Next Source of Competitive Advantage," *Harvard Business Review* (July/August 1988): 41–50; and Peter R. Dickson, "Toward a General Theory of Competitive Rationality," *Journal of Marketing* (winter 1992).

Figure 17.1 **Chapter Organization**

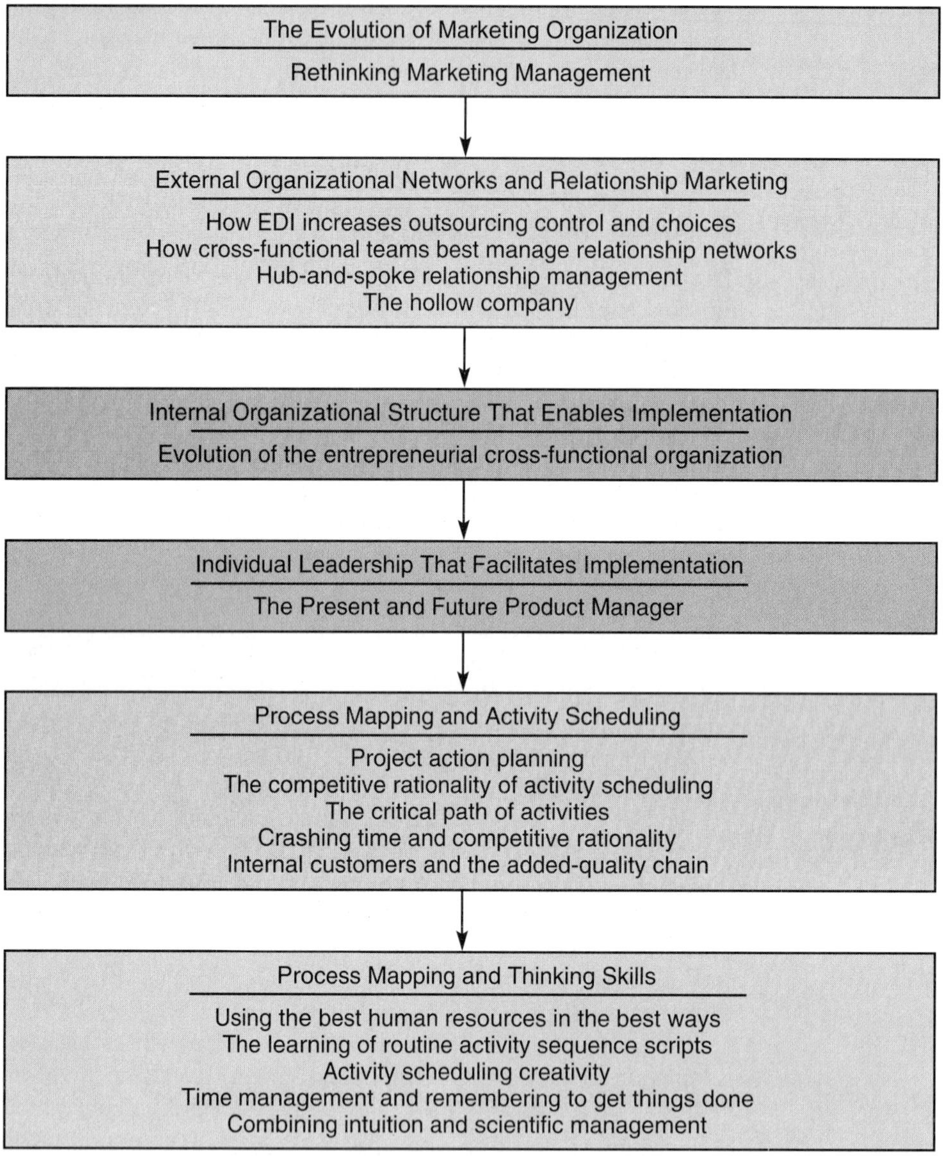

Following a discussion of the evolution of marketing organization, this chapter discusses the organization of a network of relationships, the internal organization of the company, and then focuses in on individual organization and implementation skills.

management? On the other hand, a firm can gain considerable advantages from having its sales force manage and implement regional direct marketing, advertising, and promotion programs. For many firms, the sensible move is to combine the sales and marketing functions. One senior executive is in charge of sales and marketing, and marketing executives who are experts in research, logistics, or products become staff that primarily support sales and cross-functional teams.

Second, outside marketing expertise is replacing inside marketing expertise. Market research firms, advertising agencies, public relations firms, telemarketing firms, freight-forwarders, third-party logistics services, and companies that run promotional programs are being given more complete responsibility for budgets, deadlines, and results. The reason is simple. They manage and implement better than layers of bureaucratic marketing management that, consequently, have been "reengineered" out of organizations over the past decade.

Third, while the marketing function and organization was being rationalized, senior executives addressed the problem of poor communication and cooperation among sales, marketing, R&D, engineering, manufacturing, and distribution by forming cross-functional teams consisting of representatives from each functional area.[6] These teams were conceived of as junior versions of the senior executive team that manages a small firm or a division of a larger company. Some cross-functional teams are temporary, created to address a short-term problem such as speeding up the launch of an important new product or improving cooperation between marketing and manufacturing (as discussed in Chapter 4) or between marketing and R&D (as discussed in Chapter 10). Others are permanent and are used to team manage a product market. Such cross-functional teams provide a constant and continuous interface among all the firm's functions. They have budgetary responsibility and the authority to get things done, and they develop and manage relationships with outside management service companies, such as market research firms, advertising agencies, suppliers, manufacturing subcontractors, and freight-forwarders. Successful cross-functional teams that expand a product market are the embryos for future new company divisions or separate companies. The many reasons for the superior competitive rationality of cross-functional team management are described in Chapters 2 and 3. Put most simply, cross-functional team management creates a more adaptive, responsive, customer-oriented, learning organization that can apply total quality management. Teams break down the psychological, sociological, and political resistance to change that permeates the traditional bureaucratic organizational structure. Organizations that have adopted such an integrated team-management approach include 3M, Hewlett-Packard, Ford, and British Airways. The following sections further discuss how cross-functional team management is integrated into the traditional functional structures of organizations and how it can be used to manage organizational networks.

External Organizational Networks and Relationship Marketing

The combined organization and implementation of marketing programs and tasks involves the study of the economics and politics of how to do it best.[7] It is a special competitive rationality skill that the CEO and senior executives of the modern firm must possess. This skill has become crucial because the rules of the game have changed.

[6] Chapters 2 and 3 define and discuss at some length the role of cross-functional teams in planning, intelligence gathering, and intelligence use. Appendix 1 describes some of the key mechanics of setting up and leading a cross-functional team.

[7] Ronald H. Coase, "The Nature of the Firm," *Economica* 4 (1937): 386–405; Oliver E. Williamson, *Markets and Hierarchies* (New York: The Free Press, 1975); and Robert W. Ruckert, Orville C. Walker Jr., and Kenneth J. Roering, "The Organization of Marketing Activities: A Contingency Theory of Structure and Performance," *Journal of Marketing* 49 (winter 1985): 13–25.

CEOs with the old skills of charismatic leadership, cost control, or shrewd buying and selling of assets must adapt to the new reality. The reality is that American firms that use the new information and management technologies most innovatively will flourish. The new technologies increase the *ways* a firm can implement its innovation/imitation strategies most efficiently and effectively. These new information and management technologies allow firms to reduce transaction costs dramatically while increasing control.

How EDI Increases Outsourcing Control and Choices

In earlier chapters, how electronic data interchange (EDI) can simplify and reduce negotiation, contracting, shipping, customs-processing, back-ordering, expediting, payment time and costs; inventory holding costs; obsolete inventory write-downs; and in-transit monitoring costs was explained. But EDI can do even more. Most basic, EDI increases the opportunity for outsourcing production and distribution and for implementing many other marketing activities and programs (see Figure 11.9, "A Seamless Worldwide EDI Communication System"). This opens up a greater range of "how to do it best" choices that ultimately must confer a competitive advantage. As long as one firm has *more choices* of how to produce, distribute, and implement marketing programs, it will have a competitive advantage over its rivals. Furthermore, many modern products rely on so many different technologies that even the very largest companies cannot possibly be the best in all of them. As a result, firms must form strategic alliances to remain competitive.[8] Examples of such alliances are Apple and Motorola developing a new-generation operating system and microprocessor, Xerox and Sun Microsystems creating new computer products, and Apple and IBM engineering new networking software. Such alliances require special levels of shared destiny, trust, and, in particular, the ability to communicate and share information through compatible EDI systems.[9]

How Cross-Functional Teams Best Manage Relationship Networks

Beyond the advantages of cross-functional teams described in Chapters 2 and 3, cross-functional team organization and implementation is a profound advantage when addressing the company need to form alliance networks. Once a firm has learned the organizational skill of cross-functional team decision making, it can advance to the next level of competitive rationality: selecting and managing a whole *network of relationships* with other firms in a way that results in higher customer satisfaction at a lower cost. EDI provides the potential ability to develop numerous new relationships with suppliers and customers. Cross-functional team management realizes this potential.

In essence, once a cross-functional team has learned to manage itself and completely change the firm's internal political economy, it can launch into the task of reaching out, selecting, and managing a whole set of strategic alliances, that is, managing its external political economy. Throughout, this book has discussed how a firm increases its competitive rationality by choosing to contract out important organizational functions. Firms frequently use market research firms to help scan the environment

[8] Kenichi Ohmae, *The Borderless World* (New York: Harper Business, 1990), 4.
[9] John A. Byrne, Richard Brandt, and Otis Port, "The Virtual Corporation," *Business Week*, February 8, 1993, 98–103. The term *virtual corporation* is similar in meaning to the shell or hollow corporation mentioned later.

and create executives' mental models of the market environment. Firms also work with important customers and suppliers, involving them in the decision making and working with them to improve the quality of decisions and the speed of implementing them. Advertising agencies are hired to develop communication programs. Design and engineering consultants are hired to create product and service design. Integrated freight-forwarders provide global EDI networks that reduce transaction costs and increase control and choice. Information processing firms such as EDS can install or lease information systems. Manufacturer sales reps are used to personally sell to customers. Distributors sell, educate, train, install, and inventory products and are counted on to provide after-sales service. All of these firms form a network of strategic alliances (a network of legal and social contracts) used to make decisions and manufacture, market, and service the product (see Figure 17.2).[10] Examples of other diverse functions that can be contracted out include warehousing, trucking, sales promotions, and new-product R&D undertaken by universities or research organizations such as the Battelle Memorial Institute or Bell Laboratories. In short, many firms have been outsourcing numerous and varied key organizational activities for decades. What is new is that some firms have dramatically increased their outsourcing of much of their manufacturing to new suppliers or expanded their network of alliances to include even competitors.

Hub-and-Spoke Relationship Management

At the center (or hub) of a network of strategic alliances or long-term, outsourcing relationships is the cross-functional team. Some of the alliance partners may be important enough (such as designers, suppliers, customers, or the advertising agency) to be represented on the cross-functional team or cross-functional team working parties. Other relationships will be managed through the sales force or kept in constant contact through meetings, briefings, and EDI. The critical point is that a cross-functional team can manage a network organization much better than the traditional bureaucratic organization (see Figure 17.2). Bureaucratic organizations assign authority and responsibility to manage each of the external agents shown in Figure 17.2b to different departments, which then proceed to manage them *inside* their separate silos. The result is an increase in the probability of significant communication breakdowns and political system friction in both the internal and external network, that is, a decrease in system competitive rationality. A cross-functional team forms a much stronger and more capable hub for a network of marketing alliances (see Figure 17.2a). Over the long term, these competitive realities point to a single conclusion. Firms that shift to cross-functional team management and EDI increase their own internal competitive rationality and are better able to harness the competitive rationality available from other organizations with which they have working relationships.

Why must the firm be able to use EDI and cross-functional team management to take advantage of the full forces of competition? The theory of competitive rationality demonstrates that competition creates suppliers who are skilled at serving their

[10] For an interesting discussion of network organizations, see Frederick E. Webster, "The Changing Role of Marketing in the Corporation," *Journal of Marketing* 56 (October 1992): 1–17. This book, however, goes much further with integrating marketing management into general business management (undertaken by a cross-functional team) than Professor Webster proposes. Internal organizational politics are greatly reduced by cross-functional team business management. This simplifies organizational politics down to the economics and politics of managing the strategic alliances in the network.

Figure 17.2a **A Network of Organizational Relationships Managed by a Cross-Functional Team**

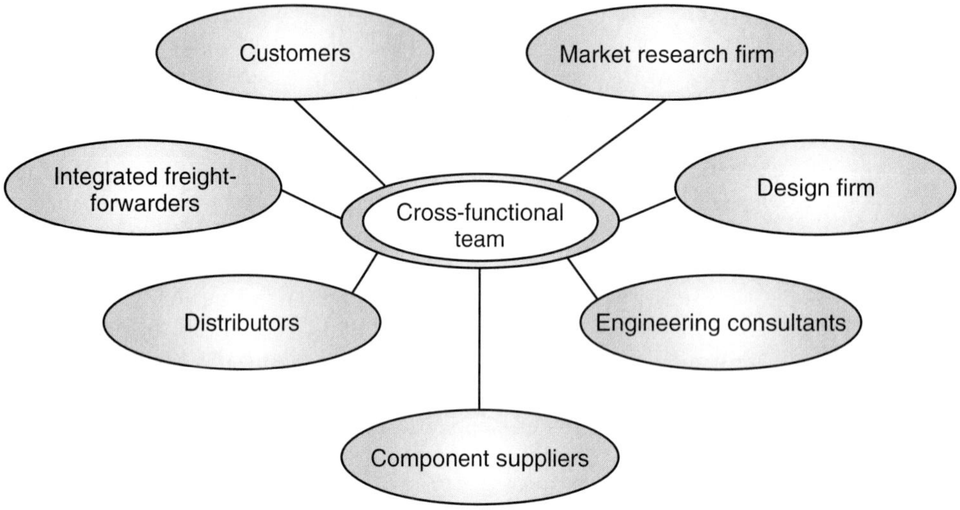

As a group, the cross-functional team must manage a whole network of strategic alliances and working relationships. However, all members of the cross-functional team are involved in the management process.

customers. Competition among suppliers of production, distribution, and marketing services illustrated in Figure 17.2 creates specially skilled executives and firms. In fact, this competition is likely to produce firms that are more efficient at certain production, distribution, and marketing functions and programs than the manufacturing or service firm can ever afford to be. It is a matter of specialization and competitive survival of the fittest. Simply put, a firm often cannot improve on the efficiency of the market.[11] If this is so, then it is important that the firm chooses a strategic alliance with a supplier most efficient and effective in the desired skill. If it does not, then a rival will choose a superior supplier. This link in the rival's organizational network will be stronger than the firm's link (perhaps because it has a better freight-forwarder, design firm, or advertising agency). But making a superior choice when forming a strategic alliance is not enough. The firm must then create a working relationship that takes the most advantage of the partner's skills.

The Hollow Company

In extreme cases, the firm's essential organization and function may be purely administrative because all of the major production functions have been subcontracted out to external suppliers. For example, the company 1-800-FLOWERS subcontracts the

[11] Coase, "The Nature of the Firm"; Williamson, *Markets and Hierarchies;* and Ruekert et al., "The Organization of Marketing Activities," 17.

Figure 17.2b **A Network of Organizational Relationships Managed by Functions**

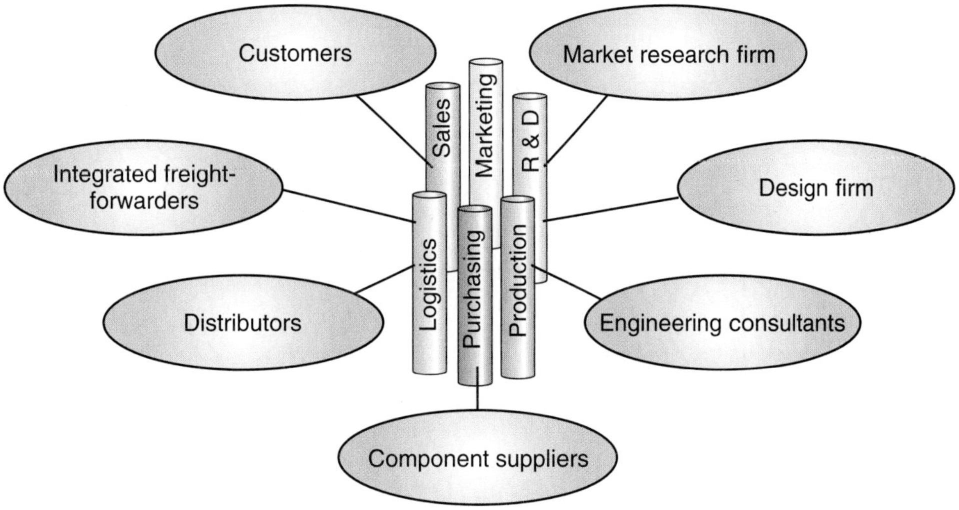

As illustrated, an organizational network managed by functional silos risks communication inefficiencies and political ineffectiveness. Brand or product management helps increase coordination but often is only a tactical solution to the strategic organization problem.

delivery of flowers to local florists (see Figure 17.3). In this case, the firm's core competency is its ability to position a product, make market decisions, implement programs, and choose the right organization network alliances and manage them. Companies such as Casio, Nike, Liz Claiborne, and Emerson Radio have moved toward such marketing organizations. They are very flexible and adaptive because the production investment risks are carried by their suppliers.[12] MS-DOS, the operating system that Microsoft sold to IBM (and that was eventually responsible for Microsoft making a name for itself) was purchased from a small Seattle computer company. The system was initially called Q-DOS (quick and dirty operating system). Microsoft changed the name, for fairly obvious reasons, positioned the product superbly, developed the trading alliances, and managed the alliances very well.

However, most start-up organizations take on a great many production, distribution, and sales functions, either because they feel they can do it more cost-effectively or because they fear a loss of control. In-house manufacturing is likely to occur when marketing complex products, particularly of innovations early in the product's life cycle, when a great deal of competitive advantage comes from secret processes, undisclosed formulas, or other information that needs to be kept confidential for as long as possible within the organization.[13] A firm that emphasizes *innovation* more than imitation is not

[12] Ravi S. Achrol, "Evolution of the Marketing Organization: New Forms for Turbulent Environments," *Journal of Marketing* 55 (October 1991): 77–93.

[13] Ruekert et al., "The Organization of Marketing Activities"; and Erin Anderson, "The Salesperson As Outside Agent or Employee: A Transaction Cost Analysis," *Marketing Science* 4, no. 3 (1985): 234–54.

Figure 17.3 **A Network Organization Ad**

Rather than sending flowers by UPS or FedEx, as some companies such as Black Tie Roses do, 1-800-FLOWERS subcontracts a network of local florists to arrange and deliver the flowers. In this way, all of the firm's manufacturing and physical distribution functions are outsourced.

likely to outsource the R&D, design, and production of key components unless it has patents on its product and process innovations. A firm that emphasizes *imitation* more than innovation may be more likely to outsource. A company that emphasizes imitation often feels less at risk in giving away its vital technological secrets and customer contacts to a supplier. However, this may be a huge mistake, for if the firm is *not* an innovator, how does it compete if its suppliers treacherously become its competitors?

In global sourcing and marketing, a firm has to constantly transfer its design and manufacturing technology to suppliers in its organizational network. This inevitably increases the skills of its offshore partners, which poses a very serious, long-term competitive risk. For example, many Asian manufacturers are being given technology by U.S. companies and other multinationals that would have cost billions of dollars and taken a generation of management to develop on their own.[14] One company, Schwinn Bicycle Co., taught its two Chinese suppliers (Giant and China) how to become its major competitors and became its own victim of global sourcing.[15] According to the theory of competitive rationality, this continuing giveaway should spur the firms who give such technology to even *greater* innovation. To stay ahead of the potential competition from errant suppliers that they create by transferring their existing technology, they always must be several steps ahead in their experimentation, learning, and implementation skills (that is, they must practice superior competitive rationality). *Thus, the cumulative effect of such global sourcing and technology transfer is to speed up the rate of innovation/imitation in the global market, and this rate of change will continue to accelerate.*

Internal Organizational Structure That Enables Implementation

To cope with today's market environment, organizations have developed a wide variety of internal organizational structures that range from the simple functional organization to the product market organization to the more complex matrix organization. Each of these structures has its advantages and disadvantages.[16] The *functional* organizational structure creates functional specialists—such as a sales manager, advertising manager, and market research manager—who all report to a marketing vice president. It is the most common form of marketing organization, and it is very simple and efficient in a stable environment. It cannot adapt to change very quickly, however, and breaks down as the number of products, market segments served, and functions increases. It is particularly unsuited for serving very different global markets. A *product market* organization adds a layer of staff positions called product, brand, or market managers whose responsibility is to coordinate all of the functional activities associated with each product brand, or specific market. A *matrix* organization is designed to form teams of functional and product market managers that can focus on a specific project.

New product development highlights the difference between functional and matrix organizational structures. The bureaucratic, functional management of new product development involves cooperation among functional departments, such as marketing, R&D, and manufacturing, who together employ formal, bureaucratic channels of authority and communication. Management guidance is provided by senior management or a product manager who is responsible for orchestrating the new product development process but lacks the authority to make it happen. Cross-functional team or matrix management, on the other hand, involves the creation of a full-time or part-time team of executives with different functional skills who have collective responsibility and authority for the project. A team whose members are temporarily transferred from their functional departments to work on the project part time is called a project matrix team. A project matrix team may be used by smaller firms that cannot commit full-time human resources to a single new product development cross-functional team. In fact, it is not unusual for a manager to be a member of several such cross-functional teams working on different projects.

---

14 Robert Neff et al., "Multinationals Have a Tiger by the Tail," *Business Week*, December 7, 1992.

15 Andrew Tanzer, "Bury Thy Teacher," *Forbes*, December 21, 1992, 90–95. Schwinn was also not a leading innovator and, in fact, missed the boat on the mountain bike fad.

16 Barton Weitz and Erin Anderson, "Organizing and Controlling the Marketing Function," in *Review of Ma[illegible]ng 1981*, ed. B. M. Enis and K. J. Roering. (Chicago: American Marketing Association, 1981), 124–42.

Figure 17.4a **Entrepreneurial, Cross-Functional Organization**

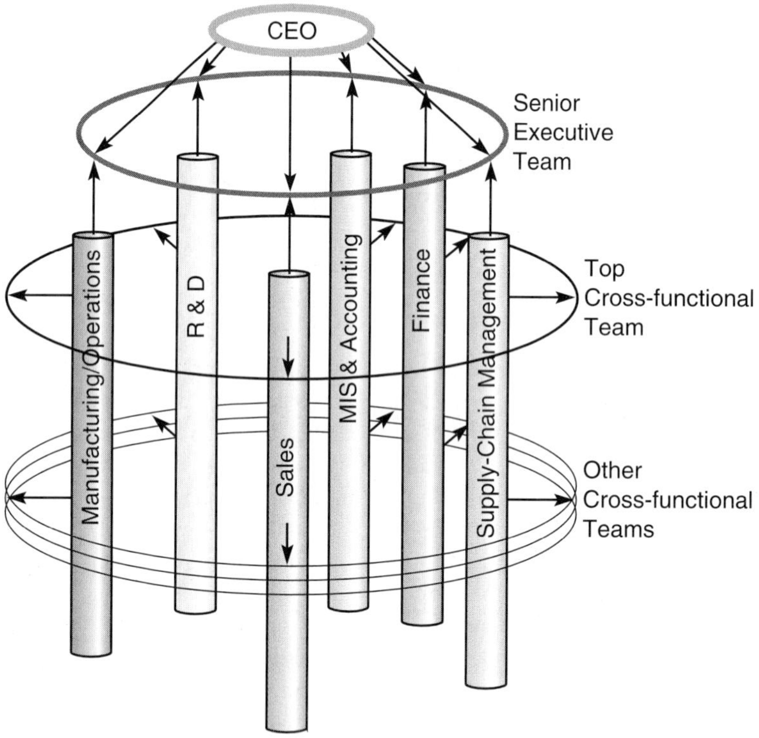

The senior cross-functional executive team is made up of the executives who head up each function. They meet weekly to manage the company or division. Each of them is also responsible for championing a cross-functional product development team. This requires them to promote the interests of this team at the highest levels of the firm. In this way, cross-functional management is inculcated throughout the organization, particularly if promotion depends on working within and leading lower level product development teams. The thickness of the cross-functional rings symbolizes the importance and responsibilities of the teams.

Evolution of the Entrepreneurial Cross-Functional Organization

A *servo-mechanism* is a mechanism that automatically brings a system back under control so it performs as it should. Examples of mechanical servo-mechanisms are cruise controls on cars or ABS braking systems. Ideally, social systems also have built-in servo-mechanisms that make them self-managing and hence much more reliable and efficient. The following social servo-mechanism processes keep the entrepreneurial, cross-functional organization illustrated in Figure 17.4 in control:

1. *Each member of the senior executive team is a champion of at least one cross-functional team, as well as responsible for a specialized functional department.* As champion, she or he is responsible for the cross-functional team delivering a quality outcome, on time and under budget. A product champion thus has an interest in assembling the most talented cross-functional team possible and to choose an excellent team leader, rather than choosing political favorites. Championing also means preserving and protecting the interests of the product

Figure 17.4b **The Twenty-First-Century High-Flying Organization Structure**

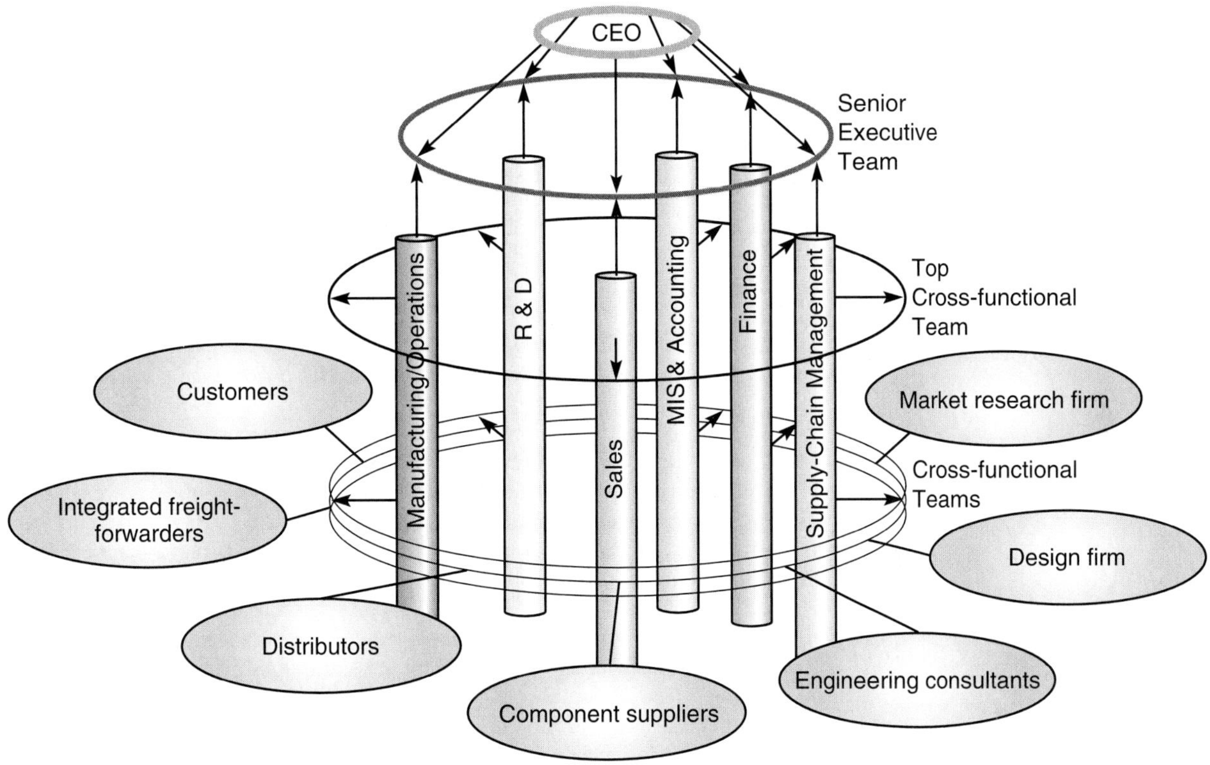

Combining Figure 17.1a and Figure 17.3a illustrates the complete modern organization. Note the critical role that each cross-functional team plays in holding the organization together and in maintaining relations with the alliance partners. Often each alliance partner has a similar entrepreneurial, cross-functional organization, so the competitive entity looks like a network of interconnected spaceships. In such an entity, it is the network of relationships among cross-functional teams that holds the whole alliance together.

development team and raising problems with the cooperation and performance of another function directly with the head of that function or at executive meetings. She or he also will have to resolve problems that cross-functional teams are having with her or his functional department. In this way, the needs and the priorities of the cross-functional teams are championed and resolved by senior management.[17] If executives are not assigned to champion such product/service development teams, a strong possibility exists that functional fiefdoms and traditional bureaucratic sluggishness will overcome cross-functional organization and destroy it.

The added responsibility of holding the reins of several cross-functional teams as well as running a functional department will force the executive to delegate more, including

[17] Brown and Eisenhardt (1995) found that product development teams are most successful when they are led or championed by leaders with power, vision, and influence in the organization: Shona L. Brown and Kathleen M. Eisenhardt, "Product Development: Past Research, Present Findings, and Future Directions," *Academy of Management Review* 20, no. 2 (1995): 370.

encouraging the number-two person in the department to help champion a more junior and less important cross-functional team. This will further reinforce the signals sent from the top of each functional department that the major mission of the functional area is to support and help implement the cross-functional product development projects, rather than fighting with other functional areas for resources.

2. *The process of selecting a CEO will be driven by how well a person has championed cross-functional teams, worked well as a senior cross-functional team member, and managed his or her functional area. Promotion through functional departments and to more important cross-functional teams will also depend on previous team performance.* With such promotion criteria, the human capital skills of developing and managing cross-functional teams will be imbued from the top down in the organization. Making promotion dependent on team performance institutionalizes team performance skills throughout the management and culture of the organization. It also will break down functional silo mentalities because team performance will depend on understanding other functions and cooperating with them. Appointment to a team will become a mark of honor within a functional department, and appointment to several teams and, finally, leadership of a team will become the desired career path.
3. *Allocation of resources will be to teams and not functions, and project priority will be established by the senior cross-functional team and ultimately by the CEO.* Such cross-functional team priorities establish the future vision and direction of the enterprise and avoid fights among cross-functional teams for resources. Functional areas will grow and shrink depending on their employment by the cross-functional teams instead of the political power of their vice president. If the cross-functional teams prefer to outsource because it is competitively more rational, then the functional area will shrink and have to raise its performance to survive. This will greatly increase the cooperation and support cross-functional teams receive from functional areas.
4. *Project teams continue to run projects, and highly successful teams become the senior executive team of new divisions.* By such an entrepreneurial process of spinning off new divisions that manage highly successful new products and services, the company rewards the entire team.[18] This creates legendary organization stories that encourage team cooperation and the drive to make every post a winning post. It thus deals with the problem of selfish individuals who, otherwise, might be prepared to destroy a team to promote or save their own careers. In such teams, top-down discipline is replaced by team self-discipline: "In a self-disciplined organization, employees come to meetings on time, work toward agreement on defined agendas, and do not question in the corridors the decisions they agreed to in the conference room. Above all, they deliver on their promises and commitments."[19]

   Team self-discipline and cooperation (putting aside self-interest, territoriality, and work-to-rule) are often exhibited when emergency workers respond to natural disasters, which is why the CEO and president of Intel, Andy Grove uses this analogy to describe how he wants his firm to work. Such an entrepreneurial process is also found at 3M, where project teams led by an entrepreneur who came up with the idea can grow into separate divisions. This "grow and divide" process encourages innovation and entrepreneurship. It also leads to a much higher return on investment in research and development.[20]
5. *Future project team leaders emerge as natural, informal team leaders and are identified as such by their peers and champions.* Ambitious, talented individuals will reveal themselves by their energy, their insights, and their willingness to be team players. Their current team leader, colleagues, and team champion will support their promotion to leadership of future teams. This reduces the promotion of political favorites or "toadies" within the organization that frequently occurs in traditional functional bureaucracies.

---

[18] See Sumantra Ghoshal and Christopher A. Bartlett, "Changing the Role of Top Management: Beyond Structure to Processes," *Harvard Business Review* (January/February 1995): 86–96.
[19] Ghoshal and Bartlett, "Changing the Role of Top Management," 91.
[20] San M. Lee, "The Pan-Pacific Age and the United States," *Pan Pacific Business Association Newsletter,* winter 1988, University of Nebraska, as quoted in Achrol, "Evolution of the Marketing Organization."

6. *The most talented junior executives will become members of several teams.* This develops and tests the executive's ability to participate in and manage several projects at once and also fosters learning across teams about new technologies and superior team processes.
7. *The senior cross-functional team is also the team that directs and develops the higher order learning processes of the organization.* Although talented, younger executives may join the team to address particular organizational learning disabilities, it is crucial that the senior management team take on this added responsibility because they can institute the learning processes, including learning to make the team's own operational processes more efficient. Thus, consistent with the process learning hierarchy described in Chapter 4, the senior-executive cross-functional team becomes the most important learning/TQM team in the organization.

   Each functional area will have its own learning teams to improve its operational processes and to improve its cooperation with the cross-functional teams. Similarly, all of the cross-functional product development teams will improve their work processes through the higher order learning processes institutionalized by the senior cross-functional team.

All of these processes are actually far more than servo-mechanism processes. Yes, they will keep an organization efficient, effective, and progressive. But they also create a new type of organization and culture. All of a firm's processes contribute to changing its wealth, resources, and, hence, structure. That is one of the laws of competitive rationality. But the above listed processes are a special category of change processes called *metamorphosis processes.* Metamorphosis processes directly transform the organization and its management. Like the metamorphosis of a grub into a butterfly, such processes can transform a slow-moving, inefficient organization into an organization whose appearance and performance are dazzling—an organization that metaphorically can fly![21] But it can take a long time for such a metamorphosis to completely occur because it will take five to ten years for the talent to rise through the ranks of the organization based on these processes.

Individual Leadership That Facilitates Implementation

Implementation is the series of steps taken by managers to gain the cooperation and compliance needed to install planned changes in an organization's behavior. One study found the best implementation approach was for the manager to:

1. Have the seniority and authority to manage the change process and appraise performance.
2. Demonstrate the need for change through unfavorable benchmark performance comparisons of existing routines or behaviors with comparable organizations.
3. Demonstrate the feasibility of change by describing ways current practices can be improved.
4. Form a participant task force to identify inefficient and ill-advised procedures or activities and to suggest ways they might be improved.
5. Approve suggested changes.

[21] See Ghoshal and Bartlett, "Changing the Role of Top Management," 86–96. Such organization metamorphosis processes are akin to Ghoshal and Bartlett's competence-building and renewal processes. The difference is that the set of metamorphosis processes described in this textbook are more than competence-building or renewal processes. They are explicitly directed at creating an entrepreneurial cross-functional firm organized as illustrated in Figure 17.4. Such an organization has embedded in it the metamorphosis processes that formed it and make it a continuousl[illegible]eri-menting, learning, improving, and evolving enterprise.

6. Monitor and demonstrate improvements in performance brought about by the implemented change.[22]

This approach was observed to be more effective than implementing by edict, by persuasion, or, at the other extreme, by more participative approaches. The successful implementer unfreezes old beliefs, norms, attitudes, and behaviors and actively supervises the change process. This approach is also consistent with decentralized, continuous, cross-functional management, which assumes the sales and marketing executives are responsible for implementing the marketing strategy and projects. Interestingly, another study notes that in Japan the marketing manager "patiently advises, guides and persuades, and the members concerned develop a feeling that the decision is their own idea."[23] Marketing managers in Japan are not market specialists but rather are experts in *implementing change* in the organization. It seems they can exert such informal influence because the whole organization shares the customer-orientation norm, a cooperative rather than adversarial norm, and a consensus decision-making norm. In U.S. firms with less of a clan culture and more of a bureaucratic structure, a senior line manager is likely to be much more effective at implementation management than a junior staff manager such as a brand or product manager.

The Present and Future Product Manager

A product or brand manager still can play a very important cajoling, educating, coordinating, and monitoring role with sales, the advertising agency, and manufacturing. In a bureaucratic organization, a product or brand manager is responsible for overseeing the development and execution of marketing plans but cannot ensure the necessary cooperation from others in the organization. Although this can be a problem even in bureaucracies, most of the time things get done through informal influence.[24] The product manager with good people skills and expertise can play a key role in ensuring the execution of product market plans (see Figure 17.5). The informal communication and leadership of such product managers act as the glue that binds the organization together. The problem is that they are often in the job for too short a time to effectively build the team or clan spirit. The role of product managers in an organization using cross-functional-team decision making is less clear because the team, as a team, takes collective responsibility for implementing its decisions. The individual with overall responsibility is the team leader, who is just as likely to be a designer or engineer as a marketer. Perhaps the product manager evolves into the team's executive assistant and will come to play a dominant role in managing the product as it matures, consulting the cross-functional team on an as-needed basis.

---

[22] Paul C. Nutt, "Tactics of Implementation," *Academy of Management Journal* 29, no. 2 (1986): 230–61.

[23] William Lazer, Shoji Murata, and Hiroshi Kosaka, "Japanese Marketing: Towards a Better Understanding," *Journal of Marketing* 49 (spring 1985): 69–81.

[24] David L. Wilemon, "Interpersonal Influence in Product Management," *Journal of Marketing* 40 (October 1976): 33–41; and Steven Lysonski, Alan Singer, and David Wilemon, "Coping with Environmental Uncertainty and Boundary Spanning in the Product Manager's Role," *Journal of Business & Industrial Marketing* 3, no. 2 (1988): 5–16.

Figure 17.5 How a Product Manager Elicits Support

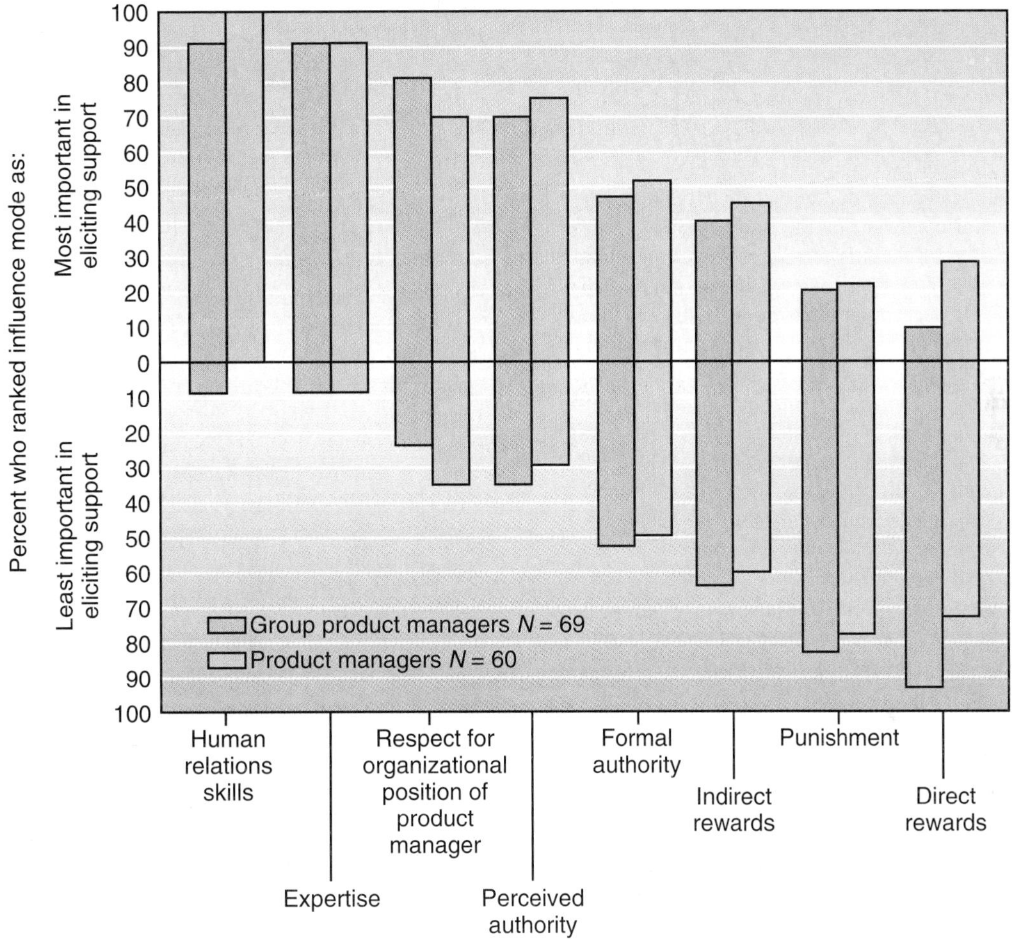

Product managers use charm, congeniality, and expertise to get things done. Often this is because they lack authority and reward control.

SOURCE: Adapted from Alladi Venkatesh and David L. Wilemon, "Interpersonal Influence in Product Management," *Journal of Marketing* 40 (October 1976): 36.

Process Mapping Activity Scheduling Techniques That Facilitate Implementation

Many implementation concerns should have been addressed in the environment-strategy meshing process. Strategy already will have been refined to handle production scheduling and capacity, the limited experience of the sales force, and other such constraints. The savvy marketing planner also will have lined up a senior manager to play the role of the *champion* or *fixer* if, as a last resort, someone needs to 'ean on

Rationality in Practice

A Comedy of Errors

For a concatenation of comedic [implementation] errors confounding a single promotion, few can top Pan Am's ill-fated "Bottle in a Basket" campaign of a few years back. To demonstrate Pan Am's superior service on the hotly competitive New York–San Juan route, the airline's ad agency, J. Walter Thompson, hit upon the idea of serving passengers with a light repast: a small bottle of Mateus wine, sliced salami, cheese, and an apple, all served in a little plastic basket on a dainty gingham tablecloth. Cute.

"We got the thing all organized," a former J. Walter Thompson account executive recalls, "when all of a sudden we get this hysterical phone call from Pan Am: 'Don't run the ad! We just received 2,000 pounds of sliced salami—but our contract with the commissary requires that all meats must be sliced by them.'" Back went the sliced salami along with a rush order for a ton of whole salamis. At length, with the salamis received and duly sliced in the commissary, the campaign was ready to kick off again when another May Day call was flashed from Pan Am. It seemed that while the little plastic baskets were in New York, the bottles of wine were in San Juan. Hence, another delay to let the bottles catch up with the baskets. No such luck. A mix up in the order resulted in the baskets being shipped to Puerto Rico at the same time that the wine was being flown to New York.

With the logistical problems involving baskets, bottles, and salamis finally straightened out, Pan Am signaled the agency to run the kick-off ad—which pulled so well that the maiden 'Bottle in a Basket' flight was a sellout. Just as airline and agency were congratulating each other, however, word came from San Juan that the wine bottles aboard the first flight had cork tops, not screw-off caps, and the flight attendants had no corkscrews to open them. "We ended up with 180 frustrated passengers ready to break the bottle over our heads," reports the ad man.

Refusing to despair, the indomitable airline thereupon shipped cases of Mateus back to Portugal in exchange for screw-capped bottles. Unfortunately, by the time all the elements of the promotion were finally in place, Pan Am had switched its Puerto Rico service to much larger 747s, and the assembly and serving of 300 baskets of food was deemed too much of a hassle for Pan Am's stewardesses. So, the entire promotion was ditched.

SOURCE: Quoted directly from Robert Levy and Lynn Adkins, "The Hypes That Failed," *Forbes*, September 1980, 74–75.

someone else to gain resources or cooperation. However, the many details necessary to execute the marketing strategy still must be worked out. The Rationality in Practice box presents an amusing story of what can happen when such action-planning steps are not taken.

Over the years, techniques such as management by objectives have come and gone, but one management approach—management by profanity (MBP)—has stood the test of time. That is about the only test that it has stood. When things go wrong, MBP becomes the management approach of choice. It can be observed when a senior executive turns to a subordinate and asks a question such as, "We did send back the packaging artwork that we approved last month, didn't *you?*" The classic reaction to MBP is an exclaimed or muted oath, normally accompanied by a sinking feeling and clammy palms. Highly contagious, MBP can trigger in others an involuntary string of colorful phrases, vigorous arm waving, hand washing, and the high-pitched shouting of directions down corridors to no one in particular. It is best avoided because it can become a chronic condition and is associated with high blood pressure, angina, short- and long-term hormonal imbalances, and premature aging. More seriously, the problems of poor execution go beyond the undermining of a particular strategy. The finger pointing that results can rip an organization's morale and harmony apart. It also can undermine an organization's confidence that it can do anything right and can lead to individual disillusionment with the company. The solution is systematic project action planning.

Project Action Planning

In our personal lives, we frequently undertake orchestrated behavioral routines in which certain activities must follow one or more others (for example, getting dressed in the morning must come *before* starting the car). If we do not perform these activities in the right order, then we do not achieve the desired goal, and not only do we end up looking stupid, but we often have to spend extra time and effort undoing the mistakes before starting over. The potential problems are even greater when organizations undertake major construction projects or attempt a major new-product launch.

The use of scientific management in project scheduling probably occurred as early as the construction of the pyramids and was certainly well understood by the railroad contractors who criss-crossed the U.S. heartland in the nineteenth century. It was further refined during World War II when U.S. shipyards were able to produce liberty ships for the convoys faster than the German U-boats could sink them, which was very fast.

The modern origins of planned project implementation are usually traced to the use of Program Evaluation Review Technique (PERT) on the Polaris Weapon Systems development in 1958 and Du Pont's development of the Critical Path Method (CPM) at about the same time.[25] These critical-path analysis techniques are commonly used in building and highway construction. They also have been used to dramatically increase the speed, efficiency, and profitability of new product launches. Few good reasons exist why they should not be used as a matter of course in implementing marketing strategy and, hence, become an integral part of the annual marketing plan. Good managers go through an intuitive path or network analysis in their action planning and control, anyway. CPM analysis can assist in planning and controlling the implementation of competitive strategy and, through a mental assimilation of the logic and structure of the process, can improve the intuitive action planning of managers. Much has been made of the need to continuously increase manufacturing productivity by improving the production process. Little has been said about continuously improving the marketing production process. Critical-path analysis assists in marketing action plans in a number of ways, listed in Table 17.1. It is not *the* answer, but it is part of an answer.[26]

The Competitive Rationality of Activity Scheduling

The first step in a CPM analysis is to break down the marketing strategy into specific activities and activity sequences. Examples of a new-product activity schedule and promotion activity schedule (AS) scripts are presented in Figure 17.6. The potential number of activities and complex sequencing emphasize why having a staff create marketing plans does not work. Line managers must prepare the marketing plan, for it is they who must develop a strategy or a project into a list of specific tasks (correctly sequenced), create milestone completion dates and progress reviews, and assign responsibility for the efficient and effective completion of each task to specific individuals.[27]

[25] As an aside, Du Pont is seldom given the accolades it deserves for the many outstanding innovations in management accounting and scientific management that its employees have developed over the past century.

[26] An excellent example of the use of CPM in implementing a marketing plan is provided by Warren Dusenberry, "CPM for New Product Introductions," *Harvard Business Review* (July/August 1967): 124–39.

[27] John M. Hobbs and Donald F. Heany, "Coupling Strategy to Operating Plans," *Harvard Business Review* (May/June 1977): 119–24.

Table 17.1 **Advantages of Using the Critical Path Method in Strategy Implementation**

1. It enables decision makers to estimate how long it will take to roll out all of the components of the marketing plan, and it can be used to calculate the chances that targeted deadlines will be met.
2. It greatly improves control over all the integrated and interdependent activities required to implement the marketing plan.
3. It reveals interdependencies and human resource bottlenecks that would not be exposed by more intuitive action planning.
4. It encourages a greater degree of honesty and accuracy in the forecasting of the time necessary to enact specific activities.
5. It enables senior executives to delegate responsibility with confidence and to manage by exception.
6. It encourages more responsible time management from external participants, such as market research firms and advertising agencies.
7. It reduces confusion, duplication, false starts, and frustration, and it can significantly improve internal communication and morale.
8. It ensures that synergy gets a chance by orchestrating the timing of interactive marketing activities.
9. It enables sound decisions to be made about where to invest extra resources to speed up overall implementation.
10. It allows the detailed information on time and costs from those responsible for implementing specific activities to be used as a final check on the feasibility of the proposed marketing strategy.
11. It enables the timely scheduling of go/no-go decisions or contingency plan reviews.

To be able to do all of these they must believe in the plan or project, own it, know all of the activities and sequences involved, and understand it enough to adapt it in ways that more efficiently and effectively achieve the desired objectives. In short, they must be involved in the initial planning. Once an activity schedule has been developed for an advertising campaign or sales promotion, it can be used as an activity sequence blueprint or script for future ad campaigns. The next step is to assign responsibility for implementing each activity to an individual or to an individual leading a team. This individual is then asked to indicate all the activities that absolutely must precede the task he or she is responsible for executing. He or she also must estimate the time needed to complete the task, given the resources that will be made available. CPM uses only one time estimate, while PERT uses a most optimistic, most likely, and most pessimistic time estimate.

The Critical Path of Activities

All the activities are now connected in their dependency sequences or paths. This produces a network of sequenced activities, as illustrated in Table 17.2 on pages 667–668, which enables the computation of the earliest possible start time of each activity (EST) and the identification of a set of sequenced activity paths. The path that will take the longest time to implement is the *critical path*. All other paths have some float or slack time (a time cushion) in that a time overrun can occur on a noncritical path activity and it will not delay the overall rollout of the marketing plan. Time overrun on the critical path is *critical* because it will push the completion of the whole project back and, in fact, may mean missing important deadlines, such as the Christmas season, an attractive media supplement, or an important trade show.

Working backward from the last activity on the critical path, a manager can compute the latest start time (LST) of all preceding activities. The difference between LST and EST gives the maximum possible slack or float for each activity. Of course, if all of the slack or float time on an implementation path is used by one activity on the path, then the rest of the activities on that path lose their slack time, and any delay in starting them or time overrun then becomes critical. Procrastinators and dawdlers

Figure 17.6a A New-Product Activity Sequence (AS) Script

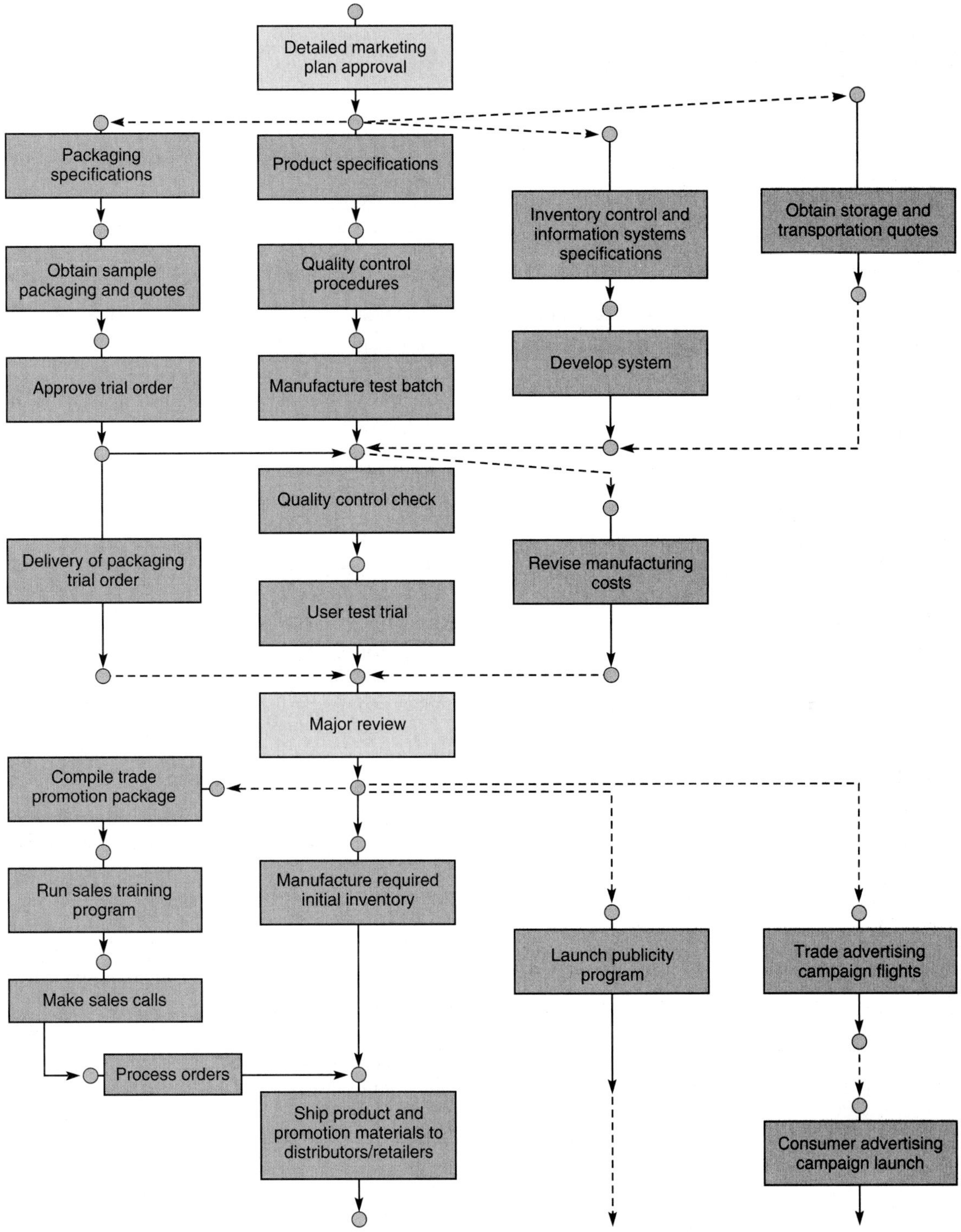

(continued)

Figure 17.6b **A New-Product Activity Sequence (AS) Script**

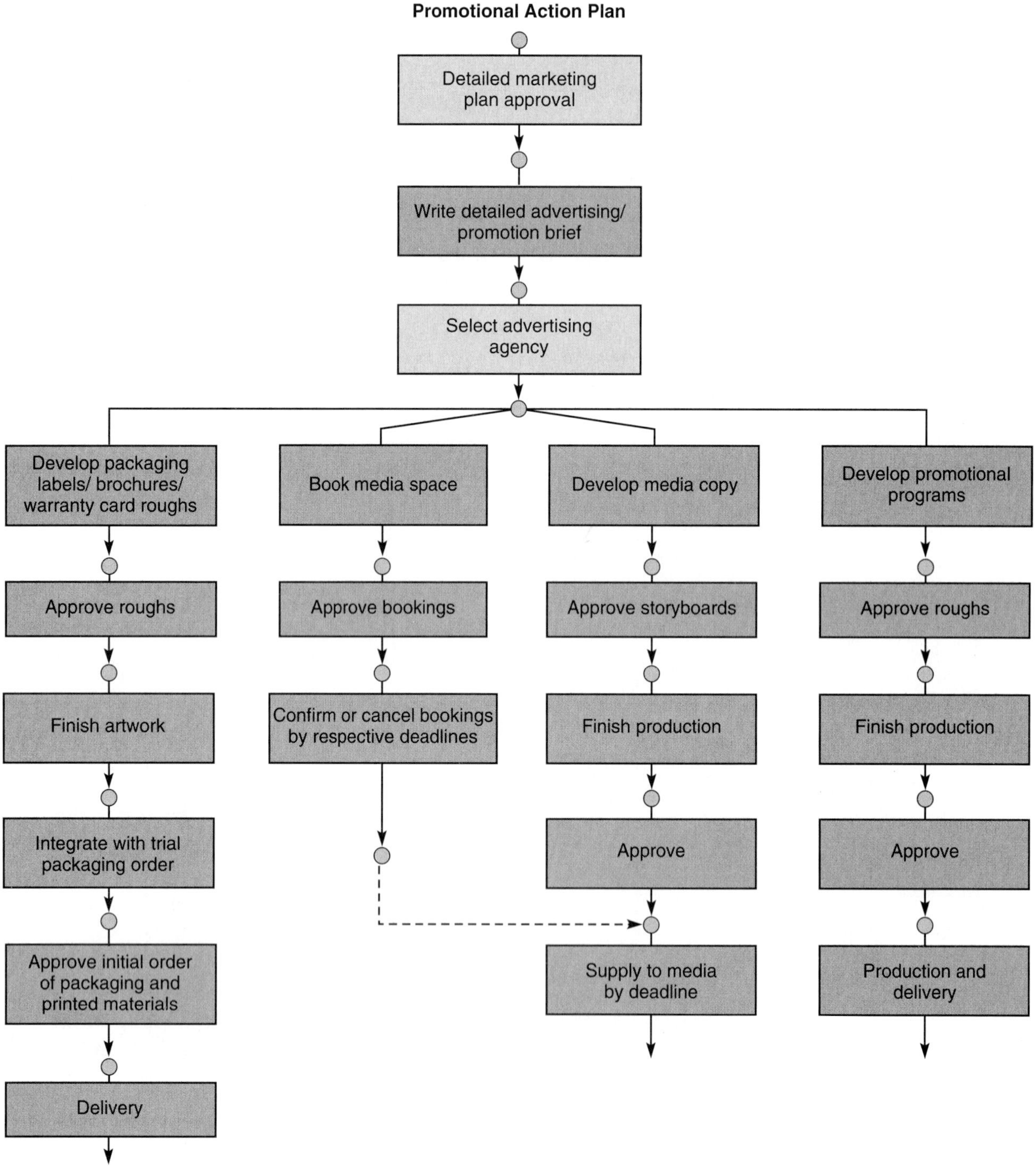

Table 17.2 Speeding Up Implementation by Project Crashing

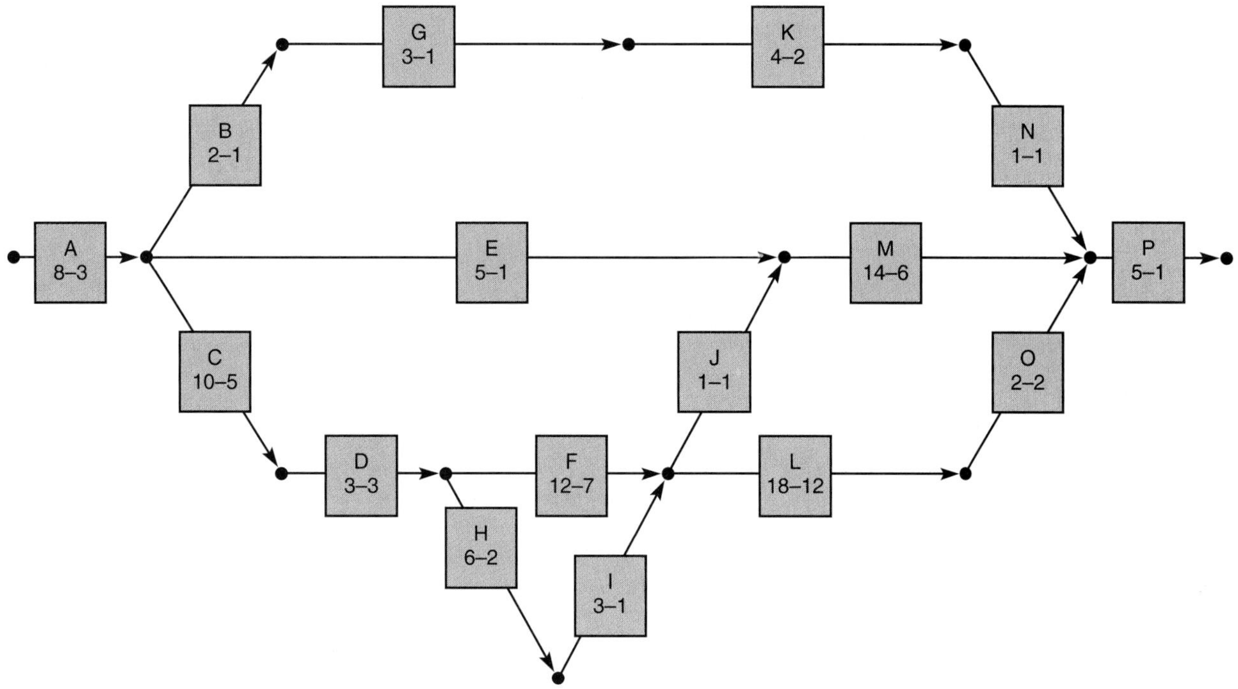

Network Plan for NCR Century Direct-Mail Campaign

ACTIVITY	ACTIVITY DURATION IN DAYS		ACTIVITY DOLLAR COST		RATE OF COST INCREASE ($/DAY)
	NORMAL	CRASH	NORMAL	CRASH	
A. Rough copy	8	3	$ 400	$ 650	$ 50
B. Copy for announcement	2	1	125	225	100
C. Layout	10	5	600	1,200	120
D. Approval	3	3	—	—	—
E. Research mailing lists	5	1	100	540	110
F. Final art	12	7	750	1,500	150
G. Approval—announcement	2	2	—	—	—
H. Final copy	6	2	250	400	38
I. Type set	3	1	350	535	88
J. OK mailing lists	1	1	—	—	—
K. Printing—announcement	4	2	150	400	125
L. Printing	18	12	2,150	3,350	200
M. Order mailing lists	14	6	500	620	15
N. Deliver to mailing center—announcement	1	1	—	—	—
O. Deliver to mailing center	2	2	—	—	—
P. Mail material	5	1	1,150	1,650	125

(continued)

Table 17.2 *(continued)*

CRASHING ANALYSIS	PROJECT DURATION (DAYS)	PROJECT COST (DIRECT)
Normal time and cost	58	$6,525
Critical path A-C-D-F-L-O-P		
a) Activity A reduced 5 days at $50/day	53	6,775
b) Activity C reduced 5 days at $120/day	48	7,375
c) Activity P reduced 4 days at $125/day	44	7,875
d) Activity F reduced 3 days at $150/day	41	8,325
Critical paths now A-C-D-F-L-O-P and A-C-D-H-I-L-O-P		
e) Activities E and F can be jointly reduced 2 days at ($38 and $150)/day	39	8,701
f) Activity L reduced 5 days at $200/day	34	9,701
Critical paths now A-C-D-F-L-O-P A-C-D-H-I-L-O-P A-C-D-F-J-M-P A-C-D-H-I-J-M-P		
g) Activities M and L can be jointly reduced 1 day at ($15 and $200)/day	33	9,916

make no friends down the implementation path because the extra time they take reduces the time cushioning of succeeding activities. When everyone is aware of the network and who is responsible for what and when, then the participants tend to come under increased peer pressure to perform on time. The system tends to be self-managing.

Crashing Time and Competitive Rationality

Often the implementation of a marketing plan requires the meeting of various externally imposed deadlines. An executive's career can depend on meeting such deadlines. After the construction of the initial CPM chart, it may become apparent that such important deadlines will not be met unless things are put into overdrive and the time taken to execute some of the activities is shortened. Reducing the time taken to execute the overall plan is called, rather colorfully, "crashing" the project. Table 17.2 presents a modified analysis of the crashing of a direct-mail campaign for the NCR Century computer.[28]

The normal and crash time for each of the sixteen activities was first estimated. The crash time is the minimum time it will take to complete the activity regardless of the cost or resources expended. The average daily cost of crashing each activity also must be estimated. This is a best estimate of the cost of saving a day on each activity. In actuality, the daily cost of crashing each activity is likely to be a discontinuous step function rather than a continuous and linear function. The activities on the initial critical-path activity sequence are crashed starting with the least expensive time savings

[28] Edward J. Feltz, "The Costs of Crashing," *Journal of Marketing* (July 1970): 64–67.

Rationality in Practice

Time-Based Competition

Atlas Door, founded in the late 1970s, became the leading door supplier in less than ten years against long-established rivals. Traditionally, the industry had a sixteen-week order-delivery activity sequence cycle. Atlas computerized its order-entry, pricing, engineering, and manufacturing so it could price and schedule 95 percent of its business while the customer was still on the phone. This saved one to two weeks. Just-in-time production cut manufacturing down to two and one-half weeks. Being able to access previous special orders on the computer greatly reduced reengineering time, and shipping only complete orders forced a very efficient just-in-time logistics system, saving time associated with completing orders after the initial shipment. Atlas positioned itself as the supplier of last resort and penetrated the market when the competition could not deliver or missed key deadlines. This enabled Atlas to charge higher prices while the simplification that led to the faster service reduced costs.* As mentioned in the discussion of company analysis in Chapter 4, firms are using benchmarking to discover ways firms in other markets have simplified routines. What is learned is imitated or modified to shorten the time necessary to complete all activity sequences, be they routine or complex. The motive for the creative "crashing" of activity sequences is the belief that time is money. Taking too much time is a competitive disadvantage in many markets today.

*George Stalk Jr., "Time—The Next Source of Competitive Advantage," *Harvard Business Review* (July/August 1988): 41–51.

(that is, activity A, followed by C, P, and F). As the critical activity sequence is crashed, it may be sufficiently shortened so it ceases to be the only critical path (that is, if F is crashed by more than three days). When this occurs, then an analysis of simultaneously crashing joint critical paths has to be taken (see Table 17.2). It should be noted that crashing all activities cost $11,060, while the selective crashing of activities on the changing critical paths produced the same effect (a thirty-three-day project) at a cost of $9,916. Whether activity schedule crashing is done using a technique, such as CPM, or done intuitively, a major component of competitive rationality is a firm's ability to speed up its implementation. Firms such as Toyota, Hitachi, Honda, Sharp, Sony, Mitsubishi, Benetton, The Limited, Federal Express, McDonald's, and Domino's Pizza have demonstrated the advantages of greatly accelerating their competitive action time (see the next Rationality in Practice box).

It has been suggested that simply compressing or crashing product development schedules is more appropriate for more certain, less competitively dynamic settings.[29] But in such situations, what is the hurry? In hypercompetitive markets the cross-functional team has to compress product development and implementation time by both crashing individual activities and planning the schedule so more tasks that are not completely dependent on each other are undertaken in parallel. As described in Chapter 4, a company can learn how to do this from other companies through best-practice benchmarking. The team also has to be prepared to adapt the tasks and product design as market realities change during product development and implementation of marketing programs. Such creative improvisation requires a special type of team and individual, creative process thinking. This process thinking is constantly being applied to thinking about coordinating *all* of the processes involved in an added-quality supply chain.

[29] Kathleen M. Eisenhardt and Behnam N. Tabrizi, "Accelerating Adaptive Processes: Product Innovation in the Global Computer Industry," *Administrative Science Quarterly* 40 (1995): 84–110.

Internal Customers and the Added-Quality Chain

In addition to forecasting and updating completion time and identifying when and what material and labor resources will be needed, process mapping activities identify internal customer links. The implementation of the "internal customer" concept requires that the teams, executives, and workers responsible for preceding activities treat the teams, executives, and workers responsible for the activities that follow as their internal customers. The quality and timeliness of the preceding-activity outcome become part of the quality and timeliness of the inputs of the internal customer's activity that follows. Internal customers are expected to blow the whistle on poor quality, cost overruns or delays and, more important, to work with their "suppliers" to solve such problems. In this way, implementation becomes self-managing, and fewer overseeing layers of management are needed.

In addition, just as process mapping works backward from the target completion time to determine when each activity must be completed and started, it can be used to determine the necessary output and input quality of each activity. To better understand this internal added-quality chain, consider the following:

$$q_1 \rightarrow q_2 \rightarrow q_3 \rightarrow \cdots q_{n-2} \rightarrow q_{n-1} \rightarrow Q_n$$

Q_n is the quality of the product or service delivered to the ultimate customer, the quality that determines customer satisfaction. It is the output quality of the final n activity that completes the finished product or service. In the case of a product, it is likely to be packaging or delivery of the product to the customer. But this n activity had the output quality of the $n - 1$ activity, q_{n-1}, as part of its input quality. The $n - 1$ activity had q_{n-2} as part of its input quality, and, working all the way back through the process map's sequence of activities, the third activity had q_2 as part of its input quality, and the second activity had the output quality q_1 of the first task in the quality chain as part of its input quality.

The careful consideration of such an added-quality chain, working backward from the targeted quality delivered to the ultimate customer, ensures that each activity's output is directed toward adding satisfaction to the ultimate customer and toward serving the next internal customer by improving the quality of the latter's process inputs. The activities whose quality inputs and outputs are crucial in determining the ultimate quality of the product or service and customer satisfaction then will be identified. By tracing back through the quality chain, tasks will be exposed whose quality output is not very important to adding to the ultimate quality of the product. The resources allocated to such activities might be greatly reduced and, perhaps, the whole task eliminated. The justification for a process can be most directly established by asking the question Would the ultimate customers pay for the process if they knew about it? In large bureaucracies in particular, many such "worthless" activities often abound and would fail the test. They include senior management reporting, reviewing, approving, and supervising tasks that are not needed when teams cooperate horizontally. The Rationality in Practice box, "Mixing and Matching Value-Added Processes," describes how a much more efficient value-added chain can be created by making each group of workers associated with a process the actual owners of the process.

In Chapter 9 an actual input/output quality-added process map is presented in Figure 9.8 that computes the causal relationship between the output quality of service tasks in the process map and ultimate customer satisfaction. Such a map identifies the

Rationality in Practice

Mixing and Matching Quality-Added Processes

In the 1970s the textile industry in Central Italy went through an extraordinary evolution forced on them by global competition. Ten to twenty thousand small businesses have replaced the few dozen monolithic textile mills.* In the old vertically integrated mills, a management hierarchy supervised in detail all of the market environment analysis processes, product development and design processes, and production and distribution. In the new system, small "shops," sometimes family businesses, are responsible for a single process skill such as high-quality dress knitting or dying garments. They own their own single process businesses. This leads to greater process expertise, low administration overheads, and compensation schemes directly tied to process input/output efficiency.

Work is contracted out by master brokers who choose the shops they think can do the best job. This creates pressing "survival" incentives for shops to benchmark their specific process against the best, to stay abreast of market trends, and to react quickly and deliver excellent service. The master brokers select, coordinate, and manage the set of outsourced processes that they mix and match together. This involves making sure each shop is informed of the needs of the next shop that is its "customer" in the value-added chain and helping solve implementation problems, from raw materials supply-chain management through sales and delivery. Often different shops are housed under the same roof with lines marking where one business ends and the other begins. It is as if the different workers who "own" specific processes in a typical business actually do own the process and their "internal customers" become their actual external customers. This system allows no room or time for company politics, opportunism, and game playing. Shops that play this way do not last. The remaining shops work together to create more efficient, innovative relationship processes, rather than fighting over who gets the biggest slice of the trading relationship (see Chapter 11).

The master brokers compete among themselves on satisfying customers and assemblying the most competitive value-added processes. As a result the productivity and performance of the new organization is light years ahead of the bureaucratic, over-supervised vertical organization it replaced. Product variety increased from 600 to 6,000 yarns, inventory velocity increased, and inventories dropped from 120 to 15 days of production. While textile production fell in the rest of Europe between 1970 and 1982, the output of the Prato, Italy, region doubled.

*Russell Johnston and Paul R. Lawrence, "Beyond Vertical Integration—the Rise of the Value-Adding Partnership," *Harvard Business Review* (July/August 1988): 94–101.

tasks whose output quality most determines or drives ultimate service quality and customer satisfaction, in a manner similar to the way critical-path analysis identifies the tasks whose completion time needs to be shortened.

Using the Best Human Resources in the Best Ways

The experienced implementer knows that a few subordinates are always clearly superior. Consequently, they are assigned to the most demanding and critical implementation activities. But a problem can arise when an organization leans too much on such individuals at critical times. Although the maxim "give a busy person the job" often holds true (they are busy because they are competent and can execute), such executives can be stretched in too many ways by too many tasks, all needing to be completed about the same time. The stress can tie them up and then break one of the most important resources an organization has: a potential leader. Such overload may also endanger the project's quality and customer satisfaction. The AS script analysis approach to action planning enables senior management to review the assignment of responsibilities to make sure key implementation bottlenecks are not created by making too many demands, at any one time, on the most conscientious and talented executives.

Process Mapping and Thinking Skills

The importance of process mapping and thinking was emphasized in the discussion in Chapter 4 on process learning and improvement. Figure 4.10 (A Process Skills Hierarchy) reveals that the highest order construct that drives process learning, the increase in a firm's competitive rationality, and accumulation of capital is the process thinking skills of the managers who develop and implement a firm's processes.

The learning process hierarchy has very important implications for the competitive rationality of management control and innovation of processes. If a marketing manager in charge of a number of processes is not constantly informed about changes in the input/output efficiency and effectiveness of the processes he or she manages, then the firm is competitively vulnerable to the firm whose similar processes are managed by an executive who is more informed. Thus a clear and indisputable objective of senior management should be to increase the quality of the processes that measure inputs, operational processes, and outputs (see Chapter 19). Furthermore, the manager must have the process thinking skills that enable him or her to digest the information and creatively adapt the processes they must manage. A manager who lacks process thinking skills cannot manage.

Jack Welch, the highly respected CEO of General Electric, calls the modern business leader a "process champion." Process champions need process thinking skills.[30] If those involved in new product development do not possess a deep understanding of the manufacturing process, then they will not design for the most efficient and highest quality manufacturing process. If those involved in setting up learning processes have neither a deep understanding of the firm's actual product development processes nor its manufacturing processes, then they will suggest hiring and training, evaluation, and reward processes that will not produce the most efficient and highest quality new product development and manufacturing processes. Such skills are particularly needed when downsizing a bloated bureaucracy to the lean, decentralized, entrepreneurial, cross-functional organization described earlier in this chapter.

The process thinking skill that managers and engineers must excel in is the imagined use and direction of human capital and machinery so as to: (1) reduce the input costs of the process, (2) increase the process efficiency characteristics, such as execution time, flow smoothness, contingency adaptability, and self-improvement, and (3) increase the output of the process as measured by the immediate and ultimate customers. Such skills are critical components of what Professor George Day calls a "market-driven" organization:

> Each process must be mapped to reveal where and how each of the activities is located. Mapping will also identify disconnects at hand-off points (where information, questions, and decisions are transferred within and between processes), delays and unnecessary work, and sequences of activities that can be done in parallel. An important

[30] See T. A. Stewart, "GE Keeps Those Ideas Coming," in R. M. Kanter et al. *The Challenge of Organizational Change* (New York: The Free Press, 1992), 475.

> consideration is the locus of responsibility for each of the activities in the process, with a view to revealing dispersed ownership and lack of focus.[31]

Process owners must be identified and have the process thinking skills and mental models to identify and eliminate sources of process delay, to link the quality of the process's output to increasing ultimate customer satisfaction, and to continuously strive to reduce input costs. In short, the three drivers of competitive rationality also must drive the process thinking of the manager. It is then up to the manager to apply his or her process thinking to imagine new ways to make the processes they manage more effective and more efficient. Such skills are particularly needed in the design and management of service processes and supply-chain logistics processes.

Experienced managers often do not prepare formal marketing action plans because marketing projects and routines are less structured than those for manufacturing. They cannot be as clearly specified in engineering terms and have to be more flexible in the face of uncontrollable events. So how do experienced managers prepare action plans? They map them out intuitively and store them in what is called the manager's *prospective memory*. Prospective memory is memory not of past events but of things to do in the future. Years of experience (making mistakes and watching others make even more) enable a manager to sequence a project's activities or tasks. A manager learns an activity sequence script by implementing or supervising the implementation of similar projects over time. Intuitive scheduling is perhaps the most underrated and neglected skill in marketing management.

The Learning of Routine Activity Sequence Scripts

Production process activity sequences executed in the past form overlapping patterns of action stored in memory. Activity-schedule memory identifies the common elements of previous projects, such as activities, actors, and physical surroundings, to form routine activity sequence scripts.[32] These scripts themselves can be stored in memory for future use in similar situations. They become the basis for action planning.

Figure 17.7 shows how the stored experiences of production processes on previous occasions may overlap, forming a common set of activities, subroutines, actors, and objects used in the production process that become a production process script. For example, the production process undertaken at time $t - 3$ overlaps with the earlier, similar production process undertaken at time $t - 4$. The sequence of activities and events of the project undertaken at time $t - 2$ is added and so are the activities of the project undertaken during time $t - 1$. When asked at time t to implement or supervise a similar project, the manager now possesses an activity sequence script he or she has learned from past experience. The very distinctive elements or outcomes of previous projects will be remembered, but they will be remembered separately and will not be part of the script. Like an experienced cook, the manager will use the AS script as a blueprint but will improvise by using the people and resources at hand. As events unfold when he or she is implementing a project's activity sequence, they will prompt recall of what happened in a specific past production process, reminding the manager of what had worked and what had not worked.

---

[31] George S. Day, "The Capabilities of Market-Driven Organizations," *Journal of Marketing* 58 (October 1994): 47.

[32] Roger Schank and Robert Abelson, *Scripts, Plans, Goals, and Understanding* (Hillsdale, NJ: Lawrence Erlbaum Associates, 1977).

Figure 17.7 How an Activity Sequence Script Is Learned

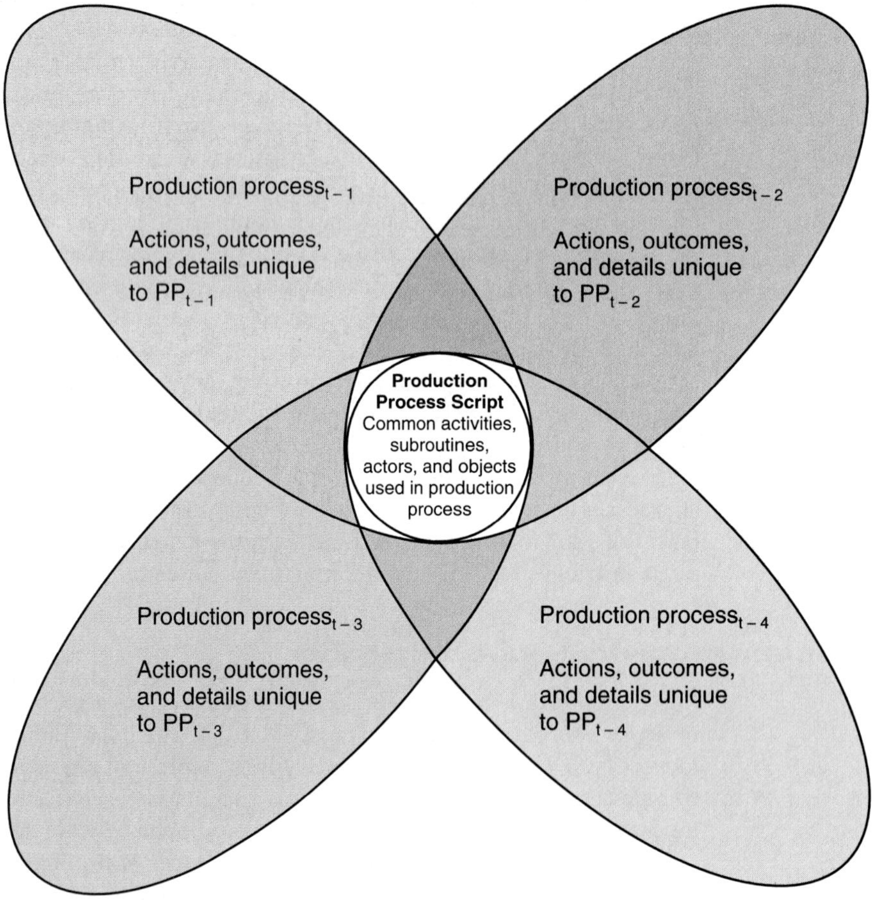

Memory of past behaviors are stacked on top of each other in our memory structure. Production process activity sequences executed in the past form overlapping patterns of action that are stored in memory. Activity schedule memory processes abstract common elements of previous projects, such as activities, actors, and physical surroundings, to form routine activity sequence scripts. These scripts themselves are stored in memory for future use in similar situations. They become the basis for action planning.

Activity Scheduling Creativity

Some managers and employees are only able to learn and follow particular production scripts.[33] The risk is that they become slaves of these routines, mindlessly executing their work-to-rule scripts. They cease to pay attention to new environmental information that suggests the market is changing and that the old way of doing things may

[33] Try reciting the alphabet backwards! For more complex examples of AS script rigidity, see Connie J. G. Gersick and J. Richard Hackman, "Habitual Routines in Task-Performing Groups," *Organizational Behavior and Human Decision Processes* 47 (1990): 65–97; and Ellen J. Langer, "Minding Matters: The Mindlessness/Mindfulness Theory of Cognitive Activity," in *Advances in Experimental Social Psychology*, ed., L. Berkowitz (New York: Academic Press, 1989).

no longer be the best way.[34] Changing conditions can upset the effectiveness of AS scripts and routines that were previously very effective and efficient. Inevitably, routines must be changed creatively to meet the new conditions. Creative adaptation of routines can be improvised while on the job. For example, Scandinavian Airlines System (SAS) and British Airways have trained twenty-four thousand and thirty-seven thousand employees, respectively, to respond creatively when it comes to pleasing the customer rather than to executive service routines mindlessly.[35]

Other managers with superior abstract thinking skills—or higher levels of curiosity, creativity, initiative, and motivation—advance beyond learning and improvising AS scripts. These managers excel at quickly identifying patterns in the dynamic environment and at foreseeing their likely implications. Their production scripts become the basis of theories about how production processes work and interact, which allow them to create rules about what to do and what not to do when implementing plans within the firm and in the market. These theories and rules are the highest order of information from past experiences stored in memory and used in the activity-schedule memory process (see Figure 17.8). Managers use these rules to adapt old scripts to new situations, to transfer what they have learned in one situation to another, and to assemble completely new scripts. Such managers also are likely to have superior prospective memory skills; they have longer memory frames, they plan further into the future, and they are superior time managers.[36] An organization that continuously strives to learn how to do everything it does better must be led by managers with such skills.

Time Management and Remembering to Get Things Done

Prospective memory is a very special aspect of memory that is needed for action planning. In contrast to stored memories of past events and experiences, it involves the deliberate planning, rehearsing, and remembering of things to do that will affect the future. Prospective memory requires recall of activities that have been done so far in an activity sequence, those that have yet to be done, the order in which they must be completed, and which activities have to be executed in the present.

The *master activity schedule (MAS)* is a manager's mental diary. It is called a master activity schedule because it is the tool for merging, integrating, and prioritizing activities from several different activity schedule (AS) scripts that a manager is currently supervising or implementing (see Figure 17.9). Every day a manager is doing several things at once, making more or less progress on several activity sequences. It is akin to juggling several balls in the air at one time. A manager organizes this perpetual juggling act with the MAS and, in the short term, with the daily master activity schedule (DMAS). First, the manager assembles the set of n (number) activity sequences he or she is currently undertaking. Then the manager chooses which activities or tasks from different projects should be done in which order. Managers with superior process thinking skills will be better at seeing how certain activities and tasks naturally flow together, at understanding causal sequences by which certain

---

[34] Howard M. Weiss and Daniel R. Ilgen, "Routinized Behavior in Organizations," *The Journal of Behavioral Economics* 14 (1985): 57–67; Meryl R. Louis and Robert I. Sutton, "Switching Cognitive Gears: From Habits of Mind to Active Thinking," *Human Relations* 44, no. 1 (1991): 55–76; and Abraham S. Luchins and Edith H. Luchins, *Wertheimer's Seminars Revisited—Problem Solving and Thinking*, vol. III (Albany, NY: State University of New York, 1970).

[35] Karl Albrecht and S. Albrecht, *The Creative Corporation* (Homewood IL: Dow Jones-Irwin, 1987).

[36] Elliott Jacques, *The Form of Time* (New York: Crane, Russak, 1982); and Walter Kiechel, "How Executives Think," *Fortune*, February 4, 1985, 127–28.

Figure 17.8 Activity-Schedule Memory Skills

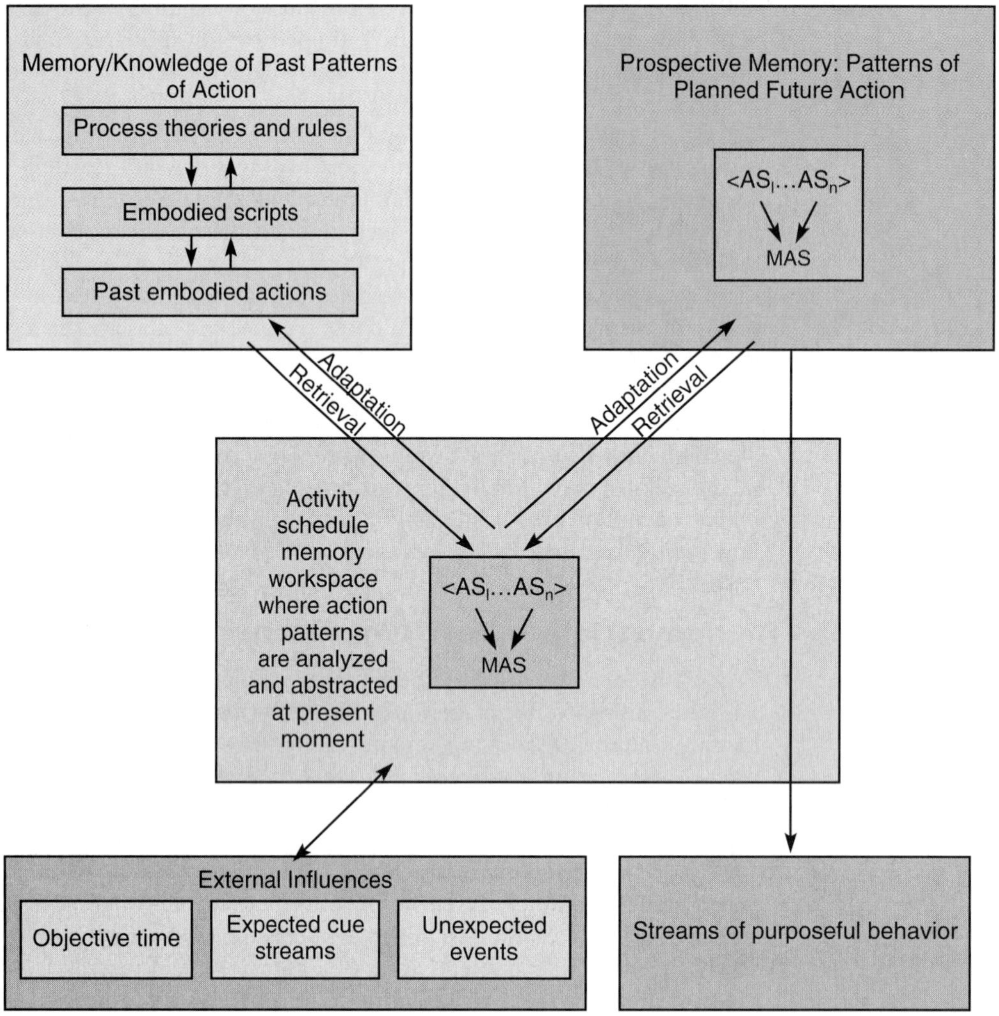

The activity-schedule memory process consists of three temporal dimensions (past, present, and future) and related memory skills essential to effective planning and implementation. Information abstracted from stored past experience and planned sequences of future actions interact and influence our present thoughts and behaviors. Past experience is stored in memory in three levels of abstraction and organization. The most basic level stores the elements of our past experience, which form the building blocks for the other two levels. The next level stores production process activity sequences, or assemblages of similar activity sequences, which become activity schedule (AS) scripts. At the highest level, managers with superior abstract thinking skills advance beyond learning and improvising activity schedule scripts. Their production scripts become the basis of their personal theories about how production processes work and interact, which allow them to create rules about what to do and what not to do when implementing plans within the firm and in the market. Such managers are also likely to have superior prospective memory skills.

activities must precede or follow others, and at estimating how much time and coordination will be required to complete each project. The MAS has to be constantly monitored and updated as projects progress at different rates and as environmental

Figure 17.9 **How a Manager's Prospective Memory Operates**

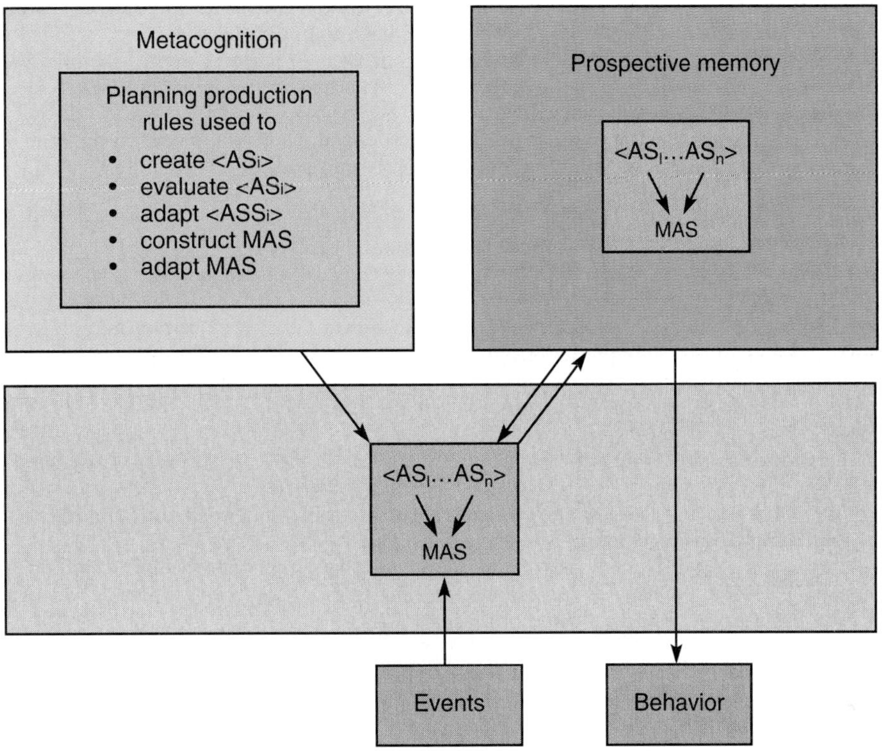

This figure illustrates how a busy manager intuitively remembers what to do next. Prospective memory is the future temporal element of our activity-schedule memory process that involves our ability to think and plan ahead. Such planned actions can be loaded into a "what I/we have to do" schedule and combined with activity sequences stored in memory to direct purposive behavior. Metacognition is our self-awareness of our implementation planning and time management skills—how we use external prompts such as lists, diaries and charts. Some managers are very aware of their skills, are able to manage time effectively, and are adept at organizing sequences of future actions in prospective memory. Other managers do not have well-developed process thinking skills, and as a result they have fuzzy prospective memories and are bad time managers, always late and forgetful. The other terms in the figure are defined below:

AS*i* = The *i* production process activity schedule
<AS*i*> = A set of production process activity schedules that the manager is responsible for executing or having executed by others.
<ASS*i*> = A set of activity schedule scripts.
MAS = The master activity schedule that merges a set of ASs.

conditions change. More alert managers will be faster and better at making these adjustments. Beyond their ability to continuously organize and coordinate the disparate elements of the MAS, successful managers also must be able to implement individual activities. This requires the ability to focus on the task at hand while blocking out other potential distractions.

A manager with a very routine job follows a single activity sequence each day, day in and day out. He or she has no variety and no need for MAS skills in prospective memory. On the other hand, the efficiency and effectiveness of a very busy executive

Table 17.3 Ten Time-Management Tips (Production Rules)

1. Develop long-range, major goals and projects and a short-run "to do" master activity schedule (MAS), which is a combination of tasks related to the activity schedules of different projects you are executing in parallel.
2. Make a list each day of the six most important things you have to do from your master activity schedule. Write them in a good pocket diary and update them each new day. Focus your day on the 20 percent of the activities that produce 80 percent of your productivity (Pareto's Principle). Concentrate your effort.
3. Group tasks around when they need to be done, and do all the most demanding thinking tasks at the time of the day you think best (for example, if you are a morning person, do them in the morning). Group other tasks around where they need to be done to avoid wasted traveling time.
4. Schedule and rehearse your day while you are exercising, washing, shaving, or applying your makeup in the morning. Think about starting and *finishing* each key activity or task. Try to anticipate and avoid problems.
5. If you are a procrastinator, do tasks you do not want to do first. They then will be off your mind, and you will have a sense of achievement and a more positive attitude the rest of the day.
6. Do not take on more than you can manage. Good time managers know when they are overcommitted; poor time managers do not and use the overload as an excuse for the lateness and sloppiness of everything they do. Reserve one or two hours a day for unexpected tasks, delays, and so forth.
7. Control interruptions. Use a muted telephone answering machine to eliminate distractions and to keep in touch with other people's activities.
8. Plan meetings, keep them focused, and conduct them with speed. Do not let the least prepared participants dictate how a meeting is run.
9. Do everything you do as well as you can. It is better to do it right the first time than waste time and effort having to undo it and do it again (a basic principle of quality management).
10. Do not wait to be told to do something. Do not ask what to do. Suggest, recommend, act, advise, and report. Take the initiative. Do not do work that can be delegated to capable subordinates. Doing tasks others can do is often a way of avoiding what you know only you can do and have to do (a form of procrastination).

involved in implementing a dozen projects at once depends on his or her master activity scheduling in prospective memory. Executives without such intuitive mental skills may be creative in terms of coming up with ideas but will be hopeless at getting things done and coping creatively with unexpected events that disturb their routines. Such coping requires changing individual AS scripts and the MAS in response to new information from the environment. A manager with excellent production rule and prospective memory skills is commonly known as a good time manager. Some of the skills (and production rules) associated with good time management are described in Table 17.3.[37]

Combining Intuition and Scientific Management

Activity-schedule memory theory also helps explain why quality circles and worker consultations are so useful in implementation. Managers and lower-level employees cannot be expected to show initiative and creativity if they do not understand how their tasks fit into the big picture, the larger production process, or the AS script. When they develop such an understanding, what they do starts to make sense, and

[37] Table 17.3 is based in part on William Oncken Jr. and Donald L. Wass, "Management Time: Who's Got the Monkey," *Harvard Business Review* (November/December 1974): 75–80; and Warren Keith Schilit, "A Manager's Guide to Efficient Time Management," *Personnel Journal* (September 1983): 736–42.

they feel much more a part of a team and interested in the overall outcome. Everyone is on the same page of the same script. Participants also are able to then step back and suggest creative ways to speed up activity sequences (crashing the critical path), reduce costs, and increase output quality. Workers and managers also become each other's customers in the activity sequence because they recognize that their success depends on working with each other, rather than warring with each other. Not all managers and employees can be expected to respond equally to becoming involved in the bigger picture, just as few second lieutenants are capable of thinking like generals. But, at worst, it is likely that most suggestions will, at least, ever-so-slightly improve the efficiency and effectiveness of implementation.

The problem with managers relying on intuition to create action plans and activity schedules, as just described, is that these internal memory structures cannot be shared readily with all the individuals and teams working on implementation. A formal action-plan path analysis allows everyone to know where, how, and at what time they fit into the rollout (see the Rationality in Practice box). It also enables the organization to pass on to future managers the wisdom and action-oriented implementation insights that the experienced manager has in his or her head.[38]

Discussion Questions and Minicases

1. Why should a chief executive of a company encourage all functional areas (such as accounting, procurement, distribution, manufacturing, employee services, R&D, and design) in a firm to contract themselves out for hire to other companies that are not direct competitors? What are the risks, and how can they be minimized?
2. What type of network organization might you set up to offer a nationwide cut-flower delivery service to compete against Teleflora or 1-800-FLOWERS, which link a network of thousands of florist stores? What other organizations and established companies might be part of the network? What would your firm actually do? What flowers would you concentrate on?
3. What sort of training should a marketing graduate be given to succeed in a company that uses cross-functional teams to manage a network of outsourcing relationships? What specific technical skills do you think a marketing graduate should have in order to excel in such an organization? What marketing courses do you think should be required to train such a marketing graduate? What courses currently required for marketing majors might be dropped or made optional?
4. How would you organize the marketing of a start-up operation in a new country? How would you staff the organization in a way that would lead to the greatest competitive rationality?
5. How should a firm organize its marketing when it does not use direct selling but relies on direct marketing through mail-order and magazine advertising? (Hint: Think about what marketing function is most important for such a firm.)
6. Banks are typically organized with their sales operations separate from marketing. Sales operations is the function that is in charge of branch management and tellers. In recent years, a number of banks have become dissatisfied with their marketing efforts. What might be the problem, and how might it be addressed?
7. How might a firm improve the effectiveness of its product managers without switching to cross-functional team management?
8. In what order are tasks crashed in an activity schedule to increase the speed of implementation (that is, to increase time competition)?

[38] Benjamin B. Tregoe and Peter M. Tobia, "An Action-Oriented Approach to Strategy," *Journal of Business Strategy* 11, no. 1 (January/February 1990): 16–21.

Rationality in Practice

Scheduling Tools

To create an activity schedule document, inexpensive computer software can be used to describe the activity sequences, estimate the time and resource needs, and generate a critical path and scheduling chart, all in less than an afternoon. It can be refined later by consulting with the parties responsible for the different activities. At most, it will take about ten to twenty work hours and is a task ideally suited to help a brand, product, or project manager with his or her planned marketing activities. In addition to the inexpensive computer software, several worksheets and visual aids are available to help implement the product market plan (see figures). The support systems exist to help a marketing manager and cross-functional team plan and implement a project's AS script. What is often absent is a greater *commitment* of time, training, and human resources to the rudimentary application of scientific management to action planning.

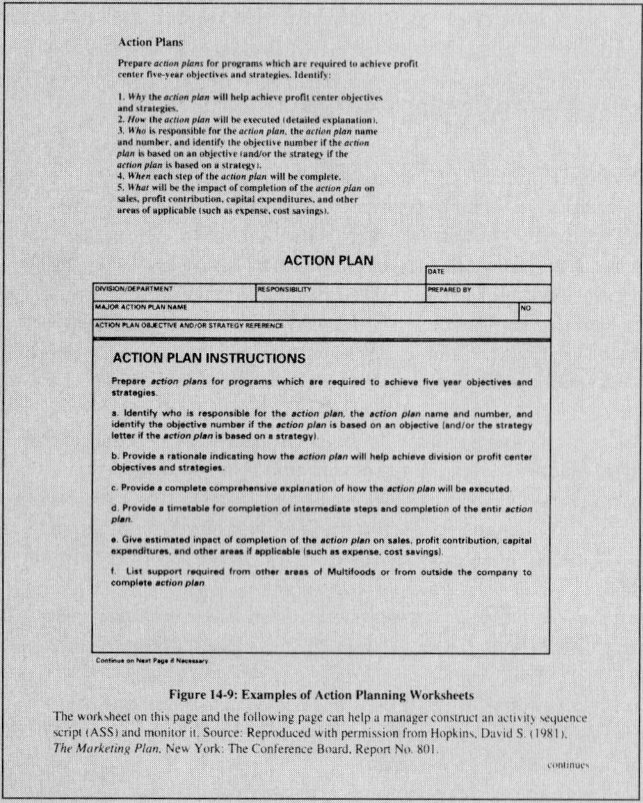
Action Plans

Prepare *action plans* for programs which are required to achieve profit center five-year objectives and strategies. Identify:

1. *Why* the *action plan* will help achieve profit center objectives and strategies.
2. *How* the *action plan* will be executed (detailed explanation).
3. *Who* is responsible for the *action plan*, the *action plan* name and number, and identify the objective number if the *action plan* is based on an objective (and/or the strategy if the *action plan* is based on a strategy).
4. *When* each step of the *action plan* will be complete.
5. *What* will be the impact of completion of the *action plan* on sales, profit contribution, capital expenditures, and other areas of applicable (such as expense, cost savings).

ACTION PLAN

DATE

DIVISION/DEPARTMENT | RESPONSIBILITY | PREPARED BY

MAJOR ACTION PLAN NAME | NO

ACTION PLAN OBJECTIVE AND/OR STRATEGY REFERENCE

ACTION PLAN INSTRUCTIONS

Prepare *action plans* for programs which are required to achieve five year objectives and strategies.

a. Identify who is responsible for the *action plan*, the *action plan* name and number, and identify the objective number if the *action plan* is based on an objective (and/or the strategy letter if the *action plan* is based on a strategy).

b. Provide a rationale indicating how the *action plan* will help achieve division or profit center objectives and strategies.

c. Provide a complete comprehensive explanation of how the *action plan* will be executed.

d. Provide a timetable for completion of intermediate steps and completion of the entir *action plan*.

e. Give estimated inpact of completion of the *action plan* on sales, profit contribution, capital expenditures, and other areas if applicable (such as expense, cost savings).

f. List support required from other areas of Multifoods or from outside the company to complete *action plan*.

Continue on Next Page if Necessary

Figure 14-9: Examples of Action Planning Worksheets

The worksheet on this page and the following page can help a manager construct an activity sequence script (ASS) and monitor it. Source: Reproduced with permission from Hopkins, David S. (1981). *The Marketing Plan*. New York: The Conference Board, Report No. 801.

continues

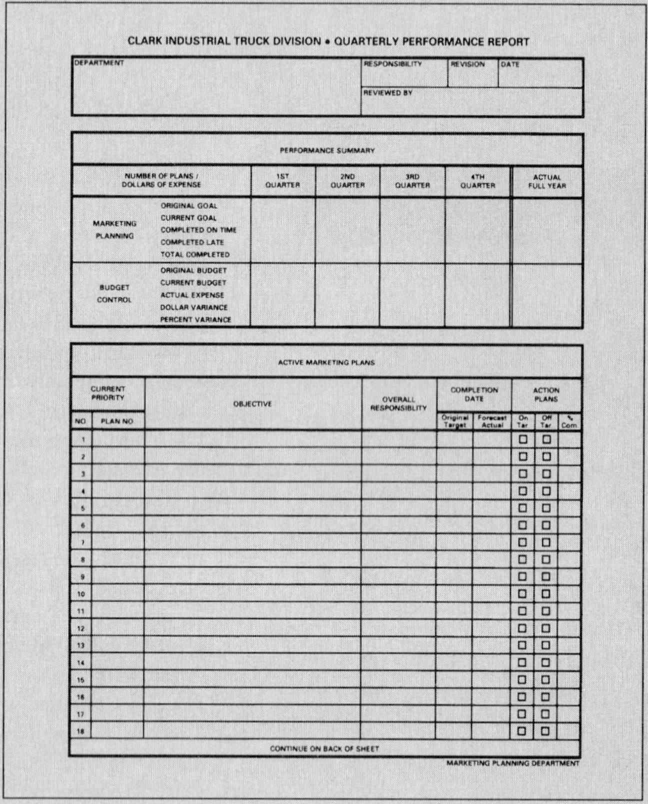
CLARK INDUSTRIAL TRUCK DIVISION • QUARTERLY PERFORMANCE REPORT

DEPARTMENT | RESPONSIBILITY | REVISION | DATE | REVIEWED BY

PERFORMANCE SUMMARY

NUMBER OF PLANS / DOLLARS OF EXPENSE		1ST QUARTER	2ND QUARTER	3RD QUARTER	4TH QUARTER	ACTUAL FULL YEAR
MARKETING PLANNING	ORIGINAL GOAL CURRENT GOAL COMPLETED ON TIME COMPLETED LATE TOTAL COMPLETED					
BUDGET CONTROL	ORIGINAL BUDGET CURRENT BUDGET ACTUAL EXPENSE DOLLAR VARIANCE PERCENT VARIANCE					

ACTIVE MARKETING PLANS

CURRENT PRIORITY		OBJECTIVE	OVERALL RESPONSIBLITY	COMPLETION DATE		ACTION PLANS		
NO	PLAN NO			Original Target	Forecast Actual	On Tar	Off Tar	% Com
1						☐	☐	
2						☐	☐	
3						☐	☐	
4						☐	☐	
5						☐	☐	
6						☐	☐	
7						☐	☐	
8						☐	☐	
9						☐	☐	
10						☐	☐	
11						☐	☐	
12						☐	☐	
13						☐	☐	
14						☐	☐	
15						☐	☐	
16						☐	☐	
17						☐	☐	
18						☐	☐	

CONTINUE ON BACK OF SHEET

MARKETING PLANNING DEPARTMENT

Examples of Action Planning Worksheets

The worksheet on this page and the tools illustrated on the following page can help a manager construct an activity sequence (AS) script and monitor it.

SOURCE: Reproduced with permission from David S. Hopkins, *The Marketing Plan* (New York: The Conference Board, 1981), Report no. 801.

9. Figure 17.7 illustrates how we learn an activity schedule script. Use the figure to describe how we learn a golf swing, a tennis serve, to turn on skis, and to swim. According to the process described by this figure, when is it best to get expert coaching? What implications does this have for organizations and individuals developing implementation routines?

Even a simple task matrix—with weeks across the top, tasks down the page, and the initials of executives responsible for implementation and supervision in the cells—is better than nothing. A firm should also require such action planning from its advertising agency and other outside contractors whose quality of service is increasingly judged on its speed as well as its content. A firm's routines are its genes. Improve its routines, and you improve its genes and its chances of future success.* A company culture that emphasizes time management and rewards activity-schedule memory skills will find that almost all of its routines will be improved. Action planning is not just necessary to execute strategy. It is a crucial competitive rationality skill that can improve a firm's production routines in all aspects of its business.

*See Richard R. Nelson and Sidney G. Winter, *An Evolutionary Theory of Economic Change* (Cambridge, MA: Harvard University Press, 1982); and the theory of competitive rationality in Chapter 1.

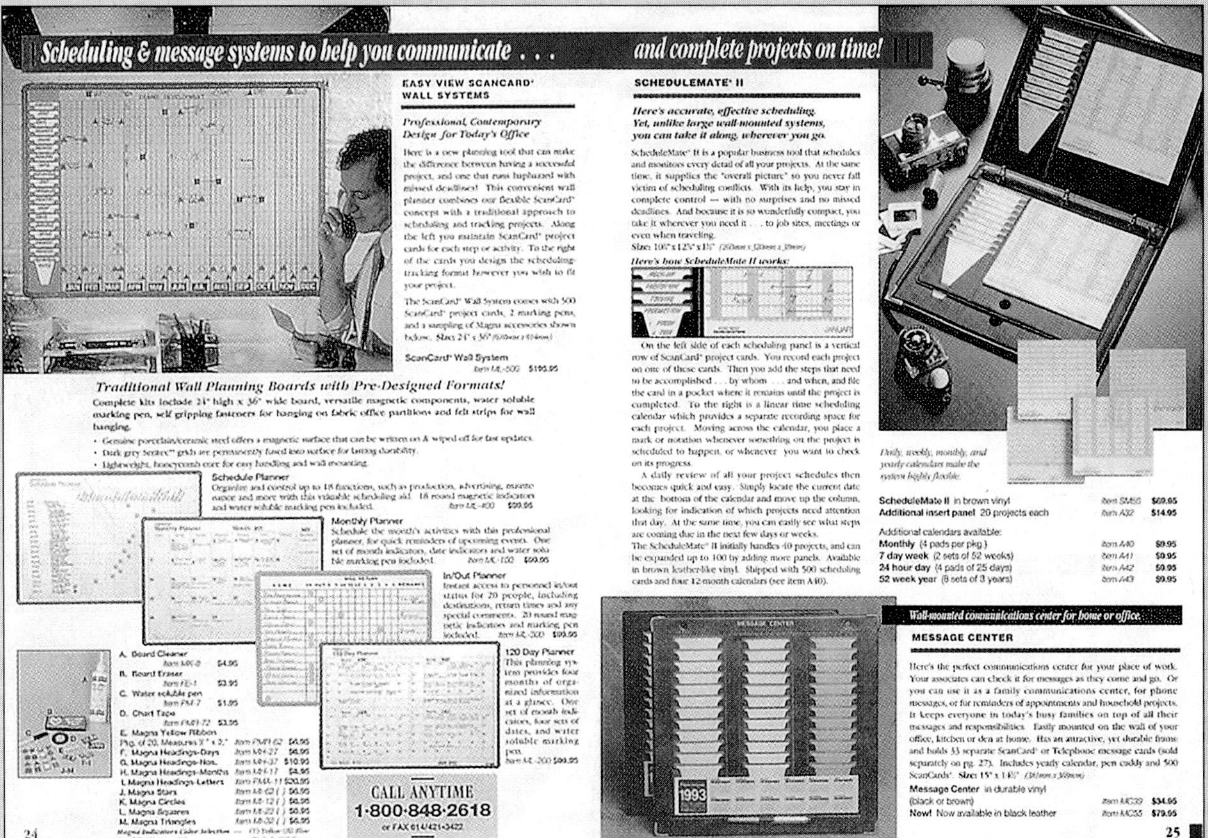

10. How might you test whether a manager has the desired intuitive action-planning skills? What in a manager's thinking, personal planning, and past behavior might provide good evidence of the presence of such skills?

11. What games do you think require prospective memory skills?

12. What are the advantages and disadvantages of a manager having a secretary keep the executive appointment diary, screen incoming calls, type, open mail, and so on?
13. The recent discovery of old takes of early Charlie Chaplin movies has revealed that cameo scenes were shot hundreds of times to produce the marvelous spontaneity and impudence of the "little tramp." Chaplin was a perfectionist who demonstrated the value of really caring about execution and implementation. What lessons might marketers learn from Chaplin's work habits? In your answer, explain the crucial difference between making a movie and making a market.
14. Why would preparing a critical path and hanging it on the wall in a public place, where progress to date on the project can be seen by all, work particularly well in a clan culture?
15. How are football coaching and directing a ballet similar to planning and implementing a competitive marketing program?

16. Some experts have argued that next to the president, the most important person in the modern organization is the vice president of Continuous Improvement, who is responsible for continuously improving organization structure, systems, and processes. Other experts disagree. Please discuss both sides of the argument.

17. As described in Chapter 1, great companies are founded by successful entrepreneurs who grow their proprietary enterprise through creative innovations in their manufacturing and product development processes. As the original proprietor, they are often the heart and soul of their organization's learning processes. The nested learning hierarchy (Figure 4.10) provides a new perspective of the problem of transition from the original entrepreneur's creative leadership and human capital to a leadership that must find a new source of process innovation and learning. When the entrepreneur leaves, the firm often "stagnates and decays" and leads to a "clogs to clogs" rise and fall of family prosperity over three generations. The gifted entrepreneur has not created a gifted learning organization.

So what should happen when the entrepreneurial leaders of family businesses start to approach retirement? The preeminent desire of most entrepreneurs who have dedicated their life to building their business is to keep the business flourishing long after their departure. In this way, their families are supported, and part of their genius lives on. With this goal in mind, how might such an entrepreneur best spend his or her time in the last few years of actively running the business?

Go as far as you can see, and when you get there, you will see farther.

Anonymous

Business more than any other occupation is a continual dealing with the future; it is a continual calculation and instinctive exercise in foresight.

Henry R. Luce

CHAPTER EIGHTEEN

Budgeting and Forecasting

Budgeting involves deciding what to spend on various marketing activities or programs. It is often calculated using rules of thumb such as budgeting next year's advertising expenditure by basing it on a percentage of this year's sales or next year's expected sales. But this rule makes no sense to a company launching a new product or service into a market. No sales exist, and the firm will have to invest in an initial marketing campaign to create a reason for consumers to change their behavior in the market. Thus, the budgeting of the advertising-to-expected-sales ratio will be much higher than established rivals.

Notice what this means for a market with an accelerating amount of innovation/imitation in products or customer services. With each new innovation, the market's advertising-to-sales ratio is likely to increase because each new entry has a much higher advertising-to-sales ratio. In addition, the existing firms with products or services also are likely to increase their advertising to drown out the innovator's voice share and to help choke up the distribution channels by coordinating a channel promotional push program with their added advertising pull.

One might think this competitive dynamic will inevitably lead to overadvertising in such a market, so how does the market correct itself? What happens is that the

profitability of all the firms will decline as they overspend in launching new products or defending their existing market share. This in turn will lead to a reduction of the types of innovation and imitation that deliver only marginally increased customer satisfaction. Instead, the market will focus on product or service research and development that hits home runs rather than singles. Thus, when a market starts to overspend on advertising questionable innovations/imitations, it creates an opportunity for innovators with truly superior innovations to deflate the sales of established competitors that are inefficiently overspending on advertising.

These market changes occur because advertising of really superior new innovations is much more effective and efficient. Why? A really compelling message theme needs less repeated exposures (often only one) to have its maximum impact. In some markets, a new innovation needs little or no traditional mass-media advertising, relying instead on the word of mouth of satisfied triers and users. For example, how much advertising for gourmet coffee have you seen? Not a lot, and yet it is taking over the premium coffee market segment, redefining the standard for a quality cup of coffee. This is occurring despite the established players spending a good deal on brand-awareness advertising. But their advertising makes weak differential-advantage claims. The recent Tasters Choice advertising mini–soap opera, tracking the progress of a relationship started by the woman running out of coffee and knocking on a neighbor's door, is cute and likely has raised Tasters Choice brand awareness and sales, but it contains no compelling message as to why Tasters Choice tastes better. Similarly, a movie can be heavily advertised, but if the critics and early viewers give it "two thumbs down," it dies after the first weekend.

The first lesson is that a genuine improvement in taste or performance sold through the right channels beats a heavily advertised, established product or questionable improvement almost every time. The second lesson is that the mindless application of a percentage-of-sales or match-the competition budgeting routine is competitively irrational because it can lead a company (and a market) down a budgeting and spending path that is inefficient and ineffective. This chapter discusses how to use more competitively rational processes for developing forecasts, budgeting, and allocating resources. ■

The Profit and Loss (P&L) Budget Statement

Budgeting is an organization process that involves making forecasts based on the proposed marketing strategy and programs. The forecasts then are used to construct a budgeted profit-and-loss statement. An important aspect of budgeting is deciding how to allocate the last available dollars across all of the proposed programs within the marketing plan.

Since each business or marketing plan should end with a summary statement of the forecast sales, costs, and bottom-line profit for the year ahead, this chapter begins with the profit-and-loss statement (see Figure 18.1 for chapter organization). In concept, the profit-and-loss (P&L) statement is simple; in practice, it is difficult to construct because its elements can only be estimated. Businesses first prepare a planned P&L statement; then at the end of the year the actual P&L will be computed, and it can be compared to the planned P&L statement. This kind of analysis contributes significantly to competitive rationality by providing the firm with an opportunity to learn about how and why actual performance varies from planned performance. A discussion of the specifics of such an analysis appears in Chapter 19, on profit and loss control. Here, discussion of how a P&L budget statement is assembled starts by using an example.

P&L projections for the ACME Company are presented in Table 18.1. The planned P&L statement requires several inputs. The projection of sales is based on forecasts of overall market size as well as company share. Planned unit price comes from the marketing plan and variable, fixed, and program costs come from company accounting records. By making such a table into a simple spreadsheet, budgeters can play "what if," changing the forecasts, price, and different costs to determine their impact on the bottom line. The "what if" process often involves making best-case, most likely, and worst-case estimates of each variable in the spreadsheet and seeing their effects on the outcome. The what-ifs that the bottom line is most sensitive to become the forecasts and estimates that staff then pay most attention to, try to forecast most accurately, and try most to account for and control.

For most teams and marketing executives, the most mysterious and, hence, uncertain part of a P&L statement is the projected costs. In past years, marketers perhaps grumbled that the accountants in their firm knew the cost of everything and the value of nothing. As shall be shown in this and the next chapter, what is closer to the truth is that no one in the firm knew either the true value or cost of anything! In today's era of increased competition, when innovation/imitation must reduce costs as well as increase quality, the team must understand costs and know the cost structure involved in designing a product or service and setting its price. Effective decision making means allocating scarce resources across product lines and within marketing programs. Cost rationality is a major part of such competitive rationality because, as discussed in Chapter 1, one of the three drivers of competitive rationality is the control and reduction of costs. Developing such a skill requires knowledge of the different types of costs presented in Table 18.1, how they are related, and how they affect profit (see Figure 18.2 on page 690). A marketing executive who brings market research, marketing strategy, *and* cost accounting skills to a cross-functional team becomes an indispensable member of the team and a much more attractive candidate for team leader.

Figure 18.1 Chapter Organization

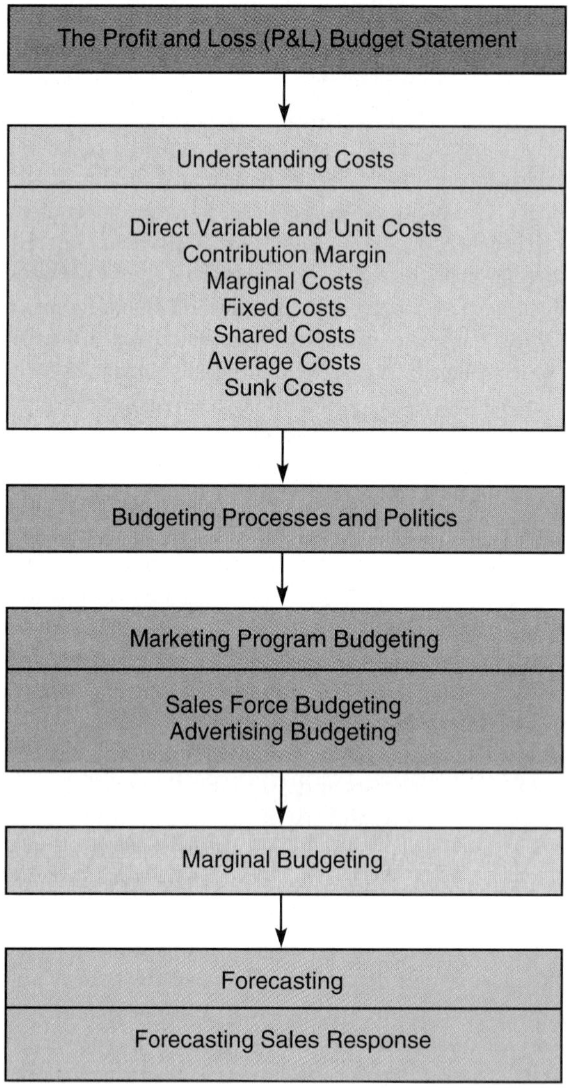

At the heart of budgeting is the Profit and Loss Statement. The first step in constructing such a statement is to fully understand all of the types and costs involved and to then appreciate the budgeting process which is often a political as well as an economic process. The second half of the chapter discusses salesforce budgeting, advertising budgeting and marginal budgeting. The chapter closes with a discussion of how to forecast changes in demand, changes in supply, changes in cost and consumer response to changes in marketing strategy, tactics and programs.

Table 18.1 **Example of a Profit-and-Loss Budget Statement for the ACME Company**

INPUTS		CURRENT YEAR (actual)	% CHANGE PROJECTED		NEXT YEAR (projected)
Market sales (units)		700,000	10.0%		770,000
Our market share		28%			28%
Our unit sales		196,000			215,600
Unit price		$100.00			$100.00
Variable manufacturing costs		$50.00			$50.00
Variable distribution costs		$15.00			$15.00
FIXED COSTS (IN $000S)					
Advertising		$1,707	0.0		$1,707
Selling		2,568	0.0		2,568
Sales promotion		300	0.0		300
R&D		175	0.0		175
Administration overhead		1,300	0.0	1,300	
PROFIT-AND-LOSS ESTIMATES (in $000s)		CURRENT YEAR (actual)			NEXT YEAR (projected)
Total revenue		$19,600			$21,560
Total variable cost		12,740			14,014
Total contribution		$ 6,860			$ 7,546
Advertising	$1,707			$1,707	
Selling	2,568			2,568	
Sales promotion	300			300	
R&D	175			175	
Administration overhead	1,300			1,300	
Total fixed costs		$ 6,050			$ 6,050
Operating profit		$ 810			$ 1,496

Understanding Costs

Direct Variable Costs and Unit Costs

Direct variable costs increase as production and sales increase. They also should decrease as production and sales decrease, but often they are more sticky on the downside than the upside. For example, part-time labor is more of a direct variable cost than full-time labor, who have to be paid even when business is slow. Variable costs typically include raw material costs, royalties, distribution costs, and sales commissions. Total direct variable cost *(TVC)* is a function of Q (the quantity sold and produced): $TVC = f(Q)$. This is an increasing function, but the rate of increase slows down as a firm takes advantage of volume economies in buying, producing, and selling.[1]

[1] As firms produce and sell more, they learn how to make and market products better and cheaper. This effect is called the *experience curve.* The cost of making calculators, computers, and hand tools, processing color film, and many other products and services has dropped dramatically in recent decades. Such superior learning from experience is a m[illegible]lement of competitive rationality.

Figure 18.2 **An Example of a Marketing Budgeting Worksheet**

Marketing Budget Proposal For: ______________________

Summary		19__ Actual	19__ Actual	19__ Original vote	19__ Estimated	19__ Proposed	19__ Approved
Sales	$						
Income before marketing	$						
Income before marketing to sales	%						
Marketing (A)	$						
Marketing to sales	%						
Marketing including allocations (B)	$						
Operating income before adjustment (D)	$						
Operating income to sales	%						
Population	M						
Sales milex ($/1000 population)	$						
Marketing milex ($/1000 population)	$						

Marketing Budget Categories

1. Magazines						
2. Newspaper rop						
3. Newspaper supplements						
4. Radio						
5. Television						
6. Posters						
7. Special media						
8. Agency fees						
9. Trade media						
11. Consumer non-price incentives						
13. Consumer price incentives						
14. Sales conferences						
15. Merchandising materials						
17. Trade allowances						
18. Trade free goods						
19. Sundries						
Marketing (A)						

Allocation of publicity						
Allocation of fgt. on unindent. merch. materials						
Allocation of military food marketing						
Marketing including allocation (B)						

Package development (C)						
Market research (C)						

(A) Marketing — Total of budget categories.
(B) Marketing including allocations — Marketing plus allocations of publicity, freight on unidentified merchandising materials, and military food marketing.
(C) Already deducted via administration expenses in arriving at income before marketing.
(D) Operating income before adjustments — "Income before marketing" less "Marketing including allocations" before corporate adjustments.

Per ______________________

Date ______________________

Note that the estimates go through several revisions, and some costs are allocated because these costs are expended on marketing several products and cannot be directly estimated.

SOURCE: Reproduced with permission from David S. Hopkins, *The Marketing Plan* (New York: The Conference Board, 1981), Report no. 801, 95.

Marketing is most interested in the average variable cost of producing and making a product to a specific segment. This is sometimes called *unit cost* and serves as an absolute floor for a product's price. In the spreadsheet in Table 18.1 the variable manufacturing unit cost is $50 and the variable distribution cost is $15, making a total variable cost of $65.

Contribution Margin

The *contribution margin (cm)* is the difference between price and average *variable* unit cost, expressed in dollars. When multiplied by sales volume, it is referred to as gross or total contribution (see Figure 18.3). In Table 18.1 the total contribution in the current year was $6,860,000. The term *contribution* is used because CM measures the contribution each sale makes toward paying for fixed costs. After fixed costs are paid, CM measures the contribution each sale makes to profits. The contribution margin percentage *(%CM)* is equal to the dollar contribution margin divided by the price. To achieve the target contribution margin percentage, either variable costs must be decreased or price must be increased.[2]

Marginal Costs

Marginal cost is the direct variable cost of producing and selling one more unit than the volume currently produced and sold. It includes only unavoidable, additional costs. Typical marginal costs include additional material, direct processing, and transportation costs and sales commissions. Fixed and other variable costs already spent on producing and marketing the product are not considered. The direct costs involved in making and selling additional units are usually less than the costs of producing what already has been sold. This is due to volume economies in the variable costs of production and selling. The decreasing slope of the TVC curve indicates such economies. The marginal costs of a product are often used to price special orders or export sales. If a firm has no better use of its resources, then any additional sale at a price above marginal cost is worthwhile, provided it does not affect existing sales demand. However, if a firm is producing at capacity, then the marginal cost of increasing production can be prohibitive because major new investments are needed to expand capacity.

Fixed Costs

Costs that are planned and incurred during the planning period no matter what the level of production and sales are called *fixed costs.* Absolute fixed costs are depreciations on plant and patent amortization. Other fixed costs are somewhat manageable over the long term, such as R&D, rents, insurance, advertising, health benefits, and administrative overheads. *Program fixed costs* are up-front costs that are committed to a program and are spent no matter what the revenues from the program. Examples are advertising, special sales training, and promotion costs. In Table 18.1 the cost of the advertising program is $1,707,00. Most costs are manageable, but fixed costs take

[2] Different industries use different terms to describe gross contribution (for example, *net earnings* or *revenues*) ... contribution margin percentage (sometimes confusingly called *margin* or *profit margin*).

Figure 18.3 **The Relationship between Costs, Profit, and Gross Contribution**

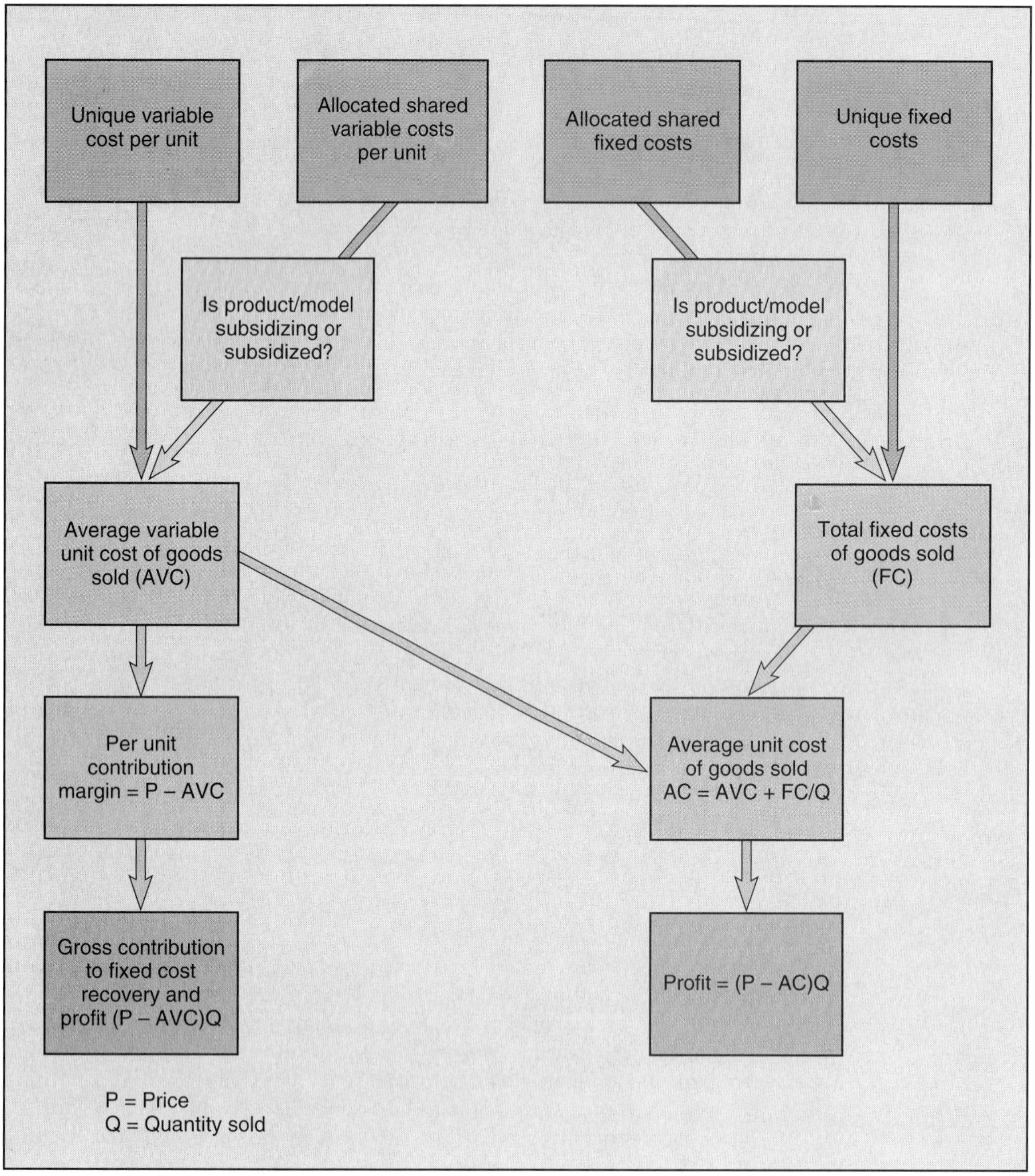

$$\begin{aligned}\text{Gross Contribution} &= (P - AVC)Q \\ &= P - (AVC + FC/Q)\,Q + FC \\ &= (P - AC)Q + FC \\ &= \text{Profit} + FC\end{aligned}$$

more effort to measure and more time to manage.[3] Profits can be earned only after all fixed costs are covered. The level of sales for a given price that covers all fixed costs is the break-even sales volume. One of the reasons why American companies facing new, high fixed costs to be spent on R&D and manufacturing are going global is that the expanded sales base makes the required break-even sales volume more attainable.

Shared Costs

Shared costs include both fixed and variable costs shared among products. Calculating the true cost of a specific product is often difficult because it requires a decision of how to allocate costs among products. It is a particular problem for service costing because a great deal of the costs of providing services are shared. This may lead to underestimating or overestimating the real costs of products or services sold to specific segments. If costs are not allocated appropriately, then one product will end up carrying (subsidizing) the cost of another. This can create serious mistakes when promoting particular products or markets at the expense of other products or segments. As many costs as possible should be sourced to a specific product or market, rather than sharing the costs among them. That way, each product or market has an incentive to find ways to reduce costs and to make sure they have been allocated fairly.

The traditional way of allocating shared costs is by a percentage of the direct labor cost involved in making a product. It can create serious cost and pricing distortions, particularly when shared costs such as factory support operations, engineering, design, distribution, marketing, and other overheads make up a significant portion of a firm's cost structure. Such distortions are avoided with activity-based costing.[4] Shared marketing and other overhead costs are first sourced to activities and processes (such as selling and service). An analysis is then done to determine how much of these activities (measured in time and cost) are spent making, marketing, and servicing specific products. The results may not be very accurate, but it is better to be within 20 percent when measuring how much of the actual organizational resources are allocated to a product than to be assuredly wrong (at times by as much as 100 percent) using outdated allocation methods. Competitive rationality depends on minimizing the biases that can obstruct the understanding of internal costs (and cost structures) just as much as minimizing the biases that obstruct an understanding of the external market environment.

Average Costs

The *average cost* of producing and selling is the sum of all fixed and variable direct and shared costs divided by Q. In Table 18.1 the average cost of goods sold for the current year was (\$12,740,000 + \$6,050,000)/196,000, or \$95.87. The greater the ratio of fixed costs to total variable costs, the faster average costs falls as Q increases.[5] This explains

---

[3] B. Charles Ames and James D. Hlavacek, "Vital Truths about Managing Your Costs," *Harvard Business Review* (January/February 1990): 140–47. This excellent article emphasizes that, over the long term, a firm must be a lower-cost supplier and must continuously reduce its costs by correctly measuring them, by allocating them sensibly to product market segments, and by making someone responsible for reducing them.

[4] Robin Cooper and Robert S. Kaplan, "Measure Costs Right: Make the Right Decisions," *Harvard Business Review* (September/October 1988): 96–103.

[5] Average variable unit costs decrease as volume increases for two reasons that are often confused. The first is *economies of scale* that come from purchasing, manufacturing, distribution, and marketing efficiencies that occur with greater sales (the average unit variable-cost curve slopes downward when plotted against volume). Second, as an organization *learns* from its accumulated production and sales experience, the whole average unit cost curve changes by shifting down (lower than the previous average unit cost curve).

why in markets where fixed costs are high, firms try very hard to increase sales and gain market share from each other. Costs fall faster and hence profits increase faster with an increase in sales. Long-distance telecommunications is a market with such a cost structure. In the example, fixed costs are low relative to variable costs, so such a strategy is less attractive.

Sunk Costs

Costs incurred in the past are called *sunk costs*. Examples are R&D and the production cost of finished goods in inventory. Sunk costs are relevant in the initial pricing decision and when estimating future profits, but they are not relevant when considering a change in price. This is because such costs will be deducted equally from the sales of each alternative pricing option. They do not vary across pricing options, and a pricing decision must focus solely on costs that vary among pricing options. For example, when considering an extra price promotion, the only costs that should be considered are for advertising and administering the price promotion and for added logistics and inventory management. These added costs may be compensated by lower average manufacturing costs that result from the higher volume of sales.

Budgeting Processes and Politics

Budgeting involves converting all of the planned programs, tactics, and tasks into costs and subtracting these costs from expected sales. Most firms have standard budgeting procedures and use standardized forms to capture information (see Figure 18.2). How a firm actually does budgeting depends on the following factors:

- *Organizational culture.* Although budgeting fundamentals are common to most firms, any given firm may have relatively unique procedures or budgeting routines.
- *Organizational politics.* A firm's political structure determines who controls total expenditures and who allocates resources by approving budgets.
- *Control over information.* Budgets cannot be constructed without the correct historical or current information.
- *Decentralization of profit responsibility.* How the budgets for operating divisions and product groups are approved is related to a firm's profit responsibility structure.
- *Composition of the senior management team.* The budgeting skills and career specialization of senior managers come into play.
- *Importance of the project.* This is related to the rewards and sanctions associated with the outcomes for key people.

No universal budgeting procedure is used by all firms. Figure 18.4 presents the results of a study on the use of three common procedures.[6] Only 7 percent of the firms use a bottom-up method, in which budgets are developed by line managers and submitted to higher-level managers. Sixty percent use a bottom-up/top-down procedure, in which a lower-level manager's initial budget recommendations are scrutinized

[6] Nigel F. Percy, "The Marketing Budgeting Process: Marketing Management Implications," *Journal of Marketing* 51 (October 1987): 45–59. This study focused on U.K. manufacturing firms. The budgeting practices of U.S. firms may be different.

Figure 18.4 **Three Different Marketing Budgeting Routines**

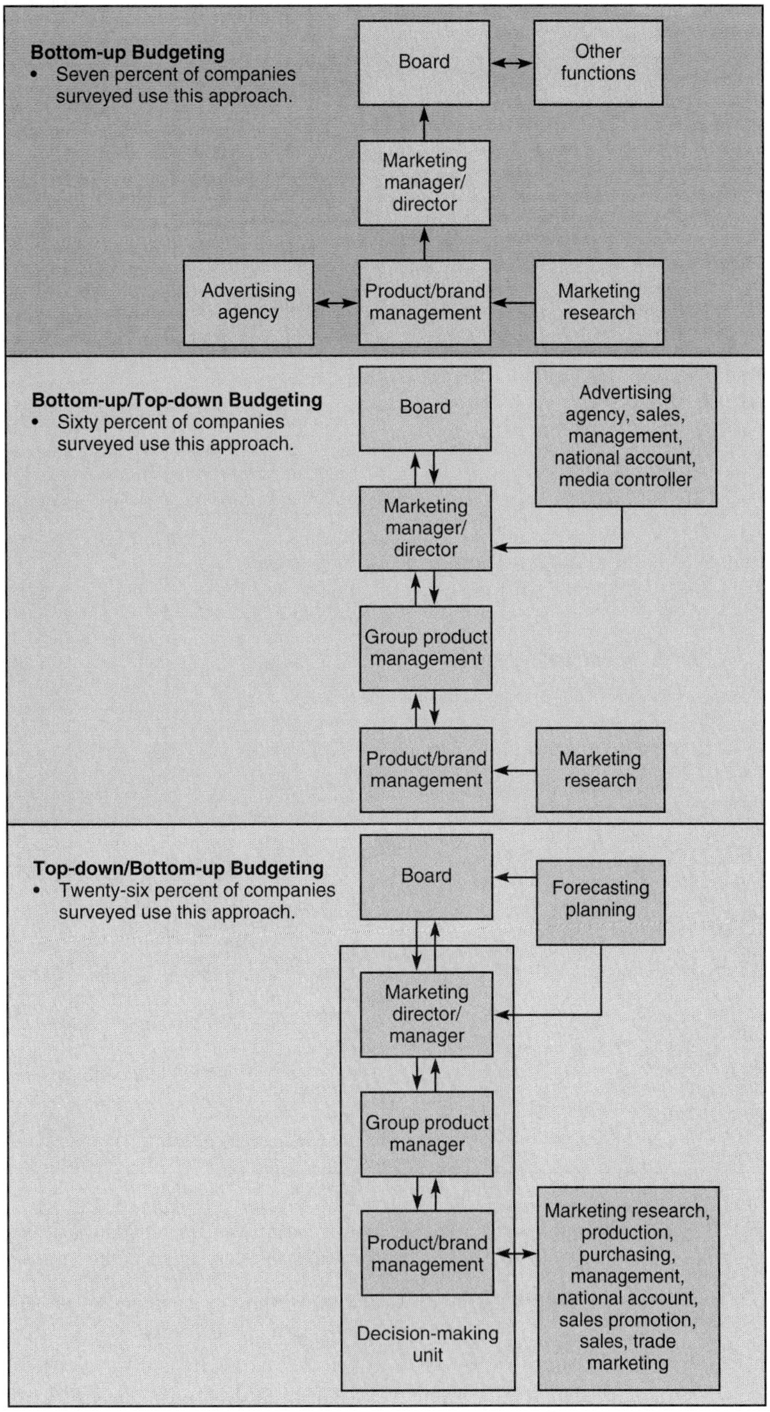

In a study of marketing budgeting, 93 percent of the firms surveyed employ a budgeting process or routine that is either bottom-up, bottom-up/top down, or top down/bottom-up. The third process is clearly the most directive, and the researchers found that this approach was related to a situation of financial stringency and other budget constraints.

Figure 18.5 **Characteristics of Bottom-up and Top-down Budgeting**

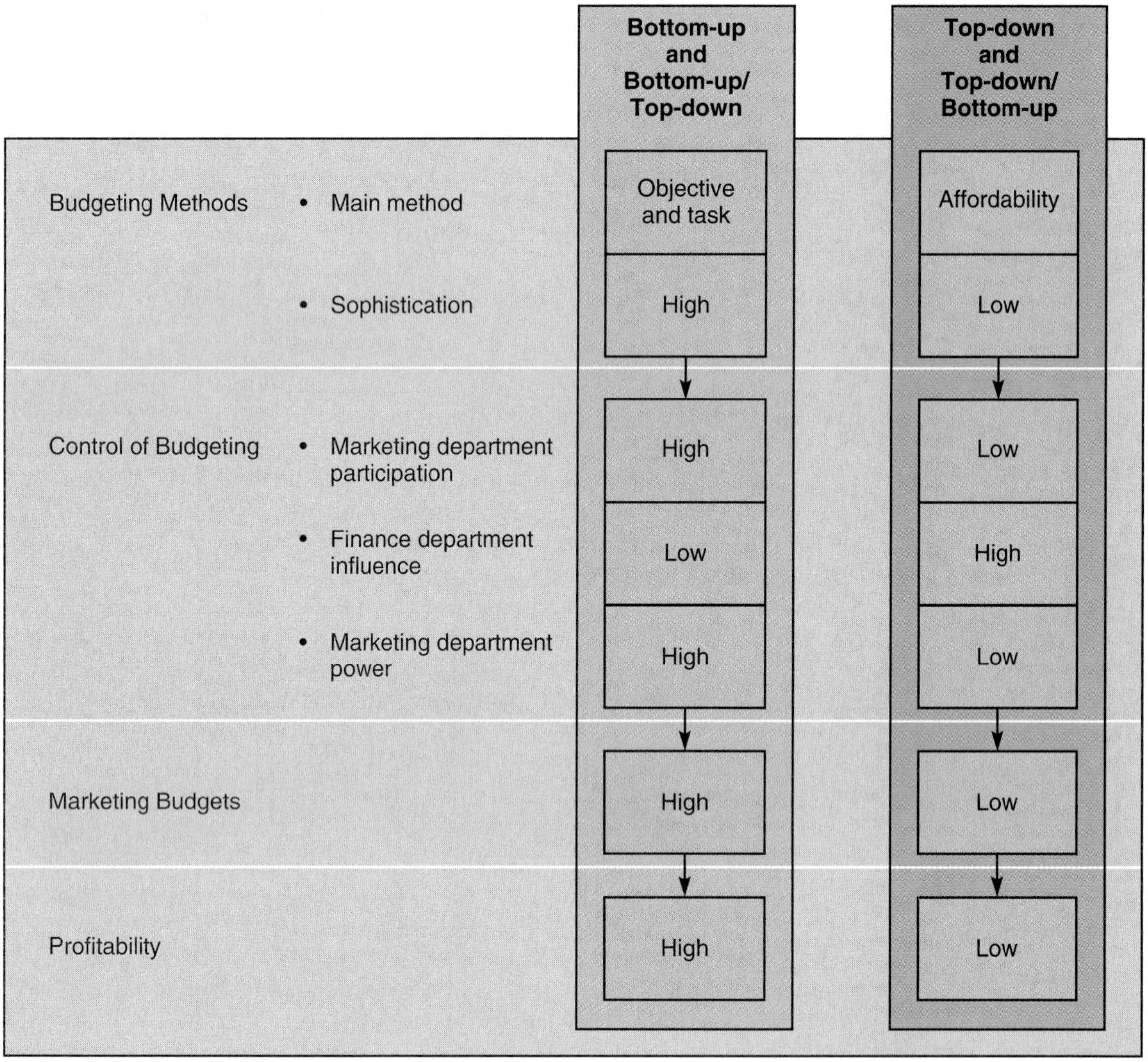
Bottom-up and Bottom-up/ Top-down
Top-down and Top-down/ Bottom-up
Budgeting Methods
• Main method
Objective and task
Affordability
• Sophistication
High
Low
Control of Budgeting
• Marketing department participation
High
Low
• Finance department influence
Low
High
• Marketing department power
High
Low
Marketing Budgets
High
Low
Profitability
High
Low

The top-down approach displayed in this figure suggests that the finance executives are either politically dominant or possess greater competitive rationality skills than the marketing executives. The bottom-up approach suggests the opposite.

by upper management before approval. About one in four of the firms surveyed use a top-down/bottom-up procedure, in which budget constraints are passed down from top management, and specific product-market budgets are then submitted by teams or managers subject to such constraints. The remainder of the firms use a different method. Figure 18.5 presents the characteristics of each of these budgeting procedures. The bottom-up/top-down approach has more of a market orientation than the top-down/bottom-up approach, because it is initially developed by executives who are closer to the market and, hence, more likely to understand the market.

Budgeting is both a rational and a political process. Rational budgeting attempts to allocate resources where they will produce the greatest contribution to financial and marketing objectives. Political budgeting enables those individuals with the most power and influence to obtain the most resources for their projects, whatever the financial or marketplace consequences. This very likely may lead to an inefficient allocation of resources.[7] Therefore, the decision maker must display a good political sense as well as management accounting skills. This also explains the great advantage of using a cross-functional team approach, where major budgeting decisions in a division are made by the CEO in consultation with a management team representing production, sales, marketing, purchasing, and finance. This approach minimizes, but does not eliminate, the politics and thus increases the chances of competitively rational budgeting.

Marketing Program Budgeting

This discussion now turns to how to set the budget for each specific marketing activity. The focus is on the two major components of marketing budgeting: sales force and advertising budgeting. Very similar issues and problems arise in setting the budgets for other marketing activities and projects.

Sales Force Budgeting

If the workload approach has been used to determine how sales territories should be staffed to meet the selling objectives, then this information also can form the basis of the sales budget. The budget can be built by estimating the likely compensation and expenses involved in servicing each territory. Historical information will help in this estimation but may have to be adjusted if call rates, call time, and other duties have changed. The cost of keeping the sales force in the field is the total cost of serving all the territories. The sales management overhead expenses and salaries must be added to estimate the overall budget. The telemarketing group may operate under a separate budget funded from the direct sales it generates.

Rather than a line-item budget, which details expenses item by item, a regional sales manager is often given an overall program budget, which enables him or her to juggle expense overruns. This approach also gives the sales manager the opportunity to spend money where he or she thinks it will produce the greatest return. In the modern U.S. economy, average personal-selling costs are about 14 percent of gross sales.[8] Because a significant percentage of personal-selling expenses are directly tied to sales, personal-selling budgets tend to be a little easier to estimate and control than other marketing expenses. Many firms compare selling-expense-to-sales ratios among regions to help control costs and to estimate future budgets (see Chapter 19).

---

[7] See Percy, "The Marketing Budgeting Process." Also see D.C. Hambrick and C.C. Snow, "A Contextual Model of Strategic Decision Making in Organizations," in *Academy of Management Proceedings*, ed. R.L. Taylor (Ada, OH: Academy of Management Journal, 1977); and Richard M. Cyert and James G. March, *A Behavioral Theory of the Firm* (Englewood Cliffs, NJ: Prentice-Hall, 1963).

[8] William A. O'Connell and William Kennan Jr., "The Shape of Things to Come," *Sales & Marketing Management*, January 1990, 36–41.

Advertising Budgeting

An unresolved (and perhaps unresolvable) argument has continued for years over how to set an advertising budget. At the heart of the problem is deciding how best to estimate the effect of advertising on sales. As discussed previously (and illustrated later in this chapter in the section on marginal budgeting), various techniques can be used to estimate sales response, but many firms are not familiar with them. Instead, they have concluded that if they cannot measure advertising's separate, unique effect on buyer behavior or sales, then what is the point of setting target performance objectives? This, in part, explains why a number of more traditional, simple rules are used, even by very large companies, to decide how much to spend on advertising during the planning period. Several of these rules are now discussed before an alternative approach based on the objective-task method is described.

Percentage of Sales

The most common way of determining how much to spend is to project sales and spend a prespecified percentage of projected sales on advertising. It is useful to find out how much, as a percentage of sales, the industry as a whole spends on advertising.[9] The amount varies considerably among product markets. In the pharmaceuticals and cosmetics industries, a company may spend 20 percent or more of its annual sales on advertising; food, soap, and cleaner manufacturers spend about 10 percent of their sales on advertising; the two major U.S. soft-drink companies (Coca-Cola or Pepsi) spend about 5 percent; retail chains spend about 2 percent; and automobile manufacturers spend between 1 percent and 5 percent, with the smaller, foreign manufacturers spending a higher percentage.

If a market is efficient, then the competitors in the industry might be expected to learn to spend about the right amount on advertising. If they were spending too little or too much, then presumably a new or established competitor would discover this through experimentation and gain a major advantage by doing something different. The Rationality in Practice box presents two such cases. Each deviated from the standard percentage-of-sales method of setting the advertising budget, but one became a success story and the other did not. Note that if the competitors in a market stick to a percentage-of-sales rule, then they are setting their advertising voice share in proportion to their current market share. This is an implicit acceptance of the competitive status quo, and it implies a tacitly agreed on "don't rock the boat" collusion.

Again, if markets are efficient, then the reason some industries spend more on advertising than others is presumably because advertising is more effective in those markets compared with other marketing expenses (such as extra services to distributors). If this is true, the percentage of sales an industry spends on advertising may tell something about both the effectiveness of advertising in that industry's market. Changes in spending, such as those revealed in Figure 18.6 on page 700 also may tell something about the changing effectiveness of different marketing tactics over time. Perhaps spending has swung too far in favor of promotions, and, in the late 1990s, spending on advertising will increase again.

Competitive Parity Plus

The problem with using the percentage of sales to determine an advertising budget is that it ignores many environmental realities. For example, a new entry attempting to

[9] Paul Farris and Mark Albion, "Determinants of the Advertising-to-Sales Ratio," *Journal of Advertising Research* (December 1981): 7–16.

Rationality in Practice

Breaking with Tradition

The possibility always exists that the established players are wrong, and the level of advertising spending in a market is too low and could be greatly expanded if aroused by an aggressive campaign. In the fall of 1976, Canon introduced its fully automatic AE-1 single-lens-reflex camera by radically departing from the industry's conventional advertising expenditure and media strategy. Using the Australian tennis pro John Newcombe, it ran pre-Christmas prime-time TV ads to demonstrate that it had solved the problem of expensive-camera complexity—"The Canon AE-1 is so advanced, it's simple." Over the next two years, Canon's spending on TV and magazine ads doubled each year to almost $10 million. Other manufacturers scrambled to keep up, and industry spending just on television in 1978 soared to $50 million. However, Canon had gained a jump on the competition and over three years gained 32 percent of the 35 mm market, catapulting itself past market leaders Minolta, Olympus, and Pentax. Canon achieved this feat by breaking with industry advertising conventions and investing in a bold new creative and media strategy that greatly expanded both total demand and its own market share. The expensive-camera market segment had been asleep until Canon woke it up.

In a very different market, Heineken broke with tradition by slashing its advertising buying in 1987 to a quarter of what it was in 1985. Senior executives believed that Heineken's image would not suffer too much and the savings would compensate for the damage to profits resulting from a weakening dollar. They were very wrong. Heineken's market share of imported beers slipped from 38 percent to 23 percent. The advertising expenditure was needed to *maintain* its advertising voice share, its mind share, and its market share. Competing Mexican brands, in particular, gained a major advantage from Heineken's mistake.

SOURCES: Courtland L. Bovee and William F. Arens, *Contemporary Advertising* (Homewood IL: Irwin, 1986); and Jeffrey A. Trachtenberg, "Beer Blunder," *Forbes*, February 8, 1988, 128–30.

penetrate a market must at least match the advertising expenditure of the competitor whose market share it is attacking. This competitive parity approach to ad budgeting means the firm with low market share will have to spend a considerably higher percentage of its sales on advertising if it is trying to increase its market share. Some experts have proposed (without any strong empirical evidence to support their figures) that a new entry should identify the market share it hopes to have at the end of two years and should spend one and one-half times that percentage during those two years on advertising. For example, if the goal is a market share of 10 percent, then the new entry should spend 15 percent of the industry's total spending on advertising during those two years. The theory is that a new entrant must gain mind share (consumer attention) before it gains market share, and it will take a higher voice share (advertising dollars spent) for a new entrant to achieve this.[10] In markets where competitive reactions are likely to be fierce, the amount spent may have to increase greatly to obtain a voice share and resulting mind share that is higher than current market share. As described in the chapter introduction, the long-term effects of using such percentage-of-sales and competitive-parity advertising budgeting logic can lead to overspending on advertising.

Objective Task

If a company does not have a strong competitive position and message theme, then it should spend less on advertising and more on R&D that will produce a more competitive

[10] James C. Schroer, "Ad Spending: Growing Market Share," *Harvard Business Review* (January/February 1990): 44–48. In mature markets, a company has to outspend the competition by a huge amount to gain share and/or develop a brilliant new creative such as Diet Pepsi's Ray Charles "uh-huh" ads. See also Chapter 6 for a discussion of voice share, mind share, and market share.

Figure 18.6 **Changes in Spending on Advertising and Promotions**

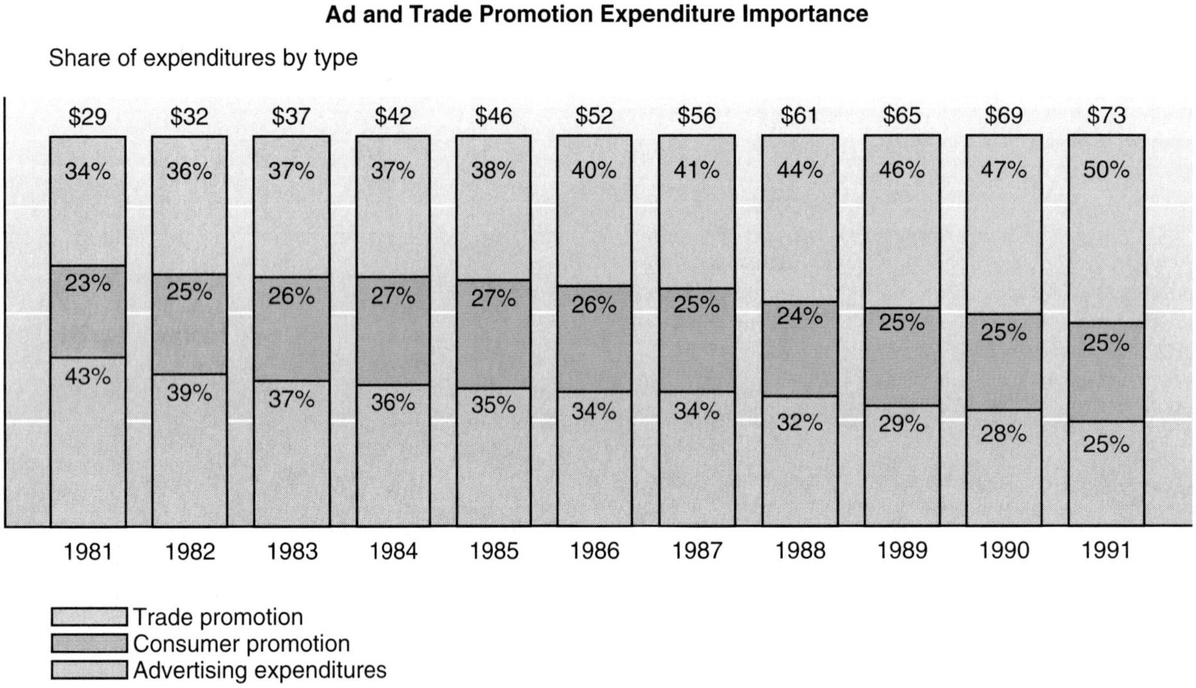

In the 1980s, consumer packaged-goods companies learned that, dollar for dollar, trade promotions were more effective at helping them achieve their goals than consumer advertising compaigns. They reallocated their spending accordingly.

SOURCE: Neilsen Marketing Research, Donnelley Marketing, 1992.

product or service. On the other hand, if it has a lot to say, then it should spend enough advertising to inform all consumers of its competitive advantages. If a company has a new product that it knows is clearly superior to the competition and will be profitable, then it should invest in a marketing campaign that includes a large enough advertising budget to reach most of the target market. In short, how much a firm spends on advertising should be based on a thorough analysis of the market environment and an assessment of the competitive potential and profitability of the product or service to be advertised. Such an *objective-task* approach is detailed in Figure 18.7.

After the initial steps, in which the environment is analyzed, communication goals, a message strategy, and a media strategy should be developed based on the positioning strategy and information about the competitors' advertising strategies and spending. The next step is to estimate the approximate cost of a campaign that will achieve the communication goals (expressed in terms of the basic message theme, timing, and the target audience's average frequency of exposure to the message). The approximate media cost and cost of developing the creatives should be estimated by the

Figure 18.7 **Objective-Task Advertising Budgeting**

1. From the environmental analysis, determine the competitor's advertising efforts and likely future efforts.
2. Determine the targeting/positioning strategy.
3. Specify new communications objectives and new basic-message and media strategies based on the above facts.
4. Determine the expenditure needed on creatives and media over the planning period to achieve the message objectives and strategy.
5. Allocate a budget to regional or particular markets. Base this budget on market potential and cost per target thousand. Revise the media budget.
6. Look at the total cost. Consider company internal resources. Can we afford this investment at this time? If not, go back to the beginning and prune.

At Step 3 in the usual objective-task method of determining the advertising budget, it is recommended that various objectives, such as a 40 percent brand awareness (mind share), be specified. The ad agency should have a gut feel for how many exposures of a particular ad are needed to create brand awareness. This judgment will determine how much needs to be spent on media to achieve the needed exposure average frequency. If the budget has to be pruned, judgment again should be used to cut out the least effective spending. Note that this is not a top-down or bottom-up process but rather is based on planned objectives and marketing programs. The above process forces the team to ask whether it might be better to spend the dollars on some marketing activity other than advertising. This concern over the incremental return for dollars spent applies to all marketing spending and is called *marginal budgeting*.

advertising agency. Step 5 in Figure 18.7 narrows down such estimates by specifying how much will be spent in specific markets.

Looking at the overall advertising budget required to achieve the advertising objectives in *all* of the geographical markets, the company must decide whether it can afford the advertising budget it has developed and whether it appears to be a good investment. If the budget is too expensive, the decision makers must decide where to trim the fat. The budget might cut back on the overall reach and frequency objectives or on the amount spent on creating the advertisements (advertising execution). But such pruning may weaken the overall campaign so much that it threatens its success in all markets. A better approach may be to cut back on the number of markets to ensure the potency of the campaign in the remaining markets (see Chapter 15). This occurred during the 1992 presidential election when, in the last two weeks of the campaign, the Democrats spent all the money they had left in about eighteen states where the polls suggested the race was close.

Marginal Budgeting

A very important element of competitive rationality is for a firm to recognize that buyer response to spending on different marketing activities varies by the activity. In other words, the response elasticity of buyers to different marketing tactics varies. The recognition of this fact is not enough. The firm with the superior insight to correctly estimate these response elasticities will, all other things being equal, end up being more competitive and profitable. This, of course, assumes that the firm follows through by investing in the activities that produce the greatest response. This type of investment decision making is called *marginal budgeting:* spending the marginal dollar so it has the greatest effect on long-term profitability. Some experts believe this is how all marketing budgets should be set.[11]

To explain the marginal budgeting process, return to the initial planned P&L statement developed by the ACME company manager in Table 18.1 which is used as a starting point for considering the relative impact of changes in the advertising and promotion budgets. The brand manager has asked several experienced managers to forecast market share for the company's product brand at different advertising and promotion budget levels (a 20 percent cut, no change, and a 20 percent increase) under each of three scenarios or future "states of the world": status quo (competition continues as usual), worst case (competitors introduce new brands), and best case (competitors cut back their marketing spending). Table 18.2 presents the forecasts obtained from the managers and the projected next-year profit obtained from plugging the market share and budget projections into the spreadsheet. The conclusion is that dollars should be shifted from promotion to advertising.

The results in Table 18.2 suggests that an increase in the advertising budget is perceived by the managers to have a positive marginal impact on profit, regardless of which scenario occurs. The worst-case estimate is that increasing advertising by 20 percent will increase profits by 190,000. The best-case estimate is that profits will increase by $730,000. Further, the 20 percent cut in promotion does not hurt profit much and even improves profitability in the status quo scenario. The manager could extend this analysis by asking her or his colleagues for market share estimates two or three years into the future and expanding the number of scenarios that might occur (for instance, scenarios that assume different economic conditions, like prosperity versus recession). The next Rationality in Practice box presents another marginal budgeting spreadsheet that can be used to allocate resources.

Forecasting

Budgeting always requires a forecast of sales and costs. Traditionally, these projections are based on the history of past sales and costs. Past performance should be the starting point of a forecast, but as discussed in many of the earlier chapters, the purpose of marketing planning and management is to make things happen, things like dramatically increasing sales and reducing costs. If the marketing plan has no impact on history, then it is very much a status quo plan. Many plans operate this way intentionally. If the marketing strategy in place is working and the company wants assured performance from the product market, then the marketing plan and competitive strategy

[11] L. M. Lodish, *Advertising and Promotion: Vaguely Right or Precisely Wrong?* (New York: Oxford University Press, 1986); and John R. Rossiter and Larry Percy, *Advertising and Promotion Management* (New York: McGraw-Hill 1987), 398.

Table 18.2 Inputs and Results for ACME's Marginal Budgeting Analysis

	Managers' Average Market-Share Estimates Given Different Scenarios		
	WORST CASE	STATUS QUO	BEST CASE
If the advertising budget is			
Cut 20%	24%	25%	26%
Maintained	28	28	30
Increased 20%	30	32	34
If the promotion budget is			
Cut 20%	26	27	27
Maintained	28	28	29
Increased 20%	29	30	31

	Profit Projections (in Millions) Using the Table 18.1 Spreadsheet		
	WORST CASE	STATUS QUO	BEST CASE
If the advertising budget is			
Cut 20%	$0.76	$1.03	$1.30
Maintained	1.50	1.50	2.04
Increased 20%	1.69	2.23	2.77
If the promotion budget is			
Cut 20%	1.47	1.74	1.74
Maintained	1.50	1.50	1.77
Increased 20%	1.25	1.52	1.79

will be very likely more of the same—with small improvements. In this situation, and assuming the external environment is not expected to change dramatically, historical projections are quite reasonable and often quite accurate.[12]

Forecasting becomes much more difficult when a sharp shift in marketing strategy is proposed, such as a shift in product positioning.[13] The other major contributors to the unreliability of historical forecasts are unexpected changes in the economy or in competitor behavior. Sales forecasts then must be generated from expert opinion as well as customer and sales force estimates (see Table 18.3 on page 706).[14] For example, the one question economists have difficulty forecasting is the one question that firms most want them to forecast: When will a recession in the economy occur? The last recession in the U.S. economy began in July 1990, but it was not until November that a majority of economic forecasters predicted a recession would take place. By April 1991

[12] For a comprehensive guide to forecasting, see David M. Georgoff and Robert G. Murdick, "Manager's Guide to Forecasting," *Harvard Business Review* (January/February 1986): 110–20.

[13] David L. Hurwood, Elliot S. Grossman, and Earl L. Bailey, *Sales Forecasting* (New York: The Conference Board, 1978), Report no. 730.

[14] Kenneth R. Evans and John L. Schlacter, "The Role of Sales Managers and Salespeople in a Marketing Information System," *The Journal of Personal Selling and Sales Management* (November 1985): 49–58; and E. Taylor, "Using the Delphi Method to Define Marketing Problems," *Business*, October/November 1984, 16–22.

Rationality in Practice

Marginal Budgeting

The following table presents a marginal budgeting (MARGINAL) spreadsheet that can help determine whether the firm's resources should be used to increase the advertising budget or for some alternative marketing activity. MARGINAL's purpose is to act as a focus for the cross-functional team working on the final stages of the entire marketing budget for a product market. Prior to the meeting, each member of the group should be asked to prepare an estimate of the likely return over the next five years of investing an additional amount (such as $10,000), more than what was tentatively planned, in each of several marketing budget items. These estimates then can be Delphied (circulated among the participants and then revised until some consensus is reached) and used in the MARGINAL analysis. Variations in the original estimates say a lot about the firm's understanding of current sales response elasticities to the different marketing tactics and programs. How a firm arrives at the final estimates also says a lot about its competitive rationality decision-making procedures.

the recession was officially recognized, but by then the recovery actually had begun![15] The reasons why economic forecasting is so off is that it cannot predict sharp shifts in government policy, international incidents that affect the political and economic outlook, and "manic-depressive" mood swings in business and consumer behavior.

Most of the forecasting techniques described in Table 18.3 are geared toward projecting demand without explicit consideration of changes in the firm's marketing strategy. The innovative manager faces the problem of estimating what the firm's share of market sales will be *if* the current strategy is changed. The spreadsheet format in Table 18.1 is an effective tool for marketing budgeting because it enables planners to conduct "what if" analyses; that is, "If the advertising budget is increased by 20 percent,

[15] Rob Norton, "Recession? What Recession," *Fortune*, June 12, 1995, 27.

MARGINAL: A Marginal Budgeting Spreadsheet

Purpose: To determine the best allocation of funds by choosing investments offering the highest potential return. The return on an investment must be higher than the minimum target return. The incremental (marginal) dollar amount should be invested in activities yielding the highest projected rate of return. All investments yielding returns above the minimum target return should be considered if funds are available.
Incremental amount available for investment: $10,000
Minimum acceptable target return on investments: 30.0%

		Estimated Gross Profit Increase ($ in 000s)						
		Year						
Incremental Investment	Cost	1	2	3	4	5	Return	Above Target?
Consumer advertising	($10.0)	$10.0	$2.0	$2.0	$3.0	$1.0	38.7%	Yes
Trade advertising	(10.0)	8.0	4.0	2.0	0.0	0.0	24.9	No
Publicity promotion	(10.0)	6.0	4.0	4.0	2.0	2.0	30.3	Yes
Sales force training	(10.0)	5.0	4.0	5.0	3.0	2.0	30.5	Yes
Sales promotions	(10.0)	12.0	0.0	2.0	0.0	0.0	31.6	Yes
Packaging redesign	(10.0)	0.0	6.0	6.0	5.0	5.0	27.3	No
Product redesign	(10.0)	0.0	8.0	7.0	6.0	5.0	35.7	Yes

Instructions
Step 1: Set incremental investment amount and target return rate.
Step 2: Develop five-year income stream estimates for various marketing activities.
Step 3: Develop what-if analyses by choosing pessimistic and optimistic income projections.

NOTE: The return is the internal rate of return (IRR), which equates the present value of the initial investment to the present value of the cash flow stream.

and market share subsequently increases to 30 percent, what is the impact on profit?" The following section briefly describes methods of estimating how market share and sales will respond to changes in marketing strategy.

Forecasting Sales Response

Market response refers to the degree of sales change that occurs in response to changes in marketing strategy. It is more commonly referred to as *elasticity*, which is defined formally as the percentage change in sales relative to the percentage change in price or some other marketing variable. How can a manager develop estimates of how sales will change if marketing strategy (price, advertising budget, sales force allocation, and so on) is adjusted? Four general techniques will be described. The advantages and disadvantages of each method are summarized in Table 18.4.

Table 18.3 A Summary of Forecasting Techniques

Expert Opinion: People who have expert knowledge about an industry are surveyed to get their opinions of the industry's outlook. Their forecasts and justifications are often then circulated among them, and experts are asked to adjust their estimates based on shared information. This is called the Delphi method of forecasting. Relative to other forecasting techniques, experts are best at scenario forecasting: estimating the effects of extraordinary events such as a change in government policy, technology, or the economy.

Survey of Buyer Intentions: Buyers are surveyed and asked to estimate their purchase intentions. This is appropriate when buyers have clear intentions and are willing to express them. Some trade associations, trade magazines, or market research firms undertake such surveys for an industry (for instance, the Annual Survey of Buying Power taken by *Sales and Marketing Management*). When the state of the economy greatly influences sales, then surveys of buying intentions are quite useful for forecasting.

Sales Force Survey: Gathering feedback from the sales force is less effective than directly surveying buyers, but it is easier to do. The problem is that salespeople can be too optimistic or too pessimistic depending on their current enthusiasm and confidence. Sales force surveys can be useful in estimating the impact of new products, services, strategies, and programs that buyers are not yet aware of and in estimating likely changes in regional demand.

Historical Sales Projections: Past sales are plotted, and statistical trend projections are made. This forecast is often broken down into trend, cycle, and seasonal components. Historical projections are best when the market is stable and past marketing strategy will be continued in the future. Most forecasts start with such an historical sales projection and then are adjusted by some other forecasting techniques.

Input-Output Modeling: Used by economists to project industry demand, a model is constructed using economic determinants of demand (inputs) that forecast sales (output). It can be very reliable in stable economic conditions but not when major changes occur in the marketplace, such as the development of new, competitive technologies or an unexpected global political event (a war in the Middle East or the collapse of the U.S.S.R., for example). The most sophisticated predictive modeling is done by experts called econometricians. In recent years they have had a hard time with their predictions because the major drivers of the economy have been very unstable.

Table 18.4 Estimating Sales Response Elasticities to Changes in Marketing Strategy

APPROACH	ADVANTAGES	DISADVANTAGES
Judgment Based on managers' past observations of how sales are related to marketing effort.	Managers have good insight and a bird's-eye view of the market. Also, low cost and easy to obtain.	Subjective estimates can be very biased because managers only remember past programs that resulted in extreme outcomes.
Consumer Surveys Direct questioning of consumers. Examples: conjoint studies, copy testing, purchase intentions.	Only moderately expensive.	Not applicable to all tactics (such as very new product concepts or ad budget decisions).
Test Market Experiments Manipulate key marketing variables to evaluate their effects on sales and profits. Random assignment of test markets/subjects to treatment conditions.	Can isolate the effects of marketing effort on sales and can examine interaction effects. High validity, if test not contaminated by competitor behavior.	Most costly. Usually outside expertise is needed. Slow.
Statistical Demand Analysis Mathematical model of demand that estimates relationships between demand and marketing.	With enough data, highly valid. Allows many factors to be considered and provides estimates of optimal effort and spending.	Extensive data needed. Very high cost. Only covers the efforts tried in the past. Usually requires outside expertise.

Subjective Judgment

Subjective judgment involves obtaining a manager's best guess of how sales or market share will change if marketing strategy is changed. Experienced managers are the most accessible source of market response information and can provide reliable sales response estimates provided they are asked properly. It is useful to interview several managers to obtain sales response figures. It is also important to provide them with explicit questions that cover all plausible customer and competitor reactions.[16]

Consumer Surveys

This method involves telephone, mail, or personal interview surveys of consumers to obtain their reactions to alternate marketing strategies (such as different prices, ad campaigns, or product descriptions). However, consumers are notorious for being much more price sensitive than they will admit to.

Experimentation

Experimentation occurs when the firm purposely manipulates marketing variables over time or in different regions to assess the impact of such changes on sales and profits. For example, a consumer goods manufacturer experimented with its price for a product over several months by using different price levels in three different groups of geographic markets. It is important to maintain as much control as possible in an experiment to eliminate the possibility of any variables other than the one being manipulated affecting sales results.

Statistical Demand Analysis

This technique involves obtaining a statistical estimate of the relationships between sales and important marketing variables using actual sales and marketing data over time. It requires the relatively sophisticated econometric modeling of a great deal of data collected for many time periods. A statistical demand analysis generally provides the most accurate information on elasticitities (because it uses actual sales data and accounts for the influence of many variables), but it is extremely complicated to implement and often very expensive.

From reading this chapter it should be clear that the budgeting, forecasting, and costing processes of firms can vary greatly. This suggests that some firms are much better at this activity than their rivals. Consequently, it is very likely that the next breakthrough in total quality management will be in improving management processes such as budgeting. It will involve learning from companies that are very good at budgeting and experimenting with new processes that replace traditional rules of thumb that are nowhere near precise enough to produce accurate estimates of costs and forecast profits. A further take-away from this chapter is that there is much room for innovation and improvement in budgeting practices and is, thus, a skill area that presents real opportunities for marketing management and marketing executives.

Discussion Questions and Minicases

1. The spreadsheet PROFIT, presented in the following table, takes standard accounting information and computes the traditional P&L budget statement and a more competitively rational P&L budget statement. Please explain the differences between the two statements.
2. A company has a choice between manufacturing its product in Mexico using a highly labor-intensive process or investing in a new robotic plant and making the product in the United States. The average unit cost of production in Mexico can be expected to stay about constant because although labor rates are expected to rise, productivity and

[16] Herman Simon, "Pricing Opportunities—and How to Exploit Them," *Sloan Management Review* (winter 1992): 55–65.

Traditional and Rational Profit and Loss Budget Statements

MANAGEMENT ACCOUNTING INFORMATION (in $000s)	
Sales	$15,000
Increase/decrease in inventory	(67)
Variable manufacturing costs	6,018
Fixed manufacturing costs	870
Variable distribution costs	774
Fixed distribution costs	100
Actual selling costs	300
Selling costs to be charged to this period	300
Actual advertising costs	1,707
Advertising costs to be charged to this period	900
Actual sales promotion costs	1,568
Sales promotion costs to be charged to this period	1,200
Actual market research and development costs	175
Market R&D costs to be charged to this period	50
Actual product management costs	210
Product management costs to be charged to this period	200
Administration overhead costs	1,300

changing exchange rates will compensate for the increase. At current sales levels, the proposed capital-intensive U.S. manufacturing unit would operate at about 50 percent capacity, and at that capacity the average unit cost would be about the same as the Mexican product's cost. From a pricing perspective, which manufacturing process would you choose? What market information would help you to make the choice?

3. A highly ambitious product manager is told that senior management is about to introduce a new competitive line that will be managed by another executive. To help launch the new line, she is informed that most of the shared costs will be allocated as costs charged to her product. She considers writing a memo to her superiors suggesting a different approach. She is not against today's breadwinners funding tomorrow's breadwinners but is concerned about fairness and her annual bonus. Please write the memo for her.
4. An airline uses old planes on one route and new planes on another. The old planes have a zero book value. How should this fact affect the airline's pricing on these routes?
5. When the president of Sony, Akio Morita, came to the United States in 1955 to sell his tiny transistor radio, a major distributor expressed interest in selling it under its own name (which Sony wisely refused to do) and asked for quotes on the cost of orders of 5,000; 10,000; 30,000; 50,000; and 100,000 units. The distributor was shocked when Sony quoted a higher per-unit price for the 100,000 order. However, when the reason for the price was explained, the distributor was impressed by the unknown Japanese company's business savvy, and it placed the order. What justification did Sony provide?
6. A producer of a well-known brand of canned goods earns a 40 percent contribution margin on its sales to supermarkets. It is approached by a supermarket chain to supply a line of lower priced canned goods marketed under the store's own brand name. The producer has excess capacity because a current recession has resulted in a slump in sales of its branded line. What factors would you consider in deciding whether to supply such a line? What price would you charge?
7. A publisher of specialized books normally sells its books for $30 average. The production cost is $20. On average, 75 percent of the production runs are sold in the first twelve

TRADITIONAL PROFIT-AND-LOSS STATEMENT (in $000s)

Sales		$15,000
Variable manufacturing costs	$ 6,018	
Variable distribution costs	774	
Inventory adjustments	(67)	6,725
Gross profit		$ 8,275
Fixed manufacturing costs	870	
Fixed distribution costs	100	
Administrative overhead costs	1,300	2,270
Profit before marketing costs		$ 6,005
Selling costs	300	
Advertising costs	1,707	
Sales promotion costs	1,568	
Market research and development costs	175	
Product management costs	210	3,960
Net profit before taxes		$ 2,045

RATIONAL PROFIT-AND-LOSS STATEMENT (in $000s)

Sales		$15,000
Variable manufacturing costs	$ 6,018	
Variable distribution costs	774	6,792
Gross manufacturing contribution		$ 8,208
Selling	300	
Advertising	900	
Sales promotion	1,200	2,400
Gross marketing earnings		$ 5,808
Market R&D costs	50	
Product management costs	200	250
Net marketing earnings		$ 5,558
Fixed manufacturing costs	870	
Fixed distribution costs	100	
Administrative overhead costs	1,300	
Inventory adjustments	(67)	2,203
Net profit before taxes		$ 3,355

COSTS CARRIED FORWARD TO BE CHARGED TO FUTURE PERIODS

Selling	$ 0
Advertising	807
Sales promotion	368
Market R&D	125
Product management	10
Total costs carried forward	$1,310

months. The remaining inventory is eventually sold, but on average it takes an additional three years to sell a book that has not sold in the first twelve months. The yearly cost of holding each book is 25 percent of cost (10 percent in warehousing and utilities, 2 percent in insurance and record keeping, and 13 percent in the cost of capital tied up in the book). The owner is thinking of instituting a clearance sale of all books held for twelve months.

After holding any book title for twelve months he offers retailers the sale price for a two-week period. What is the lowest sale price he should offer to sell the books for during the two-week period? What would be some of the long-term effects of such a sales tactic? What is the long-term solution?

8. Which of the budgeting routines in Figure 18.2 do you think shows the greatest competitive rationality? Why? What might your answer depend on?

9. The excessive construction of commercial offices in the United States and particularly in metropolitan areas such as Dallas-Forth Worth during the 1980s was an economic disaster. Could it have been avoided by better forecasts? What forecasting techniques do you think could have been used? (Hint: Think of what is needed to be forecast.)

10. Why might firms rely too much on forecasts of sales and costs based on computer-generated historical statistics?

11. What marketplace events are most likely to upset an economic forecast based on historical data?

12. The failure of almost all econometric forecasters to predict the 1990–1992 recession in the United States and Britain has added to the general skepticism about economic forecasting. A further concern is that the forecasts of different prestigious economic forecasting units often vary. How should an executive respond when fifty different economic forecasters make fifty different predictions?

13. The mental model an executive uses to think about the impact of advertising expenditure on sales is a very important determinant of advertising budget decision making. Draw a graph of the relationship that you believe exists between advertising spending and sales. On the graph, indicate the optimum amount that should be spent on advertising. Would the relationship between spending on other marketing activities and sales have a similar shape?

14. Describe what economic theory the MARGINAL spreadsheet is based on, and explain how it works (see the box on page 705). What problems may arise from using such a spreadsheet? What does the spreadsheet not consider?

15. Another way to understand the output implications of a cost structure is to use the DuPont Financial Analysis model. It breaks financial analysis into two streams: income and investment. The following table presents the DuPont spreadsheet, which enables planners to use the DuPont model in "what-if" analyses under different assumptions and forecasts of sales, costs, and investments in new assets. For example, what happens if average inventory is eliminated by logistic innovation? What are the advantages of using such a spreadsheet?

16. In 1992, on discovering that its "Uh-huh" Diet Pepsi ads were ranked number one in Video Storyboard Test's ranking of the most popular commercials for each quarter of 1991 and that Diet Coke's forced preference advantage had slipped from 70–30 percent to only 52–48 percent, PepsiCo decided to increase its ad budget spending from $70 million in 1991 to $120 million in 1992.[17] What does this tell about the competitive rationality of Pepsi's advertising budgeting and about advertising budgeting in general?

[17] Joshua Levine, "Affirmative Grunts," *Forbes*, March 2, 1992, 90–91.

RETURN: A DuPont Financial Analysis Spreadsheet

ASSUMPTIONS

Net sales	$1,000
Cost of goods sold	450
Variable expenses	150
Fixed expenses	200
Inventory	500
Accounts receivable	300
Other current assets	100
Fixed assets	2,000
Total liabilities	800

INCOME STATEMENT ACCOUNTS

Net sales		$1,000
Cost of goods sold		450
Gross margin		$ 550
Expenses		
Variable	150	
Fixed	200	
Total expenses		350
Net profit		$ 200

BALANCE SHEET ACCOUNTS

Inventory	$ 500
Accounts receivable	300
Other current assets	100
Total current assets	$ 900
Fixed assets	2,000
Total assets	$2,900
Total liabilities	800
Net worth	$2,100

FINANCIAL RATIOS

Net Profit Margin (Net Profit / Net Sales) 20.0% × Asset Turnover (Net Sales / Total Assets) 34.5%

↓

Return on Asset (Net Profit / Total Assets) 6.9% × Financial Leverage (Total Assets / Net Worth) 1.4%

↓

Return on Net Worth (Net Profit / Net Worth) 9.5%

When you are drowning in numbers you need a system to separate the wheat from the chaff.

Anthony Adams

Without measurement you cannot manage.

Anonymous

CHAPTER NINETEEN

Marketing Management Control

Control is about getting information to decision makers and implementers as accurately, directly, and quickly as possible about changes in the efficiency and effectiveness of key (driver) process input/output ratios. Note that it is about getting the information into the hands of the teams and individuals that execute the decision-making and implementation processes. It is not about getting information into the hands of management four layers above the process and four months later. The most useful information is about changes in the efficiency and effectiveness of processes such as input cost, output quality, and process time. Control is exemplified by the following two control processes: open-book accounting and tracking and analyzing customer complaints and questions on 800-number customer hot lines.

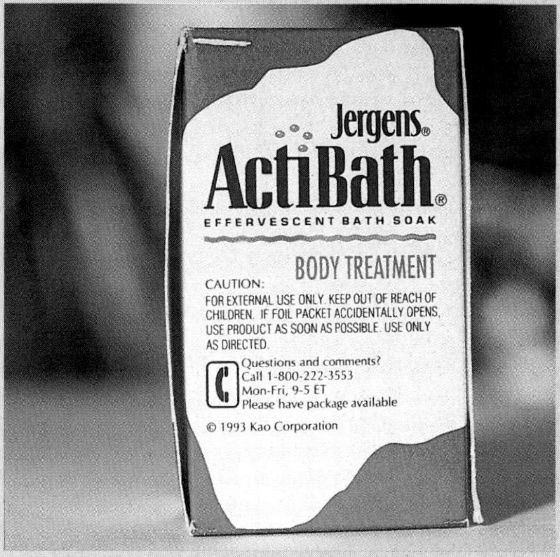

Open-book accounting is a process where key cost, time, and quantity and quality of output data are fed back to workers. Measures such as on-time shipments, customer returns, the year-to-date cash-flow statement, year-to-year revenue, average gross margin, job cost over and under, revenue per employee, and return on operating assets are posted in lunchrooms and available on E-mail notice boards.[1] The basics of the meaning and significance of the ratios have

to be explained if not already fully understood by the team or individuals. The teams and individuals should be rewarded for meeting and exceeding goals and also should share in some ownership to motivate finding long-term solutions over short-term fixes. To try to achieve and exceed their goals, the teams must be empowered with not only the information but also the resources to be able to improve their work processes.

The Mid Atlantic Medical Services HMO (Mamsi) has employed an interesting open-book approach in its relationship with its doctors. It sends a monthly printout of the doctors' average monthly patient costs by category of illness or treatment process. Two doctors have been terminated by Mamsi for cost reasons in the past five years. "Just having the facts at their fingertips is enough to get most doctors in line."[2] Some doctors have experienced a decline in their costs from 140 percent of the internist average to 110 percent in just a year. These costs were still 10 percent higher than average, but the doctors clearly had tried quite successfully to adopt several new treatment practices recommended by Mamsi that maintained the quality but reduced the costs of patient diagnosis, treatment, and care processes. Over four years the percentage of Mamsi babies born under Mamsi care by cesarean section went from 34 percent to 22 percent. Such cost savings can be passed on to the HMO member and hence reduce health care costs. In short, open-book accounting is a very clever relationship control process that relies on the power of information in the right hands. It has the capability of continuously reducing health care costs in a way that no regulatory process can.

Many appliance and computer companies use an 800-number hot line to carefully track and analyze customer inquiries and complaints to identify design weaknesses, and complaints about manufacturing quality, service, and price.[3] The information is analyzed by market researchers or quality controllers and passed on to cross-functional product development teams. It is a form of quality control aimed at continuously improving a firm's products and customer services. It also ensures that the added quality is what the customer wants to see improved. ■

---

[1] John Case, "The Open-Book Revolution," *Inc.*, June 1995, 26–43.
[2] John R. Hayes, "Knowledge is Money," *Forbes*, February 13, 1995, 188.
[3] John W. Verity, "The Gold Mine of Data in Customer Service," *Business Week*, March 21, 1994, 113–14; and David Greising, "Quality: How to Make it Pay," *Business Week*, August 8, 1994, 54–59.

An organization's control processes and systems are important to its competitive rationality because of the impact they make on its implementation and learning processes. Chapter 17 discussed organization and process controls that improve implementation effectiveness and efficiency. But the ultimate quality test of a firm's processes is the quality of its output, as measured by customer satisfaction and profitability. Such output has to be both measured and managed. Even organizations with a clan culture where everyone shares the same vision must have output performance standards that are monitored and used as important feedback to improve decision-making and implementation processes. Relevant output performance statistics keep the firm and its teams alert, able to diagnose change and to experiment, learn, and adapt. Evidence also shows that a combination of the organization and social control processes described in Chapter 17 and performance output controls create the highest job satisfaction.[4]

One of the most robust principles of behavioral learning theory, so robust it is close to a law, is that the speed and quality of learning depend on the speed and quality of the feedback. The principle also seems to apply to the learning of social systems and, particularly, firms. For instance, as the quality of feedback about the defect rate of machines and manufacturing processes improved through superior machine control systems, scientific management, and statistical process control (SPC), manufacturing has been able to accelerate its learning about how to make the manufacturing process more efficient.

When a firm has to rely on the superiority of its higher order learning processes to advance or sustain its competitiveness in the market (as described in Chapter 4), what feedback controls does it use to learn how to assess and improve, through redesign, these processes? As machine and statistical quality controls are to manufacturing processes and as customer satisfaction is to product or service design processes, what are the measurement controls for a firm's higher order learning processes? What evidence indicates that the firm is continuously improving its higher order learning and control processes? Is its benchmarking getting better? Is it imitating faster? Is its costing process control becoming more effective? Does the firm reward teams and individuals in a way that reinforces the desired outcomes? The following three sections discuss such general learning controls. Specific marketing outcome controls such as customer satisfaction are then presented, and these are followed by a discussion of how firms monitor and diagnose the causes of variance in performance measures (see Figure 19.1).

General Learning Controls

A firm should measure its learning potential through regular surveys of key employees asking their attitudes toward experimentation, benchmarking, discovery, learning, knowledge transfer, change, and how organization learning processes are improving. These surveys could be benchmarked against firms in other industries that are leaders in organization learning and continuous improvement. Also, senior management bonuses should depend on a mix of sales performance, profit, customer satisfaction ratings, and organization learning potential as measured by these employee surveys.

[4] Bernard J. Jaworski, Viasis Stathakopoulos, and Shanker Krishnan, "Control Combinations in Marketing: Conceptual Framework and Empirical Evidence," *Journal of Marketing* 57, no. 1 (January 1993): 57–69.

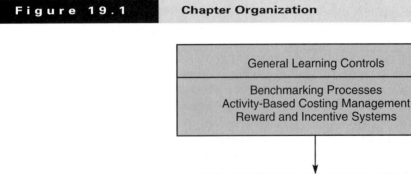

Figure 19.1 **Chapter Organization**

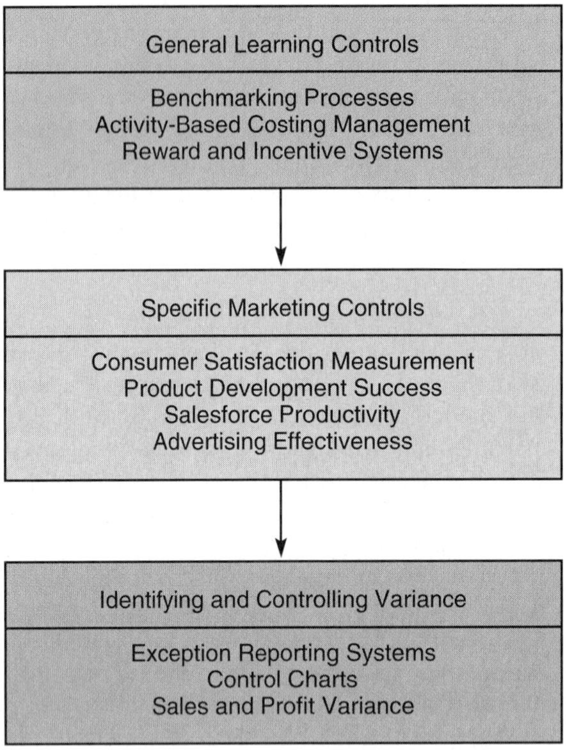

In this chapter controls are used to ensure that a marketing activity or program is being executed as planned and is not running off the rails. But in the modern company culture that emphasizes total quality management and continuous learning and improvement, control processes must do much more. They are used to learn how to improve a firm's processes, practices, and programs. This chapter starts by describing several control processes that are part of an organization's higher learning capabilities. A number of specific control processes are then described that measure a firm's customer orientation, the success of its product development processes, and the effectiveness of its two major marketing programs—its salesforce and its advertising. Control of a firm's order/delivery cycle and distribution services was discussed in Chapter 13 because logistic management systems are effectively logistic control systems. This chapter concludes with a section that describes how to identify when a process or system is out of control and how to diagnose or learn why and what might be done about it.

Without such feedback controls, the continuous improvement of a firm's learning processes is less conscious, deliberate, and rational and, indeed, is likely to progress and regress depending on chance variations in processes, uncontrolled learning experiments, and individual genius. The value of the development of such learning feedback controls goes beyond the incremental improvement in the processes. The continuous tracking of an organization's attitude to change and its learning drive can, in itself, heighten the continuous learning drive as well as suggest ways the drive can be nurtured and directed. For example, in a work-to-rule bureaucratic culture, the introduction of learning process measurement is likely to have a major effect on individual attitudes and the culture. The new, enlightened *learning* process controls replace the explicit and implicit *work-to-rule* process controls that long have suppressed the testing and learning of new work processes and rules. We now discuss three such learning process controls: *benchmarking*, *costing*, and *reward systems* processes.

Benchmarking Processes

In Chapter 4 a method of learning the best ways to increase the implementation speed of a company by imitating other companies' best practices was described. Such benchmarking learning can be used to not only speed up processes but also to increase process and product quality and reduce process and product costs (see Figure 19.2). In marketing management the most common benchmarking processes are associated with measuring customer satisfaction and financial performance.

Continuous Customer-Satisfaction Benchmarking

The best-known example of customer satisfaction benchmarking is the J.D. Power & Associates Customer Satisfaction Index for automakers. Each March, the company (which also offers similar surveys that rate airline service; see Figure 15.4 in Chapter 15) sends out a six-page detailed survey to some seventy thousand owners of new-model cars. About one-third respond. Manufacturers receive very detailed reports of problem areas and of benchmark comparisons with competitors. In the late 1980s, Honda drew a great deal of public attention to the J.D. Powers survey by promoting the fact that Honda was rated number one in customer satisfaction four years in a row. Then all of the premier brands, such as Lexus and Infiniti, strove to achieve the top rating ahead of Honda and Mercedes (see Figure 19.3). In 1991, Lexus and Infiniti succeeded. Surprisingly, General Motors's compact car, the Saturn, has scored very highly. The reason is that its dealer customer service is superb. The rest of the industry has been slow to imitate by benchmarking against Saturn dealers. The measures and weighing system that J.D. Powers uses has changed over time based on the responses of consumers and the auto industry. For example, customer handling (before and after sales service from the dealer) has accounted for 40 percent of the score, but this has been increased to 50 percent or more because dealer service has become more important to customers.[5]

Benchmarking Financial-Performance

Financial performance also can be studied relative to other firms. For example, domestic airlines benchmark themselves on their cost-per-available-seat mile. Southwest has the lowest cost (7.5 cents/mile), and USAir has the highest (11 cents/mile). Rather than comparing performance over time or against budget expectations, a firm participating in an interfirm comparison can compare performance across its own similar operating units. These units may be regions, divisions, or stores within a company; independently operated franchises; or even separate companies in the same line of business. The statistics compared are normally adjusted for sales and are performance statistics such as advertising and selling-expense-to-sales ratios, stock-turn, gross margin, and sales per employee. They provide an assessment of competitive rationality in terms of cost management and operational efficiencies.

The participants in an interfirm or interregion analysis often are surveyed beforehand or have a working party choose the operating and output ratios they wish to benchmark with each other. They may have difficulty setting a standard code of

[5] Larry Armstrong, "Who's the Most Pampered Motorist of All," *Business Week*, June 19, 1991, 90–91.

Figure 19.2 **Using Benchmarking to Continuously Improve a Firm's Competitiveness**

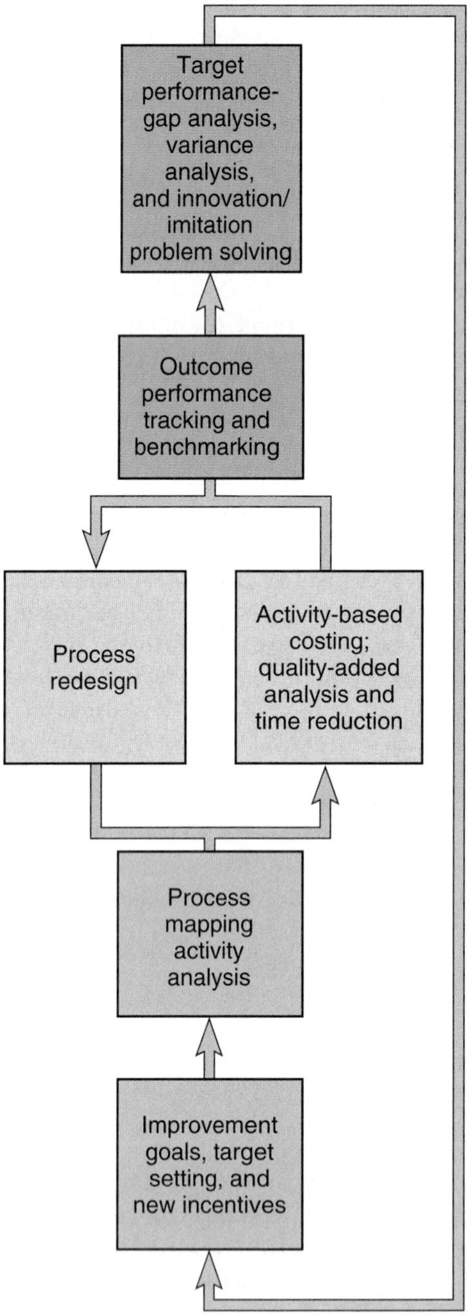

Benchmarking is best used in a management process that is continuously seeking to increase consumer satisfaction, to reduce costs, and to simplify and shorten the relevant manufacturing, logistics, or marketing process map.

SOURCE: Based on Paul Sharman, *A Tool Kit for Continuous Improvement*, May 1992, 17–20, by permission of The Society of Management Accountants of Canada.

Figure 19.3 **Promoting Customer Satisfaction**

Jeep has promoted its Total Quality Award for being recognized as number one for "Best Ownership Experience." More than 35,000 owners of 200 different nameplates rated their vehicles on areas such as craftsmanship, ride and handling, safety, luxury, ease, convenience, and dealership experience. As service and customer satisfaction have become increasingly important to consumers, ratings such as this one and the well-known J. D. Powers Customer Satisfaction Index have become increasingly important.

accounts as well as difficulty with consistency and honesty in reporting performance among the participants. Continuous benchmarking is much easier when undertaken within a company because confidentiality is critical when it is undertaken among firms. The participants receive information about the overall median, lower, and upper quartile performances on each statistic (and maybe the average of the best three as well), but no other individual firm's results are disclosed. This usually requires the participation of a trade association to gather the responses and an independent accounting firm to do the analysis. Such analyses of comparative production and accounting statistics have been undertaken in many industries for years. Comparisons of marketing performance measures are less common.

Determining where an organization ranks on various performance measures also requires an analysis of why variance exists. Reviewing the difference between the top performance and its own performance tells a firm how far it has to go to be the best (see gap analysis in Figure 19.2). But it does not explain how to get there. In fact, it simply may not be possible to get there because the top performer does not face the same internal and external environmental constraints. Analyzing sets of determinant performance ratios to diagnose the source of an inefficiency and to establish whether or not something can be done to improve a particular operating statistic is quite an art. But, at the least, a comparison of similar operating units can prompt a sobering reappraisal of current behaviors and standard operating procedures (production and marketing process routines). If the analysis was performed within an organization, high-performing units can explain to less-successful units how they managed to get to the top of the heap. For example, in the chapter introduction example, doctors whose patient care costs for a type of treatment were below average could train and mentor doctors whose equivalent costs are above average.

Activity-Based Costing Management

The competitively rational firm is continuously reducing the input costs of its processes without reducing the effectiveness or added value of the processes. The drive to reduce costs is exemplified in many Japanese companies whose cost management processes have the following characteristics:

- A price down/cost down mentality. This is driven by the belief that in the global marketplace prices will always trend down rather than up, so costs also always must be driven down.
- To be able to continuously "cost down," Japanese management accountants spend their time out in the plant or the field continuously helping to improve the processes whose costs they report. They are working in teams looking for better, cheaper, easier, and faster process improvements. Half the accountants in Japanese firms undertake such continuous process improvement; in U.S. firms the situation is very different.
- Japanese firms understand that costs are driven by and set mostly during the conceptual design stage. That is why they employ "target costing," which is designing a product to a future price and cost. Management accountants design costs out of manufacturing and distribution processes at the time the product and processes are designed and not later. They prevent rather than cure out-of-control costs. To do this they become expert thinkers about their firm's business processes and its process cost drivers.[6]

The implications of this "cost down"–driven corporate culture for other global participants is that every cross-functional team must not only understand the cost implications of its decision making and implementation but also must actively and continuously innovate/imitate to remove the costs from such processes. This also means that the modern marketing executive must be skilled in process cost management, which accountants call *activity-based cost (ABC) management.* Note that the term is not activity-based costing but the management of activity-based costs:

> Implementing ABC in my company equates to rearranging the deck chairs on the Titanic! Most companies' most pressing need is reducing costs (Activity-Based Cost

[6] Robert A. Howell and Michiharu Sakurai, "Management Accounting (and Other) Lessons from the Japanese," *Management Accounting*, December 1992, 28–34.

Management) not reallocating costs (Activity-Based Costing). *Tom Pryor, President, ICMS Software Inc.*

Modern management accountants do not simply measure costs. When they measure costs, they do so to shine a light on them, and then they seek to reduce them by placing the information in the hands of the employees responsible for a particular process, as described in the chapter introduction, or by actively suggesting themselves ways to reduce costs. But their views of process management and control are quite broad and enlightened, as is evident from the thoughts of the following leading thinkers on process cost management:

> Activities are no more than components of a process. Real benefits accrue from process improvement. *Dennis A. Loewe, Financial Services Controller, Weyerhaeuser*

> Cost management is a set of techniques and methods for planning, measuring, and providing feedback to improve a company's products and processes. . . . The emphasis must therefore be on improving processes to eliminate waste and, thus, deliver higher quality, lower-costing products or services to customers.[7]

> Companies need to map and improve customer-focused processes. . . . The long-run global imperative, of course, is to find ways to reduce costs (primarily by removing constraints that cause delay, excess, and variation) of producing what the customer wants in the form the customer wants it. . . . I envision a business as a system of interrelated processes in which people are continually learning and inventing more fulfilling ways to profitably exceed the expectations of customers (internal and external).[8]

> You first understand the way work is being performed (in other words you undertake some form of activity analysis). Then you use some criteria (either cost reduction, cycle times to be compressed, quality improvement, etc.) to evaluate that work. *R. Steven Player, Arthur Anderson & Co.*

Cost managers must understand processes and be process thinkers because they cannot measure what they do not understand and because behavior can be influenced by measures; the better the measures, the better the learning. A further implication is that a firm should hire marketing and sales executives who are skilled in activity-based cost management, or it should hire accountants who become skilled in understanding marketing processes and removing the costs from them. Clearly, the second alternative (even if practiced by the Japanese) is not only inefficient but also creates the possibility of serious responsibility conflicts with marketing executives. A third, compromise alternative is to teach executives on the job how to reduce costs by learning from expert consultants (see the Rationality in Practice box).

The ABC of Process Maps

ABC control and management are achieved through first mapping the process activities, as described in Chapter 17. This identifies all of the activities in a process. The cost of a process is the cost of undertaking all of the activities. Chapter 17 explained

[7] Barry J. Brinker, "From the Editors: The State of Cost Management," *Journal of Cost Management* (winter 1992): 3–4.
[8] H. Thomas Johnson, "It's Time to Stop Overselling Activity-Based Concepts," *Management Accounting*, September 1992, 27–35; and from a reply to letters to the editor.

Rationality in Practice

If You Can't Fish... Hire a Fisherwoman

Many firms simply lack the expertise and the will to remove unnecessary costs from all of their processes. The competitively rational action for such firms is to hire ABC management consultants who have such skills. Chandrika Tandon, a native of Madras, is such an expert. She started cutting costs in her twenties when working for Citibank in India and moved on to become a banking cost-cutting expert for McKinsey & Co. in New York. In 1990 she left with seven colleagues and started her own consulting business. With her help, her first client, Midatlantic Corp., reduced its noninterest expenses by one-third, and her second client, Riggs National Bank in Washington, reduced its costs by one-fifth. In 1994 she worked with the $48 billion Providence bank, Fleet Financial Inc., to reduce its process costs. Enlisting the help of six thousand employees who came up with twenty-eight thousand money-saving ideas, the company shrunk its workforce by 20 percent, reduced annual costs by $300 million, and increased revenues by $50 million. And such cost savings were achieved in a healthy, profitable company.

The 1994 cost-cutting project revealed hundreds of useless, expensive processes, such as 22 monthly reports prepared by eight hundred branch offices (211,200 reports a year) that were read by no one! Another four employees spent all their time collating credit-card reports that were sent by FedEx nightly to managers who already had the reports available on their desk computers! Fifty work teams drawn from across the organization to avoid conflicts of interest and to ensure fairness studied specific operations (processes), suggested cost-reduction changes, and rated the suggestions in terms of their risk to the firm's competitive services and employee morale. Low-risk recommendations were immediately implemented. For example, by changing the daily routines of tellers and adding part-time tellers in peak traffic periods, the bank saved tens of millions of dollars. Examples of the other three thousand changes in processes that were implemented are switching to recycled laser-printer toners, reducing services in little-used branches and rerouting branch calls to a central teleservicing organization, reducing the supply of company cars, and slicing away two layers of management in commercial lending by simplifying the loan process. The company could have saved $500,000 a year by getting rid of company-supplied coffee, but this was judged a cost-cutting move that would have hurt productivity and morale; instead employees now use their own mugs, and this saves $50,000 a year in throwaway coffee cups.

The lasting benefit of such a one-time drive to reduce costs is that the organization now has learned to apply the processes Tandon used to continuously reduce its costs in the future. By watching and working with the ABC management consultants, the organization taught itself how to fish.

SOURCE: Geoffrey Smith, "Fleet's Can-Do Spirit: We Can Do Without," *Business Week*, March 21, 1995, 106–7.

how to identify the critical-path activities, where any delay in completing the activity will delay completion of the whole process/project. It also explained how to trace back through the process the critical, quality-added activities that determine ultimate output quality and customer satisfaction. ABC management means identifying the activities in the process that contribute most to the cost of the process. To be most effective, this requires that the teams or individual responsible for each activity identify all of their costs and own them. Such empowerment and responsibility make them more determined to search for ways of reducing the costs without sacrificing the output quality or timeliness of the activity. As mentioned earlier, simply reducing the costs of an activity is not the goal. Reducing the cost of undertaking an activity that makes a better product or service is the goal.

When an activity involves the use of equipment, plant, or other such assets, the amount of equipment use measured in terms of associated consumables and time of use have to be recorded in a computer account. From such use accounting, the true operating and depreciation costs of using the equipment or plant materials, such as a desktop publishing computer for producing a product brochure, can be calculated.

Similarly, management time usage should be identified and accounted for to identify the actual cost of overseeing and troubleshooting particular activities and processes.

After improving accounting for the direct costs of activities, the next step is to identify activities that can trigger other costly activities. For example, to understand the cost of order processing, a firm needs to study what activities the receipt of an order triggers and to cost these activities. Understanding the true cost of a cross-functional product development team requesting a new drawing from the engineering department requires estimating the cost of the activities that the request triggers: the inspection, data processing, quality control consultation, and supervision. Similarly, the receipt of a sales lead may involve a telemarketing qualification call, an internal search of company files about the potential customer, and so on. A cost driver activity is one that leads to a sequence or subroutine of costly activities. The questions that must be asked for activity cost management are (1) Do the triggered activities need to be undertaken? How do they add to increasing customer service and satisfaction or product quality? and, (2) Can the whole subroutine be shortened and simplified (reengineered)?

ABC management coupled with open-book management, described in the chapter introduction, creates a very powerful internal control system. When employees see and come to understand the cost implications of their actions and the activities they are responsible for, they are better able to control and manage costs themselves. The results can be surprising. For example, a skeptical visitor to the Springfield Remanufacturing Corp., which uses open-book management, approached a guy who was polishing a crankshaft and asked, "I understand that most SRC employees really understand their business. I'm curious—what is the price of that crankshaft you're working on?" At his own company, such a question would provoke a grievance for trying to embarrass a union worker who only was doing his "work-to-rule" job. He also figured the worker would confuse cost with price. Instead, the guy asked, "List price or dealer net?" He then proceeded to explain both prices, the overall cost of the crankshaft, and the cost of his polishing activity.[9]

For ABC management, the costing of a product or service is relatively straightforward. The processes involved in developing, researching, manufacturing, distributing, and marketing a product or service are mapped and costed, based on the activities involved. When unusual or unexpected activities are undertaken, they are logged into a computer and assigned to the specific product or service under a specific cost code that identifies the activity and the product/service. The real problem with ABC is updating the firm's accounting system so that it can be undertaken.

Reward and Incentive Systems

Business enterprises are economic entities. Employees are also economic agents who work for economic rewards—not exclusively, but economic incentives assuredly motivate, direct, and hence, control behavior. It is therefore logical that a major part of organization control is achieved by reward processes that link financial rewards to appropriate measures of work process performance. It then becomes critical to choose the right performance criteria to reward. In 1990, Edward A. Brennan, chair of Sears Roebuck & Co., shook up the company by making all employees focus on profits. In

[9] John Case, "The Open-Book Revolution," *Inc.*, June 1995, 26–43; see also John Case, *Open-Book Management: The Coming Business Revolution* (New York: HarperBusiness, 1995).

the Sears Tire & Auto Centers, this resulted in the setting of higher sales targets and quotas; sales commissions and incentives were based on the amount of repairs done.

Two years later, Sears agreed to pay $8 million to settle civil charges that it overcharged customers for repairs in California. Undercover agents were overcharged an average of $288 for unnecessary repairs.[10] The economic control mechanism encouraged the Sears employees to cheat their customers and cost the company hundreds of millions in the loss of future business and brand equity. In another incident, an ABC news story about Food Lion highlighted a number of serious hygiene and sanitation problems in deli and meat merchandising apparently caused by the market managers' efforts to meet the company's cost and profit margin goals.[11] The next Rationality in Practice box also highlights how the wrong economic reward processes can really hurt an otherwise excellent company.

Company-wide profit sharing is a particularly effective control tactic because it encourages all sorts of initiatives to reduce costs and increase sales, it stimulates information exchange, and it encourages informal social controls among employees. An advantage of a general profit-sharing program is that it overcomes some of the problems of measuring performance in intermediary processes. As outcomes become a shared responsibility, as decision making becomes shared, as implementation requires organization-wide cooperation, and as results increasingly depend on uncontrollable factors such as competitor behavior and economic conditions, it becomes difficult to connect results to individual performance or to use bureaucratic forms of control. A firm has to rely more on collective economic incentives.

Profit sharing is usually understood to be a reward process that uses an annual bonus to reward employees based on company or corporate profit performance.[12] The employee's share is distributed either as cash or as a deferred payment into a retirement fund. Even though profit-sharing plans lack the ability to directly link individual employee or team performance to rewards, employers have successfully used profit-sharing plans to improve company performance, reduce costs, and create a more cooperative workforce. John V. Jensen, manager of employee benefits at Andersen Corporation, testifies to the effectiveness of Andersen's profit-sharing plan.[13] In 1987, Andersen's profit-sharing distribution reached 84 percent of pay, and business was booming. According to Jensen, employees do see a link between profit sharing and reducing expenses, holding down costs, and making high-quality products. Hartzell Manufacturing in St. Paul, Minnesota, also has reported positive results from its profit-sharing plan.[14] Since its implementation, employees are more willing to work together to solve problems, correct each other's mistakes, cooperate with team members, and generally work smarter.

A final profit-sharing success story comes from the service sector.[15] Southwest Airlines had outstanding operating profits in 1990, reaching $81.9 million, while only one other United States carrier reported profits. Southwest employees also were reported to be the most productive employees in the airline industry in 1990, with employee revenues reaching $137,675. Employee turnover was also low, 7.8 percent in

[10] Seth Faison, "Sears Will Pay $6 Million to Settle Repair Complaints," *New York Times*, September 3, 1992, D5; and Kevin Kelly and Eric Schine, "How Did Sears Blow This Gasket?" *Business Week*, June 29, 1992, 38.
[11] *ABC News Primetime Live*, November 5, 1992, Transcript no. 270.
[12] Robert L. Heneman, *Merit Pay: Linking Pay Increases to Performance Ratings* (Reading, MA: Addison-Wesley, 1992), 95.
[13] Polly T. Taplin, "Profit-Sharing Plans as an Employee Motivator," *Employee Benefit Plan Review* (January 1989): 10.
[14] Rebecca Sisco, "Put Your Money Where Your Teams Are," *Training* (July 1992): 42.
[15] Danna K. Henderson, "Southwest Luvs Passengers, Employees, Profits," *Air Transport World* (July 1991): 32–41.

Rationality in Practice

Outcome Goals Out of Control

In a Rationality in Practice box in Chapter 1, the spectacular way Bausch & Lomb (B&L) developed the contact lens market was showcased. For twelve straight years up to 1993, B&L achieved double-digit growth in sales and earnings, a remarkable achievement for hard-driving chair and CEO Daniel Gill. The company and he prospered. His own bonus plan was weighted 30 percent on sales growth, 30 percent on profit growth, 30 percent on return on equity, and 10 percent on improvement in customer satisfaction. In 1991 he earned $6.5 million and in 1992 $5.7 million.

But in 1994 the Securities and Exchange Commission mounted an investigation of irregularities in B&L's marketing and accounting practices. It appears that to make the annual sales growth targets, several questionable marketing programs were implemented. First, distributors were given very generous payment terms if they increased their orders and built up their inventory. Second, at the end of 1993 large quantities of unordered contact lenses were shipped to some distributors who were told they had to pay for them only when they sold them. But B&L counted them as sales, and in 1994 almost all of them were returned. Third, many managers sold contact lenses and Ray-Ban sunglasses to distributors who shipped them to other markets and undercut the prices of B&L's official distributors in those markets. Some salespeople even may have received bonuses based on how much their distributors diverted sales to foreign markets and by doing so undercut B&L's position in those markets.

CEO Gill's line was "make the numbers but don't do anything stupid." Unfortunately, it was interpreted as "I'd be stupid not to make the numbers." The pressure to make the performance goals panicked managers into constantly running end-of-month promotions to distributors and customers that overloaded distribution operations. The result was lower prices and higher costs.

The fundamental problem with these tactics was that B&L's competitiveness was slipping away. Long-term, corrective laser surgery threatened to eliminate the need for many types of contact lenses. In the short term B&L had not kept up with its competitors' innovations in soft-contact lenses, particularly Johnson & Johnson's (J&J) initiatives, and also resorted to some questionable new product launches. In 1989, the same Optima lenses it had developed in the 1970s and still sold for $70 a pair were repackaged as Sequence 2 and Medalist brands to compete in the frequent-replacement market segment that J&J had primarily developed. The new brands sold for as low as $7.50, and when some Optima customers discovered they were continuing to pay $70 for the same lenses, they filed a class-action suit against B&L claiming dishonest and deceptive practices. CEO Gill blamed poorly executed marketing plans, removed several marketing and financial executives, and ordered managers to follow the most conservative accounting practices. In his own words: "We think we are the most honorable beings on the face of the earth." For now, no more end-of-quarter wheeling and dealing is occurring, and global brand management has reduced the grey-market diverting. It is unclear how B&L's distributors and Optima customers rate the honorableness of B&L's old versus new behavior. In December 1995 Gill was fired.

One moral of this story is that even the best of firms can spin out of control when senior management focus too much on sales and profit growth and set almost impossible performance goals. Another lesson is that the best way to achieve a growth goal is from genuinely new products, and if such sales cannot be generated, do not try to fake it to make it.

SOURCE: Joyce Barnathan, "Blind Ambition," *Business Week*, October 23, 1995, 78–92.

1990, and, according to Ann Rhoades, vice president of personnel, all employees "question every change we make and watch every penny." Another type of reward process control is described in the Rationality in Practice box about employee suggestion systems.

Finally, it should be evident that all three of the above (benchmarking, costing, and reward system) control processes discussed, *when combined*, have learning and continuous improvement effects much greater than the sum of their parts. For example, ABC control provides higher quality cost information to the teams and people responsible for process improvement. Reward processes provide the motivation and incentives to improve the processes, and benchmarking against the best provides the targets and ideas that can be imitated. Together, along with the informal clan and interpersonal controls discussed in Chapter 17, they work much more effectively. This synergy probably explains why employees prefer a mix of these controls. The discussion next turns to specific marketing learning controls.

Specific Marketing Controls

The theory of competitive rationality suggests that customer satisfaction is a key output control measure. If the firm's customer satisfaction index rating is not higher or not rising faster than its rivals, then the firm is in trouble. Another output control measure that is a critical determinant of the success of a firm's competitive rationality is the percentage of its sales and profits coming from new products (products introduced in the past five years).

Customer Satisfaction Measurement

In a competitive market, customer loyalty and satisfaction are leading indicators of future sales. If they begin to decrease, then it is likely future sales also will decrease. Therefore, in an effort to avoid losing customer sales, marketers are increasingly conducting surveys of customer satisfaction.[16]

Table 19.1 on page 728 presents an example of such an analysis. It segments customers by their past loyalty. A slip in satisfaction from a company's most loyal customers is much more serious than a decline in satisfaction among customers who never have been very loyal. The most rigorous customer satisfaction index (CSI) counts the percentage of "happy" customers in the satisfaction survey. Happy customers say (1) they are *completely* satisfied, (2) they would *definitely* recommend the product or service to friends, and (3) they *definitely* plan to continue to be loyal customers.[17] Many firms would be lucky to have a score of 20 percent to 30 percent on this type of index. The advantages of such a demanding standard of satisfaction are that it leaves a lot of room for improvement, and it is very easy for everyone, particularly senior management, to understand. It is useful for tracking change and, more important, the rate of change, and it is user friendly. It is useful for benchmarking and also making a follow-up diagnosis to determine why customers are *not* happy, which customer segments are most unhappy, and how their problems can be resolved so they will become happier customers.

Other experts recommend multiple-item scales that track overall satisfaction, expectations, and ideal point to measure satisfaction.[18] Using multiple measures increases the reliability of the answers. Examples of such measures follow:

[16] Robert A. Westbrook, "A Rating Scale for Measuring Product/Service Satisfaction," *Journal of Marketing* 44 (fall 1980): 68–72; and Richard L. Oliver and John E. Swan, "Consumer Perceptions of Interpersonal Equity and Satisfaction in Transactions: A Field Survey Approach," *Journal of Marketing* 53 (April 1989): 21–35.

[17] This measure was recommended in a talk given at an American Marketing Association and American Society for Quality Control meeting, March 11–13, 1990, by D. Randall Brandt of Burke Marketing Research, "The Purpose and Prospects of Customer Satisfaction Measurement."

[18] Michael J. Ryan, Thomas Buzas, and Venkatram Ramaswamy, "Making CSM a Power Tool," *Marketing Research* 7, no. 3 (summer 1995): 11–16.

Rationality in Practice

Employee Suggestion Systems

A reward system for employees' good ideas promotes and directs the three drives to increase customer satisfaction, reduce costs, and improve the decision-making and implementation routines of a firm. According to the Employee Involvement Association, in 1991 more than $2 billion was saved by member companies who had an employee suggestion plan.* The association recommends that employees should be involved as much as possible in the creation and implementation of employee suggestion systems, thereby creating a feeling of worker ownership. This also should increase acceptance and feelings of fairness.

One method of evaluating employee suggestions comes from a nuclear generating plant of a southern utility company.† It involves two types of suggestions: tangible ideas that result in measurable increases in profitability and intangible ideas that do not directly influence profitability but may address such issues as working conditions, employee safety, public relations, and internal communications. Intangible suggestions may be rewarded financially, but the reward is usually smaller than those for tangible suggestions, which most often equal a percentage of the increased profits. Eligibility for suggestion rewards is limited to employees whose normal job responsibilities do not include suggesting improvements. For example, a quality-control employee may not receive a reward for an idea relating to quality control, but a machine tool operator could.

Once the employee has generated a tangible idea, he or she must complete a form that identifies the problem and the specific solution. This involves stating what, how, where, and when the solution can be implemented. Once the form is completed, it is given to the suggestion program administrator who judges the eligibility of the employee and the suggestion. If the employee and suggestion are both eligible, the suggestion is sent to the supervisor responsible for the area of concern. The supervisor analyzes the suggestion, estimates the costs of implementation, and determines the annual savings in operations. The supervisor then recommends or rejects the suggestion, and the decision is sent back to the program administrator. Rejected suggestions can be appealed through the program administrator, and the administrator may resubmit the idea to another supervisor for reevaluation.

If the suggestion has been accepted and the reward exceeds $1,000, it is sent to the economic analysis section for final review and approval. If the reward is less than $1,000, it is automatically approved. Tangible suggestions accepted by the economic analysis section are awarded 20 percent of the first year's increase in "measurable net savings which result directly from the suggestion," with a maximum reward of $10,000. The reward given to the employee is based on an estimate of the first year's savings, so he or she can be rewarded immediately. At the end of the first year following the actual implementation of the suggestion, the reward may be adjusted, but it never will be decreased. Potential problems of suggestion systems are a lack of management support and monetary awards that are too small. If the company cannot afford larger rewards, points could be awarded and used in an annual lottery for a grand prize.

*Formerly called the National Association of Suggestion Systems, One Illinois Center, Suite 200, 111 East Wacker Drive, Chicago, IL 60601-4298.

†P. Michael Moore, "Employee Suggestion Systems Can Work," *CMA Magazine*, November 1988, 40–42.

In general, how satisfied are you with Company/Product/Brand/Service X?

Completely dissatisfied 1 2 3 4 5 6 7 8 9 10 Completely satisfied

How well did Company/Product/Brand/Service X meet your expectations?

Did not meet my expectations 1 2 3 4 5 6 7 8 9 10 Exceeded my expectations

When thinking of your ideal company, how well does Company/Product/Brand/Service X compare?

Very far away from my ideal 1 2 3 4 5 6 7 8 9 10 Very close to my ideal

When summed, customers' answers to these three questions better predict loyalty for services and products than each individual measure. A useful follow-up question is to

Table 19.1 A Customer Loyalty and Satisfaction Matrix

	CURRENT SATISFACTION				
PAST LOYALTY	COMPLETELY SATISFIED	SOMEWHAT SATISFIED	NEUTRAL	DISSATISFIED	% OF SALES
Firm friends	7%	3%	0%	0%	10%
Core loyal	10	5	5	5	25
Loyal switchers	10	10	10	10	40
Buy-on-price customers	0	5	10	10	25
Overall	27%	23%	25%	25%	100%

Just looking at the overall result, the situation looks rather grim. An analysis of the past loyalty figures, however, provides a little more assurance and explanation. Fortunately, the customers who are most loyal are generally still satisfied. The firm should be somewhat concerned with the 20 percent of core loyal customers who are currently dissatisfied. The customers who buy on price have a tendency to be less satisfied because they have not developed a continuous cooperative relationship, and they always will be dissatisfied if they think they could have gotten a lower price.

ask the open-ended question "How can we improve?" The answers then can be used to increase the quality of the product and service and reduce dissatisfaction. For example, for several years United Parcel Service (UPS) asked customers questions about their satisfaction with the speed and reliability of their shipping service. When they asked the more general question about how the service could be improved, they discovered customers wanted more face-to-face contact with the UPS drivers; they wanted a person to front the service who they could get to know, ask for advice on shipping, and personally deal with problems and emergencies. As a result the company is now giving its sixty-two thousand drivers an additional thirty minutes a day to spend time with customers and a small commission on any leads they generate.[19] In 1994, the program cost about $6 million in extra drivers and commissions but has generated tens of millions of additional revenue.

But even before a firm undertakes regular surveys of customer satisfaction, it should first develop a program to monitor customer dissatisfaction calls, such as the program described in the chapter introduction. Consumer complaints send red-alert signals about problems with design or after-sales service. Furthermore, the section on customer service and warranties in Chapter 10 explained how a firm's responses to customer complaints are both measures of true customer orientation and baseline indicators of how much a learning organization it really is.

Tracking service requests is another way of identifying customer dissatisfaction. For example, the downtown Chicago Marriott hotel discovered that two-thirds of its guest calls to housekeeping were for an iron and ironing board. Instead of replacing the black-and-white televisions in the bathrooms of concierge-level guest rooms (housekeeping had received no calls requesting color televisions in the bathroom), the hotel spent $20,000 putting irons and ironing boards in all guest rooms.[20]

[19] David Greising, "Quality: How to Make It Pay," *Business Week*, August 8, 1995, 54–59.

[20] The bad news is that it took the hotel fifteen years to discover the ironing problem! See Leonard L. Berry, "Improving America's Service," *Marketing Management* 1, no. 3 (1992): 29–37.

Product Development Success

The percentage of current sales coming from new or modified products introduced in the past three years is called the new product ratio (NPR) and indicates how quickly and successfully the firm is reformulating itself by creating or entering new product markets or creatively destroying its established product markets. A highly innovative firm such as 3M has a goal of gaining more than 20 percent of its sales from products launched in the past five years. The new product ratios are critical measures of the market success of a firm's innovation/imitation decisions and the rate of change within the organization. When NPRs are high (and getting higher), the firm is showing sure signs of superior competitive rationality (assuming costs *also* are being controlled). Although it can be subject to fudging (small modifications to mature products are claimed to be new products), the ratio is an important internal and external indicator of a firm's ability to initiate and adapt to change. As mentioned in the discussion of corporate mission and competence in Chapter 4, a 1992 survey of high-growth companies found that a firm's commitment and investment in new product development resulted in a higher NPR. In a market with a great deal of innovation/imitation, NPR is one of the three most important outcome measures, along with customer satisfaction and overall profits.

Sales Force Productivity

Sales force control involves a great deal of the informal or clan process control. The more successful such informal control is, the less the need for output control of the sales effort. In this context, the annual sales force meetings can be seen in a very different light. Like the tribe meeting for a special religious ceremony, it is full of rites of passage, initiations, rituals, honorific recognition, the relating of legends, the creation of new legends, and, most of all, the reaffirmation of group values. Sales conferences are thus extremely important for creating and sustaining clan culture and controls.

Controlling selling performance should be relatively straightforward if the reward system of salary, commission, bonuses, and contests is properly designed to direct the behavior of salespeople. The training program should make very clear how a sales rep's performance will be measured. Ideally, it should include instructions on how to use the company computer information system (having access to the performance statistics the sales manager looks at daily or weekly can help the sales rep monitor his or her own performance on an ongoing basis). Such performance statistics should be compared to sales force averages and the individual's past performance. This approach follows a basic law of evaluation and control; self-monitoring and self-control are always more effective than externally imposed monitoring and control.

The three basic dimensions of performance direction and control that most concern sales management are (1) the allocation of effort to selling different product groups, (2) the allocation of effort to new versus old business, and (3) the control of various expense-to-sales ratios. Each of these will be discussed in turn.

Selling Different Product Groups

The information system of the modern firm now enables it to compute the contribution of individual product sales to company growth and profitability. This information should clearly direct and be used to control the individual efforts of a salesperson. However, a major constraint on directing the efforts of a salesperson toward selling a particular product line can occur. The profile of customers in the salesperson's territory may be such that little or no potential or present demand exists for the company's most profitable or high-growth product lines. In this situation, the sales manager and product managers must work with the sales rep to determine the appropriate allocation of effort across the product groups for the rep's territory. Sales performance goals and budgets are then developed, and performance is compared against these goals and past performance history.

New versus Old Products

Steering a sales force toward new versus old business is problematic because even though most companies expect their salespeople to find new business, they do not want this to happen at the expense of old business. It is almost impossible to achieve both goals in a highly competitive market where new business is someone else's old business and old business is someone else's future new business. Time spent attacking someone else's market share therefore, is time spent away from defending one's own current market share. Another problem is the uncertainty over the growth potential of a territory. A sales rep will tend to underestimate growth potential, and senior management will tend to overestimate it. That is why the conversion percentage of leads (the percentage of new accounts resulting from leads provided to the sales rep) is such an important measure of a sales rep's motivation and ability to pioneer a sale. Here, no one can question whether leads exist in the territory. They have been generated through telemarketing, trade shows, advertising, or publicity and have been passed on to the sales rep to follow up on and convert to new customers. If the conversion percentage is low because the sales rep is generating his or her own new leads and converting them into new accounts, then all is well (except it suggests the territory potential is too large for one sales rep to handle). If, however, no other reasonable explanation exists for the low conversion percentage, then the salesperson is probably misdirecting his or her efforts, is not working hard enough, or lacks the necessary selling skills.

Expense-to-Sales Ratios

Table 19.2 presents a simple sales control spreadsheet that computes some typical control statistics used to monitor the effort invested in new versus old business over time. It also monitors some selling cost ratios, the third important dimension of control. The value of such a simple spreadsheet is that it enables a sales rep, alone or with the sales manager, to observe the effect of changing his or her behavior on some of the important performance ratios.[21] This raises a common problem with sales force control. It is very rare for a sales rep to improve performance on every possible ratio that can be computed, so the picky sales manager surely can find something to express concern about. Control is not simply finding fault in the details; it is using details to recommend overall performance improvements. When overall performance is superior, then a sales manager and the company should forget the minor transgressions and be much more interested in congratulating the salesperson and learning how the rep achieved the superior performance. That way, his or her tactics can be shared with marketing and the rest of the sales force.

Advertising Effectiveness

The first and most successful way to control advertising effectiveness and spending is to include an ad agency representative in the management team. The agency person-

[21] Performance ratios measure output-to-input performance efficiency and can be compared with past performance or highest performers in the company. See Thomas V. Bonoma, *Marketing Management* (New York: The Free Press, 1984), 508.

Table 19.2 **Sales Control Statistics**

NAME: R.G. BARRY

CONTROL AND EVALUATION OF A SALESPERSON

ANNUAL PERFORMANCE	1991	1992	1993	1994	1995
Dollar sales ($000)	$900.5	$926.6	$978.2	$1,074.8	$1,121.8
Dollar sales quota ($000)	$800.0	$850.0	$900.0	$950.0	$1,000.0
Gross profit of sales mix ($000)	$198.4	$204.4	$216.8	$232.5	$263.3
Sales to new accounts ($000)	$64.7	$38.9	$55.6	$70.9	$80.6
Salary and/or commission	$35,444	$37,367	$42,378	$44,232	$44,566
Selling expenses	$19,567	$22,333	$24,678	$25,111	$30,233
Number of days worked	274	280	278	283	267
Calls on new prospects	132	105	126	135	124
Number of new accounts	17	9	12	14	18
Number of old accounts	225	235	233	238	239
Calls on old accounts	946	1115	1120	1098	1044
Number of accounts lost	7	11	7	13	20

SALES ANALYSIS RATIOS	1991	1992	1993	1994	1995
Dollar sales/dollar sales cost	$16.37	$15.52	$14.59	$15.50	$15.00
Sales/call	$835.3	$759.5	$785.1	$871.7	$960.4
Cost/call	$51.0	$48.9	$53.8	$56.2	$64.0
New sales/new account	$3,806	$4,322	$4,633	$5,064	$4,478
New accounts/prospect calls	12.9%	8.6%	9.5%	10.4%	14.5%
Average cost of new account	$396	$571	$565	$542	$441
New business cost/sales	10.4%	13.2%	12.2%	10.7%	9.9%
Old sales/old account	$3,715	$3,777	$3,960	$4,218	$4,356
Old sales/old account calls	$884	$796	$824	$914	$997
Old business cost/sales	5.8%	6.1%	6.5%	6.2%	6.4%
Gross profit percentage	22.0%	22.1%	22.2%	21.6%	23.5%
Gross profit in dollars/sales cost in dollars	$3.61	$3.42	$3.23	$3.35	$3.52
Gross profit/call	$184	$168	$174	$189	$225
Sales to quota ratio	112.6%	109.0%	108.7%	113.1%	112.2%

nel must share the values of the organization and understand its culture, its politics, and its competitive rationality. The agency must become a believer in its client, so it will exercise self-control and also can be informally controlled. The absence of such an understanding can lead to a nightmare of over-the-shoulder agency supervision and endless questions about expenses. The time and effort an organization spends monitoring the progress of its agency can be very counterproductive.

Admittedly, maintaining process control over the ad agency is not easy because an important characteristic of informal clan control is that the member feels its membership in the clan is not threatened. Members may be sanctioned but not rejected by the clan or firm. This rejection is precisely what happens when a firm changes its advertising agency. Changing the agency people who work on the account also does not help because informal personal relationships help manage and control the client-agency relationship (see Chapter 14). Moreover, the effectiveness of an advertising campaign still needs to be monitored by outcome measures. An agency's assurance that its proposed campaign will be a great success does not make it so. Evaluating effectiveness is part of most major advertising campaigns. It is how an organization learns about what advertising works and what does not.

The ads whose outcome performance can be most easily and validly tested in the field are direct-response ads sent to different samples drawn from mailing lists. The ad that generates the most orders or inquiries and keeps on pulling (after several repetitions) is clearly the most effective and should be used as the message theme and creative material in a more general advertising campaign. The standard approach to testing a TV campaign is to use day-after recall (DAR). Interviewers elicit feedback from respondents who claimed to watch the TV program the previous day and ask them to recall specific copy points. Improved versions of this approach measure the delayed effects of multiple exposures on preferences as well as awareness. The interviewers mask the brand name in an ad and ask respondents to recall it. These latter approaches are fairer tests of the effects of ads whose goal is to influence emotions rather than change beliefs.

The Starch Recognition Tests use a similar approach to determine the effectiveness of test ads placed in specific magazines. Despite some measurement problems, such recall tests do give a rough measure of the attention-grabbing or pulling power of an ad. The problem is that such tests encourage sensationalized ads. As one crusty advertising executive points out, if you want to score high on DAR or Starch ratings, "Put a gorilla in a jockstrap" in the ad. His prescription for increasing product mind share and sales is not as definitive.

Copy Pretesting

The objective of testing the potential effectiveness of an advertising campaign prior to launching it is to make sure the creatives achieve the targeting/positioning and message strategy objectives. Several approaches can be used. The minimal approach to pretesting creatives is to conduct one-on-one discussions with a small sample of consumers. The subjects are exposed to a test ad (either as a rough storyboard or in its finished form) along with several unrelated and competitive comparison advertisements. After ad exposure, the subjects are asked to recall the content of the test ad or to express thoughts about it.

If the subjects cannot "play back" the most important elements of the test ad, cannot remember the brand name, or react negatively to elements of the ad, then the creative staff must go back to the drawing board. Pretesting is most useful for newsworthy or informational-persuasive strategies but is not good for ads that use image and feeling strategies. Subjects often have difficulty expressing emotional reactions created by an ad, and one exposure of such an ad is seldom enough to register any effect.

Theater testing is a more controlled approach to evaluating a finished TV ad. Respondents are recruited by phone or mail and invited to view new TV shows with commercials embedded in the programming. A raffle or drawing held before and after the exposure to the ads offers each participant a choice of "gifts" (the test and competitive products). This enables the survey conductors to measure changes in choice preferences that result from one, two, or three exposures to the ad. Written evaluations of the show and the ads are also obtained.

These techniques are limited in their discriminative and predictive powers. Focus groups and theater tests are able to identify a *very* good and a *very* bad ad, but they do not discriminate well among good, average, and bad ads.

The most sophisticated approach to testing an ad is offered by Information Resources, Inc. (IRI). IRI's BehaviorScan approach can test various TV commercials by broadcasting them to selected homes in their test markets and tracking with retail sales data their effect at the local grocery stores. It can be used by packaged-goods manufacturers to test market a new product and to test a new advertising campaign against an old one. A.C. Nielsen Co. and Burke Marketing Services, Inc., have developed similar monitoring systems. Recent research with tracking systems has produced some fascinating insights, including the conclusion that increasing the advertising of established brands more often than not has *no* effect on sales.[22] (See also Chapter 15 figure on the effectiveness of television advertising.)

Identifying and Controlling Variance

Output control involves converting objectives into specific, measurable standards, finding ways to measure the standards, reporting the results in user-friendly ways, interpreting and diagnosing the exceptional results, taking corrective action, and documenting the diagnosis and action taken. According to quality guru Edward Deming, the first task is to focus on and eliminate the *special* causes of exceptional negative results.[23] These are the one-time performance blips related to human or system failure. When these are reduced, management then can turn to the variation in performance created by *common* causes within the organization, such as worker ability and motivation, equipment, poorly designed activity scheduling, and basic management systems. These variations are much more difficult to reduce. They are within the control limits but still differ from the average. Figure 19.4 shows how Xerox significantly reduced the common causes of its billing system errors from 5 percent to the company's goal of 0.25 percent.[24] Xerox decreased errors in each of the activities that made up its billing production routine by changing each activity so it was less prone to error and by introducing new controls on each activity.

Performance is the overall average output and *conformance* is the extent to which results do not deviate from an average. Quality control seeks to first increase conformance and then raise performance. However, it is much easier to monitor and adjust machines and production processes to eliminate common causes of variance than it is to adjust marketing control. A firm has greater control over its production process. Marketing processes do not have the same quality of feedback information, and they depend on variances in distributor and customer behavior that are very difficult to control.

The principles are, however, still the same: The firm must construct a flowchart of the activity schedule that describes how the process should work and then construct a second flowchart to describe how the process actually does work. Comparing the two activity schedules identifies the inefficiencies, makes simpler procedures more evident, and points out the sources and causes of variability in completion time or quality of output. Such flowcharts also help members of a cross-functional team organize their collective thoughts and come to a common understanding of what has been happening and what has to happen. The input/output performance and conformance of each task in the activity schedule need to be tracked. Each subsequent task results from its antecedent tasks and so has a vital interest in the antecedent tasks' performance and

---

[22] Magid M. Abraham and Leonard M. Lodish, "Getting the Most out of Advertising and Promotion," *Harvard Business Review* (May/June 1990): 50–60.

[23] Mary Walton, *The Deming Management Method* (New York: Putnam, 1986).

[24] Norman E. Rickard, "Customer Satisfaction = Repeat Business," in *Creating Customer Satisfaction*, ed. Earl L. Bailey (New York: The Conference Board, 1990), 44.

Figure 19.4 **Identifying and Reducing Common Causes of Service Error Rates**

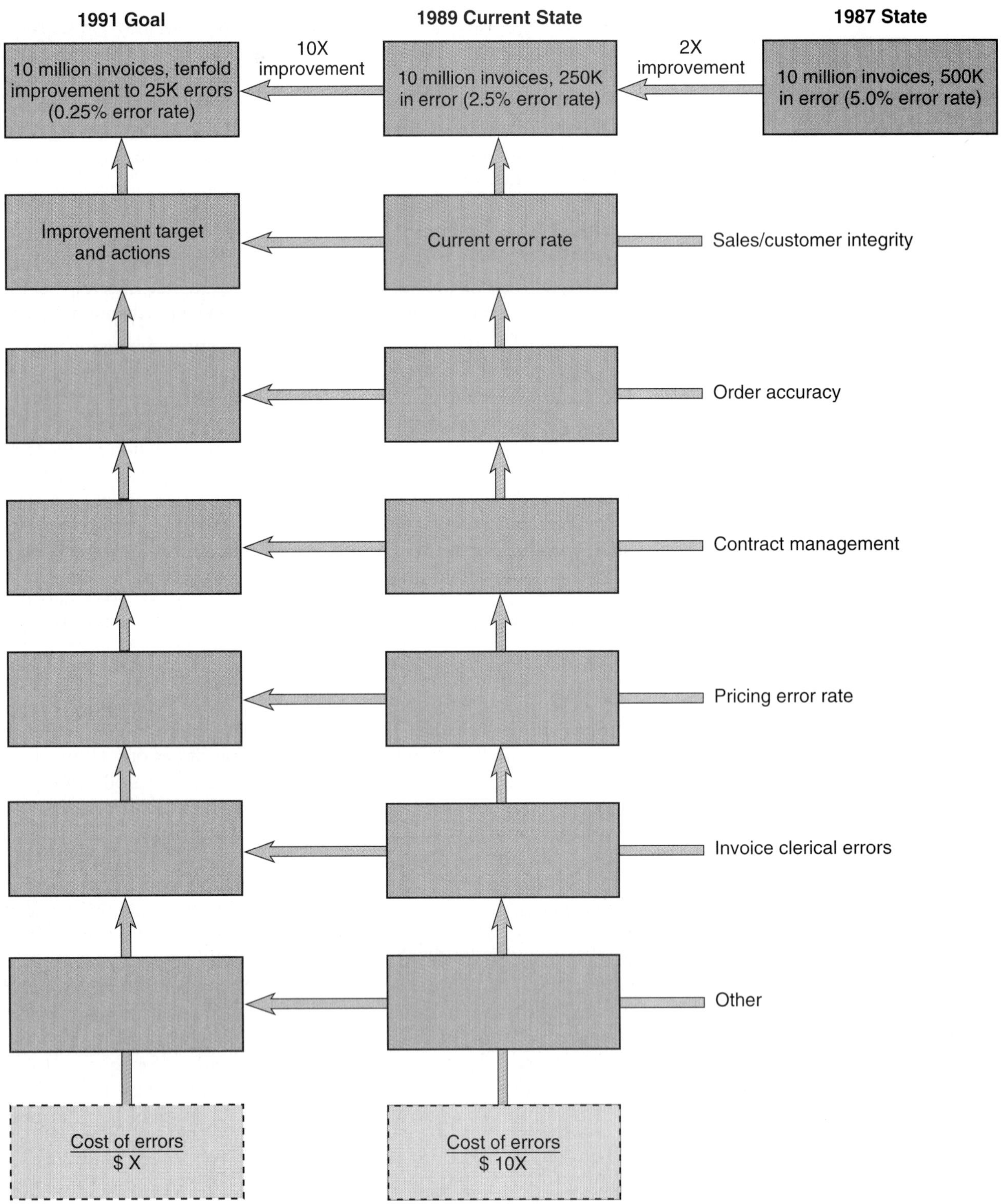

The monitoring of output error rates for the overall billing system and its specific functions or activities leads to the identification of causes and to process control by changing subroutines and systems as described in Figure 19.2.

conformance. In this sense, the system has some built-in internal controls. For example, in flute making when one craftsman hands a piece to a fellow worker, the piece is only accepted if it has the right look and feel. This hand-to-hand checking is a very effective form of built-in quality control.[25]

The Fishbone diagram or Ishikawa diagram (after its inventor Kaoru Ishikawa) is a useful tool for identifying performance variance. It is a cause-and-effect diagram where the effect is stated on the far right of the figure and the causes of the variance are presented as branches. The result is a figure that looks similar to a fish skeleton. The typical causes of variance in process output are material, machine, and manpower inputs and process methods and measurement (the 5Ms). Figure 19.5 presents two different fishbone diagrams that identify the causes of variance in salesperson effectiveness and product delivery time. The figures (based on Chapters 12 and 13) demonstrate the versatility of the tool.

Exception Reporting Systems

To avoid being buried in output data from routine, ongoing marketing activities, many marketers use an exception management reporting system. It reports only exceptional results, those that deviate significantly from what was planned or budgeted. When this occurs, the system reports the situation in detail. For example, it may present the results of the previous five reporting periods so a visual trend analysis can be taken to help diagnose the cause. The benefits to a manager are obvious. He or she can focus attention and management on the exceptions, good or bad. Many production, accounting, and marketing information systems already have this capability, and, if not, their report writing can be modified to accommodate such triggers. Immediate exception reporting is a crucial part of total quality management because TQM requires that deviations from accepted performance be corrected immediately.

For example, Cypress Semiconductor Corp. in Silicon Valley, California, has its computer-based purchasing system designed so it completely shuts down if an order fails to arrive on time and if no one has explained to senior management why it is late.[26] To start up the system again, the supplier has to be contacted, a new delivery date set, and the information reported to the chief financial officer. This system goes beyond exception reporting; it demands a response and creates so much inconvenience that it quickly eliminates such errors and increases just-in-time inventory productivity. It is an example of output control in that it responds to unfavorable information, but it is also an example of process control because it makes sure the correct process routines are followed and orders are received on time.

The way an intensive care unit operates in a hospital provides a good analogy of an effective exception-reporting marketing information system. Patients using intensive-care equipment have their vital life signs connected to several machines. The machines are preset to set off an alarm if, for example, the patient's blood pressure or pulse rate fall below a certain level. Intensive-care machines do not ring alarms when the patient's vital signs become better than normal, but an exception management system *should* do this. Such cases may identify new cost-saving efficiencies or sales initiatives that should be adopted throughout the system. Under-budget spending is also not necessarily a good sign, for it may indicate that a particular campaign is

[25] Scott D. N. Cook and Duora Yanow, "Culture and Organization Learning," *Journal of Management Inquiry* 2, no. 4 (December 1993).

[26] Richard Brandt, "Here Comes the Attack of the Killer Software," *Business Week*, December 9, 1991, 70.

Figure 19.5 **Fishbone Diagrams That Identify Sources of Variance**

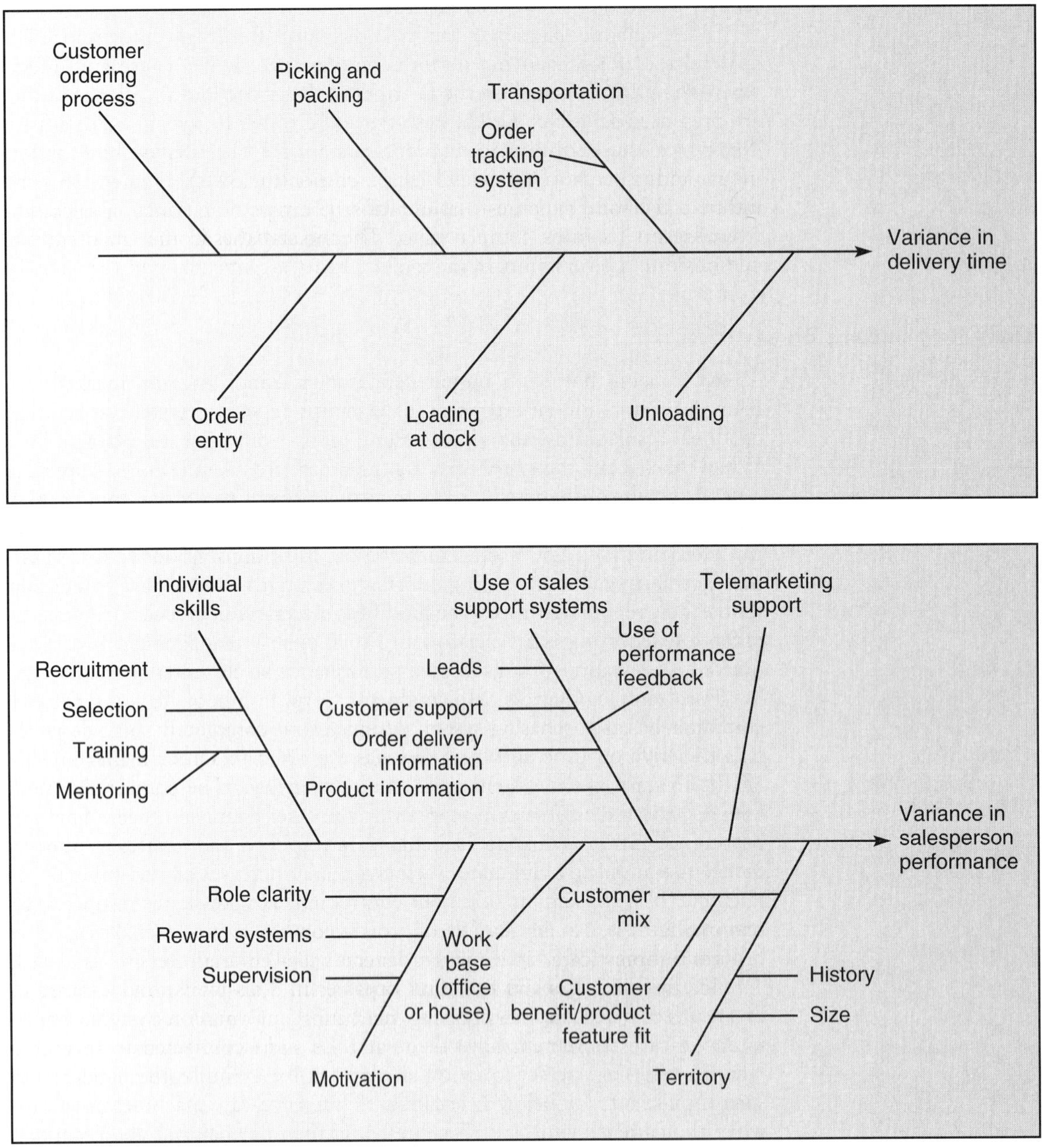

These figures are used by quality experts to identify the sources of variance and, hence, the drivers of quality conformance. For delivery time, the major sources of variance, and hence the drivers of quality delivery service, are order processing and transportation. A weak order tracking system can mean the order gets lost during transportation. Diagnosing variance in salesperson performance is much more difficult, as is evident from the complexity of the figure.

not being implemented. In seasonal business, fast exception reporting is crucial because it enables quick responses.

Choice of Measures and Accountability

It is important to spend time thinking about which performance measures and level of analysis should be reported and what other statistics should have preset exception reporting triggers. The individual or teams held accountable for particular process performance measures should make the final choice of level of analysis and trigger points. Key marketing statistics are daily, weekly, or monthly forward orders, shipments, inventory, and critical expense-to-sales ratios. The reporting system also could include ratios of returns to sales, complaints to sales, and statistics from regular consumer and trade surveys. The upper and lower alert limits around planned (expected or budgeted) performance also should be the decision of the individual or teams who must react to the information. Also, some types of trigger points (such as sales and inventory) may have to be adjusted seasonally.

Accountability should be considered when deciding on the level of analysis. If different line executives are responsible for territorial, regional, and product group performance, sales and expenses should be aggregated by sales territory, region, and product group. An executive cannot be responsible for performance if what he or she is responsible for is not measured and reported by the firm's management information system. Executive information systems developed in the mid-1980s organize and integrate the existing databases of an organization so the performance statistics an executive is responsible for managing can be tracked. Costing around $20,000 for hardware and software, they normally use a Windows-based spreadsheet such as Excel or Lotus 1-2-3 as the interface.

Control Charts

When a deviant operating statistic is flagged, a report should be produced that contains the recent operating history, perhaps in a chart similar to that illustrated in Figure 19.6. In this simple control chart, it is clear the marketing expense-to-sales ratio has been climbing steadily over time. It is not a one-time blip caused by a special event that led to underspending in a previous period, but it is a definite trend that probably can be diagnosed. It also may be useful to have the system report the previous year's performance as well as the last time the exception limits were exceeded.

Future sophisticated information systems will allow managers to record for future reference the diagnosis and remedial steps taken. This would allow future management teams to find out when previous exceptional deviations occurred, what the diagnoses revealed, which remedial steps were taken, and how everything worked out.

Exception management systems will feed crucial information into an organization's computer files recording the history of a product or sales region. Given that many people spend only five to ten years with the same company, fewer people are around for younger executives to question regarding how problems were handled in the past. The greatly expanded storage capacity of computers will make it easy to capture and attach exception or contingency management decision information to critical past operating statistics and, hence, partially (but certainly not completely) compensate for the loss of the wisdom and insights of "old salts." Such archived information also will be valuable in evaluating management performance.

Figure 19.6 An Output Performance Control Chart

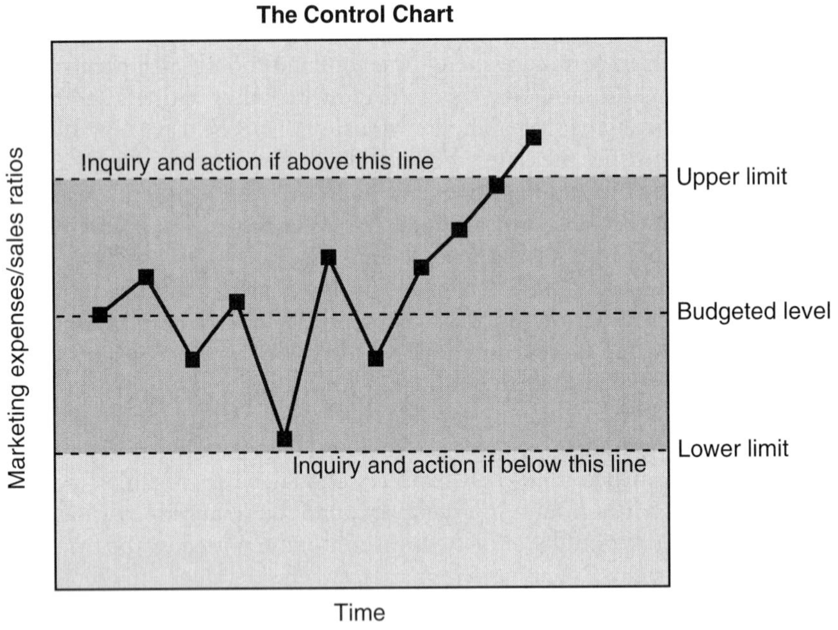

This chart reveals a clear trend in the marketing expense-to-sales ratio. It suggests a common problem that has a negative trend. An exception appears to be the drop expressed by the fifth square. Future sophisticated information systems will generate such control charts on a computer screen and allow the manager to record in a window for future reference the diagnosis and remedial steps taken. This would be a real advantage for the next brand or product manager who comes along. He or she will have access to information on when previous exceptional deviations occurred, the diagnosis of what caused them, the remedial steps taken, and the outcome.

Sales and Profit Variance

An important aspect of control is that it allows firms to compare actual, bottom-line performance to planned or budgeted performance. A profit variance may be the result of some things going right and other things going wrong. Variance analysis attempts to untangle some of these swings and roundabouts. In particular, variance analysis untangles deviations from the plan that are the result of miscalculations in estimating total market size, market share, price, and costs. It identifies problem areas and, to a lesser degree, diagnoses problems to determine possible causes.

The variance analysis section of management accounting courses traditionally has been very intimidating for marketing majors. In part, this is because the potential to make compounding computational mistakes is very great when variance analysis is done by hand. The VARIANCE spreadsheet (see Table 19.3) takes care of such concerns.[27] It extends the traditional variance analysis in two important ways. First, it separates manufacturing and marketing activity costs so researchers can determine

[27] This spreadsheet is based on James M. Hulbert and Norman E. Toy, "A Strategic Framework for Marketing Control," *Journal of Marketing* (April 1977): 12–21.

Table 19.3 Performance Compared to Plan Variance Analysis

	PLANNED	ACTUAL	VARIANCE
Market size	40,000,000	50,000,000	10,000,000
Sales volume	20,000,000	22,000,000	2,000,000
Market share	50%	44%	–6%
Price	$0.5000	$0.4773	($0.0227)
Variable unit costs			
Production	$0.2000	$0.2000	$0.0000
Marketing	0.1000	0.1000	0.0000
Total variable unit costs	$0.3000	$0.3000	$0.0000
Unit contribution margin	$0.2000	$0.1773	($0.0227)
Total revenue	$10,000,000	$10,500,600	($500,600)
Total variable costs	6,000,000	6,600,000	($600,000)
Total contribution margin	$ 4,000,000	$ 3,900,600	($ 99,400)

Variances	ACTUAL TO PLANNED
Price/Cost $[(Ca - Cp) \times Qa]$	($499,400)
Volume Variance	
Market share $[(Sa - Sp) \times Ma \times Cp]$	(600,000)
Market size $[(Ma - Mp) \times Sp \times Cp]$	1,000,000)
Total volume variance $[(Qa - Qp) \times Cp]$	$400,000)
Total contribution variance	($99,400)

C = Contribution margin per unit
S = Market share
M = Market size
Q = Quantity sold
a = Actual
p = Planned

how these costs deviated from plan-influenced profit. Second, it allows an after-the-fact adjustment of the initial plan's targets to account for totally unforeseeable events (for instance, a competitor entry or exit, bad weather, a plant strike or shutout, or a dramatic rise in raw material costs). This helps explain performance variance that was completely beyond the control of management. Such a variance from the budget does not reflect on the quality of the environmental forecasts or the implementation and control of prices and costs. The remaining performance variance then can be traced to poor estimates of market size and market share or poor price, manufacturing cost, and marketing cost control.

The following examples will show the difference between price and volume variance. Suppose planned sales are 5,000 units at $10 per unit for a total of $50,000. Actual sales equal 5,000 units at $8 per unit for a total of $40,000. The $10,000 total variance is due entirely to the actual price being $2 lower than planned. Price variance can be found by taking the difference between actual price and planned price multiplied by planned units. Now suppose actual volume sold equals 3,000 units at $10 per unit for a total of $30,000. In this case, the $20,000 variance is due entirely to the actual volume being lower than the planned volume. Volume variance is calculated by taking the difference between planned and actual volume multiplied by planned price.

Volume variance can be caused by two factors: market share and market size. To determine the share component of the total volume variance, take the difference between actual and planned share, multiplied by the product of actual market size times planned contribution per unit (see the calculation in Table 19.3). Similarly, market size variance can be found by taking the difference between actual and planned market size, multiplied by the product of planned share times contribution per unit. The sum of the market share variance and market size variance yields the total volume variance.

The first step in the variance analysis spreadsheet requires the entry into Table 19.3 of planned estimates and actual market size, market share, unit price, production variable unit costs, and marketing variable unit costs. The spreadsheet does the rest. In this example, the total contribution was $99,400 less than expected (i.e., it deviated from the plan by 2.5 percent). It can be traced to the market share being 12 percent lower than expected (44 percent rather than 50 percent) and the price being 4.8 percent lower than expected. Clearly, a deteriorating competitive position has occurred. In fact, the situation would have been much worse had not the market size turned out to be much larger (25 percent higher) than expected. Although this was a fortuitous compensating variance, it is really not good news because it may indicate a loss of new business to competitors. The only outstanding performance was the control of costs. The Fishbone diagram in Figure 19.7 illustrates this analysis.

Uncontrollable Variance

The REVISVAR spreadsheet presented in Table 19.4 on page 742 increases the sophistication of the analysis by allowing an after-the-fact adjustment of planned performance because of unforeseeable circumstances. In the example, the circumstances were an unexpected increase in market size, a drop in market share, and a drop in industry and company price. The unforeseeable increase in demand resulted from a fire in a European manufacturing plant that increased industry exports by a million units. The underestimation in demand error therefore should be reduced by 1,000,000 (see the "Revised" column). A new competitor also entered the market and, if this had been anticipated, company market share would have been reduced by a percentage point. Because of the new competitor's entry pricing strategy, the planned average unit selling price also would have been revised down two cents. The overall lower market prices caused by the new entry may, in fact, have accounted for some of the unexpected increases in demand.

Overall, actual performance was $284,400 better than the revised expected performance, largely because of the underestimation of the market. Revised performance was estimated to be $383,800 lower than the initially planned performance mainly because of the price cost variance. The net effect was a shortfall of $99,400 in the actual as compared to the initially planned contribution. The diagnosis is that the problem was not price control but the initial and revised estimates of market size and market share. This case study of the VARIANCE and REVISVAR spreadsheets demonstrates the power of variance analysis to diagnose causes and assign responsibility for variations in key performance measures.

Figure 19.7 **Diagnosing Sources of Profit Contribution Variance**

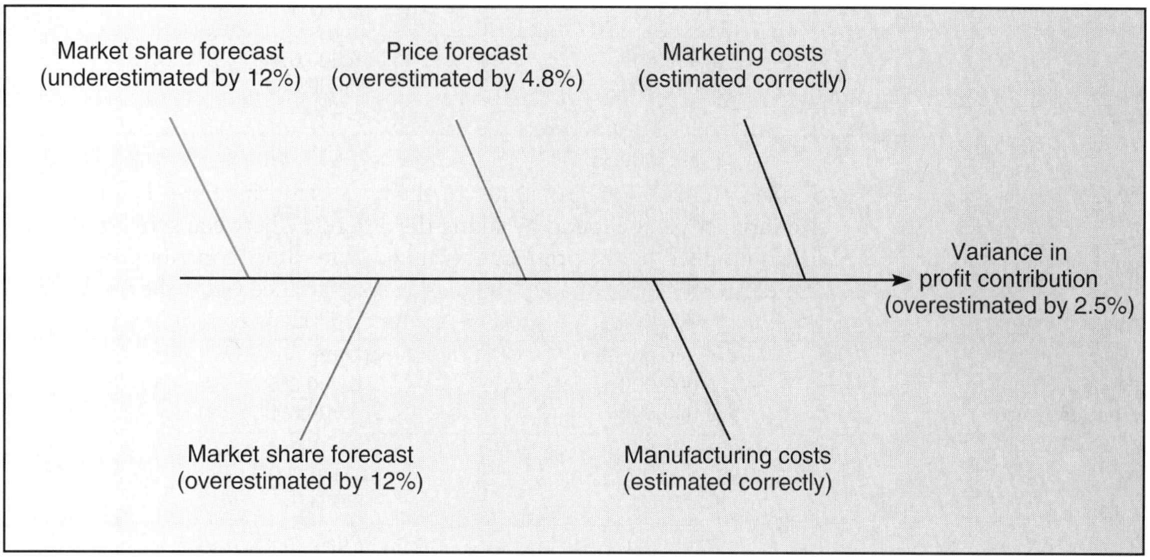

This figure presents just one time period's performance variance (see Table 19.3). The Fishbone diagram can be used to summarize variances over many periods and then these diagrams can be used to identify the typical causes of performance variance.

Discussion Questions and Minicases

1. The following is a true horror story about customer disservice. Describe the types of service process controls you would implement to make sure such an incident never would occur again.

On Thursday, 9 A.M., I made a call to CVI (Cable Vision Industries) to schedule a service call. I have two cable connections; however, only one was working. I was told the serviceman would be at my house between 8 A.M. and noon the following day (Friday). On Friday morning, I was up before 8 A.M. and ready for the serviceman. I worked on a project while sitting about fifteen feet from the front door. My seven-year-old was home and playing and I also had four dogs indoors. At *eleven* o'clock, I received a call from CVI's office saying that the serviceman was on his way. At around *12:15*, I called CVI to find out why the serviceman hadn't arrived yet. I was told to hold the line, I did —for around 18 minutes. Being put on hold for 5 minutes is a very long time; 18 minutes is an eternity. Finally, I was told by the operator that she couldn't contact the serviceman because he wasn't answering her call. She said she knew he was going home at 1:30, so he should be at my place soon.

At 1:40 P.M., I again called CVI. A different operator answered the phone. I had to explain the entire situation again. But this time, I at least got a name—Linda. She puts me on hold for around 12 minutes. Back on the line again, she tells me they still can't contact the serviceman. I tell her that I would like to talk to a supervisor. I'm back on hold now for about 8 minutes. Back on the line she (Linda) tells me that the

Table 19.4 Revised Variance Analysis: Accounting for Uncontrollable Events

	PLANNED	ACTUAL	REVISED
Market size	40,000,000	50,000,000	41,000,000
Sales volume	20,000,000	22,000,000	20,090,000
Market share	50%	44%	49%
Price	$0.5000	$0.4773	0.4800
Variable unit costs			
Production	$0.2000	$0.2000	$0.2000
Marketing	0.1000	0.1000	0.1000
Total variable unit costs	$0.3000	$0.3000	$0.3000
Unit contribution margin	$0.2000	$0.1773	$0.1800
Total revenue	$10,000,000	$10,500,600	$9,643.200
Total variable costs	6,000,000	6,600,000	6,027,000
Total contribution margin	$ 4,000,000	$ 3,900,600	$3,616,200
Variances	ACTUAL TO PLANNED	ACTUAL TO REVISED	REVISED TO PLANNED
Price/Cost $[(Ca - Cp) \times Qa]$	($499,400)	($59,400)	($401,800)
Volume Variance			
Market share $[(Sa - Sp) \times Ma \times Cp]$	(600,000	(400,000)	(82,000)
Market size $[(Ma - Mp) \times Sp \times Cp]$	1,000,000	793,800	100,000
Total volume variance $[(Qa - Qp) \times Cp]$	$400,000	$343,800	$ 18,000
Total contribution variance	($99,400)	$284,400	($383,800)

C = Contribution margin per unit
S = Market share
M = Market size
Q = Quantity sold
a = Actual
p = Planned

supervisor said they would try to contact the serviceman and let me know. I called back again around 2 P.M. and asked to talk to a supervisor. I did not go through the story again. After waiting 14 minutes, I was told that there were three supervisors on duty now and until 5 P.M. However, the operator could not get in contact with any of them. She said she would keep trying and have one of them call me.

It's now 2:45 P.M. I am talking to another operator whose name is also Linda. I go through the entire story again. I waited another 12 minutes. Then I was asked if anyone had left a message on the front door. I said he couldn't have missed me. I hadn't even left my working space by the front door long enough to take a shower, in fear of missing the serviceman. I also told her I had four dogs in the house that go crazy barking when the bell rings or someone knocks on the door. I was put back on hold. While on hold, I took the cordless phone to the door and there it was; a door-hanger message that read "Sorry We Missed You!" The serviceman wrote on the card, "Will need to be home." The time was also written in at 11:45 A.M. He never rang the bell. He just hung the note and left.

The operator came back on the line and I told her about the doorknob message. On hold again for 4 minutes and I'm finally speaking to a supervisor. I repeat the story, which is becoming a saga. The supervisor (Malena) says to me, "Wait a minute, let me check your. . ." she started saying "account" then started mumbling to herself. I could hear her punching the keys of her computer. I was saying to myself, *yes, please check my account and you will see it is flawless, a good account that you wouldn't want to lose.* I had the feeling that if our account wasn't just right (up to date payments, etc.) then she would have fluffed me off. When she came back on the line, I told her that I felt as a supervisor she should know that I was told over two hours ago that a service person would call me, and over an hour ago I was told a supervisor would contact me. I also told her that I have been given the runaround all day and that I had spent more than an hour just on hold, not counting interacting with the operators.

She then says, "We will have someone out today." I said, "Great, but when? I cannot sit here all day waiting." I asked her to give me a time and I would be back by then. She said she couldn't do that because she has no idea how long each service call would take and that they run anywhere from 5 minutes to an hour. She said she could set it for a certain time, and someone will call 30 minutes ahead of time, so we set the time at *after* 5:30 P.M. Five minutes after getting off the phone with the supervisor, the first Linda I talked to hours ago called and asked, "I'm calling about the third cable hookup you need." I thanked her and said I did not want a third hookup, but that I had two hookups, one of which was not working. Before I could say anything else, she put me on hold. After another 6-minute wait, she came back on the line. Before she could say any more, I cut in to tell her that I had just (10 minutes ago) talked to the supervisor and the matter has been resolved. The operator then wanted the name of the supervisor I talked to so that she could check with her and get her own records in order.

At 5:05 P.M., the serviceman shows at our front door. No call ahead and *before* the designated time. Would we have received another "Sorry We Missed You" had we not come home early from doing some chores? After checking a few wires and changing a few, he had the set working. In the middle of his working, he received a call from CVI's office. When he got off the phone, he asked if someone from here called the office, "irate" about the service. I said I was not irate, however, I had been on the phone all day trying to get this matter resolved. He then said, "It must have been something, because they sent me from the other side of town to do this job." He was at our home for approximately one minute. However he did leave a tool at our house and had to come back an hour later to pick it up.

2. The Geneva-based International Standards Organization has produced an extensive list of quality standards (ISO 9000) that apply to numerous functions within an organization.[28] Some examples are listed here:

- *Design:* Sets a planned approach for meeting product/service specifications.
- *Inspection and testing:* Requires workers and managers to verify that all production activities are undertaken according to process specifications.

[28] Jonathan B. Levine, "Want EC Business? You Have Two Choices," *Business Week*, October 19, 1992, 58–59.

- *Training:* Specifies methods to identify training needs and keep records.
- *Purchasing:* Specifies ways of approving suppliers and ordering procedures.

Independent ISO auditors inspect and certify that a firm meets the standards required by the Economic Community. Certification can cost hundreds of thousands of dollars and take as long as eighteen months. The ISO 9000 certification has been adopted in fifty-five countries. What impact do you think it will have on global marketing?

3. Federal Express puts a scanner code on all its packages, and the code is scanned whenever the package is moved. Experts predict that all freight will have such codes in the future. What impact will this have on logistics control and services?
4. A firm makes two types of jets for jet-skis, Widjets and Gadjets. The production costs for these two items are presented in the table on the left.

WIDJETS	GADJETS
Labor at $10/hour	
$40	$200
Materials and parts	
300	300
Processing at $20/hour	
200	40
Total	
$540	$540

The firm makes one thousand Widjets and one thousand Gadjets a year, and its total overhead costs for R&D, design, sales, and administration are $770,000. The selling price for both types of jets is $1,100.

The traditional cost accounting method of allocating overhead and processing costs involves the amount of direct labor cost. Subtract total direct labor and material costs from total costs and divide by total labor costs. This gives the allocation per dollar of labor cost to be assigned to each Widjet and Gadjet. Using this method of costing, what is the cost of producing a Widjet and Gadjet? Another way to allocate costs is to charge to each jet the direct costs of processing and then allocate the overhead as a function of processing time. Using this costing approach, what is the cost of a Widjet and a Gadjet? What is the more correct way? Does it make a difference to the Widjet and Gadjet product managers? Which is closer to activity-based costing? How could additional activity-based costing techniques be used to correctly cost the Widjets and Gadjets?

5. A well-known overnight delivery company discovered that most of its customers packaged their shipments in standard-sized cartons that could be processed by customer remote data entry, bar code generation, attachment, reading and tracking, and automated sorting technology. But some customers wished to ship uncrated bicycles, another to ship unpackaged mufflers, and yet another to ship mesh bags of beach balls. Servicing these customers required special handling, sorting, and shipping space, such special service that doing business with these customers was unprofitable. What should the company consider when deciding whether to raise its prices for these customers?
6. What fairness and motivation problems might arise with profit sharing?
7. Some consultants have suggested that a better alternative to profit sharing is a profit-related pay plan where the employee's salary is supplemented if the company makes a profit, but it is also reduced if the company makes a loss. What control problem might result from such a scheme?
8. A program to reward employee suggestions seems to be a very sound idea, but how might it be difficult to implement so as to be useful in improving a firm's marketing management?
9. Why has customer service become more important to auto buyers since the quality of American-made cars has been raised to almost the level of imports?
10. In April 1993, the Kennedy School of Government at Harvard University launched a project designed to pass legislation that gives shareholders more rights and control over management. One of its proposed regulations would require firms to track customer satisfaction surveys and publish them in quarterly and annual reports. What does this activity have to do with shareholder rights? What effect do you think such a law would have on management?
11. Using surveys to monitor customer satisfaction has become a very important marketing control measure over the past decade. But are any other satisfaction indices important?
12. Monitoring customer dissatisfaction is a key component of competitive rationality, but often customers will not report their dissatisfaction. What marketing tactic can a firm

employ to make sure dissatisfaction is reported by customers and brought to the attention of senior management?

13. Why is the percentage of new products contributing to sales such a critical measure? Should it be an absolute or comparative measure?
14. How can product managers create political problems for a sales manager who is trying to control the allocation of his or her sales effort across product groups?
15. Diagnose the performance of the sales rep reported in Table 19.2. What action would you take if you were the sales manager?
16. Why might a firm pretest its advertising creatives rather than rely on measures after it has appeared in the media? Who should do the pretesting?

Genius is 1 percent inspiration and 99 percent perspiration.

Thomas Edison

Imagination is more important than knowledge.

Albert Einstein

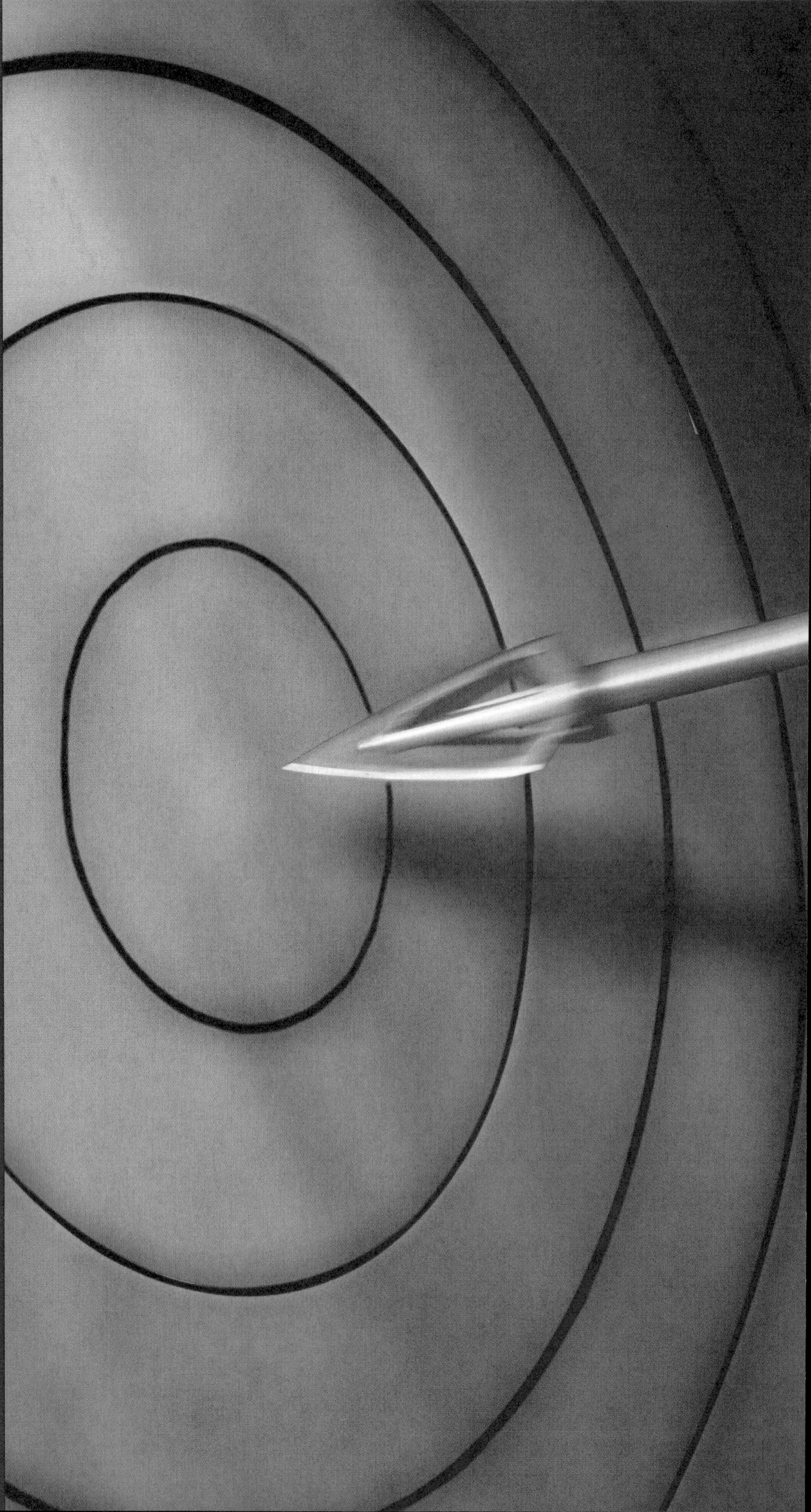

APPENDIX ONE

A Guide to Creative Decision Making

It is a Monday morning in June, show-and-tell time of the year. The brand manager has been delaying work on the annual marketing plan, rationalizing that the day-to-day implementation and firefighting problems of managing a brand must take priority. New strategy development has been postponed several times because it is such an unstructured, usually unproductive exercise. An inadequate environmental report containing various unrelated market research reports and some newspaper clippings on competitive activity and economic trends has been pushed around the desk, the way a child plays with indigestible food on a plate. The manager actually knows a lot more about the environment, but even though this internal information is somehow stored in memory, the manager cannot readily access it. First, new facts have to be absorbed, and then the manager has to start creating ideas. The outward evidence of this process may involve a lot of head scratching, ear pulling, forehead massaging, hand clenching, doodling, and gazing out the window. What is going on inside the marketing manager's mind during such moments of intense cognitive effort, and what facts, structure, and procedures will help?

The lot of marketing decision makers is not easy. First, few universal marketing laws can be applied to the unique product market each marketing manager faces. Second, a variety of factors can bias a manager's perceptions and judgments of the marketplace. Third, competing marketing managers are continually disturbing the equilibrium. The moment one manager thinks the situation is under control, some other enterprising mover and shaker changes the situation. Creative decision making is like playing chess with multiple

opponents who frequently change the rules by, for example, moving their knights four squares forward and two to the side instead of making the standard play. But at least chess is played at only arm's length. The competitive market game is played from a greater physical, temporal, and conceptual distance. Furthermore, strategies are unreliably implemented, resulting in outcomes that are difficult to measure and that extend over an indeterminant length of time. Before these results can be observed, they are affected by poorly understood competitor and facilitator actions and reactions. The overlapping factors that influence creative decision making can result in quite a quagmire—one that the manager often must face alone.

The manager's mind must absorb, structure, and create at a very abstract level of perception and imagination. This is the *art* of marketing management. However, it being an artistic skill does not mean managers cannot apply logic and science to improve their understanding and problem solving.

This appendix begins with theories of the organization and processing of information. The second section examines the use and misuse of history and experience. The third section describes the creative problem-solving process and presents suggestions on how to improve each stage of this process. The fourth section discusses the organization and management of group problem-solving situations and explains how to increase the productivity of group and team problem solving. Metacognition, an awareness of our own thought processes, was introduced in Chapter 17 in the discussion of activity-schedule memory. Metacognition theory says that the more aware we become of *how* we think, the more we will be able to improve the *way* we think. ■

How Information Is Stored in Memory

Cognitive psychologists have proposed a variety of theories of possible memory structures for storing and processing information. It is generally assumed that the content and organization of these structures is learned over time and will vary greatly among individuals. It is believed that experts, in comparison with novices, have developed much richer cognitive structures in their domain of expertise and possess a superior ability to recognize and comprehend relevant patterns of information in the environment. While some theorists have advanced the controversial assertion that people are born with some basic cognitive structures (for example, visual perception and language) or naive theories about physics and psychology, we primarily build our memory structures from direct experience and secondhand knowledge (vicarious learning). It is this capacity to learn that enables people to vary so much in knowledge and behavior and to be so creative, adaptable, and successful as a species.

The dominant metaphor in the twentieth century for describing the human mind has been the machine metaphor. In the early 1900s, the human mind was compared to the workings of an automobile, while in recent decades the mind has been commonly viewed as an information processing computer. Today, many of the standard models of memory structure and processes are based on computer models of artificial intelligence, which are favored, in part, by cognitive scientists because they are easily quantifiable. However, it has become increasingly clear that traditional structural models, based on the manipulation of meaningless, abstract symbols, cannot adequately account for the mental processes necessary to negotiate a complex, dynamic world (or market). As some psychologists have recently noted, people in the real world "face a situation in which there are several tasks operative at once, some embedded within others, some of which seem to run in parallel, all of which need to be discovered. . . . Other people with variable relations to the multiple tasks at hand are a part of the stimulus environment . . . [and] the subject is operating on an environment that simultaneously operates on the subject . . . in a continuous process of interaction."[1] Some recently developed theories of memory and cognition, referred to collectively as "embodied cognition,"[2] were designed to better account for the flexible mental processes and skills such as process thinking and activity schedule memory that are necessary for business managers to succeed in a dynamic environment.

In brief, embodied cognition views human memory as a dynamic and flexible meaning system. In such a system, categories of thought are heavily context-dependent, mental representations are rich, multisensory perceptual (that is, *embodied*) images with gestalt properties, and meaning is understood in terms of how the individual (constrained by his or her physical capabilities) can interact with an object or other person in a given situation. Generative compositional mechanisms combine the basic perceptual *(embodied)* elements stored in memory and mesh them with patterns in the environment. An individual's understanding of abstract concepts is based on the metaphorical extension of basic concepts, encoded in terms of embodied action. This type of cognitive system offers an explanation for such phenomena as creativity and prospective thought and serves as the theoretical foundation for the model of activity schedule memory skills described in Chapter 17.

In the embodied view of cognition, two types of mental abilities are central to managerial skill performance: the ability to recognize, comprehend, and match patterns of activities, including dynamic processes, spatial and temporal information, and complex causal relationships; and the ability to block out distractions and focus on the specific task at hand. The basic principles of embodied cognition can be applied to other related cognitive skills that are essential to effective managerial performance, such as multitasking, innovation, learning from experience, transfer of knowledge to

---

[1] Michael Cole, Lois Hood, and Ray McDermott, "Ecological Niche Picking," in Ulric Neisser (ed.), *Memory Observed* (New York: Freeman, 1982); 366–373.

[2] Based on Lawrence W. Barsalou, "Flexibility, Structure, and Linguistic Vagary in Concepts: Manifestations of a Compositional System of Perceptual Symbols," in A. F. Collins, S. E. Gathercole, M. A. Conway, and P. E. Morris (eds.), *Theories of Memory,* eds. (Hillsdale, NJ: Erlbaum, 1993); 29–101; and Arthur M. Glenberg, "What Is Memory For," *Behavioral and Brain Sciences* (in press). Both theories are described and applied to marketing in Alan J. Malter, "An Introduction to Embodied Cognition: Implications for Consumer Research," in Kim P. Corfman and John Lynch (eds.), *Advances in Consumer Research,* vol. 23 (Provo, UT: Association for Consumer Research, 1996); 272–276.

novel situations, planning and coordination, time management, and the ability to perform tasks under pressure.

It Is Not What You Have but How You Use It

Problem solving is directly related to memory organization and structure. The famous Gestalt school of thought in psychology emphasized the structural understanding of facts: putting facts together in the right way and organizing them to create new meaning. This means marketers must structure environmental facts so they can use them better. They must organize how they think about the marketplace. The process of organizing environmental information prescribed by the STRATMESH procedure is such an attempt. This organization was called a mental model in Chapters 2 and 3. Chapters 4 through 8 described a number of such frameworks and models. After repeated use of the same consumer, channel, competitor, public policy, and company environment frameworks or mental models described in Chapter 2, a marketing planner will adopt this general framework as his or her own way of thinking about any product market. The more frequently such an organized way of thinking is used, the easier it will be for the manager to think about the environment this way.

New theories make the distinction between declarative knowledge (facts) and procedural knowledge (the skills we have learned, both physical and mental). John McEnroe developed exceptional motor responses for playing tennis. Albert Einstein developed brilliant mental motor responses for thinking about time, mass, and energy. Investigating competitive-rationality thought procedure is important because it will help explain what gives direction to a manager's thought and behavior and how thoughts and facts are connected.

Researchers at Carnegie-Mellon University, such as John R. Anderson, have created artificial-intelligence computer programs with logic built on hundreds, even thousands of condition-action pairs, called *production rules.*[3] These rules are based on the concept of "if x then y." For example, *if* Hal is the father of Joel and Joel is the father of Paul, *then* Hal is the grandfather of Paul. For the rule to apply, the thinker must be aware of the facts contained in x (that Hal is the father of Joel and Joel is the father of Paul). This depends on whether such facts can be pulled from memory or from outside information. Systems of these production rules can model psycholinguistic mental processes, mathematics skills, and problem solving. In the Rationality in Practice box, you are asked to solve a series of problems. By completing the entire water jug exercise, you will understand better the material presented later in this appendix.

Competitive Thinking Production Rules

An example of a marketing *strategy* production rule might be the following: *If* the consumers are price sensitive and our closest competitor drops its price, *then* we should consider dropping our price. It can be made more complicated by detailing the action, such as looking at the impact of a price decrease on other participants in the marketplace and on contribution margin. The importance of studying not only what managers know (that is, what they can access in memory) but also what mental procedures

[3] John R. Anderson, *The Architecture of Cognition* (Cambridge, MA: Harvard University Press, 1983).

they apply to such knowledge now becomes clear. A particular planning process is actually a set of recommended planning production rules that should be applied to the suggested strategy and environmental information. The STRATMESH process, described in Chapter 2, uses very clear procedures that describe how information should be used. Most planning systems are not specific in regard to *how* information should be used. This means individual planners must apply whatever intuitive information-usage rules or procedures they have learned.

The Thinking Skills of Expert Marketing Decision Makers

Expert chess or marketing strategists are very different from novices on three interrelated components: They are more knowledgeable (have access to more facts) about the subject, they have superior subject knowledge structure and organization that enable them to see the facts differently, and they possess many more plays, or procedures, triggered by their views of the facts.[4] The parallels among expert chess players, great entrepreneurs, and talented senior executives now should be clear and have been confirmed by research. Several extensive field studies provide strong evidence that skilled senior executives think differently from their lesser-skilled counterparts because they have richer, more complex, and more discriminating memory structures and well-learned, often intuitive ways of searching and using information. According to Daniel Isenberg in his article "How Senior Managers Think," senior managers can sense intuitively when a strategy-environment problem exists.[5] They have well-programmed and integrated implementation responses. This intuitive fluency in analysis and response is the result of well-organized and interrelated memory structures that interrogate the environmental facts and prompt *ah-ha!* strategy and implementation solutions. Their pattern recognition is so superior that they are much better at identifying a *new* environmental fact and at drawing higher order implications from such anomalistic information.

Experienced senior executives also are capable of stepping back and seeing the big picture, a skill that comes from possessing higher-order integrated information structures. In fact, some senior managers actively test strategic hypotheses to learn about the business. What appears to be action for action's sake is adding to experience and environmental information structures. Finally, senior managers appear to see the connections among problems and how solving one problem may create others. This suggests they are better at mentally meshing new problem-solving strategy with all aspects of the environment because of the quality of their environmental information structure and their frequent use of this structure in their day-to-day thinking. To put it simply, they are paid a lot to think a lot and to put all the pieces together.

Other researchers have observed the greater cognitive power of the senior executive in terms of how perceptions and thinking are organized. Senior executives can conceptualize whole systems and reason through the multiple consequences of strategy on consumers and competitors. Like chess masters, skilled managers also are more capable of making subtle distinctions and differentiating among environmental phenomena. In particular, they are adept at seeing a strategy or fact from *someone else's* point of view (for example, the different viewpoints of the different players in a market). As Walter Kiechel suggests in "How Executives Think," "thirteen ways of

---

[4] W. G. Chase and H. A. Simon, "Perception in Chess," *Cognitive Psychology* 4 (1973): 55–81.

[5] Daniel J. Isenberg, "How Senior Managers Think," *Harvard Business Review* (November/December 1984): 81–90.

Rationality in Practice

The Water Jug Problem

This problem will test your ability to think abstractly. Imagine you are working at a kitchen sink and on the bench in front of you is a large plastic jug that, when filled to the top, has a capacity of 29 quarts and a smaller jug that, when filled to the top, has a capacity of 3 quarts. The containers have no graduated markings. How can you use these two jugs to gather 20 quarts of water? Give yourself a minute to solve the problem.

The solution is to first fill the 29-quart jug and then fill the 3-quart jug three times from the larger jug.

The next problem is a little more complicated. You are now given a jug with a capacity of 21 quarts and a second with a capacity of 127 quarts, and you get to keep the 3-quart jug. Using all or any of these three jugs, obtain 100 quarts of water. Give yourself two minutes to solve this problem.

One solution is to fill the 127-quart container once and then remove the excess by filling the 21-quart jug once and 3-quart container twice ($127 - 21 = 106$; $106 - 3 = 103$; $103 - 3 = 100$). Another solution is to remove the excess water by filling the 3-quart jug nine times ($127 - (9 \times 3) = 100$).

Now that you understand the nature of the task, solve each of the following problems. You may use any or all of the measuring jugs described in each problem. Write down your solution beside each problem using the alphabetical code for each jar. For example, the production-rule solution to problem 1 is B – 3C. Time how long it takes you to solve all the problems.

looking at a blackbird" may be routine thinking for senior executives.[6] They also can think in more dimensions and are adept at going from the abstract *down* to the particular and back *up* again. This is further support that information is hierarchically stored and integrated by levels of abstraction and that the paths in these networks are frequently traveled and restructured. Another interesting field observation is that experienced executives start to test possible strategies against environmental facts much earlier in the problem-solving process than do novices, perhaps because they already have the memory structures in place to do so.

Decision Making Is Not for Everyone

Some evidence indicates that most people, managers or not, can only cope with two abstract dimensions and about ten concepts at once.[7] When situations are described in three or more dimensions or when we have to juggle a dozen or more factors at once, we become confused and start to simplify. The limitations in our capacity to think in the abstract may be even greater. Our evolutionary heritage influences our consumption decision making. It also influences our ability to make strategic decisions.

In his famous work on developmental psychology, Jean Piaget described the highest level of cognitive development as formal, operational thinking. A person with such hypothetical-deductive skill can imagine and test possible hypothetical strategies against facts. He or she also can understand and fluently use abstract concepts, such as

[6] Walter Kiechel, "How Executives Think," *Fortune*, February 4, 1985, 127–28.

[7] G. A. Miller, "The Magical Number Seven, Plus or Minus Two: Some Limits on Our Capacity for Processing Information," *Psychological Review* 63 (1956): 81–97.

PROBLEM	A	B	C	OBTAIN	SOLUTION
	GIVEN CONTAINER WITH THESE CAPACITIES:				
1		29	3	20	______
2	21	127	3	100	______
3	14	163	25	99	______
4	18	43	10	5	______
5	9	42	6	21	______
6	20	59	4	31	______
7	23	49	3	20	______
8	15	39	3	18	______
9	28	76	3	25	______
10	18	48	4	22	______
11	14	36	8	6	______

price elasticity. The bad news is that decades of testing and research have shown that not all adults (maybe only 50 percent) are capable of such formal thinking, and even those who can often do not use the skill in their problem-solving tasks. It is clear that a planner/strategist needs such skills if he or she is going to use mental methods to test possible strategies against environmental information structures. Planning that involves the understanding of and creative development of strategy requires the skills of induction (taking specific experiences and information and generalizing, or integrating, them into a higher order structure) *and* deduction (applying the generalizations and structural understanding to specific situations). It also requires the additional prospective memory skill of thinking ahead (that is, conjecture about what will happen). Little is known about this important competitive rationality skill.

Two alternative methods of managerial problem solving are available (see Figure 1). The *reproductive* approach recalls a successful past strategy and seeks to apply the same strategy to a similar situation. Its use of what is called *transduction logic* goes from the particular to the particular. Like teaching a dog a trick, the reproductive approach is a learned stimulus response, a reflexive problem-solving response that does not employ a higher-order understanding of the situation. One problem with reproductive thinking is that a short-term change in performance, such as a monthly downturn in sales, will produce a knee-jerk, firefighting response rather than careful reflection and a wait-and-see attitude. If sales bounce back the next month, then the outcome will reinforce the manager's shoot-from-the-hip style of decision making, even if the results are unrelated to the actions the manager took. Other problems with this approach will be discussed later in this appendix.

The *productive* thinking approach uses abstract mental structures (built by using past induction and current deduction) to mentally test hypotheses to explain the environment and suggest strategies. The problem is solved through understanding,

Figure 1 **Two Methods of Managerial Decision Making**

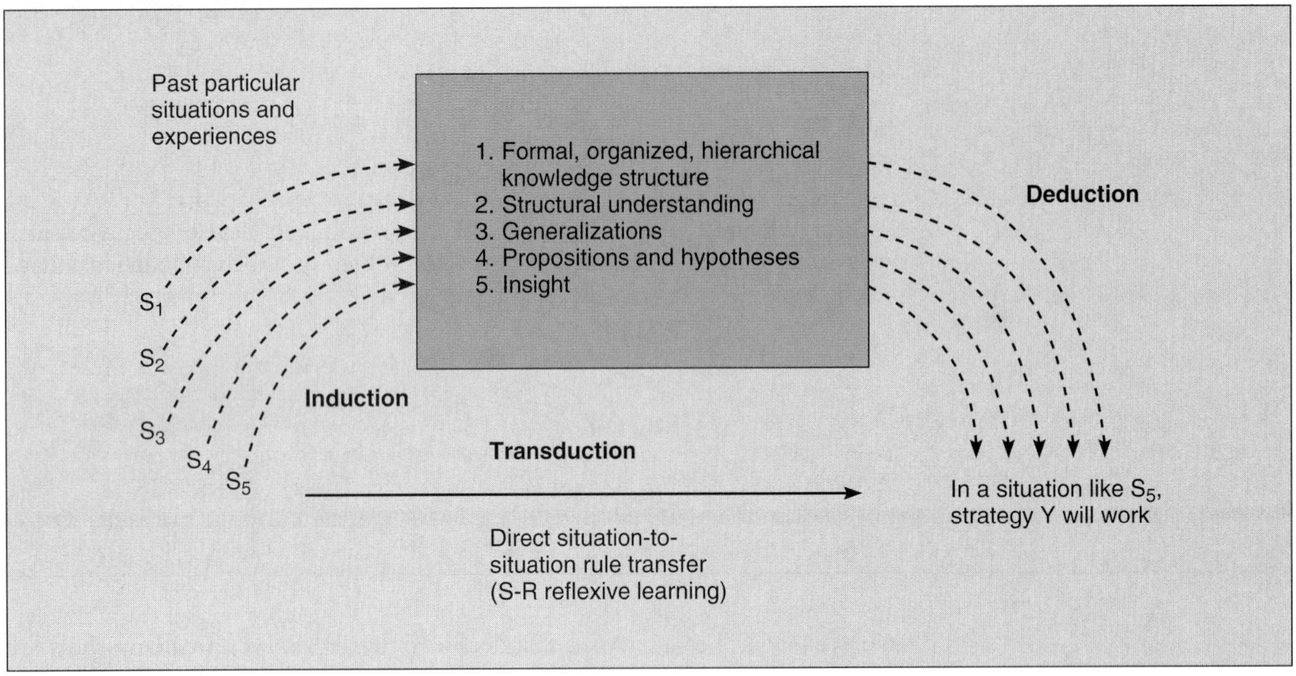

The transduction, or reproductive, approach to managerial decision making recalls a successful past strategy and seeks to apply the same strategy to a similar situation. Transduction logic, then, goes from the particular to the particular. The induction-deduction, or productive, thinking approach involves using past situations and experiences based on abstract mental models and structures to test hypotheses and suggest strategy. The problem is solved through understanding, insight, and the use of formal thinking.

insight, and formal thinking. It is a skill that not everyone has acquired or been given. Developmental concept-learning studies have shown that average and below-average children use the reproductive method to solve problems, but children with high intelligence quotients (IQs) and college students solve the same problems using more of a productive, hypothesis-testing approach. Marketing planning is, of course, a much tougher problem-solving exercise than those used by developmental psychologists.

Marketing planning is at least a two-stage hypothesis-testing exercise using incomplete and unreliable information. The first stage answers the question "What is the future operating environment?" The question answered during the second stage (which is dependent on the answer to the first question) is "What strategy best fits this future operating environment?" It is this type of demanding cognitive problem that the STRATMESH planning procedure was designed to help solve. To cope, managers often have to simplify the problem. But this may create more problems than it solves. The application of the productive problem-solving approach to marketing planning is still better than the application of the reproductive, what-did-we-do-last-time problem-solving approach.

Research suggests that a higher-order mental skill exists that may be rarer even than productive problem solving: problem *finding*.[8] Problem finding is the ability to see and anticipate problems. Compared to problem solving, this skill requires even more complicated and sensitive information structures in memory (broad and deep expertise) and the ability to imagine first-, second-, and third-order consequences. It also requires the ability to see a situation or a strategy from many different problem-*creating* perspectives and to anticipate interaction (synergy) effects among variables. This skill probably results from a combination of individual mental skills (such as multiple role playing, "what if, then that" reflection, and projection) and specific industry or product market experience. It is not necessarily related to high IQ or education. An individual with such skills is likely to have highly developed environmental and strategy memory structures, as illustrated in Figure 2. Such an individual may appear to be coldly logical. It is also possible for an individual with such skills to appear to make intuitive, almost impulsive decisions. This is because of the frequency and fluency of his or her use of such skills. Like skilled generals or creative scientists, new information indicating slight changes are seen by problem-finding managers as anomalies that may require a radical change in the way they view the situation and the mental production rules and strategy they apply to the situation.

Arthur Koestler has written about creativity in art, literature, humor, and science.[9] He has concluded that the common feature of creativity is the novel combination of ideas, the *juxtapositioning* of ideas and facts in new and surprising ways. The PC STRATMESH program attempts to foster creativity in marketing decision making by forcing managers to consider many different combinations of suggested strategic and environmental facts (see Appendix 2). It is evident, however, that many marketing managers and entrepreneurs are able to do this in their minds intuitively, Somehow, they are able to combine their information structures about the marketplace with their knowledge of alternative marketing strategies to develop new, creative strategies. They are endowed with specially creative mental processes, or production rules, that categorize and combine information.

Using Experience and History

The history of an organization describes its heritage and traditions and is useful in understanding its current culture.[10] Most managers, particularly young ones, need to know the history of the company and the background of particular product markets that predate their own experience. History can provide lessons about what strategies work and do not work in the marketplace. It also can explain the attitudes and likely reactions of competitors, distributors, and senior executives who, as junior executives, may have been responsible for some of the history. Placing past strategies in their environmental contexts helps planners understand how the organization has found ways to adapt in the past. History then can be seen as a flow of interrelated events that is still evolving.

[8] Patricia Kennedy Arlin, "Piagetian Operations in Problem Finding," *Developmental Psychology* 13, no. 3 (1977): 297–98; and "Cognitive Development in Adulthood: A Fifth Stage?" *Developmental Psychology* 11, no. 5 (1975): 602–6.

[9] Arthur Koestler, *The Act of Creation* (New York: Dell, 1964).

[10] George David Smith and Lawrence E. Steadman, "The Present Value of Corporate History." *Harvard Business Review* (November/December 1981): 164–73.

Figure 2 **The Mental Models and Memory Structures of the Strategist**

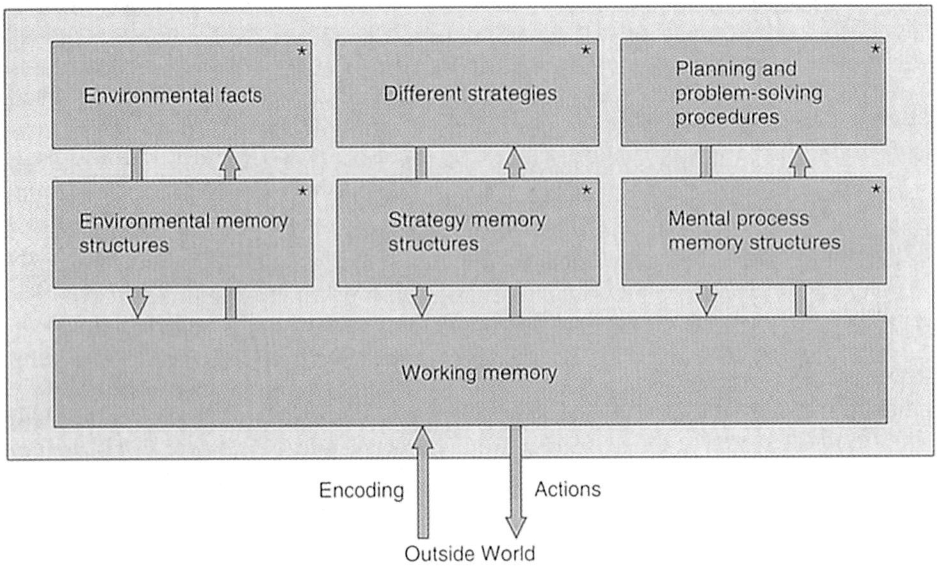

The environmental facts are stored in memory structure networks called mental models in this text. The different marketing tactics and strategies discussed in this textbook are also stored in different knowledge structures. The way Chapters 9 through 13 are organized is likely to influence both your learning and the way you store the marketing strategies and tactics described in those chapters. Managers also have memory stores that contain the problem-solving procedures such as STRATMESH they retrieve from long-term memory and use to process the environmental information and strategic information in their working memories.

*STRATMESH modifies these structures and content.

The immediate past strategy is often a useful starting point for developing new strategy. However, before a manager tests the fit of this strategy to the anticipated future environment, several issues need to be explored. First, how did the implemented strategy differ from the planned strategy? Differences between planned and actual strategies may shed light on recent environmental changes and constraints that produced the differences and may not have been adequately factored into the projected product market environmental analysis. When history is ignored, it is likely to repeat itself.

On the negative side, history taken out of context and used to rationalize rather than learn can be "bunk," as Henry Ford put it. Productive thinking uses history well by analyzing past strategy and adapting it to fit the new environment. History is likely to be misapplied by reproductive problem solvers who, in reaching for old saws and bandages, are trapped by tradition and ritual. During World War II, a British motorized, light-artillery unit sought to speed up its rate of fire. A careful, slow-motion study of film of the firing procedure revealed that two members of the five-man team snapped to attention for three-second periods while each shell was fired. Puzzled by this meaningless act, a crusty, old artillery colonel was consulted. After pondering it for some time, he finally exclaimed, "Ah-ha! I have it. They are holding the horses."

Rationality in Practice

Am I Dogmatic, Rigid, Myopic? Never!

If you have not tried the simple exercises in the box on page 753, then you might find it useful to do so before reading on. Completing those exercises will help you to better appreciate the following findings.

Problems 2 to 6 in the earlier exercise can be solved by the use of the rule B–A–2C. Two of the problems can be solved other ways: Problem 5 can be solved by using the formula A+2C poured into B, and problem 6 can be solved with B–7C. Some of you may have discovered that problems 7 through 10 could be solved using production rules that were simpler than the B–A–2C procedure (problem 7: A–C; problem 8: A+C; problem 9: A–C; problem 10: A+C; problem 11; A–C). All of the problems (except problem 9, which was the extinction task) could be solved using the habituated production rule B–A–2C. The experiments conducted by Max Wertheimer and his students from 1936 to 1937 suggest that most of you would not have used the simpler rules, particularly if you were racing the clock.

In a wonderful stream of inductive, phenomenon-oriented research led by the Socratic Wertheimer, students tested people from various age and education populations; varied the problems (jigsaw puzzles, geometry problems, mazes); concretized the problems by, for example, having subjects actually pour the water; varied the time pressure; varied the involvement and rewards; varied experimenters; varied the number of extinction tasks; varied instructions and framing; and included self-recited warnings after problem 6 that cautioned the subjects not to be blind to other solutions. They had to work very hard to moderate the Einstellung effect, which was dramatic under speedy and stressed conditions, when the number of set-creating problems was increased, when subjects were encouraged to generalize the rule that solves the problem, and when very complex water-jug problems were used.

To paraphrase the major researcher Abraham S. Luchins, whose dissertation initially was rejected because certain members of his committee could not believe the *strength* of his results, methods have to be developed to make problem solvers open to the evidence, to new problem-solving procedures, and to the testing of new hypotheses.* Otherwise, they will be slaves to the rote application of learned, mechanized rules that may work inefficiently most of the time and, when the situation changes sufficiently, may not work at all or, worse, may block the problem solver's ability to develop creative, innovative solutions. Good advice for managers, don't you think?

*See Abraham S. Luchins and Edith H. Luchins, *Wertheimer's Seminars Revisited: Problem Solving and Thinking*, vol. III (Albany, NY: Faculty-Student Association, State University of New York at Albany, Inc., 1970).

Although this is a bizarre example, many companies and executives seem unable to live in the present. A fitting epitaph for many companies, and even civilizations buried by competition, is that they did not *learn* from the past; they *lived* in the past.

Perceptual Rigidity

Einstellung, or problem-solving rigidity, is a common phenomenon (see the Rationality in Practice box). The famous philosopher David Hume called it mental inertia. It suggests that planners should be very cautious in transferring solutions or production rules from one problem to another and strategies from one environment to another. The Ryder advertisement identifies a type of marketing decision-making Einstellung: companies seeing distribution as a cost rather than a source of competitive advantage (see Figure 3).

Recent events can distort perceptions about the marketplace in the same way a driver's fear of having an accident is affected by witnessing a gruesome head-on wreck. Called a memory availability bias, it clearly has personal survival value. But it also can distort decision making that has to place events and abstract issues in perspective. Other decision biases and traps are presented in Table 1.

Figure 3 **Decision-Making Einstellung**

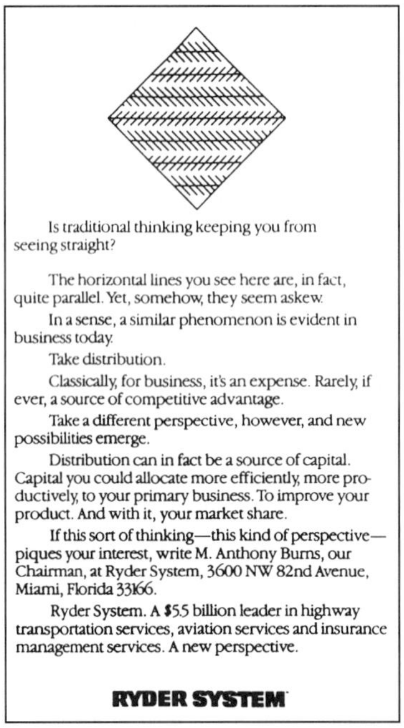
Is traditional thinking keeping you from seeing straight?
The horizontal lines you see here are, in fact, quite parallel. Yet, somehow, they seem askew.
In a sense, a similar phenomenon is evident in business today.
Take distribution.
Classically, for business, it's an expense. Rarely, if ever, a source of competitive advantage.
Take a different perspective, however, and new possibilities emerge.
Distribution can in fact be a source of capital. Capital you could allocate more efficiently, more productively, to your primary business. To improve your product. And with it, your market share.
If this sort of thinking—this kind of perspective—piques your interest, write M. Anthony Burns, our Chairman, at Ryder System, 3600 NW 82nd Avenue, Miami, Florida 33166.
Ryder System. A $5.5 billion leader in highway transportation services, aviation services and insurance management services. A new perspective.
RYDER SYSTEM

This clever ad attempts to get customers to change their conventional thinking and practices.

Table 1 **Ten Decision Traps**

1. **Plunging ahead:** Gathering conclusions; forming beliefs and conclusions without thinking about the best way to make the decision.
2. **Frame blindness:** Solving the wrong problem because you have applied the wrong mental model or framework.
3. **Tunnel vision:** Applying too limited a perspective or not applying all of the mental models needed to solve the problem (such as the STRATMESH environment models). Being too influenced by conventional thinking or the thinking of others.
4. **Judgment overconfidence:** Failing to see reality because you are too sure of your facts or beliefs.
5. **Shortsighted shortcuts:** Using rules of thumb (simple information-processing production rules), such as relying too much on a certain type of available facts.
6. **Shooting from the hip:** Winging it, rather than following a more laborious, systematic, and careful decision-making procedure such as STRATMESH.
7. **Group failure:** Assuming a group of smart people will produce a collectively smart decision without a carefully managed group decision-making process.
8. **Fooling yourself about feedback:** Not learning from past mistakes because you are defensive and attribute failure to causes other than your poor decision making.
9. **Not keeping track:** Not tracking outcomes and, hence, being unable to assess success or failure.
10. **Failure to audit decision process:** Not recording the decision process, so it is unclear what went wrong, and it is impossible to know how to make better decisions the next time.

SOURCE: Based on J. Edward Russo and Paul J. H. Schoemaker, *Decision Traps* (New York: Simon and Schuster, 1990).

Computer-based statistical analysis, decision calculus, and artificial intelligence (AI) can help managers use all the information available (particularly the most recent information) to make balanced predictions about the incidence and severity of marketplace events.[11] However, the use of artificial intelligence systems also can increase the risk of problem-solving rigidity. In most decision situations, AI is likely to reduce the perceptual and shortcut biases in decision making and improve the quality of the mediocre decision maker. However, if something new is introduced into the decision-making environment, then the task is made doubly difficult because both human and machine will have to be reprogrammed. It is yet to be established which will adapt fastest, and it may not be the machine. If this is so, then marketers face the compounded problem of human and machine Einstellung. A description of a creative problem-solving process designed to overcome rigidity in decision making follows.

Stages in Creative Problem Solving

As long ago as 1926, the stages of a creative problem-solving approach were defined as preparation, incubation, insight, and testing. Very little refinement of these steps has occurred since, but the anecdotal experiences of great minds have accumulated to provide guidance about enhancing the productivity of each of these stages.[12]

Preparation: Putting on Your Bifocals

During this stage, information about the problem is gathered and structured. In marketing management, it involves performing the environmental analysis and structuring the information in a particular way in the environment report. Information quantity, quality, type, and organization shape the spotting of problems and opportunities in the current or proposed strategy, so this is a very important stage (see Chapters 2 and 3). To encourage creativity, the problem should be restated from each player's perspective. The decision maker also should keep asking, "Has the core problem been identified, or am I still treating the symptoms?"

Incubation and Meditation

Total preoccupation with a problem is not good. Humans work best on a problem if we adopt a pulsed concentration strategy, alternating between periods of focus and concentration, the way a dog worries over a bone, followed by periods of mental relaxation, digestion, and lower level thinking. The conscientious manager probably never stops thinking about the marketing strategy, the environment, or a particular issue or problem. Instead, he or she raises and lowers it between consciousness and conscious thinking. Some only may need to change their focus to another problem, but most may need to relax completely by, for example, fishing, hunting, partying, or cooking. The initial focus and concentration gets the external environmental facts

[11] For an excellent extended discussion of the problem of overconfidence in beliefs and judgments based on past success, see J. Edward Ruso and Paul J. H. Schoemaker, "Managing Overconfidence," *Sloan Management Review* (winter 1992): 7–17. They prescribe a waiting period of critical analysis before commiting to a plan of action. The decision maker should decide cautiously and implement confidently.

[12] See also Richard E. Mayer, *Thinking, Problem Solving, Cognition* (New York: W. H. Freeman and Company, 1983); and W. A. Wickelgren, *How to Solve Problems* (San Francisco: Freeman, 1984).

and proposed strategy in their mind. The most effective next step is to turn inward and become introspective, contemplative, reflective, and projective—to daydream the problem.

Focused concentration probably is best when one is mentally fresh and at maximum alertness. Sleep-and-waking research shows that maximum periods of alertness occur early in the morning, late in the morning, early in the evening, and later in the evening. The time in between is filled with mental slumps. It is not coincidental that these slumps occur at midmorning coffee and tea breaks, at siesta time after midday lunch, and at game-show time on evening television when we put our feet up. The night owl/early bird dichotomy is a documented individual difference, so periods of maximum conscious mental effort should match one's own personal arousal cycle. In fact, the pulsed concentration approach may be a way of simply accommodating our natural physical and mental alertness cycles.

Several ways to "rev" concentration into overdrive exist. One is to write down the current solution, improved solutions, and the most novel solutions to a problem. The next step is to work these solutions over by elaborating them. Managers then take the strategy apart component by component, inspect it, clean and polish it, and then reassemble it in their mind. While doing this, they note any fringe thoughts and issues and come back to them later. Another way is to talk to a mentor or an equally involved colleague, such as a fellow cross-functional team member. The advantage of such discussion is that clearly explaining a problem to someone else often forces clarification of the issues and structure (a sounding board effect). The other individual's questioning and restructuring of the problem often will lead to a mental breakthrough. Working with someone else also can boost feelings of confidence, self-competence, and control.

When incubating a problem, it is important to stop consciously worrying about the problem, to reduce stress, and to relax. Everyone has a different method of relaxing that may include some of the following: exercise, soaking in a bath, drowning in music, taking a sauna, neck message, deep breathing, and meditation. For example, one way to build confidence and feelings of competence and control is through exercise. Physical fitness often brings feelings of mental fitness and well-being. Another approach is to view the problem as a game, a detective puzzle where just one new insight or fact may break open the case. The objective is to get the monkeys off one's back.

Successful incubation results in deep thought reorganization in memory and perhaps a slow, laborious, high-torque churning and meshing of information structures and mental models. The reason for the earlier assertion that managers never stop thinking about a problem (it just drops from internal sight) is that often a surprising thought or solution to a problem will come to mind spontaneously, even when they were not consciously thinking about it. When this happens while showering, shaving, or even sleeping, it is important to write the idea down. Nothing is more frustrating than trying to recall a brilliant, but forgotten, idea or insight.

The "Ah-Ha" Illumination

Illumination, or insight, is the exhilarating "ah-ha" or "eureka" experience that results when everything seems to fall into place. That may be literally what happens. Insight is a restructuring of perception and facts that brings new organization, perspective, hypothesis, and explanation. Tabatha Babbett, a Shaker woman, thought of the circular saw while working at her spinning wheel and watching two men saw wood using the traditional, two-person, straight saws. She connected two concepts almost subconsciously. The idea for the steel frame that enabled the building of skyscrapers came when the inventor's wife put a heavy book down on top of a fragile bird cage.

The mental meshing of disparate environmental facts into a cohesive, higher-order concept and synchronicity, the clicking together of strategy and environmental facts, are keys to skilled, competitive thinking. Much of our modern humor depends on assembling disparate facts and fitting them together in a perverse and unexpected way by the punch line. The "ha-ha" surprise of a good joke is not too different from the "ah-ha" insight that occurs during problem solving.

Insight often comes from the slow accumulation of facts, or it can be produced by exposure to a single new fact or proposition that leads to a radically new explanation. Although Darwin developed one of the great theories of modern philosophy and science, he had some fairly weird theories to explain the evolution and extinction of species before he developed his theory of the origin of species. According to his own handwritten notebooks, in July of 1837, after undertaking one of humanity's greatest around-the-world observational research programs, his explanation for what he had observed involved *monads* (not to be confused with *nomads*)! Monads were small living particles that determined the characteristics of a species but that had their own life cycles. This explained the origin and extinction of species. Species died out because their monads reached the end of their life cycles.

In September of 1838, after reading Malthus's *Essay on Population*, Darwin understood that the limits to population growth were determined by environmental resources. He then was able to develop key insights: the competition for resources among species determines the limits of a species' population growth and that adaptation to the environment is the key to survival of the fittest. In the process, he dropped his monad explanation and completely restructured how he organized all of his thoughts, perceptions, and facts. Marketing managers can experience similar dramatic insights and illuminations toward understanding their competitive marketplaces, but most of their time is spent on the labor: the 99 percent perspiration component of creativity (versus the 1 percent inspiration) that Thomas Edison described.

Testing: Shucks, Another Dead End

Ensuring that a solution or a strategy works requires screening the idea for its fit. This is what STRATMESH is designed to help do. It also may be useful to bring in independent participants to evaluate the fit. The developers of a strategy may be too close to the problem and solution to see the implementation constraints. It is important to resist getting discouraged if the flaws in a strategy are exposed. Even Einstein admitted he wasted two years on a stroke of genius that was not. It is comforting to know this happens to even the very, very best minds. Testing builds the confidence to implement the strategy, just as it exposes the overconfidence that can result from the euphoria of the initial idea.[13]

Team Decision Making

Marketing decision making often involves group consultation and team decision making. This can occur at the early stage of creative strategy development and at the

[13] See Russo and Schoemaker, "Managing Overconfidence."

senior-management review stage (see Chapter 2). Team decision making has several advantages. Judicious selection of group members who represent different internal and external constituencies and who have different marketplace experiences will encourage multiple views of the environment and strategy fit. Cross-functional teams enable the efficient accumulation of creative ideas from a number of people. Teams also can produce greater comprehension, cohesion, and focus and more effective implementation. Effective planning is the multiplicative product of *quality* decision making and *acceptance* by those who have to implement the plan. Team decision making must not achieve one to the exclusion of the other.

The disadvantages of teams are that they can be unwieldy (more than ten members may be hard to control), difficult to manage, and, because of the presence of political moles, sandbaggers, and social loafers, can increase rather than decrease discord, rivalry, and organization frustration. They also can produce social pressures to conform, can be dominated by an individual, and, through a lack of personal accountability, can produce irresponsible decisions. A group's effectiveness critically depends on the role and performance of the group leader. The leader must, through formal status and informal respect, direct and encourage the group, set the tone of discussion, maintain morale, manage meeting mechanics, and most important, make sure the team *makes* decisions.[14] One of the reasons small entrepreneurial companies can compete against large corporations may be that the commitment to quality group decision making is greater in the small enterprise, where team members are shareholders and all have a major stake in seeing the group work effectively. Some of the major group decision-making problems and suggested solutions are listed in Table 2.

Brainstorming, Blue Skying, and Beyond

In the 1960s, group brainstorming sessions were very much in vogue. The procedure encouraged off-the-wall ideas and responses, encouraged free-association and fringe thoughts, used analogy, and encouraged the unusual combination of ideas and concrete visualization of abstract ideas. The emphasis was on the production of new ideas, and any criticism was absolutely taboo. Later research showed that individuals given the same instructions, but who worked alone and then pooled their ideas were at least as productive, if not more productive, as brainstorming groups. The theory behind brainstorming is that one person's idea will spark another person's idea, and a ripple of creativity will build into a torrent. At least three things can go wrong in practice. First, the discussion can fly off on tangents that send it out of control and into the wild blue yonder. Second, adversarial competitiveness and gamesmanship among individuals and participating constituencies, such as finance versus marketing versus production, can inhibit any additive creativity that comes from group dynamics. Third, lazy individuals can hide in groups and be less productive than if they had to develop something alone.

The advantages of the two approaches can be combined by first asking individuals to work alone and allowing them to discuss and circulate their ideas. Then, others can incubate on the ideas before the meeting. This is likely to happen anyway because many executives will want to float trial balloons before the meeting. The meeting

[14] Jon R. Katzenbach and Douglas K. Smith, *The Wisdom of Teams: Creating the High Performance Organization* (Cambridge, MA: Harvard Business School, 1993). The authors emphasize the need to set specific targets for the team, such as getting a product to market in half the usual time.

Table 2 **Summary of Group/Team Decision-Making Problems and Solutions**

PROBLEM	POSSIBLE SOLUTIONS
Lack of knowledge; reinventing the wheel	Add experience to the team.
Lack of creativity	Add the best and brightest to the group; encourage the group's confidence in its own creativity.
Creative impasse	Break and incubate.
Narrow perspective	Vary the background and perspective of the team membership, even though it will increase management problems.
Groupthink	Bring in an individual, even late in the planning process, to be a perceptual heretic and a devil's advocate.
Premature closure	Separate "getting ideas out on the table" from "idea evaluation."
Paralysis by analysis	Set no-matter-what deadlines on decision making and implementation; use analysts who cut through the rhetoric rather than pile it on.
Lack of preparation	Circulate environmental report and proposed starting strategy beforehand; give plenty of notice; embarrass loafers and unseat them for second offenses.
Hidden agendas and politics	Encourage opening position statements and concerns; use heavyweights to increase cooperation and commitment to the overall planning goal.
Cheap shots in group discussions	Make team members pay $1 into a party pot for every cheap shot.
Low commitment	Make sure line and sales management implementers are heavily represented; develop a performance-incentive payment scheme for all participants; make promotions dependent on team performance.
Arguing at cross purposes	Structure and direct discussion to deal with issues in an orderly manner.
Everyone talking at once	Pass or throw a ball around. Only the person holding the ball gets to talk.
Separation of creativity and responsibility in team membership	Never embarrass the major stakeholder. Allow him or her to direct the contribution of the spark plugs.
Diffused responsibility	Identify the manager with ultimate implementation and performance responsibility, and give him or her the ultimate veto.
Top-down domination	Tell senior management to step back and play a supportive, nurturing role.
Physical distractions	Relocate, but pack the information-system supports before the suntan lotion.
Time stress	Don't make things worse by panicking; learn from your mistakes so it does not happen again in the future.
Insoluble conflicts	Return to the basics instead of constantly trying to break the deadlock.

must be artfully directed back to the topic by the discussion leader without cutting off the creative process. Some level of criticism and evaluation is also appropriate. Pointing out an environmental constraint on a new marketing strategy is a necessary start to the problem-solving process. The group's intellectual resources then must be harnessed to invent a solution. Criticism is not bad. It is essential to improve ideas and if not present will feed the concerns of group cynics who believe team decision making wastes time.

The group leader can encourage creativity by showing confidence in the group's creative ability. Research has clearly demonstrated that groups whose leaders tell them they have a reputation for being original thinkers produce better solutions to problems.[15] Instructions that ask for interesting, clever, and unusual ideas also work better than instructions that simply ask for many ideas. Another way to increase group creativity is to ask the participants to come to the meeting with solid ideas that will work and with at least one really off-the-wall suggestion. Part of the meeting should be set aside for discussing what may seem to be outrageous suggestions. It is likely that breakthrough advances in strategy, competitiveness, and profitability will come from radical rather than conservative thinking.

Good and Bad Criticism

Often it is not criticism per se but the intent and tone of criticism that create problems. At the very outset, the group discussion leader must emphasize that the superordinate goal of the group is to develop a more competitive, profitable strategy. This objective must dominate all other personal or subgroup goals. It may require bringing in a senior executive to impress the group with the importance of burying hatchets. Care must be taken, however, to not produce an under-the-gun group siege mentality. The leader must be skilled at discouraging the adversarial, tit-for-tat game of pointing out flaws in each other's ideas and in identifying and flushing out hidden agendas. The group leader must do this without undermining the legitimacy of individuals voicing the concerns of the function or outside constituency they represent. If avenues for such individual expression are not left open, then the organization runs the risk of groupthink, where people are afraid to voice criticism for fear of upsetting group cohesion. Historians consider groupthink a major reason for poor White House decision making in the early years of the Vietnam War.

The tone of the criticism can make a big difference (see Table 3). Expressing one's reaction with enthusiasm—"I quite like the idea, but I'm wondering how we can handle the concerns of distributors, who . . . "—is very different from sneering, "I've never heard a more stupid idea in my life. You want to have our distributors hate us more than they already do." Good, useful criticism is not a gushing, Pollyanna style of communication but a cooperative attempt to turn problems into advantages.

Decision Politics, Roles, and Responsibilities

Team selection and dynamics are often complicated when groups have three key players: a discussion leader, a creative leader, and the individual who is responsible for implementation and any resulting negative outcome. It is very dangerous not to have someone individually responsible for the product market plan because the alternative, collective responsibility, is often no responsibility. In group decision making, success has many followers but failure has none. Also, if the planning is important enough for the cross-functional team to consist of the top talent, then some of the participants may be more talented and creative than the person responsible for the project and may overwhelm him or her.

[15] M. A. Colgrove, "Stimulating Creative Problem Solving: Innovative Set," *Psychological Reports* 22 (1968): 1205–11.

Table 3 Idea Starters and Stoppers

IDEA STOPPERS	IDEA STARTERS
It's too much work.	It's okay
We'll look silly.	Tell me more.
We're not ready for that.	What are the options?
We've never done that before.	I'd like your ideas.
It's not practical.	What do you think?
It won't work here.	Let's give it a try.
Be realistic.	I've got a wild idea.
It's not in the budget.	What other ways are there?
We've heard it all before.	What if . . . ?
We'll never get it approved.	We might want to consider . . .
That's really weird.	Yes!
Get serious.	
Naah.	

SOURCE: Based on Susan Butruille, Stanley S. Gryskiewicz, and Robert C. Preziosi, "Kaleidoscope Thinking for Creativity," *Training and Development,* September 1991, 28.

At times it may be wise to appoint a discussion leader who is not the creative leader or person ultimately responsible for the plan because when the roles are combined such a group leader is likely to dominate the group. When this happens, decisions cease to be group decisions. For instance, a senior executive can impose the wrong decision on a group. Studies taken after World War II showed that high-status air force pilots were able to persuade the groups they led that their clearly incorrect solution was correct. Lower status pilots were less successful at such persuasion.

For uncertain choices, a weighted average of opinions based on individual expertise is superior to both simple majority voting and leaving the decision up to the acknowledged expert. In other words, experts should be given more say, but even experts can benefit from the collective decision process. For example, expert consultants, such as doctors, lawyers, accountants, and engineers, often form partnerships where the collective wisdom of the partnership can be readily provided to the client. Decisions in companies are often based on an informal weighing of group members' opinions. But this will only happen if the leader encourages the voicing of other opinions.

When a group member develops a brilliant but risky strategy that someone else will have to ultimately implement, the discussion leader's skills are likely to be stretched. The organization wants to utilize the mercurial brilliance of junior and senior executive spark plugs but cannot afford to undermine the position of the implementer, who does not want to appear to be a pedestrian thinker. Clearly, executives who manage these discussions well earn their pay.

Meeting Mechanics and Monkey Wrenches

The importance of managing the mechanics of a cross-functional team meeting are often underestimated. Frequently, group meetings get off to a bad start because the participants are given too little notice and do not have enough time to read and ponder preparatory reports. The meetings then end on a frustrating note because key participants have not scheduled enough time and have to leave the meeting early to fulfill other commitments.

The meeting surroundings can have a major effect on the process. Marketing strategy meetings are often lengthy. This means the chairs and room temperature must be comfortable, and external visual and audio distractions must be minimized. The meeting table should be designed so participants sit face-to-face and support systems such as drinks, snacks, and bathrooms are conveniently available. The farther participants have to travel for refreshments, the more likely they will be bushwhacked in the halls while the discussion is hurt or delayed by their absence. Meeting interruptions must be minimized. This all may sound trivial, but the cost of executive time spent in planning meetings can be astronomical. Chapters 2 and 3 discuss more meeting mechanics specific to the STRATMESH planning procedure. Poor meeting mechanics not only increase organizational inefficiency but also send bad signals to the participants about how seriously they should view the company's decision-making process.

Multiple Teams

For very important decisions, it may be useful to create several cross-functional teams or to split a team into several smaller teams that each address the same problem. This approach, although expensive, has been shown in controlled studies to result in more creative advertising campaigns and other marketing tactics.[16] This approach also has been successfully employed in new product development by Japanese companies such as Sharp, Casio, and NEC, who have hundreds of teams working on similar projects in the general product market of office automation.[17] The *external* competitive rationality of these firms is increased by creating an *internal* competition among teams within the firm.

Teams That Reengineer Marketing Decision and Implementation Processes

A common theme running throughout this text is the need to increase the added value and reduce the cost of organization routines, particularly the new product development procurement, sales-prospect conversion, order-delivery, and after-sales service processes. A team must harness all of the individual and group creative skills to improve the processes. Table 4 lists the additional unique requirements of an organization decision-making team given such a process reengineering task.

Companies such as Kodak, Motorola, Chrysler, and Western Digital have had considerable success using such teams to reduce the time it takes to invent a new, improved product or to imitate and improve on a competitor's new product. Also the cost to develop a new product has been greatly reduced. Even more important, the

[16] I. Gross, "The Creative Aspects of Advertising," *Sloan Management Review* 14, no. 1 (1972): 83–109; and Paul Saintilan and John R. Rossiter, "Gross' Theory of Creative Competition: The Time is Right" (Working Paper 92–001, Australian Graduate School of Management, University of New South Wales, 1992).

[17] Kenichi Ohmae, *The Borderless World* (New York: Harper Perennial, 1991), 65–71.

Table 4 **Team Requirements for New-Product-Development Process Reengineering**

1. Must be championed by a senior executive who can persuade functional barons to accept changes in the new product development process that cross their boundaries. The champion must give process reeingineering number-one priority and must be energetic, enlightened, resolute, and prepared to take the certain heat that radical change will generate (the elimination of old reward systems, jobs, standard operating procedures, rules, whole processes, and even whole departments).
2. Must be a small team of five to ten members with two or three outsiders who are not afraid to ask the dumb questions, such as "Why do we do it that way" or "Why do we do it at all?" The team should have bottom-up involvement of the best people in the organization when an organization does its own reengineering of its genes (routines). All members must have excellent activity-schedule memory (ASM) skills so they can create and critique new value-added activity sequences.
3. Must be led by a process-oriented senior executive who understands the entire value-added chain, from concept to after-sales service.
4. Must focus on changing the process and nothing else (such as changing departments). Must move quickly and decisively. The team should not accept watered-down political compromises or attempts to delay.
5. Must be concerned about implementation: changing company information systems, culture, personnel, and reward systems so they fit the new process. The team should not try to make everyone happy. It cannot be done. The objective is radical change and not consensus.
6. Must accept that fundamentally changing routines involves risk and conflict. Team members must be able to deal with both in a constructive, problem-solving way.
7. Must not quit or accept only minor improvements. The team should use examples from other firms to inspire and teach.
8. The whole team must sell the whole exercise as well as implement it. It must not be sold as yet another management fad or flavor-of-the-month.

SOURCE: Michael Hammer and James Champy, *Reengineering the Corporation: A Manifesto for Business Revolution* (New York: Harper-Collins, 1993).

quality of the output of the new product development process is greater, as measured by lower product cost and higher customer satisfaction.

The first stage of process reengineering is to create a process map, which describes the typical process, such as the new product development activity-sequence script. The second step is to reengineer the process completely to improve the quality and speed of decision making and implementation. The third step is to build into the process self-learning steps so each new product development cross-functional team is constantly finding ways to improve the new product development process. If the new process does not have such learning built in, then the process cannot continue to reengineer itself. Consequently, the competitive rationality drive to improve organization decision-making and implementation routines constantly will be frustrated because it will be, at best, intermittently satisfied.

In a world where global competition is regularly introducing new innovations and the life cycle of a new model is measured in months rather than years, a firm cannot review and overhaul its marketing routines every five years or so. It must *continuously* improve its marketing processes. In such markets, creative team decision making involves much more than inventing new products or marketing programs. It involves constantly improving marketing management processes through creative innovation and sharing the innovations throughout the organization. This is the essence of competitive rationality, and competitive rationality is the essence of competitiveness.

Discussion Questions

1. Why is the problem-solving game marketing planners must face harder than playing chess?
2. Argue the pros and cons of whether a marketing manager's creative skills are superior to that of a composer or artist.
3. How is the cognitive architecture of experts different from the cognitive architecture of novices on the subject of expertise? How does this difference enable the experts to think better about the subject?
4. What is induction and deduction? How are they used in marketing planning?
5. How can history work for and against you when problem solving?
6. Name two thinking production rules that the STRATMESH process uses. Does it use any others? (Hint: See Chapter 1.)
7. What are the basic advantages and disadvantages of group/team decision making?
8. Why is it important to distinguish among the discussion leader, the creative leader, and the person responsible for implementation?
9. Why are meeting mechanics so important?

Classic Problem-Solving Exercises

1. A Kurdish peasant woman was kneading dough in front of the center pole of her tent. She wanted more flour, and, since the bag of flour was behind the pole, she bent forward, encircling the pole with her arms, plunged her cupped hands into the flour bag, and scooped out some flour. When she pulled back to get the flour to the dough she had been kneading, she found the pole was in the way. Hearing her exclamations, a passing mullah popped his head inside the tent and, after stroking his beard for several minutes, gave her a suggestion that solved the problem. What was it?
2. A man bought a horse for $600 and sold it for $700. He then bought it back for $800 and sold it for $900. How much money did he make in the horse business? What was the value of the horse at the end of the dealing?
3. You are in a cell that is 16 ft. 8 in. long, 12 ft. 6 in. wide, and 7 ft. 9 in. high. The four walls, floor, and ceiling are made of solid concrete. Terrorist jailers open the steel door and throw in two sticks of wood and a large C-clamp. The first piece of wood is 2 in. by 1 in. and 60 in. long. The second piece is 2 in. by 1 in. and 42 in. long. You are given thirty minutes to make a hat rack on which a jailer can hang his hat, flak jacket, and submachine gun. If you cannot do this in the time allotted, you will be shot. How would you make the hat rack?
4. Count the squares.

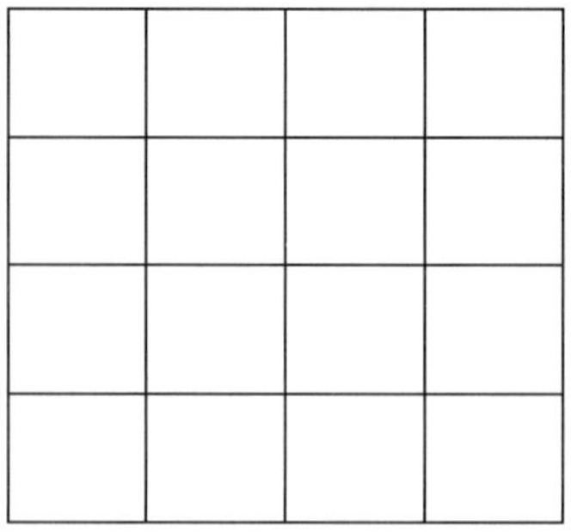

5. Link the nine dots with as few connected, straight lines as you can.

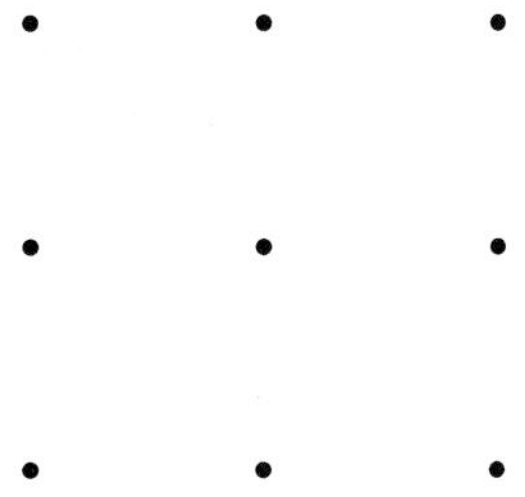

6. In a knockout tennis tournament involving only sixty-four players, how many matches will be played? If only 55 players participate, how many matches will be played?
7. A train leaves Detroit bound for Chicago every hour on the hour, and a train leaves Chicago for Detroit every hour on the hour. The trip takes six hours. How many trains will you meet coming from Chicago if you board the 8 A.M. train in Detroit bound for Chicago?
8. Divide the circle into as many parts as you can using only four straight lines.

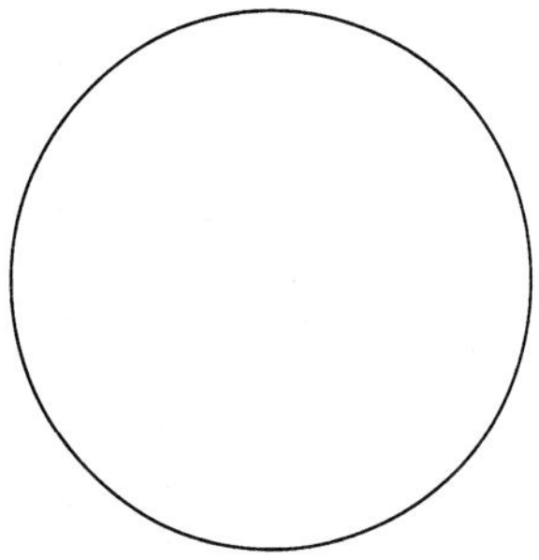

9. Twelve books stand on a bookshelf. If a bookworm eats and crawls its way from page 1 of the first book to the last page of the last book, how many books has it eaten its way through?
10. Look at the old woman in the following picture. Try to guess her nationality. Next, see the young girl in the picture.

11. If the puzzle you solved before this one was harder than the puzzle you solved after you solved the puzzle before you solved this one, was the puzzle you solved before you solved this one harder than this one?

12. Below is a plot of land owned by Solomon.

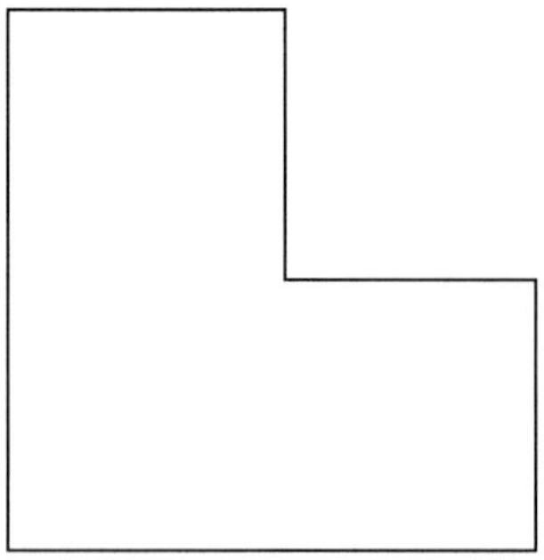

He has four sons. How can he divide the land into four plots of equal size *and* shape?

When a man's knowledge is not in order, the more of it he has the greater will be his confusion.

Herbert Spencer

Life is the continuous adjustment of internal relations to external relations.

Herbert Spencer

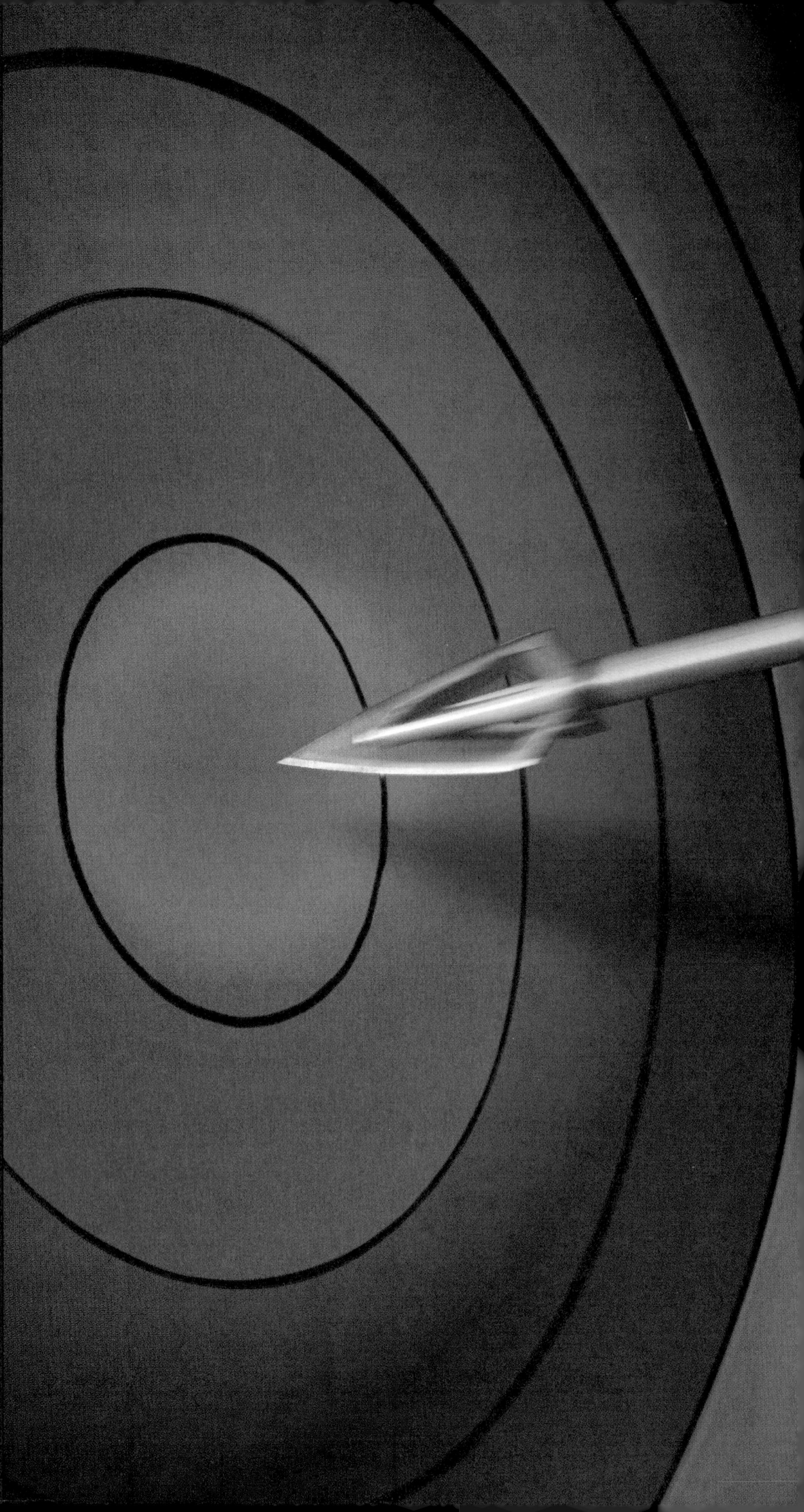

APPENDIX TWO

Sample New Venture Marketing Plan

Executive Summary

The used-car and auto-repair markets often have been associated with unfair business practices that are largely the result of consumers' lack of information and expertise. This reputation is not reflective of the majority of the sellers within these markets but is nonetheless the burden they must carry.

Automobiles are becoming more complex. This trend began with the adoption of the automatic transmission several decades ago. The state-of-the-art auto of today contains many microprocessors for control of the engine, transmission, and, most recently, the braking system. Thus the average automobile owner cannot know enough to judge the type and extent of necessary repairs to his or her vehicle, nor can he or she adequately judge the condition of a previously owned vehicle. This, when combined with the distrust of dealers and repairers, creates an opportunity for the independent auto diagnostician.

The major auto manufacturers, through their dealers, offer warranties on used autos for varying lengths of time depending on the vehicle age and condition. The independent used-car dealer generally does not offer such warranties and is therefore at a competitive disadvantage. The independent diagnostician can help by certifying the condition of a used car for the potential buyer.

The proposed AUTOTEST service to be offered in Columbus, Ohio, will require an investment of some $700,000. It is projected to earn $60,000 a year on the owners' investment of $120,000. The bank loan of $600,000 will be paid off in ten years, thus leaving the owners with the property and residual value of the premises and goodwill.

The viability of this venture, which will charge a premium price for its service, will depend crucially on the marketing campaign establishing demand for the AUTOTEST *seal of approval* among both buyers and sellers.

Environment Reports

1.00 Consumer Analysis

The mechanical condition at the time of sale is reported as the single most important factor in purchasing a used car. Most used-car buyers base their assessments of an automobile's mechanical condition and purchase value on the seller's oral representations and on the physical appearance of the car. In the Columbus, Ohio, market, demand would come from the following:

1.10 The Younger, Careful Buyer Benefit Segment

The major benefit sought from such a service is reducing the cost and time involved in repairing a recently purchased used car. A number of consumers also mentioned avoiding the feeling of having been taken. The major target markets are teenagers (first car) and young, working women. They currently rely on family and friends to undertake such inspections with variable success. Young men think they are less at risk. The young consumers who have paid for an auto diagnostic in the past also report having fewer wrecks, are better credit risks, and are generally more responsible and conscientious.

More than 50 percent of the consumers in the market for a used car would be seriously interested in such a service at the right money and time cost. More than 70 percent would prefer to have an independent firm (one that would not be doing any repair work) perform the inspection. Twenty percent of recent buyers of used cars actually did have their car inspected before the purchase. The mean expected price of diagnostic service was $50, with a large standard deviation of $10. More than 100,000 used-car sales are made in Columbus and Franklin County each year. It is estimated that more than half of them are more than four years old. Total potential demand is conservatively estimated to be 20 to 30 vehicles a day over 300 working days (7,500 vehicles).

1.20 The Quality Seller Benefit Segment

In his article "The Market for 'Lemons': Quality Uncertainty and the Market Mechanism," George A. Akerlof convincingly argues that seller reluctance to tell the buyer of poor vehicle quality occurs often enough that most buyers always discount the stated condition of the vehicle and, hence, lower the amount they are prepared to pay for a car. This hurts the seller of a quality used car. Reducing the cost of discovering the truth about a car would make the used-car market more efficient, in that used-car prices would be more related to the quality of the individual car and, hence, would benefit the seller of a 'gem,' a high-quality used car. This seller tends to be an older household who bought a new car, has owned and looked after it for more than six years and sixty-thousand miles, and trades in the car for a new one. Such sellers are likely to encourage a prospective buyer to have their 'gem' inspected.

1.30 Independent, Honest Joe Used-Car Dealers

Local used-car dealers are generally in favor of the proposed service, even if it were legally mandated, with the understanding that most of the cost could be passed on to consumers. Such diagnostic information would benefit a dealer in negotiating a trading price and helping resell the car. These benefits are particularly attractive to small

SOURCE: This STRATMESH case was prepared by P. R. Dickson with the assistance of the following group of MBA students: Matt Harlow, Bill Hunnicutt, Mark Knouff, Peter Polanski, Dale Sydnor, and Gary Wedlund. It is designed to help teach the importance of fitting proposed strategy to the reported environmental facts.

dealers who lack the capability of checking over a car and wish to position themselves as having higher integrity and higher quality cars than their competition.

Such dealers have an image disadvantage compared to the private seller. It is likely that nondisclosures of vehicle mechanical problems are as high if not higher in private sales made by "decent folks" because used-car businesses have a word-of-mouth reputation and an operating license to protect that keeps them a little more honest in their car dealing than a citizen disposing of a used car. Selling inspected vehicles would reduce the sleaze factor, which is often an illusion.

2.00 Competitor Analysis

The U.S. public has a cultural mistrust of auto repair facilities and car dealers, which will work against them. However, they can marginally price down any diagnostic service to cover the direct cost of the labor if they have slack facility capacity and if it leads to repair work. The major competitors are the following:

2.10 General Repair Service Chains: Formidable Price Competition

BP Pro-Care and Goodyear Auto Centers are fully capable of performing diagnostic services. They are well financed with significant brand recognition, placed in convenient locations, fully staffed with competent mechanics and advanced equipment, possess multibrand knowledge, and have additional capability of repairing most problems found. Their overall credibility is variable, with Sears most suspect. The cost of a full diagnostic service from these competitors is about $60.

2.20 New-Car Dealers: Credibility Problem

New-car dealers are fully capable of offering diagnostic services but hampered by long waiting periods if their current style of customer queuing is retained. Establishment of separate facilities is dependent on the strength of the individual dealership. Lack of consumer confidence would be the primary limiting factor because of the dealers' interest in selling and servicing used cars. The offering of extended warranties on their new cars and near-new cars is an indirect competitive threat to the proposed service. If a car with a one-hundred-thousand-mile, seven-year extended warranty is sold after five years with thirty-thousand miles still on the warranty, then the buyer's perceived risks are greatly reduced. The cost of a diagnostic service package from a dealer varies from about $50 to $100. The higher priced service involves following a manufacturer-prescribed diagnostic package.

3.00 Facilitator Analysis

Conventional channels do not apply to this service, but the following players in the market can act as facilitators:

3.10 Lending Institutions: Their Car, but Do They Care?

Their risk is the possibility of an automobile malfunctioning after it has been tested and approved, resulting in customer repayment problems. However, this did not seem to worry them. Perhaps more senior executives would be more appreciative of the concept since it may not only reduce lending risk but also enhance a bank's customer service if it supports its customers use of such a service. However, convincing lenders to encourage their borrowers to make more informed purchases will be no easy task. Many bank managers take a narrow and very conservative view of the service they provide customers. Indeed, they almost scoffed at the idea that banks would become a facilitating agent for such a service.

3.20 The AAA: Little Local Interest

The AAA also was judged to be an important party in the diagnostic clinic environment. A local AAA manager expressed a lack of interest toward this venture. AAA offers such diagnostic services in several states, as do its sister institutions in countries such as Australia and New Zealand. Despite the local disinterest, it should be remembered that the AAA was founded to provide automobile-related services to its members. Perhaps its members only buy new or near-new cars.

3.30 Consumer Organizations: Will They Help or Hurt?

The popularity of consumer interest groups such as those founded by Ralph Nader has been in decline in recent years, but research indicates that the issues raised by such groups are still important in consumers' minds. The problem with such groups is that they are often dead against anyone earning money and profiting from helping consumers make better choices (themselves excepted). They are chronically suspicious of the integrity and corruptibility of such a business, perhaps rightly so.

3.40 Interested Insurers Are Disinterested

The insurance industry makes a big marketing deal out of its concern over vehicle safety, but the fact is it has seldom initiated economic incentives to encourage its customers to buy safer cars or keep their cars safe. To be fair, the greatest cause of accidents is driver malfunction! The middle-level insurance executives spoken to expressed little interest in the service. They see themselves in the insurance business. They did acknowledge that the most dangerous drivers (eighteen to twenty-five-year-old males) also are likely to be buying older used cars, which may have mechanical problems that contribute to wrecks.

4.00 Public Policy and Legal Analysis

Public policy will play a vital role in determining the long-term potential of the service concept. In order to develop a successful strategy, we must identify and monitor the likely moves of the following players:

4.10 Ohio State Regulations: No Safety and Pollution Inspections

Several states require regular vehicle safety and pollution inspections for older vehicles. Most of the inspection facilities are either licensed by the state or, alternatively, are owned and run by the states, with resulting customer service and efficiencies that are typical of state-managed enterprises. The state of Ohio does not require such inspections; however, in recent years it has enacted or considered several consumer protection rules and acts governing deceptive sales practices, odometer tampering, lemon automobiles, and safety inspections. Jalopy pollution inspection regulations also may be enacted. The result is that Ohio has more malfunctioning, dangerous, dirty clunkers than, say, Florida or California, but his is likely to change.

4.20 FTC Federal Regulations: Down but Not Out

In 1984, the FTC proposed a trade regulation to discourage oral misrepresentation and unfair "omissions of material facts" by used-car dealers concerning the coverage of warranties. The rule provided for warranty information through the required usage of a "Buyers Guide" sticker. The dealers had some legitimate complaints about how the program would be implemented, but instead of suggesting an information program that might work, the industry lobbyists attacked the whole concept. Congress killed the FTC efforts to provide more used-car buyer information before the 1988 election. The used car industry was a major contributor to the 1988 political campaigns of incumbents. Future energy, pollution, safety, and consumer federal regulations are likely to encourage states to introduce new inspection programs. However, such programs will have to be very low cost and efficient, or they will be politically unacceptable to both federal and state governments trying to reduce government and costs.

4.30 Customer Lawyers Seeking Damages

Consumers and their ambulance-chasing lawyers may attempt to sue the diagnostic service, claiming that a diagnostic error on the mechanics of a vehicle contributed to the cause of an accident. Worse, some insurance companies may encourage such litigation as a way of reducing their liability.

5.00 Organization Human Resources Analysis

Initial partners involved in this entrepreneurial start-up venture are three recent MBA graduates with varying business and technical backgrounds. One partner was employed by Midas Muffler as an assistant manager; another was a store manager and partner for a local Goodyear Tire and Service Center. The remaining partner has a father who is sixty years old, ran his own garage, and would work for five years and even employ some of his mechanic friends, part-time, to provide the expertise. The three partners prefer to keep their current jobs but will accept responsibility for marketing, public relations, accounting, personnel, and financial management on a part-time gratis basis.

6.00 Financial Resources Analysis

Each of the three partners are willing to support the start-up with $40,000 from their personal resources for a total of $120,000. The current lending ratio offered by local banks for asset-based ventures of this type, which are considered viable, is six-to-one. In better times it has been as high as ten-to-one. Total capital available for the venture would therefore be $840,000. The owners agree to retain all net profit in the business for the first five years with a view to using the funds to first franchise the concept in other Ohio cities. They would like to earn interest on their investments at the same rate as the bank, which is 10 percent on a ten-year loan.

Strategy Report

1.00 Positioning: Impartial, Expert, Fast

AUTOTEST will provide diagnosis tests of the safety of the vehicle (brakes, steering, suspension) and the worthiness of its drivetrain (engine and transmission) on older cars for buyers, sellers, and owners. Successful service differentiation will involve the following:

1.10 Added Value to Private Buyer: Wins Both Ways

The service is valuable to the private buyer whatever the outcome. If the car passes the tests with flying colors, it increases the likelihood that the car is basically sound and worth the price paid. If the car does not pass the minimum test, then the buyer has avoided problems. An in-between rating enables the buyer to get quotes for the cost of repairs. The service also may be valuable as a checkup before going on a major holiday, for a do-it-yourselfer who lacks the diagnostic equipment, or for an owner who wishes to question a repair estimate. Sellers of quality used cars will have their cars tested and use it as a selling point.

1.20 Added Value to Independent Used-Car Dealers

The ratings can be used by independent used-car dealers, particularly those without workshops, to screen some prospective buys and to use as a selling feature on their cars. If forty independent dealers used this service occasionally to regularly, then they would differentiate themselves from the other two-hundred dealers in the county. We will list participating dealers in our launch advertising and offer contract rates to secure this "fleet" segment. Buyers of used cars who are prepared to pay a premium for a quality used car will seek out dealers who sell AUTOTESTED cars. Thus the positioning strategy relies a lot on self-selection segmentation creating a new type of dealer: a dealer in premium used cars.

2.00 Testing Services

A complete diagnosis of the engine, transmission, brakes, steering, and suspension will be offered as a package deal at a reasonable price. These services will be performed by friendly, skilled mechanics using state-of-the-art diagnostic equipment in a drive-through, four-station setting with an attractive lounge. Initial service will be offered by appointment (the inspection will take an hour), but a queuing service may be introduced at a later date. The features of the service are as follows:

2.10 Quality Seal: Minimum Acceptable Standards

An A (autotest) Seal will be issued only if the car meets all acceptable quality standards. Otherwise, a report will be issued without a sticker identifying the car's condition. The seal must be a very attractive, high-quality, dated decal that cannot be removed. All customers will be given computer-based, laser printer reports of their car's performance, which in reality will be a Windows-based form that includes compression test results and a series of item checks. It just looks more credible coming from a computer, which can produce a certificate-looking report and also store the record, thus minimizing paperwork. The records also can be statistically analyzed to provide information to customers and publicity releases to the press in the future about lemons. It also makes the reporting faster and more foolproof. The seal will be attached to the car by the mechanic.

2.20 Quality Mechanics with Customer Service Skills

Employees will wear a distinctive uniform, somewhat classier than normally worn by mechanics—the wear and tear will be less because no repair work will be done. The average hourly rates for good auto mechanics is $15/hour in Columbus. The head mechanic will be one of the owners' fathers who is a very street-smart, experienced mechanic. The two other mechanics paid $15/hour should prefer diagnostic work to the hard-and-dirty labor of repairs. The two junior staff paid $7.50/hour should be apprentices in their late teens. Priority should be given to hiring a woman and minority to help in customer relations.

A two-week initial training period should occur on fleet sales allowing any operational problems to be worked out in relative privacy. If initial volume warrants, the fleet diagnostic services can be established as a second-shift operation, involving a retired, experienced mechanic and a young, part-time apprentice, thus increasing capital utilization, contribution, and profits.

3.00 Price

The service will have a premium image and can therefore command a higher price than competing service centers. Our primary appeal will be to middle-income groups who are willing to pay a premium price for a fast, quality service. The key pricing tactics follow:

3.10 Consumer Prices: $60 and $35 for Safety or Drivetrain

Our services will be sold in packages and pieces at the following initial price points:

Complete Package	$59.99
Drivetrain Package	$34.95
Safety Package	$34.95

The budgeted price will be $57 after deducting credit card fees for about 67 percent of purchases.

3.20 Fleet Pricing: $45 for Complete Package

In order to receive the AUTOTEST quality seal, the dealers would have to purchase the Complete Package listed. The contract price for dealers will be $45 per vehicle. Dealers will have to pay by cash or check—no credit.

3.30 Initial Half-Price Promotion Offering for First One-Thousand

During the market introduction, we will offer a discount on a comprehensive diagnostic package in order to stimulate "first time" sales, and we will offer half price for the first month of testing private vehicles. Because capacity for the first month is five-hundred private vehicles, this will cost $15,000. We will offer half price off dealer price for the first five-hundred dealer vehicles tested. This will cost $12,000.

4.00 Location and Premises

AUTOTEST will be located in a mall near Morse Road close to many of the used-car dealers and has a design similar to Goodyear, Sears, and Firestone auto-repair centers, except smaller. The mall location is attractive because of the parking space availability (thirty spaces), and it is easy to find and get to. The four-bay building with a customer lounge will be able to be expanded to six bays. The lounge should contain the latest auto magazines, *Consumer Reports*, blue books, and three cable televisions and a coffee station for customer entertainment.

The AUTOTEST premises would be similar in design to the building here.

5.00 Personal Selling to Dealers

The founders will act as the initial sales force. Each will have twenty used-car dealers to call on and will contact each one at least once a month. Eighty percent of the dealer business is expected to come from about six to eight dealers having twenty cars tested a month. If four to five sign on initially, then we expect others to feel the competitive pressure to follow. The new-car dealerships will use their own workshops to look at cars and therefore will not use the service.

5.10 Use Parts Suppliers as Volunteer Sales Force

Auto parts outlets such as NAPA and Nationwise provide minimal car repair advice as a value-added feature. Referrals for diagnostic service will only enhance their business while a reciprocal arrangement to auto parts stores should do little harm to our unbiased image. Fifty free tests should be given out to employees of ten of these stores and the program assessed in terms of referrals (cost of $3,000 to come out of initial advertising budget).

6.00 Advertising and Publicity Campaign

The initial three-month promotion will be very heavy. It will create a great deal of publicity and word of mouth and will encourage a number of dealers to start using the AUTOTEST seal as a selling point. Once the service becomes well known, it will be sold by word of mouth and reminder advertising in the used-car classifieds. The major program elements follow:

6.10 Communication Message: Look for the Quality Seal

Based on our promotional objectives, our communication message should focus on the following key points:

1. Look for the AUTOTEST Quality Seal.
2. Know what the AUTOTEST Quality Seal means: what its *absence* means.
3. We sell "goodwill." Any firm or individual that uses our services or recommends them will be perceived as caring and trustworthy.

6.20 Media Channels: Three-Month Big Bang on Print and Radio

Over the first three months, a campaign on local radio stations and the newspaper will promote the AUTOTEST service and looking for the AUTOTEST Seal of Approval. This will include twenty-four $500 ads in the auto section of the *Columbus Dispatch* and twelve full-page ads in the twelve issues of *Tradin Times*. The cost of the special print campaign will be $20,000. A $20,000 radio campaign also will be undertaken.

Another $10,000 will be spent on brochures and seals; $10,000 will be paid to an agency for creatives, design of seal, and PR work; and $200 per week will be spent on remainder ads in the used-car classified-ad sections of *Tradin Times* and the Saturday *Columbus Dispatch*.

6.30 Publicity

We will use every opportunity to create consumer awareness of AUTOTEST by obtaining as much free publicity as possible, given the public service nature of our unique product. Some suggested outlets for free publicity will include television, radio, and newspapers as well as publications such as *Business First*, *Columbus Monthly*, *Columbus Alive*, suburban newsletters, and the AAA newsletter. Part of the publicity will be that AUTOTEST is a free-market test of whether used-car buyers are prepared to pay a fair market price to obtain important information about a car they want to buy.

7.00 Licensing and Insurance

Vendor licensing, incorporation, and zoning requirements should be dealt with immediately on firming up the grand-opening date. Required liability-insurance binders should be obtained as soon as the operational details are established. Riders for building and equipment can be added as their values become known. An additional rider for business interruption should be included, with a large initial limit to cover the damage that could be done to image building if a loss of business occurs early in the process.

A Federal Employer Identification Number (FEIN) should be obtained on receipt of the incorporation papers. Immediately following receipt of the FEIN, registration with the Workers Compensation Bureau and the Ohio Bureau of Employment Services should be accomplished.

8.00 Budget

The budgeting projects an annual profit of $60,000 on sales of $360,000 and an investment of $120,000. It is hard to see where costs can be trimmed unless inspection routines can be made even more efficient than estimated. To that end it is suggested that some of the projected profits can be used to reward employees for cost time/cost saving suggestions. Key elements of the budget follow:

8.10 Annual Sales Forecast: Seven-thousand services

4,000 private sales	at $57 =	$228,000
1,000 half sales	at $33 =	33,000
2,000 dealer sales	at $45 =	90,000
(Less $1,000 in bad debts)		(1,000)
7,000 sales		$350,000

One-shift capacity is 4 bays × 8 hours × 5 days × 50 weeks = 8,000.

8.20 Financing: Buy What Appreciates; Lease What Depreciates

Immediately after determination of the locations suitable for the initial site, options on the land should be acquired and mortgage financing sought from the bank. The building should be included in the financing, with both being owned by a separate, related corporation and leased back to AUTOTEST. This company will retain title to the property should the venture fail. Lease commitments should be sought for all equipment. Preferably the equipment manufacturers' programs should be used because they combine price discounts with market interest rates.

8.30 Annual Profit-and-Loss Budget Statement

Lease of $600,000 facility	$ 95,000
Equipment leasing	10,000
Utilities and insurance	20,000
Head diagnostic technician	30,000
Two technicians	60,000
Two junior technicians	30,000
Employee benefits	20,000
Employee suggestion incentives	5,000
Employee performance bonuses	10,000

Annual marketing expenses	10,000
Total operating costs	$290,000
Sales	$350,000
Profit	$ 60,000

8.40 Capital Expenditure of $700,000

Major spending is $600,000 needed to purchase, renovate, and lease back the facility; $60,000 on the initial advertising campaign; $10,000 on initial legal and incorporation fees; and $30,000 on initial price discounts and free services. The reserve of $20,000 will be used as initial working capital and for contingencies.

Credits

P. 3 Courtesy of Full Service Network, a division of Time Warner Cable. **P. 16** © 1996, Copyright of The Reader's Digest Association, Inc. Reader's Digest, The Digest, and the Pegasus logo are registered trademarks of the Reader's Digest Association, Inc. **P. 17** © 1996, Copyright of The Reader's Digest Association, Inc. Reader's Digest, The Digest, and the Pegasus logo are registered trademarks of the Reader's Digest Association, Inc. **P. 20** Butch Gemin/The Dryden Press. **P. 21** HGM Medical Laser Systems. **P. 35** © 1996 PhotoDisc, Inc. Table 02.01 Source: Reprinted with permission from MARKETING PLANNING by Howard Sutton (New York: The Conference Board, 1990) Table 8. Figure 02.05 Booz, Allen and Hamilton, Inc. Reprinted with permission. **P. 69** © 1996 Clifton Eoff/Wal-Mart Stores, Inc. Used with permission. Table 03.01 Source: William Dillon, Thomas J. Madden, and Neil H. Firtle, MARKETING RESEARCH IN A MARKETING ENVIRONMENT 3/e (Burr Ridge, IL: Irwin, 1994) p. 162. Reproduced with permission. **P.112** Source: Abbie Griffin and John R. Hauser, "The Voice of the Customer," *Marketing Science*, Vol. 12, No. 1, Winter 1993. **P. 115** © 1992 The Economist Newspaper Group, Inc. Reprinted with permission. Table 03.02 Source: Reprinted with permission from COMPETITIVE INTELLIGENCE by Howard Sutton (New York: The Conference Board, 1988). **P. 113** "Has Our Standard Stalled?" Copyright 1992 by Consumers Union of US, Inc., Yonkers, NY 10703-1057. Reprinted by permission from CONSUMER REPORTS, June 1992. **P. 115** Source: Reprinted with permission from CURRENT PRACTICES IN MEASURING QUALITY by Francis J. Walsh (New York: The Conference Board, 1989). Figure 03.04 © Henry Groskinsky. Figure 03.06 Courtesy of Stephen J. Bass & Partners. Figure 03.07 Courtesy of FIND/SVP. Figure 03.08 Source: Reproduced with permission from John D. C. Little, "Decision Support Systems for Marketing Managers," JOURNAL OF MARKETING 42 (Summer 1979), pp. 9–26. Figure 03.09 Reprinted by permission of the publisher form "What the Hot Marketing Tool of the 80's Offers You" by Michael Dressler, Joquin Ives Brant, and Ronald Beall, INDUSTRIAL MARKETING MANAGEMENT (March 1983), p. 54. Copyright 1983 by Elsevier Science Publishing Co., Inc. Figure 03.11 Source: Reprinted with permission from THE MARKETING PLAN by Howard Sutton (New York: The Conference Board, 1990). **P. 119** Paul Chesley/Tony Stone Images. Figure 04.02 Reprinted by permission from page 21 of STRATEGIC MARKET PLANNING: THE PURSUIT OF COMPETITIVE ADVANTAGE by George S. Day, Copyright © 1984 by West Publishing Company. All rights reserved. **P. 155** Annette Coolidge/The Dryden Press. **P. 158** Courtesy of Ford Motor Company. Figure 05.03a Courtesy of Ford Motor Company. Figure 05.03b Courtesy of Ford Motor Company. Figure 05.03c Courtesy of Ford Motor Company. Figure 05.03d Courtesy of Ford Motor Company. **P. 182** © 1996 PhotoDisc, Inc. **P. 184** © 1996 PhotoDisc, Inc. **P. 185** © 1996 PhotoDisc, Inc. **P. 172** WALL STREET JOURNAL (October 19, 1989). Reprinted by permission of THE WALL STREE JOURNAL, © 1989 Dow Jones & Company, Inc. All Rights Reserved Worldwide. Figure 05.09 Source: MARKETING NEWS (January 2, 1995) pp. 16. Reprinted with permission from American Marketing Association. Figure 05.11 Source: Reproduced with permission from Niren Vyas and Arch G. Woodside, "An Inductive Model of Supplier Choice Processes," JOURNAL OF MARKETING 48 (Winter 1984), pp. 30–45. **P. 207** Terry Vine/Tony Stone Images. **P. 213** Sources: G. Bruce Knecht, "How Bud Won the Battle," DUN'S REVIEW (February 1982) pp. 83–85; "A Shrinking Market Has Beermakers Brawling," BUSINESS WEEK (August 20, 1984) pp. 59, 63; and William Dunn, "Where the Beer Industry is Heading," AMERICAN DEMOGRAPHICS (February 1986) pp. 37–39. **P. 239** Courtesy of Blockbuster Entertainment. Figure 06.02 DILBERT reprinted by permission of United Feature Syndicate, Inc. **P. 238** Sources: "The Anatomy of RCA'S Videodisc Failure," BUSINESS WEEK (April 23, 1984) pp. 89–90; "The VCR Boom Puts Blank Tapes in Fast Forward," BUSINESS WEEK (August 6, 1984) pp. 92–93; Susan Spillman, "Videocassette Rental Sites in Darndest Spots," ADVERTISING AGE (August 30, 1984) pp. 1–5; Alex Ben Block, "Hard Dollars in Video Software," FORBES (June 17, 1985) pp. 128–132; Stephen Kindel, "Goodbye, TV Hello, Video," FORBES (July 1, 1985) pp. 100–101; Randy Pitman, "A Tale of Two Cultures: The Video Business and Libraries," WILSON LIBRARY BULLETIN (May 1988) pp. 27–28; and Peter M. Nichols, "Home Video," NEW YORK TIMES (October 10, 1995) p. B10. Figure 06.03 Source: Donald R. Lehmann and Russell S. Winer, ANALYSIS FOR MARKETING PLANNING (Burr Ridge, IL: Irwin, 1991) p. 22. Reproduced with permission. Figure 06.10 Source: FORBES (November 23, 1992) pp. 190. Reprinted by permission of FORBES Magazine © Forbes Inc., 1992. **P. 251** Courtesy of Home Shopping Network. FPO CREDIT – IMAGE NOT YET RECEIVED. **P. 271** © John Coletti/The Picture Cube, Inc. **P. 272** Courtesy of The Sharper Image. Figure 07.02a Stock Montage. Figure 07.02b Stock Montage. Figure 07.02c International Business Machines. Figure 07.02d © Guiliano Colliva/The Image Bank. Figure 07.04 From MARKETING CHANNEL MANAGEMENT: STRATEGIC PLANNING AND TACTICS by Kenneth G. Hardy and Allan J. Magrath. Copyright © 1988 by Scott, Foresman and Company. Reprinted by permission of HarperCollins Publishers. Figure 07.05 From MARKETING CHANNEL MANAGEMENT: STRATEGIC PLANNING AND TACTICS by Kenneth G. Hardy and Allan J. Magrath. Copyright © 1988 by Scott, Foresman and Company. Reprinted by permission of HarperCollins Publishers. Figure 07.07 Thomas L. Prince, "An Empirical Investigation of Market Power and Channel Conflict in the Cut-Flower Distribution Channel," unpublished master's thesis. Reprinted by permission. **P. 287** Owen Franken/Stock Boston. Figure 08.01 Sources: Lewis M. Schneider, "New Era in Transportation Strategy," HARVARD BUSINESS REVIEW (March/April 1985) pp. 118–126; Chris Welles, et al., "Is Deregulation Working," BUSINESS WEEK (December 22, 1986) pp. 50–55; Stephen Koepp, "Rolling Back Regulation," TIME (July 6, 1987) pp. 50–52; Joel A. Bleeke, "Strategic Choices for Newly Opened Markets," HARVARD BUSINESS REVIEW (September/October 1990) pp. 158–165; Richard J. Herring and Ashish C. Shah, eds., "Reforming the American Banking System," (Philadelphia, PA: The Wharton Financial Institutions Center, 1991); and Robert V. Delaney, "Cass Sixth Annual State of Logistics Report," (St. Louis, MO) 1995; Association of American Railroads (Washington, DC); and Air Transport Association of America. UNF 08.01 Image courtesy of Whirlpool. Figure 08.02 Source: Elliott H. McCleary, "How and Where You Can Save Over 50% on Prescription Drugs," CONSUMER'S DIGEST (November/December 1992). Reprinted with permission of CONSUMER'S DIGEST, INC. UNF 08.02 Adapted with permission from Paul Slovic, "Perception of Risk," SCIENCE MAGAZINE (April 17, 1987) pp. 280–285. Copyright 1987 American Association for the Advancement of Science. Figure 08.03 Source: Joan V. Bernstein, "Environmental Policy and Strategic Planning," CORPORATE STEWARDSHIP AND THE ENVIRONMENT, Barbara H. Peters and James L. Peters, eds. (New York: The Conference Board, 1991) p. 20. Reprinted with permission from The Conference Board. Figure 08.03 Source: Ronald E. Berenbeim, CORPORATE ETHICS PRACTICES (New York: The Conference Board, 1992). Reprinted with permission from The Conference Board. UNF 08. 03 Source: Ronald E. Berenbeim, CORPORATE ETHICS PRACTICES (New York: The Conference Board, 1992) p. 40. Reprinted with permission from The Conference Board. Figure 08.04 Sources: Gene R. Laczniak and Patrick E. Murphy, MARKETING ETHICS (Lexington, MA: Lexington Books, 1985) pp. 117–123; and Jan Willem Bol, Charles T. Crespy, James M. Stearns, and John R. Walton, THE INTEGRATION OF ETHICS INTO THE MARKETING CURRICULUM (Needham Heights, MA: Ginn Press, 1991) p. 27. Figure 08.07 Source: Based on a combination of ethics models developed by Craig J. Thompson, "A Contextualist Proposal for the Conceptualization and Study of Marketing Ethics," JOURNAL OF PUBLIC POLICY AND MARKETING Vol. 14 No. 2 (Fall, 1995) pp. 177–191. **P. 325** Annette Coolidge/The Dryden Press. Text item 09.01 Source: The above spreadsheet is an extension of method discussed in Roger A. Kerin, Michael G. Harvey, and James T. Rothe, "Cannibalism and New Product Development," BUSINESS HORIZONS (October 1978) pp. 25–31. Figure 09.04 Source: Greg M. Allenby, "A Unified Approach to Identifying, Estimating and Testing Demand Structures with Aggregate Scanner Data," MARKETING SCIENCE (Summer 1989) pp. 265–280. **P. 366** Source: Adapted from John W. Keon, "Product Positioning: TRINODAL Mapping of Brand Images, Ad Images, and Consumer Preference," JOURNAL OF MARKETING RESEARCH (November 1983) pp. 380–392. Figure 09.07 Source: For details see Valarie A. Zeithaml, A. Parasuraman, and Leonard L. Berry, "A Conceptual Model of Service Quality and Its Implications for Future Research," JOURNAL OF MARKETING Vol. l49 No. 4 (Fall 1985) pp. 41–50. **P. 367** Source: R.R. Batsell and J.B. Elmer, "How to Use Market-Based Pricing to Forecast Consumer Purchase Decisions," JOURNAL OF PRICING MANAGEMENT (Spring 1990) pp. 5–15. Permission granted by Faulkner & Gray, 11 Penn Plaza, NY, NY 10001. Table 9.1 Source: These eight dimensions of quality are based on David A. Garvin, "Competing on the Eight Dimensions of Quality," HARVARD BUSINESS REVIEW (November/December 1987) pp. 101–107. **P. 368** Source: Paul E. Green and Abba M. Krieger, "Recent Contributions to Optimal Product Positioning and Buyer Segmentation," EUROPEAN JOURNAL OF OPERATIONAL RESEARCH Vol. 41 (1989) pp. 127–141. **P. 370** Source: Peter R.

Dickson, "Person-Situation: Segmentation's Missing Link," JOURNAL OF MARKETING Vol. 12 (1982) pp. 56–64. **P. 372** Source: G. Lynn Shostack, "Service Positioning Through Structural Change," JOURNAL OF MARKETING (January 1987) pp. 34–43. **P. 374** WALL STREET JOURNAL (March 22, 1984). Reprinted by permission of THE WALL STREET JOURNAL, © 1984 Dow Jones & Company, Inc. All Rights Reserved Worldwide. **P. 374** Source: Adapted from AUTOMOTIVE NEWS (September 15, 1986). **P. 377** Courtesy of Ford Motor Company. Table 10.01 Sources: These charts are based on data from Dataquest, Inc., the National Institute of Standards & Technology, the Thomas Group, Inc., and the Institute for Defense Analyses. See Otis Port, Zachary Schiller, and Resa W. King, "A Smarter Way to Manufacture," BUSINESS WEEK (April 30, 1990) pp. 110–117. Figure 10.02 Source: Adapted from Robert G. Cooper, "Third-Generation New Product Process," JOURNAL OF PRODUCT INNOVATION MANAGEMENT Vol 11 (1994), pp. 3–14. Table 10.02 Source: Peter Dickson, et al., "Managing Design in Small High-Growth Companies," JOURNAL OF PRODUCT INNOVATION MANAGEMENT Vol. 12 No. 5 (November 1995) pp. 406–414. **P. 400** Sony Electronics, Inc. **P. 402** Steelcase, Inc. **P. 413** Courtesy of Landor Associates. **P. 413** Courtesy of Landor Associates. **P. 413** Courtesy of Landor Associates. Figure 10.05 Source: Karl T. Ulrich and Steven D. Eppinger, PRODUCT DESIGN AND DEVELOPMENT (New York: McGraw-Hill, 1995). Reproduced with permission of The McGraw-Hill Companies. Figure 10.06 Reprinted by permission of Harvard Business School Press from HEARING THE VOICE OF THE MARKET by Vincent P. Barabba and Gerald Zaltman. Boston: 1991, p. 54. Copyright © 1991 by the President and Fellows of Harvard College; all rights reserved. Figure 10.08 Reprinted with permission of The Free Press, a division of Simon & Schuster from MANAGING BRAND EQUITY: CAPITALIZING ON THE VALUE OF A BRAND NAME by David A. Aaker. Copyright © 1991 by David A. Aaker. CO 11. 00 David Young-Wolff/PhotoEdit. Figure 11.03 Reproduced with permission from RETAIL PREVIEW-CONSUMABLES, Issue 3, August 1992, Management Horizons, a consulting division of Price Waterhouse. Figure 11.04 Sources: V. Caster Rangan, Melvyn A.J. Menezes, and E.P. Maier, "Channel Selection for New Industrial Products: A Framework, Method and Application," JOURNAL OF MARKETING Vol 56 (July 1992) pp. 69–82; Rowland T. Moriarty and Urula Moran, "Managing Hybrid Marketing Systems," HARVARD BUSINESS REVIEW (November/December 1990) pp. 146–155; and Louis W. Stern and Frederick D. Sturdivant, "Customer-Driven Distribution Systems," HARVARD BUSINESS REVIEW (July/August 1987) pp. 34–41. Figure 11.05 Source: Adapted from Erin M. Anderson and Barton A. Weitz, A FRAMEWORK FOR ANALYZING VERTICAL INTEGRATION ISSUES IN MARKETING (Harvard Business School Press, 1991) p. 54. Figure 11.05 Source: Diana L. Haytko, "Advertising Agency Interpersonal Process and Outcome Performance Management of Client Relationships," unpublished doctoral dissertation (University of Wisconsin-Madison, School of Business, 1987). CO 12.00 Defense Distribution Region East (New Cumberland, PA). Table 12.01 Source: Douglas M. Lambert and James R. Stock, STRATEGIC LOGISTICS MANAGEMENT 3/e (Burr Ridge, IL: 1993) p. 175. Reproduced with permission. Figure 12.03 Source: Adapted from Scott A. Wagoner, "Logistics and Quality Management: Leadership and the Process Improvement Link," LOGISTICS SPECTRUM (Winter, 1989) p. 15. Figure 12.05 © 1996 PhotoDisc, Inc. Figure 12.06 Source: TRAFFIC MANAGEMENT NEWS CAPSULE (July 1990) p. 19. Reprinted with permission. Figure 12.08 Butch Gemin/The Dryden Press. Figure 12.09 © 1996 PhotoDisc, Inc. Figure 12.10 Courtesy of FedEx Corporation. All rights reserved. Figure 12.11 Source: Fritz Companies, Inc., San Francisco. CO 13.00 © Tom McCarthy/ PhotoEdit. Table 13.01 Excerpt adapted from SALES MANAGEMENT: ANALYSIS AND DECISION MAKING, Second Edition by Thomas N. Ingram and Raymond W. LaForge, copyright © 1992 by The Dryden Press, reprinted by permission of the publisher. UNF 13.01 © Keff Greenberg/ The Picture Cube, Inc. Text item 13.01 Source: C. Davis Fogg and Josef W. Rokus, "A Quantitative Method for Structuring a Profitable Sales Force," JOURNAL OF MARKETING Vol 37 (July 1973) pp. 8–17. Figure 13.02 Source: Based on William C. Moncrief, "Selling Activity and Sales Position Taxonomies for Industrial Salesforces," JOURNAL OF MARKETING RESEARCH Vol. 23 (August 1986) pp. 261–270. Table 13.02 Source: Louis A. Wallis, COMPUTERS AND THE SALES EFFORT, Report No. 884 (New York: The Conference Board, 1986). Text item 13.02 Source: C. David Shepherd and James C. Heartfield, "Discrimination Issues in the Selection of Salespeople: A Review and Managerial Suggestions," JOURNAL OF PERSONAL SELLING AND SALES MANAGEMENT Vol 11 No 4 (Fall 1991) pp. 67–75. UNF 13.02 © Larry Lawfer/The Picture Cube, Inc. Text item 13.03 Source: Rayna Skolnik, "Salespeople Sound Off on Meetings," SALES AND MARKETING MANAGEMENT (November 1987) p. 108. Figure 13.08 Source: SALES MANAGER'S DESK BOOK by Gene Garofalo. © 1989. Used by permission of the publisher, Prentice Hall/A Division of Simon & Schuster, Englewood Cliffs, New Jersey. CO 14.00 Eveready Battery Company, Inc. Table 14.01 Reprinted with permission from the September 27, 1995 issue of ADVERTISING AGE. Copyright © 1995 Crain Communications Inc. Figure 14.01a Reprinted with permission from Eastman Kodak Company. Table 14.02 Reprinted with permission from the April 10, 1995 issue of ADVERTISING AGE. Copyright © 1995 Crain Communications Inc. Figure 14.04 Source: "Impact in the Aisles," PROMO: The Magazine of Promotion Marketing (January 1996) pp. 25–28. Reprinted with permission. CO 15.00 Courtesy of HealthRider. Text item 15.01 Source: Excerpted from Stuart Elliott, "More Scenes from the Past Sell Products in the Present," NEW YORK TIMES (April 24, 1992); and Melanie Wells, "Old Ads Get Recycled by Different Retailers," ADVERTISING AGE (February 15, 1993) pp. 12. UNF 15.02 Jeff Greene/The Palm Beach Post. Figure 15.10 Source: Leonard M. Lodish et al., "How TV Advertising Works: A Meta-analysis of 389 Real World Split Cable TV Advertising Experiments," JOURNAL OF MARKETING RESEARCH (May 1995) pp. 125–139. CO 16.00 Courtesy of Southwest Airlines. Table 16.02 Source: Donnelley Marketing Inc., "13th ANNUAL SURVEY OF PROMOTIONAL PRACTICES" (1991). Figure 16.03 Source: Adapted from Robert L. Rosiello, "Managing Price, Gaining Profit," HARVARD BUSINESS REVIEW (September/October 1992) p. 86. UNF 16.04 Source: Reprinted from "Pricing Opportunities and How to Exploit Them" by Herman Simon, SLOAN MANAGEMENT REVIEW (Winter 1992) pp. 55–65, by permission of the publisher. Copyright © 1992 by The Sloan Management Review Association. All rights reserved. Figure 16.05 © 1996 Don Couch Photography. Figure 16.06 Butch Gemin/The Dryden Press. CO 17.00 Courtesy of International Rescue Corps, Patron: Her Royal Highness the Princess Royal. Text item 17.01 Source: Excerpted from Robert Levy and Lynn Adkins, "The Hypes That Failed," FORBES (September 1980) pp. 74–75. UNF 17.01 Source: THE MARKETING PLAN by David S. Hopkins (New York: The Conference Board Report No. 801, 1981). UNF 17.03a Index Stock Photography, Inc. UNF 17.03b Index Stock Photography, Inc. Figure 17.05 Source: Adapted from Alladi Venkatesh and David L. Wilemon, "Interpersonal Influence in Product Management," JOURNAL OF MARKETING Vol 40 (October 1976) p. 36. CO 18.00 © 1996 PhotoDisc, Inc. Text item 18.01 Sources: Courtland L. Bovee and William F. Arens, CONTEMPORARY ADVERTISING (Homewood, IL: Irwin, 1986); and Jeffrey A. Trachtenberg, "Beer Blunder," FORBES (February 8, 1988) pp. 128–130. Figure 18.02 Source: THE MARKETING PLAN (New York: The Conference Board Report #801, 1981) p. 95. Figure 18.06 Source: Donnally Marketing, Neilsen Marketing Research. CO 19.00 Annette Coolidge/The Dryden Press. Text item 19.01 Source: Geoffrey Smith, "Fleet's Can-Do Spirit: We Can Do Without," BUSINESS WEEK (March 21, 1996) pp. 106–107. Figure 19.02 Source: Based on Paul Sharman, "A Toolkit for Continuous Improvement," The Society of Management Accountants of Canada (May 1992) pp. 17–20. Text item 19.02 Source: Joyce Barnathan, "Blind Ambition," BUSINESS WEEK (October 23, 1995) pp. 78–92. Table App1.01 Source: Based on J. Edward Russo and Paul J.H. Schoemaker, DECISION TRAPS (New York: Simon and Schuster, 1990). Table App1.03 Source: Adapted from Susan Butruille, Stanley S. Gryskiewicz, and Robert C. Preziosi, "Kaleidoscope Thinking for Creativity," TRAINING AND DEVELOPMENT (September 1991) p. 28. Used with permission. Table App1.04 Table "Team Requirements for New Product Development," from REENGINEERING THE CORPORATION by Michael Hammer and James Champy. Copyright © 1993 by Michael Hammer and James Champy. Reprinted by permission of HarperCollins Publishers, Inc. UNF App2.02 © Peter Dickson.

Name Index

Company Index

Subject Index

A Process Skills Hierarchy

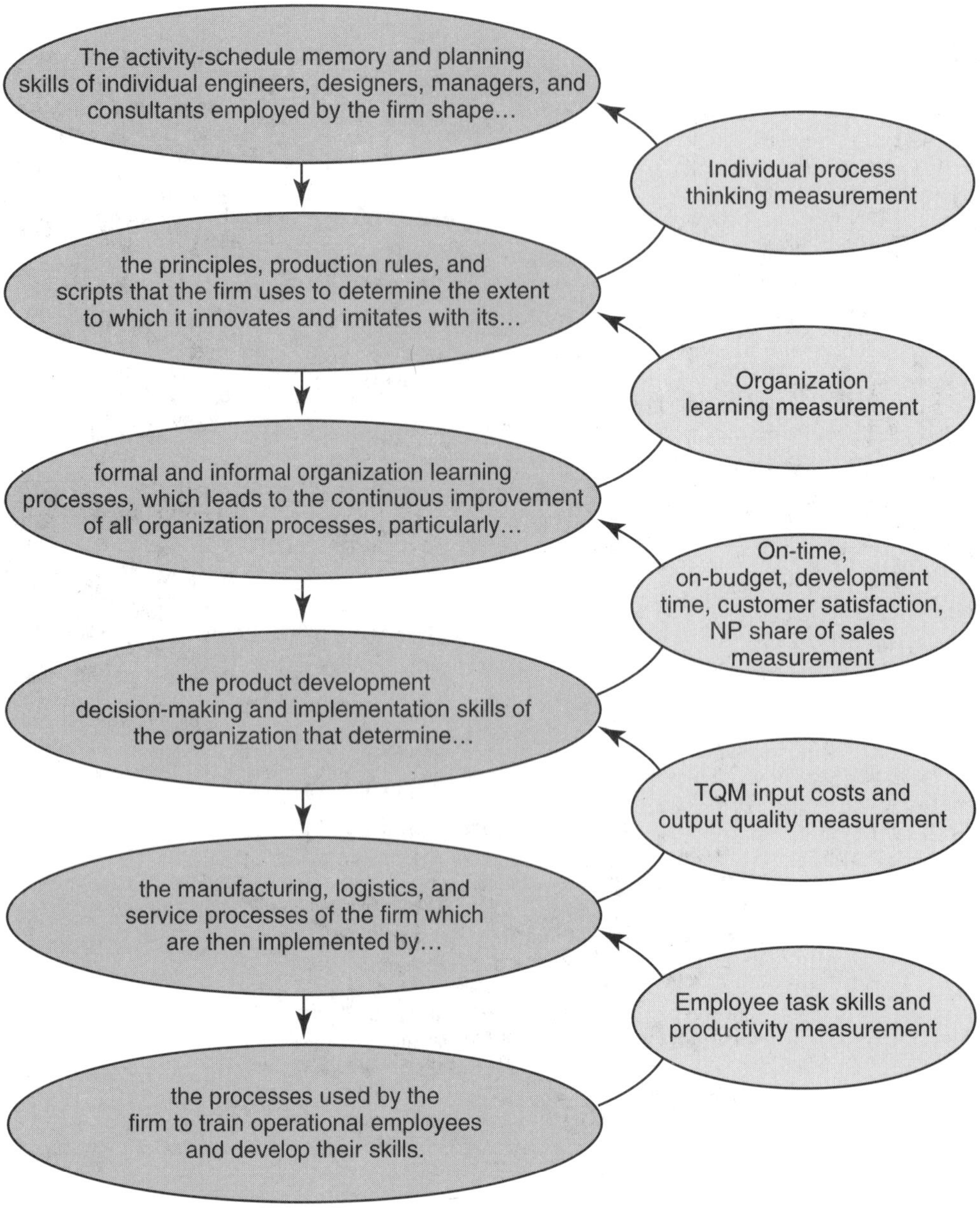
The activity-schedule memory and planning skills of individual engineers, designers, managers, and consultants employed by the firm shape…
the principles, production rules, and scripts that the firm uses to determine the extent to which it innovates and imitates with its…
formal and informal organization learning processes, which leads to the continuous improvement of all organization processes, particularly…
the product development decision-making and implementation skills of the organization that determine…
the manufacturing, logistics, and service processes of the firm which are then implemented by…
the processes used by the firm to train operational employees and develop their skills.
Individual process thinking measurement
Organization learning measurement
On-time, on-budget, development time, customer satisfaction, NP share of sales measurement
TQM input costs and output quality measurement
Employee task skills and productivity measurement